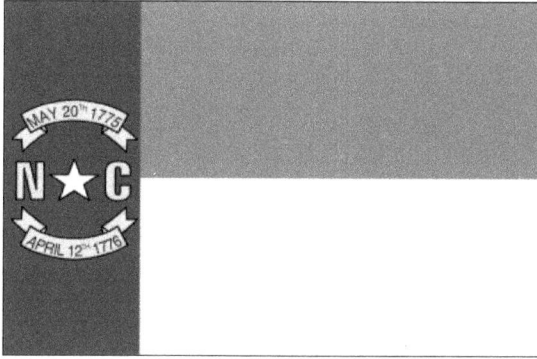

NC Patriots 1775-1783: Their Own Words

Volume 1–The NC Continental Line
2nd Edition

J.D. Lewis

Published by Carla G. Harper
Stokesdale, NC 27357

carla@carlagharper.com
www.carlagharper.com

ISBN 978-0-9971907-4-8

Table of Contents

Chapter One – 1775

The year of 1775 brings North Carolina to the forefront leading all calls for freedom–with the Mecklenburg Resolves of May 20th signed by twenty-seven Patriots, some who later serve in the North Carolina Militia, some who later serve in the North Carolina Contintental Line, and some who later serve in the formation of the North Carolina state government. A heartbeat that is tentative and tepid in other colonies soon pounds strongly in the Old North State. This is not a case of the Royal Government's representatives saying stupid

Key Events of 1775
• Patriots defy Royal Governor Josiah Martin and assemble for two Provincial Congresses.
• Mecklenburg Resolves issued May 20th.
• Most county Militias assemble.
• Fort Johnston seized by Patriots.
• Gov. Josiah Martin forced to flee to HMS *Cruizer* off Cape Fear.
• Two regiments of Provincial troops are authorized/assembled, then placed on the Continental line.
• Seven regiments of Minutemen and 37 regiments of Militia are established and fielded.
• NC Continental troops and Minutemen/ Militia assist VA at the Great Bridge near Norfolk.
• NC Continental troops and Minutemen/ Militia assist SC in the famous Snow Campaign against noted Loyalists.

things or making minor faux pas. North Carolina is boiling over with enthusiasm to "get on with it." OK, at least one-third of the population is already at that point thanks to the well-documented and well-known reasons from a decade ago–the Stamp Act, the Quartering Act, the Tea Act, etc. With plenty of highly-educated and intelligent leaders keeping their energy up, there never is a consideration of turning back now that the First Continental Congress has wrapped up a few months earlier and the Second Continental Congress is planned for May 10th, again in Philadelphia.

In preparation, the Second Provincial Congress convenes on April 3rd in New Bern. They elect their delegates to the Second Continental Congress and they elect a Committee of Safety to guide their upcoming actions. This is done much to the chagrin of the Royal Governor, Josiah Martin, sitting uncomfortably nearby at the Tryon Palace, also in New Bern. Gov. Martin instinctively knows that things are unraveling right before his very eyes, but he has not the wherewithal to do anything about the things he despises. Patriot Militias assemble in New Hanover and Brunswick counties, contrary to his orders to stand down. As mentioned above, the Mecklenburg Resolves are published soon afterwards, on May 20th, and then word arrives about the "shot heard around the world" including the actions at Lexington and Concord in Massachusetts. On

This three-volume set is dedicated to Dr. Bobby Gilmer Moss of Blacksburg, SC, whose many published efforts served to inspire this compilation. Without this inspiration, the Author probably would not have undertaken such madness as this.

Preface

With scores of books already in print about the American Revolution in North Carolina, what makes this work different? Most historians merely offer a broad-brushed canvas with an overview of a very complex human struggle, and those works are fine for those who simply want to absorb only a few highlights. Other books offer considerable details on one of a handful of selected battles, each replete with hundreds of footnotes that help the reader to get thoroughly lost and frustrated such that they struggle to retain a coherent story, or worse, they give up and stop reading. History can be boring. Furthermore, many works simply rely on the same earlier sources and seldom offer anything new, or worse, they simply repeat the many earlier inaccuracies.

This three-volume set provides a very detailed and comprehensive narrative that has never been told before and is mostly told by thousands of those who were actually there. This set is certainly intended for the serious-minded Revolutionary War "wonk" who simply cannot get enough first-hand accounts, even if some accounts often contradict one another. Since there were so many players during the eight years that North Carolina Patriots fought for their freedom, it is impossible to tell a single story with a single viewpoint. There are literally thousands of voices to be heard, each with their own small tale adding to the mosaic of the overall narrative. Although this effort is not a light read, and although it also follows the traditional sequential timelines, one quickly realizes that this is one long and complex tale, and this work ensures that the reader gets the full impact of all the many details from those who participated. As you read it, you are there.

North Carolina was the fourth most populous province at the beginning of the American Revolution with a total population of approximately 255,000, including 10,000 slaves. Many are not aware that North Carolina's population grew significantly during the American Revolution, and by the end of the war the total population was nearly 350,000, an almost forty percent increase in eight difficult years. As the crown colony evolved into a new free state, and the new state continually expanded westward, there were many new people with new points of view to incorporate into the awkwardly progressing society that would soon emerge, not without much pain and sacrifice from all of those involved. Most folks tried to simply go on with their lives, but this was impossible. Every facet of the emerging North Carolina society was embroiled in the arduous task of nation building, whether it wanted to be

or not. Historians agree that there were essentially three roughly equal groups within the state's borders—one-third were ardent Patriots willing to fight for their independence, one-third were ardent Loyalists willing to fight on behalf of the crown, and the last one-third were fence-sitters watching and waiting for one of the other two groups to win.

There is virtually no contemporaneous data available to adequately describe the last one-third of North Carolina's society during the American Revolution. Apathetic fence-sitters have been around since before history, and they will continue until history ends—and moreover, they seldom document their actions, or more accurately, their inactions. As expected, most adopted the stance that they had no control over the outcome and simply watched the events unfold around them. None were unscathed by these unfolding events, and as the months and years went by it became more difficult to sit on the fence. Very little more will be discussed herein about the fence-sitters.

For those inclined to learn more about the second group, the Loyalists (also known as Tories), there is a book entitled, *The Loyalists in North Carolina During the Revolution*, written by Robert O. DeMond and published in 1940. This definitive work leaves little to speculate about the history of the many Loyalists in North Carolina. This group played an important role in shaping the story of the Old North State during its formative years, but very little more will be discussed herein, except when absolutely necessary to keep the story moving forward.

The final one-third—the Patriots—is the subject of this work. Since one-third of 255,000 equals 85,000 Patriots, and that one-half of these would be males—roughly 42,000—then it will probably sound amazing that many historians acknowledge that North Carolina fielded between 30,000 and 36,000 Patriot soldiers over the course of the eight-year war. This means that between 70% and 80% of all Patriot males actively participated in military activities during the American Revolution. The remaining 20% to 30% were either too young, too old, or they were involved in improving the new state government. So, who produced the goods for market? Who brought the goods to market? Were there actually any markets?

The 30,000 to 36,000-man estimate includes three distinct groups of military men. There were the Provincial and State Troops that were mustered for a definite period of time, usually for six months, nine months, or twelve months—and paid for that definite period of time. Then there was the Militia that was called out for specific, usually urgent and short-term needs—and only paid for those short efforts. These two groups

were paid by the State and are fully described in Volume 2. Finally, there were the Continental soldiers that were mustered for longer periods of time–and they were paid by the Continental Congress. Well, actually, each state contributed money to the Continental Congress to in turn pay for the Continental soldiers. Not much has changed in over 235 years.

It is estimated that North Carolina provided more than 8,800 men to serve on the Continental Line over the course of the eight-year war. Simply put, that roughly equals 1,100 men per year, not an exhorbitant number by itself. However, with all that transpired during those eight years, recruiting, training, and maintaining that many soldiers quickly became a big challenge for the newly-created state government and for the families at home. Besides the marching, the biggest complaint from the state's first professional soldiers was the lack of clothing and footwear. Although the Continenal Congress paid their salaries, each state was required to furnish their soldiers' accoutrements, including their firearms, swords, ammunition, and mess kits. With no manufacturing plants of its own, North Carolina had to purchase these goods, usually from overseas, although some items were available from sister states. Transporting and distributing these purchased items were challenging as well, especially since the British ruled the high seas and closely watched most ports. Understandably, privateering was a very risky but lucrative business along the coast, including the coast of North Carolina.

There exist several sources of information about the North Carolina Continental soldiers. *The Colonial and State Records of North Carolina*– a twenty-eight volume set of books first printed in the 1890s by order of the General Assembly and compiled by William L. Saunders and Walter Clark–contains dozens of rolls and lists of the soldiers in the various North Carolina Continental regiments. These lists are fairly accurate and fairly complete–to a point. There are no complete lists for the non-commissioned officers such as corporals and sergeants, and certainly only incomplete lists for the common privates.

In 1932, the North Carolina Daughters of the American Revolution (DAR) published a significant book entitled, *Roster of Soldiers from North Carolina in the American Revolution,* with a good listing of all known Continental soldiers of the state as well as some Militia rolls and other related information. The DAR employed F.B. Heitman's *Historical Register of Officers of the Continental Army During the War of the Revolution–April 1775 to December 1783*, first printed in 1893; they employed *Pierce's Register*, a 1915 DAR compilation of the "Register of

the certificates by John Pierce, Esquire, Paymaster General and Commissioner of Army Accounts for the United States to officers and soldiers of the Continental Army under act of July 4, 1783;" and they finally employed the *Colonial and State Records* described above.

Although these works provide an enormous amount of useful information, none are considered to be anywhere near complete. First of all, there were no records kept of the Continental units established in 1775 and even some from early 1776. No satisfactory explanation has ever been supplied as to why these do not exist. Secondly, the same is true for all soldiers mustered into the NC Light Dragoons. These were at first NC Provincial Troops on April 16, 1776, but were placed on the Continental Line on March 7, 1777. However, most records do exist for the NC Artillery, which also began as Provincial Troops then added to the Continental Line on July 10, 1777, but alas some of these are also lost to the sands of time. Finally, when chaos reigned while the British invaded South Carolina in 1780 and North Carolina in 1781, some Continental records were accidentally destroyed and therefore also lost.

Although the above-described rolls and lists do contain a great amount of useful information, there is also a considerable amount of incorrect information passed along over the years. An example is–the 10th NC Regiment was completely disbanded effective on June 1st of 1778, never to be resurrected. However, one important historian of the mid-1800s asserted that the 10th NC Regiment continued until the end of the war. It just so happens that this historian was the NC Secretary of State, William Hill, who was responsible for validating all pension requests in the 1830s and 1840s. It appears that if he was not sure as to which regiment a particular captain belonged he would simply write down that he was in the 10th NC Regiment. When one looks at the totality of the rolls and lists available, it becomes quite clear that those later captains are accurately assigned to their proper regiments that continued in lieu of the 10th NC Regiment, yet so many historians fail to take that extra step because it requires extra effort.

The rolls and lists are also missing much useful information, such as a soldier's county of residence, his birth date, and anything else that could help to identify one soldier from another. John Jones of the 1st NC Regiment just might be the same man as John Jones of the 4th NC Regiment listed on a later roll. Many soldiers re-enlisted later in different regiments, but the average researcher would not know this. Most historians simply do not care for this much detailed information, so they simply ignore these details. Details, details–just give me the highlights.

In the early 1800s, the federal government authorized the payment of a small pension to men who could prove that they had served in the Continental Army without deserting, and could prove that they truly needed financial assistance. The primary law was enacted on March 18, 1818, thirty-five years after the end of the American Revolution. Those who applied for this annual stipend had to furnish certain information that had to be witnessed by a justice of local courts. Over time, these have been named "Federal Pension Applications (FPAs)" and there are three versions–"S" is for an application that was instigated by the "Survivor"–the man who actually served; "W" is for an application that was instigated by a "Widow" (authorized later); and, "R" is for an application that was "Rejected" for various reasons. Appendix C herein includes a complete listing of all known Continental soldiers from North Carolina, and those who filed a FPA are annotated with a one- to five-digit number preceded by an S, a W, or an R, e.g., S31460, W132, R4433. If none of these are provided for a solider listed in Appendix C, then there is no record–the particular soldier did not file a request for a pension.

From 1818 to after the U.S. Civil War, over 150,000 pension applications were submitted by pensioners, their widows, and later by their descendents. Of course, these 150,000 applications were from men who had served in all thirteen original states. Furthermore, in 1832 the federal government allowed pension applications from State Troops and Militiamen, as long as they could prove at least six months' service without deserting, and again proving that they truly needed financial assistance. Therefore, the 150,000 known pension applications also include non-Continental soldiers.

These 150,000 pension applications can be found in the U. S. National Archives in Washington, DC, and they are in various conditions, from excellent to virtually useless. Some contain dozens of hand-written pages, with all sorts of substantiating documents, including original discharge papers. Most are only a page or two with another page or two of supporting affadavits by friends or family. Many are very difficult to transcribe due to extremely poor hand-writing. All have been micro-filmed for posterity. Thanks to the Internet, these 150,000 pension applications have been scanned and can be viewed online. At present, these scanned images can only be seen on a couple of pay sites, but hopefully in the near future they will be added to the public domain and ultimately free.

Of the estimated 8,800 North Carolina Continentals roughly 10-15% of the men who survived the war actually applied for a federal pension after 1818. Either they were already dead, or they did not want the pension for various reasons, or they were not aware that they could even apply for a pension. As the years rolled on and the laws were amended to allow widows to apply, the number of Continental pensioners increased slightly. Some widows re-applied at the conclusion of the Civil War to have their previous payments re-instated–nearly a century after the American Revolution began. It is estimated that only approximately 5,500 North Carolina soliders and their widows applied for a pension after 1818, and the majority of these were <u>not</u> ex-Continental soldiers.

In perusing the roughly 5,500 pension applications that are available, it is interesting to see the variety of inputs found on one application versus another. One pensioner may barely recall that he was even in the war, but he could recall that he was in a specific battle. The next pensioner could attest to every officer he served under, the date he enlisted, and the date he was discharged. A very interesting theme among the pensioners was– they transferred from one unit to another quite frequently–much more often than the official rolls or lists might indicate. The most useful information would be the pensioner's county of residence when he joined. This helps many researchers in a lot of ways that the casual reviewer would ignore.

On a final note about the pension applications, one must be aware that a pensioner's recollection of thirty-five to fifty years later tends to be somewhat faulty, therefore, a large number of errors can be expected. The most common mistake was a superior officer's first name–they tended to get the last name correct, but could not recall a first name, or took a guess, usually wrong. Of course, there are plenty of other mistakes, but most of these can be interpreted to arrive at the correct information. Then, there are those that are so wrong that they amount to nothing more than trash. These are in the extreme minority, however.

As described in greater detail later herein, the North Carolina Continental Line participated in thirty-seven known battles and/or significant skirmishes. Interestingly, only seven of these occurred within the state of North Carolina, yet none of these seven battles employed large numbers of North Carolina Continentals. Most battles were in South Carolina–eighteen. Four were in Georgia, two in Virginia, two in Pennsylvania, three in New York, and one in New Jersey. This certainly indicates a lot of marching to and from North Carolina.

The final statistic to get out of the way is that the desertion rate among the North Carolina Continentals was roughly 10%, about the national average. Certainly, private soldiers deserted more than any other rank. The highest known rank of a deserter within the NC Continental Line was one Lieutenant–very early in the war. He was a true Loyalist at heart and cleared his conscience five months after enlisting. There were several sergeants, several corporals, and a handful of musicians (fifers and drummers)–the rest were privates. One Continental captain retired and later turned traitor, but he was soon captured and hanged.

The North Carolina Continental Line served from November of 1775 to the end of the war in mid-1783. Most served quietly but ably, mostly just plodding along doing what their superiors ordered. Some were placed on "his excellency's guard," a protection detail for General George Washington, an honor in itself. A few distinguished themselves greatly at the battle of Fort Lafayette in New York–the British permitted them to march out wearing their guns and swords. The rest got little recognition, if any. Each and every one of them should be honored and highly praised by all generations that follow. They contributed significantly to the freedom we all now enjoy.

Recruiting for the Continental Line primarily fell upon the county Militias over the entire course of the Revolutionary War. Once assembled, the men were turned over to specific Continental officers spread out all across the state at various times. This recruiting effort is fully described in Volume 2, as are the few times that Continental officers led Militia units. While it is impossible to completely eliminate duplicate discussions of overlap in these two separate organizations, the primary discussion is included in the volume that clearly retains the greatest part of the effort being described.

The greatest majority of the detailed information and narrative contained in this three-volume set comes from the approximately 5,500 pension applications found in the national archives. Employing the "bottom-up" technique, detailed accounts of which officers were at which battles all come from these pension applications, and these details can be found in Appendix B. As mentioned earlier, North Carolina provided approximately 8,800 Continentals in ten regiments of Infantry, four companies of Light Horse, and two companies of Artillery. Appendix C includes over 7,200 of the known men who actually participated in the North Carolina Continental Line over the eight-year war. 82% is much better than 0%, but we owe it to the remaining 18% to identify them all. What follows is mostly in "their own words."

May 31st, Gov. Martin abruptly flees New Bern and goes directly to Fort Johnston at the mouth of the Cape Fear River. By July 15th, he is aboard the HMS *Cruizer* anchored just offshore and out of small arms' reach.

It is about now that the Royal Government's representative starts saying stupid things and making major faux pas, not just minor ones. And yet, the Patriots are well prepared and moving forward. The fence-sitters (not to be mentioned much more) light up their pipes and get comfortable in their rocking chairs–to sit back and to be as neutral as possible. The Loyalists are all abuzz and transmitting stealthy notes to and from the offshore royal governor. Or, so they think. Some are intercepted by the Patriots, who pretty much have things figured out.

The standoff begins. Who is going to blink first? Three days after Gov. Martin climbs aboard the HMS *Cruizer*, the Patriots seize Fort Johnston on July 18th. Col. Robert Howe and his Militia, along with John Ashe and Cornelius Harnett, march into the abandoned fort and burn it in full view of Gov. Martin aboard the HMS *Cruizer*. Five hundred men are observed inspecting the fort the next day, but the Patriots cannot get to the guns that were earlier removed from the fort and placed along the shore since they are within range of the *Cruizer's* guns. And that is that, for now. Stalemate.

August 20th finds the Patriots convening their Third Provincial Congress in Hillsborough, well out of the reach of the offshore Royal Governor and his onshore Loyalist minions. Among all the business transacted, this congress chooses to establish two regiments of Provincial Troops–the 1st NC Regiment and the 2nd NC Regiment–to be led respectively by Col. James Moore of New Hanover County and Col. Robert Howe of Brunswick County. Also authorized are six regiments of Minutemen for six months; and, the usual county Militias are authorized to be made ready, if needed. The North Carolina Patriot government decides to be proactive instead of reactive, but mostly they decide to overtly project the prevailing attitude–"Don't Tread on Me." By October 18th, the provincial government elects its first leader–President Cornelius Harnett of Wilmington.

On November 28th, the Second Continental Congress in Philadelphia resolves to accept the two NC provincial regiments onto the Continental Line for a term of one year. Thus begins the NC Continental Line.

The 1st NC Regiment, led by Col. James Moore, is divided into two battalions–one stationed in Wilmington and one stationed in New Bern. The 2nd NC Regiment, led by Col. Robert Howe, was also divided into two battalions–one stationed in Edenton and one stationed in Salisbury.

North Carolina Continental Line
November 28, 1775

1st NC Regiment
Col. James Moore

- Lt. Col. Francis Nash
- Maj. Thomas Clark

Captains
- Thomas Allen
- George Lee Davidson
- William Davis
- Henry "Hal" Dixon
- Caleb Grainger
- William Green
- Alfred Moore
- William Pickett
- Robert Rowan
- John Walker

2nd NC Regiment
Col. Robert Howe

- Lt. Col. Alexander Martin
- Maj. John Patten

Captains
- James Armstrong
- John Armstrong
- James Blount
- Simon Bright
- Charles Crawford
- Nathaniel Keais
- William Knox
- Hardy Murfree
- Michael Payne
- Henry Irwin Toole

1st NC Regiment as of November 28, 1775

Rank	Name	Commission	County From
Colonel	James Moore	8/21/1775	New Hanover
Lt. Colonel	Francis Nash	9/1/1775	Orange
Major	Thomas Clark	9/1/1775	New Hanover
Captain	Thomas Allen	9/1/1775	
Captain	George Lee Davidson	9/1/1775	Anson
Captain	William Davis	9/1/1775	
Captain	Henry "Hal" Dixon	9/1/1775	Orange (Caswell)
Captain	Caleb Grainger	9/1/1775	New Hanover
Captain	William Green	9/1/1775	
Captain	Alfred Moore	9/1/1775	Brunswick
Captain	William Pickett	9/1/1775	Anson
Captain	Robert Rowan	9/1/1775	Cumberland
Captain	John Walker	9/1/1775	Tryon

2nd NC Regiment as of November 28, 1775

Rank	Name	Commission	County From
Colonel	Robert Howe	8/21/1775	Brunswick
Lt. Colonel	Alexander Martin	9/1/1775	Guilford
Major	John Patten	9/1/1775	Beaufort
Captain	James Armstrong	9/1/1775	Pitt
Captain	John Armstrong	9/7/1775	Surry
Captain	James Blount	9/1/1775	Edgecombe
Captain	Simon Bright	9/1/1775	Dobbs
Captain	Charles Crawford	9/1/1775	Cumberland
Captain	Nathaniel Keais	9/1/1775	Beaufort
Captain	William Knox	9/1/1775	Rowan
Captain	Hardy Murfree	9/1/1775	Hertford

Captain	Michael Payne	9/1/1775	
Captain	Henry Irwin Toole	9/1/1775	Edgecombe

Within two weeks of being elevated to the Continental Line, half of the 2nd NC Regiment, stationed at Edenton, sees its first action at the Great Bridge just north of Norfolk, Virginia. James Murray, Earl of Dunmore, and the last Royal Governor of Virginia, orders an attack against Virginia Patriots led by Col. William Woodford and his 2nd VA Regiment of Continentals. This confrontation has been simmering for some time and it erupts on December 9th. North Carolina sends the Halifax District Minutemen under Col. Nicholas Long who arrives in time to be useful to Col. Woodford. 250 men of the 2nd NC Regiment under Col. Robert Howe also arrive just in time to help end this affair, although they see very little action. The sheer number of these reinforcements helps to convince Lord Dunmore that his cause is not worth pursuing.

In his 1833 pension application, Giles Matthew (S8993) asserts:

"… in November in the year of 1775 he enlisted in Capt. Hardy Murfree's company under the command of Col. Robert Howe in the 2nd Regiment of the Continental Line from Hertford County, they marched to Edenton from thence they marched to the Long Bridge [aka Great Bridge] near Norfolk and there remained for some time and had an engagement with the enemy…" [minor edits]

As one can see, most pension applications seldom contain much more informaton than what is provided above; short and to the point. However, a select few do contain much more, as will be shown later herein.

Three weeks later, a portion of the Salisbury battalion of the 2nd NC Regiment, led by Lt. Col. Alexander Martin, join up with a contingent of NC Militia and they all march into South Carolina to help subdue a growing Loyalist faction in the backcountry at the battle of the Great Cane Brake on December 22nd. Most of the Loyalists are captured and taken to Charlestown. The next day, December 23rd, begins the famous Snow Campaign, the long march back from the Great Cane Brake in thirty hours of heavy snowfall that dumps more than two feet of snow on the miserable Patriots. The North Carolinians return just as 1775 ends.

In his 1835 pension application, Samuel Ingram (R5485) asserts:

"… he enlisted in the army of the United States as a regular soldier for the term of six months under Captain William Pickett, a recruiting officer; that during that time he marched from Salisbury in the state of North Carolina under the command of Lt. Col. Alexander Martin, a field officer, against a body of Tories under Thomas Fletchall and was out in what was then called the Snow Campaign…" [minor edits]

Although the 1st NC Regiment sees no action in 1775, they keep the homefront secure while Royal Governor Josiah Martin does his best to stir up Loyalist sentiments while securely aboard the HMS *Cruizer* offshore.

Since these troops are now on the Continental Line, the North Carolina Provincial Congress resolves to upgrade their uniforms from hunting shirts and splatterdashes. Each man is also given a haversack and ammunition cartouches. These accoutrements are to be paid by each man via monthly payroll deductions of ten shillings. It is Spring of 1776 before all North Carolina Continentals are dressed alike.

Appendix B includes a listing of all known Continental units that participated in each battle/skirmish of 1775.

Chapter Two – 1776

Key Events of 1776

- Patriots assemble for two more Provincial Congresses (April and November).
- Halifax Resolves issued April 12th.
- Battle of Moore's Creek Bridge (Feb. 27) totally subdues Loyalists in NC.
- British land forces along the Cape Fear, but are soon driven back to their ships.
- Gov. Josiah Martin still aboard the HMS *Cruizer* finally leaves in September.
- Seven more regiments are fielded for the NC Continental line.
- Three companies of Light Horse and one company of Artillery are established and fielded as Provincial troops.
- Declaration of Independence announced.
- British initiate a two-pronged attack by encouraging the Cherokee to aid them in the west and sends a large force to Charlestown, SC.
- NC Continentals and Militia respond by sending troops against the Cherokee and to Charlestown, SC; enemy defeated.
- Theater of war again goes to the North.

New Years Day brings an ominous start to 1776 for the North Carolina Continentals. Col. Robert Howe and half of the 2nd NC Regiment are in Norfolk, Virginia when Gov. Dunmore decides to bombard the town after the Patriots refuse to permit the re-provisioning of his ships offshore. Norfolk is literally destroyed by the Royal Navy bombardment and the subsequent Patriot looting and burning of the former Loyalist stronghold.

In a letter, dated January 2nd, Col. Robert Howe relates to the Virginia Convention:

"The cannonade of the town began around a quarter after three, yesterday, from upwards of one hundred pieces of cannon, and continued till near ten, at night, without intermission; it then abated a little, and continued till two, this morning. Under cover of their guns they landed, and set fire to the town in several places near the water, though our men strove to prevent them all in their power; but the houses near the water being chiefly wood, they took fire immediately, and the fire spread with amazing rapidity. It is now become general, and the whole town will, I doubt not, be consumed in a day or two. Expecting that the fire would throw us into confusion, they frequently landed; and were every time repulsed, I imagine with loss, but with what loss, I cannot tell; the burning of the town has made several avenues, which yesterday they had not, so that they may now fire with greater effect; the tide is now rising, and we expect at high water another cannonade."

In a follow-up letter, dated January 4th, Col. Howe reports that he has had no men killed during the actions on New Year's Day, but five or six are wounded. Nine-tenths of the town is destroyed, but the fire is now out.

Col. James Moore and half of the 1st NC Regiment remain vigilant of the ongoing dialogue between Royal Governor Josiah Martin, still offshore aboard the HMS *Cruizer*, and his Loyalist followers, chiefly in and around Cross Creek in Cumberland County. Col. Moore stations men along both sides of the lower Cape Fear River, fully expecting to witness many more Royal Navy sails entering the river any day now.

Although Gov. Josiah Martin does his best to transmit secret messages, many of his communiqués are intercepted and virtually all of his schemes are well known to the Patriots. Not only is he instigating Loyalists to gather up their arms and to challenge the pesky Patriots, he also convinces the British Army in the northern theater to consider sending a large force southward with the intent of retaking Wilmington and ultimately retaking the whole of North Carolina as a result.

As a result of Gov. Martin's massive letter campaign, British General William Howe instructs Maj. Gen. Henry Clinton to open a front in the American south. This plan reaches Gov. Martin on January 3rd. The prime target is Charlestown, South Carolina, and it is hoped that a show of force will rally the area's considerable Loyalist population to the British cause. Maj. Gen. Clinton's army is to arrive by sea from Boston and join a force being sent from England, in the waters off Cape Fear, North Carolina in January or early February. However, thanks to the unpredictable weather and dozens of trivial navigational problems, this fleet does not arrive until mid-March.

However, not aware of the dozens of trivial navigational problems, Gov. Martin decides it is time to implement his part of the plan. On January 10th he issues a proclamation declaring the royal standard to be raised in North Carolina and calls upon all Loyalists to assist in defeating the rebellion. He also authorizes Loyalist leaders of Anson, Bute, Chatham, Cumberland, Guilford, Mecklenburg, Rowan, and Surry counties to begin mustering their Militias and to seize Patriot arms and ammunition. He instructs them to march towards the small town of Brunswick near the mouth of the Cape Fear River and to be at a yet-to-be-announced location no later than February 15th, at which time the Royal Navy will have arrived.

Earlier, the Highland Scots of Cross Creek had assured Gov. Martin that they could assemble more than 3,000 men, but explained that they only had 1,000 stand of arms. By the time of Gov. Martin's proclamation their enthusiasm somewhat cools and the Highland Scots opine that they should wait at least until March 1st before assembling their men, unless the British fleet arrives earlier. Other Loyalists are in favor of no more delays and are ready to march at any time.

Gov. Martin commissions Donald McDonald a brigadier general of the Loyalist Militia, and Donald McLeod as second in command with the rank of lieutenant colonel. Meanwhile, in the backcountry Loyalist leaders are finding it difficult to organize. Only with the news that Cross Creek is preparing to march do they cautiously make their way towards their associates. Many enlist because they have only recently been forced to renew their oaths of allegiance to the crown.

As the backcountry Loyalists skulk away from their homes, the wary Patriots instantly realize that something is abrew. News spreads as if they all have high-speed internet. Captain William Dent of Guilford County hastily organizes his merry band of Patriots and they soon confront a band of Loyalists from Surry County making their way through his territory. A skirmish flares and Captain Dent is killed. The Guilford County Loyalists resolutely push onwards with their Surry County brethren, unsure if their ultimate goal is achievable, especially since seven of their leaders have been arrested and taken to the Halifax jail.

Acutely aware of all the Loyalists making their way towards Cross Creek, on February 10th mobilization orders are issued to all Patriot Militia and Minutemen commanders. Col. James Moore and his 1st NC Regiment quietly take the lead along the Cape Fear River, and he strategically plans to intercept the Loyalists at Rockfish Creek, close to Cross Creek–and they arrive on February 15th. Orders go out to the surrounding judicial districts and counties, and within hours thousands of Patriots are preparing themselves–just in case they are needed.

Also expecting Gov. Josiah Martin to take advantage of things, Col. William Purviance and his New Hanover County Regiment of Militia erect earthworks along the river bank in front of Wilmington to aid in the defense against a potential river assault by the HMS *Cruizer*. Small artillery is mounted on parapets along the earthworks and fire rafts are constructed and positioned along both banks of the Cape Fear River. Maj. Quince brings 50-60 men of the Brunswick County Regiment to help reinforce Col. Purviance. Finally, Col. Purviance throws a heavy boom across the Cape Fear River just above his hometown. No provisions are going up or downriver now.

Time is quickly running out for Brig. Gen. Donald McDonald and his growing Loyalist army. The British Navy is expected any day now. Worse, the Patriots are visibly encircling Cross Creek as more Militia and provincial troops arrive each hour.

Most historians paint a fairly simple picture that Col. Richard Caswell and his New Bern District Minutemen come to the rescue and almost single-handedly stop the bad Loyalists. As with all fairy tales, things are a little more complex.

It is true that Col. Richard Caswell manages to quickly assemble a very large number of men from his district and the surrounding counties, and he quickly marches them in the proper direction. But, that is about it. He has no viable plan and he does not know the local terrain well enough to select a good location at which to face his opponent.

As already mentioned, Col. James Moore stops at Rockfish Creek, just south of Cross Creek along the Cape Fear River, with a growing entourage that peaks at roughly 1,100 men. Since Col. Moore believes his army to be outnumbered, he digs in and prepares for a strong defensive approach. On February 18th, Loyalist Brig. Gen. Donald McDonald decides to make his move, hoping to bluff his way through the Patriot blockade at Rockfish Creek. The next day, he parades his troops and makes preparations for battle, all the while hoping that his opponent will back down. To avoid combat, he sends a message under a flag of truce to Col. Moore, bearing a copy of Gov. Josiah Martin's proclamation and warning the Patriots that they are disobeying the king's standard–if they do not accept the crown by noon the next day then "the necessary steps for the support of royal authority" will be undertaken.

Col. Moore plays for more time. His reply is so vague it means essentially nothing. But, he goes on to say that he must consult with all other Patriot officers in the vicinity and a final decision is promised by noon on February 20th. The stalling tactic works to a degree–the Anson County Loyalists decide to go back home and avoid this nonsense.

By then, news of Col. Richard Caswell's approaching army of 600 Patriots reaches Brig. Gen. McDonald's camp. Immediate action is required, but evasion is the ultimate goal. The Loyalists decide to fall back to Cross Creek, ford the Cape Fear River at Campbellton, and follow the river along that bank down to the coast–all before the Patriots can catch them. They are to march the next day, on February 21st.

Interestingly, Col. James Moore and his growing army, with all of its intelligence gathering abilities, do not realize what is happening. Expecting an attack at dawn the next day, he does not learn of Brig. Gen. McDonald's departure until the following day. He immediately sends out expresses to the various other commanders spread out across the region, and one express directs Col. Richard Caswell to go to Corbett's Ferry on the Black River. Others are ordered to destroy all bridges between Cross Creek and Wilmington. Col. Moore then promptly marches his men to Elizabeth Town fully expecting to intercept the Loyalists at that location.

Brig. Gen. Donald McDonald and his Loyalist army reach the Black River on February 23rd and he is soon informed that his enemy is four miles ahead at Corbett's Ferry. He quickly calls for battle formation. Then he dispatches a small group forward to distract Col. Caswell's Patriots long enough for them to repair a nearby bridge and once again avoid a fight. Not only do they succeed in avoiding Col. Richard Caswell, they also capture two wagons and twenty-one bullocks destined for the Patriots ahead. By eight p.m. on Monday, February 26th, the Loyalists cross the river and are once again marching towards the sea to link up with Royal Governor Josiah Martin.

In the meantime, as Col. John Alexander Lillington and his Wilmington District Minutemen are marching northward, they come upon Moore's Creek Bridge; Lillington instantly realizes that this will be the perfect spot to intercept Brig. Gen. McDonald's Loyalists. That is, if they are only slightly diverted from the most-traveled route.

Col. Richard Caswell soon realizes that he has been outmaneuvered by Brig. Gen. McDonald so he quickly reverses his army and begins looking for routes that will get him back ahead of his enemy. Col. James Moore also realizes that the only way his men will catch up to their enemy will be via small boats floating downriver about sixty miles from his location. He arrives at Dollison's Landing in the afternoon of February 26th and awaits for daylight to collect his horses and then to proceed.

Late that night, an express rider brings news that Col. Caswell has linked up with Col. Lillington at Moore's Creek Bridge, and their men have thrown up some decent earthworks and removed most of the planking from the bridge. Col. Lillington arrives first and fortifies a small knoll on the east bank of the small creek. Col. Caswell arrives with eight hundred men and takes command since he has the larger number of men. He then instructs that more earthworks shall be erected on the west bank of Moore's Creek, never explaining why these are important.

Before the sun sets, the Loyalists come almost within shouting distance of the Patriots' camp–actually they are about six miles back, and Brig. Gen. McDonald sends a messenger under a flag of truce urging the Patriots to lay down their arms with the usual "or else." Col. Richard Caswell immediately sends back his refusal, and the Loyalists immediately convene to decide their plan of attack–set for daybreak.

The approach actually begins at one a.m. that morning. Unfamiliar with the terrain, the Loyalists are soon lost and stumbling in the swamps. About an hour before daylight they spot the dying flames of Col. Caswell's west bank campfires. Three columns of Loyalists quietly enter Col. Caswell's camp–only to find that the Patriots have only created a "fake camp"–the Patriots have actually all slept on the east bank.

Loyalist Alexander McLean leads a patrol that stumbles upon the bridge just about the same time as the sun comes over the horizon. Lt. Col. Donald McLeod, followed by some swordsmen under Capt. Angus

Campbell, hurries forward, only to discover that the bridge is missing planks, and even worse the stringers have been greased with soap and tallow. McLeod and Campbell lead the Highland Scots on a foolish charge across the slippery bridge. As they reach the far side there is a fierce report of musket fire from the opposite side. Both Lt. Col. McLeod and Capt. Campbell fall mortally wounded. Other Loyalists are either thrown from the bridge or they jump of their own volition due to the massive amount of lead shot coming their way. Any subsequent Loyalists who actually manage to cross the slippery bridge are instantly shot down.

On the other side of the dark creek bank some Highlanders take cover and begin returning fire. Most, however, simply flee the scene. All nearby wagons are abandoned and their horses taken by the first Loyalist with a knife to cut the reins. The battle is over in less than thirty minutes. An examination of Lt. Col. Donald McLeod's body shows that he has been hit by nine musket balls and twenty-four swan shot. Col. James Moore and his men arrive several hours after the battle, and he concludes that approximately seventy Loyalist have lost their lives, while only one Patriot is killed in this crucial engagement–John Grady of Duplin County.

Patriot patrols are dispatched to round up as many prisoners as possible, and to collect any and all articles of any value thrown away by the Loyalists. Orders are sent to Lt. Col. James Martin, of the Guilford

County Regiment of Militia, to stop at Cross Creek, seize the town, and to intercept any Loyalists trying to get back home.

Brig. Gen. Donald McDonald is awakened in his tent, unaware of the disaster that has just occurred. The remaining officers immediately gather and it is decided to divide the remaining ammunition among the survivors and then to disband and to make their way home as best they can. Brig. Gen. McDonald remains in his tent and is soon captured and taken to Col. James Moore's camp where he tenders his sword. After his baggage is searched he is escorted to the Halifax, North Carolina jail.

Nearly 850 Loyalists are captured over the next few days, most simply paroled and allowed to return home. In addition to Brig. Gen. McDonald, there are about thirty other officers soon confined in the Halifax jail. Listed among the articles captured from the Loyalists are 350 gun and shot bags, almost 1,500 stand of firearms, two medicine chests, one valued at £300, thirteen wagons and their teams, and finally a chest containing £15,000 Sterling in gold coins.

Meanwhile, Royal Governor Josiah Martin learns that his army is marching to the coast to meet with him, so he orders the HMS *Cruizer* to slip upriver to aid the approaching Loyalists. When the HMS *Cruizer* gets close to the town of Wilmington with its recent defensive measures put in place, the captain of the warship quickly decides to back off and to attempt a bypass of the town through the channel on the west side of Grand Island. After a small skirmish that sends a landing party back to the ship, the HMS *Cruizer* drops anchor and heads back downstream, harassed by rifle fire all the way.

· When Gov. Josiah Martin learns of the debacle at Moore's Creek Bridge, he shrugs off the incident as only a "little check the Loyalists here have received." He clings to his position that returning North Carolina to the crown is as promising as ever.

Interestingly, most historians identify only a handful of North Carolina Patriot military units to have participated in the battle of Moore's Creek Bridge. Most agree that Col. Richard Caswell led the Patriots at this important event, while a handful of historians insist that Col. James Moore rightfully led the Patriot force. Some acknowledge that Col. John Alexander Lillington and the Wilmington District Minutemen were involved to some degree. And, some historians barely acknowledge that some Militia units arrived in time to participate in the brief encounter.

As described above, the battle of Moore's Creek Bridge lasts less than thirty minutes. The Loyalists attempted to cross a partially-destroyed bridge over a fairly small creek, and the surrounding terrain was quite swampy and heavily wooded. A normal conclusion would be that very few Patriots actually fired a shot on that fateful morning. Perhaps a hundred men crouching behind earthworks about forty to fifty yards east of the bridge fired their muskets and a small swivel gun with grape-shot. Perhaps a hundred more Patriots hotly pursued the fleeing Loyalists through the woods, and subsequently perhaps several hundred Patriots spent the next day or two chasing down remnants of the Loyalist army.

Yet, in reviewing thousands of pension applications and corroborating evidence such as Col. Richard Caswell's own list of the participants, a very different picture unfolds. Many more Patriots answered the call for men to come stop a growing Loyalist uprising–they all instinctively knew that this was important. Militia units arrived from as far west as Surry County and Tryon County, and from as far east as Northampton County. Minutemen from five of the six districts arrived–the Edenton District Minutemen were still on alert and monitoring what the Royal Governor of Virginia was doing just across the Dismal Swamp.

Most estimates conclude that the Patriots brought approximately 1,100 soliders to the battle of Moore's Creek Bridge. It turns out that Col. Richard Caswell's very large army included the following:

- New Bern District Minutemen – 11 Companies
- Wilmington District Minutemen – 5 Companies
- Halifax District Minutemen – 5 Companies
- Hillsborough District Minutemen – 7 Companies
- 1st Battalion of Salisbury District Minutemen – 1 known Company
- 2nd Battalion of Salisbury District Minutemen – 11 Companies
- New Bern District Militia – 21 Companies
- Wilmington District Militia – 26 Companies
- Halifax District Militia – 2 Companies
- Hillsborough District Militia – 10 Companies
- Salisbury District Militia – 25 Companies
- 1st NC Regiment of Continentals – 7 Companies
- 2nd NC Regiment of Continentals – 1 Company with Col. Richard Caswell, and 1 Company under Lt. Col. James Martin (Guilford County)

From this information, it becomes very clear that the Patriots brought many more men than the historical estimates of 1,100. Certainly each Minuteman and Militia company probably contained small numbers of men, but when you tally up the total number of companies–133–and use an average of 25 men per company, the total is now well over 3,300 Patriots gathered at and around Moore's Creek Bridge. It must be noted, however, that twelve of those 133 companies stopped at Cross Creek as ordered–Lt. Col. James Martin and the twelve companies of Militia from

Guilford County spent three or four days rounding up the incoming Loyalists after they had fled the battlefield. It is entirely probable that many more Militia companies were in similar circumstances–mostly involved in rounding up enemy combatants in the surrounding area.

The rest of the previously-untold story is that there were a significant number of Patriots anxiously marching towards Moore's Creek Bridge, but they simply did not make it in time. Eleven companies of the 2nd Rowan County Regiment of Militia under Lt. Col. Christopher Beekman marched via Camden, SC and reached Cross Creek when they learned of the Patriot victory. Fifty-five (55) other Minutemen and Militia companies were on their way when they learned that the battle was over. Some completed their trip and assisted in escorting prisoners to various jails across the state. Some learned of the Patriot victory and simply turned around and headed back home to be discharged from duty.

As one can surmise, the North Carolina Continentals only played a very minor role in the actual battle on February 27th, but Col. James Moore's earlier decision to set up a blocking position at Rockfish Creek and to stall Brig. Gen. Donald McDonald helped to gain valuable time for the Patriot Militias to arrive in time to guarantee victory. Although Col. Moore did make it to the battlefield a few hours after the battle, most historians fail to note that some of his men had already arrived the night before. Captain Alfred Moore was stationed at Fort Johnston in Brunswick County, keeping an eye on Royal Governor Josiah Martin aboard the HMS *Cruizer*, when he was ordered to join Col. James Moore at Rockfish Creek. His company was one of seven Continental units that joined Col. Richard Caswell on the night of February 26th. Two or three Continental companies came down in small boats from Rockfish Creek.

Among the thousands of federal pension applications less than twenty men admit to being a Continental soldier at the battle of Moore's Creek Bridge in 1776. This includes two men who admit to marching towards the battle but arriving too late.

In his 1832 pension application, William Wood (S7971) asserts:

> "I enlisted in the county of Orange, state of North Carolina in December 1775 for 12 months under Captain Alfred Moore in the First Regiment of Continentals......was marched to Cross Creek, Cumberland County North Carolina, from thence to Fort Johnston...until we were ordered to march up the country to Cross Creek against the Tories–where we were stationed for some time in Rockfish near Cross Creek, where we threw up some breast work–from thence to Negro Head Point–and from thence to Moore's Creek Bridge where we joined Colonel Caswell and had a battle with the Tories under the command of Tory leaders Donald McDonald & Hector O'Neill and where Captain Donald

McLeod was killed and the Tories defeated–in this battle I served as a Sergeant Major. After the battle I was marched back to Fort Johnston where I continued until the term of 12 months for which I enlisted expired." [minor edits]

Appendix B provides a complete listing of Continental units that participated in all thirty-seven battles/skirmishes, including this one.

The repercussions of this Patriot victory are soon felt all over the thirteen colonies. In the northern colonies, it is exaggerated to unbelievable levels. But, this is one of the first absolute decisions won entirely by American arms. Lost to most historians, however, is the simple fact that this critical engagement included absolutely no British soldiers–it was truly a civil war between two segments of North Carolina's existing populace, almost all "citizen soldiers."

Perhaps the greatest outcome of this Patriot victory is that it completely silences the state's Loyalists for several long years. This fact alone leads to several productive years all across the state. There is a downside as well. This victory over-inflates the perceived capabilities of the North Carolina Militia such that the state consistently falls short of its quota of men for the Continental Line, also for several long years. Everyone is of the opinion that "our Militia whooped 'em once and we can do it again."

Capt. Francis Parry of the HMS *Cruizer* soon tires of listening to Royal Governor Josiah Martin's rants about the loss at Moore's Creek Bridge, so he decides to use his time wisely and exercise his men and their cannons whenever opportunities present themselves. Anchored only 200 yards offshore, he orders his men to fire upon anyone they see in and around Fort Johnston. On March 10th, Capt. Parry even goes so far as to put a landing party ashore to attack the Patriots that are ever present–but, they are quickly sent back to their ship by Capt. Alfred Moore and his company of the 1st NC Regiment along with a handful of men from the Brunswick County Regiment of Militia.

On March 12th, Major General Henry Clinton finally arrives at the entrance to the Cape Fear River and quickly learns the sad news from Royal Governor Josiah Martin. There is not going to be a linkup with thousands of Loyalists as planned. Five weeks later, on May 31st, Commodore Peter Parker's fleet straggles in from Great Britain after having been widely dispersed by storms during its long Atlantic crossing.

While he is waiting for Cdr. Parker, Maj. Gen. Henry Clinton decides at first not to put his men ashore; he considers it too dangerous. However, not knowing how long he will have to wait for Cdr. Parker, he soon realizes that his men need to get off the troopships, if only to stretch their legs for a short while. Acutely aware that his men will only be targets on the mainland, he puts them ashore on Bald Head Island and Battery Island (between Bald Head Island and the mainland). As the days extend into weeks, with no word from Cdr. Parker's fleet, he drills his men in street fighting–Clinton has already decided that Charlestown will be his next target.

Meanwhile, Col. James Moore learns of the British fleet anchored at the entrance to the Cape Fear River and he assembles 449 men from his 1st NC Regiment, 120 men from the 2nd NC Regiment, and 1,278 Militia from the surrounding area, for a total of 1,847 men to face an unknown number of British regulars aboard an unknown number of troopships (the numbers are learned later). He has his men to erect two artillery batteries armed with 6-pounders and 9-pounders, then has them to sink hulks in the Cape Fear River to block the channel below Wilmington.

On April 6th, the British captures one Patriot officer with five men near Brunswick Town. The Royal Navy cruises the general area and fires salvos at anyone who exposes themselves on the shore. During this time, they also pick up a few survivors and Loyalist refugees of the battle of Moore's Creek Bridge.

In his 1834 pension application, Isham Simmons (W8725) asserts:

"That he entered the service of the Unites States as a private volunteer Militia man [no, he was in the 1st NC Regiment, and is even on official rolls] from the county of Guilford, North Carolina, under the command of Captain Henry Dixon, the number of the regiment not recollected, but was commanded by Lt. Col. Francis Nash... We were marched down near Wilmington on the Cape Fear River where we continued until the spring of the year 1777 [no, it was 1776], they rendezvoused at Captain Dixon's own house... and was marched down the Cape Fear River where we learned the Tories were embodied near Moore's [Creek] Bridge; we were marched towards them but before we reached the said bridge, General [no, Col. Richard] Caswell defeated them. Thence we were marched to Wilmington, NC. Thence to Charlestown thence to Brunswick, where we had an engagement with the British and was defeated by them after firing three or four rounds we retreated to Fort Johnston..." [minor edits]

Maj. Gen. Henry Clinton issues a proclamation urging the citizens to return to the king. He promises to pardon all those who will come in and re-affirm their allegiance–except for Robert Howe and Cornelius Harnett, two ardent Patriots from Brunswick County and New Hanover County. Howe and Harnett are named as outlaws by the British ministry since they had organized the first Militia used against the king. Howe is now a brigadier general on the Continental Line, and Harnett is already the president of the transitional state government.

On May 1st, Maj. Gen. Henry Clinton orders Fort Johnston to be demolished because Patriot riflemen have used its remains to hide among while firing upon the nearby British fleet for days. This action does not stop the sniping. The Royal Navy moves 200 yards from shore, but they are still fired upon by the marksmen. Five shots hit the armed transport *Sovereign*. Some of the shots fly over the *Sovereign* and hit men on the transport *Glasgow Packet* behind her, killing two men and wounding two. The HMS *Cruizer* and the *Sovereign* fire back with their artillery and drive the snipers away. No known pensioners mention these events.

The British ships continue to move and then anchor 400 yards from the shore, however, the sniping resumes. There are "between fifty and sixty of the Rebels well armed, and draped in caps and hunting frocks." They do not cause much damage due to the increased distance. The schooner *St. Lawrence* fires 4-pounders and swivel guns at the riflemen on shore, also with no effect.

On May 2nd, Maj. Gen. Clinton lands ten companies near Fort Johnston to try to eliminate the snipers, but they only find tracks from the Patriots' horses. Clinton's men search for four miles inland and find no one. On the morning of May 3rd, the Patriot snipers return. Again, the HMS *Cruizer* fires back with her guns, and the Patriots are silenced once again. Realizing that the British are not going away anytime soon, Capt. Alfred Moore, of the 1st NC Regiment, leaves Fort Johnston for good.

With the British fleet anchored offshore for two months awaiting others coming from Great Britain, both sides become quite anxious with the stalemate. By now, Maj. Gen. Clinton has men stationed at the remnants of Fort Johnston, as well as on Battery Island and Bald Head Island. He decides to break the monotony and personally leads a night raid on the bridge at Orton Mill. Early on May 11th, a Sunday morning, the British row upstream for fifteen miles with muffled oars. At Brig. Gen. Robert Howe's home, Kendal Plantation, they pull onshore. Maj. Gen. Clinton wants to destroy the home of the man who had organized the first North Carolina Patriot Militia units the year before.

Upon landing the British make so much noise that the Patriot sentries hear them and kill one British soldier, Private George McIntosh, of the 44th Regiment of Foot. The sentries are also able to collect their horses and throw open the fences holding the cattle to keep the British from stealing them. Maj. Gen. Clinton orders his men to fix bayonets and approach the house. His men do not find any soldiers, but they treat the women of the house quite roughly. One is shot through the hip, another stabbed with a bayonet and a third was butt-stroked with a musket. So brutal is the treatment that Maj. Gen. Clinton later provides them with financial reimbursement.

During this raid, the British have several men wounded by the Patriots hiding in the surrounding darkness, and one British sergeant is taken prisoner. After searching the house, the British march on to Orton Mill, where Maj. William Davis commands a detachment of ninety men of the 1st NC Regiment. Maj. Davis hears them approaching and withdraws with his baggage and two swivel guns. The British burn the mill and then plunder homes along the way back to their boats. All they obtain from this raid are three horses and three cows. No known pensioners later mention these events.

On May 16th, American snipers along the Cape Fear River fire upon the British sloop *Falcon*. The *Falcon* returns fire with no effect. The next day, Maj. Gen. Charles, Lord Cornwallis goes on a mission "in the most secret manner imaginable and left in the dead of the night." Nine hundred British Regulars row up the Cape Fear River with the intent to burn Brunswick Town, the base camp of many local Patriots. Lord Cornwallis surprises the sentinels on the outskirts of town and takes possession of Brunswick Town with only one man killed. Unfortunately for the British, the town has been abandoned for some time and only a small garrison is stationed here. All that Lord Cornwallis can obtain for his efforts are twenty bullocks and six horses.

By mid-May of 1776, Maj. Gen. Henry Clinton moves all of his men to Fort Johnston from the outlying areas. The British later noted that they lived off rice and "cabbage trees." The "cabbage trees" are what the British soldiers call the palmetto trees along the Southern coast. At night, the British set fire to pine trees to illuminate their camps and to watch for Patriot snipers. On the night of May 20th, the Patriots send a fire raft down the Cape Fear River in hopes that it will burn the British transport *Glasgow Packet*. The British intercept this attempt and tow it to a marshy area where it burns out. On the night of May 22nd, some Patriots on horseback approach Fort Johnston. A company of British Light Infantry surprise them and drive them off with no harm to either side.

The next night there is a violent thunderstorm that Dr. Forster of the British hospital later described as:

> "a Thunder Storm by much the most dreadful one I ever saw in my Life, it terminated in a most violent storm of Rain and Wind, several Tents were thrown down and others blown some distance from the spot where they were pitched and many of the highest Trees shiver'd to threads by Lightning and others torn up by the Roots by the violence of the Wind, it was a most shocking night to pass in Camp."

During this storm, three Patriots creep up to the camp and fire upon a British sentry. The sentinel, Private James Wilcox, is wounded in the hand but he fires back and kills one of the attackers. Private Wilcox sounds the alarm and the other two Patriots flee, leaving their fallen comrade where he fell.

Snipers continue to fire upon the British ships in the Cape Fear River throughout the month of May. On May 24th and May 27th, the schooner *St. Lawrence* returns fire, to no avail. Maj. Gen. Henry Clinton wavers on whether to invade the Chesapeake region or to move on down to Charlestown, South Carolina. On May 31st, Commodore Peter Parker's fleet finally arrives at the entrance to the Cape Fear River. Maj. Gen. Henry Clinton immediately orders all troops to their ships and for all ships to head south–Clinton has had enough of the pesky North Carolinians. It is time to take South Carolina, a much easier target.

While Maj. Gen. Clinton is keeping the Cape Fear region busy, the remainder of North Carolina moves forward on other pressing matters. On April 4th, the Fourth Provincial Congress assembles at Halifax and Samuel Johnston is elected the second president of North Carolina, succeeding Cornelius Harnett. The important question of Independence is moved, discussed, and unanimously approved by this Congress. On Monday, April 8th, Cornelius Harnett, Thomas Burke, Allen Jones, Thomas Jones, Abner Nash, John Kinchen, and Thomas Person are appointed a committee to take into consideration the usurpations and violences committed by the King and Parliament in Britain, and on April 12th, Mr. Harnett submits their report, later to be named as the "Halifax Resolves."

As can be seen on the current North Carolina state flag, the top date is for the Mecklenburg Resolves of May 20, 1775, and the lower date is for the Halifax Resolves of April 12, 1776. One must recall that the national declaration for independence is almost three months later.

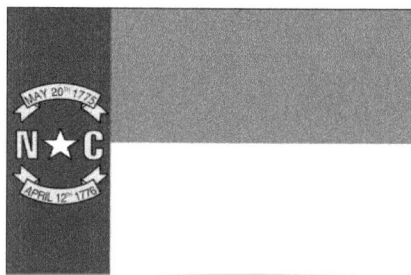

It is during this session that the North Carolina Provincial Congress decides to abolish the Minutemen of the six districts and to replace them with brigades of Militia at the district level to superintend the Militia at the county level. Each district's brigade is now assigned a brigadier general of Militia, commissioned by the Provincial Congress. This

Congress also authorizes the establishment of four more regiments of Continentals to be placed upon the line as soon as practical. By April 16th, they commission all officers of the newly-created 3rd NC Regiment, 4th NC Regiment, 5th NC Regiment, and 6th NC Regiment, plus three companies of Light Horse as Provincial Troops.

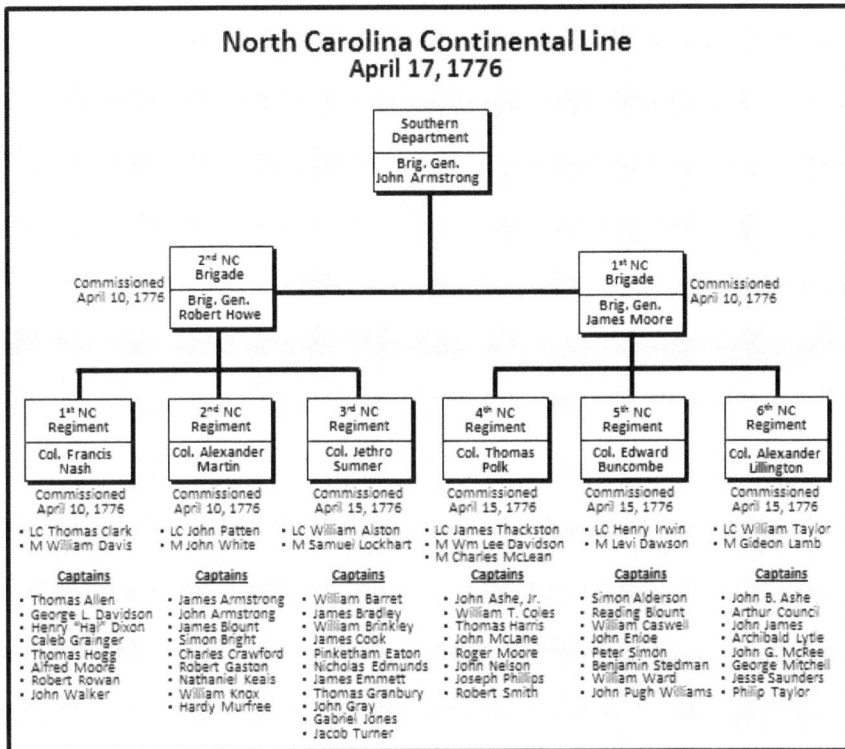

North Carolina Continental Line
April 17, 1776

Southern Department — Brig. Gen. John Armstrong

2nd NC Brigade — Brig. Gen. Robert Howe (Commissioned April 10, 1776)

1st NC Brigade — Brig. Gen. James Moore (Commissioned April 10, 1776)

1st NC Regiment	2nd NC Regiment	3rd NC Regiment	4th NC Regiment	5th NC Regiment	6th NC Regiment
Col. Francis Nash	Col. Alexander Martin	Col. Jethro Sumner	Col. Thomas Polk	Col. Edward Buncombe	Col. Alexander Lillington
Commissioned April 10, 1776	Commissioned April 10, 1776	Commissioned April 15, 1776	Commissioned April 15, 1776	Commissioned April 15, 1776	Commissioned April 15, 1776
• LC Thomas Clark • M William Davis	• LC John Patten • M John White	• LC William Alston • M Samuel Lockhart	• LC James Thackston • M Wm Lee Davidson • M Charles McLean	• LC Henry Irwin • M Levi Dawson	• LC William Taylor • M Gideon Lamb

Captains

• Thomas Allen • George L. Davidson • Henry "Hal" Dixon • Caleb Grainger • Thomas Hogg • Alfred Moore • Robert Rowan • John Walker	• James Armstrong • John Armstrong • James Blount • Simon Bright • Charles Crawford • Robert Gaston • Nathaniel Keais • William Knox • Hardy Murfree	• William Barret • James Bradley • William Brinkley • James Cook • Pinketham Eaton • Nicholas Edmunds • James Emmett • Thomas Granbury • John Gray • Gabriel Jones • Jacob Turner	• John Ashe, Jr. • William T. Coles • Thomas Harris • John McLane • Roger Moore • John Nelson • Joseph Phillips • Robert Smith	• Simon Alderson • Reading Blount • William Caswell • John Enloe • Peter Simon • Benjamin Stedman • William Ward • John Pugh Williams	• John B. Ashe • Arthur Council • John James • Archibald Lytle • John G. McRee • George Mitchell • Jesse Saunders • Philip Taylor

Also during April of 1776, the Continental Congress names Brig. Gen. John Armstrong of Virginia as the first leader of the Southern Department. His tenure is so short lived that he has no influence on military affairs within North Carolina. On April 10th, the Continental Congress promotes both James Moore and Robert Howe as brigadier generals for the state of North Carolina. The Continental Congress only asks for two more regiments from North Carolina, but the Provincials are so ardent that they authorize four more regiments instead. The rank and file are now required to enlist for 2-1/2 years.

3rd NC Regiment as of April 17, 1776			
Rank	**Name**	**Commission**	**County From**
Colonel	Jethro Sumner	4/15/1776	Bute (Warren)
Lt. Colonel	William Alston	4/15/1776	Halifax
Major	Samuel Lockhart	4/15/1776	Halifax
Captain	William Barret	4/17/1776	
Captain	James Bradley	4/16/1776	Halifax
Captain	William Brinkley	4/17/1776	Halifax
Captain	James Cook	4/17/1776	
Captain	Pinketham Eaton	4/17/1776	Halifax
Captain	Nicholas Edmunds	4/16/1776	
Captain	James Emmett	4/17/1776	Cumberland
Captain	Thomas Granbury	4/17/1776	
Captain	John Gray	4/17/1776	Edgecombe
Captain	Gabriel Jones	4/16/1776	
Captain	Jacob Turner	4/17/1776	Bertie

4th NC Regiment as of April 17, 1776			
Rank	**Name**	**Commission**	**County From**
Colonel	Thomas Polk	4/15/1776	Mecklenburg
Lt. Colonel	James Thackston	4/15/1776	Orange
Major	William Lee Davidson	4/15/1776	Mecklenburg
Major	Charles McLean	4/16/1776	Tryon (Lincoln)
Captain	John Ashe, Jr.	4/17/1776	New Hanover
Captain	William Temple Coles	4/17/1776	Rowan
Captain	Thomas Harris	4/17/1776	Anson
Captain	John McLane	4/17/1776	
Captain	Roger Moore	4/17/1776	Brunswick
Captain	John Nelson	4/17/1776	Guilford
Captain	Joseph Phillips	4/17/1776	Surry
Captain	Robert Smith	4/17/1776	Tryon (Lincoln)

5th NC Regiment as of April 17, 1776			
Rank	**Name**	**Commission**	**County From**
Colonel	Edward Buncombe	4/15/1776	Tyrrell
Lt. Colonel	Henry Irwin	4/15/1776	Edgecombe
Major	Levi Dawson	4/15/1776	Craven
Captain	Simon Alderson	4/16/1776	
Captain	Reading Blount	4/17/1776	Craven
Captain	William Caswell	4/17/1776	Dobbs
Captain	John Enloe	4/17/1776	Pitt
Captain	Peter Simon	4/17/1776	
Captain	Benjamin Stedman	4/16/1776	Hyde
Captain	William Ward	4/17/1776	
Captain	John Pugh Wiliams	4/17/1776	Bertie

6th NC Regiment as of April 17, 1776			
Rank	**Name**	**Commission**	**County From**
Colonel	John Alexander Lillington	4/15/1776	New Hanover
Lt. Colonel	William Taylor	4/15/1776	
Major	Gideon Lamb	4/15/1776	Pasquotank/Camden
Captain	John Baptiste Ashe	4/17/1776	
Captain	Arthur Council	4/17/1776	Cumberland
Captain	John James	4/17/1776	Duplin
Captain	Archibald Lytle	4/17/1776	Orange
Captain	John Griffith McRee	4/16/1776	Bladen
Captain	George Mitchell	4/17/1776	Onslow
Captain	Jesse Saunders	4/17/1776	Orange
Captain	Philip Taylor	4/17/1776	Granville

The rules and regulations for recruiting officers are worth noting here:

1. They are to enlist none but able-bodied men, fit for service, capable of marching well, and such whose attachment to American liberties they have no cause to suspect; young, hearty, robust men, whose birth, family connections, and property bind them to the interests of their country, and well-practiced in the use of firearms, are much preferred.
2. They are as much as possible to have regard to moral character, particularly sobriety.
3. They are not to enlist any imported servant, nor, without the leave of his master, any apprentice.
4. They are to be careful in enlisting such men for Sergeants and Corporals whose ability and diligence make them fit for that appointment; they are also to appoint a Fifer and Drummer.
5. They are to exert themselves to complete their companies, and punctually to report to their Colonels.
6. That the soldiers be allowed 1 shilling per day for their subsistence.
7. They are to take notice that the Colonels of their battalion (same as regiment), or some field officer appointed by him, are to inspect their men, and to reject such as are not fit for service.
8. They are to furnish the subaltern officers of their companies with a copy of their instructions.
9. They are to enlist their men according to the following form, viz:
   "I have this day voluntarily enlisted myself as a soldier in the American Continental Army, and do bind myself to conform in all instances to such rules and regulations as are or shall be established for the government of the said army; as witness my hand," etc.
10. That they enlist no soldier under 5 feet 4 inches high, able-bodied men, healthy, strong made, and well-limbed, not deaf, or subject to fits, or ulcers on their legs, or ruptures.
11. That they pay to each soldier they shall enlist 40 shilling bounty, and £3 advance; and that every recruit take the following oath:

"I _____, do swear that I will be faithful and true to the United Colonies; that I will serve the same, to the utmost of my power, in defense of the just rights of America, against all enemies whatsoever; that I will to the utmost of my abilities, obey the lawful commands of my superior officers, agreeable to the Ordinances of Congress, and the Articles of War to which I have subscribed and lay down my arms peaceably, when required so to do by the Continental Congress. So help me God."

Since money is so scarce, the Provincial Congress authorizes Lt. Col. Alexander Martin to borrow £2,000 to make partial payment for wages owed to the men of the 2nd NC Regiment, which is secured by a draft on the Continental Congress. The Continental Congress is quick to add the four new regiments on the regular establishment.

On May 7th, Nicholas Long, the former Colonel/Commandant of the Halifax District Minutemen, is commissioned as the Deputy Quarter Master General (DQMG) for the Southern Department, with the rank of colonel. Camp Quankey is established as a Continental Army depot very near the town of Halifax, NC. Disappointingly, the Continental Congress refuses North Carolina's offer of the three companies of Light Dragoons, so these remain as Provincial Troops for the time being.

As Maj. Gen. Henry Clinton and his army lay off the coast, rumors of his true intentions spread like wildfire among members of the Provincial Congress, the Continental Congress, and even within the military. One suggests that the British plan to land troops at Little River, thirty miles south of Cape Fear, and penetrate the province by way of Lake Waccamaw to make a junction with the Highland Scots, who are by no means dejected by their defeat at Moore's Creek Bridge. From Brig. Gen. Robert Howe comes the rumor, gained from recent British deserters, that Maj. Gen. Clinton is only awaiting a shipment of bombs before assaulting Wilmington and razing it to the ground.

Most of this is posturing by those who can–simply to encourage the Continental Congress to replace Brig. Gen. John Armstrong with a much stronger leader for the Southern Department–Maj. Gen. Charles Lee. The government of South Carolina also wants Maj. Gen. Charles Lee, whom they feel "was equal to a reinforcement of 1,000 men." Apparently, Gen. Lee is also maneuvering his political contacts within the state of Virginia to acquire the job that both North and South Carolina want him to have, and he is bending the ear of Brig. Gen. Robert Howe, who is in turn transmitting his desires to the North Carolina Provincial Congress.

All of this comes to a head very quickly, and Maj. Gen. Charles Lee marches from Virginia to Halifax, NC by May 20th. News arrives that there are now between sixty and seventy British ships at Cape Fear. After a lengthy stay at Halifax waiting for the Virginia Riflemen, Maj. Gen. Lee resumes his march south, first to Tarborough, then to New Bern, and he arrives in Wilmington on June 1st–the same day that most of the British fleet is sighted just off Charlestown harbor.

Maj. Gen. Charles Lee quickly dispatches a considerable army of about 700 men to go on ahead of him–the 8th Virginia Regiment and detachments from the first four North Carolina Continental regiments. Arms are so scarce that before the new North Carolina units begin their march, muskets have to be taken from the Militia. There is simply an acute shortage of any kind of weapon, from guns to swords.

As his own retinue nears Charlestown and express riders bring the news that an estimated fifty-one (51) British ships are anchored on the far side of the Charlestown Bar, Maj. Gen. Charles Lee finally sends an express to the Continental Congress for them to quickly send as many regiments as possible from Maryland and Pennsylvania.

On June 8th, after most of the British fleet cross the bar and anchor in Five Fathom Hole, Maj. Gen. Henry Clinton sends a proclamation to the Patriots on shore to lay down their arms or face military action, which South Carolina President John Rutledge immediately rejects. With a new fort on Sullivan's Island only half complete, Sir Peter Parker, now an admiral, is confident that his warships can blast the fort into pieces.

The square-shaped Fort Sullivan (renamed Fort Moultrie) is made up of only the completed seaward walls, with walls made from palmetto logs 16-feet wide and filled with sand, which rise ten feet above the wooden platforms for the artillery. A hastily-erected palisade of thick planks helps to guard the powder magazine and the unfinished northern walls. An assortment of thirty-one (31) hard-to-get cannons, ranging from 9- to 12-pounders, as well as a few English 18-pounders and French 26-pounders, line the front and rear walls. The British finally attack Fort Moultrie on June 28, 1776–in concert with a naval attack.

The British also attempt an assault from Long Island by small boats against South Carolina Col. William Thomson's Rangers on the northern end of Sullivan's Island. The attack is covered by an armed British schooner. The boats are turned back when the Americans fire at point-blank range, causing very heavy casualties in the British assault party. With this rebuff, Maj. Gen. Henry Clinton calls off the attack and no other attempts are made. By 9:30 p.m., all firing ceases. At 11:30 p.m., the British ships withdraw to Five Fathom Hole. This is known as the Breach Inlet Naval Battle.

North Carolina Continental Line
June 28, 1776

Southern Department
Maj. Gen. Charles Lee — HQ at Charlestown, SC

2nd NC Brigade — Brig. Gen. Robert Howe (At Charlestown, SC)

1st NC Brigade — Brig. Gen. James Moore (At Wilmington, NC)

1st NC Regiment	2nd NC Regiment	3rd NC Regiment	4th NC Regiment	5th NC Regiment	6th NC Regiment
Col. Francis Nash	Col. Alexander Martin	Col. Jethro Sumner	Col. Thomas Polk	Col. Edward Buncombe	Col. Alexander Lillington
• LC Thomas Clark • M William Davis • M Wm B. Williams	• LC John Patten • M John White	• LC William Alston • M Samuel Lockhart	• LC James Thackston • M Wm Lee Davidson • M Charles McLean	• LC Henry Irwin • M Levi Dawson	• LC William Taylor • M Gideon Lamb
Captains	**Captains**	**Captains**	**Captains**	**Captains**	**Captains**
• Thomas Allen • George L. Davidson • Henry "Hal" Dixon • Caleb Grainger • Thomas Hogg • Alfred Moore • Robert Rowan • John Walker	• James Armstrong • John Armstrong • Charles Crawford • William Fenner • James Gardner • Robert Gaston • James Gee • John Heritage • Nathaniel Keais • William Knox • Hardy Murfree • Joseph Tate	• William Barret • James Bradley • William Brinkley • James Cook • Pinketham Eaton • Nicholas Edmunds • James Emmett • Thomas Granbury • John Gray • Daniel Jones • Gabriel Jones • Jacob Turner.	• John Ashe, Jr. • William T. Coles • Thomas Harris • John McLane • Roger Moore • John Nelson • Joseph Phillips • Robert Smith	• Simon Alderson • Reading Blount • William Caswell • John Enloe • Peter Simon • Benjamin Stedman • William Ward • John P. Williams	• John B. Ashe • Arthur Council • William Glover • John James • Archibald Lytle • John G. McRee • George Mitchell • Philip Taylor

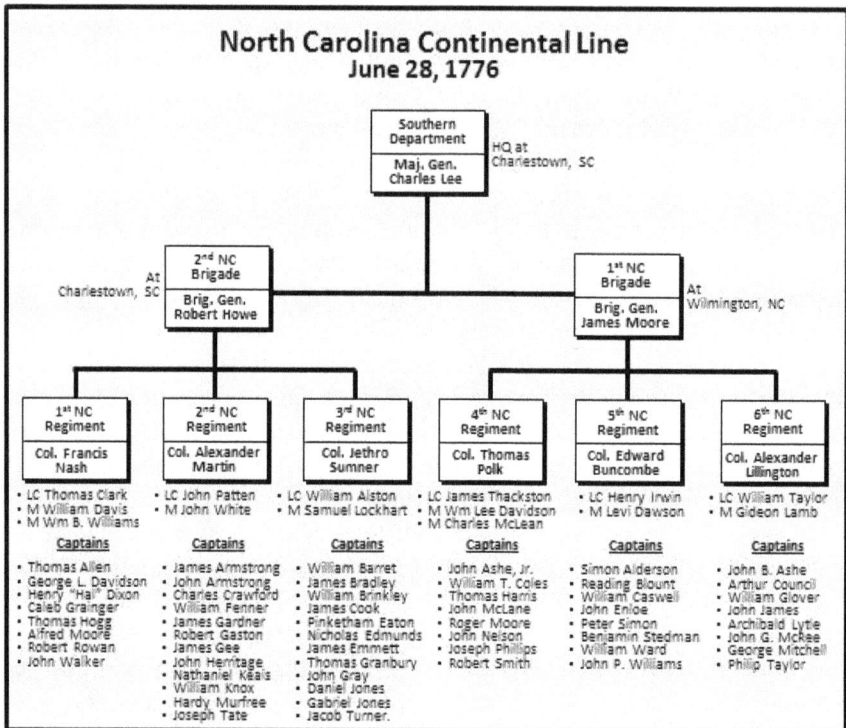

With their efforts repulsed at both ends of the island, the British halt their attack. Still, they have a major problem. Of the three ships which have run aground, the HMS *Acteon* is still unable to extract herself, despite the best efforts of her crew. The captain requests Admiral Parker's permission to abandon ship and to destroy her to keep the ship from falling into the hands of the Patriots. Approval is received and the captain sets ablaze one of the British Navy's finest ships, commissioned less than a year before. An American salvage party goes out to the *Bristol* after it is abandoned and is able to gather the ship's bell, the colors, and various stores before the spreading fire endangers their safety. Half an hour later, the ship's magazine explodes.

Brig. Gen. Robert Howe led Charlestown's defenses, and the army under his leadership included four South Carolina regiments, the 2nd NC Regiment led by Col. Alexander Martin, the 3rd NC Regiment led by Col. Jethro Sumner, and numerous South Carolina Militia units. The defenses at Haddrell's Point were led by Brig. Gen. John Armstrong (VA) and included detachments of both the 1st NC Regiment led by Col. Francis Nash with two companies, and one company of the 2nd NC Regiment led by Capt. John Armstrong. With South Carolina Col. William Thomson at the Breach Inlet Naval Battle was a detachment of the 1st NC Regiment led by Lt. Col. Thomas Clark with five companies.

Here is the model for future triumph. It is here, in a day-long battle, that a gallant and spirited band defeats, in desparate conflict, an overwhelming naval and land force and having utterly whipped them, drive them from their shores. For the new nation pride in the victory is unbounded.

For the British, the results are humiliating. A superb naval flotilla and army have been thwarted, in a large degree, due to the imprudent mistakes made by veteran officers. Poor planning and the refusal of the army and navy to cooperate sealed the doom of the British. The British lost all element of surprise and failed to take advantage of American weaknesses in early June of 1776. There were no naval officers in the fleet familiar with the Charlestown harbor. Instead, Admiral Parker relied on impressed pilots to guide the ships to their crucial anchorage.

In his 1818 pension application, Jeremiah McCartney (S42947) asserts:

"I enlisted at Wilmington in the state of North Carolina into the company commanded by Capt. Robert Smith in the regiment of Col. Thomas Polk and Lt. Col. James Thackston in the North Carolina Line on or about the 8th day of May 1776 and continued in said corps until on or about the 1st day of September 1777, when I was discharged from service at Charlestown in South Carolina; that I was in the siege of Charlestown when attacked by Sir Peter Parker & Sir Henry Clinton..." [minor edits]

In his 1818 pension application, Joseph Brown (S39225) asserts:

"That he was a resident of Camden County, North Carolina & was about 15 or 16 years of age when he entered the army; and was put into Captain James Gee's company & marched first for Edenton, then to New Bern, then to Wilmington, then to Charlestown, South Carolina; & was there at the time of the battle of Sullivan's Island in the month of June 1776. He was marched back to Wilmington..." [minor edits]

In his 1832 pension application, James McBride (S4192) asserts:

"... Capt. George Davidson's Company, in which I served, being placed under the command of Col. Alexander Martin who marched us first to Fayetteville thence by water to Wilmington thence by Brunswick & Long Bay to Waccamaw River where we took shipping & sailed to Georgetown & thence by land to Charlestown where we lay until the attack on Sullivan's Island when we were sailed across the bay to Haddrell's Point & kept during the action by the firing of the ship *Acteon*. We were taken to the island and remained until the expiration of the term of our service, when we were sailed back to Charlestown and discharged. In Charlestown I saw Maj.

Charles Cotesworth Pinckney and on Sullivan's Island, Col. William Moultrie."
[minor edits]

The British do not attempt to renew the battle or try to take the fort again this year, and by mid-August, the fleet withdraws northward to help the main British army in the campaign against New York. As described below, within two weeks after the battle, the Charlestonians learn of the signing of the Declaration of Independence in Philadelphia, which is a sign of their capacity to oppose British arms.

The Patriot victory on June 28th stood to the men who were there as their own physical Declaration, which the upsetting of the British plans in the southern colonies helped win uncommitted Americans to the struggle for independence from Great Britain. It also enabled the Southern colonies to support vital campaigns in the north. Most importantly, this victory at what would henceforth be known as the battle of "Fort Moultrie" helped keep Charlestown free from British occupation for over three more years.

Maj. Gen. Charles Lee does not spare his praise for the Patriots. He includes the North Carolina troops as "equally alert, zealous, and spirited." To General George Washington he reports that the North Carolina Line is made up of "admirable soldiers," while his report to the Continental Congress gives the South Carolina Rangers and the North Carolinians all the credit for repulsing the enemy.

The British fleet returns to their earlier anchorage across the Charlestown Bar, and there they remain for more than three weeks. Maj. Gen. Henry Clinton shifts his men from one barrier island to another, and some take it upon themselves to desert over to the Patriots. To a man, they assert "that the consequences of the action have been more decisive than we then thought."

After the fleet finally sets sail, the Patriots realize that they are now faced with two unpleasant options–go join the Northern Army, or take the fight to the British in the two Floridas that are threatening Georgia. Brig. Gen. Robert Howe is not enthusiastic about the latter. The objectives, he feels, "cannot be very important."

On August 12th, in the midst of preparations for going southward as ordered by Maj. Gen. Charles Lee, the electrifying news arrives that the Continental Congress issued the Declaration of Independence on July 4th. The plentiful military officers still within the town of Charlestown parade slowly down the streets "amidst loud acclamations of thousands who always huzza when a proclamation is read."

Brig. Gen. Robert Howe leads a contingent of mostly South Carolinians with a handful of North Carolina Continentals into Georgia– the goal is St. Augustine, Florida. The Florida Expedition (as it is called by everyone at that time) is a dismal failure almost from the start. Few have their hearts in it, and when they face minor obstacles these grow tremendously. There are many transportation breakdowns, an outbreak of Malaria, and zero cooperation from the Georgians, for whom this expedition is meant to help the most. The group soon returns to Charlestown with a sigh of relief. Howe has with him 81 men of the 1st NC Regiment, 75 men of the 2nd NC Regiment, and all but 37 men of the 3rd NC Regiment.

The only NC survivor of this expedition to actually submit a federal pension application with this expedition mentioned was Thomas Ragains of Orange County, and in his 1832 pension statement (W4502) he provides the following account:

"From Charlestown, there being a call for men to go to Saint Augustine in the Province of Florida, I entered Captain Henry "Hal" Dixon's company as a volunteer regular soldier, with the same individuals, and all the sergeants who had composed Captain Robert Rowan's company, Colonel White commanding the first regiment of North Carolina troops, taking command of us, marched us towards Saint Augustine. We went through Purrysburg, Savannah, and continued our march to Fort Barrington in Georgia; there we joined General McIntosh commanding the first regiment of Virginia troops with some others and he took command of the whole of us. We continued our march until we arrived in the Province of Florida and hearing the British had taken possession of Saint Augustine, we halted and marched back by Fort Barrington where all the troops but the North Carolina regiment, of whom I was one, under Colonel White, were left and we were marched to Sunbury where we lay some months. From thence we were marched to Wilmington, a short time before we arrived there my tour of two years for which I had entered expired, but I remained with the regiment until we arrived." [minor edits]

Before he leaves and heads northward, Maj. Gen. Charles Lee issues orders on September 8th for some men currently in North Carolina regiments to be transferred into South Carolina and Georgia regiments– both states are having extreme difficulty in recruiting fighting men for their units. A good number of men jump at the additional bounty money being offered and leave their assigned regiments long before their enlistments are up. In late October, the North Carolina Council of Safety is made aware of this scandalous situation and they immediately send orders to Brig. Gen. Robert Howe for him to reclaim these men and to return all North Carolina troops to home soil. Now the South Carolina Council wants its bounty money returned. Brig. Gen. Howe finally advises his civil government to simply resign themselves to this loss.

Earlier, when Maj. Gen. Henry Clinton and Admiral Peter Parker sailed for Charlestown on May 31st, they left behind a small garrison of about thirty soldiers on Bald Head Island at the mouth of the Cape Fear River. This garrison is protected by three British ships, and they name their small redoubt Fort George in honor of their king. Unfortunately, these thirty men only have twelve muskets among them. Soon, the three ships are joined by fifteen more, mostly empty troop ships that have discharged their men at Charlestown in early June.

Since the bulk of the British fleet have left, Brig. Gen. James Moore orders Col. Thomas Polk, of the 4th NC Regiment, to retake Fort Johnston on the mainland and to keep an eye on the small British garrison situated across the wide inlet. Col. Polk soon learns of the garrison's weaknesses and decides to put an end to their existence.

On the night of September 6th, Col. Thomas Polk sails with 150 of his men across the inlet and land on Bald Head Island. As they work their way through the woods, they are discovered. The Patriots capture five British sailors, but the alarm is sounded. The other twenty-five British sailors take refuge in the small Fort George and fire upon the North Carolinians, keeping them at a distance.

Soon, the nearby British ships hear the shots and send a relief force. The HMS *Falcon* fires her 6-pounders into the woods at the Patriots to give the relief force a chance to arrive. Col. Polk has one man killed and one man wounded, then decides to withdraw. As they leave, the NC Continentals burn a British cutter so that it cannot pursue them.

The HMS *Cruizer,* led by Capt. Francis Parry, quickly mounts four of her 3-pounders on board the sloop HMS *Defiance,* led by a Lt. Dickerson. Lt. Dickerson sails with five other boats around the island to block any escape by the Patriots. Lt. Dickerson discovers two of Col. Polk's boats at 1:00 a.m. at Buzzard's Bay near the mainland. The HMS *Defiance* and the HMS *Falcon,* led by Capt. John Linzee, fire into the woods at Buzzard's Bay, but the Patriots return fire with a 3-pounder, keeping the ships away. The British are unable to destroy the Patriots' boats and withdraw before the sun rises. Fifteen of the eighteen British ships finally sail away in early October, leaving three burned hulls no longer fit for service–one being the much-despised HMS *Cruizer*. Also sailing away is Royal Governor Josiah Martin, who goes to Long Island, New York and finally back to England. He will return, so stay tuned.

In his 1818 pension application, Joseph Curbow (S31637) asserts:

> "That he first enlisted in the United States army on the Continental establishment in the Revolutionary War for 18 months under Captain Thomas Harris of the 4th Regiment of the North Carolina troops, that James Fair was 1st Lieutenant, John Carruth the 2nd Lieutenant, and James Coots the Ensign, Colonel Thomas Polk was the first commander of the regiment and Lt. Col. James Thackston the next, in the last of March or the first of April 1776... That he served the United States in the battle of Bald Head Island below the mouth of the Cape Fear River, and was at Wilmington, New Bern, and in various scouting and guard parties..." [minor edits]

Meanwhile, the Continental Congress in Philadelphia resolves on September 3rd that two North Carolina regiments shall be sent to bolster General George Washington's army near New York. Two weeks later, this resolution is amended to permit the North Carolina Council of Safety to make the decision when their troops are ready for combat. The Council of Safety quickly determines that the units are not only far from complete in numbers, but are too "sickly and ill provided with Cloathing and by no means prepared to march to a Northern Climate."

On September 18th, the three North Carolina delegates to the Continental Congress–Joseph Hewes, William Hooper, and John Penn–pen a collaborative letter to the North Carolina Council of Safety advising them that the Continental Congress recently authorized the state of North Carolina to raise three more regiments for the Continental Line. These gentlemen also advise that these new regiments are to be filled quickly because it is quite evident that North Carolina "will no doubt be often called upon hereafter to aid the weakness of South Carolina and Georgia, and calling forth the Militia is so expensive and burdensome that it ought as much as possible to be avoided."

In October, the three Continental Congress delegates take it upon themselves to purchase rather than hire four wagons and teams to transport a large quantity of uniforms for the North Carolina Continental Line. The following items are transported on October 19th:

1. 320 Privates' Coats, Mixt Cloth, faced with Red.
2. 320 Privates' Coats, Drab, faced with Blue.
3. 264 Privates' Coats, Brown, faced with White.
4. 32 Sergeants' Coats, faced with White.
5. 16 Drums' & Fifes' Coats, faced with Brown.

6.   240 Privates' Coats, Drab, faced with Blue.
7.   32 Sergeants' Coats, Drab, faced with Blue.
8.   16 Drums' & Fifes' Coats, faced with Drab.
9.   312 Privates' Coats, Brown, faced with White.
10. 240 Pairs Drilling Breeches.
11. 280 Privates' Coats, Brown, faced with Red.
12. 296 Privates' Coats, Brown, faced with Red.
13. 266 Pairs Drilling Breeches.
14. 131 Privates' Coats, Drab, faced with Red.
15. 154 Privates' Coats, Brown, faced with Red.
16. 240 Privates' Coats, Mixt, faced with Red.
17. 21 Sergeants' Coats, Brown, faced with Red.
18. 5 Privates' Coats, Brown, faced with Red.
19. 500 Stout Oznaburgh Shirts.

The total cost is $1,664, but it is unclear just what that total covers–looks like only for the cost of the wagons and the pay for the drivers and their expenses. Needless to say, the North Carolina Continentals will soon have new clothing.

On October 19th, the Council of Safety meets at Halifax and resolves that Brig. Gen. James Moore is to enumerate the number of men under his command and provide this information to the Council. As of Monday, October 21st, Brig. Gen. James Moore identifies a total of 2,035 men under his command, including his staff (3). The breakdown is:

1st NC Regiment – 310
2nd NC Regiment – 267
3rd NC Regiment – 37 (remainder with Brig. Gen. Robert Howe in Georgia)
4th NC Regiment – 451
5th NC Regiment – 504
6th NC Regiment – 463

In early to mid-November, William Hooper, one of the North Carolina delegates sent to the Continental Congress in Philadelphia, writes home that everyone up north suspects that the British are once again loading up ships and apparently heading for Charlestown. His letters include an admonishment that North Carolina must stand tall and go to the aid of South Carolina since everyone knows that they cannot defend themselves alone.

On November 16th, the Continental Congress hastily resolves that Brig. Gen. James Moore is to take over the Southern Department at Charlestown and to station his troops in such a situation as to render aid quickly if the British fleet returns–all this based upon a rumor. Brig. Gen. James Moore's troops had missed the earlier action at Fort Moultrie and

Breach Inlet because they had been retained in the vicinity of Wilmington to guard the town against the eighteen British ships left behind that did not sail south with the others as previously described. At the same time, the Continental Congress also resolves for North Carolina to immediately raise an additional 5,000 Militia to aid South Carolina–to be paid for by the Continental Congress.

When the Fifth Provincial Congress meets at Halifax on November 12th, the 1st NC Regiment under Col. Francis Nash is marched to that town to protect the legislators. After three days at Camp Quankey along the banks of the Roanoke River, these troops return to Wilmington. This is the nearest thing to action that Brig. Gen. James Moore's brigade has yet seen. At this time, the thirty-seven men of the 3rd NC Regiment that are not with Brig. Gen. Robert Howe in Georgia are at Salisbury under Col. Alexander Martin, guarding the stores gathered at that depot.

Although considered the elite of all North Carolina troops, most of the Continentals lack the basic training required to turn them into cohesive fighting units. Not only are they poorly fed and poorly clothed until very recently, they also have insufficient arms, ammunition, blankets, and tents. To make matters worse, Brig. Gen. James Moore is forced to borrow $6,250 from Col. Thomas Polk to feed his troops. Despite these hardships, there is an undercurrent of enthusiasm among the North Carolina Continentals that helps them to believe that they are the equals of Europe's best.

On November 26th, the Fifth Provincial Congress authorizes three new regiments to be placed on the Continental service–the 7th NC Regiment, the 8th NC Regiment, and the 9th NC Regiment–and they commission the captains on November 28th.

On November 29th, the Fifth Provincial Congress resolves that Brig. Gen. James Moore is to immediately march with all troops under his command to the aid of Charlestown and that Col. Alexander Martin is to join him. They also order all North Carolina Continental Line officers that are currently on leave to catch up to their regiments as soon as possible.

One side note–on December 18th, the Fifth (and final) Provincial Congress unanimously approves the North Carolina State Constitution. During this final session, they also elect Richard Caswell as the third Provincial President, to be the first governor of the state in early 1777.

Thus ends 1776.

North Carolina Continental Line
November 28, 1776

Southern Department

Brig. Gen. James Moore

HQ at Charlestown, SC

2nd NC Brigade

Brig. Gen. Robert Howe

Returning From Florida

1st NC Brigade

Brig. Gen. James Moore

1st NC Regiment

Col. Francis Nash

- LC Thomas Clark
- M William Davis
- M Wm. B. Williams

Captains
- Joshua Bowman
- George L. Davidson
- Henry "Hal" Dixon
- Caleb Grainger
- Thomas Hogg
- Alfred Moore
- Lawrence Thompson
- John Walker

2nd NC Regiment

Col. Alexander Martin

- LC John Patten
- M John White

Captains
- John Armstrong
- Charles Crawford
- William Fenner
- James Gardner
- Robert Gaston
- James Gee
- John Herritage
- Nathaniel Kaais
- Hardy Murfree
- Joseph Tate
- Edward Vail, Jr.
- Benjamin Williams

3rd NC Regiment

Col. Jethro Sumner

- LC William Alston
- MC Samuel Lockhart

Captains
- William Barret
- James Bradley
- William Brinkley
- James Cook
- Pinketham Eaton
- Nicholas Edmunds
- James Emmett
- Thomas Granbury
- John Gray
- Daniel Jones
- Jacob Turner

Resigned 12/31/1776

6th NC Regiment

Col. Alexander Lillington

- LC William Taylor
- M Gideon Lamb

Captains
- John B. Ashe
- Arthur Council
- William Glover
- John James
- Archibald Lytle
- John G. McRee
- George Mitchell
- Philip Taylor

7th NC Regiment

Col. James Hogun

- LC Robert Mebane
- M Lott Brewster

Captains
- Green Bell (Resigned)
- Thomas Brickell
- Josiah Cotton
- Henry Dawson
- John McGlaughan
- John Poynter
- Joseph Walker
- Bennett Wood (Refused)

Commissioned Nov. 26, 1776

4th NC Regiment

Col. Thomas Polk

- LC James Thackston
- M Wm. Lee Davidson
- M Charles McLean

Captains
- John Ashe, Jr.
- William T. Coles
- William Goodman
- Thomas Harris
- John McLane
- John Nelson
- Joseph Phillips
- Robert Smith

5th NC Regiment

Col. Edward Buncombe

- LC Henry Irwin
- M Levi Dawson

Captains
- Simon Alderson
- Reading Blount
- William Caswell
- Henry Darnell
- John Enloe
- Peter Simon
- Benjamin Stedman
- William Ward
- John Pugh Williams

8th NC Regiment

Col. James Armstrong

- LC James Ingram
- M Selby Harney

Captains
- William Gurley (Refused)
- Frederick Hargett
- Simon Jones
- James May, Jr.
- Thomas Nixon
- Henry Pope
- Robert Raiford
- John Walsh
- Edward Ward

Commissioned Nov. 26, 1776

9th NC Regiment

Col. John Williams

- LC John Luttrell
- M William Polk

Captains
- Joel Brevard
- Richard D. Cook
- Michael Henderson
- Thomas McCrory
- Matthew Ramsey
- Hezekiah Rice
- John Rochelle
- Joseph John Wade

Commissioned Nov. 26, 1776

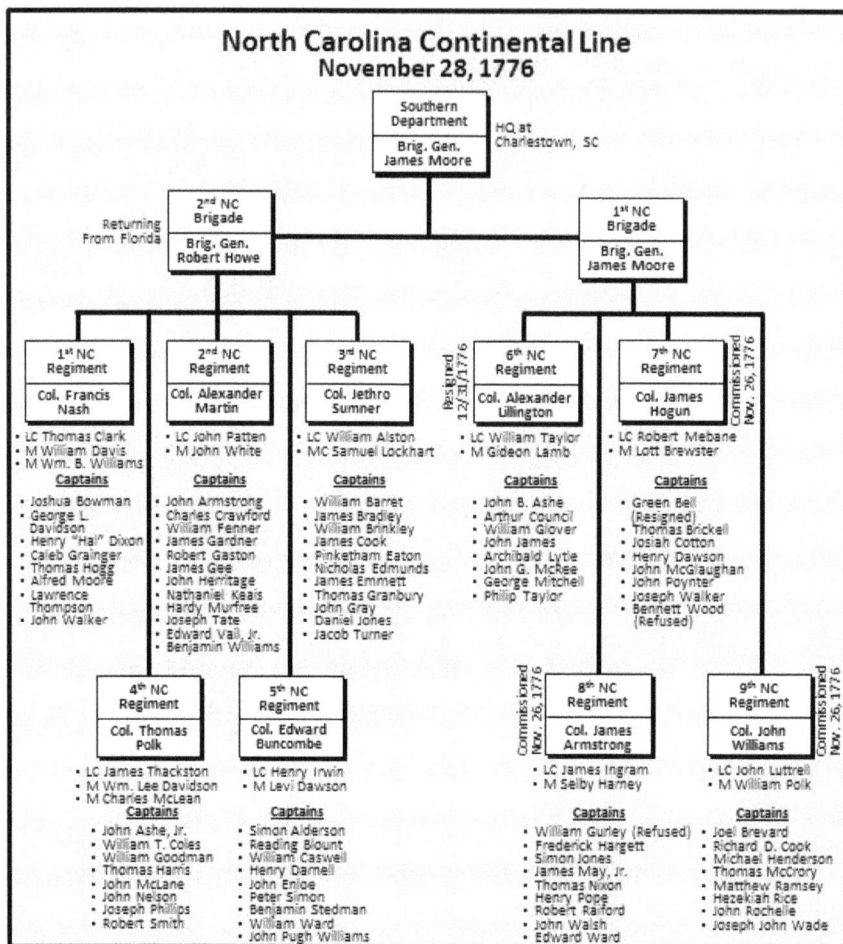

7th NC Regiment as of November 28, 1776			
Rank	**Name**	**Commission**	**County From**
Colonel	James Hogun	11/26/1776	Halifax
Lt. Colonel	Robert Mebane	11/27/1776	Orange
Major	Lott Brewster	11/26/1776	
Captain	Green Bell	11/28/1776	Edgecombe
Captain	Thomas Brickell	11/28/1776	Hertford
Captain	Josiah Cotton	11/28/1776	Northampton
Captain	Henry Dawson	11/28/1776	Halifax
Captain	John McGlaughan	11/28/1776	Hertford
Captain	John Poynter	11/28/1776	Currituck
Captain	Joseph Walker	11/28/1776	Hertford
Captain	Bennett Wood (Refused)	11/28/1776	Bute

8th NC Regiment as of November 28, 1776			
Rank	Name	Commission	County From
Colonel	James Armstrong	11/26/1776	Pitt
Lt. Colonel	James Ingram	11/26/1776	Northampton
Major	Selby Harney	11/26/1776	Pasquotank
Captain	William Gurley (Refused)	11/28/1776	Johnston
Captain	Frederick Hargett	11/28/1776	Craven (Jones)
Captain	Simon Jones	11/28/1776	Pitt
Captain	James May, Jr.	11/28/1776	Pitt
Captain	Thomas Nixon	11/28/1776	Carteret
Captain	Henry Pope	11/28/1776	Dobbs
Captain	Robert Raiford	11/28/1776	Cumberland
Captain	John Walsh	11/28/1776	Wake
Captain	Edward Ward	11/28/1776	

9th NC Regiment as of November 28, 1776			
Rank	Name	Commission	County From
Colonel	John Williams	11/26/1776	Orange (Caswell)
Lt. Colonel	John Luttrell	11/27/1776	Chatham
Major	William Polk	11/27/1776	Mecklenburg
Captain	Joel Brevard	11/28/1776	
Captain	Richard D. Cook	11/28/1776	
Captain	Michael Henderson	11/28/1776	
Captain	Thomas McCrory	11/28/1776	Guilford
Captain	Matthew Ramsey	11/28/1776	Chatham
Captain	Hezekiah Rice	11/28/1776	Dobbs
Captain	John Rochelle	11/28/1776	Wake
Captain	Joseph John Wade	11/28/1776	

Appendix B includes a listing of all known Continental units that participated in each battle/skirmish of 1776.

Chapter Three – 1777

Although there have been rumors of a British fleet sailing southward towards Charlestown since November of 1776, the North Carolina Continentals do not begin marching into its southern neighbor until January of 1777. One group under Col. Francis Nash marches via Lockwood's Folly to Little River, then to Georgetown, past Charlestown, on to Beaufort in South Carolina, where the troops then drill daily. The remainder of Brig. Gen. James Moore's brigade goes to Haddrell's Point just outside of Charlestown where the typical winter weather takes its toll on the soldiers' health. There are plenty of blankets to be had in Charlestown, but there is no money to purchase said blankets.

> ### Key Events of 1777
>
> • State Constitution is now in effect, no longer considered a Province, State's first governor elected – Richard Caswell.
> • New State General Assembly convenes twice (April & November) in New Bern.
> • Five new Counties established and their Militias fielded: Burke, Camden, Caswell, Nash, and Wilkes. Washington District reconstituted as a new County.
> • 10th NC Regiment created and placed on the Continental Line. Takes a long time to fill all companies.
> • Three Light Horse Companies and the Artillery placed on the Continental Line.
> • Continental units march northward and involved in two significant battles – Brandywine Creek, Germantown (PA)
> • Winter at Valley Forge, a bitter one.

Brig. Gen. James Moore returns to North Carolina on January 8th, while Brig. Gen. Robert Howe is now the ranking North Carolina officer stationed in Charlestown. The British never arrive, and their northern focus is to continue for the remainder of this year.

On February 5th, the Continental Congress commissions Francis Nash as the third brigadier general for the North Carolina Continentals, authorizing one brigadier per three regiments. As can be expected, there are the usual promotions within the ranks to backfill Nash's colonelcy.

By mid-February, the Continental Congress decides that all North Carolina Continental troops shall march north to support General George Washington and that they shall get there as close to March 15th as possible. At the same time, the Continental Congress begins offering a bounty of twenty dollars and a hundred acres of land to every soldier who signs up for the duration of the war. Several of the recently-authorized North Carolina regiments are still struggling to fill their ranks, and many officers use this as an excuse for staying at home instead of marching northward.

The march northward is also hampered by the lack of money to pay the troops and by the ever-changing directives from the Continental

Congress. Furthermore, Brig. Gen. Robert Howe refuses to allow the North Carolina line under his command to leave South Carolina because of constant raids upon the Georgia frontier by the Indians and Loyalists of East Florida, and again from more rumors of a British fleet sailing south. There are also shortages of provisions and firearms and the ever-present complaint of clothing and blanket shortages.

To top things off, the Continental Congress's meddling in the selection of officers and their subsequent promotions lead a few officers to resign their commissions. Some say Colonel John Alexander Lillington, of the 6th NC Regiment uses this excuse to resign his commission on December 31, 1776, yet many understand that he not only has political aspirations but also really wants to fight closer to home. He simply cites ill health. In 1779, he re-enters the military arena as a brigadier general over the Wilmington District Brigade of Militia.

Actual state records for the early months of 1777 are scant. As part of its final act in December of 1776, the previous Fifth Provincial Congress created a new body politic, the Council of State "with such powers and authority as they are respectively vested with by the form of government established by this Congress and no other whatsoever, except what is or may be given by any Resolve or Ordinance of this Congress."

The Council of State meets monthly–January 11th, February 12th, March 6th, and April 7th. Richard Caswell is sworn in as the first governor on January 16, 1777 at Tryon Palace in New Bern, which now serves temporarily as the state capitol.

On February 6th, the Council of State directs Brig. Gen. James Moore to fill the ranks of all his regiments by transfers from all the others and to march them northward. The recently-promoted Brig. Gen. Francis Nash is directed to the western part of the state to hurry up the recruiting in that region. On March 15th, Brig. Generals Moore and Nash are then ordered to take six regiments northward, no matter the numbers. The ranking Brig. Gen. James Moore orders Brig. Gen. Francis Nash to join him in Wilmington. There, unhappily, early in April, James Moore dies. Brig. Gen. Francis Nash takes command and soon has his rag-tag and saddened army marches northward.

In the meantime, the Continental Congress finally approves the three North Carolina Light Dragoon Companies to be placed on the Continental Line, effective March 7th. Formerly Provincial Troops, two new captains are commissioned on that date–Samuel Ashe, Jr. and Cosmo Medici–both previously lieutenants. Martin Phifer is one of the original captains of the Light Dragoons earlier and his company is also added to the Continental Line on this date. These companies are not assigned to any Continental regiment and are to be independently tasked

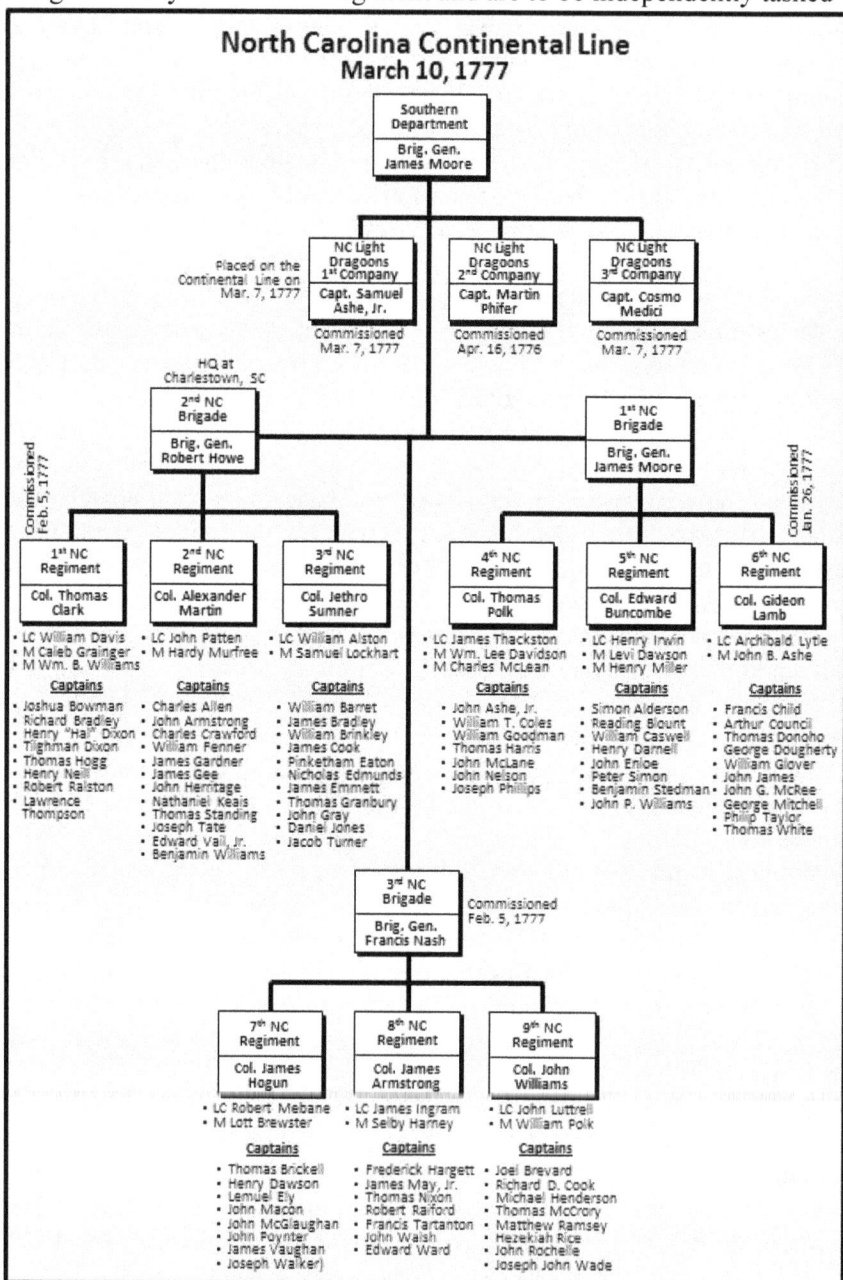

North Carolina Continental Line
March 10, 1777

Southern Department
Brig. Gen. James Moore

Placed on the Continental Line on Mar. 7, 1777

NC Light Dragoons 1st Company — Capt. Samuel Ashe, Jr. — Commissioned Mar. 7, 1777

NC Light Dragoons 2nd Company — Capt. Martin Phifer — Commissioned Apr. 16, 1776

NC Light Dragoons 3rd Company — Capt. Cosmo Medici — Commissioned Mar. 7, 1777

HQ at Charlestown, SC

2nd NC Brigade — Brig. Gen. Robert Howe — Commissioned Feb. 5, 1777

1st NC Brigade — Brig. Gen. James Moore — Commissioned Jan. 26, 1777

1st NC Regiment — Col. Thomas Clark
- LC William Davis
- M Caleb Grainger
- M Wm. B. Williams

Captains
- Joshua Bowman
- Richard Bradley
- Henry "Hal" Dixon
- Tilghman Dixon
- Thomas Hogg
- Henry Neil
- Robert Ralston
- Lawrence Thompson

2nd NC Regiment — Col. Alexander Martin
- LC John Patten
- M Hardy Murfree

Captains
- Charles Allen
- John Armstrong
- Charles Crawford
- William Fenner
- James Gardner
- James Gee
- John Herritage
- Nathaniel Keais
- Thomas Standing
- Joseph Tate
- Edward Vail, Jr.
- Benjamin Williams

3rd NC Regiment — Col. Jethro Sumner
- LC William Alston
- M Samuel Lockhart

Captains
- William Barret
- James Bradley
- William Brinkley
- James Cook
- Pinketham Eaton
- Nicholas Edmunds
- James Emmett
- Thomas Granbury
- John Gray
- Daniel Jones
- Jacob Turner

4th NC Regiment — Col. Thomas Polk
- LC James Thackston
- M Wm. Lee Davidson
- M Charles McLean

Captains
- John Ashe, Jr.
- William T. Coles
- William Goodman
- Thomas Harris
- John McLane
- John Nelson
- Joseph Phillips

5th NC Regiment — Col. Edward Buncombe
- LC Henry Irwin
- M Levi Dawson
- M Henry Miller

Captains
- Simon Alderson
- Reading Blount
- William Caswell
- Henry Darnell
- John Enloe
- Peter Simon
- Benjamin Stedman
- John P. Williams

6th NC Regiment — Col. Gideon Lamb
- LC Archibald Lytle
- M John B. Ashe

Captains
- Francis Child
- Arthur Council
- Thomas Donoho
- George Dougherty
- William Glover
- John James
- John G. McRee
- George Mitchell
- Philip Taylor
- Thomas White

3rd NC Brigade — Brig. Gen. Francis Nash — Commissioned Feb. 5, 1777

7th NC Regiment — Col. James Hogun
- LC Robert Mebane
- M Lott Brewster

Captains
- Thomas Brickell
- Henry Dawson
- Lemuel Ely
- John Macon
- John McGlaughan
- John Poynter
- James Vaughan
- Joseph Walker)

8th NC Regiment — Col. James Armstrong
- LC James Ingram
- M Selby Harney

Captains
- Frederick Hargett
- James May, Jr.
- Thomas Nixon
- Robert Raiford
- Francis Tartanton
- John Walsh
- Edward Ward

9th NC Regiment — Col. John Williams
- LC John Luttrell
- M William Polk

Captains
- Joel Brevard
- Richard D. Cook
- Michael Henderson
- Thomas McCrory
- Matthew Ramsey
- Hezekiah Rice
- John Rochelle
- Joseph John Wade

by Brig. Gen. James Moore. All are soon ordered to escort prisoners taken a year ago at Moore's Creek Bridge to Philadelphia.

As one of the new thirteen states with a new State Constitution, the North Carolina legislature does not first meet until April 7th at New Bern. Its first order of business is to enact legislation necessary to put the new government into full operation. After establishing the state Militia and other requisite Acts, on April 17th, the General Assembly authorizes a 10th NC Regiment to be placed on the Continental Line. However, with a definite lack of funding and the resulting poor organization, this regiment will not start marching northward until November 1st, and most units will not reach their destination until well into the Spring of 1778.

Colonel Abraham Sheppard of Dobbs County was in command of a Militia regiment sent to South Carolina and he successfully pled his case to be removed from "the most miserable part of God's creation, both men and lands." Many historians assert that Gov. Richard Caswell owed him for past favors and that Col. Sheppard promised to assemble a new Continental regiment post haste. He indicates that the men are practically enrolled and will form up as soon as the word is given. Col. Sheppard also assures the governor that his new regiment will be ready to march by July 1st, and that privates will not draw any pay until three hundred have been added to the rolls. He is given the privilege of selecting his own officers. It takes Gov. Richard Caswell two months to convince the Continental Congress to accept this new regiment, and the North Carolina General Assembly, however, quickly places some restrictions on Col. Abraham Sheppard's command.

As briefly mentioned earlier, on April 15th, North Carolina loses its top military commander–Brig. Gen. James Moore dies of what was diagnosed as "a fit of Gout in his Stomach." This is not just a blow to North Carolina, but also to the overall Continental Line.

Brig. Gen. Robert Howe finally returns to Charlestown from "a fatiguing, fruitless expedition into Georgia." He is ordered to remain in Charlestown and to assume command of the Southern Department, which consists of South Carolina and Georgian Continentals. He soon releases the North Carolina Continentals with reluctance, asserting that the South Carolina regiments are filling very slowly–but the previous threat of a British fleet has clearly evaporated.

Brig. Gen. Francis Nash abandons his recruiting mission in the west and hurries to Wilmington to assume command of the gathering troops. Men begin trickling in from as far away as Beaufort and Charlestown in South Carolina, and a rendezvous point is established at Halifax, North

Carolina. The march to join General George Washington is to begin as soon as all units are assembled.

Col. Jethro Sumner's 3rd NC Regiment is the first to arrive at Halifax, but is far from full strength due to being weakened by those men who had abandoned the regiment in favor of enlisting in the South Carolina and Georgia lines. Numbers in the North Carolina Line are further depleted by deserters. Gov. Richard Caswell offers to pardon all deserters who rejoin their units–few accept.

Col. Abraham Sheppard is authorized to offer new recruits an enlistment bounty of $30, a suit of clothes, and 100 acres of land for those who will sign up for three years or 250 acres if they sign up for the duration of the war. Col. Sheppard is hampered by the North Carolina General Assembly, who has him only recruit "young, hearty, robust men, whose birth, family connections, and property, bind them to the interest of their country…" Most young men with these characteristics will normally never seek to join the ranks, but prefer an officer's commission.

10th NC Regiment as of April 20, 1777			
Rank	**Name**	**Commission**	**County From**
Colonel	Abraham Sheppard	4/17/1777	Dobbs
Lt. Colonel	Adam Perkins	4/17/1777	Currituck
Major	John Sheppard	4/17/1777	Dobbs
Captain	Dempsey Gregory	4/19/1777	
Captain	Armwell Herron	4/19/1777	Pitt
Captain	John Jarvis	4/19/1777	Currituck
Captain	Isaac Moore	4/19/1777	Perquimans
Captain	Abraham Sheppard, Jr.	4/19/1777	Dobbs
Captain	John Slaughter	4/19/1777	
Captain	Silas Stevenson	4/19/1777	Craven
Captain	Andrew Vanoy	4/19/1777	Rowan
Captain	James Wilson	4/19/1777	Caswell

As the Continental troops slowly gather at Halifax, an outbreak of Smallpox prompts the officers to finally begin their march northwards in early May. Col. John Williams of the 9th NC Regiment is left at Camp Quankey just outside Halifax to organize and send forth new recruits as fast as they come in. Three officers from each of the nine existing Continental regiments are left in state to continue recruiting–most are lieutenants. Brig. Gen. Francis Nash remains long enough to establish recruiting procedures and sends about 1,500 men northward under Col. Alexander Martin.

In the meantime, on May 2nd, the North Carolina legislature resolves that Brig. Gen. Francis Nash shall punish Capt. Griffith John McRee of the 6th NC Regiment for misleading his recruits into thinking that they had signed up for six months when he enrolled them for 2-1/2 to 3 years. On that same date, the legislature resolves that Capt. Cosmo Medici of the NC Light Dragoons shall proceed with his unit northward–if his men need horses they shall stop at Halifax and contact Militia Brig. Gen. Allen Jones or Mr. Willie Jones, who have both been ordered to assist the NC Light Dragoons with whatever accoutrements they require.

On May 9th, the North Carolina legislature resolves that Gov. Richard Caswell is now empowered to fill any vacancies of officers in the North Carolina Continental Line. On that same date, the legislature resolves to recommend that the Continental Congress accept the NC Artillery into the Continental Line. This also takes over two months and on July 10th two NC Artillery companies are finally added to the Continental Line.

The North Carolina Continental Line marches through Virginia by way of Petersburg to Richmond then to Fredericksburg and Alexandria. According to a recent resolve of the Continental Congress, Alexandria is established as a station for the inoculation against Smallpox for all Continental troops. It is here that it is discovered that nearly 200 North Carolina soldiers have already had Smallpox and are thereby immune. These are sent forward under the command of Col. Jethro Sumner and Lt. Col. Archibald Lytle.

The remainder start their inoculations on May 21st, and this procedure immobilizes the troops for three to four weeks. It is claimed that only one man is lost due to inoculation at Alexandria. After the men have a mild case of the disease they cross the Potomac River about eight miles north of Georgetown and continue northward to Philadelphia to await further orders. The North Carolina Continental Line camps within a mile of the city. Brig. Gen. Francis Nash lodges in the rented house of Thomas Burke, one of North Carolina's delegates to the Continental Congress.

On July 8th, the Continental Congress orders the North Carolina Line to Billingsport, where they are to join the Militia of New Jersey and Pensylvania in completing fortifications for the defense of the Delaware River. They are soon ordered to join Gen. George Washington, but he countermands that order–they are now to go to Trenton until the next move of the British under Maj. Gen. William Howe can be ascertained. Brig. Gen. Francis Nash is given command of some of the local Militias and his troop strength is now at approximately 2,000 men.

In the meantime, the 200 advance troops under Col. Jethro Sumner have joined Gen. Washington's army, now in camp at Morristown, New Jersey. They too sit waiting to see what the British will do next. All troops in Gen. Washington's camp are drilled and drilled until they gain a semblance of military order. To instill more discipline, officers are ordered to exercise their commands in person on the parade ground rather than leaving routine drills to the sergeants as they usually do.

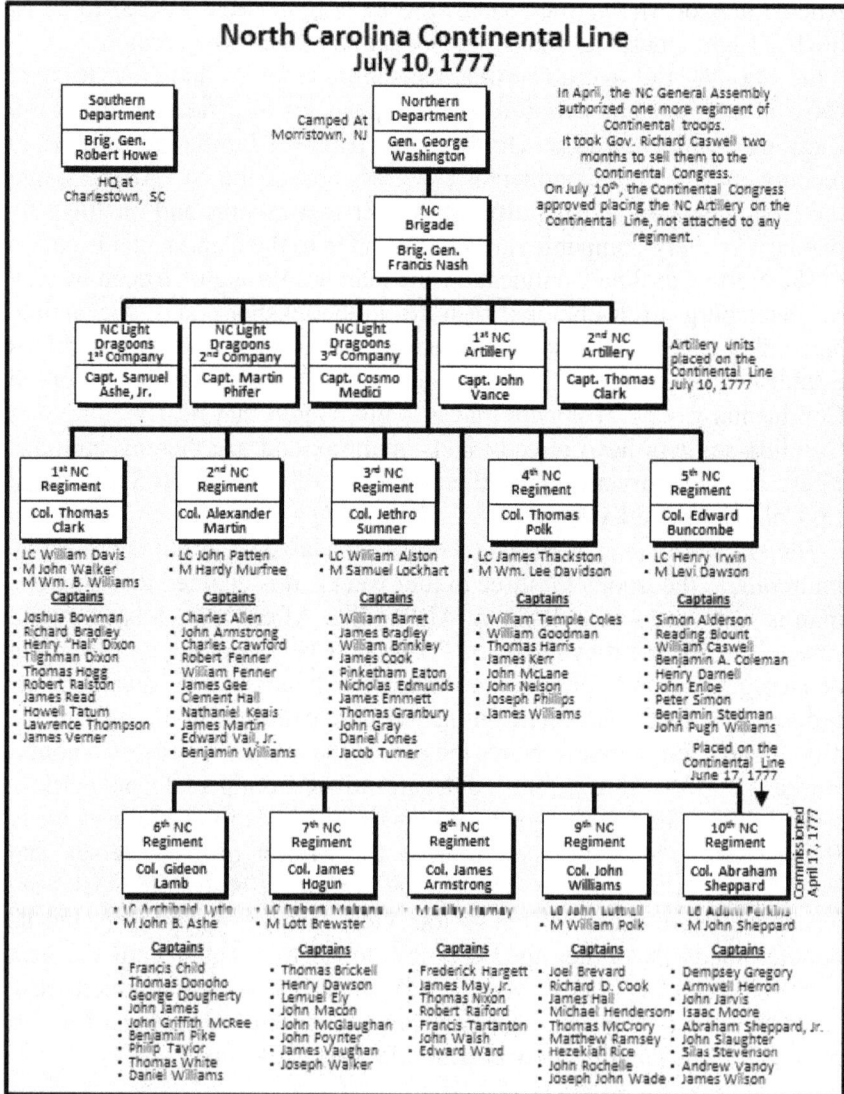

North Carolina Continental Line
July 10, 1777

Southern Department
Brig. Gen. Robert Howe
HQ at Charlestown, SC

Camped At Morristown, NJ

Northern Department
Gen. George Washington

In April, the NC General Assembly authorized one more regiment of Continental troops.
It took Gov. Richard Caswell two months to sell them to the Continental Congress.
On July 10th, the Continental Congress approved placing the NC Artillery on the Continental Line, not attached to any regiment.

NC Brigade
Brig. Gen. Francis Nash

NC Light Dragoons 1st Company
Capt. Samuel Ashe, Jr.

NC Light Dragoons 2nd Company
Capt. Martin Phifer

NC Light Dragoons 3rd Company
Capt. Cosmo Medici

1st NC Artillery
Capt. John Vance

2nd NC Artillery
Capt. Thomas Clark

Artillery units placed on the Continental Line July 10, 1777

1st NC Regiment
Col. Thomas Clark
- LC William Davis
- M John Walker
- M Wm. B. Williams

Captains
- Joshua Bowman
- Richard Bradley
- Henry "Hal" Dixon
- Tilghman Dixon
- Thomas Hogg
- Robert Ralston
- James Read
- Howell Tatum
- Lawrence Thompson
- James Verner

2nd NC Regiment
Col. Alexander Martin
- LC John Patten
- M Hardy Murfree

Captains
- Charles Allen
- John Armstrong
- Charles Crawford
- Robert Fenner
- William Fenner
- James Gee
- Clement Hall
- Nathaniel Keais
- James Martin
- Edward Vail, Jr.
- Benjamin Williams

3rd NC Regiment
Col. Jethro Sumner
- LC William Alston
- M Samuel Lockhart

Captains
- William Barret
- James Bradley
- William Brinkley
- James Cook
- Pinketham Eaton
- Nicholas Edmunds
- James Emmett
- Thomas Granbury
- John Gray
- Daniel Jones
- Jacob Turner

4th NC Regiment
Col. Thomas Polk
- LC James Thackston
- M Wm. Lee Davidson

Captains
- William Temple Coles
- William Goodman
- Thomas Harris
- James Kerr
- John McLane
- John Nelson
- Joseph Phillips
- James Williams

5th NC Regiment
Col. Edward Buncombe
- LC Henry Irwin
- M Levi Dawson

Captains
- Simon Alderson
- Reading Blount
- William Caswell
- Benjamin A. Coleman
- Henry Darnell
- John Enloe
- Peter Simon
- Benjamin Stedman
- John Pugh Williams

Placed on the Continental Line June 17, 1777

6th NC Regiment
Col. Gideon Lamb
- LC Archibald Lytle
- M John B. Ashe

Captains
- Francis Child
- Thomas Donoho
- George Dougherty
- John James
- John Griffith McRee
- Benjamin Pike
- Philip Taylor
- Thomas White
- Daniel Williams

7th NC Regiment
Col. James Hogun
- LC Robert Mebane
- M Lott Brewster

Captains
- Thomas Brickell
- Henry Dawson
- Lemuel Ely
- John Macon
- John McGlaughan
- John Poynter
- James Vaughan
- Joseph Walker

8th NC Regiment
Col. James Armstrong
- M Selby Harney

Captains
- Frederick Hargett
- James May, Jr.
- Thomas Nixon
- Robert Raiford
- Francis Tartanton
- John Walsh
- Edward Ward

9th NC Regiment
Col. John Williams
- LC John Luttrell
- M William Polk

Captains
- Joel Brevard
- Richard D. Cook
- James Hall
- Michael Henderson
- Thomas McCrory
- Matthew Ramsey
- Hezekiah Rice
- John Rochelle
- Joseph John Wade

10th NC Regiment
Col. Abraham Sheppard
- LC Adam Perkins
- M John Sheppard

Captains
- Dempsey Gregory
- Armwell Herron
- John Jarvis
- Isaac Moore
- Abraham Sheppard, Jr.
- John Slaughter
- Silas Stevenson
- Andrew Vanoy
- James Wilson

Commissioned April 17, 1777

On June 30th, the British evacuate all their posts in New Jersey, and by July 8th begin to embark an estimated 18,000 soldiers aboard a fleet of over 250 vessels in New York harbor. However, the British fleet remains anchored until July 23rd, when Gen. Washington learns they have gone downriver and have passed Sandy Hook. On July 31st, the fleet is spotted off the Delaware Capes.

Col. Jethro Sumner's men are now under Brig. Gen. Peter Muhlenberg of Virginia and are encamped near Chester, Pennsylvania. Brig. Gen. Francis Nash's brigade is still in the vincinity of Trenton, New Jersey. Gen. Washington is not convinced that the British are truly headed for Philadelphia–as late as August 21st, he is convinced that Maj. Gen. William Howe's puzzling maneuvers amount to little more than a skillful feint. After making camp in the meadows along the Neshaminy River some twenty miles north of Philadelphia he then receives the news that the British fleet is within the Chesapeake Bay, and the next day he learns that the British are well inside the Delaware Capes.

It is soon very clear that Maj. Gen. William Howe is going to disembark at the head of the Chesapeake Bay and march the fifty-five miles overland to Philadelphia. At four a.m. on August 23rd, Gen. Washington moves again toward Philadelphia and that night is in camp near Germantown, Pennsylvania.

While Washington is following Howe, Brig. Gen. Francis Nash leaves Chester, Pennsylvania for Trenton, New Jersey, where his 2,000 soldiers arrive on August 6th. While marching through Philadelphia eighty of his NC Light Dragoons and their officers are released from service; their horses are so poor and unfit for service that they are sold. The Continental Board of War refuses to purchase new horses because the men have not enlisted for the duration of the war.

As Gen. George Washington nears Philadelphia, Col. Jethro Sumner of the 3rd NC Regiment requests that his North Carolina troops be allowed to join up with Brig. Gen. Francis Nash. It is reported that the North Carolina troops under Nash at Trenton are in "high spirits," and that Brig. Gen. Nash spends the idle time drilling his brigade as a unit. During constant rains, extra whiskey rations are ordered in an attempt to keep down illness. Men desert, some are charged with theft, and some are charged with sleeping on duty, insulting officers, and disobeying orders. In general, the typical punishment for enlisted men is fifty lashes. Convicted officers are either reprimanded or cashiered out of service.

The field officers have long been quite disenchanted about the promotion policy policy employed by the North Carolina Brigade. When

Col. John Alexander Lillington resigned from the 6th NC Regiment on December 31, 1776, a few weeks later Gideon Lamb was promoted within the regiment to take his place on January 26, 1777. Archibald Lytle was likewise promoted from Major to Lt. Colonel on the same date. There are officers who had been commissioned in the earlier regiments and who strongly feel that they deserved those positions; the frustration simmers all during 1777.

Lt. Colonel James Ingram resigns his commission from the 8th NC Regiment on July 8th, but it is not until October when he is replaced by Samuel Lockhart of the 3rd NC Regiment. On June 13th, a board of general offiers of the Continental army decides that all promotions up to major shall be made from within the regiment, but higher ranks shall be made up from the State Line as a whole. Many from the North Carolina Brigade use this as the basis for their argument. When their objections are submitted to Gen. George Washington, he rules that the decision of the board is the proper policy, but that the promotions of Lamb and Lytle shall stand.

Worse is the fact that upon the death of Brig. Gen. James Moore the Continental Congress has not chosen his successor, and there are rumors that a Pennsylvanian might replace him. Sixteen field officers of the North Carolina Brigade dispatch a bitter remonstrance to the Continental Congress complaining of these rumors, along with other issues.

By the middle of July, Col. John Williams of the 9th NC Regiment, still in Halifax, North Carolina recruiting, has collected some 300 recruits for all nine regiments, including over 125 for his own regiment. At least 50 men are without arms, however. And, the 300 refuse to march until they receive their back pay. Lt. Col. Henry Irwin comes from his sick bed when about thirty Loyalists "make an attempt" on Tarborough in Edgecombe County. With about 25 Continentals, Lt. Col. Irwin disarms the malcontents and forces them to take the oath of allegiance to the United States.

Other officers become disgusted and try to resign. The 10th NC Regiment recruiting officers make promises that those who enroll in their regiment will not be required to leave the state. Militia officers purposefully hamper Continental recruiting lest their own commands be depleted. Unrest simmers in both New Hanover and Guilford counties, but these are quieted before violence actually erupts.

Col. John Williams drills his men and marches them to Cross Creek to protect the region's salt supply warehoused there. The Militia is called out to support Col. Williams and to help guard critical supply depots in the state. More of these home efforts are included in Volume 2.

In early August of 1777, the state finally receives $300,000 in Continental currency, and the men's pay is caught up on August 20th. When the men under Col. John Williams receive their pay, a number of officers resign rather than leave the state. He refuses their resignations and has them marching northward by September 1st. Lt. Col. John Luttrell is left behind to supervise all recruiting activities within the state. The 6th NC Regiment has so many deserters from fear of an Indian uprising in the west that an officer is left behind just to round them all up.

By early August, the 10th NC Regiment is still being organized at Kingston. 328 men have enlisted, but they are, in general, "the sickly offscouring of the back country." However, a few companies of the 10th NC Regiment and the remaining NC Light Dragoons are sent northward in small groups as soon as they are equipped.

On Sunday, August 24th, General George Washington reaches Philadelphia. For two hours his 16,000 men follow him down Front Street and up Chestnut Street, marching twelve abreast. Brig. Gen. Francis Nash was previously ordered to bypass Philadelphia and has camped in Chester. He is now ordered to join the main army with Col. Thomas Procter's regiment of artillery on Monday and to follow the same route as Gen. Washington's army had the day before.

Within two days, this large Patriot army is encamped at Wilmington, Delaware. By now, word arrives that Maj. Gen. William Howe has landed his troops at Head of Elk, Maryland (about eight miles below present-day Elkton) and is aiming for Philadelphia. Col. Alexander Martin of the 2nd NC Regiment is selected to lead one hundred of the best rank and file forming up a temporary "Corps of Light Infantry." Very little has been documented as to why this unit is formed at this time.

On September 7th, Gen. Washington's army marches to near Newport, less than ten miles from where Maj. Gen. William Howe is encamped at Iron Hill. On the next day they are paraded, then marched out of camp, and stationed in a battle line along Red Clay Creek to await the British that never show up. That night intelligence reports that Maj. Gen. Howe has ordered his troops to send away their baggage and tents.

At two a.m. on September 9th, Gen. Washington puts his own troops in motion and then puts Brandywine Creek between his army and the army of his enemy. He takes the high ground behind one of the likelier stream crossing, Chadds Ford. Gen. Washington can do no more than await Maj.

Gen. Howe's next move. The North Carolina Line is no different from all the other soldiers camped opposite their enemy. Some are nervous, some are scared, some are simply dazed–and all they can do is wait.

Gen. George Washington positions detachments to guard other fords above and below Chadds Ford, hoping to force the battle there. He employs Maj. Gen. John Armstrong commanding about 1,000 Pennsylvania Militia to cover Pyle's Ford, a few hundred yards south of Chadds Ford, which is covered by Maj. Gen. Anthony Wayne's and Maj. Gen. Nathanael Greene's Continental divisions. Maj. Gen. John Sullivan's division extends northward along Brandywine Creek's east banks, covering the high ground north of Chadds Ford along with Maj. Gen. Adam Stephen's division and Maj. Gen. William Alexander, Lord Stirling's divisions. Further upstream is a Continental regiment under Col. Moses Hazen, of Canada, covering Buffington's Ford and Wistar's Ford. Gen. Washington is confident that the area is secure and defensible with his now approximately 14,500 troops.

British Maj. Gen. William Howe has better information about the area than Gen. Washington and he has no intention of mounting a full-scale frontal attack against the prepared Patriot defenses. He instead employs a flanking maneuver. About 5,000 men under the command of Lt. Gen. Baron Wilhelm von Knyphausen advance to meet Gen. Washington's troops at Chadds Ford. The remainder, approximately 10,000 men under the command of Lt. Gen. Charles, Lord Cornwallis, march north to Trimble's Ford across the West Branch of Brandywine Creek, and then east to Jefferis Ford across the East Branch, (two fords that Gen. Washington has overlooked) and then turns south to flank the American forces.

September 11th begins with a heavy fog, which provides cover for the British troops. Gen. George Washington receives contradictory reports about the British troop movements and continues to believe that the main force is moving to attack at Chadds Ford. At 5:30 a.m. the British and Hessian troops begin marching east along the Great Road, from Kennett Square, PA, advancing on the Patriot troops positioned where the road crosses Brandywine Creek. The first shots of the battle take place at a tavern where the British are repulsed. The British call for reinforcements and run down the road to take cover behind the stone walls on the Old Kennett Meeting House grounds. The battle is fought at mid-morning around the meeting house while the pacifist Quakers continue to hold their midweek service.

From the church, the battle continues for three miles to what is now Battlefield Park. Eventually the British push the Patriots back, but not before suffering heavy losses. The British appear on the Americans' right flank at around 2:00 p.m. With Col. Moses Hazen's regiment outflanked, Generals Sullivan, Stephen, and Lord Stirling try to reposition their troops to meet the unexpected British threat to their right flank. Maj. Gen. William Howe is slow to attack, which buys time for the Patriots to position some of their men on high ground at Birmingham Meeting House, about a mile north of Chadds Ford. By 4:00 p.m., the British attack, with Stephen's and Lord Stirling's divisions receiving the brunt of the assault; both Patriot divisions lose ground fast.

Maj. Gen. John Sullivan attacks a group of Hessian troops trying to outflank Maj. Gen. Lord Stirling's men near Meeting House Hill and buys some time for most of Lord Stirling's men to withdraw, but returning British fire forces Sullivan's men to retreat. At this point, slightly after 4:00 p.m., General Washington and Maj. Gen. Nathanael Greene arrive with reinforcements to try to hold off the British, who now occupy Meeting House Hill. These reinforcements, combined with the remnants of Sullivan's, Stephen's, and Stirling's divisions, stop the pursuing British for nearly an hour but are eventually forced to retreat. The Patriots are also forced to leave behind many of their cannon on Meeting House Hill because almost all of the artillery horses are killed.

When Lt. Gen. Charles, Lord Cornwallis and his large army crosses Brandywine Creek and accomplishes his flanking maneuver, he first encounters Col. Moses Hazen, who is forced to retreat towards the Patriots led by Maj. Gen. John Sullivan, Maj. Gen. Adam Stephens, and Maj. Gen. Lord Stirling. The resistance of Stirling and Stephens is such as repeatedly to repulse the British attack. Their retreat is effected with some steadiness and is shown by the simple fact that they take both artillery and baggage with them.

Lt. Gen. Baron Wilhelm Knyphausen, on the east bank of Brandywine Creek, launches an attack against the weakened Patriot center across Chadds Ford, breaking through the divisions commanded by Maj. Gen. Anthony Wayne with Brig. Gen. William Maxwell and forcing them to retreat and leave behind most of their cannon. Maj. Gen. John Armstrong's Pennsylvania Militia, never engaged in the fighting, also decides to retreat from their positions. Further north, Maj. Gen. Nathanael Greene sends Brig. Gen. George Weedon's Virginia troops to cover the road just outside the town of Dilworth to hold off the British long enough for the rest of the Continental army to retreat. Darkness brings the British pursuit to a standstill, which then leaves Brig. Gen. Weedon's force to retreat. The defeated Patriots are forced to retreat to Chester where most of them arrive at midnight, with stragglers arriving well into the early morning hours. The Patriot retreat is well-organized largely due to the efforts of Maj. Gen. Gilbert du Motier, Marquis de Lafayette, who, although wounded, creates a rallying point that allows for a more orderly retreat before being treated for his wound.

The official British casualty list details 587 casualties: 93 killed (eight officers, seven sergeants and 78 rank and file); 488 wounded (49 officers, 40 sergeants, four drummers, and 395 rank and file); and six rank and file missing and unaccounted for. No casualty return for the Patriot army at Brandywine Creek survives, and no figures, official or otherwise, are ever released. Most accounts of the American loss are from the British side. One initial report, by a British officer, records American casualties at over 200 killed, around 750 wounded, and 400 prisoners taken, many of them wounded.

In addition to losses in battle, 315 men are listed as deserters from Gen. Washington's camp during this stage of the Philadelphia Campaign. Although British Maj. Gen. William Howe defeats the American army, his lack of cavalry prevents its total destruction. Gen. Washington committed a serious error in leaving his right flank wide open and nearly brought about his army's annihilation, had it not been for Sullivan, Stirling, and Stephen's divisions, which fought for time. As evening was approaching and in spite of the early start Lt. Gen. Charles, Lord Cornwallis had made in the flanking maneuver, most of the American army was able to escape.

Although the battle of Brandywine Creek receives little attention in the annals of military history, it is significant as one of the largest land battles of the American Revolution. It is the only battle in which Washington and Howe fought head-to-head, and is a great morale booster for the American army. Additionally, it is thought to be one of the first battles in which the Ferguson Rifle is used and in which the Betsy Ross flag is flown.

Almost all of the North Carolina Continental Line comes together just before this historic battle, and parts of all ten regiments participate in the battle of Brandywine Creek under Maj. Gen. William Alexander–commonly referred to as Lord Stirling from New Jersey–near the right flank of Gen. Washington's army. Only two known advance companies of the 10th NC Regiment had left the state and joined Gen. Washington in time for this battle–the remainder of the 10th NC Regiment and the NC

Artillery continued struggling to fill their ranks at home. Few historians even mention any North Carolinians at the battle of Brandywine Creek.

Within the many pension statements made much later by survivors of the North Carolina Continental Line, it is quite clear that all ten regiments (as stated before) and the three companies of NC Light Dragoons were heavily engaged in the battle of Brandywine Creek. Many from North Carolina were wounded, and some pensioners named mess-mates who were killed. It is also readily apparent from contemporaneous rolls that a small number of men were listed as either missing or as deserters soon after this battle, some never heard from again.

Notwithstanding the glaring facts from hundreds of later pension statements, historians generally state that the North Carolina Continentals "had been held in reserve" and did not see any action on that day. One historian states that the North Carolinians were within fifty yards of the enemy and were prepared to meet them with bayonets, but the British were driven back. Another historian does assert that the hastily-designated Corps of Light Infantry assigned to Col. Alexander Martin under Brig. Gen. William Maxwell of New Jersey did see action on this fateful day, but all other North Carolinians were in reserve behind the center of the Patriot lines.

In his 1818 pension application John Hudson (S41675) asserts:

"That he the said John Hudson enlisted into the service of the United States as a Continental soldier under William Ward, Captain in the 5th Regiment of the North Carolina Line in the year 1776 for two & a half years service in the county of Johnston, that he was commanded by Col. Edward Buncombe & that he marched with said regiment to Wilmington, North Carolina, that he was then marched to the state of Maryland still under the command of said Col. Buncombe, that he was at the battles of Brandywine Creek and at Germantown, that he received a contusion on the head at the battle of Brandywine Creek, and that he continued to serve as a Continental soldier for the full term of two & half years for which he was enlisted, and was honorably discharged in one of the states to the north of Baltimore." [minor edits]

Captain James Gee of the 2nd NC Regiment dies on October 12th as a result of wounds he received at Brandywine Creek a month earlier. Captain Thomas Nixon of the 8th NC Regiment resigns his commission on September 20th, clearly a result of the battle nine days earlier. Captain Henry Dawson of the 7th NC Regiment is forced to resign his commission on October 11th, one source asserting that it is because of some sort of misconduct at the battle of Brandywine Creek. Captain

Benjamin Stedman of the 5th NC Regiment is sent home to become a recruiter immediately after Brandywine Creek. Captain Jacob Turner of the 3rd NC Regiment "distinguished himself" at Brandywine Creek, but is killed less than a month later at the battle of Germantown, Pennsylvania.

Col. Gideon Lamb of the 6th NC Regiment is accused of abandoning his troops at Brandywine Creek, but a court-martial acquits him of these charges. Col. Alexander Martin of the 2nd NC Regiment is also acquitted of similar charges, but he resigns his commission on November 22nd and returns to North Carolina–to later become governor of the state in 1782.

Although defeated, the Patriots at Chester, Pennsylvania are not discouraged–the men know that they have acquitted themselves quite well, even though mistakes have certainly been made by their officers. The Continental Congress even votes thirty hogsheads of rum for the army "in compliment…for their gallant behavior," and for each soldier to receive "one gill per day, while it lasts."

Gen. George Washington spends no time whatsoever in complimenting himself on the fine showing of his army. On September 12th, he marches his army out of Chester, crosses the Schuylkill River, and then camps at the edge of Germantown, facing his enemy. Realizing that he is between the Schuylkill and Delaware rivers, the next day he recrosses the Schuylkill and on September 15th moves to the Lancaster Road between Warren's Tavern and White Horse Tavern.

British and Patriot forces dance around each other for the next several days with only comparatively minor encounters such as the Battle of Paoli on the night of September 20–21. There is very little evidence that the North Carolina Brigade is involved in this little-mentioned engagement. They may have been, but no pensioners mention it.

The Continental Congress abandons Philadelphia, first to Lancaster, Pennsylvania for a few days and then to York, Pennsylvania. Military supplies are moved out of the city to Reading, Pennsylvania. On September 26, 1777, British forces led by Lt. Gen. Charles, Lord Cornwallis march into Philadelphia unopposed. Leaving 3,000 of his finer troops in the capital city, Maj. Gen. William Howe repositions his main force to Germantown, five miles north of Philadelphia. Over the next few days, Howe detaches some of his army to strengthen an attack on the Delaware forts and others to escort supplies into Philadelphia.

As Gen. Washington learns of these detachments reducing his enemy's strength, he and his officers agree that an attack on Howe's position at Germantown is favorable. In preparation, each man is furnished rations for two days and issued forty rounds of ammunition. All units, including the North Carolina Brigade, receive a new allotment of clothing, a welcome gift after the battle of Brandywine Creek.

Germantown is a hamlet of stone houses spreading from what is now known as Mount Airy on the north to what is now Market Square in the south. Extending southwest from Market Square is Schoolhouse Lane, running 1-1/2 miles to the point where Wissahickon Creek empties from a steep gorge into the Schuylkill River. Maj. Gen. William Howe has a base camp along the high ground of Schoolhouse and Church lanes. The western wing of the British camp, under the command of the Lt. Gen. Wilhelm von Knyphausen, has a picket of two Jaëger battalions at its left flank on the high ground above the mouth of the Wissahickon. A Hessian brigade and two British brigades camp along Market Square, and east of there are two British brigades under the command of Maj. Gen. James Grant, as well as two squadrons of dragoons, and the 1st Light Infantry Battalion. The Queen's Rangers, a New York Loyalist unit, cover the right flank.

Gen. George Washington's plan is to attack the British at night using four columns from different directions with the goal of creating a double envelopment. Gen. Washington hopes to surprise the British and Hessian armies in much the same way he had surprised the Hessians at the battle of Trenton in early January of this same year.

As the sun sets on October 3rd, the Patriot army begins a 16-mile southward march to Germantown in complete darkness. As the attack is to occur before dawn, the soldiers are instructed to put a piece of white paper on their hat to identify friend from foe. The Patriots are not detected by the Jaëger pickets, and the British and Hessian forces remain unaware that American troops are advancing on them. For the Americans, it seems that their attempt to repeat their victory at the battle of Trenton is going to succeed. The darkness makes communications between the American columns very difficult, and progress is slower than expected.

At dawn, most of the Patriot forces are well short of their intended attack positions, and they have now lost the element of surprise. One American column consisting of Militia manages to reach the British camp. These troops halt near the mouth of Wissahickon Creek and fire a few rounds from their cannon at Lt. Gen. Knyphausen's camp before withdrawing. The three remaining columns continue their advance. The column under the command of Maj. Gen John Sullivan moves down Germantown Road; the column of Maryland Militia under the command of Brig. Gen William Smallwood moves down Skippack Road to

Whitemarsh Church Road and from there to Old York Road to attack the British right flank, and the column under the command of Maj. Gen. Nathanael Greene, which consists of Greene's and Maj. Gen. Adam Stephens's divisions and Brig. Gen. Alexander McDougall's brigade, moves down Limekiln Road.

A thick fog hangs over the battlefield throughout the day of October 4th. The vanguard of Sullivan's column, on Germantown Road, launches the battle when they open fire on the British pickets of light infantry at Mount Airy just as the sun is rising at around 5:00 a.m. The British pickets fire their guns in alarm and resist the Patriot advance. British Maj. Gen. William Howe rides forward, thinking that they are being attacked by foraging or skirmishing parties, and orders his men to hold their ground. It takes a substantial part of Sullivan's division to finally overwhelm the British pickets and drive them back into Germantown.

Now cut off from the main British and Hessian force, British Lt. Colonel Thomas Musgrave orders his six companies of troops from the 40th Regiment, approximately 120 men, to fortify the stone house of Chief Justice Chew, called Cliveden. The Patriots launch furious assaults against Cliveden, but the greatly outnumbered defenders beat them back, inflicting heavy casualties. Gen. George Washington calls a council of war to decide how to deal with the distraction. Some of his subordinate officers favor bypassing Cliveden and leaving a regiment behind to deal with it. However, Brig. Gen. Henry Knox recommends to Gen. Washington that it is unwise to allow a garrison in the rear of a forward advance to remain under enemy control, and Gen. Washington concurs.

Brig. Gen. William Maxwell's brigade, which had been held in the reserve of the American forces, is brought forward to storm Cliveden, while Brig. Gen. Henry Knox, who is Gen. Washington's artillery commander, positions four three-pounders out of musket range and opens fire against the mansion's defenders. However, the thick stone walls of Cliveden withstand the bombardment from the light cannons.

Patriot infantry assaults launched against the large house are cut down, causing heavy casualties. The few Patriots who manage to get inside are shot or bayoneted. It is clear that Cliveden is not going to be taken easily.

Meanwhile, Maj. Gen. Nathanael Greene's column on Limekiln Road catches up with the Patriot forces at Germantown. His vanguard engages the British pickets at Luken's Mill and drives them off after a savage skirmish. Adding to the heavy fog that already obscures the Patriots' view of the enemy is the smoke from cannons and muskets, and Maj. Gen. Greene's column is thrown into disarray and confusion. One of his brigades, under the command of Maj. Gen. Adam Stephens, veers off course and begins following Meetinghouse Road instead of rendezvousing at Market Square with the rest of Maj. Gen. Greene's forces. The wayward brigade collides with the rest of Patriot Maj. Gen. Anthony Wayne's brigade and mistakes them for the redcoats. The two Patriot brigades open heavy fire on each other, becoming badly disorganized, and both flee. The withdrawal of Maj. Gen. Wayne's reserve New Jersey Brigade, which had suffered heavy casualties attacking the Chew House (Cliveden), leaves Conway's left flank exposed to the enemy.

In the north, a Patriot column led by Brig. Gen. Alexander McDougall comes under attack by the Loyalist troops of the Queen's Rangers and the Guards of the British reserve. After a savage battle between the two, Brig. Gen. McDougall's brigade is forced to retreat, suffering heavy losses. Still convinced, however, that they can win, the 9th Virginia Regiment (Continentals) of Maj. Gen. Nathanael Greene's column launches a savage attack on the British and Hessian line as planned, managing to break through and capturing a number of prisoners. However, they are soon surrounded by two arriving British brigades led by Lt. Gen. Charles, Lord Cornwallis, who launches a devastating countercharge. Cut off completely, the 9th Virginia Regiment is forced to surrender. Maj. Gen. Greene, upon learning of the main army's defeat and withdrawal, realizes that he now stands alone against the whole British and Hessian force, so he withdraws as well.

The large, main attacks on the British camp are repulsed with heavy casualties. Gen. George Washington orders Maj. Gen. John Armstrong and Maj. Gen. William Smallwood's men to withdraw. Brig. Gen. Maxwell's brigade, still having failed to capture the Chew House, is forced to fall back. Part of the British army rushes forward and routs the retreating Patriots, pursuing them for some nine miles before giving up the chase in the face of resistance from Maj. Gen. Greene's infantry, Maj. Gen. Wayne's artillery guns, and a detachment of dragoons, as well as the nightfall.

Of the 11,000 men Gen. George Washington leads into battle, 152 are killed (30 officers and 122 men), and 521 are wounded (117 officers and 404 men). Records show "upwards of 400 were made prisoners, including Colonel Mathews and the entire 9th Virginia Regiment." British casualties are 71 killed, 448 wounded and 14 missing, only 24 casualties of whom are Hessians.

John Fiske, in *The American Revolution* (1891), writes:

"The genius and audacity shown by Washington, in thus planning and so nearly accomplishing the ruin of the British army only three weeks after the defeat at the Brandywine, produced a profound impression upon military critics in Europe. Frederick of Prussia saw that presently, when American soldiers should come to be disciplined veterans, they would become a very formidable instrument in the hands of their great commander; and the French court, in making up its mind that the Americans would prove efficient allies, is said to have been influenced almost as much by the battle of Germantown as by the surrender of Burgoyne."

Sir George Otto Trevelyan, in Volume IV of his *History of the American Revolution*, concludes that although the battle of Germantown was a defeat for the Americans, it is of "great and enduring service to the American cause," particularly in persuading Comte de Vergennes and the French to weigh in on behalf of the United States against Britain. He continues:

"That the battle had been fought unsuccessfully was of small importance when weighed against the fact that it been fought at all. Eminent generals, and statesmen of sagacity, in every European Court were profoundly impressed by learning that a new army, raised within the year, and undaunted by a series of recent disasters, had assailed a victorious enemy in his own quarters, and had only been repulsed after a sharp and dubious conflict."

Once again, Brig. Gen. Francis Nash and his North Carolina Brigade is held in reserve under Maj. Gen. William Alexander–commonly referred to as Lord Stirling, from New Jersey. Although most historians, once again, assert that the North Carolinians are not actually engaged in the battle of Germantown, in fact, they do their share "and some pushed bayonets." They are nearly all engaged in combat and "behaved well" and "with great resolution." Some assert that Brig. Gen. Francis Nash's men are in possession of sixteen pieces of enemy artillery when after the skirmish in the fog and the start of the retreat, a volley from their left rakes their line.

Maj. Gen. Anthony Wayne forms a rear guard to protect the withdrawal, and after the flight of the Pennsylvania Militia exposes the Patriot right flank, Brig. Gen. Francis Nash moves his brigade into place and begins a stubborn resistance, then slowly withdraws. Nash is forced to abandon the captured artillery pieces and to hurry his men to prevent their encirclement. He is on his horse directing his brigade when a cannon ball smashes into his left thigh, mangling his body and killing his steed. A musket ball grazes his head, blinding him. Although not instantly killed, it is apparent that he will not live much longer. A few of his men hastily make a litter and gently carry him from the field of battle.

Col. Edward Buncombe of the 5th NC Regiment is captured and made a prisoner in Philadelphia under Lt. Gen. Charles, Lord Cornwallis. In May of 1778, he falls down some stairs and opens old wounds, and dies soon thereafter. Col. Thomas Polk of the 4th NC Regiment is wounded right after exchanging farewells with Brig. Gen. Francis Nash as he is carried off the battlefield.

Lt. Colonel Henry Irwin of the 5th NC Regiment is severely wounded and captured along with his superior, Col. Edward Buncombe. He dies from his wounds before the sun sets. Maj. William Polk of the 9th NC Regiment is also seriously wounded at Germantown, but he eventually recovers. Maj. James Witherspoon, Aide-de-Camp to Brig. Gen. Francis Nash, is also killed at this battle.

Capt. John Armstrong of the 2nd NC Regiment is wounded. Capt. Jacob Turner of the 3rd NC Regiment, who had distinguished himself earlier at the battle of Brandywine Creek, is killed at Germantown. Capt. Edward Vail, Jr. of the 2nd NC Regiment is court-martialed and convicted for cowardice during the battle of Germantown–he is cashiered on December 21st.

As was the case at Brandywine Creek, nine North Carolina Regiments, two known companies of the 10th NC Regiment, and the three companies of NC Light Dragoons all participate in the battle of Germantown. Of course, due to the casualties, there are many subsequent promotions that change the landscape of the North Carolina Continental Line. Upon the death of Brig. Gen. Francis Nash, the brigade is without a leader for many months to come, a subject that clearly irritates the North Carolina state legislature and the state's delegates to the Continental Congress.

In his 1818 pension application Goodman Harris (S38801) asserts:

"... he enlisted into the service in Granville County, North Carolina in the Spring of the year one thousand seven hundred and seventy six that he was attached to the company commanded by William Glover Captain, Solomon Walker Lieut't., and of the Sixth Regiment of the North Carolina Line, the Regiment being commanded at that time by Lt. Colonel William Taylor – that he served two years and an half in the said army that he was in the battles of Brandywine, Germantown, and Monmouth Court House in the second of which he was wounded in the thigh and of which wound he has ever been greatly disabled, that he was regularly discharged on the 18th day of November in the year one thousand seven hundred and seventy eight as he believes in New England by James Read Captain." [minor edits]

On the night of the battle, the Patriots encamp at Pennypacker's Mill. For three days, Brig. Gen. Francis Nash stubbornly fights death, but he finally gives up on October 7th. Two days later, he is buried at the crossroads near General Washington's headquarters at Toemensing. Soon thereafter, the Continental Congress votes in favor of $500 for a monument to honor the memory of Francis Nash of North Carolina.

On October 13th, a survey is made to determine clothing shortages, and of course the North Carolina Continental Line is in desparate need. Fortunately, there is a brief surplus of food since over 280 cattle have recently been driven into camp and slaughtered. Thanks to the two recent battles, the NC Light Dragoons are now reduced to footmen. A year later

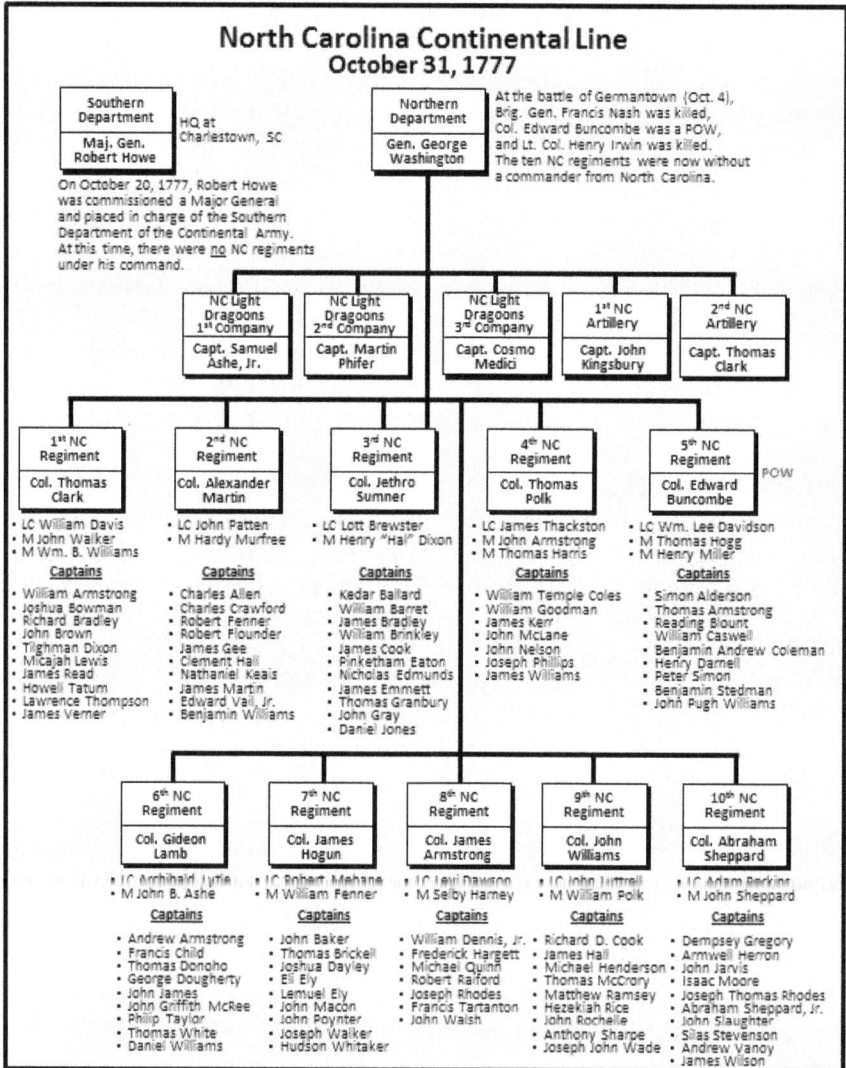

North Carolina Continental Line
October 31, 1777

Southern Department
Maj. Gen. Robert Howe

HQ at Charlestown, SC

Northern Department
Gen. George Washington

At the battle of Germantown (Oct. 4), Brig. Gen. Francis Nash was killed, Col. Edward Buncombe was a POW, and Lt. Col. Henry Irwin was killed. The ten NC regiments were now without a commander from North Carolina.

On October 20, 1777, Robert Howe was commissioned a Major General and placed in charge of the Southern Department of the Continental Army. At this time, there were no NC regiments under his command.

NC Light Dragoons 1st Company — Capt. Samuel Ashe, Jr.

NC Light Dragoons 2nd Company — Capt. Martin Phifer

NC Light Dragoons 3rd Company — Capt. Cosmo Medici

1st NC Artillery — Capt. John Kingsbury

2nd NC Artillery — Capt. Thomas Clark

1st NC Regiment — Col. Thomas Clark
- LC William Davis
- M John Walker
- M Wm. B. Williams

Captains
- William Armstrong
- Joshua Bowman
- Richard Bradley
- John Brown
- Tighman Dixon
- Micajah Lewis
- James Read
- Howell Tatum
- Lawrence Thompson
- James Verner

2nd NC Regiment — Col. Alexander Martin
- LC John Patten
- M Hardy Murfree

Captains
- Charles Allen
- Charles Crawford
- Robert Fenner
- Robert Flounder
- James Gee
- Clement Hall
- Nathaniel Keais
- James Martin
- Edward Vail, Jr.
- Benjamin Williams

3rd NC Regiment — Col. Jethro Sumner
- LC Lott Brewster
- M Henry "Hal" Dixon

Captains
- Kedar Ballard
- William Barret
- James Bradley
- William Brinkley
- James Cook
- Pinketham Eaton
- Nicholas Edmunds
- James Emmett
- Thomas Granbury
- John Gray
- Daniel Jones

4th NC Regiment — Col. Thomas Polk
- LC James Thackston
- M John Armstrong
- M Thomas Harris

Captains
- William Temple Coles
- William Goodman
- James Kerr
- John McLane
- John Nelson
- Joseph Phillips
- James Williams

5th NC Regiment — Col. Edward Buncombe POW
- LC Wm. Lee Davidson
- M Thomas Hogg
- M Henry Miller

Captains
- Simon Alderson
- Thomas Armstrong
- Reading Blount
- William Caswell
- Benjamin Andrew Coleman
- Henry Darnell
- Peter Simon
- Benjamin Stedman
- John Pugh Williams

6th NC Regiment — Col. Gideon Lamb
- LC Archibald Lytle
- M John B. Ashe

Captains
- Andrew Armstrong
- Francis Child
- Thomas Donoho
- George Dougherty
- John James
- John Griffith McRee
- Philip Taylor
- Thomas White
- Daniel Williams

7th NC Regiment — Col. James Hogun
- LC Robert Mebane
- M William Fenner

Captains
- John Baker
- Thomas Brickell
- Joshua Dayley
- Eli Ely
- Lemuel Ely
- John Macon
- John Poynter
- Joseph Walker
- Hudson Whitaker

8th NC Regiment — Col. James Armstrong
- LC Levi Dawson
- M Selby Harney

Captains
- William Dennis, Jr.
- Frederick Hargett
- Michael Quinn
- Robert Raiford
- Joseph Rhodes
- Francis Tartanton
- John Walsh

9th NC Regiment — Col. John Williams
- LC John Luttrell
- M William Polk

Captains
- Richard D. Cook
- James Hall
- Michael Henderson
- Thomas McCrory
- Matthew Ramsey
- Hezekiah Rice
- John Rochelle
- Anthony Sharpe
- Joseph John Wade

10th NC Regiment — Col. Abraham Sheppard
- LC Adam Perkins
- M John Sheppard

Captains
- Dempsey Gregory
- Armwell Herron
- John Jarvis
- Isaac Moore
- Joseph Thomas Rhodes
- Abraham Sheppard, Jr.
- John Slaughter
- Silas Stevenson
- Andrew Vanoy
- James Wilson

Cornelius Harnett charges that the NC Light Dragoons have been "shamefully neglected" with regard to equipment, as newer Continental units of other states are promptly equipped by the Continental Congress.

Before his resignation on November 22nd, Col. Alexander Martin of the 2nd NC Regiment, temporarily commanding the North Carolina Brigade since Francis Nash's death, calls a board of officers together to recommend promotions. To replace the late Lt. Col. Henry Irwin, William Lee Davidson of the 4th NC Regiment is promoted from major. Upon the resignation of Lt. Col. Samuel Lockhart on October 19th, Maj. Levi Dawson of the 5th NC Regiment is promoted in his place. Captains John Armstrong, Henry "Hal" Dixon, and Thomas Hogg are all promoted to majors. Every officer who resigns thenceforth is to be prohibited from holding either military or civil office within North Carolina.

In the meantime, while the North Carolina Continentals in Pennsylvania are without home-grown leadership, Robert Howe in Charlestown, South Carolina is promoted to Major General on October 20th and continues as the head of the Southern Department for the Continental Army at that location, mostly South Carolinians.

When the North Carolina legislature reconvenes in New Bern on November 15th, it barely concerns itself with military matters–just as it had during the Spring session of Congress. The legislature agrees to authorize a $10 bounty to any person who apprehends a deserter from the Continental army. They also agree to notify the state's delegates in the Continental Congress to nominate Jethro Sumner and Thomas Clark as brigadier generals for North Carolina. Then the legislature orders Gov. Richard Caswell to rescind his appointment of John Vance as a captain of the NC Artillery. And finally, the legislature orders a committee to investigate the officers of the 10th NC Regiment and the reasons for their delay in marching the remainder of the regiment northward.

In summary, the legislature's committee charges Col. Abraham Sheppard and his hand-picked subordinate officers with procrastination and they suggest that all are fearful of marching northward to join Gen. Washington's army. They also find that Paymaster Benjamin Sheppard and Quarter Master Alexander Outlaw are both suspected of counterfeiting, and both are discharged from their duties. Recruiting officers are accused of selling exemptions from duty. Before criminal charges can be prepared, Gov. Richard Caswell orders that money be appropriated for pay and supplies to eliminate further complaints and the remainder of the 10th NC Regiment is soon marching northward, to arrive in early 1778.

With winter rapidly approaching, General George Washington keeps his army moving around Philadelphia to keep an eye on the British encamped there. There are a couple of close calls when skirmishes almost grow into full-scale battles, and the Patriots are almost surprised by a large British foraging party when crossing the Schuylkill River at Matson's Ford on December 11th.

On December 19th, Gen. Washington's poorly fed, ill-equipped army, weary from long marches, struggles into Valley Forge, and his 12,000 Continentals prepare for winter's upcoming fury. Grounds for brigade encampments are selected, and defense lines are planned and begun. Although the construction of more than a thousand huts provides shelter, this does little to offset the critical shortages that continually plague the army. Soldiers receive irregular supplies of meat and bread, some getting their only nourishment from "fire cake," a tasteless mixture of flour and water. However, due to the talents of Baker General Christopher Ludwig, the men at Valley Forge more often than not receive fresh-baked bread, about one pound daily. So severe are conditions at times that Gen. Washington despairs "that unless some great and capital change suddenly takes place ... this Army must inevitably ... starve, dissolve, or disperse, in order to obtain subsistence in the best manner they can." Animals fare no better. Brig. Gen. Henry Knox, Washington's chief of artillery writes that hundreds of horses either starve to death or die from exhaustion.

During all this marching in weather that grows colder, the North Carolina Continental troops are not well. On November 10th about 227 rank and file are noted as sick; on December 3rd there are 258 men listed as unfit for duty–from a total of 1,033 enlisted men. The selection of a general to replace Francis Nash remains a perplexing situation. Although Col. Alexander Martin is the choice of many politicians, it is feared that his promotion will set off widespread resignations among other field officers of the North Carolina Brigade. However, as soon as he is cleared of the charges against him, Alexander Martin solves that problem by resigning on November 22nd. Lt. Col. John Patten is promoted to colonel and assumes command of the 2nd NC Regiment.

For a while, the North Carolina Brigade is under the command of Maj. Gen. Alexander McDougall of New York. The officers under him do not question his abilities, they do question whether it would appear "contemptible in the eyes of the Army, not having one General Officer from our State." According to their quota of men, they all feel that North Carolina is entitled to one major general and two brigadiers.

On December 20th, they are placed under Brig. Gen. Lachlan McIntosh of Georgia. The North Carolina Brigade now totals 1,384, and of the 1,051 on duty at Valley Forge some 353 are sick and another 164 are "unfit for want of cloaths." The year 1777 ends on "a very gloomy aspect," for an army that is in need of "breeches, shoes, stockings, blankets and… in want of flour." Will 1778 be much better?

A Return of the No. Carolina Brigade Commanded by Gen¹ McIntosh, Decemb^r 20th 1777.

Battalions.	Colonels.	Colonels	Lt.-Colonels	Majors	Captains	Lieuten'nts	Ensigns	Chaplains	Adjutants	Qr Master	Pay Master	Surgeon	Mates	Serjeants	Drummers	Fifers	Pres't fit fr d'ty	Sick present	Sick in hospital	On Command	On Furlough	Unfit for duty for want of cl'g	Total	Total Strength
1st	Clark's	1	1		4	11		1	1	1	1	1		8	8	5	41	6	13	19		18	97	140
2d	Patten's	1	1		6	10			1	1	1	1		17	11	6	118	10	27	15			170	226
3d	Sumner's	1		1	4	8	1		1	1				15	5	5	60	10	9	22			101	143
4th	Polk's		1	1	3	8	3		1		1			17	6	3	57	9	36	14	7	26	149	193
5th	Buncomb's		1	1	5	10	3	1	1	1	1	1	1	11	4	2	46	14	67	18		64	209	251
6th	Lamb's	1	1		4	5	4	1	1	1	1	1		12	5	3	45	7	42	25		22	141	181
7th	Hogun's	1	1		1	6			1	1				10	4	2	24	4	24			27	79	106
8th	Armstrong's		1		5	9			1	1		1		1			21	1	34	4			60	79
9th	Williams's			1		3	3	1	1	1				7	2	1	22	2	12	2		7	45	65
		5	7	4	32	70	14	3	9	8	6	5		98	39	27	434	63	264	119	7	164	1051	1384

Appendix B includes a listing of all known Continental units that participated in each battle/skirmish of 1777.

Chapter Four – 1778

The new year begins much as the previous year ended. The majority of North Carolina's Continental regiments are stationed at Valley Forge, a bleak and desolate location that winter. The few homes near the junction of Valley Creek and the Schuylkill River barely constitute a village. There had been a real forge at one time, but it was destroyed by the British army when it came through earlier in September of 1777. The German-born Baron Johann DeKalb, accustomed to European military practices, declares that "such a position could only have been selected by a land speculator, a traitor, or a council of idiots."

Key Events of 1778
• NC General Assembly meets twice (April & August), Gov. Richard Caswell is re-elected for his 2nd term.
• Continental Congress reduces the number of NC Continental Regiments to four, then changes its mind and wants six. NC Continental Line in terrible shape for several years to come.
• NC General Assembly responds with the creation of the "New Levies," which are hurriedly assembled, then furloughed for months, then re-activated when it is learned that the British are threatening Savannah and Charlestown again.
• The "New Levies" never show up on any Continental rolls, and most historians consider them to be Militia. Therefore, their discussion is mostly in Volume 2.
• NC Continental Line in one major battle, Monmouth Court House in New Jersey.

Some members of the Continental Congress admonish General George Washington that he should have maintained an active army in the field to constantly harass the British. His response is typically practical–not only are many men confined to the hospital for want of shoes, but blankets are so scarce that large numbers are forced to sit up by the fires all night to keep from freezing to death. In an unusual sarcastic reply, Washington notes that

"… it is a much easier and less disturbing thing to draw remonstrances in a comfortable room by a good fireside than to occupy a cold bleak hillside and sleep under frost and snow without clothes or blankets. However, although they seem to have little feeling for the naked and distressed soldiers, I feel superabundantly for them and, from my soul, I pity those miseries, which is neither in my power to relieve or prevent."

The remainder of the 10th NC Regiment, under Col. Abraham Sheppard, only makes it to Tottopomey Creek in central Virginia by mid-February. In addition to 47 men left behind at the beginning of the march in late 1777, 118 men desert along the way northward. Many fall ill and over twenty men die along the way. The skeleton of a regiment reaches Georgetown on the Potomac River in early March and begins its

Smallpox innoculation. Six soldiers die from the innoculation and many more die from a new measles epidemic that sweeps through the camp.

It is perfectly clear to many that the 10th NC Regiment will never provide great assistance to the war effort. The pitifully few who finally reach Valley Forge are disbanded and added to the ranks of the 1st NC Regiment and the 2nd NC Regiment. None of the existing North Carolina Continental Regiments contain their full quotas of 300 privates. There is an average of 88 men sick in camp, while another 219 are listed as "sick absent" in the various hospitals around Valley Forge. According to Gen. George Washington, the North Carolina Brigade is more sickly, for want

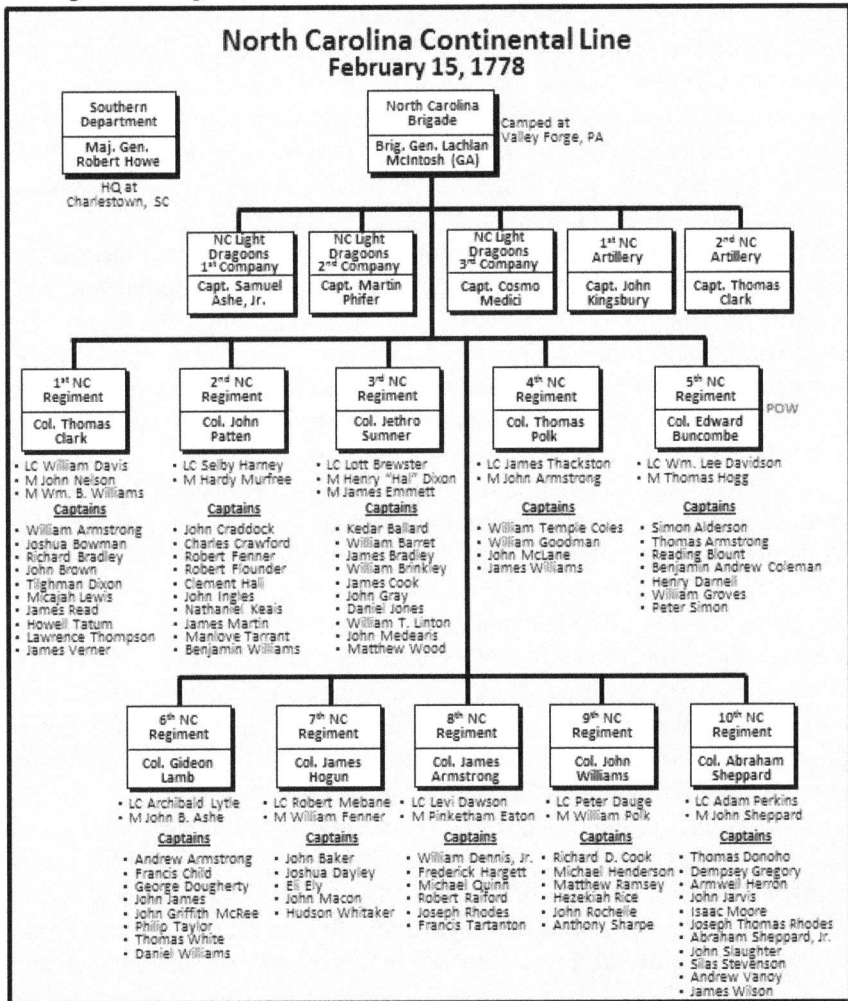

North Carolina Continental Line
February 15, 1778

Southern Department
Maj. Gen. Robert Howe
HQ at Charlestown, SC

North Carolina Brigade
Brig. Gen. Lachlan McIntosh (GA)
Camped at Valley Forge, PA

NC Light Dragoons 1st Company
Capt. Samuel Ashe, Jr.

NC Light Dragoons 2nd Company
Capt. Martin Phifer

NC Light Dragoons 3rd Company
Capt. Cosmo Medici

1st NC Artillery
Capt. John Kingsbury

2nd NC Artillery
Capt. Thomas Clark

1st NC Regiment
Col. Thomas Clark
- LC William Davis
- M John Nelson
- M Wm. B. Williams

Captains
- William Armstrong
- Joshua Bowman
- Richard Bradley
- John Brown
- Tilghman Dixon
- Micajah Lewis
- James Read
- Howell Tatum
- Lawrence Thompson
- James Verner

2nd NC Regiment
Col. John Patten
- LC Selby Harney
- M Hardy Murfree

Captains
- John Craddock
- Charles Crawford
- Robert Fenner
- Robert Flounder
- Clement Hall
- John Ingles
- Nathaniel Keais
- James Martin
- Manlove Tarrant
- Benjamin Williams

3rd NC Regiment
Col. Jethro Sumner
- LC Lott Brewster
- M Henry "Hal" Dixon
- M James Emmett

Captains
- Kedar Ballard
- William Barret
- James Bradley
- William Brinkley
- James Cook
- John Gray
- Daniel Jones
- William T. Linton
- John Medearis
- Matthew Wood

4th NC Regiment
Col. Thomas Polk
- LC James Thackston
- M John Armstrong

Captains
- William Temple Coles
- William Goodman
- John McLane
- James Williams

5th NC Regiment POW
Col. Edward Buncombe
- LC Wm. Lee Davidson
- M Thomas Hogg

Captains
- Simon Alderson
- Thomas Armstrong
- Reading Blount
- Benjamin Andrew Coleman
- Henry Darnell
- William Groves
- Peter Simon

6th NC Regiment
Col. Gideon Lamb
- LC Archibald Lytle
- M John B. Ashe

Captains
- Andrew Armstrong
- Francis Child
- George Dougherty
- John James
- John Griffith McRee
- Philip Taylor
- Thomas White
- Daniel Williams

7th NC Regiment
Col. James Hogun
- LC Robert Mebane
- M William Fenner

Captains
- John Baker
- Joshua Dayley
- Eli Ely
- John Macon
- Hudson Whitaker

8th NC Regiment
Col. James Armstrong
- LC Levi Dawson
- M Pinketham Eaton

Captains
- William Dennis, Jr.
- Frederick Hargett
- Michael Quinn
- Robert Raiford
- Joseph Rhodes
- Francis Tartanton

9th NC Regiment
Col. John Williams
- LC Peter Dauge
- M William Polk

Captains
- Richard D. Cook
- Michael Henderson
- Matthew Ramsey
- Hezekiah Rice
- John Rochelle
- Anthony Sharpe

10th NC Regiment
Col. Abraham Sheppard
- LC Adam Perkins
- M John Sheppard

Captains
- Thomas Donoho
- Dempsey Gregory
- Armwell Herron
- John Jarvis
- Isaac Moore
- Joseph Thomas Rhodes
- Abraham Sheppard, Jr.
- John Slaughter
- Silas Stevenson
- Andrew Vanoy
- James Wilson

of provisions and clothing, than any other unit under his command.

Until late February, only half of the North Carolina Brigade is fit for duty at any one time. Thanks to the recent capture of several ships at sea, their cargo of clothing has been acquired and distributed to the most destitute soldiers at Valley Forge. By the end of the month, there are less than thirty North Carolina soldiers listed as unfit for duty because of having no shoes or clothes. Nearly fifty men die of sickness in the first two months of 1778. The usually optimistic Cornelius Harnett frets that "our Continental Army will cut a poor figure in the Spring."

On February 23rd, Friedrich Wilhelm August Heinrich Ferdinand, Baron Von Steuben rides into Washington's camp at Valley Forge. Claiming to have been a lieutenant general on staff to Frederick the Great, the king of Prussia, he had actually only been a captain. This exaggeration was most likely due to a mistranslation and was included in a letter of recommendation from Benjamin Franklin while in Paris. Von Steuben speaks very little English and he often yells to his translator, "Here... come swear for me!"

With his striking combination of qualities rare among the Patriots–his high professional military reputation, forceful Prussian demeanor, and colorful personality–Von Steuben has a galvanizing effect on the downhearted and disorganized army at Valley Forge. He immediately becomes one of General George Washington's most valued and trusted officers, and he is quickly appointed as Inspector General. His mandate is to train the army to become an efficient fighting unit.

At Valley Forge, Von Steuben forms a model drill company of one hundred specially selected men and undertakes to drill them personally. As the movements progress, he begins to write the drill instructions that grow into the *Regulations for the Order and Discipline of the Troops of the United States*. This manual of drill and field service regulations becomes the foundation of military training and procedure. Commonly called the Army's "blue book," and considered only slightly less authoritative than the Bible, it remains the official United States military guide until 1812. Baron Von Steuben's regulations are officially approved by the Continental Congress on March 29, 1779.

Rigorous drill suddenly catches on with the troops and leads to what has been called "perhaps the most remarkable achievement in rapid military training in the history of the world." By Spring, Gen. Washington promotes Von Steuben to the rank of major general. From this turning point until the end of the war, the Continental Army maintains a level of discipline comparable to that of the British regulars, with their centuries-old tradition.

On February 6th, a treaty between the United States and France is signed, but General George Washington does not receive the news until May 1st, and it is announced to the troops on May 5th. There are the usual artillery salutes and the inevitable *feu de joie*. Even Washington lowers his reserve to join in a few "huzzas."

The North Carolina Brigade no longer contains more than half the men required for full strength. The 6th NC Regiment is so depleted that all officers are sent home in early February to recruit replacements, but there are no funds available to pay enlistment bounties. All of the officers for the 6th NC Regiment are listed as "dropped from the rolls" indicating that they are no longer in service and most historians assert that this regiment was completely and forever disbanded by June 1st. However, this is not the whole story, and certainly not the truth about the 6th NC Regiment.

By April 20th, the North Carolina state legislature finally gets around to military matters when it resolves that:

> "…two thousand men be raised as expeditiously as possible for that purpose to serve nine months from the time they shall appear at the place of rendezvous and that the several counties of this state furnish their proper quotas in proportion to the number of Militia in each county after deducting for such exemptions as were allowed by the Act passed the last session of the General Assembly for drafting five thousand men to go to the northward. And in order to induce men to enter as volunteers into the service, Resolved, that a bounty of one hundred dollars be given to every person who shall voluntarily enter, and the several counties shall make up their respective deficiencies out of the Militia in the following manner:
>
> "The field officers and captains shall determine how many each company shall raise in proportion to their number of Militia and the men and officers of each company shall vote and determine by ballot, being first sworn to vote for such as they think can best be spared, who shall go to make up its deficiency, and every person so voted in shall have a bounty of fifty dollars, and each company shall also furnish and provide a pair of shoes and stockings, two shirts, a hunting shirt, waistcoat with sleeves, pair of breeches and trousers, a hat and a blanket, according to the several proportions on quotas of the companies for each and every man who shall voluntarily enlist or be voted in as aforesaid, and the articles afore mentioned shall be valued on oath by three indifferent freeholders who shall grant certificates to the persons furnishing the same, and such certificates shall be received ty the tax gatherers in part of taxes. Each and every soldier who shall find a good gun of his own shall be allowed three dollars and the several captains shall have power to press for deficiency."

Soon to be known as the "New Levies," it is interesting to note that all of these soon-to-be soldiers are subsequently not considered to be on the Continental Line, even though that is the original intent of the

Continental Congress, the North Carolina General Assembly, and of the Militia recruiters from each county. More interesting is the simple fact that almost none of the enlisted men are ever found on any official rolls of the North Carolina Continental Line, and the same is true about most of the known subaltern officers.

Most official records hint that Lt. Col. Archibald Lytle of the 6th NC Regiment resigned his commission in the North Carolina Continental Line in January of 1778 and returned to his home in Orange County. However, this man shows up as the *de facto* leader of the "New Levies" as early as May of 1778, but most records indicate July of 1778. There is also some evidence that Lt. Col. James Thackston of the 4th NC Regiment is loosely associated with the "New Levies" as well, but just what his role was is unclear from the available official records.

Three known captains within the North Carolina Continental Line are also loosely mentioned with respect to the "New Levies"–George Dougherty, Micajah Lewis, and Joseph Thomas Rhodes. All of these men are transferred to the 4th NC Regiment on June 1st and all records indicate that they continued on the Continental Line for the remainder of 1778. However, for the ensuing nine months they are identified as serving under Lt. Col. Archibald Lytle of the 6th NC Regiment.

Two known officers of the 2nd NC Regiment are loosely associated with the "New Levies"–recently promoted (Jan '78) Captain Richard Graham, and Lt. Christopher Goodwin (promoted to captain in Jan. '79) are both considered part of the "New Levies." Lt. William Lytle of the 5th NC Regiment is promoted to captain in Jan. '79 and also considered part of the "New Levies."

All of the officers above are clearly listed on the official rolls of the North Carolina Continental Line. Is this because they were already in the Continental Line or because they served longer than the requisite nine months of the April 20th mandate? The reason this is important is because there are twenty-five (25) captains associated only with the state Militia who are positively identified as "New Levies" (as shown on the next page) and not one of them have ever been considered to be on the North Carolina Continental Line. Since these captains do not show up on any official rolls of the Continental Line, and the soldiers who served under them were not on any official Continental rolls, they could not apply for a federal pension in 1818 as other Continentals were allowed to do. These men had to live until 1832 when State Troops and Militiamen were permitted to apply for a pension from the federal government.

Many soldiers who later claim to have been in the "New Levies" assert that they are first marched northwards into Virginia where they stop and are furloughed at Moon's Creek with orders that they will be called out again and that their service is not yet complete. They also assert that their official start date is not until they crossed the NC-VA state line, and most claim this happens around July 20th. In December, they are recalled into service and all march to South Carolina to participate in the Purrysburg expedition, then are discharged in the middle of July of 1779. Some men fail to discuss the march northward and claim they are immediately marched into South Carolina, but this is mostly errant recall on their behalf, fifty years after the war ended.

Captain of New Levies	County From	Notes
Joseph Allen*	Craven	Captain of Militia 1776-1778.
William Bethel	Guilford	Captain of Militia 1776-1781.
James Craig	Rowan	Captain of Militia 1776-1781.
Thomas Davidson	Rowan	Captain of Militia 1780-1781.
Thomas DeVane, Jr.	New Hanover	Captain of Militia 1776-1781.
John Farrar*	Granville	No other known service.
Arthur Gatling	Hertford	No other known service.
Charles Gholson	Chatham	Captain of Militia 1776-1781.
John Griffin	Orange	Captain of Militia 1780. A Major 1781.
George Hamilton	Guilford	No other known service.
Benjamin Harrison	Dobbs	Captain of Militia 1776-1783.
Alsey High	Bute	Captain of Militia 1780-1781.
James Jack	Mecklenburg	Captain of Militia 1775-1781.
Nathaniel King	Cumberland	Major of Militia 1780-1781.
John Leak	Guilford	Captain of Militia 1776-1781.
William Lewis*	Nash	No other known service.
Matthew McCauley	Orange	Lt. in 10th NC Regiment 1777-1778. Captain of Militia 1780-1782.
Robert Moore	Caswell	Captain of Militia 1780.
Peter O'Neal	Guilford	Lt., Captain, and Major of Militia.
James Purviance	Rowan	Captain of Militia 1775-1781.
Richard Taylor	Granville	Captain of Militia 1777.
Robert Temple	Bute	Captain of Militia 1780.
Ralph Williams	Granville	Captain of Militia 1779-1780.
Theophilus Williams*	Duplin	Ensign in 6th NC Regiment 1777-1778.
William Williams*	Bertie	No other known service.
*Also identified in the NC State Records, Vol. XIII.		

In his 1833 pension application, Robert Surls (S7659) describes his service under Capt. Benjamin Harrison and marching north to join up with Gen. George Washington's army at West Point, where they build a large fort. After serving his nine months, he is put aboard a ship at Philadelphia and taken to Norfolk, then marches back home to Halifax. Several others make very similar claims. Interestingly, a few men who are clearly drafted into the "New Levies" are included in official rolls for the 3rd NC Regiment. This is not true for any other Continental regiment. More details of the "New Levies" can be found in Volume 2.

Notwithstanding, although the North Carolina General Assembly, on April 20th, authorizes these 2,000 "New Levies" and the associated cumbersome process to select them and equip them, the North Carolina Continental Line simply falls apart in late spring and early summer of 1778. The Continental Congress decides on May 29th that the existing ten (10) North Carolina Continental regiments shall be consolidated into as many regiments that best utilize the existing men. The captains with the longest terms of service are to be retained and are allowed to personally select their men from the old units. This is not exactly what transpired.

Many of the older captains decide to resign their commissions and return home. The "new and improved" regiments now contain a combination of tenured and younger officers and everything becomes official on June 1st. The 1st NC Regiment continues to be led by Col. Thomas Clark; the 2nd NC Regiment continues to be led by Col. John Patten; the 3rd NC Regiment continues to be led by Col. Jethro Sumner; and, the 4th NC Regiment is now led by Col. James Armstrong, who had previously led the 8th NC Regiment. Col. Thomas Polk, Col. James Hogun, and Col. John Williams are sent back to North Carolina to aid in recruiting and to potentially lead the "New Levies" as they are slowly being assembled. Col. Abraham Sheppard of the 10th NC Regiment is sent back with his head hung low, never to participate in the Continental Line again.

In the meantime, on May 15th, Brig. Gen. Lachlan McIntosh is reassigned to Fort Pitt on the frontier. Capt. Samuel Ashe, Jr. and his 1st Company of NC Light Dragoons go with Brig. Gen. McIntosh to Fort Pitt–where all but fourteen (14) of his men resign soon after they arrive. Col. Thomas Clark is now in command of the entire North Carolina Brigade, which is now under Maj. Gen. Gilbert du Motier, Marquis de Latayette. On May 18th, Gen. Washington dispatches Lafayette with a 2,200-man force, including the North Carolina Brigade, to reconnoitre near Barren Hill, Pennsylvania. The next day, the British hear that Lafayette has made camp nearby and sends 5,000 men to capture him. On May 20th, British Maj. Gen. William Howe leads an additional 6,000 soldiers and orders an attack on Lafayette's left flank. The flank scatters, and Lafayette organizes a retreat while the British remain indecisive. To feign numerical superiority, he orders men to appear from the woods on an outcropping known as Barren Hill (now Lafayette Hill) and to fire upon the British periodically. Lafayette's troops simultaneously escape via a sunken road. Lafayette is then able to cross Matson's Ford with the remainder of his force. Interestingly, not a single known North Carolina pensioner later describes being under Lafayette or in this brief skirmish.

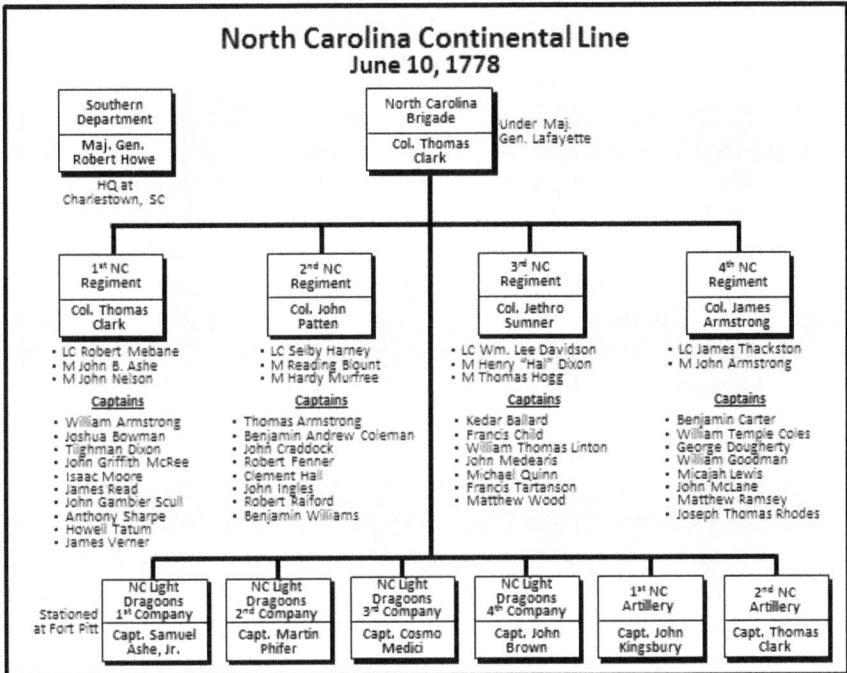

North Carolina Continental Line
June 10, 1778

		North Carolina Brigade	Under Maj. Gen. Lafayette
Southern Department		Col. Thomas Clark	
Maj. Gen. Robert Howe			
HQ at Charlestown, SC			

1ˢᵗ NC Regiment	2ⁿᵈ NC Regiment	3ʳᵈ NC Regiment	4ᵗʰ NC Regiment
Col. Thomas Clark	Col. John Patten	Col. Jethro Sumner	Col. James Armstrong
• LC Robert Mebane • M John B. Ashe • M John Nelson	• LC Selby Harney • M Reading Blount • M Hardy Murfree	• LC Wm. Lee Davidson • M Henry "Hal" Dixon • M Thomas Hogg	• LC James Thackston • M John Armstrong
Captains	**Captains**	**Captains**	**Captains**
• William Armstrong • Joshua Bowman • Tilghman Dixon • John Griffith McRee • Isaac Moore • James Read • John Gambier Scull • Anthony Sharpe • Howell Tatum • James Verner	• Thomas Armstrong • Benjamin Andrew Coleman • John Craddock • Robert Fenner • Clement Hall • John Ingles • Robert Raiford • Benjamin Williams	• Kedar Ballard • Francis Child • William Thomas Linton • John Medearis • Michael Quinn • Francis Tartanson • Matthew Wood	• Benjamin Carter • William Temple Coles • George Dougherty • William Goodman • Micajah Lewis • John McLane • Matthew Ramsey • Joseph Thomas Rhodes

	NC Light Dragoons 1ˢᵗ Company	NC Light Dragoons 2ⁿᵈ Company	NC Light Dragoons 3ʳᵈ Company	NC Light Dragoons 4ᵗʰ Company	1ˢᵗ NC Artillery	2ⁿᵈ NC Artillery
Stationed at Fort Pitt	Capt. Samuel Ashe, Jr.	Capt. Martin Phifer	Capt. Cosmo Medici	Capt. John Brown	Capt. John Kingsbury	Capt. Thomas Clark

Unable to trap Maj. Gen. Lafayette, the British resume their march north from Philadelphia to New York; the Continental Army follows and finally attacks at Monmouth Court House in New Jersey.

General George Washington recalls all outlying detachments and including the expected numbers of Militia coming to join him, he estimates that his numbers will soon swell to 20,000 troops. However, he cannot estimate how France entering the war will quickly change the complexion of the overall British strategy. He also cannot estimate what impact the departure of Maj. Gen. William Howe and his incoming replacement, Maj. Gen. Henry Clinton will have on his own war plans. He soon learns that Philadelphia is to be evacuated by the British and that New York is to be held at all cost. Gen. Washington is never certain of his enemy's intentions until on June 18th he learns that the last British soldier has left Philadephia, and they are destroying all bridges along their march towards New York.

At 5:00 a.m. the next day, Maj. Gen. Charles Lee, Maj. Gen. Anthony Wayne, Maj. Gen. Lafayette, Maj. Gen. DeKalb, and Maj. Gen. Lord Stirling of the Patriots are following their enemy towards Coryell's Ferry on the Delaware River. Lafayette's command includes the North Carolina Continentals, Brig. Gen. Charles Scott's Virginia Continentals, and Brig. Gen. William Woodford's Virginia Continentals. By June 23rd, the Patriot army crosses Coryell's Ferry and the next day they reach Hopewell, within fifteen miles of the British camp at Allentown, PA.

Already, the Patriots in the field are harassing the British column. Brig. Gen. William Maxwell and his 1,300 New Jersey Continentals and Brig. Gen. Philemon Dickinson with his 800 New Jersey Militia are following the left flank of the long British column. Brig. Gen. John Cadwalader, with about 300 Continentals and his Pennsylvania Militia, snipe at the rear of the British column. Brig. Gen. Charles Scott and his Virginia Continentals with the 2nd NC Regiment under his command are also sent out to harass the British line. These Patriots do such a great job that the British manage to crawl only thirty-four (34) miles in six days. On June 26th, the British Army bivouacs at Monmouth Court House in nearly 100 degree temperatures.

The Patriots make it to Cranbury by June 25th. The next day is miserable, a morning of steaming heat and an afternoon of "a very great gust of rain." On June 27th, the Patriots march six miles toward Englishtown and pitch their camp. Each man gathers twigs and stems from whatever they can reach to create protection from the glaring sun.

On the morning of June 28th, the Patriot scouts discover that the British are decamping and preparing themselves for another long day of marching towards New York. Gen. George Washington sends orders for Maj. Gen. Charles Lee to attack. A ragged battle line forms with Maj. Gen. Lafayette on the right, Maj. Gen. Anthony Wayne in the center, and Brig. Gen. Charles Scott with his Virginians and the North Carolina Brigade are on the left. Scott's troops repulse a British calvary charge, but when units on his right begin falling back he is forced to order his men to file off rather than to be outflanked. Maj. Gen. Lee causes additional confusion when he issues orders without notifying his subordinates of his intentions. British Maj. Gen. Henry Clinton, with artillery protection, brings up his heavy columns, and the Patriots begin to fall back. They soon run back into their own lines marching forward and there is great confusion as the two groups meet, but General Washington and his officers form up a semblance of a battle line.

Coming up to Maj. Gen. Lee, Gen. Washington demands the reason for his retreat, and Lee replies, "Sir, these troops are not able to meet British Grenadiers." The seething Washington shouts, "Sir, they are able, and by God they shall do it." Lee then requests and is granted permission to direct the holding force that will give his commander enough time to consolidate his position. This task he performs with skill and courage.

General Washington draws up his army with Maj. Gen. Nathanael Greene's division on the right, Maj. Gen. Lord Stirling's division on the left, and most of Lee's former force, now under Maj. Gen. Lafayette, in reserve. In front of his lines, Maj. Gen. Anthony Wayne commands various elements of Lee's force. Artillery is placed on both wings, with the right wing in position to enfilade the advancing British.

The British come on and attack Maj. Gen. Lord Stirling's left wing with their light infantry and the 42nd (Black Watch) Regiment in the van. They are met by a storm of fire from Lord Stirling's Continentals. The battle rages back and forth for an hour until three Patriot regiments are sent though some woods to enfilade the attacking British right flank. The attack is successful and sends the British back to reform. Thwarted on the left, Lt. Gen. Charles, Lord Cornwallis leads a violent attack against Maj. Gen. Greene's right wing, with a force comprising British and Hessian grenadiers, light infantry, the Coldstream Guards, another Guards battalion, and the 37th and 44th Regiments. The attack is met by enfilading fire from the Patriot artillery on Combs Hill, as well as accurate musket volleys from Maj. Gen. Greene's Continental regiments. The British persist up the ravine slope but within minutes five high-ranking officers and many men are down from heavy fire. The attackers recoil down the slope.

The British make no further attempts on the main Patriot line, although cannonading from both sides continue until 6:00 p.m. At this point, the British fall back to a strong position east of the ravine. Gen. Washington wants to take the offensive to the British and attack both flanks, but darkness brings an end to the battle. The British rest and then resume their march to the northeast during the night. Gen. Washington again wants to resume the battle the next day but in the morning finds that the British have withdrawn during the night, continue their march without incident to Sandy Hook, and arrive there on June 30th. The British force is then transported by the Royal Navy across Lower New York Bay to Manhattan.

The British official casualty return reports 65 killed; 59 dead of fatigue, 170 wounded, and 64 missing. The Patriot official return reports 69 killed, 161 wounded, and 132 missing (37 of whom were found to have died of heat-stroke). Other unofficial estimates increase the losses to over 1,100 British casualties and 500 American casualties.

Monmouth is the last major battle in the northern theater, and the largest one-day battle of the war when measured in terms of participants. Maj. Gen. Charles Lee is later court-martialed at the Village Inn located in the center of Englishtown, where he is found guilty and relieved of command for one year. The verdict is approved by the Continental Congress by a close vote. Many months later, Lee writes a strongly worded letter to Congress in protest but they close the affair by informing him that they have no more need of his services.

There are only two documented casualties suffered by the North Carolina Continental Line at the battle of Monmouth, New Jersey–Sgt. Stephen White of the 1st NC Regiment, and Private Willie Upton of the 2nd NC Regiment; both die from fatigue.

In his 1819 pension application, John Hargrove (S37978) asserts:

> "That he the said John Hargrove enlisted in the town of Murfreesborough in the county of Hertford in the state of North Carolina in the 2nd North Carolina Continental Battalion commanded by Colonel John Patten sometime in the year 1777, that he continued to serve in the army until the 30th of June in the year 1780 when he was discharged at Murfreesborough aforesaid. That he was in the battle at Monmouth, at the Siege of Charlestown in South Carolina, and in various skirmishes during the time of service." [minor edits]

On June 30th, General George Washington orders the first divisions of his army to resume their northward march, but there is no longer any intention of pursuing the British under Maj. Gen. Henry Clinton. The Patriots march for the Hudson River highlands where they can cover the New England states, which many guess will be Clinton's next objective. By July 1st, the Patriots cross the Raritan River at New Brunswick. It is here that the Patriots celebrate the first anniversary of the Declaration of Independence with a thirteen-gun salute, a *feu de joie*, and much cheering by all. On the morning of July 5th, the troops are paraded in column.

On July 9th, the Continental Army passes through Newark and on July 11th they bivouac at Paramus, a small Dutch settlement in the rugged hills north of Passaic. Gen. Washington then crosses the Hudson River and makes camp at White Plains, where he frets and waits for Maj. Gen. Clinton's next move. As mentioned earlier, he has no way of knowing that the British strategy has changed with France entering the war on the side of Patriots. New York is to be held, but not at the cost of all other British possessions–the British are now concerned about their Caribbean holdings as well as the two Floridas.

The Patriot camp at White Plains becomes a model of routine. On July 22nd the army is rearranged into right and left wings, each with a second line. The North Carolina Brigade is placed in the second wing under the command of Maj. Gen. Alexander McDougall of the New York Continentals. The soldiers quickly become restless, so much so that all units are assembled twice a day for roll call to prevent the men from wandering off.

Many of the enlisted men's term of enlistment begin to expire and very few are willing to re-enlist unless it is agreed that they will be furloughed and allowed to return home during the winter months. Seven known privates of the 1st NC Regiment are sentenced to 100 lashes for plundering, and one, Thomas Glover, is hanged for this offense. Two lieutenants are court-martialed for offenses brought on by the boredom.

During July and August, Col. James Hogun resurrects his 7th NC Regiment and assembles over 600 fresh troops back home, most are considered "New Levies." By the end of August they are in Philadelphia on their way to West Point, New York, where they are placed on work detail. Col. Hogun describes West Point as "disagreeably situated" between the river and the rock-studded mountains. He also really dislikes building fortifications, having his men live in tents during winter months, and he is very unhappy that Gen. Washington has ordered him to this place before all of his men have been inoculated against Smallpox. He openly complains that the new arrangement of the Continental Army is "a little mysterious." However, he has very little reason to complain–his men are too poorly armed to be considered a combat unit. Most of the weapons brought from North Carolina are in such poor condition that they must not be used in battle. General George Washington procures 400 muskets from Albany for them.

On August 8th, the North Carolina General Assembly convenes for the second time in 1778. On Monday, August 10th, Governor Richard Caswell pens an address to the General Assembly. He tells about his draw on the Continental Treasury for $500,000 to be applied in raising and marching men northward to complete the Continental regiments as demanded by the Continental Congress in May. He dispatches Maj. Reading Blount to York, Pennsylvania with this request for funds, and the Continental Congress detains Maj. Blount for three full weeks and then sends him home with a mere $100,000 and no explanation. Gov. Richard Caswell considers this to be "derogatory to the dignity of the State as well as manifest injury to the common Cause." He continues by stating that the amount received is barely sufficient to pay the authorized bounty of 1,000 volunteers–yet the same Continental Congress urgently calls upon the state to "adopt the most effectual measures for speedily reinforcing the Continental army with our quota of troops." The incongruity is astounding, not only to the governor but also to the state's legislature.

On August 14th, a joint committee of the North Carolina Senate and House of Commons, chaired by Thomas Person, reports that a board of Continental officers has been convened at Halifax and at Moore's Creek and they recommend which field officers, captains, and subalterns are to take command of the four new regiments to be fitted up from the "New Levies" raised as a result of an Act of the previous legislature. The committee further reports that it is their opinion that the remaining supernumerary Continental officers remaining shall be discharged and that the Militia captains commanding the "New Levies" shall take rank and continue with their companies unless their companies are not full, in which case such smaller companies shall be joined with other companies and one captain shall take command. This is to be accomplished without the interposition of the existing Continental officers. It is also the opinion of the joint committee that the captains of the "New Levies" shall be authorized to command Continental lieutenants and have the right to sit in court-martials and trials of the said "New Levies." The joint committee concludes that they have examined the returns of the "New Levies" now on duty from the Salisbury and Hillsborough districts and received detailed information from those at Halifax and at Duplin Court House. Based on this information, the joint committee is of the opinion that the "New Levies" together with such Continental soldiers as are now in this state on duty are fully sufficient to complete the four new battalions to be raised agreeable to the Continental Congress resolve of May 29th. Both the Senate and the House of Commons agree with this report, with only minor recommendations.

On August 18th, the North Carolina General Assembly recommends that officers under the "new arrangement" (New Levies) to use their utmost endeavors to induce the soldiers to enlist into the Continental service for the duration of the war or for three years. They also recommend that the officers grant furloughs until the first day of March 1779, should they require it, at which time the men shall be entitled to receive a bounty of fifty dollars each. It is also resolved that the officers are empowered to grant furloughs until March 1, 1779 to all soldiers who shall agree to continue in the service for nine more months after that date. If a soldier refuses to agree with either stipulation then they shall be marched immediately to headquarters. Available records do not indicate what happens next.

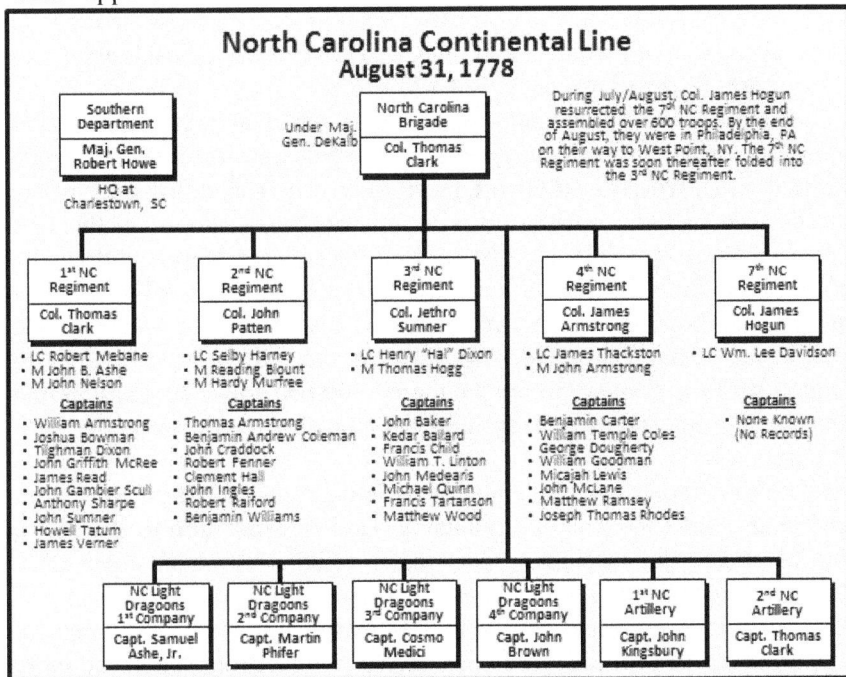

North Carolina Continental Line
August 31, 1778

Southern Department		Under Maj. Gen. DeKalb	North Carolina Brigade	During July/August, Col. James Hogun resurrected the 7th NC Regiment and assembled over 600 troops. By the end of August, they were in Philadelphia, PA on their way to West Point, NY. The 7th NC Regiment was soon thereafter folded into the 3rd NC Regiment.
Maj. Gen. Robert Howe			Col. Thomas Clark	
HQ at Charlestown, SC				

1st NC Regiment	2nd NC Regiment	3rd NC Regiment	4th NC Regiment	7th NC Regiment
Col. Thomas Clark	Col. John Patten	Col. Jethro Sumner	Col. James Armstrong	Col. James Hogun
• LC Robert Mebane • M John B. Ashe • M John Nelson	• LC Selby Harney • M Reading Blount • M Hardy Murfree	• LC Henry "Hal" Dixon • M Thomas Hogg	• LC James Thackston • M John Armstrong	• LC Wm. Lee Davidson
Captains • William Armstrong • Joshua Bowman • Tilghman Dixon • John Griffith McRee • James Read • John Gambier Scull • Anthony Sharpe • John Sumner • Howell Tatum • James Verner	**Captains** • Thomas Armstrong • Benjamin Andrew Coleman • John Craddock • Robert Fenner • Clement Hall • John Ingles • Robert Raiford • Benjamin Williams	**Captains** • John Baker • Kedar Ballard • Francis Child • William T. Linton • John Medears • Michael Quinn • Francis Tartanson • Matthew Wood	**Captains** • Benjamin Carter • William Temple Coles • George Dougherty • William Goodman • Micajah Lewis • John McLane • Matthew Ramsey • Joseph Thomas Rhodes	**Captains** • None Known (No Records)

NC Light Dragoons 1st Company	NC Light Dragoons 2nd Company	NC Light Dragoons 3rd Company	NC Light Dragoons 4th Company	1st NC Artillery	2nd NC Artillery
Capt. Samuel Ashe, Jr.	Capt. Martin Phifer	Capt. Cosmo Medici	Capt. John Brown	Capt. John Kingsbury	Capt. Thomas Clark

What is known, however, is the simple fact that the "New Levies," for the most part, are never officially placed on the North Carolina Continental Line, nor are most sent northward to join the North Carolina Brigade at White Plains and West Point. Most "New Levies" are on indefinite furlough, waiting to be recalled to active duty. North Carolina has just expended a tremendous amount of money and effort to raise 2,400 new troops for the Continental Army, but the troops are no longer wanted by the Continental Congress. With the recent "New Levies" debacle coupled with the long-standing problem of no North Carolina brigadier generals, there is now an open and acknowledged tension between the state government and the Continental Congress.

Gen. Washington's army is reorganized in early September–the North Carolina Brigade is now under Maj. Gen. Baron DeKalb at Fredericksburg (present-day Patterson, NY). Others are sent to West

Point (NY), Danbury (CT), and Maj. Gen. Lord Stirling is sent to a point between Fredericksburg and New York, NY.

On September 25th, the Continental Congress resolves that Maj. Gen. Benjamin Lincoln of Massachusetts shall take over the Southern Department headquartered at Charlestown, South Carolina–replacing Maj. Gen. Robert Howe who is ordered to join General George Washington in the northern theater. Maj. Gen. Lincoln arrives on December 10th with about 2,500 men, and he moves his headquarters to Purrysburg, SC by early January of 1779.

In October, there is a clothing windfall when a large shipment of uniforms arrives from France. Some of the coats are faced in red, some faced in blue, whereas others are faced in brown. The entire army wants those faced in blue, but the coats are distributed via lots. On the first drawing, North Carolina, New York, New Jersey, and Maryland draw the coats faced in blue. The Continental Army can now present a fully-uniformed force for once. Interestingly, also in early October, the Continental Congress decides to forward the additional $400,000 to North Carolina, making up for the mere $100,000 it had sent earlier–the tension between the two governments is now eased and essentially back to normal.

During the months of September and October, the British in New York give many hints that they are planning another expedition to the south, and of course the Patriots suspect that the target is Charlestown once again. In preparation, the Continental Congress resolves on October 17th that North Carolina shall assemble the previous order of 3,000 men for the aid of South Carolina. The news arrives with a promise to send more money to the state as soon as possible. That same day, the Continental Congress resolves that North Carolina gather yet another 2,000 men for the aid of South Carolina–now 5,000, including the "New Levies" previously requested, then placed on hold–a hold that lingers.

An interesting side note to this request is that there are numerous "back-channel communications" sent to Governor Richard Caswell that many members of the Continental Congress earnestly want Caswell to lead these new troops personally, and they are willing to provide him with a commission as a major general in the Continental Line. Several letters are passed from Philadelphia via the North Carolina delegates to the Continental Congress–Cornelius Harnett, John Penn, and John Williams. Governor Caswell handily deflects these back-channel requests by simply not responding in any official capacity. He does discuss it with a few trusted men of the state, and the legislature gives him permission to select a commanding officer with the rank of Major General of Militia. His first choice is Brig. Gen. John Ashe of the Wilmington District Brigade of Militia. Many North Carolinians, however, openly resent being called upon, once again, to help out its southern neighbor–a neighbor that has recently kicked out Maj. Gen. Robert Howe for specious allegations.

On November 8th, the British surprise no one when Maj. Gen. Henry Clinton orders an army of about 3,000 men under the command of Lt. Col. Archibald Campbell to sail southward via troop transport ships. Over a month later, they land at Tybee Island, less than two of miles from Savannah, Georgia. Campbell is met on December 29th by Maj. Gen. Robert Howe with about 550 South Carolina Continentals and about 100 Georgia Militiamen. Needless to say, the larger British army seizes Savannah on that day and they hold it well into 1782.

North Carolina responds to this new threat as it always has–gather as many men as possible and take them to the enemy quickly. Col. Gideon Lamb, of the resurrected 6th NC Regiment is charged with gathering the "New Levies" being assembled in the eastern portion of the state, while Lt. Col. Archibald Lytle is charged with assembling the "New Levies" in the western portion of the state. The North Carolina Militia is hurriedly gathered all across the state as well–now under their first ever major general over Militia–John Ashe, from Wilmington.

Brig. Gen. Griffith Rutherford of the Salisbury District Brigade of Militia is the first to respond, and he is quickly joined by Lt. Col. Archibald Lytle–both crossing together into South Carolina on December 5th. These troops, driving their own beeves and carrying their own provisions with them, reach Charlestown around Christmas. Despite Governor Richard Caswell's best exhortations, there is considerable delay in getting the troops from the eastern part of the state to move. On December 5th, Col. Gideon Lamb crosses the Neuse River with 200 "New Levies" along with about 1,000 Militiamen. However, on December 29th, these troops are still detained at Elizabeth Town–Col. Lamb is waiting for 100 more "New Levies" and a small number of Militia, both expected any hour.

None of the North Carolina "New Levies" or Militia reach Maj. Gen. Robert Howe in time to save Savannah. With the arrival of Maj. Gen. Benjamin Lincoln at Purrysburg, SC on January 3, 1779, Maj. Gen. Robert Howe soon heads to the northern theater. Not long thereafter, the British are heavily reinforced when Brig. Gen. Augustine Prevost arrives from Eastern Florida with almost 2,000 more enemy troops and assumes command of all British forces in Savannah.

In the meantime, the northern army marches into winter quarters. Each brigade is strategically placed, not only in areas with plentiful provisions, but also in locations where they can block the enemy's movements. Gen. George Washington plants his flag at Middlebrook. The army is further posted at Elizabeth and Ramapo in New Jersey; West Point and Fishkill in New York; and at Danbury in Connecticut. This semi-circle is drawn in a 40-mile radius around New York, and it allows for open routes of communications both north and south.

The North Carolina Brigade under Col. Thomas Clark is stationed at Smith's Clove until December 11th, when they move to Paramus, New Jersey. Their orders are to block communications between the locals and the British in New York. They also capture British deserters, who are beginning to come from New York in increasing numbers.

Col. James Hogun and his rag-tag 7th NC Regiment is sent to Philadelphia to support Maj. Gen. Benedict Arnold, who requested two more regiments of Continentals. Gen. George Washington explains why he sends Col. Hogun, "They are a tender set of people, but illy provided with Cloathing and therefore require warm quarters." Leaving his sick behind, Col. Hogun withdraws from the Hudson River around the middle of December and marches his regiment into Philadelphia–arriving there on January 19, 1779.

On December 5th, the Continental Congress resolves that they no longer want the services of the four companies of NC Light Dragoons as of January 1, 1779. It is also ordered that the Board of War supply these troops with such clothing as may be due to them, and pay them through January 1st. These companies are sent home and are soon thereafter converted to North Carolina State Troops as described in Volume 2.

The winter of 1778/1779 is intense, but nothing like the time spent a year earlier at Valley Forge. Just east of Col. Thomas Clark and the majority of the North Carolina Brigade, Lt. Col. Robert Mebane is stationed with about 200 men at King's Ferry to cut off enemy supplies into New York. Once again, the men build huts, but the construction pace is leisurely–their tents provide adequate protection until the huts are finished. Although there are few complaints about the lack of clothing and blankets, there is a critical shortage of shoes, and Gen. Washington fears that his army will soon be barefoot.

1778 is a tumultuous year for the North Carolina Continental Line. The implosion and reorganization of early summer is certainly painful, however, by the end of the year things are noticeably on the upswing. With the great numbers of "New Levies" brought to bear closer to home than originally planned, and the resurrection of the 7th NC Regiment to bring new recruits to the northern theater, the year ends fairly well for the NC Continentals.

Appendix B includes a listing of all known Continental units that participated in the battle of Monmouth, NJ.

Chapter Five – 1779

On January 9th, the Continental Congress finally commissions two new brigadier generals for the North Carolina Continental Line–Jethro Sumner and James Hogun. Since Jethro Sumner is in North Carolina at the time of his appointment, he remains there awaiting further orders because of the recent capture of Savannah, Georgia by the British army. With new generals comes yet another reorganization of the North Carolina Continental Line. Lt. Col. William Lee Davidson is given command of the 1st NC Regiment, and Lt. Col. Robert Mebane is given command of the 3rd NC Regiment–no explanation

> **Key Events of 1779**
>
> • NC General Assembly meets twice (May & October), Gov. Richard Caswell is re-elected for his 3rd and final term.
> • The NC Light Dragoons companies that were on the Continental Line are reconstituted as State Troops, new leadership.
> • British forces that seized Savannah, GA threaten to take Charlestown, SC. NC sends Continentals and Militia to assist.
> • NC forces are badly defeated at Briar Creek, GA, but they perform well at the battle of Stono Ferry, SC.
> • NC forces support SC and GA in other battles/skirmishes, some wins, but a big defeat again at Savannah, GA.
> • NC Continentals in the northern theater in three engagements – Near West Point, Fort Lafayette, and Stony Point, all in New York.
> • With a new British threat to bring the battle to the South, the NC Continental Line is finally ordered southward, never to return to the northern theater.

for them not being promoted to full colonels has been passed down to history. Col. Thomas Clark is ordered to take what was left of the 7th NC Regiment, plus the few "New Levies" that made it northward before orders were given for them to stop, and re-establish the 5th NC Regiment. The 6th NC Regiment is officially re-established since Col. Gideon Lamb and Lt. Col. Archibald Lytle have been fairly successful in recruiting.

The "New Levies" under Lt. Col. Archibald Lytle in South Carolina finally catch up with Maj. Gen. Benjamin Lincoln at Purrysburg soon after the general's arrival there on January 3rd. With Lt. Col. Lytle is Brig. Gen. Griffith Rutherford and a fairly large contingent of the Salisbury District Brigade of Militia. More "New Levies" and Militia are camped at Duplin Court House and Elizabeth Town with Col. Gideon Lamb, and when Maj. Gen. John Ashe of the North Carolina Militia is given command of the expedition into South Carolina, he soon marches them southward to join up with those already with Maj. Gen. Benjamin Lincoln.

By the first of February over 400 more North Carolina nine-months Continentals of the resurrected 6th NC Regiment and a large number of North Carolina Militiamen join Maj. Gen. Benjamin Lincoln at

Purrysburg along the Savannah River. Field officers command units no larger than small companies. Brig. Gen. Jethro Sumner, Lt. Col. James Thackston, Lt. Col. Archibald Lytle, Lt. Col. Henry "Hal" Dixon, and Maj. John Armstrong–all at home in late 1778 for various reasons–have assembled as many Continentals and recalled all furloughed "New Levies" as possible. These Continental officers command units ranging from thirty-eight to fifty-three men, and when new North Carolina Militia units arrive they incorporate many Militia companies into their commands. Brig. Gen. Jethro Sumner spends countless hours determining how best to structure his inexperienced commanders and men into a cohesive fighting brigade. Over the next few months he struggles to field three regiments and to remain one step ahead of his increasingly deteriorating health.

The British under Lt. Col. Archibald Campbell are not interested in merely sitting on their arms inside their recently-captured town of Savannah. By early February, with Savannah safely in the hands of Brig. Gen. Augustine Prevost, Lt. Col. Campbell ventures out and seizes the small river town of Augusta. With only a token resistance from the South Carolina Militia, Augusta is now also in British hands.

However, around the same time South Carolina Brig. Gen. William Moultrie repels the British attempting to seize the town of Beaufort, and

North Carolina Continental Line
January 30, 1779

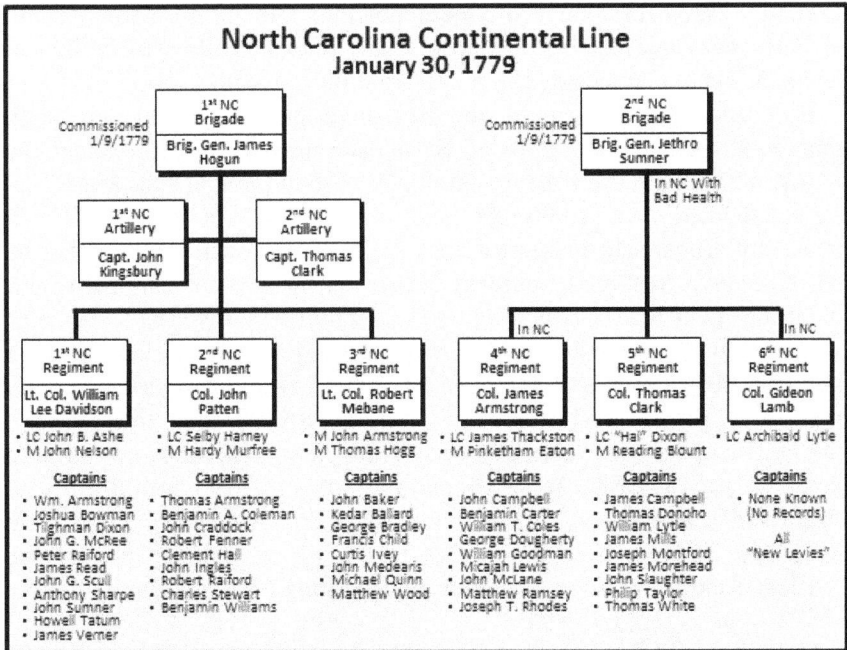

Commissioned 1/9/1779	**1st NC Brigade** — Brig. Gen. James Hogun	Commissioned 1/9/1779	**2nd NC Brigade** — Brig. Gen. Jethro Sumner (In NC With Bad Health)

1st NC Artillery — Capt. John Kingsbury
2nd NC Artillery — Capt. Thomas Clark

1st NC Regiment	2nd NC Regiment	3rd NC Regiment	4th NC Regiment	5th NC Regiment	6th NC Regiment
Lt. Col. William Lee Davidson	Col. John Patten	Lt. Col. Robert Mebane	Col. James Armstrong	Col. Thomas Clark	Col. Gideon Lamb
• LC John B. Ashe • M John Nelson	• LC Selby Harney • M Hardy Murfree	• M John Armstrong • M Thomas Hogg	• LC James Thackston • M Pinketham Eaton	• LC "Hal" Dixon • M Reading Blount	• LC Archibald Lytle

Captains	Captains	Captains	Captains	Captains	Captains
• Wm. Armstrong • Joshua Bowman • Tilghman Dixon • John G. McRee • Peter Raiford • James Read • John G. Scull • Anthony Sharpe • John Sumner • Howell Tatum • James Verner	• Thomas Armstrong • Benjamin A. Coleman • John Craddock • Robert Fenner • Clement Hall • John Ingles • Robert Raiford • Charles Stewart • Benjamin Williams	• John Baker • Kedar Ballard • George Bradley • Francis Child • Curtis Ivey • John Medearis • Michael Quinn • Matthew Wood	• John Campbell • Benjamin Carter • William T. Coles • George Dougherty • William Goodman • Micajah Lewis • John McLane • Matthew Ramsey • Joseph T. Rhodes	• James Campbell • Thomas Donoho • William Lytle • James Mills • Joseph Montford • James Morehead • John Slaughter • Philip Taylor • Thomas White	• None Known (No Records) All "New Levies"

Col. Andrew Pickens and his South Carolina Militia with a small contingent of North Carolina and Georgia Miltiamen defeat the Loyalists gathering at Kettle Creek, nearby in Georgia. More positive news comes when the Patriots learn that South Carolina Col. LeRoy Hammond with some South Carolina and Georgia Militia soundly defeat a British garrison at Herbert's Store in Georgia and seize over 200 horses.

Maj. Gen. Benjamin Lincoln wants Augusta back in Patriots' hands. He knows that all Militia units under his command are clamoring that their time is nearly up, including those from South Carolina, Georgia, and North Carolina. He sends South Carolina Brig. Gen. Andrew Williamson with over 1,200 Militia to the east bank of the Savannah River opposite Augusta. Brig. Gen. Griffith Rutherford and his 800 North Carolina Militiamen are sent to take post at Black Swamp, not far from Purrysburg. Maj. Gen. John Ashe with approximately 1,200 more North Carolina Militiamen plus 200 "New Levies" under command of Lt. Col. Archibald Lytle of the 6th NC Regiment are sent to Briar Creek on the Georgia side of the Savannah River.

Maj. Gen. Ashe is soon joined by about 75 Georgia Continentals and another 200 Georgia Militiamen under Col. Samuel Elbert. Ashe does not really want this posting, protesting that his men are still exhausted from their long march and that they are not completely armed for such an excursion. Well-rested and fully-equipped men remain in Lincoln's camp at Purrysburg because South Carolina law does not allow its Militia to leave the state without prior approval from the legislature.

To everyone's amazement, the British evacuate Augusta and begin marching back to the safety of Savannah. It is later learned that the British had received erroneous intelligence–they thought that Maj. Gen. John Ashe had over 11,000 men under his command, a force the British could not withstand. So hastily does Lt. Col. Campbell decamp that he leaves twelve freshly-slaughtered beeves on the ground. His men burn the bridge over Briar Creek after they cross hurriedly towards Savannah.

Maj. Gen. Ashe arrrives and orders the bridge to be rebuilt. Although he sends out patrols, and one even has a brief firefight with the enemy, none of the patrols send back word on the British locations. Interestingly, the British spies soon learn that Maj. Gen. John Ashe does not have so large an army as earlier reported, and this news is given both to Lt. Col. Archibald Campbell and sent to Brig. Gen. Augustine Prevost in Savannah. Prevost quickly decides to set up an ambush should the Patriots decide to march south after the retreating Lt. Col. Campbell.

On the afternoon of March 2nd, when enemy troops are sighted in their vicinity, the Patriots under Maj. Gen. John Ashe do nothing for defensive preparations. After a Council of War, the Patriots march out to disperse what they believe to be no more than a scouting party. On March 3rd, Maj. Gen. John Ashe forms his command in two lines. Precious time is lost in distributing cartridges–powder had earlier been ruined because there were no cartouche boxes, another minor military blunder by the Patriots that leads to terrible consequences. Furthermore, it is decided that Lt. Col. Archibald Lytle and his "New Levies" will not be needed so they are posted at another bridge, about a mile and a half from the other Patriots.

At three o'clock in the afternoon, mounted units on the South Carolina side of the Savannah River give an alarm, and about fifteen minutes later Brig. Gen. Augustine Prevost's army marches up to the rear of the Patriots. The British are in three columns, six abreast; and when they are within 150 yards of the Patriots they deploy into a line of battle. The Patriots hurry into a loose formation, "some carrying their cartridges under their arms, others in the bosoms of their shirts, and some tied up in the corners of their hunting shirts."

The Georgia Continentals are the first to fire. After delivering several rounds they decide to advance, but they actually drift into the line of fire of the Militia from North Carolina. The ripple effect throws everyone's aim and attention off, and a general panic ensues. Lt. Col. Archibald Lytle soon arrives with a small fieldpiece, just to see the Patriot line disintegrate as hundreds of men throw down their guns and run for cover. The Georgia Continentals hold until their situation becomes hopeless and Col. Samuel Elbert surrenders. The battle lasts no more than 15 minutes.

Maj. Gen. John Ashe and other officers on horseback ride among those fleeing and attempt to turn them back–their efforts are useless. The men surge through the woods in sheer panic and nothing is going to stop them, save a bullet in the back.

The Patriots lose 150-200 men killed. Eleven officers are captured, as are over 160 rank and file. Many place the blame directly on Maj. Gen. John Ashe, especially Brig. Gen. William Bryan of New Bern. A court-martial finds Ashe guilty of negligence–his greatest fault is that he had not laid out a route of withdrawal or designated a rendezvous point in case of defeat. Brig. Gen. William Bryan soon resigns, claiming that he is too ignorant of military matters to command such a unit.

In his 1819 pension application, Jacob Myers (S35533) asserts:

"That he the said Jacob Myers enlisted in Guilford County in the state of North Carolina in the month of June or July in the year 1777 [incorrect, it was 1778] in the company commanded by Captain William Lytle in the regiment commanded by Lt. Colonel Archibald Lytle of the North Carolina Line, that he continued to serve in said corps until September 1779 when he was honorably discharged from service in the state of South Carolina within 12 miles of Charlestown. That he was in the battle of Briar Creek and a battle within 12 miles of Charlestown [Stono Ferry] and that in the last battle he was wounded…" [minor edits]

On April 10th, Brig. Gen. Jethro Sumner writes to Governor Richard Caswell from the Patriot Camp at Black Swamp in South Carolina. Along with his return showing the numbers of men under his command, he describes that "the arrangement of three Battalions has made it necessary that each officer be supplied with another commission." He continues by asserting that he has 24 or 25 officer vacancies in the three battalions. These "battalions" are the recently recreated 4th NC Regiment, 5th NC Regiment, and 6th NC Regiment, mostly "New Levies."

As the small number of North Carolina Continentals under Brig. Gen. Jethro Sumner commiserate in South Carolina, their brethren in the northern theater now welcome warmer weather–and a surprise attack by the British. The 1st North Carolina Brigade is positioned to furnish assistance and support to several Patriot stations encircling New York. Col. John Patten and the 2nd NC Regiment receive the first spring advance by the British at his location near West Point in New York.

On May 16th, two columns with 500 British Regulars each cross the Hudson River and move to attack the North Carolina Continentals' position. They soon discover that the British have missed their designated landing sites and one column has lost its way. After a brief skirmish, and the enemy plundering several local homes, the British then fall back across the river. The Patriots suffer three men wounded in several small firefights as the British leave.

In his 1820 pension application, Asa Spellman (S42022) asserts:

"That he the said Asa Spellman enlisted in the company commanded by Captain Michael Quinn in the Tenth [Third] North Carolina Regiment, Continental Establishment, commanded by Lt. Colonel William Lee Davidson. That he enlisted for nine months and served out his term, but cannot state the day of his enlistment or discharge. He was discharged at Halifax in North Carolina. He was not in any engagement except a skirmish near West Point, and at Kings Ferry in New Jersey." [minor edits]

Two weeks later, Capt. Thomas Armstrong with 70 hand-picked men from the 2nd NC Regiment are stationed at Fort Lafayette on the east side of the Hudson River at Verplanck's Point. Another small garrison is across the river at Stony Point. Six thousand British troops disembark from ships and flatboats on both sides of the river, and it is quickly apparent that neither garrison has much of a chance. The forty men at Stony Point burn the log blockhouse and retreat before the British can arrive. The North Carolinians at Fort Lafayette are determined not to give in so easily.

British Regulars keep up a steady fire on the land side of the Patriot fort, while the ships in the river bombard the small enclosure. The Patriots eventually surrender, and every man is allowed to march out wearing their side arms, an honor given to them in admiration of their stubborn resistance. Capt. Thomas Armstrong and most of his seventy men are later exchanged in December of 1779.

In his 1832 pension application, James Gambling (W460) asserts:

"... he enlisted at first as he believes for only six months, but was returned for twelve months, which term Applicant served under Captain Edward Vail in the south, after which without leaving the service Applicant re-enlisted for three years, & was immediately marched to the north under the command of the above officers with the exception of the captain–Captain James Gee commanded the company to which Applicant belonged. Captain Gee died on the march to the north–to join the main army under General Washington. After which Captain John Craddock commanded the company. Applicant marched on with the above regiments to the commons of Philadelphia–where we remained encamped–until General Washington came on with his army, when our Brigade joined the main army. Applicant there remained with the main army in the north for less than three years–during which time, he was in the battles of Brandywine, Germantown, in which battle General Francis Nash was killed; Monmouth Court House, where the Americans were victorious. Applicant was in the fort [Ft. Lafayette] on North River, at Verplanck's Point at King's Ferry, some distance above New York. The British attacked the fort about sunrise; the engagement continued until night & was recommenced in the morning, about two o'clock p. m. the Americans had to surrender the fort, when the prisoners were taken to New York & kept in close confinement for two months & ten days in the great house called the Sugar House. Applicant was discharged from his imprisonment after the expiration of two months & ten days. The above fort was commanded by Captain Thomas Armstrong, Lieutenants Anderson & Nathaniel Lawrence–an exchange was made of prisoners, when the British put us ashore at a little place called Morristown–then we marched to West Point where we rejoined our regiment–we there remained until we received orders to march to Charlestown, South Carolina, but before this time Applicant's term of service had expired but he remained with the army until the army marched to the town of Halifax, North Carolina, where he was regularly discharged by Colonel John Patten..." [minor edits]

Those small Patriot forts are not Maj. Gen. Henry Clinton's real objective. He wants to lure Gen. George Washington into the open and crush the Patriot army. When Gen. Washington refuses to take the bait, Maj. Gen. Clinton garrisons both forts and sails back to New York. Gen. Washington moves his headquarters to Smith's Clove to reassess his situation.

Gen. Washington first thinks that attempting to retake these forts will require a larger army than he has at his disposal, but he soon alters his thinking and decides that retaking the forts is not impossible. He quickly orders Maj. Gen. Anthony Wayne to get a spy into the fort at Stony Point, which he manages to achieve. After reporting back that there are weak points and a smaller enemy presence than expected, Maj. Gen. Wayne then receives the order to retake Stony Point.

Maj. Gen. Wayne assembles an elite corps of over 1,300 men that have been drawn from troops of all regiments in the area. They are all combat veterans, 20-30 years old, and no shorter than five feet, five inches tall. This corps is hurried through an intense training that includes extensive use of the bayonet. Included are two companies of 178 men from North Carolina under the command of Maj. Hardy Murfree of the 2nd NC Regiment.

This elite corps starts out about fifteen miles upriver from the fort at Stony Point. They march a circuitous and rocky path so narrow that it becomes necessary to march in single file. Every man wears a piece of white paper in his hat so his comrades will know friend from foe. So they will rely upon the bayonet, all muskets are unloaded except for those under Maj. Hardy Murfree. If any man attempts to fire his gun, Maj. Gen. Wayne's orders are that he should be put to death immediately by the nearest officer.

At 11:30 p.m. on July 15th, the Patriots move to retake their fort. Maj. Murfree and his men approach from the front of the fort to get the enemy's attention–that's also why his men have ammunition. To mask the approach of the other Patriots his men are ordered to deliver a "perpetual and galling fire." Musket balls and grape shot rain down on them as they return a heavy fire.

As his comrades run to the ramparts, Maj. Murfree and his men increase their fire again. Maj. Gen. Anthony Wayne is grazed by an enemy musket ball and he begs his men to carry him into the fort to die. His men give a mighty shout and cross the ramparts with him on their shoulders.

It takes less than an hour to overrun the fort. The Patriots drive the defenders into each other until they begin to throw down their arms, huddling together as they collectively cry for mercy. Maj. Gen. Anthony

Wayne's artillery officers quickly turn the fort's guns and fire at the British sloop, *Vulture*, anchored nearby. The British losses are fairly heavy–63 killed, 70+ wounded, and 543 taken prisoner. The Patriots lose 15 killed and 83 wounded. Lt. William Hilton of the 1st NC Regiment is killed in this engagment. Among the wounded are Capt. Joshua Bowman of the 1st NC Regiment, Lt. John Daves of the 2nd NC Regiment, Sgt. John Harvey and Sgt. William Morgan, both of the 1st NC Regiment. Four other captains participated–Capt. John Craddock, Capt. Clement Hall, and Capt. Anthony Sharpe, all three of the 2nd NC Regiment, and Capt. John Kingsbury of the NC Artillery.

The Patriots also capture fifteen cannons and a cache of provisions, all together appraised at more than $180,000. Maj. Gen. Wayne praises Maj. Hardy Murfree for his "good conduct and intrepidity." Gen. Washington later decides that Stony Point isn't worth the force required to keep it, so he has the cannons and provisions removed and leaves it empty. He has managed to embarrass the British, which is good enough for him.

In his 1827 pension application, John Kelly (S35489) asserts:

"… he was placed in the 1st Regiment–some length of time after, he was taken with his company aforesaid & joined a regiment under General Anthony Wayne, commanded by Colonel Flury & was at the storming of Stony Point. When he & his company joined said regiment they were placed under Captain Joshua Bowman…" [minor edits]

The North Carolina Continentals are next stationed in the vicinity of West Point under the command of Maj. Gen. Alexander MacDougall. As usual, clothing is scarce–many men are nearly naked and thankful that it is now summer. Provision are scarce as well, and the men are often gripped with hunger. With an acute drought in the vicinity, there is not enough water moving to turn the grist mills to get grain ground into flour.

On April 17th, Col. Tim Pickering of the Continental War Office writes to Gov. Richard Caswell informing him that the time has expired for the men of the 3rd NC Regiment and they are on their way home. He also informs the governor that the officers have also been sent home and that Lt. Col. Robert Mebane is given orders to reform the 3rd NC Regiment while at home and then to redeploy it in the southern theater. The Continental Congress also resolves on May 7th that they still want six regiments of North Carolina Continentals and that the last four regiments shall remain in the southern theater.

On May 10th, Lt. Col. Robert Mebane informs Gov. Richard Caswell that he is now at Halifax, North Carolina, he has dismissed all of his officers, and he reminds the governor just how dissatisfied all officers are with how they are being mistreated by their state. If the legislature does not do something soon then he fears that every officer on the North Carolina Continental Line will resign their commissions.

Gov. Caswell takes immediate action and several officers who are at home on leave convince the sitting General Assembly to take their concerns to heart and to finally do something about them. On May 15th, the North Carolina legislature resolves that every officer shall receive half pay for seven years after the termination of the war, that every officer shall get a new uniform each year at the same price that they paid in 1775, that the land promised to the officers and soldiers will be tax exempt for their lifetimes, and for the officers and men who die while in service their widows shall inherit their husbands half pay for the remainder of their lives as well. This action finally stops the complaints of all active officers and their threat to resign is rescinded.

Deputy Clothier General, Thomas Craik, of North Carolina has plenty of cloth but Maj. Gen. Benjamin Lincoln refuses to allow Continental clothing to be issued to "nine-month men" because of the limited time they are to remain in the field. Brig. Gen. Jethro Sumner persuades some of the Militia to enlist for sixteen months as "substitutes." His new brigade appears even more ragged when they are paraded next to the well-clothed South Carolina Continentals. Maj. Gen. Lincoln writes to Gov. Richard Caswell that this situation is harming morale and demands that the state send proper clothing to its men, all the while continuing to forbid Thomas Craike to issue them Continental clothing.

Meanwhile, after the debacle at Briar Creek, Georgia in early spring, it soon becomes clear that the British in Savannah are not going to remain content with that singular possession. However, the same is true for the Patriots across the Savannah River. With increased Militia numbers from both South Carolina and North Carolina flowing into his camp near Purrysburg, Maj. Gen. Benjamin Lincoln grows ambitious.

Leaving about 1,000 men under Brig. Gen. William Moultrie (SC) for the defense of Purrysburg, Maj. Gen. Lincoln appoints about 4,000 men for his own objectives. When Militiamen learn that they are to cross the Savannah River, a "great mutiny" is the result and they declare they will not be forced out of their home state of South Carolina. When the sun sets roughly 400 SC Militiamen slip away in the dark–and none are ever captured as deserters. On April 23rd, Maj. Gen. Lincoln crosses the river and marches for Augusta to protect the exiled Georgia legislature, which has been summoned to meet there on May 1st.

British Brig. Gen. Augustine Prevost observes Maj. Gen. Benjamin Lincoln's movements and quickly decides to draw his enemy back out of Georgia. With over 2,400 British troops and a large number of Indians, Brig. Gen. Prevost quietly crosses the Savannah River on April 29th and attacks some South Carolina Continentals at Purrysburg. These Patriots fall back to Brig. Gen. William Moultrie's position at the Black Swamp, and they all begin a long retreat from the steadily-advancing Prevost.

Messengers are sent to Maj. Gen. Benjamin Lincoln, but it takes a few days to get the message to him and for him to make up his mind that this is not a "feint" by the wily Prevost. By May 7th, the British have pushed the Patriots very near to Charlestown, and on May 9th Brig. Gen. Augustine Prevost arrives at Charlestown Neck and demands that the Patriots surrender. Brig. Gen. William Moultrie (SC) stalls for time as he expects Maj. Gen. Lincoln to arrive soon. With Moultrie is the 2nd North Carolina Brigade under Brig. Gen. Jethro Sumner.

As Lincoln approaches, Brig. Gen. Prevost gets cold feet and abandons his siege of Charlestown. During the night of May 12th, he and his army quickly march towards the coast and set up their camp on John's Island to await for ships to arrive and haul them back to Savannah.

In his 1833 pension application, James Guthery (S21793) asserts:

"That he volunteered into the service of the United States in the year 1778 under the command of Colonel James Saunders, & chose for his Captain Robert Moore, but was soon afterwards placed under the command of Captain William Goodman in the Continental line, commanded by Lt. Col. Henry Dixon, Major John Armstrong & General Benjamin Lincoln, & received $30 bounty & continued in the Continental service from May 1778 until the 16th of August 1779, being about 15 months. When he entered the service he first marched to Peytonsburg in Pittsylvania County in the state of Virginia–thence marched back to Caswell County in North Carolina where we were discharged on furlough for six months but after the expiration of about three months we were called upon to give up the furlough, which he did & again entered the service. Thence he marched to Salisbury–thence to the 10-Mile Branch near Charlestown in South Carolina–thence to Purrysburg on Savannah River in South Carolina. Thence to a place called the Black Swamp–thence to Golphin's Mills on Savannah River–Thence to Charlestown, South Carolina, where he was engaged in the defense of Charlestown against the attack of General Prevost some time in the spring of the year 1779–Thence marched back near Stono, where he again joined General Lincoln, and soon afterwards was in the Stono battle and was commanded in that engagement by Lieutenant Joel Lewis, & Lt. Col. Dixon, this being about the 20th of June 1779..." [minor edits]

86

Meanwhile, to protect his rear, Brig. Gen. Autustine Prevost has his men to hastily throw up breastworks on the mainland at Stono Ferry. He also has his men to collect all the local boats in the vicinity and use them in the construction of a floating bridge across Stono Inlet to the island. As the days drag on, Prevost has his men to construct three solid redoubts on the mainland, each surrounded by a thick abatis of felled trees.

By June 9th, British transports and men-of-war drop anchors off John's Island. They bring supplies but no reinforcements. A week later, Brig. Gen. Prevost starts loading the booty and slaves his men have stolen during their long march through southern South Carolina. Lt. Col. John Maitland is stationed at Stono Ferry with about 800 men–a battalion of the 71st Regiment of Foot (aka Fraser's Highlanders), two Hessian regiments, and a regiment of South Carolina and North Carolina Loyalists. He also has a company of artillery with seven field guns.

The floating bridge is now disassembled to employ the boats in disembarking Prevost's troops. His sick, his spare baggage, and all horses are ferried across to John's Island for loading onto the transports.

The last of the North Carolina Militia, under Brig. Gen. John Butler of the Hillsborough District Brigade of Militia join up with Maj. Gen. Benjamin Lincoln on April 26th, and he is quite aware that their time will expire on July 10th. Brig. Gen. Jethro Sumner's nine-month "New Levies" will have to be discharged no later than August 10th. And, the Virginia Militia make it clear that they are marching home on July 15th, no matter how bad things might get. It now behooves Maj. Gen. Lincoln to make his move very soon, especially while the British are busily engaged in their embarkation efforts.

On June 19th, a council of officers decides that the Patriots shall attack the next day, and Maj. Gen. Benjamin Lincoln marches with 1,200 men shortly after midnight on the morning of June 20th. Brig. Gen. Jethro Sumner and his 2nd North Carolina Brigade command the right wing, which includes the North Carolina Militia under Brig. Gen. John Butler and two field pieces. The left wing is made up of Georgia and South Carolina Continentals and South Carolina Militia with four guns under Brig. Gen. Isaac Huger (SC). The NC Light Dragoons (now resurrected as State Troops) are led by Col. Francois DeMalmedy with thirteen known companies protecting both flanks. In reserve are Brig. Gen. Count Kasimir Pulaski and his legion, the South Carolina Light Dragoons under Col. Daniel Horry, and late-arriving Militiamen of South Carolina and Virginia.

The British troops are camped on one side with a detachment of Hessians camped on the other side. A British galley is anchored in the river to provide covering fire for the Hessians.

The battle lasts for about one hour and the Patriots seize the British redoubts. Most of the British and Hessian troops are falling back, have taken many causalities, and the Patriots are on the verge of victory when fresh British reinforcements come up. Maj. Gen. Benjamin Lincoln, realizing that his men are running short on ammunition, falls back. A British pursuit force is cut off by the quick action of Brig. Gen. Kasimir Pulaski and his cavalry units, which stop the British.

As the Patriots attack the Hessian camp they immediately come under fire from the British galley. The Patriots open fire on the ship and force it to withdraw from the fight. Being on the high ground, the Patriots overshoot the Hessians when they open fire on them. The British have gathered all the boats they can, and cross over the river to reinforce the Hessians. The British troops then charge after the Patriots.

Unknown to the British, the South Carolina Navy schooner *Rattlesnake* has come down the river. It begins to fire into the rear of the British and Hessian forces. These turn from the Patriot force and fire upon the *Rattlesnake*. The *Rattlesnake* fires back at them and repells the attack with heavy losses. The British forces lose their leader, Capt. William Wulff, and six Hessians are killed. Maj. Endemann and 37 others are wounded. Eventually, British troops try to take possession of the *Rattlesnake* in the Stono River. The attack proves unsuccessful, but the ship's commander, Capt. Frisbie (Frisby), fearing another such attack sets the ship on fire and leads his crew overland to Charlestown, not losing a man. After the battle ends, each side attempts to harass each other through long rifle shots, but these are ineffective.

Patriot casualties are 146 men killed and wounded with 155 men missing. The British have three officers killed, 23 men killed, 93 men wounded, and one man missing. The North Carolina Continental Line wounded include Col. James Armstrong of the 4th NC Regiment, Col. Thomas Clark of the 5th NC Regiment, Lt. Col. James Thackston of the 4th NC Regiment, Lt. Col. Henry "Hal" Dixon of the 5th NC Regiment, Lt. Col. Archibald Lytle of the 6th NC Regiment, Maj. John Armstrong of the 4th NC Regiment, Capt. Joseph Thomas Rhodes of the 4th NC Regiment, and Capt. James Campbell of the 5th NC Regiment, who is also taken prisoner–not exchanged until 6/14/1781. Lt. William Charlton of the 5th NC Regiment is mortally wounded, and he dies the next day, the only death of the 2nd North Carolina Brigade.

Captains of the 4th NC Regiment who also participate are: John Campbell, Benjamin Carter, Samuel Chapman, William Temple Coles, George Dougherty, William Goodman, John McLane, and Matthew Ramsey. Captains of the 5th NC Regiment who also participate are: Thomas Donoho, William Lytle, James Mills, Joseph Montford, James Morehead, John Slaughter, John Sumner, and Philip Taylor.

Captains of the "New Levies," actually serving under Lt. Col. Archibald Lytle in the recently resurrected 6th NC Regiment, but never listed on any official rolls of North Carolina Continentals, include William Bethel (Guilford), David Cowan (Rowan), William Ganns (Mecklenburg), Arthur Gatling (Gates), John Griffin (Orange), Alsey High (Warren), Matthew McCauley (Orange), Robert Moore (Caswell), Barnett Pulliam (Granville), and Robert Temple (Franklin).

Private Hugh Jackson, future U.S. President Andrew Jackson's older brother, dies from heat/fatigue in the battle of Stono Ferry, SC.

In his 1831 pension application addendum, John Redding (S41971) asserts:

"... he then was exchanged into the 3rd North Carolina Regiment, and done duty in Captain Philip Taylor's company of Infantry [1779 placed into the 5th NC Regiment] as a waiter to the Captain, and when he joined headquarters at Purrysburg in South Carolina and was present when the British took the *Congress* galley and *Lee* galley from the Americans between Savannah Town and Purrysburg, after that he was taken as a waiter and horseler to Brigadier General Jethro Sumner and under the command of General Lincoln who was head in command, he was then marched to Stono and was in the battle at that place, after that General Sumner was taken sick and brought him back with him to Halifax Town in North Carolina and was there discharged by General Sumner." [minor edits]

With the enlistment terms of all "New Levies" running out, many North Carolina Continental officers are sent home to assist in recruiting once again. And once again the Continental Congress changes its mind and resolves that North Carolina shall now field six regiments (also called battalions by many back then) and to replace all nine-month men currently in the field. For home defense the Continental Congress authorizes North Carolina to raise regiments of men who enlist for one year. These new recruits are to receive the same pay and benefits as all Continentals, plus a $200 bounty, and the promise that they will not have to serve north of Virginia. Even with the increased bounties, the recruiters have extreme difficulty in getting men to enlist. Gov. Richard Caswell presses everyone he can, but by July 1st less than 300 men have enlisted. On June 30th, Lt. Col. Robert Mebane, his health much improved, writes to the governor that the recruiting in the Salisbury District has netted zero new men as of that date. Gov. Caswell orders all Militia officers to now actively draft the remainder, bounty or no bounty. He then fires off more letters to the Continental officers in the state–be prepared to gather your men and march them per directions.

Brig. Gen. Jethro Sumner's bad health returns and he goes home to recuperate. As others follow, they all soon realize that the life of recruiting is no better than fighting. Money has depreciated so much they all find it very difficult in supporting themselves, even after the state grants them all an extra ten dollars per diem. Despite his poor health, Brig. Gen. Jethro Sumner continues diligently in building up the Continental troops, but this effort is very slow in producing results. As soon as arms can be acquired, he sends his new recruits Charlotte, then to the High Hills of the Santee, near Camden in South Carolina, for additional training. The men recruited from the Edenton, New Bern, and Halifax districts are collected at Kingston under Maj. Reading Blount and are issued "good new arms." They soon join others from the Wilmington District at Camden, South Carolina in the designated training camps.

By August 8th, it is clear that the British have withdrawn from South Carolina back to Savannah, so Gov. Richard Caswell writes to South Carolina Gov. John Rutledge that he has stood down all of his Militia– they will not be marching south. Gov. Caswell also informs Gov. Rutledge that 300 North Carolina Continentals are already in his state training at the High Hills of the Santee. On September 1st, Brig. Gen. Benjamin Lincoln writes to President John Jay in Philadelphia that he currently has only 90 North Carolina Continentals in Charlestown, but that 300 more are now on their way.

The summer of 1779 also brings many demands from the southern states for the return of their northern troops. When it is finally agreed by the Continental Congress to send them home they do not march immediately. With the growing threat of the British in Savannah planning to go after Charlestown again, Gen. George Washington finally agrees that the North Carolina 1st Brigade will be better used in defense of their southern neighbor. On August 10th, they are ordered south–but, they do not start marching until early September. Congress decides that these Continentals shall be better dressed during their long march. The officers of the brigade are so unkempt that the Continental Congress advances $100,000 to clothe them.

As the 1st North Carolina Brigade reaches Trenton, New Jersey, the

Continental Congress sends notice that they shall wait for new orders at that location. Word reaches Philadelphia that Maj. Gen. Benjamin Lincoln's southern army has expelled the British from South Carolina after the affair at Stono Ferry. Gen. Washington orders Brig. Gen. James Hogun to turn the North Carolina Brigade around and they meet the general at his headquarters in Morristown. They are ordered to retake their post at Paramus, New Jersey.

During that long, hot summer the Continental Congress appeals to the French for assistance in dislodging the British at Savannah. On September 3rd, word arrives that the French Admiral Jean Baptiste Charles Henri Hector, Comte d'Estaing with his fleet and 4,000 soldiers is just off the coast from Savannah. He sends word to Charlestown that the Patriots better get moving because he is only going to remain in this area for only two more weeks; he knows that hurricane season coming.

On September 16th, Maj. Gen. Benjamin Lincoln marches into Admiral d'Estaing's camp that is pitched about three miles south of Savannah. Lincoln quickly learns that the brazen admiral has already summoned the British to surrender. Brig. Gen. Augustine Prevost stalls until his outlying detachments can sneak back into Savannah. Then, it rains.

On October 5th, French and Patriot artillery bombard the British position–day and night they hammer Brig. Gen. Augustine Prevost's defenses with a steady fire. After days of arguing with Lincoln, Admiral d'Estaing insists on launching an all-out frontal assault on the town, and Lincoln has no choice but to go along with the mad scheme. With him are five known companies of the North Carolina Continental Line–Lt. Col. Selby Harney leading one company of the 2nd NC Regiment; Capt. John Campbell, Capt. Samuel Chapman, and Capt. Matthew Ramsey of the 4th NC Regiment; and Capt. William Lytle of the 5th NC Regiment.

To make an incredibly long story short, the planned attack on October 9th does not go well. One error after another leads to the foregone-conclusion of a disaster in the making. Admiral d'Estaing is late, and when he does arrive he proceeds to attack before any other units can get into place. The Patriots are handily driven backwards, with many "hung dead and wounded on the abatis." The allies lose 16 officers and 228 men killed, 63 officers and 521 men wounded.

Maj. Gen. Benjamin Lincoln is disappointed, but he wishes to continue the siege. The French admiral has lost his taste for land warfare, and his men remind him that hurricane season is rapidly approaching. On October 18th, the siege is lifted and the next day the Patriots are back on the other side of the Savannah River, marching slowly back to Charlestown. The day after that, the French sail away.

In his 1832 pension application, Thomas Ross (S4126) asserts:

"…was transferred to Captain Joseph Montford's company & was finally discharged under Captain Matthew Ramsey by Lt. Colonel Robert Mebane in Charlestown… he was at the Siege of Savannah in October and was in several skirmishes in South Carolina." [minor edits]

Had the British been defeated they would have been deprived of a base from which to launch a southern campaign. The news of the British victory soon reaches the ears of General Henry Clinton in New York, and he and his council soon determine that it is now time to return to Charlestown to finish off the next two southern states–South Carolina and then North Carolina. If three dominoes will fall, they can then press the other states to give in. So they think.

It is this failure at Savannah that finally prompts General George Washington to release the 1st North Carolina Brigade and order them to march southward on November 18th. Due to torrential rains, they do not depart until November 24th. By December 5th they are in Philadelphia arranging water transportation, but the Continental Congress orders them to march home. Extremely embarrassed, the Board of War does manage to have them ferried across the Chesapeake Bay. The North Carolina Continental Line of the northern theater now consists of 33 command and staff officers, 90 non-commissioned officers, and 705 rank and file. Capt. John Kingsbury and the singular NC Artillery company are also sent southward along with Brig. Gen. James Hogun.

On December 26th, a large British fleet of over 90 troopships escorted by fourteen men-of-war, sets sail to the southward out of New York harbor. Dozens of Patriot spies corroborate the fleet setting sail, and other spies agree that the ultimate destination is Charlestown. The British are weary of the prolonged stalemate in the northern theater, and with the news that Savannah has held out against a combined force of French and Continentals, the leaders in New York agree that the time is ripe for them to open up a new front in this long and boring war.

The end of 1779 finds Brig. Gen. Jethro Sumner still recruiting at home and training his small numbers in the High Hills of the Santee, just outside of Camden, South Carolina. Brig. Gen. James Hogun and the 1st North Carolina Brigade is somewhere in Virginia fighting a new battle–the damned weather again–which has turned bitter cold and in many places there are over three feet of snow and ice that cut through worn footwear like a knife. To Brig. Gen. Hogun's credit, he pushes his men hard, then demands just a bit more.

With most men's enlistment time expiring, the 5th NC Regiment and the 6th NC Regiment simply dissolve, never to be resurrected. Most of the rank and file in the 4th NC Regiment will also be ending their service soon, but the officers remain resolute and are at home beating the recruiting drum. Col. Thomas Clark soon takes over the 1st NC Regiment again when they get home in February, and Lt. Col. William Lee Davidson effectively retires from Continental service, only to be asked to take over a Militia regiment soon after returning home.

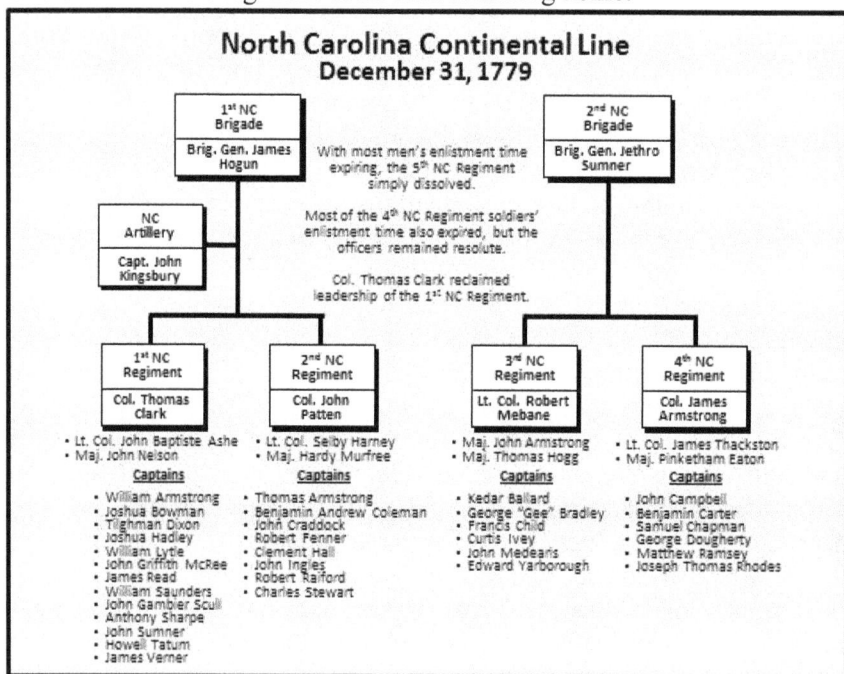

North Carolina Continental Line
December 31, 1779

1st NC Brigade
Brig. Gen. James Hogun

With most men's enlistment time expiring, the 5th NC Regiment simply dissolved.

Most of the 4th NC Regiment soldiers' enlistment time also expired, but the officers remained resolute.

Col. Thomas Clark reclaimed leadership of the 1st NC Regiment.

2nd NC Brigade
Brig. Gen. Jethro Sumner

NC Artillery
Capt. John Kingsbury

1st NC Regiment
Col. Thomas Clark
- Lt. Col. John Baptiste Ashe
- Maj. John Nelson

Captains
- William Armstrong
- Joshua Bowman
- Tilghman Dixon
- Joshua Hadley
- William Lytle
- John Griffith McRee
- James Read
- William Saunders
- John Gambier Scull
- Anthony Sharpe
- John Sumner
- Howell Tatum
- James Verner

2nd NC Regiment
Col. John Patten
- Lt. Col. Selby Harney
- Maj. Hardy Murfree

Captains
- Thomas Armstrong
- Benjamin Andrew Coleman
- John Craddock
- Robert Fenner
- Clement Hall
- John Ingles
- Robert Raiford
- Charles Stewart

3rd NC Regiment
Lt. Col. Robert Mebane
- Maj. John Armstrong
- Maj. Thomas Hogg

Captains
- Kedar Ballard
- George "Gee" Bradley
- Francis Child
- Curtis Ivey
- John Medearis
- Edward Yarborough

4th NC Regiment
Col. James Armstrong
- Lt. Col. James Thackston
- Maj. Pinketham Eaton

Captains
- John Campbell
- Benjamin Carter
- Samuel Chapman
- George Dougherty
- Matthew Ramsey
- Joseph Thomas Rhodes

Appendix B includes a listing of all known Continental units that participated in the battles of 1779.

Chapter Six – 1780

Key Events of 1780
• NC General Assembly meets twice (April & November), and elects Abner Nash as the second governor of NC.   • The British capture Charlestown, SC in May, along with over 90% of the entire NC Continental Line.   • The few Continental officers not captured at Charlestown are asked to lead NC Militia units at the battle of Camden, SC.   • A long and painful rebuilding of the NC Continental Line begins.

After a long and miserable march, the 1st North Carolina Brigade under Brig. Gen. James Hogun reaches Wilmington by February 19th. Although their stay is very short, they are provided with rum, sugar, and coffee. The soldiers are–again– badly in need of uniforms, hats, and boots, but–again –there is no money. With every man's pay already in arrears for several months, some refuse to march any further "till they had justice done them." Private Samuel Glover, earlier a sergeant, of the 2nd NC Regiment and a veteran of the battles of Brandywine Creek, Germantown, Monmouth, and Stony Point, is the ringleader of this small group of dissenters. On February 23rd, he is executed as an example to the others–who quickly resume their march to Charlestown with heads hung low.

The 2nd North Carolina Brigade already stationed in the south has essentially dissolved as their brethren are marching southward. Brig. Gen. Jethro Sumner is at home recouperating from a chronic bout of illness (history has never revealed just what he suffered from). Colonel James Armstrong of the 4th NC Regiment is at home encouraging his officers to increase their recruiting efforts on the homefront.

Although the Continental Congress has authorized four North Carolina regiments, the Old North State can barely field three regiments–those marching towards Charlestown. The officers of the now-defunct 6th NC Regiment continue to contribute to the war effort as best they can. Col. Gideon Lamb, at home in Camden County, assists throughout the year of 1780 in rounding up deserters in the eastern half of North Carolina. Lt. Col. Archibald Lytle continues to help in recruiting new men in the Hillsborough District–his home is Orange County. But, he is now leading a small group of NC Militia units already in Charlestown.

Hogun's brigade finally reaches Charlestown on the evening of March 3rd and parades through the town to give "great spirits to the Town and confidence to the Army." The 1st NC Regiment and 2nd NC Regiment combined total no more than 600 rank and file–each regiment needs another 200 men to complete their complement. Time has expired for over fifty men during the march south, and another twelve have deserted as their regiments marched through home territory. The 3rd NC Regiment is reconstituted at the High Hills of the Santee near Camden, South Carolina in the latter half of 1779 and marches under Lt. Col. Robert Mebane to Charlestown early in 1780. His early arrival somehow prompts many men to desert, and two officers are sent home to round up those who are absent without leave.

As the 1st North Carolina Brigade is still marching southward, British General Henry Clinton arrives with more than 8,500 troops at the end of January. His fleet barely escapes being caught in the ice floes of New York Harbor, but they do manage to sail directly into a gale that lasts for four days–scattering the ships across the Atlantic Ocean. One ship, the *Anna*, with thirty Hessians, Ansbach Jaëgers, and artillery, is dismasted and drifts for eleven weeks until landing at St. Ives on the coast of Cornwall, England. Most of the cavalry's horses had to be thrown overboard during the gale to save the ships.

In the early part of February of 1780, the remaining fleet finally assembles off the coast of Savannah–with eleven ships missing. In addition to the *Anna*, the transports *Judith* and the *Russia Merchant*, along with a one-masted artillery transport ship, are lost. The *Russia Merchant* is carrying most of the heavy seige artillery and ammunition needed to conquer a fortified town such as Charlestown. A voyage that normally takes only ten days ends up taking the British fleet five weeks.

General Clinton puts Brig. Gen. James Patterson ashore with 1,400 infantry and orders him to mount a diversion by the way of Augusta, Georgia and to keep the backcountry Militia tied down so they cannot reinforce Charlestown. With Brig. Gen. Patterson are Maj. Patrick Ferguson and Lt. Col. Banastre Tarleton, both who immediately set out to replace their lost cavalry horses by impressing them from local plantations around Beaufort, South Carolina.

On the evening of February 11th, Maj. Gen. Alexander Leslie lands unopposed on Simmons Island (now called Seabrook Island) with the Light Infantry and the Grenadiers. It rains heavily all that night, but Gen. Clinton also comes ashore and spends the night under a tree in the rain.

On February 12th, the rest of the invasion force is issued three days rations and they disembark. The artillery has to remain on board since there are no horses to pull the heavy cannons. On the morning of February 14th, the Jaëgers and the 33rd Regiment set out in search of Stono Ferry. Capt. Johan Ewald of the Jaëgers writes that the march is "through a wilderness of deep sand, marshland, and inpenetrable woods where human feet had never trod." They do not see any Patriots, but they do hear firing in the swamps. After investigating, the Hessians find a small group of British Grenadiers firing their muskets to attract attention since they are lost.

This group now marches to Stono Ferry and they quickly realize that they are exposed to the Patriots' cannons on the high ground on the other side of the river. They immediately turn around to get out of range, but the Patriots simply watch and do not fire a shot.

General Henry Clinton, with Lt. Gen. Charles, Lord Cornwallis, arrives at James Island early in the morning of February 15th. The night before, the Patriots quietly abandon their position nearby. As the British move across the Stono River, the defenders of Charlestown do not fire a single shot. Meanwhile, other Patriots are ordered to destroy Fort Johnson so it can no longer be a defendable position for the British.

The quiet lasts almost another week before hostilities finally have to happen. On February 22nd, a detachment of Patriot cavalry are the first to attack the British since this force has landed on American soil–at Stono.

In the meantime, Maj. Gen. Benjamin Lincoln sends express riders all across the South, and even some to Philadelphia–"send more men…NOW." He also sends a letter to François-Joseph Paul, Marquis de Grasse Tilly, Comte de Grasse pleading for help from the French fleet under his command. Maj. Gen. Lincoln also secretly sends South Carolina Lt. Col. John Tennant to Havana requesting Spanish aid in the form of men and ships. The request is refused, even though Spain has recently entered the war. Without missing a beat, Maj. Gen. Lincoln also supervises the construction of fortifications in and around Charlestown and the outlying forts guarding Charlestown Harbor, which have fallen into near ruin since the last time the British were here in 1776.

A bright spot is the the naval strength in Charlestown Harbor. Commodore Abraham Whipple commands nine armed vessels, ranging from sixteen to forty-four guns, anchored inside the breakwaters. However, three French frigates pull anchors and set sail as soon as it is obvious that the British are about to arrive.

As he approaches the entrenched Patriot city, General Henry Clinton quickly surmises that his 6,000 men will not be enough to take the town by assault. Troop transports are sent back to New York for reinforcements. Brig. Gen. James Patterson is ordered to bring up his diversionary force that has been left near Savannah. By the middle of April, General Clinton has assembled more than 10,000 troops under his command, and he has access to 5,000 sailors under Vice-Admiral Mariot Arbuthnot just offshore.

Not a great fan of the Militia, Maj. Gen. Benjamin Lincoln, however, sends multiple letters to Gov. Richard Caswell, then Gov. Abner Nash, to send every Militiaman available within North Carolina. Brig. Gen. John Alexander Lillington of the Wilmington District Brigade of Militia has actually already been in Charlestown since late January of 1780, and he has with him over 2,000 men. As with all Militias, this soon becomes a revolving door due to short enlistment periods. North Carolina law only requires that a Militiaman serve for three months at a time, then he is guaranteed the right to lay down his arms for a defined period of time before being asked to serve again. The law is the law.

On January 28th, Lt. Col. Archibald Lytle pens a letter to Gov. Richard Caswell complaining that the last General Assembly did absolutely nothing to improve the Continental Line, then he asks Brig. Gen. John Butler of the Hillsborough District Brigade of Militia if he can lead one of the Militia regiments under his command. After consulting with his subordinates, Brig. Gen. John Butler agrees that Lt. Col. Lytle can take over the Wake County Regiment of Militia in lieu of Col. Michael Rogers, who is not well. Typical for all Militia regiments, their enlistment expires after three months, and they all go home. Lt. Col. Lytle remains in Charlestown and he inherits all the small detachments of Militia companies that arrive under no field officers. He names his rag-tag band of Militia companies the "NC Light Infantry" and all are taken prisoner when Charlestown falls later, on May 12th.

As the earlier men's enlistments are expiring, former Gov. Richard Caswell is commissioned as the second and only current major general in charge of all North Carolina Militia. In early May of 1780, he marches from Kingston towards Charlestown with yet another 2,000 Militiamen, mostly from the eastern portion of the state.

During the April session of the North Carolina General Assembly, the legislature resolves to raise 3,000 new Continentals for the term of three years or for the duration of the war. Each recruit is to receive a $500 bounty at enlistment, another $500 at the end of each year of service, and when their three years are up, each soldier is to receive a slave and 200 acres of land. If a soldier is killed while in service, then his widow will receive these benefits. All Militia brigades across the state are incentivized to help in recruiting for the North Carolina Continental Line. Each Militia recruiter is to receive $250 for each man enrolled.

To defend three miles of fortifications in and around Charlestown, Maj. Gen. Benjamin Lincoln has roughly 2,650 Continental soldiers and about 2,500 Militiamen, about a third of which are from South Carolina. He also has the "expert opinions" of all the local civil authorities, who chronically complain about his decisions.

The British begin their assault in earnest on April 1st with the commencement of trenching within 1,000 yards of Patriot positions around the city. On April 8th, the handful of Patriot ships in Charlestown Harbor slips anchors and set sail, taking advantage of a brisk southern breeze. The British ships beyond the breakwaters soon take their place in the expansive harbor and prepare to begin their bombardment.

The next day, April 9th, General Henry Clinton sends his first formal demand for the city to surrender. Maj. Gen. Benjamin Lincoln politely declines. On each succeeding day, the British up the ante by shelling every section of Charlestown. Lincoln's biggest mistake is to listen to the pleas of the civil authorities that he must continue a vigorous defense, while his trusted officers advise that the Continentals, at least, should cross the Cooper River and march along the eastern shore to safety.

By April 14th, all escape routes are now closed–thanks to British Lt. Col. Banastre Tarleton scattering the SC Light Dragoons under Brig. Gen. Isaac Huger stationed at Moncks Corner. Things proceed to get worse until May 12th, when Maj. Gen. Lincoln finally surrenders all military forces in and around Charlestown. At 11 o'clock a.m., the Patriots march out with colors cased and their drums mournfully beating out the "Turk's March." One of his enemy notes that "Lincoln limped out at the head of the most ragged rabble I ever beheld." Over 5,466 Continental soldiers, Militiamen, and armed civilians finally surrender to the British army under General Henry Clinton on that day.

The North Carolina Continentals under Brig. Gen. James Hogun surrender 814 officers and men–287 of the 1st NC Regiment under Col. Thomas Clark; 301 of the 2nd NC Regiment under Col. John Patten; 162 of the 3rd NC Regiment under Lt. Col. Robert Mebane; and, 64 of the NC Artillery under Capt. John Kingsbury. The state also surrenders over 1,200 Militiamen on that day. Some of the North Carolina Continentals are imprisoned until the end of the war.

The known North Carolina Continentals killed during the Siege of Charlestown are–Capt. Joshua Bowman of the 1st NC Regiment, Lt. George Cook of the 1st NC Regiment, and Lt. William Ferrell of the 2nd NC Regiment. The known North Carolina Continentals wounded include Lt. Col. Selby Harney of the 2nd NC Regiment, Capt. John Craddock of the 2nd NC Regiment, Capt. Joseph Montford of the 1st NC Regiment, and Lieutenants James Campen, Arthur Cotgrave, and Charles Gerrard of the 2nd NC Regiment. Those who die while a prisoner of war–Brig. Gen. James Hogun dies on 1/4/1781 while in captivity at Haddrell's Point; Capt. James King of the 1st NC Regiment; Lt. Thomas Allen of the 3rd NC Regiment, and Sgt. Thomas Blanchett of the 2nd NC Regiment.

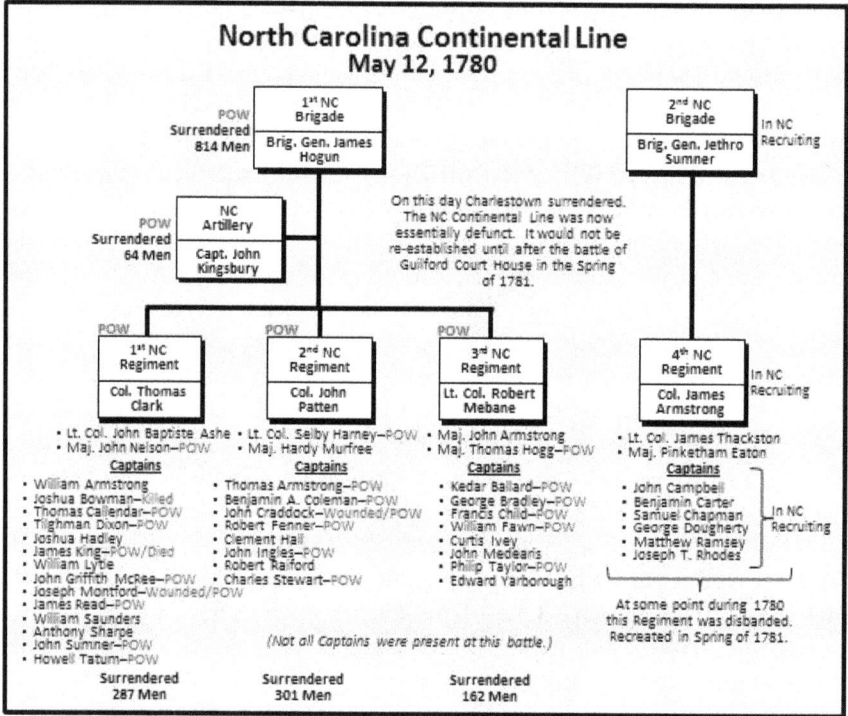

North Carolina Continental Line
May 12, 1780

POW Surrendered 814 Men — 1st NC Brigade — Brig. Gen. James Hogun

2nd NC Brigade — Brig. Gen. Jethro Sumner — In NC Recruiting

POW Surrendered 64 Men — NC Artillery — Capt. John Kingsbury

On this day Charlestown surrendered. The NC Continental Line was now essentially defunct. It would not be re-established until after the battle of Guilford Court House in the Spring of 1781.

POW 1st NC Regiment — Col. Thomas Clark

POW 2nd NC Regiment — Col. John Patten

POW 3rd NC Regiment — Lt. Col. Robert Mebane

4th NC Regiment — Col. James Armstrong — In NC Recruiting

• Lt. Col. John Baptiste Ashe
• Maj. John Nelson–POW
Captains
• William Armstrong
• Joshua Bowman–Killed
• Thomas Callendar–POW
• Tilghman Dixon–POW
• Joshua Hadley
• James King–POW/Died
• William Lytle
• John Griffith McRee–POW
• Joseph Montford–Wounded/POW
• James Read–POW
• William Saunders
• Anthony Sharpe
• John Sumner–POW
• Howell Tatum–POW

• Lt. Col. Selby Harney–POW
• Maj. Hardy Murfree
Captains
• Thomas Armstrong–POW
• Benjamin A. Coleman–POW
• John Craddock–Wounded/POW
• Robert Fenner–POW
• Clement Hall
• John Ingles–POW
• Robert Raiford
• Charles Stewart–POW

(Not all Captains were present at this battle.)

• Maj. John Armstrong
• Maj. Thomas Hogg–POW
Captains
• Kedar Ballard–POW
• George Bradley–POW
• Francis Child–POW
• William Fawn–POW
• Curtis Ivey
• John Medearis
• Philip Taylor–POW
• Edward Yarborough

• Lt. Col. James Thackston
• Maj. Pinketham Eaton
Captains
• John Campbell
• Benjamin Carter
• Samuel Chapman
• George Dougherty
• Matthew Ramsey
• Joseph T. Rhodes
In NC Recruiting

At some point during 1780 this Regiment was disbanded. Recreated in Spring of 1781.

Surrendered 287 Men

Surrendered 301 Men

Surrendered 162 Men

In his 1824 pension application, Jesse Rowell (S38337) asserts:

"That he the said Jesse Rowell enlisted for the term of the war some time in the month of October in the year 1776 in the company commanded by Captain Thomas Allen in the regiment commanded by Colonel Thomas Clark in the line of the state of North Carolina on the old Continental Establishment that he continued to serve in said corps for the term of about seven years when he was taken a prisoner by the British at Charlestown [under Capt. Joshua Bowman] in whose custody he remained until Peace, that he never obtained a written discharge." [minor edits]

Effectively, the North Carolina Continental Line is now non-existent, and with the capture of so many officers, it will take almost a year to gather enough men to field more than a company of Continentals at any given time. However bad as it is, it truly could have been worse. Several officers were at home on furlough and therefore escaped the fate of their comrades. Additionally, Brig. Gen. William Caswell with 650 Militiamen and Col. Abraham Buford of Virginia are at Lenud's Ferry in South Carolina when they learn of the surrender of Charlestown. Brig. Gen. Caswell immediately turns his large group of Militiamen home and heads to Cross Creek. Col. Buford is soon thereafter caught by British Lt. Col. Banastre Tarleton at the Waxhaws and unmercifully massacred, although Buford manages to escape with a handful of men.

On May 30th, Col. James Armstrong of the essentially defunct 4th NC Regiment writes to Brig. Gen. Jethro Sumner. Armstrong has learned of Brig. Gen. William Caswell's successful retreat from South Carolina and he informs the general that his intentions are to meet Brig. Gen. William Caswell at Cross Creek to perhaps convince some of Caswell's Militiamen to join the Continental Line. Col. Armstrong has just received $50,000 for recruiting and he is determined to make good use of it. Unfortunately, there are no further records to indicate how many men he manages to enlist. What is known is that the Continental Line is not improved much during the second half of 1780.

The real downside, other than the capture of so many Continental soldiers, is the fact that the British are back in the South, and it is increasingly clear that they not only want South Carolina, but they have definite sights on North Carolina. Soon after the Fall of Charlestown, the last Royal Governor of North Carolina–Josiah Martin–meets up with Lt. Gen. Charles, Lord Cornwallis and joins his army for the inevitable return to the Old North State. Authorities soon learn this is true when Loyalists across the state rapidly spread the news that the former governor "will be in Cross Creek within a fortnight."

The Loyalists in both South Carolina and North Carolina are now emboldened with the British spreading into the countryside away from their hub at Charlestown. Internecine warfare is soon the norm all across the two states, and will continue to be the norm for more than a year and a half.

The British offer Brig. Gen. James Hogun a parole to some other community, but he declines, asserting that he wishes to share the hardships with his men. He tries to maintain a military attitude while imprisoned at Haddrell's Point, but he is not a strong man. During the ensuing winter his health begins to fail and on January 4, 1781, James Hogun dies. North Carolina mourns another great loss.

The handful of Continental officers still pursuing deserters in North Carolina quickly realize their folly–there are no units to send them back to. Many of these officers and the few left as recruiters soon begin to submit their resignations, citing "sheer poverty" as their reason. Brig. Gen. Jethro Sumner, still not 100% healthy, takes measure of what few Continental officers he has at his disposal and he concludes that the lieutenants and captains will best be employed by continuing an active recruitment campaign. He also asks Maj. Hardy Murfree to continue his recruiting efforts at home in Hertford County.

Maj. Gen. Richard Caswell convinces Brig. Gen. Jethro Sumner that his field officers will better serve the state by leading Militia and other state units. Maj. John Armstrong of the 4th NC Regiment is given command of a unit ambiguously named the NC Light Infantry–these soldiers are a small contingent of 60 men from Halifax County who finally catch up with the North Carolina Militia in South Carolina and attach themselves to Maj. Armstrong. Lt. Col. Henry "Hal" Dixon is given command of the Caswell County Regiment of Militia. Lt. Col. John Baptiste Ashe becomes a recruiter for the 1st NC Regiment. Lt. Colonel William Lee Davidson is named the Colonel/Commandant of the Mecklenburg County Regiment of Militia. Lt. Col. Samuel Lockhart volunteers as a captain in the Halifax County Regiment of Militia. Lt. Col. James Thackston accepts command of the Orange County Regiment of Militia. Major William Polk is promoted to Lt. Colonel and assigned as the Aide-de-Camp to Maj. Gen. Richard Caswell of the North Carolina Militia. Maj. Reading Blount helps out in the Craven County Regiment of Militia. Maj. Pinketham Eaton volunteers as a major in the Halifax County Regiment of Militia. Maj. Thomas Harris becomes the Aide-de-Camp to Brig. Gen. Griffith Rutherford in the Salisbury District Brigade of Militia.

At the time of the Fall of Charlestown on May 12th, there are sixteen Continental captains still on active duty that have not been captured. All six of the active 4th NC Regiment captains are on duty recruiting new men for their regiment: John Campbell, Benjamin Carter, Samuel Chapman, George Dougherty, Matthew Ramsey, and Joseph Thomas Rhodes. Of the five captains of the 1st NC Regiment, three are assigned to recruiting new men within the state: William Lytle, William Saunders, and Anthony Sharpe; two captains choose to lead Militia companies: William Armstrong and Joshua Hadley. Both captains of the 2nd NC Regiment are assigned as recruiters for their regiment: Clement Hall and Robert Raiford. And finally, for the 3rd NC Regiment, two captains choose to lead Militia companies: Curtis Ivey and Edward Yarborough; while one captain, John Medearis is selected to lead the Public Factory recently built in Granville County.

With the British army steadily advancing across the state of South Carolina, the Militias of both South Carolina and North Carolina somehow manage to counter the enemy with unexpected victories, which also helps to squelch Loyalist gatherings that almost get out of hand in the summer of 1780. On June 20th, Col. Francis Locke, of the Rowan County Regiment with a rather large Militia contingent, defeats a large Loyalist force of over 700 men led by Lt. Col. John Moore at Ramseur's Mill in Lincoln County. On July 12th, a band of South Carolina Militia soundly defeats a British/Loyalist detachment at Williamson's Plantation in northern South Carolina. These two relatively minor incidents have a profound impact on both sides very soon thereafter.

For the Patriots these two victories convince the politicians of both states that their Militia can be used effectively against the enemy such that both states, once again, pay less attention on filling Continental regiments. For Lt. Gen. Charles, Lord Cornwallis, the British are now not quite as bold as they have been since immediately after the Fall of Charlestown on May 12th.

Since that fateful day in May, Maj. Gen. Johann DeKalb is the ranking Continental in the South. DeKalb is marching southward with a contingent of Delaware and Maryland Continentals and during a stop in Hillsborough he learns of the Patriot surrender of Charlestown. Quite aware that another general will be ordered to succeed Lincoln, DeKalb patiently waits for his new commander to arrive. His wait is not pleasant, however. Provisions are scarce thanks to a drought and crop failures, and his men almost starve to death. It is so desparate at the end of June that DeKalb decides to move his army into South Carolina along the Pee Dee River, but he goes no further than the Deep River in Randolph County. He has to place his men on short rations until food can be acquired from the surrounding countryside.

On June 14th, the Continental Congress resolves that Maj. Gen. Horatio Gates, the hero of Saratoga in 1777, shall succeed the captured Maj. Gen. Benjamin Lincoln as the new commander of the Southern Department. General George Washington is not consulted on this assignment; his choice would have been Maj. Gen. Nathanael Greene of Rhode Island.

Maj. Gen. Gates eventually stops in Hillsborough, where he finds "the most unpromising Prospect my Eyes ever beheld." He quickly learns of DeKalb's location and on July 25th he reaches the Bavarian general's camp on the Deep River. DeKalb turns over command with no hesitation, and he informs Maj. Gen. Gates of his plan to march via Salisbury and Charlotte, where provisions are known to be plentiful, then onward to Camden in South Carolina, where an opportunity might present itself.

Maj. Gen. Horatio Gates immediately dismisses Maj. Gen. DeKalb's plans and describes a more direct route towards Camden. Waiting for no further intelligence, he proceeds to lead his army into a sterile and infertile region of pine barrens that is populated mostly by Loyalists. To the astonishment of his hungry men, he issues orders that they hold themselves in readiness to march at a moment's notice.

Food is collected by the use of threats and even violence. Thomas Burke's plantation is ruined by roving foragers, which evokes a strong protest from the future governor himself. Soldiers are quartered in private homes, and wagons and horses are impressed with no guarantee of payment.

The new Southern Continental Army marches on July 27th. The Virginia Militia, marching at the rear of the "grand army" intercepts and consumes the scant provisions that have been delivered. Men are forced to forage in fields and orchards, mostly eating green corn and green peaches. Officers use their wig powder to thicken soup. Maj. Gen. Gates is concerned that Maj. Gen. Richard Caswell and his North Carolina Militia have not yet arrived, but moreso he even blames Caswell for the shortage of provisions–food destined for his Continentals must have been intercepted and consumed by the unworthy Militia, claims Maj. Gen. Gates.

The two Patriot armies join on August 7th, and Maj. Gen. Richard Caswell brings more than 2,100 North Carolina Militiamen. More impressive, he also brings an inordinately large baggage train that is hauling so many cumbersome household items that the Continentals almost laugh him off the field. This only increases Maj. Gen. Gates' disdain for Militia in general, and North Carolina Militia in specific. However, Maj. Gen. Gates manages to conceal this disdain as Brig. Gen. Edward Stevens arrives with 700 Virginia Militiamen.

Meanwhile, the British commander over the Camden garrison, Francis, Lord Rawdon, learns of Maj. Gen. Gates's entry into South Carolina and he marches his men to occupy the bridge across the western branch of Lynches Creek, known as Little Lynches Creek. The British outpost at Lynches Ferry withdraws and joins Lord Rawdon's army. Maj. Gen. Gates and his army move towards Lord Rawdon and actually succeed in flanking their enemy's force, which is much smaller than the Patriot army. The Patriots engage British sentries with long-range rifles, but never hit any of them. After a two-day wait, Maj. Gen. Horatio Gates moves up the creek and crosses over at another location.

Lord Rawdon does not want to risk a major fight at this location since he knows that Lt. Gen. Charles, Lord Cornwallis is on his way to rendezvous at Camden, so Lord Rawdon withdraws back to Camden and establishes his camp at Log Town. He orders the Loyalist Militia to harass the Patriots and to lead them away from his retreat, which they succeed in accomplishing, taking Maj. Gen. Gates 35 miles out of his way–and buying the British more time to prepare for the upcoming battle of Camden.

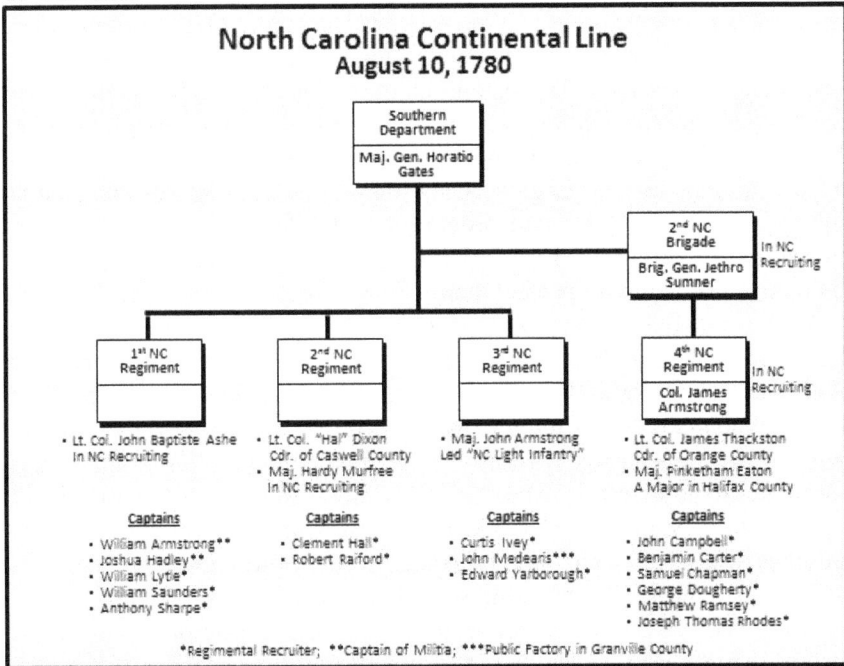

North Carolina Continental Line
August 10, 1780

Southern Department
Maj. Gen. Horatio Gates

2nd NC Brigade — In NC Recruiting
Brig. Gen. Jethro Sumner

1st NC Regiment

2nd NC Regiment

3rd NC Regiment

4th NC Regiment — In NC Recruiting
Col. James Armstrong

- Lt. Col. John Baptiste Ashe In NC Recruiting

- Lt. Col. "Hal" Dixon Cdr. of Caswell County
- Maj. Hardy Murfree In NC Recruiting

- Maj. John Armstrong Led "NC Light Infantry"

- Lt. Col. James Thackston Cdr. of Orange County
- Maj. Pinketham Eaton A Major in Halifax County

Captains
- William Armstrong**
- Joshua Hadley**
- William Lytle*
- William Saunders*
- Anthony Sharpe*

Captains
- Clement Hall*
- Robert Raiford*

Captains
- Curtis Ivey*
- John Medearis***
- Edward Yarborough*

Captains
- John Campbell*
- Benjamin Carter*
- Samuel Chapman*
- George Dougherty*
- Matthew Ramsey*
- Joseph Thomas Rhodes*

*Regimental Recruiter; **Captain of Militia; ***Public Factory in Granville County

Maj. Gen. Gates cannot move across the river so he moves his army to Rugeley's Mills by way of Hanging Rock. This takes him 35 miles from Camden, where he had been only 15 miles away beforehand. He arrives at his desired location on August 15th and waits for the arrival of Col. Thomas Sumter and his South Carolina Militia–who never arrive.

On the afternoon of August 15th, Lt. Gen. Cornwallis sends out Lt. Col. Banastre Tarleton to gain intelligence on the nearby Patriot army. He intercepts a patrol and brings back three prisoners. They tell Lt. Gen. Cornwallis that their unit is to join Maj. Gen. Gates as he marches on

Camden that night. Lt. Gen. Cornwallis orders his army to march northward at 10:00 p.m., to gain surprise against Maj. Gen. Gates.

The two fairly large armies surprise each other around 2:30 a.m. on a slight rise near Saunder's Creek called Parker's Old Field. The British Legion hail the Patriot Lt. Col. Charles Tuffin Armand's Legion, then spot Virginian Lt. Col. Charles Porterfield's light infantry on their flank by the light of the moon. A single pistol shot rings out from Armand's lead horseman, who promptly rides back to the security of the light infantry, 300 yards to the rear. Lt. Col. Charles Tuffin Armand rides over to Lt. Col. Porterfield and whispers, "There is the enemy, Sir. Must I charge him?" Lt. Col. Porterfield replies, "By all means, Sir." Armand rides back to his troops in the road, but it is too late.

Lt. Col. Tarleton's Legion charges first. He "came on at the top of his speed, every officer and soldier with a yell of an Indian savage–at every leap their horses took, crying out 'charge, charge, charge' so that their own voices and the echoes resounded in every direction through the pine forest." Lt. Col. Armand's men hold their ground and empty their pistols at the charging British Legion. Then, they draw their sabres and ride at the enemy. Lt. Col. Armand orders his right flank to come up on line instead of retreating. He knows that Lt. Col. Porterfield's light infantry is on their flanks and will protect them.

As desired, the infantry on both sides rises to expectations and catch Lt. Col. Tarleton's British Legion in a cross fire and force them to withdraw. The Virginia Militia has never been in a fight before and flees back to the main body on the road. Lt. Col. Armand's Legion withdraws with them causing confusion for a few minutes. Disorder reigns throughout the entire 1st Maryland Regiment, but Lt. Col. Porterfield's light infantry stops any possible British advantage. After about twenty minutes of disorganized battle both sides fall back to regroup.

Lt. Col. Charles Porterfield, with his horse reigned directly at the enemy, receives a terrible wound in his left leg, a little below the knee, which shatters it to pieces. Falling forward to the pommel of his saddle, he directs Capt. Drew to order retreat, which is done in an even tone. The Patriots instantly fall back obliquely from the road, which is wholly secluded from the enemy. Lt. Col. Porterfield is eventually removed from the battlefield after his horse falls and those around him are still being fired at.

Back on the road, Maj. Gen. Horatio Gates learns that his men have just stumbled upon the main British force under Lt. Gen. Charles, Lord Cornwallis, whom he thought was still in Camden. Maj. Gen. Gates retreats and takes up a defensive position across the Charlotte Road, and decides to wait until morning to commence his attack.

Meanwhile, Lord Rawdon comes down the road and dismounts to inspect a dead Patriot. He suspects that they might be Continentals due to the way they are fighting and the dead man's clothing proves him to be correct. He informs Lt. Gen. Cornwallis of his findings and advises him that they are on good ground to fight a larger force, since the swamps on each side protect their flanks. Lt. Gen. Cornwalls also decides it is best to wait until morning to launch <u>HIS</u> attack. Great minds think alike.

Early in the dawn hours of August 16th, Lt. Col. Otho H. Williams (MD) surveys the Patriot line and notices the British advancing up the road. He consults Captain Singleton of the artillery and it is determined that the British can be no more than 200 yards off. Lt. Col. Williams gives the order for an artillery barrage and the British quickly unlimber their guns and reply. The battle of Camden is now underway.

Brig. Gen. Edward Stevens, on the left, is ordered to move his Virginians forward and the inexperienced and seldom reliable Militia responds with hesitation. Lt. Col. Otho Williams calls for volunteers, leads 80 or 90 troops to within forty yards of the deploying British, and delivers a harassing fire from behind trees. Lt. Gen. Charles, Lord Cornwallis, positioned near the action and always alert, notices the Virginians' hesitation and orders Lt. Col. James Webster to advance on the right. In what is one of the worst mismatches in military history, two of the best regiments to ever serve in the British Army, the 33rd Regiment and the 23rd Regiment, with the best trained light infantry in the world, come up against untrained and unreliable Militiamen on the Patriot left.

Seeing the perfectly-formed line sweep toward them with a mighty cheer, then terrible silence, save the clanking of cold steel bayonets on musket barrels, the Virginians break and run. Some manage to get off a few shots and several of the British troops go down. However, the pell-mell panic quickly spreads to the North Carolina Militia near the road and soon that Militia breaks through the Maryland Continentals stationed in reserve, and throws that normally-reliable troop into total disarray.

Witnessing the wholesale panic of his entire left wing, Maj. Gen. Horatio Gates mounts a swift horse and takes to the road with his Militia, leaving the battle to be decided by his more brave and capable officers. Incidentally, Maj. Gen. Gates covers sixty miles in just a few short hours! Although Congress later exonerates him for his misconduct and cowardice, Gates never holds a field command again.

Maj. Gen. Baron Johann DeKalb and Brig Gen. Mordecai Gist, on the

Patriot right wing, and the Maryland Continentals are still in the field. One regiment of North Carolina Militia does not take part in the flight and falls back into the fighting alongside the Delaware Continentals. Lt. Col. Otho H. Williams and Maj. Gen. DeKalb try to bring Brig. Gen. William Smallwood's Maryland reserve to the left of the 2nd Brigade to form an "L." However, Brig. Gen. Smallwood has fled the battle and the troop is without leadership.

In the meantime, British Lt. Gen. Cornwallis has advanced strong troops into the gap and between the two brigades. At this point Lord Cornwallis sends Lt. Col. James Webster and his veteran troops against the 1st Maryland Regiment. Much to the credit of the Patriots, they stand fast and go toe-to-toe with the best regiments in the world for quite some time. However, after several breaks and rallies, they are forced from the field and into the swamps. Most of the Maryland troops, because of the inability of Lt. Col. Banastre Tarleton's horse to pursue in the terrain, escape to fight another day.

Only the 2nd Maryland Brigade, the Delaware Continentals, and Lt. Col. Henry "Hal" Dixon's North Carolina Militia continue the battle. At this point, it is some 600 Patriots against 2,000 British. The Patriots manage to check Lord Rawdon's left and even seize a few prisoners. It should be noted here that in one of those strange battlefield occurrences, the Patriots' most experienced Continentals are facing the British army's most inexperienced troops, the Royal NC Regiment of Loyalists. Maj. Gen. Baron Johann DeKalb personally leads bayonet charge after bayonet charge for over an hour. His horse is shot out from under him and he suffers a saber cut to the head. In a final assault he kills a British soldier and then goes down because of bayonet wounds and bullet wounds. His troops close around him and oppose yet another bayonet charge from the British.

However, at this point, Lt. Col. Banastre Tarleton returns with his horsemen from the pursuit of the fleeing Militiamen and Lt. Gen. Cornwallis throws his horse troops on the Patriot rear. The remaining Patriot troops stand for a few minutes and fight the onslaught from all sides but finally break and run. The battle of Camden is over.

About sixty men rally as a rear guard and manage to protect the retreating troops through the surrounding woods and swamps. It must be noted that in the manner of warfare in the 18th Century, Lord Cornwallis takes Baron DeKalb back to Camden and has him looked after by his personal physician. Unfortunately, the Baron succumbs to his wounds.

He is buried in Camden and a monument has been erected to his memory on the old battlefield.

Casualties for the battle of Camden for the British are 331 out of all ranks for 2,239 engaged. This includes two officers and 66 men killed, eighteen officers and 227 enlisted wounded, and eighteen missing. The American casualties have never been fully reckoned; however three officers die in battle and thirty are captured. Approximately 650-700 of Maj. Gen. Horatio Gates's soldiers are either killed or taken prisoner out of 3,050 effectives engaged. The loss of arms and equipment is devastating to the Patriot cause for months.

The known North Carolina Continentals that participate in the skirmish at Little Lynches Creek (August 11th), Parker's Old Field (August 15th), and at the battle of Camden (August 16th) are: Lt. Col. Henry "Hal" Dixon commanding the Caswell County Regiment of Militia, Maj. John Armstrong commanding the hastily created "NC Light Infantry," and the following two known leaders of Militia units: Capt. William Armstrong and Capt. Joshua Hadley.

In his 1832 pension application, Willoughby Blackard (S29638) asserts:

> "… then to South Carolina to Edisto River above Charlestown & then Stono River & was in the battle of Stono Ferry, Gen'l Lincoln was commander-in-chief who was there wounded. From the battle of Stono went into Charlestown & was there taken prisoner on May 26, 1780 & remained a prisoner until the 27 July same year, was then exchanged & then was put in the 6th Reg. North Carolina Line, Lt. Col Henry Dixon, Lt. Col Robert Mebane, Maj. Thomas Donoho, Capt. Edward Yarborough, served under Capt. Yarborough to the end of the war. I was at Gates's defeat on August 16, 1780." [minor edits]

Within ten days after the battle of Camden, 700 Continentals gather at Hillsborough–180 miles away. Maj. Gen. Horatio Gates covers that distance in a mere three days. No one wants to admit that the disaster has been so complete, but everyone knows it to be true. Maj. Gen. Gates's expresses to General George Washington are factual, but none reflect the gloom that hangs over North Carolina.

On August 23rd, Brig. Gen. Jethro Sumner writes from Hillsborough to Col. Gideon Lamb at Edenton asserting that Maj. Gen. Horatio Gates has ordered all North Carolina Continental officers of the 4th NC Regiment, the 5th NC Regiment, and the 6th NC Regiment to come to Hillsborough and take charge of three regiments of Militia from the Hillsborough District. All furloughs are cancelled effective immediately, and all officers shall arrive in Hillsborough no later than September 5th. Many officers refuse to serve again, citing pressing family demands and complaining that they are owed considerable sums in back pay.

In the southern part of the state, Maj. Gen. Richard Caswell tries to rally his Militia, but there is virtually no response. Those that do heed his call arrive with their heads hung low, sulking and complaining. Gov. Abner Nash inherits a terrible situation and his own apprehensions do little to improve things. The North Carolina legislature convenes in New Bern September 5-12, and it is required to devote more attention to military demands. However, they do little to encourage the rebuilding of the North Carolina Continental Line, preferring instead to depend on Militia drafts for the next three months. They also decide to appoint Brig. Gen. William Smallwood of the Maryland Line to take over all of the North Carolina Militia, astonishing every soldier belonging to the state, Continental or Militiaman. More on this in Volume 2.

Gov. Nash complains to the legislature that his Council of State will not attend called meetings, so the legislature decides to create a Board of War in its stead. Its members are given extraordinary powers in raising, organizing, and equipping all military forces of the state. They are to coordinate with ranking officers in the state to plan all military operations and for those officers to maintain accurate troop returns. Their new authority includes the right to remove or suspend any and all officers of the state and to appoint others when necessary.

The five members of the new Board of War are elected by a joint ballot of both houses of the legislature: Archibald MacLaine, Thomas Polk, Alexander Martin, John Penn, and Oroondates Davis. MacLaine and Polk refuse to serve, and their positions are never filled. Davis is a lawyer and a member of the legislature from Halifax County. John Penn has been a delegate to the Continental Congress and is considered to be a politician. Only Alexander Martin has any previous military experience as a previous Colonel/Commandant of the 2nd NC Regiment.

In early September, the North Carolina legislature commissions William Lee Davidson as Brigadier General (Pro Tempore) of the Salisbury District Brigade of Militia in place of Griffith Rutherford who was captured at the battle of Camden on August 16th. They have apparently forgotten that the Council of State has already commissioned Henry William Harrington of Richmond County as Brigadier General (Pro Tempore) in late July as Rutherford left the state to join Maj. Gen. Richard Caswell and Maj. Gen. Horatio Gates for the battle of Camden. Needless to say, Brig. Gen. (Pro Tempore) Henry William Harrington is not pleased. William Lee Davidson, also not too pleased, refuses to relinquish his Continental commission and is ever-ready to resume his command once his Continental regiment is reactivated. It never is.

On September 16th, Captain George Dougherty of the 4th NC Regiment writes to Brig. Gen. Jethro Sumner that he is "somewhat nettled" at the appointment of Brig. Gen. William Smallwood over any North Carolina troops. Two days later, Brig. Gen. (Pro Tempore) William Lee Davidson writes to Brig. Gen. Jethro Sumner that,

> "I need not tell you the dreadful effects of Gen. Gates's retreat to Hillsborough. The effects of it are, in my opinion, worse than those of his defeat. It has frightened the ignorant into despair, being left without cover or support to defend themselves against the whole force of the enemy."

On September 19th, Brig. Gen. Sumner arrives near Salisbury, and several discouraged regiments of NC Militia soon join him.

Although Maj. Gen. Horatio Gates avows that the British will not march northward any time soon, Brig. Gen. Jethro Sumner and his growing Militia march into Charlotte on the morning of September 25th – his own intelligence is quite the opposite of Gates's. Reports are coming in hourly that the British are less than fifteen miles away. Brig. Gen. Sumner orders Col. William Richardson Davie, commissioned on September 5th as the new Colonel and Commander of the NC State Cavalry–Western District (State Troops) and headquartered in Mecklenburg County, to cover his withdrawal. Brig. Gen. Sumner and his large continengent of Militiamen gather those stores and provisions that they can haul and he sees them safely to Salisbury, a little more than forty miles away.

As Lt. Gen. Charles, Lord Cornwallis approaches Charlotte on September 26th, Brig. Gen. Sumner and his Militia are on their way to Salisbury, and the local farmers are "flying before us in confusion." Col. Davie goes beyond his orders and fights an almost pitched battle with the entire British army as they march into Charlotte. Joined by Militia reinforcements, Col. Davie continues to harass Cornwallis for several hours, and it is estimated that his Patriots kill twenty and wound even more of the enemy.

Charlotte turns out to be a royal pain for Lt. Gen. Charles, Lord Cornwallis. His army, as any at the time, requires sustenance for their horses, and small foraging parties begin sweeping the countryside in ever-widening circles, stripping it of all grain and grasses. Col. William Richardson Davie with considerable support from several local Militia units constantly harass the British occupiers, with an intense focus on these foraging parties. Riflemen also hide on the outskirts of Charlotte and take every target of opportunity that comes their way.

As this continues, former Royal Governor Josiah Martin hands out paroles and certificates of protection, signing them "Governor of North Carolina." He manages to convince many that the British will soon be in control of North Carolina, as they already are in South Carolina. Lt. Gen. Charles, Lord Cornwallis issues a proclamation that the British have arrived and are offering protection to those who want to return the king's standard. Brig. Gen. Jethro Sumner finally gets his hands on Cornwallis's proclamation and Martin's parole, and forwards them to Maj. Gen. Horatio Gates on October 5th.

Meanwhile, on October 3rd, the Continental Congress in Philadelphia issues another resolve for all states to refill their Continental regiments, and that North Carolina must provide four regiments of infantry. They continue with defining that each regiment is to consist of nine companies and that each company is to consist of 64 men, including commissioned officers and privates. Three days later, Gov. Abner Nash writes back to President Samuel Huntington that:

> "I am now sorry to acquaint you that there is little prospect of our being able to fill up our Continental Battalions, owing to the perpetual calls we have for the Militia. All that part of the people who might otherwise be expected to enlist in the service are employed as substitutes, and indeed get the most extravagant premiums, far beyond anything that the public could offer."

In early October, news arrives that Maj. Patrick Ferguson has been killed and his entire Loyalist army has been captured at the battle of Kings Mountain in northern South Carolina. Lord Cornwallis and a number of his officers fall ill. The British general finally concludes that it is time to fall back into South Carolina and regroup. One of his aids writes, "Charlotte is an agreeable village but in a damned rebellious country." Col. William Richardson Davie and a growing numbr of local Militia units follow the British withdrawal and even skirmish with a large group sent back to fend them off. The British hurry to Winnsborough in South Carolina, leaving the North Carolinians jubilant and even confidently asserting that they will win this war–somehow.

Hillsborough continues to be a key rendezvous point for the Continental Army in the South. It is swarming with soldiers from several states, many who openly boast that they will soon finish off the British army. On October 7th, Lt. Col. William Washington and 100 of his 3rd

Regiment of Light Dragoons from Virginia arrive in Hillsborough. Col. Daniel Morgan, also of Virginia, is not far behind him.

The North Carolina Board of War authorizes the issuance of certificates to owners of grain taken for the army, but wandering bands of Patriot foragers often take what they want. The few arms available are issued to those Continental troops who have lost weapons at the battle of Camden, even though these arms were bought for the North Carolina Militia using state funds.

Maj. Gen. Horatio Gates grows short tempered and brooding about his future, "making everyone unhappy that had to Communicate with him." He openly and constantly blames his defeat on the "rascally behavior of the Militia," enough so that the North Carolina legislature appears to have lost faith in the ability of all home-grown officers, particularly the Militia officers, and specifically with Maj. Gen. Richard Caswell. In early September, he is removed as the commanding general of the North Carolina Militia, and is replaced by Brig. Gen. William Smallwood of the Maryland Continental Line, who in fact has done very little more than Caswell or Gates did at Camden.

At New Bern, a very angry Richard Caswell openly confronts Gov. Abner Nash, who explains that it is the legislature, in the creation of the Board of War, which has practically removed the state's Militia from executive direction. Caswell resigns from the Militia and from his position on the Board of Trade. To his credit, Gov. Abner Nash informs the Board of War that the former governor has been treated poorly, and Alexander Martin of that supercilious group suggests that a separate command be created just for Caswell.

Equally as frustrating, Maj. Gen. Horatio Gates takes it upon himself to assign the few active North Carolina Continenal officers in the field under Brig. Gen. William Smallwood as well. This is done without consulting Brig. Gen. Jethro Sumner, who is chasing Loyalists on the Yadkin River near Salisbury. Conversely, however, Gates insists that Sumner send him dispatches every six hours, if not more frequently.

Although Brig. Gen. Sumner had begrudgingly agreed earlier to serve under Maj. Gen. Richard Caswell of the Militia, he is definintely not happy that another brigadier general is now his superior, especially a brigadier general from another state. Board of War member, Alexander Martin, appeals to his patriotism, asserting,

"Should you leave the Service at this critical Juncture in the Face of the Enemy, the Board will sincerely regret it and wish the brave and virtuous Soldiers will dispense with immediate Inconveniences & will not for the little punctilio of Honour suffer his Country to be given into the Hands of a Merciless Enemy."

However, Jethro Sumner and his handful of officers are proud men, and this is an era in which pride and honor are important.

As Brig. Gen. William Smallwood leaves Hillsborough and finally takes to the field in the middle of October, Brig. Gen. Jethro Sumner sends a brief dispatch to him on October 20th, "I feel myself distressed to signify my declining any further Command of the Line of Militia." He and his other unhappy Continental officers who had been leading Militia units make their way homeward. Militia officers all across the state also began to find excuses not to serve under Brig. Gen. Smallwood of Maryland. Those in his path are not so lucky.

The Board of War decides it is time for all Continentals to leave Hillsborough and especially for Maj. Gen. Horatio Gates to move his operations "closer to his enemy." Around November 5th, the general finally leaves Hillsborough with an escort of 130 Continental mounted troops, but it is very evident that Gates's army is in no condition to fight.

On November 17th, the Board of War writes to Brig. Gen. (Pro Tempore) William Lee Davidson:

"We are sorry that your complaints are so justly founded, and that we have it not in our power at present to relieve them, as General Gates hath drawn from out of our public Store almost every Article for the Relief of the Northern Army."

Interestingly, on the same date, Maj. Gen. Horatio Gates writes a letter to the Board of War complaining that Col. Thomas Polk, Commissary General, had refused to provide him with everything he needs. As a result, Thomas Polk resigns. Another sad loss.

Not long after Gates marches out another major general rides into Hillsborough seeking the Continental Army. Gen. George Washington's personal selection is Maj. Gen. Nathanael Greene of Rhode Island, and Greene's appointment is generally popular with the army. He leaves for the South on October 23rd and stops in Philadelphia for nine days to urge the Continental Congress to provision his men for the upcoming march. On his way south, he stops at Annapolis and Richmond, both towns promising him more assistance than they ever intend to fulfill.

Maj. Gen. Greene fully expects to meet Maj. Gen. Gates at Hillsborough, but Gates had already left. Gov. Abner Nash is also not there, and this more than irritates the new general. Greene dashes off an express to the Governor suggesting that he could better utilize his talents by preparing the state's Militia to meet an invasion of the British in South Carolina.

Maj. Gen. Nathanael Greene also quickly fires off an express to Brig. Gen. Jethro Sumner on November 26th sincerely requesting his assistance in reconstructing the North Carolina Continental Line. Maj. Gen. Greene goes on to advise that all able-bodied officers are ordered back to active duty, and all known deserters and former prisoners of war who had escaped are to be reactivated as soon as possible. Brig. Gen. Sumner is authorized to pardon all deserters who will willingly rejoin, and Hillsborough is designated as the rendezvous point–once again.

Learning that Maj. Gen. Horatio Gates is in Charlotte, Maj. Gen. Nathanael Greene rides to that location and arrives on December 2nd. When Greene rides into the small village he finds an army busily constructing huts to thwart the chilling winds of the oncoming winter. Despite rumors of ill will between the two generals, Greene is cordially and respectfully greeted by Gates. On December 3rd, the troops learn of the change in command, and later that day Maj. Gen. Greene reviews the rank and file while complimenting his predecessor.

Colonel Thomas Polk, who has recently resigned as Commissary General, is received by Maj. Gen. Nathanel Greene on his first night in camp and questioned at length about the state of affairs relative to military supplies and other resources in the vicinity. Polk explains that there is only a three-day supply of provisions on hand and that ammunition is dangerously low. He later declares that Maj. Gen. Greene better understands the local situation within one hour than Gates has in over five months. Citing his advanced years, Polk refuses to withdraw his resignation, which is begrudgingly acknowledged. Soon thereafter, Col. William Richardson Davie is given the job, in January.

In public Maj. Gen. Greene says it will take "some time to inform himself of the Country, not choozing to be in surprizing Distance of Lord Cornwallis until he was strong enough to fight him." To his friend Joseph Reed, Greene complains that "General Gates has lost the Confidence of the Officers; and the Troops all their discipline; and so addicted to plundering that they were a terror to the Inhabitants." His inherited army is little more than a ragged and unruly mob. In short, Greene's army is, in his opinion, "but a shadow of an army in the midst of distress."

His first priority is to fire off dispatches to anyone that might provide assistance, but he knows that he cannot just sit around waiting for them to answer. To assert his authority, he launches his own rumor that the first deserter caught will be shot–but, the men still wander off. The next one found is executed in front of the entire army. This has a definite sobering effect, at least to the Continentals. By now–the sixth year of the war–the North Carolina Militia adroitly knows that the Continentals cannot and will not touch them, so they are not very concerned.

Acutely aware of the problems associated with William Smallwood, a brigadier general very recently promoted to major general by the Continental Congress, being in command of North Carolina troops, Maj. Gen. Nathanael Green quickly convinces Congress to recall Smallwood to the north. He marches out of Greene's camp on December 19th. Maj. Gen. Greene abruptly appoints William Lee Davidson to lead the North Carolina Militia as a brigadier general, subject to the state legislature's approval–it replies that Davidson is already in charge of all Militia in the Salisbury District since Griffith Rutherford is a prisoner of war.

On December 7th, Greene writes from Charlotte to his commander in New York, General George Washington:

> "Nothing can be more wretched and distressing than the condition of the troops, starving with cold and hunger, without tents and camp equipage... As I expected, so I find the great bodies of Militia that have been in the field and the manner in which they came out, being all on horse back, had laid waste all the country, in such a manner that I am really afraid it will be impossible to subsist the few troops we have, and if we can be subsisted at all, it must be by moving to the provisions, for they have no way of bringing it to the army. I have desired the Board of War of this State not to call out any more Militia until we can be better satisfied about the means of subsistence for the regular troops and the Militia from Virginia."

Maj. Gen. Greene soon concludes that it is wise to split his army, contrary to conventional wisdom. He orders Virginia Brig. Gen. Daniel Morgan (recently promoted) and Lt. Col. William Washington to the backcountry of South Carolina along the Broad River and to harry the enemy, collect provisions and forage, and in general "spirit up the people." Greene will take his half of the army into the Pee Dee region of South Carolina, where foraging and provisions are a little more available. On December 20th, after a steady rain for over ten days, the two armies march in different directions. Greene camps on Hick's Creek near the Pee Dee River in northeastern South Carolina on the day after Christmas. As usual, the new commanding officer complains that his men have insufficient clothing and blankets, but at least they now have food to eat. Unfortunately, this bounty is not to last very long.

On December 28th, Maj. Gen. Nathanael Greene writes his last letter of the year to his commanding officer, Gen. Washington, explaining why he has chosen his current camp's location:

> "I was apprehensive, on my first arrival, that the country around Charlotte was too much exhausted to afford subsistence for the Army at that place for any considerable time. The probability that my taking this position would discourage the enemy from attempting to possess themselves of Cross Creek, which would have given them the command of the greatest part of the provisions in the lower country, was another inducement to come to this place. It is also a camp of repose, and no army ever wanted one more, the troops having utterly lost their discipline."

All the while, Maj. Gen. Greene complains to the North Carolina Board of War that they must complete their Continental regiments rather than coddling their Militia. Their first response is that the Militiamen can be employed by Greene in partisan warfare until the Continental units are filled. The Board of War, however, does inform Greene that new Continental recruits are being raised, but they will not send them immediately "lest they disturb as to provisions." They then add insult when they announce that these new recruits will not be ordered to join Greene's army until the general has gathered enough strength to "offend the enemy."

As a new year approaches, six Continental officers decide it is in their best interest to retire on half pay effective January 1, 1781: Col. James Armstrong of the 4th NC Regiment; Col. Gideon Lamb of the 6th NC Regiment; Lt. Col. William Lee Davidson of the 1st NC Regiment; Lt. Col. James Thackston of the 4th NC Regiment; Capt. Francis Child of the 3rd NC Regiment, and Capt. Micajah Lewis of the 4th NC Regiment. The four latter men accept positions in the North Carolina Militia.

1780 ends with the North Carolina Continental Line in a state of rebuilding from virtually nothing. At this point in time, the state's Militia and State Troops are much more valued, if only to the state–and the legislature can certainly demand that these soldiers never leave the state, something it cannot demand of its Continentals. Maj. Gen. Nathanael Greene is acutely aware of these facts, but he uses every known trick to counter such thinking. Greene is not in the South to save North Carolina; he is in the South to save a nation. It will take more than a year for him to prove this.

Appendix B includes a listing of all known Continental units that participated in the battles of 1780.

Chapter Seven – 1781

As the new year of 1781 arrives, there is not a single North Carolina Continental "rank and file" soldier actually on active duty. The limited Contintental officers still on active duty are all across the state recruiting, but until a sizeable number of new recruits come together such that a reasonable period of drilling and training can take place, none are even given the precious few firearms currently available.

With the retirement of many key officers who elected to take half pay effective January 1st, and all others still prisoners of war since the Fall of Charlestown, SC back in May of 1780, there are zero colonels left on the

Key Events of 1781
• NC General Assembly meets in January.
• With 90% of all NC Continental soldiers captured at the Fall of Charleston, the Continental Congress authorizes NC to raise new men to reconstitute four new regiments of NC Continentals in January. It takes most of the year to accomplish.
• British Lt. Gen. Charles, Lord Cornwallis enters North Carolina to pursue Brig. Gen. Daniel Morgan in their "Race to the Dan" during January and February.
• British seize the town of Wilmington and establish a base there in January. They are forced to evacuate in November.
• Battle of Guilford Court House on March 15th, British victory with huge losses.
• With a large British Army presence in the State, Loyalist factions begin to resurface.
• NC Continental Line joins Maj. Gen. Nathanael Greene in South Carolina to retake all British outposts in the back-country, and to retake Augusta, GA. The British are soon left only with Charles-town and a growing Loyalist population.

Continental Line. Brig. Gen. Jethro Sumner provides a return of the officers of the North Carolina Continental Line as of January 23rd:

Rank	Present	POWs	Total
Colonel	-	2	2
Lt. Colonel/Cmdt	-	1	1
Lt. Colonel	1	2	3
Major	4	2	6
Captain	24	12	36
Capt.-Lt.	8	2	10
Lieutenant	22	28	50
Ensign	1	1	2
Surgeon	2	4	6
TOTAL	**62**	**54**	**116**

Based upon recent analysis of all available data found in the many pension applications and state records, the following officers are known to have been considered "present" in January of 1781:

Rank	Officer's Name	Assigned Regiment
Brig. Gen.	Jethro Sumner	-
Lt. Colonel	John Baptiste Ashe	1st NC Regiment
"	Henry "Hal" Dixon	2nd NC Regiment
Major	John Armstrong	3rd NC Regiment
"	Reading Blount	2nd NC Regiment
"	Hardy Murfree	2nd NC Regiment
"	Pinketham Eaton	4th NC Regiment
Captain	William Armstrong	1st NC Regiment
"	Alexander Brevard	4th NC Regiment
"	John Campbell	4th NC Regiment
"	Benjamin Carter	4th NC Regiment
"	Samuel Chapman	4th NC Regiment
"	Thomas Donoho	1st NC Regiment
"	George Dougherty	4th NC Regiment
"	William Goodman	4th NC Regiment
"	Christopher Goodwin	2nd NC Regiment
"	Joshua Hadley	1st NC Regiment
"	Clement Hall	2nd NC Regiment
"	Curtis Ivey	3rd NC Regiment
"	William Lytle	1st NC Regiment
"	Samuel Martin	2nd NC Regiment
"	John Medearis	3rd NC Regiment
"	James Mills	1st NC Regiment
"	Dennis Porterfield	3rd NC Regiment
"	Robert Raiford	2nd NC Regiment
"	Matthew Ramsey	4th NC Regiment
"	Joseph Thomas Rhodes	4th NC Regiment
"	William Saunders	1st NC Regiment
"	Anthony Sharpe	1st NC Regiment
"	Edward Yarborough	3rd NC Regiment

As can be seen, there is one more Lt. Colonel than the one identified by Brig. Gen. Jethro Sumner, and one less Captain simply because the last one cannot be identified by this author. As mentioned earlier, in January of 1781, all of these officers (and subaltern officers, such as lieutenant and ensigns) are ordered to recommence a strong recruiting effort now that Maj. Gen. Nathanael Greene has taken over the Southern Department and is stationed in northeastern South Carolina consolidating half of his forces with various new Militia units that are arriving daily from all parts of Virginia.

In the meantime, the other half of his army under Brig. Gen. Daniel Morgan severely spanks the British Army at the battle of Cowpens on January 17th in northern South Carolina. The morning after this remarkable victory, Brig. Gen. Morgan knows that Lt. Gen. Charles,

Lord Cornwallis will soon be pursuing him, so he takes his band of Continentals from Maryland and Delaware and some Virginia Militiamen and heads northward with his many British prisoners.

What later becomes known as "The Race to the Dan" begins on January 18th when Brig. Gen. Daniel Morgan breaks camp in the wee hours of that morning and avoids the few roads to keep his enemy guessing as to his whereabouts and his ultimate objective. He first goes to Gilbert Town, very near present-day Rutherfordton in North Carolina.

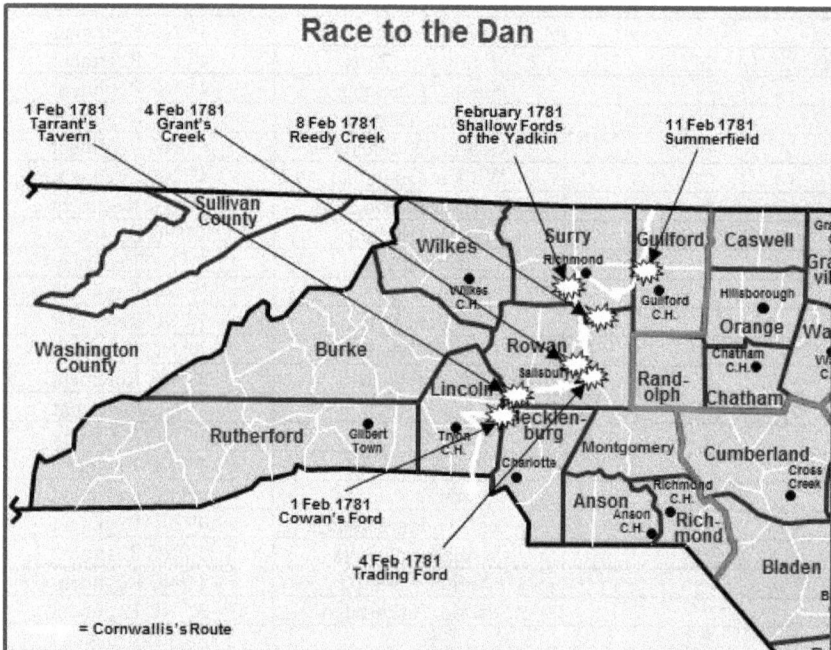

In the evening of the same Thursday that Brig. Gen. Morgan leaves the Cowpens, British Maj. Gen. Alexander Leslie arrives in Lord Cornwallis's camp with 1,200 fresh reinforcements from Charlestown. With these additions, Lord Cornwallis now fields an army of almost 2,500 soldiers, including more than 1,200 Regulars. Early the next morning, the British army breaks camp in search of the Patriots under Brig. Gen. Daniel Morgan. Although the weather and the conditions of the many rivers and streams–at this time of year unpredictable at best and impossible at worst–as well as the lack of decent roadways, Lt. Gen. Cornwallis and his men eventually average "about a mile an hour" in their quest to overtake the elusive Patriots. Amazingly, Brig. Gen. Daniel Morgan barely manages to remain one step ahead of Lord Cornwallis.

```
┌─────────────────────────────────────────────────────────────────────────┐
│                    North Carolina Continental Line                        │
│                          January 23, 1781                                 │
│                                                                           │
│                           ┌──────────────┐                                │
│                           │   Southern   │                                │
│                           │  Department  │                                │
│                           ├──────────────┤                                │
│                           │ Maj. Gen. Nathanael │                         │
│                           │    Greene    │                                │
│                           └──────────────┘                                │
│                                                                           │
│                           ┌──────────────┐                                │
│                           │      NC      │  In NC                         │
│                           │   Brigade    │  Recruiting                    │
│                           ├──────────────┤                                │
│                           │ Brig. Gen. Jethro │                           │
│                           │    Sumner    │                                │
│                           └──────────────┘                                │
└─────────────────────────────────────────────────────────────────────────┘
```

1st NC Regiment	2nd NC Regiment	3rd NC Regiment	4th NC Regiment
• Lt. Col. John Baptiste Ashe In NC Recruiting	• Lt. Col. "Hal" Dixon Cdr. of "NC Regiment" • Maj. Reading Blount In "NC Regiment" • Maj. Hardy Murfree In NC Recruiting	• Maj. John Armstrong Cdr. of Surry County Regiment of Militia Under SC Brig. Gen. Andrew Pickens	• Maj. Pinketham Eaton A Colonel in Halifax County Regiment
Captains	**Captains**	**Captains**	**Captains**
• William Armstrong* • Thomas Donoho* • Joshua Hadley* • William Lytle** • James Mills* • William Saunders* • Anthony Sharpe*	• Christopher Goodwin* • Clement Hall* • Samuel Martin* • Robert Raiford*	• Curtis Ivey* • John Medearis*** • Dennis Porterfield* • Edward Yarborough**	• Alexander Brevard* • John Campbell* • Benjamin Carter* • Samuel Chapman* • George Dougherty* • William Goodman* • Matthew Ramsey** • Joseph Thomas Rhodes*

*Regimental Recruiter; **Captain Under Lt. Col. Henry "Hal" Dixon; ***Public Factory in Granville County

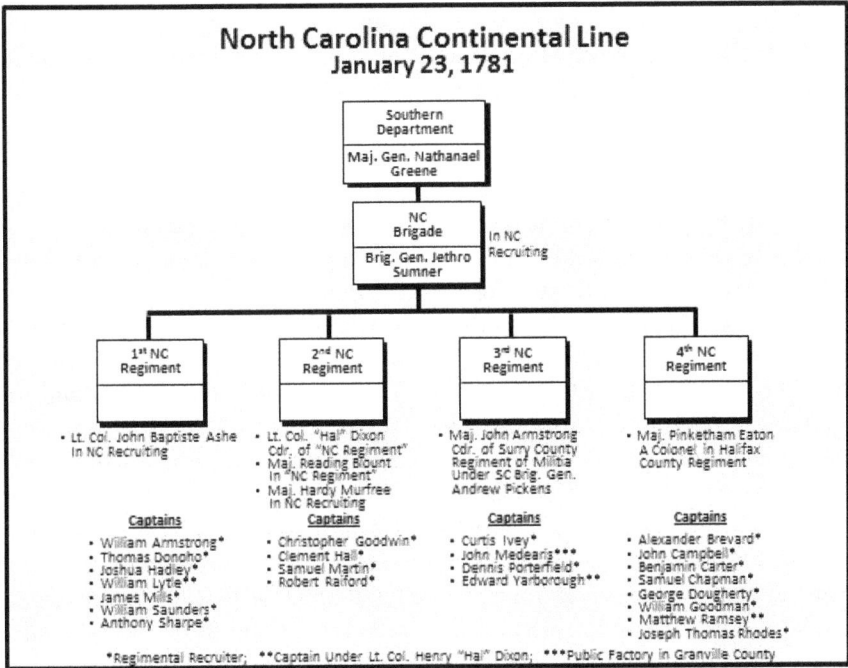

When Maj. Gen. Nathanael Greene learns of Morgan's victory at the Cowpens, he too instinctively knows that Lt. Gen. Cornwallis will do all in his power to retake the British prisoners. Expresses fly between Greene and Morgan and the commander makes it very clear–get those British prisoners to Halifax County in Virginia as soon as possible. Greene also advises his brigadier to meet him at Beattie's Ford on January 30th, which is accomplished. The two split up from there to Salisbury, then march to Guilford Court House, reaching the latter on February 7th. While there, Maj. Gen. Nathanael Greene observes that this would be a great location to take on his enemy, but not at this time. Brig. Gen. Daniel Morgan marches onward with his prisoners as Greene waits for the arrival of Brig. Gen. Isaac Huger (SC). These latter two make it to the Dan River by February 13th and complete their crossing the next day, one full day before the British arrive. The "Race to the Dan" is won by the Patriots, not a trivial accomplishment.

Although many North Carolina Militia units support both Brig. Gen. Daniel Morgan and Maj. Gen. Nathanael Greene in the "Race to the Dan," not one North Carolina Continental soldier participates. For the first time since the long war began in 1775, soldiers from other states are in North Carolina helping in her time of need. Greene has Continentals from Delaware, Maryland, and Virginia with him, as well as Militia units from Virginia. Brig. Gen. Andew Pickens of South Carolina joins up with Brig. Gen. Daniel Morgan until he reaches the Virginia line, then Pickens rejoins Maj. Gen. Greene after he returns to the Old North State on February 24th.

Frustrated with the Patriots' escape into Virginia with so many British prisoners, Lt. Gen. Charles, Lord Cornwallis turns his army and goes immediately to Hillsborough, where he sets up camp. After resting for a few days, on February 18th, he sends out Lt. Col. Banastre Tarleton into the countryside to ask around for Loyalist recruits.

In the meantime, after the battle of Cowpens in January, he sends word to Lt. Col. Nisbet Balfour in Charlestown to dispatch a detachment of the 82nd Regiment under Maj. James H. Craig to leave Charlestown and to go take Wilmington, North Carolina. This will provide the British with a port whereby Lord Cornwallis can receive supplies by way of the Cape Fear River, via Cross Creek (Cumberland County). Maj. Craig sails from Charlestown on January 21st with 300 Regular troops on board a frigate, two sloops of war, and eighteen other vessels. After sailing up the Cape Fear River, Capt. John Barclay and a contingent of Royal Marines land twelve miles from Wilmington. They march overland to the town, while the galleys continue up the river. The town leaders attempt to gain favorable terms from Capt. Barclay, to no avail. The British promptly seize the town without a shot being fired.

Earlier, on January 4th, the state's Board of War writes to Maj. Gen. Nathanael Greene apologizing that the legislature has not yet agreed on some mode of completing their Continental regiments, "but in their room have employed the Militia, a defence too transitory to place much Reliance in, who, with their Horse, unfortunate for us, we find have too much destroyed the Resources of this Country, that heretofore were great as to provision Supplies." The Board acknowledges that the state's treasury is exhausted and will continue so until taxes are collected, which translates to no new Continentals any time soon.

On January 16th, the Board of War appoints Col. William Richardson Davie as Superintendent Commissary General to oversee all provisions and supplies to the state's military, including all Continentals within her boundaries. Col. Davie is authorized up to four assistants to carry his orders into the many counties and to see his orders properly executed. All county commissaries are directed to cooperate fully with Col. Davie and his assistants. This is a good start to ensure all military units across the state are properly fed, but it takes many months to work out all of the kinks already inherent in the system.

With such a formidable enemy now in the extreme northern and southern parts of the state, the North Carolina civil authorities are barely one notch below panic-stricken. Gov. Abner Nash somehow manages to convince the legislature to convene at New Bern on January 27th, very aware of Lt. Gen. Charles, Lord Cornwallis pursuing Brig. Gen. Daniel Morgan towards the Dan River. They are not aware, however, of the imminent capture of Wilmington two days later.

On January 27th, Brig. Gen. Jethro Sumner writes to Maj. Gen. Nathanael Greene explaining that raising four new regiments–again virtually from scratch–will take a considerable length of time. The most pressing issue is to get the state's legislature to determine a lawful process for recruiting and maintaining large numbers of men. The second issue is the fact that so many high-level Continental officers are still prisoners of the British, and the mid-level officers are not in favor of promoting or commissioning new leaders for the four new regiments. This can only translate to the reality that the new regiments will have to be led by Lt. Colonels and Majors, and even determining who will be selected based upon seniority is not a simple process.

The General Assembly finally resolves on February 11th for the state to provide 2,724 new recruits for the four new Continental regiments demanded recently by the Continental Congress. Each commander of the four regiments is to order the field officers and captains to meet at some convenient location on or before March 20th and to sort out the nine-months men raised in 1778 as well as all prisoners now on parole, then to determine the remaining available recruits shall now be required to fill the Continental ranks. For any man who will willingly volunteer, he will receive a bounty of £3,000 plus three barrels of corn for his wife and two barrels of corn for each child under ten years of age to be delivered to his wife annually. The £3,000 is to be paid in either money or certificates bearing 6% interest per annum until paid–and tax free.

Each man is required to serve twelve months and is to be paid from the date of his enlistment. If insufficient numbers volunteer, then drafts are to be made of the remaining eligible men, again for twelve months, and again for the same bounty and pay as volunteers. For any man who will willingly volunteer for "the duration of the war," he will receive a bounty of £2,000 at time of enlistment, and after completing this service will additionally receive one prime slave, or the value thereof, and 640 acres of land. Each new recruit, volunteer or draftee, is also to receive two pairs of shoes, two pairs of stockings, two shirts, one pair of breeches, one pair of overalls, one waistcoat, one coat, one hunting shirt, one blanket, and one hat. These are to be delivered to each man on the day of rendezvous, or as soon thereafter as they can be acquired. Furthermore, if they fulfill their enlistment, then they will be exempted from further military service for one full year thereafter.

All new recruits are required to rendezvous on or before April 25th at either Salisbury, Hillsborough, Edenton, Halifax, Smithfield, or Duplin Court House. If they do not show up, they are to be considered as deserters and subsequently rounded up. All Militia officers employed in executing this Act are allowed full pay and rations for every day of actual service while recruiting.

During the same legislative session, the General Assembly resolves that Brig. Gen. Jethro Sumner be requested to permit his Continental officers to join Militia units and help get them organized until an arrangement of the Continental officers shall take place. Everyone is acutely aware that Lt. Gen. Charles, Lord Cornwallis and his large British army are in the state and will soon commence hostilities. The entire state Militia is on call to muster and to march their men towards Hillsborough as quickly as possible. Even some retired Continental officers are called upon during this panic-filled time. Col. James Armstrong is recalled by the General Assembly to take over the New Bern District Brigade of Militia on February 7th when they hear the rumor of Brig. Gen. William Caswell's resignation. Three days later they have to rescind that appointment when they learn the truth–Brig. Gen. William Caswell had not resigned.

During this short legislative session, the active Continental officers send one of their own to address the General Assembly about their newest complaint–their pay between 1777 and 1780 was so diminished due to inflation that they want the state to provide them with backpay to make up the difference. The General Assembly considers this request at this session and again later in 1781, but no resolution is made during this year.

As soon as he learns of the latest resolves from the legislature, Brig. Gen. Jethro Sumner fires off several letters from his home in Warren County. On February 21st, he orders Lt. Col. John Baptiste Ashe to provide him with the officers' "new arrangement" and for him to get the officers to Maj. Gen. Richard Caswell's headquarters at Kingston to assist him in organizing and commanding the Militia. On February 25th, Sumner writes to Maj. Gen. Nathanael Greene informing his commander that the temporary plan for command of the four new Continental regiments is assigned to Lt. Col. Henry "Hal" Dixon, Lt. Col. John

Baptiste Ashe, Maj. Hardy Murfree, and Maj. John Armstrong. He continues with noting that many Continental officers are already being assigned to Militia units, and his own preference is to lead the Halifax District Brigade of Militia since Brig. Gen. Allen Jones is currently ill. A week later, Brig. Gen. Thomas Eaton (Pro Tempore) insists on leading the Halifax District Brigade of Militia and Sumner is without a Militia command–he is left at home on the sidelines at this point in time.

With Maj. Gen. Nathanael Greene now back in North Carolina, he quickly marches his growing army back towards Guilford Court House, his earlier noted location for a potential face-off with his enemy, Lt. Gen. Charles, Lord Cornwallis. In late February and early March, the two opponents spar with each other in the countryside between Guilford Court House and Hillsborough. On February 25th, Lt. Col. Henry "Light Horse Harry" Lee and about 240 of his Legion from Virginia, along with nearly 500 North and South Carolina Militiamen under South Carolina Brig. Gen. Andrew Pickens surprise a large group of Loyalists under Col. (Doctor) John Pyle at Haw River and route them. On the next day, Maj. Micajah Lewis (formerly a captain in the 4th NC Regiment) leads a small group of Militiamen from Surry County and they are all surprised by Lt. Col. Banastre Tarleton and his Legion–Maj. Lewis is killed at Dickey's Farm in what is present-day Alamance County.

Since Maj. Gen. Greene is constantly on the move to keep his enemy guessing, he dispatches Col. Otho H. Williams of Maryland to keep his men between the British and Patriot camps. On March 6th, Col. Williams and his vigilant patrols spot Lt. Col. Banatre Tarleton's Legion and Lt. Col. James Webster with about 1,000 British Regulars around eight o'clock a.m. riding towards Whitesell's Mill in northeastern Guilford County. Clearly outnumbered, the Patriots give a brief skirmish then quickly withdraw from the vicinity. It is now quite apparent that Lt. Gen. Cornwallis is on the move and looking for a fight.

Several other firefights follow, all leading the opposing armies to the destined rendezvous at Guilford Court House on March 15th. Lt. Col. Henry Lee meets Lt. Col. Banastre Tarleton very early in the morning at the New Garden Meeting House, a mere few miles from the later battlefield. Skirmishes continue all the way to the ultimate battlefield.

When the British arrive in the vicinity of Guilford Court House, Maj. Gen. Nathanael Greene feels the time is right to fight. He has roughly 4,300 troops, of which 1,600 are Continental Regulars, facing nearly 2,200 British Regulars. The battle, which starts around 11:30 a.m., lasts for about two and a half hours.

Lt. Gen. Charles, Lord Cornwallis finds the Patriots in position on rising ground about one and a half miles from the Court House. He is unable to gain much information from his prisoners or the local residents about the Patriot army. To his front he sees a plantation with a large field straddling both sides of the road, with two more fields further over on the left separated by 200 yards or so of woodland. To his right beyond the fields the woodland extends for several miles. On the far side of the first field is a fenced wood, one mile in depth, through which the Salisbury Road passes into an extensive cleared area around the court house. Along the edge of this woodland is a fence forming the Patriots' first line of defense with a 6-pound cannon on each side of the dirt road.

The Patriots' front line consists mostly of North Carolina Militia, flanked on each end with riflemen and light horse. To keep the Militia anchored in the middle of a long line of men, the only remnants of the NC Continental Army is stationed in the center of that long line, supported also with a small regiment of Militia led by the Continental Lt. Colonel Archibald Lytle. This front line does precisely what it is asked to do—fire one, preferably two, shots at the oncoming British Regulars, then leave the field in an orderly manner for the second line to do a similar job. Virginia Militiaman Samuel Houston, on the second line, climbs a tree for a better view of the upcoming battlefield. He later commented that the North Carolinians waited until the British were "very near" before they began firing.

The British now focus on the second line, mostly comprised of the Virginia Militia. The Von Bose regiment (Hessian) heads to the southern flank. Brig. Gen. Charles O'Hara leads the 2nd Battalion of Guards to the center, while the 23rd Regiment of Foot and the 33rd Regiment of Foot follow. The Jaëgers and the Guards Light Infantry make it to the northern flank. The Redcoats never stop, and advance "in their eagerness to go to the Virginia line." Lord Cornwallis does not want to lose momentum, now that the wet plowed fields and fences are behind him. Having driven one Militia line out of his way, the British now face a much longer and much bloodier fight against a much more stubborn Patriot force.

The two sides exchange numerous volleys, some estimate between eighteen (18) and twenty (20) rounds each—well past the effective limits of the typical musket's flintlock. This trivial situation is what finally means that the Patriots have to retire from the second line—the alternative is to face the sharp end of a bayonet while replacing a worn out flintlock, not appealing to too many men no matter how experienced.

N

Legend:
- British Troops
- Farthest Advance
- British Artillery

1,900 – 2,200 Soldiers

93 Killed
413 Wounded
26 Missing

2nd LINE

[From 1st Line]

DE Continentals
VA Rifles
Guards Jäger's Light Infantry
RAMS... Militia
33rd Foot
EATON
23rd Foot
Guards Grenadiers
2nd Battalion of Guards
BUTLER
[Militia Left]

1st LINE

[To 2nd Line]
NC Light Dragoons
Horse Regiment
NC Light Dragoons
3rd Continental Light Dragoons
DE Continentals
VA Continentals
VA Rifles

Warren County Regiment
Franklin County Regiment
Nash County Regiment
Edgecombe County Regiment
Halifax County Regiment
Northampton County Regiment
Martin County Regiment
Hertford County Detachment
Camden County Detachment
Hyde County Detachment
Johnston County Detachment
Jones County Detachment
2nd Granville County Regiment
1st Granville County Regiment
Caswell County Regiment
1st Orange County Regiment
2nd Orange County Regiment
3rd Orange County Regiment
Singleton [To 3rd Line]

NC Regiment of Continentals
Chatham County Detachment
Wake County Detachment
Bladen County Detachment
Cumberland County Detachment
Duplin County Detachment
2nd Guilford County Regiment
1st Guilford County Regiment
Anson County Detachment
Randolph County Regiment
Washington County Detachment
Mecklenburg County Detac...
Wilkes County Detachment
Lincoln County Detachment
Rutherford County Detachm...
Burke County Detachment
Rowan County Regiment
Surry County Regiment
Surry County (NC) Rifles
VA Rifles
Lee's Legion Cavalry
Lee's Legion Infantry
VA Continentals
Fence Lines

CORNWALLIS
WEBSTER
33rd Foot
23rd Foot
Guards Jäger's
Grenadiers Guards
Light Infantry
Smith
Tarleton's Legion
2nd Battalion of Guards
McLeod
71st Foot
Hoskins
O'Hara
1st Battalion of Guards
Von Bose
LESLIE

Salisbury Road
Plowed Field
[To 2nd Line]

Yards 0 100 200 300 400

126

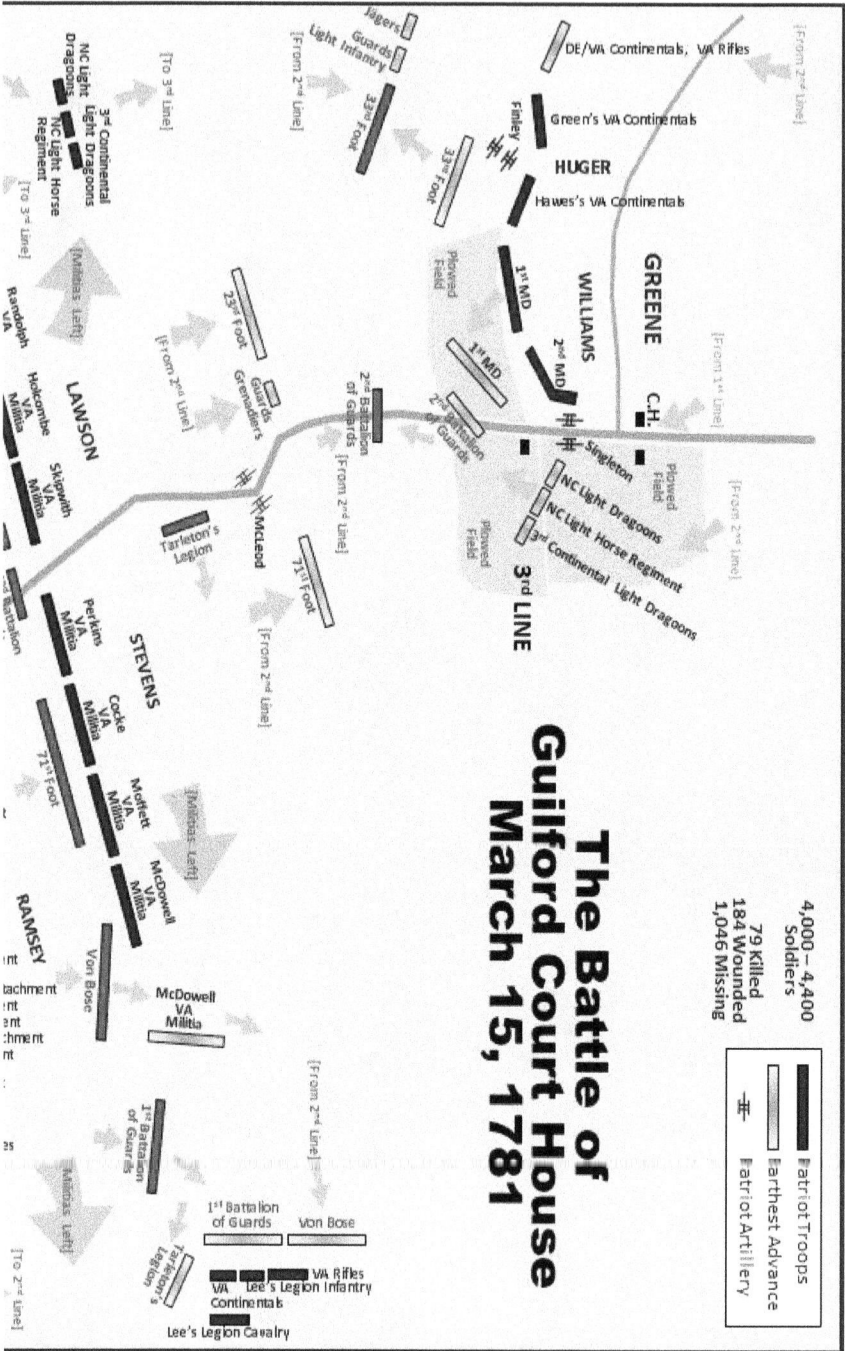

The Battle of Guilford Court House
March 15, 1781

The ground between the second and third lines includes a slight depression called "the vale" by contemporary witnesses. As the British army move past the second line they descend a few feet in elevation only to have to march up towards the well-rested Continentals, who are positioned at the peak of a short rise, along what contemporaries called "the ridge." This slight difference in elevation is what caught the eye of Maj. Gen. Nathanael Greene nine days earlier before he dashed to the Dan River and the Virginia state line.

Maj. Gen. Greene and his Continentals rest for nearly ninety minutes and quietly scan the visible vicinity. Separated by almost 600 yards of thick woodlands, the third Patriot line sees none of the fighting ahead of them. They can only wait nervously and listen to the furious sounds that somehow edge closer each ticking minute. The light horsemen of the NC Light Horse Regiment, the NC Light Dragoons, and Lt. Col. William Washington's 3rd Continental Dragoons of Virginia also survive two successful withdrawals and now position themselves on the southern flank of the third line, across the road from the Court House. With a decent road behind the Continentals, these cavalrymen are ideally situated to react to any possible crisis along the third line. Also at the third line are the Delaware, Maryland, and Virginia Continentals, as well as Col. Charles Lynch's remaining Virgnia riflemen, who have successfully withdrawn from the first and second lines. These tired warriors take a position along the northern flank for the third time today.

Finally, remnants of the second line begin to appear, and the Continentals steel themselves, knowing that the British Regulars have to soon appear as well. The British 33rd Regiment of Foot arrives first and immediately attacks the position of the Virginia Continentals led by Brig. Gen. Isaac Huger on the ridge, only to be driven back with help from Capt.-Lt. Finley's artillery. The 33rd Regiment of Foot recoils and takes a relatively high position then digs in. Next arrives the 2nd Guards Battalion who routes the 2nd Maryland Regiment (Continentals) and promptly seizes Capt. Anthony Singleton's two 6-pounders.

The 1st Maryland Regiment (Continentals) quickly counterattacks with support from the three units of cavalry–the NC Light Dragoons, the NC Light Horse Regiment, and the 3rd Continental Light Dragoons (VA). This mobile force stops the 2nd Guards Battalion and even pushes it backwards. With further assistance from the North Carolina Continentals, the Maryland Brigade retakes the captured artillery. The fighting between the 1st Maryland Regiment and the 2nd Guards Battalion is described as very intense, and often referred to as "the melee." Both units are fairly evenly matched and both have proud histories to live up to. According to Maryland Col. Otho H. Williams, "the first regiment embraced the opportunity and... they bayoneted and cut to pieces a great number of the Guards who had taken our field pieces."

During "the melee," Lt. Col. James Stuart of the 2nd Guards Battalion makes his way through a crowd to confront Capt. John Smith of the 1st Maryland Regiment, who is furiously assaulting some Grenadiers. Lt. Col. Stuart thrusts his short sword, Capt. Smith avoids it nimbly, then wheels around and gives Lt. Col. Stuart a back-handed blow to the head, killing the British officer. Capt. Smith is then shot in the back of the head, but miraculously the buckshot only stuns him. Around the same time, Brig. Gen. Charles O'Hara is rallying his 2nd Guards Battalion and he suffers his second wound of the day, being shot in the chest. This again rallies the 2nd Guards Battalion for a short spell, but they soon fall back and the Patriot dragoons charge after them.

This is when British Lt. John McLeod arrives with two 3-pounders. His crew efficiently repulses the Patriot dragoons with well-placed grapeshot. The guns fire, the Patriots withdraw, and this saves what is left of the 2nd Guards Battalion. By now, the Grenadiers have also arrived. The 1st Maryland Regiment then also withdraws back towards the court house, following the cavalry.

From the position of Lt. Gen. Charles, Lord Cornwallis, the moment of victory seems at hand. With the arrival of the 23rd Regiment of Foot, the 71st Regiment of Foot, and the rallied 2nd Guards Battalion, he now has a fairly solid line of infantry ready to attack. He orders an advance, with the 23rd Regiment of Foot and the 33rd Regiment of Foot facing Lt. Col. Samuel Hawes's 2nd Virginia Regiment (Continentals) and Lt. Finley's artillery, and the 71st Regiment of Foot and the 2nd Guards Battalion moving towards the 1st Maryland Regiment and the court house. On the northern flank, Lt. Col. James Webster and his 33rd Regiment of Foot cross a ravine and attack Lt. Col. Hawes's 2nd Virginia Regiment, which is supported by Capt. Robert Kirkwood's company. Lt. Ebenezer Finley's guns fall to the British 23rd Regiment of Foot.

The brief, bloody struggle for the northern flank results in the wounding of both commanders on each side. Lt. Col. Webster falls with a severe leg wound, a shot that destroys his kneecap and femur. Brig. Gen. Isaac Huger is shot in the right hand, and his sword falls into his lap, which he catches with his left hand, draws from his pocket a handkerchief, ties up his right hand, then moves on. Maj. Gen. Nathanael

Greene then chooses to ensure his army's survival and orders a total withdrawal.

Upon the withdrawal of Lt. Col. William Washington and the 2nd Maryland Regiment after "the melee," Maj. Gen. Greene orders Col. John Green to move his 1st Virginia Regiment back from the ridgeline and to form a rear guard across the Reedy Fork Road. The Delaware Regiment joins Lt. Col. Hawes's right flank, then they both withdraw to the east, backfilling Col. Green's previous position. Brig. Gen. Isaac Huger, with Capt. Robert Kirkwood, soon follows.

Lt. Gen. Cornwallis orders the 23rd Regiment of Foot and the 71st Regiment of Foot, with some of his cavalry, to pursue the retreating Patriots. They kill or wound as many as they can overtake, until being completely exhausted, they are obliged to halt. The British Legion dragoons continue until a sharp volley by Lt. Matthew Rhea's company of Col. Green's 1st Virginia Regiment halts them in their tracks.

Stopping about three miles from the battlefield to look at his watch, Beverly Randolph reports to his men that the "general engagement including skirmishes of picket and outpost continued 2 hours and 27 minutes." By 2:30 p.m., roughly two and a half hours after the initial cannonade, the battle of Guilford Court House ends.

The British own the battlefield and are thus the victors, as the Patriots disappear into the woods and down the Reedy Ford Road. The British have captured almost 1,300 small arms as well as the four 6-pounders. According to Lt. Gen. Cornwallis's own return, he led 1,924 men onto the battlefield; he had 93 killed, 413 wounded, and 26 missing–casualties that amounted to nearly one-quarter of his army. This is certainly a very costly victory for the proud Redcoats. The Patriots reportedly lose 79 men killed and 184 wounded.

Since the North Carolina Continentals have only recently begun to rebuild, there is but one "regiment" at the battle of Guilford Court House. Lt. Col. Henry "Hal" Dixon and Maj. Reading Blount command four small companies led by Capt. William Lytle, Capt. Griffith John McRee (who has only recently been exchanged), Capt. Matthew Ramsey, and Capt. Edward Yarborough. Lt. Col. Archibald Lytle led the small 3rd Orange County Regiment of Militia, which only consisted of two companies. These Continentals were stationed at the middle of the first line near the Salisbury Road to help anchor the North Carolina Militia.

In his 1818 pension application, Henry Martin (S41791) asserts:

"That he the said Henry Martin enlisted in the state of North Carolina, Dobbs County, in the year 1776, date not remembered, in the company commanded by

Capt. Simon Bright in the 2nd Regiment that he continued to serve in said company and in the service of the United States until the end of the war when he was discharged from service in the state aforesaid that he was in the battles of the Great Bridge in Virginia, Charlestown [Fort Moultrie 1776], Trenton in New Jersey, Brandywine Creek in Pennsylvania, and Germantown do, Monmouth NJ, Stony Point, Charlestown under General Lincoln, and at Guilford Court House. NC..." [minor edits]

After the battle, the British are spread across a large expanse of woodland without food and shelter, and during the night torrential rains start. Fifty of the wounded die before sunrise. Had the British followed the retreating Americans they might have come across their baggage and supply wagons, which had been left where the Americans had camped on the west of the Salisbury Road prior to the battle. Retiring to Hillsborough, Lt. Gen. Charles, Lord Cornwallis raises the royal standard, offers protection to the inhabitants, and for the moment appears to be master of Georgia and the two Carolinas. In a few weeks, however, he abandons the heart of the state and marches to Wilmington to recruit and refit his command.

Maj. Gen. Nathanael Greene decides not to follow his enemy to the coast; he stops and rests his men at Ramsey's Mill in Chatham County. He then turns his exhausted army back towards South Carolina with the express intent of destroying the small British outposts all along the backcountry and forcing the Redcoats back to the confines of Charlestown. By April 20th, the small and rebuilding 1st NC Regiment led by Maj. Pinketham Eaton joins him in the Pee Dee region.

Hoping to lure Lt. Gen. Charles, Lord Cornwallis back into South Carolina, Maj. Gen. Greene has the Marquis de Lafayette sent to Virginia and Maj. Gen. Anthony Wayne is soon ordered to join him. On April 6th, Greene leaves Ramsey's Mill and heads southward. Although his return is heralded with great joy in most of South Carolina, his departure is marked with gloom in most of North Carolina. Before he is even out of the state, Loyalists under the soon-to-be-notorious David Fanning commence their brutal raids against local Patriots in and around Randolph, Chatham, Cumberland, and Montgomery counties.

On April 19th, Lt. Gen. Charles, Lord Cornwallis marches out of Wilmington. Earlier, some of his men have been seen at Brunswick Town, so the rumor of a southern march is soon on everyone's lips. Brig. Gen. Jethro Sumner has orders–if Cornwalls marches towards Virginia he is to join Maj. Gen. Baron Von Steuben at Portsmouth; if Cornwallis marches south he is to join Maj. Gen. Nathanael Greene in South Carolina. Little does Greene know, the new Continentals are coming in so slowly that Brig. Gen. Jethro Sumner has no units assembled and clothed, much less trained even in the basics.

It is soon very evident that Lord Cornwallis is going to Virginia, and the rebuilding North Carolina Continentals can do absolutely nothing to slow him down, much less to stop him. All Militia units in the eastern part of the state are ordered out, and many came together under their commanders. But, none have more than two or three rounds of ammunition, so all they can do is to harass the British rear as they march through Duplin, Wayne, Johnston, Nash, Halifax, and Northampton counties and into Virginia by the middle of May.

On April 13th, Maj. Pinketham Eaton is at Chatham Court House when he writes to Brig. Gen. Jethro Sumner that he has just received 170 new recruits from Lt. Col. William Thomas Linton of the Nash County Regiment of Militia, but he has no officers to lead the new men. He also notes that he has already been commanded by Maj. Gen. Nathanael Greene to march immediately with these new recruits to his camp in South Carolina–please help. Four days later, Maj. Eaton writes to Brig. Gen. Sumner that he is now in the Pee Dee region of South Carolina and that several of his new men have already deserted.

By April 21st, Smallpox is prevalent in the town of Halifax. Col. Benjamin Seawell of the Franklin County Regiment of Militia writes to Brig. Gen. Jethro Sumner–"where do I take the new recruits now?" Similarly, Col. Nicholas Long, the Deputy Quarter Master General (DQMG) for the state headquartered at Halifax, with Lt. Gen. Cornwallis heading his direction, he advises Brig. Gen. Sumner that he is removing all Public Stores to a safe location–and to avoid the Smallpox. On April 27th, Lt. Col. Henry "Hal" Dixon writes to Brig. Gen. Sumner that he is now in Hillsborough–there are no provisions, but there are also no new recruits as yet, he doesn't expect them for another month or so, and therefore he's going back home to Caswell County. The next day, he writes to his general that he has changed his mind about going home–he is now going to visit Brig. Gen. John Butler of the Hillsborough District Brigade of Militia, where he "shall use my utmost endeavor to get everything in order for the reception of the Troops by the time they will rendezvous at this place."

Now that he is positive that Lt. Gen. Cornwallis is marching to Virginia, on April 30th, Brig. Gen. Jethro Sumner sends orders to Maj. John Armstrong in Salisbury to march all of his new recruits to the newly-designated rendezvous point at Harrisburgh in Granville County. The next day, Sumner writes to his commander, Maj. Gen. Greene, informing him of the Smallpox outbreak in Halifax, that Brig. Gen. John Alexander Lillington of the Wilmington District Brigade of Militia is at Kingston attempting to harass Lord Cornwallis, and that he is redirecting the Halifax recruits to Harrisburgh. And, "Sir, there's nothing that I can do about Lord Cornwallis going into Virginia."

On May 4th, Brig. Gen. Jethro Sumner orders Maj. Reading Blount to bring the New Bern District recruits on to Harrisburgh. On May 7th, he writes to Maj. Gen. Nathanael Greene a fairly long account of "essentially no progress" with respect to filling the Continental regiments.

On that same date, Lt. Col. Banastre Tarleton sacks the town of Halifax, North Carolina. In that town, local Patriots gather once again to try to stop Lord Cornwallis's march north to Virginia. Lt. Col. Banastre Tarleton is well ahead of Lord Cornwalls this time–and he decides to circle around the small town and to come in from the north, behind the Patriots. He strikes them while they are assembling on a bridge, but this time he loses three dragoons and a number of horses killed.

The local Militia does not disperse, but instead occupies a redoubt on the other side of the Roanoke River. Maj. Gen. Greene's engineer– Thaddeus Kosciuszko–had built the redoubt when he correctly guessed that Lord Cornwallis would come to this important town of Halifax.

Lt. Col. Banastre Tarleton observes that the redoubt is overlooked by higher ground on the other side of the river. A cannon from the main force will easily drive the Patriots away. He sends a request to dispatch the Guards on horseback since he only has light troops and about sixty infantry to hold the ground. Lord Cornwallis sends out a party of pioneers and a cannon. However, the field piece does not drive away the Patriots and they continue to fire upon the Redcoats, even as Lord Cornwallis occupies their town on May 11th. He finally sends a large detachment across the river and this group finally drives off the pesky NC Patriot Militia.

The British army does not treat the town kindly after the long standoff. There is so much looting that Lord Cornwallis has to court-martial and execute a sergeant and a dragoon. He then dispatches Lt. Col. John Hamilton and his NC Loyalists onward to find Maj. Gen. Phillips's location in Virginia–his ultimate goal. Shortly thereafter, he moves his army across the Roanoke River and into Virginia.

Lt. Gen. Cornwallis's plan to split the northern and southern colonies will most likely work as long as Maj. Gen. Phillips elects to collaborate with him. Fortunately for the Patriots, Maj. Gen. Phillips dies of a fever a few days before Lord Cornwallis makes it to Virginia.

In the meantime, Maj. Pinketham Eaton and two companies of the rebuilding 1st NC Regiment join up with Maj. Gen. Nathanael Greene in northeastern South Carolina. Greene is now determined to lay siege to the British garrison in Camden led by Francis, Lord Rawdon. He makes his new camp at a location less than two miles out of Camden at a place known as Hobkirk's Hill. He has Continentals from Maryland, Delaware, and Virginia, several companies of Light Dragoons from Lt. Col. William Washington and Lt. Col. Henry Lee, some Virginia Militia, twelve companies of North Carolina Militia, and ten companies of North Carolina State Troops led by Col. James Read, a former Continental captain–for a total of 1,200 to 1,500 men.

Col. Francis, Lord Rawdon commands about 950 men, mostly Loyalist Militia, a small detachment of the 63rd Regiment of Foot, and the Royal Regiment of Artillery, with 50 men from the 4th Battalion and two 6-pounders.

Very early in the morning of April 25th, a Continental deserter, sometimes identified as a drummer, makes his way into Camden. He is brought before Lord Rawdon and informs the British commander of the Continental Army's dispositions and that they have no artillery. Fearing that South Carolina Brigadier Generals Francis Marion and Thomas Sumter are on their way to join Maj. Gen. Nathanael Greene, and believing the Continental artillery is many miles away, Lord Rawdon decides it is a judicious time to attack

At approximately 9:00 a.m., Lord Rawdon leaves the security of his Camden fortifications with approximately 950 troops. At around 11:00 a.m., while many of the Continentals are occupied with cooking and washing clothes, their advanced pickets detect the British forces which have gained the Patriot's left flank by a long march skirting a swamp next to the ridge occupied by the Continental Army.

The advanced pickets, under Capt. Robert Kirkwood of Delaware, are able to delay the British advance giving Maj. Gen. Greene time to issue orders and line up his forces for battle. He places the 1st Virginia Regiment under Lt. Colonel Richard Campbell on the extreme right with the 2nd Virginia Regiment under Lt. Colonel Samuel Hawes to their left. On the extreme left, Maj. Gen. Greene places the 2nd Maryland under Lt Colonel Benjamin Ford, with the 1st Maryland commanded by Lt. Colonel John Gunby to their right. The artillery is placed in the center with the North Carolina State Troops and Militia in the rear.

Having extricated his forces from the woods and forced back the pickets, Lord Rawdon arranges his forces and slowly advances up the ridge towards the waiting Continentals. Maj. Gen. Greene, perceiving the British forces are presenting a narrow front, orders an attack. He instructs Lt. Col. Campbell on the right to wheel his men to the left and engage the British on their flank; he then orders Lt. Col. Ford to take his men and make a similar movement on the left. Maj. Gen. Greene orders the two remaining regiments in the center to advance with bayonets and confront the enemy head on, while Lt. Col. William Washington is to take his cavalry around the British left flank and attack the enemy in the rear. The forceful movement of the Patriots and the unexpected contribution of their artillery to the exchange inflict heavy casualties on the British, but the enemy line holds.

During the advance of the 1st Maryland Regiment on the British left, Capt. William Beatty, Jr., who is in command of the right of the 1st Maryland Regiment, is killed causing his company to stop their advance. Lt. Col. Gunby orders his men to stop their advance and fall back with the intention of reforming their line. At this time, Lt. Col. Benjamin Ford of the 2nd Maryland Regiment is mortally wounded, throwing his troops into disorder. When the Continental flank begins to fall apart, Lord Rawdon and the Volunteers of Ireland (Rawdon's Personal Regiment) charge. The Maryland troops rally briefly to fire a few rounds and then flee. Lord Rawdon, although outnumbered nearly two to one, and without artillery, takes the field.

Lt. Col. William Washington and his cavalry never make it to the action. Their circuitous route to reach the British rear takes them to Lord Rawdon's hospital and commissary area, where they capture 200 prisoners. Thus laden, they are too late to assist in the battle, and subsequently join Maj. Gen. Nathanael Greene's army on its retreat from the battlefield. The Patriot retreat does not last long. Lord Rawdon withdraws most of his forces back to Camden, leaving only a company of dragoons at the battlefield. That afternoon, Maj. Gen. Greene sends Lt. Col. William Washington and Capt. Robert Kirkwood back to Hobkirk's Hill, where they ambush and drive the dragoons away. Maj. Gen. Greene turns his army around and reoccupies the site by early evening. He soon writes to a French Minister, Chevalier La Luzerne, "We fight, get beat, rise, and fight again."

The British casualties are 39 killed, 210 wounded, and 12 missing. The total Patriot casualties are 19 killed, 113 wounded, 48 wounded prisoners, 41 unwounded prisoners, and 50 missing/unaccounted for, some of whom are killed.

The North Carolina Continental officers who participate in the battle at Hobkirk's Hill include Maj. Pinketham Eaton and Capt. Griffith John McRee of the yet-to-be-filled 1st NC Regiment, and Capt. Edward Yarborough on loan from the yet-to-be-recreated 3rd NC Regiment.

In his 1832 pension application, Jacob Brown (W2062) asserts:

> "He was then marched down near Camden, South Carolina to a creek called Sutton's Creek where there was a battle between General Greene's army and Lord Rawdon's army in which General Greene had to retreat on the opposite side of the creek and formed a line. This applicant states that he was in said battle. He states that when he joined the army at the mouth of Rocky River he was placed under the command of Colonel James Read, who was a Regular officer [now over State Troops]." [minor edits]

Soon thereafter, Maj. Gen. Nathanael Greene orders out Lt. Col. Henry "Light Horse Harry" Lee and his Legion to join up with Brig. Gen. Francis Marion of South Carolina. Attached to Lt. Col. Lee's regiment are Maj. Pinketham Eaton, Capt. Robert Smith, Lt. John Campbell and approximately 115 North Carolina Continental soldiers. This newly-combined Patriot contingent soon makes its way to Fort Motte along the Broad River in present-day Orangeburg County.

Fort Motte is erected around the mansion of Mrs. Rebecca Motte on Mount Joseph Plantation. Since only a protracted siege or cannon can reduce the fort, it becomes the principal depot for the convoys moving supplies up from Charlestown to the backcountry British outposts. It is garrisoned with the 2nd Battalion of the 84th Regiment of Foot led by Lt. Donald McPherson, with a troop of Hessian dragoons, and some Loyalist Militia. The mansion is situated on Buckhead Hill and is surrounded by a deep trench, along which have been raised a parapet. Opposite the mansion stands another hill on which there is an old farmhouse.

Brig. Gen. Francis Marion, with Lt. Col. Henry Lee, decides to take the fort on May 12th, and since Lt. Col. Lee has more experienced men, Brig. Gen. Marion gives him the honor of reducing the fort. Lt. Col. Lee places his 6-pounder such that it will rake the northern face of the enemy's defensive works. His men dig a trench towards the fort 400 yards away. Lt. McPherson has a small artillery piece, but he is never able to use it.

Lt. Col. Lee then summons Lt. McPherson and asks if he wants to surrender, which he politely declines. He is hoping that a relief column from Camden will soon come to his aid. It is not long before the retreating army of Francis, Lord Rawdon can be seen in the distance of the fort's defenders. Brig. Gen. Marion knows that Lord Rawdon can reach his position within 48 hours, so he decides upon a desperate strategy. He sends Lt. Col. Henry Lee to ask Mrs. Motte is she will allow his men to burn her fine home, and she readily agrees.

Waiting until noon when the roof is very hot and dry, Lt. Col. Lee orders the house to be set on fire. Parson Mason Locke Weems later writes that Mrs. Motte lent the Patriots a bow and "African arrows." However, William Dobein James was there and in his contemporary book about Brig. Gen. Francis Marion he writes,

> "The house was not burnt, as is stated by historians, nor was it fired by an arrow from an African bow, as sung by poets. Nathan Savage, a private in Marion's brigade, made up a ball of rosin and brimstone, to which he set fire and slung it on the roof of the house."

As the roof catches fire, Lt. McPherson sends a detail aloft to rip off the burning shingles. Capt. Samuel Finley fires grapeshot upon those on the rooftop with his 6-pounder. When Lt. McPherson's men begin jumping from the burning house, he raises the white flag.

As soon as the British and Loyalists lay down their arms, Brig. Gen. Francis Marion sends his men to the house to help put the fire out. He offers the enemy generous terms. When they march out, Lt. Col. Henry Lee accepts the surrender of the British regulars, while Brig. Gen. Marion accepts the surrender of the Loyalist Militia–this is how fractured the Patriots are at that point in time–Continentals versus Militia.

Mrs. Motte invites both the Patriot and captured British officers to dine with her that night. The dinner is marred when one of Lt. Col. Lee's officers, Cornet William Butler Harrison, orders three Loyalists to be hanged. Brig. Gen. Marion is seated at the table when Lt. McPherson receives the news of this hanging. Brig. Gen. Marion leaps up from the table and storms out of the mansion, arriving to find two dead Loyalists on the ground and one swinging from a noose. He orders the man cut down and strongly tells Lt. Col. Lee's men that he is in charge and that he will kill the next man who harms any prisoners.

Brig. Gen. Marion loses two men: Lt. Cruger and Sgt. McDonald, who had been commissioned a lieutenant before he fell.

In his 1832 pension application, Thomas Parham (W5524) asserts:

> "He had then been in the Militia in this tour but about 2 or 3 weeks, when at Ramsey's Mills he was persuaded to enlist in the Continental service which he did, under Captain Robert Smith for the space of 12 months. From Ramsey's Mills he marched under Captain Smith into South Carolina towards Camden -- and attacked a

small fort called Motts Fort on the Congaree River which was occupied by the British & negroes and Tories & took it after 8 or 10 days." [minor edits]

In the meantime, Francis, Lord Rawdon decides to evacuate Camden on May 10th, because the "whole interior country had revolted." He takes his men back to Charlestown and by July 20th he is on a ship headed back to England. However, his ship is seized by Privateers and he is soon turned over to the French, who do not exchange him until January of the next year.

Maj. Gen. Nathanael Greene's next objective is the British outpost at Ninety-Six. The British had secured Ninety-Six as a base of operations in the backcountry of South Carolina during June of 1780, and Lt. Gen. Charles, Lord Cornwallis believed Ninety-Six would be crucial to control the backcountry once the British Army moved northward out of South Carolina. Lord Cornwallis left Lt. Colonel John Harris Cruger, a Loyalist from New York, in charge of the outpost. Lt. Col. Cruger's instructions were to be "vigorous" in punishing rebels and maintaining order in the area. Lt. Col. Cruger used the fortified town of Ninety-Six as his base of operations to send forth many raids and skirmishes against local Patriots.

When the British gain control of Ninety-Six after the Fall of Charlestown in May of 1780, they then surround the town with a stockade and rebuild Fort Williamson. Beyond the town is another redoubt known as the Star Fort. It is two hundred feet in diameter and has ten salients or star points. A ditch and an abatis surround the Star Fort, which will become the principle British position during this final siege.

Lt. Col. John Harris Cruger knows that the Star Fort is the key to British defenses here and he prepares quite well for the inevitable siege that is now upon him. Additionally, the town of Ninety-Six is surrounded by tall walls built upon an elevated site that provides a clearing of one mile around the exterior. Before leaving the outpost to its own devices, Lt. Gen. Charles, Lord Cornwallis dispatches Lt. Henry Haldane of the engineers to assess the fort and to improve its defenses. Lord Cornwallis also sends a brass 3-pounder along with a wagonload of entrenching tools. Lt. Haldane constructs an additional fortification west of the town, a hornwork built upon Fort Williamson known as Holme's Fort. A covered runway extends from the jailhouse and down a slope into a ravine, where a small stream flows– the fort's water source.

An earth bank, in which an abatis has been constructed, reinforces the exterior of the stockade walls. The abatis will slow down an assaulting force so that cannon and small arms fire can eliminate them. Within the fort several blockhouses are built. A portable gun platform has been built on which the British placed their three brass 3-pounders.

When Francis, Lord Rawdon abandons Camden, he sends a message to Lt. Col. John Harris Cruger ordering him to evacuate Ninety-Six and to join Loyalist Col. Thomas Brown in Augusta, GA. South Carolina Brig. Gen. Andrew Pickens's men intercept these orders and they kindly inform Maj. Gen. Nathanael Greene, who moves his force towards Lt. Col. Cruger, arriving at Ninety-Six on May 21st.

Maj. Gen. Greene is soon joined by a large contingent of South Carolina Militia under Brig. Gen. Andrew Pickens, a fairly large group of North Carolina Militia, and a small detachment of sixty-six (66) North Carolina Continentals under Maj. Pinketham Eaton with four captains: Alexander Brevard, Thomas Donoho, Joshua Hadley, and William Lytle. Maj. Gen. Greene is forced to lift the siege a month later as British reinforcements out of Charlestown advance toward Ninety-Six. The British soon abandon Ninety-Six on July 8th and move back to the coast, just as the Patriots wanted all along.

In his 1832 pension application, Thomas Perkins (S9455) asserts:

> "He was living in Lincoln County, North Carolina when he went into service, the year he was drafted he does not recollect, he was drafted some time after the Declaration of Independence, & went into the service under the command of Captain Alexander Brevard, Major John Hampton and the regiment was commanded by Lt. Colonel Henry Dixon, and the whole of the forces was commanded by Major General Nathanael Greene. From Lincoln, North Carolina he marched to a little village whose name he does not now remember from thence to Cambridge [aka Ninety Six], South Carolina where the Americans besieged the British & Tories for several days, and he was engaged in repeated skirmishes during the siege, and was also employed in working on the ditches and mines that were dug & sunk to defeat & destroyed the enemy. A short time before the reinforcement of the British arrived he was with others dispatched, as a guard of prisoners that were sent, & he accompanied them as one of the guard to Salisbury, North Carolina." [minor edits]

Early during the siege of Ninety-Six, Maj. Gen. Nathaniel Greene dispatches part of his growing army to Augusta, Georgia, including Lt. Col. Henry Lee and his Legion and Maj. Pinketham Eaton and his small 1st NC Regiment. Some say this group was not at Ninety-Six until after Augusta. On May 23rd, the Patriot forces begin to encircle Fort Grierson in a manner intended to draw Lt. Col. James Grierson out in an attempt to reach the nearby Fort Cornwallis. Loyalist Col. Thomas Brown, aware of the danger to Lt. Col. Grierson, sallies forth from Fort Cornwallis, but when faced with Lt. Col. Henry Lee's strength, limits his support to an ineffective cannonade.

Lt. Col. James Grierson, hard pressed, throws open the gates of his fort, and endeavors to escape. Thirty of his men are killed, and forty-five wounded and captured. Lt. Col. Grierson is made a prisoner, but is later killed by a Georgia rifleman on June 6. The whole army probably knows who fired the fatal shot, and no doubt the commanders know, but their knowledge is not made official. No further notice is taken of the matter.

During this exchange, Maj. Pinketham Eaton is severely wounded and somehow captured by the Loyalists. Maj. John Armstrong later writes on June 13th to Brig. Gen. Jethro Sumner:

"I have disagreeable news to inform you of the death of Major Eaton. He was wounded at Augusta, taken prisoner and surrendered up his sword, and was afterwards put to death with his own sword. This I have by a letter from Capt. Edward Yarborough." [there is no proof Eaton was killed by his own sword]

The other known North Carolina Continental officers with Maj. Eaton are Capt. Alexander Brevard, Capt. Thomas Donoho, Capt. Joshua Hadley, Capt. William Lytle, and Robert Smith, who is promoted to captain right after Eaton's murder on May 24th, but he later resigns.

In his 1832 pension application, Jesse Webb (W18333) asserts:

"At Ramsey's Mill, he was placed under the command of Major Pinketham Eaton, a Continental officer who had charge of all the 12 months men. Under Major Eaton's orders he went to Fort Thomson on the Wateree River, which he assisted in taking, he then went to a Fort on the Congaree River which had surrendered before his arrival [Fort Motte], and he marched on to Augusta, Georgia where there were established two forts, one commanded by Lt. Col. Grierson, a Tory, and the other under the charge of the British commanded by Col. Brown [also a Tory]. That the Americans besieged the forts and finally succeeded in capturing them. Major Eaton was killed during the siege and the command of the American troops devolved upon an officer whose name is not recollected." [minor edits]

Meanwhile back at home, the ongoing recruiting effort to fill four Continental Regiments is going very slowly. On May 12th, Capt. Edward Yarborough writes to Brig. Gen. Jethro Sumner that he has left home, goes to Guilford Court House, then on to Salisbury, where he gets very sick and is put into the military hospital there.

Maj. John Armtstrong writes to Brig. Gen. Sumner on May 22nd informing his commander that he has collected about 30 new recruits in the Salisbury District:

"... and this day I expect about fifty more and by the last of this week I think will have about 200 in all if they come in according to promise."

The real purpose of his letter is to get firm orders on where to send the men. He has recently been ordered directly by Maj. Gen. Nathanael Greene to send the men immediately to South Carolina, but he has just received a note from Brig. Gen. Jethro Sumner telling him to send the men to Harrisburgh in Granville County. On May 26th, Maj. Armstrong fires off another note: "I start marching tomorrow for the southward."

Needless to say, the North Carolina Continental recruitment campaign of 1781 is not a well-oiled machine.

On June 1st, Lt. Col. John Baptiste Ashe, having recently moved his family to Halifax, writes to his general:

"I have collect'd eight or ten, among them three Villainous Deserters, Two of them Major Hogg, Captn. Chapman, and myself thought proper to chastise yesterday morning; forgiving the third. They have all Since Deserted; An Example of Death must be made, Genl., and that shortly of Such offenders."

From his home in Hertford County, Maj. Hardy Murfree writes to his general on June 9th:

"I have at Winton about 60 men which I shall send up in a few days. Lieut. Finny came from Edenton 2 days ago and informed me Captain Hall has received no men yet, that the Colonels of the Counties have not got them ready to deliver."

On June 13th, Maj. John Armstrong writes again from Salisbury providing some information about the Siege of Ninety-Six, the death of Maj. Pinketham Eaton at Augusta, Georgia, and that:

"I am almost ready to march with 200 good men of this district. I sent 180 before."

Two days later, Maj. Hardy Murfree writes once again,

"I have sent Lieuts. Andrew and Finny with the 12 months drafts that I have received from the counties of Bertie, Hertford, and Gates…The lower Counties have delivered no men yet, but am informed the commanding Officers of the Counties, are about marching them to Edenton, and as soon as they are received shall be marched up to Head Quarters."

On June 22nd, Capt. George Dougherty writes from Duplin County:

"… the draft was made in Duplin, but more than half of them have been among the Tories or so disaffected that they will not appear; the number that we ought to have here is about 70 men, & there is not above 24 yet appeared, & about 20 from Onslow."

He continues by informing Brig. Gen. Sumner that the men are not properly clothed and those responsible for providing clothing for new recruits are simply refusing to do so.

On June 25th, Brig. Gen. Jethro Sumner writes to his commander, Maj. Gen. Nathanael Greene, that retired Col. James Armstrong has been helping with the recruiting effort in New Bern District, and that those new recruits should be at headquarters within two or three days. When these recruits arrive, he plans to immediately form the 2nd NC Regiment. He also informs that he has more recruits for the existing 1st NC Regiment under Maj. Pinketham Eaton, apparently still not aware of Eaton's murder at Fort Grierson a month earlier. He includes a notice of his plans to march to Virginia soon to join up with Maj. Gen. Baron Von Steuben. Finally, he informs the general about the British in Wilmington and their forays into the countryside harassing the citizens.

Three days later, on June 28[th,] Brig. Gen. Sumner writes to Maj. Gen. Baron Von Steuben telling the Baron that the New Bern District recruits arrived yesterday. He plans to march about 600 Privates with very few arms fit for the field on June 30th, and requests advice on which route to take to avoid trouble.

On June 29th, an express arrives from Gen. Stephen Drayton of South Carolina, who is currently in Hillsborough. Drayton notifies Brig. Gen. Sumner that the British from Charlestown sent reinforcements in relief of Ninety-Six and that Maj. Gen. Greene wants all North Carolina Continentals to forget Virginia and to march immediately to help him in South Carolina. Brig. Gen. Sumner fires off expresses to Gen. Drayton, Gov. Thomas Burke, and to Maj. Gen. Baron Von Steuben–he will march soon with 500 men and 300 stand of arms via Salisbury to Maj. Gen. Nathanael Greene's camp in South Carolina.

The General Assembly meets again on June 23rd at Wake Court House, and the first item on their agenda is to reinforce their January resolve of raising Continental recruits. They now resolve to "compel the Counties which have not furnished their quota of Continental troops, as required by a late Act of the General Assembly of this State, to furnish the same." This new law stipulates that every colonel or commanding officer of every Militia regiment shall within six weeks furnish the number of men as previously required. However, there does not appear to be any punishment for falling short. When the General Assembly learns of the news that Maj. Gen. Greene needs help, they pass yet another resolve for the Militia brigades from the Salisbury District to send 1,000 men, and for the Hillsborough District to send 500 men and for all of them to march southward as soon as possible. More on this can be found in Volume 2.

On July 1st, Maj. John Armstrong writes from his camp on the Broad River in South Carolina to Brig. Gen. Sumner. He is on his way to join up with Maj. Gen. Greene–he starts out with 300 men and now has a little over 200 men. Many desert. Most are Loyalists who just signed up for the bounty, only to slip away night after night. His rather long letter goes on with the typical military complaints–no money, no clothing, no medicines for the sick, etc.

On July 8th, Maj. Hardy Murfree writes from his home in Hertford County to Brig. Gen. Jethro Sumner requesting clarification of the role that retired Col. Gideon Lamb is playing in the Continental recruitment effort. Maj. Murfree is under the impression that Col. Lamb has retired, but Col. Lamb is issuing orders to Murfree's men. He also informs his general that the recruiting effort in the "lower counties" of the Edenton District is not going very well.

By July 14th, Brig. Gen. Jethro Sumner is in Salisbury and he writes to Gov. Thomas Burke and complains about the bad state of the Commissary's stores along the route he has taken. He also complains of more desertions among the new recruits. A court-martial sentences two to death, one is shot as an example, and the other is pardoned. However, three more desert after the execution. He informs the governor that he has 500 men but only 300 have arms. In another letter three days later, Sumner writes, "I am at a loss to judge what detains Major Murfree of Edenton and Captain Dougherty of Wilmington districts…"

On July 17th, Lt. Col. Henry "Hal" Dixon writes to Col. Nicholas Long, the Deputy Quarter Master General (DQMG) in Halifax, North Carolina telling him of his recent letter from the Marquis de Lafayette in Virginia. Lafayette warns that Lt. Gen. Charles, Lord Cornwallis is likely to return to North Carolina soon and advises that all magazines and depots in his path should be removed to safer locations. He states that Maj. Gen. Nathanael Greene wants the military stores moved to the Moravian Town and the valuable horses, cattle, etc. moved to Campbellton.

The next day, Gov. Thomas Burke writes to Col. John Peasley of the Guilford County Regiment of Militia that he has ordered Continental Maj. Thomas Hogg to:

"Conduct an Expedition for reducing the disaffected who openly adhered to the Enemy, in the Condition of either Soldiers or prisoners, your Horsemen and perhaps some of your people will be essentially serviceable to him…"

On July 22nd, Maj. Hardy Murfree writes to Brig. Gen. Jethro Sumner that a group of Loyalists and perhaps a few British soldiers came to the nearby Wineoak Ferry and burned a private home, took all the horses, and:

"… plundered the inhabitants in a most cruel manner."

Murfree continues by requesting that:

"If I am not greatly wanted in camp, to let me stay in this part of the county while the enemy continues so near. As we have no army near us and liable to be plundered, &c., by those Tories who has done more mischielf than the British army."

He goes on to inform his general that Col. Gideon Lamb is marching the remaining Edenton District recruits to the general's location in South Carolina.

On that same date, Col. Gideon Lamb writes to Brig. Gen. Sumner that he is currently in Warren County and he is marching 54 new recruits and four officers to his location. He leaves Capt. Clement Hall in Edenton to gather the rest at that location, and he leaves Lt. William Ferrebee in Brig. Gen. Isaac Gregory's Militia camp to gather what he can from that location. He goes further to state that he was not consulted earlier on the disposition of the active Continental officers and that he considers himself to continue to be on active duty, as apparently does Col. James Armstrong and Lt. Col. James Thackston. Now that he has learned that he is supposed to be retired and there is no command available for him then he shall return home.

On July 29th, Maj. Reading Blount is in Salisbury and he passes on the news that the French Fleet is allegedly at New York thereby causing the British to send troops from Virginia to their relief. On August 1st, Maj. Blount follows up with another letter to his general that Capt. William Goodman arrived on July 28th with 120 men and some arms that arrived from Virginia. Although most men do not have shoes, he plans to march southward in about five days hence.

On August 28th, Maj. Thomas Hogg writes to Brig. Gen. Jethro Sumner that he has been in Halifax for three weeks and has only received twenty new recruits, but no clothing for them. Col. James Armstrong is on his way to this location with about 50 more new recruits. As soon as these are all here he plans to assemble them into "a Company & march to join you under the command of a Capt. & two Subs."

North Carolina Continental Line
September 1, 1781

```
                          Southern
                         Department

                      Maj. Gen. Nathanael
                            Greene

                             NC
                           Brigade            In NC
                                             Recruiting
                       Brig. Gen. Jethro
                            Sumner


    1st NC              2nd NC              3rd NC              4th NC
   Regiment            Regiment            Regiment            Regiment

  Lt. Col. John       Maj. Reading        Maj. John         Lt. Col. Henry
  Baptiste Ashe          Blount           Armstrong          "Hal" Dixon

• Maj. Hardy Murfree                    • Maj. Thomas Hogg
```

Captains	Captains	Captains	Captains
• William Armstrong	• Samuel Budd	• John Daves	• John Campbell
• Benjamin Bailey	• Benjamin Carter	• Clement Hall	• Samuel Chapman
• Alexander Brevard	• Tilghman Dixon	• Anthony Hart	• George Dougherty
• Thomas Callendar	• Thomas Evans	• Curtis Ivey	• William Ferrebee
• James Campbell	• William Goodman	• John Medearis*	• Matthew Ramsey
• Thomas Donoho	• Christopher Goodwin	• Dennis Porterfield	• Joseph Thomas Rhodes
• Hardy Holmes	• Joshua Hadley	• Edward Yarborough	
• William Lytle	• Charles Stewart		
• John Griffith McRee			
• James Mills			
• Robert Raiford			
• William Saunders			
• Anthony Sharpe			
• Howell Tatum	* In QM Department at Wake Court House		

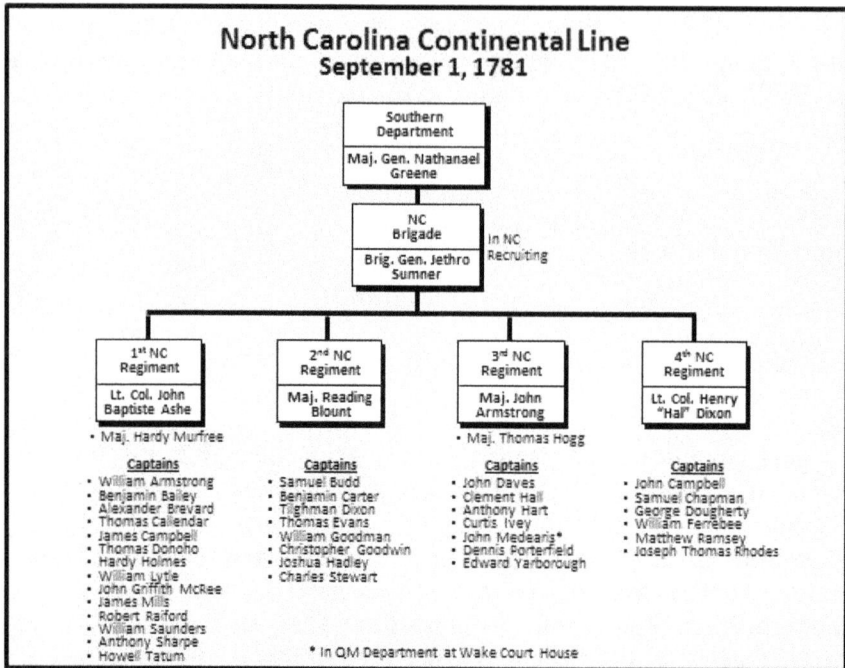

On September 9th, Maj. Hardy Murfree writes to Gov. Thomas Burke complaining that he has no command and wishes to be doing something useful. He requests of the governor that he be permitted to raise a party of horsemen and march them to Virginia.

As can be surmised, the summer of 1781 is quite chaotic for the North Carolina Continental Line. With the British in Virginia threatening to re-invade the Old North State, the heightened tensions in South Carolina, and the difficult recruiting effort going on all over the state, it should be considered "amazing" that the state actually manages to assemble four new regiments of Continental soldiers since the beginning of the year.

As it turns out, the British in Virginia never march into North Carolina. Lt. Col. Banastre Tarleton sweeps through southern Virginia on a destructive raid then returns to Lt. Gen. Charles, Lord Cornwallis's camp on the Chesapeake. Many Loyalists in Virginia use Lt. Col. Tarleton as cover for their plundering raids that eventually make their way into small communities along the NC/VA border.

To add to the chaos and confusion, Maj. James H. Craig, the British commander in Wilmington sends detachments out into the countryside during the summer of 1781 to generally harass the Patriots and to stir up Loyalist sentiment, which is increasing daily. The many Loyalists have skirmishes with local Patriot Militias all during July and August. In mid-

August, Maj. James H. Craig personally leads a detachment on a jaunt to New Bern and for two days he occupies the town and burns local plantations. On his march to and from New Bern, several North Carolina Militia units can only harry the British–they simply have limited ammunition and must avoid a general engagement.

In early August, Brig. Gen. Jethro Sumner reaches the camp of his commander, Maj. Gen. Nathanael Greene, who is clearly disappointed in the amount of time it takes North Carolina to recreate its required and much-needed four regiments of Continentals. News soon arrives in Greene's camp from South Carolina Brig. Gen. Andrew Pickens that after the British sent relief to Ninety-Six they are now withdrawing from that fortified town and marching towards Orangeburgh, perhaps on their way to Charlestown.

Not long after Brig. Gen. Sumner's march into Maj. Gen. Greene's camp, Col. François DeMalmedy arrives with over 400 mounted State Troops and Militiamen under his command. Since many North Carolina Militia leaders are apparently quite sick, Col. DeMalmedy adopts their orphan companies, and by the time he reaches Maj. Gen. Greene's camp he has twenty-four (24) companies under his command. North Carolina also sends an additional forty (40) companies of Militia and their field officers to Greene's camp in late August and early September.

Maj. Gen. Nathanael Greene immediately launches a comprehensive training program for the new Continental recruits and often includes the various Militiamen in these training exercises. Every day the men undergo drills and battlefield exercises. Fire discipline is instilled by the regular firing of blank cartridges–upon the command of their officers.

Many of the North Carolina Continental officers spend considerable time sitting in almost continuous court-martials. Men are charged with almost every known offense, but the majority are accused of desertion or leaving camp without permission. Private John Rogers, of the 1st NC Regiment, is hanged for desertion. Private Josiah Saylers is also sentenced to hang, but several officers come forward and beg that he be pardoned. Maj. Gen. Greene agrees with the pardon.

By the end of August a fairly large contingent of South Carolina Militia and State Troops meet up with Maj. Gen. Greene's growing army, which now includes almost 2,200 men under his command. On August 23rd, he breaks camp with most of the North Carolina Continentals leading the way, and the remainder detached to the rear to guard the beef that has been brought along on the hoof–to be slaughtered as needed. Greene's army only marches in the early mornings or late afternoons. He leaves several officers at Camden to bring forth those who are sick in the hospital after they recover.

Maj. Gen. Greene authorizes the numerous Militiamen to be issued only twenty rounds of ammunition, whereas each Continental is issued thirty rounds. When his army halts for any length of time they are again drilled in battlefield techniques. On August 30th, they reach Howell's Ferry on the Congaree River–marching over ninety miles in one week. The soldiers are only allowed to take their camp kettles and provisions from this point forward. It is here at Howell's Ferry that Maj. Gen. Greene learns that Lt. Col. Alexander Stewart and the British army have made camp at Eutaw Springs–less than forty miles from his current location.

Maj. Gen. Nathanael Greene stops his army at Fort Motte to wait on the arrival of more South Carolina Militiamen under Brig. Gen. Francis Marion. While resting, the men clean and repair their weapons, wash their clothes, and…drill once again. After a twenty-mile march, his army camps that night at Burdell's Plantation, only seven miles from Eutaw Springs. On that day, 100 more North Carolina Continentals under Maj. Reading Blount arrive. The more-experienced officers are re-assigned such that four regiments are constituted, although the 3rd NC Regiment and 4th NC Regiment are not much more than mere detachments of the first two regiments. Greene's orders that night are, "This Army will March at 4 o'clock tomorrow Morning by the right to attack the Enemy."

Lt. Col. Alexander Stewart feels secure at his location and therefore allows his intelligence to lag–he has no idea that the Patriots are approaching his camp. September 8th dawns fair and intensely hot, but the Patriots, on short rations and with little rest, advance in early morning light toward the cool springs. Upon their approach the surprised British leave their uneaten breakfast and quickly throw lines of battle across the road in a heavily wooded area. Behind them, in cleared fields, stands a large brick home with a high-walled garden. The woods and waters of Eutaw Creek are on the north.

Heavy firing soon crackles and booms through the shady woods. At first the center of the Patriot line caves in, but while opposing flanks are fighting separate battles, Maj. Gen. Greene restores the center with North Carolina Continentals. The whole British line then begins to give, but Lt. Col. Stewart quickly pulls up his left-flank reserves, forcing the Patriots to retreat under thunderous fire. The encouraged British shout, yell, and rush forward in disorder; whereupon Maj. Gen. Greene (according to J. P. Petit) "brings in his strongest force: the Maryland and Virginia

Continentals, Kirkwood's Delawares, and Lt. Colonel Washington's South Carolina [sic] cavalry . . . with devastating effect."

The British flee in every direction and the Patriots take over their camp. Only Maj. John Majoribanks, on the British right flank and pushed far back into the woods near Eutaw Creek, is able to hold his unit together. Maj. Henry Sheridan takes hasty refuge in the brick home; Lt. Col. Stewart gathers some of his men beyond, and from this vantage they "pick off" many Patriot officers and men.

Maj. Gen. Greene sends Lt. Col. Washington's cavalry to deal with Maj. Majoribanks, but penetrating the woods with horses is too difficult, so Lt. Col. Washington tries to encircle and rout, thus exposing himself to dangerous fire. His horse is shot from under him, he himself is wounded, and his company is practically ravaged. When a hand-to-hand fight develops, a British soldier poises his sword over the wounded Lt. Col. Washington, but Maj. Majoribanks sees this and gallantly turns it aside. Washington is now his prisoner.

In the enemy's camp, eating their deserted breakfast, and feeling the battle is won, the hungry and thirsty Patriots begin plundering the British stores of food, liquors, and equipment. Thoroughly enjoying themselves they ignore their leaders' warnings and commands. Maj. John Majoribanks, realizing the disorder, falls upon them. Maj. Henry Sheridan and Lt. Col. Stewart pound at their right and Maj. John Coffin comes in from their left. The stunned Patriots fight this impossible situation bravely, but they are quickly put to flight from the British camp.

After more than four hours of indecisive battle, under a merciless sun, both armies have had enough. Casualties are extremely high. "Blood runs ankle deep in places," and the strewn areas of dead and dying is heartbreaking. Maj. Gen. Greene collects his wounded and returns to Burdell's Plantation. Lt. Col. Stewart remains the night at Eutaw Springs but hastily retreats the next day toward Charlestown, leaving behind many of his dead unburied and seventy of his seriously wounded. The gallant Maj. John Majoribanks, wounded and on his way to Moncks Corner, dies in a slave cabin on Wantoot Plantation.

According to Benson J. Lossing in his *Pictorial Field-Book of the Revolution*–the Patriots lose 152 killed, 424 wounded, and 40 missing; the British lose 85 killed, 72 wounded, and 500 captured as prisoners. The North Carolina Continentals suffer more casualties than any other unit on the battlefield that day. Five officers and 43 rank and file are killed; eight officers and 80 rank and file are wounded; and, ten rank and file are listed as missing. Two known officers are prisoners of the British when that day ends.

The North Carolina Continental officers killed at Eutaw Springs on September 8th are: Capt. William Goodman, Capt. Christopher Goodwin, and Lt. James Dillon–all of the 2nd NC Regiment; and, Capt. Dennis Porterfield of the 3rd NC Regiment. Officers wounded are: Lt. Hardy Holmes, Lt. Abner Lamb, and Lt. James Moore of the 1st NC Regiment; Capt. Joshua Hadley, Lt. Richard Andrews, and Lt. James Scurlock of the 2nd NC Regiment; and, Lt. Charles Dixon and Lt. Thomas Dudley of the 3rd NC Regiment. Capt. Samuel Budd and Lt. Jesse Read, both of the 2nd NC Regiment, are taken prisoner that day.

In his 1833 pension application, Absalom Knight (S4483) asserts:

> "In the month of August 1780 [no] or 1781[yes] he volunteered for a tour of five months but before he entered the service he exchanged places with Joseph Matthews who had enlisted for a tour of twelve months in the regular service & he entered the service in company commanded by Capt. Benjamin Carter & Lieut. Thomas Dudley in the First [no, Second] Regiment, commanded by Lt. Col. Archibald Lytle [No] and Maj. John Armstrong—he recollects having been some time at a place called the Round O and Pon Pon and also being a considerable time at Bacon's Bridge as he was also during that campaign at the battle of the Eutaw Spring & was wounded with a bayonet in the left arm. He frequently saw Genl Nathanael Greene during the battle but does not recollect any other of the regular officers in command on that day. A portion of the twelve months he was ordered to take charge of a wagon & was employed in hauling forage to the cavalry which was commanded by Lt. Col. William Washington before the battle. He served his twelve months and was discharged near Bacon's Bridge & went home." [minor edits]

Although the British retain the battlefield on that day, Maj. Gen. Nathanael Greene is quite pleased with how things turned out. He praises all of his troops, and the North Carolina Continentals find a confidence they had not felt for years.

The day after the battle, Maj. Gen. Greene decides to attack Lt. Col. Alexander Stewart's weakened army for a second time in two days. He dispatches Lt. Col. Henry "Light Horse Harry" Lee and Brig. Gen. Francis Marion to intercept reinforcments or to slow the British march should they head towards Charlestown. However, Lt. Col. Stewart expects as much so he has his men to destroy over a thousand stand of arms and throw what is left into the nearby Eutaw Springs. Stores that cannot be easily transported are also destroyed. Some of the Patriots follow Lt. Col. Stewart until he is reinforced by 400 fresh troops from Charlestown.

Maj. Gen. Nathanael Greene rests his army for a few days then returns to the High Hills of the Santee after a series of leisurely marches. He sends his prisoners to Salisbury and these are escorted by a detachment of North Carolina Continentals under Capt. Thomas Donoho. From Salisbury, the North Carolina Militia escorts them to Virginia.

Meanwhile back at home, the recruiting effort for additional Continentals drops off significantly after Brig. Gen. Jethro Sumner left the state earlier in August. The recently-convened General Assembly apparently has a change of heart and concludes that the act of conscripting fugitives of the over-exaggerated Militia retreat at Guilford Court House in March has not been applied justly. On July 4th, the legislature implores Maj. Gen. Greene:

> "... to discharge those unhappy men and permit them to return to their families as soon as the situation of affairs will admit of such an act of benevolence."

The few Continentals left at home during the Eutaw Springs mission continue their recruitment efforts, no matter how difficult the results. By the end of August, Maj. Thomas Hogg and the semi-retired Col. James Armstrong manage to bring seventy men to Harrisburgh, but once again, they cannot get their allocated clothing to materialize. A recently-elected Gov. Thomas Burke seems to bring a new energy to the state from his headquarters at Halifax, North Carolina. In early September, Gov. Burke returns to his home in Hillsborough to better organize his planned campaign against the state's growing Loyalist problem.

Aware that his life has been threatened by several Loyalist leaders, Gov. Burke sends orders to Brig. Gen. John Butler of the Hillsborough District Brigade of Militia, who is camped on the south side of the Haw River, to return to Hillsborough. As he complies, the Loyalist leader, Col. David Fanning, follows—and he learns that his target is now within his reach and is protected by only a small guard detail.

On September 12th, in a heavy fog, Col. David Fanning and 500 Loyalists creep into Hillsborough and completely surprise the sleepy citizens, their civil leadership, and a small group of Patriot troops stationed near the court house. Fanning's men gradually make their way to Gov. Burke's home in the eastern part of Hillsborough, and the governor puts up a vigorous defense along with his personal Life Guard, Capt. John DeCoin of Edgecombe County. The Patriots are quickly overpowered, and upon the word of a British officer accompanying the boisterous Loyalists that no harm will come to them if they surrender, then does Gov. Burke give up his sword. In addition, Col. David Fanning and his Loyalist regiment take nearly 200 prisoners on that day. They also manage to free thirty Loyalists who have been scheduled to be hanged on that same day as well.

Among the 200 prisoners taken that day are five known Continental soldiers, who essentially are in the wrong place at the wrong time: Privates Thomas Bowles, Hugh Catchum, and William Douglas of the 1st NC Regiment; and, Private Joseph Brown and Corporal Marmaduke Maples of the 2nd NC Regiment. Actually, these five men are the only names known of a 70-man detachment of Continentals led by Lt. Col. Archibald Lytle, who just happens to be in Hillsborough on that fateful day. He too is taken prisoner, marched to Wilmington along with the governor and the other prisoners, and turned over to Maj. James H. Craig of the British garrison. Lt. Col. Archibald Lytle is exchanged on February 9th of the next year (1782).

In his 1818 pension application, Marmaduke Maples (S41802) asserts:

"… in the fall of 1779 and reached Charlestown, South Carolina the spring following before the commencement of the siege of that garrison by the British forces under the command of Sir Henry Clinton. He the deponent fought there in defense of the garrison under General Lincoln during the siege was surrendered a prisoner of war with the rest of the troops of the garrison to the forces by the capitulation taking place. He the deponent remained a prisoner at that place 15 months, 10 of which was confined in a prison ship. In July 1781, agreeable to a cartel agreed on for the exchange of prisoners of the two armies he the deponent with a number of other prisoners taken in the garrison before mentioned and elsewhere was conveyed by British ships to a place called the Old Jamestown, state of Virginia, where they were received by the Marquis de Lafayette who then commanded the American forces near that place. He the deponent with about 40 others (being all the North Carolina line that had remain prisoners to that period out of 1000 when captured the rest being dead or enlisted with the British with the exception of a few that made their escape) was marched under the command of Lt. Col. Robert Mebane of the North Carolina line to Hillsborough in this state. Shortly after arriving there was with others late exchanged taken prisoner by a band of people called Tories under the command of McNeill and David Fanning who had made an expedition against that place it being the time when, Thomas Burke, Esquire, then goveror of this state was captured. On their retreat toward Wilmington in the state I reason that the deponent was in a low state of health and not able to travel he was admitted to remain on parole as a prisoner of war." [minor edits]

Upon the invitation to join Maj. Gen. Nathanael Greene for breakfast, Brig. Gen. Jethro Sumner learns of Gov. Thomas Burke's capture on September 25th. As soon as breakfast is over, Sumner leaves Greene's camp and is in Salisbury by October 2nd. He reaches his home in Warren County on October 10th, and is in Halifax by October 20th. Maj. Gen.

Greene instinctively knows that North Carolina will probably devolve into near chaos with the governor now a prisoner of the Loyalists, and he wants his seasoned brigadier to be quickly available should the civil government need his assistance. Lt. Col. John Baptiste Ashe is left in charge of the North Carolina Brigade as Brig. Gen. Sumner goes home.

New flares of violence between the Patriots and the Loyalists soon erupt between Hillsborough and Wilmington, immediately after Loyalist Col. David Fanning marches his prisoners to his British protectors. With the Continental Army entrenched in South Carolina to prevent any new thrusts by the British, soon to be confined to Charlestown, the state of North Carolina once again calls upon their Militia to regain control of the embroiled countryside. And also once again, the heightened Loyalist sentiments and activities further complicate the Continental recruiting efforts.

Many new recruits simply refuse to take the field. The contractors filling the roles of local commissaries also refuse to leave their homes unprotected, therefore, no supplies are moving anywhere in the state. Maj. Gen. Nathanael Greene predicts before Brig. Gen. Jethro Sumner leaves his camp, "as I fear all things will get into confusion from this untoward event." Brig. Gen. Sumner soon falls ill again, but he stays on the job when he is able.

The North Carolina Continentals attached to the army of Maj. Gen. Nathanael Greene and stationed at the High Hills of the Santee are not a particularly happy bunch, especially the officers in the field. Lt. Col. John Baptiste Ashe is granted permission to go home and command now devolves to Maj. John Armstrong. The officers under Armstrong sulk–they have once again served without pay, without a full complement of arms, and without sufficient clothing. Provisions sent to them mysteriously disappear before they arrive. On October 25th, Maj. John Armstrong writes to Brig. Gen. Jethro Sumner along with his monthly return of his men that Capt. George Dougherty has been granted leave "to wait on the Assembly with the remonstrance of the Officers of our State now in the Southern Army."

Among other issues, the officers want their legislature to make good on its promises of land grants as a reward for their service, and they want the state to begin surveying these grants very soon. Although the General Assembly convenes at Salem on November 8th, no actual business is completed during this session, and there are scant records to indicate why this is so.

Although they are no longer marching "to and fro," the Southern Army is not living the high life while situated at the High Hills of the Santee. An epidemic of dysentery and camp fever hits with great force. In some companies, every man is in his tent with a fever. Over one-half of the North Carolina Brigade is confined to their tents. The November nights begin to get quite cold, and most of the rank and file–once again–have no blankets. However, the news of Lt. Gen. Charles, Lord Cornwallis's capitulation is soon raising their spirits–enough so that many leave their tents long enough to parade and fire a celebratory salute.

The Patriot victory at Yorktown, Virginia is great news to North Carolina. It also means that Maj. Gen. Nathanael Greene will soon have many more troops in his camp, from Pennsylvania, Maryland, Delaware, and Virginia. The mountain men from across the Appalachians follow Col. Isaac Shelby and Col. John Sevier to Greene's camp, and he quickly assigns these Militia units to support SC Brig. Gen. Francis Marion along the Pee Dee River.

Thanks to a recent prisoner exchange and now back at home, Brig. Gen. Griffith Rutherford assembles a very large contingent of Militiamen and State Troops from all across the state–he is determined to drive the British out of Wilmington once and for all. By mid-October he is in Bladen County skirmishing with Loyalists all the way down the Cape Fear River. It is not until nearly mid-November when Brig. Gen. Rutherford learns of the Patriot victory at Yorktown from Lt. Col. Henry "Light Horse Harry" Lee, who has just arrived to assist the Militia in taking Wilmington.

On November 17th, Brig. Gen. Rutherford stops the celebrations and orders his men to move across the Cape Fear River and to march towards the occupied town. That night, his large army camps within four miles of Wilmington. There is no resistance, since the British are preparing to leave. Within the Patriot ranks are men who still want revenge for the destruction of their homes, and for the murders of their friends. After sunrise on November 18th, the British form columns and march down to the transport ships, leaving their horses behind.

On that same day, Maj. Gen. Nathanael Greene breaks camp and moves his army over to Fort Motte. He is fretful that the British in Charlestown might want to break out and move their headquarters down to Savannah, and he wants to be in a better position to thwart this. Although his army is not large enough to attempt a siege against the enemy entrenched in Charlestown, Maj. Gen. Greene is not adverse to striking his enemy at every opportunity and with every resource at his disposal. He mostly relies upon the cavalry of Lt. Col. Henry Lee and Lt. Col. William Washington (who is still a prisoner, but his men are still active) to work with other Light Horse of South Carolina. He adds a few units of the Maryland and Virginia Continentals and creates a "flying party" of over 400 men to be led by Col. Otho Williams of the Maryland Line again.

After a few skirmishes with the British at Dorchester and the Quarter House, Maj. Gen. Nathanael Greene once again moves his army–this time to the tiny community of Round O–a mere dot on a map in southern South Carolina. Once again, supplies are critical. Although hunting is typically forbidden, a number of hunters are issued permits to kill wild fowl for the officers.

On November 25th, Maj. John Armstrong forwards his monthly return to Brig. Gen. Jethro Sumner. He thanks the general for the account of the defeat of Lord Cornwallis at Yorktown. He tells of Col. Isaac Shelby and Brig. Gen. Francis Marion surprising the enemy at Moncks Corner in October, and that the commandant at Charlestown has discharged over 400 Loyalists who will not enlist under him. He ends with a request for news on Capt. George Dougherty's meeting with the General Assembly.

Winter camp conditions in South Carolina are much more favorable than "up north" as the North Carolina Continentals have seen on several occasions. All Continentals are on the drill field daily, and all troops are kept busy cleaning their equipment and their scant clothes. On Christmas Day, Capt. Clement Hall arrives with 160 gallons of rum and a barrel of coffee for the North Carolina Brigade. An angry Maj. Gen. Greene brings him before a court-martial to determine why so many provisions are disappearing before they reach his camp. Capt. Hall is merely the recipient of Maj. Gen. Nathanael Greene's ire on this day.

Thus 1781 ends for the North Carolina Continental Line.

Appendix B includes a listing of all known Continental units that participated in each battle/skirmish of 1781.

Chapter Eight – 1782

The New Year arrives with a detachment of the North Carolina Continental Line under Maj. Reading Blount getting assigned, on January 2nd, to assist Lt. Col. Henry "Light Horse Harry" Lee's cavalry. Maj. Blount's detachment consists of three captains, six lieutenants, ten sergeants, nine corporals, and 150 men. This unit is carved out of the existing North Carolina Brigade for a special mission.

Upon the return of British Maj. James H. Craig from Wilmington, he is promoted to Lt. Colonel and his men are assigned to John's Island outside of

> ### Key Events of 1782
>
> • NC General Assembly meets twice (January and April). In April, they elect Alexander Martin as the state's fourth governor.
> • Officers of the NC Continental Line issue their recommendation for reorganization on April 24th, approved by the General Assembly on April 30th.
> • The Partisan warfare between the Patriots and Loyalists finally subsides and is all but ended by Summer of 1782.
> • NC Continental Line in two skirmishes: St. John's Island in January, and Combahee Ferry in August.
> • Preliminary Peace terms are signed in Paris on November 13, 1782.
> • Completely hemmed in by Maj. Gen. Nathanael Greene, the British army in Charlestown consolidate their holdings, then finally evacuate in December 1782. Both Carolinas are now rid of the enemy.

Charlestown, where he is then given even more men under his command. His orders are to tend to the British cattle there and to command the garrison of 500 British troops on John's Island. Lt. Col. Craig is housed on the eastern end of John's Island at Gibbes's Plantation. His men are stationed at Fenwick Hall and some British dragoons are stationed four miles away. Lt. Colonel Craig's presence offers a threat to the upcoming South Carolina legislature, which is scheduled to convene in nearby Jacksonborough in early January, and Maj. Gen. Nathanael Greene prefers to be rid of this threat, if at all possible.

Never missing a chance for advance planning and extra training, Maj. Gen. Greene orders this new unit to be led jointly by South Carolina Lt. Col. John Laurens and Lt. Col. Henry Lee. Detailed plans are soon developed and each company is drilled in what is expected of them. Since the Patriots have no boats they can only approach John's Island by a narrow canal to the Stono River called the "New Cut." The canal can only be crossed two times each month, shortly after midnight when "the depth of water is not more than waist high."

The British know about the strategic value of the "New Cut" and they place a galley and two gunboats four hundred yards apart to guard the waterway. The galleys have to remain apart so they can still stay afloat at low tide, and this leaves a gap that the Patriots can pass through. The tide gives them only small window to get in, strike the British, and get out.

On the cold and rainy night of January 12th, Lt. Col. Lee and Lt. Col. Laurens rendezvous at a point less than a mile from the "New Cut." Maj. Gen. Greene and the main army broke camp the day before and marched towards John's Island in case the British try to send reinforcements to assist Lt. Col. James H. Craig. As Lt. Col. Laurens waits, he addresses his men, appealing to their honor and their patriotism. He issues instructions to them on how to cross the waist deep water without getting their arms or ammunition wet. He tells them that no one is "to fire or advance without orders, confusion only can arise from unconnected individual efforts."

Lt. Col. John Laurens then divides his force into two columns. Lt. Col. Henry "Light Horse Harry" Lee commands one and Maj. James Hamilton of the Pennsylvania Line commands the other. At one o'clock in the morning the crossing begins. Lt. Col. Lee sends Capt. John Rudolph across first with his Legion Infantry. As they move they can hear the British sentries in the boats call out "All's safe." Lt. Col. Lee's column easily makes the crossing onto John's Island.

The second column under Maj. Hamilton soon breaks contact in the darkness and disappears. Lt. Col. Laurens searches for an hour and finally finds Maj. Hamilton. Maj. Hamilton's guide has deserted him leaving his troops to find their way on their own. The hour they are lost has seemed like an eternity. When the tide comes in Lt. Col. Laurens has no choice but to call off the operation and recall Lt. Col. Lee's troops who have made it onto the island. On the march back across the "New Cut," Lt. Col. Lee's men find themselves waist deep in "mud, weeds and water." Several soldiers become stuck in the mud and "are obliged to be pulled out."

On January 14th, Maj. Gen. Greene has his men search the riverbank for a boat to ferry Lt. Col. Laurens' troops back across the inlet to try again. To cover their withdrawal he brings up his cannon to fire on the galleys as they cross. The artillery fires on the British vessels throughout the day, but the boats refuse to withdraw. That night Lt. Col. Craig evacuates John's Island and the British galleys withdraw from the "New Cut."

On January 15th, Lt. Col. Laurens with a small force of cavalry and infantry crosses the "New Cut" in a boat and finds the remains of the British camp. It has been hurriedly abandoned. Lt. Col. Laurens captures a few stragglers, but the British commandant of Charlestown, Maj. Gen.

Alexander Leslie, has learned of Maj. Gen. Greene's raid and has moved all his men to nearby James Island.

Lt. Col. Laurens does find a schooner that the British have loaded all their supplies onto. He orders his men to attack the schooner and his men fire a volley at her. This "throws the Crew into great confusion," almost making the schooner run aground. The British crew on the schooner stack the baggage and use it as protection against the incoming musket balls. They return fire as their ship moves slowly away. Lt. Col. Laurens remarks, "If I had a three pounder…perhaps she might still be taken."

Lt. Col. James H. Craig's new position is now at Perroneau's on James Island. Maj. Gen. Greene remarks, "We have got the territory but we missed the great objective of the enterprise." He withdraws to an encampment at Skirving's Plantation, six miles in front of Jacksonborough on the road to Charlestown. The expedition is considered a failure, but it does eliminate the British threat to the legislature meeting in Jacksonborough.

For the rest of 1782, the British army remains bottled up in and around Charlestown, with forage parties making frequent raids into the countryside every now and then. They continue to have garrisons at the Quarter House just outside of town, and another garrison at Moncks Corner. There are rumors every now and then that they are going to march to Savannah to consolidate their forces, but these rumors never bear any fruit. Of course, there are often rumors that a British fleet has left New York with 5,000 or 10,000 reinforcements to the Charlestown garrison, but these too never materialize. The rumors, however, do keep Maj. Gen. Nathanael Greene's army constantly on edge.

Meanwhile, other than the raid on John's Island, the New Year is brought in by the North Carolina Continentals like most every earlier New Year. Again, the officers want new clothes. Maj. John Armstrong, writing from the camp at Round O on January 3rd, complains, "We appear ridiculous among those that we are not acquainted with. We are fed up with promises until we can swallow no more of them." On January 16th, Maj. Griffith John McRee, writing from Wilmington, complains, "…I had collected about one hundred men, mostly all recruits…They are very likely young men and very naked, which prevents me from marching them to the Southward…"

On January 16th, the previously-captured Gov. Thomas Burke escapes from the British camp on James Island and makes his way to Maj. Gen. Nathanael Greene's camp by January 20th. After a band of Loyalist refugees were allowed to camp on the same island, the governor felt that his life was in grave danger. The Loyalists were determined to let him know that they despise him and all Whigs, and one night his quarters were fired upon. Gov. Burke sent a request to Maj. Gen. Alexander Leslie to allow him a parole within Patriot lines, but the general never bothered to reply.

As soon as he makes it to Maj. Gen. Greene's camp, he requests a court of inquiry to determine if his course of action was proper. Led by Maj. Gen. Arthur St. Clair, the council reportedly agrees that Gov. Burke is justified in breaking his parole. But, this is not the end of it. British Maj. Gen. Alexander Leslie insists that he be returned unconditionally, while the governor insists that he be exchanged just like any other paroled officer. So severe is the criticism from his political enemies back at home, Gov. Thomas Burke later writes to Maj. Gen. Greene that the British "unfortunately place a higher value on me than my own country did..." The criticism slows as he resumes his executive duties, but he makes it very clear–he does not want to be re-elected as governor.

Although the British influence in both Carolinas has been severely reduced, the Continental recruiting effort for 1782 is no more effective than it had been during 1780 and 1781. Continental officers are stationed all across the state and rendezvous points are established with dates designated for new men to assemble, but few show up voluntarily. Maj. Griffith John McRee is in Wilmington–not only does he have no clothing to provide his recruits, he also has no arms to give to them–and he just might have to march them through hostile Loyalist territory to get to headquarters. Brig. Gen. Jethro Sumner sends expresses all over the state looking for guns and ammunition, only to get the typical run-around.

By February 2nd, Maj. Gen. Nathanael Greene's patience runs out. Sumner has been gone for over three months and Greene has not heard from him since he left. Maj. Gen. Greene orders Brig. Gen. Sumner to get the clothing situation fixed immediately–and to do the same with his state's supply problems. Not only is his commander pressing him, so are his officers. On February 3rd, Maj. John Armstrong writes, "We are very desirous to hear from you and what success Capt. Dougherty had."

The North Carolina General Assembly is supposed to covene in Salem during January, but a quorum never shows, so the assembly is cancelled. Capt. George Dougherty has been sent as the official representative of the North Carolina Continental officers to implore the state legislature to provide them with back-pay for the years when money was devalued, and for the legislature to authorize the surveyors to commence laying off the lands promised to the officers and men.

158

On February 6th, Lt. Col. Henry "Hal" Dixon writes to Brig. Gen. Jethro Sumner from near Jacksonborough in South Carolina and provides the North Carolina Brigade's proposed new reorganization, taking into account all prisoners and those who retired in 1781. This "interim" restructuring goes into effect immediately, even though two key leaders are still prisoners. Those in camp have already learned that Lt. Col. Archibald Lytle is soon to be exchanged, so he is listed as the new commander for the 4th NC Regiment. Hardy Murfree is now identified as a Lt. Colonel and commander of the 1st NC Regiment. Lt. Col. Henry "Hal" Dixon now commands the 2nd NC Regiment, and Lt. Col. Selby Harney now commands the 3rd NC Regiment, even though he too is still a prisoner.

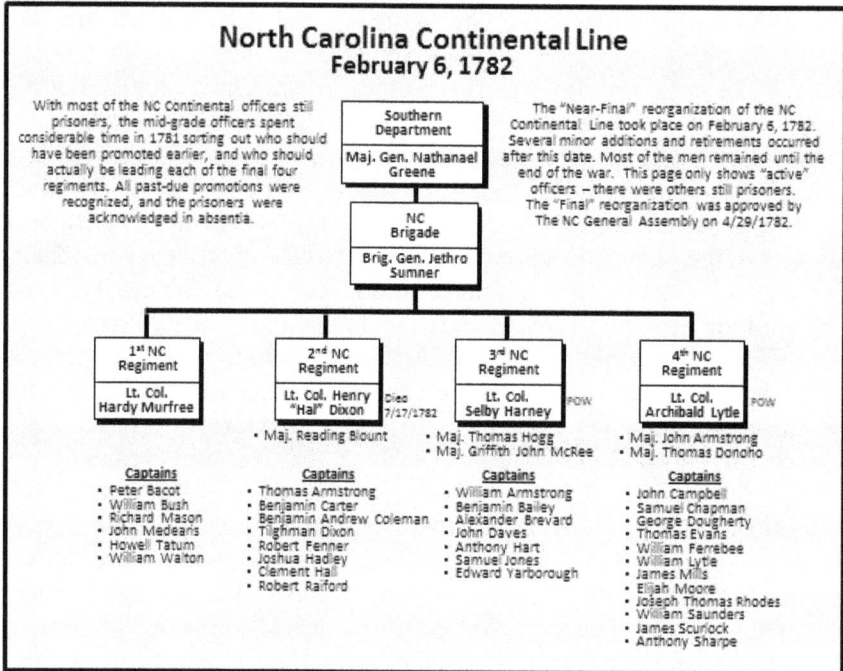

North Carolina Continental Line
February 6, 1782

With most of the NC Continental officers still prisoners, the mid-grade officers spent considerable time in 1781 sorting out who should have been promoted earlier, and who should actually be leading each of the final four regiments. All past-due promotions were recognized, and the prisoners were acknowledged in absentia.

The "Near-Final" reorganization of the NC Continental Line took place on February 6, 1782. Several minor additions and retirements occurred after this date. Most of the men remained until the end of the war. This page only shows "active" officers – there were others still prisoners. The "Final" reorganization was approved by The NC General Assembly on 4/29/1782.

Southern Department
Maj. Gen. Nathanael Greene

NC Brigade
Brig. Gen. Jethro Sumner

1st NC Regiment
Lt. Col. Hardy Murfree

Captains
- Peter Bacot
- William Bush
- Richard Mason
- John Medearis
- Howell Tatum
- William Walton

2nd NC Regiment
Lt. Col. Henry "Hal" Dixon — Died 7/17/1782
- Maj. Reading Blount

Captains
- Thomas Armstrong
- Benjamin Carter
- Benjamin Andrew Coleman
- Tilghman Dixon
- Robert Fenner
- Joshua Hadley
- Clement Hall
- Robert Raiford

3rd NC Regiment
Lt. Col. Selby Harney — POW
- Maj. Thomas Hogg
- Maj. Griffith John McRee

Captains
- William Armstrong
- Benjamin Bailey
- Alexander Brevard
- John Daves
- Anthony Hart
- Samuel Jones
- Edward Yarborough

4th NC Regiment
Lt. Col. Archibald Lytle — POW
- Maj. John Armstrong
- Maj. Thomas Donoho

Captains
- John Campbell
- Samuel Chapman
- George Dougherty
- Thomas Evans
- William Ferrebee
- William Lytle
- James Mills
- Elijah Moore
- Joseph Thomas Rhodes
- William Saunders
- James Scurlock
- Anthony Sharpe

As predicted, Lt. Col. Archibald Lytle is exchanged on February 9th, but it takes a considerable time to notify him and for him to make his way to Maj. Gen. Nathanael Greene's camp in South Carolina. This reorganization is by no means approved–it is merely the active duty officers' interpretation of who shall be promoted based on who resigned and when. It is not long before other Continental units learn of what has taken place, and their complaints go all the way to Philadelphia, even though it is none of their business nor does it materially affect them. Since the North Carolina legislature is not in session, Brig. Gen. Jethro

Sumner can only fend off (or ignore) all criticisms until the legislature reconvenes in April–a long two months away.

On February 19th, Maj. Griffith John McRee notifies his commander that he begins marching to the southward tomorrow with 180 new recruits. Maj. McRee almost begs his commander to really "represent the deplorable situation of this party to the Legislature and endeavor to procure them some supplies of clothing." He leaves Capt. Joshua Hadley in Wilmington to continue with recruiting in that location.

On February 20th, Capt. William Ferrebee of the 4th NC Regiment writes from Edenton to Brig. Gen. Jethro Sumner "in hopes of having it in my power to give a better account than I am able to presently." He complains that the county colonels are negligent in sending in their quotas of new recruits, and the delinquents are determined not to come in until they are forced to show up. He takes it upon himself to extend the deadline until March 10th, hoping that this will make a difference.

On March 15th, Lt. Col. Archibald Lytle learns that his exchange is a fact, but being at home in Hillsborough with no horse, he has no way to rejoin the army. Again typically, he has to wait more than a month for the legislature to convene and to approve the purchase of a new horse for the Continental officer.

In the meantime, Gov. Thomas Burke decides to employ Maj. Thomas Hogg, of the 3rd NC Regiment, as a commander over some State Troops in pursuit of the Loyalists who are really making life difficult in central North Carolina. Col. David Fanning, the notorious Loyalist who had captured the governor six months ago, now wants a conditional truce. Gov. Burke simply wants Col. David Fanning–no truce. However, none of the state's Militia or State Troops feel they are strong enough to take on the dreaded Tory commander and his band of Loyalists.

As with all things militarily within the state, nothing is accomplished easily or efficiently. One of the officers of the State Troops feels slighted that a Continental is placed over him and he takes his case all the way to the General Assembly–of course, it will not convene for yet another month. Extremely frustrated, on March 23rd, Gov. Burke orders Maj. Hogg to ignore the man and to get on with his assigned task. Everyone will just have to wait and see what the legislature might do in a month.

Another frustrated man, Maj. Griffith John McRee decides to write to the governor on March 31st–he's now at Bacon's Bridge in South Carolina and his men don't have suitable clothing. One of his men forged his signature to send a man home to get clothes–he had given the order but simply had not signed the pass. He is now afraid that several of his officers will resign because they were not recently provided new uniforms, as others had received. The system just isn't fair, but cannot the governor apply pressure on the legislature or whomever?

Interestingly, Lt. Col. Hardy Murfree writes a very similar letter to the governor on the same day:

> "I applied to General Greene to know in what manner the clothing should be issued…I then ordered a Board of Officers to sit and inquire who were entitled to the clothing, agreeably to the instructions."

It turns out that several Continental officers who were prisoners were authorized new uniforms, but active duty officers were not.

> "I should, therefore, be glad if your Excellency thinks proper that those gentlemen might have some satisfaction made them in order that matters might be accommodated without injuring the service as much as to lose several valuable officers."

Also on March 31st, Lt. Col. Hardy Murfree writes to Brig. Gen. Jethro Sumner,

> "Applicable to your instructions I met the Officers of your Brigade and made the arrangement which I have sent to you with two Copies which I hope will meet with your approbation."

The only version that survives is very similar to the earlier one, dated February 6th, only it shows all prisoners in their assigned regiments, and it only includes three regiments. Therefore, it is not shown herein.

Lt. Col. Murfree continues with news that two captains–John Medearis and Matthew Ramsey–choose to take retirement rather than reorganization, and that he has appointed Capt. Thomas Armstrong as the general's Aide-de-Camp. Maj. John Armstrong and Maj. Reading Blount are going to take leave for a while and go home. And, finally:

> "Capt. George Dougherty arrived in camp a few days ago with new clothing for the officers."

On April 8th, Maj. Gen. Nathanael Greene writes to Gov. Thomas Burke:

> "I hope to Heaven your Legislature will adopt some decisive measures for filling up your Continental Line. Short enlistments are the bane of service. By the time men are formed for soldiers their service expires, which makes the composition of our

Army unfit for the purposes of Military glory or National security. Besides, which we are never able to have our men decently clad, for no sooner is clothing issued than part of it goes immediately home.... It is true they are better than no force, but far inferior to those who are voluntarily enlisted... Your State, by neglecting me, may bring me into distress, and perhaps disgrace, but that will not mend their situation."

On April 9th, Lt. Col. Hardy Murfree is encamped at Bacon's Bridge in South Carolina and he writes to Brig. Gen. Jethro Sumner that several Continental officers have been released in Charlestown on parole, and these men report that they were fed fairly well. Lt. Col. Murfree relates that he has very recently discharged 100 men whose time has expired. His final note is about once again sending Capt. George Dougherty to call on Gov. Thomas Burke and the legislature about the land previously promised to all Continental soldiers.

On April 17th, Lt. Thomas Pasteur writes to Gov. Thomas Burke that several Continental officers were recently exchanged in Virginia and:

"A number of them were obliged on their landing to sell part of their clothing in order to enable them to proceed to their respective homes, and to discharge the bills of taylors and washerwomen."

He goes on to report that two officers in camp consider themselves injured because they are not on the list to receive new uniforms.

On April 13th, the North Carolina General Assembly convenes at Hillsborough. It is not until April 24th that the legislature finally gets around to matters regarding the North Carolina Continental Line.

"Agreeable to order of the Honorable Major General Greene to Brigadier General Sumner to convene, as soon as may be, the Officers of the North Carolina Line, who were to arrange and form themselves into Regiments, Agreeable to Resolves of Congress of the 3rd and 21st October, 1780, Boards of the said Line were Assembled in Halifax the 23rd Jany., '81, Camp Pon Pon S. Carolina, 6th February, '82, Camp near Bacon's Bridge, 30th March, and at Hillsborough, the 24th April, when the Arrangement was concluded to be just and fair, and the Regiments as follows [see graphic on the next page]"

However, it is not until April 30th that each house of the General Assembly final issue their approval:

"Resolved, that this House to approve of the within arrangement and do accordingly recommend for Continental Commissions the officers therein mentioned."

North Carolina Continental Line
April 24, 1782

"Agreeable to order of the Honorable Major General Greene to Brigadier General Sumner to convene, as soon as may be, the Officers of the North Carolina Line, who were to arrange and form themselves into Regiments, agreeable to Resolves of Congress of the 3rd and 21st October, 1780.

Southern Department

Maj. Gen. Nathanael Greene

NC Brigade

Brig. Gen. Jethro Sumner

Boards of the said Line were assembled at Halifax the 23rd January, 1781, Camp Pon Pon South Carolina, 6th February, 1782, Camp near Bacon's Bridge 30th March, and at Hillsborough, the 24th April, when the arrangement was concluded to be just and fair, and the Regiments as follows:"

Approved by NC General Assembly April 30th.

1st NC Regiment	2nd NC Regiment	3rd NC Regiment	4th NC Regiment
POW Col. Thomas Clark	POW Col. John Patten	POW Lt. Col. Selby Harney	Lt. Col. Archibald Lytle

• Lt. Col. Hardy Murfree
• Maj. John Nelson – POW

• Lt. Col. Henry "Hal" Dixon
• Maj. Reading Blount

• Maj. Thomas Hogg
• Maj. Griffith John McRee

• Maj. John Armstrong
• Maj. Thomas Donoho

Captains	Captains	Captains	Captains
• Peter Bacot	• Thomas Armstrong	• William Armstrong	>> • John Campbell
• Thomas Callendar–POW	• Benjamin Carter	• Kedar Ballard–POW	• Samuel Chapman
• Tilghman Dixon	• Benjamin A. Coleman	• Benjamin Bailey	• George Dougherty
• Joshua Hadley	• John Craddock–POW	• George Bradley–POW	• Thomas Evans
• Samuel Jones	• Robert Fenner	• Alexander Brevard	• William Ferrebee
• James Read–POW*	• Clement Hall	• John Daves	• William Lytle
• John Sumner–POW	• John Ingles–POW	• William Fawn–POW	• James Mills
• Howell Tatum	• Robert Raiford	• Joseph Montford–POW	• Elijah Moore
• William Walton	• Charles Stewart–POW	• Edward Yarborough	>> • Joseph Thomas Rhodes
			>> • William Saunders
			>> • James Scurlock
			• Anthony Sharpe

*A Colonel of NC State Troops
>> On 4/24/1782 Roll as a Lieutenant

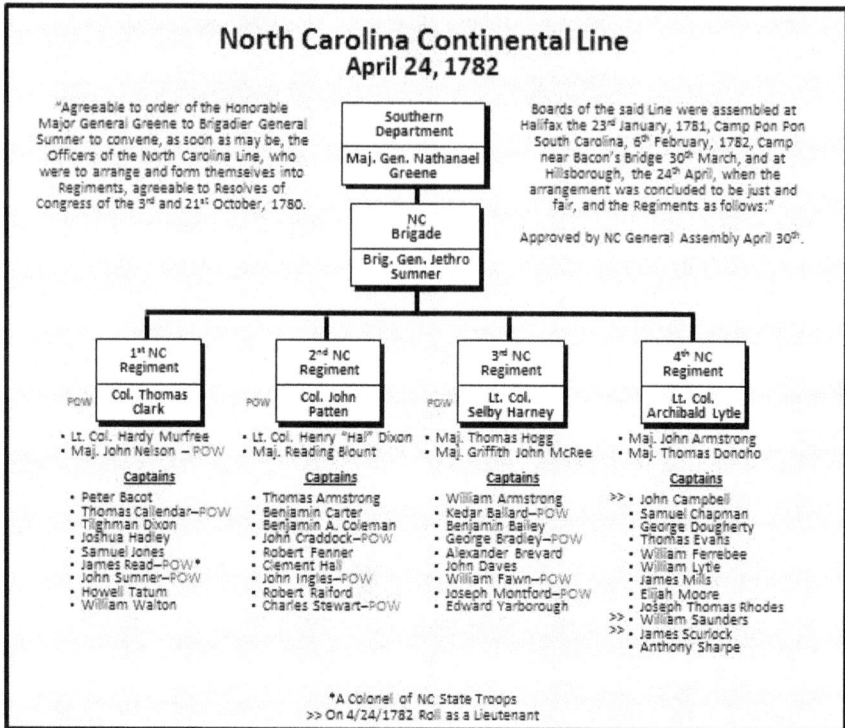

In the meantime, Lt. Col. Hardy Murfree writes to Brig. Gen. Jethro Sumner that he will have 276 men to discharge on May 1st:

"… which will make the Brigade look small… I should be much obliged to you to inform me by the first opportunity what the Assembly are about doing for the Army, and what plan they have fell on to raise troops."

On May 1st, Lt. Col. Murfree writes again to inform his commander that Maj. Gen. Nathanael Greene approves of allowing the discharged men to enlist in South Carolina units or in Lt. Col. Henry Lee's Legion. Lt. Col. Murfree requests from Maj. Gen. Greene to learn if he can get some money to enlist the men back into North Carolina units, but Maj. Gen. Greene says there is no money to be had. Later reports indicate that very few men actually accept the enticing bounties offered by both South Carolina and Virigina. They all know that they are now legally exempt from all military duty for at least the next twelve months, and most simply want to go home. They all know the war is winding down.

On May 7th, the General Assembly in Hillsborough reviews the petition of retired-Col. James Armstrong. He claims that he was never consulted in the re-arrangement of the officers since the beginning of that effort over a year ago, and that he has since provided a considerable amount of time and expenses in the past year's recruiting effort. The legislature agrees that they considered him to be on active duty all that time and agrees to pay him through April 24th, the arbitrary, but somewhat official date when they consider him to have retired.

On May 10th, the newly-elected Governor Alexander Martin writes to the General Assembly:

"... to draw your attention to the officers and soldiers of the North Carolina Line who are now looking up to your Honorable Body to ascertain their lands with precision which you have heretofore granted them as a reward for their military services... At the same time permit me to recommend to your generous notice the officers and soldiers of the states of Maryland and Delaware, who, with cheerfulness, marched to our relief at a time of our captured troops could afford to us no assistance against an unrestrained and conquering enemy, who, with unremitting perseverance in hardship and toil, have followed their gallant leaders thro' every hazardous enterprise, and with prodigality of life have copiously bled for us in every conflict." [minor edits]

The General Assembly does take up more Continental matters, but it chooses to defer any discussion about setting aside North Carolina lands for Maryland and Delaware Continentals. On May 11th, the General Assembly passes an Act for raising troops to complete the Continental Battalions,

"Whereas the time of service of the troops raised to complete the Continental Battalions of this state by an Act of Assembly passed at Halifax in February, one thousand seven hundred and eighty one, is nearly expired; and whereas it is absolutely necessary the said battalions be immediately completed, and the common mode of recruiting being found ineffectual..."

The legislature requires that all men between the ages of sixteen and fifty years old (with minor exceptions) shall be divided into classes of twenty men each–and for each class to furnish one able-bodied man who shall serve in the Continental service for eighteen months. If not enough men are selected in this manner, then each county commandant shall draft the rest. All county officers are required to make accurate returns of the men drafted and volunteered–this time with penalties for not doing so. These returns are to include name, size, age, complexion, and occupation of the men raised, as well as the captain's name from whose company they are taken. All men are to rendezvous by August 1ˢᵗ at either Salisbury, Hillsborough, Winton, Warrenton, Kingston, Duplin Court House, or Ramseur's Mill. All men are to receive a proper allotment of clothing–to be provided by the class of twenty men who selected them. More recruiting details can be found in Volume 2.

On May 16ᵗʰ, the legislature finally passes an Act for the relief of the officers and soldiers of the Continental Line:

"Whereas the officers and soldiers of the Continental Line of this state, have suffered very much by the depreciation of paper currency, as well as by the deficiency of clothing and other supplies… and the honorable Continental Congress have resolved that such depreciation shall be made good to the eighteenth day of August, one thousand seven hundred and eighty, agreeable to a scale of depreciation established."

The legislature also provides that each soldier who shall continue to the end of the war shall receive a bounty of land ranging from 640 acres for a private up to 12,000 acres for a brigadier general. Absalom Tatum, Isaac Shelby, and Anthony Bledsoe are appointed commissioners on behalf of the state to examine and superintend the laying off the land– along with any agent(s) appointed by the officers. In this Act, the General Assembly also provides 25,000 acres for Maj. Gen. Nathanael Greene "as a mark of the high sense this State entertains of the extraordinary services of that brave and gallant officer."

Over the summer, almost every enticement is offered to fill the Continental regiments. Pardons are offered to all deserters and delinquent draftees who willingly rejoin at the designated rendezvous points–few do. Men who are drafted can "purchase" a substitute. Or, two classes (40 men) can avoid service by sending one good wagon with team–to serve the army for eighteen months.

Men are assembled slowly, but as they gather it is soon realized that there are not enough muskets available, and the North Carolina Militia simply refuse to help their brethren out. To further complicate things, new recruits who show up are to be supplied by the Continental Quarter Master department, however, draftees and substitutes are to be supplied by their local Militia. And, many new recruits arrive at their designated rendezvous point only to find no Continental officer there to officially receive them–many immediately desert soon thereafter.

On June 28ᵗʰ, Maj. Reading Blount–in New Bern–writes to Brig. Gen. Jethro Sumner:

"There is no provision made for their subsistence between this and camp on any route that I can hear of, and the nature of the law is such from what I can learn that no officer will (willingly) undertake to march them; there is one or two & twenty of them when all collected."

Ironically, down in South Carolina at Maj. Gen. Greene's camp, there is very little for the soldiers to actually do, other than fight boredom. Much of the time is spent drilling. A parade is held in April and it is noted that the North Carolina Brigade "makes a very bad fire." Both officers and men in camp are getting quite irritated–many blame the civil authorities. Capt. Samuel Jones of the 1st NC Regiment is brought before a court-martial charged with using strong language against Gov. Alexander Martin. However, Maj. Gen. Greene has the time to write to Brig. Gen. Jethro Sumner:

"Many of the troops of your Line will shortly go home, besides those that have already been discharged, I beg you, therefore, to exert yourself in collecting and forwarding the drafts that are to replace them."

On July 4th, the Independence Day celebration breaks the monotony of camp routine for a day, at least. At five o'clock in the afternoon, the army draws up in a single line to salute Maj. Gen. Nathanael Greene. Thirteen cannon are fired, followed by a twenty-one gun salute to honor the recent birth of the Dauphin of France, then a *feu de joie* of running fire from one end of the long line to the other. The line then passes in review and that night the officers are entertained by Maj. Gen. Greene and South Carolina Gov. John Rutledge.

Apparently boredom also affects those who are not in camp that summer. On July 15th, Maj. John Armstrong writes to Brig. Gen. Jethro Sumner that he has recently been wounded in a duel with Maj. Joel Lewis of the North Carolina State Regiment (State Troops):

"If I am able to ride I will be at Salisbury at the time of bringing in the drafts. Capts. Yarborough and Gamble [a Militia officer] is there now and receives the deserters, delinquents, and others sent to them. Capt. Brevard superintends the district of Morgan. Lieut. Campbell, Guilford, Capt. Carter the three counties on Pee Dee and myself in Surry."

By summer's end, word leaks out of Charlestown that Maj. Gen. Alexander Leslie is planning to evacuate the town soon. It is also rumored that New York will be evacuated as well. Savannah is now free of the British, although some Regulars and Hessians are still ashore waiting to board their transports home. On August 15th, Maj. Gen. Anthony Wayne marches his troops back to Maj. Gen. Greene's camp.

Meanwhile, on August 7th, the Continental Congress resolves that the many Continental Lines shall be rearranged into regiments of not less than 500 men each. Any additional men are to be assigned to company-sized units until there are enough recruits assembled to create a full regiment. Officers are to be assigned based upon seniority. Surplus officers are to retire, but can be recalled if necessary. This new plan is to go into effect on January 1, 1783. Once again, the North Carolina Brigade assigns a group of officers, led by Maj. Reading Blount, to ascertain what–if anything–needs to be rearranged. They meet many times before a final solution is offered.

Back home, on August 5th, Col. Nicholas Long–Deputy Quarter Master General (DQMG) for the North Carolina Continental Line, stationed at Halifax, NC–writes to Brig. Gen. Jethro Sumner,

"I inform you that there is not an Assistant Deputy Quarter Master in this state subject to my command at present. Those who have heretofore served have all resigned, nor have I one to assist me in any branch whatever."

It is clear that many within the state now consider the war to be over.

The General Assembly's target date of August 1st for all new recruits to be at their rendezvous point passes quietly. On August 5th, recently-promoted Lt. Col. John Armstrong writes to Brig. Gen. Jethro Sumner:

"We have at this place at present between fifty & sixty men & believe there will be very few more before the 15th instant…"

But, he goes on to complain that officers are scarce, and one officer plans to take leave soon.

On August 7th, Maj. Thomas Donoho writes to his general from Hillsborough:

"I have been here ten days and have received no men but from Caswell and Granville counties, and only twenty-five from each of them (fifty in all) and am informed the other counties are not to rendezvous till the 20th of the month, of course it will be out of my power to march agreeable to your orders, except to go without men, which I don't conceive to be your intention."

He continues by noting that provisions are scarce, and one of his captains must stay in the area to settle some personal business.

On August 14th, Capt. Alexander Brevard of the 3rd NC Regiment writes from Ramseur's Mill to Brig. Gen. Jethro Sumner:

"I have attended at this place since the first of this month. Orders from Genl. [Charles] McDowell to the Colonels for the troops of Morgan District to rendezvous at this place the 20th instant."

He continues by telling his commanding officer that he feels he needs at least one more officer here to help him when the southward march begins.

On August 15th, Capt. Joshua Hadley of the 1st NC Regiment writes from Cross Creek to Brig. Gen. Jethro Sumner:

"Capt. [Robert] Raiford has directed me to meet at Duplin immediately, in order to receive the eighteen months men to be delivered there, in consequence of which I have ordered the men from this county to march thither today, & expect to get to Duplin Court House on Sunday next. Captain [Joseph Thomas] Rhodes is now in Duplin & I beg leave to make known to you that there are now in this county a number of delinquents and deserters, who with a little trouble & the assistance of some State Horse, who have been lately ordered into this neighborhood might be collected... I might meet the troops at Wilmington or elsewhere as you shall direct." [minor edits]

On August 18th, Capt. Thomas Evans of the 4th NC Regiment writes from Kingston to Brig. Gen. Jethro Sumner:

"... we have no news, the recruits come in slowly only to the amount of [torn out] as yet joined, but we expect the whole of the Pitt men in today."

On the same date, Lt. Col. Hardy Murfree writes from his home in Hertford County to Brig. Gen. Jethro Sumner:

"Captain [Tilghman] Dixon has been waiting at Winton since the 1st of the month, and has had no men delivered. They classed the men in Hertford & Gates counties yesterday, and are to be drafted nine days hence. Some of the lower counties have drafted their men, but have got none of them clothed, and don't appear to be in a hurry about it. Col. [George] Wynns informs Captain Dixon that he cannot have his men ready to deliver before a month from this time."

He continues by informing his commanding officer that Capt. Tilghman Dixon has since gone to Hillsborough on personal business and that Capt. William Walton remains behind to collect any new recruits.

On August 22nd, Maj. Thomas Donoho of the 4th NC Regiment writes from Hillsborough to Brig. Gen. Jethro Sumner:

168

"Before I recd. yours I had sent Capt. [Elijah] Moore and Lieut. [William] Saunders off with a party of seventy men unarmed but on the receipt of your sent an express to stop them at Salisbury till they can be armed; the men come in very slow and numbers desert. I am doubtful we shall make but poor returns from this district. Randolph County has not sent any of their men yet, and I am informed they expect to join on the march and have just sent to the Col. to march them here immediately and suppose they will be down in a few days. We are very scarce of provisions and under the necessity of impressing of it from the inhabitants who have been greatly distressed already by the State Troops." [minor edits]

Also on August 22nd, Capt. Robert Raiford of the 2nd NC Regiment writes from Duplin Court House to Brig. Gen. Jethro Sumner:

Also on August 22nd, Capt. Robert Raiford of the 2nd NC Regiment writes from Duplin Court House to Brig. Gen. Jethro Sumner:

"I have Inclos'd you a Return of the Men received, by which you will see the deficiencies of the Countys of Duplin, Bladen, and Cumberland, and the utter inattention of the commanding officers of the Countys of New Hanover, Brunswick, and Onslow... Capts. Rhodes, Hadley, Lieuts. Ashe and Hill are here with me. I shall in a week or so send you another return by which time I hope the other Countys will Join, & these send the remainder of their Quotas. Till then, I shall use all the possible means of collecting the 18 months men, delinquents, & deserters."

RETURN OF THE MEN FROM WILMINGTON DISTRICT, AUG. 22ND, '82.

COUNTIES.	Volunteers.	Drafts.	Substitutes.	Delinquents.	Deserters.	Total.	Coats.	Vest Coats.	Shirts.	Overalls.	Breeches	Hunting Shirts.	Stockings.	Shoes.	Hats.	Blankets.	Stocks	Yards Tent Cloath.	Waggons.	Horses.
Duplin recd. 1st Augt.....	22	5	6	6		39	13	13	37	37	17	15	37	36	14	14	18	70¼	1	8
Bladen recd. the 20th......	..	1	20	4	2	27	5	6	23	18	5	2	11	13	4	5	3	5	..	...
Cumberland recd. the 22..	1	..	5	2	2	10	3	2	10	6	2	2	6	6	2	2	4	5	..	...
Total.	23	6	31	12	4	76	21	21	70	61	24	19	54	55	20	21	25	80¼	1	8

On August 25th, Brig. Gen. Mordecai Gist (MD) with a unit of Continental Cavalry under Col. George Baylor and a unit of Continental Light Infantry under Lt. Col. John Laurens (SC) is detached by Maj. Gen. Nathanael Greene to stop the British and Loyalist forces from plundering plantations of the Beaufort and Colleton districts of South Carolina. This detachment finds 300 British Regulars and 200 Loyalists with 18 vessels already on the Combahee River. Brig. Gen. Gist sends part of his forces across the Combahee Ferry to drive them off, and sends Lt. Col. Laurens downriver to intercept any that might attempt to flee.

At Tar Bluff, Lt. Col. Laurens throws up a hasty earthwork with fifty men and a howitzer. This small group stops the British flotilla. British Maj. William Brereton arrives and quickly dislodges the small Patriot group, killing Lt. Col. John Laurens and several of his men. The British forces escape Brig. Gen. Gist's follow-up. Forty men from the North Carolina Continental Line are detached to support Lt. Col. John Laurens in this expedition–none have been identified to date. This is the last known conflict with any North Carolina Continentals participating.

On September 1st, Gov. Alexander Martin writes to all brigadier generals of the seven NC Militia districts,

> "... several Colonels and Commanding Officers of counties have failed or refused to order the late nine months and other exempted persons to be classed and drafted... You will therefore please to order all the nine months men, and other classes in your brigade lately claiming exemptions to be immediately classed as the law directs..."

On September 10th, Gov. Alexander Martin writes from New Bern to the North Carolina delegates in Philadelphia:

> "Our eighteen months men are ready to march, but on receiving orders at present are halted."

As can be seen, sometimes they are referred to as nine-month men, and other times they are called eighteen-month men (which is correct).

Also on September 10th, Lt. Col. Hardy Murfree writes from his home in Hertford County to Brig. Gen. Jethro Sumner:

> "I recd. your favour and observed the contents, in the beginning of the year 1778 Colo. Polk, Williams, and Brewster resigned, which entitled Ashe, self, and Dixon to Lieutn. Colonelcys."

The matter of "seniority" within the North Carolina Brigade seems to never get resolved. Other Continental regiments are aware and voicing their criticism of how North Carolina decides who gets which promotion. Lt. Col. Murfree continues by complaining that he wishes some kind of "board" will settle it and get it over with. Ask and ye shall receive...

On September 14th, the Continental Congress in Philadelphia:

> "Resolves, that the commander in chief & the commanding officers of the Southern Army direct the officers of the line of each state respectively to meet together & agree & determine upon the officers as are inclinable to repair within the British lines, or any other who shall remain in service to command the troops, arranged as aforesaid, provided that where it cannot be done by voluntary agreement, the junior

officers of each grade will retire, so as to leave complete corps of officers in proportion to the number of men, and to be adjusted upon the principles of the acts of the 3rd and the 21st of October, 1780, and the fifth resolution of the act passed the 23rd day of April, 1782." [minor edits]

On September 17th, Brig. Gen. Jethro Sumner writes to the North Carolina delegates in Philadelphia:

"My instructions for making the arrangements I received from General Greene, to whom I transmitted the arrangements approv'd by resolve of the General Assembly, and who have acknowledged the receipt of the enclosures by Lieut. [Thomas] Pasteur. I make no doubt but Genl. Greene was made acquainted of Lieut. Colonel Stewart's complaint to the War Office of Lieut. Colos. [Hardy] Murfree and [Henry] Dixon's claim for the dates of their Commissions issuing." [minor edits]

He continues,

"I am satisfied you are acquainted of many of the distresses we labor under for some pay, when two, three, and four years are due, not a clothier that has a yard of any thing, no magazine of provisions, seldom any rations, travelling expenses, &c., &c., &c, takes more money than we can command by any means consistent." [minor edits]

On September 20th, Maj. J. Burnett–Aide-de-Camp to Maj. Gen. Nathanael Greene–writes to both Lt. Col. Archibald Lytle and to Brig. Gen. Jethro Sumner. He directs Lt. Col. Archibald Lytle:

"... to proceed to the state of North Carolina and take the most effectual measures for bringing forward the recruits from that state... You will take with you a copy of the return of the officers of your line now serving with this army, made out agreeable to the general orders & resolutions of Congress for reforming the establishment of the army, and endeavor to have it completed by Genl. Sumner and the officers of the Line who are in the state. It will be necessary that the officers should be assembled, their rank settled and ascertained, with their desire either to continue or retire, agreeable to the resolution of Congress and the general orders, a copy of which you will take with you." [minor edits]

To Brig. Gen. Jethro Sumner he writes:

"The General desires you will have the officers assembled and their rank settled, and then make out a list of their names &c., agreeable to a form which he thinks best, a copy of which Lt. Col. Lytle will also deliver."

Very few records exist for the month of October 1782. On October 2nd, Gov. Alexander Martin writes to the commissioners overseeing the

171

surveying of Continental soldiers and officers' lands:

"Tho' the Assembly have omitted making a land provision for the heirs of the officers who have been killed or died in the service of this state the present war, I make no doubt as generosity & humanity dictate the measure there will be a provision for them next Assembly. You will therefore reserve as much land for officers' heirs, of whom you have information as aforesaid, equal to their respective ranks." [minor edits]

Governor Martin also asks for three copies of all lands surveyed–one for the General Assembly, one to be lodged in the Secretary of State's office, and one for the inspection of the Governor and Council of State.

On October 28th, an agreement is reached between the Southern Department, represented by Maj. J. Burnett, and the British army, represented by Maj. James Wemyss for the exchange of all prisoners:

1st. That all non-commissioned officers and privates who have been delivered previous to the date hereof be considered as exchanged and properly accounted for.

2nd. That all the British prisoners of War now in the American Army, including those lately at Georgetown, be sent to Charlestown, as early as possible, and be considered as exchanged.

3rd. That an immediate exchange of regular officers, as far as similar rank will apply shall be effected and the paroles of the unexchanged officers be extended agreeable to their wishes.

4th. That all Militia and citizens, both American and British, taken as Prisoners of War, by either army in the Southern Department previous to the date of this agreement, be considered as hereby exchanged, and those who may now be in confinement, be immediately liberated.

On October 31st, Maj. Gen. Nathanael Greene writes to Gov. Alexander Martin,

"The troops have not been supplied with rice or bread for upwards of thirty days, and a great part of that time they were without any kind of meal. Unless the pork can be had from North Carolina our prospects will appear very unfavorable."

On November 9th, the North Carolina delegates in Philadelphia write to Gov. Alexander Martin, that on November 4th, the Continental Congress resolves:

"That the Commander in the Southern Army be instructed to retain in the public service so many of the eighteen months drafts of the state of North Carolina as he shall think the public safety may require, and that a proportional number of officers shall be continued in full pay for the Command of those troops while they are in the field, the resolution of the 7th of August nothwithstanding, and they retire on the same principles or emoluments on which they would have retired had not the operation of the said Resolve been postponed." [minor edits]

On November 10th, Lt. Col. Archibald Lytle documents the results from a Board of Officers and their recommendation for which officers to retain in the existing four regiments–the ideal situation:

"The Board of Officers convened by order of Lt. Col. Lytle are of the opinion the following officers are entitled to commands in the No. Carolina Line from their rank, viz... That if any officer nominated to a command agreeable to rank, do not serve but is permitted to retire by exchange, or quit the service the next senior officer as here arranged shall be call'd into the service. And as a number of officers entitled to command in the Line are absent on duty, and others are prisoners of war, it is necessary to nominate the following officers present to do duty, until the proper officers can take command, on the foregoing principles."

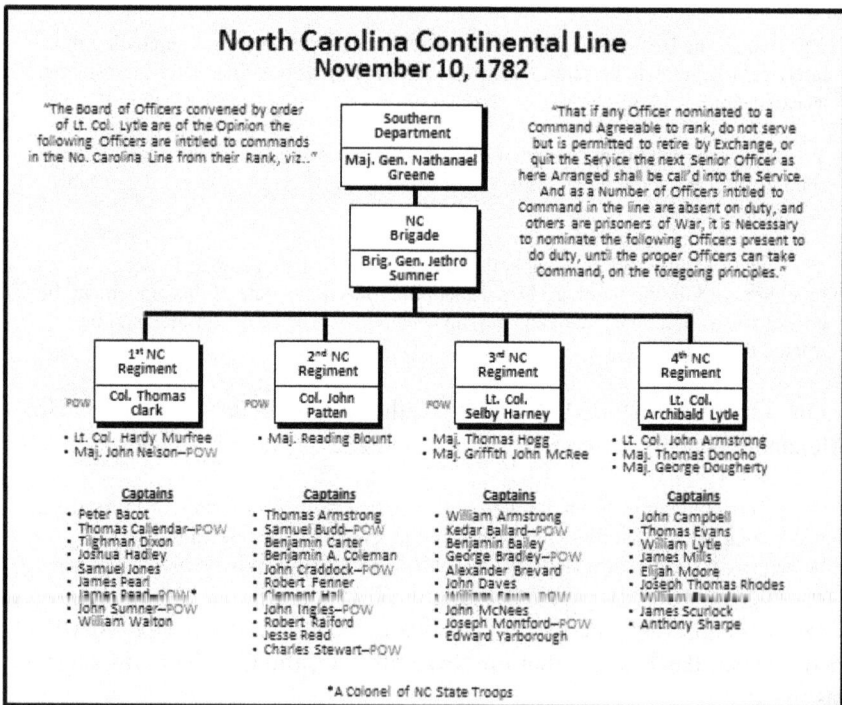

North Carolina Continental Line
November 10, 1782

"The Board of Officers convened by order of Lt. Col. Lytle are of the Opinion the following Officers are intitled to commands in the No. Carolina Line from their Rank, viz..."

Southern Department
Maj. Gen. Nathanael Greene

NC Brigade
Brig. Gen. Jethro Sumner

"That if any Officer nominated to a Command Agreeable to rank, do not serve but is permitted to retire by Exchange, or quit the Service the next Senior Officer as here Arranged shall be call'd into the Service. And as a Number of Officers intitled to Command in the line are absent on duty, and others are prisoners of War, it is Necessary to nominate the following Officers present to do duty, until the proper Officers can take Command, on the foregoing principles."

1st NC Regiment	2nd NC Regiment	3rd NC Regiment	4th NC Regiment
POW Col. Thomas Clark	POW Col. John Patten	POW Lt. Col. Selby Harney	Lt. Col. Archibald Lytle
• Lt. Col. Hardy Murfree • Maj. John Nelson–POW	• Maj. Reading Blount	• Maj. Thomas Hogg • Maj. Griffith John McRee	• Lt. Col. John Armstrong • Maj. Thomas Donoho • Maj. George Dougherty
Captains • Peter Bacot • Thomas Callendar–POW • Tilghman Dixon • Joshua Hadley • Samuel Jones • James Pearl • James Pearl–POW* • John Sumner–POW • William Walton	**Captains** • Thomas Armstrong • Samuel Budd–POW • Benjamin Carter • Benjamin A. Coleman • John Craddock–POW • Robert Fenner • Clement Hall • John Ingles–POW • Robert Raiford • Jesse Read • Charles Stewart–POW	**Captains** • William Armstrong • Kedar Ballard–POW • Benjamin Bailey • George Bradley–POW • Alexander Brevard • John Daves • William Faron–POW • John McNees • Joseph Montford–POW • Edward Yarborough	**Captains** • John Campbell • Thomas Evans • William Lytle • James Mills • Elijah Moore • Joseph Thomas Rhodes • William Saunders • James Scurlock • Anthony Sharpe

*A Colonel of NC State Troops

Since all officers are not present, the Board of Officers nominates six captains to active duty until the proper officers can take command:

Captain Present in Camp	Ultimate Captain – When Available
Benjamin Carter	James Read
Alexander Brevard	Joseph Thomas Rhodes
Thomas Evans	William Armstrong
Joshua Hadley	Robert Fenner
William Lytle	Benjamin Andrew Coleman
James Mills	Tilghman Dixon

"The surplus will be continued as at present."

No records from 1782 exist that describe in detail the results of this Board of Officers' recommendations.

On Novemer 12th, Lt. Col. John Armstrong writes from camp at Ashley Hill near Charlestown to Brig. Gen. Jethro Sumner,

"A new arrangement hath taken place in our line which will be handed to you by Lt. Col. Lytle. The officers in general here wish that you would not suffer any partial appointments by the Assembly, in case reduction takes place in our line, or filling up the vacancies of the prisoners of war, which is now arranged. We have suffered by those impositions before and came off 2nd best. Nothing but adhering strictly to the resolves of Congress can be satisfactory to the officers of the army. I am now without a command or money. How to get home I know not, my certificate is blank and protested at home and abroad." [minor edits]

The day before, on November 11th, Maj. Gen. Nathanael Greene writes to Brig. Gen. Jethro Sumner:

"Lt. Colonel Lytle who waits on the Legislature to represent some abuses which have been practiced in furnishing the last drafts from your state will hand you the arrangement of troops from N. Carolina who are with this army. I must request you will order those officers who are arranged to those men, to join the army without a moment's delay. Lt. Col. Lytle will give you a list of their names. The troops are so raw & undisciplined that every exertion & attention of their officers will barely fit them for the field before the opening of the spring campaign. It is of the utmost consequence therefore that every officer of them should be in camp immediately... Our prospects of obtaining the necessary supplies of provision for this army during the winter are very gloomy, and unless we can get some stall-fed beef or salted pork from N. Carolina we shall be much distressed." [minor edits]

On November 16th, Governor Alexander Martin writes from Hillsborough to Maj. Gen. Nathanael Greene:

"...I am waiting for the meeting of the Legislature, who stood adjourned to the first of this instant; but I am doubtful a session will not be made at this time as few members have appeared..."

Since no other legal provisions have been made to acquire cattle for the Southern Army, Governor Martin goes on to tell Maj. Gen. Greene that he is endeavoring to raise cattle "by Contribution," and has succeeded fairly well until the Commissary General Department was abolished. He is doing everything in his power to secure beef stock and salted pork for the army this winter.

On November 20th, Lt. Col. Selby Harney writes from Camden County to Brig. Gen. Jethro Sumner:

> "Lieut. Colonel Lytle has just acquainted me by a line of my exchange. He desires me to apply to you for orders, but I hope Sir my inability of body will for the present excuse me from being called to camp. Add to this I have neither horses nor money to carry me there. If there should be any duty to do in the district I should use utmost endeavor to do it." [minor edits]

The musket ball that wounded him at the Fall of Charlestown has never been removed, therefore, he will soon have that surgery so he can return to active duty.

On November 22nd, Lt. Col. Hardy Murfree writes from Halifax, NC to Brig. Gen. Jethro Sumner,

> "I came to this place today on my way to Hillsborough, but was informed the Assembly did not meet so shall return home... My circumstances you are not unacquainted with, so shall be very glad to retire when the arrangement takes place."

On November 26th, with little fanfare, all Patriot prisoners taken in the Southern Department are officially exchanged, including the following remaining North Carolina Continental officers:

Rank*	Name	Battle Taken	Date Taken
Colonel	Thomas Clark	Charlestown	5/12/1780
"	John Patten	Charlestown	5/12/1780
Lt. Colonel	Selby Harney	Charlestown	5/12/1780
Major	John Nelson	Charlestown	5/12/1780
Captain	Kedar Ballard	Charlestown	5/12/1780
"	George Bradley	Charlestown	5/12/1780
"	John Craddock	Charlestown	5/12/1780
"	John Ingles	Charlestown	5/12/1780
"	Joseph Montford	Charlestown	5/12/1780
"	James Read	Hillsborough	9/12/1781
"	John Sumner	Charlestown	5/12/1780
Capt.-Lt.	Thomas Callendar	Charlestown	5/12/1780
"	William Fawn	Charlestown	5/12/1780
"	Phil Jones	Charlestown	5/12/1780

Rank*	Name	Battle Taken	Date Taken
"	Charles Stewart	Charlestown	5/12/1780
Lieutenant	Samuel Budd	Eutaw Springs	9/8/1781
"	John Clendenan	Eutaw Springs	9/8/1781
"	William Hargrave	Charlestown	5/12/1780
"	Jesse Read	Eutaw Springs	9/8/1781
"	James Tatum	Charlestown	5/12/1780
Surgeon	James W. Greene	Charlestown	5/12/1780
*Rank at the time of capture. Some are promoted during their detention.			

All British prisoners taken in the Southern Department are also exchanged on this date, except for those taken at Yorktown in Virginia.

Since the Continental Congress wants no troops to remain in the field except for those who have enlisted for three years, Maj. Gen. Nathanael Greene decides to send all North Carolina Continentals home except for one regiment. Officers are directed to furlough their men until further notice. Maj. Gen. Greene's objective is to keep the men on active duty, but to allow them to remain at home with no pay, no clothing issued, and no ration allowance. This offers him the most options at the lowest cost.

The day that all of South Carolina, North Carolina, and even Georgia has been long awaiting finally arrives on Saturday, December 14th, when the British army finally evacuates the city of Charlestown. Maj. Gen. Alexander Leslie agrees not to destroy the city if the Patriots will allow his troops to depart safely. Upon the firing of the morning cannon the British, their allies, their Loyalists, and 5,000 slaves move out of the forward works, while the Continentals of Maj. Gen. Anthony Wayne move in–keeping a respectful distance.

South Carolina Brig. Gen. William Moultrie later writes in his memoirs:

"This fourteenth day of December, 1782, ought never to be forgotten by the Carolinians; it ought to be the day of festivity with them, as it is the real day of their deliverance and independence."

By three o'clock in the afternoon, Maj. Gen. Nathanael Greene and South Carolina Gov. John Matthews, his council, and other prominent citizens–escorted by 150 cavalry–ride into Charlestown. The balconies, doors, and windows are crowded, as are all streets. Even with all of the festivities, Maj. Gen. Greene sees little but trouble for the future–he is not convinced the war is yet over. However, he ends the year with:

"I believe both the people and the Army are tired of war. The one from the expense, the other from getting no pay."

176

Chapter Nine – 1783

By the first of 1783, news has finally reached North Carolina that there is now a provisional treaty in work between the United States and Great Britain. However, there are no celebrations, no thirteen gun salutes, and no *feu de joie* by any troops within the state. Moreover, there are no more frantic demands for new recruits into the North Carolina Continental Line.

With the reorganization of the entire Continental Line in late 1782, the Continental Congress only wants men who have

Key Events of 1783

- In January, the NC Continental Line is reduced to a single regiment, led by Lt. Col. Archibald Lytle.
- NC General Assembly meets in April at Hillsborough and re-elects Governor Alexander Martin.
- In May, Maj. Gen. Nathanael Greene sends the last NC Continental company home on furlough, to be recalled if necessary. They are never recalled.
- Some historians assert that all Military operations cease when Maj. Gen. Nathanael Greene sends the Continentals home in May. Others say the NC units remain vigilant until the end of the year. Pensioners later assert they were on active duty as late as June of 1783.
- On September 3rd, the Treaty of Paris is signed and the War is over.

enlisted for at least three years or preferably for the duration of the war. Since North Carolina's legislature has recently only required new recruits to enlist for a maximum of eighteen months, Maj. Gen. Nathanael Greene is given the option–retain those you want, send home the rest. In December of 1782, he sends home all North Carolina Continentals except for one regiment.

The following known captains remain in service and are active during the remaining time in 1783:

Captains Active in 1783	Regiment as of 11/10/1782
Peter Bacot	1st NC Regiment
Alexander Brevard	3rd NC Regiment
Benjamin Andrew Coleman	2nd NC Regiment
Joshua Hadley	1st NC Regiment
Clement Hall	2nd NC Regiment
William Lytle	4th NC Regiment
Robert Raiford	2nd NC Regiment
Joseph Thomas Rhodes	4th NC Regiment
Anthony Sharpe	4th NC Regiment

Most evidence indicates that Lt. Col. Archibald Lytle commands the North Carolina Regiment during 1783, but some sources assert that he is forced to retire at the end of 1782. Most consider this final regiment to be the last incarnation of the 1st NC Regiment. Others could care less.

On January 5th, Maj. Gen. Nathanael Greene writes from his new headquarters in Charlestown to Gov. Alexander Martin:

"In consequence of an enclosed copy of a Resolution of Congress and from the difficulty of clothing and feeding the troops in the Southern Department, I have sent home all those belonging to your state, except one complete regiment... I have directed the officers marching home the troops to furlough the men until your futher orders." [minor edits]

Although available records are not complete, the following known officers either elect, or are forced, to retire effective January 1, 1783:

Rank	Name	Last Regiment
Colonel	Thomas Clark	1st NC Regiment
"	John Patten	2nd NC Regiment
Lt. Colonel	John Armstrong	4th NC Regiment
"	Hardy Murfree	2nd NC Regiment
Major	John Nelson	1st NC Regiment
Captain	Thomas Armstrong	Sumner's Aide-de-Camp
"	William Armstrong	3rd NC Regiment
"	Benjamin Bailey	3rd NC Regiment
"	Kedar Ballard	3rd NC Regiment
"	George "Gee" Bradley	3rd NC Regiment
"	Samuel Budd	2nd NC Regiment
"	John Campbell	4th NC Regiment
"	John Craddock	2nd NC Regiment
"	John Daves	3rd NC Regiment
"	Tilghman Dixon	1st NC Regiment
"	Thomas Evans	4th NC Regiment
"	William Fawn	3rd NC Regiment
Captain/Paymaster	Robert Flounder	2nd NC Regiment
Captain	John Ingles	2nd NC Regiment
"	Samuel Jones	1st NC Regiment
"	John McNees	3rd NC Regiment
"	James Mills	4th NC Regiment
"	Joseph Montford	3rd NC Regiment
"	Elijah Moore	4th NC Regiment
"	James Pearl	1st NC Regiment
"	Jesse Read	2nd NC Regiment
"	William Saunders	4th NC Regiment
"	James Scurlock	4th NC Regiment
"	William Walton	1st NC Regiment
"	Edward Yarborough	3rd NC Regiment

There is conflicting information about Lt. Col. Selby Harney, Maj. Thomas Hogg, and Capt. Robert Fenner–some sources say all are forced to retire on 1/1/1783, whereas other sources indicate they are active until mid-1783.

The official rolls found in *The State Records of North Carolina* and other similar sources indicate that many soldiers "deserted" in early 1783, mostly during May and June. However, the men who survived long enough to apply for a federal pension as early as 1818 claim that they were "properly furloughed" by their captains in May and June of 1783. Several men claim that they were "discharged" as late as October 1, 1783, some say as late as August 1, 1783, but again, most claim they were "furloughed" during May and June of 1783.

On January 5th, Maj. Gen. Nathanael Greene writes a second letter to Governor Alexander Martin:

> "Your letter of the 17th of November containing charges against Captain [Robert] Raiford, who I ordered immediately to attend your summons, I have received, but from its being recommended by Lt. Colonel Lytle and others that the arrival of your letter was too late to afford time for him to go to Wilmington before the court would rise, I permitted him to continue with the army... Upon inquiry into the matter I hope your Excellency will find his conduct far less blamable than it has been represented to you, but be that as it may, he shall be forthcoming at any time you may think proper, if the proposed is not agreeable." [minor edits]

It is alleged that Capt. Robert Raiford burst into the Bladen County Court House at the head of thirty men in September of 1782. He attacked an attorney, Archibald MacLaine, with his sword, for defending a Loyalist who was on trial that day. The mob beat the court clerk for no apparent reason and then moved the riot out into the street. After electing "field officers," the mob marched around the county apprehending Loyalists without any orders from a higher commanding officer. A warrant was issued for Capt. Raiford's arrest, but he had returned to Maj. Gen. Greene's army where he had been put in command of the light infantry. A year later, Capt. Robert Raiford is brought to trial, and he is acquitted.

On February 2nd, Maj. Gen. Nathanael Greene writes to Brig. Gen. Jethro Sumner, who is at home in Warren County:

> "I have written to Lieut. Col. [Hardy] Murfree to let him know that I have no objection, if his private affairs require it, to his being put upon the half pay establishment. I suppose he is apprised of a late resolution of Congress, by which officers in his situation are precluded from the right of ever being called into service hereafter. Were there any probability of active scenes I should be anxious to have your services in this army, but from the situation of your line, and the probable inactivity of the army for some time to come, from the expense you must incur, and

as I am sensible your private concerns must call for your attention, after having been so long engaged in public business, I have no objection to your continuing in North Carolina, where you can superintend the recruiting service, & your own private concerns at the same time." [minor edits]

That same week, things get interesting in North Carolina. On February 7th, Governor Alexander Martin writes from his home at Danbury, NC to Maj. Gen. Nathanael Greene in South Carolina:

"I have the pleasure to say that on the 29th ultimo Lord Charles Montague was conducted into this state as a prisoner of war, with his son and four other British officers... His lordship is very uneasy in his present situation and requests to be paroled to New York; this I have declined, and have informed him that I must first consult you on a representation made to me by some officers and other gentlemen of character that the regiment lately raised for his Lordship's command was chiefly composed of captive soldiers of the Virginia and North Carolina Continental Lines, being compelled to enlist into the British service under his Lordship's direction on the severest penalties." [minor edits]

Also interesting is the fact that it takes Maj. Gen. Nathanael Greene over six weeks to pen a response to Governor Martin, and on March 28th, he writes:

"Your letter of February 16th [?] giving an account of Lord Charles Montague's being a prisoner at Wilmington was handed me at the beginning of this month and I would have given it an early answer; but before it came to hand Lord Charles was paroled at large, with permission to go to New York. I could not recall what had been granted. I made enquiry into the complaint against Lord Charles and find that he did enlist American soldiers into the British service but the conditions on which they engaged show it to be a voluntary act... I understand your state have some heavy cannon lying useless in your state. Will you be so obliging as to lend them to this state or a part of them." [minor edits]

On May 5th, Governor Alexander Martin writes to the North Carolina General Assembly,

"In the last letter from General Greene, now before you, I am requested to furnish the state of South Carolina with cannon at Edenton, on loan or purchase; in either case they will be gladly received by that state. You will please to signify your pleasure respecting those Guns, that I may communicate the same to General Greene."

The North Carolina General Assembly gathers in Hillsborough on April 18th, and it is clear that their focus is now on peacetime projects. Two new counties are established in what would later become the state of Tennessee–Davidson and Greene–and both are named for men the state admires greatly. Almost like "parting shots," the legislature does pass two new Acts on behalf of the state's Continental Line.

On May 16th, the General Assembly passes "An Act for emitting One Hundred Thousand Pounds in Paper Currency…and advancing to the Continental officers and soldiers part of their pay and substance…" Among other considerations, this Act provides that "any officer or soldier who is, or hath been, of the continental line of this state, and have demands against the same for services, shall be intitled to have and receive from the commissioners…"

On May 17th, the General Assembly passes "An Act for the relief of the Officers and Soldiers of the Continental Line, and for other purposes." This Act provides instructions on how each Continental soldier "shall on application being made to the Secretary of the State, obtain and receive from him a warrant of survey for such quantities of land" as each solider is entitled to. No warrant is to be issued before October 1st, and each soldier must secure their assigned lands within three years thereafter.

The military life in Charlestown is slowly winding down. The rank and file, mostly stationed on James Island, is often exercised on the drill field, that is, when they are not digging out stumps or repairing their huts. Off-duty officers often go into the city for relaxation. In rotation, officers also dine with Maj. Gen. Nathanael Greene at the home of South Carolina Gov. John Rutledge, Greene's headquarters. He later writes that the local politicians have grown so jealous of the military that he fears "we shall starve or feed ourselves by force."

On April 23rd, Maj. Gen. Greene finally receives official news of last November's provisional treaty signed in Paris. His army, which includes men from the Pennsylvania, Maryland, South Carolina, and North Carolina Continental lines celebrate with a "grand review," followed by a feast, fireworks, and dances. A number of the elite in Charlestown come to James Island to join in the festivities.

As expected, with this joyous news Greene's army grows restless. In early May, the 1st Regiment of Virginia Cavalry ride home. Around the first of June, the Maryland Continentals threaten to leave. Soon, grumbling is heard from all remaining troops in South Carolina. The 476 men of the North Carolina Regiment remain comparatively quiet, although 22 men are reported to have deserted between April and May.

On June 26th, Maj. Gen. Greene receives a resolution from the Continental Congress–go ahead and furlough all troops as quickly as possible and place all military stores in appropriate magazines. The remaining North Carolina Continentals begin their relatively-short march northward. The end comes quietly; there is only a gradual disappearance of the few remaining soldiers, mostly from South Carolina. There are no more grand parades or twenty-one gun salutes.

The final treaty between the United States and Great Britain is signed on September 3rd in Paris. By then, the Southern Army is dissolved and Maj. Gen. Nathanael Greene is marching homeward. He stops in Wilmington on August 11th, and the townfolk honor him with bonfires and the firing of guns. After staying much longer than he really wants, he resumes his ride northward on August 24th, escorted by Maj. Reading Blount. At every stop along the way in North Carolina, including Tarborough and Halifax, he is lavishly entertained.

Chapter Ten – After the War

There are no precise records available to provide us with the exact number of men who participated in the North Carolina Continental Line, and the scant rolls and other lists that have been handed down over the past two centuries contain so many errors that they are merely a starting point for historians to employ, as they deem appropriate. With that said, there are fairly-decent estimates as to the number of North Carolina Continental soldiers killed, wounded, and taken prisoner over the course of the eight-year war. Certainly, better records exist for known officers than for non-commissioned officers and for private soldiers.

In 1908, historian Samuel A'Court Ashe, in his *History of North Carolina–Volume I–1584 to 1783*, provides his painstakingly detailed estimate of the number of North Carolina Continental soldiers whereby he ends up with the number of 8,800. Based upon all other available evidence, such as survivor pension applications and consolidating available rolls that have survived history, Ashe's estimate must be considered to be reasonable and fairly accurate.

During the war, the North Carolina General Assembly is petitioned many times by wounded survivors and widows of men killed for financial assistance after the fact. In most instances these requests are granted and very nominal compensations are provided. When these requests are made in late 1782 and early 1783, the state's financial situation is extremely dire and the General Assembly can only offer twenty to thirty barrels of corn to help each of those in need.

As mentioned earlier herein, the state of North Carolina provides several legislative Acts to assist her soldiers financially over the course of the war, but the state never passes a comprehensive pension program. In 1780, the state does, however, offer each Continental soldier a bounty of land in the western section of the state–in what is today Tennessee. This Act is extended in 1782 and more specifics are included:

Rank	# of Acres Authorized
Major General	25,000
Brigadier General	12,000
Colonel / Chaplain	7,200
Lieutenant Colonel	5,760
Major / Surgeon	4,800
Captain	3,840
Subaltern / Surgeon's Mate	2,560
Non-Commissioned Officer	1,000
Privates / Fifers / Drummers	640

A special provision in the previously-mentioned 1780 law soon causes problems for the Continental soldiers. Under the 1780 Act, inhabitants already living in the area set aside as the military district are allowed to remain and apply for grants as one would in any of the state's other counties. Unfortunately for the soldiers, the area set aside for bounty land claims contains many inhabitants and a small amount of cultivable land. In 1783, the North Carolina General Assembly attempts to alleviate this problem by passing a law that sets aside another tract of land for the men who have served in the Continental Line. Paragraph VII of this Act reserves a tract of land in the sparsely populated area of present-day north-central Tennessee and sets the boundaries of the new Military District as follows:

> "Beginning at the Virginia Line where Cumberland River intersects the same, thence south fifty-five miles, thence west to the Tennessee River, thence down the Tennessee to the Virginia Line, thence with the said Virginia Line east to the beginning."

The law establishes allotments of land, on a proportional scale, for any soldier who serves less than three years. Although the General Assembly gives preference to men who served at least two and a half years, a claim can be made on service of at least two years. The legislature appoints Colonel Martin Armstrong, of the Surry County Regiment of Militia, as chief surveyor for the Military District bounty lands.

The 1782 Act appoints three commissioners, Absalom Tatom, Isaac Shelby, and Anthony Bledsoe, any two of whom are to examine and superintend the laying off of the land allotted to the soldiers. Prior to this appointment, Tatom had served in the North Carolina House of Commons and was also a Lieutenant and a Captain of the 1st NC Regiment. Later he would serve as an Auditor for Hillsborough District in settling Revolutionary War claims. Isaac Shelby was a Colonel and Commandant of the Sullivan County Regiment of Militia, and had participated in many battles and skirmishes during the war, including the battle of Kings Mountain. Anthony Bledsoe, a surveyor by profession, had lived in the western lands since around 1760, had established outposts on the Holston River, and represented Sullivan County in the 1782 North Carolina General Assembly. He had also earlier been a Major, a Lt. Colonel, and in 1783, the Colonel and Commandant of the newly-created Davidson County–the county designated for all Continenal soldier land bounties.

The law empowers the commissioners to appoint surveyors and chain carriers to lay off the Military District and to hire a guard for the surveying team. Finally, the law places limits on the number of men employed in each capacity. As payment for their services, these men are also to receive land in the following manner:

Position	Number	Allotment
Commissioner	3	5,000 acres each
Surveyor	1-3	2,000 acres each
Chain Carrier/Marker/Hunter	6 or less	640 acres each
Guards	100 or less	320 acres each

In 1784, the North Carolina General Assembly establishes a land office in Nashville for the registration of bounty land warrants and again selects Martin Armstrong to head that office. His duties include hiring the surveyors and returning the completed surveys to the Secretary of State. William Polk, William Terrell Lewis, and Stockley Donelson are elected by the legislature as surveyors for the middle, western, and eastern districts respectively. Donelson and Lewis, along with William Terrell, a clerk in James Glasgow's office and uncle to William Terrell Lewis, soon become central figures in speculation in the Military District.

To secure a claim in the bounty land district, a soldier first receives a warrant from the Secretary of State–James Glasgow–based on proof of his length of service. Upon receiving his warrant, the soldier delivers it, in person, to the land office in Nashville. Martin Armstrong then appoints a surveyor to locate, survey, and plot the appropriate amount of land. The completed plats are then returned to the Secretary of State. James Glasgow then prepares a grant for the governor's signature, which is witnessed by Glasgow himself, or Willoughby Williams, a Deputy Secretary of State who is also Glasgow's son-in-law. Once signed and sealed, the soldier has a completed grant for land in the Military District.

Variations in this process eventually cause problems. One issue is the verification of a soldier's service. Instead of proving his service or having the Secretary of State prove service by checking vouchers and muster rolls, former officers can produce a list of former soldiers. Officers prove to be the most qualified to know service records, and such lists often give a soldier's length of service and provide other information, such as death, wounds, promotions, capture, or discharge. These lists, instead of a soldier's individual affidavit of service, can then be submitted to the Secretary of State's office. The men named on the lists, their heirs, or assignees now have the proof of service to claim bounty land warrants. The process of producing such lists is later abused as unscrupulous speculators coerce drunken officers to sign lengthy lists.

Another issue is the ability of a soldier or his heirs to assign warrants to others. Many men, released from service without adequate food, clothing, or pay, quickly sell their rights to these lands for a paltry sum. Assignments constitute one such method by which a soldier or his heirs can sell their right to the land. Through this process, a person obtains a warrant and assigns or sells it to whomever he chooses. The remote location of the bounty land district discourages many people from claiming their grants. A lack of money also persuades some soldiers to use their land rights for settling debts. Those who receive warrants but choose not to travel such a distance often assign their warrants to others. This ability to assign land later aids greedy land speculators in the area.

To assign this land bounty, a soldier or his heirs endorse the warrant to another interested person. Warrants are often assigned several times before the land is finally surveyed. A typical assignment reads:

Mr. James Glasgow, Secretary of State
I have received of "Name Surname" valuable and full consideration for my Right, Title, Interest & Claim in and to the land within mentioned to whom you will please issue the Grant accordingly - May 23d 1784
Name Surname2
Witness
Name Surname3

Many of these assignments, however, are forged.

It is not until 1796 that Andrew Jackson, then a United States Congressman, accidentally discovers wholesale frauds in the land office, and he claims that these frauds involve Martin Armstrong, James Glasgow, and most likely also Governor John Sevier of the newly-formed state of Tennessee. Andrew Jackson lays his findings before North Carolina Governor Samuel Ashe, who immediately sends a request to Governor Sevier to forward all records of Martin Armstrong's office to him in Raleigh for investigation–but, Governor Sevier refuses.

While a North Carolina General Assembly committee begins investigating the matter, the papers and books of James Glasgow are stored in the Comptroller's office for that committee's use. This office is soon broken into and a large chest and trunk containing incriminating evidence are stolen. The robbery, however, is stopped and most of the papers are recovered. All of the robbers, except for one slave, manage to escape.

Back in Nashville, a group of deeply-involved land speculators meet in the home of William Blount to review plans to prevent implication of Governor John Sevier–these include three Blount brothers, Stockley

Donelson, and William Tyrrell. William Tyrrell is dispatched to Raleigh to attempt another theft of the incriminating papers, and in case of failure, to burn the State House in which they are deposited. This plot is betrayed to Judges John McNairy and Howell Tatum of Tennessee, the latter who sends an express rider to inform Governor Samuel Ashe, who foils the plot by doubling the guards in the Comptroller's office. The committee is soon able to reveal "one of the most comprehensive records of fraud and land thievery in the history of public lands."

With an Act of the General Assembly backing him, the new Governor William Richardson Davie, in 1799, commissions John Willis of Robeson County and Francis Locke of Rowan County to go to Tennessee and obtain from Governor John Sevier the books and papers related to this case. Should Governor Sevier refuse to relinquish them, they are then to remain in Tennessee and make exact copies "carefully transcribing them from their face original entries, interlineations, erasures by blotting or strokes of the pen." Willis and Locke reach Nashville on April 20th and immediately go to see the governor.

The North Carolina commissioners, "strongly & properly urged the right of the State," but Governor John Sevier replies that, "it is not in his power, nor is he at liberty to comply." The following day, Governor Sevier announces that he needs his state's legislature to decide the matter. Willis and Locke then propose that they simply transcribe a copy, and Governor Sevier "readily agrees."

The books have not only been "abused and worn by time and use, so as to be in many parts obliterated and unintelligible," but there are "the Most Atrocious frauds." In the first book of locations, which is "in a Mangled State Sewed Together," many names have been entirely erased and others inserted in their place. They also discover that persons have been allowed to file a number of locations, without names, with a blank left to be filled in later. Another method of "a most scandalous nature" is the removal of about 150 pages involving about 500 false claims of the first book.

This arduous task of transcription, with the assistance of three young men, is completed on July 13th and deposited in the office of the Secretary of State in Raleigh on August 2, 1799. On the basis of six categories of fraudulent practices, the commissioners conclude that "much injury had been suffered & done in the office in Nashville by neglect and want of judgement in those who superintend'd it, as by frauds & design; that many individuals have and will be injured and deprived of their rights by the irregularities of these books."

Governor Davie calls a meeting of his Council of State for their advice. After much deliberation, this august group can only recommend that the governor bring the evidence to the General Assembly, which will not convene until November, when Davie is already on his way to France as the new ambassador under President John Adams.

The General Assembly brings the matter into the court system in June of 1800. Not only is the long-time Secretary of State, James Glasgow, involved, but also the great criminal lawyer and jurist, John Haywood, cousin of State Treasurer John Haywood. The attorney Haywood seals his political future in the state by resigning from the Superior Court bench to handle the defense of James Glasgow for a fee of $1,000.

Samuel A'Court Ashe, in his *History of North Carolina,* later describes, "Seldom has a trial so greatly shocked public attention–the chief defendant was a public character whose long career had until this period been marked with particular excellence and now, singularly enough, defenced by one who had with unusual luster worn the judicial ermine, while the issues were of the highest concern to the people of the state."

Despite John Haywood's able defense, James Glasgow is convicted and fined £2,000; the slave who attempted to burn the State House is executed, and all others managed, somehow, to escape punishment. This relatively mild punishment of Glasgow, and the failure to fully convict all other offenders, remains as one of the blackest spots in the Old North State's history.

In later pension applications, many men of the "rank and file" assert that they have applied for and are granted their bounty lands, and they soon learn that their new property is essentially worthless pine barrens. It is a fact that the officers are assigned the choicest of all lands, and many North Carolina Continental officers move to their new lands and many become noteworthy men in the creation of the new state of Franklin and eventually the state of Tennessee.

North Carolina never establishes a formal pension program primarily because of its sad financial state of affairs, but also because the legislators truly feel that the bounty land is the only way the state can afford to assist their men in arms. They are also keenly aware of all proceedings that transpire at the Federal level, even as early as 1776.

The first national pension law, on August 26, 1776, promises half pay for life or during disability to every officer, soldier, or sailor losing a limb in any engagement, or being so disabled in the service of the United States as to render him incapable of earning a livelihood. Proportionate relief is promised to those who are only partially disabled. However, the Continental Congress is without money or real executive power, and is obliged to trust execution of this Act to the individual states.

General George Washington is a strong advocate of a "half pay and pensionary establishment." On January 28, 1778, during the hard winter at Valley Forge, he sends to Congress a gloomy account. He says that, on the part of his officers, there are frequent resignations. To reanimate the languishing zeal of the officers he urges Congress to pass half pay and pensions:

> "This would not only dispel the apprehension of personal distress at the termination of the war, from having thrown themselves out of professions and employments they might not have it in their power to resume; but would in a great degree relieve the painful anticipation of leaving their widows and orphans, a burthen on the charity of the country, should it be their lot to fall in its defense."

As a result of Gen. Washington's appeal, after several weeks of deliberation, the Continental Congress, on May 15, 1778, unanimously votes to all commissioned officers, who shall continue in the service of the United States until the end of the war, half pay for seven years after its conclusion. On August 24, 1780, this resolution is modified to extend the half pay priveleges to widows or orphan children of such officers who have died while in service to their country. This is the first national pension law on behalf of widows and orphans. The Continental Congress recommends to the state legislatures to make the necessary payments on behalf of the United States of America.

On October 21, 1780, the Continental Congress extends the half pay for life instead of for just seven years. This decision causes many states to object since the money is essentially coming from them. On April 23, 1782, a provision is made for the sick and wounded–any found unfit for duty in the field or in garrison are to receive a discharge and a pension in the amount of five dollars per month. The states are to discharge such pensions annually, and to draw upon the Superintendent of Finance for the money advanced.

Compelled by a critical state of affairs, on March 22, 1783, nine states vote in favor of commutation of the half pay for life to five years full pay, in money, or in securities bearing interest at six percent per annum, as Congress shall find most convenient. This resolution, known as the Commutation Act, gives great satisfaction to the army. The remaining four states fight this law for a year, but their issues eventually subside.

On June 7, 1785, the Congress of the Confederation adopts a resolve to uniformly provide for invalid pensioners. Commissioned officers, so disabled as to be wholly incapable of earning a livelihood, are to be allowed a half pay pension. Non-commissioned officers and privates are provided a fixed five dollars per month pension.

On June 11, 1788, the Congress of the Confederation passes its last resolution on the subject of invalid pensions:

"That no person shall be entitled to a pension as an invalid who has not, or shall not before the expiration of six months from this time, make application therefor, and produce the requisite certificates and evidence to entitle him thereto."

In September of 1789, the first Congress under the new Federal Constitution provides for the continuance by the United States of the pensions which, under Congressional authority, have been granted and paid by the states to Revolutionary invalids. In 1790, the United States also undertakes the payment of certain arrears to March 4, 1789, due to Revolutionary pensioners, and unpaid through the neglect or refusal of the states to act.

In March of 1792, there are 1,358 non-commissioned officers and privates on the general pension list, none of whom receive more than five dollars per month. The entire number of invalid pensioners at that point in time is 1,472. These numbers include men from all states.

On March 23, 1792, Congress enacts a general pension law, but it is not to last very long since it is repealed. Its only significance is found in the fact that it furnishes the first occasion for a disagreement between Congress and the Judiciary as to their respective powers under the Federal Constitution. Congress yielded to a contention of the Judiciary by passing the act of February 28, 1793, which repealed the objectional sections of the 1792 act and established new regulations. All evidence relative to invalids is to be taken upon oath before the judge of the district in which the invalid resided, or before any three persons commissioned by the judge.

Between 1793 and 1803, no significant modifications to existing Revolutionary War pension laws are made. The most important change in 1803 is the endowment of the Secretary of War with the power of final decision in the allowance of claims. A supplementary Act of March 3, 1805 extends benefits to those who, in consequence of known wounds received in the military service during the Revolution, have at any period since the war become and continued disabled so as to render them unable to procure a subsistence by manual labor.

Invalid pension legislation on behalf of soldiers of the Revolution reaches its most comprehensive form in the Act of April 10, 1806 and supplementary provisions. This liberal law repeals all former enactments, and from the date of passage it becomes the fundamental provision upon which the claims of such invalids are thereafter based. It does not affect pensions already granted, however. This Act adds a provision for all volunteers, Militia, and State Troops, who have received wounds in the line of duty. Desertion is now a question.

On April 25, 1808, an Act directs the Secretary of War to place on the pension list of the United States all persons who remain on the pension lists of any of the states. This completes the assumption by the United States of the payment of all Revolutionary War invalid pensioners in all states. This Act expires in 1812, but is extended for another six years on April 25, 1812. It is extended again for one year on May 15, 1820, and for six years each by the Acts of February 4, 1822 and May 24, 1828.

On April 24, 1816, Congress approves a pay increase for all ranks of men receiving pensions. A private is increased from $5 to $8 per month. Pensions for 1st Lieutenants and all officers of lower rank receive another $3 per month, as well.

A new principle is introduced into national pension legislation by the enactment of the Revolutionary Service Pension Law of March 18, 1818. In his message of December, 1817, President James Monroe recommends to Congress some provision for the indigent survivors of the Revolutionary army, of whom he thought there are but a few. Some within Congress want a pure service pension law, whereas others advocated a measure based upon "service and poverty." No one has a clue about what numbers they might be facing.

The Act that ultimately passes provides that every person who had served in the Revolutionary War until its close, or for the term of nine months or longer at any period of the war, on the Continental establishment or in the navy, and who as a resident citizen of the United States, and is by reason of his reduced circumstances in life, "in need of assistance from his country for support," shall receive a pension. Officers start at $20 per month; non-commissioned officers and privates reveive $8 per month—all for the duration of their natural lives. Pensions, if allowed, commence from the date of the applicant's declaration.

The entire country is soon surprised and also quite indignant about the numbers who quickly apply for this federal pension. By the middle of September, the number of applications is so great that it is not possible to process them all. Flagrant abuses are the subject of severe comments in many of the nation's newspapers of 1818.

At the first session of the Sixteenth Congress in December of 1819, the question of pension fraud demands and receives attention. Many simply want to repeal the Act of 1818, but this is quickly determined to be inexpedient. Public indignation at exposures of fraud and abuses lead Congress to enact remedial legislation on May 1, 1820. This Act requires pensioners–all before and all to come–to submit sworn schedules of their whole estate and income, exclusive of personal clothing and bedding. They are also required to take an oath that they have not disposed of any part of their property with the intention of bringing themselves within the provision of the law, and that they have not in person or in trust property or income of any kind other than that shown in the schedules subscribed by them.

The Act of 1820 causes the names of thousands of pensioners to be stricken from the rolls. Many of those who apply for a continuance suffer a rejection of their claims without hope of favorable action and are consequently dropped.

On March 1, 1823, Congress passes an Act that provides for the restoration to the pension list of those persons who have been dropped on account of the evidence afforded by their schedules of property, but have since become so reduced in circumstances as to need a pension.

The pension business is now so extensive and cumbersome that Congress finally abandons the attempt to participate in the detailed administration of general laws. They grant all powers to the Secretary of War.

In his message of December 1827, President John Quncy Adams recommends to Congress that they consider "the debt, rather of justice than gratitude, of the surviving warriors of the Revolutionary War." They pass an Act on May 15, 1828 granting full pay for life, beginning on March 3, 1826, to the surviving Revolutionary officers in the Continental Line, who have been entitled to half pay for life by the resolution of October 21, 1780. The same allowance is also made for non-commissioned officers and soldiers who enlisted for the war and also served until its end, and thereby become entitled to receive the reward of $80 promised by the resolution of May 15, 1778. All beneficiaries under this Act are required to give up other pensions which they might be receiving under the laws of the United States, but, under later amendments, are permitted to retain invalid pensions.

The Act of 1828 is not at first regarded as an ordinary pension law, and it is executed by the Secretary of the Treasury. In 1835, this function is transferred to the Secretary of War. By the end of 1828, it is estimated that about 850 men have been allowed full pay for life.

Around 1830, the rapid retirement of the public debt brings about a considerable surplus in the United States Treasury. President Andrew Jackson, in his December, 1829 message, suggests the extension of the benefits of the pension laws to all Revolutionary War soldiers who are unable to maintain themselves in comfort. Not everyone agrees. After two years of debate and arm-twisting, Congress passes an Act on June 7, 1832, probably the most important Act passed for Revolutionary War pensions.

This Act grants to all who had completed, at one or more terms, a total service of two years during the Revolutionary War, whether in the Continental Line or State Troops, volunteers, or Militia, or in the navy, and who are not entitled to any benefit under the Act of May 15, 1828, full pay for life according to rank, not to exceed a captain's pay, to commence from March 4, 1831. All who had completed a total service of not less than six months are to receive for life an annuity bearing the same proporation to the amount granted those who had served the full two years.

The Secretary of the Treasury is originally charged with the execution of the act of 1832, but this duty is transferred to the Secretary of War in a resolution dated June 28, 1832. Evidence in support of claims is taken in the form of declarations upon oath before a court of record in the county where the applicant resides. The lack of authentic rolls necessitates, in the consideration of a large number of applications, entire reliance in so far as a man's narrative of service can be compared with the known events of the period of the alleged service. Much importance is attached to traditionary evidence, such as a general belief in the man's neighborhood that the claimant had truly been a Revolutionary soldier. This is also to be established by evidence from a nearby clergyman and other persons of character and standing in the community.

In the fall of 1834, most startling frauds under the 1832 Act come to light. Numerous indictments for perjury and forgery in the prosecution of pension claims are found at a session of the federal court in western Virginia, and men of the accused are said to have fled to Texas. Similar stories come from Vermont, Kentucky, and New York.

On July 4, 1836, Congress passes an Act that provides if any Revolutionary War soldier who would have been entitled to a pension under the Act of 1832, had died, leaving a widow whose marriage took place before the expiration of his last period of service, such widow, so long as she remained unmarried, shall be entitled to receive the pension which might have been allowed to her husband, if living at the time the Act was passed. This Act of 1836 is the first of many laws for the benefit of Revolutionary War widows. These grow more and more liberal as the years pass.

The Act of April 1, 1864 grants $100 additional annual pension to each of the surviving soliders of the Revolution then on the pension rolls. By November of that year, seven of the number who are intended recipients of this special award have died at an average age of about one hundred years, and but five are still living. For the benefit of these five, Congress passes the private Act of February 27, 1865, granting each of them a gratuity of $300 annually during his natural life, in addition to their existing pension payments.

By June 30, 1867, all Revolutionary War soldiers on the pension rolls have died, but during the following year, two other Revolutionary War soldiers are pensioned by special Act at $500 per annum. Daniel F. Bakeman, the last survivor, dies on April 5, 1860. On June 30, 1869, the names of 887 Revolutionary War widows are still on the pension rolls.

In 1874, the Commissioner of Pensions, J. H. Baker, reports that a total of 289,715 soldiers served during the Revolutionary War. Of this number, 57,623 filed for pensions–less than 20 percent. 20,485 filed under the 1818 Act; 1,200 filed under the 1828 Act; 33,425 filed under the 1832 Act; and the remainder [2,513] filed under minor and special Acts. Under the general laws from July 4, 1836 to June 30, 1874, 39,295 Revolutionary War widows are pensioned. Of these, 5,446 were married prior to the end of the war; 28,837 were married prior to 1794; 1,242 were married between 1794 and 1800; and, 3,750 were married after 1800.

As mentioned earlier in the Preface, North Carolina contributed approximately 8,800 men to the Continental Line, and only about 10%-15% of those survived until 1818 (or afterwards) AND bothered to apply for a federal pension. Most officers accepted the half-pay pension at the end of the war, which grew to full pay in 1826 if they were still alive, so there are even less than 10% of the officers who bothered to apply for a federal pension, which occurred prior to 1826 in most cases.

Most of the Continental non-commissioned officers and privates (and fifers, and drummers) who did apply for a federal pension in or after 1818 were approved. However, this was not the case for most widows who filed for her husband's pension in 1836–most simply could not prove their marriage, a heart-breaking situation caused by moving so far from North Carolina and having no documentation with them in their new home, be it in Kentucky, Ohio, or even Missouri.

Appendix A

**North Carolina Laws Pertaining to
The NC Continental Line
1778-1783
(There Were None 1775-1777)**

NC Laws Pertaining to the NC Continental Line
1778

Chapter I. An Act for raising Men to Compleat the Continental Battalions Belonging to this State (April 1778).

I. Whereas it is absolutely necessary that the continental Battalions belonging to this State be completed, and it is found impracticable to obtain that End in the common Mode of recruiting;

II. Be it therefore Enacted by the General Assembly of the State of North Carolina, and it is hereby Enacted by the Authority of the same, That Two Thousand Six Hundred and Forty Eight Men shall be raised and detached from the Militia of this State towards completing the same, in the following Proportion and Manner, viz. From the County of Craven Eighty-Six, Carteret Thirty, Beaufort Twenty-Six, Johnston Thirty-Four, Hyde Twenty-Eight, Dobbs One Hundred and Three, Pitt Thirty-Five, New Hanover Thirty-Two, Onslow Forty-Seven, Bladen Sixty-Three, Duplin Sixty-Two, Cumberland Seventy-Three, Brunswick Thirteen, Rowan One Hundred and Seventy-Four, Mecklenburg One Hundred, Tryon Eighty-Three, Anson Seventy-Eight, Surry Eighty-Eight, Guilford One Hundred and Fifty-Six, Burke Sixty-Two, Washington Sixty-Two, Wilkes Thirty-Five, Orange One Hundred, Granville Seventy, Wake Sixty, Chatham Sixty-Six, Caswell Seventy-Seven, Halifax Eighty-Six, Northampton Sixty-Two, Edgecombe Sixty-Three, Bute One Hundred and Five, Martin Thirty-Seven, Nash Fifty-Six, Chowan Thirty-Three, Perquimons Thirty-Three, Pasquotank Forty-Five, Currituck Fifty, Bertie Seventy-Six, Tyrrell Thirty-Four, Hertford Sixty-Two, and Camden Forty-One. And the Colonel or Commanding Officer in each County is hereby directed to order the Field Officers and Captains to his Regiment belonging to meet at the Court House on or before the Twenty-Fifth Day of May next, and the Field Officers and Captains shall then and there apportion the Men to be raised in the County to the several Companies, in Proportion to the Number of Militia, including Officers of every Rank, his Excellency the Governor only excepted, in each Company respectively, after deducting for such Militia Men only as shall have heretofore actually enlisted good and able bodied Men as regular Soldiers, or cause such to be enlisted, to serve in the Continental Army agreeable to the Act passed in May One Thousand Seven Hundred and Seventy Seven, for encouraging the recruiting Service, which said enlistments they shall prove by their own Oath, and the Testimony of an indifferent Person, to be obtained without Fraud or Collusion in due Time, and without the Procurement of Assistance of any Continental Officer or Soldier, and the commanding Officer in each and every County shall, within Five Days after such Meeting, order a General Muster at the Place or Places by Law appointed, and he is hereby authorized to offer a Bounty of One Hundred Dollars to every able bodied Man who shall voluntarily enter into the Service, and if a sufficient Number of Volunteers do not turn out, then the several Companies shall immediately proceed to determine by Ballot who shall go out of each Company, to make up its particular Quota; and the Persons so voted in shall go themselves, or provide able bodied Men to serve in their Stead, and shall be entitled to a Bounty of Fifty Dollars each.

III. And be it further Enacted, by the Authority aforesaid, That if any Company shall refuse to appear and ballot agreeable to this Act, that in that Case the Field Officers shall point out the Men who shall serve. Provided, That it shall not be lawful to vote for any

Person who shall produce Certificates of having actually enlisted regular Soldiers, by themselves, or some others for them, to serve in the Continental Army, agreeable to the Act passed in May One Thousand Seven Hundred and Seventy Seven, for encouraging the recruiting Service, if such Certificates were granted and obtained fairly and without Fraud, and the Men whose Names are therein mentioned were actually enlisted by or on Account of the Persons claiming such Exemptions, the Proof thereof made agreeable to the Directions of this Act.

IV. And be it further Enacted, by the Authority aforesaid, That each and every Person who shall voluntarily enter or be voted into the Service as aforesaid, shall be entitled to have and receive from the commanding Officer of the County a Pair of Shoes and Stockings, two Shirts, a Hunting Shirt, Waistcoat with Sleeves, a Pair of Breeches and Trousers, a Hat and a Blanket, and Five Yards of Tent Cloth; and every Six Men shall be entitled to have and receive from the said commanding Officer One Axe, and a Pot or Camp Kettle.

V. And in order to procure the Clothing aforementioned, Be it Enacted by the Authority aforesaid, That every Company shall furnish and provide One Pair of Shoes and Stockings, Two Shirts, a Hunting Shirt, a Waistcoat with Sleeves, a Pair of Breeches and Trousers, a Hat and a Blanket, Five Yards of Tent Cloth for each and every Man, and One Axe, and a Pot or Camp Kettle, for every six Men raised out of such Company respectively; and the said Articles shall be valued on Oath by Three Freeholders or Householders, who shall grant Certificates of Valuation to the Persons furnishing the same, which Certificates, with Receipts endorsed from the commanding Officer of the County for Delivery thereof, shall be received by the Taxgatherers in Part of Public Taxes: And if any Company shall fail to furnish its Quota of Clothing, Tent Cloth, Camp Kettles, and Axes, or any Part thereof, the commanding officer of the County shall have Power to cause so much of the property of any Person or Persons belonging to such Company, refusing to furnish his or their quota of the aforesaid Articles, to be seized and sold, as will procure the Clothing and other Articles wanted, and shall grant Certificates of the Amount, which shall also be received by the Taxgatherers in Part of Public Taxes.

VI. And be it further Enacted, by the Authority aforesaid, That the Brigadier Generals of each District shall take into their Possession, and distribute to the Troops so raised, such Guns as belong to the Public, and are good and sufficient; and in case there should not be Arms for every Man, then, and in that Case, the Colonel or commanding Officer of each County shall purchase Guns for the Men marching from the same, and shall give Certificates to those from whom the Guns are bought; which Certificates, countersigned by the Clerks of the respective Counties, shall be paid by the Treasurer of either District, and allowed in the Settlement of their Accounts with the Public.

VII. And be it Enacted, by the Authority aforesaid, That the Men who shall be raised in Manner aforesaid in the Districts of Halifax, Edenton, New Bern, and Wilmington, shall march to Halifax, and from thence to Petersburg in Virginia, and those who shall be raised in the Districts of Hillsborough and Salisbury, shall rendezvous at Peytonsburg in Pittsylvania, with all possible Expedition, under the command of such Continental Officer or Officers as the commanding officer in the Continental Service in this State shall appoint for that Purpose; and if there be none such appointed in any County then the commanding Officer of the Militia in such County shall appoint a Person to conduct the Men thereto belonging either to Halifax, or to Peytonsburg in Virginia, as the Case may require, there to be delivered to the Continental Officer appointed to receive them, and such Person shall be allowed Captain's Pay and Rations during the Time of his Employment; and the Men who shall be raised in Manner aforesaid, shall serve in the Continental Battalions of this State for the Space of Nine Months from the Time that they shall arrive at either of the Places aforesaid, unless sooner discharged, and shall be subject to the same Rules and Discipline and have the same Pay and Rations, as the Continental Troops, from the Day of their being voted in or enlisted.

VIII. And be it Enacted, by the Authority aforesaid, That in case any Person so voted in, or voluntarily entering as a Soldier agreeable to the Directions of this Act, shall fail to appear in due Time at the Place of general Rendezvous, or shall desert his Duty during the Time specified in this Act, such Person shall from thenceforward be held and deemed a Continental Soldier during the present War, and shall be liable to be taken as such; and every Person who shall voluntarily enlist, or be voted into the Service, in Consequence of this Act, and shall well and faithfully serve as a Soldier, agreeable to the true Intent and Meaning of this Act, shall be free and exempt from serving again as a Soldier for the Space of Three Years next after the Time of his procuring a Certificate of his having served as aforesaid. And if any Person shall harbor or conceal any of the Men who shall voluntarily enter or be voted into the Service as aforesaid, such Person, on Conviction thereof before any Justice of Peace in the County wherein the Offence shall be committed, shall be deemed a Continental Soldier, and shall be turned over by the said Justice to a Continental Officer, or committed to Gaol for that Purpose, and shall serve for Three Years, or during the War.

IX. And be it Enacted, by the Authority aforesaid, That the Captains of each and every Company shall return descriptive Lists of the Men raised in such Company, specifying the Name, Size, Age, Complexion and Occupation, of the Men so raised, and also the Name and Number of the Company from whence they were taken: And the said commanding Officer shall make two fair Copies of such descriptive Lists, one of which he shall deliver to the Continental or other Officer appointed to take Charge of the Men, and he shall take a Receipt for the Delivery of the Men on the other.

X. And be it further Enacted, That the Quakers, Dunkers, Moravians, and Menonists, shall furnish Men in Proportion to their respective Numbers in each County, and in Default thereof, the commanding officer of each and every County is hereby empowered to hire Men instead of the Men to be by them furnished, and by Warrant under his Hand, directed to the Sheriff of the County, to levy the Sum given for such Man or Men on the Goods and Chattels, Lands and Tenements, of any Person belonging to such Sect, as shall refuse or fail to find a Man or Men agreeable to this Act.

XI. And be it Enacted, by the Authority aforesaid, That the Men raised in the County of Rowan, and those raised in the County of Guilford, shall have the Liberty of electing two Captains for each County, and the Men raised in New Hanover County and Brunswick shall elect One Captain jointly; and in such Counties as raise more than Fifty Men, the Men so raised shall and may elect a Captain in every County, and in the Counties which raise a smaller Number than Fifty, the Men shall and may elect One Lieutenant for every County; and the Persons so elected, shall be commissioned accordingly by the Governor, and shall march and continue with their respective Companies, with the Rank of Militia, and the Pay and Rations of regular Captains and Lieutenants, during the Time of their continuing in Service.

XII. And be it Enacted, by the Authority aforesaid, That James Roper and William Shepherd be appointed Contractors for the District of Salisbury, Thomas Hart for the District of Hillsborough, to contract for and purchase Provisions, and issue them to the Men raised in the said Districts until their Arrival at Peytonsburg in Virginia; and that William Bennett be appointed for the District of Edenton, Hardy Bryan for the District of New Bern, Thomas Amis for the District of Wilmington, and William Amis for the District of Halifax, for the like Purposes, until the Men raised in the said District respectively shall arrive at Halifax, and then that William Amis be appointed to take Charge of all those who rendezvous at Halifax, and conduct them as far as Petersburg: And the said Contractors, and every of them, shall grant Certificates to the Owners for the Provisions by them respectively furnished, and shall have full Power to seize Provisions of every Kind from any Persons who shall or may have more Provisions than may be necessary for their own Use or Family Consumption, if the Owners shall refuse to sell the same, and shall grant Certificates as aforesaid; and the said Certificates shall be redeemed at the next Session of Assembly: And the said Contractors shall keep regular Accounts of their Disbursements or Purchases, and of all Certificates by them granted, that the Assembly may not be defrauded by Claimants, and may more easily settle with the said Contractors, who shall be allowed One Hundred and Twenty Dollars per Month for their Trouble, over and above all Sums of Money by them expended for the Purposes aforesaid.

XIII. And be it Enacted, by the Authority aforesaid, That the Colonel or commanding Officer of the Militia in each County be, and he is hereby empowered and required, to furnish the necessary Wagons and Carts for marching the Troops raised in such County, agreeable to the Militia Law.

XIV. And be it further Enacted, by the Authority aforesaid, That the Owners of said Wagons shall be allowed Forty Shillings per Day, and Forage and Shoes for their Horses, and every Cart the Sum of Twenty Shillings per Day, with Forage and Shoes for their Horses; and the said Wagons and Carts with Teams, before marching, shall be appraised by Three Freeholders, that in case of Loss or Death, the Owner may be paid for the same.

XV. And be it Enacted, by the Authority aforesaid, That the Continental Deputy Paymaster General be, and he is hereby directed to pay the Troops aforesaid; and that his Excellency the Governor be, and he is hereby empowered to grant Warrants on the Treasury to the said Paymaster for the necessary Sums, taking Security for due Application of the same.

NC Laws Pertaining to the NC Continental Line
1779

Third Session of 1778 (1/19/1779) Chapter II. An Act for Raising Forces for the Defence of this and the Neighbouring States and other purposes therein mentioned.

I. Whereas it is necessary for the support of this and the neighboring States that a force should be immediately embodied and marched to the seasonable relief of the Militia of this Government who are now in actual service and whose time of service will expire in the month of April next,

II. Be it therefore enacted by the General Assembly of this State, and by the authority of the same, that the Governor do immediately issue orders to the Colonels of the respective Counties, directing them to call a general Muster of the Militia of the several counties, and such Colonels are hereby empowered to enlist all such able-bodied men who will engage to serve this State for three months from the time of leaving the limits thereof, and shall pay as a bounty to all such able bodied volunteers the sum of three hundred dollars and such volunteers shall be further entitled to the daily pay and subsistence which the militia when in actual service are authorized to receive and shall be further entitled to draw upon the public Commissary daily and every day for a Gill of Spirits.

III. And be it further enacted that in case a sufficient number of volunteers cannot be had the Colonels of the respective Regiments shall direct drafts to be made in such manner and in such proportions as has been heretofore directed by the Law of this State for regulating the mode of drafts.

IV. And be it further enacted by the authority aforesaid that the Governor shall allot to each and every County of this State its respective proportion of fifteen hundred men, which proportion such County is hereby enjoined to furnish; and the Colonels of the respective regiments are empowered and directed to raise their proportionable number in the first Instance by the enlistment of volunteers as aforesaid and in case of their deficiency to complete the Quota by drafts and such drafted soldiers shall be entitled to a bounty of One Hundred and Fifty Dollars, the pay and subsistance of Militia and a Gill of Spirits; and such drafted soldier shall be bound to serve for three months from the time of leaving the limits of this State.

V. And be it further Enacted by the authority aforesaid, That the Governor shall immediately order the men commonly called nine-months men and heretofore raised by virtue of an act of Assembly of this State, to march immediately to join the army under the command of General [Benjamin] Lincoln.

VI. And whereas many persons lately drafted to march to the Southward to reinforce the army under General Lincoln, have failed or refused to march accordingly or after marching and continuing in service for some time have deserted and returned home, be it therefore enacted by the authority aforesaid that the Colonels or Commanding Officers in their respective Counties shall order all such persons to march agreeable to the orders issued by his Excellency the Governor, and if any person so ordered shall fail to comply, he shall be subject to the pains and penalties in such case by the Laws provided for regulating the militia of this State.

VII. And be it further Enacted by the authority aforesaid, that the volunteers and drafted men by this act directed to be raised shall be formed into two Regiments to be commanded by Militia officers and that the Field Officers and other Officers necessary for the command of one of the said Regiments shall be taken out of the Districts of Hillsborough and Salisbury, and the officers necessary for the other Regiments from the Districts of Halifax, Edenton, New Bern, and Wilmington agreeable to the Militia Law.

VIII. And be it further Enacted by the Authority aforesaid, That his Excellency the Governor be Directed to grant Warrants on the Treasurer's or either of them to the Colonels or Commanding Officers in their respective Counties for so much money as shall appear to him to be necessary to pay the bounty proposed and held out by this Act to Volunteers and Drafted men taking bond and security for faithfully applying and accounting for the same.

IX. And be it further Enacted by the authority aforesaid, that if any Colonel or commanding officer shall advance the bounty by this Act directed to be paid to the Volunteers and drafted men, such Colonel or Commanding Officer shall be entitled to receive the sum by him so advanced with six per centum Interest thereon out of the public Treasury on Settlement of his account with the General Assembly.

X. And be it further Enacted by the Authority aforesaid, That the Governor with the advice of the Counsel shall be empowered to order the drafted men and also the Volunteers hereby directed to be raised, to the Assistance of our neighboring State and without the limits of this Government whenever our own safety or the necessary defense of our neighboring States shall require.

XI. Provided always, That this Authority so invested in the Governor and Council of State shall not be considered longer to continue than during the term this act shall be in force and this act shall continue in force for the term of six months and no longer.

First Session (5/3/1779) Chapter I. An Act for Raising Regular Forces for the Defense of this and the Neighboring States, and for other purposes.

I. Be it Enacted by the General Assembly of the State of North Carolina, and it is hereby Enacted by the Authority of the same, That any ten of the Militia, who shall, on or before the 1st day of July next, enlist one able bodied man into the Continental service for the space of eighteen months, or a longer period, they shall during the time of such enlistment be cleared from all military duties or drafts whatsoever, except when this state shall be invaded, or in case of domestic insurrection; but to entitle themselves to this exemption, they shall by their own oaths, and likewise by the oath of an indifferent person, prove such enlistment to have been bonafide made, agreeable to the true intent and meaning of this act, and shall likewise produce on oath from the Colonel or commanding officer of any county within this state, a receipt for such soldier to him actually delivered; which requisites being performed, the field officers of the county in which they reside are hereby ordered and directed to grant them a discharge, under the penalty of forfeiting one thousand pounds each for every refusal, to be recovered in any court of record having cognizance thereof by the parties grieved, and applied to their own use; And the field officers of any county within this state, who shall grant a discharge to any person or persons contrary to the directions of this act, shall forfeit five hundred pounds each for every offence, to be recovered by any person suing for the same, and applied to his own use; and each of them shall be for ever after incapable of holding any office, either civil or military, within this state.

II. And be it further enacted, by the authority aforesaid, That the Colonel or commanding officer of any county to whom such enlisted soldiers shall be delivered over, shall cause such soldiers to be marched to a place of rendezvous within the county in, which such officer shall command; and the governor of this state is hereby empowered and directed to appoint such place of rendezvous, and to direct one or more officers of such regular troops to give attendance and receive such recruits.

III. And be it further enacted, by the authority aforesaid, That the Captain of each respective company, or any other person or persons by him or them authorized, shall have full power and authority, and are hereby expressly required and commanded, to apprehend and secure every person of the nine-months regulars, as also of the three months Militia, or any other deserter from the regular service, who have deserted or refused to march in either of the services aforesaid, which they shall know to be lurking within the limits of their command or elsewhere, and shall for that purpose take to his or their assistance so many of their company as he or they shall think necessary; and every person who shall refuse or neglect, when called upon, to aid and assist in apprehending such deserter or delinquent, for every such offense shall forfeit the sum of fifty pounds, to be recovered by warrant under the hand of the commanding officer, and applied to the use of the county.

IV. And be it further enacted, by the authority aforesaid, That in case two thousand men should not be raised agreeable to this act before the first day of July next, that then, and in that case, the governor, with the advice of the council, shall be empowered to embody a number of Militia equal to the deficiency; and such deficiency shall be made up from all the counties of the state, proportionately to the numbers which they shall have furnished by enlistment under this act, and with a respect to the number of which they may be delinquent of their respective portions of the whole two thousand.

V. And be it further enacted, by the authority aforesaid, That the Militia so to be embodied shall be entitled to the same pay, bounty, and rations as the Militia now in service in the Southern states, and shall be subject to perform the same duty, and serve the same space of time, and subject to the like rules and regulations; and all drafts which may be made shall be agreeable to the militia law, and the practice heretofore had under it.

VI. And be it further enacted, by the authority aforesaid, That all soldiers enlisted by virtue of this law shall be subject to the articles of war which are binding upon the Continental army, and shall incur similar pains and penalties for similar offences; and every soldier enlisting shall sign articles of enlistment, agreeable to the Continental regulation.

NC Laws Pertaining to the NC Continental Line
1780

First Session (4/17/1780) Chapter XXV. An Act for Raising men to Compleat the Continental Battalions belonging to this State, and Other Purposes.

I. Whereas by reason of the short enlistment of a great number of soldiers of the continental army, the Continental battalions of this State are very incomplete;

II. Be it therefore enacted by the General Assembly of the State of North Carolina, and it is hereby enacted by the authority of the same, that three thousand men shall be immediately recruited within this State for the term of three years, or during the war, and each and every soldier so enlisted shall have five hundred dollars at the time of such enlistment, and shall receive the same clothing, pay and rations, that the Continental soldiers are now, or may hereafter be entitled to.

III. And as a farther consideration, be it enacted, by the authority aforesaid, that each and every soldier who shall well and truly serve and perform his duty as a soldier, shall be entitled to receive at the expiration of every year the sum of five hundred dollars, to be paid him by the proper officer appointed for that purpose, and each and every soldier who shall serve out his three years, or to the end of the present war, shall have and receive one prime slave between the age of fifteen and thirty years, or the value thereof in current money, and two hundred acres of land, to be laid off as herein after located and described; and every soldier enlisted as aforesaid, who may die in the service of his country by the fate of war, sickness, accident, or otherwise, his heirs shall be entitled to receive his pay, together with the slave and land intended to be given him in virtue of this Act.

IV. And be it enacted, by the authority aforesaid, that every soldier who may be disabled in the service, and shall obtain a discharge, shall be intituled to receive the same consideration as if he had served out his full time.

V. Be it enacted, by the authority aforesaid, that all that tract or territory of land situate between the Virginia line and the rivers Tenasee and Holston, as far up as the mouth of French Broad river; thence a direct course to the mouth of Powell's river; thence a direct course to a great gap in Cumberland mountain, about twenty miles south west of the Kentucky road, where it strikes Cumberland mountain; thence a north course to the Virginia line; shall be kept and reserved to and for the use of the said State, and that it shall not be lawful for any person or persons to make entry of, or settle on any of the said lands, until they shall have permission so to do by the Legislature of the said State; and it is hereby declared that the whole of the said lands above recited are held and reserved for the express purpose of laying out therefrom such lands as this State have engaged and promised to the officers and soldiers of their several Continental battalions already raised, or which may hereafter be raised.

VI. And be it further enacted, by the authority aforesaid, that if any person or persons shall presume to make entry of, or settle on any of the before recited lands, contrary to this Act, that he, she or they, so entering or settling, shall not thereby be intituled to any pre-emption of or to such lands.

204

VII. And be it further enacted, that no assignment of transfer made by any soldier of any thing allowed by virtue of this Act, during the continuance of the time for which such soldier may be enlisted, shall be valid.

VIII. And be it further enacted, that his excellency the Governor, upon application to him made, from time to time, may grant warrants on the treasury for all such sums of money as he may deem necessary to Brigadier General Sumner, and the brigadier general of the several districts (and in case of the absence of any brigadier, then, and in that case, to the commanding officer of the respective counties in such district) within this State, for the purpose of carrying this Act into effect; which said brigadiers shall appoint as many recruiting officers in their respective districts, for the purpose of enlisting soldiers agreeable to this Act, as they may think proper, and may parcel out such portions of the money as they may draw for the purpose aforesaid to such recruiting officers, first taking bond, with sufficient security, for the due application and accounting for the same: And the said brigadiers, on receiving such warrants as aforesaid, shall also give bond, with approved security, to the Governor, for the due application of all money to be by them received in consequence of such warrants, and shall make an accurate return of the whole amount of the sums received, and the number of men recruited therewith, to the next Assembly; and the Militia and Continental officers so employed in recruiting, shall be intituled to two hundred and fifty dollars for each and every able bodied man they may inlist by virtue of this Act; and a drum and fife shall be allowed each officer employed in the said service. Provided nevertheless, that this Act shall not extend to authorize any recruiting officer to inlist any sailor, seaman, or foreigners, not citizens of this State, or the United States, previous to the passing of this Act.

IX. And whereas it hath been represented to this General Assembly, that sundry of the subjects of this State have, contrary to the laws, and in direct violation of the treaties subsisting between this State and the Cherokee Indians, settled beyond the boundary line, on the lands reserved for the said Indians' hunting ground, to their great uneasiness; Be it therefore enacted, by the authority aforesaid, that none of the said persons so unlawfully settled shall be entitled to enter, survey, or take up, any of the said lands, but that they remove themselves therefrom before the first day of January next; and if they shall refuse or delay to remove themselves, and are found on the said lands after the day aforesaid, they, and every one of them, shall forfeit and pay the sum of five hundred pounds; to be recovered in any court having cognizance of the same, to the use of the State, and be liable to be forcably removed therefrom; and the Governor, or commander in chief for the time being, is hereby authorized and required to order out such force from any of the neighboring counties as may be sufficient to effect the same.

NC Laws Pertaining to the NC Continental Line
1781

Third Session of 1780 (1/18/1781). Chapter II. An Act to Reduce the Six Continental Battalions Belonging to this State to Four, to Compleat the said four Battalions, and for other purposes therein mentioned (February 1781).

I. Whereas the honorable the Congress have resolved that the Continental Battalions belonging to this State shall be reduced to four, and have requested that the said battalions be immediately completed; and as it has been found impracticable to fill up the same by the common mode of recruiting, and the pressing necessity for their being immediately completed being evident, recourse must be had to other methods for effecting the same:

II. Be it therefore enacted by the General Assembly of the State of North Carolina, and it is hereby enacted by the authority of the same, that the said six battalions be, and they are hereby reduced to four.

III. And be it further enacted, by the authority aforesaid, that two thousand seven hundred and twenty four men shall be raised from the Militia of this State to complete the said battalions, in the following manner: The Colonel or commanding officer of each and every battalion is hereby directed to order the field officers and Captains of his battalion to meet at the place by law appointed for the general muster of his said battalion, or at some other convenient place, on or before the twentieth day of March next, and the field officers and Captains shall then and there divide the said battalion, officers and men of every rank included (his excellency the Governor, Judges of the Superior Courts of Law, Continental Delegates, Attorney General, and Public Secretary, excepted) into classes of fifteen men, after deducting all such who, by themselves or substitutes, faithfully served for the space of nine months, agreeable to Act of Assembly passed at New Bern in May, one thousand seven hundred and seventy eight, and who shall produce their discharge, regularly and fairly obtained, to the commanding officer of the battalion to which they respectively belong, and all such as were captured and made prisoners when in the actual defense of the United States, and are now on parole, or prisoners with the enemy; provided that this Act shall not be construed so as to exempt any persons who have served or hired substitutes under an Act passed at Smithfield in May, one thousand seven hundred and seventy nine, or any other Act not herein mentioned, such Acts not having exempted any person from military duty in cases of actual invasion or insurrection: And whereas it may happen that a number not sufficient to make a class may be left after dividing the battalions into classes of fifteen, then, and in that case, it shall be lawful for the said commissioned officers, field officers and Captains, by lot, to determine what men shall be of the said number, and to which class each of them shall be added, therein to stand a draft, provided the class to which he may belong do not produce a volunteer on the day of the general muster: And the Colonel or commanding officer of each battalion of militia shall within fifteen days after such meeting order a general muster at the place by law appointed, or other convenient place, and is hereby authorized there to offer a bounty of three thousand pounds to every able-bodied man, over and above a bounty of three barrels of corn for his wife, and two for each of his children who shall be in his family, and shall be under ten years of age, such corn to be delivered annually to his wife or assignee, or her order, by the commissioner of the county wherein she may reside, or by some other person appointed for that purpose, for and during the term the said volunteer or draft may continue in service, and the commissioner shall be allowed for the same in the settlement of his public accounts; the said three thousand pounds to be paid either in money or certificates upon the public treasury, bearing an interest of six percent per annum till paid, and free from taxation, and shall be a tender in payment of public taxes, the sum for which such certificates may be granted to be payable to the person to whom they are granted, or his assigns, within twelve months after the enlistment, to every able-bodied man who shall enlist, or be drafted in the said Continental Battalions for the space of twelve months; and the said volunteers shall be subject to the same rules and discipline, and have the same pay and rations, as the Continental troops belonging to this State, from the day of their being enlisted: And in case a sufficient number of volunteers do not then enlist, the commanding officer shall immediately order one man to be drafted from each of the classes which have failed to produce a volunteer; and each of the men so drafted shall be intituled to receive the same bounty, pay, and rations as if they had enlisted, and shall be obliged to serve in the Continental Battalions of this State for the same term, and be subject to the same rules and discipline, as the said volunteer, or produce an able-bodied substitute on the day, and at the place appointed by this law for the district rendezvous; which substitute on being approved of by the field officer delivering, and the Continental officer receiving him, shall be entitled to the bounty, pay, and rations, and shall be obliged to serve for the same term, and be subject to the same rules and discipline, as the said drafted man would have been, had he not hired such substitute; all the taxable property within the district of each battalion, whose owners are neither in the Continental service or liable to be classed as by this Act directed, shall be subject to a tax of three pounds upon every hundred pounds value of the same (the property of orphans excepted) an exact list of the names of the owners of which property shall be returned by the respective Captains and commanding officers of the companies of each battalion to the collectors and county treasurers aforesaid, on or before the twentieth day of April next.

IV. And be it further enacted, by the authority aforesaid, that the collectors of the pecuniary tax in the respective districts, collect and pay into the hands of the county treasurers, all the tax payable by virtue of this Act, on or before the first day of October next; and any collector who shall fail to collect the aforesaid tax, or to pay the same to the treasurers of the respective counties, and the county treasurer neglecting to pay the same to the respective district treasurers, shall forfeit double their commissions.

V. And be it further enacted, by the authority aforesaid, that every person who shall voluntarily enlist himself into the Continental service during the war, shall be entitled to have and receive as a bounty the sum of two thousand pounds, to be paid in the same manner as the three thousand pounds herein before directed to be paid as a bounty to such persons as shall voluntarily enlist or be drafted into the Continental service for the space of twelve months, to be paid him on the day upon which he shall arrive at the place of general rendezvous appointed for the troops raised in the district wherein such person shall so enlist, and be entitled to the same clothing as the Continental soldiers now in the service of the United States are entitled to; and every person enlisting in the war as aforesaid, upon his producing a certificate of having so served from the Colonel of the regiment to which he belonged, shall be entitled to have and receive, as a recompence for such service, one prime slave, or the value thereof, and six hundred and forty acres of land, under the same rules and restrictions as the additional bounty given to soldiers enlisting in the Continental service under the Act for that purpose passed the first session

207

of the present General Assembly, that is to say, no disposition or transfer of lands or negroes by this Act allowed to drafts or volunteers, made by the said drafts or volunteers during the time of their service, shall be in any wise good, except where they shall transfer or dispose of the same by will; and in case any of the said drafts or volunteers shall die intestate before the expiration of the time of their enlistment, the said negroes and lands to which they are entitled respectively, shall go and descend to their legal representatives.

VI. And be it further enacted, by the authority aforesaid, that the men so raised shall rendezvous on or before the twenty fifth day of April next at the following places, to wit, those from the district of Salisbury at Salisbury, from the district of Hillsborough at Hillsborough, from the district of Edenton at Edenton, and Halifax at Halifax, from the district of New Bern at Smithfield, and Wilmington at Duplin Court House, unless otherwise ordered by the brigadier general of the respective districts; and in case any of the said volunteers and drafts should fail to appear at the day and place appointed for the district rendezvous, or at any time, place or places, that may hereafter be appointed by the commanding officer for the time being, they being considered by this law as Continental soldiers from the day of the drafts or enlistments, shall be treated as deserters by a Court-Martial composed of Continental officers.

VII. And be it further enacted, by the authority aforesaid, that any volunteer or draft faithfully serving, either by himself or substitute, the aforesaid term, shall be exempted from all drafts whatever for twelve months from the date of his or his substitute's discharge, provided it be certified on the back of said discharge, by the commanding officer of the Militia battalion to which such volunteer or draft belonged at the time of his entering the said service, that he has reason to believe the said volunteer or draft has faithfully served as aforesaid, and been legally discharged; and in case of the death of any of the said volunteers, drafts or substitutes, when in the service of this State, their families shall be provided for in the same manner as during their service.

VIII. And be it further enacted, by the authority aforesaid, that if any person shall harbor, conceal or abet, any soldier deserting from the Continental army, the person so harboring, concealing or abetting, such soldier, where the circumstances of such harboring, concealing or abetting furnish a sufficient presumption that the person so harboring knew him to be a deserter, on conviction before three justices of any county in this State, shall be deemed a Continental soldier during the war, and shall serve in one of the battalions belonging to this State, or deliver an able-bodied substitute to the commanding officer of the Militia battalion of the district wherein he resided at the time of his so harboring, concealing or abetting, any Continental deserter as aforesaid, or to the commanding officer of the Continental battalion to which he may be turned over; and in case the person so harboring, concealing or abetting, such soldier, and convicted as aforesaid, should not be sufficiently able bodied to serve as a soldier, and should neglect to deliver an able-bodied substitute to the commanding officer of the Militia battalion as aforesaid within ten days after such conviction, or being able-bodied should abscond, or having joined the Continentals belonging to this States should desert, the commanding officer of the said Militia battalion is hereby authorized and commanded to hire a substitute in the stead of the person not being able bodied, and neglecting to deliver a substitute as aforesaid, or being able bodied, and absconding or deserting, and to cause the hire and expense of such substitute to be levied by warrant under his hand and seal on the goods and chattels, lands and tenements, of the person so offending.

IX. And be it further enacted, by the authority aforesaid, that the Captains shall return descriptive lists of the volunteers and drafts raised in and from the several classes apportioned to them to their Colonel or commanding officer within two days after such draft, therein specifying the name, size, age, complexion, and occupation, of the men so raised, and also the name of the captain from whose company they were taken; and the said commanding officer shall make two fair copies of such descriptive lists, one of which, by him or one of his field officers, to be delivered with the men so raised, on or before the twenty fifth day of April next, at the district rendezvous, to the Continental officer, or other person appointed to receive and take charge of the said men, and shall take a receipt for the delivery of the men on the other, and shall then take a descriptive list, of all substitutes there offered by drafted men of the battalion to which he belongs, and approved by the persons appointed for that purpose; one fair copy of which list he is required to deliver with the said substitutes to the Continental officer, or other person appointed to receive and take charge of the said men, and shall take a receipt for the said substitutes, in like manner as for the said drafts; and one other fair copy of the descriptive list of such substitutes, together with receipts for the volunteers, drafts and substitutes as aforesaid, shall be returned to, if not taken by, the Militia Colonel or commanding officer of the battalion.

X. And be it further enacted, by the authority aforesaid, that the commanding officers of the battalions shall send a list of the volunteers, drafts and substitutes, to the brigadiers general of their respective districts, within fifteen days from the district rendezvous; and the brigadiers general shall, within one month from the receipt of such list, transmit copies thereof to his excellency the Governor for the time being.

XI. And be it further enacted, by the authority aforesaid, that each and every person who shall voluntarily enter or be drafted into the said service, or be received as a substitute by the persons appointed for the purposes aforesaid, shall be entitled to have and receive two pair of shoes, two pair of stockings, two shirts, two stocks, one pair of breeches, one pair of overalls, one waistcoat, one coat, one hunting shirt, one blanket, and one hat; which clothing shall, if possible, be delivered to each volunteer; draft and substitute, on the day and place of the district rendezvous, or as soon after as they can be made up.

XII. And in order to procure the clothing afore-mentioned, Be it enacted, by the authority aforesaid, that every class shall furnish, provide and deliver, to the Colonel or commanding officer of the battalion to which such class belongs, two pair of good strong shoes, one pair of good warm yarn or cotton stockings, one pair of good thread or cotton stockings, two good and strong linen shirts, two black leather stocks, one pair of good buckskin or good thick and strong woollen cloth breeches, one pair of good and strong linen overalls, one waistcoat of good thick and strong woollen cloth lined with linen, one coat of the same with the waistcoat lined with linen, with capes and cuffs of blue cloth of the same quality, one good and strong hunting shirt with a blue linen cape, one good and well made wool hat, for the volunteers, drafts or substitutes, of their own class, and in proportion to the assessment of their taxable property for the year one thousand seven hundred and eighty; and the Colonel or commanding officer is hereby required to cause the said clothing to be appraised by two freeholders, and to give certificates to the persons furnishing the same, which shall be received in payment of taxes; and in case any class should fail to deliver the same to the Colonel or commanding officer of the battalion to which the said class belongs within twenty days after the day of general muster of the battalion as aforesaid, the commanding officer is hereby authorized and commanded to appoint a proper person or persons to purchase said articles of clothing, and by warrant under his hand and seal to levy the cost and expense attending the purchasing the same in due proportion to their taxable property aforesaid.

XIII. And be it further enacted, by the authority aforesaid, that the Colonel or commanding officer who may attend at the district rendezvous take proper methods to have the clothing at the said rendezvous, and see it delivered to the soldiers for whom it may be provided; and the County Commissioners are hereby required to deliver, by order of the commanding officer of the county battalion, to the soldiers raised as aforesaid, rations sufficient to serve them to the district rendezvous, allowing fifteen miles for a day's march.

XIV. And be it further enacted, by the authority aforesaid, that every Militia officer employed in carrying this Act into execution, shall be allowed full pay and rations for every day of actual service: And each and every Militia officer neglecting or refusing to do any or every of the duties by this Act required, shall forfeit a sum equal to three months pay, to be collected in the same manner as fines and forfeitures inflicted by the Militia laws are collected; which fines and the money arising from such forfeitures shall be immediately paid to the county treasurer for the use of the county.

XV. And whereas it may happen that some counties of this State may be prevented by means of invasion from making the draft hereby directed to be made on the time aforesaid, Be it further enacted by the authority aforesaid, that if any of the counties of this State shall be prevented by invasion thereof from making the said draft on the time aforesaid, in that case the commanding officer of the battalion of such counties shall make the draft as soon as the said hindrance shall be removed; saving in all cases to persons who may at the time of such draft be in the actual Militia service of this State, all penalties for failing to appear as drafted soldiers during the continuance in the said Militia service. Provided that such drafted soldier shall make his appearance at headquarters and deliver himself to a Continental officer within forty days after the expiration of his said service.

XVI. And be it further enacted by the authority aforesaid, that all persons liable to Militia duty, and who have resided ten days in any part of this State before the day of drafting, shall be considered as liable to stand draft, and subject to the operations of this Act, and that any Militia man who shall after the passing this Act, and before the day of drafting, absent himself, or remove with intent to evade the operations of this Act, shall be held and deemed a Continental soldier for twelve months from the day he may be taken thereafter, and the real and personal estates of all such persons shall be liable to be sold by the colonel of the county, or so much thereof as will be sufficient to procure a Continental soldier for the term of twelve months, in the room and stead of such person so removing; and that any draft, volunteer, substitute, or other soldier, under this Act, deserting or failing to appear when called on, shall be held and deemed a Continental soldier during the war. Provided, that refugees from Georgia and South Carolina shall not be considered as within the meaning of this Act.

XVII. And be it further enacted, by the authority aforesaid, that James Coor and William Pasteur be appointed commissioners to print, or cause to be printed or written, three thousand five hundred certificates of seven thousand five hundred dollars each, of the following form, viz. 'State of North Carolina. This may certify that the bearer is entitled to seven thousand five hundred dollars, to be paid out of the public treasury of this State, with six per cent. interest at any time after the first day of March, in the year one thousand seven hundred and eighty two, agreeable to Act of Assembly. Given under my hand this —— day of —— one thousand seven hundred and eighty one.' And shall in the most frugal and expeditious manner deliver, or cause to be delivered, the said certificates to the several district treasurers on or before the first day of April next, in the proportions following, that is to say, to the Treasurer of the district of New Bern five hundred, Wilmington five hundred, Salisbury nine hundred, Hillsborough six hundred, Halifax five hundred, and the remaining five hundred of the said certificates to the Treasurer of the District of Edenton, taking receipts for the same: And the said Commissioners shall, previous to their entering on the printing or writing the same, take an oath not to print or write, or cause to be printed or written, any greater number of certificates than are hereby directed to be printed or written; and the treasurers of each district are required to attend in person, or otherwise, at the place of general rendezvous in their respective districts, and after signing the said certificates, to deliver one of them to each volunteer and draft who by virtue of this Act shall appear at such place of rendezvous, taking a receipt from each individual, for which trouble and expense the said treasurers shall be allowed in the settlement of their public accounts: And the Treasurer of the District of New Bern shall advance to the said Commissioners the sum of three thousand pounds out of the public treasury, to enable them, if necessary, to hire expresses, and purchase paper, for the purpose of procuring and delivering the said certificates as directed by this act; for which sum the said Commissioners shall account with the board of auditors, who are hereby directed to allow them a reasonable compensation for their services and expenses in performing the several duties required of them by this Act.

XVIII. And be it further enacted, by the authority aforesaid, that whosoever shall by printing, writing, engraving, or by any other way or means, pass or counterfeit or attempt to pass or counterfeit, any of the certificates by this Act directed to be granted, or any part, word or letter, name, emblem or device of the same, or shall make or construct any die, press, type, or other instrument, for imitating any of the said certificates, or any part, word, letter, name, emblem or device thereof, or shall alter or deface any of the said certificates with intent to change the value or denomination thereof, or shall knowingly pass or utter any counterfeit likeness of any of the said certificates, being thereof lawfully convicted by confession or verdict, or on arraignment or trial shall stand mute, or challenge peremptorily more than thirty five jurymen, every such person shall receive judgment of death, without benefit of clergy, and shall suffer as in case of felony.

First Session (6/23/1781). Chapter V. An Act to Compel the Counties which have not Furnished their Quota of Continental troops, as Required by a late Act of the General Assembly of this State, to Furnish the Same (July 1781).

I. Whereas many of the counties of this State have not furnished their quota of Continental troops, as ordered by an Act of the General Assembly of this State, intituled, An Act to reduce the six Continental Battalions belonging to this State to four, to complete the said four battalions, and for other purposes;' and whereas it is necessary that the said quota of Continental troops should be immediately raised, and employed in the defense of the State;

II. Be it therefore enacted by the General Assembly of the State of North Carolina, and it is hereby enacted by the authority of the same, that the colonel or commanding officer of every Militia batallion in this State which hath not already been classed, or being classed, have not furnished their proportion of Continental troops as aforesaid, shall within six weeks after passing this Act proceed to class, if not already classed, his battallion, and in either case to draft, if drafting should be necessary, from such classes their full quota of troops, in the manner directed by the aforesaid Act; and where any class of any batallion already made have not furnished a volunteer or draft as the said law directs, the Colonel or commanding officer shall within the time aforesaid, if volunteers do not offer, make a draft from each of the said classes agreeable to the aforesaid Act; and that this Act shall not be construed so as to oblige any class that have drafted, or provided a volunteer agreeable to law, to furnish again.

III. And be it further enacted, that the officer who shall cause the said Continental troops to be drafted as aforesaid, shall under the penalties of the before recited Act, cause the same to be marched as soon as may be to such place as is by the said appointed Act for the district rendezvous of the troops to be raised from his batallion, or to such other place as shall be appointed by the Brigadier General [Jethro] Sumner, or the commanding officer in the Southern army.

IV. And be it further enacted, that the men so drafted shall serve twelve months after their arrival at the place of rendezvous afore-mentioned, and shall be subject to the same rules, regulations and penalties, and entitled to the same emoluments, as the Continental troops already raised in virtue of the above recited Act. Provided nevertheless, that any county or counties who have furnished any number of men since the sitting of the last Assembly for the southern army, to serve ten months under the command of [SC] [Brig.] General [Thomas] Sumter, shall be considered as having furnished one man in the Continental draft, for every three men in the said service from said county. Provided also, that this Act shall not be construed so as to excuse any county or batallion from furnishing their quota in any future draft, under similar circumstances.

NC Laws Pertaining to the NC Continental Line
1782

First Session (4/13/1782). Chapter I. An Act for Raising Troops to Compleat the Continental Battalions of this State, and Other Purposes (May 1782).

I. Whereas the time of service of the troops raised to complete the Continental Battalions of this State by an Act of Assembly passed at Halifax in February, one thousand seven hundred and eighty one, is nearly expired; and whereas it is absolutely necessary the said battalions be immediately completed, and the common mode of recruiting being found ineffectual;

II. Be it therefore enacted by the General Assembly of the State of North Carolina, and it is hereby enacted by the authority of the same, That the colonel or commanding officer of each battalion in this State is hereby directed to order the field officers and captains of his battalion to meet at the place by law appointed for the general muster of his battalion, or at some other convenient place, on or before the fifteenth day of June next, and the field officers and captains shall then and there divide the said battalion, officers and men of every rank between the ages of sixteen and fifty included, (his excellency the Governor, Judges of the Superior Courts of Law, Attorney General, Continental Delegates, the Speakers of both Houses of the General Assembly, and Moravians, Quakers, Menonists and Dunkards, who are by law subject to a three fold tax, in lieu of all drafts and military duty, excepted) into classes of twenty men each, after deducting all such as have been captured and made prisoners when in actual service of this or the United States and are now on parole, and all such as have been lately drafted, or have turned out as volunteers in behalf of classes and have performed their respective tours of duty either by personal service, or by hiring a substitute who shall have performed his tour of duty agreeable to law, and all such who are now in the service of this State under an Act for raising troops out of the Militia of this State for the defense thereof, provided such exemption be agreeable to the said Act; and provided that all delinquents who have been turned over to the Continental service for desertion or other military offence, within twelve months preceeding the fifteenth day of March last, shall not be included in any class for raising the aforesaid Continental troops if they have actually served the time prescribed by law, and shall produce a discharge from the proper Continental officer certifying the same.

III. And be it further enacted by the authority aforesaid, That the commanding officer of the several regiments within their respective counties in this State shall cause all the inhabitants of their counties between the ages of sixteen and fifty to be enrolled, no respect being had to any exemptions, and hold a court of enquiry to exempt such who are unfit for service, previous to the day directed by this Act for the classing the Militia as aforesaid, and whereas it may happen that a number not sufficient to make a class may be left, after dividing the battalions into classes of twenty, then and in that case, it shall be lawful for the said commissioned officers, field officers and captains, by lot to determine what men shall be of the said number, and to which class each of them shall be added, therein to stand a draft, provided the class to which he may belong do not produce a volunteer on the day of the general muster; and the commanding officer of each battalion of Militia shall, within ten days after classing his battalion as aforesaid, order a general muster of his said battalion at the place aforesaid, and shall then and there require each class to furnish one able-bodied man, who shall serve in the Continental battalion; belonging to this State for eighteen months from the day of their meeting at such place of rendezvous as is hereafter appointed: And the said volunteers shall be subject to the same rules and discipline, and have the same pay and rations as the Continental troops belonging to this State, from the day of their being enlisted. And in case a sufficient number of volunteers do not then enlist, the commanding officer shall immediately order one man to be drafted from each of the classes who have failed to produce a volunteer, and each of the men so drafted shall be entitled to receive the same pay and rations as if they had enlisted, and shall be obliged to serve in the Continental battalions of this State for the same term, and be subject to the same rules and discipline as the said volunteer, or produce an able-bodied substitute on the day, and at the place appointed by this Act for the district rendezvous, which substitute on being approved of by the field officer delivering, and the Continental officer receiving him, shall be entitled to the same pay and rations, and shall be obliged to serve for the same term, and be subject to the same rules and discipline, as the drafted man would have been had he not hired such substitute.

IV. Provided always, That no British or Hessian deserter who hath not been a resident of this State twelve months, or orphan or apprentice under eighteen years of age, Indian, sailor, or negro slave, shall be received as a substitute for any class volunteer or draft whatever: And provided further, That no Militia officer shall take or receive any person offered as a substitute for any person, then being himself a substitute for any person or class under this Act, on pain of forfeiting for every such offense, the sum of fifty pounds specie, to be recovered by action of debt in any court of record in this State, by any person who will sue for the same, and applied one half to his own use, the other half to the use of the State, and becoming moreover liable to be removed from office.

V. And be it further enacted, by the authority aforesaid, That the field officers and Captains shall class the men in such manner that each class may be of equal value, as near as may be, agreeable to the assessment of their taxable property for the year one thousand seven hundred and eighty one.

VI. And be it further enacted, That each and every Captain, or other officer commanding the respective companies of Militia in this State, shall, previous to the time of classing their battalion, make return on oath to the Colonel or commanding officer of their regiment of all the effective men belonging to their companies respectively, under pain of forfeiting fifty pounds specie for each and every neglect or refusal, to be recovered by any person suing for the same, in any court of record in this State, and applied one half to his own use, and the other half to the use of the State.

VII. And be it further enacted, by the authority aforesaid, That the Captains shall return descriptive lists of the volunteers and drafts raised in and from the several classes apportioned to them, to the Colonel or commanding officer within five days after such draft, therein specifying the name, size, age, complexion and occupation, of the men so raised, and also the name of the captain from whose company they were taken; and the said commanding officer shall make two fair copies of such descriptive lists, one of which by him, or one of his field officers, to be delivered with the men so raised, on or before the first day of August next, at the district rendezvous, to the Continental officer or other person appointed to receive and take charge of the said men, and shall take a receipt for the delivery of the men on the other; and shall also take a descriptive list in manner aforesaid of all substitutes there offered by drafted men of the battalion to which he belongs, and approved by the persons appointed for that purpose, one fair copy of which list he is required to deliver with the said substitutes to the Continental officer, or other person appointed to receive and take charge of the said men, and shall take a receipt for the said substitutes in like manner as for the said drafts, and one other fair copy of the descriptive list of such substitutes, together with receipts for the volunteers, drafts and substitutes as aforesaid, shall be returned to, if not taken by, the Militia Colonel or commanding officer of the battalion.

VIII. And be it further enacted by the authority aforesaid, That the men so raised shall rendezvous on or before the first day of August next at the following places, to wit: Those from the District of Salisbury, at Salisbury; from the District of Hillsborough, at Hillsborough; from the District of Edenton, at Winton; from the District of Halifax, at Warrenton; from the District of New Bern, at Kingston; from the District of Wilmington, at Duplin Court House; and those from the District of Morgan, at Ramseur's Mill. And in case any of the said volunteers and drafts should fail to appear at the day and place appointed for the district rendezvous, they shall be considered as deserters, and treated accordingly.

IX. And be it further enacted, That the commanding officer of the battalions shall send a list of the volunteers, drafts and substitutes, to the brigadiers general of their respective districts within fiften days from the district rendezvous, and the brigadiers general shall, within one month from the receipt of such list, transmit copies thereof to his excellency the Governor for the time being.

X. And be it further enacted by the authority aforesaid, That each and every person who shall voluntarily enter, or be drafted into the said service, or be received as a substitute by the persons appointed for the purposes aforesaid, shall be entitled to have and receive two pair of shoes, two pair of stockings, two shirts, two stocks, one pair of leather or woollen breeches, two pair of overalls, one waistcoat, one coat, one hunting-shirt, one blanket, one hat, and five yards of tent cloth; which clothing shall be good and new, and shall be delivered to the said volunteer, draft or substitute, on the day and place of the district rendezvous. And in order to procure the aforesaid clothing,

XI. Be it enacted by the authority aforesaid, That the said clothing shall be furnished by the respective classes to the volunteer, draft or substitute, belonging to the said class, in proportion to the assessment of their taxable property for the year one thousand seven hundred and eighty one as aforesaid, on the day, and at the place of the district rendezvous, or before. And in case the said clothing shall not be delivered to the said volunteer, draft or substitute, on the time aforesaid, the Colonel or commanding officer of the county to which such class so deficient belongs, shall by warrant under his hand appoint two of the ablest men in property in the said class, to procure from the class their quota of clothing so deficient and in case the said men so appointed, do not collect the said clothing in the foregoing proportion, with respect to their assessment, within twenty days from their appointment, then and in that case, the Colonel or commanding officer shall issue his warrant to the lieutenant or ensign of the company to which such class belongs, to levy of the goods and chattels of the person so appointed, a sum sufficient to procure such deficient articles of clothing as aforesaid by sale of the goods and chattels of the said persons, which clothing shall be appraised by two freeholders on oath, and certificates given to the parties furnishing the same in specie, and shall be received by the sheriff or collector in payment of taxes.

215

XII. And be it further enacted by the authority aforesaid, That every volunteer or draft faithfully serving, either by himself or substitute the aforesaid term, shall be exempted from all drafts whatsoever for twelve months from the date of his, or his substitute's discharge, provided it be certified on the back of the discharge by the commanding officer of the Militia battalion to which such volunteer or draft belonged at the time of his entering the said service, that he has reason to believe the said volunteer or draft has faithfully served as aforesaid.

XIII. And be it further enacted by the authority aforesaid, That any person who shall apprehend or deliver, or cause to be apprehended or delivered to a Continental officer, any deserter from the Continental, State Troops, or delinquent from the Militia service, on producing a receipt for the delivery of such deserter or delinquent to the Colonel or commanding officer of the county wherein he shall reside, shall be entitled to receive the sum of four pounds specie, as a reward for apprehending and delivering such deserter or delinquent in full, and it is hereby declared, that no exemptions whatever shall in future be allowed for such service.

XIV. And be it further enacted by the authority aforesaid, That the volunteers and drafts raised as aforesaid, shall be forwarded without delay to their respective places of rendezvous by the commanding officer of the battalions from whence they shall be raised, or by some field officer of his said battalion, by him to be appointed for that purpose as herein before directed, on penalty of one hundred pounds specie, to be recovered by any person for the use of the person so suing.

XV. Provided nevertheless, That any two classes in each regiment who shall produce to the commanding officer of the regiment one good wagon, and team of four good horses, geers and every thing compleat for the road, fit to carry one ton at least, and deliver the same as public property, for the use of the North Carolina brigade, shall be exempt from the draft. And provided also, That if it should happen in any case that more than four classes in any battalion should be desirous of furnishing their proportion of wagons and teams, the preference shall be determined by lot, on the day the men are classed.

XVI. And be it further enacted by the authority aforesaid, That every Militia officer employed in carrying this Act into execution shall be allowed full pay and rations for every day he may be in actual service; and each and every Militia officer neglecting or refusing to do any or every of the duties by this Act required, shall forfeit a sum equal to three months pay, to be collected in the same manner as fines and forfeitures inflicted by the Militia law, which fines and forfeitures shall be paid to the county treasurer for the use of the county.

XVII. And be it further enacted, that the County Commissioners shall, by order of the commanding officer of the county, deliver to the soldiers raised as aforesaid, rations sufficient to serve them to the district rendezvous, allowing fifteen miles for a days march.

XVIII. And whereas sundry persons employed in the quarter master, commissary, and in other the staff department of the Continental army, claim exemptions from Militia duty, and other drafts; Be it therefore enacted by the authority aforesaid, That no person whatever shall claim, or be entitled to the exemption from this draft, under color of being in the staff department of this, or the United States, except the deputy quarter master general, and deputy commissary general.

XIX. And be it enacted, That the Continental officer receiving the drafts and volunteers in the several districts respectively, shall within twenty days after the first day of August next, make returns to the Governor of the said drafts and volunteers by them respectively received, showing the numbers for each particular county within such district, as also a particular account of the clothing and tent cloth with which the said drafts and volunteers are furnished.

XX. And whereas the commanding officers of sundry battalions have failed to deliver their full quota of troops which were to be raised by an Act of Assembly passed at Halifax in February, one thousand seven hundred and eighty one, intituled, An Act to reduce the six Continental Battalions belonging to this State to four, to complete the said four battalions, and for other purposes, and amended by an Act passed at Wake County, the last session of the General Assembly, intituled, An Act to compel the counties which have not furnished their quota of Continental troops as required by a late Act of the General Assembly of this State, to furnish the same; Be it therefore enacted by the authority aforesaid, That in addition to the troops to be raised by virtue of this Act, the commanding officer in each battalion which have failed to deliver their full quota of troops on the last twelve months draft, to the Continental officer agreeable to the directions in the before recited Act, are hereby authorized and directed to raise a number of able bodied men sufficient to complete the whole number apportioned to the battalions respectively of the delinquent classes, under the same rules and regulations, and subject to the same pains and penalties, as are prescribed in the Acts aforesaid.

Chapter III. An Act for the Relief of the Officers and Soldiers in the Continental Line, and for Other Purposes Therein Mentioned (May 1782).

I. Whereas the officers and soldiers of the Continental line of this State, have suffered very much by the depreciation of paper currency, as well as by the deficiency of clothing and other supplies, that have been due them according to sundry acts and resolves of the General Assembly of this State; and whereas, the honorable the Continental Congress have resolved, that such depreciation shall be made good to the eighteenth day of August, one thousand seven hundred and eighty, agreeable to a scale of depreciation established;

II. Be it enacted by the General Assembly of the State of North Carolina, and it is hereby enacted by the authority of the same, That all depreciation of pay and subsistance, due to any officer or soldier before the said eighteenth day of August, one thousand seven hundred and eighty, be made good to them agreeable to the resolution of Congress, and that they shall be paid for all deficiency of clothing, and that John Hawks, James Coor, and William Blount, Esquires, or any two of them, be, and they are hereby appointed a board to liquidate, and finally settle the same in specie.

III. And for the more immediate relief of the parties, Be it Enacted That each officer and soldier shall receive indented certificates, one or more being for twelve months pay and subsistance, which shall be negotiable in prompt payment for any public property that may be immediately sold, and shall receive another certificate or certificates, for the balance, which shall be paid off by any treasurer of the State, as soon as the situation of the finances will permit.

217

IV. And be it enacted, That the balance, or arrearages, due to any officer or soldier who has been killed in action, or died in service, since the eighteenth day of August, one thousand seven hundred and eighty, shall be paid to the heirs of such officer or soldier deceased, and that such widows of officers and soldiers deceased, as are by resolve of the Assembly of North Carolina, entitled to half pay, shall have the depreciation made good to them, and have their certificates issued accordingly.

V. And be it further enacted, That the Commissioners aforesaid shall each receive twenty four shillings per day for their trouble in liquidating, and finally settling the aforesaid accounts, and that any person who shall counterfeit any certificate issued in consequence of this law, shall be deemed guilty of forgery, and suffer accordingly.

VI. And whereas it is proper that some effectual and permanent reward should be rendered for the signal bravery, and persevering zeal, of the Continental officers and soldiers in the service of the State; Be it enacted, That each Continental soldier of the line of this State, who is now in service, and continues to the end of the war, or such as from wounds or bodily infirmities, have been, or shall be rendered unfit for service, which shall be ascertained by a certificate from the commanding officer, shall have six hundred and forty acres of land, and every officer who is now in service, and shall continue in service during the war, as well as those officers who from wounds or bodily infirmities, have left, or may be obliged to leave the service, shall have a greater quantity, in proportion to his pay, as followeth: A private six hundred and forty acres of land, and each non-commissioned officer one thousand acres, a subaltern two thousand five hundred and sixty acres, a captain three thousand eight hundred and forty acres, a major four thousand eight hundred acres, a lieutenant colonel five thousand seven hundred and sixty acres, a lieutenant colonel commandant seven thousand two hundred acres, a colonel seven thousand two hundred acres, a brigadier twelve thousand acres, a chaplain seven thousand two hundred acres, each surgeon four thousand eight hundred acres, each surgeons mate two thousand five hundred and sixty acres; and where any officer or soldier has fallen, or shall fall in the defense of his country, his heirs or assigns shall have the same quantity of land that such officer or soldier would have been entitled to, had they served during the war; and the aforesaid grants of land to each officer and soldier, shall be free from taxation during the term they respectively shall continue in actual service, unless by them sooner disposed of.

VII. And whereas in May, one thousand seven hundred and eighty, an act passed at New Bern, reserving a certain tract of country to be appropriated to the aforesaid purposes, and it being represented to this present Assembly that sundry families had, before the passing the said act, settled on the said tract of country; Be it enacted, That six hundred and forty acres of land shall be granted to each family, or head of a family, and to every single man of the age of twenty one years and upwards, (to include their improvements) settled on said land before the first day of June, one thousand seven hundred and eighty, for which they shall have the right of pre-emption; Provided, no such grant shall include any salt lick, or salt spring, which are hereby declared to be reserved as public property, together with six hundred and forty acres of the adjoining lands, for the common use and benefit of the inhabitants of that country, and not subject to future appropriations; and all the remainder of the aforesaid tract of country, shall be considered as subject to partition, as by this act directed.

VIII. And be it further enacted, That Absalom Tatom, Isaac Shelby, and Anthony Bledsow, Esquires, or any two of them, are appointed commissioners in behalf of the State, to examine and superintend the laying off the land in one or more tracts allotted to the officers and soldiers, and they shall be accompanied by one or more agents, whom the officers may appoint, to assist in the business; and in case any commissioner so appointed shall die, or refuse to act, his excellency the Governor shall fill up the vacancy.

IX. And whereas it is proper that an early opportunity should be taken to explore, and lay off those lands; Be it therefore enacted, That his excellency the Governor, or his successor, shall be empowered in the course of the present year, or as soon as the situation of the public affairs shall render it practicable and expedient, to direct the commissioners to proceed in the execution of their duty, and he shall appoint them a proper guard, not exceeding one hundred men, properly officered, which said officers shall be appointed and commissioned by the Governor. And that each commissioner shall receive, in one survey, five thousand acres of land for his service.

X. And be it further enacted by the authority aforesaid, That twenty five thousand acres of land shall be allotted for, and given to Major General Nathanael Greene, his heirs or assigns, within the bounds of the lands reserved for the use of the army, to be laid off by the aforesaid commissioners, as a mark of the high sense this State entertains of the extraordinary services of that brave and gallant officer.

XI. And be it further enacted by the authority aforesaid, That the said commissioners are hereby authorized and empowered, to appoint one or more surveyors, not exceeding three, as they may find necessary, for the more speedy and effectual laying off, and surveying the said lands, and also to employ the usual number of chain carriers and markers, and such number of hunters (not exceeding six) as may be absolutely necessary to supply the persons concerned in this business with provisions, which said surveyors shall be allowed two thousand five hundred acres of land each for their services, the chain carriers, markers and hunters, six hundred and forty acres each for their services, and the private men of the guard three hundred and twenty acres each, and the officers of the guard in proportion to their militia pay respectively.

XII. And be it further enacted by the anthority aforesaid, That the commissioners shall be empowered, from time to time, during the execution of this business, to administer an oath or oaths in cases where doubts may arise respecting any settler claiming a right to pre-emption under this act, and to grant certificates to such persons as shall appear to them to have a right to the same; and the said commissioners are directed and required to note down, in a book to be kept by them for that purpose, the names of such persons to whom certificates of pre-emption may be granted, a copy of which certificates they shall return to the General Assembly, also an accurate draft of the country they may explore, and the tracts of land they may lay off.

XIII. And be it further enacted by the authority aforesaid, That the commissioners hereby appointed shall take an oath, to do equal right and justice in determining preference to the settled, as by this act admitted.

NC Laws Pertaining to the NC Continental Line
1783

First Session (4/18/1783). Chapter I. An Act for Emitting One Hundred Thousand Pounds in Paper Currency, for the Purposes of Government for Seventeen Hundred and Eighty Three, for the Redemption of Paper Currency now in Circulation, and advancing to the Continental Officers and Soldiers Part of their Pay and Subsistance, and for Levying a Tax, and Appropriating the Confiscated Property for the Redemption of the Money now to be Emitted.

I. Whereas the necessity for money for the purposes aforesaid, is indispensable; Be it enacted by the General Assembly of the State of North Carolina, and it is hereby enacted by the authority of the same, That one hundred thousand pounds be emitted in paper bills of credit, on the faith and credit of this State, in bills of the following denominations, to-wit: Twenty thousand bills of forty shillings each, forty thousand bills of twentty shillings each, twenty thousand bills of ten shillings each, twenty thousand bills of five shillings each, forty thousand bills of two shillings each, ten thousand bills of one shilling each, and twenty thousand bills of six pence each; that the same be printed in a printing press, and that John Geddie and James Gillispie be appointed commissioners to superintend the press and number the bills; and that John Hunt and Benjamin McCulloch be appointed commissioners to sign and deliver the same to the public treasurers, to be by them applied as hereafter by this Act directed.

II. And be it further enacted by the authority aforesaid, That the general form of the bills hereby directed to be emitted, shall be as follows, to wit: "This bill of —— shillings shall be a tender in all payments whatever, agreeable to Act of Assembly passed at Hillsborough, the seventeenth day of May, Anno Domini, seventeen hundred and eighty three." And such bills shall be impressed and printed, the whole of them, on thin paper of the same fabrication, both in the face and the reverse thereof, on the edges as well as the body thereof, with diverse letters, marks, devices and words, which may be difficult of imitation, and which in the opinion of the said superintendants, may most effectually secure the same from attempts to counterfeit.

III. And be it further enacted by the authority aforesaid, That each pound of the emission aforesaid shall be deemed and held equal to two and an half Spanish Milled Dollars, and shall be a tender in all payments whatever.

IV. And be it further enacted by the authority aforesaid, That each and every person appointed by this Act to superintend the press, number, sign, and pay the bills into the public treasury, shall take an oath well and truly to execute the duties, and discharge the trust by this Act required; and each and every one of them shall enter into bond to the Governor for the time being, with sufficient security, to be by him approved, in the sum of one hundred thousand pounds, for the faithful and due performance of the duties by this Act required.

V. And be it further enacted by the authority aforesaid, That each and every commissioner for superintending the press, and numbering or signing, and paying into the public treasury, shall receive twelve shillings for every thousand bills by them signed or numbered, and delivered into the public treasury, to be paid out of the money by them paid into the public treasury.

VI. And be it further enacted by the authority aforesaid, That the commissioners by this Act appointed shall be, and are empowered to purchase paper and materials, and to employ a printer to print the said bills, and may draw on the treasury into which the aforesaid bills shall be paid, for the money necessary for the same, and their drafts shall be admitted as vouchers in the settlement of the treasurers' public accounts.

VII. And be it further enacted by the authority aforesaid, That the superintendants of the press, as soon as they have struck the sum of money hereby directed to be emitted, shall break and destroy, or cause to be broken or otherwise destroyed, such types, dies, or other emblems, as they shall have used in printing and impressing the same.

VIII. And be it further enacted by the authority aforesaid, That whoever shall by printing, writing, engraving, or by any ways and means counterfeit any of the said bills of credit, emitted by virtue of this Act, or any part, word, letter, name, emblem or device of the same, or shall make or construct any die, press, type, or other instrument for emitting or counterfeiting any of the said bills, or any part, letter, name, emblem or device thereof, except by authority of law, (or in case where such may be signed in order to bring suspected persons to justice) or shall alter or deface any of the said bills with intention to change the value and denomination thereof, or shall knowingly pass or utter any counterfeit likeness of any of the said bills, being thereof lawfully convicted by confession or verdict, or on arraignment on trial shall stand mute, or challenge peremptorily more than thirty-five jurymen, every such person shall be subject to, and suffer the same pains and penalties as are provided by an Act passed at Halifax, in the year seventeen hundred and seventy nine, intituled, An Act for punishing persons concerned in any of the several species of counterfeiting in this State.

IX. And be it further enacted by the authority aforesaid, That if any commissioner appointed by this Act to sign the said bills of credit, or superintend and number the same, shall die, refuse to act or resign, remove or become disabled or disqualified, it shall and may be lawful for the Governor to appoint one in his stead, and such commissioner shall give bond, and be subject to the same rules and regulations as commissioners appointed by this Act.

X. And be it further enacted by the authority aforesaid, That the treasurer of the district wherein the money shall be struck, shall attend upon notice from the commissioners, at the place where the same may be impressed and signed, for the purpose of receiving it, and shall be allowed for every thirty miles he shall travel in going to, and returning from such place, and for every day's attendance for that purpose, the sum of twenty shillings.

XI. And be it further enacted by the authority aforesaid, that the bills of credit to be emitted in virtue of this Act, shall be impressed, signed and numbered, at Halifax town.

XII. And be it further enacted by the authority aforesaid, that the treasurer to whom the commissioners before named shall pay the money emitted by virtue of this Act, is hereby directed and required to pay the same out of the treasury for the purposes, and in manner hereafter mentioned, and for no other purposes or manner; that is to say, to the warrant of the commissioners for the paper and printing; to the warrant of the Governor for the allowance of the commissioners for superintending the press, numbering, signing, and delivering the bills into the public treasury; to the order of the General Assembly for allowances given to their members and officers for their attendance and service; and to the warrant of the Governor for the salary or allowance of the civil list, for their services performed, or to be performed; all such allowances to be for services performed in the year seventeen hundred and eighty-three, and for no other time preceeding.

XIII. And be it further enacted by the authority aforesaid, that the several district treasurers respectively, shall have and receive from the treasurer of Halifax district, the sum of two thousand five hundred pounds out of the monies to be emitted in virtue of this Act, to be by them applied to the express purposes mentioned in this Act, and to no other use or purpose whatsoever; and the said treasurer of Halifax district is hereby required to deliver the aforesaid sum to the other district treasurers or their orders respectively; and the sum of seventy-two thousand pounds to pay into the hands of Willie Jones, Henry Montfort, and Benjamin McCulloch, esquires, who shall respectively give bond, with good and sufficient security, payable to the Governor for the time being, in the sum of fifty thousand pounds, for the faithful application of the said monies to the purposes appointed by this Act to be by them paid to the Continental officers and soldiers of this State, in part discharge of the arrears due them, in such manner as shall be directed hereafter, any law, usage or custom to the contrary, notwithstanding.

XIV. And be it further enacted, by the authority aforesaid, that any officer or soldier who is, or hath been, of the Continental line of this State, and have demands against the same for services, shall be entitled to have and receive from the commissioners aforesaid, out of the monies emitted by virtue of this Act, the one fourth part of the balance which on a settlement with the commissioners appointed for that purpose, shall appear to be justly due and owing to such officer or soldier respectively; and the said commissioners are hereby authorized and required to grant to each of the officers and soldiers aforesaid, one or more printed certificates under their hands, for the balance which on a full settlement shall be due in specie, which certificates so issued, shall bear an interest of six per cent. per annum, until paid, from the date thereof.

XV. And be it further enacted, by the authority aforesaid, that for the year seventeen hundred and eighty-three, a tax of three pence for each and every pounds value of taxable property in this State shall be levied, and paid in the bills as before directed by this Act to be emitted, or in gold or silver at the rates established by law, in currency or currency certificates, as rated by the Act for the sale of confiscated property, or in specie certificates at their nominal value. Provided, the late currency, currency certificates, and specie certificates, shall not be received for more than two thirds of the said tax.

XVI. And be it further enacted by the authority aforesaid, that the above tax shall be collected, paid and accounted for, as directed by an Act, intituled, An Act for ascertaining what property in this State shall be deemed taxable property, the method of assessing the same, and of collecting public taxes.

XVII. And be it further enacted, by the authority aforesaid, that each and every public treasurer be, and hereby is directed and required to retain in his hands, all such bills of credit emitted by virtue of this Act, as may be paid him for the taxes for the year seventeen hundred and eighty-three also all the gold or silver that may be paid him for the taxes for the year seventeen hundred and eighty-three, until otherwise directed by the General Assembly, any law, usage or custom to the contrary notwithstanding.

XVIII. And be it further enacted, by the authority aforesaid, that all the property belonging to this State which has been confiscated by and under the several laws commonly called confiscation laws, is hereby expressly reserved as a fund for the redemption of the said bills of credit emitted by virtue of this Act.

XIX. And be it further enacted by the authority aforesaid, that each of the treasurers from the several districts within this State shall attend the General Assembly whenever they shall meet, and lay before them all certificates and monies they shall have received in their respective districts, to be disposed of in such manner as the General Assembly may judge proper, and any treasurer failing or neglecting to comply with this Act, shall forfeit the sum of two hundred pounds, to be sued for and recovered in any court of record, by action of debt, by the comptroler, and applied to the use of the State.

Chapter III. An Act to Amend an Act, intituled, An Act for the Relief of the Officers and Soldiers of the Continental Line, and for Other Purposes.

I. Whereas, by the above mentioned law, certain quantities of land are allowed to sundry persons, officers and soldiers, and to the heirs of sundry officers and soldiers who have fallen in the course of the war, for obtaining titles to which no mode is pointed out;

II. Be it therefore enacted by the General Assembly of the State of North Carolina, and it is hereby enacted by the authority of the same, that each and every person and persons entitled to land by virtue of the aforesaid law, shall on application being made to the Secretary of the State, obtain and receive from him a warrant of survey for such quantities of land, within the limits of the land reserved by the aforesaid law for the said officers and soldiers, as he, she, or they, by the aforesaid law shall be entitled to, which shall be directed to Colonel Martin Armstrong, who is hereby appointed surveyor for this purpose, and is authorized and required, by himself or deputy, to execute and return the same into the secretary's office within the same time, and in the same manner as is required in other cases; and for which services he shall be entitled to the same fees, and be subject to the same pains and penalties for neglect or breach of duty; and shall also, previous to his entering upon the exercise of that office, take the same oath in presence of the Governor, as is by law appointed to be taken by other surveyors, and shall also administer to every chain-carrier who shall be employed with him in running out any of the said tracts, the same oath as is usually administered to chain carriers in other cases.

III. And least disputes should or may arise between two or more persons by each wishing or claiming to have his warrant or warrants located on the same piece of land; be it enacted by the authority aforesaid, That in such case the parties contending or claiming the same, shall cast lots for the choice, and the person in whose favor the lot falls, shall have the preference to such tract or parcel of land so claimed.

IV. And be it further enacted by the authority aforesaid, that no warrant shall be issued by the secretary in virtue of this Act, before the first day of October next; and the officers and soldiers aforesaid shall be allowed the term of three years from the first day of October next, to secure the lands hereby reserved for them.

V. And be it further enacted by the authority aforesaid, that where a warrant shall be hereafter located, without any person making objections to such location, that such location shall be good and valid, notwithstanding the claim that may be afterwards set up by any other person.

VI. And be it further enacted by the authority aforesaid, that the secretary shall make out grants for all surveys returned to his office, which grants shall be authenticated by the Governor, countersigned by the secretary, and recorded in his office ready to be delivered to the parties to whom the same shall be made.

VII. And for prevention of disputes, be it enacted by the authority aforesaid, that the officers and soldiers aforesaid shall enter and survey the lands within the following lines, that is to say; beginning in the Virginia line where Cumberland river intersects the same, thence south fifty miles, thence west to the Tenasee river, thence down the Tenasee to the Virginia line, thence with the said Virginia line east to the beginning.

VIII. And be it further enacted by the authority aforesaid, That no person or persons but the officers and soldiers of the Continental line (except those who are now settled on Cumberland river and have a right of pre-emption, whose claims are hereby reserved to them) shall enter any lands within the said bounds within three years after the passing of this Act; and all entries hereafter made within that time, by any except officers or soldiers entitled by law, are hereby declared void.

IX. Provided nevertheless, that Anthony Bledsoe, Absalom Tatom, and Isaac Shelby, late commissioners to lay off the lands for the Continental officers and soldiers, and the surveyors guards, and others who accompanied the said commissioners on that duty, shall each obtain titles to such quantity of land within the bounds aforesaid, as they or each of them are entitled to by the Act under which they were appointed, by entering the said lands with the entry-taker of Davidson County, who is required to receive their claims without any purchase money, and to grant them warrants for the same.

X. And be it further enacted by the authority aforesaid, that the surveyor by this Act appointed shall have the same fees, as by law are appointed for public surveyors, and shall be, and hereby is allowed and permitted to lay off for himself, within the bounds of the aforesaid tract of land, equal to the amount of his fees rating the said lands, at ten pounds the hundred acres, anything in this Act notwithstanding.

XI. And be it further enacted by the authority aforesaid, that the scale of depreciation established by an Act, intituled, An Act for establishing a scale of depreciation, with a provision for suits commenced for paper currency, and for suspending the operation of the laws therein mentioned, shall be the scale by which the Continental officers and soldiers of this State shall account for all such sums of money as they have received in part of their pay and subsistence, and by which they shall account for such balances as may be due from them on the sums by them received for the purpose of recruiting.

XII. And be it further enacted by the authority aforesaid, that all officers who have served with reputation two years and upwards, and either resigned, or were left out of the line on the reduction of their respective corps, and their heirs shall be entitled to grants of land proportionate (having respect to their time of service) to those grants that officers who have served during the war are entitled to by law, computing their time of service at

224

seven years; and also all soldiers who have served two years or upwards, shall be entitled to grants of lands proportionate (having respect to their time of service) to those grants of land that soldiers who have served two years and an half are entitled to by law.

XIII. And be it further enacted by the authority aforesaid, That his excellency Alexander Martin, Esquire, and David Wilson, Esquire, be entitled, agreeable to report of the committee, to two thousand acres of land each, adjacent to lands allotted for the officers and soldiers, for which they shall have and receive titles in the same manner as is directed by this Act, for the officers and soldiers to obtain titles to their lands, any law, or custom to the contrary, notwithstanding.

XIV. And whereas it will be more convenient for the officers and soldiers to attend at Halifax than at New Bern to have their accounts liquidated and settled; be it enacted by authority aforesaid, that Willie Jones, Benjamin McCulloch, and Henry Montfort, Esquires, be, and are hereby appointed commissioners in the room and stead of James Coor, John Hawks, and William Blount; and in case of the death of the said Willie Jones, Benjamin McCulloch, or Henry Montfort, or refusal to act, the Governor is hereby empowered to appoint one or more persons in his or their place, as the case may be, to liquidate and settle the officers and soldiers accounts to the first day of January, one thousand seven hundred and eighty-two, who are hereby empowered to allow interest on all accounts by them settled, agreeable to a resolution of this General Assembly of the fifteenth of May.

XV. And whereas it is absolutely necessary that some mode be adopted for the speedy recovery of monies due from any delinquent, superintendant commissioner, or county commissioner of confiscated property, sheriffs, treasurers, and tax-gatherers; Be it enacted by the authority aforesaid, that if any superintendant commissioner, or county commissioner of confiscated property, sheriff, treasurer or tax-gatherer, who have been, or shall be appointed by virtue of any Act of Assembly, shall fail or neglect to account for all monies which they respectively have been, now are, or hereafter shall be empowered and authorized to receive, it shall and may be lawful for any court of record in this State, on motion of the attorney general, or any other attorney, to grant judgment against such superintendant commissioner, or county commissioner of confiscated property, sheriff, treasurer or tax-gatherer, for all sums which he may have in his hands unaccounted for, with interest thereon from the day of receipt till the same is paid, and to award execution against the body, goods and chattels, lands and tenements, of such delinquent, or his securities; provided such delinquent have ten days previous notice of such motion; any law to the contrary, notwithstanding.

Appendix B

**The Known NC Continental Line Units
At Each Battle/Skirmish**

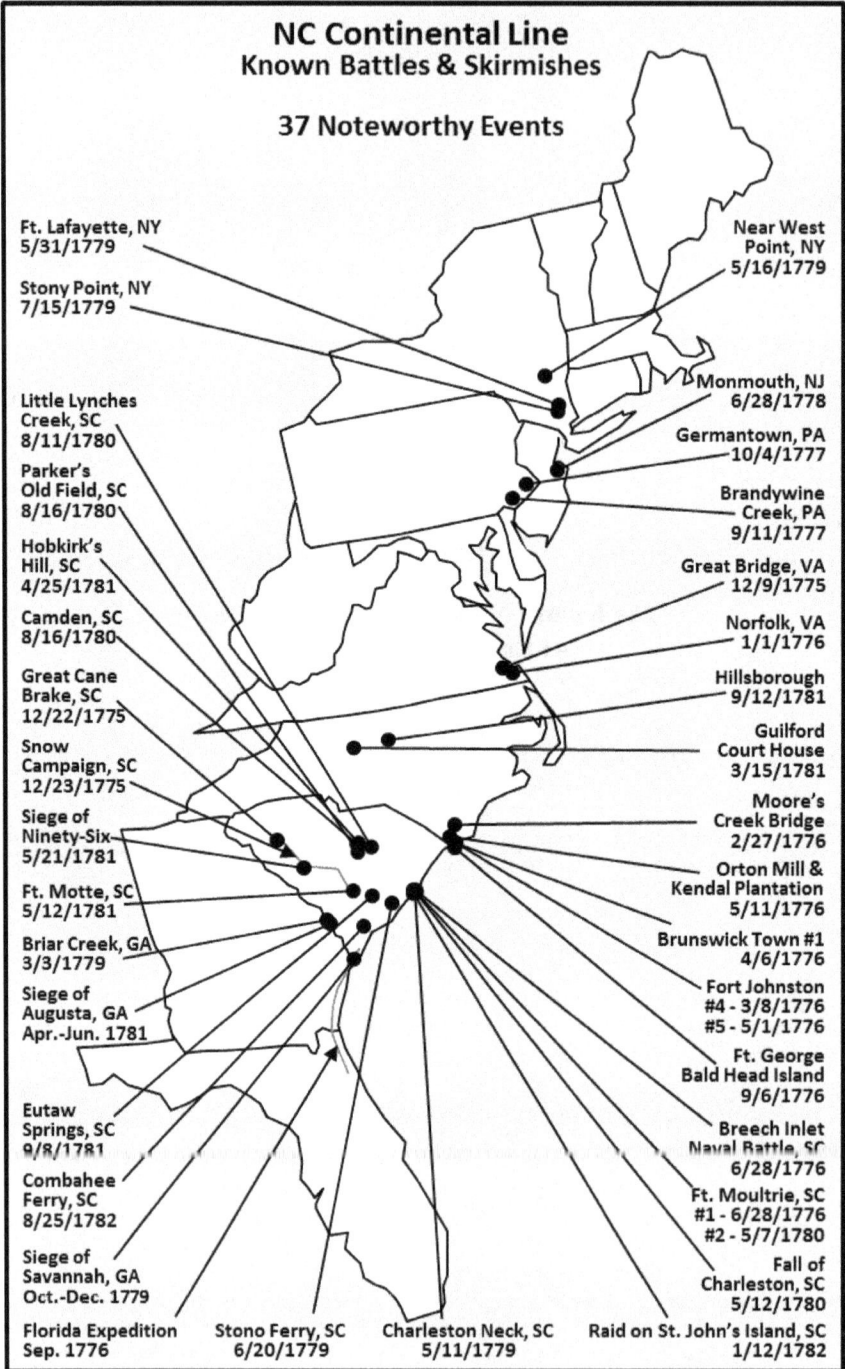

NC Continental Line
Known Battles & Skirmishes

37 Noteworthy Events

Ft. Lafayette, NY
5/31/1779

Stony Point, NY
7/15/1779

Little Lynches
Creek, SC
8/11/1780

Parker's
Old Field, SC
8/16/1780

Hobkirk's
Hill, SC
4/25/1781

Camden, SC
8/16/1780

Great Cane
Brake, SC
12/22/1775

Snow
Campaign, SC
12/23/1775

Siege of
Ninety-Six
5/21/1781

Ft. Motte, SC
5/12/1781

Briar Creek, GA
3/3/1779

Siege of
Augusta, GA
Apr.-Jun. 1781

Eutaw
Springs, SC
9/8/1781

Combahee
Ferry, SC
8/25/1782

Siege of
Savannah, GA
Oct.-Dec. 1779

Florida Expedition
Sep. 1776

Stono Ferry, SC
6/20/1779

Charleston Neck, SC
5/11/1779

Near West
Point, NY
5/16/1779

Monmouth, NJ
6/28/1778

Germantown, PA
10/4/1777

Brandywine
Creek, PA
9/11/1777

Great Bridge, VA
12/9/1775

Norfolk, VA
1/1/1776

Hillsborough
9/12/1781

Guilford
Court House
3/15/1781

Moore's
Creek Bridge
2/27/1776

Orton Mill &
Kendal Plantation
5/11/1776

Brunswick Town #1
4/6/1776

Fort Johnston
#4 - 3/8/1776
#5 - 5/1/1776

Ft. George
Bald Head Island
9/6/1776

Breech Inlet
Naval Battle, SC
6/28/1776

Ft. Moultrie, SC
#1 - 6/28/1776
#2 - 5/7/1780

Fall of
Charleston, SC
5/12/1780

Raid on St. John's Island, SC
1/12/1782

Date	Battle/Skirmish	Regiment(s) Involved
12/9/1775	Great Bridge (VA)	2nd NC Regiment – Howe's Battalion
12/22/1775	Great Cane Break (SC)	2nd NC Regiment – Martin's Battalion; 1 company of the 1st NC Regiment on loan
12/23/1775	Snow Campaign (SC)	2nd NC Regiment – Martin's Battalion; 1 company of the 1st NC Regiment on loan
1/1/1776	Norfolk (VA)	2nd NC Regiment – Howe's Battalion
2/27/1776	Moore's Creek Bridge	1st NC Regiment – 7 Companies; 2nd NC Regiment – 2 Companies supporting Militia
3/8/1776	Ft. Johnston #4	1st NC Regiment – 1 Company
4/6/1776	Brunswick Town #1	1st NC Regiment – Moore's Battalion; 2nd NC Regiment – 2 Companies
5/1/1776	Ft. Johnston #5	1st NC Regiment – 1 Company
5/11/1776	Orton Mill & Kendal Plantation	1st NC Regiment – 1 Company
6/28/1776	Ft. Moultrie #1 (SC)	1st NC Regiment – Nash's Battalion, 2nd NC Regiment, 3rd NC Regiment, 4th NC Regiment
6/28/1776	Breech Inlet Naval Battle	1st NC Regiment – Clark's Battalion of 5 Companies
Sept. 1776	Florida Expedition	1st NC Regiment – 1 Company; 2nd NC Regiment – 1 Company; 3rd NC Regiment – All except 1 Company (in NC)
9/6/1776	Ft. George-Bald Head Island	4th NC Regiment – 2 Companies
9/11/1777	Brandywine Creek (PA)	All 10 NC Regiments, 3 Cos. of Dragoons
10/4/1777	Germantown (PA)	All 10 NC Regiments, 3 Cos. of Dragoons
6/28/1778	Monmouth (NJ)	1st NC Regiment, 2nd NC Regiment, 3rd NC Regiment, 3 Cos. of Dragoons, NC Artillery
3/3/1779	Briar Creek (GA)	4th NC Regiment, 5th NC Regiment
5/11/1779	Charleston Neck (SC)	Unknown – Under SC Lt. Col. John Laurens.
5/16/1779	Near West Point (NY)	1st NC Regiment, 2nd NC Regiment
5/31/1779	Ft. Lafayette (NY)	2nd NC Regiment
6/20/1779	Stono Ferry (SC)	4th NC Regiment, 5th NC Regiment, 6th NC Regiment
7/15/1779	Stony Point (NY)	1st NC Regiment, 2nd NC Regiment, Artillery
Oct-Dec 1779	Siege of Savannah (GA)	4th NC Regiment – 3 companies, 5th NC Regiment – 1 company.
5/7/1780	Ft. Moultrie #2 (SC)	1st NC Regiment (2 men), 2nd NC Regiment (2 men)
5/12/1780	Siege of Charleston (SC)	1st NC Regiment, 2nd NC Regiment, 3rd NC Regiment, NC Artillery
8/11/1780	Little Lynches Creek (SC)	2 Continental officers not captured at Charleston, leading some NC militia units
8/16/1780	Parker's Old Field (SC)	Maj. John Armstrong led NC light infantry
8/16/1780	Camden (SC)	2 Continental officers not captured at Charleston, leading some NC militia units

Date	Battle/Skirmish	Regiment(s) Involved
3/15/1781	Guilford Court House	Continentals not captured at Charleston, leading some NC militia units
4/25/1781	Hobkirk's Hill (SC)	1st NC Regiment + 1 Captain from 3rd NC Reg.
5/12/1781	Ft. Motte (SC)	1st NC Regiment detachment
5/21/1781	Siege of Ninety-Six 1781 (SC)	1st NC Regiment detachment
5/24/1781	Siege of Augusta (GA)	1st NC Regiment detachment
9/8/1781	Eutaw Springs (SC)	1st NC Regiment, 2nd NC Regiment, 3rd NC Regiment, 4th NC Regiment
9/12/1781	Hillsborough	Handful of Continentals surprisingly caught by Loyalist Col. David Fanning
1/12/1782	Raid on St. John's Island (SC)	Unknown – under SC Lt. Col. John Laurens
8/25/1782	Combahee Ferry (SC)	Unknown – under SC Lt. Col. John Laurens

The Known NC Continentals at Great Bridge (VA) – 12/9/1775

2nd NC Regiment – Howe's Battalion of five (5) known companies, led by:
- Capt. James Blount
- Capt. Simon Bright
- Capt. Charles Crawford
- Capt. Hardy Murfree
- Capt. Henry Irwin Toole

The Known NC Continentals at Great Cane Brake (SC) – 12/22/1775

2nd NC Regiment – Martin's Battalion of four (4) known companies, led by:
- Capt. John Armstrong
- Capt. George Lee Davidson
- Capt. William Knox
- Capt. William Pickett (on loan from the 1st NC Regiment)

The Known NC Continentals in the Snow Campaign (SC) – 12/23/1775 to 12/30/1775

2nd NC Regiment – Martin's Battalion of four (4) known companies, led by:
- Capt. John Armstrong
- Capt. George Lee Davidson
- Capt. William Knox
- Capt. William Pickett (on loan from the 1st NC Regiment)

The Known NC Continentals at Norfolk (VA) – 1/1/1776

2nd NC Regiment – Howe's Battalion of four (4) known companies, led by:

- Capt. James Blount
- Capt. Simon Bright
- Capt. Charles Crawford
- Capt. Henry Irwin Toole

The Known NC Continentals at Moore's Creek Bridge – 2/27/1776

1st NC Regiment detachment of seven (7) known companies, led by:
- Capt. Thomas Allen (little evidence)
- Capt. George Lee Davidson (little evidence)
- Capt. William Davis (boated from Cross Creek)
- Capt. Henry "Hal" Dixon (maybe, maybe not)
- Capt. Alfred Moore (marched from Brunswick)
- Capt. Robert Rowan (marched from Cross Creek)
- Capt. John Walker (marched from Wilmington)
2nd NC Regiment detachment of two (2) known companies supporting Militia:
- Capt. James Armstrong – in New Bern District Minutemen under Col. Caswell
- Capt. William Knox – in Guilford County Regiment of Militia under Lt. Col. James Martin

The Known NC Continentals at Ft. Johnston #4 – 3/8/1776

1st NC Regiment detachment of one (1) known company, led by:
- Capt. Alfred Moore

The Known NC Continentals at Brunswick Town #1 – 4/6/1776

1st NC Regiment detachment – Moore's Battalion
2nd NC Regiment detachment of two (2) companies

The Known NC Continentals at Ft. Johnston #5 – 5/1/1776

1st NC Regiment detachment of one (1) known company, led by:
- Capt. Alfred Moore

The Known NC Continentals at Orton Mill & Kendal Plantation – 5/11/1776

1st NC Regiment detachment of one (1) known company, led by:
- Maj. William Davis

The Known NC Continentals at Ft. Moultrie #1 (SC) – 6/28/1776

Defending Charlestown:
Brig. Gen. Robert Howe

2nd NC Regiment led by Col. Alexander Martin with seven (7) known companies:
- Capt. Robert Gaston
- Capt. James Gee
- Capt. John Herritage
- Capt. Nathaniel Keais
- Capt. William Knox
- Capt. Hardy Murfee
- Capt. Joseph Tate

3rd NC Regiment led by Col. Jethro Sumner, with seven (7) known companies:
- Capt. William Barrett
- Capt. William Brinkley
- Capt. Pinketham Eaton
- Capt. James Emmett
- Capt. Thomas Granbury
- Capt. John Gray
- Capt. Jacob Turner

Haddrell's Point Defenses:
1st NC Regiment detachment led by Col. Francis Nash with two (2) known companies:
- Capt. Henry "Hal" Dixon
- Capt. Thomas Hogg

2nd NC Regiment detachment of one (1) known company:
- Capt. John Armstrong with 100 men

4th NC Regiment detachment of three (3) known companies:
- Capt. John Nelson
- Capt. Joseph Phillips
- Capt. Robert Smith

NC Light Dragoons Detachment of one (1) known company:
- Capt. James Jones - 3rd Troops with 41 men

The Known NC Continentals at the Breech Inlet Naval Battle – 6/28/1776

NC 1st Regiment detachment led by Lt. Col. Thomas Clark with 200 men in five (5) known companies:
- Capt. Thomas Allen
- Capt. George Lee Davidson
- Capt. Alfred Moore
- Capt. Robert Rowan
- Capt. John Walker

The Known NC Continentals in the Florida Expedition – Sept. 1776

Brig. Gen. Robert Howe, leading SC troops, GA troops, and NC troops:

1st NC Regiment detachment of one (1) known company:
- Capt. Henry "Hal" Dixon
2nd NC Regiment detachment of one (1) company (unknown)
3rd NC Regiment – all but one (1) company (unknown)

The Known NC Continentals at Ft. George-Bald Head Island – 9/6/1776

4th NC Regiment detachment led by Col. Thomas Polk, with two (2) companies:
- Capt. Thomas Harris
- Capt. Robert Smith

The Known NC Continentals at Brandywine Creek (PA) – 9/11/1777

NC Brigade of all ten (10) regiments led by Brig. Gen. Francis Nash, Maj. James Witherspoon (Aide-de-Camp).
1st NC Regiment led by Col. Thomas Clark, Lt. Col. William Davis, Maj. John Walker, Maj. William B. Williams, and the following known companies:
- Capt. William Armstrong (probable)
- Capt. Joshua Bowman
- Capt. Richard Bradley (probable)
- Capt. John Brown
- Capt. Henry "Hal" Dixon
- Capt. Tilghman Dixon
- Capt. Thomas Hogg (probable)
- Capt. Micajah Lewis
- Capt. James Read
- Capt. Howell Tatum
- Capt. Lawrence Thompson
2nd NC Regiment led by Col. Alexander Martin, Lt. Col. John Patten, Maj. Hardy Murfree, and the following known companies:
- Capt. Charles Allen
- Capt. John Armstrong
- Capt. Charles Crawford
- Capt. Robert Fenner
- Capt. William Fenner
- Capt. James Gee (mortally wounded – died 11/12/1777)
- Capt. Clement Hall
- Capt. Nathaniel Keais (probable)
- Capt. James Martin (probable)
- Capt. Edward Vail, Jr.
- Capt. Benjamin Williams
3rd NC Regiment led by Col. Jethro Sumner, Lt. Col. William Alston, Maj. Samuel Lockhart, and the following known companies:
- Capt. William Barrett (probable)
- Capt. James Bradley (probable)

- Capt. William Brinkley
- Capt. James Cook (probable)
- Capt. Pinketham Eaton
- Capt. Nicholas Edmunds (probable)
- Capt. James Emmett
- Capt. Thomas Granbury
- Capt. John Gray (probable)
- Capt. Daniel Jones
- Capt. Jacob Turner

4th NC Regiment led by Col. Thomas Polk, Lt. Col. James Thackston, Maj. William Lee Davidson, and the following known companies:
- Capt. William Temple Coles
- Capt. William Goodman
- Capt. Thomas Harris
- Capt. James Kerr (probable)
- Capt. John McLane (probable)
- Capt. John Nelson
- Capt. Joseph Phillips
- Capt. James Williams

5th NC Regiment led by Col. Edward Buncombe, Lt. Col. Henry Irwin, Maj. Levi Dawson, and the following known companies:
- Capt. Simon Alderson
- Capt. Reading Blount
- Capt. William Caswell
- Capt. Benjamin Andrew Coleman
- Capt. Henry Darnell
- Capt. John Enloe
- Capt. Peter Simon (probable)
- Capt. Benjamin Stedman
- Capt. John Pugh Williams

6th NC Regiment led by Col. Gideon Lamb, Lt. Col. Archibald Lytle, Maj. John Baptiste Ashe, and the following known companies:
- Capt. Francis Child (probable)
- Capt. Thomas Donoho
- Capt. George Dougherty
- Capt. John James (probable)
- Capt. John Griffith McRee
- Capt. Benjamin Pike
- Capt. Philip Taylor
- Capt. Thomas White
- Capt. Daniel Williams

7th NC Regiment led by Col. James Hogun, Lt. Col. Robert Mebane, Maj. Lott Brewster, and the following known companies:
- Capt. Thomas Brickell
- Capt. Henry Dawson

- Capt. Lemuel Ely
- Capt. John Macon (probable)
- Capt. John McGlaughan
- Capt. John Poynter
- Capt. Joseph Walker

8th NC Regiment led by Col. James Armstrong, Maj. Selby Harney, and the following known companies:
- Capt. Frederick Hargett
- Capt. Thomas Nixon
- Capt. Robert Raiford
- Capt. Francis Tartanson
- Capt. John Walsh

9th NC Regiment led by Col. John Williams, Maj. William Polk, and the following known companies:
- Capt. Richard D. Cook
- Capt. James Hall (probable)
- Capt. Michael Henderson (probable)
- Capt. Thomas McCrory
- Capt. Matthew Ramsey (probable)
- Capt. Hezekiah Rice
- Capt. John Rochelle (probable)
- Capt. Anthony Sharpe
- Capt. Joseph John Wade (probable)

10th NC Regiment detachment of the following known companies:
- Capt. Abraham Sheppard, Jr.
- Capt. Andrew Vanoy

NC Light Dragoons:
- Capt. Samuel Ashe, Jr. – 1st Troop
- Capt. Cosmo Medici – 3rd Troop
- Capt. Martin Phifer – 2nd Troop

The Known NC Contientals at Germantown (PA) – 10/4/1777

NC Brigade of all ten (10) regiments led by Brig. Gen. Francis Nash (killed), Maj. James Witherspoon (Aide-de-Camp - killed).

1st NC Regiment led by Col. Thomas Clark, Lt. Col. William Davis, Maj. John Walker, Maj. William B. Williams, and the following known companies:
- Capt. William Armstrong (probable)
- Capt. Joshua Bowman
- Capt. Richard Bradley (probable)
- Capt. John Brown
- Capt. Henry "Hal" Dixon
- Capt. Tilghman Dixon
- Capt. Thomas Hogg (probable)
- Capt. Micajah Lewis

- Capt. James Read
- Capt. Howell Tatum
- Capt. Lawrence Thompson

2nd NC Regiment led by Col. Alexander Martin, Lt. Col. John Patten, Maj. Hardy Murfree, and the following known companies:
- Capt. Charles Allen
- Capt. John Armstrong
- Capt. Charles Crawford
- Capt. Robert Fenner
- Capt. William Fenner
- Capt. Clement Hall
- Capt. Nathaniel Keais (probable)
- Capt. James Martin (probable)
- Capt. Edward Vail, Jr.
- Capt. Benjamin Williams

3rd NC Regiment led by Col. Jethro Sumner, Lt. Col. William Alston, Maj. Samuel Lockhart, and the following known companies:
- Capt. William Barrett (probable)
- Capt. James Bradley (probable)
- Capt. William Brinkley
- Capt. James Cook (probable)
- Capt. Pinketham Eaton
- Capt. Nicholas Edmunds (probable)
- Capt. James Emmett
- Capt. Thomas Granbury
- Capt. John Gray (probable)
- Capt. Daniel Jones
- Capt. Jacob Turner (killed)

4th NC Regiment led by Col. Thomas Polk, Lt. Col. James Thackston, Maj. William Lee Davidson, and the following known companies:
- Capt. William Temple Coles
- Capt. William Goodman
- Capt. Thomas Harris
- Capt. James Kerr (probable)
- Capt. John McLane (probable)
- Capt. John Nelson
- Capt. Joseph Phillips
- Capt. James Williams

5th NC Regiment led by Col. Edward Buncombe (POW), Lt. Col. Henry Irwin (POW/Killed), Maj. Levi Dawson, and the following known companies:
- Capt. Simon Alderson
- Capt. Reading Blount
- Capt. William Caswell
- Capt. Benjamin Andrew Coleman
- Capt. Henry Darnell

- Capt. John Enloe
- Capt. Peter Simon (probable)
- Capt. John Pugh Williams

6th NC Regiment led by Col. Gideon Lamb, Lt. Col. Archibald Lytle, Maj. John Baptiste Ashe, and the following known companies:
- Capt. Francis Child (probable)
- Capt. Thomas Donoho
- Capt. George Dougherty
- Capt. John James (probable)
- Capt. John Griffith McRee
- Capt. Benjamin Pike
- Capt. Philip Taylor
- Capt. Thomas White
- Capt. Daniel Williams

7th NC Regiment led by Col. James Hogun, Lt. Col. Robert Mebane, Maj. Lott Brewster, and the following known companies:
- Capt. Thomas Brickell
- Capt. Henry Dawson
- Capt. Lemuel Ely
- Capt. John Macon (probable)
- Capt. John McGlaughan
- Capt. John Poynter
- Capt. Joseph Walker

8th NC Regiment led by Col. James Armstrong, Maj. Selby Harney, and the following known companies:
- Capt. Frederick Hargett
- Capt. Robert Raiford
- Capt. Francis Tartanson
- Capt. John Walsh

9th NC Regiment led by Col. John Williams, Maj. William Polk, and the following known companies:
- Capt. Richard D. Cook
- Capt. James Hall (probable)
- Capt. Michael Henderson (probable)
- Capt. Thomas McCrory
- Capt. Matthew Ramsey (probable)
- Capt. Hezekiah Rice
- Capt. John Rochelle (probable)\
- Capt. Anthony Sharpe
- Capt. Joseph John Wade (probable)

10th NC Regiment detachment of the following known companies:
- Capt. Abraham Sheppard, Jr.
- Capt. Andrew Vanoy

NC Light Dragoons:
- Capt. Samuel Ashe, Jr. – 1st Troop

- Capt. Cosmo Medici – 3rd Troop
- Capt. Martin Phifer – 2nd Troop

The Known NC Continentals at Monmouth (NJ) – 6/28/1778

1st NC Regiment led by Col. Thomas Clark, Lt. Col. Robert Mebane, Maj. John Baptiste Ashe, Maj. John Nelson, and the following known companies:
- Capt. William Armstrong
- Capt. Joshua Bowman
- Capt. Tilghman Dixon
- Capt. John Griffith McRee
- Capt. Isaac Moore
- Capt. James Read
- Capt.-Lt. John Gambier Scull
- Capt. Anthony Sharpe
- Capt. Howell Tatum
- Capt. James Verner

2nd NC Regiment led by Col. John Patten, Lt. Col. Selby Harney, Maj. Hardy Murfree, and the following known companies:
- Capt. Thomas Armstrong
- Capt. Benjamin Andrew Coleman
- Capt. John Craddock
- Capt. Robert Fenner
- Capt. Clement Hall
- Capt. John Ingles
- Capt. Robert Raiford
- Capt. Benjamin Williams

3rd NC Regiment led by Col. Jethro Sumner, Lt. Col. William Lee Davidson, Lt. Col. Henry "Hal" Dixon, Maj. Thomas Hogg, and the following known companies:
- Capt. Kedar Ballard (probable)
- Capt. Francis Child
- Capt. William Thomas Linton
- Capt. John Medearis (probable)
- Capt. Michael Quinn (probable)
- Capt. Francis Tartanson
- Capt. Matthew Wood

NC Light Dragoons (Capt. Medici in NC):
- Capt. Samuel Ashe, Jr.
- Capt. John Brown
- Capt. Martin Phifer

NC Artillery:
- Capt. John Kingsbury

The Known NC Continentals at Briar Creek (GA) – 3/3/1779

4th NC Regiment detachment led by Maj. Pinketham Eaton, with two (2) known companies, led by:
- Capt. George Dougherty
- Capt. William Goodman

5th NC Regiment detachment led by Maj. Reading Blount, with four (4) known companies, led by:
- Capt. Thomas Donoho
- Capt. William Lytle
- Capt. Joseph Montford
- Capt. John Sumner

6th NC Regiment of "New Levies" led by Lt. Col. Archibald Lytle. None of his six (6) known captains have ever been considered by official records to be Continentals; they were considered to be NC Militia:
- Capt. James Craig (Rowan)
- Capt. Thomas Davidson (Rowan)
- Capt. John Griffin (Orange)
- Capt. Matthew McCauley (Orange)
- Capt. Robert Moore (Caswell)
- Capt. Richard Taylor (Granville)

Plus, six (6) NC Militia captains claim to have served under Lt. Col. Archibald Lytle at the battle of Briar Creek (GA).

NC Regiment of Militia led by Lt. Alexander Brevard (4th NC Regiment) acting as a Lt. Colonel.

The Known NC Continentals at Charleston Neck – 5/11/1779

NC Light Infantry – 250 men led by SC Lt. Col. John Laurens, unit(s) unknown

The Known NC Continentals at Near West Point (NY) – 5/16/1779

1st NC Regiment. Only known company was led by:
- Capt. Howell Tatum

Very likely that other active companies participated, but no definitive evidence.

2nd NC Regiment led by Col. John Patten. Only known company was led by:
- Capt. Clement Hall

Very likely that other active companies participated, but no definitive evidence.

The Known NC Continentals at Ft. Lafayette (NY) – 5/31/1776

2nd NC Regiment detachment of one (1) company led by Capt. Thomas Armstrong with 70 hand-picked men.

The Known NC Continentals at Stono Ferry (SC) – 6/20/1779

Brig. Gen. Jethro Sumner
4th NC Regiment led by Col. James Armstrong, Lt. Col. James Thackston, Maj. John Armstrong, Maj. Pinketham Eaton, and the following known companies:
- Capt. John Campbell
- Capt. Benjamin Carter
- Capt. Samuel Chapman
- Capt. William Temple Coles
- Capt. George Dougherty
- Capt. William Goodman
- Capt. John McLane
- Capt. Matthew Ramsey
- Capt. Joseph Thomas Rhodes (wounded)
5th NC Regiment led by Col. Thomas Clark, Lt. Col. Henry "Hal" Dixon, Maj. Reading Blount, and the following known companies:
- Capt. James Campbell (POW)
- Capt. Thomas Donoho
- Capt. William Lytle
- Capt. James Mills
- Capt. Joseph Montford
- Capt. James Morehead
- Capt. John Slaughter
- Capt. John Sumner
- Capt. Philip Taylor
6th NC Regiment of "New Levies" led by Lt. Col. Archibald Lytle. None of his eleven (11) known captains have ever been considered by official records to be Continentals, but considered by all to have been NC Militia officers:
- Capt. William Bethel (Guilford)
- Capt. David Cowan (Rowan)
- Capt. William Ganns (Mecklenburg)
- Capt. Arthur Gatling (Gates)
- Capt. John Griffin (Orange)
- Capt. Alsey High (Warren)
- Capt. John Leak (Guilford)
- Capt. Matthew McCauley (Orange)
- Capt. Robert Moore (Caswell)
- Capt. Barnett Pulliam (Granville)
- Capt. Robert Temple (Franklin)

The Known NC Continentals at Stony Point (NY) – 7/15/1779

Maj. Hardy Murfree led 178 hand-picked men from the 1st NC Regiment and 2nd NC Regiment, and the NC Artillery – in the following five (5) known companies:
- Capt. Joshua Bowman (1st NC Regiment) (wounded)
- Capt. John Craddock (2nd NC Regiment)
- Capt. Clement Hall (2nd NC Regiment)
- Capt. John Kingsbury (NC Artillery)
- Capt. Anthony Sharpe (1st NC Regiment)

The Known NC Continentals at the Siege of Savannah (GA) – Oct.-Dec. 1779

2nd NC Regiment detachment of one (1) company led by Lt. Col. Selby Harney
4th NC Regiment detachment of three (3) known companies led by:
- Capt. John Campbell
- Capt. William Lytle
- Capt. Matthew Ramsey
5th NC Regiment detachment of one (1) known company led by:
- Capt. Samuel Chapman

The Known NC Continentals at Ft. Moultrie #2 (SC) – 5/7/1780

1st NC Regiment detachment of Artificers - 2 men
2nd NC Regiment detachment of Artificers - 2 men

The Known NC Continentals at the Fall of Charleston (SC) – 5/12/1780

NC Brigade led by Brig. Gen. James Hogun (POW) and three (3) regiments:
1st NC Regiment led by Col. Thomas Clark (POW), Maj. John Nelson (POW), and the following nine (9) known companies:
- Capt. Joshua Bowman (killed)
- Capt.-Lt. Thomas Callendar (Lt. Colonel's Company) (POW)
- Capt. Tilghman Dixon (POW)
- Capt.-Lt. James King (Colonel's Company) (POW)
- Capt. John Griffith McRee (POW)
- Capt. Joseph Montford (POW)
- Capt. James Read (POW)
- Capt. John Sumner (POW at Williamson's Plantation on 7/12/1780)
- Capt. Howell Tatum (POW)
2nd NC Regiment led by Col. John Patten (POW), Lt. Col. Selby Harney (POW) and the following eight (8) known companies:
- Capt. Thomas Armstrong (POW)
- Capt. Benjamin Andrew Coleman (POW)

- Capt. John Craddock (Colonel's Company) (POW)
- Capt. Robert Fenner (POW)
- Capt. John Ingles (POW)
- Capt.-Lt. Charles Stewart (Lt. Colonel's Company) (POW)
- Lt. Jesse Read (leading Clement Hall's Company) (POW)
- Lt. John Daves (Major's Company) (POW)
3rd NC Regiment led by Lt. Col. Robert Mebane (POW), Maj. Thomas Hogg (POW) and the following five (5) known companies:
- Capt. Kedar Ballard (POW)
- Capt. George "Gee" Bradley (POW)
- Capt. Francis Child (POW)
- Capt.-Lt. William Fawn (POW)
- Capt. Philip Taylor (POW)
NC Artillery led by Capt. John Kingsbury (POW) with:
- Capt.-Lt. Philip Jones (POW)

The Known NC Continentals at Little Lynches Creek (SC) – 8/11/1780

- Lt. Col. Henry "Hal" Dixon of the 5th NC Regiment led the Caswell County Regiment of Militia
- Maj. John Armstrong of the 4th NC Regiment led the NC Light Infantry, a temporary unit of NC State Troops/Militia

The Known NC Continentals at Parker's Old Field (SC) – 8/16/1780

Maj. John Armstrong of the 4th NC Regiment led the NC Light Infantry, a temporary unit of NC State Troops

The Known NC Continentals at the battle of Camden (SC) – 8/16/1780

- Lt. Col. Henry "Hal" Dixon of the 5th NC Regiment led the Caswell County Regiment of Militia
- Maj. John Armstrong of the 4th NC Regiment led the NC Light Infantry, a temporary unit of NC Militiamen

The Known NC Continentals at Guilford Court House – 3/15/1781

NC Regiment led by Lt. Col. Henry "Hal" Dixon and Maj. Reading Blount, with five (5) known companies led by:
- Capt. Joshua Hadley (1st NC Regiment)
- Capt. William Lytle (4th NC Regiment)
- Capt. John Griffith McRee (1st NC Regiment)
- Capt. Matthew Ramsey (4th NC Regiment)
- Capt. Edward Yarborough (3rd NC Regiment)

The Known NC Continentals at Hobkirk's Hill (SC) – 4/25/1781

1st NC Regiment (currently being reconstituted from scratch) detachment led by Maj. Pinketham Eaton, with two (2) known companies, led by:
- Capt. John Griffith McRee (recently exchanged)
- Capt. Edward Yarborough (of the 3rd NC Regiment)

The Known NC Continentals at Ft. Motte (SC) – 5/12/1781

1st NC Regiment detachment led by Maj. Pinketham Eaton with three (3) known companies, led by:
- Lt. John Campbell
- Capt. Joshua Hadley
- Capt. Robert Smith

The Known NC Continentals at the Siege of Ninety-Six 1781 – 5/21/1781 to 6/19/1781

1st NC Regiment detachment led by Maj. Pinketham Eaton (one source asserts he was not at Ninety-Six) with four (4) known companies, led by:
- Capt. Alexander Brevard
- Capt. Thomas Donoho
- Capt. Joshua Hadley
- Capt. William Lytle

The Known NC Continentals at the Siege of Augusta (GA) – 5/24/1781 to 6/1/1781

1st NC Regiment detachment led by Maj. Pinketham Eaton (killed), with four (4) known companies, led by:
- Capt. Alexander Brevard
- Capt. William Lytle
- Capt. Joseph Thomas Rhodes
- Capt. Robert Smith

The Known NC Continentals at Eutaw Springs (SC) – 9/8/1781

Brig. Gen. Jethro Sumner
1st NC Regiment led by Lt. Col. John Baptiste Ashe, with ten (10) known companies, led by:
- Capt. William Armstrong
- Capt. Benjamin Bailey
- Capt. Alexander Brevard
- Capt. Thomas Donoho
- Capt. William Lytle

- Capt. Griffith John McRee
- Capt. James Mills
- Capt. Robert Raiford
- Capt. Anthony Sharpe

2nd NC Regiment led by Maj. Reading Blount, with eight (8) known companies, led by:
- Capt. Samuel Budd (POW)
- Capt. Benjamin Carter
- Capt. Tilghman Dixon
- Capt. Thomas Evans
- Capt. William Goodman (killed)
- Capt. Christopher Goodwin (killed)
- Capt. Joshua Hadley (wounded)
- Capt. Charles Stewart

3rd NC Regiment led by Maj. John Armstrong, with five (5) known companies, led by:
- Capt. John Daves
- Capt. Clement Hall
- Capt. Curtis Ivey
- Capt. Dennis Porterfield (killed)
- Capt. Edward Yarborough

4th NC Regiment led by Lt. Col. Henry "Hal" Dixon, with two (2) known companies, led by:
- Capt. George Dougherty
- Capt. Joseph Thomas Rhodes

The Known NC Continentals at Hillsborough – 9/12/1781

Lt. Col. Archibald Lytle (POW)
1st NC Regiment:
- Private Thomas Bowles (POW)
- Private Hugh Catchum (POW)
- Private William Douglas (POW)
2nd NC Regiment:
- Private Joseph Brown (POW)
- Corporal Marmaduke Maples (POW)

The Known NC Continentals at the Raid on St. John's Island (SC) – 1/12/1782

NC Light Infantry – 150 men led by SC Lt. Col. John Laurens, unit(s) unknown

The Known NC Continentals at Combahee Ferry (SC) – 8/25/1782

NC Light Infantry – 40 men led by SC Lt. Col. John Laurens, unit(s) unknown

Appendix C

**All Known NC Continental Soldiers
In Alphabetical Order**

Name	1st Unit	Year / Rank / Served Under / Notes	Known Battles
Aaron, George	DQMG	1780, a Wagoner under Col. Nicholas Long (Deputy QM General)	
Aaronheart, John	1st NC Regiment	4/28/1781, a Private under Capt. Alexander Brevard for 12 months. Discharged on 4/28/1782. aka John Aronhart.	
Abbitt, Ezekiel	5th NC Regiment	1776, a Musician under Capt. Simon Alderson. Dropped from the rolls in Jan. 1778.	
Abbot, John	1st NC Regiment	7/20/1778, a Musician under Maj. Thomas Hogg.	
Abbot, John	3rd NC Regiment	6/24/1779, a Private under Capt. Michael Quinn, then a Sergeant under Capt. Edward Yarborough. S39925.	Eutaw Springs (SC).
Abbott, John	1st NC Regiment	6/1/1781, a Private under Capt. William Lytle. Attached to Lee's Legion. Discharged 6/1/1782. From Guilford County. S32089.	Eutaw Springs (SC).
Abute, John	1st NC Regiment	A Private under Capt. William Lytle, dates unknown.	
Acock, Moses	3rd NC Regiment	1777, a Private under Capt. Jacob Turner. Died in May 1778.	
Acock, Robert	3rd NC Regiment	4/20/1776, a Private under Capt. Jacob Turner for 2-1/2 years. 9/10/1778, a known Private under Capt. Thomas Armstrong (2nd NC Regiment). Discharged on 11/10/1778 in CT. S35168.	Brandywine Creek (PA), Germantown (PA).
Acock, Samuel	2nd NC Regiment	Apr. 1781, a Private under Capt. Benjamin Carter for 12 months. Discharged on 4/25/1782.	
Adams, Arthur	10th NC Regiment	8/12/1777, a Private under Capt. Abraham Shepherd, Jr.	
Adams, David	1st NC Regiment	6/6/1781, a Private under Capt. William Lytle for 12 months. Discharged on 6/6/1782 (4th NC Regiment). Earlier in NC Militia. S34622.	Siege of Ninety-Six 1781 (SC), Eutaw Springs (SC).
Adams, Ezekiel	6th NC Regiment	1777, a Private under Capt. Thomas Donoho. Deserted on 8/25/1777.	
Adams, James	4th NC Regiment	1782, a Private under Capt. Anthony Sharpe for 18 months. Earlier in NC Militia. From Halifax County, NC. S8007.	
Adams, Jeremiah	4th NC Regiment	Aug. 1782, a Private under Capt. Anthony Sharpe for 18 months. Discharged at Ten-Mile Spring, SC. From Surry County. W8093.	
Adams, John	10th NC Regiment	7/5/1777, a Sergeant under Capt. Armwell Herron. A Private in June 1778. Died on 7/10/1778.	
Adams, Lanier	2nd NC Regiment	1777, a Private under Capt. Benjamin Williams. Dropped from the rolls in Jan. 1778.	
Adams, Niper	1st NC Regiment	1777, a Private under Capt. Henry "Hal" Dixon. Died on 7/27/1777.	
Adams, Philip	3rd NC Regiment	7/20/1778, a Private under Lt. Joseph Montford for nine months. From Halifax County, NC. Earlier and later in NC Militia. Spring of 1781, joined under Capt. Robert Raiford (1st NC Regiment) for 12 months. Discharged at Hillsborough, NC. S8008.	Eutaw Springs (SC).

Name	1st Unit	Year / Rank / Served Under / Notes	Known Battles
Adams, William	1st NC Regiment	4/28/1781, a Wagoner under Capt. Alexander Brevard. Discharged on 4/12/1782. Stationed at Salisbury.	
Adams, William	1st NC Regiment	6/6/1781, a Private under Capt. Griffith John McRee for 12 months.	
Adams, William	1st NC Regiment	1782, a Private under Capt. Peter Bacot for 18 months. Died on 5/28/1783.	
Adams, Zach'l	1st NC Regiment	A Private under Capt. William Lytle, dates unknown.	
Adcock, Edmund	3rd NC Regiment	1782, a Private under Capt. Alexander Brevard for 18 months. Died on 6/7/1783.	
Adcock, George	1st NC Regiment	A Private under Capt. James Read. Died on 8/21/1778.	
Adcock, John	10th NC Regiment	5/6/1777, a Private under Capt. James Wilson for three years. 9/8/1778, a known Private in the Major's Company (Maj. John Baptiste Ashe) (1st NC Regiment).	
Adcock, Joshua	10th NC Regiment	5/5/1777, a Private under Capt. James Wilson for three years. June of 1778, in 1st NC Regiment under Lt. Thomas Callender, then Lt. Daniel Shaw. 9/8/1778, a known Private in the Major's Company (Maj. John Baptiste Ashe) (1st NC Regiment) - sick in camp on that date. POW at the Fall of Charleston, escaped after a few weeks, went home. From Caswell County, NC. S6467.	Siege of Charleston 1780 (SC).
Addams, Philip	1st NC Regiment	5/2/1781, a Private under Capt. Robert Raiford for 12 months. Discharged 5/2/1782 (2nd NC Regiment).	
Addleman, John	3rd NC Regiment	6/22/1779, a Private under Capt. Kedar Ballard for three years. 1781, a Private under Capt. Clement Hall (3rd NC Regiment). Discharged on 9/29/1782 (2nd NC Regiment).	
Adkerson, Richard		6/5/1779, a Private, unit unknown. Joined for nine months. Possibly Richard Adkinson as shown below.	
Adkins, Benjamin	10th NC Regiment	12/10/1777, a Private, unit unknown. A Benjamin Atkins joined the 5th NC Regiment on same date. Same man?	
Adkins, David	NC Artillery	8/24/1776, a Matross under Capt. John Vance as NC Provincial Troops. 7/10/1777, on Continental Line. 11/16/1777, under Capt. John Kingsbury. 5/1/1778, in same unit. 9/16/1778, in same unit. Deserted 4/1/1779.	
Adkins, Gideon	3rd NC Regiment	6/16/1778, a Musician under Capt. Kedar Ballard. 1781, a Musician under Capt. Edward Yarborough Discharged 4/1/1782. aka Gideon Akins.	
Adkins, Richard	3rd NC Regiment	1781, a Private under Capt. Edward Yarborough for 12 months. Discharged on 6/17/1782.	
Adkins, Samuel	4th NC Regiment	1782, a Private under Capt. Anthony Sharpe for 18 months.	
Adkins, Thomas	10th NC Regiment	5/22/1777, a Private under Capt. Dempsey Gregory. 9/8/1778, a known Private under Capt.	

246

Name	1st Unit	Year / Rank / Served Under / Notes	Known Battles
		Howell Tatum (1st NC Regiment).	
Adkins, William	6th NC Regiment	May 1776, a Private under Capt. William Glover. Very sick in Dec. 1776, hired a substitute. Earlier a Minuteman. From Granville County when he enlisted. S6469.	
Adkinson, James	1st NC Regiment	1782, a Private under Capt. Peter Bacot for 18 months. Earlier, in NC Militia, unit(s) unknown. Enlisted in Edgecombe County, NC. Discharged in the Fall of 1782 at Halifax, NC. aka James Atkison, James Atkinson. S41399.	
Adkinson, Joel	1st NC Regiment	8/1/1782, a Private under Capt. Joshua Hadley for 18 months.	
Adkinson, John	6th NC Regiment	4/24/1776, a Corporal under Lt./Capt. Thomas White for three years. A Private in June 1778. 9/8/1778, a known Private under Capt. John Sumner (1st NC Regiment). Dropped from the rolls in Nov. 1778. aka John Adkerson, John Atkinson. From Johnston County, NC.	
Adkinson, John	10th NC Regiment	5/26/1777, a Private under Capt. Andrew Vanoy. A Musician in June 1778. A Private in Sept. 1778. 3/12/1779, re-enlisted under Capt. Thomas Armstrong (2nd NC Regiment). aka John Adkerson.	
Adkinson, Richard	2nd NC Regiment	April 1781, a Private under Capt. Benjamin Carter for 12 months. Died 10/18/1781. aka Richard Adkison.	
Aged, Benjamin	3rd NC Regiment	5/11/1776, a Private under Capt. Jacob Turner. 9/9/1778, under Capt. Benjamin Andrew Coleman (2nd NC Regiment). Discharged on 11/10/1778.	
Ager, John		10/7/1777, rank and unit unknown, enlisted for three years. 9/8/1778, a known Tailor in the Major's Company (Maj. Griffith John McRee) (1st NC Regiment) - stationed at Lancaster, PA on that date.	
Aikens, James	1st NC Regiment	1781, a Private under Capt. Thomas Donoho. Discharged at Bacon's Bridge, SC. From Granville County, NC. Earlier in NC Militia. W26780.	Eutaw Springs (SC).
Airs, Ezekiel	3rd NC Regiment	1781, a Private under Capt. Clement Hall for 12 months. Discharged on 4/21/1782 (2nd NC Regiment).	
Airs, Patt	1st NC Regiment	4/28/1781, a Private under Capt. Griffith John McRee for 12 months.	
Albarty, Frederick	4th NC Regiment	April 1776, an Ensign under Capt. Joseph Phillips. Served 5 years and 3 months. Discharged in Mecklenburg County, NC. From Surry County, NC. aka Frederick Alberty. W3749.	Brandywine Creek (PA), Germantown (PA).
Albertson, Caleb	10th NC Regiment	5/10/1777, a Private under Capt. Isaac Moore. Dropped from the rolls in Jan. 1778.	
Albertson, Henry	5th NC Regiment	10/24/1776, a Private under Capt. John Enloe. 9/10/1778, a Private under Capt. Thomas Armstrong (2nd NC Regiment). Deserted on	

Name	1ˢᵗ Unit	Year / Rank / Served Under / Notes	Known Battles
		2/29/1780.	
Albright, John	4ᵗʰ NC Regiment	1782, a Private under Capt. Thomas Evans for 18 months.	
Albritton, Matthew	4ᵗʰ NC Regiment	Spring of 1782, a Private under Capt. Thomas Evans for 18 months. The official records indicate that he deserted on 4/20/1783. He claims he was honorably discharged by Capt. Benjamin Coleman. From Pitt County, NC. R72.	
Albrooks, William	1ˢᵗ NC Regiment	4/28/1781, a Private under Capt. Griffith John McRee. Discharged 4/28/1782. Then, under Capt. Robert Raiford (2nd NC Regiment) for 18 months.	
Alcock, William	10ᵗʰ NC Regiment	8/31/1777, a Private under Capt. Silas Stevenson. Deserted on 1/20/1778.	
Alderman, Daniel	2ⁿᵈ NC Regiment	4/15/1781, a Corporal under Capt. Benjamin Andrew Coleman for 12 months. aka Daniel Addleman. W9696.	
Alderson, Simon	2ⁿᵈ NC Regiment	1777, a Private under Capt. Edward Vail, Jr. 9/9/1778, a Private in the Colonel's Company (Col. John Patten) led by Capt. John Craddock. A Sergeant on 5/20/1779. A POW on 6/1/1779. Also a POW at the Fall of Charleston, SC. aka Simon Anderson.	Ft. Lafayette (NY), Siege of Charleston 1780 (SC).
Alderson, Simon	5ᵗʰ NC Regiment	First, a Captain in the New Bern District Minutemen. 4/16/1776, a Captain in the 5th NC Regiment. Retired 6/1/1778. aka Simeon Alderson.	Brandywine Creek (PA).
Alderson, Thomas	5ᵗʰ NC Regiment	5/3/1776, an Ensign. Rescinded 5/9/1776.	
Aldridge, Francis	4ᵗʰ NC Regiment	March or April of 1782, a Private under Capt. Anthony Sharpe for 18 months. May have also served under Capt. Robert Raiford (2nd NC Regiment). Discharged at James Island, SC. Earlier in NC Militia, unit unknown. S35170.	
Aldridge, Gess	3ʳᵈ NC Regiment	7/20/1778, a Private under Lt./Capt. George "Gee" Bradley for nine months.	
Aldridge, Joseph	5ᵗʰ NC Regiment	12/18/1776, a Private under Capt. Simon Alderson. 9/9/1778, a Private in the Colonel's Company (Col. John Patten) (2nd NC Regiment) led by Capt. John Craddock. Discharged on 5/20/1779.	
Aldridge, William		4/19/1776, a Private, regiment and unit unknown. 9/8/1778, a known Private in the Colonel's Company (Col. Thomas Clark) (1st NC Regiment) led by Capt. John Gambier Scull. aka William Auldridge.	
Alexander, Anthony	1ˢᵗ NC Regiment	4/3/1781, a Private under Lt./Capt. Benjamin Bailey for 12 months. Discharged on 4/3/1782.	
Alexander, Benjamin	2ⁿᵈ NC Regiment	3/1/1782, a Private under Capt. Clement Hall for 12 months. May be same man as directly below.	
Alexander, Benjamin	7ᵗʰ NC Regiment	1777, a Private under Capt. Joseph Walker. 9/8/1778, a known Private under Capt.	

Name	1st Unit	Year / Rank / Served Under / Notes	Known Battles
		Tilghman Dixon (1st NC Regiment). Discharged on 2/27/1780.	
Alexander, Charles	4th NC Regiment	11/27/1776, a 2nd Lieutenant under Capt. Robert Smith, then 1st Lieutenant on 1/20/1777. Mid-1777, under Capt. Micajah Lewis. Dropped from the rolls in Jan. 1778.	
Alexander, Ezekiel	2nd NC Regiment	3/1/1782, a Private under Capt. Clement Hall for 12 months.	
Alexander, Hezekiah	4th NC Regiment	4/17/1776. Paymaster Appointment Rescinded 4/18/1776. A Lieutenant on 1/20/1777. Retired 6/1/1778.	
Alexander, John	3rd NC Regiment	6/22/1779 to 12/1/1779, a Private under Capt. Kedar Ballard. Also in the NC Militia. From Mecklenburg County, NC. W20586.	
Alexander, Joseph	2nd NC Regiment	Apr. 1777, a Private under Capt. William Fenner for three years. 9/9/1778, a Private in the Lt. Colonel's Company (Lt. Col. Selby Harney). Deserted on 1/1/1780.	
Alexander, Levy	6th NC Regiment	1777, a Private under Capt. Thomas Donoho. Died in Aug. 1777.	
Alexander, William		5/10/1781, an Ensign, unit unknown. 9/8/1781, a Lieutenant. Transferred to 4th NC Regiment as a Lieutenant on 2/6/1782 until the end of the war.	
Alexander, William	2nd NC Regiment	1777, a Private under Capt. Charles Allen. Died on 3/14/1778.	
Alexander, William	2nd NC Regiment	1777, a Musician under Capt. William Fenner. A Private in Sep. 1777. Back to Musician in June 1778.	
Alfin, William	4th NC Regiment	August 1782, a Private under Capt. Joseph T. Rhodes, then under Capt. Joshua Hadley (1st NC Regiment) for 18 months. Served about 11 months. From Onslow County, NC. Earlier in NC Militia. aka William Alphin, William Olfin. S8018.	
Alford, William	10th NC Regiment	1777, an Assistant Commissary. Discharged 3/4/1778. From what is now Wayne County, NC.	
Allen, Arthur	1st NC Regiment	4/12/1782, a Private under Capt. William Lytle. Deserted on 7/7/1782 (4th NC Regiment). aka Arthur Allens.	
Allen, Benjamin	1st NC Regiment	Jan. 1782, a Private under Lt. Abner Lamb for 12 months. From Pasquotank County, NC. S41407.	
Allen, Charles	2nd NC Regiment	10/20/1775, an Ensign under Capt. John Armstrong. 6/8/1776, a 2nd Lieutenant under Capt. Nathaniel Keais. Promoted to Captain in 1777. Transferred to 5th NC Regiment, date unknown. Died 1/7/1778.	Great Cane Brake (SC), Snow Campaign (SC), Moore's Creek Bridge, Brandywine Creek (PA), Germantown (PA).

Name	1st Unit	Year / Rank / Served Under / Notes	Known Battles
Allen, Elijah	3rd NC Regiment	12/1/1781, a Private under Capt. Samuel Jones for 12 months.	
Allen, Hardy	3rd NC Regiment	7/20/1778, a Private under Capt. Kedar Ballard for nine months.	
Allen, James	1st NC Regiment	4/25/1781, a Private under Capt. Robert Raiford. Discharged on 2/14/1782.	
Allen, Jesse	6th NC Regiment	Enlisted 4/16/1776 under Lt./Capt. Francis Child. A PC (?) in June 1778. A Sergeant in Sep. 1778. 9/8/1778, a known Private under Capt. Griffith John McRee (1st NC Regiment) - sick on that date at Valley Forge. Discharged 11/10/1778.	
Allen, John	5th NC Regiment	9/9/1775, a 2nd Lieutenant in the New Bern District Minutemen. 4/17/1776, a 2nd Lieutenant under Capt. Reading Blount and Col. Edward Buncombe. 5/9/1776, a Lieutenant under Capt. John Vance (NC Artillery). 10/1/1776, a Lieutenant under Capt. William Caswell. Died in Sep. 1780. From Craven County.	
Allen, Jonathan	3rd NC Regiment	2/1/1782, a Private under Capt. Samuel Jones.	
Allen, Joseph	3rd NC Regiment	6/24/1779, a Private under Capt. Michael Quinn for nine months.	
Allen, Joseph	4th NC Regiment	1782, a Private under Capt. Thomas Evans for 18 months.	
Allen, Joseph	10th NC Regiment	7/3/1777, a Sergeant, unit unknown. A Lieutenant on 3/31/1782, unit unknown.	
Allen, Michael	3rd NC Regiment	1782, a Private under Capt. Alexander Brevard for 18 months. Deserted 6/18/1783.	
Allen, Thomas	1st NC Regiment	9/1/1775, a Captain under Col. James Moore. Resigned 8/15/1776.	Moore's Creek Bridge [4], Breech Inlet Naval Battle (SC).
Allen, Thomas	3rd NC Regiment	7/20/1778, a Corporal under Capt. John Baker for nine months.	
Allen, Thomas	3rd NC Regiment	1st Lieutenant on 3/17/1778. POW at the Fall of Charleston, died in prison on 8/25/1780.	Siege of Charleston 1780 (SC).
Allen, Thomas	5th NC Regiment	1777, a Private under Capt. Benjamin Stedman.	
Allen, Thomas	5th NC Regiment	1777, a 2nd Lieutenant under Capt. Benjamin Stedman. From Johnston County, NC. R105. Probably the same man as directly above.	
Allen, Walter	1st NC Regiment	A Sergeant under Capt. Anthony Sharpe, dates unknown.	
Allen, Walter	5th NC Regiment	3/28/1777, an Ensign under Capt. Reading Blount. 10/4/1777, a Lieutenant. Dropped from the rolls in January 1778.	
Allen, William		6/5/1779, a Private, regiment and unit unknown. Joined for nine months.	
Allen, William	2nd NC Regiment	1777, a Private under Capt. Charles Allen. Died on 1/7/1778.	
Allison,	5th NC	1777, a Private under Capt. Henry Darnell.	Ft. Lafayette

Name	1st Unit	Year / Rank / Served Under / Notes	Known Battles
Achis	Regiment	POW at Ft. Lafayette, NY on 6/1/1779.	(NY).
Allison, Andrew	1st NC Regiment	5/7/1776, a Private under Lt./Capt. John Sumner for three years. 9/8/1778, a known Private under Capt. John Sumner.	
Allison, Peter	2nd NC Regiment	1782, a Private under Capt. Robert Raiford for 18 months. aka Peter Alison.	
Almonds, James	1st NC Regiment	9/8/1778, a known Private under Capt. Joshua Bowman.	
Alsbrook, Amos	3rd NC Regiment	7/20/1778, a Private under Lt. Joseph Montford for nine months.	
Alsbrook, Clayborn	1st NC Regiment	1782, a Private under Capt. Peter Bacot for 18 months.	
Alsobrook, Jesse	1st NC Regiment	4/25/1781, a Private and a Corporal under Capt. Robert Raiford for 12 months. From Halifax Co., NC. Earlier in the Militia. On some rolls as Jesse Alsbrook. S16600.	Eutaw Springs (SC).
Alston, William	3rd NC Regiment	A Lt. Colonel under Col. Jethro Sumner from April 15, 1776 to Oct. 25, 1777, when he resigned. Several sources indicate his last name was Ashton, but most assert it was Alston.	Brandywine Creek (PA), Germantown (PA).
Alsworth, Joseph	7th NC Regiment	1777, a Private under Capt. Joseph Walker. Deserted on 9/17/1777.	
Altman, Garret	3rd NC Regiment	7/20/1778, a Private under Lt./Capt. George "Gee" Bradley for nine months.	
Altorn, James	4th NC Regiment	1779, a Private under Capt. Samuel Chapman for nine months. Earlier in NC Militia. From Guilford County, NC. W21611.	Stono Ferry (SC).
Ambrose, David	2nd NC Regiment	May 1776, a Private under Capt. William Fenner, then under Capt. Joseph Tate. June 1777, a Private under Capt. Charles Allen. 9/10/1778, a known Private under Capt. Thomas Armstrong. A Musician in 1781. Enlisted near New Bern, NC. Discharged at Wilmington, NC. S37667.	Brandywine Creek (PA), Germantown (PA), Monmouth (NJ), Eutaw Springs (SC).
Ames, John	7th NC Regiment	1777, a Private under Capt. John McGlaughan. Died 11/15/1777.	
Ames, Thomas	7th NC Regiment	2/1/1777, a Private under Capt. John McGlaughan for three years. 2/26/1778, a known Private under Capt. Howell Tatum (1st NC Regiment). 9/8/1778, a known Private under Capt. Howell Tatum. Deserted on 2/12/1779. 3/12/1779, re-enlisted for the duration of the war in the same unit - must've returned.	
Amis, James	DQMG	1780, a Wagon Maker under Col. Nicholas Long (Deputy QM General). 1780, also a Private under Capt. Solomon Wood (NC Light Dragoons). Also serving as of 8/23/1781.	
Amis, Thomas	3rd NC Regiment	12/22/1776, a Commissary, replacing William Amis who had resigned. Then a Captain in NC Militia. From Bladen County, NC.	
Amis, William	3rd NC Regiment	5/6/1776, a Commissary. Resigned 12/1/1776. 12/9/1777, appointed a Contractor to provision Continental troops coming through Halifax, NC.	
Ammins,	1st NC	6/1/1778, a Sergeant under Capt. Griffith John	

Name	1st Unit	Year / Rank / Served Under / Notes	Known Battles
George	Regiment	McRee.	
Ammis, James	3rd NC Regiment	5/25/1776, a Private under Capt. Thomas Granbury. Discharged 11/10/1778.	
Ammons, James	9th NC Regiment	5/10/1777, a Private under Capt. Joseph J. Wade for three years. 3/12/1779, re-enlisted for the duration of the war under Capt. Griffith John McRee (1st NC Regiment). Dropped from the rolls in July 1779. aka James Ammonds.	
Ammons, Jordan	5th NC Regiment	4/20/1777, a Private under Capt. William Caswell. 9/9/1778, a Private under Capt. Robert Fenner (2nd NC Regiment).	
Ammons, Mark	1st NC Regiment	4/12/1781, a Private under Capt. William Lytle for 12 months. Deserted on 7/5/1782 (4th NC Regiment).	
Ammons, Thomas	3rd NC Regiment	7/20/1778, a Private under Lt. Joseph Montford for nine months.	
Ammons, Wood	1st NC Regiment	4/12/1781, a Private under Capt. William Lytle. Deserted on 7/5/1782.	
Amos, James	2nd NC Regiment	5/25/1777 and 9/9/1778, under Capt. Clement Hall. S12924.	
Amos, John	4th NC Regiment	April 1781, a Private under Capt. Joseph T. Rhodes for 12 months. Discharged 4/12/1782 at Bacon's Bridge, SC. Enlisted at Ramsey's Mill, NC. Earlier in NC Militia. S41414.	Siege of Augusta (GA).
Amsley, James	10th NC Regiment	A Private, unit and dates unknown. 3/12/1779, re-enlisted under Capt. Benjamin Williams (2nd NC Regiment). aka James Ansley.	
Anderson, George	1st NC Regiment	4/12/1781, a Private under Capt. Alexander Brevard for 12 months. Discharged on 4/12/1782. Earlier in NC Militia. From Edgecombe County. aka George Aderson. S46684.	Siege of Augusta (GA), Siege of Ninety-Six 1781 (SC).
Anderson, George	3rd NC Regiment	6/24/1779, a Private under Capt. Michael Quinn for nine months.	
Anderson, Isaac	3rd NC Regiment	6/22/1779, a Private under Capt. Kedar Ballard for nine months.	
Anderson, James	1st NC Regiment	May 1778, a Private under Capt. Tilghman Dixon. Upon the Fall of Charleston, he escaped capture and joined MG Richard Caswell's Militia as they were marching south.	Brandwine Creek (PA), Siege of Charleston (SC).
Anderson, James	4th NC Regiment	1/25/1777, a Drum Major. Died on 6/12/1778.	
Anderson, James	5th NC Regiment	1777, a Private under Capt. William Caswell. Died on 11/14/1777.	
Anderson, John	1st NC Regiment	4/28/1781, a Private under Capt. Griffith John McRee for 12 months.	
Anderson, John	5th NC Regiment	5/6/1776, a Private under Capt. John Enloe for one year. 10/24/1776, re-enlisted for another 3 years in the same unit. 10/25/1777, Capt. Enloe resigned, and his company was taken over by Capt. Thomas Armstrong (2nd NC Regiment). 9/10/1778, a known Private under Capt. Thomas Armstrong (2nd NC Regiment). Deserted on	Brandwine Creek (PA), Germantown (PA), Monmouth (NJ).

Name	1st Unit	Year / Rank / Served Under / Notes	Known Battles
		2/9/1780 (?). From Pitt County, NC.	
Anderson, Robert	1st NC Regiment	1781, a Private under Capt. William Armstrong for 12 months. Discharged on 5/22/1782.	
Anderson, Thomas	1st NC Regiment	4/28/1781, a Private under Capt. Alexander Brevard for 12 months. Discharged on 5/28/1782.	
Anderson, Thomas	5th NC Regiment	12/18/1776, a Musician under Capt. William Caswell. A Private in Jan. 1778. 9/9/1778, a Private under Capt. John Ingles (2nd NC Regiment). 3/12/1779, re-enlisted under Capt. John Ingles. Deserted on 4/30/1779.	
Anderson, William	3rd NC Regiment	1776, a Private under Capt. John Gray. 7/20/1778, a Private under Maj. Reading Blount (2nd NC Regiment) soon assigned to Lt./Capt. George "Gee" Bradley (3rd NC Regiment). A Sergeant on 10/25/1778. Apparently in NC Militia from late 1778 to Spring of 1779. Re-enlisted on 5/20/1779, appointed a Corporal. POW at the Fall of Charleston (SC), escaped after six weeks. From Edgecombe County, NC. S6512.	Siege of Charleston 1780 (SC).
Anderson, William	7th NC Regiment	1777, a Private under Capt. John McGlaughan. Deserted in Apr. 1777.	
Anderson, Wilson	5th NC Regiment	1777, a Corporal under Capt. John Enloe. Died 3/15/1778.	
Andress, Evan	4th NC Regiment	Aug. 1781, a Private under Capt. Joseph T. Rhodes for 12 months. Earlier in NC Militia. From Franklin County, NC. S45832.	
Andrews, Abiel	4th NC Regiment	1777, a Lieutenant under Capt. James Williams. Dropped from the rolls in Jan. 1778.	
Andrews, Alfred	1st NC Regiment	1781, a Corporal under Capt. William Armstrong for 12 months. Discharged on 3/27/1782. aka Alford Andrews.	
Andrews, Isaac	5th NC Regiment	6/5/1779, a Private under Maj. Reading Blount.	
Andrews, Joseph	1st NC Regiment	4/25/1781, a Private under Capt. William Walton for 12 months. Discharged 4/1/1782.	
Andrews, Richard	2nd NC Regiment	1777, an Ensign under Capt. James Gee. March 1778, a 2nd Lieutenant. POW at Ft. Lafayette 6/1/1779, exchanged 3/26/1781. While in prison, promoted to 1st Lieutenant on 5/10/1780. Wounded at Eutaw Springs on 9/8/1781, no further service. Resigned 8/18/1782.	Ft. Lafayette (NY), Eutaw Springs (SC).
Angel, Benjamin	3rd NC Regiment	A Private under Capt. James Emmett. Discharged 3/27/1778.	
Angel, Thomas	4th NC Regiment	1782, a Private under Capt. Thomas Evans for 18 months.	
Angel, Thomas	5th NC Regiment	5/12/1777, a Private under Capt. William Caswell. 9/9/1778, a known Private under Capt. Robert Fenner (2nd NC Regiment). POW at Ft. Lafayette, NY on 6/1/1779. aka Thomas Angle.	Ft. Lafayette (NY).
Angline, Cornelius	1st NC Regiment	1777, a Private under Capt. Henry "Hal" Dixon. Died in July 1777.	

Name	1st Unit	Year / Rank / Served Under / Notes	Known Battles
Anthony, James	9th NC Regiment	5/4/1777, a Private under Capt. Hezekiah Rice for three years. 9/8/1778, a known Private in the Lt. Colonel's Company (Lt. Col. Robert Mebane) (1st NC Regiment) led by Capt. Joshua Bowman - sick on that date at Valley Forge. 3/12/1779, re-enlisted for the duration of the war in the same unit. POW at the Fall of Charleston, eventually escaped. From Caswell County, NC. aka James Antoney. W3914.	Stony Point (NY), Siege of Charleston 1780 (SC).
Antony, John	3rd NC Regiment	6/22/1779, a Corporal under Capt. Kedar Ballard.	
Antrican, Francis	1st NC Regiment	4/25/1781, a Private under Capt. Thomas Donoho. After the battle of Eutaw Springs, transferred to Capt. Edward Yarborough (3rd NC Regiment). Discharged 5/22/1782. From Orange County, NC. Later in NC Militia. aka Francis Enderkin, Francis Andriken. S4261.	Siege of Ninety-Six 1781 (SC), Eutaw Springs (SC).
Apperson, William	1st NC Regiment	6/13/1777, a Private under Capt. John Brown. 9/8/1778, a known Private under Capt. Joshua Bowman. Discharged on 3/16/1779. From Surry County. aka William Epperson. His widow claims he was under Capt. Joseph Phillips (4th NC Regiment), but that was later in the NC Militia. W3915.	Brandywine Creek (PA), Germantown (PA), Monmouth (NJ).
Arbuckle, John	9th NC Regiment	1777, a Private under Capt. Thomas McCrory. Deserted on 12/2/1777. aka John Arnbuckle.	
Archdeacon, Richard	4th NC Regiment	8/1/1782, a Private under Capt. Joseph T. Rhodes for 18 months.	
Archer, Dempsey	7th NC Regiment	Nov. 1777, a Private under Capt. Lemuel Ely. Died 2/14/1778.	
Argoe, Levin	5th NC Regiment	1776, a Private under Capt. Reading Blount for 12 months. From Dobbs County. NC. Born 1754 in Johnston (what would become Dobbs) County, NC. Moved to SC during the war, joined SC Militia. aka Levin Argor. S17825.	
Armistead, Westwood	1st NC Regiment	Feb. 1781, a Private under Lt. John McNees. From Northampton County, NC. Captured by British while marching from Augusta to Ninety-Six, SC in March 1781 - held until the end of the war. W8100.	Hobkirk's Hill (SC), Siege of Augusta (GA).
Armstrong, Abel	2nd NC Regiment	Sep. 1775, a Lieutenant under Capt. William Knox. Later, a Captain in NC Militia.	Great Cane Brake (SC), Snow Campaign (SC), Ft. Moultrie #1 (SC).
Armstrong, Andrew	6th NC Regiment	1775, a 2nd Lieutenant in the Salisbury District Minutemen. 4/17/1776, a 2nd Lieutenant under Capt. John Baptiste Ashe and Col. John Alexander Lillington. 9/19/1776, a 1st Lieutenant under Capt. Griffith John McRee. Promoted to Captain on 10/12/1777. Retired 6/1/1778.	
Armstrong,	3rd NC	1781, a Private under Capt. Clement Hall.	

Name	1st Unit	Year / Rank / Served Under / Notes	Known Battles
Benjamin	Regiment	Deserted on 4/1/1782 (2nd NC Regiment).	
Armstrong, James	NC Light Dragoons	April 16, 1776, a Cornet under Capt. James Jones. 1777, a Lieutenant.	
Armstrong, James	2nd NC Regiment	9/1/1775, a Captain under Col. Robert Howe. 11/26/1776, Colonel over 8th NC Regiment. 6/1/1778, commander of 4th NC Regiment. Wounded at Stono Ferry, NC. Retired on half pay in Jan. 1781. Little known about him between Stono and his retirement - he did help recruit new men, and most considered him to be on active duty. From Pitt County, NC.	Moore's Creek Bridge [4], Brandywine Creek (PA), Germantown (PA), Stono Ferry (SC).
Armstrong, John	2nd NC Regiment	9/7/1775, a Captain under Col. Robert Howe. Wounded at Germantown. Promoted to Major and transferred to 4th NC Regiment on 10/4/1777. A Lt. Colonel in the 3rd NC Regiment on 7/17/1778 (back-dated - happened on 7/17/1782). 1780, in militia leading a unit simply called the NC Light Infantry. Early 1781, leading a Surry County Regiment attached to BG Andrew Pickens (SC), chasing Lt. Col. Lord Cornwallis. Mid-1781, commander of the newly-recreated 3rd NC Regiment - at battle of Eutaw Springs (SC). 2/6/1782, back in recreated 4th NC Regiment under Lt. Col. Archibald Lytle. Resigned on 1/1/1783.	Great Cane Brake (SC), Snow Campaign (SC), Ft. Moultrie #1 (SC), Brandywine Creek (PA), Germantown (PA), Stono Ferry (SC), Parker's Old Field (SC), Camden (SC), Eutaw Springs (SC).
Armstrong, Thomas	1st NC Regiment	3/28/1782, an Adjutant.	
Armstrong, Thomas	6th NC Regiment	1775, a 2nd Lieutenant in NC Militia. 4/17/1776, a 2nd Lieutenant under Capt. Arthur Council and Col. John Alexander Lillington. Also a Lieutenant under Capt. John Pugh Williams (5th NC Regiment). 10/25/1777, promoted to Captain. Transferred to 2nd NC Regiment on 6/1/1778. Captured at Ft. Lafayette, NY on May 31, 1779. Men allowed to march out wearing their side arms, an honor accorded them in admiration of the stubborn resistance. Exchanged Dec. 1779. Again, taken prisoner at the Fall of Charleston, exchanged July 1781. Aide-de-Camp to BG Jethro Sumner 3/28/1782 until the end of the war. Retired on 1/1/1783.	Monmouth (NJ), Ft. Lafayette (NY), Siege of Charleston 1780 (SC).
Armstrong, Thomas	6th NC Regiment	4/17/1776, a Lieutenant, Captain unknown.	
Armstrong, William	1st NC Regiment	1/4/1776, an Ensign. 4/10/1776, a 2nd Lieutenant. Promoted to 1st Lieutenant on 1/1/1777 under Capt. Thomas Hogg. Promoted to Captain on 8/29/1777 or 10/1/1777 (two sources). Transferred to 3rd NC Regiment on 2/6/1782. Retired 1/1/1783.	Monmouth (NJ), Eutaw Springs (SC).
Arnold, Aaron	2nd NC Regiment	4/1/1782, a Private under Capt. Robert Fenner, then Capt. Clement Hall for 12 months. Sick, sent home in Dec. 1782. From Orange County.	

Name	1st Unit	Year / Rank / Served Under / Notes	Known Battles
		S21051.	
Arnold, Arthur	5th NC Regiment	A Private under Capt. Reading Blount. Dropped from the rolls in Feb. 1778.	
Arnold, John	10th NC Regiment	4/21/1777, a Private under Capt. Silas Stevenson. Dropped from the rolls in Jan. 1778.	
Arnold, William	2nd NC Regiment	3/15/1781, a Private under Capt. Benjamin Carter for 12 months. Discharged on 4/25/1782 in SC. S37684.	Eutaw Springs (SC).
Arnot, David	1st NC Regiment	1778-1780, a Private under Capt. Joshua Bowman. During most of this time, he was removed from his unit and assigned as an Armourer under Col. Nicholas Long (Deputy QM General). Rejoined his unit on their way south to Charleston. Discharged there in April 1780. 8/23/1781, an Armourer again under Col. Nicholas Long. From Halifax County, NC. aka David Arnold. S41417.	
Arrington, John	3rd NC Regiment	3/1/1782, a Private under Capt. Samuel Jones.	
Arters, Stephen	3rd NC Regiment	1781, a Private under Capt. Clement Hall for 12 months. Discharged on 11/21/1782 (2nd NC Regiment).	
Arthur, John Lawson	5th NC Regiment	3/27/1777, a Private under Capt. William Caswell. 9/9/1778, a known Private under Capt. Robert Fenner (2nd NC Regiment). A Corporal in Nov. 1779.	
Arthur, William	6th NC Regiment	1777, a Sergeant under Capt. Philip Taylor. Deserted on 8/25/1777.	
Artis, John	3rd NC Regiment	May 1781, a Private under Capt. Clement Hall. Discharged on 11/1/1782 (2nd NC Regiment). From Cumberland County, NC. S41416.	
Asbett, James	5th NC Regiment	7/20/1778, a Private under Maj. Reading Blount for nine months. Dropped from the rolls in October 1778.	
Ash, Charles	1st NC Regiment	1782, a Private under Capt. Peter Bacot for 18 months.	
Ashe, Cincinatus	1st NC Regiment	4/19/1781, Lt. Col. John Baptiste Ashe asks HQ for a certificate of commission for this man.	
Ashe, John Jr.	4th NC Regiment	First, a Captain in the Wilmington District Minutemen. 4/17/1776, a Captain in 4th NC Regiment. Resigned ~4/3/1777.	
Ashe, John Baptiste	6th NC Regiment	First, a Captain in the Salisbury District Minutemen. 4/17/1776, a Captain in the 6th NC Regiment. A Major on 1/26/1777. He was also a Major in the 1st NC Regiment from 6/1/1778 to 11/2/1778, when he was promoted to Lt. Colonel (1st NC Regiment). Resigned after the battle of Eutaw Springs (SC).	Brandywine Creek (PA), Germantown (PA), Monmouth (NJ), Eutaw Springs (SC).
Ashe, Samuel	1st NC Regiment	POW at the Fall of Charleston, exchanged Summer of 1781 at Jamestown, VA. Marched home, rejoined, served to the end of the war. From New Hanover County, NC. W514.	Siege of Charleston 1780 (SC).
Ashe, Samuel	3rd NC Regiment	1/23/1781, a Lieutenant under Capt. Clement Hall. Resigned on 1/1/1783 (2nd NC Regiment).	

Name	1st Unit	Year / Rank / Served Under / Notes	Known Battles
Ashe, Samuel Jr.	1st NC Regiment	9/1/1775 to 4/15/1776, a Lieutenant and Paymaster. Paymaster Appointment Rescinded 4/18/1776. April 16, 1776, a Lieutenant under Capt. John Dickerson (NC Light Dragoons). Retired. 3/7/1777, a Captain of the First Troop of NC Light Dragoons - on that date, this unit was placed on the NC Continental Line. May 1777, sent to Fort Pitt under BG. McIntosh. Jan. 1779, a Captain under Col. Francois DeMalmedy (State Troops). One source claims he was a Major.	Moore's Creek Bridge [4], Brandywine Creek (PA), Germantown (PA), Monmouth (NJ).
Ashe, William	1st NC Regiment	4/19/1781, Lt. Col. John Baptiste Ashe asks HQ for a certificate of commission for this man.	
Ashlock, Jesse	2nd NC Regiment	5/15/1781, a Private under Capt. Tilghman Dixon then Capt. Joshua Hadley for 12 months. Discharged 5/21/1782 (1st NC Regiment) at Guilford Court House. From Caswell County, NC. S1160.	Eutaw Springs (SC).
Askins, John	4th NC Regiment	5/25/1781, a Private under Capt. George Dougherty for 12 months.	
Aspley, John	NC Light Dragoons	1777, a Sergeant under Capt. Samuel Ashe for 2-1/2 years. Discharged in 1780 in NC. 5/5/1781, reenlisted as a Sergeant Major under Capt. Thomas Donoho (1st NC Regiment) for one year. Discharged 5/5/1782 at Pon Pon, SC. aka John Apsley, John Ashley. W2903.	
Atkins, Benjamin	1st NC Regiment	1782, a Sergeant under Capt. Peter Bacot for 18 months.	
Atkins, Benjamin	5th NC Regiment	12/10/1777, a Private under Capt. Reading Blount. 9/9/1778, under Capt. Benjamin Andrew Coleman (2nd NC Regiment).	
Atkins, David	1st NC Regiment	1777, a Sergeant under Capt. Joshua Bowman. Discharged Nov. 1777.	
Atkins, James	4th NC Regiment	4/5/1777, a Chaplain. Resigned on 8/10/1777.	
Atkins, Shadrick	1st NC Regiment	1777, a Private under Capt. Joshua Bowman.	
Atkinson, John	2nd NC Regiment	5/26/1777, a Private, Captain unknown. 9/10/1778, a known Private under Capt. Thomas Armstrong.	
Attwood, John	3rd NC Regiment	1782, a Private under Capt. Alexander Brevard for 18 months.	
Austin, Absalom	9th NC Regiment	1777, a Private under Capt. Thomas McCrory. Died on 3/7/1778. aka Absolem Austin.	
Avarette, Thomas	3rd NC Regiment	7/20/1778, a Sergeant under Capt. Francis Child. Died on 11/28/1778.	
Avent, James		5/15/1776, a Private, regiment and unit unknown. Discharged on 11/10/1778.	
Averitt, Lewis	6th NC Regiment	A Private who enlisted for six months under an officer of Capt. Griffith John McRee's company. Petitioned the NC General Assembly for discharge - granted on 12/5/1777.	
Avery, George	1st NC Regiment	Aug. 1782, under Capt. Peter Bacot. Discharged 8/1/1783. From Edgecombe County,	

Name	1st Unit	Year / Rank / Served Under / Notes	Known Battles
		NC. Earlier in NC Militia. W8335.	
Avery, Isom	3rd NC Regiment	1782, a Private under Capt. Alexander Brevard for 18 months.	
Avery, James	9th NC Regiment	1777, a Private under Capt. Thomas McCrory. Deserted on 12/28/1777.	
Axum, Elijah	4th NC Regiment	2/7/1782, a Private under Capt. James Mills for 12 months.	
Axum, Philip	3rd NC Regiment	7/20/1778, a Private under Capt. Kedar Ballard for nine months.	
Babb, Joshua	2nd NC Regiment	6/19/1776, a Private under Capt. John Armstrong. A Musician in Apr. 1778. Back to Private in June 1778 under Capt. Robert Fenner. aka Joseph Babb.	
Bable, John	1st NC Regiment	Jan. 1782, a Private under Capt. William Armstrong.	
Bacchus, Joshua	2nd NC Regiment	5/25/1778, a Private under Capt. Armstrong.	
Bacchus, Joshua	1st NC Regiment	8/1/1782, a Private under Capt. Joshua Hadley for 18 mos. Possibly the same man as directly above.	
Bacchus, William	3rd NC Regiment	May 1781, a Private under Capt. Clement Hall for 12 months. Discharged on 8/1/1782 (2nd NC Regiment). From Chowan County, NC. aka William Bachus. W67.	
Backingham, William	3rd NC Regiment	7/20/1778, a Private under Capt. John Baker. Died on 11/25/1778.	
Bacot, Peter	1st NC Regiment	9/19/1776, an Ensign. 2/8/1777, a 2nd Lieutenant. Promoted to 1st Lieutenant on 10/4/1777. 9/8/1778, a 1st Lieutenant under Capt. James Read. POW at the Fall of Charleston, exchanged 6/14/1781. Promoted to Captain on 9/8/1781.	Siege of Charleston 1780 (SC).
Badget, Samuel	10th NC Regiment	8/24/1777, a Private under Capt. Silas Stevenson. Deserted on 1/20/1778.	
Bagby, John	1st NC Regiment	1775, a Private under Capt. Caleb Grainger for six months. Later in NC Militia. From Halifax County, NC. S31532.	
Baggett, Drew	2nd NC Regiment	1781, a Musician under Capt. Tilghman Dixon for 12 months. Discharged 5/25/1782 (1st NC Regiment).	
Baggett, Jesse	3rd NC Regiment	7/20/1778, a Corporal in the Lt. Colonel's Company (Lt. Col. William Lee Davidson) led by Lt. Capt. George "Gee" Bradley. 4/23/1779, a known Corporal in the Lt. Colonel's Company (Lt. Col. Robert Mebane) led by Capt. George "Gee" Bradley. aka Jesse Badgett.	
Baggett, John	1st NC Regiment	4/5/1781, a Private under Capt. Anthony Sharpe. Discharged on 4/5/1782.	
Baggot, Allen	3rd NC Regiment	6/5/1779, a Private under Capt. Michael Quinn. Dropped from the rolls in Oct. 1779.	
Bagley, Isaac	3rd NC Regiment	7/20/1778, a Corporal under Maj. Thomas Hogg for nine months.	
Bagley, Nathan	5th NC Regiment	8/5/1779, a Private under Maj. Reading Blount. Deserted in Oct. 1779.	

Name	1st Unit	Year / Rank / Served Under / Notes	Known Battles
Bagley, William H.	1st NC Regiment	9/8/1778, a known Private under Capt. Joshua Bowman.	
Bagnell, John	1st NC Regiment	1777, a Private, unit unknown. Dropped from the rolls in Feb. 1778. aka John Bagnel.	
Bagwell, John	1st NC Regiment	1782, a Private under Capt. Benjamin Carter for 18 months. From Bute, what is now Warren County. Earlier in NC Militia. S6571.	
Bailee, John	1st NC Regiment	2/7/1781, a Private under Capt. James Mills for 12 months. Discharged on 1/7/1782.	
Bailey, Benjamin	5th NC Regiment	10/1/1776, a 2nd Lieutenant under Capt. John Pugh Williams.	
Bailey, Benjamin	6th NC Regiment	10/20/1777, a Lieutenant. Dec. 1778, in 2nd NC Regiment.	
Bailey, Benjamin	5th NC Regiment	1775, an Ensign in the Edenton District Minutemen. 4/17/1776, an Ensign under Capt. Peter Simon and Col. Edward Buncombe. 11/28/1776, an Ensign under Capt. Henry Dawson (7th NC Regiment). 12/22/1776, a 2nd Lieutenant. Transferred to 1st NC Regiment on 6/1/1778. Promoted to Captain on 9/8/1781. Transferred to 3rd NC Regiment on 1/1/1782. Retired 1/1/1783.	Eutaw Springs (SC).
Bailey, H. William	1st NC Regiment	11/5/1776, a Sergeant under Capt. Thomas Hogg. A Private on 10/22/1777. Back to Sergeant on 3/21/1779. Dropped from the rolls in Nov. 1779.	
Bailey, Isaac	1st NC Regiment	Feb. 1779, a Private under Capt. Anthony Sharpe. Deserted on 4/22/1779.	
Bailey, John	4th NC Regiment	Jan. 1782, a Private under Capt. George Dougherty. From Anson County, NC. Born 1757 in Anson County, NC.	
Bailey, Joshua	2nd NC Regiment	12/1/1776, a Private under Capt. Edward Vail, Jr. 9/9/1778, a known Private in the Colonel's Company (Col. John Patten), led by Capt. John Craddock. A Sergeant on 7/1/1779. Discharged on 2/16/1780.	
Bailey, Joshua	4th NC Regiment	1782, a Private under Capt. Thomas Evans for 18 months. Dropped from the rolls in Jan. 1783 - transferred to (?).	
Bailey, Lewis	3rd NC Regiment	4/10/1776, a Private under Capt. Thomas Granbury for 2-1/2 years. Discharged in Oct. 1778.	
Bailey, Richard	3rd NC Regiment	Dec. 1781, a Private under Capt. Samuel Jones. Discharged in Oct. 1782 (1st NC Regiment).	
Bailey, Robert	3rd NC Regiment	7/20/1778, a Private under Capt. John Baker for nine months.	
Bailey, Stephen	1st NC Regiment	6/14/1781, a Private under Capt. Thomas Donoho for 12 months. Discharged on 6/14/1782 at Camden, SC. S41420.	
Bailey, William	3rd NC Regiment	6/21/1779, a Corporal under Capt. George "Gee" Bradley for 18 months.	
Bailey, William	5th NC Regiment	1779, a Private under Maj. Reading Blount. Deserted in Sep. 1779.	
Bain, John	9th NC Regiment	1777, a Private under Capt. Anthony Sharpe.	Brandywine

Name	1st Unit	Year / Rank / Served Under / Notes	Known Battles
	Regiment	Badly wounded at the battle of Brandywine Creek, PA. Earlier and later in PA units. Enlisted in Guilford County, NC. Born 1738 in DE. S22110.	Creek (PA).
Baker, Benjamin	2nd NC Regiment	4/15/1781, a Private under Capt. Tilghman Dixon. Discharged on 4/25/1782. From Hertford County, NC.	
Baker, Dempsey	3rd NC Regiment	9/10/1782, a Private under Capt. Benjamin Bailey for 18 months. Deserted on 6/21/1783 (?).	
Baker, George	6th NC Regiment	1775, in NC Militia. May 1776, a Private under Capt. John Baptiste Ashe, then Capt. George Dougherty. August 1777, hired Humphrey Price as a substitute since he was sick. Later, in NC Militia again. From Wilkes County, NC. S17249.	
Baker, Enos	3rd NC Regiment	7/20/1778, a Private under Capt. John Baker for nine months.	
Baker, Isaac	2nd NC Regiment	10/1/1782, a Private under Capt. Benjamin Andrew Coleman, then under Capt. Samuel Jones (1st NC Regiment) for 12 months. Discharged on 10/1/1783. R435.	
Baker, James	3rd NC Regiment	1781, a Private under Capt. Edward Yarborough for 12 months. Discharged on 4/22/1782. Enlisted in Rowan County. Earlier, lived in Hertford County - and in NC Militia, dates unknown. W9338.	
Baker, John	1st NC Regiment	5/25/1781, a Private under Capt. Thomas Donoho. Discharged 5/25/1782.	
Baker, John	1st NC Regiment	8/1/1782, a Private under Capt. Joshua Hadley for 18 months.	
Baker, John	3rd NC Regiment	6/1/1778, a known Sergeant Major.	
Baker, John	3rd NC Regiment	1777-1778, a Surgeon's Mate.	
Baker, John	5th NC Regiment	1777, a Private under Capt. John Enloe. Deserted on 3/15/1777.	
Baker, John	7th NC Regiment	11/28/1776, a 1st Lieutenant under Capt. Joseph Walker. 7/6/1777, a Captain and a Paymaster under Col. James Hogun. Retired 6/1/1778. Joined the 3rd NC Regiment in July 1778. Resigned 8/1/1779, leg wound. Then, a Colonel in the Georgia State Militia.	
Baker, Joshua	1st NC Regiment	11/10/1778, a Private under Capt. Anthony Sharpe for nine months.	
Baker, Joshua	1st NC Regiment	Dec. 1782, a Private under Capt. Peter Bacot. Died on 6/16/1783.	
Baker, Norris	3rd NC Regiment	4/18/1776, a Private under Capt. Pinketham Eaton. 9/9/1778, under Capt. Benjamin Andrew Coleman (2nd NC Regiment). Discharged 11/30/1778. Rejoined 2/20/1780.	
Baker, Peter	1st NC Regiment	2/8/1777, a 2nd Lieutenant under Capt. Joshua Bowman.	
Baker, Peter	5th NC	1778, a Private under Capt. William Lytle for	Stono Ferry

Name	1st Unit	Year / Rank / Served Under / Notes	Known Battles
	Regiment	nine months. From Caswell County. Discharged at Salisbury, NC. Earlier in the NC Militia. Enlisted in Caswell County, NC, moved to Guilford County, NC. Then joined SC unit. W277.	(SC).
Baker, Thomas	4th NC Regiment	2/14/1777, a Private under Capt. John Nelson for three years. 6/1/1778, a Private under Capt. Griffith John McRee (1st NC Regiment). 3/12/1779, re-enlisted for the duration of the war in the same unit. Deserted on 12/10/1779.	
Baker, William	2nd NC Regiment	7/20/1778, a Musician under Capt. Reading Blount for nine months.	
Baker, William	6th NC Regiment	6/26/1776, a Private under Lt./Capt. Thomas White for three years. 9/8/1778, a known Private under Capt. John Sumner (1st NC Regiment). Discharged on 4/1/1779. From Nash County. Later in NC Militia. R405.	
Baker, William	10th NC Regiment	A Private, unit and dates unknown. 9/9/1778, a known Private under Capt. Robert Fenner (2nd NC Regiment) - sick at Georgetown. Dropped from the rolls in Feb. 1779.	
Baker, William	10th NC Regiment	A Private, unit and dates unknown. 9/9/1778, a known Private under Capt. Robert Fenner (2nd NC Regiment) - sick at Valley Forge. Dropped from the rolls in Feb. 1779. Yes, two of 'em.	
Baldry, Isaac	5th NC Regiment	1776, a Private under Capt. John Enloe and Capt. William Caswell. From Pitt County. Earlier and later in NC Militia. W27543.	
Baldwin, Edward	4th NC Regiment	August 1782, a Private under Capt. Joseph T. Rhodes, then under Capt. Alexander Brevard (3rd NC Regiment) for 18 months. Furloughed in August 1783 at James Island, SC. Born 10/26/1766 in Spotsylvania County, VA. Enlisted in Caswell County, NC. R445A. aka Edward Bauldwin.	
Baler, Norris	3rd NC Regiment	4/18/1776, a Private under Capt. Pinketham Eaton for 2-1/2 years. Discharged on 11/30/1778.	
Ball, Hosea	2nd NC Regiment	5/10/1781, a Sergeant under Capt. William Goodman, then under Capt. Benjamin Bailey (1st NC Regiment) for 12 months. Earlier in NC Militia. From Currituck County, NC. S2365.	Eutaw Springs (SC).
Ballard, Dudley	1st NC Regiment	4/12/1781, a Private under Capt. William Lytle. Discharged on 4/12/1782.	
Ballard, Joel	1st NC Regiment	8/1/1782, a Corporal under Capt. Joshua Hadley for 18 months.	
Ballard, Kedar	3rd NC Regiment	4/17/1776, a 1st Lieutenant under Capt. Thomas Granbury, then Capt. James Emmett, then Capt. Jacob Turner. Promoted to Captain on 10/4/1777. 10/1/1779, also a Paymaster. POW at the Fall of Charleston - exchanged on 11/26/1782. Retired on 1/1/1783. From Gates County. Born 1753.	Siege of Charleston 1780 (SC).
Ballard,	3rd NC	1781, a Corporal under Capt. Edward	

Name	1ˢᵗ Unit	Year / Rank / Served Under / Notes	Known Battles
Lewis	Regiment	Yarborough for 12 months. Discharged on 4/22/1782.	
Ballard, Wyatt	2ⁿᵈ NC Regiment	6/6/1781, a Private under Capt. Benjamin Carter for 12 months. Discharged 4/7/1782 at Bacon's Bridge, SC. From Warren County, NC. S44327.	Fort Watson (SC), Friday's Ferry (SC), Siege of Augusta (GA), Eutaw Springs (SC) (wounded).
Ballentine, Alexander	10ᵗʰ NC Regiment	A Private, unit and dates unknown, enlisted for the duration of the war. 6/1/1778, a Private under Capt. Griffith John McRee (1st NC Regiment). A Sergeant in May 1779. Back to Private in Jan. 1780.	
Ballentine, James	4ᵗʰ NC Regiment	4/20/1777, a Sergeant Major. Dropped from the rolls in Jan. 1778. aka James Bollentine.	
Ballentine, Malachi	10ᵗʰ NC Regiment	6/2/1777, a Private under Capt. John Jarvis for three years. A Musician on 3/8/1779. 9/8/1778, a known Private in the Major's Company (Maj. John Baptiste Ashe) (1st NC Regiment). 3/12/1779, re-enlisted for the duration of the war in the same unit.	
Bane, John		7/9/1777, regiment, unit, and rank unknown, enlisted for three years. 9/8/1778, a known Private in the Lt. Colonel's Company (Lt. Col. Robert Mebane) (1st NC Regiment) led by Capt. Joshua Bowman - sick on that date at Valley Forge.	
Baney, Lyon	3ʳᵈ NC Regiment	7/20/1778, a Private under Capt. Kedar Ballard. Dropped from the rolls in Oct. 1778.	
Banks, Joseph	3ʳᵈ NC Regiment	9/13/1782, a Private under Capt. Benjamin Bailey for 18 months.	
Banks, Joseph	4ᵗʰ NC Regiment	July 1782, a Private under Capt. William Lytle for 18 months. Discharged in August 1783 at James Island, SC. From Pasquotank County, NC. S41426.	
Banks, William	3ʳᵈ NC Regiment	1781, a Private under Capt. Edward Yarborough for 12 months. Discharged on 4/1/1782.	
Banks, William	5ᵗʰ NC Regiment	1777, a Private under Capt. Benjamin Stedman. 9/9/1778, under Capt. Clement Hall (2nd NC Regiment). A Corporal on 11/10/1778. Deserted on 4/1/1779.	
Barber, John	2ⁿᵈ NC Regiment	7/20/1778, a Private under Capt. Reading Blount for nine months.	
Barber, William	1ˢᵗ NC Regiment	1777, a Private under Capt. Henry "Hal" Dixon. POW 4/14/1779 (?).	
Barber, William	3ʳᵈ NC Regiment	1779, a Private under Capt. Kedar Ballard. Probably the same man as directly above.	
Barbere, Isaac	3ʳᵈ NC Regiment	7/20/1778, a Private under Capt. Kedar Ballard for nine months.	
Barbre, Stansell	DQMG	1781-1783, a Blacksmith under Jesse Potts, Col. Nicholas Long. From Edgecombe County, NC. aka Stansell Barber. R20207.	

Name	1st Unit	Year / Rank / Served Under / Notes	Known Battles
Barco, John	10th NC Regiment	5/24/1777, a Drummer under Capt. Dempsey Gregory. Transferred to 1st NC Regiment under Capt. Howell Tatum. A Private in June 1778. POW at the Fall of Charleston, exchanged after five months. 1781, a Private under Capt. Clement Hall (3rd NC Regiment) for 12 months. Discharged on 7/10/1782 (2nd NC Regiment). From Camden County, NC. aka John Barko, John Barker. S34640.	Siege of Charleston 1780 (SC).
Barco, Leaman	10th NC Regiment	6/9/1777, a Private under Capt. Dempsey Gregory. 9/8/1778, a known Private under Capt. Howell Tatum (1st NC Regiment). A Corporal in Apr. 1782. aka Lemond Barker.	
Barco, Thomas	7th NC Regiment	1/10/1777, a Corporal under Capt. John Poynter. A Private in Jan. 1778. Back to Corporal in June 1778. 9/8/1778, a known Corporal under Capt. Tilghman Dixon (1st NC Regiment). Official records claim he deserted on 12/11/1779. He claims that he broke his arm marching south and was left behind. aka Thomas Barho, Thomas Barko, Thomas Barker. S33253.	Brandywine Creek (PA), Germantown (PA), Monmouth (NJ).
Barco, Wyllis	10th NC Regiment	12/17/1777, a Private, unit unknown. See Willis Barko below. Hard to believe there were two with such similar names, but slightly different start dates and units.	
Bardon, Christ.	1st NC Regiment	2/26/1778, a known Private under Capt. Howell Tatum.	
Barfield, James	10th NC Regiment	6/20/1777, a Private under Capt. Abraham Sheppard, Jr. POW at Ft. Lafayette, NY on 6/1/1779. Rejoined in Nov. 1779.	Ft. Lafayette (NY).
Barfield, Marmaduke	10th NC Regiment	5/4/1777, a Corporal under Capt. Abraham Sheppard, Jr. A Private in June 1778. 9/10/1778, a known Private under Capt. Thomas Armstrong (2nd NC Regiment). Deserted on 9/17/1778. aka Marmask Barfield.	
Barfield, Shadrack	10th NC Regiment	5/18/1777, a Private under Capt. Abraham Sheppard, Jr.	
Barfield, Stephen	4th NC Regiment	1776, a Private under Capt. Micajah Lewis. Died on 2/1/1778. From Duplin County, NC. aka Stephen Bearfield..	
Bargoner, John	3rd NC Regiment	5/15/1776, a Private under Capt. James Emmett for 2-1/2 years. 9/10/1778, a known Wagoner under Capt. Thomas Armstrong (2nd NC Regiment). Discharged on 11/10/1778. aka John Darganicar.	
Barker, Daniel	6th NC Regiment	1777, a Private under Capt. Thomas Donoho. Deserted in Aug. 1777.	
Barker, James	7th NC Regiment	1777, a Private under Capt. Thomas Brickell. Deserted in July 1777.	
Barker, Jesse	6th NC Regiment	1777, a Private under Capt. Thomas Donoho. Deserted in Aug. 1777.	
Barker, Joseph	4th NC Regiment	1781, a Private under Capt. George Dougherty for 12 months. Discharged 5/25/1782.	

Name	1st Unit	Year / Rank / Served Under / Notes	Known Battles
Barker, William	10th NC Regiment	4/19/1777, a Lieutenant under Capt. Isaac Moore. Dropped from the rolls in June 1778. aka William Barber.	
Barkley, Robert	2nd NC Regiment	1775, a Private under Capt. William Knox for six months. From Rowan County, NC. Discharged on 5/30/1776 at Wilmington, NC. Later in NC Militia in Lincoln County. W17252.	Great Cane Brake (SC), Snow Campaign (SC).
Barko, Willis	1st NC Regiment	9/23/1777, a Private under Capt. Henry "Hal" Dixon. 9/8/1778, a known Private under Capt. Tilghman Dixon (1st NC Regiment) - sick at Valley Forge. Died in Nov. 1778. aka Wyllis Barco, Willis Barco.	
Barksdale, Henry	1st NC Regiment	9/8/1778, a known Private in the Colonel's Company (Col. Thomas Clark) led by Capt. John Gambier Scull.	
Barksdale, Henry	4th NC Regiment	4/26/1776, a Sergeant under Capt. Micajah Lewis. A Corporal in June 1778. 9/8/1778, a known Corporal in the Colonel's Company (Thomas Clark - 1st NC Regiment) led by Capt. John Gambier Scull. Back to Sergeant on 11/10/1778. Discharged on 5/1/1779.	
Barler, William	1st NC Regiment	1777, a Private under Capt. Tilghman Dixon. POW on 4/14/1779 (?). Rejoined in 1779. W17232.	
Barlow, Christopher	7th NC Regiment	12/19/1776, a Private under Capt. John Poynter. Dropped from the rolls in Feb. 1778.	
Barlow, Robert	9th NC Regiment	1777, a Private under Capt. Joseph J. Wade. Died on 3/12/1778. aka Robert Barrlow.	
Barlow, William	1st NC Regiment	9/8/1778, a known Baggage Guard under Capt. James Read - stationed at that time in Lancaster, PA.	
Barnard, Peter	1st NC Regiment	1777, a Private under Capt. Henry "Hal" Dixon. Deserted 9/14/1778.	
Barnes, Britton	1st NC Regiment	1777, a Private under Capt. Joshua Bowman. Deserted in Sept. 1777.	
Barnes, Hezekiah	6th NC Regiment	4/16/1776, a Private under Capt. Thomas Donoho for 2-1/2 years. A Corporal in Sep. 1777. 6/1/1778, a Corporal under Capt. Griffith John McRee (1st NC Regiment). Discharged on 11/10/1778. aka Hezekiah Barns.	
Barnes, James	2nd NC Regiment	1776, a Private under Capt. John Armstrong. A Sergeant in Aug. 1777. Back to Private on 7/1/1778. 9/9/1778, a known Private under Capt. Robert Fenner (2nd NC Regiment). Deserted on 10/25/1778.	
Barnes, John	NC Artillery	10/1/1776, a Gunner under Capt. John Vance as NC Provincial Troops. 7/10/1777, on Continental Line. 11/16/1777, under Capt. John Kingsbury. 5/1/1778, in same unit. 9/16/1778, in same unit. A Sergeant on 4/1/1779.	
Barnes, John	1st NC Regiment	5/26/1776, a Private, unit unknown. 9/8/1778, a known Private in the Colonel's Company (Col. Thomas Clark) led by Capt. John Gambier	

Name	1st Unit	Year / Rank / Served Under / Notes	Known Battles
		Scull. 3/12/1779, in same unit. aka John Burns.	
Barnes, Moses	4th NC Regiment	1782, a Private under Capt. Thomas Evans for 18 months.	
Barnes, Thomas	3rd NC Regiment	5/24/1779, a Private under Capt. Michael Quinn. A Corporal in 1780.	
Barnes, William	3rd NC Regiment	6/24/1779, a Private under Capt. Michael Quinn.	
Barnes, William	5th NC Regiment	1777, a Private under Capt. Benjamin Stedman. Missing on 10/4/1777 (battle of Germantown). aka William Barns.	Germantown (PA).
Barnet, James	1st NC Regiment	6/1/1781, a Private under Capt. Griffith John McRee. Discharged on 6/1/1782. First name might be John.	
Barnett, Sion	2nd NC Regiment	1782, a Corporal under Capt. Benjamin Carter for 18 months. Discharged at 10-Mile Spring, SC outside Charleston. From Warren County, NC. Earlier in NC Militia. R531.	
Barnhill, David	4th NC Regiment	1781, a Private under Capt. George Dougherty for 12 months. Discharged 5/25/1782.	
Barnhill, Henry Jr.	3rd NC Regiment	7/20/1778, a Private under Capt. Francis Child for nine months. Discharged 5/4/1779 at Halifax, NC. From Pitt County, NC. Earlier in NC Militia. S6579.	
Barnhill, James	1st NC Regiment	1781, a Private under Capt. William Lytle for 12 months. Discharged on 6/10/1782.	
Barrer, Moses	1st NC Regiment	1782, a Private under Capt. Peter Bacot for 18 months.	
Barret, William	3rd NC Regiment	4/17/1776, a Captain under Col. Jethro Sumner. June 1778, joined the 3rd Continental Dragoons (VA) as a Lieutenant, promoted to Captain. Served until the end of the war. Born 1760 in Louisa County, VA [6].	Ft. Moultrie #1 (SC).
Barrett, John	DQMG	1780, a Wagoner under Col. Nicholas Long (Deputy QM General). 1780, a Wagon Maker on the roll of Capt. Solomon Wood (NC Light Dragoons) - this seems to be for bookkeeping only. 8/23/1781, a Timber Getter for Wagons, Gunstocks, etc. under Col. Nicholas Long. aka John Barrot.	
Barron, James	2nd NC Regiment	9/9/1778, a known Private in the Colonel's Company (Col. John Patten) led by Capt. John Craddock.	
Barrot, Joseph	1st NC Regiment	6/14/1781, a Private under Capt. Thomas Donoho. Deserted on 7/19/1781. Rejoined in Jan. 1782. Discharged on 6/14/1782.	
Barrow, Daniel	3rd NC Regiment	7/20/1778, a Private under Lt./Capt. George "Gee" Bradley for nine months.	
Barrow, Jacob	7th NC Regiment	11/28/1776, a 2nd Lieutenant under Capt. Henry Dawson. 12/22/1776, a 1st Lieutenant under Capt. Henry Dawson. From Halifax County, NC.	
Barrow, James	2nd NC Regiment	5/10/1776, a Private, unit unknown. 9/9/1778, a Private in the Colonel's Company (Col. John Patten) led by Capt. John Craddock. Discharged	

Name	1st Unit	Year / Rank / Served Under / Notes	Known Battles
		on 11/10/1778.	
Barrow, James	3rd NC Regiment	1777, a Drummer under Capt. Pinketham Eaton. A Drum Major in Sep. 1777. Dropped from the rolls in Sept. 1778.	
Barrow, John	4th NC Regiment	4/20/1776, a Private under Capt. John McLane, then under Capt. Micajah Lewis for 2-1/2 years. 9/8/1778, a known Private in the Colonel's Company (Col. Thomas Clark) (1st NC Regiment) led by Capt. John Gambier Scull. Discharged on 11/10/1778 in NY. Enlisted in Bertie County, NC. Later lived in Hertford County, NC. R566.	Brandywine Creek (PA), Germantown (PA).
Barrow, Samuel	7th NC Regiment	11/28/1776, a 2nd Lieutenant under Capt. Josiah Cotton, then under Capt. James Vaughan. From Northampton County, NC.	
Barrow, Willis	2nd NC Regiment	9/9/1778, a known Private in the Lt. Colonel's Company (Lt. Col. Selby Harney).	
Bartholo-mew, John	3rd NC Regiment	4/20/1776, a Private under Capt. Jacob Turner. 9/9/1778, a Private in the Lt. Colonel's Company (Lt. Col. Selby Harney) (2nd NC Regiment). Discharged in Oct. 1778. Apparently re-enlisted, dates and unit unknown (probably in NC Militia). From Bute County, what is now Warren County. W4880.	Ft. Moultrie #1 (SC), Brandywine Creek (PA), Monmouth (NJ), Savannah (GA), Camden (SC).
Bartlett, Hastin	6th NC Regiment	1776, a Private under Capt. Archibald Lytle for two years. Later in VA unit. From Orange County (what is now Person County), NC.	
Bartley, Henry	7th NC Regiment	3/13/1777, a Private under Capt. John Poynter. 2/26/1778, a known Private under Capt. Howell Tatum (1st NC Regiment).	
Basker, John		5/4/1777, unit and rank unknown. 9/8/1778, a known Private under Capt. Howell Tatum (1st NC Regiment).	
Basket, William	5th NC Regiment	6/15/1779, a Private under Capt. Joseph Montford for 18 months.	
Basmore, David	1st NC Regiment	8/6/1777, a Private, unit unknown. 9/8/1778, a known Private in the Colonel's Company (Col. Thomas Clark) led by Capt. John Gambier Scull.	
Bass, Aaron	3rd NC Regiment	6/24/1779, a Private under Capt. Michael Quinn. Deserted in Dec. 1779.	
Bass, Council	3rd NC Regiment	7/20/1778, a Fifer in the Lt. Colonel's Company (Lt. Col. William Lee Davidson) led by Lt./Capt. George "Gee" Bradley. 4/23/1779, a known Fifer in the Lt. Colonel's Company (Lt. Col. Robert Mebane) led by Capt. George "Gee" Bradley.	
Bass, Dred	1st NC Regiment	5/18/1781, a Private under Capt. Robert Raiford. Aug. 1781, transferred to the Legion (State Legion vs. Lee's Legion - which one, currently unknown).	
Bass, Elijah	1st NC Regiment	Spring of 1779, a Private under Lt./Capt. Benjamin Bailey. Killed at the battle of Eutaw	Eutaw Springs (SC).

Name	1st Unit	Year / Rank / Served Under / Notes	Known Battles
		Springs, SC on 9/8/1781. From Bute County, NC.	
Bass, Ezdras	10th NC Regiment	4/22/1777, a Private under Capt. Abraham Sheppard, Jr. Dropped from the rolls in June 1778.	
Bass, Hardy	1st NC Regiment	6/14/1781, a Private under Capt. Thomas Donoho. Discharged on 6/14/1782.	
Bass, Isaac	10th NC Regiment	5/18/1777, a Private under Capt. Abraham Sheppard, Jr.	
Bass, Moses	3rd NC Regiment	7/5/1779, a Private under Lt./Capt. George "Gee" Bradley. Deserted in Sep. 1779.	
Bass, Richard	1st NC Regiment	5/18/1781, a Private under Capt. Thomas Donoho. Dropped from the rolls sometime during 1781.	
Bass, Uriah	3rd NC Regiment	7/20/1778, a Private in the Lt. Colonel's Company (Lt. Col. William Lee Davidson) led by Lt./Capt. George "Gee" Bradley. 4/23/1779, a known Private in the Lt. Colonel's Company (Lt. Col. Robert Mebane) led by Capt. George "Gee" Bradley.	
Bateman, Jonathan	2nd NC Regiment	5/15/1777, a Private under Capt. Edward Vail, Jr. Died on 4/8/1778.	
Bateman, Nary	3rd NC Regiment	7/20/1778, a Private under Capt. Francis Child for nine months.	
Bateman, Peter	10th NC Regiment	7/12/1777, a Private under Capt. Abraham Sheppard, Jr. 9/10/1778, a known Private under Capt. Thomas Armstrong (2nd NC Regiment). Dropped from the rolls in June 1779. Re-enlisted in Nov. 1779.	
Bateman, William	2nd NC Regiment	1782, a Private under Capt. Robert Raiford for 18 months.	
Bates, Edward	3rd NC Regiment	1779, a Private under Capt. Kedar Ballard.	
Bates, Frederick	2nd NC Regiment	1777, a Private under Capt. Charles Allen. 9/10/1778, a known Private under Capt. Thomas Armstrong.	
Bates, James	1st NC Regiment	4/15/1781, a Private under Capt. Anthony Sharpe. Discharged on 4/15/1782.	
Bates, Luke	10th NC Regiment	4/27/1777, a Private under Capt. Abraham Sheppard, Jr. for three years. 9/8/1778, a known Private under Capt. Howell Tatum (1st NC Regiment). 3/12/1779, re-enlisted for the duration of the war in the same unit.	
Bates, William	2nd NC Regiment	April or May 1781, a Private under Capt. Tilghman Dixon for 18 months. Discharged in Dec. '81 or Jan. 82 in Wilmington, NC. Earlier in Militia for about two years, unit and dates unknown. S32105.	Eutaw Springs (SC)
Batesta, John	NC Artillery	6/5/1777, a Matross under Capt. John Vance as NC State Troops. 7/10/1777, on Continental Line. 11/16/1777, under Capt. John Kingsbury. Deserted on 4/8/1778. aka John Babtists.	
Batey, Hugh	1st NC Regiment	1777, a Private under Capt. Robert Ralston. A Corporal in Nov. 1777. Died 8/6/1778.	

267

Name	1st Unit	Year / Rank / Served Under / Notes	Known Battles
Bation, David	5th NC Regiment	5/20/1779, a Private under Capt. Joseph Montford. Deserted in Sep. 1779.	
Batstaff, Frederick	1st NC Regiment	1782, a Private under Capt. Peter Bacot for 18 months.	
Battiss, John	3rd NC Regiment	7/20/1778, a Private in the Lt. Colonel's Company (Lt. Col. William Lee Davidson) led by Lt./Capt. George "Gee" Bradley. 4/23/1779, a known Private in the Lt. Colonel's Company (Lt. Col. Robert Mebane) led by Capt. George "Gee" Bradley. Died at Philadelphia Hospital. aka John Batliss.	
Baxley, Joshua	1st NC Regiment	8/1/1782, a Private under Capt. Joshua Hadley. Died on 6/6/1783. aka Joshua Backsley.	
Baxter, David	1st NC Regiment	5/26/1781, a Private under Capt. Alexander Brevard.	
Baxter, Samuel	2nd NC Regiment	11/22/1776, a Sergeant under Capt. Benjamin Williams. A Private on 1/1/1778. 9/9/1778, a known Private in the Major's Company (Maj. Hardy Murfree). 3/12/1779, re-enlisted in the Major's Company (Maj. Hardy Murfree). POW at Ft. Lafayette, NY on 6/1/1779. Promoted to Corporal in Nov. 1779. A Musician Sergeant in Jan. 1782.	Ft. Lafayette (NY).
Baxter, Thomas	1st NC Regiment	1782, a Private under Capt. Alexander Brevard for 18 months.	
Baxter, William	1st NC Regiment	4/12/1781, a Private under Capt. Benjamin Bailey for 12 months. Discharged on 4/12/1782.	
Bay, Andrew	9th NC Regiment	Jan. 1777, a Private under Capt. Thomas McCrory, enlisted for three years, served 2-1/2 years. 5/1/1777, a Sergeant Major. From Guilford County, NC. S2940.	Brandywine Creek (PA), Germantown (PA), Briar Creek (GA).
Bayley, William Henry	1st NC Regiment	1776, a Private under Capt. Joshua Bowman.	
Bayne, John	9th NC Regiment	7/9/1777, a Private under Capt. Thomas McCrory. Dropped from the rolls in Feb. 1779.	
Beach, Robert	3rd NC Regiment	7/20/1778, a Private under Capt. Francis Child for nine months.	
Beal, Jonathan	2nd NC Regiment	8/7/1777, a Private under Capt. James Martin for 2-1/2 years. Died on 5/16/1778. aka John Beal.	
Bealey, Archibald	3rd NC Regiment	1782, a Private under Capt. Edward Yarborough for 12 months. Discharged on 6/17/1782. aka Archibald Bealy.	
Beaman, Jeremiah	2nd NC Regiment	1777, a Private under Capt. James Gee. 9/9/1778, a known Private under Capt. John Ingles. aka Jeremiah Beamon.	
Beard, Andrew	1st NC Regiment	1775, a known Sergeant under Capt. Robert Rowan. 7/31/1779, letter from R. Rowan to Gov. R. Caswell.	
Beard, Valentine	NC Light Dragoons	April 16, 1776, a Cornet under Capt. Martin Phifer.	

Name	1st Unit	Year / Rank / Served Under / Notes	Known Battles
Beasley, Samuel	3rd NC Regiment	Jan. 1779, a Private under Capt. John Medearis for nine months.	
Beasley, Samuel	5th NC Regiment	5/20/1777, a Private under Capt. Reading Blount.	
Beasley, William	2nd NC Regiment	5/17/1781, a Corporal under Capt. William Goodman, then Capt. Benjamin Bailey (1st NC Regiment). Discharged 5/17/1782 (3rd NC Regiment) at Edenton, NC. Enlisted in Currituck County, NC. S41432.	Eutaw Springs (SC).
Beasley, William	3rd NC Regiment	1/2/1782, a Private under Capt. Samuel Jones for 12 months.	
Beausnaut, Joseph	6th NC Regiment	1777, a Sergeant under Capt. Thomas Donoho. Dropped from the rolls in Jan. 1778.	
Beavans, Robert	2nd NC Regiment	1776, a 1st Lieutenant, unit unknown.	
Beaver, John	5th NC Regiment	3/1/1779, a Corporal under Maj. Reading Blount. Discharged on 12/1/1779.	
Beayous, George	3rd NC Regiment	1778, a Private under Lt./Capt. Joseph Montford. aka George Beavens.	
Beck, Frederick	9th NC Regiment	1777, a Private under Capt. Richard D. Cook. Deserted on 10/10/1777.	
Beddlehizer, Lewis	4th NC Regiment	1/1/1777 or 6/17/1777 (two sources), a Private under Capt. Robert Smith for three years. 9/8/1778, a known Private in the Colonel's Company (Col. Thomas Clark) (1st NC Regiment) led by Capt. John Gambier Scull - assigned to QM General's department. Dropped from the rolls in Feb. 1779. aka Lewis Biddlehizer.	
Bedo, John	3rd NC Regiment	Feb. 1779, a Private under Capt. John Medearis.	
Beeks, William	7th NC Regiment	1777, a Master Sergeant. A Lieutenant and an Adjutant 11/22/1777 to 6/1/1778 (retired).	
Beeney, Joseph	5th NC Regiment	6/1/1779, a Private under Capt. Joseph Montford. Dropped from the rolls in Oct. 1779.	
Belch, Philip	5th NC Regiment	1777, a Private under Capt. Henry Darnell. Died on 11/21/1777.	
Belew, Charles	4th NC Regiment	5/20/1776, a Private under Capt. Joseph Phillips. A Sergeant in April 1778. 9/8/1778, a Sergeant under Capt. James Read (1st NC Regiment). aka Charles Ballew, Charles Ballen. Dropped from the rolls in Dec. 1778.	
Belew, John	4th NC Regiment	1782, a Private under Capt. William Lytle for 18 months.	
Bell, Benjamin	DQMG	1780, a Tailor on the roll of Capt. Solomon Wood (NC Light Dragoons) - this seems to be for convenience only. 8/23/1781, a Tailor under Col. Nicholas Long (Deputy QM General).	
Bell, Benjamin	2nd NC Regiment	1777, a Corporal under Capt. Clement Hall. Died on 4/17/1778.	
Bell, Elias	3rd NC Regiment	7/20/1778, a Private under Capt. John Baker for nine months.	
Bell, George	1st NC Regiment	4/25/1781, a Private under Capt. Griffith John McRee. Discharged on 4/25/1782.	

Name	1st Unit	Year / Rank / Served Under / Notes	Known Battles
Bell, Green	7th NC Regiment	11/28/1776, a Captain under Col. James Hogun. Resigned before 12/17/1776. From Edgecombe County, NC.	
Bell, James	1st NC Regiment	8/1/1782, a Corporal under Capt. Joshua Hadley for 18 months.	
Bell, John	1st NC Regiment	5/3/1777, a Private under Capt. Tilghman Dixon. 9/8/1778, a known Private under Capt. Tilghman Dixon.	
Bell, John	1st NC Regiment	1777, a Musician under Capt. Joshua Bowman. A PC (?) in June 1778.	
Bell, Josiah	3rd NC Regiment	1781, a Private under Capt. Clement Hall for 12 months. Discharged on 7/10/1782 (2nd NC Regiment) at Bacon's Bridge, SC. Enlisted in Virginia. Claims to have been under Capt. William Ferrebee during 1779, but Ferrebee was not a captain (4th NC Regiment) until July 1781. S41433.	
Bell, Robert	1st NC Regiment	5/18/1781, an Ensign under Capt. Robert Raiford. 9/8/1781, a Lieutenant. Transferred to 2nd NC Regiment on 2/6/1782. Served until the end of the war.	
Bell, Samuel	2nd NC Regiment	2/7/1782, a Private under Capt. Benjamin Andrew Coleman for 12 months. Furloughed in Dec. 1782. From Duplin County (what is now Sampson County). Born in Surry County, VA in 1749. S6598.	
Bell, William	1st NC Regiment	1777, a Private under Capt. Joshua Bowman.	
Bell, William	2nd NC Regiment	5/15/1781, a Private under Capt. Benjamin Andrew Coleman for 12 months. Re-enlisted on 8/1/1782 for 12 months.	
Belsire, Thomas	6th NC Regiment	1777, a Private under Capt. George Dougherty. Missing on 10/4/1777 at the battle of Germantown, PA. Rejoined in July 1778 under Capt. Griffith John McRee (1st NC Regiment). 9/8/1778, a known Private under Capt. Griffith John McRee (1st NC Regiment) - sick on that date. aka Thomas Bellsire.	Germantown (PA).
Benbury, Thomas	5th NC Regiment	4/17/1776, a Paymaster. Paymaster Appointment Rescinded 4/18/1776.	
Bencham, Hodges	8th NC Regiment	1777, a Sergeant under Capt. Francis Tartanson. Died 3/30/1778.	
Bennett, Benjamin	10th NC Regiment	6/16/1777, a Private under Capt. John Jarvis. Dropped from the rolls in June 1778.	
Bennett, Jacob	10th NC Regiment	9/8/1777, a Private under Capt. John Jarvis for three years. 9/8/1778, a known Private in the Major's Company (Maj. John Baptiste Ashe) (1st NC Regiment). 3/12/1779, re-enlisted for the duration of the war in the same unit.	
Bennett, James	7th NC Regiment	1777, a Private under Capt. Henry Dawson. Died in July 1777.	
Bennett, James	7th NC Regiment	1777, a Private under Capt. Joseph Walker. Died on 1/26/1778.	
Bennett, John	2nd NC	1782, a Private under Capt. Robert Raiford.	

270

Name	1st Unit	Year / Rank / Served Under / Notes	Known Battles
	Regiment	The official records indicate that he deserted on 6/11/1783. He claims he left because of rampant illness, along with many others. From New Hanover County, NC. Earlier in NC Militia. R760.	
Bennett, Moses	3rd NC Regiment	A Private under Capt. Pinketham Eaton. Discharged on 11/10/1778.	
Bennett, Nehemiah	3rd NC Regiment	7/20/1778, a Private under Lt./Capt. George "Gee" Bradley for nine months. On the official rolls as Nehemiah Bennell.	
Bennett, Reuben	1st NC Regiment	5/5/1781, a Private under Capt. Robert Raiford for 12 months. Discharged 5/5/1782 at Round O, SC. Enlisted in Warren County, NC. S18714.	Eutaw Springs (SC).
Bennett, Sion	2nd NC Regiment	1782, a Corporal under Capt. Benjamin Carter.	
Bennett, Solomon	3rd NC Regiment	6/29/1779, a Private under Capt. Kedar Ballard. Deserted on 8/5/1779.	
Bennett, Thomas	3rd NC Regiment	5/8/1776, a Private under Capt. Jacob Turner. A Corporal in June 1778. A Sergeant on 10/25/1778. Discharged on 11/10/1778.	
Bennett, William	3rd NC Regiment	7/20/1778, a Private under Lt./Capt. George "Gee" Bradley for nine months.	
Bennett, William	3rd NC Regiment	7/20/1778, a Private under Capt. Francis Child for nine months.	
Benson, Bagley	2nd NC Regiment	9/9/1778, a known Private under Capt. Robert Fenner.	
Benson, Bailey	5th NC Regiment	12/18/1777, a Private under Capt. William Caswell. Discharged 2/8/1780. aka Benson Bailey.	
Bently, Thomas	3rd NC Regiment	1781, a Private under Capt. Clement Hall for 12 months. Discharged on 4/1/1782 (2nd NC Regiment). Drafted while living in Pitt County. aka Thomas Bentley. S8063.	
Benton, David	4th NC Regiment	6/15/1776, a Private under Capt. John Nelson for three years. 9/8/1778, a known Private under Capt. Joshua Bowman (1st NC Regiment). Then, under Capt. Griffith John McRee. Discharged on 5/15/1779 at West Point, NY. Later in NC Militia, unit unknown. S39195.	
Benton, Dempsey	2nd NC Regiment	1782, a Private under Capt. Robert Raiford for 18 months.	
Benton, Edom	3rd NC Regiment	7/20/1778, a Private under Maj. Thomas Hogg. Died on 11/7/1778.	
Benton, Elkanah	1st NC Regiment	5/16/1782, a Private under Lt. Aber Lamb. Enlisted at Nixonton, NC. Discharged at Georgetown, SC. From Pasquotank County, NC. S41429.	
Benton, Jesse	3rd NC Regiment	5/11/1776, a Sergeant under Capt. James Emmett. Dropped from the rolls in Oct. 1777.	
Benton, Jesse	4th NC Regiment	1777, a Private under Capt. James Williams. Dropped from the rolls in Feb. 1778.	
Benton, Jethro	3rd NC Regiment	4/14/1777, a known Ensign under Capt. Thomas Granbury.	

Name	1st Unit	Year / Rank / Served Under / Notes	Known Battles
Benton, John	4th NC Regiment	1781, a Private under Capt. Joseph T. Rhodes for 12 months. Wounded at Eutaw Springs. Discharged on 2/17/1782. From Wake County, NC.	Eutaw Springs (SC).
Benton, Joshua	4th NC Regiment	1781, a Private under Capt. George Dougherty for 12 months. Discharged 5/25/1782.	
Benton, Kedar	3rd NC Regiment	4/16/1776, a Private under Capt. James Emmett. 9/9/1778, a Private in the Major's Company (Maj. Hardy Murfree - 2nd NC Regiment). Discharged on 10/16/1778. aka Kadar Banton.	
Benton, Nathan	3rd NC Regiment	1/1/1782, a Private under Capt. Samuel Jones for 12 months.	
Bernell, Nehemiah	3rd NC Regiment	7/20/1778, a Private under Lt./Capt. George "Gee" Bradley.	
Berry, Amos	10th NC Regiment	1/10/1778, a Private, unit unknown. Died on 4/10/1778.	
Berry, Caleb	3rd NC Regiment	Jan. 1779, a Private under Capt. John Medearis.	
Berry, James	1st NC Regiment	4/28/1781, a Private under Capt. Alexander Brevard. Discharged on 4/25/1782.	
Berry, James	2nd NC Regiment	1782, a Private under Capt. Benjamin Carter for 18 months. Deserted on 12/25/1782.	
Berry, John	1st NC Regiment	1777, a Private under Capt. Joshua Bowman. Deserted in Sept. 1777.	
Berry, John	2nd NC Regiment	1777, a Private recruited by Capt. Manlove Tarrant, then under ?. Enlisted in Camden County, NC. Wounded, POW at the Fall of Charleston (SC), escaped soon thereafter. S41428.	Brandywine Creek (PA), Germantown (PA), Monmouth (NJ), Siege of Charleston (SC).
Berry, John	2nd NC Regiment	11/9/1777, a Private under Capt. James Gee for three years. 9/9/1778, a known Private under Capt. John Ingles. A Corporal in Dec. 1778. A Sergeant in Nov. 1779. Back to Private on 2/10/1780.	
Berry, Robert	1st NC Regiment	1778, an Artificer under Capt. Joshua Bowman. 9/8/1778, a known Artificer under Capt. Tilghman Dixon (1st NC Regiment).	
Berry, Robert	6th NC Regiment	1777, a Private under Capt. George Dougherty. Dropped from the rolls in July 1779 (4th NC Regiment).	
Berry, Solomon	2nd NC Regiment	1777, a Sergeant under Capt. James Gee for three years. 9/9/1778, a known Sergeant under Capt. John Ingles. Re-enlisted as a Private on 1/31/1780.	
Berryhill, William	1st NC Regiment	9/1/1775, a Lieutenant, unit unknown.	
Bertie, John	10th NC Regiment	8/7/1777, a Private under Capt. Isaac Moore for three years. 9/8/1778, a known Private in the Lt. Colonel's Company (Lt. Col. Robert Mebane) (1st NC Regiment) led by Capt. Joshua Bowman. 3/12/1779, re-enlisted for the duration	

Name	1ˢᵗ Unit	Year / Rank / Served Under / Notes	Known Battles
		of the war in the same unit. Deserted on 1/1/1783. aka John Bartie, John Bartee.	
Bertie, Thomas	8ᵗʰ NC Regiment	11/28/1776, an Ensign under Capt. William Gurley. Resigned Feb. 1777. From Hyde County, NC.	
Beseley, John	4ᵗʰ NC Regiment	1777, a Corporal under Capt. William Goodman for three years.	
Best, John	4ᵗʰ NC Regiment	1781, a Private under Capt. Joseph T. Rhodes for 12 months. Born in Dobbs County, living in Duplin County when he enlisted. Discharged in 1782 at Long Bay. S6614.	
Best, Thomas	2ⁿᵈ NC Regiment	1/15/1777, a Private under Capt. Charles Allen. 9/10/1778, a known Private under Capt. Thomas Armstrong. Deserted on 2/17/1780.	
Betts, Mathias	3ʳᵈ NC Regiment	9/14/1781, a Private under Capt. Samuel Jones for 12 months.	
Betts, Matthew	4ᵗʰ NC Regiment	1776, a Private under Capt. Joseph Phillips. Discharged on 11/25/1777.	
Betts, William	3ʳᵈ NC Regiment	3/6/1782, a Private under Capt. Samuel Jones for 12 months.	
Beverhouse, Abraham	1ˢᵗ NC Regiment	June 1781, a Private under Lt./Capt. Benjamin Bailey. Discharged on 6/26/1782.	
Bexley, James	1ˢᵗ NC Regiment	4/5/1781, a Private under Capt. Anthony Sharpe. Discharged on 4/5/1782.	
Bibber, Daniel	2ⁿᵈ NC Regiment	6/6/1781, a Private under Capt. Benjamin Carter for 12 months. Discharged on 6/6/1782.	
Bibby, Absalom	2ⁿᵈ NC Regiment	5/18/1781, a Private under Capt. Tilghman Dixon. Discharged on 5/21/1782 (1ˢᵗ NC Regiment).	
Bibby, Solomon	3ʳᵈ NC Regiment	5/17/1781, a Private under Capt. Edward Yarborough. Dropped from the rolls on 4/1/1782. A free man of color from Franklin County. aka Solomon Bibbie. S6644.	Eutaw Springs (SC).
Biby, Thomas	3ʳᵈ NC Regiment	1779, a Private under Capt. Kedar Ballard. Discharged on 12/1/1779.	
Bickerstaff, John	2ⁿᵈ NC Regiment	6/8/1776, an Ensign.	
Bido, John		A Private, regiment and unit unknown. Deserted in Sep. 1779.	
Bilbry, Nathaniel	3ʳᵈ NC Regiment	4/20/1776, a Private under Capt. Thomas Granbury and Capt. William Brinkley. Discharged in Oct. 1778. Rejoined the 2nd NC Regiment under Capt. Benjamin Williams. aka Nathaniel Bilbory, Bilberry. From Edgecombe County. Later, a Lieutenant in NC Militia. S6645.	Brandywine Creek (PA), Germantown (PA), Monmouth (NJ)
Billings, Abraham	1ˢᵗ NC Regiment	4/28/1781, a Private under Capt. John McRees. Deserted on 7/13/1781.	
Billips, Richard	3ʳᵈ NC Regiment	1781, a Private under Capt. Edward Yarborough for 12 momths. Discharged on 4/22/1782.	
Billups, Thomas	7ᵗʰ NC Regiment	3/11/1777, a Musician under Capt. John McGlaughan for three years. 2/26/1778, a Private under Capt. Howell Tatum (1st NC Regiment). 9/8/1778, a known Musician under	

Name	1st Unit	Year / Rank / Served Under / Notes	Known Battles
		Capt. Howell Tatum). 4/15/1781, a Musician under Capt. Robert Raiford (1st NC Regiment). Discharged 4/15/1782. From Bertie County, NC. aka Thomas Billops, Thomas Billips. W3927.	
Bingham, John	4th NC Regiment	1782, a Private under Capt. Anthony Sharpe for 18 months.	
Binham, Drury	2nd NC Regiment	12/16/1776, a Private, unit unknown. 9/10/1778, a known Private under Capt. Thomas Armstrong.	
Binum, William	1st NC Regiment	4/12/1781, a Private under Capt. William Lytle. Discharged on 4/12/1782.	
Bird, Hardy	10th NC Regiment	7/1/1777, a Private under Capt. Abraham Sheppard, Jr. 9/9/1778, a known Private in the Major's Company (Maj. Hardy Murfree) (2nd NC Regiment). 3/12/1779, re-enlisted in the Major's Company (Maj. Hardy Murfree). POW at Ft. Lafayette, NY on 6/1/1779. Rejoined in Nov. 1779. From Johnston County, NC. W18597.	Ft. Lafayette (NY).
Bird, Jacob	1st NC Regiment	4/28/1781, a Private under Capt. Griffith John McRee. Deserted on 6/18/1781.	
Bird, Moses	4th NC Regiment	1776, a Musician under Capt. Micajah Lewis. Dropped from the rolls in Jan. 1778. Jan. 1779, a Musician under Capt. Philip Taylor (5th NC Regiment) for 2-1/2 years.	
Bird, Thomas	DQMG	1780, a Shoemaker on the roll of Capt. Solomon Wood (NC Light Dragoons) - this seems to be for convenience only. 8/23/1781, a Shoemaker under Col. Nicholas Long (Deputy QM General).	
Birgay, William	5th NC Regiment	Jan. 1779, a Private under Capt. Philip Taylor. A Corporal in May 1779.	
Bishop, Christopher	4th NC Regiment	1777, a Musician under Capt. James Williams. Discharged on 11/8/1777.	
Bishop, Moses	3rd NC Regiment	7/20/1778, a Sergeant in the Colonel's Company (Col. Jethro Sumner) for nine months.	
Bishop, William	1st NC Regiment	1781, a Private under Capt. William Armstrong for 12 months. Discharged on 12/1/1782.	
Bissel, Enos	10th NC Regiment	9/10/1777, a Private, unit unknown. 9/9/1778, a known Private in the Colonel's Company (Col. John Patten) (2nd NC Regiment) led by Capt. John Craddock. aka Enos Bizzel.	
Biznard, Peter	1st NC Regiment	9/8/1778, a known Private under Capt. Joshua Bowman.	
Black, George	4th NC Regiment	1782, a Sergeant under Capt. William Lytle for 18 months. Deserted on 12/10/1782.	
Black, Giren	3rd NC Regiment	8/1/1782, a Private under Capt. Benjamin Bailey for 12 months.	
Black, Guin	1st NC Regiment	1782, a Private under Capt. Peter Bacot for 18 months.	
Black, James	1st NC Regiment	Aug. 1782, a Private under Capt. Joshua Hadley, then under Capt. William Lytle for 18 months. Discharged (4th NC Regiment) in Jan.	

Name	1st Unit	Year / Rank / Served Under / Notes	Known Battles
		1783 in Wilmington, NC. Born in Scotland. Living in what is now Robeson County when he enlisted (Bladen County at that time).	
Black, James	3rd NC Regiment	9/1/1782, a Private under Capt. Benjamin Bailey for 12 months.	
Black, John	9th NC Regiment	1777, a Private under Capt. Thomas McCrory. Deserted in Nov. 1777.	
Black, Martin	10th NC Regiment	5/16/1777, a Private under Capt. Silas Stevenson. June 1778, under Capt. Clement Hall (2nd NC Regiment). 9/9/1778, a known Private under Capt. Clement Hall (2nd NC Regiment). POW at the Fall of Charleston, escaped after seven days. Re-enlisted for 18 months under Capt. Benjamin Coleman (2nd NC Regiment). Discharged in Dec. 1782 in Charleston, SC. Enlisted at New Bern, NC. S41441.	Monmouth (NJ), Stony Point (NY), Near West Point (NY), Siege of Charleston 1780 (SC).
Black, Martin	4th NC Regiment	1782, a Private under Capt. Thomas Evans for 18 months.	
Blackard, Willoughby	3rd NC Regiment	Fall of 1778, a Private under Lt./Capt. William Saunders. POW at the Fall of Charleston (SC), exchanged quickly. Rejoined under Capt. Edward Yarborough. Discharged on 11/15/1781. From Bute County, NC. S29638.	Stono Ferry (SC), Siege of Charleston (SC), Camden (SC), Guilford Court House, Hobkirk Hill (SC), Eutaw Springs (SC).
Blackleach, Thomas	8th NC Regiment	1777, a Sergeant under Capt. John Walsh. A Private in Jan. 1778. Dropped from the rolls in Feb. 1778.	
Blackley, Ebenezer	10th NC Regiment	4/20/1778, a Surgeon's Mate. Dropped from the rolls in Oct. 1778.	
Blackstone, Henry	1st NC Regiment	6/20/1780, a Musician under Capt. William Lytle for 12 months. 4/1/1782, a Private under Capt. Benjamin Andrew Coleman (2nd NC Regiment) for 12 months.	
Blackwell, James	NC Light Dragoons	1777, a Horseman under Capt. John Dickerson for three years. 3/7/1777, this unit was on the Continental Line (earlier - NC State Troops). Discharged 5/10/1777 in Northampton County, NC. From Granville County, NC. W18613.	
Blackwell, James	3rd NC Regiment	7/20/1778, a Private under Lt./Capt. George "Gee" Bradley for nine months.	
Blago, Moses	1st NC Regiment	7/20/1778, a Private under Maj. Thomas Hogg for nine months.	
Blake, Christopher	5th NC Regiment	1777, a Private under Capt. Simon Alderson. Died on 4/30/1778.	
Blake, William	1st NC Regiment	1777, a Private under Capt. Robert Ralston. A Sergeant in Oct. 1777. A Private in May 1778. 9/8/1778, a known Private under Capt. John Sumner (1st NC Regiment). A Corporal in Nov. 1779. A Sergeant 2/10/1780.	
Blalock,	9th NC	1777, a Private under Capt. Joseph J. Wade.	

Name	1st Unit	Year / Rank / Served Under / Notes	Known Battles
William	Regiment	Deserted on 8/6/1777.	
Blamer, John	4th NC Regiment	1782, a Corporal under Capt. Thomas Evans. Died on 6/13/1783.	
Blanchard, John	2nd NC Regiment	10/11/1776, a Private, unit unknown. 9/10/1778, a known Private under Capt. Thomas Armstrong.	
Blanchard, Micajah	3rd NC Regiment	1781, a Private under Capt. Clement Hall for 12 months. Discharged on 8/1/1782 (2nd NC Regiment).	
Blanchett, Frederick	10th NC Regiment	8/20/1777, a Musician under Capt. Andrew Vanoy. 9/9/1778, a known Private in the Colonel's Company (Col. John Patten) (2nd NC Regiment) led by Capt. John Craddock.	
Blanchett, James	2nd NC Regiment	7/20/1778, a Private under Capt. Reading Blount for nine months. aka James Blanchets.	
Blanchett, John	3rd NC Regiment	10/11/1776, a Musician under Capt. James Emmett. Transferred to 2nd NC Regiment on 3/27/78 under Capt. Reading Blount.	
Blanchett, Thomas	2nd NC Regiment	6/21/1777, a Sergeant under Capt. Andrew Vanoy. A Private in June 1778 under Capt. Robert Fenner (2nd NC Regiment). POW at the Fall of Charleston, SC - died in captivity. aka Thomas Blanchet. W20395.	Siege of Charleston 1780 (SC).
Blango, Benjamin	3rd NC Regiment	7/20/1778, a Private under Maj. Thomas Hogg for nine months.	
Blango, Moses	3rd NC Regiment	7/20/1778, a Private under Maj. Thomas Hogg for nine months.	
Blanks, Nicholas	6th NC Regiment	5/2/1776, a Private under Lt./Capt. George Dougherty for 2-1/2 years. 9/8/1778, a known Private under Capt. Griffith John McRee (1st NC Regiment) - sick on that date at Valley Forge. Discharged on 11/10/1778.	
Blanton, Kadar	2nd NC Regiment	9/9/1778, a known Private in the Major's Company (Maj. Hardy Murfree).	
Blanton, Levy	3rd NC Regiment	6/2/1779, a Private under Capt. George "Gee" Bradley.	
Blanton, Rowland	7th NC Regiment	11/28/1776, an Ensign under Capt. John Glaughan. From Edenton District.	
Bletcher, Jacob	1st NC Regiment	1781, a Private under Capt. William Armstrong for 12 months. Discharged on 12/23/1782. From Orange County, NC. Earlier, in NC Militia. S39198.	
Blocksom, Sovereign	5th NC Regiment	11/29/1776, a Private under Capt. John Enloe. 9/10/1778, a known Private under Capt. Thomas Armstrong (2nd NC Regiment). Discharged on 1/30/1780. aka Sovvain Blocksom. aka Sovereign Blokam. aka Sovrain Blocksom.	
Blockwell, James	3rd NC Regiment	7/20/1778, a Private under Lt./Capt. George "Gee" Bradley.	
Blount, Benjamin	1st NC Regiment	4/15/1781, a Private under Capt. Anthony Sharpe. Re-enlisted in March 1782. Deserted in June 1783 (?).	
Edmond Blount	2nd NC Regiment	4/15/1781, a Private under Capt. Tilghman Dixon. Dropped from the rolls sometime during	

Name	1st Unit	Year / Rank / Served Under / Notes	Known Battles
		1781.	
Blount, Frederick	2nd NC Regiment	7/15/1782, a Private under Capt. Clement Hall.	
Blount, Jacob	2nd NC Regiment	4/17/1776, a Paymaster. Paymaster Appointment Rescinded 4/18/1776. 1777, PM of militia.	
Blount, James	2nd NC Regiment	9/1/1775, a Captain under Col. Robert Howe. Resigned before 6/1/1778. From Edgecombe County, NC.	Great Bridge (VA).
Blount, James	5th NC Regiment	1777, a Private under Capt. Simon Alderson. Discharged on 10/6/1777.	
Blount, Jesse	8th NC Regiment	12/11/1776, a Paymaster.	
Blount, John	6th NC Regiment	1777, a Private under Capt. George Dougherty. Died on 1/24/1778.	
Blount, Reading	5th NC Regiment	1775, a Captain in the New Bern District Minutemen. 4/17/1776, a Captain. 5/12/1778, a Major. 6/1/1778, a Major in 2nd NC Regiment. Summer of 1778, returned home to help recruit new Continentals. Early 1779, a Major in the Craven County Regiment attached to Col. William Caswell (Dobbs County) for a very short while. Early 1779, also a Major under Col. Thomas Clark in the "new" 5th NC Regiment. Mid-1781, a Major who commanded the newly-recreated 2nd NC Regiment until 2/6/1782, when Lt. Col. Henry "Hal" Dixon took over. When Dixon died on 7/17/1782, he re-assumed command of the regiment.	Brandywine Creek (PA), Germantown (PA), Briar Creek (GA), Stono Ferry (SC), Guilford Court House, Eutaw Springs (SC).
Blount, Thomas	3rd NC Regiment	7/20/1778, a Private under Maj. Thomas Hogg for nine months. 6/29/1779, a Private under Capt. Kedar Ballard for 18 months. aka Thomas Blunt.	
Blount, Thomas	4th NC Regiment	1781, a Private under Capt. George Dougherty for 12 months. Discharged 5/25/1782.	
Blount, Thomas	5th NC Regiment	1775, an Ensign in the New Bern District Minutemen. 4/17/1776, an Ensign under Capt. Reading Blount and Col. Edward Buncombe. 4/28/1777, a Lieutenant under Capt. Benjamin Stedman. Dropped from the rolls in Jan. 1778. 1780, a Militia Colonel as Adjutant General to MG Richard Caswell in the NC Militia. Younger brother of Capt./Maj. Reading Blount.	
Blount, Warren	1st NC Regiment	11/10/1778, a Sergeant under Capt. Anthony Sharpe for nine months. 1795, living in Duplin County, NC.	
Blount, Whitmel	4th NC Regiment	1775, a 2nd Lieutenant in the Edenton District Minutemen. 11/20/1776, a Lieutenant in the 4th NC Regiment.	
Blount, William	3rd NC Regiment	12/11/1776, a Paymaster.	
Blue, Neil	1st NC Regiment	1777, a Private under Capt. Joshua Bowman. 7/1/1779, a Corporal. Deserted 12/7/1779. aka Neal Blue.	

Name	1st Unit	Year / Rank / Served Under / Notes	Known Battles
Blurton, Edward	5th NC Regiment	April 1776, a Private under Capt. William Ward, then under Capt. Benjamin Andrew Coleman for 18 months. Discharged in Nov. 1777 at Valley Forge, PA. Later in NC Militia. W5223.	Brandywine Creek (PA).
Blurton, Henry	5th NC Regiment	1777, a Sergeant under Capt. Benjamin Andrew Coleman. Dropped from the rolls in Jan. 1778.	
Blythe, Joseph		7/2/1779, a Sergeant, unit unknown.	
Blythe, Joseph	1st NC Regiment	7/12/1776, a Surgeon. POW at the Fall of Charleston, exchanged 6/14/1781. Feb. 1782, in 4th NC Regiment until the end of the war.	Siege of Charleston 1780 (SC).
Blythe, Samuel	1st NC Regiment	3/28/1776, an Ensign. 7/7/1776, a 2nd Lieutenant. 2/5/1777, a 1st Lieutenant under Capt. Joshua Bowman. Resigned 4/16/1778.	
Bogart, Tunis	2nd NC Regiment	3/1/1779, a Private under Capt. Robert Fenner. aka Junis Bogart.	
Bogas, Benajah	2nd NC Regiment	Dec. 1782, a Private under Capt. Benjamin Carter.	
Boggs, Ezekiel	4th NC Regiment	7/26/1776, a Private, unit unknown. 1777, under Capt. William Goodman. 9/8/1778, a known Private in the Colonel's Company (Col. Thomas Clark) (1st NC Regiment) led by Capt. John Gambier Scull - at Tarrytown on that date. Discharged 7/25/1779.	
Boggs, John	4th NC Regiment	7/15/1776, a Private under Capt. William Goodman for three years. 9/8/1778, a known Private in the Colonel's Company (Col. Thomas Clark) (1st NC Regiment) led by Capt. John Gambier Scull. Discharged on 7/15/1779. From Orange County, NC. W18627.	Brandywine Creek (PA), Germantown (PA), Monmouth (NJ).
Bogle, Archibald	2nd NC Regiment	A Sergeant under Capt. Charles Allen, dates unknown. 9/8/1778, a known Sergeant under Capt. Thomas Armstrong.	
Bolin, Thomas	4th NC Regiment	1782, a Private under Capt. William Lytle for 18 months. From Wilkes County, NC. Furloughed in Aug. 1783 in Wilmington, NC. Born 1/12/1766 in Orange County, what is now Caswell County, NC. aka Thomas Boling. S32126.	
Bolton, Benjamin	1st NC Regiment	1781, a Private under Capt. William Armstrong for 12 months. Discharged on 12/1/1782 at Ashley Hill, SC. From Richmond County, NC. S37795.	
Bolton, Richard	3rd NC Regiment	7/20/1778, a Sergeant under Capt. Kedar Ballard for nine months.	
Bond, Elisha	9th NC Regiment	1/1/1777, a Private under Capt. Richard D. Cook for three years. 9/8/1778, a known Private in the Lt. Colonel's Company (Lt. Col. Robert Mebane) (1st NC Regiment) led by Capt. Joshua Bowman. Discharged on 1/27/1780.	
Bond, James	2nd NC Regiment	1/15/1777, a Private, unit unknown. 9/10/1778, a known Private under Capt. Thomas	

278

Name	1ˢᵗ Unit	Year / Rank / Served Under / Notes	Known Battles
		Armstrong.	
Bond, Richard	1ˢᵗ NC Regiment	8/1/1782, a Sergeant under Capt. Joshua Hadley for 18 months.	
Bond, Richard	5ᵗʰ NC Regiment	1777, a Private under Capt. Reading Blount. Dropped from the rolls in Feb. 1778.	
Bond, Thomas	9ᵗʰ NC Regiment	1777, a Private under Capt. Richard D. Cook. Died on 12/13/1777.	
Bone, Archibald	1ˢᵗ NC Regiment	March 1776, a Private under Capt. Robert Rowan then Capt. Joshua Bowman for 12 months. Discharged March 1777 at Wilmington, NC. Later in NC Militia. From Cumberland County, NC. S41456.	Breech Inlet Naval Battle (SC).
Bone, James	2ⁿᵈ NC Regiment	1/15/1777, a Corporal under Capt. Charles Allen for three years. A Private in Jan. 1778. Died 6/17/1783.	
Bonner, William	1ˢᵗ NC Regiment	4/15/1781, a Corporal under Capt. Anthony Sharpe. Dropped from the rolls sometime during 1781.	
Bonny, Gideon	4ᵗʰ NC Regiment	1777, a Corporal under Capt. William Goodman. Dec. 1778, a Lieutenant, Captain not known. Sources claim 6th Regiment, but it was folded into the 2nd Regiment in June 1778.	
Booling, William	1ˢᵗ NC Regiment	6/14/1781, a Private under Capt. Thomas Donoho. Dropped from the rolls sometime during 1781.	
Boomer, William	5ᵗʰ NC Regiment	Jan. 1779, a Private under Maj. Pinketham Eaton.	
Boon, David	1ˢᵗ NC Regiment	1781, a Private under Capt. William Lytle for 12 months. Discharged on 5/19/1782. From Hertford County, NC.	
Boon, David	3ʳᵈ NC Regiment	7/20/1778, a Private under Capt. Kedar Ballard for nine months.	
Boon, Elisha	3ʳᵈ NC Regiment	7/20/1778, a Private under Capt. John Baker for nine months. Discharged in April 1779 at Halifax, NC. 5/4/1781, re-enlisted as a Private under Capt. Tilghman Dixon (2nd NC Regiment). Discharged on 5/4/1782 (1ˢᵗ NC Regiment). Then in NC Militia for six months - unit unknown. From Nash County, NC. S35196.	Eutaw Springs (SC).
Boon, James	3ʳᵈ NC Regiment	7/20/1778, a Private under Lt./Capt. George "Gee" Bradley for nine months.	
Boon, John	1ˢᵗ NC Regiment	Jan. 1782, a Private under Capt. James Mills for 12 months.	
Boon, Joseph	4ᵗʰ NC Regiment	1776, a Private under Capt. Micaiah Lewis. Dropped from the rolls in Jan. 1778.	
Boon, Lewis	2ⁿᵈ NC Regiment	7/20/1778, a Private under Capt. Reading Blount for nine months. Discharged in April 1779. From Bertie County, NC. S6683.	
Boon, Willis	5ᵗʰ NC Regiment	1776, a Private under Capt. John Pugh Williams for 2-1/2 years. Dropped from the rolls in Feb. 1778. Claims to have served the full term, then re-enlisted for another year under Maj. Hardy Murfree (2nd NC Regiment). Then, joined VA	Brandywine Creek (PA), Germantown (PA), Guilford Court House

Name	1st Unit	Year / Rank / Served Under / Notes	Known Battles
		unit under Lt. Col. William Washington. aka Whylis Boon. S41455.	(under Lt. Col. W. Washington). Claims to have been at battle of Camden, but Maj. H. Murfree not there.
Boon, William	8th NC Regiment	1/1/1777, a Private under Capt. John Walsh. 9/9/1778, a known Private under Capt. Clement Hall (2nd NC Regiment).	
Boons, William		A Private, regiment and unit unknown. Deserted in Sep. 1779.	
Bootey, Caudel	3rd NC Regiment	7/20/1778, a Private under Capt. Michael Quinn for nine months. aka Candel Bootey.	
Booth, John	8th NC Regiment	2/19/1777, a Private under Capt. Robert Raiford. Dropped from the rolls in Feb. 1778. aka John Boothe.	
Bootle, Thomas	4th NC Regiment	5/20/1776, a Private under Capt. Joseph Phillips for three years. Deserted on 10/26/1777. Rejoined in Feb. 1778. 9/8/1778, a known Private under Capt. James Read (1st NC Regiment). Discharged on 5/26/1779 at Paramus, NJ. Then joined a MA unit. aka Thomas Booth. W16507.	
Boozman, Ethelredge	3rd NC Regiment	7/20/1778, a Private under Capt. Kedar Ballard. Dropped from the rolls in Oct. 1778. aka Ethelredge Bozman.	
Boozman, Jesse	3rd NC Regiment	7/20/1778, a Private under Capt. Kedar Ballard for nine months. Enlisted at Tarborough, NC. Discharged 4/15/1779 at Halifax, NC. From Edgecombe County, NC. aka Jesse Bozman. S41447.	
Boren, Jacob	2nd NC Regiment	11/29/1776, a Sergeant under Lt./Capt. James Martin. aka Jacob Bosen.	
Borows, John	2nd NC Regiment	1777, a Private under Capt. William Fenner. Dropped from the rolls in April 1778.	
Bostian, Andrew	NC Light Dragoons	April 1776, a Private of the 2nd Company of Light Horse under Capt. Martin Phifer. 3/7/1777, on Continental Line. Discharged 4/18/1778. aka Andrew Boston, Andrew Bostain. S6680.	Germantown (PA).
Bostian, Jacob	NC Light Dragoons	April 1776, a Private of the 2nd Company of Light Horse under Capt. Martin Phifer. 3/7/1777, on Continental Line. Discharged in 1778. From Rowan County, NC. aka Jacob Boston. S6675.	Brandywine Creek (PA), Germantown (PA).
Boston, Andrew	1st NC Regiment	4/28/1781, a Private under Capt. Griffith John McRee. Discharged 4/28/1782.	
Boston, Christopher	1st NC Regiment	4/28/1781, a Private under Capt. Griffith John McRee, then under Capt. Alexander Brevard. Discharged 4/28/1782 in Salisbury, NC. W12323.	Siege of Ninety-Six 1781 (SC), Eutaw Springs

Name	1st Unit	Year / Rank / Served Under / Notes	Known Battles
			(SC).
Boswell, William	10th NC Regiment	6/17/1777, a Sergeant under Capt. Isaac Moore for three years. A Private in June 1778. 9/8/1778, a known Private in the Lt. Colonel's Company (Lt. Col. Robert Mebane) (1st NC Regiment) led by Capt. Joshua Bowman. A Corporal in Oct. 1778. POW at the Fall of Charleston, SC. Enlisted in Perquimans County, NC. aka William Baswell. W18639.	Monmouth (NJ), Siege of Charleston 1780 (SC).
Bowen, James	5th NC Regiment	Jan. 1779, a Private under Maj. Pinketham Eaton.	
Bowen, Stephen	1st NC Regiment	7/28/1778, a Sergeant under Capt. Anthony Sharpe for three years. Furloughed Jan.-May 1780 due to illness. Discharged in August 1781. Then joined NC Militia. From Duplin County, NC. W5853.	Stono Ferry (SC) (?).
Bowers, Giles	3rd NC Regiment	7/20/1778, a Private under Lt./Capt. George "Gee" Bradley. Deserted in Oct. 1778. 1782, a Private under Capt. Robert Raiford (2nd NC Regiment). Deserted on 6/8/1783 (?).	
Bowers, Solomon	1st NC Regiment	4/5/1781, a Private under Capt. Anthony Sharpe. Discharged on 4/15/1782.	
Bowers, William	5th NC Regiment	1777, a Private under Capt. Benjamin Stedman. Died in June 1778.	
Bowles, Benjamin	1st NC Regiment	4/10/1781, a Private under Capt. Robert Smith then Capt. Alexander Brevard for 12 months. Discharged 4/12/1782 in Chatham County, NC. Later lived in Montgomery County, NC. aka Benjamin Boles, Benjamin Bowels. S41448.	Siege of Augusta (GA).
Bowles, Jesse	1st NC Regiment	4/12/1781, a Private under Capt. Alexander Brevard for 12 months. Discharged on 4/12/1782.	
Bowles, Thomas	1st NC Regiment	1781, a Private under Capt. Thomas Donoho for 12 months. Furloughed due to getting Smallpox, recovered and went to Hillsborough to join up with his unit - captured by Col. David Fanning on 9/12/1781, POW for 13 months. Rejoined his unit at Round O, SC and was soon thereafter discharged. Earlier in Militia. From Orange County, NC. W5857.	Hillsborough.
Bowles, William	1st NC Regiment	4/12/1781, a Private under Capt. Alexander Brevard for 12 months. Discharged on 4/12/1782. Born 6/6/1752. R1076.	
Bowlin, Baxter	1st NC Regiment	Nov. 1777, a Private under Capt. Robert Ralston. Dropped from the rolls in Jan. 1778.	
Bowlin, Jeremiah	1st NC Regiment	1777, a Private under Capt. Robert Ralston. Deserted on 8/4/1777.	
Bowman, John		A Private, regiment and unit unknown. From Rowan County, NC. POW at the Fall of Charleston, SC - Paroled 5/19/1780. Born 11/15/1762. W397.	Siege of Charleston 1780 (SC).
Bowman, Joshua	1st NC Regiment	9/1/1775, a 2nd Lieutenant. 11/15/1775, a 1st Lieutenant. Acted as a Captain at the battle of Moore's Creek Bridge (?). 9/18/1776, a Captain	Moore's Creek Bridge [4], Brandywine

Name	1st Unit	Year / Rank / Served Under / Notes	Known Battles
		under Col. Thomas Clark. Wounded at Stony Point (NY). Killed on March 30, 1780 during the Siege of Charleston. Some records list him as Joseph Bowman.	Creek (PA), Germantown (PA), Monmouth (NJ), Stony Point (NY), Siege of Charleston 1780 (SC).
Bowman, Robert	1st NC Regiment	A Private under Capt. Henry "Hal" Dixon. Deserted in 1776.	
Boyakin, James	1st NC Regiment	A Private under Capt. Peter Bacot for 18 months.	
Boyce, Arthur	2nd NC Regiment	June 1778, a QM Sergeant in the Colonel's Company (Col. John Patten) led by Capt. John Craddock. June 1779, a Sergeant. Deserted on 12/2/1779.	
Boyce, John	1st NC Regiment	1781, a Private under Capt. Anthony Sharpe. Died on 7/25/1782.	
Boyce, Seth	8th NC Regiment	1777, a Private under Capt. John Walsh. Died on 10/5/1777.	Germantown (PA).
Boyce, William	1st NC Regiment	1781, a Private under Capt. William Armstrong for 12 months. Discharged on 10/1/1782. Earlier in SC Militia. From Randolph County, NC. W9361.	
Boyd, Adam	1st NC Regiment	Oct. 1777, a Private, unit unknown.	
Boyd, Adam	1st NC Regiment	Oct. 1777, a Judge Advocate.	
Boyd, Adam	1st NC Regiment	1/4/1776, an Ensign. 3/3/1776, a 2nd Lieutenant. A Chaplain in the 2nd NC Regiment in Oct. 1777. Another source claims it was the 5th NC Regiment (wrong). 8/18/1778, Chaplain of the entire NC Brigade until June 1780.	Moore's Creek Bridge [4].
Boyd, Benjamin	2nd NC Regiment	1782, a Corporal under Capt. Benjamin Carter for 18 months.	
Boyd, Benjamin	4th NC Regiment	1781, a Private under Capt. Joseph T. Rhodes for 12 months. Discharged on 1/23/1782.	
Boyd, Hugh	4th NC Regiment	4/17/1776, a Surgeon.	
Boyd, James	3rd NC Regiment	7/20/1778, a Private in the Lt. Colonel's Company (Lt. Col. William Lee Davidson) led by Lt./Capt. George "Gee" Bradley. 4/23/1779, a known Private in the Lt. Colonel's Company (Lt. Col. Robert Mebane) led by Capt. George "Gee" Bradley.	
Boyd, John	1st NC Regiment	1775, a Private under Capt. Alfred Moore for six months. Re-enlisted for 12 months as a Sergeant. Discharged at Charleston, joined the SC 1st Regiment as a Sergeant for another 12 months. S41446.	
Boyd, John	6th NC Regiment	1777, a Sergeant under Capt. Griffith John McRee. A Private in June 1778 under Capt. Tilghman Dixon. Back to Sergeant in Nov.	

Name	1st Unit	Year / Rank / Served Under / Notes	Known Battles
		1779 (1st NC Regiment). From Rowan County, NC. Born 8/3/1758. W24708.	
Boyd, John	10th NC Regiment	6/14/1777, a Private under Capt. Silas Stevenson. Died on 3/22/1778.	
Boyd, Joseph	3rd NC Regiment	7/20/1778, a Corporal under Lt./Capt. George "Gee" Bradley for nine months.	
Boyd, Samuel	3rd NC Regiment	7/20/1778, a Private in the Lt. Colonel's Company (Lt. Col. William Lee Davidson) led by Lt./Capt. George "Gee" Bradley. 4/23/1779, a known Private in the Lt. Colonel's Company (Lt. Col. Robert Mebane) led by Capt. George "Gee" Bradley.	
Boyd, William	1st NC Regiment	1775, a Private under Capt. John Walker, Lt. Absalom Tatum. From Guilford County. Later in NC Militia in Guilford County and Wilkes County. This man and the next man are probably father and son, or perhaps the same exact person. S30881.	Moore's Creek Bridge (?).
Boyd, William	1st NC Regiment	1775, a Private under Capt. John Walker, Lt. Absalom Tatum. From Guilford County. Later in NC Militia in Mecklenburg County and Surry County. S45878.	Moore's Creek Bridge (?).
Boyd, William	10th NC Regiment	6/14/1777, a Private under Capt. Silas Stevenson. 9/9/1778, a known Private in the Lt. Colonel's Company (Lt. Col. Selby Harney) (2nd NC Regiment).	
Boyes, Jesse	4th NC Regiment	4/22/1776, a Private under Capt. Micajah Lewis. 9/8/1778, a known Private in the Colonel's Company (Col. Thomas Clark) (1st NC Regiment) led by Capt. John Gambier Scull. Discharged on 11/10/1778. aka Jesse Boyce, Jesse Boice.	
Boyle, Archibald	2nd NC Regiment	9/10/1778, a Private under Capt. Thomas Armstrong.	
Boyles, Benjamin	1st NC Regiment	1781, a Private under Capt. Alexander Brevard. Discharged on 4/12/1782.	
Boyles, William	1st NC Regiment	1781, a Private under Capt. Alexander Brevard. Discharged on 4/12/1782.	
Bozar, Thomas	1st NC Regiment	1777, a Private under Capt. Lawrence Thompson.	
Bozer, Thomas	1st NC Regiment	1776, a Private under Capt. Joshua Bowman. 9/8/1778, a known Private under Capt. Joshua Bowman. Probably the same man as directly above - two not listed in 1st NC Regiment.	
Brabble, James	10th NC Regiment	5/17/1777, a Private under Capt. John Jarvis for three years. 9/8/1778, a known Private in the Major's Company (Maj. John Baptiste Ashe) (1st NC Regiment). aka James Brable.	
Brabsy, Jacob	5th NC Regiment	5/9/1776, a Private under Capt. John Pugh Williams. 9/9/1778, a known Private in the Major's Company (Maj. Hardy Murfree) (2nd NC Regiment). Discharged on 11/10/1778. aka Jacob Braboy.	
Bracell,	2nd NC	1782, a Private under Capt. Benjamin Carter for	

Name	1st Unit	Year / Rank / Served Under / Notes	Known Battles
George	Regiment	18 months.	
Bracher, Samuel	4th NC Regiment	1777, a Private under Capt. James Williams. Discharged in Nov. 1777.	
Bracker, Isaac	4th NC Regiment	2/7/1782, a Private under Capt. James Mills. Died on 9/18/1782.	
Braddy, Benjamin	3rd NC Regiment	7/20/1778, a Private under Maj. Thomas Hogg for nine months.	
Braddy, Henry	3rd NC Regiment	7/20/1778, a Private under Maj. Thomas Hogg for nine months.	
Braddy, John	1st NC Regiment	11/10/1778, a Private under Capt. Anthony Sharpe for nine months.	
Bradford, John	1st NC Regiment	3/12/1779, a known Private under Capt. John Sumner. aka John Broadford.	
Bradford, William Jr.	NC State	1778, as a Lt. Colonel, the Deputy Quartermaster General for State troops.	
Bradley, Francis	9th NC Regiment	Spring of 1778, a Private under Capt. Matthew Ramsey for 2-1/2 years. From Chatham County, NC. Stationed at Halifax, NC for all of his service - since he was blind in one eye. Born 3/9/1752 in Bute County, NC. S6740.	
Bradley, George "Gee"	3rd NC Regiment	4/17/1776, a 1st Lieutenant under Capt. Pinketham Eaton. 9/19/1778, a Captain under Lt. Col. Robert Mebane. POW at the Fall of Charleston, paroled June 1781. Finally exchanged on 11/26/1782. Retired 1/1/1783.	Siege of Charleston 1780 (SC).
Bradley, James	NC Artillery	5/9/1776, a Lieutenant under Capt. John Vance.	
Bradley, James	3rd NC Regiment	4/16/1776, a Captain under Col. Jethro Sumner. Retired 6/1/1778. Later in NC Militia as a Private and a Captain.	
Bradley, James	4th NC Regiment	5/16/1776, a Private under Capt. John Nelson for three years. 9/8/1778, a known Private under Capt. Griffith John McRee (1st NC Regiment) - assigned to His Excy's Guard. Discharged in May 1779. aka James Bradly.	
Bradley, Richard	1st NC Regiment	3/5/1777, a Captain and a Paymaster under Col. Thomas Clark. Retired 6/1/1778.	
Bradley, Richard	2nd NC Regiment	4/1/1782, a Private under Capt. Clement Hall. Dropped from the rolls in Sept. 1782.	
Bradley, Richard	7th NC Regiment	8/9/1777, a Corporal under Capt. Henry Dawson, then under Capt. James Read (1st NC Regiment) around the first of 1778. 9/8/1778, a known Corporal still under Capt. James Read (1st NC Regiment). POW at the Fall of Charleston, SC, escaped in August 1782. Married in Duplin County, NC in 1783. W896.	Siege of Charleston 1780 (SC).
Bradley, Robert	NC Artillery	5/9/1776, a Matross under Capt. John Vance as NC Provincial Troops. 7/10/1777, on Continental Line. 11/16/1777, under Capt. John Kingsbury. 5/1/1778, in same unit. 9/16/1778, in same unit.	
Bradley, Samuel	5th NC Regiment	1777, a Private under Capt. Reading Blount. Dropped from the rolls in June 1778.	
Bradsher,	8th NC	1777, a Private under Capt. John Walsh. Died	

Name	1st Unit	Year / Rank / Served Under / Notes	Known Battles
John	Regiment	on 1/28/1778. aka John Broadsher.	
Brady, Benjamin	1st NC Regiment	4/15/1781, a Corporal under Capt. Anthony Sharpe. A Sergeant in Jan. 1782. Discharged on 4/15/1782 (4th NC Regiment).	
Brady, James	5th NC Regiment	1/3/1777, a Private under Capt. Benjamin Andrew Coleman for 2-1/2 years. A Corporal on 9/1/1777 until Jan. 1778. Discharged in June 1779. From Johnston County, NC. S8090.	Stono Ferry (SC).
Brady, John	2nd NC Regiment	1782, a Private under Capt. Robert Raiford for 18 months.	
Brains, Michael	10th NC Regiment	6/20/1777, a Private under Capt. Isaac Moore. Died on 9/9/1777.	
Braly, John	1st NC Regiment	1775, a Private under Capt. George Davidson for six months. Then, in NC Militia. From Rowan County, NC. R1149.	Great Cane Brake (SC), Snow Campaign (SC).
Branch, Burrell	4th NC Regiment	1781, a Private under and Capt. George Dougherty then Capt. Joseph T. Rhodes for 12 months. Discharged on 5/25/1782. From Duplin County, NC. Earlier in NC Militia.	
Branch, Job	2nd NC Regiment	11/29/1776, a Corporal under Lt./Capt. James Martin. A Private in June 1778. 9/9/1778, known Private under Capt. Benjamin Andrew Coleman. Discharged on 1/29/1780.	
Brand, John	5th NC Regiment	1777, a Private under Capt. Henry Darnell. Deserted in Aug. 1777.	
Brandon, Thomas	1st NC Regiment	4/28/1781, a Private under Capt. Griffith John McRee. Discharged 4/28/1782.	
Brandon, Thomas	9th NC Regiment	1/12/1777, a Private under Capt. Joel Brevard, then under Capt. Anthony Sharpe. June 1778, this unit was in the 1st NC Regiment. Discharged on 1/27/1780 in Charleston, SC. Apparently in the NC Militia afterwards, unit and dates unknown. S38211.	Monmouth (NJ), Stony Point (NY).
Brandon, William	1st NC Regiment	9/1/1775, a Lieutenant under Capt. George Davidson for three years. Official records claim he resigned 3/8/1776. In his Pension Application, he asserts that he served between two and three years. From Rowan County, NC. Later a Private in the NC Militia. aka William Brannon. S3082.	Great Cane Brake (SC), Snow Campaign (SC). At Moore's Creek Bridge [4].
Brandon, William	3rd NC Regiment	5/1/1777, a Private under Capt. Jacob Turner. Dropped from the rolls in Jan. 1778.	
Brandon, William	10th NC Regiment	Jan.-Jun. 1778, a Private, unit unknown. Joined the 5th NC Regiment in Jan. 1779, unit unknown.	
Brannon, Christian	1st NC Regiment	1777, a Private under Capt. John Brown. A Corporal in April 1778. Dropped from the rolls in June 1778. aka Christian Brennon.	
Brannon, James	6th NC Regiment	4/15/1776, a Private under Lt./Capt. Thomas White for three years. A Sergeant in Nov. 1777. Back to Private in Sept. 1778. 9/8/1778, a known Sergeant under Capt. John Sumner (1st NC Regiment). Discharged 5/17/1779 as a	

Name	1st Unit	Year / Rank / Served Under / Notes	Known Battles
		Private.	
Brannon, Jesse	5th NC Regiment	1779, a Private under Maj. Reading Blount. Died on 8/25/1779.	
Brannon, Thomas	9th NC Regiment	1/12/1777, a Private under Lt./Capt. Anthony Sharpe for three years. 9/8/1778, a known Private in the Lt. Colonel's Company (Lt. Col. Robert Mebane) (1st NC Regiment) led by Capt. Joshua Bowman.	Monmouth (NJ), Stony Point (NY), Eutaw Springs (SC).
Brant, James	1st NC Regiment	5/17/1781, a Private under Capt. Benjamin Bailey. Discharged on 5/17/1782.	
Brantley, Amos	1st NC Regiment	May 1782, a Corporal under Capt. Peter Bacot for 18 months. Discharged in August 1783 at Wilmington, NC. S38569.	
Brantley, Britton	3rd NC Regiment	7/20/1778, a Corporal under Capt. John Baker for nine months. aka Brittin Brantley.	
Brantley, John	1st NC Regiment	1782, a Private under Capt. Peter Bacot for 18 months.	
Brantley, John	3rd NC Regiment	7/20/1778, a Private under Capt. John Baker for nine months. 6/30/1779, a Private under Capt. George "Gee" Bradley for 18 months. 8/1/1782, a Private under Capt. Samuel Jones (1st NC Regiment). Discharged on same date (?).	
Brantley, John	6th NC Regiment	5/1/1776, a Private under Lt./Capt. George Dougherty. 9/8/1778, a known Private under Capt. Tilghman Dixon (1st NC Regiment). Discharged in Nov. 1778.	
Brantley, William	1st NC Regiment	1776, a Private under Capt. Joshua Bowman.	
Branton, Ephraim	7th NC Regiment	1777, a Private under Capt. Thomas Brickell. A Corporal in Oct. 1777. 2/26/1778, a known Private under Capt. Howell Tatum (1st NC Regiment). Died on 5/12/1778.	
Branton, Levi	3rd NC Regiment	6/2/1779, a Private under Capt. George "Gee" Bradley for 18 months.	
Braoly, Richard	1st NC Regiment	A Private, unit and dates unknown. Also shows up in some accounts of the 3rd NC Regiment.	
Brasfield, James	2nd NC Regiment	7/5/1777, a Private, unit unknown. 9/9/1778, under Capt. Benjamin Andrew Coleman.	
Bratcher, Samuel	4th NC Regiment	1776, a Private under Lt./Capt. James Williams for 18 months. Discharged 11/27/1777. S39227.	
Braunon, Joseph	6th NC Regiment	4/15/1776, a Private under Capt. Thomas White. A Sergeant in Nov. 1777. Back to Private in Sep. 1778. Discharged on 5/17/1778.	
Bray, Cornelius	10th NC Regiment	8/16/1777, a Private, unit unknown. One source claims he joined in April 1778. 9/9/1778, a known Private in the Colonel's Company (Col. John Patten) (2nd NC Regiment) led by Capt. John Craddock.	
Brayboy, John	3rd NC Regiment	8/27/1778, a Private under Capt. Kedar Ballard. Deserted on 10/29/1779.	
Brazel, John	10th NC Regiment	A Private, unit and dates unknown. Mustered out in June 1778.	
Brazil, Benjamin	3rd NC Regiment	1778, a Private under Capt. John Baker. Deserted on 7/9/1778.	

Name	1st Unit	Year / Rank / Served Under / Notes	Known Battles
Brazil, Byrd	3rd NC Regiment	5/5/1776, a Private under Capt. William Brinkley for 2-1/2 years. Early '78, under Capt. Philip Taylor (6th NC Regiment). June 1778, under Capt. Benjamin Williams (2nd NC Regiment). Discharged in Oct. 1778. Enlisted in Chatham County, where he lived. On the official rolls as Byrd Brazle. S31571.	
Breacher, John	3rd NC Regiment	7/20/1778, a Corporal under Lt./Capt. George "Gee" Bradley for nine months.	
Brees, Thomas	6th NC Regiment	5/2/1777, a Private under Capt. Francis Child. A Corporal in Feb. 1778. Back to Private in June 1778. 6/1/1778, a Private under Capt. Griffith John McRee (1st NC Regiment). aka Thomas Breece.	
Brevard, Adam	3rd NC Regiment	7/20/1778, a Private in the Lt. Colonel's Company (Lt. Col. William Lee Davidson) led by Lt./Capt. George "Gee" Bradley. 4/23/1779, a known Private in the Lt. Colonel's Company (Lt. Col. Robert Mebane) led by Capt. George "Gee" Bradley.	
Brevard, Alexander	4th NC Regiment	11/27/1776, an Ensign under Capt. Robert Smith. 12/9/1776, a Lieutenant in 1st NC Regiment then under the 4th NC Regiment (under Capt. Robert Smith, then under Capt. William Goodman). A Lt. Colonel of Militia at Briar Creek (1779). Returned to 4th NC Regiment. A Captain on 10/20/1780. 1781, a Captain under Lt. Col. John Baptiste Ashe (1st NC Regiment). 2/6/1782, in 3rd NC Regiment. Retired 1/1/1783. From Lincoln County, NC.	Siege of Ninety-Six 1781 (SC), Siege of Augusta (GA), Eutaw Springs (SC).
Brevard, Ephraim	1st NC Regiment	Surgeon, start date unknown. POW at the Fall of Charleston, SC.	Siege of Charleston 1780 (SC).
Brevard, Joel	9th NC Regiment	11/28/1776, a Captain under Col. John Williams. Resigned in Aug. 1777. From Salisbury District.	
Brevard, John	9th NC Regiment	A Private, unit and dates unknown.	
Brevard, John	9th NC Regiment	11/28/1776, a 1st Lieutenant under Capt. Joel Brevard. Also served under Capt. Joseph J. Wade. Dropped from the rolls in Jan. 1778. From Salisbury District.	
Brevard, Joseph	1st NC Regiment	5/9/1781, an Ensign under Capt. Robert Raiford. 8/1/1781, a Lieutenant. Regimental QM on 3/13/1782 (2nd NC Regiment).	
Brewer, Benjamin	7th NC Regiment	1777, a Private under Capt. Henry Dawson. Died on 10/25/1777.	
Brewer, Benjamin	10th NC Regiment	A Private, unit unknown. Died on 8/1/1778.	
Brewer, Henry	10th NC Regiment	5/12/1777, a Private under Capt. James Wilson for three years. 9/8/1778, a known Private in the Major's Company (Maj. John Baptiste Ashe) (1st NC Regiment) - sick in the flying hospital on that date. Discharged in August 1781.	

Name	1st Unit	Year / Rank / Served Under / Notes	Known Battles
		S39213.	
Brewer, Joshua	1st NC Regiment	11/10/1778, a Private under Capt. Anthony Sharpe for nine months.	
Brewer, Lewis	3rd NC Regiment	7/20/1778, a Private under Capt. Kedar Ballard for nine months.	
Brewer, Moses	1st NC Regiment	1782, a Private under Capt. Peter Bacot for 18 months.	
Brewer, Rice	3rd NC Regiment	1/1/1781, a Private under Capt. Samuel Jones for 12 months.	
Brewer, Robert	5th NC Regiment	1779, a Private under Capt. Joseph Montford. Dropped from the rolls in Oct. 1779.	
Brewer, William	1st NC Regiment	1782, a Private under Capt. Peter Bacot for 18 months. From Halifax County, NC. S41458.	
Brewington, Benjamin	3rd NC Regiment	7/20/1778, a Private under Capt. Michael Quinn for nine months. On the official rolls as Benjamin Bruington.	
Brewington, Joshua	1st NC Regiment	11/10/1778, a Private under Capt. Anthony Sharpe for nine months. On the official rolls as Joshua Bruington. From Duplin (what is now Sampson) County, NC. Later in NC Militia. S8091.	Stono Ferry (SC).
Brewster, Lott	7th NC Regiment	11/24/1776 or 11/27/1776, a Major (two sources). A Lt. Colonel in 3rd SC Regiment on 10/25/1777 to 3/15/1778 (resigned).	Brandywine Creek (PA), Germantown (PA).
Brice, John		A Private, regiment and unit unknown. Deserted in Sep. 1779.	
Brickall, Mathias	7th NC Regiment	Dec. 1777, a Master Sergeant. Dropped from the rolls in Jan. 1778. Probably the same man as the two below.	
Brickell, Matthew	7th NC Regiment	12/8/1776, a Sergeant under Capt. Thomas Brickell. Dropped from the rolls in Jan. 1778.	
Brickell, Thomas	7th NC Regiment	11/28/1776, a Captain under Col. James Hogun. Dropped from the rolls in Jan. 1778. From Hertford County, NC. aka Thomas Brickle.	Brandywine Creek (PA), Germantown (PA).
Brickle, Mathias	1st NC Regiment	An Ensign under Lt. Col. Hardy Murfree, dates unknown. From Hertford County, NC.	
Bridges, Benjamin	3rd NC Regiment	4/20/1776, a Private under Capt. Jacob Turner. 9/9/1778, a known Private in the Lt. Colonel's Company (Lt. Col. Selby Harney) (2nd NC Regiment). Discharged in Oct. 1778. S35199.	Brandywine Creek (PA), Germantown (PA).
Bridges, George	6th NC Regiment	3/10/1777, a Drummer under Capt. Griffith John McRee. Then, a Private under Capt. Christopher Goodwin (3rd NC Regiment). Discharged in October 1778. Later in NC Militia. From Rowan County, NC. S32139.	
Bridget, William	10th NC Regiment	5/11/1778, a Private, unit unknown. Died in July 1778.	
Briggs, Robert	1st NC Regiment	5/9/1781, a Private under Capt. Griffith John McRee. A Sergeant in Aug. 1781. Discharged 5/9/1782.	
Bright, Charles	1st NC Regiment	4/1/1781, a Private under Capt. Benjamin Bailey for 12 months. Discharged 4/1/1782.	

288

Name	1st Unit	Year / Rank / Served Under / Notes	Known Battles
Bright, Charles	2nd NC Regiment	8/7/1777, a Private under Capt. James Martin for three years. 9/9/1778, a known Private under Capt. Benjamin Andrew Coleman. A Corporal in Nov. 1778. A Sergeant on 2/21/1779.	
Bright, Jesse	3rd NC Regiment	1781, a Corporal under Capt. Clement Hall for 12 months. Discharged on 7/10/1782 (2nd NC Regiment).	
Bright, Job	3rd NC Regiment	1779, a Private under Capt. Kedar Ballard. A Corporal in Dec. 1779.	
Bright, John	2nd NC Regiment	1781, a Private under Capt. Benjamin Carter for 12 months. Discharged on 4/10/1782.	
Bright, Simon	2nd NC Regiment	9/1/1775, a Captain under Col. Robert Howe. Resigned 5/1/1776 due to bad health. Died in Dec. 1776. From Dobbs County, NC.	Great Bridge (VA).
Bright, Simon	2nd NC Regiment	1/1/1782, a Private under Capt. Benjamin Andrew Coleman for 12 months (per Feds). He claims to have been under Capt. James Mills (1st NC Regiment) starting in 1781, then under Maj. George Dougherty (4th NC Regiment) making ammunition in Salisbury while recuperating from an illness. From Bladen County, later lived in Columbus County. S6725 & S9293.	
Bright, William		A Private, regiment and unit unknown. Deserted in Sep. 1779.	
Bright, Willis	4th NC Regiment	5/22/1778, a Wyllis Bright enlisted as a Private in the Lt. Colonel's Company of the 10th NC Regiment for three years, mustered Feb. 1779. Preceding is from the official records. He claims to have been under Capt. William Goodman (4th NC Regiment) AND under Col. Gideon Lamb (6th NC Regiment) at the same time. From Pasquotank County, NC. aka Willis Brite. S41459.	Briar Creek (GA), Stono Ferry (SC).
Brigman, Thomas	3rd NC Regiment	1/22/1780, a Private under Capt. George "Gee" Bradley.	
Brinkle, William	3rd NC Regiment	1781, a Forage Master under Capt. Edward Yarborough for 12 months. Dropped from the rolls on 4/1/1782. aka William Brikle.	
Brinkley, Michael	3rd NC Regiment	7/20/1778, a Private in the Colonel's Company (Col. Jethro Sumner). aka Malachi Brinkley.	
Brinkley, Michael	4th NC Regiment	1781, a Private under Capt. Joseph T. Rhodes for 12 months. Discharged on 1/23/1782.	
Brinkley, Thomas	1st NC Regiment	6/14/1781, a Private under Capt. Thomas Donoho. A Sergeant in Jan. 1782. Discharged on 3/19/1782.	
Brinkley, William	3rd NC Regiment	1775, a Captain in the Halifax District Minutemen. 4/17/1776, a Captain under Col. Jetro Sumner. Retired 6/1/1778.	Ft. Moultrie #1 (SC), Brandywine Creek (PA), Germantown (PA).
Brintley, Michael	1st NC Regiment	1782, a Sergeant under Capt. Peter Bacot for 18 months.	

Name	1st Unit	Year / Rank / Served Under / Notes	Known Battles
Brinton, John	3rd NC Regiment	7/20/1778, a Private under Capt. Francis Child. Deserted on 8/1/1778.	
Brister, Philemon	4th NC Regiment	1781, a Private under Capt. Joseph T. Rhodes for 12 months. Discharged on 5/14/1782.	
Britnell, James	9th NC Regiment	5/28/1777, a Private under Capt. Richard D. Cook for three years. 9/8/1778, a known Private in the Lt. Colonel's Company (Lt. Col. Robert Mebane) (1st NC Regiment) led by Capt. Joshua Bowman. aka James Britnal.	
Britt, Arthur	2nd NC Regiment	7/20/1778, a Private under Capt. Reading Blount. Died on 10/28/1778.	
Brittain, Philip	9th NC Regiment	12/3/1776, a Musician under Capt. John Rochelle, then under Capt. Thomas McCrory, then under Capt. Joseph John Wade for three years. A Private in Jan. 1778. 9/8/1778, a known Private in the Lt. Colonel's Company (Lt. Col. Robert Mebane) (1st NC Regiment) led by Capt. Joshua Bowman, then Capt. Thomas Callendar. Discharged on 1/27/1780 at Halifax, NC. From Orange County, NC. On some official rolls as Philip Briton or Philip Britton. S39243.	Monmouth (NJ).
Brittle, Benjamin	3rd NC Regiment	7/20/1778, a Private in the Lt. Colonel's Company (Lt. Col. William Lee Davidson) led by Lt./Capt. George "Gee" Bradley. 4/23/1779, a known Private in the Lt. Colonel's Company (Lt. Col. Robert Mebane) led by Capt. George "Gee" Bradley. Died at Philadelphia Hospital.	
Brittle, William	1st NC Regiment	4/12/1781, a Private under Capt. William Lytle. Discharged on 4/5/1782. First name might be Britton (?).	
Britton, James	9th NC Regiment	12/1/1776, a Private under Capt. Richard D. Cook for three years. 9/8/1778, a known Private in the Lt. Colonel's Company (Lt. Col. Robert Mebane) (1st NC Regiment) led by Capt. Joshua Bowman. Discharged 2/1/1780.	
Broadbent, Richard	8th NC Regiment	1777, a Private under Capt. John Walsh. Deserted on 2/11/1779.	
Broadstreet, James	3rd NC Regiment	7/20/1778, a Corporal under Capt. Kedar Ballard for nine months.	
Broadwell, David	7th NC Regiment	5/4/1776 (?), a Private under Capt. John Baker (?). Dropped from the rolls in 1779.	
Brock, James	3rd NC Regiment	6/30/1779, a Private under Capt. George "Gee" Bradley for 18 months.	
Brock, John	5th NC Regiment	Jan. 1779, a Private under Capt. Philip Taylor.	
Brocky, William	1st NC Regiment	1782, a Private under Capt. Peter Bacot for 18 months.	
Brookin, Thomas	1st NC Regiment	1/7/1782, a Sergeant under Capt. James Mills. Died on 8/5/1782 (4th NC Regiment).	
Brooks, Asa	5th NC Regiment	1777, a Sergeant under Capt. William Caswell. A QM Sergeant in Jan. 1778. Died 6/3/1778.	
Brooks, George	10th NC Regiment	6/2/1777, a Sergeant under Capt. Andrew Vanoy. A Private in June 1778 under Capt.	

Name	1st Unit	Year / Rank / Served Under / Notes	Known Battles
		Robert Fenner (2nd NC Regiment). A Corporal in Oct. 1778. Back to Sergeant in Sep. 1779.	
Brooks, John	10th NC Regiment	5/11/1777, a Private, unit unknown. 9/9/1778, a known Private under Capt. John Ingles (2nd NC Regiment). Discharged on 11/10/1778.	
Brooks, Thomas	10th NC Regiment	7/1/1777, a Private under Capt. James Wilson for three years. 9/8/1778, a known Wagoner in the Major's Company (Maj. Griffith John McRee) (1st NC Regiment). 3/27/1780, a Private under Maj. John Nelson (1st NC Regiment). Most likely a POW at the Fall of Charleston, SC. Probably in other battles. Probably from Chatham County, NC. R1257.	Siege of Charleston 1780 (SC).
Broom, Mason	5th NC Regiment	4/2/1776, a Private under Capt. Reading Blount. 9/9/1778, a known Private in the Lt. Colonel's Company (Lt. Col. Selby Harney) (2nd NC Regiment). Discharged in Oct. 1778. S41457.	Brandywine Creek (PA), Germantown (PA).
Brothers, David	1st NC Regiment	A Private under Capt. William Lytle for 12 months. Discharged on 4/15/1782.	
Brower, Henry	10th NC Regiment	5/20/1777, a Private under Capt. James Wilson.	
Brown, Arthur	1st NC Regiment	4/15/1781, a Private under Capt. Anthony Sharpe. Discharged on 4/15/1782 (4th NC Regiment). Wounded at the battle of Eutaw Springs (SC). Enlisted in Pitt County, NC. S39222.	Eutaw Springs (SC).
Brown, Benjamin	3rd NC Regiment	9/17/1782, a Private under Capt. Benjamin Bailey for 18 months. From Wake County, NC. Earlier in NC Militia. S31564.	
Brown, Benjamin	7th NC Regiment	1777, a Corporal under Capt. Joseph Walker. Died in Feb. 1778.	
Brown, Collin	1st NC Regiment	10/12/1780, a Corporal under Capt. William Lytle. Dropped from the rolls sometime during 1781.	
Brown, Collins	1st NC Regiment	1777, a Private under Capt. Henry "Hal" Dixon. Died on 4/14/1778.	
Brown, David	9th NC Regiment	1/8/1777, a Private under Capt. Richard D. Cook for three years. POW on 10/4/1777 at the battle of Germantown, PA. 9/8/1778, a known Private in the Lt. Colonel's Company (Lt. Col. Robert Mebane) (1st NC Regiment) led by Capt. Joshua Bowman - sick on that date. Died on 11/18/1778.	Germantown (PA).
Brown, David E.	5th NC Regiment	5/1/1776, a Private under Lt./Capt. Henry Darnell for 2-1/2 years. Wounded at the battle of Brandywine Creek (PA). Then under Capt. Benjamin Andrew Coleman (2nd NC Regiment). Discharged in April 1778 at the Camp on the Schuylkill River, PA. S39239.	Brandywine Creek (PA),
Brown, Henry	1st NC Regiment	6/6/1781, a Private under Capt. Robert Raiford. Died in Oct. 1781.	
Brown, Henry	3rd NC Regiment	1/9/1782, a Private under Capt. Samuel Jones for 12 months.	
Brown, Isaac	4th NC	1782, a Private under Capt. Thomas Evans for	

Name	1st Unit	Year / Rank / Served Under / Notes	Known Battles
	Regiment	18 months.	
Brown, Jacob	3rd NC Regiment	1780, a Private under Capt. Edward Yarborough for nine months, stationed at Salisbury building and repairing wagons most of his time served. From Rowan County, NC. Earlier in NC Militia. W2062.	Hobkirk's Hill (SC).
Brown, James	1st NC Regiment	4/15/1781, a Private under Capt. Anthony Sharpe. Discharged on 2/14/1782. One source claims his first name was John (?).	
Brown, James	1st NC Regiment	6/14/1781, a Private under Capt. Thomas Donoho. Discharged on 6/14/1782. aka Joseph Brown.	
Brown, James	2nd NC Regiment	4/25/1781, a Private under Capt. Robert Raiford, then under Capt. Tilghman Dixon for 12 months. Discharged on 5/26/1782 (1st NC Regiment) at Hillsborough, NC. Enlisted while living in Granville County, NC. Later lived in Wake County, NC. Born 11/20/1752 in MD. S6702.	Eutaw Springs (SC).
Brown, James	3rd NC Regiment	6/10/1779, a Private under Capt. Michael Quinn. Deserted in Oct. 1779. One source claims his first name was Joseph.	
Brown, James	5th NC Regiment	1779, a Private under Capt. Reading Blount. Deserted in Sep. 1779.	
Brown, James	5th NC Regiment	Jan. 1779, a Private under Capt. Philip Taylor.	
Brown, James	6th NC Regiment	5/8/1776, a Private under Lt./Capt. Thomas White for three years. 9/8/1778, a known Private under Capt. John Sumner (1st NC Regiment). Discharged 5/10/1779 at Reading, PA. S40753.	
Brown, James	10th NC Regiment	7/1/1777, a Private, unit unknown. 9/9/1778, a known Private under Capt. Robert Fenner (2nd NC Regiment). Deserted on 1/1/1780.	
Brown, John	1st NC Regiment	10/20/1775, an Ensign. 1/4/1776, a 2nd Lieutenant. 4/26/1777, a Captain. June 1778, a Captain of the NC Dragoons. Discharged in 1779. Then, a Captain in NC Militia. From Bladen County, NC. W9746.	Moore's Creek Bridge [4], Brandywine Creek (PA), Germantown (PA), Monmouth (NJ).
Brown, John	2nd NC Regiment	1782, a Private under Capt. Robert Raiford. Deserted on 6/10/1783 (?).	
Brown, John	2nd NC Regiment	4/25/1781, a Private under Capt. Tilghman Dixon. Discharged on 4/25/1782. From Caswell County, NC. W18651.	
Brown, John	3rd NC Regiment	7/20/1778, a Sergeant under Capt. Francis Child for nine months.	
Brown, John	4th NC Regiment	1782, a Sergeant under Capt. William Lytle for 18 months.	
Brown, Joseph	2nd NC Regiment	1776, a Private under Lt. Manlove Tarrant then Capt. James Gee. Then under Capt. John Ingles. POW at the Fall of Charleston (SC), held 18	Ft. Moultrie #1 (SC), Brandywine

Name	1st Unit	Year / Rank / Served Under / Notes	Known Battles
		months, exchanged at Jamestown, VA. Went to Hillsborough, captured by Col. David Fanning on 9/12/1781, sent to Wilmington then back to Charleston where he was a POW again for another year - exchanged just before the British evacuated Charleston. Then under Capt. Clement Hall until peace was announced. Discharged at Edenton, NC. From Camden County, NC. Born 12/4/1758. S39225.	Creek (PA), Germantown (PA), Monmouth (NJ), Siege of Charleston 1780 (SC), Hillsborough.
Brown, Joseph	2nd NC Regiment	11/9/1776, a Private under Capt. James Gee for three years. 11/12/1777, a Private under Capt. John Ingles. Discharged in Nov. 1779, returned home. A Musician Corporal in Sep. 1782, re-enlisted for the duration of the war. From Halifax County, NC. W3931.	
Brown, Joseph	4th NC Regiment	4/4/1777, a Private under Capt. Joseph Phillips. 9/8/1778, a known Private under Capt. James Read (1st NC Regiment). Deserted on 9/10/1778.	
Brown, Joseph	6th NC Regiment	5/8/1776, a Private under Capt. Thomas White. Discharged on 5/10/1779.	
Brown, Mark	DQMG	1780, a Tailor under Col. Nicholas Long (Deputy QM General).	
Brown, Morgan W.	9th NC Regiment	First, in SC units. 11/28/1776, a 1st Lieutenant under Capt. Joseph John Wade, then Capt. Richard D. Cook until 10/12/1777 (resigned). Then, an Assistant Commissary. Later volunteered in NC Militia, POW at the Fall of Charleston, unit unknown. From Anson County, NC. Born 1/13/1753 (or 1758 - two sources) in Anson County, NC. S3063.	Brandywine Creek (PA), Siege of Charleston 1780 (SC).
Brown, Moses	10th NC Regiment	7/28/1777, a Private under Capt. Abraham Sheppard, Jr. 9/9/1778, a known Private in the Lt. Colonel's Company (Lt. Col. Selby Harney) (2nd NC Regiment). 3/12/1779, re-enlisted under Capt. Benjamin Williams (2nd NC Regiment).	
Brown, Park	10th NC Regiment	5/12/1777, a Sergeant under Capt. Abraham Sheppard, Jr. Deserted on 5/1/1779. aka Pond Brown.	
Brown, Peter	4th NC Regiment	1776, a Private under Capt. Robert Smith. Dropped from the rolls in May 1778.	
Brown, Patrick	2nd NC Regiment	3/12/1779, re-enlisted in the Major's Company (Maj. Hardy Murfree).	
Brown, Robert	10th NC Regiment	8/30/1777, a Private, unit unknown for three years. 9/8/1778, a known Private under Capt. Howell Tatum (1st NC Regiment) - sick on that date in camp hospital. Discharged on 9/10/1778. Later in NC Militia. From Guilford County, NC. S6714.	
Brown, Samuel	3rd NC Regiment	7/20/1778, a Private in the Colonel's Company (Col. Jethro Sumner) for nine months. Probably same man as directly below.	
Brown,	3rd NC	7/20/1778, a Private under Capt. Kedar Ballard.	

Name	1st Unit	Year / Rank / Served Under / Notes	Known Battles
Samuel	Regiment	Dropped from the rolls in Oct. 1778.	
Brown, Solomon	1st NC Regiment	5/2/1781, a Private under Capt. Anthony Sharpe. Jan. 1782, a Musician. Discharged on 5/21/1782 (4th NC Regiment).	
Brown, Thomas	1st NC Regiment	8/1/1776, a Sergeant under Capt. Thomas Hogg. A Private in May of 1778. Dropped from the rolls in March 1779.	
Brown, Thomas	2nd NC Regiment	9/9/1778, a known Private under Capt. John Ingles.	
Brown, Thomas	3rd NC Regiment	7/20/1778, a Private under Maj. Thomas Hogg for nine months.	
Brown, Thomas	5th NC Regiment	A Private under Capt. Reading Blount, dates unknown.	
Brown, Thomas	7th NC Regiment	A Private under Capt. Henry Dawson. Deserted in Apr. 1777.	
Brown, Thomas	10th NC Regiment	5/12/1777, a Private under Capt. James Wilson for three years. 9/8/1778, a known Private in the Major's Company (Maj. John Baptiste Ashe) (1st NC Regiment) - sick in the flying hospital on that date. 3/12/1779, re-enlisted for the duration of the war in the same unit.	
Brown, Thomas	10th NC Regiment	8/25/1777, a Private under Capt. Abraham Sheppard, Jr. Dropped from the rolls in June 1778.	
Brown, Warren	3rd NC Regiment	1781, a Private under Capt. Edward Yarborough for 12 months. Discharged on 5/1/1782. 9/7/1782, a Private under Capt. Benjamin Bailey for 18 months.	
Brown, William	1st NC Regiment	9/4/1777, a Private under Capt. Howell Tatum for three years. 9/8/1778, a known Private in the Lt. Colonel's Company (Lt. Col. Robert Mebane) led by Capt. Joshua Bowman. 3/12/1779, re-enlisted for the duration of the war in the same unit. From Bute (Warren) County, NC. W17354.	
Brown, William	9th NC Regiment	9/1/1776 (?), a Private under Capt. Thomas McCrory.	
Brownfield, William	4th NC Regiment	1775, a 1st Lieutenant in the 2nd Salisbury District Minutemen. 4/17/1776, a 1st Lieutenant under Capt. Robert Smith and Col. Thomas Polk. From Mecklenburg County.	
Browning, Mark	1st NC Regiment	4/23/1781, a Private under Capt. Robert Raiford. Discharged 4/25/1782.	
Browning, George	2nd NC Regiment	9/9/1778, a known Private under Capt. Clement Hall. 3/12/1779, re-enlisted under Capt. Clement Hall. aka George Brownrigg.	
Browning, George	10th NC Regiment	7/1/1777, a Corporal, unit unknown. A Sergeant in Jan. 1779.	
Browning, William	5th NC Regiment	Jan. 1779, a Private under Capt. Philip Taylor. A Sergeant in Apr. 1779.	
Brownlay, Robert	5th NC Regiment	1777, a Corporal under Capt. Benjamin Stedman. A Sergeant in Nov. 1778. Probably the same man as directly below.	
Brownley,	2nd NC	9/9/1778, a known Private under Capt. Clement	

Name	1st Unit	Year / Rank / Served Under / Notes	Known Battles
Robert	Regiment	Hall. aka Robert Brownby.	
Brownum, Elijah	1st NC Regiment	6/6/1781, a Private under Capt. William Lytle. Discharged on 6/6/1782.	
Bruce, George	9th NC Regiment	3/9/1776, a Private under Lt./Capt. Hezekiah Rice. 3/15/1777, a Private under Capt. Richard D. Cook for three years. 9/8/1778, a known Private in the Lt. Colonel's Company (Lt. Col. Robert Mehane) (1st NC Regiment) led by Capt. Joshua Bowman. POW at Fall of Charleston, escaped after six months. From Guilford County, NC. S39212.	Brandywine Creek (PA), Monmouth (NY), Stony Point (NY), Siege of Charleston 1780 (SC).
Bruce, Peter	9th NC Regiment	11/28/1776, an Ensign under Capt. John Rochelle. Resigned in Dec. 1776. From Hillsborough District.	
Bruce, Thomas	2nd NC Regiment	5/22/1777, a Private under Capt. Benjamin Williams for three years. One source asserts that he was dropped from the rolls in Jan. 1778. Another source asserts that on 9/8/1778, he was a known Private under Capt. Griffith John McRee (1st NC Regiment).	
Brummager, Edward	1st NC Regiment	8/1/1782, a Private under Capt. Joshua Hadley for 18 months.	
Brutus, "Unknown"	2nd NC Regiment	A Private under Capt. Benjamin Williams. Dropped from the rolls in Jan. 1778. aka ? Bruties.	
Bryan, Benjamin	7th NC Regiment	4/27/1777, an Ensign under Capt. John McGlaughan. 7/15/1777, a 2nd Lieutenant. Dropped from the rolls in Nov. 1777. aka Benjamin Bryar, Bryer.	
Bryan, David	1st NC Regiment	11/10/1778, a Private under Capt. Anthony Sharpe for nine months.	
Bryan, Hardy	7th NC Regiment	12/11/1776, a Commissary.	
Bryan, Hezekiah	2nd NC Regiment	6/15/1781, a Private under Capt. Tilghman Dixon. Discharged on 6/16/1782 (1st NC Regiment) at Guilford Court House, NC. From Wake County, NC. Earlier in NC Militia, unit and regiment unknown. Born 1759 or 1760 in SC. W895.	Eutaw Springs (SC) (in the rear guard).
Bryan, Isaac	10th NC Regiment	12/11/1777, a Paymaster. Replaced Benjamin Sheppard.	
Bryan, John	1st NC Regiment	5/20/1781, a Private under Capt. Griffith John McRee for 12 months. Discharged on 5/25/1782. The previous is per official records. In his pension application, he claims he enlisted in 1782 under Capt. Robert Raiford (2nd NC Regiment) for 18 months, and that he was furloughed on 7/7/1783. A friend (James Moore) says he signed up under Capt. Thomas Evans (2nd NC Regiment) and was transferred to Capt. Benjamin Coleman (2nd NC Regiment). From Duplin County, NC. aka John Brien. W9747.	
Bryan, John	7th NC	1777, a Musician under Capt. John	

Name	1st Unit	Year / Rank / Served Under / Notes	Known Battles
	Regiment	McGlaughan. Deserted in Aug. 1777.	
Bryan, John	7th NC Regiment	1777, a Private under Capt. Joseph Walker. Deserted on 9/17/1777.	
Bryan, John Council	New Levies	4/21/1778, appointed Commissary for new Continentals that may be raised in New Bern.	
Bryan, Keedar	3rd NC Regiment	2/1/1782, a Private under Capt. Clement Hall (2/6/1782 - 2nd NC Regiment) for 12 months.	
Bryan, Randle	1st NC Regiment	10/1/1776, a Private under Capt. Joshua Bowman. 9/8/1778, a known Private under Capt. Tilghman Dixon. Dropped from the rolls in Nov. 1779. aka Randol Brian, Randal Brian.	
Bryan, Thomas	10th NC Regiment	6/1/1777, a Musician under Capt. Silas Stevenson. A Private in June 1778. Mustered in July 1779.	
Bryan, William	4th NC Regiment	12/11/1776, a Paymaster.	
Bryan, William	8th NC Regiment	2/8/1777, a Sergeant under Capt. John Walsh. A Private in Apr. 1778. 9/10/1778, a known Private under Capt. Thomas Armstrong (2nd NC Regiment). aka William Brian.	
Bryant, Ambrose	10th NC Regiment	6/16/1777, a Private under Capt. James Wilson. Dropped from the rolls in June 1778.	
Bryant, Charles	1st NC Regiment	1781, a Private under Capt. Benjamin Bailey for 12 months. 3/1/1782, joined Lee's Legion.	
Bryant, Darby	3rd NC Regiment	7/20/1778, a Private under Capt. Michael Quinn for nine months.	
Bryant, Dempsey	4th NC Regiment	1782, a Musician under Capt. Anthony Sharpe.	
Bryant, James	1st NC Regiment	5/17/1781, a Private under Lt./Capt. Benjamin Bailey for 12 months. Discharged on 5/17/1782.	
Bryant, John	1st NC Regiment	8/1/1782, a Private under Capt. Joshua Hadley for 18 months.	
Bryant, John	3rd NC Regiment	9/7/1782, a Private under Capt. Benjamin Bailey for 18 months.	
Bryant, John	4th NC Regiment	7/4/1776, a Private under Capt. Micajah Lewis for three years. A Sergeant on 11/1/1777. Back to Private in April 1778. 9/8/1778, a known Private in the Colonel's Company (Col. Thomas Clark) (1st NC Regiment) led by Capt. John Gambier Scull. Dropped from the rolls in Jan. 1779.	
Bryant, John	7th NC Regiment	1/28/1777, a Sergeant under Capt. Thomas Brickell. Dropped from the rolls in Oct. 1777.	
Bryant, John Jr.	7th NC Regiment	11/28/1776, a 1st Lieutenant under Capt. Green Bell, then under Capt. Lemuel Ely. From Edgecombe County, NC.	
Bryant, Nicholas	DQMG	1780, a Tailor on the roll of Capt. Solomon Wood (NC Light Dragoons) - this seems to be for convenience only. 8/23/1781, a Tailor under Col. Nicholas Long (Deputy QM General).	
Bryant, Thomas	2nd NC Regiment	6/1/1777, a Private, unit unknown. 9/9/1778, a known Private in the Colonel's Company (Col. John Patten) led by Capt. John Craddock.	
Bryant,	3rd NC	June 1778, a Private under Capt. Michael	

Name	1st Unit	Year / Rank / Served Under / Notes	Known Battles
Thomas	Regiment	Quinn. Deserted on 6/14/1778.	
Bryant, William	DQMG	1780, a Wagoner under Col. Nicholas Long (Deputy QM General). Said to be an ex-Continental soldier.	
Bryant, William	2nd NC Regiment	1/15/1777, a Musician under Capt. Charles Allen. A Private in June 1778. 9/9/1778, a known Private under Capt. Clement Hall. Hired his brother, Samuel, to finish his tour. From Nash County, NC. aka William Bryan. W5916.	
Bryant, William	5th NC Regiment	4/26/1776, a Private under Capt. John Pugh Williams, then under Capt. Reading Blount. Enlisted at Orangeburgh, SC. Wounded at the battle of Brandywine Creek (PA). Dropped from the rolls in 1779 (2nd NC Regiment) - discharged at White Plains, NY. S31215.	Brandywine Creek (PA).
Bryant, William	10th NC Regiment	7/12/1777, a Private under Capt. Abraham Sheppard, Jr. Dropped from the rolls in Aug. 1778.	
Bryley, Charles	1st NC Regiment	1777, a Private under Capt. John Brown. Killed on 9/17/1777.	
Bryly, William	4th NC Regiment	7/26/1776, a Private under Capt. Thomas Harris. Discharged 10/31/1777.	
Bubby, Edward	1st NC Regiment	6/2/1781, a Private under Capt. Robert Raiford. Discharged 6/3/1782.	
Buck, Abraham	3rd NC Regiment	7/20/1778, a Private under Capt. John Baker for nine months.	
Bucoe, Abraham	4th NC Regiment	1782, a Private under Capt. Anthony Sharpe for 18 months. Deserted on 6/13/1783 (?).	
Budd, Samuel	2nd NC Regiment	11/22/1777, a 1st Lieutenant under Capt. Charles Allen. 9/9/1778, under Capt. Benjamin Andrew Coleman. POW at the Fall of Charleston (SC), exchanged on 6/14/1781. Also a POW at the battle of Eutaw Springs, SC on 9/8/1781 - exchanged on 11/26/1782. Retired 1/1/1783. R20171.	Siege of Charleston 1780 (SC), Eutaw Springs (SC).
Buford, William	NC Light Dragoons	1776, a Cornet. 5/15/1777, a 2nd Lieutenant under Capt. Edward Vail, Jr. Transferred to NC Dragoons on 7/16/1777 under Capt. Samuel Ashe. Promoted to Captain in 1781 (NC State Troops). Wounded at Eutaw Springs, SC on 9/8/1781.	Eutaw Springs (SC).
Bugg, William	3rd NC Regiment	5/25/1776, a Private under Capt. James Emmett for 2-1/2 years. 9/9/1778, a known Private under Capt. Clement Hall (2nd NC Regiment) - sick at Yellow Swamp. Discharged on 11/26/1778 in New York. From Wake County, NC. W898.	
Bull, Michael	2nd NC Regiment	1777, a Musician under Capt. Benjamin Williams for three years. A Private in Jan. 1778. 9/9/1778, a known Private in the Major's Company (Maj. Hardy Murfree). Died in Jan. 1779.	
Bull, Thomas	1st NC Regiment	Dec. 1780 to 1782, a Surgeon's Mate. His commission dated 7/22/1781 per NC State	

Name	1st Unit	Year / Rank / Served Under / Notes	Known Battles
		Records in 2nd NC Regiment (Vol. XVI, page 576). Resigned 8/19/1782.	
Bullard, Thomas	1st NC Regiment	11/10/1778, a Private under Capt. Anthony Sharpe for nine months. Earlier and later in NC Militia. From Duplin County, NC.	
Bullen, Michael	NC Artillery	5/17/1776, a Matross under Capt. John Vance as NC Provincial Troops. 7/10/1777, on Continental Line. 11/16/1777, under Capt. John Kingsbury. April 1778, a known Corporal. 5/1/1778, in same unit. 9/10/1778, in same unit. aka Michael Bulling.	
Bullock, Balaam	2nd NC Regiment	1777, a Private under Capt. James Gee. 9/9/1778, a known Private under Capt. John Ingles. POW at Ft. Lafayette on 6/1/1779. Rejoined in Nov. 1779 as a Musician.	Ft. Lafayette (NY).
Bullock, Daniel	3rd NC Regiment	7/20/1778, a Private under Capt. Francis Child for nine months.	
Bullock, Daniel	9th NC Regiment	11/28/1776, a Lieutenant under Capt. Matthew Ramsey. Dropped from the rolls in Jan. 1778.	
Bullock, Daniel	9th NC Regiment	3/23/1777, a Private under Capt. Richard D. Cook for three years. A Corporal in Nov. 1777. A Sergeant in Jan. 1778. Back to Private in June 1778. 9/8/1778, a known Private in the Lt. Colonel's Company (Lt. Col. Robert Mebane (1st NC Regiment) led by Capt. Joshua Bowman - sick on that date. Dropped from the rolls in Nov. 1779.	
Bullock, David		3/23/1777, regiment, unit, and rank unknown. 9/8/1778, a known Private in the Lt. Colonel's Company (Lt. Col. Robert Mebane) (1st NC Regiment) led by Capt. Joshua Bowman - sick on that date.	
Bullock, John	5th NC Regiment	4/20/1776, a Private under Capt. John Enloe. 9/10/1778, a known Private under Capt. Thomas Armstrong (2nd NC Regiment). Discharged on 11/10/1778.	
Bullock, John	8th NC Regiment	1777, a Private under Capt. Francis Tartanson. Dropped from the rolls in Sept. 1777.	
Bullock, Martin	4th NC Regiment	2/20/1777, a Corporal under Capt. John Nelson for three years. A Private in June 1778. 6/1/1778, a Private under Capt. Griffith John McRee (1st NC Regiment). Deserted in Dec. 1778.	
Bullock, Moses	8th NC Regiment	1777, a Private under Capt. Francis Tartanson. Dropped from the rolls in Sept. 1777.	
Bullock, Nathaniel	2nd NC Regiment	1782, a Private under Capt. Robert Raiford for 18 months.	
Bullock, Thomas	4th NC Regiment	1777, a Sergeant under Capt. John Nelson. Dropped from the rolls in Feb. 1778.	
Bunbardy, John	3rd NC Regiment	6/22/1779, a Private under Capt. Kedar Ballard. Deserted on 10/3/1779. aka John Bumbardy.	
Bunch, Clement	4th NC Regiment	1782, a Private under Capt. William Lytle for 18 months.	
Buncombe,	5th NC	April 15, 1776, a Colonel. Captured at	Brandywine

Name	1st Unit	Year / Rank / Served Under / Notes	Known Battles
Edward	Regiment	Germantown 10/4/1777, POW in Philadelphia, paroled. May 1778, fell down a flight of stairs, reopened old wounds, died as a result. From Tyrrell County (what is now Washington County), NC.	Creek (PA), Germantown (PA).
Bundy, James	8th NC Regiment	3/13/1777, a Private under Capt. Francis Tartanson. A Corporal in June 1778 in the Lt. Colonel's Company (Lt. Col. Selby Harney) (2nd NC Regiment). aka James Bunday.	
Bunn, Jesse	2nd NC Regiment	1782, a Private under Capt. Robert Raiford for 18 months.	
Burch, John	3rd NC Regiment	7/20/1778, a Musician under Capt. John Baker.	
Burd, Benjamin	3rd NC Regiment	June 1777, a Private under Capt. Kedar Ballard for 12 months. Discharged in July 1778 at Halifax, NC. On the official rolls as Benjamin Bird. He signed his last name as Burd. R21880.	
Burch, William	NC Artillery	7/15/1776, a Corporal under Capt. John Vance as NC Provincial Troops. 7/10/1777, on Continental Line. 11/16/1777, under Capt. John Kingsbury. 5/1/1778, in same unit. May 1778, sick in camp. 9/16/1778, in same unit. aka William Burk.	
Burden, Thomas	3rd NC Regiment	6/18/1779, a Private under Capt. Kedar Ballard. Deserted on 10/27/1779.	
Burdenton, John	3rd NC Regiment	6/29/1779, a Private under Capt. Kedar Ballard. Deserted on 11/19/1779. aka John Burtenton.	
Burges, George	4th NC Regiment	1/1/1777, a Private under Capt. William Goodman for three years. 9/8/1778, a known Private in the Colonel's Company (Col. Thomas Clark) (1st NC Regiment) led by Capt. John Gambier Scull. Discharged on 1/28/1780.	
Burges, Isaac	1st NC Regiment	8/15/1777, a Private under Capt. Anthony Sharpe. Died on 7/10/1778.	
Burges, John	10th NC Regiment	A Private, unit and dates unknown. Dropped from the rolls in Feb. 1778.	
Burges, Joseph	6th NC Regiment	1777, a Private under Capt. Thomas Donoho. Died in Aug. 1777.	
Burges, Peter	4th NC Regiment	1/1/1777, a Private under Capt. William Goodman for three years. 9/8/1778, a known Private in the Colonel's Company (Col. Thomas Clark) (1st NC Regiment) led by Capt. John Gambier Scull. Deserted on 2/3/1780.	
Burges, Zephaniah	3rd NC Regiment	4/17/1776, an Ensign under Capt. Thomas Granbury and Col. Jethro Sumner. From the Edenton District.	
Burgess, Abram	2nd NC Regiment	9/9/1778, a known Sergeant under Capt. Benjamin Andrew Coleman.	
Burgess, Absalom	5th NC Regiment	1777, a Sergeant under Capt. Henry Darnell. POW at Ft. Lafayette, NY on 6/1/1779. Rejoined in Nov. 1779. aka Absalom Burges.	Ft. Lafayette (NY).
Burgess, Bryant	1st NC Regiment	1782, a Private under Capt. Peter Bacot for 18 months.	
Burgess,	NC	1777, a Matross under Capt. John Kingsbury.	

Name	1st Unit	Year / Rank / Served Under / Notes	Known Battles
Philip	Artillery	Dropped from the rolls prior to May 1778. Probably the same man as directly below.	
Burgess, Philip	10th NC Regiment	A Private, unit and dates unknown. 9/9/1778, a known Private under Capt. John Ingles (2nd NC Regiment).	
Burk, Charles	8th NC Regiment	5/27/1777, a Private under Capt. Robert Raiford for three years. 6/1/1778, in 2nd NC Regiment. 9/9/1778, a known Private in the Lt. Colonel's Company (Lt. Col. Selby Harney) (2nd NC Regiment). 3/12/1779, re-enlisted in the Lt. Colonel's Company (Lt. Col. Selby Harney) (2nd NC Regiment). POW on 6/20/1779 at the battle of Stono Ferry (SC), held about four months. Rejoined in Nov. 1779. From Johnston County, NC. aka Charles Bourk, Charles Bourke. W18474.	Stono Ferry (SC).
Burke, Charles	2nd NC Regiment	A Private, unit unknown.	
Burke, David	1st NC Regiment	5/28/1781, a Private under Capt. Alexander Brevard. Discharged on 5/25/1782. aka David Burk.	
Burke, Elihu	1st NC Regiment	6/6/1781, a Private under Capt. Alexander Brevard. Discharged on 6/7/1782. aka Elihu Burk. W8233.	
Burke, Jacob	5th NC Regiment	1777, a Private under Capt. Benjamin Stedman. 9/9/1778, a known Private under Capt. Clement Hall (2nd NC Regiment). aka Jacob Burk.	
Burke, Meredith	3rd NC Regiment	7/20/1778, a Private under Lt./Capt. George "Gee" Bradley for nine months. aka Meredy Burk, Meredy Burke.	
Burkett, Uriah	4th NC Regiment	1781, a Corporal under Capt. Joseph T. Rhodes for 12 months. Discharged on 4/25/1782 as a Sergeant. R20316.	
Burn, David	5th NC Regiment	Jan. 1779, a Private under Capt. Philip Taylor. Discharged in Apr. 1779 at the Two Sisters Ferry, SC. 1782, a Private under Capt. Peter Bacot (1st NC Regiment) for 18 months. Discharged on 7/1/1783 at James Island, SC. aka David Burns. S9299.	
Burnett, Charles	5th NC Regiment	6/1/1779, a Private under Capt. Joseph Montford.	
Burnett, David	5th NC Regiment	1777, a Private under Capt. Reading Blount. Dropped from the rolls in Feb. 1778.	
Burnett, John	4th NC Regiment	1781, a Private under Capt. George Dougherty for 12 months. Discharged 5/25/1782.	
Burnett, William	2nd NC Regiment	4/25/1781, a Private under Capt. Tilghman Dixon. Discharged on 4/25/1782.	
Burnett, William	10th NC Regiment	9/5/1777, a Private under Capt. Abraham Sheppard, Jr. 9/9/1778, a known Private under Capt. Clement Hall (2nd NC Regiment). 3/12/1779, re-enlisted under Capt. Clement Hall. Deserted on 1/15/1780.	
Burnham, Jesse	7th NC Regiment	1777, a Private under Capt. Thomas Brickell. Deserted in Apr. 1777.	

Name	1ˢᵗ Unit	Year / Rank / Served Under / Notes	Known Battles
Burnham, Samuel		A Private, unit unknown. Deserted in Sep. 1779.	
Burns, David	1ˢᵗ NC Regiment	1782, a Private under Capt. Peter Bacot for 18 months.	
Burns, Frederick	3ʳᵈ NC Regiment	1781, a Private under Capt. Edward Yarborough for 12 months. Discharged on 4/15/1782.	
Burns, Jesse	3ʳᵈ NC Regiment	1781, a Private under Capt. Edward Yarborough for 12 months. POW on 4/1/1782 (?).	
Burns, John	4ᵗʰ NC Regiment	5/20/1776, a Sergeant under Capt. Robert Smith for three years. A Private in June 1778. Back to Sergeant on 11/10/1778. 3/12/1779, re-enlisted as a Sergeant in the Colonel's Company (1st NC Regiment) led by Capt. John Gambier Scull. The official rolls assert he deserted on 12/25/1779, but he was actually furloughed due to illness. His unit was at the Fall of Charleston, so afterwards he rejoined under Capt. William Lytle. Discharged in Feb. 1783 at Hillsborough, NC. aka John Burus. R1501.	
Burns, Philip	1ˢᵗ NC Regiment	1781, a Private under Capt. Alexander Brevard for 18 months - joined after the battle of Eutaw Springs (SC). Furloughed after serving seven or eight months. From Lincoln County, NC. Earlier in NC Militia. S20909.	
Burns, Sterral	6ᵗʰ NC Regiment	1777, a Private under Capt. Thomas Donoho. Deserted in Aug. 1777. aka Sterral Burus.	
Burns, William	10ᵗʰ NC Regiment	5/20/1777, a Private under Capt. Dempsey Gregory for three years. A Musician in June 1778. 9/8/1778, a known Drummer under Maj. John Baptiste Ashe (1st NC Regiment) - sick in camp on that date. Deserted on 2/10/1779. aka William Burus.	
Burnsides, David	6ᵗʰ NC Regiment	1777, a Sergeant under Capt. George Dougherty. Dropped from the rolls in Jan. 1778.	
Burris, Aaron	4ᵗʰ NC Regiment	1782, a Private under Capt. William Lytle for 18 months.	
Burris, George	2ⁿᵈ NC Regiment	Dec. 1782, a Private under Capt. Robert Raiford. Deserted on 4/2/1783 (?).	
Burrow, Willey	1ˢᵗ NC Regiment	1777, a Private under Capt. Caleb Grainger, then under Capt. Howell Tatum. A Corporal in March 1778, back to Private in July 1778. 9/8/1778, a known Private under Capt. Howell Tatum. POW at the Fall of Charleston (SC), held 15 months. From Northampton County, NC. aka Wyly Burrow, Willie Burrow, Wilie Burroughs, William Burrow. S41466.	Brandywine Creek (PA), Germantown (PA), Monmouth (NJ), Siege of Charleston (SC).
Burrows, Samuel	3ʳᵈ NC Regiment	6/24/1779, a Private under Capt. Michael Quinn. Dropped from the rolls in Oct. 1779.	
Burrus, John	1ˢᵗ NC Regiment	4/28/1781, a Private under Capt. Alexander Brevard. Discharged on 4/28/1782. aka John Burris.	
Burshaw, John	3ʳᵈ NC Regiment	6/30/1779, a Private under Capt. Kedar Ballard. Deserted on 9/26/1779.	
Burt, John	4ᵗʰ NC	1781, a Private under Capt. George Dougherty	

Name	1st Unit	Year / Rank / Served Under / Notes	Known Battles
	Regiment	for 12 months. Discharged 5/25/1782. aka John Bert.	
Burton, John	3rd NC Regiment	1781, a Private under Capt. Edward Yarborough for 12 months. Discharged on 5/1/1782.	
Burton, John	8th NC Regiment	Early 1777, a Private, unit unknown. From Hertford County, NC. Discharged at Halifax, NC in the Spring of 1783. W4140.	Brandywine Creek (PA), Guilford Court House, Eutaw Springs (SC).
Burton, Julius	10th NC Regiment	5/20/1777, a Corporal under Capt. James Wilson for three years. A Private in June 1778. 9/8/1778, a known Private in the Major's Company (Maj. John Baptiste Ashe) (1st NC Regiment). 3/12/1779, re-enlisted for the duration of the war under Capt. James Read (1st NC Regiment). Received 50 lashes for stealing a pair of shoes. aka Julius Burden.	
Burtonshell, Joshua	5th NC Regiment	1777, a Private under Capt. William Caswell. Deserted in Nov. 1777.	
Burtson, Jesse	4th NC Regiment	1776, a Private under Capt. Thomas Harris. Discharged 10/31/1777.	
Burwick, Edward	3rd NC Regiment	7/20/1778, a Private under Maj. Thomas Hogg. Deserted on 8/2/1778.	
Bush, Chany	4th NC Regiment	1777, a Private under Capt. William Goodman. Died on 1/2/1778.	
Bush, John	5th NC Regiment	1775, an Ensign in the New Bern District Minutemen. 4/17/1776, an Ensign under Capt. William Caswell and Col. Edward Buncombe. Resigned in June 1776. 11/28/1776, an Ensign again in the 5th NC Regiment. 2/8/1777, a Lieutenant under Capt. Frederick Hargett (8th NC Regiment). An Adjutant 8/2/1777 under Capt. John Walsh. Dropped from the rolls in Jan. 1778. From Johnston County, NC. W4626.	
Bush, William	7th NC Regiment	1777, a Private under Capt. Thomas Brickell. Deserted in April 1777.	
Bush, William	8th NC Regiment	4/10/1777, an Ensign under Capt. Francis Tartanson. 8/15/1777, a 2nd Lieutenant. Transferred to 1st NC Regiment on 6/1/1778. 2/1/1779, a 1st Lieutenant. 5/12/1781, an Adjutant. Allegedly, after the battle of Eutaw Springs (SC), a Captain until the end of the war – no record thereof.	
Busler, John	2nd NC Regiment	4/15/1781, a Private under Capt. Tilghman Dixon. Discharged on 4/25/1782.	
Bussell, William	1st NC Regiment	8/1/1782, a Private under Capt. Joshua Hadley for 18 months.	
Butler, Charles	5th NC Regiment	4/20/1776, a Private under Capt. John Enloe for 2-1/2 years. 9/10/1778, a known Private under Capt. Thomas Armstrong (2nd NC Regiment). Discharged on 11/10/1778. Later in NC Militia, unit unknown. S41464.	Brandywine Creek (PA), Germantown (PA), Monmouth (NJ).
Butler, Isaac	2nd NC	5/5/1776 (?), a Private under Capt. John Baker	

Name	1st Unit	Year / Rank / Served Under / Notes	Known Battles
	Regiment	(?). Discharged on 5/8/1779.	
Butler, James	2nd NC Regiment	7/20/1778, a Private under Capt. Reading Blount for nine months.	
Butler, Jethro	2nd NC Regiment	4/15/1781, a Private under Capt. Tilghman Dixon for 12 months. Discharged on 4/25/1782 at Bacon's Bridge, SC. From Bertie County, NC when he enlisted. S41465.	
Butler, Joel	3rd NC Regiment	7/20/1778, a Private under Lt./Capt. George "Gee" Bradley for nine months.	
Butler, John	2nd NC Regiment	4/15/1781, a Private under Capt. Tilghman Dixon. Discharged on 4/25/1782.	
Butler, John	4th NC Regiment	5/4/1776, a Private under Capt. Robert Smith then Capt. Jerome MacLaine for 2-1/2 years. Discharged at Halifax, NC. From Bertie County. S41463.	Ft. Moultrie #1 (SC).
Butler, John	7th NC Regiment	5/5/1776 (?), a Private under Capt. John Baker (?). Dropped from the rolls in 1779.	
Butler, Lawrence	2nd NC Regiment	6/1/1781, a Private under Capt. Tilghman Dixon. Died on 3/24/1782.	
Butler, William	2nd NC Regiment	7/20/1778, a Private under Capt. Reading Blount for nine months. From Hertford County, NC.	
Butt, Archibald	10th NC Regiment	4/1/1778, a Private under Capt. William Shepherd. 9/9/1778, a known Private under Capt. Clement Hall (2nd NC Regiment). Oct. 1778, a Musician. 3/12/1779, re-enlisted under Capt. Benjamin Andrew Coleman. POW at the Fall of Charleston (SC), escaped and joined MD Line. First enlisted in Prince George County, MD into NC Line. aka Archibald Butes, Archibald Butts. S39252.	Monmouth (NJ), Siege of Charleston (SC).
Butts, Jacob	3rd NC Regiment	1776, a Sergeant under Capt. Thomas Granbury. Discharged on 10/17/1777.	
Butts, Job	3rd NC Regiment	1776, a Corporal under Capt. Thomas Granbury. Discharged in Oct. 1778.	
Butts, Jonathan	3rd NC Regiment	1776, a Sergeant under Capt. Thomas Granbury. Discharged on 10/17/1777.	
Butts, Jonathan	3rd NC Regiment	4/14/1777, a known Ensign under Capt. William Brinkley.	
Butts, William	10th NC Regiment	7/23/1777, a Private under Capt. Abraham Sheppard, Jr. 9/9/1778, under Capt. Clement Hall (2nd NC Regiment). Dropped from the rolls in March 1779.	
Bynum, Drury	5th NC Regiment	12/16/1776, a Corporal under Capt. John Enloe for 2-1/2 years. A Sergeant in Sep. 1777. 6/1/1778, re-enlisted as a Private under Capt. Thomas Armstrong (2nd NC Regiment) for the duration of the war. Back to Corporal on 5/15/1779. Back to Sergeant on 7/25/1779. Later served under Capt. Robert Raiford. Discharged in Washington, NC. On the official rolls as Drury Benham. S37815.	Brandywine Creek (PA), Monmouth (NY).
Bynum, William	1st NC Regiment	1781, a Private, unit unknown. Confined four nights for desertion during July 1781.	

Name	1st Unit	Year / Rank / Served Under / Notes	Known Battles
Byrum, Lawrence	NC Light Dragoons	5/15/1776, a Private under Capt. John Dickerson, then Capt. Samuel Ashe. 3/7/1777, this unit was placed on the NC Continental Line until Jan. 1779. 1781, in the NC Militia. Born on 11/15/1759 in Surry County, VA. S9125.	Germantown (PA), Monmouth (NJ).
Cade, Waddell	10th NC Regiment	5/18/1777, a Private under Capt. Abraham Sheppard, Jr.	
Cadle, Zackariah	2nd NC Regiment	7/19/1781, a Private under Capt. Benjamin Carter. Deserted on 10/15/1782.	
Caesar, Francis	3rd NC Regiment	6/19/1779, a Private under Capt. Michael Quinn. Deserted in Dec. 1779. aka Francis Ceaser.	
Cahoon, Jonathan	8th NC Regiment	3/1/1777, a Musician, unit unknown. A Private in Jan. 1778. Dropped from the rolls in Feb. 1778.	
Cail, Amo.	7th NC Regiment	2/1/1777, a Private under Capt. James Vaughan. Died in Dec. 1777.	
Caile, William	4th NC Regiment	May or June, 1782, a Musician under Capt. Anthony Sharpe. Enlisted at Kingston, NC. Discharged in August 1783 by Capt. Joseph T. Rhodes at James Island, SC. On the official rolls as William Cale. Born in Dobbs County, NC. W5241.	
Cain, John	3rd NC Regiment	6/14/1779, a Private under Capt. Michael Quinn for 18 months.	
Cain, Joseph	3rd NC Regiment	8/27/1778, a Private under Lt./Capt. George "Gee" Bradley for three years.	
Cain, Richard	2nd NC Regiment	1782, a Private under Capt. Benjamin Carter.	
Cain, William	3rd NC Regiment	7/20/1778, a Private under Lt. Joseph Montford for nine months.	
Cake, Philip	NC Artillery	4/17/1777, a Corporal under Capt. John Vance as NC State Troops. 3/7/1777, on Continental Line. 11/16/1777, under Capt. John Kingsbury. 5/1/1778, in same unit. 9/16/1778, in same unit.	
Cake, Philip	3rd NC Regiment	2/1/1780, a Sergeant under Lt./Capt. Samuel Jones. Deserted on 4/1/1782. Probably the same man as directly above.	
Calaghan, Cornelius	8th NC Regiment	2/14/1777, a Private under Capt. John Walsh. POW at Ft. Lafayette, NY on 6/1/1779. Discharged in 2/14/1780. aka Cornels Calaghan.	Ft. Lafayette (NY).
Calahan, Humphrey	2nd NC Regiment	Aug. 1778, a Private, unit unknown. 9/9/1778, a known Private in the Major's Company (Maj. Hardy Murfree) (2nd NC Regiment). Deserted on 10/6/1778. aka Humphrey Callahan, Humphy Calahan.	
Calahan, William	5th NC Regiment	Jan. 1779, a Corporal under Capt. Philip Taylor.	
Caldwell, William	4th NC Regiment	1775, a 2nd Lieutenant in the 2nd Salisbury District Minutemen. 4/17/1776, a 2nd Lieutenant under Capt. Robert Smith and Col. Thomas Polk. From Mecklenburg County.	
Cale, Abner	3rd NC Regiment	1781, a Private under Capt. Clement Hall. Discharged on 8/16/1782 (2nd NC Regiment).	

Name	1st Unit	Year / Rank / Served Under / Notes	Known Battles
Cale, John	1st NC Regiment	4/16/1777, a Private, unit unknown. 9/8/1778, a known Private in the Colonel's Company (Col. Thomas Clark) led by Capt. John Gambier Scull. aka John Call.	
Calf, Robert	2nd NC Regiment	Sep. 1777, a Private under Capt. William Fenner. Dropped from the rolls in June 1778.	
Callahan, Valentine	1st NC Regiment	A Private under Capt. George Lee Davidson for one year, dates unknown. Later in NC Militia. R20338.	
Callaway, Peter	8th NC Regiment	Summer of 1777, a Private under Capt. William Dennis for nine months. Then in NC Light Dragoons under Lt./Capt. Edmund Gamble. A Continental for a total of three years. Then, in NC Militia. From Carteret County, NC. W10564.	
Callender, Thomas	1st NC Regiment	6/11/1776, an Ensign. 1/1/1777, a 2nd Lieutenant under Capt. Henry "Hal" Dixon. 9/8/1778, a known Lieutenant under Maj. John Baptiste Ashe. Promoted to Captain-Lieutenant on 3/30/1780. Promoted to full Captain on 5/12/1780 (one source says 8/8/1780). POW at the Fall of Charleston, exchanged 6/14/1781. Retired 1/1/1783. From Wilmington, NC. aka Thomas Calendar.	Siege of Charleston 1780 (SC).
Callum, Frederick	10th NC Regiment	5/17/1777, a Private under Capt. John Jarvis. Died 1/12/1779.	
Calvard, John	5th NC Regiment	8/3/1779, a Private under Capt. Reading Blount. Deserted in Oct. 1779.	
Calvert, Stephen	2nd NC Regiment	12/18/1781, a Corporal under Capt. Benjamin Andrew Coleman. A Private in Apr. 1782.	
Cameron, Alexander	1st NC Regiment	4/24/1781, a Private under Capt. Anthony Sharpe. Discharged on 4/24/1782.	
Cameron, Daniel	3rd NC Regiment	1/4/1782, a Private under Capt. Samuel Jones for 13 months. aka Daniel Cammeron. Born 1740.	
Cameron, John	1st NC Regiment	9/26/1775, a Private under Capt. Henry "Hal" Dixon. Discharged 3/26/1778 at Wilmington, NC.	
Campain, Thomas	2nd NC Regiment	4/18/1776, a Private, unit unknown. 9/9/1778, a known Private under Capt. Benjamin Andrew Coleman.	
Campbell, Angus	4th NC Regiment	1782, a Private under Capt. Anthony Sharpe for 18 months.	
Campbell, George	3rd NC Regiment	7/20/1778, a Private under Capt. Michael Quinn for nine months.	
Campbell, George	4th NC Regiment	April 1776, a Private under Capt. Robert Smith for 12 months. From Mecklenburg County, NC. Born 1755 in PA. S31590.	Ft. Moultrie #1 (SC).
Campbell, Israel	1st NC Regiment	1781, a Private under Capt. William Lytle. Discharged on 5/12/1782.	
Campbell, James	2nd NC Regiment	4/25/1781, a Private under Capt. Tilghman Dixon. Dropped from the rolls sometime during 1781.	
Campbell,	4th NC	1775, a Lieutenant in Rowan County, NC. 1776,	Stono Ferry

Name	1st Unit	Year / Rank / Served Under / Notes	Known Battles
James	Regiment	an Ensign in the 4th NC Regiment, unit unknown. 4/19/1777, a Lieutenant under Capt. Andrew Vanoy (10th NC Regiment). Transferred to 2nd NC Regiment on 6/1/1778. A QM on 9/10/1778. 12/14/1778, a Captain under Col. Thomas Clark. Jan. 1779, transferred to 5th NC Regiment. Wounded and taken prisoner at Stono Ferry, SC (5th NC Regiment), exchanged 6/14/1781. Apparently retired soon thereafter.	(SC).
Campbell, Jesse	3rd NC Regiment	1781, a Private under Capt. Edward Yarborough. Discharged on 4/22/1782.	
Campbell, John	5th NC Regiment	4/20/1779, a Lieutenant under Maj. Reading Blount. By 1781, in the 1st NC Regiment.	Ft. Motte (SC).
Campbell, John	6th NC Regiment	A Private under Capt. George Dougherty. Dropped from the rolls in Feb. 1778.	
Campbell, John	10th NC Regiment	4/20/1777, a Lieutenant. Transferred to 4th NC Regiment on 6/1/1778. Promoted to Captain on 4/5/1779 under Col. James Armstrong. However, the 4/24/1782 roll claims he was still a Lieutenant. Retired 1/1/1783.	Stono Ferry (SC), Siege of Savannah (GA).
Campbell, Laughlin	NC Artillery	6/5/1776, a Sergeant under Capt. John Vance as NC Provincial Troops. 7/10/1777, placed on Continental Line. 11/16/1777, under Capt. John Kingsbury. 5/1/1778, in same unit. 9/16/1778, in same unit. Deserted on 4/1/1779. aka Lachlin Campbell, Lauchlin Campbell, Lachlan Campble.	
Campbell, Martin	4th NC Regiment	6/1/1777, a Private under Capt. William Goodman for three years. 9/8/1778, a known Private in the Colonel's Company (Col. Thomas Clark) (1st NC Regiment) led by Capt. John Gambier Scull. 3/12/1779, re-enlisted for the duration of the war in the same unit.	
Campbell, Neil	2nd NC Regiment	11/25/1781, a Private under Capt. Benjamin Andrew Coleman for 12 months.	
Campbell, Patrick	2nd NC Regiment	8/18/1776, a Private under Capt. William Fenner. A Sergeant in Sep. 1777. Discharged on 5/1/1779.	
Campbell, Solomon	10th NC Regiment	8/4/1777, a Private under Capt. John Jarvis. Died in April 1778.	
Campbell, Thomas	10th NC Regiment	6/18/1777, a Private under Capt. John Jarvis for three years. 9/8/1778, a known Private in the Major's Company (Maj. John Baptiste Ashe) (1st NC Regiment).	
Campbell, Walter	4th NC Regiment	Jan. 1782, a Private under Capt. George Dougherty for the war.	
Campbell, William	DQMG	1780, served under Capt. Solomon Wood (NC Light Dragoons). 1780, also a Blacksmith under Col. Nicholas Long (Deputy QM General). Also on 8/23/1781.	
Campbell, William	NC Artillery	8/15/1776, a Bombardier under Capt. John Vance as NC Provincial Troops. 7/10/1777, on Continental Line. 11/16/1777, under Capt. John	

Name	1st Unit	Year / Rank / Served Under / Notes	Known Battles
		Kingsbury. 5/1/1778, in same unit. 9/16/1778, in same unit. A Private in Oct. 1778.	
Campbell, William	1st NC Regiment	9/10/1776, a Private under Lt./Capt. John Brown. 9/8/1778, a known Private under Capt. Howell Tatum.	
Campbell, William	1st NC Regiment	May 1781, a Private under Capt. Alexander Brevard for 12 months. Discharged on 4/28/1782 (a Shoemaker attached to the 3rd NC Regiment) at the Continental Factory in Rowan County, NC. He was from Rowan (what would later be Iredell) County, NC. S32162.	
Campbell, William	6th NC Regiment	1777, a Corporal under Capt. Thomas Donoho. 6/1/1778, a Corporal under Capt. Griffith John McRee (1st NC Regiment). Died in Feb. 1780.	
Campen, James	2nd NC Regiment	12/11/1776, an Ensign under Capt. James Gee. 12/21/1777, a 1st Lieutenant under Capt. Benjamin Williams. 9/9/1778, a 1st Lieutenant under Capt. Robert Fenner. Wounded/POW at the Siege of Charleston - exchanged 6/14/1781. March 1782, a 1st Lieutenant under Capt. Robert Raiford (2nd NC Regiment). His Bounty Land Warrant (BLWt485-300) shows he was a Captain (?). aka James Campin, Campaigne.	Siege of Charleston 1780 (SC).
Campen, John	4th NC Regiment	1782, a Private under Capt. Anthony Sharpe.	
Canaday, Thomas	4th NC Regiment	5/25/1781, a Private under Capt. George Dougherty then under Capt. Joseph T. Rhodes for 12 months. Discharged 6/1/1782 while serving under Capt. Benjamin Andrew Coleman (2nd NC Regiment) at Wilmington, NC. Born in Currituck County on August 20, 1763, moved to and enlisted from Duplin County. On the official rolls as Thomas Canady. aka Thomas Kenneday - signed his last name Canaday and Kenneday. W3561.	Eutaw Springs (SC).
Canady, Richard	2nd NC Regiment	4/15/1781, a Private under Capt. Benjamin Andrew Coleman for 12 months.	
Candy, William	10th NC Regiment	2/16/1778, a Private under Capt. William Shepherd. Deserted on 9/14/1778.	
Cannon, Benjamin	3rd NC Regiment	Apr. 1776, a Musician under Capt. Pinketham Eaton. Died on 5/1/1778.	
Cannon, Bind	1st NC Regiment	5/8/1781, a Private under Capt. Griffith John McRee. Deserted on 6/1/1781.	
Cannon, David	2nd NC Regiment	12/18/1781, a Private under Capt. Benjamin Andrew Coleman for 12 months. First name might be Edward (?).	
Cannon, Henry	5th NC Regiment	9/9/1775, a 2nd Lieutenant in the New Bern District Minutemen. 4/17/1776, a 2nd Lieutenant under Capt. John Enloe and Col. Edward Buncombe. 1776, also a Captain in NC Militia. From Craven County.	
Cannon, John	4th NC Regiment	2/7/1782, a Private under Capt. James Mills. Died on 8/25/1782.	
Cannon,	10th NC	4/19/1777, a 1st Lieutenant under Capt.	

Name	1st Unit	Year / Rank / Served Under / Notes	Known Battles
Lewis	Regiment	Armwell Herron. Dropped from the rolls in June 1778. Joined the 5th NC Regiment in May 1779.	
Caper, Robert	1st NC Regiment	Oct. 1777, a Private under Capt. Tilghman Dixon. Died on 10/25/1777.	
Cappell, Charles	1st NC Regiment	1782, a Private under Capt. Peter Bacot for 18 months.	
Capps, Dempsey	5th NC Regiment	5/20/1777, a Private under Capt. Reading Blount. POW at the Fall of Charleston (SC), exchanged at Jamestown, VA after fifteen months - ~August 1781 - discharged. Born 9/7/1760. W22735.	Siege of Charleston 1780 (SC).
Capps, Francis	1st NC Regiment	4/7/1781, a Private under Capt. Alexander Brevard. Discharged on 4/12/1782 (3rd NC Regiment). aka Francis Kapps.	
Capps, William	2nd NC Regiment	Sep. 1775, a Private under Capt. Nathaniel Keais. 5/27/1777, a Private under Capt. William Caswell (5th NC Regiment) for 2-1/2 years. 9/9/1778, under Capt. Clement Hall (2nd NC Regiment), then under Capt. Benjamin Andrew Coleman. POW at the Fall of Charleston, SC, held 15 months and exchanged at Jamestown, VA. From Johnston County, NC. On the official rolls as William Caps. S6772.	Stony Point (NY), Siege of Charleston 1780 (SC).
Capps, William	10th NC Regiment	6/14/1777, a Private under Capt. Silas Stevenson. 9/9/1778, a Private in the Colonel's Company (Col. John Patten) (2nd NC Regiment) led by Capt. John Craddock.	
Caraway, Francis	3rd NC Regiment	5/12/1781, a Corporal under Capt. Edward Yarborough. Discharged on 4/25/1782.	
Carbett, James	5th NC Regiment	6/29/1779, a Corporal under Capt. Joseph Montford.	
Card, Joshua	8th NC Regiment	1777, a Private under Capt. John Walsh. Died on 10/4/1777 at the battle of Germantown, PA.	Germantown (PA).
Card, William	3rd NC Regiment	1781, a Sergeant under Capt. Edward Yarborough. Discharged on 4/22/1782.	
Carey, Arthur	3rd NC Regiment	7/20/1778, a Private under Capt. Francis Child for nine months.	
Carey, H. Andrew	3rd NC Regiment	Apr. 1776, a Sergeant under Capt. Pinketham Eaton. Died in Sep. 1777.	
Carey, John	2nd NC Regiment	1777, a Private under Capt. Benjamin Williams. Dropped from the rolls in Jan. 1778.	
Carlisle, James	DQMG	1780, a Shoemaker on the roll of Capt. Solomon Wood (NC Light Dragoons) - this seems to be for convenience only. 8/23/1781, a Shoemaker under Col. Nicholas Long (Deputy QM General).	
Carlton, David	1st NC Regiment	12/7/1781, a Private under Capt. Peter Bacot, then transferred under Capt. Samuel Jones (1st NC Regiment). Discharged on 12/3/1782 at Ashley Hill, SC. On the official rolls as David Carleton. Earlier in NC Militia. From Craven County, NC. Born 1757 in Craven County, NC. S8170.	

Name	1st Unit	Year / Rank / Served Under / Notes	Known Battles
Carlton, James	10th NC Regiment	5/5/1777, a Corporal under Capt. John Jarvis. A Private in June 1778. aka James Calton.	
Carlton, John	3rd NC Regiment	12/7/1781, a Private under Capt. Samuel Jones. Discharged on 1/1/1783 (1st NC Regiment). On the official rolls as John Carleton.	
Carmack, James	8th NC Regiment	A Corporal under Capt. John Walsh. A Private in Jan. 1778. Dropped from the rolls in Feb. 1778.	
Carmack, John	3rd NC Regiment	11/1/1781, a Private under Capt. Clement Hall for 12 months. Discharged on 11/1/1782 (2nd NC Regiment) in SC. Enlisted in Orange County, NC. W3772.	
Carmady, James	5th NC Regiment	1778, a Corporal under Capt. William Caswell. A Private in Jan. 1778. Died on 5/12/1778.	
Carman, Stephen	2nd NC Regiment	1777, a Corporal under Capt. James Martin. A Sergeant in Oct. 1777. Deserted on 2/20/1779.	
Carmichael, Duncan	2nd NC Regiment	5/15/1781, a Private under Capt. Tilghman Dixon. Discharged on 5/28/1782 (1st NC Regiment) in Mecklenburg County, NC. Drafted in Caswell County, NC. Born 5/11/1754. S41467.	Siege of Ninety-Six 1781 (SC), Eutaw Springs (SC).
Carmichael, Robert	1st NC Regiment	1777, a Private under Capt. John Brown. 9/8/1778, a known Private under Capt. John Sumner - sick in camp on that date.	
Carnelison, John	4th NC Regiment	June 1778, a Private under Capt. Matthew Ramsey, Maj. John Armstrong. Later in NC Militia.	Stono Ferry (SC).
Carner, Anthony	1st NC Regiment	1776, a Private, and in 1777, a Sergeant under Capt. Lawrence Thompson. Discharged on 1/20/1778. Re-enlisted as a Private in March 1778. 9/8/1778, a known Private under Capt. Tilghman Dixon. Dropped from the rolls in July 1779. From Orange County, NC. aka Anthony Carney. W2753.	Brandywine Creek (PA), Germantown (PA), Monmouth (NJ).
Carnes, Thomas J.	NC Artillery	1/1/1777, a Capt.-Lt. under Capt. Thomas Clark. 7/10/1777, on Continental Line. Resigned 3/8/1779.	
Carney, John	1st NC Regiment	4/5/1781, a Private under Capt. Anthony Sharpe. Badly wounded at the battle of Eutaw Springs, SC - furloughed. From Caswell County, NC. R1710	Eutaw Springs (SC).
Carns, Joshua	2nd NC Regiment	5/15/1781, a Private under Capt. Tilghman Dixon. Dropped from the rolls sometime during 1781.	
Carol, John	7th NC Regiment	1778, a Private under Capt. John Baker. Deserted on 7/23/1778 (3rd NC Regiment).	
Carothers, James	4th NC Regiment	5/1/1776, a Corporal under Capt. John Nelson for three years. A Private in June 1778. 6/1/1778, a Wagoner under Capt. Griffith John McRee (1st NC Regiment). Discharged on 5/1/1779 at Paramus, NJ. aka James Caruthers. S10428.	Brandywine Creek (PA), Monmouth (NJ).
Carpenter, James	3rd NC Regiment	A Private under Capt. Pinketham Eaton for 2-1/2 years. From Wake County, NC. Later in NC	Stono Ferry (SC).

Name	1st Unit	Year / Rank / Served Under / Notes	Known Battles
		Militia. R1717.	
Carpenter, Peter	1st NC Regiment	Sep. 1775, a 1st Sergeant under Capt. William Davis. 11/28/1776, an Ensign under Capt. Edward Ward (8th NC Regiment).	
Carpenter, Thomas	3rd NC Regiment	1781, a Private under Capt. Clement Hall. Discharged on 4/12/1782 (2nd NC Regiment).	
Carr, James	4th NC Regiment	1775, a 1st Lieutenant in the Salisbury District Minutemen. 4/17/1776, a 1st Lieutenant under Capt. William Temple Coles and Col. Thomas Polk.	
Carr, James	4th NC Regiment	1781, a Sergeant under Capt. George Dougherty. Discharged 5/25/1782.	
Carr, Solomon	7th NC Regiment	1/6/1777, a Private under Capt. John Macon for three years. 9/8/1778, a known Private under Capt. Joshua Bowman (1st NC Regiment). Discharged on 2/1/1780 near Halifax, NC. Enlisted in Bute County, NC. W5893.	Germantown (PA), Stony Point (NY).
Carrall, Butler	10th NC Regiment	1777, an Ensign under Capt. John Jarvis. Dropped from the rolls in June 1778. aka Butler Carroll, Butler Cawall.	
Carraway, Gideon	8th NC Regiment	11/28/1776, a 1st Lieutenant under Capt. Frederick Hargett. Resigned in Feb. 1777. From Craven County, NC. aka Gideon Carroway.	
Carraway, John	3rd NC Regiment	7/20/1778, a Private under Capt. Michael Quinn for nine months.	
Carraway, Thomas	10th NC Regiment	5/5/1777, a Private under Capt. Abraham Sheppard, Jr. 9/9/1778, a known Private under Capt. Robert Fenner (2nd NC Regiment). 3/12/1779, re-enlisted under Capt. Robert Fenner.	
Carrell, Benjamin	5th NC Regiment	1777, a Private under Capt. Benjamin Andrew Coleman. Died in Aug. 1777.	
Carrell, Daniel	3rd NC Regiment	1776, a Private under Capt. Jacob Turner for 2-1/2 years. From Bute County, NC. Later in SC Militia. R1726. aka Daniel Carrol.	Ft. Moultrie #1 (SC).
Carrell, Hardy	4th NC Regiment	8/1/1782, a Private under Capt. Joseph T. Rhodes for 18 months. Furloughed in July 1783 at James Island, SC, taken to Wilmington, NC. Enlisted in Duplin County, NC. S41469.	
Carrell, John	1st NC Regiment	6/11/1781, a Private under Capt. Robert Raiford. Discharged on 6/11/1782.	
Carrier, John	9th NC Regiment	5/5/1777, a Private under Capt. Richard D. Cook for three years. 3/12/1779, re-enlisted for the duration of the war as a Private in the Lt. Colonel's Company (Lt. Col. Robert Mebane) (1st NC Regiment) led by Capt. Joshua Bowman. A Corporal in Nov. 1779.	
Carrin, Emanuel	3rd NC Regiment	9/7/1782, a Private under Capt. Benjamin Bailey for 18 months.	
Carrington, James	9th NC Regiment	11/28/1776, a 2nd Lieutenant under Capt. Matthew Ramsey. From Hillsborough District.	
Carroll, Benjamin	3rd NC Regiment	1781, a Private under Capt. Clement Hall. Discharged on 11/10/1782 (2nd NC Regiment). Re-enlisted again under Capt. James Mills (4th	

Name	1st Unit	Year / Rank / Served Under / Notes	Known Battles
		NC Regiment), discharged in the Fall of 1783. Earlier in NC Militia. From Orange (what is now Durham) County. W10587.	
Carroll, Britton	3rd NC Regiment	7/20/1778, a Private under Maj. Thomas Hogg.	
Carroll, Douglas	2nd NC Regiment	June 1778, a Private, unit unknown. 9/9/1778, under Capt. Clement Hall (2nd NC Regiment).	
Carroll, William	3rd NC Regiment	1781, a Private under Capt. Clement Hall. Discharged on 11/10/1782 (2nd NC Regiment). Born in Fairfax County, VA. Lived in Granville County, NC when he enlisted. W6640.	
Carroll, William	6th NC Regiment	A Private under Capt. George Dougherty. Dropped from the rolls in Jan. 1778.	
Carroner, Christopher	3rd NC Regiment	1/15/1782, a Private under Capt. Samuel Jones for 13 months.	
Carson, Alexander	2nd NC Regiment	Sep. 1775, a Private under Capt. William Knox for six months. Re-enlisted under Capt. John Armstrong. Discharged 8/21/1778 at Moon's Creek due to illness. R1737.	
Carson, John	2nd NC Regiment	3/18/1776, a Sergeant under Capt. John Armstrong. A Private in Nov. 1778. POW at Ft. Lafayette on 6/1/1779. aka Jonathan Carson, John Cason.	Ft. Lafayette (NY).
Carstarphen, James	7th NC Regiment	11/28/1776, an Ensign under Capt. Henry Dawson. Dropped from the rolls in Oct. 1777. One source asserts he enlisted as a Lieutenant. From Halifax County, NC. aka James Caustaphan, James Canstanphin, James Caustauphen, James Casstaphen.	
Carter, Abraham	5th NC Regiment	1779, a Private under Maj. Reading Blount for nine months. Dropped from the rolls in Oct. 1779.	
Carter, Benjamin	8th NC Regiment	11/22/1776, a Lieutenant under Capt. William Temple Coles. 11/27/1776, a 1st Lieutenant under Capt. Robert Smith. 3/10/1778, a Captain under Col. James Armstrong. 6/1/1778, transferred to the 4th NC Regiment. Mid-1781, a Captain under Maj. Reading Blount (2nd NC Regiment). Resigned sometime during 1782. S46541.	Stono Ferry (SC), Eutaw Springs (SC).
Carter, Charles	1st NC Regiment	4/28/1781, a Private under Capt. Alexander Brevard. Deserted on 5/7/1781.	
Carter, Charles	3rd NC Regiment	1782, a Private under Capt. John Daves, then under Capt. Robert Raiford (2nd NC Regiment). Earlier in NC Militia. From Rowan County, NC. R1752.	
Carter, Daniel	3rd NC Regiment	1781, a Private under Capt. Clement Hall. Deserted on 4/1/1782 (from 2nd NC Regiment).	
Carter, David	10th NC Regiment	8/20/1777, a Corporal under Capt. James Wilson. Died in July 1778.	
Carter, Edward	5th NC Regiment	1777, a Sergeant under Capt. Simon Alderson. Dropped from the rolls in Jan. 1778.	
Carter, Giles	3rd NC Regiment	3/1/1777, a Private under Capt. Jacob Turner. 9/9/1778, a known Private under Capt. John	

Name	1st Unit	Year / Rank / Served Under / Notes	Known Battles
		Ingles (2nd NC Regiment). From Hertford County, NC.	
Carter, Henry	3rd NC Regiment	1782, a Private under Capt. Alexander Brevard for 18 months.	
Carter, Hibbard	6th NC Regiment	A Private under Capt. George Dougherty. Died on 4/11/1778.	
Carter, Hubart	1st NC Regiment	1776, a Private under Capt. Joshua Bowman.	
Carter, Isaac	1st NC Regiment	5/25/1781, a Private under Lt./Capt. Benjamin Bailey. Discharged on 5/25/1782 (3rd NC Regiment).	
Carter, Isaac	4th NC Regiment	1782, a Private under Capt. Thomas Evans. Deserted on 6/11/1783 (?).	
Carter, Isaac	8th NC Regiment	2/5/1777, a Private under Capt. John Walsh. 9/9/1778, a known Private under Capt. Robert Fenner (2nd NC Regiment). POW at Ft. Lafayette, NY on 6/1/1779. Discharged on 2/20/1780 at Lockwood's Folly, NC. July 1781, re-enlisted under Capt. Dennis Porterfield (3rd NC Regiment) for 12 months. Wounded at Eutaw Springs (SC). From Cumberland County, NC. Born 10/29/1756. S8147.	Brandywine Creek (PA), Germantown (PA), Monmouth (NJ), Ft. Lafayette (NY), Eutaw Springs (SC).
Carter, Isaac	8th NC Regiment	9/1/1777, a Private under Capt. John Walsh for three years. POW at Ft. Lafayette, NY on 6/1/1779. Discharged on 2/14/1780. From Gates County, NC. W4912.	Ft. Lafayette (NY).
Carter, Isaac	10th NC Regiment	9/1/1777, a Private under Capt. Silas Stevenson. 9/9/1778, a known Private under Capt. Clement Hall (2nd NC Regiment). Deserted on 6/13/1783 (?).	
Carter, John	1st NC Regiment	5/30/1777, a Private under Capt. Anthony Sharpe for three years. 9/8/1778, a known Private in the Lt. Colonel's Company (Lt. Col. Robert Mebane) (1st NC Regiment) led by Capt. Joshua Bowman - sick on that date at Valley Forge. Discharged on 5/1/1779.	
Carter, John	3rd NC Regiment	7/10/1778, a Private under Capt. Michael Quinn for nine months. Discharged at Halifax, NC. Probably from Craven County, NC. R1749.	
Carter, John	3rd NC Regiment	7/20/1778, a Private in the Lt. Colonel's Company (Lt. Col. William Lee Davidson) led by Lt./Capt. George "Gee" Bradley. 9/9/1778, under Capt. Clement Hall (2nd NC Regiment). Died at New Windsor Hospital on 11/18/1778.	
Carter, John	3rd NC Regiment	6/30/1779, a Private under Capt. George "Gee" Bradley for 18 months.	
Carter, John	3rd NC Regiment	2/1/1781, a Private under Capt. Samuel Jones.	
Carter, John	5th NC Regiment	1777, a Private under Capt. Benjamin Stedman.	
Carter, John	6th NC Regiment	6/25/1776, a Sergeant under Capt. Thomas Donoho. Discharged on 5/16/1779.	
Carter, John Jr.	6th NC Regiment	1777, a Private under Capt. Thomas Donoho.	

Name	1st Unit	Year / Rank / Served Under / Notes	Known Battles
Carter, John Sr.	6th NC Regiment	6/26/1776, a Private under Capt. Thomas Donoho for 2-1/2 years. 6/1/1778, a Private under Capt. Griffith John McRee (1st NC Regiment).	
Carter, Moses	3rd NC Regiment	7/19/1782, a Private under Capt. Alexander Brevard then under Capt. Joseph T. Rhodes (4th NC Regiment). Discharged on 7/1/1783. S41470.	
Carter, Robert	5th NC Regiment	5/4/1776, a Private under Capt. John Pugh Williams for 2-1/2 years. 9/9/1778, a known Private under Capt. Clement Hall (2nd NC Regiment). Discharged on 11/10/1778.	
Carter, Samuel	5th NC Regiment	4/26/1776, a Private under Capt. John Pugh Williams. A Corporal in Nov. 1777. Back to Private in Apr. 1778. 9/9/1778, a known Private in the Major's Company (Maj. Hardy Murfree) (2nd NC Regiment). Discharged 10/16/1778.	
Carter, Sewall	1st NC Regiment	1781, a Private under Capt. Robert Raiford. Discharged on 4/1/1782.	
Carter, Stephen	1st NC Regiment	8/26/1778, a Private under Capt. Anthony Sharpe. Deserted in Jan. 1779.	
Carter, William	1st NC Regiment	4/26/1781, a Private under Capt. Robert Raiford. Discharged 4/26/1782.	
Carter, William	7th NC Regiment	1777, a Private under Capt. Joseph Walker. Died on 4/17/1778.	
Cartwright, Joseph	3rd NC Regiment	1/1/1782, a Private under Capt. Samuel Jones for 12 months. Enlisted in Bladen County, NC on 12/12/1781. Discharged 12/12/1782 (1st NC Regiment). Born 10/26/1761 in Duplin (would become Sampson) County, NC. S8161.	
Cartwright, Josiah	10th NC Regiment	5/31/1777, a Private under Capt. Dempsey Gregory. 9/8/1778, a known Private under Capt. Howell Tatum (1st NC Regiment). aka Joseph Casteright.	
Cartwright, Robert	1st NC Regiment	11/10/1777, a Private under Capt. William Armstrong for three years. 9/8/1778, a known Private under Capt. John Sumner (1st NC Regiment). aka Robert Carteright.	
Cartwright, Robert	6th NC Regiment	11/10/1777, a Private under Ensign Joseph Richardson.	
Cartwright, Thomas	1st NC Regiment	9/20/1777, a Private under Capt. William Armstrong for three years. 9/8/1778, a known Private under Capt. John Sumner (1st NC Regiment). 3/12/1779, re-enlisted for the duration of the war in the same unit. A Corporal in July 1779.	
Cartwright, Thomas	6th NC Regiment	9/20/1777, a Private under Ensign Joseph Richardson. 3/12/1779, a known Private under Capt. John Sumner (1st NC Regiment).	
Caruthers, Hugh	10th NC Regiment	1777, a Private under Capt. James Wilson for 12 months. From Orange County, NC. Also served in NC Militia.	
Caruthers, Thomas	4th NC Regiment	4/27/1776, a Private under Capt. John Nelson for three years. 6/1/1778, a Wagoner under	

Name	1st Unit	Year / Rank / Served Under / Notes	Known Battles
		Capt. Griffith John McRee (1st NC Regiment). Discharged on 5/1/1779. Later in NC Militia, unit and dates unknown - at Kings Mountain (SC), unit unknown. aka Thomas Carruthers, Thomas Carothers. S35809.	
Carver, James	1st NC Regiment	Sep. 1775, a 2nd Sergeant under Capt. William Davis.	
Carvin, Thomas	5th NC Regiment	11/26/1776, a Private under Capt. William Caswell.	
Carvin, William	2nd NC Regiment	5/12/1781, a Private under Capt. Tilghman Dixon. Deserted on 7/20/1781.	
Cary, John	2nd NC Regiment	1777, a Private under Capt. Benjamin Williams. Dropped from the rolls in Jan. 1778. aka Jonathan Cary.	
Case, Jonathan	1st NC Regiment	5/17/1781, a Private under Lt./Capt. Benjamin Bailey. Discharged on 5/17/1782 (3rd NC Regiment).	
Case, Joseph	3rd NC Regiment	8/27/1778, a Private under Lt./Capt. George "Gee" Bradley.	
Case, Joseph	4th NC Regiment	1777, a Private under Capt. William Goodman for three years. Enlisted in Bertie County, NC. Discharged at Richmond, VA. S41472.	
Casey, John	DQMG	1780, a Wagoner under Col. Nicholas Long (Deputy QM General). Said to be an ex-Continental soldier (?).	
Casey, William	3rd NC Regiment	A servant to BG Jethro Sumner for 13 months, dates unknown. Earlier in VA unit. Enlisted in Warren County. A free colored man. aka William Kersey. W29906.5	
Cashway, Joshua	2nd NC Regiment	3/26/1776, a Private, unit unknown. 1777, a Private under Capt. Clement Hall. POW at Ft. Lafayette on 6/1/1779. aka Joseph Casway.	Ft. Lafayette (NY).
Casidy, John	6th NC Regiment	1777, a Private under Capt. Thomas Donoho. Died on 1/28/1778.	
Casman, Benjamin		7/21/1777, unit and rank unknown. 9/8/1778, a known Sergeant under Capt. Howell Tatum (1st NC Regiment).	
Cason, Cannon	1st NC Regiment	6/12/1780, a Private under Lt./Capt. Benjamin Bailey. 1/1/1782, a Private under Capt. Samuel Jones (3rd NC Regiment) for 12 months.	
Cason, Hilly	1st NC Regiment	6/12/1780, a Corporal under Lt./Capt. Benjamin Bailey. 4/1/1782, a Private under Capt. Samuel Jones (3rd NC Regiment/1st NC Regiment) for 12 months. Died on 8/12/1782 (1st NC Regiment).	
Cason, William	5th NC Regiment	A Private under Capt. John Enloe. Died on 3/5/1778.	
Cassels, Thomas	4th NC Regiment	7/15/1776, a Private under Capt. Roger Moore, then under Capt. William Goodman. A Corporal in Dec. 1778. Discharged on 6/16/1779 at Ft. Constitution on Kings River. Enlisted in Orange County, NC. On the official rolls as Thomas Caswell. S41473.	Monmouth (NJ).
Casteen,	3rd NC	2/3/1782, a Private under Capt. Samuel Jones.	

Name	1ˢᵗ Unit	Year / Rank / Served Under / Notes	Known Battles
William	Regiment	Died on 9/14/1782 (1ˢᵗ NC Regiment).	
Casten, Francis	3ʳᵈ NC Regiment	7/20/1778, a Private under Capt. John Baker for nine months.	
Caster, Jacob	3ʳᵈ NC Regiment	7/20/1778, a Private under Capt. Michael Quinn for nine months.	
Caster, John	3ʳᵈ NC Regiment	7/20/1778, a Private under Capt. Michael Quinn for nine months.	
Castle, Thomas	1ˢᵗ NC Regiment	6/15/1776, a Private, unit unknown. 9/8/1778, a known Private in the Colonel's Company (Col. Thomas Clark) led by Capt. John Gambier Scull.	
Caswell, William	2ⁿᵈ NC Regiment	9/1/1775, an Ensign under Capt. Simon Bright. 4/17/1776, a Captain under Col. Edward Buncombe (5ᵗʰ NC Regiment). Feb. 1778, back in NC mostly recruiting new Continentals. Then, a Colonel and BG in NC Militia.	Great Bridge (VA), Brandywine Creek (PA), Germantown (PA).
Catchum, Hugh	1ˢᵗ NC Regiment	1781, a Private under Capt. William Lytle for 12 months. Captured right after enlisting at Hillsborough (9/12/1781), taken to Wilmington then Charleston, SC, exchanged after about nine months. Discharged soon thereafter at MG Nathanael Greene's camp. Earlier in NC Militia. From Orange County, NC. S166690.	Hillsborough.
Cates, Matthew	6ᵗʰ NC Regiment	6/30/1776, a Private under Lt./Capt. Thomas White for 2-1/2 years. From Johnston County, NC. R1806.	
Cates, Matthias	10ᵗʰ NC Regiment	6/30/1776, a Corporal, unit unknown, enlisted for three years. A Private in Aug. 1778. 9/8/1778, a known Private under Capt. John Sumner (1st NC Regiment).	
Caton, Francis	1ˢᵗ NC Regiment	5/15/1781, a Private under Capt. Tilghman Dixon. Deserted on 7/18/1781. Received clothing on 5/24/1782. From Caswell County. aka Frank Caton.	
Caton, James		5/5/1777, a Private, regiment and unit unknown, enlisted for three years. 9/8/1778, a known Private in the Major's Company (Maj. John Baptiste Ashe) (1st NC Regiment). aka James Caten.	
Caton, Thomas	10ᵗʰ NC Regiment	6/12/1777, a Private under Capt. John Jarvis for three years. 9/8/1778, a known Private in the Major's Company (Maj. John Baptiste Ashe) (1st NC Regiment). A Corporal on 12/1/1778. Back to Private on 3/20/1779. aka Thomas Caten.	
Caudle, Absalom	1ˢᵗ NC Regiment	1775, a Private under Capt. Robert Rowan for twelve months. Discharged in Dec. 1776 at Wilmington, NC. From Bladen County, NC. Later in NC Militia. W10589.	
Causeway, Joseph	2ⁿᵈ NC Regiment	3/12/1779, re-enlisted under Capt. Clement Hall.	
Cavender, James	1ˢᵗ NC Regiment	5/28/1781, a Private under Capt. Alexander Brevard. Discharged on 5/25/1782 (3rd NC	

Name	1st Unit	Year / Rank / Served Under / Notes	Known Battles
		Regiment).	
Cavender, William	1st NC Regiment	5/28/1781, a Private under Capt. Alexander Brevard. Discharged on 5/25/1782 (3rd NC Regiment).	
Cavender, William	4th NC Regiment	Sep. 1777, a Private under Capt. William Goodman. Discharged on 10/31/1777.	
Ceeley, Tobias	1st NC Regiment	1777, a Private under Capt. Joshua Bowman. Deserted in Sep. 1777.	
Chace, Blake	2nd NC Regiment	Dec. 1778, a known Lieutenant. Sources claim 6th Regiment, but it was folded into the 2nd Regiment in June 1778.	
Chace, Blake	3rd NC Regiment	5/22/1778, a Private under Maj. Pinketham Eaton.	
Chalco, William	7th NC Regiment	1777, a Private under Capt. Thomas Brickell. Deserted in Apr. 1777.	
Chalk, William	1st NC Regiment	12/29/1776, a Private under Lt./Capt. Howell Tatum. 9/8/1778, a known Private under Capt. Howell Tatum. A Sergeant in March of 1780. Born in England. Enlisted from Hertford County, NC.	
Chamberlain, Christopher	2nd NC Regiment	1777, a Private under Capt. James Martin. Died on 5/22/1778.	
Chamberlain, Dixon	4th NC Regiment	2/7/1782, a Private under Capt. James Mills for 12 months.	
Chamberlain, Malachi	2nd NC Regiment	7/20/1778, a Private under Capt. Reading Blount for nine months.	
Chambers, James	1st NC Regiment	4/28/1781, a Private under Capt. Griffith John McRee for 12 months. Dropped from the rolls after April 1782.	
Champion, Thomas	3rd NC Regiment	4/18/1776, a Private under Capt. Jacob Turner. Discharged on 11/10/1778.	
Chance, Philemon	10th NC Regiment	7/1/1777, a Private under Capt. Armwell Herron. 9/10/1778, a known Private under Capt. Thomas Armstrong (2nd NC Regiment). POW at Ft. Lafayette, NY on 6/1/1779. 1781, a Private under Capt. Edward Yarborough (3rd NC Regiment). A Corporal in Apr. 1782. Discharged 10/1/1783.	Ft. Lafayette (NY).
Chance, Stephen	10th NC Regiment	7/1/1777, a Musician under Capt. Armwell Herron. A Private in June 1778. 9/10/1778, a known Private under Capt. Thomas Armstrong (2nd NC Regiment).	
Chandler, Thomas	1st NC Regiment	March 1780, a Private under Capt. William Lytle for the war. Discharged 1/7/1782 near Camden, SC. Enlisted at Wilkes Court House, NC. S39314.	
Chapell, Edward	3rd NC Regiment	7/20/1778, a Private under Capt. Kedar Ballard for nine months.	
Chapman, Samuel	8th NC Regiment	11/28/1776, a 2nd Lieutenant under Capt. James May, Jr., then under Capt. Francis Tartanson. 4/5/1779, a Captain under Col. James Armstrong. 1781, mostly in NC recruiting. Resigned 11/2/1782. From Carteret County, NC.	Stono Ferry (SC), Siege of Savannah (GA).

Name	1ˢᵗ Unit	Year / Rank / Served Under / Notes	Known Battles
Chappell, Samuel	9ᵗʰ NC Regiment	12/25/1776, a Private under Capt. John Rochelle, then under Capt. Joseph J. Wade for three years. 9/8/1778, a known Private in the Lt. Colonel's Company (Lt. Col. Robert Mebane) (1st NC Regiment) led by Capt. Joshua Bowman. Discharged on 2/1/1780 at Halifax, NC. 4/24/1781, re-enlisted and appointed a Sergeant under Capt. Tilghman Dixon (2nd NC Regiment) for 12 months. Discharged 4/25/1782 at Bacon's Bridge, SC. W6671.	Monmouth (NJ), Stony Point (NY), Eutaw Springs (SC).
Charborough, Stephen	1ˢᵗ NC Regiment	6/6/1781, a Private under Capt. Griffith John McRee. Discharged on 6/26/1782.	
Chardick, Benjamin	3ʳᵈ NC Regiment	6/20/1779, a Private under Capt. George "Gee" Bradley. Deserted in Sep. 1779.	
Charles, Winoke	5ᵗʰ NC Regiment	Dec. 1776, a Private under Capt. John Pugh Williams. Deserted on 8/28/1777. 7/20/1778, a known Private under Maj. Thomas Hogg (3rd NC Regiment) for 9 months. aka Wynnick Charles.	
Charlescroft, Stephen	3ʳᵈ NC Regiment	5/1/1776, a Private under Capt. Thomas Hogg. Discharged 11/2/1778 (3rd NC Regiment).	
Charleton, George	3ʳᵈ NC Regiment	1781, a Private under Capt. Edward Yarborough. Dropped from the rolls on 4/1/1782.	
Charleton, William	10ᵗʰ NC Regiment	6/3/1777, a Private under Capt. Silas Stevenson. 9/9/1778, a known Private in the Colonel's Company (Col. John Patten) (2nd NC Regiment) led by Capt. John Craddock. POW at Ft. Lafayette, NY on 6/1/1779. Rejoined in Nov. 1779.	Ft. Lafayette (NY).
Charlton, William	3ʳᵈ NC Regiment	3/14/1779, an Ensign under Maj. Pinketham Eaton. Sep. 1779, a 2nd Lieutenant. Wounded at Stono Ferry, died 6/21/1779. aka William Charleton.	Stono Ferry (SC).
Charn, John	1ˢᵗ NC Regiment	9/8/1778, a known Private under Capt. Howell Tatum.	
Charney, David	4ᵗʰ NC Regiment	A Private under Capt. Robert Smith. Dropped from the rolls in Sep. 1777.	
Chase, Blake	3ʳᵈ NC Regiment	5/21/1778, a Private under Capt. Michael Quinn for 3 years.	
Chase, Joseph	NC Artillery	1/1/1777, a Musician under Capt. Thomas Clark. Deserted in June 1778.	
Chavers, Drury	1ˢᵗ NC Regiment	1781, a Private under Capt. Alexander Brevard. Discharged on 4/12/1782 (3rd NC Regiment).	
Chavis, Caezer	2ⁿᵈ NC Regiment	5/19/1781, a Private under Capt. Benjamin Carter. Discharged 4/25/1782. From Hertford County, NC.	
Chavons, Drury	1ˢᵗ NC Regiment	6/14/1781, a Private under Capt. Thomas Donoho. Dropped from the rolls sometime during 1781.	
Cheesbor-ough, John	6ᵗʰ NC Regiment	7/3/1777, a Paymaster. 4/25/1778, an Ensign. Retired on 6/1/1778.	
Cheese, John	1ˢᵗ NC Regiment	6/11/1776, an Ensign. 1/20/1777, a 2nd Lieutenant. Resigned 4/1/1777.	

Name	1st Unit	Year / Rank / Served Under / Notes	Known Battles
Cherry, Daniel	5th NC Regiment	1777, a Private under Capt. Henry Darnell. Died on 10/18/1777.	
Cherry, Joshua	3rd NC Regiment	7/20/1778, a Private under Capt. Francis Child for nine months. Born 2/15/1761 in what would become Martin County, NC. Enlisted in Martin County. Later in NC Militia. S32174.	
Cheshire, Hardy	2nd NC Regiment	1777, a Drum Major under Capt. James Gee. Dropped from the rolls in Nov. 1777.	
Cheshire, John	1st NC Regiment	4/28/1781, a Private under Capt. Alexande Brevard. Discharged on 5/28/1782 (3rd NC Regiment). aka John Chesheir.	
Chesson, Joshua	7th NC Regiment	2/4/1777, a Private under Capt. Joseph Walker. 9/8/1778, a known Private under Capt. Tilghman Dixon (1st NC Regiment). Discharged on 2/8/1780.	
Chester, David	1st NC Regiment	10/23/1776, a Sergeant under Lt./Capt. Robert Ralston. 9/8/1778, a known Sergeant under Capt. John Sumner. 1779, a QM Sergeant.	
Chester, John	7th NC Regiment	1778, a Private under Capt. Benjamin Harrison (?) for nine months (at the end of this tour he was in the 3rd NC Regiment). 1782, a Private under Capt. Benjamin Coleman (2nd NC Regiment) for 18 months. From Dobbs County. Born in 1748 in Hyde County, NC. S1897.	
Chester, John	3rd NC Regiment	7/20/1778, a Private under Lt./Capt. George "Gee" Bradley for nine months.	
Chester, John	4th NC Regiment	1782, a Private under Capt. Thomas Evans for 18 months.	
Chetry, Alexander	4th NC Regiment	7/15/1776, a Private under Capt. William Goodman. Died in May 1778.	
Chew, Malachi	10th NC Regiment	6/25/1777, a Private under Capt. Isaac Moore for three years. 9/8/1778, a known Private in the Lt. Colonel's Company (Lt. Col. Robert Mebane) (1st NC Regiment) led by Capt. Joshua Bowman. 3/12/1779, re-enlisted for the duration of the war in the same unit. A Corporal in May 1779. A Sergeant in Nov. 1779.	
Child, Francis	6th NC Regiment	1775, a 1st Lieutenant in the Wilmington District Minutemen. 4/17/1776, a 1st Lieutenant under Capt. Griffith John McRee and Col John Alexander Lillington. 1/26/1777, promoted to Captain. Transferred to 3rd NC Regiment on 6/1/1778. POW at the Fall of Charleston. Jan. 1781, accepted 1/2 pay to retire. Some sources assert he was a Captain in the 1st NC Regiment late 1777/early 1778 - no proof seen.	Monmouth (NJ), Siege of Charleston 1780 (SC).
Child, James	1st NC Regiment	9/1/1775, an Ensign. Resigned in October. aka James Childs.	
Childas, William	1st NC Regiment	5/5/1781, a Corporal under Capt. Robert Raiford. A Private on 1/5/1782. Discharged 5/5/1782. Probably William Childers below.	
Childers, Abraham	NC Light Dragoons	April 16, 1776, a Cornet under Capt. John Dickerson. 1777, an Ensign under Capt. Samuel Ashe.	

318

Name	1st Unit	Year / Rank / Served Under / Notes	Known Battles
Childers, Robert	3rd NC Regiment	1782, a Musician under Capt. Alexander Brevard. Deserted in March 1783 (?).	
Childers, William	1st NC Regiment	11/1/1778, a Private under Capt. Anthony Sharpe for nine months. From Lincoln County, NC. aka William Childress. W6666. Widow pretty sure he also served in NC Militia.	
Chinn, Jim	1st NC Regiment	2/26/1778, a known Private under Capt. Howell Tatum (1st NC Regiment).	
Chitham, Thomas	3rd NC Regiment	7/20/1778, a Private under Capt. Kedar Ballard for nine months.	
Choves, Solomon	3rd NC Regiment	7/20/1778, a Private under Capt. Kedar Ballard for nine months.	
Christian, James	2nd NC Regiment	5/19/1777, a Private under Capt. James Martin for three years. 9/9/1778, a known Private under Capt. Benjamin Andrew Coleman. aka James Christain.	
Christian, James	9th NC Regiment	1777, a Sergeant under Capt. Richard D. Cook. Discharged on 1/29/1778. S12699.	
Christian, John	3rd NC Regiment	5/11/1776, a Fifer under Capt. James Emmett for 2-1/2 years. A Fife Major on 8/17/1777. A Private in June 1778. Discharged in Oct. 1778. From Chatham County, NC. Later in NC Militia, unit unknown - at battle of Lindley's Mill. W6668.	Brandywine Creek (PA), Germantown (PA).
Christie, John	3rd NC Regiment	7/20/1778, a Private under Lt. Joseph Montford for nine months.	
Christmas, John	1st NC Regiment	9/1/1775, a Drum Major, unit unknown. A Private in July 1779.	Moore's Creek Bridge [4].
Christmas, Joseph D.	1st NC Regiment	1775, a Fife Major. Reenlisted in July of 1779 as a Private.	
Christopher, Simon	1st NC Regiment	1777, a Private under Capt. Joshua Bowman. Dropped from the rolls in Feb. 1778.	
Chubbock, Jeremiah	4th NC Regiment	1781, a Private under Capt. George Dougherty. Discharged 5/25/1782.	
Chumney, John	10th NC Regiment	6/27/1777, a Private under Capt. Andrew Vanoy. Dropped from the rolls in June 1778.	
Chumney, Robert	10th NC Regiment	6/27/1777, a Private under Capt. Andrew Vanoy. 9/9/1778, a known Private in the Lt. Colonel's Company (Lt. Col. Selby Harney) (2nd NC Regiment). aka Robert Chumner.	
Church, William	5th NC Regiment	5/12/1776, a Private under Capt. John Pugh Williams. 9/9/1778, a known Private in the Major's Company (Maj. Hardy Murfree) (2nd NC Regiment). Discharged on 11/12/1778.	
Churn, John	1st NC Regiment	1777, a Private under Capt. Howell Tatum.	
Civil, David	3rd NC Regiment	3/1/1782, a Private under Capt. Samuel Jones for 12 months.	
Clack, William	4th NC Regiment	5/20/1776, a Private under Capt. Joseph Phillips. A Sergeant in Sep. 1777. Back to Private in June 1778. 9/8/1778, a Private under Capt. James Read (1st NC Regiment). POW 4/14/1779 (?). aka William Clark.	
Clagburn,	5th NC	10/28/1776, a Private under Capt. Reading	

Name	1st Unit	Year / Rank / Served Under / Notes	Known Battles
Shubal	Regiment	Blount. A Corporal in Dec. 1777. 9/9/1778, a known Private in the Lt. Colonel's Company (Lt. Col. Selby Harney) (2nd NC Regiment). 1780, a Wagoner under Col. Nicholas Long (DQMG). aka Shubal Claghorn, Shubal Claughurn, Shubal Claghorn, Shoebill Clegghorn.	
Clampett, Govey	10th NC Regiment	4/1/1777, a Private under Lt. Matthew McCauley and Capt. Andrew Vanoy. 9/8/1778, a known Private under Capt. Tilghman Dixon (1st NC Regiment). Dropped from the rolls in Mar. 1779. Enlisted at Hillsborough, NC. aka Govey Clampet, Govea Clampitt. W18.	Monmouth (NJ).
Clanghorn, Timothy	2nd NC Regiment	7/20/1778, a Private under Capt. Reading Blount for nine months.	
Clark, Abner	5th NC Regiment	1777, a Private under Capt. John Pugh Williams. Died on 1/28/1778.	
Clark, Abraham	10th NC Regiment	5/3/1777, a Private under Capt. Abraham Sheppard, Jr. Dropped from the rolls in June 1778.	
Clark, H.	2nd NC Regiment	7/20/1778, a Private under Capt. Reading Blount for nine months.	
Clark, Isaac	1st NC Regiment	May 1777, a Private under Capt. John Brown. 9/8/1778, a known Private under Capt. Tilghman Dixon. POW at the Fall of Charleston, SC - escaped. Enlisted in Halifax County, NC. Discharged in July 1783 near Charleston, SC. S41488.	Brandywine Creek (PA), Germantown (PA), Siege of Charleston 1780 (SC).
Clark, Isaac	6th NC Regiment	2/20/1777, a Private under Capt. Francis Child. After 6/1/1778, this unit was in the 3rd NC Regiment.	
Clark, Jacob	1st NC Regiment	1777, a Private under Capt. John Walker, then under Capt. John Brown. 9/8/1778, a Private under Capt. James Read. POW at the Fall of Charleston, taken to St. Augustine until the end of the war. Enlisted in Wilmington, NC. W4155.	Brandywine Creek (PA), Germantown (PA), Siege of Charleston 1780 (SC).
Clark, James	8th NC Regiment	2/1/1777, a Corporal under Capt. John Walsh. A Private in June 1778. 9/9/1778, under Capt. Benjamin Andrew Coleman (2nd NC Regiment). Back to Corporal in March 1779. Discharged on 2/1/1780.	
Clark, John		2/14/1777, a Private, regiment and unit unknown, enlisted for three years. 9/8/1778, a known Private under Capt. Griffith John McRee (1st NC Regiment) - sick on that date in Valley Forge. 3/12/1779, re-enlisted for the duration of the war in the same unit.	
Clark, John	3rd NC Regiment	4/16/1776, a Private under Capt. Jacob Turner, Capt. Matthew Wood, then Capt. Robert Fenner (2nd NC Regiment) for 2-1/2 years. Discharged in Oct. 1778 at Camp Frederickborough, NY. Enlisted in Bute County, NC. S42124.	Germantown (PA).
Clark, John	3rd NC	7/20/1778, a Private in the Lt. Colonel's	

Name	1st Unit	Year / Rank / Served Under / Notes	Known Battles
	Regiment	Company (Lt. Col. William Lee Davidson) led by Lt./Capt. George "Gee" Bradley. 4/23/1779, a known Private in the Lt. Colonel's Company (Lt. Col. Robert Mebane) led by Capt. George "Gee" Bradley. Died at Philadelphia Hospital.	
Clark, John	4th NC Regiment	Oct. 1777, a Corporal under Capt. John Nelson. A Private in June 1778.	
Clark, John	4th NC Regiment	1777, a Private under Capt. Thomas Harris. A Corporal in Sep. 1777. Discharged on 11/1/1777. aka John Clarke.	
Clark, Osborn	10th NC Regiment	6/1/1777, a Sergeant under Capt. Silas Stevenson. A Private in June 1778 under Capt. Benjamin Andrew Coleman (2nd NC Regiment). Probably in engagements up north. POW at the Fall of Charleston (SC), exchanged at Jamestown, VA in 1781. Served earlier, unit(s) unknown. aka Osbern Clark, Ozborn Clark. S41489.	Siege of Charleston 1780 (SC).
Clark, Thomas	NC Artillery	1/1/1777, a Matross under Capt. Thomas Clark as NC Provincial Troops. 7/10/1777, on Continental Line. 9/9/1778, in same unit.	
Clark, Thomas	NC Artillery	1/1/1777, a Captain of Artillery, State Troops. 7/10/1777, this unit was placed on the Continental Line, not attached to any regiment. A known Captain of Artillery on 9/9/1778. Unit disbanded June 1779. From Hyde County, NC.	
Clark, Thomas	1st NC Regiment	9/1/1775, a Major. 4/10/1776, a Lt. Colonel. 2/5/1777, a full Colonel when Francis Nash promoted to Brig. Gen. Early 1778, 6th NC Regiment folded into 1st NC Regiment. Thomas Clark given command. On May 15th, 1778, he was given command of the entire NC Brigade now with Maj. Gen. George Washington. 1779, commander of the "new" 5th NC Regiment under BG Jethro Sumner. Wounded at Stono Ferry, SC. 1780, back in command of 1st NC Regiment. Surrendered 287 men at Charleston. POW at the Fall of Charleston, imprisoned until 11/26/1782. Retired 1/1/1783.	Moore's Creek Bridge [4], Breach Inlet Naval Battle (SC), Brandywine Creek (PA), Germantown (PA), Monmouth (NJ), Near West Point (NY), Stono Ferry (SC), Siege of Charleston (SC).
Clark, Thomas	3rd NC Regiment	2/20/1782, a Private under Capt. Samuel Jones for 12 months.	
Clark, Thomas	4th NC Regiment	1781, a Musician under Capt. George Dougherty. Discharged 5/25/1782.	
Clark, Thomas	9th NC Regiment	11/28/1776, an Ensign under Capt. Richard D. Cook. 2/1/1777, a 2nd Lieutenant. Transferred to 4th NC Regiment on 6/1/1778. Promoted to 1st Lieutenant on 2/10/1779. Some sources say he was later a Captain. From Hyde County, NC.	
Clark, Thomas	10th NC Regiment	4/21/1777, a Private under Capt. Silas Stevenson. Deserted in Apr. 1778.	
Clark,		5/20/1776, regiment, unit, and rank unknown.	

Name	1st Unit	Year / Rank / Served Under / Notes	Known Battles
William		9/8/1778, a Private under Capt. James Read (1st NC Regiment) - sick on that date in Trenton.	
Clark, William	NC Artillery	1/1/1777, a Sergeant under Capt. Thomas Clark. Also on 9/9/1778.	
Clarke, Neil	6th NC Regiment	A Private under Capt. Griffith John McRee. Dropped from the rolls in June 1778.	
Clarke, John	4th NC Regiment	1777, a Private under Capt. Thomas Harris. A Corporal in Sep. 1777. Discharged on 11/1/1777.	
Clarkson, Thomas	3rd NC Regiment	1781, a Sergeant under Capt. Clement Hall. Discharged on 4/21/1782 (2nd NC Regiment).	
Clay, David	4th NC Regiment	1782, a Private under Capt. Thomas Evans for 18 months. From Duplin County, NC. W6690.	
Clayton, Coleman	2nd NC Regiment	5/15/1781, a Private under Capt. Tilghman Dixon. Discharged on 5/28/1782 (1st NC Regiment). Earlier in NC Militia. From Caswell County, NC. On the official rolls as Coleman Cleaton. aka Coliman Cleaton, Clayton Coleman. W6692.	Eutaw Springs (SC).
Clayton, Joseph	5th NC Regiment	9/9/1775, a 2nd Lieutenant in the Edenton District Minutemen. 4/17/1776, a 2nd Lieutenant under Capt. John Pugh Williams and Col. Edward Buncombe. From Bertie County.	
Clayton, Lambert	1st NC Regiment	4/28/1781, a Sergeant under Capt. Griffith John McRee. Discharged on 4/28/1782.	
Cleaver, Jacob	6th NC Regiment	5/6/1776, a Sergeant under Capt. Thomas White for 2-1/2 years. A Private in May 1778. 9/8/1778, a known Tailor under Capt. John Sumner - stationed at Philadelphia. Discharged on 10/20/1778. aka Jacob Cleaner, aka Jacob Clever.	
Clements, Curtis	10th NC Regiment	6/1/1777, a Private, unit unknown, enlisted for three years. 9/8/1778, a known Private under Capt. John Sumner (1st NC Regiment) - sick in camp on that date.	
Clements, David	2nd NC Regiment	Sep. 1775, a Private under Capt. William Knox for six months. Nov. 1778, a Private under Capt. Matthew Ramsey (4th NC Regiment) for nine months. S35840.	Great Cane Brake (SC), Snow Campaign (SC), Ft. Moultrie #1 (SC), Stono Ferry (SC).
Clements, John	10th NC Regiment	4/21/1777, a Sergeant under Capt. Silas Stevenson. A Private in June 1778 in the Colonel's Company (Col. John Patten) (2nd NC Regiment) led by Capt. John Craddock. 3/12/1779, re-enlisted under Capt. Benjamin Williams (2nd NC Regiment). aka John Clemmons.	
Clements, William	2nd NC Regiment	Sep. 1775, a Private under Capt. William Knox for six months. April 1776, re-enlisted for another six months, discharged. Then joined NC Militia. From Rowan County, NC. S30942.	Great Cane Brake (SC), Snow Campaign (SC), Ft. Moultrie #1

Name	1st Unit	Year / Rank / Served Under / Notes	Known Battles
			(SC).
Clements, William	6th NC Regiment	9/9/1775, a 1st Lieutenant in the Hillsborough District Minutemen. 4/17/1776, a 1st Lieutenant under Capt. James Emmett and Col. John Alexander Lillington (6th NC Regiment).	
Clemmens, John	5th NC Regiment	7/1/1779, a Private under Capt. Joseph Montford for 18 months.	
Clendenan, John	3rd NC Regiment	Earlier, a Private in NC Militia. 4/15/1776, an Ensign under Capt. James Emmett. 6/18/1777, a 2nd Lieutenant. 12/23/1777, a 1st Lieutenant. A QM on 12/14/1779. POW at the Fall of Charleston, paroled, then exchanged on 6/14/1781. Broke his parole and raised a company of Militia in Orange County. Taken POW at Hillsborough on 9/12/1781, exchanged on 11/26/1782. aka John Clendenin, John Clendennen, John Clandennan.	Siege of Charleston (SC), Hillsborough.
Cleveland, Benjamin	2nd NC Regiment	9/1/1775, an Ensign. Declined commission, became a Lieutenant in the Surry County Regiment of Militia. Later, a Captain and Colonel of NC Militia.	
Cleveland, James	3rd NC Regiment	7/20/1778, a Private under Lt. Joseph Montford for nine months.	
Clifton, Clay	2nd NC Regiment	1782, a Private under Capt. Benjamin Carter.	
Clifton, Daniel	3rd NC Regiment	6/5/1779, a Sergeant under Capt. Michael Quinn for 18 months. From Dobbs County, NC.	
Clifton, Richard	3rd NC Regiment	1776, a Private under Capt. James Emmett. Died in Feb. 1778.	
Clifton, William	3rd NC Regiment	1781, a Private under Capt. Edward Yarborough. Discharged on 4/22/1782.	
Clifton, William	9th NC Regiment	12/24/1776, a Sergeant under Capt. Richard D. Cook. Dropped from the rolls in Jan. 1778.	
Clinch, James	2nd NC Regiment	9/1/1775, an Ensign. Resigned in October 1775.	
Clinch, Joseph	3rd NC Regiment	4/17/1776, a 1st Lieutenant under Capt. John Gray. 4/14/1777, a known 1st Lieutenant under Capt. Pinketham Eaton.	
Clinton, John	1st NC Regiment	4/19/1776, a Sergeant under Ens. James Read. A Private in June 1778. 9/8/1778, a known Private in the Colonel's Company (Col. Thomas Clark) led by Capt. John Gambier Scull. Discharged on 10/28/1778.	
Close, George	5th NC Regiment	5/26/1779, a Private under Capt. Joseph Montford. Dropped from the rolls in Oct. 1779,	
Clower, Daniel	1st NC Regiment	1/13/1782, a Private under Capt. James Mills for 12 months. 2/6/1782, this would be in the 4th NC Regiment. Enlisted in Orange County, NC. Discharged in April 1783 in SC. S37865.	
Clower, John	1st NC Regiment	1781, a Private under Capt. William Walton. Discharged 5/25/1782.	
Clower, Jonathan	1st NC Regiment	5/25/1781, a Private under Maj. Thomas Donoho for one year. Transferred to Lt. Col. Henry "Light Horse Harry" Lee (VA). From	Eutaw Springs (SC).

Name	1st Unit	Year / Rank / Served Under / Notes	Known Battles
		Orange County, NC. Born on 12/3/1763 in Burke County, PA. W22802.	
Clower, William	1st NC Regiment	1/13/1782, a Private under Capt. James Mills for 12 months. 2/6/1782, this would be in the 4th NC Regiment. In his pension application, he asserts that he joined in 1779 under Capt. Jones, then re-enlisted in 1780 under Capt. James Mills at the Siege of Charleston. Discharged, then re-enlisted again. These are not listed in the "official record." Earlier in NC Militia. S34690.	
Clubb, Samuel	3rd NC Regiment	3/6/1782, a Private under Capt. Samuel Jones for 13 months.	
Coats, Benjamin	10th NC Regiment	9/1/1777, a Private under Capt. James Wilson for three years. 9/8/1778, a known Private in the Major's Company (Maj. John Baptiste Ashe) (1st NC Regiment) - sick in camp on that date. 1781, a Private under Capt. William Armstrong. Discharged on 12/23/1782.	
Coats, Ezekiel	3rd NC Regiment	7/20/1778, a Private under Capt. Francis Child for nine months.	
Cobb, Henry	3rd NC Regiment	1781, a Private under Capt. Clement Hall. Discharged on 9/1/1782 (2nd NC Regiment).	
Cobb, Nathaniel	2nd NC Regiment	7/20/1778, a Private under Capt. Reading Blount for nine months.	
Cobb, William	7th NC Regiment	1777, a Private under Capt. Henry Dawson. Died on 1/26/1778.	
Coble, Shadrack	5th NC Regiment	1777, a Private under Capt. Simon Alderson. Killed 10/4/1777.	Germantown (PA).
Cochran, John	6th NC Regiment	5/19/1776, a Private under Capt. Philip Taylor for 2-1/2 years. 1/8/1778, transferred to Capt. John Sumner (1st NC Regiment). Discharged 11/19/1778. Enlisted from Caswell County, NC. Later in NC Militia. Born 1757 in Hanover County, VA. S2140.	Brandywine Creek (PA), Germantown (PA).
Cockburn, John	3rd NC Regiment	7/20/1778, a Private under Lt./Capt. George "Gee" Bradley for nine months.	
Cocker, Henry	1st NC Regiment	9/8/1778, a known Private under Capt. Joshua Bowman.	
Coddle, Richard	2nd NC Regiment	11/1/1776, a Private, unit unknown. 9/9/1778, a known Private under Capt. John Ingles.	
Coffield, Benjamin	6th NC Regiment	5/17/1777 to 6/1/1778, an Adjutant. aka Benjamin Caffield.	
Cofield, Samuel	4th NC Regiment	1782, a Private under Capt. William Lytle for 18 months.	
Cogdell, William	1st NC Regiment	4/28/1781, a Private under Capt. Alexander Brevard. Discharged on 4/25/1782 (3rd NC Regiment). An Orderly stationed at Salisbury, NC. aka William Cogdill.	
Coggin, Robert	1st NC Regiment	4/17/1781, a Private under Capt. Anthony Sharpe, then Capt. Benjamin Carter (2nd NC Regiment) for 12 months. Discharged on 4/19/1782 at Bacon's Bridge, SC. Enlisted at Ramsey's Mill, NC. S41492.	
Coggins,	5th NC	1777, a Private under Capt. Benjamin Stedman.	

Name	1st Unit	Year / Rank / Served Under / Notes	Known Battles
James	Regiment	9/9/1778, a known Private under Capt. Clement Hall (2nd NC Regiment). aka James Coggin.	
Coker, Hardy	10th NC Regiment	7/1/1777, a Private under Capt. James Wilson. From Craven County, NC. aka Hy. Cocker. See Henry Cocker above - might be same man.	
Coker, Joshua	1st NC Regiment	5/9/1781, a Private under Capt. Alexander Brevard. 3/20/1782, transferred from the 3rd NC Regiment to the Virginia Artillery. aka Jos. Koker.	
Colbreath, Archibald	4th NC Regiment	1782, a Sergeant under Capt. Thomas Evans for 18 months.	
Colbreath, Daniel	3rd NC Regiment	5/30/1778, a Private under Lt./Capt. George "Gee" Bradley for 18 months. Deserted on 10/16/1779.	
Cole, Charles	1st NC Regiment	5/18/1781, a Private under Capt. Thomas Donoho. Discharged on 5/18/1782 at Bacon's Bridge, SC. Enlisted in Granville County, NC. Claims he was at the battle of Cowpens, SC - that was before this enlistment - probably in NC Militia under Capt. William Bennett. S41493.	Eutaw Springs (SC).
Cole, George	2nd NC Regiment	Spring of 1776, a Private under Capt. Nathaniel Keais, then Capt. Charles Crawford, then Capt. Benjamin Williams, then Capt. Charles Allen for 2-1/2 years. Re-enlisted for six more months. 9/10/1778, a known Private under Capt. Thomas Armstrong. POW at Ft. Lafayette (NY) on 6/1/1779. Discharged on 1/30/1780 at Halifax, NC. S41491.	Ft. Lafayette (NY).
Cole, Henry	1st NC Regiment	Sep. 1775, a Private under Capt. John Walker for 12 months. S39359.	Breech Inlet Naval Battle (SC).
Cole, Jesse	5th NC Regiment	1779, a Private under Capt. Reading Blount. Deserted in Sep. 1779.	
Cole, John	1st NC Regiment	1781, a Private under Lt. James Pearl for 12 months. Earlier in NC Militia. Then joined Col. Henry Lee's Legion (VA). From Orange County, NC. R2131.	
Cole, Martin	1st NC Regiment	Sep. 1775, a Private under Capt. Alfred Moore for six months. Re-enlisted under Capt. John Walker for the duration of the war. 11/18/1776, a Private under Lt./Capt. John Brown. 9/8/1778, a known Private under Capt. Tilghman Dixon. 3/19/1778, assigned to His Excellency's Guards under a Capt. Gibbs. 1779, returned to his old unit. POW at the Fall of Charleston, SC - exchanged at Williamsburg, VA. At some time, he was a Sergeant Major. Re-enlisted as a Sergeant in 1782. Discharged in August 1783 at James Island, SC. S39345.	Breech Inlet Naval Battle (SC), Brandywine Creek (PA), Germantown (PA), Siege of Charleston 1780 (SC).
Cole, Robert	1st NC Regiment	A Private under Capt. Anthony Sharpe. Died on 4/28/1778.	
Cole, Thomas	5th NC Regiment	1776, a Private under Capt. William Caswell. From Johnston County. W5824.	
Cole,	5th NC	11/26/1776, a Corporal under Capt. William	Brandywine

Name	1st Unit	Year / Rank / Served Under / Notes	Known Battles
Thomas	Regiment	Caswell. A Private in June 1778 under Capt. Robert Fenner (2nd NC Regiment). Discharged on 2/8/1780. From Johnston Co., NC. Later in NC Militia. S39348.	Creek (PA), Germantown (PA), Monmouth (NJ).
Cole, William	3rd NC Regiment	12/25/1777, a Private under Lt./Capt. George "Gee" Bradley. Discharged prior to 3/30/1780.	
Coleman, Benjamin Andrew	5th NC Regiment	9/9/1775, a 1st Lieutenant in the New Bern District Minutemen. 4/17/1776, a 1st Lieutenant under Capt. Reading Blount and Col. Edward Buncombe. 4/30/1777, a Captain in the 5th NC Regiment. Transferred to NC 2nd Regiment on 6/1/1778. POW at the Fall of Charleston.	Brandywine Creek (PA), Germantown (PA), Monmouth (NJ), Siege of Charleston 1780 (SC).
Coleman, Charles	3rd NC Regiment	1777, a QM Sergeant. On 10/14/1777, Regimental QM. Dropped from the rolls in Sep. 1778. aka Charles Colman.	
Coleman, Charles	3rd NC Regiment	4/14/1777, a known Ensign under Capt. James Emmet. Probably the same man as directly above.	
Coleman, John	DQMG	1780, an Armourer under Col. Nicholas Long (Deputy QM General). Also on 8/23/1781.	
Coleman, John	1st NC Regiment	5/15/1781, a Private under Lt./Capt. Benjamin Bailey. Discharged on 5/15/1782 (3rd NC Regiment).	
Coleman, John	2nd NC Regiment	2/10/1782, a Private under Capt. Benjamin Andrew Coleman for 12 months.	
Coleman, John	9th NC Regiment	11/28/1776, an Ensign under Capt. Joseph John Wade. From Salisbury District.	
Coleman, Levy	1st NC Regiment	4/25/1781, a Private under Capt. Thomas Donoho. Discharged on 5/25/1782.	
Coleman, Theophilus	7th NC Regiment	11/28/1776, a 2nd Lieutenant under Capt. Green Bell, then under Capt. Lemuel Ely. From Edgecombe County, NC.	
Coleman, William	4th NC Regiment	1777, a Private under Capt. Thomas Harris. Deserted in Aug. 1777.	
Coles, Alexander	9th NC Regiment	A Private under Capt. Joseph J. Wade. A Corporal in Jan. 1778. Died on 4/4/1778.	
Coles, William Temple	4th NC Regiment	1775, a Captain in the Salisbury District Minutemen. 4/17/1776, a Captain in the 4th NC Regiment. Retired in Dec. 1779. aka William Temple Cole, aka I. William Cole.	Brandywine Creek (PA), Germantown (PA), Stono Ferry (SC).
Coleson, Benjamin	10th NC Regiment	5/18/1777, a Private under Capt. Abraham Sheppard, Jr.	
Colihorn, Robert	2nd NC Regiment	1777, a Private under Capt. Charles Allen. Died on 5/16/1778. Another source claims he was discharged on 1/30/1780.	
Colley, William	1st NC Regiment	1777, a Corporal under Capt. Henry "Hal" Dixon. A Sergeant on 1/1/1778. A Sergeant Major on 3/19/1778. Later in SC Militia, units and dates unknown. R2168.	
Collins,	8th NC	9/8/1776 (?), a Private under Capt. Robert	

Name	1st Unit	Year / Rank / Served Under / Notes	Known Battles
Benjamin	Regiment	Raiford. A Corporal in Nov. 1777. Back to Private in June 1778 in the Lt. Colonel's Company (Lt. Col. Selby Harney) (2nd NC Regiment). Discharged on 2/16/1780.	
Collins, Caleb	1st NC Regiment	1782, a Private under Capt. William Walton for 18 months. Earlier, in NC State Troops (Light Dragoons in '79). From Tyrrell County, NC. S41490.	
Collins, Charles	10th NC Regiment	5/6/1777, a Private under Capt. James Wilson for three years. 9/8/1778, a known Private in the Major's Company (Maj. John Baptiste Ashe) (1st NC Regiment). 3/12/1779, re-enlisted for the duration of the war in the same unit.	
Collins, Hezekiah	1st NC Regiment	5/28/1781, a Private under Capt. Alexander Brevard. Discharged on 5/25/1782 (3rd NC Regiment).	
Collins, Jeremiah	3rd NC Regiment	1781, a Corporal under Capt. Clement Hall. Discharged on 8/16/1782 (2nd NC Regiment).	
Collins, John	2nd NC Regiment	1782, a Private under Capt. Robert Raiford for 18 months.	
Collins, John	2nd NC Regiment	3/18/1776, a Private under Capt. James Gee. 9/9/1778, a known Private under Capt. John Ingles. Discharged on 9/30/1778.	
Collins, John	2nd NC Regiment	7/20/1778, a Private under Capt. Reading Blount for nine months. Dropped from the rolls in Oct. 1778.	
Collins, John	3rd NC Regiment	1781, a Private under Capt. Clement Hall. Discharged on 8/1/1782 (2nd NC Regiment).	
Collins, John	4th NC Regiment	2/6/1782, a Private under Capt. James Mills for 12 months.	
Collins, John	4th NC Regiment	1782, a Private under Capt. Anthony Sharpe. Died on 3/26/1783.	
Collins, John	5th NC Regiment	1777, a Private under Capt. John Pugh Williams. Discharged on 3/1/1779.	
Collins, John	8th NC Regiment	2/11/1776 (?), a Private under Capt. Edward Ward, then under Capt. Robert Raiford for three years. 1778, a Sergeant under Capt. Benjamin Williams (2nd NC Regiment). Discharged in March 1779. S41496.	Brandywine Creek (PA), Germantown (PA).
Collins, Joshua	4th NC Regiment	1777, a Musician under Capt. William Temple Coles. Deserted on 2/15/1778.	
Collins, Matthew	6th NC Regiment	Oct. 1777, a Private under Capt. Griffith John McRee. Discharged on 6/4/1778.	
Collins, Samuel	2nd NC Regiment	1777, a Musician under Capt. James Martin. Died on 4/18/1778,	
Collins, Shadrack	2nd NC Regiment	1782, a Private under Capt. Benjamin Carter.	
Collins, Shadrack	3rd NC Regiment	7/20/1778, a Private under Capt. Kedar Ballard for nine months.	
Collins, Thomas	8th NC Regiment	1777, a Private under Capt. John Walsh. Dropped from the rolls in Jan. 1778.	
Colnel, John	8th NC Regiment	3/12/1777, a Private under Capt. Francis Tartanson.	
Colston,		6/7/1776, a Private, regiment and unit unknown,	

Name	1st Unit	Year / Rank / Served Under / Notes	Known Battles
Henry		enlisted for three years. 6/1/1778, a Private under Capt. Griffith John McRee (1st NC Regiment).	
Colston, James	3rd NC Regiment	5/13/1782, a Private under Capt. Benjamin Bailey.	
Colter, Levi		2/1/1777, a Private, regiment and unit unknown, enlisted for 2-1/2 years. 9/8/1778, a known Private in the Major's Company (Maj. John Baptiste Ashe) (1st NC Regiment).	
Colwell, David	2nd NC Regiment	1782, a Private under Capt. Benjamin Carter.	
Colwell, John	8th NC Regiment	3/12/1777, a Private under Capt. Francis Tartanson for three years. 9/10/1778, a known Private under Capt. Thomas Armstrong (2nd NC Regiment). aka John Caldwell. R1590.	
Comber, Hugh	3rd NC Regiment	1782, a Corporal under Capt. Alexander Brevard for 18 months.	
Combs, George	1st NC Regiment	5/9/1781, a Private under Capt. Alexander Brevard. Discharged on 5/9/1782 (3rd NC Regiment). S41497.	Siege of Ninety-Six 1781 (SC), Eutaw Springs (SC).
Combs, John	4th NC Regiment	1782, a Private under Capt. Thomas Evans. Deserted on 6/21/1783 (?).	
Combs, Robert	2nd NC Regiment	5/2/1781, a Private under Capt. Benjamin Carter. Discharged 4/2/1782.	
Comer, James	NC Light Dragoons	May 1776, a Private in the NC Light Dragoons (State Troops) for 2-1/2 years. On 3/7/1777, these were placed on the NC Continental Line - at that time under Capt. Samuel Ashe. From Granville County, NC. Later in NC Militia. R20350.	
Cominel, Francis	3rd NC Regiment	6/30/1779, a Private under Capt. George "Gee" Bradley. Deserted in Dec. 1779.	
Cominger, John	4th NC Regiment	6/17/1776, a Private under Capt. John Nelson for three years. 9/8/1778, a known Private under Capt. Griffith John McRee (1st NC Regiment) - sick on that date at Reading, PA. Dropped from the rolls in Feb. 1779. aka John Cumminger.	
Conaway, William	1st NC Regiment	1782, a Private under Capt. Peter Bacot for 18 months.	
Condon, John	1st NC Regiment	Oct. 1777, a Private under Capt. Lawrence Thompson. Dropped from the rolls in Jan. 1778.	
Cone, W.	3rd NC Regiment	1777, a Private under Capt. Thomas Granbury. Died on 9/16/1777.	
Conger, Jonathan	4th NC Regiment	1/25/1777, a QM Sergeant. Promoted 9/11/1777 - to what, not known. Maybe regimental QM.	
Conger, Stephen	1st NC Regiment	10/10/1776, a Sergeant Major. 1/29/1778, an Adjutant. Retired 6/1/1778.	
Conn, Benjamin	2nd NC Regiment	1782, a Private under Capt. Robert Raiford. Deserted on 4/2/1783 (?). R2316.	
Conn, David	7th NC Regiment	1777, a Private under Capt. Joseph Walker. Dropped from the rolls in Sep. 1777.	
Conn, John	1st NC	5/20/1781, a Private under Capt. Alexander	

328

Name	1st Unit	Year / Rank / Served Under / Notes	Known Battles
	Regiment	Brevard. Discharged on 5/28/1782 (3rd NC Regiment). Earlier in NC Militia. From Guilford (what is now Rockingham) County, NC. S17890.	
Conner, Charles	1st NC Regiment	1777, a Private under Capt. Howell Tatum. 9/8/1778, a known Private under Capt. Howell Tatum - manning a row galley at Trenton on that date.	
Conner, Edward	1st NC Regiment	Sept. 1775, a Private under Capt. William Davis. From what is now Horry County, SC - went to New Hanover County, NC and enlisted. Born on 12/31/1757 in Duplin County, NC. Later in NC Militia and SC Continental line. S21123.	Moore's Creek Bridge [4].
Conner, James	1st NC Regiment	Sep. 1775, a Private under Capt. George Davidson for six months. From Mecklenburg County, NC. Then in NC Militia. S8237.	Great Cane Brake (SC), Snow Campaign (SC).
Conner, John Sr.	2nd NC Regiment	8/15/1776, a Private under Lt./Capt. Thomas White for three years. 6/1/1778, a Private under Capt. Griffith John McRee (1st NC Regiment). Discharged in Feb. 1780.	
Conner, William	1st NC Regiment	2/26/1778, a known Private under Capt. Howell Tatum.	
Conneway, John	9th NC Regiment	6/19/1777, a Private under Capt. Joel Brevard for three years. A Sergeant in Jan. 1778. A Corporal in June 1778. Back to Private in Aug. 1778. 9/8/1778, a known Private in the Lt. Colonel's Company (Lt. Col. Robert Mebane) (1st NC Regiment) led by Capt. Joshua Bowman. Deserted on 12/15/1779. Received clothing on 5/24/1782. From Caswell County. On some rolls as John Conaway.	
Connor, Benjamin	4th NC Regiment	1782, a Private under Capt. Anthony Sharpe for 18 months.	
Connor, Doshey	2nd NC Regiment	1782, a Private under Capt. Benjamin Carter. Died on 6/14/1783.	
Connor, Jacob	7th NC Regiment	1777, a Private under Capt. John McGlaughan. Died on 2/6/1778.	
Connor, James	1st NC Regiment	4/7/1781, a Private under Capt. William Lytle. Discharged on 4/7/1782.	
Connor, John	10th NC Regiment	6/28/1777, a Private under Capt. Silas Stevenson. 9/9/1778, a known Private under Capt. Clement Hall (2nd NC Regiment) - sick at Valley Forge on that date. Died in Dec. 1778. aka John Conner.	
Connor, Mordecai	3rd NC Regiment	1782, a Private under Capt. Alexander Brevard for 18 months.	
Connor, William	1st NC Regiment	6/14/1781, a Private under Capt. Thomas Donoho. Dropped from the rolls sometime during 1781.	
Connor, William	2nd NC Regiment	1782, a Private under Capt. Benjamin Carter.	
Connor,	5th NC	7/1/1779, a Private under Capt. Joseph	

Name	1st Unit	Year / Rank / Served Under / Notes	Known Battles
William	Regiment	Montford. Deserted on 11/10/1779.	
Connor, William	7th NC Regiment	1777, a Private under Capt. John McGlaughan. Died on 4/21/1778.	
Connor, William	8th NC Regiment	1777, a Musician under Capt. John Walsh. Dropped from the rolls in Jan. 1778.	
Connolly, John	1st NC Regiment	1777, a Private under Capt. Howell Tatum. Dropped from the rolls in Jan. 1778.	
Conver, John	6th NC Regiment	8/15/1776, a Private under Lt./Capt. Thomas White.	
Conver, William	8th NC Regiment	1777, a Musician under Capt. John Walsh.	
Cook, Allen	3rd NC Regiment	3/5/1782, a Private under Capt. Samuel Jones.	
Cook, George	10th NC Regiment	4/19/1777, a 2nd Lieutenant under Capt. John Jarvis. Promoted to 1st Lieutenant on 7/10/1777. Transferred to 1st NC Regiment on 6/1/1778 under Capt. Tilghman Dixon. Killed during the Siege of Charleston in May of 1780.	Siege of Charleston 1780 (SC).
Cook, James	2nd NC Regiment	9/1/1775, an Ensign. Resigned 10/21/1775. 4/17/1776, a Captain of the 3rd NC Regiment under Col. Jethro Sumner. Retired 6/1/1778.	
Cook, John	1st NC Regiment	1777, a Private under Capt. Thomas Hogg. Deserted in Jan. 1777.	
Cook, John	1st NC Regiment	9/8/1778, a known Private under Capt. Joshua Bowman.	
Cook, John	6th NC Regiment	1777, a Corporal under Capt. Philip Taylor. Dropped from the rolls in Nov. 1778.	
Cook, John	10th NC Regiment	4/21/1777, a Corporal under Capt. Silas Stevenson. Dropped from the rolls in Feb. 1779.	
Cook, Joseph	2nd NC Regiment	1777, a Private under Capt. William Fenner. Dropped from the rolls in Sept. 1777.	
Cook, Richard Donaldson	9th NC Regiment	11/28/1776, a Captain under Col. John Williams. Retired 6/1/1778. From Hillsborough District.	Brandywine Creek (PA), Germantown (PA).
Cook, Robert	1st NC Regiment	Sep. 1775, a Private under Capt. William Davis, then under Capt. Thomas Hogg for six months. From New Hanover County, NC. Discharged in March 1776 (signed 5/14/1776). S8233.	
Cook, Robert	2nd NC Regiment	7/20/1778, a Private under Capt. Reading Blount for nine months.	
Cook, Sanders	10th NC Regiment	5/31/1777, a Private under Capt. Dempsey Gregory. 9/8/1778, a known Private under Capt. Howell Tatum (1st NC Regiment). aka Saunders Cook.	
Cook, Stephen	2nd NC Regiment	12/20/1776, a Private under Capt. John Armstrong. 9/9/1778, a known Private under Capt. Robert Fenner. Died on 11/19/1779.	
Cook, Thomas	1st NC Regiment	1781, a Private under Capt. Alexander Brevard.	
Cook, Thomas	9th NC Regiment	1777, a Sergeant under Capt. Richard D. Cook. Dropped from the rolls in Dec. 1777.	
Cook, William	4th NC Regiment	1782, a Private under Capt. Anthony Sharpe for 18 months.	

330

Name	1st Unit	Year / Rank / Served Under / Notes	Known Battles
Cooke, John	2nd NC Regiment	4/21/1777, a Private, unit unknown. 9/9/1778, a known Private in the Colonel's Company (Col. John Patten) led by Capt. John Craddock. aka John Cook.	
Cookey, Isaac	2nd NC Regiment	4/1/1782, a Private under Capt. Clement Hall for 12 months.	
Cooksey, Hezekiah	1st NC Regiment	1781, a Private under Capt. Anthony Sharpe. Discharged 2/2/1783.	
Cooksey, Thomas	1st NC Regiment	1781, a Musician under Capt. Anthony Sharpe. Discharged 2/2/1783.	
Cooley, Gabriel	3rd NC Regiment	7/20/1778, a Private under Lt./Capt. George "Gee" Bradley for nine months. 1779, a Private under Capt. Reading Blount (5th NC Regiment). Died in Sep. 1779. aka Gabriel Cooly.	
Cooley, Jeffrey	3rd NC Regiment	7/20/1778, a Private under Lt./Capt. Joseph Montford for nine months. Deserted the next day (7/21/1778). Taken and compelled to serve three years as a consequence of his desertion in the 5th NC Regiment, starting in Jan. 1779. From Halifax County, NC. aka Jeffrey Coley. W4160.	
Cooley, Samuel	5th NC Regiment	4/16/1776, a Surgeon. Retired 6/1/1778. 1780, a Surgeon in VA Militia.	
Cooley, William	3rd NC Regiment	7/20/1778, a Private under Lt./Capt. George "Gee" Bradley for nine months.	
Cooper, Benjamin	1st NC Regiment	5/17/1781, a Private under Lt./Capt. Benjamin Bailey. Discharged on 5/17/1782 (3rd NC Regiment).	
Cooper, Frederick	1st NC Regiment	4/28/1781, a Private under Capt. Griffith John McRee. A Corporal in Aug. 1781. Discharged on 4/28/1782. Earlier in PA and in NC Militia in Rowan County, NC. W3001.	Siege of Ninety-Six 1781 (SC), Eutaw Springs (SC).
Cooper, Henry	7th NC Regiment	1777, a Sergeant under Capt. John McGlaughan. A QM Sergeant on 12/18/1777. Back to Sergeant in June 1778 (3rd NC Regiment). Back to QM Sergeant on 2/12/1779.	
Cooper, Jeremiah	5th NC Regiment	1777, a Private under Capt. John Pugh Williams. Dropped from the rolls in Apr. 1778.	
Cooper, John	4th NC Regiment	1777, a Corporal under Capt. William Temple Coles. Died on 4/16/1778.	
Cooper, John	7th NC Regiment	1777, a Private under Capt. John McGlaughan. Died in July 1777.	
Cooper, Joshua	5th NC Regiment	11/1/1776, a Private under Capt. Henry Darnell. POW at Ft. Lafayette, NY on 6/1/1779. Rejoined in Nov. 1779.	Ft. Lafayette (NY).
Cooper, Joseph	2nd NC Regiment	11/17/1777, a Private, unit unknown. 9/9/1778, under Capt. Benjamin Andrew Coleman.	
Cooper, Josiah	1st NC Regiment	2/26/1778, a known Private under Capt. Howell Tatum.	
Cooper, Josiah	7th NC Regiment	1777, a Private under Capt. John McGlaughan. Died on 11/29/1777.	
Cooper, Nathaniel	5th NC Regiment	5/5/1776, a Private under Capt. John Pugh Williams. 7/20/1778, a Private under Capt.	

Name	1st Unit	Year / Rank / Served Under / Notes	Known Battles
		Reading Blount. 9/9/1778, a known Private in the Major's Company (Maj. Hardy Murfree) (2nd NC Regiment). Discharged on 11/10/1778.	
Cooper, Solomon	10th NC Regiment	1/20/1778, a Private under Capt. William Shepherd.	
Cooper, Solomon	10th NC Regiment	1/20/1778, a Lieutenant under Capt. William Shepherd. Retired 6/1/1778.	
Cooper, William	4th NC Regiment	4/26/1776, a Private under Capt. Lewis (?) for 2-1/2 years. 9/8/1778, a known Private in the Colonel's Company (Col. Thomas Clark) (1st NC Regiment) led by Capt. John Gambier Scull. Discharged on 11/10/1778.	
Cooper, William	5th NC Regiment	4/16/1776, a Lieutenant, later to serve under Capt. Henry Darnell. 6/12/1776, a 2nd Lieutenant under Capt. John Enloe. Dropped from the rolls in Oct. 1777.	
Coops, Francis	8th NC Regiment	3/29/1777, a Musician under Capt. Francis Tartanson. A Private in June 1778. aka Francis Cook.	
Coops, William	8th NC Regiment	1777, a Private under Capt. Francis Tartanson. Dropped from the rolls in Sept. 1777.	
Coots, James	4th NC Regiment	1775, an Ensign in NC Militia 4/17/1776, an Ensign under Capt. Thomas Harris and Col. Thomas Polk. 11/30/1776, a Lieutenant under Capt. William Goodman. Dropped from the rolls in June 1778. From Guilford County. 1780, a Lieutenant in NC Militia.	
Copeland, Cader	5th NC Regiment	9/11/1777, a Private under Capt. Benjamin Andrew Coleman (6/1/1778, in 2nd Regiment). 9/9/1778, under Capt. Clement Hall (2nd NC Regiment). 3/12/1779, re-enlisted under Capt. Clement Hall. POW at the Fall of Charleston. Afterwards, joined Capt. Charles Stewart (5th NC Regiment). Discharged at Georgetown, SC. From Halifax County. aka Cadar Copeland, Keeder Copeland, Cato Copeland, Kadar Copeland. W17665.	Monmouth (NJ), Stoney Point (NY), Siege of Charleston (SC).
Copeland, John	6th NC Regiment	April 1776, a Private and a Sergeant under Capt. Archibald Lytle for 2-1/2 years. Jan. 1778, furloughed at Hillsborough, NC due to disease in his leg. Enlisted in Orange County, NC. S40052.	
Copeland, Richard	3rd NC Regiment	5/17/1776, a Private under Capt. James Emmett for 2-1/2 years. Discharged in Oct. 1778 in the state of CT while serving under Capt. Benjamin Williams (2nd NC Regiment). Enlisted at Chatham Court House, NC. S39335.	
Copes, Francis	2nd NC Regiment	3/29/1777, a Private, unit unknown. 9/9/1778, a known Private in the Major's Company (Maj. Hardy Murfree).	
Copland, James	3rd NC Regiment	1779, a Private under Capt. Michael Quinn. Discharged in Dec. 1779.	
Copland, John	1st NC Regiment	5/7/1781, a Private under Capt. Anthony Sharpe. Dropped from the rolls sometime	

Name	1st Unit	Year / Rank / Served Under / Notes	Known Battles
		during 1781.	
Copland, Richard	3rd NC Regiment	1779, a Private under Capt. Michael Quinn. Discharged in Dec. 1779.	
Copland, Richard	5th NC Regiment	8/5/1779, a Private under Maj. Reading Blount. Deserted in Oct. 1779.	
Copland, Ripley	9th NC Regiment	3/10/1777, a Private under Capt. Matthew Ramsey for three years. 9/8/1778, a known Private in the Lt. Colonel's Company (Lt. Col. Robert Mebane) (1st NC Regiment) led by Capt. Joshua Bowman - sick on that date. Discharged on 3/15/1780 at Charleston, SC. Enlisted in Chatham County, NC. aka Ripley Copeland. W9811.	Monmouth (NJ), Stony Point (NY).
Coplin, Job	4th NC Regiment	1782, a Private under Capt. William Lytle. Died on 3/7/1782.	
Coplin, Reuben	4th NC Regiment	A Corporal under Capt. Thomas Harris. Discharged 10/31/1777.	
Corbett, Alexander	5th NC Regiment	1777, a Private under Capt. Simon Alderson. Deserted on 8/28/1777. aka Alexander Corbitt.	
Corbett, James	1st NC Regiment	12/14/1778, a Corporal under Capt. Anthony Sharpe. 6/29/1779, a Corporal under Capt. Joseph Montford (5th NC Regiment).	
Corbin, Arthur	7th NC Regiment	12/30/1776, a Private under Capt. James Vaughan. 2/26/1778, a known Private under Capt. Howell Tatum (1st NC Regiment). 9/8/1778, a known Private under Capt. Howell Tatum. Discharged on 2/1/1780.	
Corbit, Richard	3rd NC Regiment	7/20/1778, a Private under Lt./Capt. George "Gee" Bradley for nine months.	
Cordle, Richard	3rd NC Regiment	11/1/1776, a Private under Capt. Pinketham Eaton. Dropped from the rolls in June 1779.	
Corey, John	3rd NC Regiment	7/20/1778, a Private under Capt. Francis Child for nine months.	
Corinth, William	6th NC Regiment	Oct. 1777, a Private under Capt. Griffith John McRee. Died on 2/27/1778. aka William Cornish.	
Cornelison, John	5th NC Regiment	3/1/1779, a Private under Capt. Joseph Montford. Discharged on 11/30/1779 by Lt. Col. Robert Mebane. S35209.	Stono Ferry (SC).
Cornelius, Isaac	5th NC Regiment	5/14/1776, a Private under Capt. John Pugh Williams. 9/9/1778, a known Private under Capt. Clement Hall (2nd NC Regiment). Discharged on 11/10/1778.	
Cornelius, John	1st NC Regiment	5/2/1781, a Private under Lt./Capt. Benjamin Bailey. Discharged on 5/15/1782 (3rd NC Regiment).	
Cornelius, William	NC Artillery	7/14/1776, a Matross under Capt. John Vance as NC Provincial Troops. 7/10/1777, on Continental Line. 11/16/1777, under Capt. John Kingsbury. April 1778, AWOL. 5/1/1778, in same unit. Dropped from the rolls in June 1778.	
Cornett, Bird	3rd NC Regiment	7/20/1778, a Private in the Lt. Colonel's Company (Lt. Col. William Lee Davidson) led by Lt./Capt. George "Gee" Bradley. 4/23/1779,	

NC Patriots 1775-1783: Their Own Words

Name	1st Unit	Year / Rank / Served Under / Notes	Known Battles
		a known Private in the Lt. Colonel's Company (Lt. Col. Robert Mebane) led by Capt. George "Gee" Bradley.	
Coroband, Wyllis	4th NC Regiment	1782, a Private under Capt. Thomas Evans. Deserted Sept. ?.	
Cortslow, Thomas	4th NC Regiment	1777, a Private under Capt. James Williams. Discharged in Aug. 1777.	
Coston, Henry	1st NC Regiment	1777, a Private under Capt. John Brown. 9/8/1778, a Private under Capt. Tilghman Dixon. aka Henry Costen.	
Cotanch, John	3rd NC Regiment	7/20/1778, a Private under Capt. Francis Child for nine months. 1782, listed on the rolls "dead" (?) in Capt. William Lytle's Company (4th NC Regiment).	
Cotanch, Malachi	5th NC Regiment	1/11/1777, a Private under Capt. Henry Darnell. 9/9/1778, a known Private under Capt. Benjamin Andrew Coleman (2nd NC Regiment). 3/12/1779, re-enlisted under Capt. Benjamin Andrew Coleman. Deserted on 1/30/1780. aka Mala Cotouch.	
Cotgrave, Arthur	2nd NC Regiment	3/26/1777, a 1st Lieutenant under Capt. James Martin. 9/9/1778, a Lieutenant under Capt. John Ingles. Wounded, taken prisoner at the Fall of Charleston. Exchanged 6/14/1781. Resigned on 8/1/1782. aka Arthur Colgrove. One source claims he was commissioned on 3/26/1778 and he resigned on 10/1/1781 (wrong).	Siege of Charleston 1780 (SC).
Cottle, John	2nd NC Regiment	1778, a Private under Capt. Benjamin Andrew Coleman. Dropped from the rolls in Aug. 1778.	
Cotton, Elijah	10th NC Regiment	7/1/1777, a Private under Capt. Abraham Sheppard, Jr. 9/9/1778, a known Private in the Lt. Colonel's Company (Lt. Col. Selby Harney) (2nd NC Regiment).	
Cotton, Henry	1st NC Regiment	9/8/1778, a known Private under Capt. Tilghman Dixon.	
Cotton, John	10th NC Regiment	6/13/1777, a Private, unit unknown. 9/10/1778, a known Private under Capt. Thomas Armstrong (2nd NC Regiment). Deserted in June 1779.	
Cotton, Josiah	7th NC Regiment	11/28/1776, a Captain under Col. James Hogun. Resigned in Dec. 1776. From Northampton County, NC. aka Joseph Cotton.	
Coulson, Hardy	4th NC Regiment	6/7/1776, a Private under Capt. John Nelson. Discharged on 6/1/1779. aka Hy. Conlson.	
Coulter, Levy	6th NC Regiment	2/1/1777, a Private under Maj. John Baptiste Ashe.	
Council, Arthur	6th NC Regiment	1775, a Captain in the Cumberland County Regiment of Militia. 4/17/1776, a Captain under Col. John Alexander Lillington. Died in April of 1777. His company was taken over by Thomas White. From Cumberland County, NC.	
Council, Robert	1st NC Regiment	1/4/1776, an Ensign. 7/7/1776, a 2nd Lieutenant. Resigned, re-enlisted as Ensign again on 3/28/1777. Promoted to 2nd Lieutenant	Moore's Creek Bridge [4].

334

Name	1st Unit	Year / Rank / Served Under / Notes	Known Battles
		again on 7/8/1777. 1st Lieutenant on 8/20/1777 under Capt. Joshua Bowman. 7/1/1778, a Captain in NC Light Dragoons.	
Covington, James	9th NC Regiment	11/28/1776, a Lieutenant, unit unknown.	
Covington, William	4th NC Regiment	3/28/1777, an Adjutant. Died on 4/13/1778.	
Covry, Shadrack	10th NC Regiment	5/30/1777, a Private under Capt. Andrew Vanoy.	
Cowan, David	4th NC Regiment	3/20/1779, a Lieutenant under Capt. Matthew Ramsey. Then, a Captain in NC Militia.	Stono Ferry (SC).
Cowan, Joseph	4th NC Regiment	May 1776, a Private under Capt. Robert Smith for 12 months. Enlisted in Mecklenburg County. Discharged at Wilmington, NC. Later in NC Militia. W25444.	Ft. George - Bald Head Island.
Cowan, Robert	7th NC Regiment	1/7/1777, a Private under Capt. John McGlaughan. Deserted in Apr. 1777. Rejoined in June 1778. A Corporal in Nov. 1778. A Sergeant in Sep. 1779.	
Coward, Ephraim	2nd NC Regiment	7/20/1778, a Private under Capt. Reading Blount for nine months.	
Coward, Zadock	2nd NC Regiment	7/20/1778, a Private under Capt. Reading Blount for nine months.	
Cowny, Shade	2nd NC Regiment	5/30/1777, a Private, unit unknown. 9/9/1778, a known Private under Capt. John Ingles.	
Cox, Edward	10th NC Regiment	6/12/1777, a Musician under Capt. Abraham Sheppard, Jr. Dropped from the rolls in Jan. 1778.	
Cox, Jesse	4th NC Regiment	1782, a Private under Capt. William Lytle for 18 months.	
Cox, Jesse	10th NC Regiment	6/10/1777, a Private under Capt. John Jarvis. 9/8/1778, a known Private in the Colonel's Company (Col. Thomas Clark) (1st NC Regiment) led by Capt. John Gambier Scull - sick at Princeton on that date. A Sergeant on 6/15/1779. Dropped from the rolls in Nov. 1779.	
Cox, John	1st NC Regiment	4/28/1781, a Private under Capt. Alexander Brevard. Discharged on 4/28/1782 (3rd NC Regiment). Enlisted in Rowan County, NC. S35847.	Siege of Ninety-Six 1781 (SC), Eutaw Springs (SC).
Cox, John	2nd NC Regiment	10/19/1781, a Private under Capt. Benjamin Coleman, then under Capt. Samuel Jones (1st NC Regiment) for 13 months. Discharged at Ashley Hill, SC. S41495.	
Cox, Joseph	2nd NC Regiment	1776, a Private under Capt. John Armstrong. Discharged at the High Hills of the Santee in SC. From Surry County, NC. Later in NC Militia, unit unknown. S41494.	Stono Ferry (SC).
Cox, Joseph	2nd NC Regiment	1777, a Private under Capt. William Fenner. A Corporal in Jan. 1778. Died on 4/23/1778.	
Cox, Philip	4th NC Regiment	1777, a Private under Capt. James Williams. Discharged in Aug. 1777.	

Name	1st Unit	Year / Rank / Served Under / Notes	Known Battles
Cox, Thomas	10th NC Regiment	6/12/1777, a Private under Capt. Abraham Sheppard, Jr. 6/1/1778, a Private under Capt. Clement Hall (2nd NC Regiment). A Corporal on 11/1/1782. Deserted on 6/13/1783 (?). Enlisted while living in Randolph County, NC. R2399.	
Cox, William	1st NC Regiment	8/22/1776, a Private under Lt./Capt. Joshua Bowman. Deserted on 8/31/1777.	
Cox, William	5th NC Regiment	4/17/1776, a Private under Capt. William Caswell. Discharged on 11/10/1778. Enlisted at Halifax, NC, where he lived. Born 1762 in VA. S8225.	
Cox, William	7th NC Regiment	12/11/1777, a Paymaster.	
Cox, William	10th NC Regiment	6/3/1777, a Private under Capt. Silas Stevenson. 9/9/1778, a known Private in the Colonel's Company (Col. John Patten) (2nd NC Regiment) led by Capt. John Craddock. Died in Nov. 1778.	
Cox, William Armon	1st NC Regiment	6/10/1776, a Private, unit unknown. Dropped from the rolls in Nov. 1777.	
Coxey, Thomas	1st NC Regiment	1782, a Private under Capt. James Mills for 12 months. Discharged 1/1/1783.	
Cozzart, David	9th NC Regiment	12/18/1776, a Sergeant under Capt. Richard D. Cook for three years. A Private in Feb. 1778. 9/8/1778, a known Private in the Lt. Colonel's Company (Lt. Col. Robert Mebane) (1st NC Regiment) led by Capt. Joshua Bowman. Discharged on 1/27/1780. aka David Cozzorte, David Corzzorte.	
Crabb, Benjamin	1st NC Regiment	5/20/1776, a Private under Capt. Roger Moore. 12/1/1776, re-enlisted and made a Sergeant under Capt. William Goodman for 2-1/2 years. 9/8/1778, a known Sergeant in the Colonel's Company (Thomas Clark - 1st NC Regiment) led by Capt. John Gambier Scull. Enlisted in Currituck County, NC. Discharged on 11/18/1778. S39368.	Brandywine Creek (PA), Germantown (PA).
Crabb, Hilly	3rd NC Regiment	7/20/1778, a Private under Capt. Kedar Ballard for nine months.	
Crabb, Jarrot	1st NC Regiment	11/1/1778, a Private under Capt. Anthony Sharpe for nine months. Enlisted at Halifax, NC. On the official rolls as Jairah Crabb. S41499.	
Craben, Charles	6th NC Regiment	A Private under Capt. George Dougherty. Missing on 9/11/1777 at the battle of Brandywine Creek, PA.	Brandywine Creek (PA).
Crable, Daniel	4th NC Regiment	1782, a Private under Capt. Thomas Evans. Deserted in Sept ?.	
Craddock, John	2nd NC Regiment	5/3/1776, an Ensign. 5/16/1776, a 2nd Lieutenant. Then, a 1st Lieutenant under Capt. Benjamin Williams. 12/21/1777, a Captain of the Colonel's Company (Col. John Patten). Wounded and taken prisoner at the Fall of	Monmouth (NJ), Stony Point (NY), Siege of Charleston

Name	1st Unit	Year / Rank / Served Under / Notes	Known Battles
		Charleston. A POW until 11/26/1782. Retired 1/1/1783.	1780 (SC).
Craford, John	4th NC Regiment	1781, a Private under Capt. Joseph T. Rhodes. Discharged 4/25/1782.	
Craft, James	6th NC Regiment	1777, a Private under Capt. Thomas Donoho. Dropped from the rolls in Jan. 1778.	
Craft, Stephen	6th NC Regiment	1777, a Private under Capt. Thomas Donoho. Dropped from the rolls in Jan. 1778.	
Crafton, Bennett	6th NC Regiment	1775, an Adjutant in the Granville County Regiment. 4/17/1776, an Adjutant in 6th NC Regiment. 1781, a Major in the NC State Troops.	
Craig, David	4th NC Regiment	1775, a 2nd Lieutenant in the Salisbury District Minutemen. 4/17/1776, a 2nd Lieutenant under Capt. William Temple Coles and Col. Thomas Polk. From Rowan County. Accused of being involved with counterfeiting, outcome unknown.	
Craig, George	5th NC Regiment	1777, a Private under Capt. John Pugh Williams. Died in Nov. 1777.	
Craig, Gerald	6th NC Regiment	5/24/1776 or 5/24/1777 (two sources), a Sergeant under Lt./Capt. George Dougherty for 2-1/2 years. A Private in June 1778. 9/8/1778, a known Private in the Lt. Colonel's Company (Lt. Col. Robert Mebane) (1st NC Regiment) led by Capt. Joshua Bowman - sick on that date at Reading, PA. Dropped from the rolls in Oct. 1778. aka Jareed Craig, Jarrerd Craig, Gerrard Craig.	
Craige, Archibald	6th NC Regiment	A Private under Capt. Griffith John McRee. Killed at the battle of Germantown, PA on 10/4/1777.	Germantown (PA).
Craige, James	1st NC Regiment	4/28/1781, a Private under Capt. Alexander Brevard.	
Craike, Thomas	NC State	11/23/1776, Deputy Commissary General, to replace Nathaniel Rochester, who resigned. 6/14/1779, Deputy Clothier General. aka Thomas Craick, Thomas Craik.	
Crain, Stephen	3rd NC Regiment	4/25/1781, a Private under Capt. Edward Yarborough for 12 months. Discharged on 4/22/1782 at Bacon's Bridge, SC. From Halifax County, NC. W9823.	
Craven, James	1st NC Regiment	6/11/1776, an Ensign. 1/1/1777, a 2nd Lieutenant under Capt. Thomas Hogg. 9/8/1778, a known Lieutenant under Capt. John Sumner. Dishonorably discharged on 11/20/1779.	
Crawford, Charles	2nd NC Regiment	9/1/1775, a Captain under Col. Robert Howe. Retired 6/1/1778. 1779, in NC Militia. From Cumberland County, NC.	Great Bridge (VA), Brandywine Creek (PA), Germantown (PA), Monmouth (NJ).

Name	1st Unit	Year / Rank / Served Under / Notes	Known Battles
Crawford, David	1st NC Regiment	6/10/1776, an Ensign under Capt. George Davidson. Promoted to Lieutenant, date unknown.	
Crawford, James	3rd NC Regiment	7/20/1778, a Private under Lt. Joseph Montford for nine months.	
Crawford, William	1st NC Regiment	1/4/1776, an Ensign. 3/28/1776, a 2nd Lieutenant. Resigned 8/15/1776.	Moore's Creek Bridge [4].
Crawley, David	5th NC Regiment	3/1/1779, a Sergeant under Capt. Joseph Montford. Dropped from the rolls in Dec. 1779.	
Creed, Hazard	3rd NC Regiment	7/20/1778, a Private under Lt. Joseph Montford for nine months.	
Creekman, Mathias		Mar. 1779, a Private, regiment and unit unknown.	
Creemer, James	1st NC Regiment	4/15/1781, a Private under Capt. Anthony Sharpe for 12 months. Discharged on 4/15/1782. From Pitt County, NC. Earlier in NC Militia. On the official rolls as James Craimor. S2480.	Eutaw Springs (SC).
Crenshaw, Arthur		An Ensign, unit and dates unknown. POW at the Fall of Charleston, exchanged 6/14/1781.	Siege of Charleston 1780 (SC).
Cresson, Andrew	2nd NC Regiment	1775, a Private under Capt. John Armstrong. 1776, joined an SC unit. 1778, in VA unit. From Surry County, NC. aka Andrew Crison. 1781, rejoined 2nd NC Regiment under Capt. Tilghman Dixon.	Eutaw Springs (SC).
Crether, Jeremiah	7th NC Regiment	1777, a Private under Capt. Thomas Brickell. Died on 3/14/1778.	
Crews, Etheldred	4th NC Regiment	1782, a Private under Capt. William Lytle for 18 months.	
Crider, Jacob	4th NC Regiment	1777, a Corporal under Capt. William Temple Coles. Deserted on 10/3/1777.	
Crief, Thomas	10th NC Regiment	5/14/1777, a Musician under Capt. John Jarvis for three years. A Private in June 1778. 9/8/1778, a known Private in the Major's Company (Maj. John Baptiste Ashe) (1st NC Regiment). aka Thomas Creef.	
Criswell, Thomas	3rd NC Regiment	3/8/1782, a Private under Capt. Samuel Jones.	
Croe, William	3rd NC Regiment	1782, a Private under Capt. Alexander Brevard. Discharged on 3/1/1783.	
Cronister, James	2nd NC Regiment	Jan. 1782, a Private under Capt. Thomas Armstrong. Enlisted at Orangeburgh, SC - therefore, probably from SC. Discharged at Bacon's Bridge, SC in 1783. aka James Cronstler. S34989.	
Crosby, William	1st NC Regiment	5/9/1781, a Private under Capt. Alexander Brevard, then in Jan. 1782 under Capt. William Armstrong. Deserted on either 5/7/1782 or 6/20/1782 (two different sources). aka William Crosbey.	
Cross, Anthony	3rd NC Regiment	6/14/1779, a Private under Capt. George "Gee" Bradley. Dropped from the rolls in Oct. 1779. From Dobbs County, NC.	

Name	1st Unit	Year / Rank / Served Under / Notes	Known Battles
Cross, Martin	1st NC Regiment	1777, a Drummer under Capt. John Brown. 9/8/1778, a Drummer under Capt. James Read. 1779, a Fife Major. Deserted on 12/9/1779.	
Cross, Stephen	2nd NC Regiment	5/19/1781, a Private under Capt. Benjamin Carter. Discharged 4/19/1782.	
Crover, Peter	1st NC Regiment	1781, a Private under Capt. William Walton. Discharged 5/20/1782.	
Crow, James	1st NC Regiment	4/28/1781, a Private under Capt. Griffith John McRee. Discharged on 4/28/1782.	
Crumety, William	2nd NC Regiment	12/5/1781, a Private under Capt. Benjamin Andrew Coleman for 12 months.	
Crump, Edward	4th NC Regiment	3/1/1776, a Private under Capt. William Goodman. 9/8/1778, a known Private under Capt. Joshua Bowman (1st NC Regiment). 3/12/1779, re-enlisted for the duration of the war under Capt. Griffith John McRee (1st NC Regiment). Deserted on 3/24/1779.	
Crumpton, James	2nd NC Regiment	1782, a Private under Capt. Robert Raiford for 18 months.	
Crumpton, Thomas	4th NC Regiment	1782, a Private under Capt. William Lytle for 18 months.	
Crunk, John W.	2nd NC Regiment	March 1776, a Private under Capt. John Armstrong. May 1776, a Sergeant. Sept. 1776, an Ensign. June 1777, joined SC unit. Had enlisted from Guilford County, NC. S38646.	
Crutcher, Anthony	5th NC Regiment	5/14/1777, a Sergeant under Capt. Benjamin Andrew Coleman. 9/9/1778, a Sergeant in the Major's Company (Maj. Hardy Murfree) (2nd NC Regiment). 2/27/1780, an Ensign. 5/18/1781, a Lieutenant in the 5th NC Regiment. Retired 1/1/1783. aka Anthony Crutches, Croutchor, Croutcher.	
Crutcher, Henry	5th NC Regiment	8/20/1777, an Ensign under Capt. Benjamin Stedman. Resigned on 12/11/1777. aka Henry Crutches.	
Cubert, "Unknown"	1st NC Regiment	1777, a Drummer under Capt. John Brown. Dropped from the rolls in Jan. 1778. aka ? Cubet.	
Cullum, Israel	4th NC Regiment	1777, a Private under Capt. William Goodman. Died on 7/7/1777.	
Cullum, Thomas	DQMG	1780, an Artificer under Col. Nicholas Long (Deputy QM General). Made Cartouch Boxes. 8/23/1781, a Leather worker, making saddles, harnesses, caps, etc. aka Thomas Collom.	
Cummings, Benjamin	5th NC Regiment	A Private under Capt. Reading Blount. Died 5/5/1778.	
Cummings, Edward	3rd NC Regiment	7/20/1778, a Private under Capt. Michael Quinn for nine months.	
Cummings, George	6th NC Regiment	4/16/1776, a Sergeant under Lt./Capt. Thomas Donoho for 2-1/2 years. A Private in Dec. 1777. A Sergeant Major in 1778. 9/8/1778, a known Sergeant under Capt. Griffith John McRee (1st NC Regiment). Back to Private in Oct. 1778. Discharged on 11/3/1779. aka George	

Name	1st Unit	Year / Rank / Served Under / Notes	Known Battles
		Cummins.	
Cummings, John	4th NC Regiment	A Private under Capt. John Nelson, dates unknown.	
Cummings, John	10th NC Regiment	7/25/1777, a Private under Capt. Silas Stevenson. 9/9/1778, a known Private in the Major's Company (Maj. Hardy Murfree) (2nd NC Regiment). Died in Oct. 1778. aka John Cummin.	
Cummings, Shadrack	10th NC Regiment	6/6/1777, a Private under Capt. Silas Stevenson. 9/9/1778, a known Private in the Lt. Colonel's Company (Lt. Col. Selby Harney) (2nd NC Regiment). 3/12/1779, re-enlisted in the Lt. Colonel's Company (Lt. Col. Selby Harney) led by Capt. Charles Stewart. Deserted on 3/1/1783 (?).	
Cunningham, William	1st NC Regiment	5/15/1781, a Private under Lt./Capt. Benjamin Bailey. Discharged on 5/15/1782 (3rd NC Regiment). 9/7/1782, re-enlisted as a Private under Capt. Benjamin Bailey (3rd NC Regiment) for 18 months.	
Curbow, Joseph	4th NC Regiment	April 1776, a Private under Capt. Thomas Harris for 18 months. Re-enlisted for another 18 months, but got very sick and had his brother, William, to serve out the remainder of his time. Then three tours in NC Militia, unit(s) not named. aka Joseph Kerbo. S31637.	Ft. George - Bald Head Island.
Curby, William	5th NC Regiment	8/5/1779, a Private under Capt. Reading Blount. Deserted in Oct. 1779.	
Curl, John	3rd NC Regiment	7/20/1778, a Private under Capt. Kedar Ballard for nine months.	
Curlew, William	DQMG	1780, a Timber Getter on the roll of Capt. Solomon Wood (NC Light Dragoons) - this seems to be for convenience only. 8/23/1781, a Timber Getter under Col. Nicholas Long (Deputy QM General) - for the making of Wagons, Gunstocks, etc.	
Curling, William	1st NC Regiment	Jan. 1779, a Private under Capt. William Armstrong.	
Curry, Duncan	10th NC Regiment	10/24/1777, a Private under Capt. Andrew Vanoy. 9/9/1778, a known Private in the Lt. Colonel's Company (Lt. Col. Selby Harney) (2nd NC Regiment).	
Curry, John	2nd NC Regiment	1777, a Private under Capt. James Gee. 9/9/1778, a known Private under Capt. John Ingles (2nd NC Regiment). Discharged on 11/10/1778. aka Jonathan Curry.	
Curry, John	4th NC Regiment	1777, a Private under Capt. James Williams. Missing 9/16/1777.	
Curry, John	4th NC Regiment	10/4/1782, a Private under Capt. James Mills. A QM Sergeant in Dec. 1782. Discharged 10/4/1783. S8266.	
Curry, Robert	1st NC Regiment	5/28/1776, a Private under Lt./Capt. Joshua Bowman. Deserted on 6/15/1777.	
Curry,	10th NC	6/27/1777, a Private under Capt. Silas	

340

Name	1st Unit	Year / Rank / Served Under / Notes	Known Battles
Robert	Regiment	Stevenson. Deserted in Apr. 1778. Probably the same man as directly above.	
Curry, Thompson	2nd NC Regiment	5/4/1776, a Private, unit unknown. 9/10/1778, a known Private under Capt. Thomas Armstrong.	
Curry, Thompson	3rd NC Regiment	5/4/1776, a Corporal under Capt. Thomas Granbury. A Sergeant in Nov. 1777. Discharged in Oct. 1778.	
Curtis, Bartholomew	2nd NC Regiment	1777, a Private under Capt. John Armstrong. Dropped from the rolls in Dec. 1777.	
Curtis, John	5th NC Regiment	9/9/1775, a 2nd Lieutenant in the New Bern District Minutemen. 4/17/1776, a 2nd Lieutenant under Capt. Simon Alderson and Col. Edward Buncombe. Dropped from the rolls in Sept. 1777. aka John Custin, John Custis.	
Curtis, Joshua	2nd NC Regiment	Sep. 1775, a Private under Capt. John Armstrong for nine months. 7/1/1777, an Ensign in 4th NC Regiment under Capt. John Nelson. Promoted to 2nd then 1st Lieutenant under Capt. Micajah Lewis (1st NC Regiment). Resigned 2/20/1778. S39392.	Germantown (PA).
Curtis, Moses	1st NC Regiment	5/9/1781, a Private under Capt. Alexander Brevard, then Capt. Griffith John McRee. Deserted on 5/28/1781.	
Curtis, Peter	2nd NC Regiment	Feb. 1776, a Private under Capt. John Armstrong. Nov. 1776, furloughed due to illness, stayed at home longer than thought proper, listed as deserted. Rejoined under Capt. Benjamin Williams - how long unclear. From Guilford County, NC. Later, in NC Militia. Might be same man as directly below. W3005.	
Curtis, Peter	4th NC Regiment	1777, a Musician under Capt. John Nelson. Deserted in Sep. 1777.	
Curtis, Reuben	2nd NC Regiment	Sep. 1775, a Private under Capt. John Armstrong for nine months. Also a Sergeant, dates unknown. Sep. 1777, an Ensign under Capt. William Fenner. Dropped from the rolls in June 1778.	
Custis, Thomas	3rd NC Regiment	7/20/1778, a Private under Capt. Michael Quinn. Discharged on 7/24/1778.	
Custis, Thomas	8th NC Regiment	11/28/1776, an Ensign under Capt. Henry Pope. 1/16/1777, under Capt. Francis Tartanson. From Beaufort County, NC. aka Thomas Custice.	
Daffell, Thomas	2nd NC Regiment	2/10/1777, a Private, unit unknown. 9/9/1778, a known Private under Capt. John Ingles.	
Dail, John	10th NC Regiment	8/5/1777, a Private under Capt. Isaac Moore for three years. 9/8/1778, a known Private in the Lt. Colonel's Company (Lt. Col. Robert Mebane) (1st NC Regiment) led by Capt. Joshua Bowman - sick on that date, then by Capt. John Griffith McRee. POW at the Fall of Charleston, SC, escaped within a month. On the official rolls as John Deal. From Perquimans County, NC. S6783.	Siege of Charleston 1780 (SC).
Dailey,	4th NC	5/1/1776, a Private under Capt. James Williams	

Name	1st Unit	Year / Rank / Served Under / Notes	Known Battles
Jeremiah	Regiment	for 2-1/2 years. 9/8/1778, a known Private in the Colonel's Company (Col. Thomas Clark) (1st NC Regiment) led by Capt. John Gambier Scull - sick at Valley Forge on that date. Discharged on 11/10/1778.	
Dailey, John	4th NC Regiment	1/8/1777, a Sergeant under Capt. John Poynter. A Private in Jan. 1778. Died on 12/15/1778.	
Danagan, Thomas	2nd NC Regiment	9/9/1778, a known Private under Capt. John Ingles.	
Dance, Etheldred	3rd NC Regiment	4/14/1777, a known 2nd Lieutenant under Capt. James Emmet.	
Daniel, James	9th NC Regiment	11/28/1776, a Lieutenant under Capt. John Rochelle then Capt. Joseph John Wade. Resigned in Nov. 1777. One source asserts his first name was Joseph. From Hillsborough District.	
Daniel, Jeptha	4th NC Regiment	1781, a Private under Capt. George Dougherty. Discharged 5/26/1782.	
Daniel, Job	1st NC Regiment	8/1/1782, a Private under Capt. Joshua Hadley for 18 months. From Craven County, NC. Earlier in NC Militia. aka Joab Daniels. R2645.	
Daniel, John	5th NC Regiment	1777, a Corporal under Capt. Benjamin Stedman. A Private in 1777. Died on 11/30/1777.	
Daniel, Joshua	7th NC Regiment	1777, a Musician under Capt. Henry Dawson. Died in July 1777.	
Daniel, Sion	NC Light Dragoons	1777, a Private for 18 months, Captain unknown. Later in NC Militia. Enlisted while attending school in Wake County, NC. Home was Halifax County, NC.	Brandywine Creek (PA).
Daniel, Thomas	3rd NC Regiment	1778, a Private under Capt. Francis Child. Deserted on 8/2/1778.	
Daniels, John	1st NC Regiment	4/12/1781, a Private under Capt. William Lytle. Deserted on 6/1/1781. aka John Daniel.	
Daniels, Thomas	4th NC Regiment	1782, a Corporal under Capt. James Mills for 12 months. Discharged 3/1/1783.	
Danolson, Jesse	5th NC Regiment	6/5/1779, a Private under Capt. Joseph Montford. Deserted on 5/27/1783 (?).	
Darby, John	4th NC Regiment	5/15/1777, a Private under Capt. James Williams. Dropped from the rolls in Sept. 1777. aka John Darley.	
Darnald, Anthony	3rd NC Regiment	4/20/1778, a Private under Lt./Capt. George "Gee" Bradley. Deserted in Oct. 1778.	
Darnell, Henry	5th NC Regiment	1775, a 1st Lieutenant under Capt. William Caswell and Col. Richard Caswell in the New Bern District Minutemen. From Dobbs County. 4/17/1776, a 1st Lt./Adjutant under Capt. William Caswell and Col. Edward Buncombe (5th NC Regiment). 10/1/1776, a Captain in the 5th NC Regiment. Retired 6/1/1778. aka Henry Darnall.	Brandywine Creek (PA), Germantown (PA).
Darren, John	2nd NC Regiment	6/28/1777, a Fifer, unit unknown. 9/9/1778, a known Fifer in the Colonel's Company (Col. John Patten) led by Capt. John Craddock.	

Name	1st Unit	Year / Rank / Served Under / Notes	Known Battles
Dasher, Christian	1st NC Regiment	3/29/1777, a Private, unit unknown. 9/8/1778, a known Tailor under Capt. James Read, stationed at Lancaster, PA.	
Dauge, John	NC Artillery	11/1/1777, a known Captain of Artillery - in John Vance's Company (?).	
Dauge, Peter	10th NC Regiment	5/7/1777, a Private under Capt. John Jarvis. Dropped from the rolls in Sep. 1778. From Currituck County, NC. On the official rolls as Peter Doug. aka Peter Daug, aka Peter Dang. S41511.	
Dauge, Peter	9th NC Regiment	Dec. 1777, a Lt. Colonel when John Luttrell resigned. Retired on 6/1/1778. Some sources claim he was In the 10th NC Regiment, but doesn't make sense. Earlier and later a Colonel in the NC Militia. From Camden County.	
Daughtry, Dempsey	2nd NC Regiment	1777, a Private under Capt. Clement Hall. Dropped from the rolls in Jan. 1778. aka Dempsey Doughtry.	
Daughty, Jesse	10th NC Regiment	Aug. 1778, a Private under Capt. Andrew Vanoy. Deserted on 1/8/1780.	
Davant, Barnabas	2nd NC Regiment	8/31/1777, a Private, unit unknown. 9/10/1778, a known Private under Capt. Thomas Armstrong.	
Davenport, Asahel	7th NC Regiment	1777, a Corporal under Capt. Joseph Walker. A Private in Oct. 1777. Dropped from the rolls in Dec. 1777.	
Davenport, Daniel	5th NC Regiment	1776, a Private that served his six months as of 11/21/1776. Unit unknown.	
Davenport, Ephraim	1st NC Regiment	1781, a Private under Capt. Alexander Brevard for 12 months. Discharged 5/2/1782.	
Davenport, William	3rd NC Regiment	7/20/1778, a Private under Capt. Michael Quinn for nine months. Discharged at Halifax, NC. From Pitt County, NC. Earlier in NC Militia. S2507.	
Daves, John	2nd NC Regiment	6/7/1776, a QM. 9/30/1776, an Ensign under Capt. Charles Crawford. 10/4/1777, a 1st Lieutenant under Maj. Hardy Murfree. Wounded at Germantown. Wounded at Stony Point 7/16/1779. Led the Major's Company at the Siege of Charleston. POW at the Fall of Charleston, exchanged in June of 1781. Transferred to 3rd NC Regiment while in prison (1/1/1781). A Captain in 3rd NC Regiment on 9/8/1781. Retired 1/1/1783. aka John Davis.	Germantown (PA), Stony Point (NY), Siege of Charleston 1780 (SC).
Davey, James	1st NC Regiment	7/9/1781, a Private under Capt. William Lytle for 12 months. Dropped from the rolls sometime during 1781.	
Davidson, Emanuel	1st NC Regiment	12/14/1778, a Private under Capt. Anthony Sharpe.	
Davidson, George Lee	1st NC Regiment	9/1/1775, a Captain under Col. James Moore. Resigned 2/5/1777. Later in NC Militia.	Great Cane Brake (SC), Snow Campaign (SC), Moore's Creek

Name	1st Unit	Year / Rank / Served Under / Notes	Known Battles
			Bridge [4], Breech Inlet Naval Battle (SC).
Davidson, James	1st NC Regiment	1781, a Private under Capt. William Armstrong. Discharged on 4/21/1782.	
Davidson, James	1st NC Regiment	4/15/1781, a Private under Capt. Robert Raiford. Deserted in Aug. 1781. Rejoined on 12/25/1781. Dropped from the rolls in Jan. 1782. aka James Davison.	
Davidson, John	1st NC Regiment	5/25/1781, a Private under Capt. Griffith John McRee. Discharged on 5/25/1782.	
Davidson, Joseph	4th NC Regiment	4/26/1776, a Private under Capt. Roger Moore, then Capt. William Goodman for 2-1/2 years. 9/8/1778, a known Private in the Colonel's Company (Col. Thomas Clark) (1st NC Regiment) led by Capt. John Gambier Scull. Discharged on 11/10/1778 at White Plains, NY. aka Joshua Davidson, Josh. Davison. W4175.	Brandywine Creek (PA), Germantown (PA), Monmouth (NJ).
Davidson, Thomas	2nd NC Regiment	6/1/1778, a Private in the Lt. Colonel's Company (Lt. Col. Selby Harney). Discharged on 10/1/1778. From Hertford County, NC.	
Davidson, William Lee	4th NC Regiment	4/15/1776, a Major. 10/4/1777, a Lt. Colonel. Transferred to 3rd NC Regiment on 6/1/1778. 1/9/1779, commanded the 1st NC Regiment (should have been promoted to full Colonel, why not unknown). Dec. 1779, effectively retired. June 1780, a Colonel of the Mecklenburg County Regiment of Militia. Sep. 1780, a BG (ProTempore) of the Salisbury District Brigade of Militia - still considered on active duty as a Lt. Colonel in the 1st NC Regiment until he retired on 1/1/1781. Killed in action on 2/1/1781 at Cowan's Ford, NC.	Brandywine Creek (PA), Germantown (PA), Monmouth (NJ).
Davie, William Richardson	Southern Department	Jan. 1781, Superintendent Commissary General. Also a full Colonel. Earlier in NC Militia.	
Davies, Daniel	1st NC Regiment	4/28/1781, a Private under Capt. Alexander Brevard. Deserted on 5/17/1781.	
Davies, John	4th NC Regiment	7/1/1777, a Private under Capt. William Goodman. Deserted in Dec. 1777. Rejoined in Aug. 1778. Deserted again on 9/22/1778.	
Davies, Leonard	1st NC Regiment	5/25/1781, a Private under Capt. Alexander Brevard. Deserted on 7/1/1781. Apparently rejoined in Jan. 1782. aka Leonard Davis.	
Davis, Aaron	2nd NC Regiment	12/12/1781, a Private under Capt. Benjamin Andrew Coleman for 12 months. Discharged on 12/21/1782 at Ashley Hill, SC. Enlisted at Elizabethtown in Bladen County, NC. W6968.	
Davis, Aaron	3rd NC Regiment	7/20/1778, a Private under Capt. Kedar Ballard for nine months.	
Davis, Aaron	5th NC Regiment	1777, a Private under Capt. John Pugh Williams. Dropped from the rolls in Jan. 1778.	
Davis,	1st NC	8/1/1782, a Musician under Capt. Joshua	

Name	1st Unit	Year / Rank / Served Under / Notes	Known Battles
Archibald	Regiment	Hadley. A Private in Dec. 1782.	
Davis, Archibald	6th NC Regiment	A Private under Capt. Philip Taylor. Dropped from the rolls in Feb. 1778.	
Davis, Asa	2nd NC Regiment	1777, a Musician under Capt. Clement Hall. A Private in June 1778.	
Davis, Bartley	3rd NC Regiment	7/20/1778, a Private under Lt./Capt. George "Gee" Bradley for nine months.	
Davis, Benjamin	1st NC Regiment	1776, a Private under Capt. Joshua Bowman.	
Davis, Benjamin	1st NC Regiment	Nov. 1777, a Private under Capt. Lawrence Thompson. Discharged on 2/28/1778.	
Davis, Benjamin	10th NC Regiment	5/2/1777, a Private under Capt. Abraham Sheppard, Jr. for three years. 9/9/1778, a known Private under Capt. Robert Fenner (2nd NC Regiment). From Chatham County, NC. Later in NC Militia. W3783.	
Davis, Burrel	1st NC Regiment	6/20/1781, a Private under Capt. Anthony Sharpe. Dropped from the rolls sometime during 1781.	
Davis, Cage	10th NC Regiment	10/1/1777, a Private under Capt. James Wilson for three years. 9/8/1778, a known Private in the Major's Company (Maj. John Baptiste Ashe) (1st NC Regiment) - sick in camp on that date. aka Case Davis.	
Davis, Cyrus	6th NC Regiment	4/29/1776, a Corporal under Capt. William Glover, then Capt. Thomas Donoho for 2-1/2 years. A Private in June 1778. Discharged on 9/9/1778. Wounded at the battle of Germantown (PA). Enlisted in Granville County, NC. S41500.	Brandywine Creek (PA), Germantown (PA), Monmouth (NJ).
Davis, David	7th NC Regiment	1/15/1777, a Private under Capt. John Poynter. Deserted in Aug. 1777. aka David Dairs.	
Davis, Edward	3rd NC Regiment	12/12/1781, a Private under Capt. Samuel Jones for 12 months. Earlier in NC Militia. From Bladen County, what is now Columbus County, NC. Discharged on 12/12/1782 (1st NC Regiment) in Brunswick County, NC. S8284.	
Davis, Elisha	10th NC Regiment	5/31/1777, a Sergeant under Capt. Dempsey Gregory. A Private in June 1778. 9/8/1778, a known Private under Capt. Howell Tatum (1st NC Regiment).	
Davis, Frederick	2nd NC Regiment	12/12/1776, a Private under Capt. James Gee for three years. 9/9/1778, a known Private under Capt. John Ingles. Discharged on 1/31/1780.	
Davis, Granville	6th NC Regiment	4/28/1776, a Sergeant under Capt. Philip Taylor for 2-1/2 years. A Private in Aug. 1778. 9/8/1778, a known Private under Capt. John Sumner (1st NC Regiment). Dropped from the rolls in Sept. 1778.	
Davis, Hugh	4th NC Regiment	6/10/1777, a Private under Capt. William Temple Coles for three years. 9/8/1778, a known Private under Capt. John Sumner (1st NC Regiment). Deserted on 12/7/1779.	
Davis, James	1st NC	1776, a Private under Capt. Joshua Bowman.	

Name	1st Unit	Year / Rank / Served Under / Notes	Known Battles
	Regiment	Discharged on 5/28/1778.	
Davis, James	1st NC Regiment	6/15/1777, a Private under Capt. Lawrence Thompson for three years. 9/8/1778, a known Fifer under Maj. John Baptiste Ashe. 3/12/1779, re-enlisted for the duration of the war in the same unit.	
Davis, James	1st NC Regiment	6/6/1781, a Private under Capt. William Lytle. Discharged on 6/6/1782. aka Joseph Davis.	
Davis, James	3rd NC Regiment	7/1/1779, a Private under Capt. Kedar Ballard. Deserted on 10/19/1779.	
Davis, Jehu		5/6/1781, an Ensign, regiment and unit unknown.	
Davis, Joel	4th NC Regiment	6/12/1781, a Private under Capt. George Dougherty. Discharged 7/3/1782. Earlier and later in NC Militia. From Johnston County, NC. W351.	Eutaw Springs (SC).
Davis, John		5/6/1781, an Ensign, regiment and unit unknown.	
Davis, John	1st NC Regiment	7/1/1777, a Private, unit unknown. 9/8/1778, a known Private in the Colonel's Company (Col. Thomas Clark) (1st NC Regiment) led by Capt. John Gambier Scull.	
Davis, John	1st NC Regiment	8/1/1782, a Private under Capt. Joshua Hadley for 18 months.	
Davis, John	2nd NC Regiment	1777, a Private under Capt. Edward Vail, Jr. 9/9/1778, a known Private in the Colonel's Company (Col. John Patten) led by Capt. John Craddock.	
Davis, John	3rd NC Regiment	6/30/1779, a Private under Capt. Kedar Ballard and Capt. John Daves for the duration of the war. From Johnston County, NC. W19156.	
Davis, John	3rd NC Regiment	10/3/1781, a Private under Capt. Samuel Jones. A Corporal in Apr. 1782 (1st NC Regiment). Discharged 10/1/1782.	
Davis, John	10th NC Regiment	Jan. 1778, a Private, unit unknown. Died in May 1778.	
Davis, Joseph	1st NC Regiment	8/1/1782, a Private under Capt. Joshua Hadley for 18 months. Enlisted while living in Burke County, NC. R2717.	
Davis, Joseph	1st NC Regiment	8/1/1782, a Private under Capt. Joshua Hadley for 18 months. Enlisted while living in Rowan County, NC. Claims his true name was Joseph Nothern, reason unexplained. S7274.	
Davis, Joshua		6/10/1779, a Private, regiment and unit unknown.	
Davis, Josiah	2nd NC Regiment	4/25/1776, a Private, unit unknown. 9/9/1778, a known Private in the Colonel's Company (Col. John Patten) led by Capt. John Craddock. Discharged on 10/30/1778.	
Davis, Lee		Sep. 1779, a Private, regiment and unit unknown.	
Davis, Micajah	1st NC Regiment	1776, a Fifer and a Drummer - unit and regiment unknown. 5/5/1781, a Private under Capt. Robert Raiford. Promoted to ? on	Brandywine Creek (PA), Monmouth

Name	1st Unit	Year / Rank / Served Under / Notes	Known Battles
		1/8/1782 (2nd NC Regiment). Discharged on 4/23/1782. From what is now Franklin County, then Bute County.	(NJ), Guilford Court House, Eutaw Springs (SC).
Davis, Richard	10th NC Regiment	5/15/1777, a Private under Capt. James Wilson for three years. 9/8/1778, a known Private in the Major's Company (Maj. John Baptiste Ashe) (1st NC Regiment). POW at the Fall of Charleston, SC, held 14 months, exchanged at Jamestown, VA. S41502.	Monmouth (NJ), Siege of Charleston (SC).
Davis, Robert	1st NC Regiment	August 1781, a Private under Capt. Elijah Moore for 18 months, marched to SC and placed under Capt. Alexander Brevard (3rd NC Regiment), then under Capt. Joseph T. Rhodes (4th NC Regiment). Lived in Caswell County when he joined. Furloughed in July 1782 at James Island, SC to escort the sick home. R2744.	
Davis, Samuel	3rd NC Regiment	April 1776, a Private under Capt. Jacob Turner for 2-1/2 years. 10/5/1777, served under Capt. Kedar Ballard. 6/1/1778, a Private under Capt. Benjamin Williams (2nd NC Regiment). Discharged in Oct. 1778 at Frederickstown, NY. Later in SC Militia. Born in Sep. 1757 in Craven County, NC. Enlisted while living in Bute County, NC. S39406.	
Davis, Samuel	3rd NC Regiment	7/20/1778, a Private in the Lt. Colonel's Company (Lt. Col. William Lee Davidson) led by Lt./Capt. George "Gee" Bradley. 4/23/1779, a known Private in the Lt. Colonel's Company (Lt. Col. Robert Mebane) led by Capt. George "Gee" Bradley. Living in Northampton County, NC when he enlisted. Moved to Pitt County. Later, lived in Jones County, NC. Discharged in April 1779. Later in NC Militia. S8285.	
Davis, Samuel	6th NC Regiment	4/29/1776, a Musician under Capt. Archibald Lytle, then under Capt. Thomas White. A Corporal in Nov. 1777. Dropped from the rolls in Jan. 1778. Enlisted while living in Orange County, NC. Discharged at Halifax, NC. W4938.	Brandywine Creek (PA), Germantown (PA).
Davis, Stephen	1st NC Regiment	Jan. 1779, a Private under Capt. Anthony Sharpe.	
Davis, Stephen	3rd NC Regiment	1779, a Private under Capt. Michael Quinn. Probably the same man as directly above.	
Davis, Thomas		Sep. 1779, a Private, regiment and unit unknown. Deserted in Sep. 1779.	
Davis, Thomas	1st NC Regiment	7/6/1781, a Private under Capt. Alexander Brevard. Discharged on 7/7/1782.	
Davis, Thomas	2nd NC Regiment	1777, a Sergeant under Capt. Clement Hall. A Sergeant Major in Nov. 1777. A Private in Feb. 1778. Back to Sergeant in Nov. 1778.	
Davis, Thomas	3rd NC Regiment	1781, a Private under Capt. Clement Hall. Deserted on 4/1/1782 (2nd NC Regiment).	

Name	1st Unit	Year / Rank / Served Under / Notes	Known Battles
		Rejoined in Dec. 1782. Deserted again on 1/15/1783 (?).	
Davis, Thomas	3rd NC Regiment	2/1/1782, a Private under Capt. Samuel Jones. Deserted on 4/1/1782.	
Davis, William	1st NC Regiment	1776, a known Private under Capt. John Walker [4].	Moore's Creek Bridge [4].
Davis, William	1st NC Regiment	4/28/1781, a Sergeant under Capt. Griffith John McRee. Discharged on 4/25/1782.	
Davis, William	1st NC Regiment	9/1/1775, a Captain under Col. James Moore. A Major on 4/10/1776. 2/5/1777, a Lt. Colonel. Retired 6/1/1778. aka William Daves.	Moore's Creek Bridge [4], Orton Mill & Kendal Plantation, Brandywine Creek (PA), Germantown (PA).
Davis, William	2nd NC Regiment	11/7/1776, a Corporal under Capt. Clement Hall. A Private in June 1778. Back to Corporal on 4/1/1779.	
Davis, William	3rd NC Regiment	3/1/1782, a Private under Capt. Samuel Jones for 12 months.	
Davis, William	6th NC Regiment	1777, a Private under Capt. Thomas White. Deserted in May 1778. Joined the 5th NC Regiment - discharged in Apr. 1779.	
Davis, Wyllis	5th NC Regiment	1777, a Private under Capt. John Pugh Williams. Dropped from the rolls in June 1778.	
Davis, Zachariah	2nd NC Regiment	11/3/1776, a Private under Capt. William Fenner. 9/9/1778, a known Private in the Lt. Colonel's Company (Lt. Col. Selby Harney). aka Zachary Davis.	
Dawby, I. William	1st NC Regiment	1782, a Private under Capt. Peter Bacot for 18 months. aka I. William Dawky.	
Dawes, Abraham	7th NC Regiment	12/22/1776, an Adjutant. Resigned 11/22/1777. aka Abraham Davis, Abraham Daws.	
Dawley, David	10th NC Regiment	4/29/1777, a Corporal under Capt. Armwell Herron. A Private in June 1778 under Capt. Robert Fenner (2nd NC Regiment). Back to Corporal in Nov. 1779.	
Dawson, Henry	7th NC Regiment	11/28/1776, a Captain under Col. James Hogun. One source claims he was in the 2nd NC Regiment at some time. Resigned on 10/11/1777. From Halifax County, NC.	Brandywine Creek (PA), Germantown (PA).
Dawson, John	1st NC Regiment	1781, a Private under Capt. Alexander Brevard for 12 months. Discharged on 5/25/1782.	
Dawson, Levi	5th NC Regiment	4/15/1776, a Major. 10/19/1777, a Lt. Colonel in the 8th NC Regiment. Retired on 6/1/1778.	Brandywine Creek (PA), Germantown (PA).
Dawson, Matthew	2nd NC Regiment	1777, a Private under Capt. Clement Hall. Transferred to the "Invalids Regiment" on 1/1/1779.	
Dawtry, Jacob	3rd NC Regiment	1779, a Private under Capt. Michael Quinn.	

348

Name	1st Unit	Year / Rank / Served Under / Notes	Known Battles
Dawtry, Lewis	3rd NC Regiment	7/20/1778, a Private under Lt./Capt. George "Gee" Bradley for nine months.	
Dawtry, Thomas	3rd NC Regiment	7/20/1778, a Private under Lt./Capt. George "Gee" Bradley for nine months.	
Day, John	2nd NC Regiment	1777, a Private under Capt. John Armstrong. Died on 1/14/1778.	
Dayley, Joshua	7th NC Regiment	12/18/1776, a 1st Lieutenant under Capt. John Poynter to replace William Snowden, who resigned. 10/12/1777, a Captain under Col. James Hogun. Retired 6/1/1778. aka Joshua Daly, Joshua Dailey, Daily.	
Deacon, James	NC Light Dragoons	Oct.-Dec. 1777, a known Private under Capt. Martin Phifer. May have served longer.	
Deal, Isaac	2nd NC Regiment	1777, a Private under Capt. Clement Hall. Deserted on 1/1/1779.	
Deal, John	1st NC Regiment	1782, a Private under Capt. Peter Bacot for 18 months.	
Deal, Reuben	2nd NC Regiment	1777, a Private under Capt. James Martin. Died on 4/28/1778.	
Deal, William	2nd NC Regiment	1777, a Private under Capt. Clement Hall. Died on 3/5/1778.	
Dean, Abraham	1st NC Regiment	Jan. 1782, a Private under Capt. William Armstrong.	
Dean, Benjamin	5th NC Regiment	4/2/1777, a Private under Capt. John Enloe.	
Dean, John	3rd NC Regiment	7/20/1778, a Private under Capt. Michael Quinn for nine months.	
Dean, Moses	1st NC Regiment	4/15/1781, a Private under Capt. Anthony Sharpe. Wounded at the battle of Eutaw Springs (SC). Discharged on 2/1/1782. From Beaufort County, NC. W4664.	Eutaw Springs (SC).
Dean, Philip	2nd NC Regiment	Jan. 1779, a Private under Capt. Benjamin Andrew Coleman. From Warren County, NC. W19165.	
Dean, Philip	10th NC Regiment	5/18/1777, a Private under Capt. Abraham Sheppard, Jr. Deserted in Sep. 1779.	
Dean, Richard	3rd NC Regiment	7/20/1778, a Private under Capt. John Baker for nine months. Discharged at Halifax, NC. S38658.	
Dean, Robert	1st NC Regiment	9/1/1782, a Private under Capt. William Walton. Died on 11/11/1782.	
Dean, Sterling	10th NC Regiment	7/5/1777, a Private under Capt. Abraham Sheppard, Jr. 3/12/1779, re-enlisted under Capt. Thomas Armstrong (2nd NC Regiment). POW at Ft. Lafayette, NY on 6/1/1779. Rejoined in Nov. 1779.	Ft. Lafayette (NY).
Deberry, Solomon	3rd NC Regiment	7/20/1778, a Private in the Lt. Colonel's Company (Lt. Col. William Lee Davidson) led by Lt./Capt. George "Gee" Bradley. 4/23/1779, a known Private in the Lt. Colonel's Company (Lt. Col. Robert Mebane) led by Capt. George "Gee" Bradley. aka Solomon Duberry.	
Debow, Frederick	1st NC Regiment	Spring of 1777, a Wagon Master under Capt. Tilghman Dixon. Also had a commission as	

Name	1st Unit	Year / Rank / Served Under / Notes	Known Battles
		Commissary. From Caswell County, NC. Also in NC Militia. W7005.	
Debush, Jacob	2nd NC Regiment	4/15/1781, a Private under Capt. Benjamin Andrew Coleman for 12 months. aka Jacob Debusk.	
DeCamp, Ezekiel	NC Artillery	1/1/1777, a Gunner under Capt. Thomas Clark as NC Provincial Troops. 7/10/1777, on Continental Line. Also on 9/9/1778.	
Dedrick, Jacob	1st NC Regiment	8/27/1782, a Private under Capt. Joshua Hadley for 12 months.	
Dedrick, Jacob	5th NC Regiment	1779, a Private under Capt. Reading Blount. Dec. 1779, joined Pulaski's Legion.	
DeEll, William		5/1/1779, a Private, regiment and unit unknown. Dropped from the rolls in Nov. 1779.	
Defnall, David	10th NC Regiment	4/21/1777, a Private under Capt. Silas Stevenson for three years. 9/9/1778, a known Private in the Lt. Colonel's Company (Lt. Col. Selby Harney - 2nd NC Regiment) under Capt. Charles Stewart. On official records as David Defnel. Aka David Dufnel. S37887.	Siege of Charleston 1780 (SC).
Defnel, William	10th NC Regiment	5/21/1777, a Corporal under Capt. Silas Stevenson. A Private in June 1778 in the Lt. Colonel's Company (Lt. Col. Selby Harney - 2nd NC Regiment). aka William Dufnel.	
Degnum, Thomas	1st NC Regiment	9/8/1778, a known Private in the Colonel's Company (Col. Thomas Clark) led by Capt. John Gambier Scull.	
Dego, Ere		Jan. 1779, a Private, unit unknown.	
DeKeyser, Lehancius	1st NC Regiment	10/20/1775, an Ensign and an Adjutant. 1/4/1776, a 2nd Lieutenant. Resigned on 12/10/1776. Later, a Captain and Lt. Colonel in GA Militia. From New Hanover County, NC.	Moore's Creek Bridge [4].
Delaney, Atichl. (?)	8th NC Regiment	1777, a Sergeant under Capt. John Walsh. A Private in Nov. 1778.	
Delaney, John	8th NC Regiment	4/1/1777, a Private under Capt. John Walsh. 9/9/1778, a known Private under Capt. Clement Hall (2nd NC Regiment). 3/12/1779, re-enlisted under Capt. Clement Hall. POW at Ft. Lafayette, NY on 6/1/1779. Rejoined in Nov. 1779.	Ft. Lafayette (NY).
Delaney, Michael	2nd NC Regiment	9/9/1778, a known Private in the Lt. Colonel's Company (Lt. Col. Selby Harney).	
Delany, Michael	4th NC Regiment	Feb. 1779, a Private under Capt. George Dougherty. Deserted on 4/10/1779.	
Delerase, Peter		Sep. 1779, a Private, regiment and unit unknown. Deserted in Sep. 1779.	
Delidge, Peter		Jan. 1779, a Private, regiment and unit unknown.	
Delong, Francis	7th NC Regiment	9/13/1777, a Musician (Fifer) under Capt. Henry "Hal" Dixon then under Capt. Joseph Walker for three years. May 1778, a Musician under Capt. John Sumner (1st NC Regiment). 3/12/1779, re-enlisted for the duration of the war in the same unit. POW at the Fall of	Siege of Charleston 1780 (SC).

Name	1st Unit	Year / Rank / Served Under / Notes	Known Battles
		Charleston, SC for nine months. From Pasquotank County, NC. aka Francis Dellong. S34741.	
Dempsey, Hezekiah	3rd NC Regiment	7/20/1778, a Private under Capt. Kedar Ballard. Deserted on 8/30/1778.	
Dempsey, John	3rd NC Regiment	7/20/1778, a Private under Maj. Thomas Hogg. Deserted the next day on 7/21/1778.	
Dempsey, Luke	3rd NC Regiment	Confined 41 nights for desertion and "found in the arms of the enemy" during July 1781.	
Dempsey, Squire	5th NC Regiment	1777, a Private under Capt. John Pugh Williams. Died on 3/17/1778.	
Dempsey, William	3rd NC Regiment	7/20/1778, a Private under Capt. John Baker for nine months. Deserted on 8/30/1778.	
Demry, Allen	1st NC Regiment	4/12/1781, a Private under Capt. Alexander Brevard. Discharged on 5/25/1782.	
Demry, Jehu	1st NC Regiment	1/20/1782, a Private under Capt. James Mills. 2/6/1782, in 4th NC Regiment. aka John Demry.	
Dennis, Abner	6th NC Regiment	1777, a Private under Capt. Daniel Williams. Died in Sep. 1778.	
Dennis, Charles	8th NC Regiment	1777, a 2nd Lieutenant under Capt. Simon Jones, dates unknown.	
Dennis, Hezekiah	5th NC Regiment	1777, a Private under Capt. Simon Alderson. Died on 1/12/1778.	
Dennis, John	8th NC Regiment	1777, a Private under Capt. Francis Tartanson. Went home on 11/25/1777.	
Dennis, Robert	1st NC Regiment	1777, a Private under Capt. Henry "Hal" Dixon. 1777, in 9th NC Regiment under Capt. Richard D. Cook. Died on 3/6/1778.	
Dennis, William	5th NC Regiment	1779, a Private under Capt. Reading Blount. Died 9/1/1779.	
Dennis, William Jr.	8th NC Regiment	11/28/1776, a 1st Lieutenant under Capt. James May, Jr. 1777, a Lieutenant under Capt. Francis Tartanson. 9/20/1777, a Captain under Col. James Armstrong. Retired 6/1/1778. Later, a Captain under Col. Enoch Ward (Carteret County Regiment), dates unknown. One source asserts that he was in the 1st NC Regiment during 1781 (wrong). From Carteret County, NC.	
Dennis, William	6th NC Regiment	4/16/1776, a Private under Lt./Capt. Daniel Williams for 2-1/2 years. 6/1/1778, a Private under Capt. Griffith John McRee (1st NC Regiment). Discharged on 11/10/1778.	
Denny, Abraham	10th NC Regiment	5/5/1777, a Private under Capt. Abraham Sheppard, Jr. for three years. 9/9/1778, a known Private in the Lt. Colonel's Company (Lt. Col. Selby Harney) (2nd NC Regiment). From Dobbs County, now Greene County, NC. R2882.	
Denny, David	10th NC Regiment	5/18/1777, a Private under Capt. Abraham Sheppard, Jr.	
Denson, William	5th NC Regiment	1779, a Private under Capt. Reading Blount. Died 9/1/1779.	
Dent,	4th NC	1775, a 1st Lieutenant in the Salisbury District	

Name	1st Unit	Year / Rank / Served Under / Notes	Known Battles
William Jr.	Regiment	Minutemen. 4/17/1776, a 1st Lieutenant under Capt. John Nelson and Col. Thomas Polk. 1780, a Captain in NC Militia. From Guilford County.	
Derryberry, Andrew	1st NC Regiment	1782, a Private under Capt. Peter Bacot for 18 months. 1781, in NC Militia. From Burke County, NC. aka Andrew Deberry, Andrew Devreberry. W10312.	
Derrum, Nathaniel	4th NC Regiment	6/20/1776, a Private under Capt. John Nelson for three years. Discharged on 6/20/1779.	
Desern, Frederick	6th NC Regiment	July 1776, a Private under Lt./Capt. George Dougherty, then under Capt. Francis Child. 6/1/1778, a Private under Capt. Griffith John McRee (1st NC Regiment). Discharged on 1/20/1780. From Surry County, NC. S38660.	Monmouth (NJ), Stony Point (NY).
Dew, John	10th NC Regiment	5/13/1777, a Private under Capt. Silas Stevenson. 9/9/1778, a known Private in the Lt. Colonel's Company (Lt. Col. Selby Harney) (2nd NC Regiment).	
Dewise, Hezekiah	1st NC Regiment	June 1778, a Private under Capt. Tilghman Dixon. From Halifax County, VA. Then, in NC Militia. 1781, back under Capt. Tilghman Dixon (now in the 2nd NC Regiment). aka Hezekiah Deweese, Hezekiah Dewese.	
Dickens, Thomas	1st NC Regiment	1782, a Private under Capt. Peter Bacot for 18 months. aka Thomas Dickons. S41509.	
Dickerson, Nathaniel	9th NC Regiment	11/28/1776, a Lieutenant under Capt. Joseph John Wade. May 1779, joined the 5th NC Regiment.	
Dickings, James	1st NC Regiment	5/25/1781, a Private under Capt. Thomas Donoho. Discharged 5/25/1782.	
Dickinson, George	1st NC Regiment	8/8/1777, a Private under Capt. James Read. 9/8/1778, in same unit. 3/12/1779, re-enlisted for the duration of the war in the same unit. Deserted on 5/11/1779. aka George Dickenson.	
Dickinson, Henry	4th NC Regiment	1782, a Private under Capt. Thomas Evans for 18 months.	
Dickinson, Richard	6th NC Regiment	4/2/1777, an Ensign under Capt. George Dougherty. 10/10/1777, a Lieutenant. Transferred to 1st NC Regiment on 6/1/1778. Cashiered on 11/20/1779. aka Richard Dickenson.	
Dickinson, William	3rd NC Regiment	7/20/1778, a Private under Capt. Kedar Ballard. Deserted four days later on 7/24/1778.	
Dickson, Joel	6th NC Regiment	6/2/1777, a Private under Capt. Benjamin Pike for three years. 10/11/1777, a Private under Capt. Francis Child. 6/1/1778, a Private under Capt. Griffith John McRee (1st NC Regiment). POW at the Fall of Charleston, SC - never exchanged. On the official rolls as Joel Dixon. From Carteret County, NC. S41508.	Monmouth (NJ), Siege of Charleston (SC).
Dickson, Joseph	1st NC Regiment	5/2/1781, a Private under Capt. Griffith John McRee for 12 months. Wounded at the battle of Eutaw Springs, SC. Transferred to VA Continental Line in 1782. From Lincoln	Siege of Ninety-Six 1781 (SC), Eutaw Springs

Name	1st Unit	Year / Rank / Served Under / Notes	Known Battles
		County, NC. On the official rolls as Joseph Dixon. S41505.	(SC).
Diggins, Edmund	5th NC Regiment	1777, a Private under Capt. William Caswell. Deserted in Nov. 1777. aka Edward Diggins.	
Diggs, Anthony	5th NC Regiment	8/20/1777, an Ensign. Also a Lieutenant. Retired 6/1/1778. aka Anthony Deggs.	
Dignam, Thomas	4th NC Regiment	A Private under Capt. James Williams, dates unknown. 9/9/1778, a known Private in the Colonel's Company (Col. Thomas Clark) (1st NC Regiment) led by Capt. John Gambier Scull - sick at Valley Forge on that date. Discharged on 11/10/1778. aka Thomas Digman.	
Dikes, Isom	1st NC Regiment	1777, a Private under Capt. Robert Ralston. 9/8/1778, a known Private under Capt. John Sumner. aka Isom Dyches, Isham Dikes.	
Dikons, Edward	3rd NC Regiment	6/2/1779, a Private under Capt. Michael Quinn. A Corporal in 1780.	
Dillain, John		One source claims he was a Lieutenant in the 10th NC Regiment in 1779, but that regiment was disbanded in 1778. Unknown which regiment he was actually in. Killed at Eutaw Springs on September 8, 1781. James Dillon?	Eutaw Springs (SC).
Dillany, Francis	1st NC Regiment	9/13/1777, a Musician under Capt. Henry "Hal" Dixon.	
Dillard, George	DQMG	1780, an Armourer under Col. Nicholas Long (Deputy QM General). Also on 8/23/1781.	
Dillard, James	1st NC Regiment	5/28/1781, a Private under Capt. Alexander Brevard for twelve months. Discharged on 5/9/1782. W7020.	
Dillard, John	3rd NC Regiment	Feb. 1779, a Lieutenant under Maj. Pinketham Eaton.	
Dillard, John	4th NC Regiment	2/10/1777, a Sergeant under Capt. James Williams for 2-1/2 years. Dropped from the rolls in Sept. 1777. From Bute County, what is now Warren County, NC. S3286.	
Dillard, Osborn	4th NC Regiment	5/15/1777, a Private under Capt. James Williams for 2-1/2 years. 9/8/1778, a Private in the Colonel's Company (Col. Thomas Clark) (1st NC Regiment) led by Capt. John Gambier Scull - at Tarrytown on that date. Discharged 11/10/1778.	
Dillard, Sampson	2nd NC Regiment	1778, a Corporal under Capt. James Gee. 9/9/1778, a Corporal under Capt. John Ingles. A Private in Dec. 1778.	
Dillard, William	4th NC Regiment	5/2/1776, a Private under Capt. James Williams for 2-1/2 years. 9/8/1778, a known Private in the Colonel's Company (Col. Thomas Clark) (1st NC Regiment) led by Capt. John Gambier Scull. Discharged on 11/10/1778.	
Dillard, Zachary	DQMG	1780, a Timber Getter on the roll of Capt. Solomon Wood (NC Light Dragoons) - this seems to be for convenience only. An Artificer under Col. Nicholas Long (Deputy QM General). Made Gunstocks. 8/23/1781, a Timber	

Name	1st Unit	Year / Rank / Served Under / Notes	Known Battles
		Getter for the making of Wagons, Gunstocks, etc.	
Dillon, Benjamin	7th NC Regiment	11/28/1776, an Ensign under Capt. Joseph Walker. 10/12/1777, a Lieutenant under Capt. Joseph Walker. Joined the 4th NC Regiment in Feb. 1779. From Edenton District.	
Dillon, James	7th NC Regiment	1/1/1777, a 2nd Lieutenant. 10/12/1777, a 1st Lieutenant. Transferred to 2nd NC Regiment on 6/1/1778. Killed at Eutaw Springs, SC on 9/8/1781. Probably same as John Dillain above.	Eutaw Springs (SC).
Disarn, Francis	1st NC Regiment	1777, a Private under Capt. Joseph Brown. Died on 3/12/1778.	
Disharoon, John	5th NC Regiment	11/10/1778 to 8/10/1779, a Private under Lt./Capt. William Lytle. From Orange County, NC. W9524.	Stono Ferry (SC).
Dixon, Caswell	4th NC Regiment	1782, a Private under Capt. Thomas Evans for 18 months.	
Dixon, Charles	6th NC Regiment	4/2/1777, an Ensign under Capt. Griffith John McRee. 1/19/1778, a Paymaster. 2/8/1779, a Lieutenant in the 3rd NC Regiment. Wounded at Eutaw Springs on September 8, 1781. Transferred to 4th NC Regiment on 2/6/1782. Retired 1/1/1783. From Caswell County, NC. Son of Lt. Col. Henry "Hal" Dixon.	Eutaw Springs (SC).
Dixon, George	3rd NC Regiment	July 1776, a Musician under Capt. Thomas Granbury. Dropped from the rolls in June 1778.	
Dixon, Henry	6th NC Regiment	A Private under Capt. Thomas Donoho. Died in Aug. 1777.	
Dixon, Henry "Hal"	1st NC Regiment	9/1/1775, a Captain under Col. James Moore and Col. Francis Nash. 10/4/1777, promoted to Major in 3rd NC Regiment. 5/12/1778, a Lt. Colonel under Col. Jethro Sumner. 1779, a Lt. Colonel under Col. Thomas Clark (5th NC Regiment). Wounded at Stono Ferry (SC). 11/9/1779, appointed Inspector General of NC Militia. In the Summer of 1780, Maj. Gen. Richard Caswell convinced BG Jethro Sumner to allow Lt. Col. Henry Dixon to accept a temporary command in the NC militia - in the Caswell County Regiment. Retained his commission as Lt. Col. and effectively commanded the 2nd NC Regiment (2/6/1782) since Col. Patten was still in captivity. From Caswell County. Died 7/17/1782 in camp at Round O, SC.	Brunswick Town #1, Moore's Creek Bridge [4], Ft. Moultrie #1 (SC), Florida Expedition 1776, Brandywine Creek (PA), Germantown (PA), Stono Ferry (SC), Little Lynches Creek (SC), Camden (SC), Wetzall's Mill, Guilford Court House, Eutaw Springs (SC).
Dixon, Jeremiah	1st NC Regiment	4/15/1781, a Private under Capt. Anthony Sharpe. Discharged on 4/15/1782. From Pitt County, NC. Earlier in NC Militia. S10565.	Eutaw Springs (SC).
Dixon, Jeremiah	4th NC Regiment	1777, a Private under Capt. John Nelson for three years.	
Dixon, John	6th NC	6/2/1777, a Private under Capt. Francis Child	

Name	1st Unit	Year / Rank / Served Under / Notes	Known Battles
	Regiment	for three years. 9/8/1778, a known Private under Capt. Griffith John McRee (1st NC Regiment) - sick on that date at Valley Forge. Dropped from the rolls in Sept. 1778.	
Dixon, Michael	3rd NC Regiment	1782, a Sergeant under Capt. Alexander Brevard for 18 months.	
Dixon, Retson	3rd NC Regiment	7/20/1778, a Private under Capt. Kedar Ballard for nine months.	
Dixon, Robert	1st NC Regiment	4/28/1781, a Private under Capt. Griffith John McRee. Deserted on 6/1/1781.	
Dixon, Thomas	1st NC Regiment	5/25/1781, a Private under Lt./Capt. Benjamin Bailey. Discharged on 7/26/1782.	
Dixon, Tilghman	1st NC Regiment	10/20/1775, a 1st Lieutenant. 2/5/1777, a Captain under Col. Thomas Clark. POW at the Fall of Charleston, exchanged 6/14/1781. 1781, a Captain under Maj. Reading Blount (2nd NC Regiment). Retired 1/1/1783. From Edgecombe County, NC.	Moore's Creek Bridge [4], Brandywine Creek (PA), Germantown (PA, Monmouth (NJ), Siege of Charleston 1780 (SC), Eutaw Springs (SC).
Dixon, William	1st NC Regiment	4/15/1781, a Private under Capt. Anthony Sharpe. Dropped from the rolls during 1781.	
Dixon, William	6th NC Regiment	4/20/1778, a Private under Capt. Francis Child.	
Dixon, Wynne	1st NC Regiment	3/1/1781, an Ensign under Capt. William Lytle. 7/5/1781, a 2nd Lieutenant under Capt. William Lytle (2/6/1782 in 4th NC Regiment), till the end of the war. Earlier in 1781, in Caswell County Regiment (militia) as a Lieutenant. S46000.	
Dobbins, Hugh	9th NC Regiment	1777, a Lieutenant under Capt. Thomas McCrory. Recommended by Col. John Williams on 8/16/1777. Retired 6/1/1778.	
Dobbins, James	1st NC Regiment	5/25/1781, a Private under Lt./Capt. Benjamin Bailey. Discharged on 5/25/1782.	
Dobbins, William	3rd NC Regiment	1782, a Corporal under Capt. Alexander Brevard. Died on 6/28/1783.	
Dobey, Nathaniel	2nd NC Regiment	4/23/1776, a Private, unit unknown. 9/10/1778, a known Private under Capt. Thomas Armstrong. Discharged on 11/10/1778.	
Dobey, Nathaniel	3rd NC Regiment	June 1776, a Sergeant under Capt. Thomas Granbury. Dropped from the rolls in June 1778. aka Nathaniel Doley.	
Dobson, Joseph	4th NC Regiment	1782, a Private under Capt. Anthony Sharpe for 18 months.	
Docan, John	10th NC Regiment	6/28/1777, a Private under Capt. Silas Stevenson. Dropped from the rolls in June 1778.	
Dodd, David	4th NC Regiment	5/6/1776, a Sergeant under Capt. Thomas Harris for three years. A Private in June 1778 under	Brandywine Creek (PA),

Name	1st Unit	Year / Rank / Served Under / Notes	Known Battles
		Capt. John Sumner (1st NC Regiment). A Corporal in Aug. 1778. 9/8/1778, a known Corporal under Capt. John Sumner. Discharged on 5/10/1779 at Paramus, NJ. From Anson County, NC. S38670.	Germantown (PA).
Dodd, Jesse	4th NC Regiment	5/6/1776, a Private under Capt. Thomas Harris for three years. Dropped from the rolls in Sept. 1777. Rejoined in Jan. 1778. 9/8/1778, a known Wagoner under Capt. John Sumner (1st NC Regiment). Discharged on 5/10/1779 at Paramus, NJ.	Monmouth (NJ).
Dodd, Robert	5th NC Regiment	5/4/1776, a Private under Capt. William Ward for 18 months. Discharged after 12 months on 5/4/1777, the same day that Capt. Ward resigned, at Warwick, VA. Earlier in NC Militia. Enlisted in Johnston County, NC. S41510.	
Dodd, Thomas	3rd NC Regiment	1782, a Sergeant under Capt. Alexander Brevard for 18 months.	
Doddriel, James	2nd NC Regiment	7/20/1778, a Private under Capt. Reading Blount. A Corporal on 10/3/1778.	
Dodge, Jonah	2nd NC Regiment	1777, a Musician under Capt. Clement Hall. Deserted on 2/10/1779.	
Dodson, Charles	4th NC Regiment	1776, a Private under Capt. Joseph Phillips. 9/8/1778, a Private under Capt. James Read (1st NC Regiment).	
Doherty, John	9th NC Regiment	1777, a Private under Capt. Richard D. Cook. Deserted in Aug. 1777.	
Doherty, Richard	3rd NC Regiment	7/20/1778, a Private under Capt. Michael Quinn for nine months.	
Doiland, Benjamin	1st NC Regiment	5/21/1781, a Private under Capt. Anthony Sharpe. Dropped from the rolls during 1781.	
Dollar, Jonathan	1st NC Regiment	1781, a Private under Capt. William Armstrong. Discharged 7/1/1782. From what is now Durham County. Earlier in NC Militia.	
Dolly, Caleb	10th NC Regiment	2/3/1778, a Sergeant, unit unknown. A Private in June 1778. 9/10/1778, a known Private under Capt. Thomas Armstrong (2nd NC Regiment). Deserted in June 1779.	
Dolohide, Silas	1st NC Regiment	1777, a Private under Capt. Henry "Hal" Dixon. 6/1/1778, a Private under Capt. Griffith John McRee. Deserted on 1/19/1780. aka Sylas Dollerhide.	
Doming, Speakman	10th NC Regiment	6/20/1777, a Private under Capt. Abraham Sheppard, Jr.	
Donagin, David	1st NC Regiment	1782, a Sergeant under Capt. Peter Bacot for 18 months.	
Donaldson, David	9th NC Regiment	2/15/1778, a Private under Capt. Anthony Sharpe for three years. 9/8/1778, a known Private in the Lt. Colonel's Company (Lt. Col. Robert Mebane) (1st NC Regiment) led by Capt. Joshua Bowman. Deserted on 5/20/1779.	
Donaldson, Francis	1st NC Regiment	1777, a Private under Capt. Henry "Hal" Dixon. Deserted on 5/6/1777.	

356

Name	1st Unit	Year / Rank / Served Under / Notes	Known Battles
Donaldson, Jacob	4th NC Regiment	1782, a Private under Capt. William Lytle for 18 months.	
Donaldson, Spencer	10th NC Regiment	5/18/1777, a Musician under Capt. Isaac Moore for three years. 9/8/1778, a known Private in the Lt. Colonel's Company (Lt. Col. Robert Mebane) (1st NC Regiment) led by Capt. Joshua Bowman - sick on that date.	
Donally, Hugh	2nd NC Regiment	4/25/1781, a Private under Capt. Tilghman Dixon. Died on 1/24/1782.	
Donally, John	4th NC Regiment	5/7/1776, a Private under Capt. John Nelson for three years. 6/1/1778, a Wagoner under Capt. Griffith John McRee (1st NC Regiment). Dropped from the rolls in Oct. 1778. On some rolls as John Donaldley, John Donaldby.	
Dondalout, Henry	1st NC Regiment	1/26/1777, a Private under Lt./Capt. Howell Tatum. 9/8/1778, a known Private under Capt. Howell Tatum. A Corporal in Feb. 1779. Discharged on 1/27/1780. aka Henry Dunnelloe.	
Doniho, Henry	7th NC Regiment	1/26/1777, a Private under Capt. John McGlaughan. Deserted in Apr. 1777.	
Donoho, Thomas	6th NC Regiment	1775, a 1st Lieutenant in the Hillsborough District Minutemen. 4/17/1776, a 1st Lieutenant under Capt. Archibald Lytle, then under Capt. George Mitchell. 9/10/1776, a Captain. Retired. Recalled and assigned to 10th NC Regiment. 1779, a Captain under Col. Thomas Clark (5th NC Regiment). Spring of 1781, a Captain in the 1st NC Regiment. Promoted to Major on 10/13/1781. 2/6/1782, a Major in the 4th NC Regiment, until the end of the war. From what is now Caswell County, NC. W9838.	Brandywine Creek (PA), Germantown (PA), Briar Creek (GA), Stono Ferry (SC), Siege of Ninety-Six 1781 (SC), Eutaw Springs (SC).
Dorner, John	1st NC Regiment	1777, a Private under Capt. Joshua Bowman. Deserted on 8/28/1777.	
Doty, Isaac	2nd NC Regiment	1782, a Sergeant under Capt. Benjamin Carter for 18 months. Earlier in NJ Continental Line. S38668.	
Doudon, Samuel	3rd NC Regiment	1777, a Private under Capt. Jacob Turner. POW at the battle of Brandywine Creek, PA on 9/11/1777. aka Samuel Dondon.	Brandywine Creek (PA).
Dougan, Francis	10th NC Regiment	8/14/1777, a Musician under Capt. Isaac Moore for three years. 9/8/1778, a known Private in the Lt. Colonel's Company (Lt. Col. Robert Mebane) (1st NC Regiment) led by Capt. Joshua Bowman. 3/12/1779, re-enlisted for the duration of the war in the same unit. aka Francis Dugan.	
Douge, Griffin	7th NC Regiment	5/5/1777, a Corporal under Capt. John Poynter. 9/8/1778, a known Corporal under Capt. Tilghman Dixon (1st NC Regiment).	
Douge, James	7th NC Regiment	A Private under Capt. Eli Ely. Died on 5/3/1778.	
Douge, James	7th NC Regiment	1/16/1777, a Sergeant under Capt. John Poynter. 9/8/1778, a known Sergeant under Capt. Tilghman Dixon (1st NC Regiment).	

Name	1st Unit	Year / Rank / Served Under / Notes	Known Battles
		Discharged on 1/28/1780.	
Douge, Joab	7th NC Regiment	5/11/1777, a Musician under Capt. John Poynter. 9/8/1778, a known Musician under Capt. Tilghman Dixon (1st NC Regiment).	
Douge, Josiah	2nd NC Regiment	9/9/1778, a known Private under Capt. Clement Hall.	
Douge, Richard	NC Artillery	8/19/1776, a Sergeant under Capt. John Kingsbury as NC Provincial Troops. 7/10/1777, placed on Continental Line. May 1, 1778, a known private under Capt. John Kingsbury.	
Douge, Richard	NC Artillery	8/19/1776, a Matross under Capt. John Vance as NC Provincial Troops. 7/10/1777, on Continental Line. 11/16/1777, under Capt. John Kingsbury. April 1778, a Sergeant. 5/1/1778, in same unit. 9/16/1778, in same unit.	
Douge, Zachariah	10th NC Regiment	5/13/1777, a Musician under Capt. John Jarvis for three years. A Private in Aug. 1778. 9/8/1778, a known Private in the Major's Company (Maj. John Baptiste Ashe) (1st NC Regiment). aka Zachariah Daug, aka Zachariah Dang.	
Dougherty, George	6th NC Regiment	1775, a 1st Lieutenant in the Salisbury District Minutemen. 4/17/1776, a 1st Lieutenant under Capt. John Baptiste Ashe and Col. John Alexander Lillington.10/28/1776, a Captain in the 6th NC Regiment. Transferred to 4th NC Regiment on 6/1/1778. A Major on 10/13/1782. From what is now Caswell County, NC. W9838. aka George Doherty, Daugherty.	Brandywine Creek (PA), Germantown (PA), Briar Creek (GA), Stono Ferry (SC), Eutaw Springs (SC).
Doughty, Jesse	1st NC Regiment	9/8/1778, a known Private in the Colonel's Company (Col. Thomas Clark) led by Capt. John Gambier Scull. Deserted on 1/8/1780.	
Douglas, Alexander	2nd NC Regiment	6/8/1776, a Regimental Drum Major.	
Douglas, John	1st NC Regiment	5/20/1776, a Private under Ens./Lt./Capt. James Read. 9/8/1778, a known Private under Capt. James Read (1st NC Regiment). Discharged on 5/28/1779.	
Douglas, John	4th NC Regiment	5/15/1777, a Private under Capt. James Williams. Dropped from the rolls in April 1778.	
Douglas, John	6th NC Regiment	A Private under Capt. Philip Taylor. Dropped from the rolls in Sep. 1777.	
Douglas, Robert	NC Artillery	11/16/1777, a 3rd Lieutenant under Capt. John Kingsbury.	
Douglas, William	1st NC Regiment	A Private under Capt. Henry "Hal" Dixon. 9/8/1778, a known Private under Capt. James Read. POW at the Fall of Charleston (SC). After being exchanged and on the way home, he was again taken POW at Hillsborough by Loyalist Col. David Fanning on 9/12/1781.	Siege of Charleston 1780 (SC), Hillsborough.
Douglas, William	2nd NC Regiment	1782, a Corporal under Capt. Robert Raiford.	
Dove, William	10th NC Regiment	6/14/1777, a Private under Capt. Silas Stevenson. 9/9/1778, a known Private in the	

358

Name	1st Unit	Year / Rank / Served Under / Notes	Known Battles
		Colonel's Company (Col. John Patten) (2nd NC Regiment) led by Capt. John Craddock.	
Dowd, John	2nd NC Regiment	Sept. 1782, a Private under Capt. Clement Hall. Deserted on 6/1/1783 (?). From Duplin (what is now Sampson) County, NC. Earlier in NC Militia. On the official rolls as John Doude. R13793.	
Dowdle, John	4th NC Regiment	1782, a Private under Capt. Anthony Sharpe for 18 months.	
Dowdy, Francis	1st NC Regiment	5/19/1781, a Private under Capt. Robert Raiford. Deserted in Nov. 1781.	
Dowdy, George	10th NC Regiment	1778, a Private, unit unknown. Died in Apr. 1778.	
Dowell, James	1st NC Regiment	1775, a Private under Capt. John Walker. May 1778, a Private under Capt. John Brown. 9/8/1778, a known Private under Capt. Tilghman Dixon.	
Dowling, Dennis	6th NC Regiment	4/29/1776, a Private under Lt./Capt. Thomas White. Dropped from the rolls in Nov. 1777.	
Downams, Richard	2nd NC Regiment	9/10/1778, a known Private under Capt. Thomas Armstrong.	
Downing, George	10th NC Regiment	5/18/1777, a Private under Capt. Abraham Sheppard, Jr. for three years.	
Downing, James	1st NC Regiment	1776, a Private under Capt. Robert Rowan, Capt. Absalom Tatum, and Capt. Henry Dixon for a total of one year, ending 4/30/1777. From Cumberland County, NC. Later, in NC Militia as a Sergeant. W25536.	Ft. Moultrie (SC).
Downing, Richard	10th NC Regiment	6/20/1777, a Private under Capt. Abraham Sheppard, Jr. for three years. From Johnston County, NC. W19185.	
Downing, Thomas	2nd NC Regiment	1782, a Private under Capt. Clement Hall for 12 months. Discharged 1/29/1783.	
Downing, William		Sep. 1779, a Private, regiment and unit unknown.	
Downs, John	4th NC Regiment	A Private under Capt. James Williams. 9/8/1778, a known Private in the Colonel's Company (Col. Thomas Clark) (1st NC Regiment) led by Capt. John Gambier Scull - sick at Valley Forge on that date. A Corporal on 11/10/1778. A Sergeant in Jan. 1780. aka John Downes.	
Downum, Speakman	10th NC Regiment	6/20/1777, a Private under Capt. Abraham Sheppard, Jr. Wounded in the thigh at Georgetown, MD. From Dobbs (what is now Wayne) County, NC. W128.	
Drake, Axom	1st NC Regiment	1781, a Private under Capt. William Armstrong. Discharged on 4/1/1782.	
Drake, Cove	2nd NC Regiment	1777, a Sergeant under Capt. James Gee. Discharged on 8/2/1778 from His Excy. Guards. aka Com. Drake (?).	
Drake, Ely	3rd NC Regiment	7/20/1778, a Private under Lt./Capt. Joseph Montford for nine months.	
Draper,	5th NC	1777, a Private under Capt. Reading Blount.	

Name	1st Unit	Year / Rank / Served Under / Notes	Known Battles
Roger	Regiment	Died on 4/16/1778.	
Drew, William	2nd NC Regiment	1777, a Private under Capt. James Gee. 9/9/1778, a known Private under Capt. John Ingles.	
Dring, Thomas	2nd NC Regiment	1777, a Private under Capt. Charles Allen. Died on 9/11/1777.	
Drischall, David	10th NC Regiment	8/9/1777, a Musician under Capt. Andrew Vanoy. A Private in June 1778.	
Drury, John	1st NC Regiment	Nov. 1779, a Private under Capt. Griffith John McRee.	
Drury, Morgan	1st NC Regiment	Nov. 1779, a Private under Capt. Griffith John McRee.	
Dubois, Nicholas	3rd NC Regiment	6/18/1779, a Private under Capt. George "Gee" Bradley. Deserted on 10/26/1779.	
Duckworth, John	2nd NC Regiment	1776, a Private under Capt. William Knox for six months. From Burke County, NC. Later in NC Militia. S6805.	Ft. Moultrie (SC).
Dudley, Ambrose	3rd NC Regiment	7/20/1778, a Private under Capt. John Baker for nine months. Deserted on 7/9/1778.	
Dudley, George	6th NC Regiment	May 1776, a Private under Capt. Arthur Council. Originally from Duplin County, enlisted at Cross Creek (Fayetteville) in Cumberland County. Promoted to Corporal and Sergeant. S41514.	Brandywine Creek (PA), Germantown (PA), Monmouth (NJ).
Dudley, John	2nd NC Regiment	4/7/1777, a Private under Capt. Clement Hall. A Sergeant in Sep. 1777. Back to Private in Jan. 1778. Deserted on 1/15/1780.	
Dudley, Thomas	6th NC Regiment	1776, a Musician under Capt. Thomas Donoho. May 1778, an Ensign. Transferred to 3rd NC Regiment on 6/1/1778. 6/20/1779, a 2nd Lieutenant. 3/10/1781, a 1st Lieutenant. Wounded at Eutaw Springs on September 8, 1781.	Eutaw Springs (SC).
Due, John	4th NC Regiment	1782, a Sergeant under Capt. Thomas Evans for 18 months.	
Duert, Hezekiah	2nd NC Regiment	5/15/1781, a Private under Capt. Tilghman Dixon. Discharged on 5/21/1782 (1st NC Regiment). Received clothing on 5/24/1782. From Caswell County. aka Hezekia Duest.	
Duffell, Thomas	8th NC Regiment	3/17/1777, a Private under Capt. Robert Raiford.	
Duggin, Jesse	5th NC Regiment	1777, a Private under Capt. Henry Darnell. Killed at the battle of Germantown, PA on 10/4/1777.	Germantown (PA).
Duggin, Thomas	5th NC Regiment	1777, a Private under Capt. Henry Darnell. Missing on 10/4/1777.	Germantown (PA).
Duke, Andrew	5th NC Rgiment	9/9/1775, a 1st Lieutenant in the Edenton District Minutemen. 4/17/1776, a Private under Capt. Peter Simon and Col. Edward Buncombe.	
Duke, Buckner	7th NC Regiment	1777, a Private under Capt. John Macon. Deserted in Aug. 1777.	
Duke, Hardeman	6th NC Regiment	10/10/1776, a Private under Capt. Archibald Lytle. 9/8/1778, a known Private under Capt.	

Name	1st Unit	Year / Rank / Served Under / Notes	Known Battles
		Tilghman Dixon (1st NC Regiment). Discharged in Nov. 1778. From Orange (what is now Durham) County, NC. aka Hardy Duke, Hardmond Dukes. W783.	
Duke, James	7th NC Regiment	12/25/1777, a Private under Capt. Henry Dawson for three years. 3/12/1779, re-enlisted for the duration of the war under Capt. James Read (1st NC Regiment). aka James Dukes.	
Duke, John	2nd NC Regiment	5/19/1781, a Private under Capt. Benjamin Carter. Discharged on 5/19/1782. From Hertford County, NC.	
Duke, Sherard	1st NC Regiment	5/5/1781, a Private under Capt. Robert Raiford. Died in Oct. 1781.	
Duke, William	1st NC Regiment	5/5/1781, a Sergeant under Capt. Robert Raiford. A Private on 2/1/1782. Discharged 4/27/1782 (2nd NC Regiment).	
Duke, William	6th NC Regiment	5/6/1776, a Private under Capt. Archibald Lytle for 2-1/2 years. 9/8/1778, a known Private under Capt. Tilghman Dixon (1st NC Regiment). Discharged in Nov. 1778. 5/5/1781, a Sergeant under Capt. Robert Raiford (1st NC Regiment). A Private on 2/1/1782. Discharged 4/27/1782 (2nd NC Regiment). From what is now Durham County, NC. Enlisted in Orange County, NC. Older brother of Hardeman Duke. S6808.	
Dukemore, Marina	10th NC Regiment	Apr. 1778, a Private, unit unknown. Dropped from the rolls in June 1778.	
Dukes, James	1st NC Regiment	Enlisted 12/23/1776, unit unknown. 9/8/1778, a known Private under Capt. James Read. 3/12/1779, in same unit. aka James Dakes.	
Dunbar, Dunn	DQMG	1780, a Wagoner under Col. Nicholas Long (Deputy QM General). Probably the same man as directly below.	
Dunbar, Dunn	2nd NC Regiment	1/12/1776, a Corporal under Capt. James Gee. A Private in Nov. 1778. Deserted on 4/30/1779.	
Duncan, Elijah	10th NC Regiment	1777, a Private under Capt. James Wilson. Feb. 1779, a Private under Capt. Philip Taylor (5th NC Regiment). Also served under Capt. Thomas Donoho (1st NC Regiment). Alleged to have deserted in Apr. 1779 (statement says Elijah Johnson, not Duncan). From Caswell County, NC. S3309.	
Duncan, George	1st NC Regiment	5/2/1781, a Private under Lt./Capt. Benjamin Bailey. Discharged on 5/29/1782. Probably the same man as directly below.	
Duncan, George	6th NC Regiment	4/20/1776, a Private under Capt. William Glover. Also served under Capt. Thomas Hogg (1st NC Regiment). Discharged on 10/19/1778. Apparently re-enlisted. From Granville County, NC. S41513.	
Duncan, Jesse	1st NC Regiment	5/20/1776, a Private under Capt. James Read. 9/8/1778, a known Private under Capt. James Read again. Discharged on 5/28/1779.	

Name	1st Unit	Year / Rank / Served Under / Notes	Known Battles
Duncan, Peter	1st NC Regiment	5/30/1781, a Sergeant under Capt. Anthony Sharpe. Dropped from the rolls during 1781.	
Duncan, Robert	4th NC Regiment	12/1/1777 or 2/10/1777 (two sources), a Paymaster. Retired 6/1/1778.	
Duncan, William	6th NC Regiment	4/20/1776, a Private under Capt. William Glover. Also served under Capt. Thomas Hogg (1st NC Regiment). Discharged on 10/19/1778. Apparently re-enlisted. Later in NC Militia. From Granville County, NC. W21015.	Stono Ferry (SC).
Dunham, John	5th NC Regiment	6/25/1779, a Private under Capt. Reading Blount for 18 months.	
Dunn, Benjamin	2nd NC Regiment	4/2/1777, a Private, unit unknown. 9/10/1778, a known Private under Capt. Thomas Armstrong. aka Benjamin Dun.	
Dunn, Jacob	3rd NC Regiment	7/20/1778, a Private under Capt. Kedar Ballard for nine months.	
Dunn, Jacob	10th NC Regiment	12/3/1777, a Private under Capt. John Jarvis for three years. 9/8/1778, a known Private in the Major's Company (Maj. John Baptiste Ashe) (1st NC Regiment) - sick in camp on that date.	
Dunn, Jeffrey	10th NC Regiment	11/11/1777, a Private under Capt. John Jarvis for three years. 9/8/1778, a known Private in the Major's Company (Maj. John Baptiste Ashe) (1st NC Regiment). Died on 1/12/1779. aka Jeffery Dunn.	
Dunn, Malachi	10th NC Regiment	12/3/1777, a Private under Capt. John Jarvis for three years. 9/8/1778, a known Private in the Major's Company (Maj. John Baptiste Ashe) (1st NC Regiment). Died in Dec. 1778.	
Dunn, Nicholas	5th NC Regiment	6/7/1779, a Private under Maj. Reading Blount.	
Dunn, Sterling	2nd NC Regiment	6/5/1777, a Private, unit unknown. 9/10/1778, a known Private under Capt. Thomas Armstrong. aka Sterling Dun.	
Dunnick, Peter	NC Artillery	1777, a Matross under Capt. John Kingsbury. Dropped from the rolls prior to May 1778. Probably the same man as directly below.	
Dunnick, Peter	10th NC Regiment	5/11/1778, a Sergeant, unit unknown. A Corporal in June 1778 in the Colonel's Company (Col. John Patten) led by Capt. John Craddock. Back to Sergeant on 5/24/1779. Transferred in Apr. 1782 to ?	
Dunnigan, Thomas	10th NC Regiment	Jan. 1778, a Private, unit unknown.	
Dunning, James	3rd NC Regiment	5/15/1776, a Private under Capt. James Emmett. Discharged in Oct. 1778.	
Dunning, Uriah	2nd NC Regiment	7/20/1778, a Private under Maj. Reading Blount. A Sergeant on 10/25/1778.	
Dunsee, Edward	1st NC Regiment	1777, a Sergeant under Capt. Joshua Bowman. Deserted on 9/28/1777.	
Dunson, William	5th NC Regiment	7/4/1779, a Private under Capt. Joseph Montford for 18 months.	
Dunstand, Charles	2nd NC Regiment	5/12/1781, a Corporal under Capt. Tilghman Dixon. Discharged on 5/21/1782 (1st NC	

Name	1st Unit	Year / Rank / Served Under / Notes	Known Battles
		Regiment).	
Dupree, James	1st NC Regiment	6/10/1776, a Private, unit unknown. Dropped from the rolls in Nov. 1777.	
Dupriest, James	1st NC Regiment	11/1/1778, a Private under Capt. Anthony Sharpe. Dec. 1782, a Private under Capt. Benjamin Carter (2nd NC Regiment). aka James Depriest.	
Durden, Benjamin	3rd NC Regiment	7/20/1778, a Private under Lt./Capt. George "Gee" Bradley for nine months.	
Durden, Cornelius	3rd NC Regiment	7/20/1778, a Private under Lt./Capt. George "Gee" Bradley for nine months.	
Durden, Mills	5th NC Regiment	Aug. 1777, a Private under Capt. Benjamin Andrew Coleman. 1782, a Private under Capt. Thomas Evans (4th NC Regiment) for 18 months. Enlisted in Bute (what would become Warren) County, NC. aka Mills Durdon. W17736.	Wappoo Cut (SC).
Durham, Humphrey	1st NC Regiment	5/28/1781, a Private under Capt. Alexander Brevard. Discharged on 5/25/1782. aka Humphy Durham.	
Durham, John	10th NC Regiment	6/28/1777, a Musician under Capt. Silas Stevenson. Late 1778, re-enlisted in 2nd NC Regiment under Capt. John Craddock. POW at the Fall of Charleston - retained until the end of the war. S42677.	Siege of Charleston 1780 (SC).
Durham, Joseph	1st NC Regiment	1782, a Wagoner and a Courier under Capt. John Sumner. Only 14 years old when he joined from Caswell County, NC. R3158.	
Durham, Nathan		6/20/1776, a Private, unit unknown, enlisted for three years. 6/1/1778, a Private under Capt. Griffith John McRee (1st NC Regiment).	
Durham, William	4th NC Regiment	7/5/1781, a Private under Capt. Joseph T. Rhodes. Discharged 4/12/1782.	
Durnegan, John	5th NC Regiment	6/4/1779, a Private under Capt. Joseph Montford. Deserted in Sep. 1779.	
Durremfiss, John	2nd NC Regiment	3/12/1779, re-enlisted in the Colonel's Company (Col. John Patten) led by Capt. John Craddock.	
Dyches, Isom	1st NC Regiment	1777, a Private under Capt. Robert Ralston.	
Dye, Hopkins	8th NC Regiment	1/5/1777, a Private under Capt. John Walsh. 9/9/1778, a known Private under Capt. John Ingles (2nd NC Regiment). Discharged on 1/31/1780.	
Dyson, Thomas	8th NC Regiment	1/19/1777, a Private under Capt. John Walsh. 9/9/1778, a known Private in the Major's Company (Maj. Hardy Murfree) (2nd NC Regiment). 3/12/1779, re-enlisted in the Major's Company (Maj. Hardy Murfree). A Musician on 2/1/1780.	
Eager, John	10th NC Regiment	10/1/1777, a Private under Capt. James Wilson.	
Eagle, George	1st NC Regiment	4/28/1781, a Private under Capt. Griffith John McRee. Discharged on 4/10/1782.	
Eagle, Joseph	4th NC	1/4/1776, an Ensign. Resigned 3/20/1776.	Moore's Creek

Name	1st Unit	Year / Rank / Served Under / Notes	Known Battles
	Regiment		Bridge [4].
Earhart, Philip	1st NC Regiment	1781, a Private under Capt. Alexander Brevard. 2/6/1782, in 3rd NC Regiment. Transferred to ? in March 1783.	
Earl, James	4th NC Regiment	1777, a Private under Capt. James Williams. Dropped from the rolls in Sep. 1777.	
Early, James	5th NC Regiment	1777, a Private under Capt. Henry Darnell. Deserted in Aug. 1777.	
Earp, Edward	5th NC Regiment	1776, enlisted in Wake County as a Private under Capt. William Ward for 18 months. Re-enlisted for another 12 months. Then, in NC Militia. S41468.	
Easeley, Roderick	1st NC Regiment	4/25/1781, a Private under Capt. Robert Raiford. Discharged on 5/14/1782 (2nd NC Regiment).	
Eason, William	3rd NC Regiment	7/20/1778, a Private under Maj. Thomas Hogg for nine months.	
Easter, David	9th NC Regiment	1777, a Private under Capt. Richard D. Cook. Died on 2/22/1778.	
Easter, Michael	4th NC Regiment	A Private under Capt. Robert Moore, dates unknown. From Rowan County, NC.	
Eastman, Benjamin	10th NC Regiment	7/21/1777, a Private under Capt. Dempsey Gregory. A Sergeant in June 1778. Back to Private in 11/7/1778.	
Eastmead, John	7th NC Regiment	1777, a Private under Capt. Joseph Walker. Died in Aug. 1777. aka John Estmead.	
Easton, Seth	7th NC Regiment	11/28/1776, a 1st Lieutenant under Capt. Thomas Brickell. Resigned in Aug. 1777. From Edenton District. aka Seth Eason.	
Eaton, Christopher	4th NC Regiment	November 1777, a Private under Capt. Joseph Phillips. Transferred to 2nd NC Regiment under Col. Alexander Martin. Discharged May 1780. Then in NC Militia. From Surry County, NC. R3214.	Brandywine Creek (PA), Monmouth (NJ).
Eaton, Pinketham	3rd NC Regiment	1775, a Captain in the Halifax District Minutemen. 4/17/1776, a Captain under Col. Jetro Sumner. A Major on 11/22/1777 in the 8th NC Regiment - regiment disbanded on 6/1/1778. Joined the 4th NC Regiment as a Major in Jan. 1779. Wounded at Briar Creek, GA in 1779. A Major and a Colonel of Militia between the Fall of Charleston and the battle of Guilford Court House - April 1781, back as a Major in the newly recreated 1st NC Regiment. Captured and killed at Ft. Grierson, GA on 5/24/1781.	Ft. Moultrie #1 (SC), Brandywine Creek (PA), Germantown (PA), Briar Creek (GA), Stono Ferry (SC), Hobkirk's Hill (SC), Fort Watson #2 (SC), Fort Motte (SC), Siege of Ninety-Six 1781 (SC), Siege of Augusta (GA) (Killed).
Eborne, John	5th NC	9/9/1775, a 2nd Lieutenant in the New Bern	

Name	1st Unit	Year / Rank / Served Under / Notes	Known Battles
	Regiment	District Minutemen. 4/17/1776, a 2nd Lieutenant under Capt. Benjamin Stedman and Col. Edward Buncombe. 10/1/1776, a Lieutenant under Capt. John Pugh Williams (5th NC Regiment). Dropped from the rolls in Jan. 1778. 1779, a Captain and a Lt. Colonel under Col. Rotheas Latham. Served until the end of the war. aka John Eborn, John Eburn, John Ebarn.	
Eborne, Thomas	5th NC Regiment	4/17/1776, a Lieutenant under Capt. Benjamin Stedman. Dropped from the rolls in Oct. 1777. aka Thomas Eburn.	
Echols, James	2nd NC Regiment	9/9/1778, a known Private under Capt. Clement Hall.	
Eckles, Frederick	10th NC Regiment	5/18/1777, a Private under Capt. Abraham Sheppard, Jr.	
Eckles, William	2nd NC Regiment	1781, a Sergeant under Capt. Thomas Evans. 2/6/1782, in 4th NC Regiment.	
Eckols, William	5th NC Regiment	May 1776, a Private under Capt. Simon Alderson for 12 months. 7/20/1778, a Private under Maj. Thomas Hogg (3rd NC Regiment) for nine months. 5/15/1779, re-enlisted as a Sergeant under Capt. Joseph Montford (5th NC Regiment then 1st NC Regiment). POW at the Fall of Charleston (SC), escaped after eight months. 1781, rejoined as a Sergeant under Capt. Benjamin Coleman (2nd NC Regiment) until the end of the war. Discharged at James Island, SC. From Beaufort County, NC. aka William Equals. S41517.	Siege of Charleston 1780 (SC).
Ecret, Robert	1st NC Regiment	9/1/1775, a Regimental Fife Major. Dropped from the rolls in Jan. 1778.	Moore's Creek Bridge [4].
Ector, Samuel	4th NC Regiment	1782, a Private, unit unknown. Hired a substitute who deserted, so he had to resume his service. From Orange County, NC. Born 1744. W19216.	
Edens, John	3rd NC Regiment	7/20/1778, a Private under Capt. John Baker for nine months. Enlisted at Onslow Court House, NC. Discharged in May 1779. W4945.	
Edenton, Nicholas	3rd NC Regiment	1779, a Sergeant under Capt. Michael Quinn. Discharged in Jan. 1780.	
Edge, Thomas	1st NC Regiment	1776, a Private under Capt. Joshua Bowman.	
Edge, Thomas	1st NC Regiment	1777, a Private under Capt. Lawrence Thompson. Discharged on 2/28/1778.	
Edgner, Matthias	1st NC Regiment	1782, a Private under Capt. Peter Bacot. Deserted on 6/15/1783 (?).	
Edlow, John	2nd NC Regiment	8/1/1781, a Private under Capt. Benjamin Carter. aka John Edloe.	
Edmonds, David	3rd NC Regiment	7/20/1778, a Private under Capt. Kedar Ballard for nine months.	
Edmons, Abel	2nd NC Regiment	2/1/1777, a Private under Capt. Benjamin Williams. 9/9/1778, a known Private in the Major's Company (Maj. Hardy Murfree) (2nd NC Regiment). Discharged on 2/1/1780. aka	

Name	1st Unit	Year / Rank / Served Under / Notes	Known Battles
		Abel Edmunds.	
Edmons, William	4th NC Regiment	1782, a Private under Capt. William Lytle for 18 months. Deserted on 5/5/1783 (?).	
Edmonson, John	1st NC Regiment	8/1/1782, a Private under Capt. Joshua Hadley for 18 months. Deserted on 5/13/1783 (?).	
Edmunds, Nicholas	3rd NC Regiment	4/16/1776, a Captain under Col. Jethro Sumner. Nov. 1777, left in NC as recruiter for 3rd NC Regiment. Dropped from the rolls in Jan. 1778. aka Nicholas Edmonds.	
Edoc, James	3rd NC Regiment	7/20/1778, a Private under Capt. Kedar Ballard for nine months.	
Edules, Thomas	5th NC Regiment	1777, a Musician under Capt. Benjamin Stedman. Dropped from the rolls in Jan. 1778. aka Thomas Edulus.	
Edwards, Benjamin	3rd NC Regiment	1777, a Private under Capt. Jacob Turner. Dropped from the rolls in June 1778.	
Edwards, Brown	3rd NC Regiment	7/20/1778, a Private under Capt. Michael Quinn, then under Capt. Joseph Montford (5th NC Regiment) for nine months. Earlier and later in NC Militia. From Halifax County, NC. S35910.	
Edwards, David	1st NC Regiment	4/25/1781, a Sergeant under Capt. Benjamin Bailey. Discharged on 4/25/1782. From Dobbs County, now Wayne County, NC. Earlier in NC Militia. S6812.	
Edwards, John	1st NC Regiment	May 1781, a Private under Capt. Anthony Sharpe for 12 months. From Montgomery County, NC. Enlisted at Salisbury, NC. Discharged in May 1782 at James Island, SC. Born 8/17/1766 in VA. R3258.	
Edwards, John Jr.	1st NC Regiment	Jan. 1782, a Private under Capt. William Lytle. 2/6/1782, would be in the 4th NC Regiment.	
Edwards, John	1st NC Regiment	4/12/1781, a Sergeant under Capt. William Lytle. Deserted in July 1781. Rejoined in Jan. 1782. Discharged on 4/12/1782 (4th NC Regiment).	
Edwards, John	2nd NC Regiment	6/1/1776, a Private under Capt. John Armstrong for three years. Died on 2/15/1778 in Valley Forge.	
Edwards, John	3rd NC Regiment	Oct. 1781, a Private under Capt. Samuel Jones for 12 months. Discharged 10/1/1782 (1st NC Regiment).	
Edwards, John	4th NC Regiment	1782, a Private under Capt. Anthony Sharpe for 18 months. Deserted on 4/30/1783 (?).	
Edwards, John	6th NC Regiment	1777, a Corporal under Capt. Francis Child. Dropped from the rolls in Feb. 1778.	
Edwards, Lemuel	1st NC Regiment	1782, a Private under Capt. Peter Bacot. Discharged on 1/10/1783.	
Edwards, Lemuel	3rd NC Regiment	7/20/1778, a Private under Capt. Kedar Ballard for nine months. Dropped from the rolls in Oct. 1778.	
Edwards, Reuben	4th NC Regiment	May 1778 to September 1779, a Private under Capt. Joseph Thomas Rhodes. From Wake County, NC. Later in NC Militia. S16376.	

Name	1st Unit	Year / Rank / Served Under / Notes	Known Battles
Edwards, Simon	1st NC Regiment	5/4/1781, a Private under Capt. Robert Raiford. Discharged on 5/4/1782 (2nd NC Regiment). R3264.	
Edwards, Solomon	3rd NC Regiment	7/20/1778, a Private under Capt. Francis Child for 18 months.	
Edwards, Stephen	3rd NC Regiment	7/20/1778, a Private under Lt./Capt. Joseph Montford for nine months.	
Eggerton, Jesse	3rd NC Regiment	7/20/1778, a Private under Maj. Thomas Hogg for nine months.	
Egner, Matthias	1st NC Regiment	7/25/1782, a Private under Capt. Alexander Brevard, then under Capt. Peter Bacot. Discharged in Dec. 1783. From Lincoln County, NC. S21745.	
Elder, William	2nd NC Regiment	5/1/1781, a Private under Capt. Benjamin Carter. Discharged on 6/1/1782.	
Eldridge, Levy	4th NC Regiment	1777, a Private under Capt. Joseph Phillips. Deserted on 11/20/1777.	
Elkins, Joshua	6th NC Regiment	1777, a Corporal under Capt. George Dougherty. Missing on 10/4/1777 at the battle of Germantown, PA. Discharged in 1779. 1780, joined NC Militia. From Chatham County, NC. W17755.	Germantown (PA).
Elkins, Shadrack	6th NC Regiment	3/23/1777, a Musician under Capt. George Dougherty for three years. A Private in June 1778. 9/8/1778, a known Private under Capt. Joshua Bowman (1st NC Regiment). POW in Jan. 1779 at Hackensack Ferry, NJ - held till after the Fall of Charleston, SC. Exchanged, joined Lt. Col. Henry "Light Horse Harry" Lee's Legion. From Chatham County, NC. R3286.	Germantown (PA), Monmouth (NJ).
Elks, William	5th NC Regiment	1777, a Private under Capt. Benjamin Stedman. Dropped from the rolls In Feb. 1778.	
Eller, John	3rd NC Regiment	1/15/1782, a Private under Capt. Benjamin Bailey for 12 months.	
Eller, Joseph	3rd NC Regiment	1/15/1782, a Private under Capt. Benjamin Bailey for 12 months.	
Elleums, James	3rd NC Regiment	1781, a Private under Capt. Edward Yarborough for 12 months. Discharged on 4/22/1782.	
Ellick, Joshua	3rd NC Regiment	7/20/1778, a Private under Capt. Kedar Ballard for nine months.	
Elliot, Jabesh	2nd NC Regiment	11/10/1776, a Private, unit unknown. 9/9/1778, a known Private in the Lt. Colonel's Company (Lt. Col. Selby Harney).	
Elliot, Jabez	8th NC Regiment	11/10/1776, a Private under Lt./Capt. Michael Quinn. Discharged on 1/5/1779. aka Jabez Eliot.	
Elliot, Zachary	3rd NC Regiment	1781, a Private under Capt. Edward Yarborough for 12 months. Discharged on 7/10/1782. From Pitt County, NC. His pension application does not match up with the official records, so it is difficult to assess. He claims much more service, mixing Militia with Continental service - not coherent. R3287.	Eutaw Springs (SC).
Elliott, John	1st NC Regiment	2/6/1776, a Private under Capt. George Davidson. 7/10/1776, a Private under Capt.	Breech Inlet Naval Battle

Name	1st Unit	Year / Rank / Served Under / Notes	Known Battles
		Robert Smith (4th NC Regiment). Discharged 7/10/1777. Re-enlisted under Capt. William Goodman (4th NC Regiment). From Guilford County, NC. Born 11/6/1755 in Augusta County, VA. S32232.	(SC), Briar Creek (GA), Stono Ferry (SC).
Elliott, John	10th NC Regiment	6/16/1777, a Sergeant under Capt. Andrew Vanoy. A Private in June 1778. 9/9/1778, a known Private under Capt. John Ingles (2nd NC Regiment). POW at Ft. Lafayette, NY on 6/1/1779. Rejoined in Nov. 1779. aka John Ellet.	Ft. Lafayette (NY).
Elliott, Joseph	10th NC Regiment	5/21/1777, a Private under Capt. Isaac Moore. Deserted in Apr. 1778.	
Ellis, Aaron	1st NC Regiment	5/19/1781, a Private under Capt. Robert Raiford. Discharged on 5/19/1782 (2nd NC Regiment).	
Ellis, Absalom	3rd NC Regiment	7/20/1778, a Private under Lt./Capt. George "Gee" Bradley for nine months. Also served under Capt. William Harrison, dates unknown. S41519.	
Ellis, Bartholomew	1st NC Regiment	5/2/1781, a Private under Capt. Robert Raiford. Discharged on 5/2/1782 (2nd NC Regiment).	
Ellis, James	4th NC Regiment	1781, a Private under Capt. George Dougherty for 12 months. Discharged on 5/25/1782.	
Ellis, John	1st NC Regiment	1781, a Private under Capt. Robert Raiford.	
Ellis, John	2nd NC Regiment	4/27/1776, a Private, unit unknown. 9/9/1778, a known Private under Capt. Robert Fenner (2nd NC Regiment). Discharged on 7/1/1779. From Wake County, NC. State Records and Pension asserts he was in 10th NC Regiment in early 1776, but that wasn't created until April/May 1777. Born 1754 in VA. S32233.	
Ellis, John	6th NC Regiment	1777, a Private under Capt. Thomas Donoho. Deserted in Aug. 1777.	
Ellis, Robert	1st NC Regiment	April 1776, a Private under Capt. Thomas Allen. 9/3/1776, a Private under Capt. William Fenner (2nd NC Regiment). 9/9/1778, a known Private in the Lt. Colonel's Company (Lt. Col. Selby Harney). 1781, under Capt. James Mills (1st NC Regiment). S41518.	Eutaw Springs (SC).
Ellis, Robert	2nd NC Regiment	1/1/1782, a Private under Capt. Benjamin Andrew Coleman.	
Ellis, Thomas	2nd NC Regiment	1781, a Private under Capt. Tilghman Dixon. Discharged on 4/25/1782.	
Ellis, William	7th NC Regiment	1777, a Private under Capt. Thomas Brickell. Deserted in Apr. 1777.	
Ellison, Akis	2nd NC Regiment	9/9/1778, a Private under Capt. Benjamin Andrew Coleman.	
Ellison, Andrew	4th NC Regiment	5/7/1776, a Private under Capt. William Temple Coles. POW on 4/14/1779 (?). 5/11/1779, a known Private under Capt. Sumner (1st NC Regiment) - probably discharged on that date.	
Ellison,	3rd NC	7/20/1778, a Private under Capt. Kedar Ballard	

Name	1st Unit	Year / Rank / Served Under / Notes	Known Battles
Cornelius	Regiment	for nine months.	
Ellison, Peter	2nd NC Regiment	5/19/1781, a Private under Capt. Benjamin Carter. Discharged on 5/19/1782.	
Ellums, James	2nd NC Regiment	1782, a Private under Capt. Benjamin Carter. A Corporal in Dec. 1782.	
Elmer, Eli	NC Artillery	1/1/1777, a Lieutenant under Capt. Thomas Clark. Resigned 2/13/1780.	
Elmore, Daniel	3rd NC Regiment	7/20/1778, a Private under Lt./Capt. George "Gee" Bradley for 18 months.	
Elmore, James	1st NC Regiment	5/25/1781, a Private under Capt. Thomas Donoho. Discharged on 5/25/1782.	
Elmore, Morgan	3rd NC Regiment	7/20/1778, a Private under Lt./Capt. George "Gee" Bradley for 18 months.	
Elms, Charles	3rd NC Regiment	10/28/1776, a Private under Capt. Jacob Turner for 2-1/2 years. After Capt. Turner was killed, he was under Capt. Kedar Ballard. He lost an eye at the battle of Germantown, PA. 9/9/1778, a known Private under Capt. Clement Hall (2nd NC Regiment). Discharged on 5/1/1779. 1781, a Private under Capt. Joseph T. Rhodes (4th NC Regiment) for 12 months. Discharged on 4/12/1782. When enlisted, lived in Bute County (now Warren County), NC. Later, lived in Mecklenburg County, NC. aka Charles Elloms, Charles Ellums, Charles Elmes. S8413.	Germantown (PA).
Elridge, Charles	1st NC Regiment	5/25/1781, a Private under Capt. Alexander Brevard. Deserted on 7/1/1781.	
Elridge, William	1st NC Regiment	5/25/1781, a Private under Capt. Alexander Brevard. Deserted on 7/1/1781.	
Elsmore, Ephraim	4th NC Regiment	1782, a Private under Capt. William Lytle for 18 months.	
Ely, Eli	7th NC Regiment	11/28/1776, a 2nd Lieutenant under Capt. Bennett Wood. 12/11/1776, a 1st Lieutenant under Capt. John Macon. 10/12/1777, a Captain under Col. James Hogun. Retired on 6/1/1778. From Bute County, NC.	
Ely, Lemuel	7th NC Regiment	12/17/1776, a Captain under Col. James Hogun to replace Green Bell, who resigned. Resigned 2/14/1778. From Bute County. NC.	Brandywine Creek (PA), Germantown (PA).
Emason, Henry	1st NC Regiment	1781, a Private under Capt. Alexander Brevard. 2/6/1782, in 3rd NC Regiment. Deserted on 6/23/1783 (?).	
Embry, John	10th NC Regiment	7/25/1777, a Private under Capt. Andrew Vanoy. 9/9/1778, a known Private under Capt. John Ingles (2nd NC Regiment). POW at Ft. Lafayette, NY on 6/1/1779. Rejoined in Nov. 1779. aka John Ember.	Ft. Lafayette (NY).
Emerson, Henry	1st NC Regiment	May 1781, a Private under Capt. Anthony Sharpe, then Capt. Joseph T. Rhodes (4th NC Regiment). From Chatham County, NC. Earlier in NC Militia. S21747.	
Emerson, Samuel	3rd NC Regiment	Jan. 1779, a Private in the Colonel's Company (Col. Jethro Sumner).	

Name	1st Unit	Year / Rank / Served Under / Notes	Known Battles
Emery, William	1st NC Regiment	1781, a Private under Capt. Alexander Brevard for 12 months. 1782, rejoined for 18 months under Capt. Alexander Brevard (3rd NC Regiment). From Caswell County, NC. aka William Emory. W7107.	
Emley, David	1st NC Regiment	1781, a Private under Capt. Alexander Brevard. 2/6/1782, in 3rd NC Regiment. Transferred to ? on 4/20/1783.	
Emmett, James	3rd NC Regiment	1775, a Captain in the Hillsborough District Minutemen. 4/17/1776, a Captain under Col. Jethro Sumner. Then, a Major on 2/15/1778 to 6/1/1778. One source claims he was also a Major in 1st NC Regiment from 12/22/1777 to 6/1/1778. Retired 6/1/1778. Later a Major and a Colonel in the NC Militia.	Ft. Moultrie #1 (SC), Brandywine Creek (PA), Germantown (PA).
Emory, John	5th NC Regiment	3/1/1779, a Private under Capt. Joseph Montford. Discharged on 12/1/1779.	
Emory, Stephen	2nd NC Regiment	2/1/1777, a Private under Capt. Benjamin Williams. 9/9/1778, a known Private in the Major's Company (Maj. Hardy Murfree). Died in Oct. 1778. aka Stephen Emery.	
Engavis, William	2nd NC Regiment	12/10/1781, a Sergeant under Capt. Benjamin Andrew Coleman for 12 months.	
Engram, Tobias	2nd NC Regiment	1781, a Private under Capt. Benjamin Carter for 12 months. Discharged on 4/22/1782.	
Enloe, John	5th NC Regiment	1775, a Captain in the New Bern District Minutemen. 4/17/1776, a Captain in the 5th NC Regiment. Resigned on 10/25/1777. 1779, a Major in NC Militia.	Brandywine Creek (PA), Germantown (PA).
Ephland, David	4th NC Regiment	1776, a Private under Capt. William Goodman. Enlisted in Orange County, NC. S32239.	Brandywine Creek (PA), Guilford Court House, Eutaw Springs (SC).
Epps, John	9th NC Regiment	1777, a Private under Capt. Richard D. Cook. Discharged on 1/27/1780.	
Epps, William	9th NC Regiment	1/24/1777, a Private under Capt. Richard D. Cook for three years. 9/8/1778, a known Private in the Lt. Colonel's Company (Lt. Col. Robert Mebane) (1st NC Regiment) led by Capt. Joshua Bowman. Discharged on 1/27/1780.	
Erricks, David	1st NC Regiment	6/14/1781, a Private under Capt. Thomas Donoho. Discharged on 6/14/1782.	
Erven, James	2nd NC Regiment	9/9/1778, a Private in the Colonel's Company (Col. John Patten) led by Capt. John Craddock.	
Erwin, James	1st NC Regiment	1/1/1777, a Private under Capt. Joshua Bowman for three years. 9/8/1778, a known Private in the Major's Company (Maj. John Baptiste Ashe). aka James Irvin.	
Erwin, James	5th NC Regiment	A Private, unit unknown. Deserted in Sep. 1778. aka James Ervin.	
Erwin, John	1st NC Regiment	3/28/1777, an Ensign under Capt. Henry "Hal" Dixon. Resigned on 8/25/1777.	
Erwin, John	4th NC	1777, a Private under Capt. Robert Smith.	

Name	1st Unit	Year / Rank / Served Under / Notes	Known Battles
	Regiment	Dropped from the rolls in Sep. 1777.	
Eslick, James	4th NC Regiment	1777, a Private under Capt. James Williams. Dropped from the rolls in Feb. 1778.	
Essins, Thomas	2nd NC Regiment	12/13/1781, a Private under Capt. Benjamin Andrew Coleman for 12 months.	
Esteridge, Thomas	3rd NC Regiment	3/1/1782, a Private under Capt. Samuel Jones for 12 months.	
Esterlege, Ephraim	3rd NC Regiment	4/5/1781, a Private under Capt. William Lytle. Discharged on 4/5/1782.	
Etheridge, Daniel	8th NC Regiment	1777, a Corporal under Capt. John Walsh. Deserted in Oct. 1777. Rejoined on 12/1/1777. Died on 1/19/1778. aka Daniel Ethridge.	
Etheridge, John	3rd NC Regiment	Summer 1776, a Private under Capt. Henry "Hal" Dixon for three years. 9/8/1778, a known Private under Capt. James Read. Then under Capt. Peter Bacot. Wounded/POW at the Fall of Charleston. From Halifax County, NC. aka John Etherage. R3376A.	Siege of Charleston 1780 (SC).
Etheridge, William	3rd NC Regiment	1775, an Ensign in the Halifax District Minutemen. 4/17/1776, an Ensign under Capt. William Brinkley and Col. Jethro Sumner. From Halifax County.	
Ethrington, William	4th NC Regiment	1782, a Private under Capt. William Lytle for 18 months.	
Euman, William	3rd NC Regiment	1782, a Private under Capt. Edward Yarborough.	
Evans, Burrell	3rd NC Regiment	7/20/1778, a Private under Lt./Capt. Joseph Montford for nine months.	
Evans, Charles	1st NC Regiment	4/25/1781, a Private under Capt. Robert Raiford. Discharged on 4/15/1782 (2nd NC Regiment).	
Evans, Charles	2nd NC Regiment	7/20/1778, a Private under Maj. Reading Blount for nine months.	
Evans, Charles	3rd NC Regiment	7/20/1778, a Private under Capt. John Baker for nine months.	
Evans, Edward	10th NC Regiment	5/18/1777, a Private under Capt. Abraham Sheppard, Jr.	
Evans, George	7th NC Regiment	12/20/1776, a Private under Capt. Joseph Walker. Deserted in Aug. 1777. Rejoined in Sep. 1779. Deserted again in Sep. 1779.	
Evans, James	5th NC Regiment	3/1/1779, a Private under Capt. Joseph Montford. Discharged on 12/1/1779.	
Evans, John	2nd NC Regiment	1782, a Private under Capt. Robert Raiford. Deserted on 6/11/1783 (?).	
Evans, John	2nd NC Regiment	1/13/1782, a Private under Capt. Benjamin Andrew Coleman for 12 months.	
Evans, John	3rd NC Regiment	7/20/1778, a Private under Capt. John Baker for nine months. Deserted on 7/23/1778.	
Evans, John	4th NC Regiment	4/15/1776, a Private under Capt. Robert Smith for three years. 9/8/1778, a known Private in the Colonel's Company (Col. Thomas Clark) (1st NC Regiment) led by Capt. John Gambier Scull - sick at Reading, PA on that date. Discharged on 5/1/1779.	

Name	1st Unit	Year / Rank / Served Under / Notes	Known Battles
Evans, John	7th NC Regiment	1777, a Private under Capt. James Baker for nine months. Earlier in VA units, moved to NC. Then, back to VA. Born 7/16/1757. aka John Evins. R3387.	
Evans, Joseph	4th NC Regiment	1777, a Musician under Capt. William Goodman. Died in April 1778.	
Evans, Murin	1st NC Regiment	1781, a Private under Capt. William Armstrong for 12 months. Discharged on 10/1/1782.	
Evans, Reuben	2nd NC Regiment	5/12/1781, a Private under Capt. Tilghman Dixon. Discharged on 5/26/1782 (1st NC Regiment). From Wake County, NC. S41524.	
Evans, Richard	3rd NC Regiment	5/31/1779, a Private under Capt. George "Gee" Bradley for 18 months.	
Evans, Thomas	2nd NC Regiment	1775, a Lieutenant in NC Militia. 6/6/1776, an Ensign. 7/19/1776, a 2nd Lieutenant. 5/15/1777, a 1st Lieutenant under Capt. James Martin, Col. John Patten. 9/9/1778, a known Lieutenant in the Major's Company (Maj. Hardy Murfree). Taken prisoner at Tappan (NY) on 9/28/1778, exchanged on 11/4/1780. Promoted to Adjutant on 11/22/1778 (while imprisoned). Transferred to 1st NC Regiment on 1/1/1781. 7/1/1781, a Captain under Maj. Reading Blount. Transferred to 4th NC Regiment on 2/6/1782. Retired 1/1/1783. From Surry County, NC.	Eutaw Springs (SC).
Evans, Thomas	6th NC Regiment	Oct. 1777, a Private under Capt. Thomas White. Died on 4/30/1778.	
Everet, John	1st NC Regiment	A Private under Capt. Howell Tatum. Died in Aug. 1778.	
Everet, Matthew	1st NC Regiment	4/5/1781, a Private under Capt. William Lytle. Dropped from the rolls sometime during 1781.	
Everett, Nathaniel	6th NC Regiment	May 1778, a Private under Capt. Clement Hall. Then under Capt. William Goodman. Served a total of about 7 months. Became so sick that he hired a substitute. From Tyrrell County, NC. S6829.	
Everidge, Isaac	3rd NC Regiment	1779, a Musician under Capt. Kedar Ballard. aka Isaac Everedge.	
Everington, Edward	10th NC Regiment	5/21/1777, a Private under Capt. Dempsey Gregory. 9/8/1778, a known Private under Capt. Howell Tatum (1st NC Regiment).	
Eves, William	4th NC Regiment	1777, a Private under Capt. Robert Smith. Discharged on 8/10/1777.	
Ewell, Caleb	1st NC Regiment	1781, a Private under Capt. Anthony Sharpe for 12 months. Confined for "insolence and wilfull breaking of a pot." Discharged 4/15/1782 (4th NC Regiment).	
Ewell, Nathaniel	10th NC Regiment	8/29/1777, a Private, unit unknown. 9/9/1778, a known Private under Capt. John Ingles (2nd NC Regiment). Discharged on 9/15/1778.	
Ewell, Stephen	10th NC Regiment	6/6/1777, a Private, unit unknown.	
Ewell, William	3rd NC Regiment	7/20/1778, a Sergeant under Capt. Francis Child for 18 months. Probably the same man as	

Name	1st Unit	Year / Rank / Served Under / Notes	Known Battles
		directly below.	
Ewell, William	5th NC Regiment	4/20/1777, a Lieutenant under Capt. Reading Blount. Dropped from the rolls in Jan. 1778. aka William Hewell.	
Ewing, George	1st NC Regiment	4/28/1781, a Private under Capt. Alexander Brevard. Discharged on 4/28/1782 (3rd NC Regiment).	
Ewmen, Christopher	1st NC Regiment	4/25/1781, a Private under Capt. William Walton. Discharged on 5/25/1782.	
Ezell, Timothy	3rd NC Regiment	3/6/1782, a Private under Capt. Samuel Jones for 12 months. Enlisted at Salisbury, NC. Discharged in Dec. 1782 (1st NC Regiment) at Wilmington, NC. S38686.	
Faddles, James	1st NC Regiment	1782, a Private under Capt. Alexander Brevard for 18 months. Died on 12/17/1783.	
Fagety, James	9th NC Regiment	12/25/1776, a Private under Capt. Richard D. Cook. A Corporal in Nov. 1777. Back to Private in Jan. 1779, regiment unknown. Discharged on 1/27/1780.	
Fail, Thomas	10th NC Regiment	5/1/1777, a Private under Capt. Abraham Sheppard, Jr.	
Fair, Noah	2nd NC Regiment	9/9/1778, a Private in the Colonel's Company (Col. John Patten).	
Faircloth, John	1st NC Regiment	11/10/1778, a Private under Capt. Anthony Sharpe for nine months. Probably the same man as directly below.	
Faircloth, John	3rd NC Regiment	5/20/1778, a Sergeant under Lt./Capt. George "Gee" Bradley.	
Faircloth, John	10th NC Regiment	5/18/1777, a Private under Capt. Abraham Sheppard, Jr.	
Faircloth, William	10th NC Regiment	1/20/1778, a Lieutenant under Capt. William Shepherd. Retired 6/1/1778.	
Faison, James	5th NC Regiment	5/7/1778, a Private under Maj. Reading Blount.	
Faithful, William	2nd NC Regiment	Jan. 1781, a Private under Capt. Benjamin Carter. Discharged on 4/25/1782.	
Falconer, James		June 1778, a Private, unit and regiment unknown. A Corporal in Nov. 1778. A Sergeant on 7/15/1779.	
Fann, William	1st NC Regiment	4/12/1781, a Corporal under Lt./Capt. Benjamin Bailey. Discharged on 4/12/1782 (3rd NC Regiment).	
Fanning, Peter	5th NC Regiment	7/1/1779, a Private under Maj. Reading Blount. Deserted in Dec. 1779. aka Peter Fauning.	
Farmer, Benjamin	1st NC Regiment	6/1/1781, a Private under Capt. William Lytle. Discharged on 6/1/1782 (4th NC Regiment).	
Farmer, Henry	5th NC Regiment	6/7/1779, a Private under Maj. Reading Blount. Deserted in Dec. 1779.	
Farmer, James	1st NC Regiment	9/10/1782, a Private under Capt. Joshua Hadley for 18 months.	
Farmer, Jesse	1st NC Regiment	9/10/1782, a Private under Capt. Joshua Hadley for 18 months.	
Farmer, John	5th NC	7/20/1778, a Private under Maj. Reading	

Name	1ˢᵗ Unit	Year / Rank / Served Under / Notes	Known Battles
	Regiment	Blount. A Corporal in Oct. 1778. 8/1/1779, a Private under Maj. Reading Blount again. Deserted in Dec. 1779.	
Farmer, William	1ˢᵗ NC Regiment	6/1/1781, a Private under Capt. William Lytle. Discharged on 6/1/1782 (4th NC Regiment).	
Farmer, William	5ᵗʰ NC Regiment	4/29/1776, a Private under Capt. John Pugh Williams for 2-1/2 years. 9/9/1778, a known Private in the Major's Company (Maj. Hardy Murfree) (2nd NC Regiment). Discharged on 10/24/1778. Enlisted in Bertie County, NC. S35919.	Germantown (PA).
Farr, George	NC Light Dragoons	Oct.-Dec. 1777, a known Sergeant under Capt. Martin Phifer.	
Fair, James	4ᵗʰ NC Regiment	1775, a 2ⁿᵈ Lieutenant in NC Militia. 4/17/1776, a 2ⁿᵈ Lieutenant under Capt. Thomas Harris and Col. Thomas Polk. From Anson County. aka James Fair, James Fare, James Farr.	
Farrar, William	NC Light Dragoons	A Private for 2-1/2 years, Captain unknown. Discharged at Fort Pitt in 1781. Born 3/19/1751. From Granville County, NC. After his service, moved to Guilford County, what is now Rockingham County, NC. W3968.	
Farrow, Thomas	2ⁿᵈ NC Regiment	1782, a Private under Capt. Benjamin Carter. Deserted on 6/14/1783 (?).	
Farrow, Thomas	6ᵗʰ NC Regiment	1777, a Private under Capt. Francis Child. Died on 2/8/1778.	
Faucett, James	DQMG	1780, a Wagon Maker on the roll of Capt. Solomon Wood (NC Light Dragoons) - this seems to be for convenience only. A Wagon Maker under Col. Nicholas Long (Deputy QM General). Also on 8/23/1781. aka James Fawcett.	
Faucett, Robert	2ⁿᵈ NC Regiment	Sep. 1775, a Private under Capt. Henry Irwin Toole for six months. 11/20/1776, a Private under Capt. James Gee until his death. 11/12/1777, a Private under Capt. John Ingles. POW at the Fall of Charleston, soon escaped. From Edgecombe County, NC. aka Robert Fossett, Forsett, Foisett.	Great Bridge (VA), Brandywine Creek (PA), Germantown (PA), Siege of Charleston 1780 (SC).
Faulkner, Francis	4ᵗʰ NC Regiment	5/25/1776, a Private under Capt. Joseph Phillips. A Sergeant in Sep. 1777. Back to Private in June 1778. Discharged on 5/25/1779. aka Francis Faulkener.	
Fawn, William	3ʳᵈ NC Regiment	4/16/1776 or 4/15/1777 (two sources), a 2nd Lieutenant under Capt. Jacob Turner. 10/4/1777, a 1st Lieutenant. 3/10/1780, a Captain-Lieutenant under Lt. Col. Robert Mebane. POW at the Fall of Charleston, not exchanged until 11/26/1782. 6/1/1781, a full Captain. Retired 1/1/1783. aka William Fain. W7237.	Siege of Charleston 1780 (SC).
Fearle, Ansol	1ˢᵗ NC Regiment	4/6/1781, a Corporal under Capt. William Lytle. Dropped from the rolls sometime during 1781.	

374

Name	1st Unit	Year / Rank / Served Under / Notes	Known Battles
Fearless, Elisha	3rd NC Regiment	7/20/1778, a Private under Lt./Capt. George "Gee" Bradley. Dropped from the rolls in Oct. 1778.	
Feasley, John	3rd NC Regiment	4/23/1779, a known Private in the Lt. Colonel's Company (Lt. Col. Robert Mebane) led by Capt. George "Gee" Bradley. Died at West Point.	
Fee, Thomas	9th NC Regiment	A Private under Capt. Thomas McCrory. 9/8/1778, a known Private in the Lt. Colonel's Company (Lt. Col. Robert Mebane) (1st NC Regiment) led by Capt. Joshua Bowman. Deserted on 6/30/1779.	
Fellows, John	3rd NC Regiment	4/16/1776, a 2nd Lieutenant.	
Felps, Garret	2nd NC Regiment	1777, a Private under Capt. James Gee. Died on 1/30/1778.	
Felton, Samuel	4th NC Regiment	1782, a Corporal under Capt. William Lytle. Deserted on 3/31/1783 (?).	
Fenna, John	1st NC Regiment	5/19/1781, a Corporal under Capt. Robert Raiford. Sep. 1781, transferred to SC Line. From Gates County, NC. aka John Fauney, John Fanney. W4194.	
Fennell, Morris	5th NC Regiment	5/15/1778, a Private under Capt. Thomas White for nine months. Discharged 8/5/1779. Lt. William Lord stated that Fennell was a Sergeant. aka Maurice, Morice. W7257.	Stono Ferry (SC).
Fennell, Nicholas	1st NC Regiment	Earlier in NC Militia. 1778, a Private under Capt. Anthony Sharpe for nine months. Born 2/16/1762. W3970.	Stono Ferry (SC).
Fenner, Richard	2nd NC Regiment	1777, a Paymaster. 1/10/1780, an Ensign under Capt. Robert Fenner, his brother. POW at the Fall of Charleston, exchanged on 6/14/1781. 5/12/1781, a Lieutenant. Served till the end of the war. aka Richard Finner. W789.	Siege of Charleston 1780 (SC).
Fenner, Robert	2nd NC Regiment	A Private, unit unknown. POW at the Fall of Charleston, SC.	Siege of Charleston 1780 (SC).
Fenner, Robert	2nd NC Regiment	5/2/1776, a 2nd Lieutenant. 5/20/1777, a Captain under Lt. Col. John Patten. POW at the Fall of Charleston. Exchanged prior to 1/24/1782. A brevet Major on 9/30/1783. Served to the end of the war.	Brandywine Creek (PA), Germantown (PA), Monmouth (NJ), Siege of Charleston 1780 (SC).
Fenner, William	2nd NC Regiment	9/1/1775, a 1st Lieutenant. 5/1/1776, a Captain under Col. Alexander Martin. Promoted to Major on 10/24/1777 and transferred to 7th NC Regiment. Retired 6/1/1778.	Brandywine Creek (PA), Germantown (PA).
Fentice, Moses	3rd NC Regiment	1781, a Private under Capt. Clement Hall for 12 months. Discharged 7/10/1782 (2nd NC Regiment).	
Fenton, Joshua	7th NC Regiment	1777, a Private under Capt. Thomas Brickell. 2/26/1778, a known Private under Capt. Howell Tatum (1st NC Regiment). Died on 3/24/1778.	

Name	1st Unit	Year / Rank / Served Under / Notes	Known Battles
Fenton, Thomas	10th NC Regiment	5/14/1777, a Private under Capt. John Jarvis for three years. 9/8/1778, a known Private in the Major's Company (Maj. John Baptiste Ashe) (1st NC Regiment). 3/12/1779, re-enlisted for the duration of the war in the same unit. 1780, a Private under Capt. William Lytle.	
Fereby, Robert	3rd NC Regiment	1781, a Sergeant under Capt. Clement Hall. Discharged on 7/10/1782 (2nd NC Regiment).	
Fergus, James	1st NC Regiment	5/24/1776, a Surgeon. Resigned April 1777. Surgeon's Mate in 1st NC Regiment again on 2/21/1782. 4/24/1782, back in 2nd NC Regiment. A Surgeon again on 8/20/1782, till the end of the war. From Wilmington, NC. aka Janus Fergus, John Fergus.	
Ferguson, John	1st NC Regiment	9/8/1778, a known Private under Capt. James Read.	
Ferns, William	2nd NC Regiment	6/28/1777, a Private, unit unknown. 9/9/1778, a known Private under Capt. John Ingles. aka William Ferus.	
Ferrebee, Joseph	10th NC Regiment	5/5/1777, a Lieutenant under Capt. John Jarvis. Dropped from the rolls in June 1778. From Currituck County, NC. aka Joseph Ferebee.	
Ferrebee, William	7th NC Regiment	11/28/1776, a 2nd Lieutenant under Capt. John Poynter, then under Capt. John Macon. Transferred to 4th NC Regiment on 6/1/1778. Promoted to Captain on 8/1/1781. Retired mid-1782. From Edenton District. aka William Ferrabee.	
Ferrell, Clement	4th NC Regiment	1782, a Private under Capt. William Lytle for 18 months.	
Ferrell, Enoch	10th NC Regiment	5/8/1777, a Private under Capt. James Wilson for three years. 9/8/1778, a known Private in the Major's Company (Maj. John Baptiste Ashe) (1st NC Regiment). aka Enoch Ferril.	
Ferrell, Gabriel	3rd NC Regiment	1781, a Private under Capt. Edward Yarborough. Dropped from the rolls 4/1/1782. Received clothing on 5/24/1782. He claims he was under Capt. Tilghman Dixon in Oct. 1780, but Capt. Dixon was a POW at that time. From Caswell County, NC. R3514A.	
Ferrell, James	1st NC Regiment	5/25/1781, a Private under Capt. Thomas Donoho. Discharged 5/25/1782.	
Ferrell, James	9th NC Regiment	12/15/1777, a Private under Capt. Thomas McCrory. A Corporal in Jan. 1778. Back to Private in June 1778. 9/8/1778, a known Private in the Lt. Colonel's Company (Lt. Col. Robert Mebane) (1st NC Regiment) led by Capt. Joshua Bowman. 5/25/1781, joined under Maj. Thomas Donoho (1st NC Regiment) - retired 5/25/1782. Enlisted in Wake County, NC. aka James Ferrill. W23029.	
Ferrell, John	2nd NC Regiment	March 1782, a Private under Capt. Tilghman Dixon for two three-month tours. Sources say this was in 1781, but descriptions of events	

Name	1st Unit	Year / Rank / Served Under / Notes	Known Battles
		clearly indicate 1782. From Caswell County, NC. Earlier in NC Militia.	
Ferrell, John	5th NC Regiment	Jan. 1779, a Private under Capt. Philip Taylor.	
Ferrell, Luke	5th NC Regiment	Jan. 1779, a Private under Capt. Thomas White.	
Ferrell, Luke L..	5th NC Regiment	Jan. 1779, a Lieutenant under Capt. Thomas White.	
Ferrell, Micajah	9th NC Regiment	11/28/1776, an Ensign under Capt. Joseph J. Wade. Resigned in Nov. 1778. From Wake County, NC. Later in NC Militia. aka Micajah Farrall. S31676.	
Ferrell, William	3rd NC Regiment	7/20/1778, a Private under Lt./Capt. George "Gee" Bradley for nine months. Enlisted at Kinston - Dobbs County at the time. S6831.	
Ferrell, William	8th NC Regiment	9/8/1777, an Ensign. 10/10/1777, a 2nd Lieutenant. Transferred to 2nd NC Regiment on 6/1/1778 under Capt. John Craddock. Killed on 5/10/1780 during Siege of Charleston, SC. aka William Ferrill.	Siege of Charleston 1780 (SC).
Fields, John	2nd NC Regiment	9/20/1775, a Sergeant under Capt. John Armstrong. Discharged 9/20/1776 at Salisbury, NC. From what is now Rockingham County, NC. Born 4/2/1752 in Hanover County, VA. W3971.	
Fields, John	3rd NC Regiment	7/20/1778, a Private under Capt. Francis Child for nine months.	
Fields, John	3rd NC Regiment	9/10/1782, a Private under Capt. Benjamin Bailey for 18 months.	
Fields, Lewis	2nd NC Regiment	1777, a Private under Capt. Clement Hall. Deserted in Aug. 1777. Rejoined in Sep. 1778. Deserted again in Nov. 1778. A Wagon Master on 8/22/1779. Dropped from the rolls in Oct. 1779.	
Fields, Timothy		1777, a Private, regiment and unit unknown. Died in Sep. 1779.	
Fields, William	2nd NC Regiment	Sep. 1775, a Private under Capt. William Knox for six months. Later in NC Militia and wounded in the battle of Stono Ferry (SC), Captain unknown. S25088.	
Fight, Conrad	3rd NC Regiment	1781, a Private under Capt. Clement Hall. Discharged on 12/27/1782 (2nd NC Regiment). From Rowan County, NC. W3973.	
Fikes, James	1st NC Regiment	1777, a Sergeant under Capt. Lawrence Thompson. Died in Jan. 1778.	
Fillips, John	10th NC Regiment	8/26/1777, a Private under Capt. Abraham Sheppard, Jr. Dropped from the rolls in June 1778.	
Fillips, Joshua	10th NC Regiment	8/26/1777, a Private under Capt. Abraham Sheppard, Jr. Dropped from the rolls in June 1778.	
Filman, William	4th NC Regiment	1781, a Musician under Capt. George Dougherty for 12 months. Discharged on 5/25/1782.	

Name	1st Unit	Year / Rank / Served Under / Notes	Known Battles
Filsby, Richard	4th NC Regiment	2/14/1777, a Musician under Capt. John Nelson for three years. A 6/1/1778, a Private under Capt. Griffith John McRee (1st NC Regiment). Re-enlisted in Oct. 1778. Discharged in Feb. 1780. On some rolls as Richard Philsby.	
Finch, Isham	3rd NC Regiment	7/20/1778, a Private under Capt. John Baker for nine months. Discharged in May 1779 at Halifax, NC. Enlisted in Nash County, NC. Later in NC Militia. aka Isom Finch. S41538.	
Finley, Abraham	7th NC Regiment	12/23/1776, a Private under Capt. Joseph Walker. 9/8/1778, a known Private under Capt. Tilghman Dixon (1st NC Regiment).	
Finley, Samuel	4th NC Regiment	1778, a Private under Capt. John Nelson. R3556.	
Finney, Thomas	2nd NC Regiment	1777, a Sergeant Major under Capt. John Armstrong. Promoted to Ensign on 11/12/1777. POW at the Fall of Charleston, exchanged 6/14/1781. 1/23/1781, a Lieutenant under Capt. Thomas Armstrong. Served until the end of the war.	Siege of Charleston 1780 (SC), Eutaw Springs (SC).
Fisher, James	10th NC Regiment	5/5/1777, a Private under Capt. John Jarvis for three years. 9/8/1778, a known Private in the Major's Company (Maj. John Baptiste Ashe) (1st NC Regiment). 3/12/1779, re-enlisted for the duration of the war in the same unit. 1780, a Private under Capt. William Lytle. Deserted on 2/6/1780.	
Fisher, John	3rd NC Regiment	7/20/1778, a Private under Capt. John Baker for nine months.	
Fisher, William	5th NC Regiment	3/1/1779, a Private under Capt. Joseph Montford. Discharged on 12/1/1779.	
Fist, Samuel	1st NC Regiment	1781, a Private under Capt. William Walton.	
Fitzgerald, John	DQMG	1780, a Gunstocker on the roll of Capt. Solomon Wood (NC Light Dragoons) - this seems to be for convenience only. An Artificer under Col. Nicholas Long (Deputy QM General). Made Gunstocks. Also on 8/23/1781.	
Fleetwood, Francis	10th NC Regiment	A Private, unit unknown. Deserted on 7/15/1778, regiment unknown.	
Fleming, James	1st NC Regiment	6/14/1781, a Private under Capt. Thomas Donoho. Discharged on 6/14/1782. aka James Flemming. W8819.	
Fleming, John	3rd NC Regiment	7/20/1778, a QM Sergeant for nine months.	
Fleming, Joseph	NC Artillery	8/12/1776, a Bombardier under Capt. John Vance as NC Provincial Troops. 7/10/1777, on Continental Line. 11/16/1777, under Capt. John Kingsbury. 5/1/1778, in same unit. 9/16/1778, in same unit - Sick in camp. Dropped from the rolls in Jan. 1779.	
Fleming, Samuel	2nd NC Regiment	Sep. 1775, a Private under Capt. William Knox. Discharged April 1776 in Wilmington, NC. Later in NC Militia. Born 4/1/1757 in Rowan	Great Cane Brake (SC), Snow

Name	1st Unit	Year / Rank / Served Under / Notes	Known Battles
		County, NC. S1952.	Campaign (SC).
Fleming, William	1st NC Regiment	6/14/1781, a Private under Capt. Thomas Donoho. Dropped from the rolls sometime during 1781. aka William Flemming.	
Fletcher, John	NC Artillery	5/26/1778, a Matross under Capt. Thomas Clark. Also on 9/9/1778. Deserted on 12/1/1778. Discharged on 2/28/1779 (?).	
Fletcher, Thomas	10th NC Regiment	5/5/1777, a Private under Capt. John Jarvis for three years. 9/8/1778, a known Sergeant under Maj. John Baptiste Ashe (1st NC Regiment). Jan. 1779, a Private under Capt. William Lytle (5th NC Regiment).	
Fletcher, William	10th NC Regiment	5/5/1777, a Sergeant under Capt. John Jarvis for three years. 9/8/1778, a known Sergeant under Maj. John Baptiste Ashe (1st NC Regiment). Died on 1/20/1779.	
Flewellin, William	3rd NC Regiment	May 1776, a Wagon Master under Capt. Pinketham Eaton, Capt. William Brinkley, and Capt. Jacob Turner for 2-1/2 years. From Halifax County, NC. Later in NC Militia. S3366.	Ft. Moultrie #1 (SC).
Fling, Thomas	3rd NC Regiment	6/20/1779, a Private under Capt. George "Gee" Bradley for 18 months.	
Flinn, David	6th NC Regiment	1777, a Private under Capt. Francis Child. 6/1/1778, a Private under Capt. Griffith John McRee (1st NC Regiment). Deserted 9/7/1778.	
Flinn, John	2nd NC Regiment	5/21/1781, a Private under Capt. Tilghman Dixon. Discharged on 5/21/1782 at Camden, SC. Received clothing on 5/24/1782. Enlisted while living in Caswell County, NC. Earlier in NC Militia. W4953. aka John Flyn, Flynn.	Eutaw Springs (SC).
Flinn, William	1st NC Regiment	5/14/1778, a Private under Lt. William Lytle. Died on 7/6/1778.	
Flood, Alexander	2nd NC Regiment	7/4/1777, a Private, unit unknown. 9/9/1778, a known Private in the Major's Company (Maj. Hardy Murfree).	
Flood, Benjamin	10th NC Regiment	7/10/1777, a Private, unit unknown.	
Flood, Enoch	2nd NC Regiment	4/12/1781, a Private under Capt. Benjamin Carter. Discharged on 4/10/1782.	
Flood, Frederick	4th NC Regiment	1782, a Private under Capt. William Lytle for 18 months. aka Frederick Floor.	
Flood, Samuel	2nd NC Regiment	1782, a Private under Capt. Benjamin Carter for 18 months.	
Flood, William	10th NC Regiment	7/5/1777, a Private under Capt. Abraham Shepard, Jr. 9/10/1778, a known Private under Capt. Thomas Armstrong (2nd NC Regiment).	
Flora, Lazarus	10th NC Regiment	9/4/1777, a Private under Capt. John Jarvis for three years. 9/8/1778, a known Private in the Major's Company (Maj. John Baptiste Ashe) (1st NC Regiment). From Currituck County, NC. W3975.	
Flora, Richard	10th NC Regiment	8/14/1777, a Private under Capt. John Jarvis for three years. 9/8/1778, a known Private in the	

Name	1st Unit	Year / Rank / Served Under / Notes	Known Battles
		Major's Company (Maj. John Baptiste Ashe) (1st NC Regiment). A Private under Capt. William Lytle, dates unknown.	
Florida, Francis	1st NC Regiment	1782, a Private under Capt. Peter Bacot. Deserted on 6/27/1783 (?).	
Flounder, Robert	2nd NC Regiment	1/1/1776 (?), a 1st Lieutenant under Capt. William Fenner. Promoted to Captain on 10/4/1777. Paymaster 6/1/1778. Retired 1/1/1783.	
Flowers, William	1st NC Regiment	1781, a Private under Capt. William Armstrong. Discharged on 9/15/1782 (3rd NC Regiment).	
Floyd, Buckner	3rd NC Regiment	7/20/1778, a Private in the Lt. Colonel's Company (Lt. Col. William Lee Davidson) led by Lt./Capt. George "Gee" Bradley. 4/23/1779, a known Private in the Lt. Colonel's Company (Lt. Col. Robert Mebane) led by Capt. George "Gee" Bradley.	
Floyd, John	3rd NC Regiment	7/20/1778, a Private in the Lt. Colonel's Company (Lt. Col. William Lee Davidson) led by Lt./Capt. George "Gee" Bradley. 4/23/1779, a known Private in the Lt. Colonel's Company (Lt. Col. Robert Mebane) led by Capt. George "Gee" Bradley. Died at Philadelphia Hospital.	
Flury, William	5th NC Regiment	1777, a Sergeant under Capt. Benjamin Stedman. Died on 3/16/1778.	
Fly, Charles	3rd NC Regiment	1781, a Private under Capt. Edward Yarborough. Dropped from the rolls 4/1/1782.	
Foakes, Yelverton	1st NC Regiment	2/3/1776, a Lieutenant and Regimental QM. Resigned 8/1/1776. aka Yelverton Fowkes.	Moore's Creek Bridge [4].
Foard, Hezekiah	5th NC Regiment	4/20/1777, a Chaplain. Retired 6/1/1778. aka Hezekiah Ford.	
Foard, John	3rd NC Regiment	9/1/1778, a Sergeant in the Lt. Colonel's Company (Lt. Col. William Lee Davidson) led by Lt./Capt. George "Gee" Bradley. 11/3/1778, an Ensign. 3/29/1780, a Lieutenant. aka John Ford.	
Foley, John	4th NC Regiment	1782, a Private under Capt. William Lytle for 18 months.	
Folks, James	3rd NC Regiment	1781, a Private under Capt. Clement Hall. Died on 9/14/1782 (2nd NC Regiment).	
Folks, James	3rd NC Regiment	1/1/1782, a Private under Capt. Samuel Jones for 12 months.	
Fontain, Jesse	3rd NC Regiment	1779, a Private under Capt. Michael Quinn. Discharged in Dec. 1779.	
Fonvielle, Isaac	2nd NC Regiment	4/21/1777, a Private, unit unknown. 9/9/1778, a known Private in the Lt. Colonel's Company (Lt. Col. Selby Harney). aka Isaac Fonville.	
Fonville, Isaac	10th NC Regiment	4/21/1777, a Corporal under Capt. Silas Stevenson.	
Fooks, James	5th NC Regiment	1777, a Private under Capt. William Caswell. Dropped from the rolls in Oct. 1777.	
Fooks, John	5th NC Regiment	5/24/1776, a Private under Capt. William Caswell. 9/9/1778, a known Private under Capt. Robert Fenner (2nd NC Regiment). Discharged	

Name	1st Unit	Year / Rank / Served Under / Notes	Known Battles
		on 12/1/1778. aka John Fook.	
Foorms, Arthur	2nd NC Regiment	7/12/1777, a Private, unit unknown. 9/9/1778, a known Private in the Major's Company (Maj. Hardy Murfree).	
Forbes, Joshua	1st NC Regiment	8/18/1776, rank and unit unknown. 2/26/1778, a known Private under Capt. Howell Tatum. 9/8/1778, a known Private under Capt. Howell Tatum. Assigned to His Excy's Guard.	
Forbes, William	1st NC Regiment	4/24/1781, a Corporal under Lt./Capt. Benjamin Bailey. Discharged on 4/24/1782 (3rd NC Regiment).	
Forbus, Joshua	7th NC Regiment	1777, a Sergeant under Capt. Joseph Walker. Transferred to His Excellency's Guards in Apr. 1778. Discharged on 12/18/1779.	
Forbush, Robert	1st NC Regiment	1782, a Private under Capt. Peter Bacot. Died on 6/15/1783.	
Ford, Abraham	10th NC Regiment	5/10/1777, a Private under Capt. James Wilson for three years. 9/8/1778, a known Private in the Major's Company (Maj. Griffith John McRee) (1st NC Regiment) - sick in camp on that date.	
Ford, Elias	7th NC Regiment	4/11/1777, a Private under Capt. John McGlaughan. A Corporal in Sep. 1777. 2/26/1778, a known Private under Capt. Howell Tatum (1st NC Regiment). 9/8/1777, a known Corporal under Capt. Howell Tatum. A Sergeant on 11/7/1778. aka Elias Fort.	
Ford, Lewis	5th NC Regiment	6/18/1779, a Private under Capt. Joseph Montford for 18 months.	
Ford, William	9th NC Regiment	1777, a Private under Capt. Richard D. Cook. Dropped from the rolls in Feb. 1778.	
Forehand, Jarvis	3rd NC Regiment	1781, a Private under Capt. Clement Hall. Discharged on 4/21/1782 (2nd NC Regiment).	
Foreman, Caleb	8th NC Regiment	11/28/1776, a Lieutenant under Capt. William Gurley (who refused to serve). Immediately placed under Capt. Robert Raiford. Dropped from the rolls In Jan. 1778. From Hyde County, NC.	
Forms, John	8th NC Regiment	5/14/1776 (?), a Private under Capt. Michael Quinn. Dropped from the rolls sometime during 1779 (3rd NC Regiment).	
Fornes, William	10th NC Regiment	6/28/1777, a Private under Capt. Silas Stevenson.	
Forrester, Thomas	6th NC Regiment	1777, a Private under Capt. Griffith John McRee. Killed at the battle of Germantown, PA on 10/4/1777.	Germantown (PA).
Forsyth, Hugh	4th NC Regiment	1779, a Private under Col. James Armstrong for nine months. W7315.	
Fortner, Francis	1st NC Regiment	Enlisted 5/25/1776, unit unknown. 9/8/1778, a known Private under Capt. James Read.	
Fortune, William	4th NC Regiment	1782, a Private under Capt. Thomas Evans. 12/1/1782, transferred - to where unknown.	
Fosdick, West	3rd NC Regiment	1778, a Private under Capt. George "Gee" Bradley. Deserted in Sep. 1779.	
Fossett,	9th NC	1777, a Private under Capt. Thomas McCrory.	

Name	1st Unit	Year / Rank / Served Under / Notes	Known Battles
Edward	Regiment	Dropped from the rolls in June 1778.	
Foster, Daniel	DQMG	1780, a Wagoner under Col. Nicholas Long (Deputy QM General). Said to be an ex-Continental soldier of White's Corps (?).	
Foster, David	1st NC Regiment	1782, a Private under Capt. Peter Bacot. Deserted on 6/19/1783 (?).	
Foster, David	3rd NC Regiment	7/20/1778, a Private under Capt. John Baker for nine months.	
Foster, Richard	4th NC Regiment	1781, a Private under Capt. George Dougherty for 12 months. Discharged on 5/25/1782.	
Foster, Robert	10th NC Regiment	9/10/1777, a Private under Capt. John Jarvis for three years. 9/8/1778, a known Private in the Major's Company (Maj. John Baptiste Ashe) (1st NC Regiment) - sick in camp on that date. A Private under Capt. William Lytle, dates unknown.	
Foster, William	1st NC Regiment	5/2/1781, a Corporal under Lt./Capt. Benjamin Bailey for 12 months. Discharged 5/2/1782 (3rd NC Regiment). 8/27/1782, a Private again under Capt. Benjamin Bailey (3rd NC Regiment) for 18 months.	
Foster, William	3rd NC Regiment	6/15/1779, a Private under Capt. Kedar Ballard for 18 months.	
Fountain, David	1st NC Regiment	1781, a Private under Capt. Robert Raiford. Discharged 6/1/1782.	
Fountain, James	1st NC Regiment	4/12/1781, a Private under Capt. William Lytle. A Corporal in Jan. 1782. Discharged on 4/12/1782 (4th NC Regiment). aka Joseph Fountain.	
Fountain, Jesse	4th NC Regiment	April 1779, a Sergeant under Capt. Joseph T. Rhodes.	
Fountain, Solomon	3rd NC Regiment	7/20/1778, a Private under Capt. Kedar Ballard for nine months. Enlisted at Tarborough, NC. Discharged at Philadelphia, PA. From Edgecombe County, NC. S41544.	
Fowler, Abraham	5th NC Regiment	5/6/1776, a Private under Capt. Reading Blount.	
Fowler, Abram	2nd NC Regiment	9/9/1778, under Capt. Benjamin Andrew Coleman.	
Fowler, Ashly		A Private, regiment, unit, and dates unknown.	
Fowler, Daniel	1st NC Regiment	6/1/1776, a Private under Lt./Capt. William Armstrong for 2-1/2 years. 9/8/1778, a known Private under Capt. John Sumner (1st NC Regiment). Discharged on 6/28/1779.	
Fowler, George	4th NC Regiment	1782, a Private under Capt. Thomas Evans for 18 months.	
Fowler, John	1st NC Regiment	Earlier in NC Militia. 1776, a Private under Capt. Alfred Moore. 1777, back in NC Militia. From Duplin County, NC. S16809.	
Fowler, William	9th NC Regiment	1777, a Private under Capt. Thomas McCrory. Died on 3/16/1778.	
Fox, Francis	8th NC Regiment	2/8/1777, a Private under Capt. John Walsh. 9/9/1778, a known Private under Capt. Robert	Brandywine Creek (PA),

382

Name	1st Unit	Year / Rank / Served Under / Notes	Known Battles
		Fenner (2nd NC Regiment). Discharged on 2/20/1780 at Wilmington, NC. Enlisted in Duplin County, NC. S41543.	Germantown (PA).
Fox, Joseph	3rd NC Regiment	1781, a Sergeant under Capt. Clement Hall. Discharged on 7/10/1782 (2nd NC Regiment).	
Fox, William	7th NC Regiment	1/11/1777, a Sergeant under Capt. John Poynter. Dropped from the rolls in May 1778.	
Foxa, John	2nd NC Regiment	1777, a Private under Capt. James Gee.	
Foy, Patrick	1st NC Regiment	6/29/1777, a Private under Capt. William Lytle for three years. 9/8/1778, a known Private under Capt. John Sumner - sick in camp on that date. A Corporal in Nov. 1778. Back to Private in Jan. 1779. 3/12/1779, re-enlisted for the duration of the war as a Private under Capt. John Sumner.	
Frailey, John	4th NC Regiment	1782, a Corporal under Capt. Anthony Sharpe for 18 months.	
Francis, Anthony	4th NC Regiment	1782, a Private under Capt. Thomas Evans for 18 months.	
Francis, John		Nov. 1779, a Private, regiment and unit unknown.	
Francis, Samuel	2nd NC Regiment	1782, a Private under Capt. Benjamin Carter. Deserted on 4/10/1783 (?).	
Francisco, Thomas	9th NC Regiment	1777, a Private under Capt. Richard D. Cook. Died on 3/23/1778.	
Franklin, John	6th NC Regiment	/1/1777, a Fife Major, unit unknown. A Musician in Nov. 1779. Deserted on 12/11/1779.	
Franks, John	NC Artillery	10/20/1777, a Cadet under Capt. John Vance. 11/16/1777, a Cadet under Capt. John Kingsbury. 5/1/1778, in same unit. 9/16/1778, in same unit. Probably a Matross, recorded thusly for April '78.	
Frazer, Alexander	7th NC Regiment	12/8/1776, a Sergeant under Capt. Thomas Brickell. Deserted in Aug. 1777.	
Frazier, Thomas	3rd NC Regiment	7/20/1778, a Private under Capt. Michael Quinn for nine months. Discharged at Halifax, NC. Drafted in Craven County, NC. Later in NC Militia and aboard several privateers. W34.	
Frazzle, Daniel	5th NC Regiment	4/23/1776, a Sergeant under Capt. John Pugh Williams. A Private in April 1778. Discharged in Oct. 1778. aka Daniel Frazle.	
Freazer, Daniel	1st NC Regiment	1781, a Private under Capt. Anthony Sharpe for 12 months. Discharged 9/1/1782 (4th NC Regiment).	
Frederick, Christian	1st NC Regiment	4/28/1781, a Private and a Corporal under Capt. Alexander Brevard. Discharged on 4/28/1782 (3rd NC Regiment).	
Free, Thomas	1st NC Regiment	9/8/1778, a known Private in the Lt. Colonel's Company (Lt. Col. Robert Mebane) led by Capt. Joshua Bowman.	
Freeman, Aaron	2nd NC Regiment	8/1/1781, a Private under Capt. Thomas Armstrong for one year. Discharged in August	

Name	1st Unit	Year / Rank / Served Under / Notes	Known Battles
		1782 at Ashley Hill, SC. From Dobbs County, NC. Born on 1/30/1758 in Bertie County, NC. Did Sergeant duty - not sure if he was promoted to Sergeant or not. W8833.	
Freeman, Daniel	4th NC Regiment	5/3/1776, a Private under Capt. James Williams for 2-1/2 years. 9/8/1778, a Private in the Colonel's Company (Col. Thomas Clark) (1st NC Regiment) let by Capt. John Gambier Scull. Discharged on 11/10/1778. Earlier in NC Militia. S31681.	Brandywine Creek (PA), Germantown (PA).
Freeman, Edward	1st NC Regiment	1781, a Corporal under Capt. Alexander Brevard. Discharged on 7/11/1782 (3rd NC Regiment).	
Freeman, Howell	2nd NC Regiment	4/25/1781, a Private under Capt. Benjamin Carter. Discharged on 4/25/1782. From Franklin County, NC. Earlier in NC Militia. W19296.	
Freeman, Jesse	3rd NC Regiment	7/20/1778, a Private under Capt. Michael Quinn for nine months.	
Freeman, Moses	2nd NC Regiment	4/25/1782, a Private under Capt. Benjamin Carter for 12 months.	
Freeman, Nathaniel	6th NC Regiment	1777, a Corporal under Capt. George Dougherty. A Private in Jan. 1778. 6/1/1778, a Wagoner under Capt. Griffith John McRee (1st NC Regiment). Discharged, and died on the way home at Williamsburg, VA, date unknown.	
Freeman, Roger	2nd NC Regiment	1/1/1782, a Private under Capt. Benjamin Andrew Coleman for 12 months.	
Freeman, Samuel	7th NC Regiment	5/29/1777, a Private under Capt. Joseph Walker. 9/8/1778, a known Private under Capt. Tilghman Dixon (1st NC Regiment). POW at the Fall of Charleston, SC. Earlier in NC Militia, unit unknown.	Siege of Charleston 1780 (SC).
Freeman, William	3rd NC Regiment	7/20/1778, a Private under Capt. Francis Child for nine months. Enlisted at Halifax, NC. From Bertie County, NC. Earlier and later, in NC Militia. W10042.	
Frieze, John	1st NC Regiment	4/28/1781, a Private under Capt. Griffith John McRee. Discharged on 4/28/1782.	
Frost, Miller	3rd NC Regiment	1/1/1782, a Private under Capt. Benjamin Bailey for 12 months.	
Fryar, Josiah	2nd NC Regiment	1777, a Private under Capt. James Gee. Died on 6/18/1778.	
Fryar, William	3rd NC Regiment	5/3/1776, a Private under Capt. James Emmett. 9/9/1778, a Private under Capt. John Ingles. Discharged on 11/10/1778.	
Fryar, Willis	1st NC Regiment	9/10/1782, a Private under Capt. Joshua Hadley for 18 months.	
Fulcher, Cason	4th NC Regiment	1782, a Private under Capt. Thomas Evans for 18 months.	
Fulkes, William	10th NC Regiment	5/18/1777, a Private under Capt. Abraham Sheppard, Jr.	
Fuller, George	2nd NC Regiment	5/2/1781, a Private under Capt. Tilghman Dixon for 12 months. Discharged 5/21/1782 (1st NC Regiment) at Charlotte, NC. Received clothing	Eutaw Springs (SC).

Name	1st Unit	Year / Rank / Served Under / Notes	Known Battles
		on 5/24/1782. Enlisted in Caswell County, NC. S38715.	
Fuller, John	1st NC Regiment	1782, a Private under Capt. Alexander Brevard for 18 months.	
Fuller, William	4th NC Regiment	5/20/1778, a Private under Lt./Capt. Benjamin Carter.	
Furguson, Isom	1st NC Regiment	6/11/1781, a Private under Capt. William Lytle. Discharged on 6/21/1782 (4th NC Regiment).	
Furguson, John	1st NC Regiment	1777, a Private under Capt. Henry "Hal" Dixon.	
Furguson, Peter	3rd NC Regiment	8/1/1782, a Private under Capt. Benjamin Bailey for 18 months.	
Furguson, Robert	1st NC Regiment	6/11/1781, a Private under Capt. William Lytle. Discharged on 6/21/1782 (4th NC Regiment).	
Furnavil, Richard	2nd NC Regiment	1782, a Private under Capt. Benjamin Carter for 18 months. aka Richard Farnavil.	
Furney, Peter	3rd NC Regiment	6/1/1779, a Private under Capt. George "Gee" Bradley. Dropped from the rolls in Oct. 1779. From Dobbs County, NC.	
Fussell, Samuel	1st NC Regiment	8/28/1778, a Private under Capt. Anthony Sharpe. Died on 4/5/1779.	
Futch, Martin	4th NC Regiment	Dec. 1782, a Private under Capt. William Lytle. Deserted on 6/11/1783 (?).	
Futrell, Dempsey	1st NC Regiment	4/12/1781, a Private under Capt. William Lytle. Deserted on 7/7/1781. aka Dempsey Futril.	
Futrell, Joseph	3rd NC Regiment	7/20/1778, a Private in the Lt. Colonel's Company (Lt. Col. William Lee Davidson) led by Lt./Capt. George "Gee" Bradley. 4/23/1779, a known Private in the Lt. Colonel's Company (Lt. Col. Robert Mebane) led by Capt. George "Gee" Bradley.	
Futrell, Joshua	2nd NC Regiment	1782, a Private under Capt. Benjamin Carter for 18 months.	
Gaddy, Thomas	5th NC Regiment	5/21/1776, a Private under Lt./Capt. Henry Darnell. A Corporal in Aug. 1777. Back to Private in June 1778. 9/9/1778, a known Private under Capt. Benjamin Andrew Coleman (2nd NC Regiment). 3/12/1779, re-enlisted under Capt. Benjamin Williams (2nd NC Regiment). aka Thomas Geddy.	Ft. Lafayette (NY).
Gainer, Samuel	5th NC Regiment	1777, a Private under Capt. Henry Darnell. 9/9/1778, under Capt. Benjamin Andrew Coleman (2nd NC Regiment).	
Gainer, Stephen	3rd NC Regiment	8/1/1778, a Private under Lt./Capt. George "Gee" Bradley.	
Gale, George	3rd NC Regiment	6/25/1779, a Private under Capt. George "Gee" Bradley. Died in Dec. 1779.	
Galespy, David	1st NC Regiment	1781, a Private under Capt. William Armstrong. Discharged on 7/1/1782 (3rd NC Regiment). aka David Galesby.	
Gallamore, John	1st NC Regiment	6/14/1781, a Corporal under Capt. Thomas Donoho. A Private in Jan. 1782. Discharged on 6/14/1782. Joined Lee's Legion (VA). From Granville County, NC. Earlier in NC Militia.	

Name	1st Unit	Year / Rank / Served Under / Notes	Known Battles
		aka John Gallimore. W10051.	
Gallop, Isaac	2nd NC Regiment	5/22/1777, a Private under Capt. Edward Vail, Jr, then Capt. Manlove Tarrant for three years. 9/9/1778, a known Private in the Colonel's Company (Col. John Patten) led by Capt. John Craddock. POW at the Fall of Charleston, escaped. From Camden County, NC. S41560.	Brandywine Creek (PA), Monmouth (NJ), Siege of Charleston (SC).
Gallop, Matthew	2nd NC Regiment	1777, a Corporal under Capt. James Gee. A Sergeant in June 1778. 9/8/1778, a known Sergeant under Capt. John Ingles. POW at Ft. Lafayette on 6/1/1779. Back to Private in Nov. 1779. Deserted on 12/6/1779.	Ft. Lafayette (NY).
Gamalion, Abraham	3rd NC Regiment	7/20/1778, a Private under Lt./Capt. George "Gee" Bradley for nine months.	
Gamble, Edmund	1st NC Regiment	3/28/1776, an Ensign. 7/7/1776, a 2nd Lieutenant. 1/20/1777, a 1st Lieutenant under Capt. Lawrence Thompson. 6/1/1778, transferred to NC Light Dragoons under Capt. Cosmo Medici, which were removed from the NC Continental Line in January 1779. January 1779, in the NC State Troops. aka Edmund Gambell, Edward Gamble.	
Gamble, Edmund	1st NC Regiment	1781, a known QM stationed at Salisbury. Probably the same man as directly above.	
Gambling, James	2nd NC Regiment	12/14/1776, a Corporal under Capt. Edward Vail, Jr., then under Capt. James Gee for three years. 12/21/1777, a Private in the Colonel's Company (Col. John Patten) led by Capt. John Craddock. POW at Ft. Lafayette, NY on 6/1/1779 for two months and ten days. Rejoined in Nov. 1779. Discharged on 1/30/1780 at Halifax, NC. aka James Gamberlin. W460.	Brandywine Creek (PA), Germantown (PA), Monmouth (NJ), Ft. Lafayette (NY).
Gamewell, William	10th NC Regiment	6/13/1777, a Private under Capt. John Jarvis for three years. 9/8/1778, a known Private in the Major's Company (Maj. John Baptiste Ashe) (1st NC Regiment) - sick in camp on that date. aka William Gamwell, William Gammell.	
Gammon, Jesse	1st NC Regiment	July 1782, a Private under Capt. Peter Bacot. Discharged 7/7/1783 at Wilmington, NC. Earlier in NC Militia. From Halifax County, NC. aka Jesse Gammond. W1.	
Gammon, Joshua	DQMG	1780, a Canteen Maker on the roll of Capt. Solomon Wood (NC Light Dragoons) - this seems to be for convenience only. An Artificer under Col. Nicholas Long (Deputy QM General). Made Canteens. Also on 8/23/1781. aka Joshua Gammond.	
Gandy, Ephraim	1st NC Regiment	1782, a Private under Capt. Peter Bacot for 18 months.	
Gandy, John	1st NC Regiment	2/20/1777, a Musician under Capt. Lawrence Thompson. A Private in Feb. 1778.	
Dempsey, Gardner		1778, a Private, regiment and unit unknown. POW at Ft. LaFayette, NY on 6/1/1779.	Ft. Lafayette (NY).
Gardner,	3rd NC	7/20/1778, a Private under Lt./Capt. George

Name	1st Unit	Year / Rank / Served Under / Notes	Known Battles
George	Regiment	"Gee" Bradley for nine months.	
Gardner, James	2nd NC Regiment	May 1776, a Captain. Resigned 5/15/1777.	
Gardner, John	4th NC Regiment	1782, a Corporal under Capt. Thomas Evans. Deserted on 6/8/1783 (?).	
Gardner, John	5th NC Regiment	Jan. 1779, a Private under Capt. Philip Taylor. Deserted same month.	
Gardner, John	5th NC Regiment	A Sergeant under Capt. Benjamin Andrew Coleman. Nothing more known. R20372.	
Gardner, Moy	2nd NC Regiment	5/22/1777, a Private, unit unknown. 9/9/1778, under Capt. Benjamin Andrew Coleman.	
Gardner, Thomas	3rd NC Regiment	7/1/1779, a Private under Capt. Kedar Ballard. Deserted on 10/1/1779.	
Gardner, William	1st NC Regiment	9/1/1775, an Ensign. 10/20/1775, a Lieutenant.	
Garey, George		4/16/1776, a Private, regiment and unit unknown, enlisted for 2-1/2 years. 9/8/1778, a known Private under Capt. Griffith John McRee (1st NC Regiment).	
Garey, Thomas		6/2/1777, a Private, regiment and unit unknown, enlisted for three years. 6/1/1778, a Private under Capt. Griffith John McRee (1st NC Regiment).	
Gargis, Job	2nd NC Regiment	1782, a Private under Capt. Robert Raiford. Official records indicate he deserted on 6/11/1783 (?). He claims he was honorably furloughed on 6/21/1783 at St. James Island, SC. From Halifax County, NC. Earlier in NC Militia. aka Job Gargas. S8547.	
Garland, Elisha	3rd NC Regiment	1/4/1777, a Private under Capt. Pinketham Eaton for 2-1/2 years. Discharged on 11/10/1778. Later, joined NC Militia, unit unknown. From Halifax County, NC. W926.	
Garland, Henry	1st NC Regiment	4/2/1781, a Private under Capt. William Lytle. Deserted on 7/5/1781. Might be Humphrey Garland.	
Garland, Humphrey	6th NC Regiment	A Private under Capt. Philip Taylor for 2-1/2 years. Discharged at Camden, SC. Dropped from the rolls in Jan. 1778. S38716.	
Garland, John	3rd NC Regiment	4/29/1776, a Private under Capt. Pinketham Eaton for 2-1/2 years. 9/9/1778, a known Private under Capt. Benjamin Andrew Coleman (2nd NC Regiment). Wounded at the battles of Brandywine Creek (PA) and Germantown (PA). Discharged on 11/10/1778 at Savannah, GA. Enlisted at Halifax, NC. W3011.	Brandywine Creek (PA), Germantown (PA), Monmouth (NJ).
Garland, Thomas	1st NC Regiment	1781, a Private under Capt. William Armstrong for 12 months. Discharged on 12/1/1782 (3rd NC Regiment).	
Garland, William	3rd NC Regiment	1781, a Private under Capt. Edward Yarborough. Discharged 4/22/1782.	
Garner, Dempsey	1st NC Regiment	1781, a Private under Lt./Capt. Benjamin Bailey. Discharged on 4/1/1782 (3rd NC Regiment).	

Name	1st Unit	Year / Rank / Served Under / Notes	Known Battles
Garner, Thomas	3rd NC Regiment	1781, a Private under Capt. Edward Yarborough. Discharged 6/1/1782.	
Garnes, Anthony	7th NC Regiment	7/14/1777, a Private under Capt. Lemuel Ely for three years. 9/8/1778, a known Private under Capt. Tilghman Dixon (1st NC Regiment) (actually since 6/1/1778). 3/12/1779, re-enlisted for the duration of the war in the same unit. POW at the Fall of Charleston (SC), escaped. Discharged in the Spring of 1782 at Murfreesboro, NC. A free man of color. aka Anthony Garns, Anthony Games. S38723.	Brandywine Creek (PA), Monmouth (NJ), Siege of Charleston (SC).
Garnes, Gabriel	2nd NC Regiment	5/25/1781, a Private under Capt. Tilghman Dixon. Dropped from the rolls sometime during 1781.	
Garnes, Jeffrey	7th NC Regiment	Nov. 1777, a Private under Capt. Lemuel Ely. Died 1/22/1778.	
Garrel, John	7th NC Regiment	1/10/1777, a Sergeant under Capt. John Poynter.	
Garret, Daniel	5th NC Regiment	1777, a Corporal under Capt. Henry Darnell. Discharged on 10/15/1777.	
Garret, James	5th NC Regiment	1777, a Private under Capt. Benjamin Stedman. Dropped from the rolls in Feb. 1778.	
Garret, Samuel	3rd NC Regiment	1781, a Private under Capt. Clement Hall. Discharged on 8/1/1782 (2nd NC Regiment).	
Garret, Thomas	2nd NC Regiment	1777, a Private under Capt. Edward Vail, Jr. 9/9/1778, a known Private in the Colonel's Company (Col. John Patten) led by Capt. John Craddock. Deserted on 12/11/1779.	
Garret, Thomas	5th NC Regiment	1777, a Private under Capt. Henry Darnell. Deserted in Aug. 1777.	
Garret, William	9th NC Regiment	1777, a Private under Capt. Joel Brevard. Dropped from the rolls in Feb. 1778.	
Garrick, Black	4th NC Regiment	1777, a Musician under Capt. Robert Smith. Dropped from the rolls in Jan. 1778.	
Garris, Bedford	10th NC Regiment	5/4/1777, a Private under Capt. Armwell Herron for 3 years. 9/10/1778, a known Private under Capt. William Armstrong (1st NC Regiment). 1781, a Private under Capt. William Armstrong (1st NC Regiment). Discharged on 1/21/1782. Lived in Dobbs County, NC when he enlisted. aka Begford Garris, Bigford Garris, Rigford Garris. S6876.	Monmouth (NJ), Siege of Charleston (SC).
Garris, Hardy	2nd NC Regiment	4/25/1781, a Private under Capt. Benjamin Carter. Discharged on 4/25/1782.	
Garris, Sikes	10th NC Regiment	5/4/1777, a Private under Capt. Armwell Herron. Then, served under Capt. Benjamin Andrew Coleman (2nd NC Regiment). POW at the Fall of Charleston (SC). Forced to join British Navy. War Department considered him to have deserted. Official sources have him listed as Sykes Garvis. aka Sykes Garris, Sykes Garress. His own pension statement has himself as Sike Garris. S13130.	Siege of Charleston 1780 (SC).
Garrison,	4th NC	1782, a Private under Capt. Anthony Sharpe for	

Name	1st Unit	Year / Rank / Served Under / Notes	Known Battles
Stephen	Regiment	18 months. Evidence shows he also enlisted in August 1779, unit and regiment unknown. S46444.	
Garrott, Thomas	2nd NC Regiment	A Sergeant, unit and dates unknown. From Bute County, NC. W19488.	
Garvey, Matthew	6th NC Regiment	1777, a Private under Capt. George Dougherty. Died in Mar. 1778.	
Garvey, Thomas	6th NC Regiment	6/2/1776, a Private under Lt./Capt. Francis Child, then Capt. Benjamin Pike. Enlisted in Currituck County, NC. POW at the Fall of Charleston, kept until the end of the war. S41556.	Germantown (PA), Monmouth (NJ), Siege of Charleston (SC).
Garvis, Pigford	10th NC Regiment	5/4/1777, a Private under Capt. Armwell Herron. A Musician in June 1778.	
Garvis, Wylley	2nd NC Regiment	5/12/1781, a Private under Capt. Tilghman Dixon. Discharged on 5/26/1782 (1st NC Regiment).	
Gasey, George		4/16/1776, a Private, regiment and unit unknown. 6/1/1778, a Private under Capt. Griffith John McRee (1st NC Regiment).	
Gaskin, Joseph	3rd NC Regiment	7/20/1778, a Private under Capt. Michael Quinn for nine months.	
Gaskins, Herman	2nd NC Regiment	A Private under Capt. Charles Crawford, dates unknown. S13124.	
Gaskins, William	2nd NC Regiment	5/12/1781, a Private under Capt. Benjamin Carter. Discharged 4/25/1782.	
Gaskins, William	5th NC Regiment	1777, a Sergeant under Capt. Benjamin Stedman. A Private in Aug. 1778. 9/9/1778, a known Private under Capt. Clement Hall (2nd NC Regiment). A Corporal in March 1779.	
Gass, John	5th NC Regiment	A Sergeant Major under Capt. William Lytle. From Orange County, NC. Earlier in NC Militia. On the official rolls as John Glass. W7492.	Stono Ferry (SC).
Gaston, Robert	2nd NC Regiment	Feb. 1776, a Captain under Lt. Col. Alexander Martin. Left the service before Dec. 1776.	Ft. Moultrie #1 (SC).
Gatlin, Edward	1st NC Regiment	5/11/1781, a Private under Capt. Robert Raiford. Discharged on 5/17/1782 (2nd NC Regiment).	
Gatlin, Jesse	2nd NC Regiment	1775, a Private under Capt. Hardy Murfree. Then, in NC Militia. August 1781, a Private under Capt. William Lytle (1st NC Regiment, then 4th NC Regiment) for 18 months. From Randolph County, NC. W10047.	
Gatlin, Levi	10th NC Regiment	1777, an Ensign under Capt. Silas Stevenson. 2/12/1778, a Lieutenant. Dismissed for neglect of duty and disobedience of orders on 8/22/1778 (while in 2nd NC Regiment).	
Gatree, Matthew	3rd NC Regiment	8/17/1782, a Private under Capt. Benjamin Bailey for 12 months.	
Gattery, Henry		11/1/1777, a Private, regiment and unit unknown. 9/8/1778, a known Private in the Major's Company (Maj. John Baptiste Ashe)	

Name	1st Unit	Year / Rank / Served Under / Notes	Known Battles
		(1st NC Regiment).	
Gaudy, Ephraim	1st NC Regiment	1782, a Private under Capt. Peter Bacot for 18 months. From Darlington District, SC, first in SC unit. Went to Nash County with his brother (Brittain) who was drafted, he took his brother's place. S17971.	
Gaudy, John	1st NC Regiment	9/8/1778, a known Private under Capt. Joshua Bowman.	
Gaudy, William	1st NC Regiment	1777, a Private under Capt. Joshua Bowman.	
Gaunt, Giles	1st NC Regiment	6/6/1781, a Corporal under Capt. William Lytle. Discharged on 6/6/1782 (4th NC Regiment).	
Gay, Allen	1st NC Regiment	6/2/1781, a Private under Capt. Robert Raiford. Discharged on 6/3/1782 (2nd NC Regiment). From Franklin County, NC. Born 1765 in Northampton County, NC. W1033.	Eutaw Springs (SC).
Gay, Henry	1st NC Regiment	4/15/1781, a Private under Capt. William Lytle. Discharged on 4/12/1782 (4th NC Regiment).	
Gay, James	1st NC Regiment	4/28/1781, a Sergeant under Capt. Alexander Brevard. Discharged on 4/28/1782 (3rd NC Regiment).	
Gay, James	1st NC Regiment	1782, a Private under Capt. Peter Bacot for 18 months.	
Gay, Joshua	1st NC Regiment	6/9/1781, a Private under Capt. Robert Raiford. Discharged on 5/17/1782 (2nd NC Regiment).	
Gay, Richard	1st NC Regiment	4/15/1781, a Private under Capt. William Lytle. Discharged on 4/12/1782 (4th NC Regiment).	
Gay, Simon	3rd NC Regiment	7/20/1778, a Private under Lt./Capt. George "Gee" Bradley for nine months.	
Gay, Solomon	1st NC Regiment	4/15/1781, a Private under Capt. William Lytle. Dropped from the rolls sometime during 1781.	
Gay, William	1st NC Regiment	July 1782, a Private under Capt. Peter Bacot for 18 months. From Edgecombe County, NC. S45842.	
Gay, William	3rd NC Regiment	7/20/1778, a Private in the Lt. Colonel's Company (Lt. Col. William Lee Davidson) led by Lt./Capt. George "Gee" Bradley. 4/23/1779, a known Private in the Lt. Colonel's Company (Lt. Col. Robert Mebane) led by Capt. George "Gee" Bradley. Died at New Windsor Hospital.	
Gay, Zerobabel	1st NC Regiment	5/17/1781, a Private under Capt. Robert Raiford, Lt. Col. Hardy Murfree for 12 months. Discharged 5/17/1782 (2nd NC Regiment). From Northampton County, NC. Earlier in NC Militia. On the official rolls as Babel Gay. aka Zarobabel Gay, Sarobabel Gay, Zorobabel Gay, Boble Gay. W7490. See Zerobabel Gray below.	
Gaylor, James	2nd NC Regiment	1/1/1782, a Private under Capt. Benjamin Andrew Coleman for 12 months.	
Gean, Sherod	2nd NC Regiment	Aug. 1782, a Private under Capt. Benjamin Carter for 18 months. Deserted 6/21/1783 (?). He says he was furloughed. From Franklin County, NC. Earlier in NC Militia. On the official rolls as Sherrod Jeane. R3960.	

Name	1st Unit	Year / Rank / Served Under / Notes	Known Battles
Geary, George	6th NC Regiment	4/16/1776, a Private under Lt./Capt. Thomas Donoho. Discharged on 11/10/1778.	
Geary, Joshua	6th NC Regiment	1777, a Private under Capt. Thomas Donoho. Died in Aug. 1777.	
Gee, Howell	7th NC Regiment	4/15/1777, an Ensign under Capt. John Macon. Nov. 1777, a Lieutenant. Dropped from the rolls in Jan. 1778.	
Gee, James	2nd NC Regiment	9/1/1775, a Lieutenant. 5/2/1776, a Captain under Col. Alexander Martin. Died 11/12/1777 of wounds he received at the battle of Brandywine Creek, PA.	Ft. Moultrie #1 (SC), Brandywine Creek (PA).
Gee, Jesse	5th NC Regiment	3/1/1779, a Private under Capt. Joseph Montford for nine months. Discharged on 12/1/1779.	
Gee, William	3rd NC Regiment	4/23/1776, a Corporal under Capt. Thomas Granbury. A Sergeant in Nov. 1777. A Private in June 1778. Discharged in Oct. 1778.	
Geekie, James	1st NC Regiment	12/21/1775, a Surgeon. Resigned May 1776. aka James Geikee, Gakae.	Moore's Creek Bridge [4].
Geeslin, Charles	4th NC Regiment	1782, a Private under Capt. Anthony Sharpe for 18 months. Discharged near Charleston, SC. Earlier in NC Militia, unit unknown. On the "offical rolls" as Charles Goseley. aka Charles Guslin. S37951.	
Gelden, Isaac	2nd NC Regiment	11/7/1776, a Fife Major. 9/9/1778, a Fifer under Capt. John Ingles. A Private in Nov. 1778. From Johnston County, NC. aka Isaac Geldin, Isaac Gerldin, Isaac Geldon, Isaac Geedin. W17943.	
Geniens, Miles	3rd NC Regiment	6/21/1779, a Private under Capt. Kedar Ballard for 18 months.	
George, Brittain	1st NC Regiment	Late 1775 or early 1776, a Private under Capt. Henry "Hal" Dixon. 9/8/1778, a known Private under Capt. James Read. Wounded twice at the battle of Germantown (PA). Enlisted in Bute County, NC. Discharged at Charleston, SC. aka Breton George, Britton George, Brittan George. S38725.	Moore's Creek Bridge [4], Brunswick Town #1, Ft. Moultrie #1 (SC), Germantown (PA).
George, Lewis	1st NC Regiment	1782, a Private under Capt. Alexander Brevard for 18 months.	
German, Benjamin		April 1779, a Private in the Colonel's Company, regiment unknown.	
German, Emory	4th NC Regiment	1782, a Private under Capt. Anthony Sharpe. Deserted on 5/5/1783 (?).	
Germany, Thomas	1st NC Regiment	9/4/1777, a Private under Capt. Howell Tatum for three years. 9/8/1778, a known Private under Capt. Howell Tatum.	
Gerns, James	2nd NC Regiment	1781, a Private under Capt. Tilghman Dixon. Discharged 4/15/1782.	
Gerrard, Charles	5th NC Regiment	4/30/1777, an Ensign under Capt. John Pugh Williams. 12/19/1777, a 2nd Lieutenant. 6/1/1778, a 1st Lieutenant under Capt. Thomas Armstrong (2nd NC Regiment). Wounded and POW at the Fall of Charleston, exchanged	Siege of Charleston 1780 (SC).

Name	1st Unit	Year / Rank / Served Under / Notes	Known Battles
		6/14/1781. While in captivity (or on parole), transferred to 1st NC Regiment on 1/1/1781. 1782, a Paymaster. Born 12/11/1753. aka Charles Gerald, Garrard, Gerrerd. W3999.	
Gerrel, John	7th NC Regiment	1/10/1777, a Sergeant under Capt. John Poynter. Dropped from the rolls in Jan. 1778.	
Gerrel, William	7th NC Regiment	1/10/1777, a Private under Capt. John Poynter. Dropped from the rolls in Sep. 1777.	
Gessum, Robert		6/1/1777, a Musician, regiment and unit unknown, enlisted for three years. 6/1/1778, a Musician under Capt. Griffith John McRee (1st NC Regiment).	
Gibbs, Joel	7th NC Regiment	Nov. 1777, a Private under Capt. John Macon for three years.	
Gibson, Charles	3rd NC Regiment	7/20/1778, a Private in the Lt. Colonel's Company (Lt. Colonel William Lee Davidson) led by Lt./Capt. George "Gee" Bradley for nine months. 4/23/1779, a known Private in the Lt. Colonel's Company (Lt. Col. Robert Mebane) led by Capt. George "Gee" Bradley. Enlisted in Northampton County, NC. Discharged at Philadelphia, PA. S41575.	
Gibson, Colin	1st NC Regiment	4/28/1781, a Private under Capt. Alexander Brevard. Jan. 1782, a Corporal.	
Gibson, David	1st NC Regiment	5/9/1781, a Private under Capt. Alexander Brevard. Deserted in Apr. 1782 (from 3rd NC Regiment).	
Gibson, Henry	1st NC Regiment	5/17/1781, a Private under Lt./Capt. Benjamin Bailey. Discharged on 5/17/1782 (3rd NC Regiment).	
Gibson, Jacob	5th NC Regiment	6/20/1779, a Private under Maj. Reading Blount. POW at the Fall of Charleston, taken to Jamaica until the end of the war. From Guilford County, NC. Born 1762 in Frederick County, VA. S10744.	Siege of Charleston 1780 (SC).
Gibson, Joel	1st NC Regiment	9/9/1775, a Private under Capt. Henry Dixon until January 1777. S35968.	
Gibson, John	1st NC Regiment	2/20/1777, a Private under Capt. Lawrence Thompson. Dropped from the rolls in Feb. 1778.	
Gibson, Thomas	2nd NC Regiment	2/20/1780 - an Ensign in the Lt. Colonel's Company (Lt. Col. Selby Harney) led by Capt. Charles Stewart. POW at the Fall of Charleston, exchanged 6/14/1781. Died Jan. 1782.	Siege of Charleston 1780 (SC).
Gibson, William	1st NC Regiment	9/8/1778, a known Private under Capt. Joshua Bowman.	
Gibson, William	6th NC Regiment	June 1776 or 5/6/1777 (two sources), a Musician under Capt. Philip Taylor. A Private in Apr. 1778. Dropped from the rolls in June 1778. 3/12/1779, re-enlisted for the duration of the war under Capt. Griffith John McRee (1st NC Regiment). POW at the Fall of Charleston - forced to join British Army, deserted and joined VA Militia. S38728.	Brandywine Creek (PA), Germantown (PA), Monmouth (NJ), Siege of Charleston 1780 (SC).

Name	1st Unit	Year / Rank / Served Under / Notes	Known Battles
Gidcomb, Joshua	1st NC Regiment	1782, a Private under Capt. Peter Bacot. Deserted on 6/15/1783.	
Gideon, Lewis	7th NC Regiment	1777, a Private under Capt. John McGlaughan. Deserted in Apr. 1777.	
Gifford, James	1st NC Regiment	1777, a Private under Capt. Henry "Hal" Dixon. Missing 9/12/1777, after the battle of Brandywine Creek, PA.	Brandywine Creek (PA).
Gifford, James	8th NC Regiment	12/30/1776, a Sergeant under Capt. Robert Raiford. A Private in June 1778. 9/9/1778, a known Private under Capt. Clement Hall (2nd NC Regiment). Deserted on 12/1/1779.	
Gilaspy, David	8th NC Regiment	1777, a Private under Capt. John Walsh. Dropped from the rolls in June 1778. Jan. 1779, joined the 5th NC Regiment, unit unknown. Discharged on 3/14/1780.	
Gilbert, James	2nd NC Regiment	9/9/1778, a known Private under Capt. Robert Fenner. Probably the same man as directly below.	
Gilbert, James	8th NC Regiment	1777, a Private under Capt. Francis Tartanson. Dropped from the rolls in Feb. 1778. aka Joseph Gilbert.	
Gilbert, John	2nd NC Regiment	5/19/1781, a Private under Capt. Benjamin Carter. Discharged 5/19/1782.	
Gilbert, John		A Private, regiment and unit unknown. Dead or deserted on 5/6/1778.	
Gilbert, Peter	6th NC Regiment	A Private under Capt. Thomas Donoho. Deserted in Aug. 1777.	
Giles, John	5th NC Regiment	8/22/1777, a QM Sergeant. Dropped from the rolls in Jan. 1778.	
Giles, John	5th NC Regiment	1776, a Lieutenant under Capt. William Ward.	
Gilespy, Isaac	3rd NC Regiment	1782, a Private under Capt. Alexander Brevard for 18 months. March 1783, transferred - to what, unknown.	
Gilgo, Fabin	1st NC Regiment	1781, a Private under Capt. Anthony Sharpe. Discharged on 4/15/1782 (4th NC Regiment) at Bacon's Bridge, SC. Enlisted in Craven County, NC. On the official rolls as Fibin Gilgo. S41573.	
Giligan, John	10th NC Regiment	4/1/1778, a Private under Capt. James Wilson. Deserted on 4/22/1778.	
Gill, Alexander	3rd NC Regiment	8/1/1782, a Private under Capt. Benjamin Bailey. Died on 6/18/1783.	
Gill, John	4th NC Regiment	1782, a Private under Capt. William Lytle.	
Gill, Robert	1st NC Regiment	1782, a Private under Capt. Alexander Brevard for 18 months.	
Gilleham, Howell	10th NC Regiment	5/6/1777, a Private under Capt. Isaac Moore for three years. 9/8/1778, a known Private in the Lt. Colonel's Company (Lt. Col. Robert Mebane) (1st NC Regiment) led by Capt. Joshua Bowman. 3/12/1779, re-enlisted for the duration of the war in the same unit. A Sergeant in May 1779. aka Howell Gilliam.	

Name	1st Unit	Year / Rank / Served Under / Notes	Known Battles
Gillenham, James	1st NC Regiment	9/22/1777, a Private under Capt. James Read. 9/8/1778, in same unit - sick in camp. aka James Gillearham.	
Gillespie, Robert	4th NC Regiment	1777, an Ensign under Capt. William Goodman. Aug. 1777, a Lieutenant under Capt. William Goodman. Dropped from the rolls in June 1778.	
Gilmore, Thomas	4th NC Regiment	5/16/1777, a Private under Capt. Robert Smith for three years. 9/8/1778, a known Private in the Colonel's Company (Col. Thomas Clark) (1st NC Regiment) led by Capt. John Gambier Scull - sick at Valley Forge on that date. 3/12/1779, re-enlisted for the duration of the war in the same unit.	
Gilmore, William	1st NC Regiment	6/14/1781, a Private under Capt. Thomas Donoho. Discharged on 6/14/1782.	
Gilston, Samuel	7th NC Regiment	10/4/1777, a Sergeant under Capt. Ely. A QM Sergeant on 6/17/1779.	
Ginew, William	10th NC Regiment	11/6/1777, a Private under Capt. James Wilson. Dropped from the rolls in June 1778.	
Ginn, Hardy	3rd NC Regiment	7/20/1778, a Private under Lt./Capt. George "Gee" Bradley for nine months. 4/25/1781, a Private under Capt. Tilghman Dixon (2nd NC Regiment) for 12 months. Discharged on 4/25/1782. aka Hardy Giun.	
Ginn, Jacob	3rd NC Regiment	12/11/1781, a Private under Capt. Samuel Jones. Discharged on 12/1/1782 (1st NC Regiment) as Elijah Ginn.	
Ginn, Rowland	4th NC Regiment	1781, a Private under Capt. Joseph T. Rhodes. Discharged on 7/16/1782. aka Roland Giun.	
Ginn, William		Feb. 1779, a Private in the Colonel's Company - regiment unknown. Deserted in Apr. 1779. aka William Gion.	
Ginnings, George	4th NC Regiment	1782, a Private under Capt. Anthony Sharpe. Died in Jan. 1783.	
Gipson, William	1st NC Regiment	A Private under Capt. Joshua Bowman, dates unknown.	
Gist, Robert	1st NC Regiment	1781, a Private under Capt. William Armstrong for 12 months. Discharged on 12/1/1782 (3rd NC Regiment).	
Glanden, Major	10th NC Regiment	9/30/1777, a Private under Capt. Abraham Sheppard, Jr. for three years. 9/9/1778, a known Private under Capt. John Craddock (2nd NC Regiment). POW at the Fall of Charleston (SC), escaped after four months. Re-enlisted for 12 months under Capt. Alexander Brevard (4th NC Regiment, then 1st NC Regiment). From Edgecombe County, NC. aka Major Glanders, Major Glandon. S41583.	Monmouth (NJ), Stony Point (NY), Siege of Charleston 1780 (SC).
Glasgow, Caleb	2nd NC Regiment	1777, a Private under Capt. Edward Vail, Jr. Discharged Sep. 1778.	
Glasgow, Cornelius	1st NC Regiment	Summer of 1781, a Sergeant under Lt./Capt. William Walton for 18 months. Served 16 months - all in Scouting Parties to round up Loyalists in and around Gates, Hertford, etc.	

394

Name	1st Unit	Year / Rank / Served Under / Notes	Known Battles
		Counties. This service was not recognized by many officials. Earlier in NC Militia. From Currituck County, NC. S1905.	
Glasgow, Lemuel	4th NC Regiment	Dec. 1776, a Private under Capt. William Goodman for three years. At the Fall of Charleston, escaped capture and went home. From Pasquotank County, NC. Earlier and later in NC Militia. R4056R	Siege of Charleston 1780 (SC).
Glass, James	2nd NC Regiment	1777, a Private under Capt. Clement Hall. Deserted in Aug. 1777.	
Glass, Lemuel		Aug. 1779, a Private, regiment and unit unknown. Deserted Aug. 1779.	
Glass, Levi	1st NC Regiment	8/20/1782, a Private under Capt. Joshua Hadley for 18 months. Enlisted in Cumberland County, NC. Discharged at James Island, SC. S10749.	
Glasscow, Samuel		Jan. 1779, a Private in the Lt. Colonel's Company - regiment unknown.	
Glaughan, Daniel	5th NC Regiment	1777, a Private under Capt. Henry Darnell. Dropped from the rolls in Jan. 1778. aka Daniel Gladhan, Daniel Glauhan.	
Glaughan, Jeremiah	5th NC Regiment	1777, a Sergeant under Capt. Henry Darnell. Died on 4/12/1778. aka Jeremiah Glauhan, Jeremiah Glanhan.	
Glenn, George	4th NC Regiment	5/15/1777, a Private under Capt. William Goodman for three years. 9/8/1778, a known Private in the Colonel's Company (Col. Thomas Clark) (1st NC Regiment) led by Capt. John Gambier Scull - sick at Valley Forge on that date. Dropped from the rolls in Nov. 1779.	
Glenn, Tobias	2nd NC Regiment	1777, a Musician under Capt. John Armstrong. Dec. 1777, transferred to 4th NC Regiment under Capt. James Williams. Dropped from the rolls in Jan. 1778.	
Glisson, Arthur	2nd NC Regiment	7/20/1778, a Private under Maj. Reading Blount for nine months.	
Gliston, James	1st NC Regiment	10/6/1777, a Sergeant under Capt. Tilghman Dixon for three years. 9/8/1778, a known Sergeant under Capt. Tilghman Dixon.	
Glover, Allen	1st NC Regiment	4/12/1781, a Private under Capt. William Lytle. Deserted on 7/7/1781.	
Glover, Benjamin	1st NC Regiment	4/12/1781, a Private under Capt. William Lytle. Deserted on 7/7/1781. Re-enlisted in Jan. 1782.	
Glover, John	1st NC Regiment	5/2/1781, a Private under Capt. Robert Raiford. Discharged on 5/2/1782 (2nd NC Regiment).	
Glover, John	3rd NC Regiment	4/27/1776, a Private under Capt. Thomas Granbury. 9/9/1778, a known Private under Capt. John Ingles (2nd NC Regiment). Discharged on 11/10/1778.	
Glover, John	6th NC Regiment	May 1776, an Ensign under Capt. William Glover (his brother) for 18 months. From Granville County, NC. S38734.	
Glover, Samuel	2nd NC Regiment	1777, a Sergeant under Capt. Charles Allen. 9/10/1778, a known Sergeant under Capt. Thomas Armstrong (2nd NC Regiment). A	Brandywine Creek (PA), Germantown

Name	1st Unit	Year / Rank / Served Under / Notes	Known Battles
		Private in July 1779. 2/23/1780, executed at Wilmington, NC for refusing to march any further.	(PA), Monmouth (NJ), Stony Point (NY).
Glover, Thomas	1st NC Regiment	1777, a Private under Capt. Henry "Hal" Dixon. 9/8/1778, a known Private under Capt. James Read. Hanged for plundering on 10/24/1778.	
Glover, William	6th NC Regiment	4/17/1776, a 1st Lieutenant under Capt. Jesse Saunders and Col. John Alexander Lillington. 5/7/1776, a Captain. Resigned 4/1/1777.	
Godden, Martin	1st NC Regiment	1782, a Private under Capt. Peter Bacot for 18 months.	
Godett, John	1st NC Regiment	4/5/1781, a Private under Capt. Anthony Sharpe. Discharged on 4/5/1782 (4th NC Regiment). Possibly the same man as John Goodat below.	
Godfrey, Anthony	5th NC Regiment	12/2/1779, a Private under Maj. Reading Blount.	
Godfrey, Clement	6th NC Regiment	12/16/1776, a Private under Capt. George Dougherty. 9/9/1778, a known Private under Capt. Clement Hall (2nd NC Regiment). From Duplin County, NC.	
Godfrey, Francis	7th NC Regiment	1777, a Private under Capt. Thomas Brickell. Died on 11/28/1777.	
Godfrey, William	6th NC Regiment	1777, a Private under Capt. Griffith John McRee. Dropped from the rolls in Jan. 1778. Re-enlisted as a Corporal in Jan. 1779 in the 5th NC Regiment, unit unknown, for three years.	
Godfrey, William	8th NC Regiment	11/28/1776, a 2nd Lieutenant under Capt. Edward Ward. Resigned 8/15/1777.	
Godwin, John	3rd NC Regiment	7/20/1778, a Corporal in the Lt. Colonel's Company (Lt. Colonel William Lee Davidson). 4/23/1779, a known Sergeant in the Lt. Colonel's Company (Lt. Col. Robert Mebane) led by Capt. George "Gee" Bradley.	
Goff, Thomas	4th NC Regiment	1777, a Private under Capt. Robert Smith. Dropped from the rolls in Sep. 1777.	
Goforth, Zachariah	5th NC Regiment	1779, a Private under Capt. William Lytle for nine months. Later in NC Militia. From Caswell County, NC. S3405.	Stono Ferry (SC).
Goggard, William	2nd NC Regiment	9/9/1778, a known Private in the Major's Company (Maj. Hardy Murfree).	
Goings, William	2nd NC Regiment	5/25/1781, a Private under Capt. Tilghman Dixon. Discharged on 5/21/1782 (1st NC Regiment). Received clothing on 5/24/1782. From Caswell County. aka William Goin, William Going. W930.	Eutaw Springs (SC).
Gold, David	7th NC Regiment	1/7/1777, a Private under Capt. John McGlaughan. 2/26/1778, a known Private under Capt. Howell Tatum (1st NC Regiment). 9/8/1778, a known Private under Capt. Howell Tatum. Died in Oct. 1778. aka Davis Gold.	
Goldin, Andrew	2nd NC Regiment	Aug. 1781, a Private under Capt. Benjamin Carter. Deserted on 8/17/1781.	

Name	1ˢᵗ Unit	Year / Rank / Served Under / Notes	Known Battles
Goldsbury, William	5ᵗʰ NC Regiment	1777, a Private under Capt. John Enloe. Dropped from the rolls in June 1778.	
Goldsmith, Jesse	1ˢᵗ NC Regiment	1777, a Musician under Capt. Henry "Hal" Dixon. A Private in June of 1778. 9/8/1778, a known Private under Capt. James Read.	
Gonsalez, Ferdinando de	1ˢᵗ NC Regiment	4/28/1781, a Corporal under Capt. Griffith John McRee. A Private in Aug. 1781. Discharged on 4/28/1782. Re-enlisted in 1782 for 18 months.	
Good, John	3ʳᵈ NC Regiment	7/20/1778, a Private under Lt./Capt. Joseph Montford for nine months.	
Good, John	4ᵗʰ NC Regiment	1782, a Private under Capt. Anthony Sharpe for 12 months.	
Good, William	3ʳᵈ NC Regiment	7/20/1778, a Private under Lt./Capt. Joseph Montford for nine months.	
Goodat, John	3ʳᵈ NC Regiment	7/20/1778, a Private under Capt. Michael Quinn for nine months. Possibly the same man as John Godett above.	
Goodman, Samuel	6ᵗʰ NC Regiment	5/12/1776, a Corporal under Capt. Philip Taylor for 2-1/2 years. A Private in June 1778. Back to Corporal in Sep. 1778. 9/8/1778, a known Corporal under Capt. John Sumner (1st NC Regiment). Dropped from the rolls in Nov. 1778.	
Goodman, William	4ᵗʰ NC Regiment	Earlier a 1ˢᵗ Lieutenant in the Edenton District Minutemen. 4/17/1776, a 1ˢᵗ Lieutenant under Capt. Roger Moore and Col. Thomas Polk. 10/1/1776 or 11/27/1776 (two sources), a Captain under Col. Thomas Polk (4ᵗʰ NC Regiment) then Col. James Armstrong until Dec. 1778. Jan. 1779, in NC Light Dragoons (State Troops) under Col. Francois DeMalmedy. Spring of 1781, a Captain under Maj. Reading Blount (2ⁿᵈ NC Regiment). Killed at Eutaw Springs, SC on September 8, 1781.	Brandywine Creek (PA), Germantown (PA), Briar Creek (GA), Stono Ferry (SC), Eutaw Springs (SC).
Goodnight, Henry	NC Light Dragoons	1777, a Horseman under Capt. Martin Phifer. 3/7/1777, this unit was on the NC Continental Line until Jan. 1779. S38743.	
Goodrick, Matthew	3ʳᵈ NC Regiment	4/14/1777, a known Ensign under Capt. Nicholas Edmunds.	
Goodridge, Lewis	3ʳᵈ NC Regiment	7/20/1778, a Private under Lt./Capt. George "Gee" Bradley. Discharged on 12/5/1778.	
Goodridge, Matthew	3ʳᵈ NC Regiment	4/25/1776, a Sergeant under Capt. Jacob Turner. Deserted in Oct. 1777.	
Goods, Israel	1ˢᵗ NC Regiment	1781, a Private under Capt. William Armstrong for 12 months. Discharged on 7/1/1782 (3rd NC Regiment).	
Goodson, James	3ʳᵈ NC Regiment	4/23/1779, a known Private in the Lt. Colonel's Company (Lt. Col. Robert Mebane) led by Capt. George "Gee" Bradley. Died at New Windsor Hospital, date unknown.	
Goodson, John	3ʳᵈ NC Regiment	12/11/1781, a Private under Capt. Samuel Jones for 12 months.	
Goodson, John	10ᵗʰ NC Regiment	5/18/1777, a Private under Capt. Abraham Sheppard, Jr.	

Name	1st Unit	Year / Rank / Served Under / Notes	Known Battles
Goodson, Uzal	2nd NC Regiment	1782, a Private under Capt. Robert Raiford. Deserted on 6/10/1783 (?).	
Goodwin, Christopher	6th NC Regiment	1775, a 2nd Lieutenant under Capt. Griffith John McRee and Col. John Alexander Lillington in the Wilmington District Minutemen. 4/17/1776, a 2nd Lieutenant under Capt. Griffith John McRee and Col. John Alexander Lillington. 9/19/1776, a 1st Lieutenant under Capt. Philip Taylor. Transferred to 3rd NC Regiment on 6/1/1778. Jan. 1779, a Captain in "New Levies," under Lt. Col. Archibald Lytle, then Col. Francois DeMalmedy. 1781, a Captain under Maj. Reading Blount (2nd NC Regiment). Killed at the battle of Eutaw Springs, SC on September 8, 1781. aka Christopher Gooding, Goodin, Godwin, Christopher Gooden.	Briar Creek (GA), Eutaw Springs (SC).
Goodwin, Edward	3rd NC Regiment	6/24/1779, a Private under Capt. Michael Quinn. aka Edward Goodin.	
Goodwin, John	1st NC Regiment	5/19/1781, a Private under Capt. Robert Raiford. Discharged on 2/14/1782 (2nd NC Regiment). Earlier in NC Militia. From Perquimans County, NC. S6908.	Eutaw Springs (SC).
Goodwin, Lemuel	1st NC Regiment	March 1776, a Sergeant under Capt. Thomas Allen, then under Capt. Lawrence Thompson. Discharged in Feb. 1777 at Wilmington, NC. From Halifax County, NC. Later in NC Militia. S8588.	Breech Inlet Naval Battle (SC).
Goodwin, Robison	4th NC Regiment	A Private, enlisted under Capt. Anthony Sharpe for 18 months - actually served 15 months. Living in Montgomery County, NC when he enlisted. Born in Beaufort County, NC. aka Robertson Goodwin. S6894.	
Goodwin, Thomas	3rd NC Regiment	3/15/1782, a Private under Capt. Samuel Jones for 12 months.	
Goodwin, Tiney	7th NC Regiment	1777, a Private under Capt. Thomas Brickell. Deserted on 7/25/1777.	
Goodwin, Wiley	2nd NC Regiment	1782, a Private under Capt. Benjamin Carter for 18 months. aka Wyly Gooden. S37952.	
Goodwin, William	7th NC Regiment	3/10/1777, a Private under Capt. Joseph Walker. 9/8/1778, a known Private under Capt. Tilghman Dixon (1st NC Regiment). 3/12/1779, re-enlisted for the duration of the war in the same unit. aka William Goodin.	
Gordon, Alexander	6th NC Regiment	1777, a Private under Capt. Griffith John McRee. 9/8/1778, a known Private under Capt. Joshua Bowman (1st NC Regiment). Deserted on 1/10/1780.	
Gordon, Solomon	DQMG	1780, a Wagoner under Col. Nicholas Long (Deputy QM General). Possibly the same man as directly below.	
Gordon, Solomon	2nd NC Regiment	4/12/1781, a Private under Capt. Benjamin Carter for 12 months. Badly wounded at the battle of Eutaw Springs, SC. Discharged on 4/25/1782 at Halifax, NC. S41584.	Eutaw Springs (SC).

Name	1st Unit	Year / Rank / Served Under / Notes	Known Battles
Goref, William	1st NC Regiment	1776, a Private under Capt. Joshua Bowman.	
Goren, John	3rd NC Regiment	6/29/1779, a Corporal under Capt. Kedar Ballard. aka John Goven.	
Goslin, Ambrose	2nd NC Regiment	1777, a Private under Capt. William Fenner. Died on 9/1/1777.	
Goslin, Simon	2nd NC Regiment	5/15/1781, a Private under Capt. Tilghman Dixon. Discharged on 5/21/1782 (1st NC Regiment). Received clothing on 5/24/1782. From Caswell County.	
Gothrop, John	10th NC Regiment	5/25/1777, a Private under Capt. Abraham Sheppard, Jr. Discharged in Sep. 1778.	
Gotson, James	3rd NC Regiment	7/20/1778, a Private in the Lt. Colonel's Company (Lt. Colonel William Lee Davidson) led by Lt./Capt. George "Gee" Bradley.	
Gouch, John	6th NC Regiment	A Private under Capt. Philip Taylor, dates unknown. 9/8/1778, a known Private under Capt. John Sumner (1st NC Regiment). aka John Gooch.	
Gouch, Rowland	6th NC Regiment	A Private under Capt. Philip Taylor, dates unknown (early). From Wake County, NC. Then, in NC Militia. aka Rollin Gouch.	
Gouch, William	6th NC Regiment	A Private under Capt. Philip Taylor. Dropped from the rolls in Feb. 1778. Killed in service. Brother of Rowland Gouch.	
Gough, William	1st NC Regiment	Sep. 1777, a Private, unit unknown. 11/15/1777, a Corporal under Capt. Thomas Hogg for three years. 9/8/1778, a known Private in the Lt. Colonel's Company (Lt. Col. Robert Mebane) led by Capt. Joshua Bowman - sick at Valley Forge on that date. Dropped from the rolls in Feb. 1779. Rejoined in Nov. 1779.	
Graft, Anthony	3rd NC Regiment	3/6/1782, a Private under Capt. Samuel Jones for 12 months.	
Graham, Arthur	1st NC Regiment	1781, a Private under Capt. Alexander Brevard. Discharged on 6/15/1782 (3rd NC Regiment). aka Arthur Gragham. W4068.	
Graham, Francis	1st NC Regiment	4/28/1781, a Private under Capt. Alexander Brevard. Discharged on 4/28/1782 (3rd NC Regiment).	
Graham, Francis	2nd NC Regiment	1782, a Private under Capt. Robert Raiford for 18 months. May be same man as directly above.	
Graham, George	1st NC Regiment	9/1/1775, an Ensign. 1/4/1776, a 2nd Lieutenant. Resigned 4/15/1776. Later, a Captain in the NC Rangers (Militia). aka George Grayham.	
Graham, Hugh	2nd NC Reigment	1775, a Lieutenant under Capt. William Knox. Not on any official rolls.	
Graham, John	2nd NC Regiment	1781, a Private under Capt. Tilghman Dixon. Discharged 4/15/1782.	
Graham, John	2nd NC Regiment	12/13/1781, a Private under Capt. Benjamin Andrew Coleman, then under Capt. Samuel Jones (1st NC Regiment), and finally under Capt. Clement Hall (2nd NC Regiment) for 18	

Name	1st Unit	Year / Rank / Served Under / Notes	Known Battles
		months. Furloughed in Aug. 1783 at Wilmington, NC. From Cumberland County, NC. S3422.	
Graham, Joseph	4th NC Regiment	May 1777, a Sergeant under Capt. William Goodman for nine months. Also a QM Sergeant. Discharged in August 1778. Enlisted in Mecklenburg County, NC. Later, a QM Sergeant, Captain, and Major in NC Militia. Born 10/13/1759 in Chester County, PA. S6937.	
Graham, Peter	2nd NC Regiment	1781, a Private under Capt. Tilghman Dixon. Discharged 4/15/1782.	
Graham, Richard	2nd NC Regiment	1775, a Lieutenant under Capt. William Knox. 6/8/1776, a 2nd Lieutenant under Capt. Hardy Murfree. A Captain in Jan. 1778. April 1778, in the "New Levies," considered by some not on the Continental Line. Official rolls assert he retired 6/1/1778. See Richard Grimes below.	Ft. Moultrie #1 (SC).
Graham, William	9th NC Regiment	1777, a Sergeant under Capt. Richard D. Cook. Supposed deserted in Nov. 1777. He asserts that he took sick after nine or twelve months service, and hired William Hobbs to serve the remainder of his term. From Caswell County, NC. Also in the NC Militia. R4182.	
Grainger, Caleb	1st NC Regiment	9/1/1775, a Captain under Col. James Moore. Promoted to Major on 2/5/1777 to 4/26/1777 (resigned). From New Hanover County, NC.	
Grainger, John	2nd NC Regiment	9/1/1775, a Lieutenant. Also, an Ensign in NC Militia [4].	Moore's Creek Bridge [4].
Granbury, John	3rd NC Regiment	1775, a 1st Lieutenant in the Edenton District Minutemen. 4/17/1776, a 2nd Lieutenant under Capt. Thomas Granbury, then under Capt. Pinketham Eaton. Dropped from the rolls in May 1778. aka John Grandbury, John Granberry.	
Granbury, Thomas	3rd NC Regiment	1775, a Captain in the Edenton District Minutemen. 4/17/1776, a Captain under Col. Jethro Sumner. Court-martialed for forging and selling discharges. Cashiered and resigned on 12/27/1777. A prisoner in May 1779 as a volunteer in VA unit, held two years. aka Thomas Granberry, Thomas Grandbury. S41592.	Ft. Moultrie #1 (SC), Brandywine Creek (PA), Germantown (PA).
Grandy, Davis	7th NC Regiment	1777, an Ensign. 8/26/1777, left in NC as a recruiter.	
Grandy, Obediah	7th NC Regiment	1/18/1777, a Private under Capt. John Poynter. Dropped from the rolls in Sep. 1777.	
Grant, David	2nd NC Regiment	Feb. 1776, a Private under Capt. John Armstrong. 9/9/1778, a known Private under Capt. Robert Fenner. Listed as a deserter on 1/1/1780. He claims that he was honorably discharged at West Point (NY) due to an illness, certified by Dr. John Cochran (Surgeon General). S38766.	Brandywine Creek (PA), Germantown (PA).
Grant, Elisha	2nd NC	First served under Capt. Simon Bright, dates	Brandywine

Name	1st Unit	Year / Rank / Served Under / Notes	Known Battles
	Regiment	unknown. 8/20/1777, a Private under Capt. Abraham Sheppard, Jr. (10th NC Regiment). 3/12/1779, re-enlisted under Capt. Benjamin Williams (2nd NC Regiment). POW at Ft. Lafayette, NY on 6/1/1779. Rejoined in Nov. 1779. aka Elijah Grant. S41587.	Creek (PA), Monmouth (NJ), Ft. Lafayette (NY), Siege of Charleston 1780 (SC).
Grant, Ephraim	3rd NC Regiment	7/20/1778, a Corporal under Lt./Capt. George "Gee" Bradley for nine months.	
Grant, John	3rd NC Regiment	1781, a Private under Capt. Alexander Brevard for 18 months. From Wilkes County, NC. Signed up under Capt. Jesse Hardin Franklin (militia), then soon transferred to NC Continentals and marched south. S6930.	
Grant, John	3rd NC Regiment	7/20/1778, a Private under Lt./Capt. George "Gee" Bradley. Died on 11/16/1778.	
Grant, Reuben	6th NC Regiment	1775, an Ensign in the Salisbury District Minutemen. 4/17/1776, an Ensign under Capt. George Mitchell and Col. John Alexander Lillington. 6/6/1776. a Lieutenant. From Onslow County.	
Grant, Thomas	6th NC Regiment	1775, an Ensign in the Hillsborough District Minutmen. 4/17/1776, an Ensign under Capt. Jesse Saunders and Col. John Alexander Lillington. Resigned within 2 weeks.	
Grant, William	3rd NC Regiment	7/20/1778, a Private in the Lt. Colonel's Company (Lt. Col. William Lee Davidson) led by Lt./Capt. George "Gee" Bradley. 4/23/1779, a known Private in the Lt. Colonel's Company (Lt. Col. Robert Mebane) led by Capt. George "Gee" Bradley.	
Grant, William	6th NC Regiment	1777, a Private under Capt. Thomas Donoho. Died in Aug. 1777.	
Graves, Francis	8th NC Regiment	9/1/1777, a Regimental QM. Transferred to NC 10th Regiment on 10/26/1777 as a 2nd Lieutenant. Transferred to 3rd NC Regiment on 6/1/1778. A 1st Lieutenant on 7/14/1779. POW at the Fall of Charleston, exchanged 6/14/1781. Transferred to 1st NC Regiment in July 1780 - while a prisoner. 2/6/1782, back in 3rd NC Regiment. Served until the end of the war.	Siege of Charleston 1780 (SC).
Gray, Archibald	NC Artillery	12/17/1776, a Sergeant under Capt. John Vance as NC Provincial Troops. 7/10/1777, placed on Continental Line. 11/16/1777, under Capt. John Kingsbury. 5/1/1778, in same unit. 9/16/1778, in same unit.	
Gray, Cox	3rd NC Regiment	7/20/1778, a Private under Capt. Michael Quinn for nine months. 4/25/1781, a Private under Capt. Benjamin Carter. Discharged 4/25/1782. aka Cocks Gray.	
Gray, Henry	3rd NC Regiment	7/20/1778, a Private under Lt./Capt. Joseph Montford for nine months.	
Gray, Henry	4th NC Regiment	1781, a Sergeant under Capt. Joseph T. Rhodes. Discharged 1/21/1782.	

Name	1st Unit	Year / Rank / Served Under / Notes	Known Battles
Gray, Isom	3rd NC Regiment	7/20/1778, a Private under Capt. Kedar Ballard for nine months.	
Gray, James	10th NC Regiment	5/15/1777, a Sergeant under Capt. James Wilson for three years. 9/8/1778, a known Sergeant under Maj. John Baptiste Ashe (1st NC Regiment) - sick in camp on that date. aka James Grey.	
Gray, John	3rd NC Regiment	1775, a Captain in the Halifax District Minutemen. 4/17/1776, a Captain under Col. Jethro Sumner. Retired 6/1/1778. One source asserts he died while in service in late 1777.	Ft. Moultrie #1 (SC).
Gray, Morton	3rd NC Regiment	1781, a Private under Capt. Robert Smith for five months. Earlier and later in NC Militia. From Granville County, NC.	Hobkirk's Hill (SC), Fort Motte (SC), Siege of Augusta (GA).
Gray, M. William	10th NC Regiment	4/27/1777, a Private under Capt. Armwell Herron.	
Gray, Samuel	10th NC Regiment	6/2/1777, a Private under Capt. Armwell Herron. A Drummer in June 1778 under Capt. Robert Fenner (2nd NC Regiment). POW at Ft. Lafayette, NY on 6/1/1779. Rejoined in Nov. 1779. aka Samuel Grey.	Ft. Lafayette (NY).
Gray, Thomas	NC Light Dragoons	1780, a Cornet under Capt. Solomon Wood. At this time, these were State Troops.	
Gray, William	1st NC Regiment	9/8/1778, a known Private under Capt. Howell Tatum (1st NC Regiment). Dropped from the rolls in Oct. 1779.	
Gray, William	10th NC Regiment	6/10/1777, a Private under Capt. Dempsey Gregory. 9/9/1778, a known Private under Capt. Robert Fenner (2nd NC Regiment). POW at the Fall of Charleston (SC). From Camden County, NC. aka William Grey. S41586.	Monmouth (NJ), Stony Point (NY), Siege of Charleston 1780 (SC).
Gray, Willis	1st NC Regiment	1780, a Private under Capt. Griffith John McRee for 18 months. From Johnston County, NC. W19554.	
Gray, Zerobabel	1st NC Regiment	5/17/1781, a Private under Capt. Robert Raiford. Discharged on 5/17/1782 (2nd NC Regiment). From Northampton County, NC. Earlier in NC Militia. aka Babel Gray.	
Grayham, William	4th NC Regiment	1781, a Sergeant under Capt. Joseph T. Rhodes. Discharged 6/17/1782.	
Greece, Thoplus	2nd NC Regiment	1/10/1782, a Private under Capt. Benjamin Andrew Coleman for 12 months. First name is probably Theophilus.	
Green, Abraham	7th NC Regiment	1777, a Private under Capt. Thomas Brickell. Dropped from the rolls in Jan. 1778.	
Green, Frederick	1st NC Regiment	5/9/1781, a Private under Capt. Griffith John McRee. Deserted on 7/1/1781.	
Green, Hobart	1st NC Regiment	8/1/1782, a Private under Capt. Joshua Hadley. Deserted on 4/29/1783 (?).	
Green, James	3rd NC Regiment	1782, a Private under Capt. Alexander Brevard. Deserted on 12/7/1782.	

Name	1st Unit	Year / Rank / Served Under / Notes	Known Battles
Green, James West	2nd NC Regiment	6/10/1778, a Surgeon. 12/7/1779, a Surgeon in 2nd NC Regiment. From Halifax County, NC. POW at the Fall of Charleston, paroled 6/14/1781. Transferred to 1st NC Regiment on 2/6/1782, till the end of the war. Still considered a POW as of 11/26/1782.	Siege of Charleston 1780 (SC).
Green, John	5th NC Regiment	1777, a Private under Capt. Benjamin Stedman. Died on 8/20/1777.	
Green, Joseph	8th NC Regiment	12/11/1776, a Commissary.	
Green, Josiah	3rd NC Regiment	1777, a Private under Capt. James Emmett. Dropped from the rolls in Sep. 1777.	
Green, Randolph	4th NC Regiment	1782, a Private under Capt. Thomas Evans.	
Green, Solomon	9th NC Regiment	1777, a Musician under Capt. Richard D. Cook. Deserted in Aug. 1777. aka Samuel Green.	
Green, Sutton	1st NC Regiment	6/16/1781, a Private under Capt. William Lytle. Discharged on 6/16/1782.	
Green, Thomas	3rd NC Regiment	7/20/1778, a Corporal under Maj. Thomas Hogg for nine months.	
Green, William	1st NC Regiment	2/20/1777, a Private under Capt. Lawrence Thompson. Dropped from the rolls in Jan. 1778.	
Green, William	1st NC Regiment	9/1/1775, a Captain under Col. James Moore. Resigned 1/4/1776 (Company dissolved).	
Green, William	2nd NC Regiment	7/2/1777, a Private, unit unknown. 9/10/1778, a known Private under Capt. Thomas Armstrong.	
Green, William	6th NC Regiment	6/6/1776, an Ensign under Capt. Archibald Lytle. 10/28/1776, a 2nd Lieutenant under Capt. Philip Taylor. 8/27/1777, a 1st Lieutenant under Capt. Philip Taylor. Dropped from the rolls in Sep. 1777.	
Green, Wilson		Jan. 1778, a Corporal, unit unknown. Died on 4/18/1778.	
Greenman, Caleb	1st NC Regiment	6/1/1781, a Private under Lt./Capt. Benjamin Bailey. Discharged on 6/1/1782 (3rd NC Regiment).	
Greenwood, John	7th NC Regiment	1777, a Sergeant under Capt. Joseph Walker. POW on 9/11/1777 at the battle of Brandywine Creek, PA.	Brandywine Creek (PA).
Greer, John	5th NC Regiment	Jan. 1779, a Private under Capt. Thomas White. Deserted in June 1779.	
Greer, Robert	8th NC Regiment	11/28/1776, a 2nd Lieutenant under Capt. John Walsh. 4/24/1777, a 1st Lieutenant. Court Martialed on 8/20/1777, charges unknown. Found guilty and sentenced to be cashiered, but the sentence was waived by a general officer (unnamed). Retired on 6/1/1778.	
Gregory, Abraham	4th NC Regiment	1778, a Private under Capt. William Goodman for nine months. From Caswell County (what is now Person Co.), NC. 1780, in NC Militia. aka Abram Gregory. W7600.	
Gregory, Dempsey	10th NC Regiment	4/19/1777, a Captain under Col. Abraham Sheppard. Resigned on 5/20/1778.	
Gregory,	2nd NC	Apr. 1778, a Private under Capt. Manlove	Siege of

Name	1st Unit	Year / Rank / Served Under / Notes	Known Battles
Isaac	Regiment	Tarrant, then under Capt. Clement Hall. 9/9/1778, a known Private under Capt. Robert Fenner. POW at the Fall of Charleston (SC), exchanged in 1781 at Jamestown, VA. Enlisted in Pasquotank County, NC. Discharged at Charleston, SC. S38771.	Charleston 1780 (SC).
Gregory, James	1st NC Regiment	6/14/1781, a Private under Capt. Thomas Donoho. Dropped from the rolls during 1781.	
Gregory, Robert	2nd NC Regiment	7/20/1778, a Private under Maj. Reading Blount for nine months.	
Gregory, Thomas	1st NC Regiment	11/10/1778, a Private under Capt. Anthony Sharpe for nine months. From Duplin, what is now Sampson County, NC. S41589.	
Gregory, Thomas	2nd NC Regiment	A Private under Capt. James Gee. 9/9/1778, a known Private under Capt. John Ingles. Earlier in NC Militia. From Currituck County, NC. S41588.	Stono Ferry (SC).
Gregory, William	1st NC Regiment	6/12/1777, a Sergeant under Capt. James Read. Dropped from the rolls in Nov. 1779.	
Gregory, Willis	1st NC Regiment	6/12/1777, a Private, unit unknown. 9/8/1778, a known Private under Capt. James Read.	
Grice, Gabriel	3rd NC Regiment	8/15/1782, a Private under Capt. Benjamin Bailey for 12 months.	
Griffin, Daniel	10th NC Regiment	5/20/1777, a Private under Capt. Armwell Herron. Dropped from the rolls in June 1778.	
Griffin, Dempsey	1st NC Regiment	6/20/1781, a Private under Capt. Anthony Sharpe. Discharged on 6/20/1782 (4th NC Regiment).	
Griffin, Edmund	2nd NC Regiment	11/7/1776, a Private under Capt. Benjamin Williams. 9/9/1778, a known Private in the Lt. Colonel's Company (Lt. Col. Selby Harney). Transferred to His Excy's Guards in 1778. Discharged 1/31/1780.	
Griffin, Edward	1st NC Regiment	1781, a Private under Capt. Alexander Brevard. Discharged on 7/11/1782 (3rd NC Regiment). Two men with same name listed for same dates.	
Griffin, Ezekiel	4th NC Regiment	1781, a Private under Capt. George Dougherty. Discharged 9/1/1782.	
Griffin, Ezekiel	10th NC Regiment	4/21/1777, a Private under Capt. Silas Stevenson. Dropped from the rolls in June 1778.	
Griffin, James	1st NC Regiment	1781, a Corporal under Capt. Anthony Sharpe for 12 months. Discharged 4/15/1782.	
Griffin, James	2nd NC Regiment	12/1/1776, a Private, unit unknown. 9/9/1778, a known Private in the Lt. Colonel's Company (Lt. Col. Selby Harney).	
Griffin, James	3rd NC Regiment	8/1/1782, a Private under Capt. Benjamin Bailey for 12 months.	
Griffin, James	5th NC Regiment	12/1/1776, a Corporal under Capt. Reading Blount. Discharged on 2/1/1780 at Halifax, NC. From Edgecombe County, NC. W7586.	Brandywine Creek (PA), Germantown (PA), Monmouth (NJ).
Griffin,	6th NC	1777, a Private under Capt. Thomas Donoho.	

Name	1st Unit	Year / Rank / Served Under / Notes	Known Battles
James	Regiment	Deserted in Aug. 1777.	
Griffin, Jesse	3rd NC Regiment	7/20/1778, a Private under Capt. Michael Quinn for nine months.	
Griffin, Joshua	1st NC Regiment	1777, a Private under Capt. John Brown. Died on 3/4/1778.	
Griffin, Martin	3rd NC Regiment	7/20/1778, a Private under Capt. Francis Child for nine months.	
Griffin, Robert	6th NC Regiment	5/15/1777, a Sergeant Major. Dropped from the rolls in Nov. 1778.	
Griffin, Timothy	1st NC Regiment	4/28/1781, a Private under Capt. Alexander Brevard.	
Griffin, William	2nd NC Regiment	1777, a Private under Capt. James Gee. 9/9/1778, a known Private under Capt. John Ingles (2nd NC Regiment). POW at Ft. Lafayette, NY on 6/1/1779. 1781, re-enlisted as a Private under Capt. William Lytle (1st NC Regiment) for the duration of the war.	Ft. Lafayette (NY).
Griffin, William	7th NC Regiment	1777, a Private under Capt. Henry Dawson. Dropped from the rolls in Feb. 1778.	
Griffis, Allen	1st NC Regiment	1777, a Private under Capt. Howell Tatum. Dropped from the rolls in Jan. 1778.	
Griffith, Edward	7th NC Regiment	12/28/1776, a Sergeant under Capt. James Vaughan. Died in Jan. 1777.	
Griffith, Isaac	7th NC Regiment	3/1/1777, a Musician under Capt. James Vaughan. 5/21/1777, a Private under Capt. Dempsey Gregory (10th NC Regiment). A Sergeant in Nov. 1777. 2/26/1778, a known Private under Capt. Howell Tatum (1st NC Regiment). 9/8/1778, a known Sergeant under Capt. Howell Tatum (1st NC Regiment). Discharged as a Sergeant on 3/1/1780. aka Isaac Griffin.	
Griffiths, John	1st NC Regiment	1777, a Private under Capt. Henry "Hal" Dixon. Transferred to His Excy Guards in March 1778. 9/8/1778, listed under Capt. James Read, although still with His Excy's Guards. aka John Griffis, John Griffin.	
Grifford, James	1st NC Regiment	1777, a Private under Capt. Henry "Hal" Dixon.	
Griggs, Charles	10th NC Regiment	5/18/1777, a Private under Capt. John Jarvis for three years. June 1778, a Private under Capt. Griffith John McRee (1st NC Regiment). Discharged 8/31/1781. From Currituck County, NC. aka Charles Greggs. S6933.	
Grimes, Elisha	1st NC Regiment	1777, a Private under Capt. Thomas Hogg. Deserted on 5/28/1777.	
Grimes, Richard	2nd NC Regiment	Sep. 1775, a Lieutenant under Capt. William Knox. Accidentally killed his Captain - dates, circumstances unknown. Probably the same man as Richard Graham above.	Snow Campaign (SC), Moore's Creek Bridge [4], Ft. Moultrie #1 (SC).
Grimes, William	1st NC Regiment	Spring of 1779, a Private under Capt. Tilghman Dixon. From Johnston County, NC. W19249.	

Name	1st Unit	Year / Rank / Served Under / Notes	Known Battles
Grinage, John	3rd NC Regiment	1782, a Private under Capt. Alexander Brevard. Died on 6/20/1783.	
Grinder, John	10th NC Regiment	1778, a Private under Capt. Isaac Moore. Died on 6/29/1779.	
Grindstaff, Michael	1st NC Regiment	6/6/1781, a Corporal under Capt. Alexander Brevard, then Capt. William Lytle. Discharged on 6/7/1782 (4th NC Regiment) at Camden, SC. Earlier in NC Militia, unit unknown. aka Michael Grinstaff. S35995.	Siege of Ninety-Six 1781 (SC), Eutaw Springs (SC).
Grisham, Major	4th NC Regiment	Feb. 1779, a Private under Capt. Joel Lewis.	
Grissel, Willy	1st NC Regiment	1782, a Private under Capt. Peter Bacot for 18 months.	
Grissom, Robert	6th NC Regiment	6/1/1776, a Musician under Lt./Capt. Francis Child. A Private in Oct. 1778. Deserted on 6/6/1779.	
Griswit, Thomas	4th NC Regiment	1777, a Private under Capt. Robert Smith. Died in Jan. 1778.	
Gro, James	3rd NC Regiment	7/20/1778, a Private under Capt. John Baker. Died on 11/16/1778.	
Grogan, John	5th NC Regiment	6/24/1779, a Private under Capt. Joseph Montford. Deserted on 11/8/1779.	
Grogan, James	10th NC Regiment	5/24/1777, a Private under Capt. Dempsey Gregory. 9/8/1778, a known Private under Capt. Howell Tatum (1st NC Regiment). Dropped from the rolls in Feb. 1779. aka James Grozan, James Grogin.	
Groover, Peter	1st NC Regiment	1781, a Private under Capt. Thomas Donoho for 12 months. Earlier in NC Militia. From Randolph County, NC.	Eutaw Springs (SC).
Groves, William	5th NC Regiment	1775, a 1st Lieutenant under Capt. Simon Alderson and Col. Richard Caswell in the New Bern District Minutemen. 4/17/1776, a Lieutenant under Capt. Simon Alderson, then under Capt. William Caswell. Promoted to Captain on 8/17/1777. Retired 6/1/1778. aka William Graves.	
Guard, John	10th NC Regiment	6/24/1777, a Private under Capt. Silas Stevenson. Died on 3/23/1778. aka John Gaurd.	
Guard, Joshua	4th NC Regiment	2/7/1782, a Private under Capt. James Mills for 12 months.	
Guin, Samuel	4th NC Regiment	1782, a Private under Capt. Anthony Sharpe for 18 months.	
Guion, Isaac	1st NC Regiment	9/1/1775, a Surgeon. Resigned. Dec. 1775. Re-enlisted into the 9th NC Regiment as a Paymaster on 12/11/1776. Transferred to 7th NC Regiment in 1777 as its Paymaster. Retired 6/1/1778. aka Isaac Ginon.	
Gunn, Alexander	6th NC Regiment	1777, a Sergeant under Capt. Griffith John McRee. Dropped from the rolls in Jan. 1778.	
Gunn, James		A Private Jan. to Feb. 1778, regiment and unit unknown.	
Gunn, James	2nd NC Regiment	4/15/1781, a Sergeant under Capt. Benjamin Carter. Discharged 4/10/1782.	

406

Name	1st Unit	Year / Rank / Served Under / Notes	Known Battles
Gunnell, John	2nd NC Regiment	Jan. 1779, a Private, unit unknown. 3/12/1779, re-enlisted in the Lt. Colonel's Company (Lt. Col. Selby Harney). Deserted on 1/30/1780.	
Gunns, Isaac	3rd NC Regiment	7/20/1778, a Private in the Lt. Colonel's Company (Lt. Col. William Lee Davidson) led by Lt./Capt. George "Gee" Bradley. 4/23/1779, a known Private in the Lt. Colonel's Company (Lt. Col. Robert Mebane) led by Capt. George "Gee" Bradley. Died at New Windsor Hospital. aka Isaac Gums.	
Gunston, James	1st NC Regiment	1781, a Private under Capt. Alexander Brevard for 18 months. From Surry County, NC. Earlier in NC Militia. S6939.	Siege of Ninety-Six 1781 (SC).
Gunter, Joel	6th NC Regiment	12/6/1776, a Private under Capt. William Glover for three years. 6/1/1778, a Private under Capt. Griffith John McRee (1st NC Regiment), then Capt. Francis Child. Discharged on 1/29/1780 near Halifax, NC. S38780.	
Gurganus, Reuben	3rd NC Regiment	7/20/1778, a Private under Capt. Francis Child for nine months. Discharged on 5/4/1779 at Halifax, NC. From Pitt County, NC. Later in NC Militia. S8638.	
Gurley, Joseph	1st NC Regiment	Sep. 1781, a Private under Capt. Robert Raiford. Discharged 9/13/1782 (2nd NC Regiment). Re-enlisted for the duration of the war, date unknown. From Johnston Co., NC. W4973.	
Gurley, Simon	2nd NC Regiment	1777, a Private under Capt. Edward Vail, Jr. Died on 5/6/1778.	
Gurley, William	8th NC Regiment	11/28/1776, a Captain under Col. James Armstrong. Refused to serve. From Johnston County, NC.	
Guthery, James	4th NC Regiment	5/16/1778, a Private under Capt. William Goodman. Discharged 8/10/1779 at Martin's Tavern, SC. Rejoined in Feb. 1781 for five weeks - very sick, discharged. Born 1756 in Hanover County, VA. aka James Guthrie. S21793.	Charleston Neck (SC), Stono Ferry (SC).
Guthrie, Levi	DQMG	1780, a Blacksmith under Col. Nicholas Long (Deputy QM General). Also on 8/23/1781.	
Guttery, Henry	10th NC Regiment	11/1/1777, a Private under Capt. James Wilson for three years. 9/8/1778, a known Private in the Major's Company (Maj. John Baptiste Ashe) (1st NC Regiment) - sick in the Flying Hospital on that date. Died in Oct. 1778. On some rolls as Hardy Guttery.	
Gutry, John	1st NC Regiment	Sep. 1775, a Private under Capt. Alfred Moore for six months. From Orange (soon to be Caswell) County, NC. Discharged at Wilmington, NC. Later in NC Militia. R4398.	
Guy, William	10th NC Regiment	5/18/1777, a Private under Capt. Isaac Moore. Dropped from the rolls in June 1778.	
Gwinn, William	4th NC Regiment	A Private under Capt. Roger Moore, then under Capt. William Goodman for three years. From	

Name	1st Unit	Year / Rank / Served Under / Notes	Known Battles
		Orange County, NC. Later in NC Militia. R4402.	
Habbet, Ezekiel		A Private, regiment and unit unknown. Discharged on 5/1/1778.	
Haddock, Andrew	1st NC Regiment	1778, a Sergeant under Capt. James Read. Discharged on 4/8/1778.	
Haddock, Andrew	4th NC Regiment	1782, a Sergeant under Capt. William Lytle for 18 months.	
Haddock, Richard	4th NC Regiment	1782, a Private under Capt. William Lytle for 18 months.	
Hadley, Joshua	6th NC Regiment	1775, an Ensign in the Salisbury District Minutemen. 4/17/1776, an Ensign under Capt. John Baptiste Ashe and Col. John Alexander Lillington. 4/17/1777, a 1st Lieutenant under Capt. Philip Taylor. Wounded at the battle of Germantown, PA. Transferred to 1st NC Regiment on 6/1/1778. 6/13/1779, a Captain in the 1st NC Regiment. One source asserts it was the 6th NC Regiment (No). Several sources assert he was in the Militia during 1780 and early 1781 while the NC Continental Line was rebuilding. Mid-1781, a Captain under Maj. Reading Blount (2nd NC Regiment). Wounded at the battle of Eutaw Springs, SC on September 8, 1781.	Brandywine Creek (PA), Germantown (PA), Monck's Corner #1 (SC), Lenud's Ferry (SC), Little Lynches Creek (SC), Camden (SC), Guilford Court House, Fort Motte (SC), Siege of Ninety-Six 1781 (SC), Eutaw Springs (SC).
Hadley, William	4th NC Regiment	1782, a Private under Capt. William Lytle for 18 months.	
Hadnot, West	6th NC Regiment	1777, a Sergeant under Capt. Thomas Donoho. A Private in Nov. 1777. Dropped from the rolls in Feb. 1778.	
Hafner, Jacob	1st NC Regiment	6/1/1781, a Private under Capt. William Lytle for 12 months.	
Hagenton, Jesse	3rd NC Regiment	1781, served under Capt. Edward Yarborough for 12 months. Discharged on 4/10/1782.	
Haile, Joseph	2nd NC Regiment	1775, a Private under Capt. Simon Bright for six months. 1777, a Private under Capt. Abraham Sheppard, Jr. (10th NC Regiment). 7/20/1778, a Private under Capt. Michael Quinn (3rd NC Regiment) for nine months. On the official rolls as Joseph Hale. From Wayne County, NC. S38814.	
Haines, William	1st NC Regiment	1781, a Private under Capt. Anthony Sharpe for 12 months. Discharged 2/3/1783 (4th NC Regiment).	
Hainey, Anthony	2nd NC Regiment	5/15/1781, a Private under Capt. Tilghman Dixon. Discharged 5/21/1782 (1st NC Regiment). Received clothing on 5/24/1782. From Caswell County.	
Hainey, Anthony	2nd NC Regiment	5/15/1781, a Corporal under Capt. Tilghman Dixon. Discharged on 5/21/1782 (1st NC Regiment). Probably the same man as directly above.	

Name	1st Unit	Year / Rank / Served Under / Notes	Known Battles
Hainey, John	2nd NC Regiment	5/15/1781, a Corporal under Capt. Tilghman Dixon. Discharged on 5/21/1782 (1st NC Regiment). Received clothing on 5/24/1782. From Caswell County.	
Hair, James	1st NC Regiment	5/2/1781, a Private under Lt./Capt. Benjamin Bailey. Discharged on 5/2/1782 (3rd NC Regiment).	
Hair, L. John	1st NC Regiment	8/16/1777, a Lieutenant under Capt. Anthony Sharpe. Dropped from the rolls in June 1778.	
Hair, Robert	2nd NC Regiment	1777, a Private under Capt. William Fenner. Deserted in Dec. 1777.	
Hair, Robert	4th NC Regiment	1779, a Private under Capt. Matthew Ramsey for nine months. From Rowan County, NC. 1780, in NC Militia. S9567.	
Hair, Thomas	1st NC Regiment	11/10/1778, a Private under Capt. Anthony Sharpe for nine months.	
Hair, Thomas	3rd NC Regiment	5/20/1778, a Private under Lt./Capt. George "Gee" Bradley. Deserted on 10/16/1779.	
Hair, William	3rd NC Regiment	7/20/1778, a Private under Capt. Kedar Ballard for nine months.	
Hale, Thomas	1st NC Regiment	1775, a Private under Lt. Lawrence Thompson, Capt. Alfred Moore. Enlisted in Orange County, NC. Discharged at Charleston, SC. Joined SC unit. S37975.	Moore's Creek Bridge [4], Breech Inlet Naval Battle (SC).
Hale, Thomas	1st NC Regiment	6/20/1777 to Sep. 1777, Deputy Muster Master General.	
Hale, William	1st NC Regiment	9/9/1775, a Private under Lt. Lawrence Thompson, Capt. Alfred Moore for nine months. Enlisted in Orange County, NC. Discharged in March 1776 at Wilmington, NC. S1522.	Moore's Creek Bridge [4].
Hall, Anthony	1st NC Regiment	6/10/1778, a Private under Capt. Thomas Donoho. POW at the Fall of Charleston (SC), exchanged near the end of the war. Earlier in VA Continentals. Resided in Caswell County, NC when he enlisted. W1764.	Siege of Charleston 1780 (SC).
Hall, Clement	2nd NC Regiment	9/1/1775, a 1st Lieutenant under Capt. Michael Payne. 4/19/1777, a Captain. Wrongfully blamed for seizing cider and whiskey. Mid-1781, a Captain under Maj. John Armstrong (3rd NC Regiment). 2/6/1782, moved back to 2nd NC Regiment. A brevet Major on 9/30/1783. S38790.	Brandywine Creek (PA), Germantown (PA), Monmouth (NJ), Near West Point (NY), Stony Point (NC), Eutaw Springs (SC).
Hall, David	3rd NC Regiment	Jan. 1779, a Private in the Lt. Colonel's Company (Lt. Col. Robert Mebane) led by Capt. George "Gee" Bradley. aka Davis Hall.	
Hall, David	8th NC Regiment	1777, a Sergeant under Capt. John Walsh. A Private in Jan. 1778. Back to Sergeant in Feb. 1779. Back to Private in Aug. 1779. Discharged on 2/1/1780.	

Name	1st Unit	Year / Rank / Served Under / Notes	Known Battles
Hall, Delany	3rd NC Regiment	1777, a Private under Capt. William Brinkley. Died on 3/13/1778.	
Hall, Edward	3rd NC Regiment	7/20/1778, a Private under Capt. John Baker for nine months.	
Hall, Futrill	5th NC Regiment	Jan. 1779, a Private under Capt. Philip Taylor.	
Hall, Ignatius	DQMG	1781, an Express Rider under AQMG Jesse Potts and Col. Nicholas Long for 12 months. Discharged in Nov. 1782. From Halifax County, NC. R4464.	
Hall, James	1st NC Regiment	1/1/1778, a Private under Capt. James Read. 9/8/1778, a known Private under Capt. James Read. Discharged on 2/1/1780.	
Hall, James	1st NC Regiment	4/15/1781, a Private under Lt./Capt. Benjamin Bailey. Discharged on 4/15/1782 (3rd NC Regiment). From Hertford County, NC.	
Hall, James	3rd NC Regiment	1779, a Private under Capt. Michael Quinn. Discharged in Dec. 1779. 1781, served under Capt. Edward Yarborough for 12 months. Discharged on 4/10/1782 at Bacon's Bridge, SC. From Wake County, NC. R4458.	
Hall, James	7th NC Regiment	1777, a Private under Capt. Henry Dawson. Dropped from the rolls in Oct. 1777.	
Hall, James	9th NC Regiment	1777, a Private under Capt. Joseph J. Wade. Dropped from the rolls in Jan. 1778.	
Hall, James	9th NC Regiment	May 1777, a Captain under Col. John Williams. Dropped from the rolls in Jan. 1778. One source asserts his first name was Joseph (wrong). Later, a Captain and a Lt. Colonel in the Rowan County Regiment of Militia.	
Hall, Jesse	1st NC Regiment	1781, a Corporal under Capt. Alexander Brevard for 12 months. Discharged on 5/9/1782 (3rd NC Regiment).	
Hall, Jesse	5th NC Regiment	1779, a Private under Maj. Reading Blount for nine months. Deserted in Sep. 1779.	
Hall, Jesse	6th NC Regiment	1776, a Private under Lt. George Dougherty, Capt. John Baptiste Ashe for 2-1/2 years. From Wilkes County, NC. POW at the Fall of Charleston, paroled. Rejoined under Capt. Alexander Brevard (4th NC Regiment, transferred to 1st NC Regiment in 1781). W21258.	Briar Creek (GA), Siege of Charleston 1780 (SC), Guilford Court House, Siege of Ninety-Six 1781 (SC), Eutaw Springs (SC).
Hall, John	1st NC Regiment	Sep. 1781, a Private under Capt. Anthony Sharpe. Discharged in Sep. 1782 at James Island, SC. From Richmond County, NC. S41621.	
Hall, John	1st NC Regiment	8/1/1782, a Private under Capt. Joshua Hadley for 18 months.	
Hall, John	2nd NC Regiment	4/25/1781, a Private and a Quartermaster under Capt. Tilghman Dixon. Discharged on 4/25/1782. From Warren County, NC. R14699.	Eutaw Springs (SC).

410

Name	1st Unit	Year / Rank / Served Under / Notes	Known Battles
Hall, John	3rd NC Regiment	1778, a Sergeant, unit unknown.	
Hall, John	4th NC Regiment	1782, a Corporal under Capt. Anthony Sharpe for 18 months.	
Hall, Joshua	2nd NC Regiment	4/25/1781, served under Capt. Benjamin Carter. Discharged on 4/25/1782.	
Hall, Joshua	3rd NC Regiment	Jan. 1779, a Private in the Lt. Colonel's Company (Lt. Col. Robert Mebane) led by Capt. George "Gee" Bradley.	
Hall, Nathan	5th NC Regiment	1779, a Musician under Maj. Reading Blount. Died on 8/24/1779.	
Hall, Robert	3rd NC Regiment	4/17/1776, a Surgeon. Resigned 2/28/1777.	
Hall, Thomas	1st NC Regiment	12/24/1776, an Ensign. 2/8/1777, a 2nd Lieutenant under Capt. Henry "Hal" Dixon. Resigned on 4/10/1777.	
Hall, Thomas	5th NC Regiment	3/1/1779, a Private under Capt. Joseph Montford. Discharged on 12/1/1779. Found guilty of desertion, received 100 lashes.	
Hall, William	2nd NC Regiment	4/12/1781, served under Capt. Benjamin Carter. Discharged on 4/7/1782.	
Hall, William	4th NC Regiment	1778, a Private under Capt. Matthew Ramsey for nine months. Discharged on 9/5/1779 at Bacon's Bridge, SC. From Rowan County, NC. Wounded at the battle of Stono Ferry (SC). R21886.	Stono Ferry (SC).
Hall, William	4th NC Regiment	1778, a Private under Capt. Robert Moore, then Capt. William Goodman. 1780, in NC Militia. From Caswell County, NC. S16859.	Stono Ferry (SC).
Halladay, John	1st NC Regiment	1776, a Private under Capt. George Davidson for nine months. Then, in NC Militia. From Guilford County, NC. S41627.	Breech Inlet Naval Battle (SC).
Halling, Solomon	4th NC Regiment	In his Bounty Land application, he asserts he was a Jr. Surgeon, or Surgeon's Mate, at the General Hospital in 1776. August 1779, he was promoted to Sr. Surgeon until May 1782. He was taken prisoner at the battle of Briar Creek (GA), apparently exchanged soon thereafter. BLWt54-450.	Briar Creek (GA).
Halstead, Jolly	10th NC Regiment	5/28/1777, a Private under Capt. John Jarvis for three years. 9/8/1778, a known Private in the Major's Company (Maj. John Baptiste Ashe) (1st NC Regiment). aka Jolly Holstead.	
Halstead, Samuel	10th NC Regiment	5/5/1777, a Corporal under Capt. John Jarvis for three years. A Private in June 1778. 9/8/1778, a known Private in the Major's Company (Maj. Griffith John McRee) (1st NC Regiment) - sick on that date. Died on 1/12/1779. aka Samuel Holstead, Lemuel Halstead.	
Halten, Brazil	1st NC Regiment	8/1/1782, a Private under Capt. Joshua Hadley for 18 months.	
Halyon, Willis	DQMG	1780, a Private under Capt. Solomon Wood (NC Light Dragoons) - this appears to be for convenience only. 8/23/1781, a Shoemaker	

Name	1st Unit	Year / Rank / Served Under / Notes	Known Battles
		under Col. Nicholas Long (Deputy QM General).	
Ham, Drury	2nd NC Regiment	5/15/1776, a Private, unit unknown. 9/10/1778, a known Private under Capt. Thomas Armstrong.	
Hamb, William	3rd NC Regiment	7/20/1778, a Private under Capt. Michael Quinn for nine months.	
Hamilton, Hanse	7th NC Regiment	April 1777, a Surgeon. Died in Jan. 1778.	
Hamilton, John	1st NC Regiment	1777, a Sergeant under Capt. Joshua Bowman. Dropped from the rolls in Jan. 1778. 1779, enlisted as a Private in the 4th NC Regiment, unit unknown.	
Hamilton, John	5th NC Regiment	1777, a Private under Capt. Benjamin Stedman. 9/9/1778, a known Private under Capt. Clement Hall (2nd NC Regiment) - sick at Brunswick. aka John Hambleton.	
Hamilton, Stewart	1st NC Regiment	5/25/1781, a Private under Lt./Capt. Benjamin Bailey. Discharged on 5/25/1782 (3rd NC Regiment).	
Hamm, John	3rd NC Regiment	1776, a Private under Capt. James Emmett for 18 months. Then moved to SC and joined SC Militia there. Enlisted in Chatham County, NC. S31095.	Ft. Moultrie #1 (SC).
Hamm, Philip	NC Light Dragoons	Oct.-Dec. 1777, a known Private under Capt. Martin Phifer. Not on any official rolls.	
Hammock, Samuel	1st NC Regiment	1782, a Private under Capt. Peter Bacot for 18 months.	
Hammon, Isaac	2nd NC Regiment	11/1/1781, a Private under Capt. Benjamin Andrew Coleman. Died on 8/1/1782.	
Hammon, Isaac	3rd NC Regiment	8/1/1781, served under Capt. Samuel Jones.	
Hammon, John	2nd NC Regiment	5/9/1778, a Private under Capt. Clement Hall for 2-1/2 years.	
Hammond, B. John	5th NC Regiment	5/7/1776, a Sergeant under Capt. Benjamin Stedman. Discharged on 11/10/1778. aka B. John Hammon.	
Hammond, Judah	6th NC Regiment	1777, a Private under Capt. Thomas Donoho. Died in Aug. 1777.	
Hammonds, Edward	6th NC Regiment	1777, a Corporal under Capt. Thomas Donoho. Deserted in Aug. 1777.	
Hamontree, Griffith	1st NC Regiment	4/15/1781, a Corporal under Capt. Anthony Sharpe. Discharged on 4/15/1782 (4th NC Regiment).	
Hampton, Adam	3rd NC Regiment	1775, a 1st Lieutenant in the Salisbury District Minutemen. From Tryon (what became Rutherford County). 4/17/1776, a 1st Lieutenant under Capt. James Cook and Col. Jethro Sumner. 1776, also a Captain in NC Militia.	
Hampton, Zachariah	1st NC Regiment	6/6/1781, a Private under Capt. William Lytle. Dropped from the rolls sometime during 1781.	
Hanberry, Jesse	1st NC Regiment	1781, a Private under Capt. William Armstrong for 12 months. Discharged on 11/1/1782 (3rd NC Regiment).	

Name	1st Unit	Year / Rank / Served Under / Notes	Known Battles
Hancock, Henry	2nd NC Regiment	4/25/1781, a Private under Capt. Tilghman Dixon. Dropped from the rolls during 1781.	
Hancock, Isaac	1st NC Regiment	1777, a Corporal under Capt. Henry "Hal" Dixon. A Sergeant on 10/12/1777. A Private on 2/1/1780.	
Hand, Joseph	2nd NC Regiment	1782, a Private under Capt. Robert Raiford for 18 months. From Guilford County, NC. Discharged in July 1783 at Ashley Hill, SC. Earlier in NC Militia. W7625.	
Handcock, William	6th NC Regiment	4/28/1777, an Ensign. 4/28/1777, a 2nd Lieutenant under Capt. Benjamin Pike. Resigned on 8/28/1777. aka William Hancock.	
Handley, William	10th NC Regiment	6/28/1777, a Private under Capt. Abraham Sheppard, Jr. 9/9/1778, a known Private under Capt. Benjamin Andrew Coleman (2nd NC Regiment). 3/12/1779, re-enlisted under Capt. Benjamin Andrew Coleman.	
Hanish, Elijah	2nd NC Regiment	4/20/1776, a Private, unit unknown. 9/10/1778, a known Private under Capt. Thomas Armstrong.	
Hanners, Henry	10th NC Regiment	9/18/1777, a Corporal under Capt. Dempsey Gregory. A Private in June 1778. Died 8/3/1778.	
Hanson, Paul	1st NC Regiment	5/9/1781, a Private under Capt. Alexander Brevard.	
Harback, John	5th NC Regiment	Jan. 1779, a Private under Maj. Pinketham Eaton.	
Harbert, Benjamin	5th NC Regiment	7/26/1779, a Private under Capt. Joseph Montford. aka Benjamin Harbut.	
Harbourd, John		A Private, regiment and unit unknown. Deserted in Sep. 1779.	
Hardee, Isaac	10th NC Regiment	1777, a 2nd Lieutenant.	
Hardee, William	5th NC Regiment	5/3/1776, a Private under Capt. Reading Blount for one year. Discharged on 5/3/1777 at Halifax, NC. From Pitt County, NC. W9054.	
Harden, William	NC Light Dragoons	Oct.-Dec. 1777, a known Private under Capt. Martin Phifer. Not on any official rolls.	
Hardick, Richard	2nd NC Regiment	7/31/1781, served under Capt. Benjamin Carter. Discharged on 7/25/1782.	
Hardin, Lewis	7th NC Regiment	July 1777, a Private under Capt. Henry Dawson for one year. 7/20/1778, a Private under Lt./Capt. George "Gee" Bradley and Lt./Capt. Joseph Montford (3rd NC Regiment) for nine months. 1782, re-enlisted as a Corporal under Capt. Peter Bacot (1st NC Regiment) for one year. On the official rolls as Lewis Harden. aka Lewis Harding. S38799.	Brandywine Creek (PA), Germantown (PA), Monmouth (NJ).
Harding, Abraham	1st NC Regiment	4/15/1781, a Private under Capt. Anthony Sharpe. Dropped from the rolls during 1781.	
Harding, Israel	1st NC Regiment	4/15/1781, a Sergeant under Capt. Anthony Sharpe. Discharged on 4/15/1782 (4th NC Regiment).	
Hardison,	7th NC	4/14/1777, a QM Sergeant. Died on 12/18/1777.	

Name	1st Unit	Year / Rank / Served Under / Notes	Known Battles
Hardy	Regiment		
Hardison, Jesse	3rd NC Regiment	7/20/1778, a Sergeant under Capt. John Baker for nine months.	
Hardison, Joseph	3rd NC Regiment	7/20/1778, a Private under Lt./Capt. George "Gee" Bradley for nine months.	
Hardy, John	5th NC Regiment	Sergeant under Capt. John Enloe. Missing 10/4/1777 at the battle of Germantown, PA.	Germantown (PA).
Hardy, Joseph	1st NC Regiment	4/5/1781, a Private under Capt. Anthony Sharpe. Dropped from the rolls sometime during 1781. Possibly the same man as directly below.	
Hardy, Joseph	4th NC Regiment	1781, a Private under Capt. Joseph T. Rhodes for 12 months. Discharged on 4/25/1782.	
Hardy, Robert	1st NC Regiment	5/28/1781, a Sergeant under Capt. Alexander Brevard. Discharged on 5/28/1782 (3rd NC Regiment).	
Hardy, Thomas	3rd NC Regiment	1777, a Private under Capt. Pinketham Eaton. Discharged in Oct. 1778.	
Hardy, William	NC Light Dragoons	9/10/1777, a Paymaster.	
Hare, John L.	7th NC Regiment	1777, an Ensign. 8/26/1777, left in NC as a recruiter.	
Hare, Nicholas	3rd NC Regiment	7/20/1778, a Private under Capt. Kedar Ballard for nine months.	
Hargett, Frederick	8th NC Regiment	11/28/1776, a Captain under Col. James Armstrong. Regiment disbanded 6/1/1778. Earlier and later in NC Militia. From Craven (what became Jones) County, NC. aka Frederick Harjett.	Brandywine Creek (PA), Germantown (PA).
Hargis, Abraham		A Private for 2-1/2 years, Captain and Regiment unknown. Probably in Militia afterwards. From Caswell County, NC. In Philadelphia during battle of Brandywine Creek, PA. W4480.	Germantown (PA).
Hargrave, Hezekiah	3rd NC Regiment	1782, a Private under Capt. Alexander Brevard for 18 months.	
Hargrave, William	10th NC Regiment	1/20/1778 or 2/16/1778 (two sources), an Ensign under Capt. William Shepherd. Transferred to 1st NC Regiment on 6/1/1778 under Capt. James Read. 9/8/1778, a known Ensign under Capt. James Read. 3/30/1780, a Lieutenant under Capt. Howell Tatum. POW at the Fall of Charleston, paroled 6/14/1781, but not exchanged until 11/26/1782. Retired 1/21/1783. S37980.	Siege of Charleston 1780 (SC).
Hargrove, John	10th NC Regiment	5/19/1777, a Private, unit unknown. 9/8/1778, a known Private in the Major's Company (Maj. Hardy Murfree) (2nd NC Regiment). Enlisted at Murfreesborough in Hertford County, NC. Discharged on 6/30/1780 at Murfreesborough, NC. On the official rolls as John Hargrave. aka John Harigrooves, John Hargave. S37978.	Monmouth (NY), Siege of Charleston 1780 (SC).
Harman, John	10th NC Regiment	Jan. 1778, a Private, unit unknown. Dropped from the rolls in June 1778.	
Harman,	4th NC	12/30/1776, a Musician under Capt. Robert	

Name	1st Unit	Year / Rank / Served Under / Notes	Known Battles
Robert	Regiment	Smith. A Private in June 1778. 3/12/1779, re-enlisted for the duration of the war in the Colonel's Company (Col. Thomas Clark) (1st NC Regiment) led by Capt. John Gambier Scull. Deserted 4/17/1779. aka Robert Harmon.	
Harmon, James	3rd NC Regiment	1781, a Corporal under Capt. Clement Hall for 12 months. Discharged on 8/16/1782 (2nd NC Regiment).	
Harmond, John	1st NC Regiment	4/28/1779, a Private under Capt. Griffith John McRee for 12 months. Died in Sep. 1781.	
Harney, Selby	8th NC Regiment	1775, a Captain in NC Militia. 11/26/1776, a Major in the 8th NC Regiment. A Lt. Colonel on 11/22/1777 of the 2nd NC Regiment. POW at the Fall of Charleston - wounded at Haddrell's Point. Transferred to 3rd NC Regiment on 2/6/1782. Exchanged on 11/26/1782. A full Colonel on 9/30/1783, no mention of brevet. One source claims he retired 1/1/1783. aka Selby Harvey.	Brandywine Creek (PA), Germantown (PA), Monmouth (NJ), Siege of Savannah (GA), Siege of Charleston 1780 (SC).
Harp, Joseph	4th NC Regiment	1780, a Private under Capt. Joseph T. Rhodes for 18 months. R4624.	
Harp, Matthew	1st NC Regiment	Jan. 1779, a Sergeant Major under Capt. William Armstrong.	
Harp, Richard	5th NC Regiment	3/1/1779, a Private under Capt. Reading Blount for nine months. Discharged on 12/1/1779.	
Harper, Andrew	NC Brigade	1779, Brigade Major to BG James Hogun.	
Harper, Frederick	3rd NC Regiment	7/20/1778, a Private under Lt./Capt. George "Gee" Bradley for nine months.	
Harper, Jethro	1st NC Regiment	1782, a Private under Lt. John Foard, Capt. Peter Bacot for 18 months. From Halifax County, NC. aka Jett Harper.	
Harper, John	1st NC Regiment	6/4/1781, a Private under Capt. Anthony Sharpe. Discharged 6/5/1782 (4th NC Regiment). From Dobbs (what is now Lenoir) County, NC. W4977.	
Harper, Joseph	4th NC Regiment	1781, a Private under Capt. Joseph T. Rhodes for 12 months. Discharged on 5/14/1782.	
Harper, Nathan	1st NC Regiment	6/4/1781, a Private under Capt. William Armstrong, then under Capt. Anthony Sharpe. Discharged 6/5/1782 (4th NC Regiment). Born on 11/8/1764 in Dobbs County, NC. S31091.	Eutaw Springs (SC).
Harper, Robert	10th NC Regiment	4/21/1777, a Private under Capt. Silas Stevenson. Dropped from the rolls in June 1778.	
Harper, William	4th NC Regiment	1781, a Private under Capt. Joseph T. Rhodes for 12 months. Discharged on 6/14/1782.	
Harrard, James	10th NC Regiment	5/13/1777, a Private, unit unknown.	
Harrell, Holland	5th NC Regiment	1777, a Private under Capt. Henry Darnell. Died on 8/28/1777.	
Harrell, John	1st NC Regiment	4/4/1776, a Private under Capt. John Brown for 2-1/2 years. 9/8/1778, a known Private under Capt. John Sumner. Discharged on 10/6/1778.	

Name	1st Unit	Year / Rank / Served Under / Notes	Known Battles
		aka John Harrold.	
Harrell, Peter	10th NC Regiment	5/20/1777, a Sergeant under Capt. Abraham Sheppard, Jr. 9/10/1778, a known Private under Capt. Thomas Armstrong (2nd NC Regiment). Back to Sergeant in Nov. 1778. POW at Ft. Lafayette, NY on 6/1/1779. aka Peter Harril.	Ft. Lafayette (NY).
Harrick, Elisha		5/20/1776, a Private, regiment and unit unknown. Discharged on 1/16/1779.	
Harrill, James	5th NC Regiment	Summer 1776, a Private under Capt. John Pugh Williams. Then under Capt. Robert Fenner (2nd NC Regiment). POW at the Fall of Charleston, escaped after a few months, jumped on Spanish ship and went to Cuba then Nova Scotia. Born 1757 in Halifax County, NC. aka James Harrell, James Harrold. R4634.	Brandywine Creek (PA), Germantown (PA), Monmouth (NJ), Siege of Charleston 1780 (SC).
Harris, Abner	3rd NC Regiment	7/20/1778, a Private under Lt./Capt. George "Gee" Bradley for nine months.	
Harris, Abraham	3rd NC Regiment	7/20/1778, a Private under Capt. John Baker for nine months.	
Harris, Benjamin	4th NC Regiment	8/1/1782, a Private under Capt. Joseph T. Rhodes. A Sergeant on 8/1/1783. From Duplin County, NC. Earlier in NC Militia. W5295.	
Harris, David		1779, a Private, regiment and unit unknown. Deserted in Sep. 1779.	
Harris, Edward	5th NC Regiment	1776, a Private under Capt. William Ward for eighteen months. From Johnston County, NC. Later in NC Militia.	
Harris, Edward	9th NC Regiment	6/10/1777, a Private under Capt. Richard D. Cook for three years. 9/8/1778, a known Private in the Lt. Colonel's Company (Lt. Col. Robert Mebane) (1st NC Regiment) led by Capt. Joshua Bowman - sick on that date at English Town. Dropped from the rolls in Sep. 1778.	
Harris, Elijah	1st NC Regiment	6/1/1781, a Private under Capt. William Lytle. Discharged on 6/1/1782. From Hyde Co., NC.	
Harris, George	3rd NC Regiment	1777, a Private under Capt. James Emmett. Missing on 10/4/1777.	Germantown (PA).
Harris, Goodman	6th NC Regiment	5/9/1776, a Private under Lt./Capt. Daniel Williams and Capt. William Glover. Wounded at the battle of Germantown, PA. 9/8/1778, a Private under Capt. James Read (1st NC Regiment). Discharged on 11/18/1778. Enlisted in Granville County, NC. aka Goleman Harris, Yoleman Harris. S38801.	Brandywine Creek (PA), Germantown (PA), Monmouth (NJ).
Harris, Henry	3rd NC Regiment	1781, served under Capt. Edward Yarborough for 12 months. Discharged on 4/10/1782.	
Harris, Henry	4th NC Regiment	1782, a Private under Capt. William Lytle for 18 months.	
Harris, Henry	10th NC Regiment	6/7/1777, a Private under Capt. Isaac Moore for three years. 9/8/1778, a known Private in the Lt. Colonel's Company (Lt. Col. Robert Mebane) (1st NC Regiment) led by Capt. Joshua Bowman - sick on that date.	

416

Name	1st Unit	Year / Rank / Served Under / Notes	Known Battles
Harris, Hugh	4th NC Regiment	5/20/1776, a Private under Capt. Roger Moore for three years. 9/8/1778, a known Private in the Colonel's Company (Col. Thomas Clark) (1st NC Regiment) led by Capt. John Gambier Scull. A Corporal on 11/10/1778. Discharged on 5/20/1779. Enlisted in Orange County, NC. W25743.	Germantown (PA), Monmouth (NJ).
Harris, James	5th NC Regiment	5/27/1776, a Private under Capt. Benjamin Stedman. 9/9/1778, a known Private under Capt. Clement Hall (2nd NC Regiment).	
Harris, Jesse	3rd NC Regiment	7/20/1778, a Private under Lt./Capt. George "Gee" Bradley for nine months.	
Harris, Jesse	4th NC Regiment	8/1/1782, a Private under Capt. William Lytle, then under Capt. Joshua Hadley (1st NC Regiment) for 18 months. W1277.	
Harris, John	1st NC Regiment	1777, a Private under Capt. Henry "Hal" Dixon. Dropped from the rolls in Jan. 1778.	
Harris, John	2nd NC Regiment	1777, a Private under Capt. James Martin. Dropped from the rolls in Nov. 1777. Rejoined April 1778. Discharged May 1778.	
Harris, John	6th NC Regiment	1777, a Private under Capt. Philip Taylor. Dropped from the rolls in Nov. 1777.	
Harris, Nelson	1st NC Regiment	9/18/1780, a Sergeant under Capt. William Lytle for 12 months. Discharged on 4/12/1782. From Warren County, NC. R4668.	
Harris, Robert	1st NC Regiment	5/5/1781, a Private under Capt. Robert Raiford for 12 months. Discharged on 4/28/1782 (2nd NC Regiment). From Guilford County, NC. Earlier in NC Militia. W23240.	
Harris, Stephen	5th NC Regiment	1777, a Private under Capt. Henry Darnell. Dropped from the rolls in Nov. 1777.	
Harris, Stephen	5th NC Regiment	1777, a Private under Capt. Benjamin Stedman. Dropped from the rolls in Sep. 1777.	
Harris, Thomas	1st NC Regiment	4/28/1776, a Corporal under Capt. Thomas Hogg. Discharged on 11/1/1778.	
Harris, Thomas	2nd NC Regiment	3/1/1782, a Private under Capt. Clement Hall for 12 months.	
Harris, Thomas	4th NC Regiment	1775, a Captain in the Anson County Regiment. 4/17/1776, a Captain under Col. Thomas Polk. 10/4/1777, a Major. Dropped from the rolls in Jan. 1778. 1780, a Major in NC Militia. S13312.	Ft. George - Bald Head Island, Brandywine Creek (PA), Germantown (PA).
Harris, West	9th NC Regiment	11/28/1776, a 2nd Lieutenant under Capt. Joseph John Wade. 1777, a Lieutenant in the NC Light Dragoons under Capt. Martin Phifer until Jan. 1780. From Salisbury District.	
Harris, William	2nd NC Regiment	11/7/1776, a Private under Lt./Capt. James Martin for 3 years. 9/9/1778, a known Private under Capt. Benjamin Andrew Coleman. 3/12/1779, re-enlisted under Capt. Benjamin Andrew Coleman. Wounded at the battle of Monmouth, NJ. Discharged at Trenton, NJ in	Monmouth (NJ).

Name	1st Unit	Year / Rank / Served Under / Notes	Known Battles
		1779. From Bute County, what is now Franklin County, NC. 1781, a Lieutenant in the NC Militia. S5441.	
Harrison, Daniel	3rd NC Regiment	8/20/1777, a Private under Lt./Capt. George "Gee" Bradley.	
Harrison, Dempsey	10th NC Regiment	8/21/1777, a Private under Capt. Dempsey Gregory. 9/8/1778, a known Private under Capt. Howell Tatum (1st NC Regiment). A Corporal in 1779. POW at the Fall of Charleston, SC (escaped). S41623.	Monmouth (NJ), Stony Point (NY), Siege of Charleston 1780 (SC).
Harrison, Francis	1st NC Regiment	4/15/1781, a Private under Lt./Capt. Benjamin Bailey. Discharged on 4/15/1782 (3rd NC Regiment).	
Harrison, George	4th NC Regiment	5/20/1776, a Private under Capt. Joseph Phillips. 9/8/1778, a known Private under Capt. James Read (1st NC Regiment) - sick at Princeton at that time. Dropped from the rolls in Jan. 1779.	
Harrison, Henry	1st NC Regiment	12/31/1781, a Private under Capt. William Armstrong. Died on 9/20/1782.	
Harrison, James	1st NC Regiment	1777, a Private under Capt. John Brown. 9/8/1778, a known Private under Capt. Tilghman Dixon.	
Harrison, James	3rd NC Regiment	4/20/1776, a Private under Capt. Thomas Granbury. Discharged in Oct. 1777.	
Harrison, James	7th NC Regiment	1777, a Sergeant under Capt. Lemuel Ely. Died in Aug. 1777.	
Harrison, Jesse	10th NC Regiment	8/21/1777, a Private under Capt. Dempsey Gregory. June 1778, a Private under Capt. Howell Tatum (1st NC Regiment). 9/8/1778, a known Private under Capt. Howell Tatum (1st NC Regiment). Escaped at the Fall of Charleston (SC). From Halifax County, NC. Joined NC Militia. S41620.	Siege of Charleston 1780 (SC).
Harrison, John	10th NC Regiment	5/24/1777, a Musician under Capt. Dempsey Gregory. 6/1/1778, a Private under Capt. Howell Tatum (1st NC Regiment). Discharged on 9/9/1778 at White Plains, NY. From Currituck County, NC. S41601.	
Harrison, Joseph	3rd NC Regiment	3/1/1781, a Private under Lt. Col. John Armstrong for 12 months. Served his tour at the Laboratory in Salisbury, NC. Discharged on 3/6/1782 (4th NC Regiment). From Surry County, NC. Born 5/18/1765. R4676.	
Harrison, Joshua	5th NC Regiment	1777, a Private under Capt. Reading Blount. A Sergeant in Sep. 1777. Deserted in Sep. 1779.	
Harrison, Thomas	1st NC Regiment	4/12/1781, a Private under Capt. William Lytle. Discharged on 4/12/1782. Confined four nights for desertion during July 1781.	
Harrison, Thomas	5th NC Regiment	5/21/1776, a Private under Capt. Reading Blount. 9/9/1778, a known Private in the Lt. Colonel's Company (Lt. Col. Selby Harney) (2nd NC Regiment). Discharged 2/1/1780.	

418

Name	1st Unit	Year / Rank / Served Under / Notes	Known Battles
Harrison, William	1st NC Regiment	5/18/1779, a Private under Capt. Robert Raiford for 12 months. Discharged on 5/18/1782 (2nd NC Regiment).	
Harrison, William	3rd NC Regiment	7/20/1778, a Private under Capt. John Baker. Deserted on 8/2/1778.	
Harrison, William	5th NC Regiment	1777, a Private under Capt. Henry Darnell. Dropped from the rolls in Sep. 1777. aka William Harson.	
Harrison, William	7th NC Regiment	12/11/1776, an Ensign under Capt. John Macon. 12/19/1776, a 2nd Lieutenant. 7/15/1777, a 1st Lieutenant under Capt. John Macon. Dropped from the rolls in Jan. 1778. A Captain in 1779, regiment unknown.	
Harry, Thomas	2nd NC Regiment	A volunteer Free Negro, wounded at the Siege of Charleston on 4/5/1780. Per his own pension statement, he was assigned to 2nd NC Regiment, no other source available.	Siege of Charleston 1780 (SC).
Hart, Adam	1st NC Regiment	1776, a Wagoner under Capt. Henry "Hal" Dixon. 5/25/1781, a Private under Capt. Thomas Donoho. From Guilford County, NC. S46576.	
Hart, Anthony	3rd NC Regiment	4/16/1776, a 2nd Lieutenant under Capt. Pinketham Eaton. 11/22/1777, a 1st Lieutenant under Capt. Thomas Granbury. 1778, an Adjutant. POW at the Fall of Charleston, exchanged 6/14/1781. 7/1/1781, a Captain. Resigned 4/1/1782.	Siege of Charleston 1780 (SC).
Hart, James	1st NC Regiment	9/9/1775, a Private under Capt. John Walker for six months. Later in NC Militia. From Orange County, NC. S9555.	
Hart, John	6th NC Regiment	5/7/1776, a 2nd Lieutenant. Then, a 1st Lieutenant. Promoted to Captain on 8/6/1779, regiment unknown.	
Hart, John	8th NC Regiment	1777, a Private under Capt. John Walsh. Dropped from the rolls in Feb. 1778.	
Hart, Samuel	2nd NC Regiment	1782, a Private under Capt. Benjamin Carter for 18 months.	
Hart, Samuel	6th NC Regiment	5/6/1776, a Musician under Lt./Capt. Thomas White for 2-1/2 years. Wounded at the battle of Brandywine Creek, PA. A Private in June 1778. 9/8/1778, a known Private under Capt. John Sumner (1st NC Regiment). Dropped from the rolls in Nov. 1778. He claims he was discharged in Connecticut and he then joined a VA Continental unit.He apparently re-enlisted in 1782 as a Private under Capt. Benjamin Carter (2nd NC Regiment) for 18 months. S41619.	Brandywine Creek (PA), Germantown (PA).
Hart, Samuel	9th NC Regiment	11/28/1776, a 2nd Lieutenant under Capt. Hezekiah Rice. From Hillsborough District.	
Hart, Thomas	3rd NC Regiment	1777, a Private under Capt. Pinketham Eaton. Died in June 1778.	
Hart, Thomas	6th NC Regiment	4/23/1776, a Commissary. Resigned 1/28/177.	
Hartley, John	5th NC	A Private under Capt. Benjamin Andrew	

Name	1st Unit	Year / Rank / Served Under / Notes	Known Battles
	Regiment	Coleman. Died on 6/20/1778 (2nd NC Regiment).	
Hartley, Joseph	10th NC Regiment	6/27/1777, a Sergeant under Capt. Silas Stevenson. A Private in June 1778 in the Colonel's Company (Col. John Patten) (2nd NC Regiment) led by Capt. John Craddock.	
Harvey, Absalom	3rd NC Regiment	1781, served under Capt. Edward Yarborough for 12 months. Discharged 4/1/1782.	
Harvey, James	1st NC Regiment	11/1/1778, a Private under Capt. Anthony Sharpe. From Hyde County, NC.	
Harvey, James	7th NC Regiment	11/28/1776, a Paymaster. Died in Oct. 1777.	
Harvey, John	2nd NC Regiment	9/17/1776, a Private under Capt. Benjamin Williams for three years. 9/9/1778, a known Private in the Major's Company (Maj. Hardy Murfree). Wounded at the battle of Stony Point (NY). Deserted on 1/1/1780. 5/28/1781, a Sergeant under Capt. Alexander Brevard. 1/9/1782 or 1/20/1782 (two sources), transferred to Pennsylvania Line. From Surry County, NC. W249.	Brandywine Creek (PA), Stony Point (NY).
Harvey, Joshua	2nd NC Regiment	1781, a Private under Capt. Tilghman Dixon. 7/29/1781, transferred to Lee's Legion.	
Harvey, Joshua	2nd NC Regiment	A Private under Capt. Charles Allen, dates unknown. 9/10/1778, a Private under Capt. Thomas Armstrong (2nd NC Regiment). POW at Ft. Lafayette on 6/1/1779.	Ft. Lafayette (NY).
Haslip, Charles	6th NC Regiment	1777, a Private under Capt. Thomas Donoho. Dropped from the rolls in Sep. 1777.	
Hassell, Joseph	1st NC Regiment	5/2/1781, a Sergeant under Capt. Clement Hall. 1782, a Private under Capt. Benjamin Bailey. Earlier in NC Militia. From Tyrrell County, NC. S41602.	
Hassle, Stephen	1st NC Regiment	4/5/1781, a Private under Capt. William Lytle. Dropped from the rolls sometime during 1781.	
Hastings, Carter	3rd NC Regiment	7/1/1779, a Musician under Capt. Kedar Ballard for 18 months.	
Hastings, Willis	3rd NC Regiment	1/27/1777, a Private under Capt. Jacob Turner. 9/9/1778, a known Private in the Lt. Colonel's Company (Lt. Col. Selby Harney) (2nd NC Regiment). aka Wylis Hastings.	
Hataway, Thomas	1st NC Regiment	1781, a Private under Capt. Anthony Sharpe.	
Hatch, Alexander	1st NC Regiment	4/15/1781, served under Capt. William Lytle, then under Capt. Benjamin Carter (2nd NC Regiment). Discharged on 4/10/1782 at Guilford Court House, NC. Earlier in VA units. On the official rolls as Alexander Hack (actually Alexander Hach). Born on 11/15/1764 in Dinwiddie County, VA. S8648.	
Hatchcock, Isom	3rd NC Regiment	7/20/1778, a Private under Lt./Capt. Joseph Montford for nine months.	
Hatchcock, William	3rd NC Regiment	7/20/1778, a Private in the Lt. Colonel's Company (Lt. Col. William Lee Davidson) led	

Name	1st Unit	Year / Rank / Served Under / Notes	Known Battles
		by Lt./Capt. George "Gee" Bradley for nine months. Probably the same man as William Hathcock below.	
Hatcher, David		1779, a Private, regiment and unit unknown. Died in Sep. 1779.	
Hatcock, Edward	3rd NC Regiment	7/20/1778, a Private under Lt./Capt. Joseph Montford for nine months.	
Hathaway, John	7th NC Regiment	1777, a Private under Capt. Henry Dawson. Dropped from the rolls in Feb. 1778.	
Hathcock, Frederick	2nd NC Regiment	4/20/1776, a Private, unit unknown. 9/9/1778, a known Private in the Lt. Colonel's Company (Lt. Col. Selby Harney).	
Hathcock, William	3rd NC Regiment	4/23/1779, a known Private in the Lt. Colonel's Company (Lt. Col. Robert Mebane) led by Capt. George "Gee" Bradley. Probably the same man as William Hatchcock above.	
Hathcock, Zachariah	2nd NC Regiment	9/9/1778, a known Private in the Lt. Colonel's Company (Lt. Col. Selby Harney). 3/12/1779, re-enlisted in the Lt. Colonel's Company (Lt. Col. Selby Harney). aka Zachariah Hatchcock.	
Hatsock, Peter		6/25/1777, regiment, unit, and rank unknown. 9/8/1778, a known Private in the Lt. Colonel's Company (Lt. Col. Robert Mebane) (1st NC Regiment) led by Capt. Joshua Bowman - sick on that date. 3/12/1779, re-enlisted for the duration of the war in the same unit. aka Peter Hatrock.	
Haulborn, David	2nd NC Regiment	11/29/1776, a Private, unit unknown. 9/10/1778, a known Private under Capt. Thomas Armstrong.	
Havigrooves, John	2nd NC Regiment	5/19/1777, a Private, unit unknown. 9/9/1778, a known Private in the Major's Company (Maj. Hardy Murfree).	
Hawes, Ezekiel	4th NC Regiment	1779, a Private under Capt. George Dougherty for nine months - recruited in Bladen County by Capt. James Morehead (5th NC Regiment). Discharged in August 1780 at Strawberry Ferry, SC. Earlier and later in NC Militia. From Duplin County, NC. R4760.	
Hawkins, Ephraim	1st NC Regiment	1781, a Private under Capt. Anthony Sharpe for 18 months. Earlier in NC Militia. From Rowan County, NC when he was drafted. W3987.	Eutaw Springs (SC).
Hawkins, Henry	3rd NC Regiment	7/20/1778, a Private under Capt. Kedar Ballard for nine months.	
Hawkins, Joseph	DQMG	1780, a Saddler on the roll of Capt. Solomon Wood (NC Light Dragoons) - this seems to be for convenience only. 8/23/1781, a Leather Worker under Col. Nicholas Long (Deputy QM General), making saddles, harnesses, caps, etc.	
Hawkins, Leweston	3rd NC Regiment	7/20/1778, a Private under Maj. Thomas Hogg for nine months. aka Loeston Hawkins.	
Hawkins, Lorton	4th NC Regiment	1782, a Private under Capt. William Lytle for 18 months. Possibly the same man as directly above.	

Name	1st Unit	Year / Rank / Served Under / Notes	Known Battles
Hawkins, Richard	3rd NC Regiment	7/20/1778, a Private under Capt. Kedar Ballard for nine months.	
Hawkins, William	10th NC Regiment	5/12/1777, a Private under Capt. James Wilson for three years. 9/8/1778, a known Private in the Lt. Colonel's Company (Lt. Col. Robert Mebane) (1st NC Regiment) led by Capt. Joshua Bowman. 3/12/1779, re-enlisted for the duration of the war in the same unit.	
Hawks, John	NC Artillery	5/17/1776, a Matross under Capt. John Vance as NC Provincial Troops. 7/10/1777, on Continental Line. 11/16/1777, under Capt. John Kingsbury. Died on 2/17/1778.	
Hawley, William	3rd NC Regiment	7/20/1778, a Private under Capt. Michael Quinn for nine months.	
Haws, John	1st NC Regiment	Jan. 1782, a Sergeant under Capt. James Mills. Discharged 1/1/1783 (4th NC Regiment).	
Hawthorn, John	5th NC Regiment	3/1/1779, a Musician under Maj. Reading Blount for nine months. Discharged Dec. 1779.	
Hay, Abraham	10th NC Regiment	5/4/1777, a Private under Capt. Abraham Sheppard, Jr. for three years. 9/9/1778, a known Private in the Colonel's Company (Col. John Patten) (2nd NC Regiment) led by Capt. John Craddock. POW at the Fall of Charleston, SC - held 14 months. Exchanged at Williamsburg, VA - died within hours afterwards. On the official rolls as Abraham Hays. W17262.	Siege of Charleston 1780 (SC).
Hay, Isaac	10th NC Regiment	5/31/1777, a Private under Capt. Abraham Sheppard, Jr. for three years. Spring of 1778, under Capt. Thomas Armstrong (2nd NC Regiment). 9/10/1778, a known Private under Capt. Thomas Armstrong (2nd NC Regiment). POW at the Fall of Charleston, SC - held until Aug. 1781. Exchanged at Richmond, VA, discharged by Lt. Col. Robert Mebane. The official records claim he died in Sep. 1782 (wrong). On the official rolls as Isaac Hayes. R4779.	Siege of Charleston 1780 (SC).
Hay, William	4th NC Regiment	8/1/1782, a Private under Capt. Joseph Thomas Rhodes, then under Capt. Joshua Hadley (1st NC Regiment) for 18 months. Furloughed in Aug. 1783. Earlier in NC Militia. From New Hanover County, NC. On the official rolls as William Hays. S8670.	
Haycraft, Mark	6th NC Regiment	1777, a Private under Capt. Thomas Donoho. Deserted in Aug. 1777. Possibly the same man as directly below.	
Haycraft, Mark	10th NC Regiment	7/13/1777, a Private under Capt. Armwell Herron. 3/12/1779, re-enlisted in the Major's Company (Maj. Hardy Murfree) (2nd NC Regiment). POW at Ft. Lafayette, NY on 6/1/1779. Rejoined in Nov. 1779.	Ft. Lafayette (NY).
Hayes, John	8th NC Regiment	Nov. 1777, a Private under Capt. Michael Quinn. Jan. 1782, a Private under Capt. Clement Hall (3rd NC Regiment, then 2nd NC	

Name	1st Unit	Year / Rank / Served Under / Notes	Known Battles
		Regiment).	
Hayes, Southy	1st NC Regiment	2/7/1782, a Private under Capt. James Mills for 12 months.	
Hayes, Thomas	6th NC Regiment	5/9/1776, a Private under Lt./Capt. Daniel Williams. 9/8/1778, a Private under Capt. James Read (1st NC Regiment). Discharged on 11/10/1778. He claims he was discharged in May of 1779 in Connecticut. From Granville County, NC. On the official rolls as Thomas Hays. S41600.	
Haygood, William	4th NC Regiment	3/1/1779, a Private under Capt. Joseph Thomas Rhodes for nine months. Discharged on 12/1/1779 at Charleston, SC. Earlier and later in NC Militia. 1781, re-enlisted under Capt. Thomas Evans (2nd NC Regiment) for 12 months - sent to Halifax, NC to work under Col. Nicholas Long (DQMG). From Johnston County, NC. S4314.	Stono Ferry (SC).
Haynes, Bythell	7th NC Regiment	4/9/1777, a Sergeant under Capt. Henry Dawson. Deserted on 9/17/1777.	
Haynes, Christopher	7th NC Regiment	4/15/1777, a Sergeant under Capt. Henry Dawson for three years. Discharged on 11/3/1777. From Halifax County, NC. W4227.	
Haynes, John	1st NC Regiment	A Private under Capt. William Armstrong. Discharged in June 1778. Born c.1753 in Maryland. Moved to Warren County, then to Sampson County, NC.	
Haynes, William	1st NC Regiment	1777, a Private under Capt. Henry "Hal" Dixon. Died on 3/23/1778.	
Hays, James	7th NC Regiment	11/28/1776, a 2nd Lieutenant under Capt. Henry Dawson. Dropped from the rolls in Oct. 1777.	
Hays, John	1st NC Regiment	5/9/1779, a Private under Capt. Griffith John McRee for 12 months. Deserted on 6/1/1781.	
Hays, John	9th NC Regiment	1777, a Private under Capt. Richard D. Cook. Deserted in Aug. 1777. Jan. 1782, joined 3rd NC Regiment under Capt. Clement Hall (2/6/1782, would be the 2nd NC Regiment).	
Hays, Robert	4th NC Regiment	8/16/1777, an Ensign under Capt. William Temple Coles. 10/9/1777, a 2nd Lieutenant. 6/1/1778, transferred to the 1st NC Regiment - unit unknown. 9/8/1778, a known 2nd Lieutenant under Capt. John Sumner. A 1st Lieutenant on 2/16/1780. POW at the Fall of Charleston, exchanged 6/14/1781. Served until the end of the war. On the official rolls as Robert Hayes. S38792.	Siege of Charleston 1780 (SC).
Hays, Theophilus	10th NC Regiment	3/3/1777, a Private, unit unknown. 9/9/1778, a known Private in the Major's Company (Maj. Hardy Murfree) (2nd NC Regiment).	
Haywood, Edward	3rd NC Regiment	7/20/1778, a Private under Capt. Michael Quinn for nine months.	
Hazle, Thomas	2nd NC Regiment	1777, a Private under Capt. John Armstrong. Died on 2/28/1778.	
Headwright,	1st NC	6/1/1781, a Private under Capt. William Lytle.	

Name	1st Unit	Year / Rank / Served Under / Notes	Known Battles
John	Regiment	Discharged on 6/1/1782.	
Heal, Elisha	2nd NC Regiment	7/20/1778, a Private under Maj. Reading Blount for nine months.	
Hearn, Benjamin	3rd NC Regiment	7/20/1778, a Private under Lt./Capt. George "Gee" Bradley. Discharged on 5/7/1779.	
Hearn, Drury	3rd NC Regiment	5/15/1776, a Private under Capt. James Emmett for 2-1/2 years. Discharged on 11/10/1778. Later in NC Militia. aka Drury Hern. W3548.	Brandywine Creek (PA), Germantown (PA), Monmouth (NJ).
Hearn, James	3rd NC Regiment	7/20/1778, a Private under Capt. Kedar Ballard for nine months. Discharged on 4/10/1779 at Halifax, NC. Later in NC Militia, unit unknown. From Edgecombe County, NC. Claims to have been at the Siege of Charleston, SC and at Guilford Court House, but does not name his Captain or regiment. aka James Hearne. S41631.	
Heath, William	2nd NC Regiment	1782, a Private under Capt. Robert Raiford for 18 months.	
Heathcock, Aaron	3rd NC Regiment	6/22/1779, a Private under Capt. Michael Quinn for two years.	
Hedgeman, George	1st NC Regiment	11/10/1778, a Private under Capt. Anthony Sharpe for nine months.	
Hedgeman, Lewis	1st NC Regiment	11/10/1778, a Private under Capt. Anthony Sharpe for nine months.	
Hedgpeth, Abraham	1st NC Regiment	1782, a Private under Capt. Peter Bacot for 18 months. From Nash County, NC. Born 5/1/1761 in Nansemond County, VA. S6989.	
Hedspeth, John	1st NC Regiment	4/12/1781, a Private under Capt. William Lytle. Discharged on 4/12/1782.	
Hedspeth, Marmaduke	3rd NC Regiment	1778, a Private under Capt. Francis Child. 6/1/1778, a known Private under Capt. Griffith John McRee (1st NC Regiment).	
Hedspeth, Peter	3rd NC Regiment	1781, served under Capt. Edward Yarborough for 12 months. Discharged on 5/7/1782.	
Heimbergh, Fred	1st NC Regiment	3/13/1778, a Sergeant, unit unknown. Probably Frederick Helmberg, see below.	
Helderman, Nicholas	1st NC Regiment	1781, a Private under Capt. William Armstrong for 12 months. Discharged on 5/25/1782 (3rd NC Regiment).	
Helmberg, Frederick	1st NC Regiment	3/15/1778, a Surgeon. aka Fred. Heimbergh (see above).	
Henderson, Archibald	2nd NC Regiment	12/1/1775, a Musician, unit unknown. 2/3/1778, re-enlisted as a Musician, unit unknown. A Private in June 1778. Back to Musician in Sep. 1778. 9/9/1778, a known Private in the Major's Company (Maj. Hardy Murfree).	
Henderson, Michael	9th NC Regiment	11/28/1776, a Captain under Col. John Williams. From Salisbury District.	
Henderson, Pleasant	6th NC Regiment	Was a Sergeant Major in NC Militia. 4/17/1776, a 2nd Lieutenant under Capt. Jesse Saunders and Col. John Alexander Lillington. Resigned in	

Name	1st Unit	Year / Rank / Served Under / Notes	Known Battles
		early May 1776. Later, a Lieutenant, a Captain, and a Major in the NC Militia. From Granville County.	
Henderson, Robert	2nd NC Regiment	1782, a Sergeant under Capt. Robert Raiford for 18 months.	
Hendrick, Albert	1st NC Regiment	4/28/1779, a Corporal under Capt. Griffith John McRee for 12 months. A Sergeant in Aug. 1781. Discharged on 4/28/1782.	
Hendrick, Samuel	4th NC Regiment	1782, a Private under Capt. William Lytle for 18 months.	
Hendricks, Thomas	10th NC Regiment	7/25/1777, a Private under Capt. Isaac Moore for three years. 9/8/1778, a known Private in the Lt. Colonel's Company (Lt. Col. Robert Mebane) (1st NC Regiment) led by Capt. Joshua Bowman. Died in Oct. 1778.	
Hendry, John	1st NC Regiment	9/8/1778, a known Private under Capt. Joshua Bowman.	
Henry, Burrel	1st NC Regiment	1782, a Private under Capt. Peter Bacot for 18 months.	
Henry, John	1st NC Regiment	1777, a Private under Capt. Joshua Bowman. Probably the same man as John Hendry above.	
Henry, John	4th NC Regiment	A Private under Capt. William Goodman. Died in Jan. 1778.	
Henry, Michael	7th NC Regiment	3/2/1777, a Private under Capt. James Vaughan. Deserted in Aug. 1777.	
Henry, William	1st NC Regiment	1776, a Private under Capt. Joshua Bowman.	
Henry, William	3rd NC Regiment	1/25/1782, served under Capt. Samuel Jones for 12 months.	
Hensley, William	4th NC Regiment	1782, a Private under Capt. Thomas Evans for 18 months.	
Henson, William	3rd NC Regiment	1782, a Private under Capt. Alexander Brevard then Capt. Samuel Jones (1st NC Regiment) for 18 months. Discharged at the Court House in Surry County, NC. His pension application contains a lot of erroneous recall. W8923.	
Herbert, William	6th NC Regiment	1777, a Sergeant under Capt. Thomas Donoho. Dropped from the rolls in Jan. 1778. Jan. 1779, re-enlisted in the 4th NC Regiment.	
Herman, John		Jan. 1778, a Private, regiment and unit unknown.	
Herman, Robert	1st NC Regiment	12/23/1776, a Private, unit unknown. 9/8/1778, a known Private in the Colonel's Company (Col. Thomas Clark) led by Capt. John Gambier Scull.	
Hern, Howell	1st NC Regiment	5/21/1781, a Private under Capt. Anthony Sharpe. Dropped from the rolls during 1781.	
Hern, John	1st NC Regiment	4/5/1781, a Private under Capt. Anthony Sharpe. Died on 2/20/1782.	
Herrard, James	2nd NC Regiment	9/9/1778, a known Private under Capt. Robert Fenner.	
Herring, John	1st NC Regiment	5/25/1781, a Private under Capt. Alexander Brevard. Deserted on 6/3/1781 (?).	
Herrington,	2nd NC	1782, a Private under Capt. Robert Raiford for	

Name	1st Unit	Year / Rank / Served Under / Notes	Known Battles
Giles	Regiment	18 months. aka Giles Harrington.	
Herrington, Peter	8th NC Regiment	1777, a Corporal under Capt. Francis Tartanson. A Private in Jan. 1778. Dropped from the rolls in Feb. 1778.	
Herrington, Samuel	2nd NC Regiment	1782, a Private under Capt. Benjamin Carter for 18 months.	
Herrington, Thomas	2nd NC Regiment	8/1/1782, a Corporal under Capt. Robert Raiford for 18 months. aka Thomas Harrington.	
Herrington, Thomas	4th NC Regiment	1781, a Private under Capt. George Dougherty for 12 months. Discharged on 5/25/1782.	
Herritage, John	2nd NC Regiment	9/1/1775, a 1st Lieutenant under Capt. Simon Bright. Promoted to Captain on 5/3/1776 upon the resignation of Capt. Bright. Resigned 5/15/1777. 1779, a Colonel over the newly-created NC State Regiment. From Johnston County, NC. aka John Heritage.	Great Bridge (VA), Ft. Moultrie #1 (SC).
Herron, Armwell	10th NC Regiment	Earlier, a Lieutenant in NC Militia. 4/19/1777, a Captain under Col. Abraham Sheppard. Retired on 6/1/1778. 1779, a Captain in NC State Regiment.	
Herron, Matthew	10th NC Regiment	7/8/1777, a Corporal under Capt. Armwell Herron. A Private in June 1778. 9/9/1778, a known Private in the Major's Company (Maj. Hardy Murfree) (2nd NC Regiment). 3/12/1779, re-enlisted in the Major's Company (Maj. Hardy Murfree). POW at Ft. Lafayette, NY on 6/1/1779. Rejoined in Nov. 1779. aka Matthew Herring, Matthew Hevring.	Ft. Lafayette (NY).
Hertsock, Peter	10th NC Regiment	6/25/1777, a Private under Capt. Isaac Moore. Re-enlisted in Jan. 1782 for the remainder of the war, regiment and unit unknown.	
Hessian, Peter	DQMG	1780, a Wagoner under Col. Nicholas Long (Deputy QM General). Said to be an ex-Continental soldier (?).	
Hester, Benjamin	2nd NC Regiment	5/15/1781, a Private under Capt. Tilghman Dixon. Dropped from the rolls sometime during 1781. Earlier in NC Militia. From Granville County. NC.	
Hester, John	1st NC Regiment	6/14/1779, a Private under Capt. Thomas Donoho for 12 months. Discharged on 6/16/1782.	
Hester, John	3rd NC Regiment	1/1/1782, served under Capt. Samuel Jones for 12 months.	
Hester, Joseph	3rd NC Regiment	1/1/1782, served under Capt. Samuel Jones for 12 months. Earlier in the NC Militia. From Granville County, NC. W19762.	
Hewell, Caleb	1st NC Regiment	4/5/1781, a Private under Capt. Anthony Sharpe. Dropped from the rolls during 1781.	
Hewell, William	5th NC Regiment	3/28/1777, a Lieutenant under Capt. Henry Darnell. Dropped from the rolls in Sep. 1777. aka William Huell.	
Hewes, Joseph	1st NC Regiment	5/25/1779, a Sergeant under Capt. Thomas Donoho for 12 months. Discharged on 5/25/1782.	

426

Name	1st Unit	Year / Rank / Served Under / Notes	Known Battles
Hewett, Ebenezer	6th NC Regiment	4/2/1777, a Private under Capt. Griffith John McRee for the duration of the war. 9/8/1778, a known Private in the Lt. Colonel's Company (Lt. Col. Robert Mebane) (1st NC Regiment) led by Capt. Joshua Bowman. POW at the Fall of Charleston (SC), soon escaped. 1781, in SC Militia. Enlisted at Wilmington, NC. From Brunswick County, NC. aka Ebenezer Hewitt. S41632.	Brandywine Creek (PA), Monmouth (NJ), Siege of Charleston (SC).
Hewett, Jeremiah	5th NC Regiment	6/24/1779, a Private under Capt. Joseph Montford. Deserted in Sep. 1779. From Dobbs County, NC. aka Jeremiah Hewlet.	
Hewings, Thomas	6th NC Regiment	1777, a Private under Capt. Thomas White. Dropped from the rolls in Oct. 1777.	
Hewlett, Charles	3rd NC Regiment	7/1/1779, a Private under Capt. Kedar Ballard for 18 months.	
Hewlett, Robert	7th NC Regiment	1777, a Private under Capt. John McGlaughan. Deserted in July 1777.	
Hewling, Jacob	2nd NC Regiment	9/9/1778, a known Private in the Lt. Colonel's Company (Lt. Col. Selby Harney).	
Hews, Burrel	7th NC Regiment	1777, a Private under Capt. Joseph Walker. Dropped from the rolls in Jan. 1778.	
Hews, James	1st NC Regiment	5/25/1781, a Private under Lt./Capt. Benjamin Bailey. Discharged on 5/25/1782 (3rd NC Regiment).	
Hews, John	DQMG	1780, a Saddler on the roll of Capt. Solomon Wood (NC Light Dragoons) - this seems to be for convenience only. A Saddle Maker under Col. Nicholas Long (Deputy QM General).	
Hews, William	4th NC Regiment	1782, a Private under Capt. William Lytle for 18 months.	
Hews, Willis	3rd NC Regiment	9/17/1782, a Private under Capt. Benjamin Bailey for 12 months.	
Hickman, Corbin	2nd NC Regiment	5/12/1781, a Private under Capt. Tilghman Dixon. Discharged on 5/26/1782 (1st NC Regiment). Probably the same man as directly below.	
Hickman, Corbin	5th NC Regiment	1779, a Private under Maj. Reading Blount for nine months. Dropped from the rolls in Oct. 1779.	
Hickman, Corbin	8th NC Regiment	1777, a Private under Capt. Michael Quinn. Discharged on 11/22/1779. aka Corbin Kickman.	
Hickman, Jacob	3rd NC Regiment	1782, a Private under Capt. Benjamin Coleman, then under Capt. Thomas Evans (4th NC Regiment) for 18 months. Discharged at Haddrell's Point, SC. From Pitt County, NC. S41643.	
Hickman, John	4th NC Regiment	1778, in the "New Levies" under Lt./Capt. William Lytle for nine months. Later in NC Militia. From Anson County, NC. W7745.	
Hickman, William	4th NC Regiment	1777, a Lieutenant under Capt. William Goodman. Resigned 8/25/1777.	
Hicks, C.	9th NC	1778, a Sergeant under Capt. Joseph J. Wade.	

427

Name	1st Unit	Year / Rank / Served Under / Notes	Known Battles
Tubel	Regiment	Died on 1/27/1778.	
Hicks, Charles	1st NC Regiment	11/1/1778, a Private under Capt. Anthony Sharpe for nine months.	
Hicks, Dempsey	2nd NC Regiment	Sep. 1782, a Private under Capt. Clement Hall. Deserted on 12/10/1782.	
Hicks, Hasell	5th NC Regiment	1779, a Private under Maj. Reading Blount for nine months. Deserted in Sep. 1779.	
Hicks, Henry	3rd NC Regiment	2/4/1782, a Private under Capt. Benjamin Bailey for 12 months.	
Hicks, Henry	6th NC Regiment	1777, a Private under Capt. Thomas White. Died in Dec. 1777.	
Hicks, Isaac	NC Light Dragoons	April 1776, a Private under Capt. John Dickerson in NC State Troops. Mar. 1777, this unit was led by Capt. Samuel Ashe. 3/7/1777, this unit was placed on the NC Continental Line. Discharged on 10/16/1778 at Halifax, NC. From what is now Durham County, NC. S38024.	
Hicks, James	5th NC Regiment	1777, a Private under Capt. John Pugh Williams. Dropped from the rolls in Feb. 1778.	
Hicks, John	5th NC Regiment	1777, a Private under Capt. John Pugh Williams for 2-1/2 years. From Orange County, NC. W4695.	
Hicks, Micajah	2nd NC Regiment	1782, a Private under Capt. Benjamin Carter for 18 months.	
Hicks, Micajah	4th NC Regiment	1781, a Private under Capt. Joseph T. Rhodes. Then, under Capt. William Lytle. Discharged on 4/25/1782. Earlier in MD and VA units. Probably the same man as directly above. W7738.	Cowpens (SC), Guilford Court House, Eutaw Springs (SC).
Hicks, Thomas	9th NC Regiment	1777, a Private under Capt. Hezekiah Rice. Dropped from the rolls in Jan. 1778.	
Hicks, William	9th NC Regiment	11/28/1776, an Ensign under Capt. Richard Donaldson Cook. 1781, a Captain in the NC Militia. From Hillsborough District.	
Hicksman, Charles	3rd NC Regiment	1779, a Private under Capt. Michael Quinn. Discharged in Dec. 1779.	
Hide, Sal.	5th NC Regiment	1779, a Private under Maj. Reading Blount for nine months. Dropped from the rolls in Oct. 1779.	
Higdon, Daniel	4th NC Regiment	1781, a Private under Capt. Matthew Ramsey for 12 months. Earlier in NC Militia. From Chatham County, NC. W25769.	Guilford Court House.
Higgins, Peter	6th NC Regiment	1777, a Private under Capt. Daniel Williams. Died on 3/24/1778.	
Higgins, Thomas	1st NC Regiment	A Private under Capt. Joshua Bowman, dates unknown.	
Higgins, Thomas	6th NC Regiment	1777, a Private under Capt. George Dougherty. Died on 3/27/1778.	
Highfield, Hezekiah	3rd NC Regiment	1782, a Private under Capt. Alexander Brevard for 18 months.	
Hilbert, John	1st NC Regiment	5/4/1779, a Private under Capt. Robert Raiford for 12 months. Died in Dec. 1781.	

Name	1st Unit	Year / Rank / Served Under / Notes	Known Battles
Hill, George	2nd NC Regiment	5/12/1781, a Private under Capt. Tilghman Dixon. Dropped from the rolls during 1781.	
Hill, Green	1st NC Regiment	6/20/1781, a Private under Capt. Anthony Sharpe. Dropped from the rolls during 1781.	
Hill, Jesse	1st NC Regiment	5/2/1781, a Private under Lt./Capt. Benjamin Bailey. Discharged on 5/2/1782 (3rd NC Regiment).	
Hill, John	1st NC Regiment	2/28/1778, a Private under Capt. Howell Tatum. 9/8/1778, a known Private under Capt. Howell Tatum. Re-enlisted on 9/20/1778 in same unit for 20 months. Discharged on 1/28/1780.	
Hill, John	1st NC Regiment	4/5/1781, a Private under Capt. Anthony Sharpe. A Corporal in Jan. 1782. Discharged on 4/5/1782 (4th NC Regiment).	
Hill, John	2nd NC Regiment	3/17/1776, a Private, unit unknown. 9/9/1778, a known Private in the Lt. Colonel's Company (Lt. Col. Selby Harney). Discharged on 2/1/1780.	
Hill, John	5th NC Regiment	4/4/1779, an Ensign under Maj. Reading Blount. 7/8/1781, a Lieutenant. Transferred to 4th NC Regiment on 2/6/1782, till the end of the war.	
Hill, Joseph	5th NC Regiment	1779, a Private under Maj. Reading Blount for nine months. Died on 8/15/1779.	
Hill, Moses	3rd NC Regiment	7/20/1778, a Private under Lt./Capt. George "Gee" Bradley for nine months.	
Hill, Richard	1st NC Regiment	4/12/1781, a Private under Capt. Alexander Brevard. Discharged on 4/12/1782 (3rd NC Regiment). From Franklin County, NC. Earlier in NC Militia. Tended to the sick during battle of Eutaw Springs (SC). R5006.	
Hill, Robert	3rd NC Regiment	1781, enlisted under Capt. Edward Yarborough for 12 months. Dropped from the rolls during 1781.	
Hill, Samuel	2nd NC Regiment	1781, a Private under Capt. Tilghman Dixon. Earlier in VA unit, then NC Militia. From Fairfax County, VA. S9577.	
Hill, Solomon	3rd NC Regiment	1782, a Private under Capt. Alexander Brevard. Mar. 1783, transferred to ?	
Hill, Thomas	4th NC Regiment	Jan. 1782, a Private under Capt. George Dougherty. Dropped from the rolls on 4/1/1782. From Duplin County, NC.	
Hill, Thomas	5th NC Regiment	4/26/1776, a Private under Capt. John Pugh Williams. A Corporal in Nov. 1777. Discharged in Oct. 1778.	
Hill, William	1st NC Regiment	9/1/1775, a 1st Lieutenant.	Moore's Creek Bridge [4].
Hill, William	3rd NC Regiment	7/20/1778, a Corporal under Capt. Michael Quinn for nine months.	
Hill, William	3rd NC Regiment	1/2/1782, served under Capt. Samuel Jones for 12 months.	
Hill, William	5th NC Regiment	1779, a Private under Maj. Reading Blount for nine months. Dropped from the rolls in Oct. 1779.	

Name	1st Unit	Year / Rank / Served Under / Notes	Known Battles
Hillard, James	5th NC Regiment	4/16/1776, a Private under Capt. William Caswell. Dropped from the rolls in Sep. 1777.	
Hills, Samuel	2nd NC Regiment	1781, a Private under Capt. Tilghman Dixon. Discharged 4/1/1782.	
Hilton, Arnold	1st NC Regiment	5/28/1781, a Private under Capt. Alexander Brevard. Discharged on 5/9/1782 (3rd NC Regiment). aka Arnold Hillton.	
Hilton, William	6th NC Regiment	4/1/1777, a 2nd Lieutenant under Capt. Thomas White. 10/13/1777, a 1st Lieutenant. Dropped from the rolls in June 1778. Re-enlisted into the 1st NC Regiment on 7/1/1778. He joined the 5th NC Regiment in Jan. 1779. Killed at Stony Point, NY on 7/15/1779.	Briar Creek (GA), Stono Ferry (SC), Stony Point (NY).
Hinds, Daniel	1st NC Regiment	Dec. 1782, a Private under Capt. Peter Bacot.	
Hinds, Lewis	4th NC Regiment	1781, a Private under Capt. Joseph T. Rhodes for 12 months. Discharged on 7/16/1782.	
Hines, Benjamin	1st NC Regiment	1782, a Private under Capt. Peter Bacot for 18 months.	
Hines, Thomas	DQMG	1780, an Express Rider on the roll of Capt. Solomon Wood (NC Light Dragoons) - this seems to be for convenience only. 8/23/1781, an Express Rider under Col. Nicholas Long (Deputy QM General).	
Hinnings, Michael	3rd NC Regiment	1782, hired as a substitute for William Patton - served out 17 months under Capt. Edward Yarborough at Public Factory in Salisbury, NC.	
Hinson, David	3rd NC Regiment	7/20/1778, a Private under Lt./Capt. George "Gee" Bradley for nine months.	
Hinson, Elijah	3rd NC Regiment	7/20/1778, a Sergeant under Lt./Capt. George "Gee" Bradley for nine months.	
Hinton, Jonas	3rd NC Regiment	6/1/1779, a Private under Capt. Michael Quinn for 18 months.	
Hinton, Joseph	7th NC Regiment	1777, a Musician under Capt. Thomas Brickell. Died 10/10/1777.	
Hislip, Kendle	NC Artillery	8/22/1777, a Bombardier under Capt. John Vance. 11/16/1777, under Capt. John Kingsbury. 5/1/1778, in same unit. 9/16/1778, in same unit. aka Kendle Heslop, Kindle Hiselip, Kendle Hislop.	
Hissett, Moses	5th NC Regiment	1777, a Private under Capt. Reading Blount. Died 5/3/1778.	
Hitchcock, Frederick	3rd NC Regiment	4/20/1776, a Private under Capt. William Brinkley. Discharged in Oct. 1778.	
Hitchcock, Zachariah	10th NC Regiment	6/4/1777, a Private under Capt. Abraham Sheppard, Jr. Deserted on 2/1/1780.	
Hizzs, John	1st NC Regiment	5/26/1781, a Private under Capt. Alexander Brevard.	
Hoard, Micajah	2nd NC Regiment	4/15/1781, served under Capt. Benjamin Carter. Discharged on 4/25/1782.	
Hobbs, Isaac	7th NC Regiment	1777, a Private under Capt. Joseph Walker. Died in Aug. 1777.	
Hobbs, Jacob	3rd NC Regiment	1781, a Private under Capt. Clement Hall for 12 months. Discharged on 8/1/1782 (2nd NC	

Name	1st Unit	Year / Rank / Served Under / Notes	Known Battles
		Regiment).	
Hobbs, Joseph	1st NC Regiment	1781, a Private under Capt. William Walton. Discharged on 7/1/1782.	
Hobbs, Moses	7th NC Regiment	1777, a Private under Capt. Henry Dawson. Dropped from the rolls in Feb. 1778.	
Hobbs, Peter	3rd NC Regiment	7/20/1778, a Private under Capt. Michael Quinn for nine months.	
Hobbs, Reuben	3rd NC Regiment	1781, a Private under Capt. Clement Hall for 12 months. Discharged on 8/1/1782 (2nd NC Regiment).	
Hobgood, John	3rd NC Regiment	7/20/1778, a Private under Lt./Capt. Joseph Montford for nine months.	
Hoby, William	3rd NC Regiment	7/20/1779, a Private under Capt. George "Gee" Bradley. Deserted in Sep. 1779.	
Hockammer, Philip	1st NC Regiment	1777, a Private under Capt. Henry "Hal" Dixon. Deserted on 10/12/1777. Re-enlisted in April 1778. 9/8/1778, a known Private under Capt. James Read. aka Philip Hochammer, Philip Hochommer.	
Hodge, John	5th NC Regiment	5/4/1776, an Ensign under Capt. John Enloe. 10/1/1776, a Lieutenant under Capt. John Pugh Williams. Dropped from the rolls in Jan. 1778.	
Hodges, Benjamin	5th NC Regiment	5/6/1776, a Sergeant under Capt. John Enloe. 9/8/1778, a known Sergeant in the Lt. Colonel's Company (Lt. Col. Robert Mebane) (1st NC Regiment) led by Capt. Joshua Bowman. 3/12/1779, re-enlisted for the duration of the war in the same unit as a Private. One source claims he first enlisted on 8/23/1777 for three years.	
Hodges, James	1st NC Regiment	4/12/1781, a Private under Capt. William Lytle. Confined four nights for desertion during July 1781. Dropped from the rolls sometime during 1781.	
Hodges, Joseph	5th NC Regiment	6/1/1779, a Private under Capt. Joseph Montford. Dropped from the rolls in Oct. 1779.	
Hodges, Robert	1st NC Regiment	4/12/1781, a Private under Capt. William Lytle. Deserted on 7/5/1781.	
Hodges, William	1st NC Regiment	6/15/1781, a Private under Capt. Anthony Sharpe. Discharged on 6/15/1782 (4th NC Regiment) at Bacon's Bridge, SC. Tending to a burned soldier during battle of Eutaw Springs, SC. Earlier in NC Militia. From Pitt County, NC. aka William Hodgs. S21826.	
Hodges, William	3rd NC Regiment	7/30/1779, a Private under Capt. George "Gee" Bradley. Deserted on 10/20/1779.	
Hodges, Willis	1st NC Regiment	4/12/1781, a Private under Capt. William Lytle. Confined four nights for desertion during July 1781. Discharged on 4/12/1782 (4th NC Regiment) at Bacon's Bridge, SC. Earlier in NC Miltia. From Halifax County, NC. On the official rolls as Wyllis Hodges. W7775.	Siege of Augusta (GA), Siege of Ninety-Six 1781 (SC), Eutaw Springs (SC).
Hodgton,	3rd NC	4/16/1776, a 2nd Lieutenant and an Adjutant.	

Name	1st Unit	Year / Rank / Served Under / Notes	Known Battles
Alvery	Regiment	Dropped from the rolls in Jan. 1778. aka Oliver Hodgson.	
Hofstaler, George	3rd NC Regiment	March 1779, a Private under Capt. Christopher Goodwin, then under Capt. William Goodman (4th NC Regiment). Discharged in September 1779. Earlier and later in NC Militia. From Rowan County, NC. S15176.	Briar Creek (GA), Stono Ferry (SC).
Hogan, Prosser	9th NC Regiment	5/10/1777, a Musician under Capt. Joseph J. Wade for three years. 9/8/1778, a known Private in the Lt. Colonel's Company (Lt. Col. Robert Mebane) (1st NC Regiment) led by Capt. Joshua Bowman. 3/12/1779, re-enlisted for the duration of the war in the same unit. Back to Musician in Nov. 1779. Back to Private on 3/1/1780 under Capt. Thomas Callendar. POW at the Fall of Charleston, escaped. Enlisted in Guilford County, NC. aka Proctor Hogan, Proster Hogan. S36592.	Siege of Charleston 1780 (SC).
Hogg, Andrew	3rd NC Regiment	2/8/1782, a Private under Capt. Samuel Jones for 12 months.	
Hogg, Elisha	2nd NC Regiment	1778, a Private under Capt. Benjamin Andrew Coleman for three years. From Johnston County, NC. W19808.	
Hogg, Thomas	1st NC Regiment	9/1/1775, a 1st Lieutenant. 3/1/1776, a Captain under Col. Francis Nash. Promoted to Major on 10/19/1777. 6/1/1778, a Major in 3rd NC Regiment under Lt. Col. Robert Mebane. POW at the Fall of Charleston, exchanged March 1781. Served till the end of the war. One source claims he retired on 1/1/1783. His son later asserts that he was promoted to Lt. Colonel near the end of the war.	Moore's Creek Bridge [4], Ft. Moultrie #1 (SC), Monmouth (NJ), Siege of Charleston 1780 (SC).
Hoggard, John	2nd NC Regiment	7/20/1778, a Private under Capt. Reading Blount for nine months. Discharged 4/30/1779 at Halifax, NC. Born in 1761 in Bertie County, NC where he also lived when he enlisted. aka John Hoggart. R4804.	
Hoggard, Patrick	2nd NC Regiment	7/20/1778, a Private under Capt. Reading Blount for nine months. aka Patrick Hoggart.	
Hoggard, William	5th NC Regiment	4/29/1776, a Private under Capt. John Pugh Williams. 9/9/1778, a known Private in the Major's Company (Maj. Hardy Murfree - 2nd NC Regiment). Discharged on 10/29/1778.	
Hogh, Gideon	2nd NC Regiment	Aug. 1781, a Private under Lt. James Pearl and Capt. Tilghman Dixon, then under Capt. Benjamin Andrew Coleman for 12 months. Discharged at Salisbury, NC. From Caswell County, NC. On the official rolls as Gideon Hogg. Probably Gideon Hogue, see Andrew Hogue below. S38846.	
Hogue, Andrew	3rd NC Regiment	2/8/1782, a Private under Capt. Samuel Jones for 12 months. On the official rolls as Andrew Hogg. He identifies himself as Andrew Hogh in his brother's 1819 pension application - Gideon	

Name	1st Unit	Year / Rank / Served Under / Notes	Known Battles
		Hogh. In his pension application of 1829, he identifies himself as Andrew Hogue. From Caswell County, NC. R5108..	
Hogun, David	3rd NC Regiment	6/24/1779, a Private under Capt. Michael Quinn. Dropped from the rolls in Oct. 1779. Rejoined in 1780.	
Hogun, James	3rd NC Regiment	4/17/1776, a Paymaster. Appointment Rescinded 4/18/1776. Also Paymaster of the three companies of NC Light Dragoons.	
Hogun, James	7th NC Regiment	Earlier, a Major in the Halifax County Regiment of Militia. 11/26/1776, Colonel/Commandant over the 7th NC Regiment. Early 1778, the 7th NC Regiment was disbanded due to low numbers. Col. James Hogun was sent back to NC to aid in recruiting. August 1778, the 7th NC Regiment was reinstated with over 600 men, returned to New York - folded into 3rd NC Regiment. Promoted to Brigadier General on January 9, 1779. Commandant of Philadelphia from January to November 1779. POW at the Fall of Charleston. Died at Haddrell's Point on January 4, 1781 due to ill health.	Brandywine Creek (PA), Germantown (PA), Siege of Charleston 1780 (SC).
Holden, James	5th NC Regiment	1777, a Corporal under Capt. John Pugh Williams. Dropped from the rolls in Jan. 1778.	
Holdin, William	2nd NC Regiment	5/12/1781, a Private under Capt. Tilghman Dixon. 7/29/1781, transferred to Lee's Legion.	
Holland, Brazil	4th NC Regiment	1782, a Private under Capt. Anthony Sharpe for 18 months.	
Holland, Daniel	1st NC Regiment	1782, a Private under Capt. Peter Bacot for 18 months.	
Holland, Henry	2nd NC Regiment	9/14/1781, a Private under Capt. Benjamin Andrew Coleman for 12 months.	
Holland, John	1st NC Regiment	1781, a Private under Capt. Hardy Holmes for 18 months. R5142.	
Holland, Josiah	5th NC Regiment	1777, a Private under Capt. John Pugh Williams. Died in June 1777.	
Holland, Reason	4th NC Regiment	Oct. 1777, a Private under Capt. Thomas Harris. Dec. 1777, a Private under Capt. Reading Blount (5th NC Regiment). Dropped from the rolls in Jan. 1778.	
Holland, Spier	5th NC Regiment	3/24/1776, commissioned as an Ensign to be placed under Capt. Benjamin Stedman (4/17/1776). 10/25/1777, a 1st Lieutenant. Dropped from the rolls in Jan. 1778. aka Spear Holland.	
Holland, William	7th NC Regiment	2/9/1777, a known Private under Capt. Thomas Brickell. 9/8/1778, a known Private under Capt. Howell Tatum (1st NC Regiment).	
Hollenbeck, John	5th NC Regiment	1777, a Corporal under Capt. John Pugh Williams. A Private in Nov. 1777. Dropped from the rolls in Feb. 1778.	
Holley, Joseph	1st NC Regiment	1/9/1777, a Private under Capt. Anthony Sharpe. Died 9/1/1778. Probably the same man as directly below.	

Name	1st Unit	Year / Rank / Served Under / Notes	Known Battles
Holley, Joseph	1st NC Regiment	6/9/1777, a Lieutenant under Capt. Anthony Sharpe. Died on 9/1/1778.	
Hollin, Jeremiah	2nd NC Regiment	1782, a Private under Capt. Benjamin Carter. Deserted on 6/9/1783 (?).	
Hollingshead, Benjamin	4th NC Regiment	1782, a Private under Capt. Anthony Sharpe for 18 months. Furloughed after about 13 months of service at 10-Mile Spring, SC. Earlier in NC Militia. From Rowan County, NC. On the official rolls as Benjamin Hollenhead. S16883.	
Hollingshead, Thomas	4th NC Regiment	1782, a Private under Capt. Anthony Sharpe for 18 months. Furloughed on 5/12/1783. On the official rolls as Thomas Hollenhead. R5151.	
Hollings-worth, Charles	4th NC Regiment	1775, a 1st Lieutenant in the Wilmington District Minutemen. 4/17/1776, a 1st Lieutenant under Capt. John Ashe, Jr. and Col. Thomas Polk.	
Hollis, James	4th NC Regiment	Dec. 1782, a Musician under Capt. Joseph T. Rhodes then Capt. Clement Hall. Discharged at Wilmington, NC. Earlier in British Army, deserted, moved to Duplin County, NC, joined there. S21290.	
Holloman, Kinchen	3rd NC Regiment	5/4/1776, a Private under Capt. Thomas Granbury for 2-1/2 years. 9/9/1778, a known Private under Capt. John Ingles (2nd NC Regiment). Discharged on 11/10/1778. From Hertford County, NC. R20383.	
Holloway, David	5th NC Regiment	3/1/1779, a Corporal under Maj. Reading Blount for nine months. Discharged in Dec. 1779.	
Hollowell, Samuel	8th NC Regiment	9/20/1777, a Lieutenant under Capt. Michael Quinn. Retired on 6/1/1778.	
Holly, Benjamin	1st NC Regiment	Jan. 1782, a Private under Capt. William Lytle. 2/6/1782, would be in the 4th NC Regiment. aka Benjamin Holley.	
Holly, Jacob	1st NC Regiment	4/12/1781, a Private under Capt. William Lytle. From Halifax County, NC. aka Jacob Holley. W21388.	
Holly, John	2nd NC Regiment	1/10/1782, a Private under Capt. Benjamin Andrew Coleman. Died on 9/16/1782. aka John Holley.	
Holmes, Hardy	1st NC Regiment	Nov. 1776, a 2nd Lieutenant. 1777, a 1st Lieutenant. 1778-1781, a Captain in NC Militia. 7/3/1781, a Lieutenant under Capt. Samuel Jones (3rd NC Regiment). Wounded at the battle of Eutaw Springs (SC). Allegedly, a Captain – no records thereof. BLWT1099-200.	Eutaw Springs (SC).
Holmes, John	1st NC Regiment	12/18/1781, a Private under Capt. James Mills for 12 months.	
Holmes, Josiah	1st NC Regiment	12/18/1781, a Private under Capt. James Mills for 12 months.	
Holmes, Robert	10th NC Regiment	5/8/1777, a Sergeant under Capt. Isaac Moore for three years. 9/8/1778, a known Sergeant in the Lt. Colonel's Company (Lt. Col. Robert Mebane) (1st NC Regiment) led by Capt.	

Name	1st Unit	Year / Rank / Served Under / Notes	Known Battles
		Joshua Bowman. POW on 4/14/1779 (?). Discharged on 2/1/1780. aka Robert Homes.	
Holmes, Shadrack	5th NC Regiment	5/14/1776, a Private under Capt. Reading Blount. A Sergeant on 7/1/1778. Discharged on 10/25/1778 (2nd NC Regiment).	
Holmes, Shadrack	5th NC Regiment	1777, a Private under Capt. John Pugh Williams. Dropped from the rolls in Feb. 1778.	
Holmes, Willis	DQMG	1780, a Wagoner under Col. Nicholas Long (Deputy QM General).	
Holston, Salathiel	1st NC Regiment	8/1/1782, a Sergeant under Capt. Joshua Hadley for 18 months. Deserted on 6/18/1783 (?).	
Holt, Thomas	1st NC Regiment	8/5/1777, a Private under Capt. Joshua Bowman. Dropped from the rolls in Nov. 1777.	
Holt, Thomas	1st NC Regiment	1781, a Private under Capt. Alexander Brevard. Discharged on 4/12/1782 (3rd NC Regiment).	
Honycutt, John	5th NC Regiment	8/5/1779, a Private under Capt. Reading Blount. Deserted in Oct. 1779.	
Hood, Archibald	3rd NC Regiment	5/2/1776, a Private under Capt. William Brinkley. 9/9/1778, a known Private in the Lt. Colonel's Company (Lt. Col. Selby Harney) (2nd NC Regiment). Discharged in Oct. 1778.	
Hood, Charles	1st NC Regiment	A Private under Capt. Thomas Donoho, then Capt. Clement Hall (3rd NC Regiment). Enlisted in Caswell County, NC. A free man of color. S41659.	Siege of Charleston 1780 (SC), Eutaw Springs (SC).
Hood, Charles	3rd NC Regiment	1782, a Private under Capt. Alexander Brevard for 18 months.	
Hood, Ephraim	3rd NC Regiment	6/7/1779, a Private under Capt. Michael Quinn for 18 months.	
Hood, William	1st NC Regiment	A Private under Capt. William Armstrong. Died on 2/14/1778.	
Hood, William	1st NC Regiment	1781, a Private under Capt. Alexander Brevard for 18 months. 2/6/1782, would be in the 3rd NC Regiment. W25781.	Eutaw Springs (SC).
Hooke, George	4th NC Regiment	1776, a Sergeant under Capt. John Nelson. Discharged on 5/7/1778. Then joined a VA unit. Resided in Augusta County, VA when he enlisted. Born 1751. On the official rolls as George Hook. aka George Hood. W10112.	Ft. Moultrie #1 (SC).
Hooker, John	1st NC Regiment	4/5/1781, a Private under Capt. Anthony Sharpe. Discharged on 4/5/1782 (4th NC Regiment).	
Hooker, Robert	9th NC Regiment	1777, a Private under Capt. Thomas McCrory. Deserted in Nov. 1777.	
Hooks, Ephraim	5th NC Regiment	5/9/1776, a Private under Capt. John Pugh Williams. 9/9/1778, a known Private in the Major's Company (Maj. Hardy Murfree) (2nd NC Regiment). Discharged on 11/9/1778.	
Hooks, Willoughby	3rd NC Regiment	7/20/1778, a Private under Capt. John Baker for nine months. Earlier and later in NC Militia. From Rowan County, NC. On the official rolls as Willowby Hooks. S1533.	
Hooper,	10th NC	5/16/1777, a Private under Capt. James Wilson.	

Name	1st Unit	Year / Rank / Served Under / Notes	Known Battles
Anthony	Regiment	Deserted 7/28/1778.	
Hoover, Henry	3rd NC Regiment	7/20/1778, a Private under Capt. Michael Quinn. Died on 11/2/1778.	
Hoover, Jacob	NC Light Dragoons	Oct.-Dec. 1777, a known Private under Capt. Martin Phifer. Not on any official rolls.	
Hoover, Samuel	3rd NC Regiment	7/20/1778, a Private under Capt. Michael Quinn for nine months.	
Hope, William	4th NC Regiment	Dec. 1782, a Private under Capt. William Lytle.	
Hopkins, Daniel	2nd NC Regiment	7/20/1778, a Corporal under Capt. Reading Blount for nine months. This is per the official records. In his pension application, he shows evidence (a discharge) that he had been under Lt. William Knott and Capt. Jeremiah McClure (actually John McLane) of the 4th NC Regiment for one year and was discharged on 3/31/1777. He was from Bertie County, NC. S41660.	
Hopkins, Isaac	6th NC Regiment	1777, a Private under Capt. Thomas Donoho. Deserted in Aug. 1777. Feb. 1779, re-enlisted into the 5th NC Regiment, unit unknown. Probably the same man as directly below.	
Hopkins, Isaac	6th NC Regiment	5/10/1777, a Private under Capt. Benjamin Pike. Dropped from the rolls in Jan. 1778. Re-enlisted in Jan. 1779 under Capt. Philip Taylor (5th NC Regiment, 1780 in 3rd NC Regiment). POW at the Fall of Charleston (SC) - paroled. From Granville County, NC. Born on 1/9/1756 in Orange County, VA. S7043.	Germantown (PA), Monmouth (NJ), Siege of Charleston 1780 (SC).
Hopkins, Jonathan	5th NC Regiment	11/21/1776, a Corporal under Capt. William Caswell. 9/9/1778, a known Corporal under Capt. Robert Fenner (2nd NC Regiment). Deserted on 7/3/1779. Rejoined in Nov. 1779.	
Hopkins, Joseph	3rd NC Regiment	1781, served under Capt. Edward Yarborough for 12 months. Discharged on 4/15/1782.	
Hopkins, Joseph	5th NC Regiment	6/25/1779, a Private under Maj. Reading Blount. Deserted in Oct. 1779.	
Hopkins, Richard	6th NC Regiment	5/9/1776, a Private under Capt. Philip Taylor for 2-1/2 years. 9/8/1778, a known Private under Capt. John Sumner (1st NC Regiment). Dropped from the rolls in Nov. 1778.	
Hopkins, Thomas	5th NC Regiment	1779, a Private under Maj. Reading Blount for nine months. Dropped from the rolls in Oct. 1779.	
Hopper, John	1st NC Regiment	1781, a Private under Capt. Alexander Brevard. Discharged on 4/12/1782 (3rd NC Regiment).	
Hopper, Moses	1st NC Regiment	5/25/1781, a Private under Capt. Thomas Donoho. Discharged 5/25/1782. Real name was Moses Edwards, from Guilford County, NC. Earlier in NC Militia. W25559.	Siege of Ninety-Six 1781 (SC), Eutaw Springs (SC).
Hopper, William	1st NC Regiment	Nov. 1775, a Private under Capt. Henry "Hal" Dixon. A Sergeant on 9/20/1777. A QM Sergeant in Dec. 1777. Discharged on 6/11/1778 due to the loss of one eye by disease.	

436

Name	1st Unit	Year / Rank / Served Under / Notes	Known Battles
		aka William Happer. S37995.	
Hopson, John	5th NC Regiment	1775, an Ensign in the Salisbury District Minutemen. Lived in the Hillsborough District. 4/17/1776, an Ensign under Capt. William Ward and Col. Edward Buncombe.	
Horn, Henry	3rd NC Regiment	1781, served under Capt. Edward Yarborough for 12 months. Discharged 4/22/1782.	
Hornsby, Thomas	1st NC Regiment	4/28/1781, a Private under Capt. Alexander Brevard. Probably the same man as directly below.	
Hornsby, Thomas	1st NC Regiment	1781, a QM Sergeant under Capt. Alexander Brevard for 12 months. Discharged on 4/28/1782 (3rd NC Regiment).	
Horpus, Basford	3rd NC Regiment	1778, a Private under Capt. John Baker. Deserted on 7/9/1778.	
Horseford, James	1st NC Regiment	1777, a Private under Capt. Henry "Hal" Dixon. 9/8/1778, a known Private under Capt. James Read. A Corporal on 2/1/1780.	
Horton, James	1st NC Regiment	4/6/1777, a Private under Capt. Howell Tatum. 9/8/1778, a known Private under Capt. Howell Tatum. Died on 6/3/1778 (?).	
Horton, John	3rd NC Regiment	10/1/1778, a Corporal in the Lt. Colonel's Company (Lt. Col. William Lee Davidson) led by Capt. George "Gee" Bradley. 4/23/1779, a known Sergeant in the Lt. Colonel's Company (Lt. Col. Robert Mebane) led by Capt. George "Gee" Bradley.	
Horton, Levi	1st NC Regiment	May 1778, a Private under Capt. Howell Tatum. 9/8/1778, a known Private under Capt. Howell Tatum.	
Hoskins, Ebenezer	2nd NC Regiment	4/1/1777, a Private under Capt. John Armstrong. Deserted on 9/1/1778 from Capt. Robert Fenner's company.	
House, Job	1st NC Regiment	4/19/1781, Lt. Col. John Baptiste Ashe asks HQ for a certificate of commission for this man as an Ensign.	
Houston, Abraham	2nd NC Regiment	3/12/1779, re-enlisted under Capt. Benjamin Williams.	
Houston, Archibald	1st NC Regiment	Sep. 1775, a Private under Capt. George Davidson for six months. Then in NC Militia. From Rowan County, NC. W295.	
Houston, Hugh	4th NC Regiment	7/5/1776, a Private under Capt. Robert Smith. 9/8/1778, a known Private in the Colonel's Company (Col. Thomas Clark) (1st NC Regiment) led by Capt. John Gambier Scull - sick at Princeton on that date. Discharged on 7/5/1779 at West Point, NY. aka Hugh Huston. W8928.	Brandywine Creek (PA), Germantown (PA), Monmouth (NJ).
Houstory, Henry	NC Light Dragoons	Oct.-Dec. 1777, a known Private under Capt. Martin Phifer. Not on any official rolls.	
Howard, Edward	1st NC Regiment	6/14/1781, a Private under Capt. Thomas Donoho. Discharged on 6/14/1782.	
Howard, Edward	3rd NC Regiment	7/20/1778, a Corporal under Capt. Michael Quinn for nine months.	

Name	1st Unit	Year / Rank / Served Under / Notes	Known Battles
Howard, George	4th NC Regiment	5/5/1776, a Private under Capt. Thomas Harris for three years. 9/8/1778, a known Private under Capt. John Sumner (1st NC Regiment). Discharged on 5/15/1779.	
Howard, Isaac	9th NC Regiment	2/15/1777, a Private under Capt. Richard D. Cook for three years. 9/8/1778, a known Private in the Lt. Colonel's Company (Lt. Col. Robert Mebane) (1st NC Regiment) led by Capt. Joshua Bowman - sick on that date. Discharged on 3/8/1780.	
Howard, James	NC Light Dragoons	Oct.-Dec. 1777, a known Private under Capt. Martin Phifer. Not on any official rolls.	
Howard, Joseph	4th NC Regiment	1781, a Private under Capt. George Dougherty for 12 months. Discharged on 5/25/1782.	
Howard, Joseph	7th NC Regiment	4/1/1777, a Musician under Capt. James Vaughn. 2/26/1778, a known Private under Capt. Howell Tatum (1st NC Regiment). 9/8/1778, a known Private under Capt. Howell Tatum.	
Howard, Patrick	2nd NC Regiment	1777, a Private under Capt. James Gee. Deserted, date unknown.	
Howard, Solomon	5th NC Regiment	4/28/1776, a Sergeant under Capt. John Pugh Williams. A Private in Jan. 1778. Discharged on 10/30/1778 in New York from the 2nd NC Regiment. From Bertie County, NC. S31757.	Brandywine Creek (PA), Monmouth (NJ).
Howard, William	1st NC Regiment	4/12/1781, a Private under Capt. William Lytle. Discharged on 4/12/1782 at Salisbury, NC. From Edgecombe County, NC. Earlier in NC Militia. Born 1753 in Edgecombe County, NC. S7032.	Siege of Augusta (GA), Siege of Ninety-Six 1781 (SC), Eutaw Springs (SC).
Howard, William	6th NC Regiment	1777, a Private under Capt. Thomas Donoho. Deserted in Aug. 1777.	
Howard, Willis	1st NC Regiment	4/12/1781, a Private under Capt. William Lytle. Confined four nights for desertion during July 1781. Discharged on 4/12/1782.	
Howard, Wilson	1st NC Regiment	4/12/1781, a Private under Capt. William Lytle. Confined four nights for desertion during July 1781. Discharged on 4/12/1782. Earlier in NC Militia. From Edgecombe County, NC.	
Howe, Robert	2nd NC Regiment	1775, Colonel/Commandant of Brunswick County Regiment of Militia. 9/1/1775, Colonel/Commandant of 2nd NC Regiment, first provincial troops, then Continental troops. Promoted to Brigadier General (3/1/1776 - another source says 4/10/1776). 10/20/1777, promoted to Major General, commanding all Southern Department Continentals. From Brunswick County, NC.	Great Bridge (VA), Ft. Johnston #1, Norfolk (VA), Ft. Moultrie #1.
Howe, William	1st NC Regiment	9/8/1778, a known Fifer in the Colonel's Company (Col. Thomas Clark) led by Capt. John Gambier Scull.	
Howell,	1st NC	5/2/1779, a Private under Capt. Thomas Donoho	

438

Name	1st Unit	Year / Rank / Served Under / Notes	Known Battles
Dempsey	Regiment	for 12 months. Discharged on 5/2/1782.	
Howell, Edward	4th NC Regiment	5/6/1776 (?), a Corporal under Capt. William Goodman. 9/8/1778, a known Corporal in the Colonel's Company (Col. Thomas Clark - 1st NC Regiment) led by Capt. John Gambier Scull. Discharged on 11/10/1779.	
Howell, Elias	8th NC Regiment	11/12/1776, an Ensign under Capt. Frederick Hargett. 7/12/1777, a 2nd Lieutenant. Retired 7/1/1778.	
Howell, Frederick	7th NC Regiment	8/6/1777, a Private under Capt. Lemuel Ely for three years. 3/12/1779, re-enlisted for the duration of the war under Capt. Griffith John McRee (1st NC Regiment). Dropped from the rolls in July 1779. Re-enlisted in Nov. 1779, regiment and unit unknown.	
Howell, Henry	3rd NC Regiment	1777, a Private under Capt. Thomas Granbury. Deserted in Aug. 1777.	
Howell, John	2nd NC Regiment	6/17/1777, a Private under Capt. Clement Hall for three years. 3/12/1779, re-enlisted under Capt. Benjamin Williams.	
Howell, John	3rd NC Regiment	1778, a Private under Capt. Kedar Ballard. Died on 9/28/1778.	
Howell, Silas	9th NC Regiment	1777, a Private under Capt. Richard D. Cook. Deserted in Aug. 1777.	
Howell, Stephen	9th NC Regiment	1/28/1777, a Musician under Capt. Thomas McCrory. A Private in May 1778. Died on 7/8/1778.	
Howington, William	3rd NC Regiment	5/5/1776, a Private under Lt./Capt. Kedar Ballard. Dropped from the rolls sometime during 1779.	
Hubbard, Elisha	6th NC Regiment	Nov. 1777, a Sergeant under Capt. Philip Taylor. Dropped from the rolls in Dec. 1777.	
Hubbard, James	2nd NC Regiment	7/20/1778, a Private under Maj. Reading Blount for nine months.	
Hubbard, John	1st NC Regiment	1781, a Private under Capt. Anthony Sharpe for 12 months. Discharged 9/8/1782 (4th NC Regiment). From Franklin County, NC. Earlier in NC Militia. W19841.	
Hubbard, Warburton	5th NC Regiment	1777, a Sergeant under Capt. William Caswell. Died on 5/5/1778.	
Huddy, William	3rd NC Regiment	1779, a Private under Capt. Kedar Ballard.	
Hudlar, John	3rd NC Regiment	7/24/1779, a Private under Lt. John McNees and Capt. Michael Quinn. From Jones County, NC. W8450.	
Hudler, Lemuel	10th NC Regiment	7/7/1777, a Private under Capt. Armwell Herron. Died on 4/19/1778.	
Hudley, Joseph	3rd NC Regiment	6/20/1779, a Private under Capt. George "Gee" Bradley. Died on 1/28/1780.	
Hudson, Chamberlain	3rd NC Regiment	5/7/1776, a Corporal under Capt. Jacob Turner. A Sergeant on 10/25/1777. A Private in June 1778. Discharged in Oct. 1778.	
Hudson, Ezekiel	5th NC Regiment	1777, a Private under Capt. Reading Blount. Died on 4/8/1778.	

Name	1st Unit	Year / Rank / Served Under / Notes	Known Battles
Hudson, Isaac	3rd NC Regiment	5/24/1777, a Sergeant Major. Dropped from the rolls in Sep. 1778.	
Hudson, James	5th NC Regiment	May 1776, a Private under Capt. Peter Simon then Capt. Henry Darnell for twelve months. From Martin County, NC. Discharged on 5/13/1777. S38852.	
Hudson, John	3rd NC Regiment	7/20/1778, a Private under Lt./Capt. George "Gee" Bradley for nine months.	
Hudson, John	3rd NC Regiment	1779, a Private under Capt. Michael Quinn. Discharged in Dec. 1779.	
Hudson, John	5th NC Regiment	Spring of 1776, a Private under Capt. William Ward for 2-1/2 years. Wounded at the battle of Brandywine Creek, PA. Discharged in the Fall of 1778 near Baltimore, MD. From Johnston County, NC. S41675.	Brandywine Creek (PA), Germantown (PA).
Hudson, Thomas	1st NC Regiment	1777, a Private under Capt. Micajah Lewis. Dropped from the rolls in Sep 1778 (4th NC Regiment).	
Hudson, Thomas	6th NC Regiment	1777, a Sergeant under Capt. Thomas Donoho. Died on 4/3/1778.	
Huggin, Jeff	6th NC Regiment	1777, a Private under Capt. Thomas Donoho. Dropped from the rolls in Sep. 1777.	
Huggins, James	2nd NC Regiment	4/25/1781, a Private under Capt. Tilghman Dixon. Discharged on 4/25/1782. From Jones County, NC. S46449.	
Huggins, James	8th NC Regiment	12/4/1776, a Private under Capt. John Walsh.	
Huggins, Luke	2nd NC Regiment	4/25/1781, a Private under Capt. Tilghman Dixon. Discharged on 4/25/1782.	
Huggins, Michael	2nd NC Regiment	4/25/1781, a Private under Capt. Tilghman Dixon. Discharged on 4/25/1782.	
Huggins, Nehemiah	1st NC Regiment	1778, a Private under Capt. Anthony Sharpe.	
Hughes, Francis	3rd NC Regiment	1776, a Private, unit unknown. Enlisted in Burke County, NC. Later, in Militia	
Hughes, Henry	8th NC Regiment	6/28/1777, a Corporal under Capt. John Walsh. A Private in Jan. 1778. Back to Corporal in June 1778. Back to Private in Sep. 1778.	
Hughes, John	DQMG	8/23/1781, a Leather worker under Col. Nicholas Long (Deputy QM General), making saddles, harnesses, caps, etc. aka John Hews.	
Hughes, John	4th NC Regiment	5/1/1776, a Private under Capt. Robert Smith for three years. A Corporal in Oct. 1777. Back to Private in June 1778. 9/8/1778, a known Private in the Colonel's Company (Col. Thomas Clark) (1st NC Regiment) led by Capt. John Gambier Scull. Discharged on 5/14/1779.	
Hughes, John	4th NC Regiment	12/20/1776, a Sergeant under Capt. William Temple Coles for three years. 9/8/1778, a known Sergeant under Capt. John Sumner (1st NC Regiment). Discharged on 6/28/1779. W8954.	Monmouth (NJ).
Hughes, Samuel	2nd NC Regiment	1782, a Private under Capt. Benjamin Carter for 18 months.	

Name	1st Unit	Year / Rank / Served Under / Notes	Known Battles
Hughkins, Hardy	5th NC Regiment	5/1/1776, a Private under Capt. Reading Blount. 9/9/1778, under Capt. Benjamin Andrew Coleman (2nd NC Regiment). Discharged on 3/1/1779. aka Hardy Hukins.	
Hughkins, James	2nd NC Regiment	12/4/1776, a Private, unit unknown. 9/9/1778, a known Private under Capt. Benjamin Andrew Coleman. 3/12/1779, re-enlisted under Capt. Benjamin Andrew Coleman. aka James Hukins.	
Huling, W. Jacob	2nd NC Regiment	1777, a Sergeant under Capt. William Fenner. A Private in Sep. 1777.	
Hull, Jackson	3rd NC Regiment	1777, a Private under Capt. William Brinkley. Died in Jan. 1778.	
Hull, Nathaniel	2nd NC Regiment	1782, a Private under Capt. Benjamin Carter. Deserted on 6/21/1783 (?).	
Human, Alexander	1st NC Regiment	5/5/1778, a Private for two months, furloughed. Nov. 1778, a Private under Capt. Thomas Donoho. Then, in NC Militia. From Caswell County, NC. W7849.	Briar Creek (GA), Stono Ferry (SC).
Humphrey, James	NC Light Dragoons	Oct.-Dec. 1777, a known Private under Capt. Martin Phifer. Not on any official rolls.	
Humphreys, Daniel	2nd NC Regiment	3/18/1776, a Private under Capt. James Gee for 2-1/2 years. 9/9/1778, a known Private under Capt. John Ingles. Discharged on 9/30/1778.	
Humphreys, Randal	6th NC Regiment	1777, a Private under Capt. Griffith John McRee. 9/8/1778, a known Private under Capt. Tilghman Dixon (1st NC Regiment). aka Randle Humphreys.	
Hunsucker, Abram	1st NC Regiment	6/6/1781, a Private under Capt. Alexander Brevard. Discharged on 6/7/1782 (3rd NC Regiment). Enlisted in Burke County, NC. Earlier in NC Militia. aka Abraham Hunsucker. S5258.	Siege of Ninety-Six 1781 (SC), Eutaw Springs (SC).
Hunt, David	3rd NC Regiment	7/20/1778, a Private under Capt. John Baker for nine months. Enlisted in Edgecombe County, NC. Discharged at Halifax, NC.	
Hunt, Elisha	2nd NC Regiment	9/9/1778, under Capt. Benjamin Andrew Coleman. Wounded, lost his right arm at the Fall of Charleston - POW. Free man of color. Feds listed him as Elijah Hunt, pension has Elisha. S13486.	Siege of Charleston 1780 (SC).
Hunt, Elisha	5th NC Regiment	1777, a Private under Capt. Henry Darnell.	
Hunt, John	4th NC Regiment	2/6/1782, a Private under Capt. James Mills for 12 months.	
Hunter, Asa	4th NC Regiment	1781, a Private under Capt. George Dougherty for 12 months. Discharged on 5/25/1782.	
Hunter, George	2nd NC Regiment	4/12/1781, a Private under Capt. Tilghman Dixon. Deserted on 7/20/1781.	
Huntston, Abraham	3rd NC Regiment	4/29/1776, a Private under Capt. Jacob Turner. Deserted on 12/1/1779. aka Abin Hutson.	
Hurley, David	4th NC Regiment	August 1782, a Private under Capt. Elijah Moore, then under Capt. Alexander Brevard (3rd NC Regiment) for 18 months. Discharged in NC in 1783 after peace was announced.	

Name	1st Unit	Year / Rank / Served Under / Notes	Known Battles
		S38051.	
Hurley, John	2nd NC Regiment	1/10/1782, a Private under Capt. Benjamin Andrew Coleman for 12 months. Probably the same man as directly below.	
Hurley, John	2nd NC Regiment	Sep. 1782, a Private under Capt. Clement Hall.	
Hurley, John	4th NC Regiment	1777, a Private under Capt. Thomas Harris. Died in July 1777.	
Hurley, Joseph	4th NC Regiment	7/1/1782, a Sergeant under Capt. Elijah Moore, then under Capt. Alexander Brevard (3rd NC Regiment), then under Capt. Joseph Thomas Rhodes (4th NC Regiment) for 18 months. Discharged on 7/1/1783 at Charleston, SC. S38050.	
Hurley, William	6th NC Regiment	1777, a Corporal under Capt. Thomas Donoho. Dropped from the rolls in Feb. 1778.	
Hurt, William	6th NC Regiment	1777, a Private under Capt. Thomas Donoho. Killed on 10/4/1777 at the battle of Germantown, PA.	Germantown (PA).
Hurton, Hugh	4th NC Regiment	7/5/1776, a Private under Capt. Robert Smith. 9/8/1778, a known Private in the Colonel's Company (Col. Thomas Clark) (1st NC Regiment) led by Capt. John Gambier Scull. Discharged on 7/5/1779. aka Hugh Huston.	
Hussar, Francis	5th NC Regiment	1779, a Private under Maj. Reading Blount for nine months. Dropped from the rolls in Oct. 1779.	
Hussey, John	3rd NC Regiment	1781, served under Capt. Edward Yarborough for 12 months. Discharged on 4/22/1782.	
Hussey, John		Aug. 1779, a Private, regiment and unit unknown.	
Huste, John	2nd NC Regiment	Nov. 1776, a Private under Capt. Benjamin Williams for three years. 9/9/1778, a known Private in the Major's Company (Maj. Hardy Murfree) (2nd NC Regiment). aka John Husk.	
Hutchins, Edward	2nd NC Regiment	Sept. 1775, a Private under Lt. William Fenner and Capt. William Knox for six months. 11/21/1776, a Private under Capt. William Caswell (5th NC Regiment). 9/9/1778, a known Private under Capt. Robert Fenner (2nd NC Regiment). Wounded at the battle of Germantown (PA). POW at Ft. Lafayette, NY on 6/1/1779. Discharged on 2/8/1780. July 1781, re-enlisted as a Sergeant under Capt. Alexander Brevard (1st NC Regiment) for 12 months. Discharged on 7/11/1782 (3rd NC Regiment). S38052.	Brandywine Creek (PA), Germantown (PA), Ft. Lafayette (NY).
Hutchins, Jesse	5th NC Regiment	7/26/1779, a Private under Maj. Reading Blount.	
Hutchins, Robert	3rd NC Regiment	7/20/1778, a Private under Lt./Capt. George "Gee" Bradley for nine months.	
Hutchison, Elijah	3rd NC Regiment	8/1/1782, a Private under Capt. Benjamin Bailey for 18 months. Deserted on 5/5/1783 (?). aka Elizah Hutchinson.	

442

Name	1st Unit	Year / Rank / Served Under / Notes	Known Battles
Hutson, David	2nd NC Regiment	1782, a Private under Capt. Benjamin Carter. Deserted on 11/26/1782.	
Hutson, Miles	1st NC Regiment	12/14/1778, a Private under Capt. Anthony Sharpe.	
Hutson, Miles	2nd NC Regiment	1782, a Private under Capt. Robert Raiford for 18 months.	
Hutson, Miles	4th NC Regiment	1781, a Private under Capt. George Dougherty for 12 months. Discharged on 5/25/1782.	
Hutson, Miles		1779, a Private, regiment and unit unknown.	
Huttleston, Robert	1st NC Regiment	6/14/1781, a Private under Capt. Thomas Donoho. Discharged on 6/14/1782. aka Robert Huttliston.	
Hyde, Andrew	4th NC Regiment	6/20/1777, a Musician under Capt. Thomas Harris for three years. A Private in Dec. 1777. 9/8/1778, a known Private under Capt. John Sumner (1st NC Regiment). Dropped from the rolls in Sep. 1778. aka Andrew Hide.	
Hyman, Joseph	6th NC Regiment	1777, a Private under Capt. Philip Taylor. Dropped from the rolls in June 1778.	
Hyner, Lewis	4th NC Regiment	1782, a Private under Capt. Anthony Sharpe. Deserted on 6/17/1783 (?).	
Hynes, Hardy	5th NC Regiment	4/16/1776, a Private under Capt. William Caswell. 9/9/1778, a known Private under Capt. Robert Fenner (2nd NC Regiment). Discharged on 11/10/1778. From Dobbs County, NC. On the official rolls as Hardy Hinds. aka Hardy Hines. R5468.	
Hysaw, Henry	1st NC Regiment	6/6/1781, a Private under Capt. Alexander Brevard.	
Ingles, John	2nd NC Regiment	5/3/1776, an Adjutant. 1777, a 1st Lieutenant under Capt. James Gee. 11/12/1777, a Captain under Col. John Patten. POW at the Fall of Charleston, paroled June 1781, but not exchanged until 11/26/1782. On 4/24/1782, his commission was back-dated to 10/24/1777. Retired 1/1/1783 (?). A brevet Major on 9/30/1783. aka John Inglas.	Brandywine Creek (PA), Germantown (PA), Monmouth (NJ), Siege of Charleston 1780 (SC).
Inglish, John	2nd NC Regiment	Aug. 1782, a Private under Capt. Clement Hall. Deserted on 6/15/1783 (?).	
Inglish, Joseph	5th NC Regiment	1777, a Musician under Capt. Simon Alderson. Died on 12/17/1777.	
Ingraham, John		June 1779, a Private, regiment and unit unknown. A Sergeant on 1/1/1780.	
Ingraham, John	1st NC Regiment	1777, a Sergeant under Capt. Henry "Hal" Dixon. Deserted in Sep. 1777.	
Ingram, Edwin	1st NC Regiment	1775, a Sergeant that was almost immediately promoted to Ensign under Capt. William Pickett, served six months - unit disbanded on 1/4/1776. Then, joined NC Militia. From Anson County, NC. S9741.	Great Cane Brake (SC), Snow Campaign (SC).
Ingram, James	8th NC Regiment	11/27/177, a Lt. Colonel. Resigned 7/8/1777. From Northampton County, NC.	
Ingram,	1st NC	Sep. 1775, a Private under Capt. William	Great Cane

Name	1st Unit	Year / Rank / Served Under / Notes	Known Battles
Samuel	Regiment	Pickett for six months. From Anson County, NC. Later in NC Militia. R5485.	Brake (SC), Snow Campaign (SC).
Inman, William	3rd NC Regiment	8/1/1779, a Private under Capt. George "Gee" Bradley. 1781, a Private under Capt. Edward Yarborough for 12 months. Discharged on 4/22/1782. aka William Enman.	
Ireland, James	2nd NC Regiment	1775, a Sergeant under Capt. William Knox for six months. From Rowan County, NC. Later in NC Militia. R5491.	Great Cane Brake (SC), Snow Campaign (SC), Moore's Creek Bridge [4].
Irwin, Henry	5th NC Regiment	1775, a Lt. Colonel in the Halifax District Minutemen. April 15, 1776, a Lt. Colonel in 5th NC Regiment. POW/killed at Germantown on Oct. 4, 1777. From Edgecombe County, NC.	Brandywine Creek (PA), Germantown (PA).
Irwin, James	1st NC Regiment	1/1/1777, a Musician under Capt. Thomas Hogg. A Private in Jan. 1778.	
Irwin, John	1st NC Regiment	3/28/1777, an Ensign. 4/4/1777, a 2nd Lieutenant. Resigned 8/28/1777. Later, a Lt. Colonel in NC Militia. From Mecklenburg County, NC.	
Irwin, Nicholas	2nd NC Regiment	10/7/1776, a Private under Capt. Clement Hall. Deserted on 4/29/1779. aka Nicholas Irvin.	
Isdall, George	4th NC Regiment	1782, a Private under Capt. William Lytle. Deserted on 5/5/1783 (?).	
Ives, James	5th NC Regiment	11/15/1776, a Private under Capt. Simon Alderson. 9/9/1778, a known Private in the Colonel's Company (Col. John Patten) (2nd NC Regiment) led by Capt. John Craddock. 3/12/1779, re-enlisted in the Colonel's Company (Col. John Patten) led by Capt. John Craddock.	
Ivey, Curtis	5th NC Regiment	4/23/1777, an Ensign under Capt. John Pugh Williams. 10/10/1777, a 1st Lieutenant. Transferred to 3rd NC Regiment on 6/1/1778. 2/1/1779, a Captain under Maj. John Armstrong. Transferred to 4th NC Regiment on 2/6/1782, served till the end of the war – however, he is listed as a Lieutenant on the 4/24/1782 roll (?). Some sources assert he was an Adjutant of the 1st NC Regiment in 1781. aka Curtis Ivory, Curtis Ivy.	Eutaw Springs (SC).
Ivey, David	10th NC Regiment	5/12/1777, a Musician under Capt. James Wilson for three years. June 1778, in the 1st NC Regiment. 9/8/1778, a known Wagoner in the Major's Company (Maj. Griffith John McRee) (1st NC Regiment). A Waggoner in 1781. aka David Ivy. W26156.	
Ivey, Reuben	1st NC Regiment	5/25/1781, a Private under Lt./Capt. Benjamin Bailey. Discharged on 5/25/1782 (3rd NC Regiment).	
Ivy, James	5th NC Regiment	11/15/1776, a Private under Capt. Simon Alderson.	

444

Name	1st Unit	Year / Rank / Served Under / Notes	Known Battles
Jack, Francis	5th NC Regiment	6/24/1779, a Private under Capt. Joseph Montford for 18 months. Dropped from the rolls in Oct. 1779.	
Jackson, Basil	7th NC Regiment	1777, a Private under Capt. Thomas Brickell. 2/26/1778, a known Private under Capt. Howell Tatum (1st NC Regiment). 9/8/1778, a known Private under Capt. Howell Tatum. aka Bazzle Jackson.	
Jackson, Colby	3rd NC Regiment	1782, a Private under Capt. Alexander Brevard for 18 months. aka Coleby Jackson.	
Jackson, Edmund	7th NC Regiment	3/29/1777, a Private under Capt. John Macon. 9/8/1778, a known Private under Capt. Tilghman Dixon (1st NC Regiment). Died on 4/30/1779. aka Edward Jackson.	
Jackson, Edward	3rd NC Regiment	7/20/1778, a Private under Capt. John Baker for nine months.	
Jackson, Frederick	3rd NC Regiment	7/20/1778, a Private under Capt. Kedar Ballard for nine months.	
Jackson, Hugh		A Private, regiment and unit unknown. Died from heat/fatigue at battle of Stono Ferry, SC on June 20, 1779. Future President Andrew Jackson's older brother.	Stono Ferry (SC).
Jackson, James	1st NC Regiment	1781, a Private under Capt. Anthony Sharpe. Discharged on 8/21/1782 (4th NC Regiment).	
Jackson, Jeremiah	3rd NC Regiment	10/15/1778, a Private under Capt. Michael Quinn. Re-enlisted on 6/24/1779. Dropped from the rolls in Nov. 1779. Re-enlisted in 1780.	
Jackson, John	6th NC Regiment	A Private under Capt. George Dougherty. 6/1/1778, a Private under Capt. Griffith John McRee (1st NC Regiment). Deserted on 7/12/1779.	
Jackson, John	10th NC Regiment	5/18/1777, a Private under Capt. Abraham Sheppard, Jr.	
Jackson, Levi	1st NC Regiment	5/9/1781, a Private under Capt. Alexander Brevard.	
Jackson, Robert	2nd NC Regiment	6/1/1777, a Private under Capt. Charles Allen for three years. 9/10/1778, a known Private under Capt. Thomas Armstrong. 3/12/1779, re-enlisted under Capt. Thomas Armstrong. POW at Ft. Lafayette on 6/1/1779. Mustered out in Nov. 1779.	Ft. Lafayette (NY).
Jackson, Thomas	8th NC Regiment	1777, a Private under Capt. John Walsh. Dropped from the rolls in Feb. 1778.	
Jackson, William	4th NC Regiment	5/1/1776, a Private under Capt. John Nelson for three years. 6/1/1778, a Private under Capt. Griffith John McRee (1st NC Regiment). Discharged on 5/1/1779. From Halifax County, NC. Later in NC Militia, unit unknown. W21448.	
Jackson, William	4th NC Regiment	8/1/1782, a Private under Anthony Sharpe, then under Capt. Benjamin Bailey (3rd NC Regiment) for 18 months. Discharged in Dec. 1783 (?) at James Island, SC. From Wilkes County, GA. S4433.	

Name	1st Unit	Year / Rank / Served Under / Notes	Known Battles
Jackson, William	10th NC Regiment	5/18/1777, a Private under Capt. Abraham Sheppard, Jr.	
Jackson, Zachariah	1st NC Regiment	6/30/1777, a Private under Capt. Joshua Bowman. 9/8/1778, a known Private under Capt. Tilghman Dixon. Assigned to His Excellency's Guard.	
Jackson, Zachariah	6th NC Regiment	6/13/1776, a Sergeant under Capt. George Dougherty. Transferred to Gen'l Guards on 5/22/1778. Discharged on 7/13/1779.	
Jacobs, Benjamin	10th NC Regiment	2/16/1777, a Private under Capt. Andrew Vanoy for 2-1/2 years. 9/8/1778, a known Private in the Major's Company (Maj. John Baptiste Ashe) (1st NC Regiment). A Corporal on 5/19/1779.	
Jacobs, Henry	3rd NC Regiment	1781, a Private under Capt. Clement Hall for 12 months. Discharged on 8/1/1782 (2nd NC Regiment).	
Jacobs, Hezekiah	1st NC Regiment	12/18/1781, a Private under Capt. James Mills for 12 months.	
Jacobs, John	6th NC Regiment	6/6/1776, an Ensign. 11/1/1776, a 1st Lieutenant under Capt. Charles Allen. Resigned on 3/1/1778.	
Jacobs, Joshua	1st NC Regiment	1782, a Private under Capt. Peter Bacot for 18 months.	
Jacobs, Joshua	5th NC Regiment	1777, a Private under Capt. Simon Alderson. Killed at the battle of Brandywine Creek, PA on 9/11/1777.	Brandywine Creek (PA).
Jacobs, Peter	1st NC Regiment	1777, a Private under Capt. Joshua Bowman.	
Jacobs, Peter	1st NC Regiment	1/1/1777, a Private under Capt. Thomas Hogg for three years. 9/8/1778, a known Private under Capt. Tilghman Dixon (1st NC Regiment). 3/12/1779, re-enlisted for the duration of the war in the same unit. aka Peter Jacob.	
Jacobs, Primus	4th NC Regiment	August 1782, a Private under Capt. Joseph T. Rhodes for 18 months. Furloughed in August 1783 at Wilmington, NC. A free man of color. S41688.	
Jacobs, William	4th NC Regiment	2/20/1782, a Private under Capt. James Mills.	
Jacobs, Zachariah	1st NC Regiment	12/18/1781, a Private under Capt. James Mills for 12 months. Discharged in Dec. 1782 (4th NC Regiment). From Brunswick County, NC. 1778-1781, in NC Militia. W5304.	
Jaene, Sherrod	2nd NC Regiment	1782, a Private under Capt. Benjamin Carter. Deserted on 6/21/1783 (?).	
James, Benjamin	3rd NC Regiment	1781, a Private under Capt. Clement Hall for 12 months. Discharged on 8/16/1782 (2nd NC Regiment).	
James, David	2nd NC Regiment	7/20/1778, a Private under Maj. Reading Blount for nine months.	
James, Edwin	5th NC Regiment	5/4/1776, a Private under Capt. John Pugh Williams. Discharged on 10/6/1778.	
James, Jeremiah	1st NC Regiment	1781, a Private under Capt. Robert Raiford. Discharged on 4/15/1782 (2nd NC Regiment).	

Name	1st Unit	Year / Rank / Served Under / Notes	Known Battles
James, Jeremiah	2nd NC Regiment	7/20/1778, a Private under Maj. Reading Blount for nine months.	
James, John	6th NC Regiment	1775, a Captain in the Wilmington District Minutemen. 4/17/1776, a Captain in 6th NC Regiment. One source asserts he was a Captain in 1st NC Regiment 1781-1782 (little or no evidence).	
James, Micajah	3rd NC Regiment	7/20/1778, a Private under Capt. Francis Child for nine months.	
James, Noah	2nd NC Regiment	11/7/1776, a Corporal under Capt. James Gee. 9/9/1778, a known Corporal under Capt. John Ingles.	
James, Thomas	2nd NC Regiment	7/20/1778, a Private under Capt. Thomas Armstrong. Born c.1750 in New Hanover County, NC. Enlisted from Duplin County, NC.	
James, Thomas	2nd NC Regiment	7/20/1778, a Private under Maj. Reading Blount for nine months.	
James, William	3rd NC Regiment	9/10/1782, a Private under Capt. Benjamin Bailey for 18 months.	
James, William	10th NC Regiment	12/1/1777, a Private, unit unknown. 9/8/1778, a known Private under Capt. James Read (1st NC Regiment). Died on 10/31/1778.	
Jameson, Thomas	6th NC Regiment	4/24/1776, a Private under Lt./Capt. Thomas White for 2-1/2 years. 9/8/1778, a known Artificer under Capt. John Sumner (1st NC Regiment). Dropped from the rolls in Nov. 1778. aka Thomas Jamison.	
Jamison, James	NC Artillery	8/26/1777, a Matross under Capt. John Vance. 11/16/1777, under Capt. John Kingsbury. 5/1/1778, in same unit. 9/16/1778, in same unit. aka James Jawoson, James Jarmason.	
Jarman, Emory	4th NC Regiment	1782, a Private under Capt. Anthony Sharpe for 18 months. Discharged at James Island, SC. From Anson County, NC. Earlier in NC Militia. R5555.	
Jarmin, Benjamin	3rd NC Regiment	Jan. 1779, a Private in the Colonel's Company (Col. Jethro Sumner).	
Jarvis, John	2nd NC Regiment	5/12/1781, a Private under Capt. Tilghman Dixon. Discharged on 6/12/1782 (1st NC Regiment).	
Jarvis, John	3rd NC Regiment	1782, a Private under Capt. Alexander Brevard. Died on 11/29/1782.	
Jarvis, John	10th NC Regiment	4/19/1777, a Captain under Col. Abraham Sheppard. Dropped from the rolls in June 1778. From Currituck County, NC.	
Jarvis, Levi	4th NC Regiment	5/25/1776, a Private under Capt. Joseph Phillips. 9/8/1778, a known Private under Capt. James Read (1st NC Regiment). Dropped from the rolls in Dec. 1778. aka Levi Jervoice.	
Jarvis, Thomas	5th NC Regiment	1775, a Private under Capt. Benjamin Stedman. Enlisted in Hyde County, NC. 1779, moved to Currituck County, NC. Later in NC Militia. S2649.	
Jarvis,	6th NC	A Sergeant under Capt. George Dougherty.	

Name	1st Unit	Year / Rank / Served Under / Notes	Known Battles
Thomas	Regiment	Dropped from the rolls in Jan. 1778.	
Jarvis, Willoughby	10th NC Regiment	5/5/1777, a Private under Capt. John Jarvis for three years. A Corporal in June 1778. Back to Private in Aug. 1778. 9/8/1778, a known Private in the Major's Company (Maj. John Baptiste Ashe) (1st NC Regiment). aka Willobey Jarvis.	
Jason, Henry	10th NC Regiment	5/29/1777, a Private under Capt. Andrew Vanoy. Dropped from the rolls in June 1778.	
Jean, Nathan	3rd NC Regiment	1779, a Private under Capt. Kedar Ballard for nine months. Discharged on 12/1/1779. aka Nathan Jeanes, Nathan Jeans. S41692.	Stono Ferry (SC).
Jeffrey, Drewry	1st NC Regiment	7/9/1781, a Private under Capt. William Lytle. Discharged on 6/26/1782 (4th NC Regiment). From Burke County, NC. S7067.	
Jeffrey, John		1779, a Private, regiment and unit unknown. Died on 8/15/1779.	
Jeffrey, John	5th NC Regiment	1777, a Private under Capt. Benjamin Andrew Coleman.	
Jeffries, Jacob	1st NC Regiment	5/25/1781, a Private under Capt. Thomas Donoho. Discharged 5/25/1782.	
Jeffries, John	2nd NC Regiment	9/9/1778, a Butcher under Capt. Benjamin Andrew Coleman.	
Jeffries, Thomas	3rd NC Regiment	1777, a Private under Capt. Jacob Turner. Dropped from the rolls in Jan. 1778.	
Jenkins, Abraham	5th NC Regiment	4/27/1776, a Private under Capt. John Pugh Williams. 5/15/1778, a Sergeant. A Corporal in June 1778. Discharged in Oct. 1778. Enlisted in Bertie County, NC. W20180.	Brandywine Creek (PA), Germantown (PA), Monmouth (NJ).
Jenkins, Dempsey	2nd NC Regiment	6/19/1777, a Private under Capt. Clement Hall for three years. A free black man. aka Demsey Jarkins.	
Jenkins, Elijah	1st NC Regiment	4/15/1781, a Private under Capt. Thomas Donoho for nine months.	
Jenkins, Lewis	5th NC Regiment	1776, a Private under Capt. William Ward for three years. From Wake County, NC. S31771.	
Jenkins, Robert	5th NC Regiment	4/29/1776, a Private under Capt. John Pugh Williams. 9/9/1778, a known Private in the Major's Company (Maj. Hardy Murfree) (2nd NC Regiment). Discharged on 10/29/1778. aka Robert Jinkins.	
Jenkins, William	5th NC Regiment	1777, a Private under Capt. Reading Blount. Dropped from the rolls in April 1778.	
Jenks, Thomas	3rd NC Regiment	1779, a Corporal under Capt. Michael Quinn for nine months. Discharged in Dec. 1779. From Wake County, NC. aka Thomas Jinks.	
Jennet, Solomon	2nd NC Regiment	2/1/1777, a Private under Capt. Benjamin Williams. 9/9/1778, a known Private in the Major's Company (Maj. Hardy Murfree) (2nd NC Regiment). At sometime, in His Excellency's Guards. aka Solomon Jinnitt, Jinnet.	
Jennings,	1st NC	5/25/1781, a Private under Capt. Thomas	

Name	1st Unit	Year / Rank / Served Under / Notes	Known Battles
James	Regiment	Donoho. Dropped from the rolls sometime during 1781.	
Jennings, John	10th NC Regiment	5/21/1777, a Corporal under Capt. Dempsey Gregory. A Private in June 1778. 9/8/1778, a known Private under Capt. Howell Tatum (1st NC Regiment).	
Jennings, Thomas	2nd NC Regiment	12/20/1776, a Private under Capt. Charles Allen, then Capt. Thomas Armstrong. A Corporal on 4/30/1779. Discharged on 1/28/1780 at Halifax, NC. From Pasquotank County, NC. S41694.	Monmouth (NJ).
Jennings, William	10th NC Regiment	11/6/1777, a Private, unit unknown, enlisted for three years. 9/8/1778, a known Private in the Major's Company (Maj. John Baptiste Ashe) (1st NC Regiment) - sick in the Flying Hospital on that date. Died in Oct. 1778.	
Jerrald, Hugh Pugh	2nd NC Regiment	1776, a Private under Capt. Simon Bright. Then in SC unit. Then in GA unit. S41691.	
Jervoice, Levi		5/25/1776, regiment, unit, and rank unknown. 9/8/1778, a known Private under Capt. James Read (1st NC Regiment).	
Jesse, John	3rd NC Regiment	1781, a Musician under Capt. Edward Yarborough for 12 months. Discharged on 4/22/1782.	
Jethro, Josiah	7th NC Regiment	2/13/1777, a Corporal under Capt. James Vaughan. Dropped from the rolls in Jan. 1778.	
Jew, James	3rd NC Regiment	7/20/1778, a Private under Capt. Kedar Ballard for nine months. 3/1/1779, a Private under Capt. Joseph Montford (5th NC Regiment) for nine months. Discharged on 12/1/1779. aka James Jet, James Yew.	
Jewell, Samuel	2nd NC Regiment	1/27/1777, a Private under Capt. Benjamin Williams. A free black man.	
Jiers, John	1st NC Regiment	5/25/1781, a Sergeant under Capt. Alexander Brevard.	
Jimes, Vachel	4th NC Regiment	1782, a Sergeant under Capt. Anthony Sharpe for 18 months.	
Jinks, Thomas	1st NC Regiment	1779, a Private under Capt. Thomas Donoho for nine months. Soon transferred to Capt. Matthew Ramsey (4th NC Regiment). Then transferred to Capt. Michael Quinn (3rd NC Regiment). Drafted in Wake County, NC. Discharged in Dec. 1779 at Charleston, SC. S41696.	Stono Ferry (SC), Siege of Savannah (GA).
Jirmins, Thomas	2nd NC Regiment	12/20/1776, a Private, unit unknown. 9/10/1778, a known Private under Capt. Thomas Armstrong.	
Johnson, Absalom	4th NC Regiment	1781, a Private under Capt. George Dougherty for 12 months. Discharged on 5/25/1782.	
Johnson, Andrew	1st NC Regiment	1782, a Private under Capt. Alexander Brevard, then under Capt. Joseph T. Rhodes (4th NC Regiment). From Guilford County, NC. Earlier in NC Militia. R5599.	
Johnson, Balaam	3rd NC Regiment	7/20/1778, a Private under Maj. Thomas Hogg for nine months.	

Name	1st Unit	Year / Rank / Served Under / Notes	Known Battles
Johnson, Barnaby	3rd NC Regiment	7/20/1778, a Private in the Lt. Colonel's Company (Lt. Col. William Lee Davidson) led by Lt./Capt. George "Gee" Bradley for nine months. 4/23/1779, a known Private in the Lt. Colonel's Company (Lt. Col. Robert Mebane) led by Capt. George "Gee" Bradley. From Hertford County, NC. aka Barns Johnson.	
Johnson, Benjamin	2nd NC Regiment	12/26/1776, a Corporal under Capt. Edward Vail, Jr. 9/9/1778, a known Corporal in the Colonel's Company (Col. John Patten) led by Capt. John Craddock. Discharged on 1/30/1780.	
Johnson, Benjamin	6th NC Regiment	5/9/1776, a Private under Lt. Kedar Parker and Capt. William Glover for 2-1/2 years. 4/1/1777, under Capt. Daniel Williams. 6/1/1778, a Private under Capt. Griffith John McRee (1st NC Regiment). Discharged on 11/10/1778. Enlisted in Granville County, NC. Later in NC Militia, unit and dates unknown. W13.	Monmouth (NJ).
Johnson, Brutus	10th NC Regiment	Jan. 1778, a Private, unit unknown. Died 2/15/1778.	
Johnson, Crawford	4th NC Regiment	4/11/1776, a Private under Capt. William Temple Coles for three years. 9/8/1778, a known Private under Capt. John Sumner (1st NC Regiment). Enlisted in Edgecombe County, NC. aka Crawford Johnston, Crafford Johnston. W21486.	Brandywine Creek (PA), Germantown (PA), Monmouth (NJ), Guilford Court House, Eutaw Springs (SC).
Johnson, Daniel	1st NC Regiment	5/17/1781, a Private under Capt. Robert Raiford. Discharged on 5/15/1782 (2nd NC Regiment).	
Johnson, Daniel	10th NC Regiment	9/16/1777, a Private, unit unknown. 9/9/1778, a known Private under Capt. Robert Fenner (2nd NC Regiment). aka Daniel Johnston.	
Johnson, Dempsey	3rd NC Regiment	7/20/1778, a Private in the Lt. Colonel's Company (Lt. Col. William Lee Davidson) led by Lt./Capt. George "Gee" Bradley for nine months. 4/23/1779, a known Corporal in the Lt. Colonel's Company (Lt. Col. Robert Mebane) led by Capt. George "Gee" Bradley.	
Johnson, Edward	9th NC Regiment	1777, a Private under Capt. Thomas McCrory. Deserted in Nov. 1777.	
Johnson, Ephraim	3rd NC Regiment	6/15/1781, a Private under Capt. Samuel Jones for 12 months.	
Johnson, Frederick	2nd NC Regiment	1782, a Private under Capt. Robert Raiford for 18 months.	
Johnson, Gideon	2nd NC Regiment	July 1776, a Private under Capt. John Armstrong, then Capt. Samuel Martin. Sick, discharged Oct. 1777. From Guilford County, NC. Later in NC Militia, unit and dates unknown. Born on 11/7/1754 in Amelia County, VA. S4456.	
Johnson,	2nd NC	5/29/1777, a Musician under Capt. Clement	

450

Name	1st Unit	Year / Rank / Served Under / Notes	Known Battles
Henry	Regiment	Hall. A Corporal in May 1778. 9/9/1778, a known Private under Capt. John Ingles. Deserted on 4/1/1779. aka Henry Johnston.	
Johnson, Henry	3rd NC Regiment	6/1/1779, a Sergeant under Capt. Kedar Ballard. March 1780, transferred to 2nd NC Regiment, unit unknown.	
Johnson, Henry	10th NC Regiment	9/29/1777, a Private, unit unknown. A Musician in Nov. 1779.	
Johnson, Holland	5th NC Regiment	5/20/1776, a Sergeant under Capt. Simon Alderson. A Corporal in Jan. 1778. A Private in June 1778 under Capt. Thomas Armstrong (2nd NC Regiment). Discharged on 5/20/1779. aka Holland Johnston.	
Johnson, Jacob	1st NC Regiment	1781, a Private under Capt. William Walton. Discharged on 4/1/1782.	
Johnson, James	1st NC Regiment	1777, a Private under Capt. Robert Ralston. Dropped from the rolls in Sep. 1777.	
Johnson, James	3rd NC Regiment	1779, a Private under Capt. Kedar Ballard. Discharged on 12/1/1779.	
Johnson, James	6th NC Regiment	4/2/1777, a Regimental QM. Retired 6/1/1778. Later, a Captain in NC Militia. One source asserts his first name was Joseph.	
Johnson, Jesse	1st NC Regiment	6/14/1781, a Private under Capt. Thomas Donoho. After two or three months, he joined under Capt. Michael Rudolph in Lt. Col. Henry Lee's Legion (VA). Discharged on 6/14/1782. S38884.	Eutaw Springs (SC).
Johnson, John	1st NC Regiment	6/14/1781, a Private under Capt. Thomas Donoho. A Sergeant in Jan. 1782. Discharged in June 1782.	
Johnson, John	1st NC Regiment	1/1/1782, a Private under Capt. James Mills. 2/6/1782, would be in the 4th NC Regiment.	
Johnson, John	2nd NC Regiment	11/20/1776, a Private under Capt. William Fenner for three years. Dropped from the rolls in Feb. 1778.	
Johnson, John	5th NC Regiment	1777, a Private under Capt. Reading Blount. Dropped from the rolls in Feb. 1778.	
Johnson, Joseph	9th NC Regiment	11/28/1776, an Ensign under Capt. Matthew Ramsey. Transferred to 1st NC Regiment on 6/1/1778. 2/1/1779, a 1st Lieutenant. POW at the Fall of Charleston, exchanged June 1781. Resigned 5/15/1782. From Hillsborough District. aka Joshua Johnson, Joseph Johnston. S7093.	Siege of Charleston 1780 (SC).
Johnson, Joshua	3rd NC Regiment	7/20/1778, a Sergeant under Capt. Michael Quinn for nine months.	
Johnson, Littleton	6th NC Regiment	A Sergeant under Capt. Francis Child. Dropped from the rolls in Feb. 1778. aka Lytleton Johnson.	
Johnson, Mathias	3rd NC Regiment	7/20/1778, a Private under Capt. Francis Child for nine months.	
Johnson, Reuben	4th NC Regiment	Spring of 1776, a Private under Capt. Joseph Phillips. 9/8/1778, a known Private under Capt. James Read (1st NC Regiment). POW at the	Brandywine Creek (PA), Germantown

Name	1st Unit	Year / Rank / Served Under / Notes	Known Battles
		Fall of Charleston, SC. From Surry County, NC. W10156.	(PA), Monmouth (NJ), Siege of Charleston (SC).
Johnson, Richard	8th NC Regiment	2/9/1777, a Private under Capt. John Walsh. 9/9/1778, a known Private under Capt. Benjamin Andrew Coleman (2nd NC Regiment). A Sergeant in July 1779. Discharged on 2/9/1780. From Hertford County, NC.	
Johnson, Samuel	10th NC Regiment	A Lieutenant, unit and dates unknown. Later, a Lieutenant in Militia, wounded at Kings Mountain, SC on 10/7/1780.	
Johnson, Soasby	3rd NC Regiment	1781, a Private under Capt. Samuel Jones for 12 months.	
Johnson, Solomon	1st NC Regiment	Spring of 1777, a Private under Capt. Thomas Hogg. Official records indicate that he died on 9/15/1778 (?). Born 1757 in Spotsylvania County, VA. Enlisted in Caswell County, NC.	
Johnson, Solomon	3rd NC Regiment	1/15/1782, a Private under Capt. Samuel Jones for 12 months. From Johnston County, NC. W20204.	
Johnson, Thomas	1st NC Regiment	A Private under Capt. Lawrence Thompson, then Capt. Tilghman Dixon. 9/8/1778, a known Private under Capt. James Read. In Jan. 1780, Thomas Llewellen seized him out of the army and claimed him as his indentured servant. The military had no choice but to discharge him and list him as a deserter. Later, all this was recognized and he received his land warrant and pension. S41698.	
Johnson, Thomas	3rd NC Regiment	A Private under Capt. Pinketham Eaton. Died on 5/20/1778.	
Johnson, Thomas	3rd NC Regiment	1779, a Private under Capt. Michael Quinn for nine months. Discharged in Dec. 1779.	
Johnson, William	3rd NC Regiment	1781, a Private under Capt. Clement Hall for 12 months. Discharged on 8/16/1782 (2nd NC Regiment).	
Johnson, William	4th NC Regiment	1777, a Private under Capt. James Williams. Dropped from the rolls in Sep. 1777.	
Johnson, William	5th NC Regiment	7/1/1779, a Private under Maj. Reading Blount.	
Johnson, Willoughby	1st NC Regiment	1777, a Private under Capt. Lawrence Thompson. Deserted in Sep. 1777. Found guilty in a court-martial, sentenced to be shot to death. aka Willeby Johnson.	
Johnson, Zachariah	2nd NC Regiment	1776, a Private, unit and dates unknown. Then in the Independent French Corps. From Northampton County, NC. S32344.	
Johnston, Francis	3rd NC Regiment	1779, a Private under Capt. Michael Quinn for six months. Earlier and later in the NC Militia. From Rowan County, NC. S13585.	
Johnston,	9th NC	12/22/1776, a Surgeon. Retired 6/1/1778.	

Name	1st Unit	Year / Rank / Served Under / Notes	Known Battles
Launcelot	Regiment	8/15/1778, appointed Surgeon for "New Levies." Later, a Surgeon in NC Militia 1779-1780. From Caswell County, NC. aka Lancelot Johnston. W5114.	
Johnston, William	NC Artillery	1/1/1777, a Corporal under Capt. Thomas Clark. 7/10/1777, on Continental Line. Also on 9/9/1778. aka William Johnson.	
Joiner, Benjamin	4th NC Regiment	Jan. 1782, a Private under Maj. George Dougherty.	
Joiner, Henry	3rd NC Regiment	7/20/1778, a Sergeant in the Colonel's Company (Col. Jethro Sumner) for nine months.	
Joiner, Nathaniel	3rd NC Regiment	1778, a Private under Capt. John Baker. Deserted on 7/14/1778.	
Jolly, Malachi	2nd NC Regiment	1777, a Private under Capt. Benjamin Williams. Transferred to 8th NC Regiment in Dec. 1777 under Capt. Robert Raiford. Jan. 1779, re-enlisted as a Sergeant in the 4th NC Regiment, unit unknown.	
Jones, Abraham	4th NC Regiment	2/6/1782, a Private under Capt. James Mills for 12 months. Died in Jan. 1783.	
Jones, Benjamin	3rd NC Regiment	A Private under Capt. Clement Hall. Discharged on 7/25/1782 (2nd NC Regiment).	
Jones, Berry	1st NC Regiment	7/9/1781, a Private under Capt. William Lytle. Discharged on 6/26/1782 (4th NC Regiment).	
Jones, Brinson	2nd NC Regiment	1777, a Corporal under Capt. Benjamin Williams. Died in June 1778.	
Jones, Britton	2nd NC Regiment	4/25/1781, a Private under Capt. Benjamin Carter for 12 months. Discharged on 4/25/1782 at Camden, SC. From Pitt County, NC. On the official rolls as Britain Jones. R5739.	
Jones, Broton	3rd NC Regiment	6/10/1779, a Private under Capt. George "Gee" Bradley for 18 months. Dropped from the rolls in Oct. 1779.	
Jones, Charles	5th NC Regiment	1777, a Private under Capt. John Pugh Williams. Died on 3/2/1778.	
Jones, Daniel	3rd NC Regiment	5/12/1776, a Captain in the 3rd NC Regiment. Found guilty of disobeying orders and being absent without leave, 1/31/1778. Retired 6/1/1778. One source indicates he was a 1st Lieutenant under Capt. Jacob Turner earlier (4/17/1776).	Brandywine Creek (PA), Germantown (PA).
Jones, David		1779, a Private, regiment and unit unknown. Dropped from the rolls in Oct. 1779.	
Jones, David	NC Artillery	6/15/1776, a Corporal under Capt. John Vance as NC Provincial Troops. 7/10/1777, on Continental Line. 11/16/1777, under Capt. John Kingsbury. 5/1/1778, in same unit. 9/16/1778, in same unit.	
Jones, David	2nd NC Regiment	12/12/1781, a Private under Capt. Benjamin Andrew Coleman for 12 months.	
Jones, David	4th NC Regiment	1775, an Ensign in the Wilmington District Minutemen. 4/17/1776, an Ensign under Capt. John Ashe, Jr. and Col. Thomas Polk. 11/27/1776, a 2nd Lieutenant under Capt. John	

Name	1ˢᵗ Unit	Year / Rank / Served Under / Notes	Known Battles
		Nelson. 4/3/1777, a 1ˢᵗ Lieutenant under Capt. John Nelson. Dropped from the rolls in Jan. 1778. Jan. 1779, re-enlisted in the 4ᵗʰ NC Regiment, unit unknown.	
Jones, Ezekiel	4ᵗʰ NC Regiment	1782, a Private under Capt. Anthony Sharpe for 18 months. Born on 4/3/1764. W5005.	
Jones, Francis	4ᵗʰ NC Regiment	1782, a Private under Capt. Elijah Moore and Capt. Anthony Sharpe. Earlier in NC Militia, unit unknown. S36653.	
Jones, Frederick	1ˢᵗ NC Regiment	1781, a Private under Capt. Anthony Sharpe. Discharged on 8/5/1782 (4th NC Regiment).	
Jones, Frederick	4ᵗʰ NC Regiment	1781, a Private under Capt. George Dougherty for 12 months. Discharged on 5/25/1782.	
Jones, Freeman	1ˢᵗ NC Regiment	7/9/1781, a Private under Capt. William Lytle. Discharged on 6/26/1782 (4th NC Regiment). Earlier in NC Militia. From Rutherford County, NC. W7900.	Eutaw Springs (SC).
Jones, Gabriel	3ʳᵈ NC Regiment	4/16/1776, a Captain under Col. Jethro Sumner. Resigned before 6/1/1776.	
Jones, Griffith	1ˢᵗ NC Regiment	1781, a Private under Capt. Robert Raiford. An Artificer in 1782 (2nd NC Regiment).	
Jones, Hardy	2ⁿᵈ NC Regiment	10/17/1778, a Private under Maj. Reading Blount. POW at the Fall of Charleston (SC). Enlisted in Jones County, NC. S41699.	Stono Ferry (SC), Siege of Charleston (SC).
Jones, Henry	4ᵗʰ NC Regiment	1781, a Private under Capt. George Dougherty for 12 months. Discharged on 5/25/1782.	
Jones, Hezekiah	3ʳᵈ NC Regiment	4/11/1776, a Private under Capt. James Emmett. 9/9/1778, a known Private in the Major's Company (Maj. Hardy Murfree) (2nd NC Regiment). Discharged on 10/16/1778.	
Jones, Isaac	1ˢᵗ NC Regiment	5/20/1781, a Private under Capt. Alexander Brevard. Discharged on 5/10/1782 (3rd NC Regiment).	
Jones, Isham	3ʳᵈ NC Regiment	7/20/1778, a Private in the Lt. Colonel's Company (Lt. Col. William Lee Davidson) led by Lt./Capt. George "Gee" Bradley for nine months. 4/23/1779, a known Private in the Lt. Colonel's Company (Lt. Col. Robert Mebane) led by Capt. George "Gee" Bradley. aka Isom Jones.	
Jones, Jacob	3ʳᵈ NC Regiment	4/20/1776, a Private under Capt. Thomas Granbury. 9/10/1778, a known Private under Capt. Thomas Armstrong (2nd NC Regiment). Discharged on 11/10/1778.	
Jones, Jacob	3ʳᵈ NC Regiment	May 1776, a Private under Capt. William Brinkley for 2-1/2 years. Discharged in New York, after serving his term. From Bute County, NC. S9363.	Brandywine Creek (PA), Germantown (PA), Monmouth (NJ).
Jones, James	1ˢᵗ NC Regiment	5/9/1781, a Private under Capt. Alexander Brevard.	
Jones, James	3ʳᵈ NC	1781, a Private under Capt. Edward Yarborough	

Name	1st Unit	Year / Rank / Served Under / Notes	Known Battles
	Regiment	for 12 months. Discharged on 4/13/1782.	
Jones, James	3rd NC Regiment	May 1781, a Private under Capt. Edward Yarborough for 12 months. Discharged on 4/27/1782 in NC. (Yep, two of 'em under Yarborough at the same time). From Halifax County, NC. S41701.	Eutaw Springs (SC).
Jones, James	4th NC Regiment	1781, a Private under Capt. Joseph T. Rhodes for 12 months. Discharged on 2/17/1782.	
Jones, James	5th NC Regiment	11/18/1776, a Private under Capt. John Enloe for three years. 9/10/1778, a known Private under Capt. Thomas Armstrong (2nd NC Regiment), then under Capt. John Craddock. Enlisted at New Bern, NC. Discharged in Feb. 1780 at Georgetown, VA. S41700.	Brandywine Creek (PA), Monmouth (NJ), Stony Point (NY).
Jones, John	1st NC Regiment	1781, a Private under Capt. William Armstrong. Discharged on 11/1/1782 (3rd NC Regiment).	
Jones, John	2nd NC Regiment	5/27/1778, a Private under Capt. Robert Raiford. Discharged 8/19/1779. From Guilford County, NC. Earlier and later in NC Militia. S13542.	Stono Ferry (SC).
Jones, John	3rd NC Regiment	1779, a Private under Capt. Kedar Ballard. Discharged on 2/1/1780.	
Jones, John	4th NC Regiment	2/6/1782, a Private under Capt. James Mills for 12 months.	
Jones, John	5th NC Regiment	1777, a Private under Capt. William Caswell. Killed at the battle of Germantown, PA on 10/4/1777.	Germantown (PA).
Jones, John	6th NC Regiment	9/8/1777, a Sergeant under Capt. Francis Child for three years. 6/1/1778, a Sergeant under Capt. Griffith John McRee (1st NC Regiment).	
Jones, John	7th NC Regiment	1/14/1777, a Private under Capt. James Vaughan. 2/26/1778, a known Private under Capt. Howell Tatum (1st NC Regiment). 9/8/1778, a known Private under Capt. Howell Tatum (1st NC Regiment). Died on 9/12/1778.	
Jones, John	10th NC Regiment	1/14/1777, a Private, unit unknown. Died 10/15/1778.	
Jones, Jones Lytleton	5th NC Regiment	1777, a Private under Capt. Simon Alderson. Died on 9/20/1777.	
Jones, Jonathan	1st NC Regiment	1/10/1777, a Private, unit unknown. 9/8/1778, a known Private under Capt. Tilghman Dixon.	
Jones, Jonathan	2nd NC Regiment	12/12/1781, a Sergeant under Capt. Benjamin Andrew Coleman, then under Capt. James Mills (4th NC Regiment). Furloughed on 1/7/1783 at Wilmington, NC. Earlier in NC Militia. From Onslow County, NC. S31778.	
Jones, Jonathan	7th NC Regiment	1/10/1777, a Corporal under Capt. John Poynter. Discharged on 1/29/1780. Probably the same man as in 1st NC Regiment above.	
Jones, Joshua	DQMG	1780, a Canteen Maker on the roll Capt. Solomon Wood (NC Light Dragoons) - this seems to be for convenience only. An Artificer under Col. Nicholas Long (Deputy QM General). Made Canteens. Also on 8/23/1781.	

Name	1st Unit	Year / Rank / Served Under / Notes	Known Battles
Jones, Josiah	3rd NC Regiment	4/17/1776, a Private under Capt. James Emmett. Discharged in Oct. 1778.	
Jones, Josiah	3rd NC Regiment	7/20/1778, a Drummer under Lt./Capt. George "Gee" Bradley for nine months. Wounded, a POW at the Fall of Charleston (SC). Re-enlisted in Jan. 1782 for the duration of the war. From Winton, NC (Hertford County). Born 1/26/1756. S18065.	Siege of Charleston 1780 (SC).
Jones, Lazarus	5th NC Regiment	A Private under Capt. Joseph Montford, dates unknown. W26796.	
Jones, Maurice	6th NC Regiment	6/15/1776, a 2nd Lieutenant under Capt. George Mitchell. Resigned by 7/1/1776.	
Jones, Moses	1st NC Regiment	9/17/1782, a Private under Capt. William Walton, Capt. Benjamin Bailey, then Capt. Alexander Brevard. Attached to a Maryland unit for a while. From Gates County, NC. S32347.	
Jones, Nathan	1st NC Regiment	1781, a Private under Capt. William Lytle, then under Capt. James Mills. Discharged on 4/12/1782 (4th NC Regiment). Enlisted in Duplin County, NC. R5707.	
Jones, Peter	3rd NC Regiment	7/20/1778, a Private under Capt. John Baker for nine months.	
Jones, Philip	1st NC Regiment	2/1/1782, a Private under Capt. James Mills. 2/6/1782, this unit would be in the 4th NC Regiment. Discharged on 3/1/1783.	
Jones, Philip	3rd NC Regiment	1781, a Private under Capt. Clement Hall for 12 months. Discharged on 11/1/1782 (2nd NC Regiment).	
Jones, Philip	8th NC Regiment	11/28/1776, a Lieutenant. Promoted to Captain-Lieutenant on 11/16/1777 in Kingsbury's NC Artillery Company. POW at the Fall of Charleston. Still a POW as of 11/26/1782.	Siege of Charleston 1780 (SC).
Jones, Philip	10th NC Regiment	9/4/1777, a Private, unit unknown. 9/9/1778, a known Private in the Lt. Colonel's Company (Lt. Col. Selby Harney) (2nd NC Regiment).	
Jones, Richard	3rd NC Regiment	4/15/1776, a Private under Capt. Jacob Turner for 2-1/2 years. Discharged in Oct. 1778. R1554.	
Jones, Robert	2nd NC Regiment	1777, a Private under Capt. Clement Jones. Dropped from the rolls in Jan. 1779. A free black man.	
Jones, Samuel	2nd NC Regiment	An Ensign. Died 7/7/1778. Same man as below?	
Jones, Samuel	6th NC Regiment	6/6/1776, an Ensign under Capt. George Mitchell. 1/1/1777, a Lieutenant under Capt. Thomas Donoho. Died in July 1778.	
Jones, Samuel	8th NC Regiment	11/28/1776, an Ensign under Capt. Thomas Nixon. Resigned in Feb. 1777. 10/4/1777, re-enlisted as 1st Lieutenant in 10th NC Regiment. Transferred to 3rd NC Regiment on 6/1/1778. Promoted to Captain on 9/11/1781. Court-martialed for using strong language against Governor Alexander Martin. From Franklin County, NC. Retired 1/1/1783. W230.	Eutaw Springs (SC).

Name	1st Unit	Year / Rank / Served Under / Notes	Known Battles
Jones, Simon	8th NC Regiment	11/28/1776, a Captain under Col. James Armstrong. Resigned fairly soon after being commissioned.	
Jones, Thomas	1st NC Regiment	1776-1777, a Private under Capt. Joshua Bowman. 9/8/1778, a known Private in the Major's Company (Maj. Griffith John McRee) (1st NC Regiment) - sick on that date at Valley Forge, supposedly dead.	
Jones, Thomas	1st NC Regiment	1777, a Private under Capt. Thomas Hogg. Dropped from the rolls in June 1778.	
Jones, Thomas	1st NC Regiment	1781, a Private under Capt. Anthony Sharpe. Discharged on 7/16/1782 (4th NC Regiment).	
Jones, Thomas	2nd NC Regiment	9/28/1777, a Private, unit unknown. 9/9/1778, a known Private under Capt. Benjamin Andrew Coleman. 3/12/1779, re-enlisted under Capt. Benjamin Andrew Coleman.	
Jones, Thomas	3rd NC Regiment	5/10/1776, a Private under Capt. Thomas Granbury. Discharged in Nov. 1778.	
Jones, Thomas	6th NC Regiment	A Private under Capt. George Dougherty. Jan. 1779, joined the 5th NC Regiment, unit unknown. Deserted in Apr. 1779.	
Jones, Thomas	7th NC Regiment	4/17/1777, an Ensign under Capt. John Mason. 8/15/1777, a 1st Lieutenant under Capt. John Macon. Resigned on 5/17/1778.	
Jones, Thomas	10th NC Regiment	9/28/1777, a Private, unit unknown. 9/9/1778, a known Private in the Lt. Colonel's Company (Lt. Col. Selby Harney) (2nd NC Regiment). A Sergeant on 1/1/1780.	
Jones, Timothy	10th NC Regiment	4/19/1777, a Lieutenant under Capt. Dempsey Gregory. Resigned in Apr. 1778.	
Jones, William	1st NC Regiment	9/10/1777, a Private under Capt. Tilghman Dixon. 9/8/1778, a known Private under Capt. Tilghman Dixon.	
Jones, William	1st NC Regiment	9/21/1777, a Private under Capt. Howell Tatum. 9/8/1778, a known Private under Capt. Howell Tatum. Deserted on 6/28/1779.	
Jones, William	1st NC Regiment	2/5/1782, a Private under Capt. James Mills. The next day, 2/6/1782, this unit would be in the 4th NC Regiment.	
Jones, William	1st NC Regiment	8/1/1782, a Private under Capt. Joshua Hadley for 18 months.	
Jones, William	3rd NC Regiment	1781, a Private under Capt. Edward Yarborough for 12 months. Discharged on 5/22/1782. Received clothing on 5/24/1782. From Caswell County.	
Jones, William	5th NC Regiment	6/1/1779, a Private under Maj. Reading Blount.	
Jones, William	7th NC Regiment	1777, a Private under Capt. Thomas Brickell. Deserted in Apr. 1777.	
Jones, William	10th NC Regiment	7/2/1777, a Private, unit unknown. Listed separately, but most likely the same man as directly below.	
Jones, William	10th NC Regiment	7/22/1777, a Private under Capt. Armwell Herron. 9/9/1778, a known Private in the	

Name	1st Unit	Year / Rank / Served Under / Notes	Known Battles
		Major's Company (Maj. Hardy Murfree) (2nd NC Regiment).	
Jones, Zachariah	3rd NC Regiment	1781, a Corporal under Capt. Edward Yarborough for 12 months. Discharged on 7/1/1782	
Jordan, Caleb	3rd NC Regiment	6/29/1779, a Private under Capt. Kedar Ballard. Deserted on 8/5/1779. Re-enlisted in Jan. 1782.	
Jordan, Fountain	3rd NC Regiment	2/1/1782, a Private under Capt. Clement Hall (2/6/1782 - 2nd NC Regiment). Sep. 1782, re-enlisted for the duration of the war. Discharged near Charleston, SC. S38084.	
Jordan, Hezekiah	5th NC Regiment	April 1776, a Private under Capt. William Ward. Sept. 1776, furloughed due to extreme illness - hired John Jordan to take his place. From Johnston County, NC. Earlier in NC Militia. R5766A.	
Jordan, James	10th NC Regiment	5/18/1777, a Private under Capt. Abraham Sheppard, Jr.	
Jordan, John	10th NC Regiment	5/5/1777, a Private under Capt. Abraham Sheppard, Jr. Died on 3/17/1778.	
Jordan, Nathan	3rd NC Regiment	1781, a Private under Capt. Clement Hall for 12 months. Discharged on 8/16/1782 (2nd NC Regiment).	
Jordan, Nathaniel	2nd NC Regiment	1777, a Private under Capt. John Armstrong. Died on 1/24/1778.	
Jordan, River	4th NC Regiment	1782, a Corporal under Capt. Thomas Evans. Deserted on 6/4/1783 (?). aka Rives Jordan.	
Jordan, Robert	1st NC Regiment	1777, a Private under Capt. James Read. Died on 8/24/1778.	
Jordan, Stephen	3rd NC Regiment	1781, a Private under Capt. Edward Yarborough for 12 months. Discharged on 5/1/1782.	
Jordan, Zebulon	3rd NC Regiment	1781, a Private under Capt. Edward Yarborough for 12 months. Discharged on 5/1/1782.	
Josea, William	7th NC Regiment	3/2/1777, a Private under Capt. James Vaughan. Deserted in Aug. 1777.	
Journekin, David	3rd NC Regiment	7/20/1778, a Private in the Lt. Colonel's Company (Lt. Col. William Lee Davidson) led by Lt./Capt. George "Gee" Bradley for nine months. 4/23/1779, a known Private in the Lt. Colonel's Company (Lt. Col. Robert Mebane) led by Capt. George "Gee" Bradley. aka David Jonican.	
Joyner, Eli	3rd NC Regiment	7/20/1778, a Private in the Colonel's Company (Col. Jethro Sumner) for nine months. From Halifax County, NC. aka Ely Joiner. W7925.	
Judge, James	3rd NC Regiment	A Private under Capt. Thomas Granbury. Discharged in Oct. 1778.	
Jumper, Richard	3rd NC Regiment	A Private under Capt. Pinketham Eaton for 12 months. Dropped from the rolls in Jan. 1778.	
Kail, Joab	2nd NC Regiment	7/20/1778, a Private under Capt. Reading Blount for nine months. One source identifies him as Jacob Kail. Beats me which is correct.	
Kail, John	10th NC Regiment	4/16/1777, a Private under Capt. Isaac Moore. Discharged on 12/31/1778.	

458

Name	1st Unit	Year / Rank / Served Under / Notes	Known Battles
Kariker, George	3rd NC Regiment	A Private under Lt./Capt. Christopher Goodwin for nine months - 11/5/1778 to 8/5/1779. From Mecklenburg (what would become Cabarrus) County, NC. Also in NC Militia. W9488.	Briar Creek (GA), Stono Ferry (SC).
Keais, Nathaniel	2nd NC Regiment	9/1/1775, a Captain under Col. Robert Howe then Col. Alexander Martin. Retired 6/1/1778.	Ft. Moultrie #1 (SC).
Kean, Caleb	10th NC Regiment	4/19/1777, a 1st Lieutenant under Capt. Silas Stevenson. aka Caleb Koen.	
Kean, Jacob	1st NC Regiment	2/4/1782, a Private under Capt. James Mills. On 2/6/1782, this unit was transferred to the 4th NC Regiment. Discharged on 5/23/1783.	
Keates, Thomas	2nd NC Regiment	1/10/1782, a Sergeant under Capt. Benjamin Andrew Coleman. A Corporal on 4/1/1782. A Private in Sep. 1782.	
Kee, Jonathan	6th NC Regiment	1777, a Musician under Capt. Thomas Donoho. A Private in June 1778. Discharged on 8/21/1778.	
Keel, Charles	1st NC Regiment	6/1/1781, a Private under Lt./Capt. Benjamin Bailey. Discharged on 6/1/1782 (3rd NC Regiment).	
Keel, Hardy	1st NC Regiment	4/15/1781, a Private under Capt. Anthony Sharpe. Discharged on 4/15/1782 (4th NC Regiment).	
Keel, Hardy	7th NC Regiment	12/26/1776, a Sergeant under Lt./Capt. John Baker for 3 years.	
Keeling, Leonard	1st NC Regiment	5/9/1781, a Private under Capt. Alexander Brevard. Deserted on 6/2/1781. aka Leonard Keling.	
Keen, Saucer	2nd NC Regiment	Feb. 1782, a Private under Capt. Clement Hall. Discharged 2/22/1783.	
Keen, William	2nd NC Regiment	1/25/1782, a Private under Capt. Benjamin Andrew Coleman. From what is now Sampson County, NC. One source asserts he was a Private, Corporal, and Sergeant - also under Capt. Hardy Holmes and Capt. James Mills. Discharged 1/25/1783 at Wilmington, NC. S41715.	
Keener, John	3rd NC Regiment	8/1/1782, a Private under Capt. Benjamin Bailey for 12 months.	
Keener, Martin	3rd NC Regiment	8/1/1782, a Private under Capt. Benjamin Bailey for 12 months.	
Kees, Joseph	6th NC Regiment	5/5/1776, a Sergeant under Capt. Thomas Donoho. A Private in Nov. 1777. Discharged in Nov. 1778.	
Keeter, Nehemiah	1st NC Regiment	12/18/1781, a Private under Capt. James Mills On 2/6/1782, this unit was transferred to the 4th NC Regiment. Died on 9/6/1782.	
Keeton, James	2nd NC Regiment	11/19/1777, a Private under Capt. Edward Vail, Jr. Dropped from the rolls in Feb. 1778.	
Keith, John	1st NC Regiment	9/8/1778, a known Private under Capt. James Read. A Musician, sick on 2/10/1780. aka John Keath.	
Kellahan, Martin	1st NC Regiment	8/1/1782, a Private under Capt. Joshua Hadley for 18 months.	

Name	1st Unit	Year / Rank / Served Under / Notes	Known Battles
Keller, Michael	10th NC Regiment	6/6/1777, a Private under Capt. Isaac Moore for three years. 9/8/1778, a known Private under Capt. John Sumner (1st NC Regiment).	
Kelley, Charles	10th NC Regiment	6/15/1777, a Private. 8/4/1777, a Sergeant under Capt. James Wilson. A Private in June 1778. A Corporal on 8/1/1778. 9/8/1778, a known Corporal under Maj. John Baptiste Ashe (1st NC Regiment). Back to Sergeant on 2/26/1779. POW at the Fall of Charleston, SC, held until around 9/1/1781 - exchanged at Jamestown, VA. Discharged at Richmond, VA. Enlisted at Hillsborough, NC. aka Charles Cally, Charles Kelly. W948.	Siege of Charleston 1780 (SC).
Kellihan, Isaac	4th NC Regiment	1782, a Private under Capt. William Lytle for 18 months.	
Kellion, Jacob	4th NC Regiment	5/25/1782, a Private under Maj. Thomas Donoho. Discharged on 5/25/1783.	
Kellion, John	4th NC Regiment	5/25/1782, a Private under Maj. Thomas Donoho. A Corporal in Jan. 1783. Discharged on 5/25/1783.	
Kellum, Frederick	10th NC Regiment	5/17/1777, a Private under Capt. John Jarvis for three years. 9/8/1778, a known Private in the Major's Company (Maj. Griffith John McRee) (1st NC Regiment). Died on 1/12/1779. aka Frederick Callum.	
Kellum, George	2nd NC Regiment	1782, a Private under Capt. Robert Raiford for 18 months.	
Kellum, John	2nd NC Regiment	1782, a Private under Capt. Robert Raiford for 18 months. Died on 6/28/1783.	
Kelly, Edward	6th NC Regiment	1777, a Private under Capt. Thomas Donoho. 6/1/1778, a Private under Capt. Griffith John McRee (1st NC Regiment).	
Kelly, James	3rd NC Regiment	1782, a Private under Capt. Alexander Brevard for 18 months.	
Kelly, James	3rd NC Regiment	5/20/1778, a Private under Lt./Capt. George "Gee" Bradley for nine months. Deserted in Sep. 1779.	
Kelly, James	6th NC Regiment	1777, a Private under Capt. Thomas Donoho. Died on 4/15/1778.	
Kelly, John	1st NC Regiment	3/10/1777, a Private under Capt. Tilghman Dixon. Apparently recruited by a Captain in 7th NC Regiment, various mentions of Capt. Ely and Capt. Walker. 9/8/1778, a known Private under Capt. Tilghman Dixon. Then, under Capt. Joshua Bowman. POW at the Fall of Charleston, escaped after five months. 1780, A Wagon Maker under Col. Nicholas Long (Deputy QM General) at Halifax, NC until the end of the war. From Halifax County, NC. Born 8/22/1755. aka John Kelley. S35489.	Stony Point (NY), Siege of Charleston 1780 (SC).
Kelly, John	1st NC Regiment	8/1/1782, a Private under Capt. Joshua Hadley for 18 months.	
Kelly, Oliver	NC Artillery	1/1/1777, a Matross under Capt. Thomas Clark as NC Provincial Troops. 7/10/1777, on	

460

Name	1st Unit	Year / Rank / Served Under / Notes	Known Battles
		Continental Line. Also on 9/9/1778.	
Kelly, Patrick	8th NC Regiment	1777, a Private under Capt. Francis Tartanson. Died on 11/26/1777.	
Kelly, Thomas	10th NC Regiment	1777, a Private under Capt. Isaac Moore. 9/8/1778, a known Private in the Colonel's Company (Col. Thomas Clark) (1st NC Regiment) led by Capt. John Gambier Scull. Deserted on 9/12/1778. Re-enlisted and discharged in Jan. 1779.	
Kelly, William	1st NC Regiment	1777, a Private under Capt. John Brown. Dropped from the rolls in June 1778.	
Kelly, William	3rd NC Regiment	7/20/1778, a Private under Capt. John Baker for nine months.	
Kelve, James	NC Artillery	7/9/1779, a Matross under Capt. John Kingsbury for 3 years.	
Kemmy, Jonathan	2nd NC Regiment	5/1/1777, a Private under Capt. Benjamin Williams. Dishcarged 2/1/1780.	
Kenan, William	1st NC Regiment	9/23/1776, an Ensign. Also a Commissary. Resigned in April of 1777. aka William Kennon.	
Kennedy, Archibald	5th NC Regiment	8/1/1777, a Sergeant Major. Dropped from the rolls in Sep. 1777.	
Kennedy, Benjamin	5th NC Regiment	1777, Sergeant under Capt. Henry Darnell. Dropped from the rolls in Jan. 1778. Jan. 1779, re-enlisted in the 5th NC Regiment, unit unknown.	
Kennedy, Benjamin	9th NC Regiment	1777, a Private under Capt. Matthew Ramsey for nine months. Dropped from the rolls in Oct. 1779.	
Kennedy, George	5th NC Regiment	1777, a Private under Capt. Henry Darnell. Deserted in Aug. 1777.	
Kennedy, Isaac	1st NC Regiment	1777, a Private under Capt. Joshua Bowman. Deserted in Aug. 1777.	
Kennedy, James	1st NC Regiment	4/28/1781, a Private under Capt. Alexander Brevard. Deserted on 6/16/1781.	
Kennedy, John	1st NC Regiment	9/10/1782, a Private under Capt. Joshua Hadley for 18 months. Earlier in NC Militia. From Dobbs County, NC. W10170.	
Kennedy, John	3rd NC Regiment	8/1/1782, a Private under Capt. Benjamin Bailey for 12 months.	
Kennedy, John	5th NC Regiment	1777, a Private under Capt. Henry Darnell. Deserted in Aug. 1777.	
Kennedy, Michael	1st NC Regiment	June 1779, a Private under Capt. William Armstrong.	
Kennedy, William	9th NC Regiment	A Sergeant under Capt. Matthew Ramsey for nine months. Dropped from the rolls in Oct. 1779.	
Kenney, William	1st NC Regiment	1781, a Private, unit unknown. Confined for being insolent to his Sergeant.	
Kennon, John	6th NC Regiment	1775, a 1st Lieutenant in the Hillsborough District Minutemen. 4/17/1776, a 1st Lieutenant under Capt. Philip Taylor and Col. John Alexander Lillington. aka John Kenan.	
Kenny,	3rd NC	7/1/1779, a Private under Capt. Kedar Ballard	

Name	1st Unit	Year / Rank / Served Under / Notes	Known Battles
Robert	Regiment	for 18 months. Deserted 10/1/1779. aka Robert Kenney.	
Kenny, Thomas	1st NC Regiment	6/6/1781, a Private under Capt. William Lytle for 12 months. Dropped from the rolls sometime during 1781.	
Kent, Levi	2nd NC Regiment	8/1/1782, a Private under Capt. Benjamin Coleman, then Capt. Joshua Hadley (1st NC Regiment), then Capt. Joseph T. Rhodes (4th NC Regiment) for 18 months. Furloughed after 17 months at Charleston, SC. S41714.	
Kent, Thomas	9th NC Regiment	1777, a Private under Capt. Matthew Ramsey for nine months. Died in Sep. 1779.	
Kent, Thomas	9th NC Regiment	1777, a Private under Capt. Matthew Ramsey for nine months. Dropped from the rolls in Oct. 1779. Yep, two of 'em.	
Kerby, James	4th NC Regiment	5/6/1776, a Private under Capt. Thomas Harris for three years. July 1778, transferred to serve under Capt. John Sumner (1st NC Regiment). 3/12/1779, re-enlisted for the duration of the war under Capt. Griffith John McRee (1st NC Regiment). Deserted on 1/1/1780. From Anson County, NC. On some rolls as James Kirbo or James Curbow.	Brandywine Creek (PA), Germantown (PA), Monmouth (NJ).
Kerby, William	4th NC Regiment	4/20/1776 or 9/29/1776 (two sources), a Private under Capt. Thomas Harris. Wounded at the battle of Brandywine Creek (PA). July 1778, transferred to serve under Capt. John Sumner (1st NC Regiment). Discharged 5/10/1779. Later in NC Militia. From Anson County, NC. aka William Curbow, William Kurbo. S4470.	Brandywine Creek (PA), Germantown (PA), Monmouth (NJ).
Kerr, David	1st NC Regiment	1776, an Ensign under Capt. George Davidson.	
Kerr, James	1st NC Regiment	1775, a Sergeant under Capt. George Davidson, then a Sergeant Major. From Orange County, NC. 4/17/1776, a 1st Lieutenant under Capt. William Temple Coles (4th NC Regiment). April 1777, a Captain for eight months. In six engagements, wounded twice. aka James Carr. W9093.	
Kerr, William	4th NC Regiment	1776, a Private under Ensign Patrick McGibbony, Lt. William Dent, Capt. John Nelson for 18 months. From Guilford County, NC. Later in NC Militia. R5892.	
Kersey, Jacob	NC Light Dragoons	Oct.-Dec. 1777, a known Private under Capt. Martin Phifer. Not on any official rolls.	
Kersey, James	1st NC Regiment	8/20/1782, a Private under Capt. Joshua Hadley for 18 months. Discharged 8/1/1783 at Wilmington, NC. From Bladen (what is now Robeson) County, NC. S8788.	
Kesley, Richard	1st NC Regiment	6/11/1781, a Private under Capt. Griffith John McRee. Discharged on 6/11/1782.	
Key, James	1st NC Regiment	8/1/1782, a Private under Capt. Joshua Hadley for 18 months.	
Key, William	1st NC	1782, a Private under Capt. Peter Bacot for 18	

Name	1st Unit	Year / Rank / Served Under / Notes	Known Battles
	Regiment	months.	
Keys, Joseph	1st NC Regiment	5/5/1776, a Private under Lt./Capt. Joshua Bowman for 2-1/2 years. 9/8/1778, a known Private in the Lt. Colonel's Company (Lt. Col. Robert Mebane) led by Capt. Joshua Bowman.	
Kidd, John	2nd NC Regiment	8/1/1782, a Private under Capt. Benjamin Carter for 18 months. Served ten months and ten days. Furloughed on 6/10/1783 at Ten Mile House, SC. Born 5/2/1759. On the official rolls as John Kid R5908.	
Kidwell, Elijah	4th NC Regiment	5/1/1776, a Private under Capt. William Temple Coles for three years. 9/8/1778, a known Private under Capt. John Sumner (1st NC Regiment) - sick at Valley Forge on that date. Dropped from the rolls in April 1779. aka Elisha Kidwell. S13643.	
Kidwell, John	4th NC Regiment	1776, a Private under Capt. William Temple Coles. From Rowan County, NC. Later in NC Militia. S13638.	
Kight, Charles	3rd NC Regiment	Jan. 1779, a Private in the Lt. Colonel's Company (Lt. Col. Robert Mebane) led by Capt. George "Gee" Bradley for three years.	
Kight, Dempsey	3rd NC Regiment	Jan. 1779, a Private in the Lt. Colonel's Company (Lt. Col. Robert Mebane) led by Capt. George "Gee" Bradley for three years.	
Kilby, William Tyler	2nd NC Regiment	6/6/1776, an Ensign. Died 4/6/1777. One source claims he made it to 2nd Lieutenant prior to his death. aka William Tyler Kilby, William Kirby, William Killeby.	
Kilgo, James	4th NC Regiment	1777, a Musician under Capt. Thomas Harris. Discharged on 10/31/1777.	
Killebrew, Lawrence	1st NC Regiment	July 1779, served 11 months under Capt. William Armstrong. Hired a substitute - Micajah Whitley - to serve remaining seven months. From Edgecombe County, NC. Earlier in NC Militia. W24816.	
Killet, Joseph	3rd NC Regiment	7/20/1778, a Private under Lt./Capt. George "Gee" Bradley. Deserted in Oct. 1778.	
Killingsworth, John	5th NC Regiment	1777, a Musician under Capt. Henry Darnell. A Private in Jan. 1778. 9/9/1778, under Capt. Benjamin Andrew Coleman (2nd NC Regiment).	
Killion, Jacob	1st NC Regiment	1781, a Private under Maj. Thomas Donoho for 12 months. Discharged at the hospital in Camden, SC. S32382.	
Kilpatrick, Hugh	4th NC Regiment	1782, a Private under Capt. William Lytle for 18 months.	
Kilpatrick, Robert	7th NC Regiment	8/9/1777, a Musician under Capt. Joshua Dayley. 3/12/1779, re-enlisted for the duration of the war under Capt. James Read (1st NC Regiment).	
Kime, David	4th NC Regiment	1782, a Private under Capt. Anthony Sharpe for 18 months.	
Kincaid,	1st NC	1776, a Private under Capt. Joshua Bowman.	

Name	1st Unit	Year / Rank / Served Under / Notes	Known Battles
William	Regiment	9/8/1778, a known Private under Capt. Joshua Bowman.	
King, Anthony	3rd NC Regiment	April 1781, a Private under Capt. Edward Yarborough for 12 months. Discharged 5/1/1782. From Granville County, NC. W439.	Eutaw Springs (SC).
King, David	3rd NC Regiment	1781, a Private under Capt. Edward Yarborough for 12 months. Discharged 4/23/1782. S46055.	
King, Edward	3rd NC Regiment	8/1/1782, a Private under Capt. Alexander Brevard and Capt. Joseph T. Rhodes for 18 months. S38895.	
King, Edward	3rd NC Regiment	7/20/1778, a Private under Lt./Capt. George "Gee" Bradley for nine months. 1782, re-enlisted under Capt. Joshua Hadley (1st NC Regiment) for the duration of the war. From Wilkes County, NC. R5942.	
King, Elijah	3rd NC Regiment	1776, a known Private under Capt. William Brinkley. 9/23/1776, apprehended as a deserter.	
King, Enoch	10th NC Regiment	6/15/1777, a Private under Capt. Isaac Moore for three years. 9/8/1778, a known Private in the Lt. Colonel's Company (Lt. Col. Robert Mebane) (1st NC Regiment) led by Capt. Joshua Bowman - sick on that date at Princeton.	
King, James	1st NC Regiment	6/1/1776, an Ensign. 8/15/1776, a 2nd Lieutenant. 4/3/1777, a 1st Lieutenant under Capt. Howell Tatum. 9/8/1778, under Capt. Griffith John McRee. Promoted to Captain-Lt. on 3/30/1780 under Col. Thomas Clark. One source claims it was 4/1/1780. POW at the Fall of Charleston, died in captivity (9/8/1780).	Siege of Charleston 1780 (SC).
King, James	2nd NC Regiment	6/30/1776, a Private under Capt. James Armstrong for 2-1/2 years. Died of Camp Fever on 6/2/1778 at Monmouth, NJ. From Surry County, NC. W10139.	
King, James	6th NC Regiment	1777, a Private under Capt. Daniel Williams.	
King, James	9th NC Regiment	5/1/1776 (?), a Private under Capt. Matthew Ramsey for three years. 9/8/1778, a known Private under Capt. Griffith John McRee (1st NC Regiment) - sick on that date at Yellow Springs. Died in Sep. 1779.	
King, James	10th NC Regiment	8/1/1777, a Private under Capt. Silas Stevenson. 9/9/1778, a known Private under Capt. Benjamin Andrew Coleman (2nd NC Regiment). 3/12/1779, re-enlisted under Capt. Benjamin Andrew Coleman.	
King, John	2nd NC Regiment	9/9/1778, a known Private in the Colonel's Company (Col. John Patten) led by Capt. John Craddock.	
King, John	3rd NC Regiment	1777, a Private under Capt. James Emmett. Dropped from the rolls in June 1778.	
King, John	10th NC Regiment	10/4/1777, a Private under Capt. Isaac Moore.	
King, Joseph	4th NC Regiment	1/1/1777, a Musician under Capt. William Goodman for three years. A Private in Jan.	

464

Name	1st Unit	Year / Rank / Served Under / Notes	Known Battles
		1778. 9/8/1778, a known Private in the Colonel's Company (Col. Thomas Clark) (1st NC Regiment) led by Capt. John Gambier Scull. Discharged on 1/28/1780.	
King, Mason	3rd NC Regiment	7/20/1778, a Private under Maj. Thomas Hogg. Deserted the next day on 7/21/1778.	
King, Thomas	3rd NC Regiment	7/20/1778, a Private under Capt. John Baker for nine months.	
King, Vincent	1st NC Regiment	1781, a Private under Capt. Alexander Brevard for 18 months. From Wake County, NC. Earlier in NC Militia. W4007.	
King, William	2nd NC Regiment	6/7/1777, a Private, unit unknown. 9/9/1778, a known Private in the Colonel's Company (Col. John Patten) led by Capt. John Craddock. 3/12/1779, re-enlisted under Capt. Benjamin Williams.	
King, Woody	3rd NC Regiment	1781, a Private under Capt. Clement Hall for 12 months. Discharged on 4/21/1782 (2nd NC Regiment).	
Kingsbury, John	NC Artillery	1775, in New Bern District Minutemen. 5/9/1776, an Ensign under Capt. John Vance. 7/19/1777, a Capt.-Lt. Full Captain on 11/16/1777 after John Vance resigned. NC Continental, not attached to any NC regiment. POW/Surrendered 64 men at the Fall of Charleston. Brevetted as a Major, date unknown.	Monmouth (NJ), Stony Point (NY), Siege of Charleston 1780 (SC).
Kingston, Samuel	4th NC Regiment	1782, a Private under Capt. William Lytle. Deserted on 6/12 /1783 (?).	
Kinkaid, William	6th NC Regiment	1777, a Private under Capt. George Dougherty. Dropped from the rolls in Nov. 1778.	
Kinsey, William	1st NC Regiment	8/1/1782, a Private under Capt. Joshua Hadley for 18 months.	
Kippey, Peter	3rd NC Regiment	Jan. 1778, a Private under Capt. James Emmett. Dropped from the rolls in Feb. 1778.	
Kirk, John	4th NC Regiment	5/19/1777, a Private under Capt. John Nelson for three years. 6/1/1778, a Private under Capt. Griffith John McRee (1st NC Regiment).	
Kirk, Roger	3rd NC Regiment	7/20/1778, a Private under Capt. Kedar Ballard for nine months.	
Kirkpatrick, Robert	1st NC Regiment	8/9/1777, a Musician under Capt. James Read. 9/8/1778, same unit.	
Kissey, Thomas	1st NC Regiment	5/26/1781, a Private under Capt. Alexander Brevard.	
Kitchen, Benjamin	7th NC Regiment	Nov. 1776, a Sergeant under Capt. William Lewis (?), then under Lt./Capt. John Baker. 7/20/1778, a Sergeant under Capt. John Baker (3rd NC Regiment) for nine months. From Nash County, NC. Early 1776, a Sergeant in Militia. 1779, back in Militia as a Captain. aka Benjamin Kithen. S31797.	
Kite, George	3rd NC Regiment	1781, a Private under Capt. Edward Yarborough for 12 months. Discharged 4/22/1782.	
Kite, James	3rd NC	7/20/1778, a Private under Capt. Francis Child	

Name	1st Unit	Year / Rank / Served Under / Notes	Known Battles
	Regiment	for nine months.	
Kittle, Benjamin	5th NC Regiment	8/10/1779, a Private under Capt. Joseph Montford for 18 months. Deserted in Sep. 1779.	
Kittrell, Jonathan	4th NC Regiment	3/8/1782, a Private under Capt. James Mills for 12 months.	
Knight, Absalom	2nd NC Regiment	August 1781, a Private under Capt. Benjamin Carter. Wounded at the battle of Eutaw Springs, SC. Discharged on 7/1/1782. S4483.	Eutaw Springs (SC).
Knight, Jesse	1st NC Regiment	A Private under Lt. Col. Hardy Murfree, dates unknown. From Hertford County, NC.	
Knight, John	DQMG	1780, a Shoemaker on the roll of Capt. Solomon Wood (NC Light Dragoons) - this seems to be for convenience only. 8/23/1781, a Shoemaker under Col. Nicholas Long (Deputy QM General).	
Knight, Miles	10th NC Regiment	11/1/1777, a Private under Capt. Isaac Moore. 9/9/1778, a known Private in the Major's Company (Maj. Hardy Murfree) (2nd NC Regiment). 3/12/1779, re-enlisted in the Major's Company (Maj. Hardy Murfree). POW at Ft. Lafayette, NY on 6/1/1779. A Sergeant on 2/16/1780.	Ft. Lafayette (NY).
Knight, Morgan	5th NC Regiment	1777, a Private under Capt. Reading Blount. Dropped from the rolls in Jan. 1778.	
Knight, Reuben	3rd NC Regiment	4/16/1776, a Musician under Capt. James Emmett. A Private in June 1778. 9/9/1778, a known Private in the Major's Company (Maj. Hardy Murfree) (2nd NC Regiment). Discharged on 10/16/1778.	
Knight, Samuel	9th NC Regiment	3/30/1777, a Sergeant under Capt. Joel Brevard. A Private on 5/21/1778. 9/8/1778, a known Private under Capt. Howell Tatum (1st NC Regiment).	
Knight, William	2nd NC Regiment	Dec. 1780, a Private under Capt. Christopher Goodwin. From Orange County, NC. Then in NC Militia. S31800.	Cowpens (SC), Hobkirk Hill (SC), Eutaw Springs (SC).
Knop, Adam	4th NC Regiment	1777, a Private under Capt. William Temple Coles. Discharged on 8/10/1777. aka Adam Knup.	
Knott, William	1st NC Regiment	A Private under Lt. Col. Hardy Murfree, dates unknown. From Hertford County, NC.	
Knott, William	4th NC Regiment	1775, an Ensign in the Edenton District Minutemen. 4/17/1776, an Ensign under Capt. John McLane and Col. Thomas Polk. 1777, a Lieutenant under Capt. Joseph Phillips. Dropped from the rolls in Jan. 1778. Feb. 1779, a Lieutenant in the 5th NC Regiment, unit unknown.	
Knox, William	2nd NC Regiment	Sep. 1775, a Captain under Col. Robert Howe. Accidentally killed by one of his lieutenants (Lt. Richard Graham). His deathbed wish was for his entire company to be discharged, and this wish was honored. Not on any official	Great Cane Brake (SC), Snow Campaign (SC), Moore's Creek

Name	1st Unit	Year / Rank / Served Under / Notes	Known Battles
		Continental rolls. From Rowan (what would now be Burke) County, NC.	Bridge [4], Ft. Moultrie #1 (SC).
Koen, John	10th NC Regiment	5/30/1777, a Sergeant under Capt. Dempsey Gregory, then under Capt. Issac Moore. June 1777, demoted to Corporal. 9/8/1778, a known Corporal under Capt. Howell Tatum (1st NC Regiment). POW at the Fall of Charleston, SC - exchanged in July 1782 at Jamestown, VA. Discharged in July 1782 at Richmond, VA. From Pasquotank County, NC. Born 1/27/1757 in Pasquotank County, NC. S8804.	Monmouth (NJ), Siege of Charleston 1780 (SC).
Kytle, Jacob	1st NC Regiment	10/9/1777, a Private under Capt. William Armstrong for three years. 9/8/1778, a known Private under Capt. John Sumner. Re-enlisted on 5/25/1781 under Capt. Thomas Donoho as a Corporal, then a Sergeant. Discharged 5/25/1782. From Caswell County, NC. Early 1781, in NC Militia. aka Jacob Kettle, Jacob Kittle, Jacob Kitle. S21338.	Stony Point (NY), Monmouth (NJ), Eutaw Springs (SC).
Labiel, Francis	3rd NC Regiment	6/18/1779, a Private under Capt. Kedar Ballard. Dropped from the rolls in Oct. 1779.	
Lacey, John	2nd NC Regiment	9/19/1775, a Sergeant under Capt. Nathaniel Keais, then Capt. Edward Vail, Jr. A Sergeant Major in Feb. 1778. A Sergeant in June 1778 in the Colonel's Company (Col. John Patten) led by Capt. John Craddock. Promoted to Ensign on 5/20/1779. Enlisted in Pitt County, NC. Discharged in March 1780 in Pitt County, NC. S41750.	Brandywine Creek (PA), Germantown (PA), Monmouth (NJ).
Lacey, John	3rd NC Regiment	7/20/1778, a Private under Capt. John Baker. Deserted on 8/30/1778.	
Lackey, Christopher	5th NC Regiment	5/3/1776, a 2nd Lieutenant under Capt. William Brinkley then under Capt. John Enloe, then back to Capt. Brinkley on 5/6/1776. A 1st Lieutenant in 1777 under Capt. Thomas Granbury (3rd NC Regiment) before 4/14/1777. Dropped from the rolls in Dec. 1777.	
Lackey, Thomas	3rd NC Regiment	11/4/1782, a Private under Capt. Benjamin Bailey for 18 months. Earlier in NC Militia. From Mecklenburg County, NC. W21557.	
Lacy, Burwell	3rd NC Regiment	1777, a Private under Capt. Thomas Granbury. A Corporal on 4/1/1782.	
Lacy, Frederick	1st NC Regiment	1777, a Private under Capt. Howell Tatum.	
Ladon, Thomas	7th NC Regiment	4/11/1777, a Private under Capt. Thomas Brickell. 2/26/1778, a known Private under Capt. Howell Tatum (1st NC Regiment). 9/8/1778, a known Private under Capt. Howell Tatum.	
Lafferty, John	4th NC Regiment g	6/10/1776, a Private under Capt. Robert Smith for three years. 9/8/1778, a known Private in the Colonel's Company (Col. Thomas Clark) (1st NC Regiment) led by Capt. John Gambier Scull.	Monmouth (NJ).

467

Name	1st Unit	Year / Rank / Served Under / Notes	Known Battles
		Discharged on 6/15/1779. aka John Laferty. S42813.	
Lafton, Cannon	1st NC Regiment	6/15/1781, a Private under Capt. Anthony Sharpe. Discharged on 6/15/1782 (4th NC Regiment).	
Laighton, William	4th NC Regiment	1781, a Private under Capt. George Dougherty for three years.	
Lamb, Abner	1st NC Regiment	An Ensign in 1780. 1781, a Private under Lt. Benjamin Bailey. A Lieutenant on 6/1/1781. Wounded at Eutaw Springs on September 8, 1781. Served until the end of the war. Son of Col. Gideon Lamb. From what is now Camden County, NC.	Eutaw Springs (SC).
Lamb, Gibbs	1st NC Regiment	1777, a Private under Capt. Henry "Hal" Dixon. 9/8/1778, a known Private under Capt. James Read. A Corporal on 4/1/1782.	
Lamb, Gideon	6th NC Regiment	4/15/1776, a Major of the 6th NC Regiment. Dec. 1776, a Lt. Colonel. 1/26/1777, a Colonel. Tried for abandoning his troops at battle of Brandywine Creek, acquitted. The 6th NC Regiment was folded into the 1st NC Regiment on 6/1/1778. He returned home on 6/1/1778. Summer and Fall of 1778, was charged to assemble the Eastern "New Levies" and get them ready to march asap. 6th NC Regiment recreated. Fell apart again in late 1779. Spent much of his time in 1780 and 1781 rounding up deserters. Accepted 1/2 pay in Jan. 1781 to retire, but kept working until his health fell apart. Died 11/8/1781. From what is now Camden County, NC.	Ft. Moultrie #1 (SC), Brandywine Creek (PA), Germantown (PA).
Lamb, John	1st NC Regiment	Jan. 1782, a Private under Capt. James Mills for 12 months. Discharged in Jan. 1783.	
Lambert, Aaron	10th NC Regiment	4/21/1777, a Private under Capt. Silas Stevenson. 9/9/1778, a known Private under Capt. Robert Fenner (2nd NC Regiment). POW at Ft. Lafayette, NY on 6/1/1779. Rejoined in Nov. 1779.	Ft. Lafayette (NY).
Lambert, Enoch	2nd NC Regiment	1781, a Sergeant under Capt. Robert Raiford for 18 months.	
Lambert, John	1st NC Regiment	1776, a 2nd Lieutenant. [46].	
Lambert, John	3rd NC Regiment	7/20/1778, a Private under Capt. Francis Child for nine months.	
Lambert, John	3rd NC Regiment	7/20/1778, a Private under Capt. Michael Quinn for nine months. Enlisted in Craven County, NC. Discharged 5/6/1779 at Halifax, NC. S41753.	
Lambeth, Moses	2nd NC Regiment	1781, a Private under Capt. Benjamin Andrew Coleman for 12 months. Earlier in NC Militia. From Craven County, NC.	
Lambley, Philip	4th NC Regiment	1782, a Private under Capt. Anthony Sharpe for 18 months. From Rowan County, NC. aka Philip Lambpey, Philip Lambly. W4712.	

Name	1st Unit	Year / Rank / Served Under / Notes	Known Battles
Land, Henry	2nd NC Regiment	1/13/1782, a Private under Capt. Benjamin Andrew Coleman for 18 months. Discharged on 7/1/1783.	
Land, John	4th NC Regiment	1781, a Private under Capt. George Dougherty for 12 months. Discharged on 5/25/1782.	
Land, Lemon	3rd NC Regiment	4/23/1779, a known Waiter in the Lt. Colonel's Company (Lt. Col. Robert Mebane) led by Capt. George "Gee" Bradley.	
Landus, John	6th NC Regiment	A Private under Capt. Griffith John McRee, dates unknown. 9/8/1778, a known Private under Capt. Tilghman Dixon (1st NC Regiment). aka John Landers.	
Lane, Benjamin	3rd NC Regiment	1781, a Private under Capt. Clement Hall for 12 months. Discharged on 8/16/1782 (2nd NC Regiment).	
Lane, Cityzen	3rd NC Regiment	1781, a Private under Capt. Clement Hall for 12 months. Discharged on 8/1/1782 (2nd NC Regiment).	
Lane, Isaac	3rd NC Regiment	6/29/1779, a Private under Capt. Kedar Ballard. Deserted on 8/22/1779.	
Lane, Jacob	10th NC Regiment	May 1777, a Private under Capt. Isaac Moore. 8/2/1777, a Corporal under Capt. Isaac Moore for three years. A Private in June 1778. 9/8/1778, a known Private in the Lt. Colonel's Company (Lt. Col. Robert Mebane) (1st NC Regiment) led by Capt. Joshua Bowman - sick on that date. 1781, a Corporal under Capt. William Armstrong for 12 months. Discharged on 11/1/1782. From Perquimans County, NC. aka Jacob Lain. S41751.	Monmouth (NJ), Siege of Charleston 1780 (SC).
Lane, James	3rd NC Regiment	6/29/1779, a Private under Capt. Kedar Ballard. Deserted on 8/5/1779.	
Lane, Jesse	3rd NC Regiment	3/1/1777, a Private under Capt. Jacob Turner. 9/9/1778, a known Private in the Lt. Colonel's Company (Lt. Col. Selby Harney) (2nd NC Regiment). 3/12/1779, re-enlisted in the Lt. Colonel's Company (Lt. Col. Selby Harney). 1780, a Gunstocker and a Wagon Maker on the roll of Capt. Solomon Wood (NC Light Dragoons) - this seems to be for convenience only. A Wagon Maker under Col. Nicholas Long (Deputy QM General). Also on 8/23/1781.	
Lane, Jethro	2nd NC Regiment	6/26/1777, a Private under Capt. Robert Fenner. May be the same man as directly below.	
Lane, Jethro	3rd NC Regiment	7/20/1778, a Private in the Lt. Colonel's Company (Lt. Col. William Lee Davidson) led by Lt./Capt. George "Gee" Bradley for nine months. 4/23/1779, a known Private in the Lt. Colonel's Company (Lt. Col. Robert Mebane) led by Capt. George "Gee" Bradley. Left at Trenton (?). aka Lithro Lane.	
Lane, Thomas	5th NC Regiment	5/1/1777, a Private under Capt. Benjamin Andrew Coleman. 9/8/1778, in 2nd NC Regiment.	

Name	1st Unit	Year / Rank / Served Under / Notes	Known Battles
Lane, Timothy	3rd NC Regiment	1781, a Private under Capt. Clement Hall for 12 months. Discharged on 8/1/1782 (2nd NC Regiment).	
Lane, William	5th NC Regiment	1779, a Private under Maj. Reading Blount for four months. Earlier and later, in NC Militia. 1782, a Private under Capt. Thomas Evans (4th NC Regiment) for 18 months. From Craven County, NC. R6140.	
Lanfield, Joseph	1st NC Regiment	5/9/1781, a Private under Capt. Griffith John McRee. Deserted on 7/2/1781.	
Langford, Alloway	8th NC Regiment	2/8/1777, an Ensign under Capt. Thomas Nixon. 8/1/1777, a 2nd Lieutenant. 10/12/1777, a 1st Lieutenant under Capt. John Walsh. Retired 6/1/1778.	
Langston, Elisha	3rd NC Regiment	7/20/1778, a Private under Capt. Kedar Ballard for nine months.	
Lanier, James Jr.	8th NC Regiment	11/28/1776, an Ensign under Capt. Francis Tartanson. 8/26/1777, a 2nd Lieutenant. Resigned on 10/12/1777.	
Lapsley, James	1st NC Regiment	1777, a Private under Capt. Joshua Bowman. Deserted on 8/15/1777.	
Larey, Patrick	4th NC Regiment	1782, a Private under Capt. Thomas Evans for 18 months.	
Largent, James	4th NC Regiment	First in SC unit. 1777, moved to what is now Rutherford County, NC. A Private under Capt. Micajah Lewis for nine months. Pension statement a bit confusing - name at top is James, but is signed Joseph. Later, rejoined a SC Militia unit. Born 1752 in Anson County, NC. S8824.	Stono Ferry (SC).
Larko, Francis	1st NC Regiment	Jan. 1782, a Sergeant under Capt. William Armstrong.	
Larouse, Joshua	5th NC Regiment	6/18/1779, a Private under Capt. Joseph Montford. Dropped from the rolls in Oct. 1779.	
Larry, Cornelius	4th NC Regiment	A Private under Capt. Micajah Lewis, dates unknown. 9/8/1778, a known Private in the Colonel's Company (Col. Thomas Clark) (1st NC Regiment) led by Capt. John Gambier Scull. Deserted on 6/23/1779.	
Lashley, William	3rd NC Regiment	1780, a Private for three years under Capt. John Medearis (2/6/1782, in 1st NC Regiment). From Wake County, NC. W20425.	
Lashorn, James	3rd NC Regiment	1781, a Private under Capt. Edward Yarborough for 12 months. Discharged on 4/1/1782.	
Lasiter, Jacob	2nd NC Regiment	Feb. 1778, a Private under Capt. Robert Fenner. Died 3/16/1778.	
Lasiter, James	1st NC Regiment	9/10/1782, a Private under Capt. Joshua Hadley for 18 months.	
Lasiter, James	2nd NC Regiment	5/12/1781, a Private under Capt. Tilghman Dixon. Discharged on 5/20/1782 (1st NC Regiment). First name might be Jonas.	
Lasiter, James	5th NC Regiment	6/15/1779, a Private under Capt. Joseph Montford. Dropped from the rolls in Oct. 1779.	
Lasiter, Jesse	3rd NC	1781, a Private under Capt. Clement Hall for 12	

Name	1st Unit	Year / Rank / Served Under / Notes	Known Battles
	Regiment	months. Discharged on 4/12/1782 (2nd NC Regiment).	
Lasiter, Josiah	3rd NC Regiment	7/20/1778, a Private under Maj. Thomas Hogg. Died on 9/15/1778.	
Lasiter, Luke	1st NC Regiment	6/13/1781, a Private under Capt. Robert Raiford. Discharged on 6/13/1782 (2nd NC Regiment).	
Lasley, John	1st NC Regiment	1776, a Private under Capt. Robert Rowan and Capt. Joshua Bowman for one year. Discharged at Wilmington, NC. S38904.	
Lassiter, Jethro	7th NC Regiment	11/28/1776, an Ensign under Capt. Thomas Brickell. Dec. 1776, a 2nd Lieutenant. 10/12/1777, a 1st Lieutenant. Retired 6/1/1778. From Edenton District.	
Later, Ambrose	6th NC Regiment	1777, a Private under Capt. Thomas Donoho. Deserted in Aug. 1777.	
Latham, Phineas	2nd NC Regiment	1775, a Private under Capt. Nathaniel Keais. 1777, a Sergeant under Capt. Edward Vail, Jr. 9/9/1778, a known Sergeant in the Colonel's Company (Col. John Patten) led by Capt. John Craddock. Λ Private on 5/24/1779. POW at Ft. Lafayette on 6/1/1779. Rejoined in Nov. 1779. POW at the Fall of Charleston, escaped. From Beaufort County, NC. S41752.	Ft. Lafayette (NY), Siege of Charleston (SC).
Laughing-house, John	1st NC Regiment	4/15/1781, a Private under Capt. Anthony Sharpe. Discharged on 2/14/1782 (4th NC Regiment).	
Laughing-house, Thomas	5th NC Regiment	1777, a Private under Capt. John Enloe. Dropped from the rolls in Jan. 1778. aka Thomas Laughinhouse.	
Law, John	3rd NC Regiment	1782, a Private under Capt. Alexander Brevard for 18 months.	
Lawhorn, Samuel	5th NC Regiment	7/26/1779, a Private under Capt. Joseph Montford for 18 months.	
Lawrence, Isaac	NC Artillery	1/1/1777, a Corporal under Capt. Thomas Clark. Also on 9/9/1778.	
Lawrence, Joseph	2nd NC Regiment	7/20/1778, a Private under Maj. Reading Blount for nine months.	
Lawrence, Joseph	2nd NC Regiment	4/25/1781, a Private under Capt. Benjamin Carter for 12 months. Discharged on 4/25/1782.	
Lawrence, Nathaniel	3rd NC Regiment	6/1/1777, an Ensign. 6/1/1778, transferred to 2nd NC Regiment as a 2nd Lieutenant under Capt. Robet Fenner. POW at Ft. Lafayette on 6/1/1779, exchanged 4/18/1781. 1/23/1781, a 1st Lieutenant. Retired on 1/1/1783.	Ft. Lafayette (NY).
Lawrence, William	2nd NC Regiment	5/12/1781, a Private under Capt. Tilghman Dixon. Discharged on 5/21/1782 (1st NC Regiment).	
Laws, David	NC Artillery	11/22/1776, a Bombardier under Capt. John Vance as NC Provincial Troops. 7/10/1777, on Continental Line. 11/16/1777, under Capt. John Kingsbury. 5/1/1778, in same unit. 9/16/1778, in same unit. aka David Lowe.	
Laws, John	6th NC	A Private under Capt. George Dougherty. A	

Name	1st Unit	Year / Rank / Served Under / Notes	Known Battles
	Regiment	Sergeant in Feb. 1778. Died on 3/7/1778.	
Lawson, Richard	1st NC Regiment	1777, a Private under Capt. Henry "Hal" Dixon. Killed at Germantown, PA on 10/4/1777.	Germantown (PA).
Lawson, William	3rd NC Regiment	10/5/1781, a Private under Capt. Samuel Jones for 12 months. Discharged on 10/1/1782 (1st NC Regiment).	
Leach, John	2nd NC Regiment	11/25/1776, a Corporal under Capt. William Fenner for 2-1/2 years. A Sergeant on 11/1/1777. A Private in Jan. 1778. Back to Corporal in June 1778. Re-enlisted in 1781.	
Leak, James	1st NC Regiment	Feb. 1781, hired as a Substitute, a Private under Capt. Elijah Moore for three months. Earlier and later in Militia from Caswell County, NC. S31822.	
Leathers, Moses	6th NC Regiment	4/27/1776, a Private under Capt. Thomas White for 2-1/2 years. 9/8/1778, a known Private under Capt. John Sumner (1st NC Regiment). Dropped from the rolls in Nov. 1778. Later, in NC Militia, unit unknown. From what is now Durham County, NC. Born on 7/25/1754. On some rolls as Moses Lathers. R6230.	Brandywine Creek (PA), Germantown (PA).
Ledum, John	1st NC Regiment	12/14/1777, a Private under Maj. Henry "Hal" Dixon. 9/8/1778, a known Private under Capt. Tilghman Dixon. Dropped from the rolls in May 1779. aka John Leedum.	
Lee, Aaron	1st NC Regiment	1782, a Sergeant under Capt. Peter Bacot for 18 months.	
Lee, Abraham	2nd NC Regiment	7/20/1778, a Private under Maj. Reading Blount for nine months.	
Lee, Bryan	3rd NC Regiment	7/20/1778, a Private under Capt. Kedar Ballard. Dropped from the rolls in Oct. 1778.	
Lee, Bryant	3rd NC Regiment	1778, a Sergeant, unit and dates unknown. Possibly the same man as directly above.	
Lee, Charles	3rd NC Regiment	7/20/1778, a Private under Capt. Kedar Ballard. Dropped from the rolls in Oct. 1778.	
Lee, James	2nd NC Regiment	1782, a Private under Capt. Robert Raiford for 18 months. Earlier in NC Militia. From New Hanover County, NC. W4013.	
Lee, Jesse	3rd NC Regiment	7/20/1778, a Private under Capt. Kedar Ballard. Dropped from the rolls in Oct. 1778.	
Lee, John	2nd NC Regiment	1777, a Private under Capt. James Martin. Deserted on 12/25/1777. Rejoined in Jan. 1782 under Capt. William Goodman and Capt. Clement Hall for 12 months. From Currituck County, NC. S7144.	
Lee, Joseph	3rd NC Regiment	1778, a Private under Maj. Pinketham Eaton. From Martin County, NC.	Briar Creek (GA).
Lee, Philip	2nd NC Regiment	5/12/1781, a Private under Capt. Tilghman Dixon. 7/29/1781, transferred to Lee's Legion (VA).	
Lee, Richard	3rd NC Regiment	1781, a Private under Capt. Edward Yarborough for 12 months. Discharged on 4/1/1782.	
Lee, Thomas	2nd NC Regiment	4/29/1781, a Private under Capt. Tilghman Dixon. Discharged on 4/25/1782. S41784.	Eutaw Springs (SC).

Name	1st Unit	Year / Rank / Served Under / Notes	Known Battles
Lee, William	3rd NC Regiment	5/20/1778, a Private under Lt./Capt. George "Gee" Bradley. Deserted in Sep. 1779.	
Lee, William	3rd NC Regiment	6/15/1779, a Musician under Capt. George "Gee" Bradley.	
Lee, William Jr.	1st NC Regiment	4/28/1781, a Private under Capt. Alexander Brevard, then Capt. Griffith John McRee. Deserted on 5/2/1781.	
Leept, Edmond	2nd NC Regiment	5/12/1781, a Private under Capt. Tilghman Dixon. Discharged on 5/21/1782 (1st NC Regiment). His name could be Edmond Leet.	
Leftyear, Uriah	7th NC Regiment	3/19/1777, a Private under Lt. John Baker and Capt. Joseph Walker for three years. 9/8/1778, a known Private under Capt. Tilghman Dixon (1st NC Regiment). 3/12/1779, re-enlisted for the duration of the war in the same unit. Deserted on 3/26/1779. From Hertford County, NC. aka Uriah Leftler, Uriah Leftter. R6271.	Germantown (PA), Monmouth (NJ).
Legar, James	6th NC Regiment	12/11/1776 or 12/11/1777 (two sources), a Private under Capt. George Dougherty for three years. 9/8/1778, a known Private under Capt. Griffith John McRee (1st NC Regiment). Dropped from the rolls in Nov. 1779.	
Leggett, Absalom	2nd NC Regiment	1782, a Private under Capt. Robert Raiford for 18 months.	
Leggett, Lewis	2nd NC Regiment	7/20/1778, a Private under Maj. Reading Blount for nine months.	
Leigh, Lewis	1st NC Regiment	2/2/1782, a Sergeant under Capt. James Mills. 2/6/1782, this unit was transferred to 4th NC Regiment. Died on 7/17/1782.	
Leir, James	4th NC Regiment	1782, a Private under Capt. Anthony Sharpe for 18 months. Deserted on 5/14/1782.	
Lemon, Land.	3rd NC Regiment	7/20/1778, a Private in the Lt. Colonel's Company (Lt. Col. William Lee Davidson) led by Lt./Capt. George "Gee" Bradley.	
Lemmy, Joseph	1st NC Regiment	1/4/1776, an Ensign. 1/18/1776, a 2nd Lieutenant. Died in July 1776. aka Joseph McLemmy.	
Lennihan, John	1st NC Regiment	1781, a Private under Capt. William Lytle for 12 months. Discharged 5/28/1782 (4th NC Regiment).	
Lenoir, James Jr.	8th NC Regiment	11/28/1776, an Ensign under Capt. James May, Jr. Resigned 10/13/1777. From Pitt County, NC. aka James Lenear, James Lanier.	
Leony, Michael	8th NC Regiment	Dec. 1777, a Sergeant Major. Dropped from the rolls in Jan. 1778.	
Leopard, William	2nd NC Regiment	1/82, a Private under Capt. Benjamin Carter for 18 months.	
Lesley, John	2nd NC Regiment	9/1/1782, a Private under Capt. Benjamin Andrew Coleman for 18 months.	
Lester, William	10th NC Regiment	4/24/1777, a Private under Capt. Silas Stevenson. Discharged in April 1778.	
Lethgo, William	1st NC Regiment	4/9/1781, a Private under Capt. Robert Raiford. Died on 4/1/1782 (2nd NC Regiment).	
Lett, James	1st NC Regiment	6/20/1780, a Private under Capt. William Lytle.	Eutaw Springs

Name	1st Unit	Year / Rank / Served Under / Notes	Known Battles
	Regiment	Wounded at the battle of Eutaw Springs, SC on 9/8/1781. S38912.	(SC).
Lewallen, Thomas	2nd NC Regiment	1777, a Private under Capt. Benjamin Williams. Discharged 5/31/1778.	
Lewis, Amos	5th NC Regiment	5/14/1776, a Private under Capt. Reading Blount for 2-1/2 years. Wounded at the battle of Germantown (PA). 9/9/1778, a Private in the Lt. Colonel's Company (Lt. Col. Selby Harney) (2nd NC Regiment). Discharged on 11/4/1778 at West Point, NY. From Edgecombe County, NC. S41767.	Germantown (PA).
Lewis, Benjamin	2nd NC Regiment	4/29/1781, a Private under Capt. Tilghman Dixon. Discharged on 4/25/1782.	
Lewis, Benjamin	4th NC Regiment	1782, a Private under Capt. Thomas Evans. Deserted on 6/8/1783 (?).	
Lewis, Charles	3rd NC Regiment	7/20/1778, a Private under Maj. Thomas Hogg for nine months. Later, a Sergeant in NC Militia. From what is now Rutherford County, NC. W4012.	
Lewis, David	1st NC Regiment	4/12/1781, a Private under Lt./Capt. Benjamin Bailey for 12 months. Discharged on 4/12/1782. aka David Louis.	
Lewis, Edward	10th NC Regiment	5/7/1776, a Private under Capt. Silas Stevenson. 9/9/1778, a known Private under Capt. Clement Hall (2nd NC Regiment). Died in May 1779.	
Lewis, Elisha	10th NC Regiment	6/29/1777, a Private under Capt. Silas Stevenson. One year later, furloughed due to sickness. 9/9/1778, a known Private under Capt. Robert Fenner (2nd NC Regiment). Dropped from the rolls in Feb. 1779. Claims to have been in NC Militia afterwards, but no mention of when or where. Born 1760 in NC. S34961.	
Lewis, Ephraim	3rd NC Regiment	7/20/1778, a Private under Maj. Thomas Hogg for nine months.	
Lewis, Francis	NC Artillery	3/20/1777, a Matross under Capt. John Vance as NC State Troops. 7/10/1777, on Continental Line. 11/16/1777, under Capt. John Kingsbury. 5/1/1778, in same unit. 9/16/1778, in same unit.	
Lewis, Frederick	4th NC Regiment	1781, a Corporal under Capt. George Dougherty for 12 months. Discharged on 5/25/1782.	
Lewis, Hardy	2nd NC Regiment	Jan. 1782, a Private under Capt. Robert Raiford, substituting for the remaining time of James Davison. Discharged 4/15/1782.	
Lewis, Isaac	2nd NC Regiment	Apr. 1782, a Private under Capt. Clement Hall.	
Lewis, Jacob	3rd NC Regiment	7/20/1778, a Private under Capt. John Baker for nine months.	
Lewis, James	3rd NC Regiment	1781, a Private under Capt. Edward Yarborough for 12 months. Discharged on 4/1/1782. Earlier in NC Militia. From Wake County, NC. W5022.	
Lewis, Joel		1779, a Private, regiment and unit unknown.	
Lewis, Joel		1776, an Ensign - regiment unknown. 8/1/1779, a known Lieutenant under Capt. Robert Raiford. Later, a Captain and a Major in NC Militia and	Brandywine Creek (PA), Germantown

Name	1st Unit	Year / Rank / Served Under / Notes	Known Battles
		State Troops. From Surry County, NC. Born 8/28/1760 in Albemarle County, VA.	(PA).
Lewis, John	3rd NC Regiment	7/20/1778, a Private under Lt./Capt. James Montford for 9 months. Then in NC Militia. 1/13/1782, re-enlisted as a Private under Capt. James Mills (1st NC Regiment) for 12 months. From Guilford (what is now Rockingham) County, NC. R6328.	
Lewis, John	3rd NC Regiment	7/20/1778, a Private under Lt./Capt. Joseph Montford.	
Lewis, John	9th NC Regiment	1777, a Private under Capt. Richard D. Cook. Killed on 10/4/1777 at the battle of Germantown, PA.	Germantown (PA).
Lewis, John	10th NC Regiment	8/1/1777, a Private under Silas Stevenson. 9/9/1778, a known Private under Capt. Benjamin Andrew Coleman (2nd NC Regiment). POW at Ft. Lafayette, NY on 6/1/1779.	Ft. Lafayette (NY).
Lewis, Jonathan	3rd NC Regiment	10/5/1781, a Corporal under Capt. Samuel Jones for 12 months. Discharged on 10/1/1782 (1st NC Regiment).	
Lewis, Joseph	8th NC Regiment	11/28/1776, a 2nd Lieutenant under Capt. Robert Raiford.	
Lewis, Joshua	3rd NC Regiment	7/20/1778, a Private in the Lt. Colonel's Company (Lt. Col. William Lee Davidson) led by Lt./Capt. George "Gee" Bradley for nine months. 4/23/1779, a known Private in the Lt. Colonel's Company (Lt. Col. Robert Mebane) led by Capt. George "Gee" Bradley. Died at New Windsor Hospital.	
Lewis, Joshua	3rd NC Regiment	7/1/1779, a Private under Capt. Kedar Ballard. Deserted on 10/29/1779.	
Lewis, Joshua	7th NC Regiment	1777, a Private under Capt. Joseph Walker. Dropped from the rolls in Jan. 1778.	
Lewis, Marshall	1st NC Regiment	1781, a Private under Capt. Alexander Brevard for 12 months. Discharged on 4/28/1782 (3rd NC Regiment).	
Lewis, Marshall	1st NC Regiment	4/20/1781, a Corporal under Capt. Alexander Brevard.	
Lewis, Marshall	5th NC Regiment	6/22/1779, a Private under Maj. Reading Blount. Deserted in Oct. 1779.	
Lewis, Micajah	4th NC Regiment	1774, a 2nd Lieutenant in the Salisbury District Minutemen. 4/17/1776, a 2nd Lieutenant under Capt. Joseph Phillips and Col. Thomas Polk. 7/21/1777, a Captain in the 1st NC Regiment. Transferred back to 4th NC Regiment on 6/1/1778. Furloughed in early 1779. Then, a Captain and a Major in NC Militia. Accepted 1/2 pay on 1/23/1781 to retire. Killed while in Militia service in 1781. Born 1755 in Albemarle County, VA.	Brandywine Creek (PA), Germantown (PA).
Lewis, Morgan	3rd NC Regiment	7/20/1778, enlisted as a Private under Lt./Capt. George "Gee" Bradley, then Capt. Joseph Montford (5th NC Regiment then 1st NC	

Name	1st Unit	Year / Rank / Served Under / Notes	Known Battles
		Regiment) for nine months. Served two years. S41766.	
Lewis, Nathan	3rd NC Regiment	7/20/1778, a Private under Capt. Kedar Ballard for nine months.	
Lewis, Richard	1st NC Regiment	1781, a Private under Capt. Anthony Sharpe for 12 months. Discharged 10/10/1782 (4th NC Regiment).	
Lewis, Richard	1st NC Regiment	6/1/1781, a Sergeant under Capt. William Lytle. Discharged 6/1/1782 (4th NC Regiment).	
Lewis, Thomas	4th NC Regiment	1781, a Private under Capt. Joseph T. Rhodes for 12 months. Discharged 5/16/1782.	
Lewis, W. Samuel	5th NC Regiment	May 1778, a Private under Capt. Benjamin Andrew Coleman. Dropped from the rolls in June 1778.	
Lewis, William	1st NC Regiment	Sep. 1777, a Musician, and June 1778, a Private under Capt. Henry "Hal" Dixon. 9/8/1778, a known Private under Capt. James Read. From Hertford County, NC.	
Lewis, William	3rd NC Regiment	7/20/1778, a Private under Capt. Francis Child for nine months. From Pitt County, NC.	
Lewis, William	7th NC Regiment	12/19/1776, a Musician under Capt. Joseph Walker for three years. A Drum Major in 1779. Discharged in Dec. 1779.	
Lewis, William	10th NC Regiment	1777, a Private under Capt. Abraham Sheppard, Jr. for nine months. 1778, also in NC Militia. From Dobbs County, NC. S8842.	
Lewis, William T.	9th NC Regiment	March 1777, a Lieutenant under Capt. Hezekiah Rice. Dropped from the rolls in Jan. 1778. June 1779, re-enlisted in the 4th NC Regiment under Capt. William Lytle.	
Lewis, Willis	3rd NC Regiment	7/20/1778, a Corporal under Capt. Francis Child for nine months. On the official rolls as Wyllis Lewis. S41768.	
Lezar, James		2/11/1776, a Private, regiment and unit unknown. 6/1/1778, a Private under Capt. Griffith John McRee (1st NC Regiment).	
Ligget, Daniel	5th NC Regiment	1777, a Private under Capt. Henry Darnell. Deserted in Aug. 1777. Rejoined in Jan. 1779.	
Liles, John	2nd NC Regiment	5/12/1781, a Private under Capt. Tilghman Dixon. 7/29/1781, transferred to Lee's Legion.	
Lille, John	2nd NC Regiment	1777, a Private under Capt. James Martin. Deserted on 12/25/1777.	
Lille, Lewis	2nd NC Regiment	5/19/1781, a Private under Capt. Benjamin Carter for 12 months. Discharged on 5/19/1782. From Hertford County, NC. aka Lewis Lilly.	
Lille, Lewis	4th NC Regiment	A Private under Capt. Micajah Lewis. Discharged on 8/13/1779.	
Lilley, Josiah	2nd NC Regiment	11/7/1776 under Lt./Capt. James Martin for three years. 9/9/1778, a known Private under Capt. Benjamin Andrew Coleman. 3/12/1779, re-enlisted under Capt. Benjamin Williams. Promoted to Corporal on 3/1/1780. aka Joseph Lilley, Jossia Lille, Josia Lille.	
Lillington,	1st NC	9/1/1775, a Lieutenant. Resigned in May 1776.	Moore's Creek

Name	1st Unit	Year / Rank / Served Under / Notes	Known Battles
John	Regiment		Bridge [4].
Lillington, John Alexander	6th NC Regiment	1775, Colonel/Commandant of the Wilmington District Minutemen. April 15, 1776, commissioned a Colonel, commander of the 6th NC Regiment. Resigned 12/31/1776 citing ill health. 2/12/1779, a Brigadier General in NC Militia. From New Hanover County, NC.	
Lilly, Isaac	3rd NC Regiment	1781, a Private under Capt. Clement Hall for 12 months. Discharged on 8/16/1782 (2nd NC Regiment).	
Linch, John	2nd NC Regiment	1777, a Sergeant under Capt. James Gee. A Private in Feb. 1778. Transferred to 2nd VA Regiment on 7/1/1779.	
Linch, Thomas	5th NC Regiment	8/10/1779, a Private under Capt. Joseph Montford. Dropped from the rolls in Oct. 1779.	
Lindenham, Isaac	1st NC Regiment	6/20/1780, a Private under Capt. William Lytle for three years. aka Isaac Liddenham.	
Lindon, Patrick	2nd NC Regiment	1782, a Private under Capt. Benjamin Carter for 18 months.	
Lindsey, James	1st NC Regiment	Oct. 1781, a Corporal under Capt. Elijah Moore, then Capt. Alexander Brevard (3rd NC Regiment), then Capt. Joseph T. Rhodes (4th NC Regiment). Furloughed around Nov. 1782 at James Island, SC. Earlier in NC Militia. From Orange County, NC. S10992.	
Lindsey, Walter	4th NC Regiment	6/23/1777, a Private under Capt. William Temple Coles for three years. Deserted on 9/12/1777. 9/8/1778, a known Private under Capt. John Sumner (1st NC Regiment) - sick at Valley Forge on that date. aka Walter Linsey.	
Liner, Thomas	3rd NC Regiment	5/22/1779, a Private under Capt. George "Gee" Bradley for 18 months. Deserted on 10/28/1779. Rejoined in Dec. 1779.	
Link, Paul	1st NC Regiment	5/25/1781, a Private under Capt. Thomas Donoho. Discharged 5/21/1782. aka Paul Sink.	
Linn, Robert	4th NC Regiment	5/19/1776, a Private under Capt. John Nelson. Discharged on 5/16/1779.	
Linnican, John	1st NC Regiment	5/28/1781, a Sergeant under Capt. Alexander Brevard.	
Linton, Hezekiah	2nd NC Regiment	1777, a Private under Capt. Charles Allen. Transferred to His Excy's Guards in April 1778. 9/10/1778, a known Private under Capt. Thomas Armstrong. From what is now Camden County, NC. The four Lintons herein are brothers.	
Linton, Jehu	2nd NC Regiment	1777, a Sergeant under Capt. William Fenner. A Private in Nov. 1777. Died on December 3, 1777 at Valley Forge. From what is now Camden County, NC. aka Theheu Linton. The four Lintons herein are brothers.	
Linton, Jesse	2nd NC Regiment	8/7/1776, a private under Capt. James Martin for three years. Dropped from the rolls in June 1778. Rejoined 11/19/1779. Promoted to Sergeant in March 1780. From what is now Camden County, NC. The four Lintons herein	

Name	1st Unit	Year / Rank / Served Under / Notes	Known Battles
		are brothers.	
Linton, Silas	2nd NC Regiment	8/7/1776, a private under Capt. James Martin. 9/9/1778, under Capt. Benjamin Andrew Coleman. From what is now Camden County, NC. The four Lintons herein are brothers.	
Linton, William Thomas	3rd NC Regiment	1775, an Ensign in the Halifax District Minutemen. 4/17/1776, an Ensign and a 2nd Lieutenant under Capt. Jacob Turner and Capt. William Barret. 4/14/1777, a 1st Lieutenant under Capt. Daniel Jones. 1778, a Captain. Resigned 11/1/1778. 1780, a Lt. Colonel of NC Militia. From Edgecombe/Nash County. Born on 1/8/1758 in Westmoreland County, VA. W8046.	Ft. Moultrie #1 (SC), Brandywine Creek (PA), Germantown (PA), Monmouth (NJ).
Lippincott, William	10th NC Regiment	5/8/1777, a Musician under Capt. Isaac Moore for three years. 9/8/1778, a known Fifer in the Lt. Colonel's Company (Lt. Col. Robert Mebane) (1st NC Regiment) led by Capt. Joshua Bowman. 3/12/1779, re-enlisted for the duration of the war in the same unit. aka William Lippencott.	
Lipscombe, Willis	4th NC Regiment	4/24/1776, a Private under Capt. William Goodman for 2-1/2 years. Discharged on 11/10/1778. aka Wyllis Liscomb.	
Lipscombe, Wilson	4th NC Regiment	4/24/1776, a Private under Capt. William Goodman for 2-1/2 years. 9/8/1778, a known Private in the Colonel's Company (Col. Thomas Clark) (1st NC Regiment) led by Capt. John Gambier Scull. Discharged on 7/31/1779. aka Wilson Liscombe.	
Liscombe, John	6th NC Regiment	4/28/1777, an Ensign under Capt. Daniel Williams. Dropped from the rolls in Jan. 1778.	
Lisk, James	5th NC Regiment	1777, a Private under Capt. John Enloe. Dropped from the rolls in Jan. 1778.	
Litten, Abell	2nd NC Regiment	12/1/1776, a Private under Capt. James Gee for three years. A Musician in Nov. 1777. 9/9/1778, a known Drummer under Capt. John Ingles. A Drum Major on 11/1/1778.	
Litten, Isaac	5th NC Regiment	6/20/1777, a Sergeant under Capt. Reading Blount.	
Litten, Samuel	2nd NC Regiment	12/18/1776, a Private under Capt. James Gee for three years. 9/9/1778, a known Private under Capt. John Ingles. Discharged 1/31/1780. aka Samuel Littin.	
Litter, George	3rd NC Regiment	1781, a Private under Capt. Edward Yarborough for 12 months. Discharged on 4/22/1782.	
Litter, William	3rd NC Regiment	1781, a Private under Capt. Edward Yarborough for 12 months. Discharged on 4/22/1782.	
Little, Guin	1st NC Regiment	1781, a Private under Capt. William Lytle for 12 months. Discharged 4/12/1782 (4th NC Regiment).	
Little, John	2nd NC Regiment	9/25/1776, a Private under Capt. William Fenner. 6/1/1778, a known Private in the Lt. Colonel's Company (Lt. Col. Selby Harney).	

Name	1st Unit	Year / Rank / Served Under / Notes	Known Battles
		Deserted on 8/15/1778.	
Little, John	5th NC Regiment	3/1/1779, a Private under Maj. Reading Blount for nine months. Discharged on 12/1/1779.	
Little, Nathaniel	NC Artillery	1/1/1777, a Matross under Capt. Thomas Clark as NC Provincial Troops. 7/10/1777, on Continental Line. Also on 9/9/1778.	
Little, Thomas	1st NC Regiment	4/15/1781, a Private under Capt. Anthony Sharpe. Dropped from the rolls during 1781.	
Little, William	9th NC Regiment	12/6/1776, an Ensign under Capt. John Rochelle.	
Littleton, William	4th NC Regiment	7/1/1782, a Private for 12 months under Capt. Elijah Moore, Capt. Alexander Brevard (3rd NC Regiment), and Capt. Joseph T. Rhodes (4th NC Regiment). Discharged on 7/1/1783 at Charleston, SC. S38142.	
Lloyd, Thomas	1st NC Regiment	4/19/1781, Lt. Col. John Baptiste Ashe asks HQ for a certificate of commission as a Lieutenant for this man.	
Lock, John	6th NC Regiment	4/25/1776, a Sergeant under Capt. William Glover, then Capt. Daniel Williams for 2-1/2 years. A Private in June 1778 under Capt. Joshua Bowman (1st NC Regiment). 9/8/1778, a known Private in the Lt. Colonel's Company (Lt. Col. Robert Mebane) led by Capt. Joshua Bowman - sick on that date. Discharged 11/18/1778 at King's Ferry, NY. Later in NC Militia. From Granville County, NC. S41782.	
Lock, William	6th NC Regiment	1777, a Private under Capt. Thomas Donoho. Died on 5/22/1778.	
Locke, William	1st NC Regiment	1776, a Private under Capt. Joshua Bowman.	
Lockhart, John	5th NC Regiment	5/24/1779, a Sergeant under Capt. Joseph Montford. A QM Sergeant on 12/15/1779.	
Lockhart, Samuel	3rd NC Regiment	4/15/1776, a Major under Col. Jethro Sumner. Promoted to Lt. Colonel on 10/12/1777 and transferred to 8th NC Regiment. Resigned two weeks after (10/19/1777) the battle of Germantown. One source claims he was a POW at the Fall of Charleston 5/12/1780 (not), while others assert he was a POW at the battle of Camden, SC on 8/16/1780 (yes), as a Militia captain. 1780, a Captain in the Halifax County Regiment - attached his unit under Lt. Col. Charles Porterfield (VA). Another source claims he attached his unit to Maj. John Armstrong - another NC Continental leading part of the NC State Troops. Finally, yet another source claims he did not attach his company to any other leader - he led them on his own.	Brandywine Creek (PA), Germantown (PA).
Lodge, Lewis	5th NC Regiment	10/1/1776, a Private under Capt. Reading Blount. Dropped from the rolls in Feb. 1778. From Edgecombe County, NC.	
Logan, Philip	4th NC Regiment	1777, a Capt. William Temple Coles. Deserted 9/12/1777. Rejoined in January 1779. S38155.	Brandywine Creek (PA).

Name	1st Unit	Year / Rank / Served Under / Notes	Known Battles
Logan, William	1st NC Regiment	12/15/1777, a Private under Capt. Anthony Sharpe for three years. 9/8/1778, a known Private in the Lt. Colonel's Company (Lt. Col. Robert Mebane) led by Capt. Joshua Bowman. 3/12/1779, re-enlisted for the duration of the war in the same unit.	
Lohar, John	3rd NC Regiment	6/20/1779, a Sergeant under Capt. Kedar Ballard for nine months.	
Lollar, John	4th NC Regiment	1782, a Sergeant under Capt. Anthony Sharpe for 18 months.	
Lollard, John	10th NC Regiment	3/18/1778, a Private under Capt. Isaac Moore for three years. 6/1/1778, a Private under Capt. Griffith John McRee (1st NC Regiment).	
Lolley, William	8th NC Regiment	1777, a Private under Capt. Francis Tartanson. Deserted on 8/20/1777.	
Lomack, William	5th NC Regiment	1779, a Private under Maj. Reading Blount. Dropped from the rolls in Nov. 1779. In his pension application (S41783), there are affadavits attesting that this man was in the 2nd NC Regiment under Capt. Anthony Sharpe (who was never in the 2nd), however, Maj. Reading Blount was after 1779.	
Lomax, William	1st NC Regiment	5/9/1781, a Private under Capt. Griffith John McRee, then Capt. Elijah Moore. Discharged on 5/9/1782 (3rd NC Regiment). From Guilford County, NC. W5028.	Siege of Ninety-Six 1781 (SC).
Long, Henry	2nd NC Regiment	1779, a Private under Capt. Benjamin Andrew Coleman for nine months.	
Long, James	1st NC Regiment	1782, a Private under Capt. Peter Bacot for 18 months.	
Long, James	3rd NC Regiment	7/20/1778, a Private under Capt. Kedar Ballard for nine months.	
Long, John	1st NC Regiment	1781, a Private under Capt. Alexander Brevard for 12 months. Discharged on 7/21/1782 (3rd NC Regiment).	
Long, John	7th NC Regiment	1777, a Private under Capt. Thomas Brickell. Died on 2/24/1778.	
Long, Nehemiah	5th NC Regiment	1775, a 2nd Lieutenant in the Edenton District Minutemen. 4/17/1776, a 2nd Lieutenant under Capt. Peter Simon and Col. Edward Buncombe. 10/1/1776, a Lieutenant under Capt. Reading Blount. Dropped from the rolls in Jan. 1778.	
Long, Nicholas	DQMG	1775, the Colonel/Commandant of the Halifax District Minutemen. 5/7/1776, appointed as Deputy Quartermaster General (DQMG) for the Southern Department. His HQ was at Halifax, NC. Retained this position until the end of the war.	
Long, William	2nd NC Regiment	Apr. 1782, a Private under Capt. Clement Hall. A Corporal on 11/1/1782. S18953.	
Loomis, Abner	8th NC Regiment	2/8/1777, an Ensign under Capt. Simon Jones. 8/27/1777, a 2nd Lieutenant. Resigned on 11/15/1777.	
Loomis,	8th NC	11/26/1776, a Surgeon. Transferred to 3rd NC	

Name	1st Unit	Year / Rank / Served Under / Notes	Known Battles
Jonathan	Regiment	Regiment on 6/1/1778. POW at the Fall of Charleston, paroled, then exchanged 6/14/1781. Served to the end of the war in the 3rd NC Regiment. Resigned 8/19/1782. aka Jonathan Lumos, Lumas.	
Lorain, Henry	4th NC Regiment	1777, a Sergeant under Capt. James Williams. A Corporal in June 1778. Died on 7/13/1778.	
Lord, William	1st NC Regiment	12/11/1776, a Paymaster. Resigned on 2/28/1777. 8/1/1779, a Lieutenant under Capt. Thomas White (5th NC Regiment).	Stono Ferry (SC) (?).
Lord, William	5th NC Regiment	1779, a Private under Maj. Pinketham Eaton.	
Lote, George	1st NC Regiment	1777, a Private under Capt. Joshua Bowman.	
Lott, George	6th NC Regiment	12/22/1776, a Private under Capt. George Dougherty. 9/8/1778, a known Private under Capt. Tilghman Dixon (1st NC Regiment).	
Lott, Job	5th NC Regiment	1777, a Private under Capt. John Pugh Williams. Died in June 1777.	
Loughry, William	1st NC Regiment	1775, a Private under Capt. Robert Rowan. 1777, a Private in the 10th NC Regiment, unit unknown. From Bladen (what is now Robeson) County, NC. W8263.	
Love, Amos	6th NC Regiment	1775, a 1st Lieutenant in the Salisbury District Minutemen. Lived in the Wilmington District. 4/17/1776, a Lieutenant under Capt. George Mitchell and Col. John Alexander Lillington. Resigned in June 1776.	
Love, David	NC Brigade	8/18/1779 to 8/1/1781, a Surgeon. A Prisoner at some time.	
Love, Edmund	2nd NC Regiment	10/15/1775, a Private under Capt. James Blount. Living in Currituck County, NC when he enlisted. Later in VA units. Born on 6/1/1760 in Pasquotank County, NC. S4563.	
Love, Samuel	3rd NC Regiment	3/8/1781, a Private under Capt. Samuel Jones for 12 months. Discharged on 3/1/1782.	
Love, Thomas	7th NC Regiment	3/20/1777, a Private under Capt. John Poynter. 9/8/1778, a known Private under Capt. Tilghman Dixon (1st NC Regiment). POW at the Fall of Charleston, paroled after 14 months at Jamestown, VA. Enlisted in Camden County, NC. S36048.	Germantown (PA), Brandywine Creek (PA), Siege of Charleston 1780 (SC).
Love, Thomas	10th NC Regiment	6/20/1777, a Private under Capt. Isaac Moore. 9/8/1778, a known Private under Capt. James Read (1st NC Regiment).	
Lovell, John	3rd NC Regiment	6/29/1779, a Private under Capt. Kedar Ballard. Deserted on 11/14/1779.	
Lovell, William	5th NC Regiment	6/5/1779, a Private under Capt. Reading Blount. Deserted in Oct. 1779.	
Lovesy, Boling	4th NC Regiment	1782, a Private under Capt. Thomas Evans. Jan. 1783, transferred - to where unknown.	
Lovet, Moses	3rd NC Regiment	7/20/1778, a Private under Lt./Capt. George "Gee" Bradley for nine months.	

481

Name	1st Unit	Year / Rank / Served Under / Notes	Known Battles
Lovett, John	6th NC Regiment	1776, a Private under Capt. George Mitchell for 2-1/2 years. From Carteret County, NC. R20398.	
Lovin, Arthur	2nd NC Regiment	4/24/1781, a Private under Capt. Tilghman Dixon. Deserted on 7/15/1781.	
Loving, John	3rd NC Regiment	1782, a Private under Capt. Alexander Brevard. Deserted on 6/23/1783.	
Low, Abraham	5th NC Regiment	5/10/1779, a Private under Maj. Reading Blount for 18 months.	
Low, Christopher	1st NC Regiment	2/26/1778, a known Private under Capt. Howell Tatum.	
Low, George	2nd NC Regiment	1777, a Private under Capt. Edward Vail, Jr. Deserted on 8/15/1779.	
Low, Richard	10th NC Regiment	A Private under Capt. Isaac Moore. Discharged on 6/14/1778.	
Low, Thomas	4th NC Regiment	1782, a Private under Capt. Anthony Sharpe for 18 months.	
Low, William	2nd NC Regiment	1779, a Private under Capt. Benjamin Andrew Coleman for 3 years.	
Low, William	4th NC Regiment	4/21/1776, a Musician under Capt. Micajah Lewis. 9/8/1778, a known Musician in the Colonel's Company (Thomas Clark - 1st NC Regiment) led by Capt. John Gambier Scull. Discharged on 5/1/1779. aka William Lowe.	
Lowe, James	3rd NC Regiment	1779, a Private under Capt. Michael Quinn.	
Lowe, John Sr.	10th NC Regiment	4/19/1777, a 2nd Lieutenant under Capt. James Wilson. Dropped from the rolls in Jan. 1778. He states that he resigned in the Fall of 1778 due to extended bad health. From Caswell County, NC. aka John Low. S38916.	
Lowe, Philip	2nd NC Regiment	9/1/1775, an Ensign. 5/2/1776, a 1st Lieutenant under Capt. John Herritage. Resigned 2/1/1777. Then, a Major and Lt. Col. in GA. Retired 10/1/1780.	
Lowry, Samuel	2nd NC Regiment	A Private under Capt. William Knox for six months. Later in NC Militia. From Rowan County, NC. R6495.	Great Cane Brake (SC), Snow Campaign (SC).
Loyd, Burrell	5th NC Regiment	1777, a Private under Capt. Henry Darnell. 9/9/1778, under Capt. Benjamin Andrew Coleman (2nd NC Regiment). Dropped from the rolls in Feb. 1779.	
Loyd, Henry	3rd NC Regiment	7/20/1778, a Private under Capt. Francis Child for nine months.	
Loyd, Jesse	3rd NC Regiment	7/20/1778, a Private under Capt. Francis Child for nine months.	
Loyd, Leonard	4th NC Regiment	1777, a Private under Capt. Joseph Phillips. Dropped from the rolls in Jan. 1778.	
Loyd, Thomas	6th NC Regiment	1777, a Sergeant under Capt. Thomas Donoho. Dropped from the rolls in Jan. 1778.	
Lucas, Ambrose	10th NC Regiment	4/14/1776, a Private, unit unknown. 1777, a Private under Capt. Isaac Moore. 9/8/1778, a known Private under Capt. James Read (1st NC	

Name	1st Unit	Year / Rank / Served Under / Notes	Known Battles
		Regiment). 3/12/1779, re-enlisted for the duration of the war in the same unit. Deserted on 2/1/1780.	
Lucas, Arthur	3rd NC Regiment	7/20/1778, a Private under Capt. John Baker for nine months.	
Lucas, Billing	5th NC Regiment	1779, a Private under Maj. Reading Blount. Died on 9/5/1779.	
Lucas, Charles	3rd NC Regiment	7/20/1778, a Private under Capt. John Baker for nine months.	
Lucas, David		An Adjutant killed at Germantown. Unit unknown.	Germantown (PA).
Lucas, Edward	1st NC Regiment	1777, a Private under Capt. Henry "Hal" Dixon. Deserted on 2/18/1778. Re-enlisted in 2nd NC Regiment in June 1778. 9/9/1778, under Capt. Benjamin Andrew Coleman (2nd NC Regiment). Dropped from the rolls in Feb. 1779.	
Lucas, Famoth	3rd NC Regiment	7/20/1778, a Private under Lt./Capt. Joseph Montford for nine months.	
Lucas, Matthew	5th NC Regiment	1777, a Private under Capt. Benjamin Andrew Coleman. Killed at the battle of Germantown, PA on 10/4/1777.	Germantown (PA).
Lucas, Richard	3rd NC Regiment	7/20/1778, a Private under Capt. Michael Quinn for nine months.	
Lucas, Thomas	3rd NC Regiment	1781, a Private under Capt. Edward Yarborough for 12 months. Discharged on 4/1/1782.	
Lucas, Thomas	4th NC Regiment	1782, a Private under Capt. Thomas Evans. Jan. 1783, transferred - to where unknown.	
Lucas, Valentine	3rd NC Regiment	4/22/1776, a Private under Capt. James Emmett. 9/9/1778, a known Private in the Lt. Colonel's Company (Lt. Col. Selby Harney) (2nd NC Regiment). Discharged in Oct. 1778. From Granville County, NC. aka Valentine Locus. W20497.	Ft. Moultrie #1 (SC).
Lucey, Isom	3rd NC Regiment	1777, a Private under Capt. James Emmett for 2-1/2 years.	
Luck, Paul	1st NC Regiment	1781, a Private under Capt. Thomas Donoho.	
Lucy, Burwell	DQMG	1780, a Wagoner under Col. Nicholas Long (Deputy QM General). Said to be an ex-Continental soldier (?).	
Lucy, Frederick	1st NC Regiment	1777, a Private under Capt. Howell Tatum. 9/8/1778, a known Private under Capt. Howell Tatum. aka Frederick Lucey.	
Ludwick, Lewis	3rd NC Regiment	1782, a Private under Capt. Alexander Brevard for 18 months.	
Lufman, John	4th NC Regiment	7/30/1776, a Private under Capt. William Goodman for three years. 9/8/1778, a known Private in the Colonel's Company (Col. Thomas Clark) (1st NC Regiment) led by Capt. John Gambier Scull. POW in 1779 for about 9 months - taken between Charleston and Savannah. Discharged on 8/21/1779 at Constitution Island, NY. aka John Luffman. S42901.	Brandywine Creek (PA), Monmouth (NJ), Stony Point (NY).

Name	1st Unit	Year / Rank / Served Under / Notes	Known Battles
Lumberly, Simon	7th NC Regiment	3/13/1777, a Private under Capt. James Vaughan. 2/26/1778, a known Private under Capt. Howell Tatum (1st NC Regiment). Died in Feb. 1778.	
Luten, Lemuel	7th NC Regiment	1777, a Corporal under Capt. John McGlaughan. Died in Sep. 1777.	
Luton, James	2nd NC Regiment	4/1/1777, an Ensign under Capt. Benjamin Williams. 10/4/1777, a 2nd Lieutenant under Capt. Benjamin Williams. Resigned on 3/3/1778. One source says 3/10/1778. Another source says 2/28/1778.	
Luttrell, John	9th NC Regiment	11/27/1776, a Lt. Colonel under Col. John Williams. 9/1/1777, left behind in NC to supervise all Continental recruiting in the state. Resigned in writing on 1/10/1778. Later, a Lt. Colonel and full Colonel in the Chatham County Regiment of Militia. aka John Lutzell.	
Lutts, John	10th NC Regiment	5/25/1777, a Private under Capt. John Jarvis for three years. A Corporal in June 1778. 9/8/1778, a known Corporal under Maj. John Baptiste Ashe (1st NC Regiment). Died 11/10/1778. aka John Luts.	
Lye, John	1st NC Regiment	4/28/1781, a Private under Capt. Alexander Brevard.	
Lyerly, Christopher	1st NC Regiment	4/28/1781, a Private under Capt. Griffith John McRee. Discharged on 4/28/1782 (3rd NC Regiment).	
Lynch, John	2nd NC Regiment	9/9/1778, a known Private under Capt. John Ingles.	
Lynch, John	7th NC Regiment	11/28/1776, an Ensign under Capt. Green Bell, then under Capt. Lemuel Ely. Also a Lieutenant under Capt. Lemuel Ely. Dropped from the rolls in Nov. 1778. From Bute County, NC. aka John Linch.	
Lynch, Joshua	5th NC Regiment	Spring of 1776, a Private under Capt. William Caswell for 12 months. Earlier and later in NC Militia. From Johnston County, NC. S4179	
Lynch, Lawrence	1st NC Regiment	1777, a Private under Capt. Howell Tatum. 2/26/1778, a known Private under Capt. Howell Tatum. 9/8/1778, a known Private under Capt. Howell Tatum. aka Lawrence Linch.	
Lynn, Robert		5/16/1776, a Private, regiment and unit unknown, enlisted for three years. 6/1/1778, a Private under Capt. Griffith John McRee (1st NC Regiment). Discharged on 5/15/1779.	
Lynn, Stephen	NC Artillery	11/25/1776, a Sergeant under Capt. John Vance as NC Provincial Troops. 7/10/1777, placed on Continental Line. 11/16/1777, under Capt. John Kingsbury. 5/1/1778, in same unit. 9/16/1778, in same unit. aka Stephen Lin, Stephen Linn.	
Lyon, William	4th NC Regiment	1781, a Private under Capt. William Lytle for 18 months. Discharged at 10-Mile House, SC. S31829.	Eutaw Springs (SC).
Lytle,	6th NC	1775, a Captain in the Hillsborough District	Brandywine

Name	1st Unit	Year / Rank / Served Under / Notes	Known Battles
Archibald	Regiment	Minutemen. 4/17/1776, a Captain in 6th NC Regiment. 1/26/1777, a Lt. Colonel in 6th NC Regiment, replaced Lt. Col. William Taylor, who resigned. Sent home in Jan. 1778 to recruit new men. Wounded at the battle of Stono Ferry (SC). Little known between mid-1779 and 1781. 1782, commanded the 4th NC Regiment. One source claims he was a full Colonel on 9/30/1783. From Orange County, NC. aka Archibald Lyttle, Anthony Lytle.	Creek (PA), Germantown (PA), Briar Creek (GA), Stono Ferry (SC), Hillsborough (POW-exchanged 2/9/1782).
Lytle, Micajah	5th NC Regiment	5/3/1776, a Lieutenant under Capt. William Brinkley then under Capt. John Enloe on 5/6/1776. Earlier in 1776, a Captain of NC Militia. From Martin County, NC. aka Micajah Little.	
Lytle, William	6th NC Regiment	1775, an Ensign in the Hillsborough District Minutemen. 4/17/1776, an Ensign under Capt. Archibald Lytle and Col. John Alexander Lillington. 6/6/1776, a 2nd Lieutenant under Capt. Philip Taylor and then under Capt. Archibald Lytle. 6/1/1778, in the "New Levies." A Captain on 1/28/1779. Some sources assert he was in the 3rd NC Regiment during 1779 (wrong). Late 1779, placed into 1st NC Regiment. At Guilford Court House under Maj. Reading Blount - in what was called the NC Regiment. Transferred to 4th NC Regiment 2/6/1782. Served until the end of the war. aka William Little. S46228.	Briar Creek (GA), Stono Ferry (SC), Siege of Savannah (GA), Guilford Court House, Siege of Augusta (GA), Siege of Ninety-Six 1781 (SC), Eutaw Springs (SC).
Mabry, Benjamin	1st NC Regiment	4/12/1781, a Private under Capt. William Lytle. Discharged on 4/12/1782 (4th NC Regiment). aka Benjamin Mabury, Benjamin Maberry. S38926.	
Mabry, John	1st NC Regiment	5/5/1781, a Private under Capt. Robert Raiford. 8/31/1781, transferred to Lt. Col. Henry "Light Horse Harry" Lee's Legion (VA). Earlier in NC Militia. From Franklin County, NC. S13832.	
Mabry, Philip	4th NC Regiment	1782, a Private under Capt. Anthony Sharpe. Deserted on 4/30/1783 (?). aka Philip Maybry.	
MacLean, William	1st NC Regiment	A Surgeon's Mate from 1779 to 1783. aka William MacLaine, aka William McLane. W3572.	
Macon, John	7th NC Regiment	11/28/1776, a 1st Lieutenant under Capt. Bennett Wood. Promoted to Captain on 12/11/1776, when Bennett Wood refused his commission. Retired 6/1/1778. 1780, a Captain in NC Militia. From Bute (would become Warren) County, NC. aka John Mason.	
Madara, John	2nd NC Regiment	5/18/1781, a Private under Capt. Tilghman Dixon. Discharged on 1/18/1782.	
Maddin, Bryan	8th NC Regiment	6/16/1777, a Private under Capt. Robert Raiford. Dropped from the rolls in Jan. 1778.	
Maddry, Bryan	3rd NC Regiment	7/20/1778, a Private under Maj. Thomas Hogg for nine months. Dropped from the rolls in Oct.	

Name	1ˢᵗ Unit	Year / Rank / Served Under / Notes	Known Battles
		1778.	
Maddry, Darling	2ⁿᵈ NC Regiment	4/26/1776, a Private, unit unknown for 2-1/2 years. 9/9/1778, a known Private under Capt. John Ingles. Discharged on 11/10/1778. 1782, a Sergeant under Capt. Benjamin Carter for 18 months. aka Darlin Mardray, Darling Madree.	
Maddry, John	5ᵗʰ NC Regiment	5/13/1776, a Corporal under Capt. John Pugh Williams for 2-1/2 years. Discharged on 11/13/1778. Possibly the same man as directly below.	
Madry, John	3ʳᵈ NC Regiment	6/6/1779, a Private under Capt. Michael Quinn for nine months. Discharged in Dec. 1779.	
Magell, Edward	2ⁿᵈ NC Regiment	7/28/1777, a Private, unit unknown. 9/9/1778, a known Private under Capt. Benjamin Andrew Coleman. 3/12/1779, re-enlisted under Capt. Benjamin Andrew Coleman. aka Edward Majett.	
Mahaney, William	4ᵗʰ NC Regiment	7/28/1776, a Private under Capt. William Goodman for three years. Discharged on 7/28/1779.	
Maines, William	1ˢᵗ NC Regiment	7/28/1776, a Private, unit unknown. 9/8/1778, a known Private in the Colonel's Company (Col. Thomas Clark) led by Capt. John Gambier Scull.	
Mainor, Josiah	4ᵗʰ NC Regiment	1781, a Private under Capt. George Dougherty. Discharged on 5/25/1782 at Wilmington, NC. Enlisted at Duplin Court House. aka Josiah Mainer. S41801.	
Mains, Samuel	2ⁿᵈ NC Regiment	1776, a Private under Capt. James Blount for six months. 5/5/1777, a Sergeant under Capt. John Jarvis (10th NC Regiment) for three years. A Corporal in June 1778. 9/8/1778, a known Corporal under Maj. John Baptiste Ashe (1st NC Regiment). POW at the Fall of Charleston. On some rolls as Samuel Mahans. aka Samuel Maines. S38163.	Monmouth (NJ), Siege of Charleston 1780 (SC).
Mallet, Daniel	4ᵗʰ NC Regiment	12/16/1776, a Commissary.	
Mallet, Peter	6ᵗʰ NC Regiment	4/23/1776, a Commissary. Transferred to the 4th NC Regiment on 12/16/1776. Transferred to 5th NC Regiment on 4/23/1777. Retired on 6/1/1778.	
Mallison, John	9ᵗʰ NC Regiment	1777, a Private under Capt. Richard D. Cook. A Sergeant in Nov. 1777. Dropped from the rolls in Jan. 1778.	
Mallot, Jacob	3ʳᵈ NC Regiment	1782, a Private under Capt. Alexander Brevard for 18 months.	
Malone, Isaac	3ʳᵈ NC Regiment	Feb. 1780, a Private under Capt. Kedar Ballard.	
Malphus, Henry	2ⁿᵈ NC Regiment	3/1/1782, a Private under Capt. Clement Hall for 12 months.	
Maltimore, William	3ʳᵈ NC Regiment	6/10/1779, a Private under Capt. George "Gee" Bradley for 18 months.	
Manchester,	1ˢᵗ NC	1777, a Fifer under Capt. John Brown.	

Name	1st Unit	Year / Rank / Served Under / Notes	Known Battles
Isaac	Regiment	9/8/1778, a known Private under Capt. Joshua Bowman. Deserted on 5/21/1779.	
Manders, William	2nd NC Regiment	1782, a Private under Capt. Benjamin Carter for 18 months.	
Mandley, William	2nd NC Regiment	Jan. 1779, a Private under Capt. Clement Hall.	
Manewell, Jesse	3rd NC Regiment	7/15/1782, a Private under Capt. Benjamin Bailey for 12 months.	
Manis, Frederick	4th NC Regiment	1782, a Private under Capt. Anthony Sharpe for 18 months.	
Manley, Allen	1st NC Regiment	1781, a Private under Capt. William Armstrong. Discharged on 4/1/1782 (3rd NC Regiment). One source claims his first name was Adam.	
Manley, Littleton	4th NC Regiment	1782, a Private under Capt. William Lytle for 18 months.	
Manley, Moses	3rd NC Regiment	9/7/1782, a Private under Capt. Benjamin Bailey for 18 months.	
Manly, Moses	1st NC Regiment	5/2/1781, a Private under Capt. Thomas Donoho, then under Capt. William Walton, then under Capt. Peter Bacot. Discharged on 5/2/1782 at Charleston, SC. From Hertford County, NC. aka Moses Manley. S41796.	
Manly, Southey	3rd NC Regiment	7/20/1778, a Private in the Lt. Colonel's Company (Lt. Col. William Lee Davidson) led by Lt./Capt. George "Gee" Bradley for nine months. 4/23/1779, a known Private in the Lt. Colonel's Company (Lt. Col. Robert Mebane) led by Capt. George "Gee" Bradley. From Hertford County, NC. aka Southam Manley, Sothey Manley.	
Mann, John	1st NC Regiment	5/25/1781, a Private under Capt. Robert Raiford. Discharged on 5/25/1782 (2nd NC Regiment).	
Mann, John	2nd NC Regiment	June 1778, a Private under Capt. Clement Hall then Capt. Robert Fenner. Dropped from the rolls in Feb 1779. aka John Man.	
Mann, Thomas	7th NC Regiment	12/18/1776, a Private under Capt. Joseph Walker for three years. 9/8/1778, a known Private under Capt. Tilghman Dixon (1st NC Regiment). 3/12/1779, re-enlisted for the duration of the war in the same unit. A Corporal later in March 1779. Deserted on 2/14/1780. aka Thomas Maun.	
Manning, Charles	7th NC Regiment	1/3/1777, a Private under Capt. James Vaughan. Deserted on 9/12/1777. aka Charles Mauning.	
Manning, John	2nd NC Regiment	1782, a Private under Capt. Benjamin Carter for 18 months. From Martin County, NC. R6877.	
Manning, John	3rd NC Regiment	7/20/1778, a Private under Lt./Capt. George "Gee" Bradley for nine months.	
Manning, Thomas	3rd NC Regiment	7/20/1778, a Private under Lt./Capt. Joseph Montford for nine months.	
Manning, Timothy	3rd NC Regiment	1777, a Private under Capt. Thomas Granbury.	
Manning,	4th NC	1782, a Private under Capt. Anthony Sharpe for	

487

Name	1st Unit	Year / Rank / Served Under / Notes	Known Battles
William	Regiment	18 months. Deserted on 2/27/1783 (?).	
Manora, Nicholas	4th NC Regiment	1777, a Private under Capt. Thomas Harris. Deserted on 6/6/1777.	
Manuel, Jesse	3rd NC Regiment	7/15/1782, a Private under Capt. Benjamin Bailey for 12 months. Jan. 1783, furloughed at Washington, NC. S41808.	
Maples, Marmaduke	8th NC Regiment	Jan. 1777, a Private under Capt. John Walsh, then Capt. Frederick Hargett, then Capt. Francis Tartanson (3rd NC Regiment). 6/7/1777, a Private under Capt. Robert Fenner (2nd NC Regiment). 9/9/1778, a known Private under Capt. Clement Hall (2nd NC Regiment). A Corporal in Jan. 1779. 3/12/1779, re-enlisted under Capt. Clement Hall. POW at the Fall of Charleston (SC), held 15 months - upon his return to NC, was taken prisoner on 9/12/1781 at Hillsborough by Loyalists, paroled. Then, under Capt. James Pearl (1st NC Regiment) until the end of the war. Enlisted at Cumberland County, NC. S41802.	Brandywine Creek (PA), Germantown (PA), Monmouth (NJ), Siege of Charleston 1780 (SC), Hillsborough.
March, Barnet	1st NC Regiment	5/19/1781, a Private under Capt. Robert Raiford. Discharged on 5/19/1782 (2nd NC Regiment).	
Mardsay, John	2nd NC Regiment	5/13/1776, a Corporal, unit unknown. 9/9/1778, a known Corporal in the Major's Company (Maj. Hardy Murfree).	
Marion, Philip	1st NC Regiment	9/8/1778, a known Private under Capt. James Read - sick with Yellow Fever at that time. aka Phillip Marrian.	
Marley, William	4th NC Regiment	1782, a Private under Capt. William Lytle for 18 months.	
Marlin, Michael	4th NC Regiment	1782, a Private under Capt. Anthony Sharpe for 18 months. Deserted on 5/26/1783 (?).	
Marlow, Dempsey	2nd NC Regiment	7/1/1777, a Private under Capt. Robert Fenner. 9/9/1778, a known Private under Capt. Clement Hall. 3/12/1779, re-enlisted under Capt. Clement Hall.	
Marlow, Robert	1st NC Regiment	5/20/1781, a Private under Capt. Griffith John McRee. Deserted on 5/28/1781. Jan. 1782, re-enlisted (3rd NC Regiment). Deserted again in June 1783 (?).	
Maroney, Anthony	2nd NC Regiment	2/15/1782, a Private under Capt. Benjamin Andrew Coleman for 12 months.	
Marr, John	NC Light Dragoons	Feb. or March 1777, a Private under Capt. Cosmo Medici for 18 months. Discharged in the Fall of 1778 at Halifax, NC. From Wake County, NC. S41798.	
Marsh, John	1st NC Regiment	8/2/1777, found guilty of desertion in a court-martial and sentenced to be shot to death.	
Marshall, Adam	1st NC Regiment	5/4/1781, a Private under Capt. Robert Raiford. Discharged on 5/4/1782 (2nd NC Regiment).	
Marshall, Dixon	1st NC Regiment	Dec. 1775, a Cadet. 3/28/1777, an Ensign under Capt. Henry "Hal" Dixon, then under Capt. Lawrence Thompson. 4/26/1777, a 2nd	Monmouth (NJ), Siege of Charleston

Name	1st Unit	Year / Rank / Served Under / Notes	Known Battles
		Lieutenant under Capt. John Brown. 9/8/1778, under Capt. Howell Tatum. Promoted to 1st Lieutenant on July 4, 1779 under Capt. Tilghman Dixon. POW at the Fall of Charleston, exchanged 6/14/1781. Retired 1/1/1783. S38921.	1780 (SC).
Marshall, Emanuel	1st NC Regiment	Mar. 1778, a Private under Capt. Howell Tatum. Died on 4/5/1778.	
Marshall, George	3rd NC Regiment	4/22/1776, a Private under Capt. Pinketham Eaton. 9/10/1778, a known Private under Capt. Thomas Armstrong (2nd NC Regiment). Deserted on 7/10/1779.	
Marshall, Robert	2nd NC Regiment	1777, a Private under Capt. Benjamin Williams. Deserted in Aug. 1777.	
Marshall, Willis	1st NC Regiment	1/16/1777, a Sergeant under Capt. Henry "Hal" Dixon. 9/8/1778, a known Sergeant under Capt. Tilghman Dixon. A Private in Nov. 1778. Dropped from the rolls in May 1779. aka Wyllis Marshall.	
Martin, Abraham	1st NC Regiment	5/25/1781, a Private under Capt. Griffith John McRee. Discharged 4/28/1782 (3rd NC Regiment).	
Martin, Absalom	1st NC Regiment	4/25/1781, a Private under Capt. Griffith John McRee for 12 months. Enlisted at Beaufort, NC. 4/28/1782, discharged at Wilmington, NC. From Carteret County, NC. S41800.	Eutaw Springs (SC).
Martin, Alexander	2nd NC Regiment	9/1/1775, a Lt. Colonel under Col. Robert Howe. 4/10/1776, a full Colonel. Resigned Nov. 22, 1777 after being cleared of all charges stemming from the battle of Brandywine Creek, PA. 1782, elected the 4th Governor of NC.	Great Cane Brake (SC), Snow Campaign (SC), Ft. Moultrie #1 (SC), Brandywine Creek (PA), Germantown (PA)
Martin, Andrew	6th NC Regiment	June 1776, a Private under Capt. John Baptiste Ashe. Later in NC Militia. From Guilford County, NC. S11029.	
Martin, Archibald	4th NC Regiment	1777, a Private under Capt. Robert Smith. Dropped from the rolls in Sep. 1777.	
Martin, Gabriel	3rd NC Regiment	9/17/1782, a Private under Capt. Benjamin Bailey for 18 months.	
Martin, Henry	2nd NC Regiment	1775, a Private under Capt. Simon Bright. 11/7/1776, a Corporal under Lt./Capt. Clement Hall. Back to Private in June 1778. 3/12/1779, re-enlisted under Capt. Benjamin Williams. Enlisted in Dobbs County, NC. S41791.	Ft. Moultrie #1 (SC), Brandywine Creek (PA), Germantown (PA), Monmouth (NJ), Stony Point (NY), Siege of Charleston

Name	1st Unit	Year / Rank / Served Under / Notes	Known Battles
			1780 (SC), Guilford Court House.
Martin, James	1st NC Regiment	1781, a Private under Capt. Anthony Sharpe. Discharged on 4/12/1782 (4th NC Regiment).	
Martin, James	2nd NC Regiment	1775, an Ensign under Capt. James Blount. 5/3/1776, a Lieutenant under Capt. Charles Crawford. 4/20/1777, a Captain. Retired on 6/1/1778. One source claims he was transferred to the 5th NC Regiment.	
Martin, James	5th NC Regiment	7/15/1776, a Musician under Capt. John Pugh Williams for 2-1/2 years. A Private in Jan. 1778. 9/9/1778, a known Private under Capt. Clement Hall (2nd NC Regiment). Discharged on 11/10/1778.	
Martin, James	10th NC Regiment	8/4/1777, a Sergeant under Capt. William Shepherd.	
Martin, James	10th NC Regiment	5/4/1777, a Private under Capt. Abraham Sheppard, Jr. for three years. 9/9/1778, a known Private under Capt. Clement Hall (2nd NC Regiment). POW at the Fall of Charleston, escaped after two months. Enlisted in Dobbs County, NC. S38164.	Siege of Charleston 1780 (SC).
Martin, Jesse	1st NC Regiment	8/10/1782, a Private under Capt. Joshua Hadley for 18 months.	
Martin, Joel	1st NC Regiment	1777, a Private under Capt. Joshua Bowman.	
Martin, Joel	1st NC Regiment	1777, a Private under Capt. Lawrence Thompson. Dropped from the rolls in Aug. 1778.	
Martin, Joel	8th NC Regiment	1777, a Private under Capt. Francis Tartanson. Dropped from the rolls in Sep. 1777.	
Martin, John	1st NC Regiment	6/11/1781, a Private under Capt. William Lytle.	
Martin, Joshua	1st NC Regiment	4/15/1781, a Private under Capt. Anthony Sharpe. Dead or deserted on 1/31/1782.	
Martin, Joshua	4th NC Regiment	5/1/1776, a Private under Captain John Nelson for three years. 9/8/1778, a known Private under Capt. Griffith John McRee (1st NC Regiment) - sick on that date at Valley Forge. Discharged on 7/31/1779 near Albany, NY. From Guilford County, NC. S41793.	
Martin, Michael	4th NC Regiment	1782, a Private under Capt. Anthony Sharpe. Deserted on 5/26/1783 (?).	
Martin, Richard	1st NC Regiment	8/8/1776, a Private in the Colonel's Company (Col. Thomas Clark). Discharged on 4/1/1779.	
Martin, Richard	4th NC Regiment	5/7/1776, a Private under Capt. Roger Moore, then under Capt. William Goodman for 2-1/2 years. 9/8/1778, a known Private in the Colonel's Company (Col. Thomas Clark) (1st NC Regiment) led by Capt. John Gambier Scull. Discharged on 11/10/1778 at Kings Ferry on North River (NY). From Caswell County, NC. Born 1/29/1755. R6944A.	Brandywine Creek (PA), Germantown (PA), Monmouth (NJ).

Name	1ˢᵗ Unit	Year / Rank / Served Under / Notes	Known Battles
Martin, Richard	4ᵗʰ NC Regiment	1777, a Private under Capt. Thomas Harris. 9/8/1778, a known Private under Capt. John Sumner (1st NC Regiment). 5/11/1779, a known Private under Capt. John Sumner (1st NC Regiment) - probably discharged on that date.	
Martin, Robert	1ˢᵗ NC Regiment	A Private under Capt. Henry "Hal" Dixon for six months, re-enlisted for 12 months, re-enlisted for three years. Enlisted in Caswell County, NC. Discharged at Halifax, NC. Later in NC Militia, unit(s) unknown. W1907.	Monmouth (NJ).
Martin, Robert	1ˢᵗ NC Regiment	12/13/1776, a Corporal under Capt. Henry "Hal" Dixon. 9/8/1778, a Corporal under Capt. James Read. Discharged on 2/1/1780.	
Martin, Robert	1ˢᵗ NC Regiment	4/28/1781, a Sergeant under Capt. Alexander Brevard.	
Martin, Samuel	6ᵗʰ NC Regiment	6/6/1776, a 2nd Lieutenant under Capt. George Mitchell. 6/8/1776, a 1st Lieutenant under Capt. James Gee, then Capt. Benjamin Williams (2nd NC Regiment). June of 1780, a Captain mostly recruiting new men. Retired in mid-1781. Earlier in NC Militia.	Ft. Moultrie #1 (SC), Kings Mountain (SC), Cowpens (SC).
Martin, William	5ᵗʰ NC Regiment	1779, a Private under Maj. Reading Blount for nine months. Discharged on 12/1/1779.	
Martin, William	10ᵗʰ NC Regiment	5/18/1777, a Private under Capt. Abraham Sheppard, Jr.	
Marton, Jacob	3ʳᵈ NC Regiment	1779, a Private under Capt. Kedar Ballard.	
Mascal, James	1ˢᵗ NC Regiment	4/28/1781, a Private under Capt. Alexander Brevard. Deserted on 6/18/1781.	
Mash, Ely	1ˢᵗ NC Regiment	1777, a Private under Capt. Joshua Bowman. Deserted in Aug. 1777.	
Mash, John	1ˢᵗ NC Regiment	1777, a Private under Capt. Howell Tatum. Under sentence in Aug. 1777. Probably same man as directly below.	
Mash, John	1ˢᵗ NC Regiment	A Private under Capt. Joshua Bowman. Deserted in Aug. 1777.	
Mashborne, Edward	8ᵗʰ NC Regiment	2/9/1777, a Private under Capt. Robert Raiford for 3 years. Dropped from the rolls in Feb. 1778.	
Mashburn, William	2ⁿᵈ NC Regiment	5/19/1781, a Private under Capt. Benjamin Carter. Discharged on 5/19/1782.	
Mason, Caleb	2ⁿᵈ NC Regiment	Sep. 1775, a Private under Capt. Hardy Murfree for six months. Discharged in March 1776 at Edenton, NC. From Hyde County, NC. Later in NC State Troops. S1917.	
Mason, John	3ʳᵈ NC Regiment	7/20/1778, a Private under Capt. John Baker. Died on 11/24/1778.	
Mason, John	10ᵗʰ NC Regiment	7/1/1777, a Private under Capt. Andrew Vanoy. Dropped from the rolls in June 1778.	
Mason, Patrick	2ⁿᵈ NC Regiment	5/15/1781, a Private under Capt. Tilghman Dixon. Discharged on 5/21/1782 (1ˢᵗ NC Regiment). Received clothing on 5/24/1782. From Caswell County. S41810.	
Mason,	1ˢᵗ NC	6/6/1781, a Corporal under Capt. Alexander	

Name	1st Unit	Year / Rank / Served Under / Notes	Known Battles
Philip	Regiment	Brevard.	
Mason, Philip	2nd NC Regiment	1777, a Drum Major under Capt. Edward Vail, Jr. 9/9/1778, a known Drum Major in the Colonel's Company (Col. John Patten) led by Capt. John Craddock.	
Mason, Richard	2nd NC Regiment	9/4/1778, an Ensign. 1779, a Lieutenant. Allegedly, after the battle of Eutaw Springs (SC), a Captain – no record thereof. Served until the end of the war.	
Massey, John	3rd NC Regiment	Feb. 1777, a Private under Capt. Jacob Turner for 2-1/2 years. Discharged on 2/3/1778. Then joined a GA unit. From Granville County, NC. W4724.	
Massey, Joseph	4th NC Regiment	4/23/1781, a Private under Capt. Joseph T. Rhodes, serving as a substitute for Robert Shannon (R9420) for 12 months. From Duplin County, NC. R7005.	
Massey, Thomas	3rd NC Regiment	1777, a Sergeant under Capt. James Emmett. Died on 3/12/1779.	
Masten, Thomas	4th NC Regiment	1781, a Private under Capt. George Dougherty. Discharged on 5/25/1782.	
Masterson, James	2nd NC Regiment	1775, a Private under Capt. Nathaniel Keais, then Capt. William Caswell for nine months. From Beaufort County, NC. Later in NC Militia. W8422.	
Matchet, Edward	10th NC Regiment	7/28/1777, a Private under Capt. Abraham Sheppard, Jr.	
Mathias, Stephen	2nd NC Regiment	4/1/1782, a Private under Capt. Clement Hall for 12 months.	
Mathis, Moses	1st NC Regiment	1781, a Private under Capt. William Armstrong. Discharged on 4/23/1782 (3rd NC Regiment).	
Matlock, John	4th NC Regiment	4/18/1776 or 5/11/1776 (two sources), a Private under Capt. John Nelson for three years. A Corporal in Feb. 1778. 6/1/1778, a Corporal under Capt. Griffith John McRee (1st NC Regiment). A Sergeant in Dec. 1778. Discharged on 5/1/1779 at Paramus, NJ. From Guilford (what is now Rockingham) County, NC. aka John Mattlock. W4723.	Brandywine Creek (PA), Germantown (PA).
Matlock, Nathaniel	1st NC Regiment	6/6/1781 Private under Capt. William Lytle. Earlier in NC Militia. From Granville County, NC. aka Nathaniel Medlock. S8409.	Eutaw Springs (SC).
Matterson, George	1st NC Regiment	1781, a Corporal under Capt. Alexander Brevard. Discharged on 4/28/1782 (3rd NC Regiment).	
Matthews, Charles	4th NC Regiment	1777, a Private under Capt. James Williams. Discharged on 11/1/1777.	
Matthews, Daniel	1st NC Regiment	5/6/1781, a Private under Capt. Griffith John McRee. Discharged on 5/6/1782 (3rd NC Regiment).	
Matthews, Edward	3rd NC Regiment	8/8/1777, a Musician under Capt. Jacob Turner. Discharged on 8/10/1778.	
Matthews, Gilbert	NC Light Dragoons	April 1776, a Private under Capt. Martin Phifer for 2-1/2 years. 3/7/1777, this unit was placed	Brandywine Creek (PA),

Name	1ˢᵗ Unit	Year / Rank / Served Under / Notes	Known Battles
		on the Continental Line. Wounded at battle of Germantown, and in another skirmish. Discharged in Oct. 1778 at Ft. Pitt, PA. 6/6/1779, a Private under Capt. Michael Quinn (3rd NC Regiment) for two years. Enlisted at Halifax, NC. Discharged in June 1781 at Halifax, NC. aka Gilbert Mathis. S41803.	Germantown (PA), Monmouth (NJ), Siege of Savannah (GA), Siege of Charleston (SC).
Matthews, Giles	2ⁿᵈ NC Regiment	Nov. 1775, a Private under Capt. Hardy Murfree for seven months. Then, in NC Militia. From Hertford County, NC. S8993.	Great Bridge (VA).
Matthews, Jacob	2ⁿᵈ NC Regiment	1777, a Musician under Capt. James Gee. A Private in June 1778. 9/9/1778, a known Private under Capt. John Ingles.	
Matthews, James	5ᵗʰ NC Regiment	1779, a Private under Capt. William Lytle for nine months, discharged near Savannah, GA. 6/14/1781, a Private under Capt. Thomas Donoho (1st NC Regiment) for three months, then under Capt. William Lytle. Discharged on 6/14/1782 (4th NC Regiment). Then joined a VA unit. Enlisted while living in Granville County, NC. S41818.	Briar Creek (GA), Siege of Savannah (GA), Guilford Court House, Eutaw Springs (SC).
Matthews, James	5ᵗʰ NC Regiment	8/5/1779, a Private under Maj. Reading Blount. Deserted in Oct. 1779.	
Matthews, John	2ⁿᵈ NC Regiment	3/1/1782, a Private under Capt. Clement Hall for 12 months.	
Matthews, John	8ᵗʰ NC Regiment	12/25/1776, a Private under Capt. James May, Jr., then under Capt. Simon Alderson (5th NC Regiment) for three years. A Corporal in March 1778. A Private in June 1778. Back to Corporal on 8/28/1778 under Capt. Robert Fenner (2nd NC Regiment). Discharged on 1/1/1780. From Halifax County, NC. S31839 & W4725.	Monmouth (NJ).
Matthews, Joseph	3ʳᵈ NC Regiment	7/20/1778, a Private under Capt. Kedar Ballard for nine months.	
Matthews, Reps.	3ʳᵈ NC Regiment	1781, a Private under Capt. Edward Yarborough for 12 months. Discharged on 4/22/1782.	
Maudley, William		Jan. 1779, a Private, regiment and unit unknown.	
Maulborn, David	5ᵗʰ NC Regiment	1777, a Sergeant under Capt. John Enloe for 3 years. Discharged on 1/30/1780. aka David Moulborn.	
Maulborn, Solomon	5ᵗʰ NC Regiment	1777, a Sergeant under Capt. John Enloe. Died 2/27/1778. aka Solomon Moulborn.	
Mauley, Sothy		7/20/1778, a Private in the Lt. Colonel's Company. Either 2nd or 3rd NC Regiment.	
May, James Jr.	8ᵗʰ NC Regiment	11/28/1776, a Captain under Col. James Armstrong. Resigned 8/5/1777. From Pitt County, NC.	
May, John	4ᵗʰ NC Regiment	1782, a Private under Capt. Anthony Sharpe for 18 months. 1779, in the "New Levies." Enlisted and discharged at Salisbury, NC. S36690.	
May, Joseph	3ʳᵈ NC Regiment	1781, a Private under Capt. Clement Hall. Discharged on 7/10/1782 (2nd NC Regiment).	

Name	1st Unit	Year / Rank / Served Under / Notes	Known Battles
May, Major	9th NC Regiment	12/10/1776, a Corporal under Capt. Richard D. Cook. Died on 11/27/1777.	
May, Michael	2nd NC Regiment	1782, a Private under Capt. Benjamin Carter for 18 months. Deserted on 4/4/1783 (?).	
May, Thomas	9th NC Regiment	12/1/1776, a Private under Capt. Richard D. Cook for three years. 9/8/1778, a known Private in the Lt. Colonel's Company (Lt. Col. Robert Mebane) (1st NC Regiment) led by Capt. Joshua Bowman. Discharged on 1/27/1780.	
Maynor, Henry	4th NC Regiment	1782, a Private under Capt. William Lytle for 18 months. Enlisted in Onslow County, NC. On the official rolls as Henry Mayner. W8268.	
Mays, Shadrack	3rd NC Regiment	7/20/1778, a Private under Capt. Francis Child for nine months.	
McAffee, Azariah	3rd NC Regiment	2/1/1782, a Private under Capt. Clement Hall (2/6/1782 - 2nd NC Regiment) for 12 months. First name might be John (?).	
McAllister, James	5th NC Regiment	1777, a Private under Capt. Henry Darnell. Died on 3/7/1778.	
McAllister, John	3rd NC Regiment	1782, a Private under Capt. Alexander Brevard for 18 months.	
McAllister, Joseph		6/15/1777, a Private, regiment and unit unknown, enlisted for three years. 9/8/1778, a known Private in the Major's Company (Maj. John Baptiste Ashe) (1st NC Regiment).	
McAllister, Neil	1st NC Regiment	9/1/1775, an Ensign. 1/4/1776, a 2nd Lieutenant. 6/29/1776, a 1st Lieutenant under Capt. Robert Rowan. Resigned on 6/20/1777.	Moore's Creek Bridge [4].
McAlpin, Robert	3rd NC Regiment	7/20/1778, a Private under Capt. Michael Quinn for nine months.	
McAltree, Barnabas	5th NC Regiment	1777, a Private under Capt. Henry Darnell. Dropped from the rolls in Sep. 1777.	
McBane, Daniel	5th NC Regiment	8/4/1779, a Sergeant under Maj. Reading Blount. POW at the Fall of Charleston. From Chatham County, NC. W4735.	Siege of Charleston 1780 (SC).
McBride, Duncan	1st NC Regiment	1777, a Private under Capt. Joshua Bowman. 9/8/1778, a known Private under Capt. Tilghman Dixon.	
McBride, Duncan	6th NC Regiment	1777, a Private under Capt. George Dougherty. A Corporal in Nov. 1777. Dropped from the rolls in Nov. 1778.	
McBride, James	1st NC Regiment	1775, a Private under Capt. George Davidson. Then, in NC Militia. From Guilford County, NC. Born in August 1750 in County Down, Ireland. S4192.	Breech Inlet Naval Battle (SC).
McCaleb, James	1st NC Regiment	Nov. 1777, a Private under Capt. John Brown. 9/8/1778, a known Private under Capt. James Read. aka James McCalib.	
McCall, Daniel	2nd NC Regiment	11/1/1781, a Private under Capt. Benjamin Andrew Coleman for 12 months - this per official records. In his wife's application for widow's pension, she asserts that he served under Capt. James Mills (1st NC Regiment then 4th NC Regiment). From Cumberland County,	

494

Name	1st Unit	Year / Rank / Served Under / Notes	Known Battles
		NC. W4734.	
McCallister, John	10th NC Regiment	8/8/1777, a Private under Capt. James Wilson for 12 months. Aug. 1778, discharged at White Plains, NY. S36111.	
McCann, Hugh Jr.	2nd NC Regiment	9/1/1782, a Private under Capt. Clement Hall for 12 months. Deserted on 6/13/1783 (?). From Duplin County, NC. In Pierce's Register. Born c.1765. aka Hugh McCan.	
McCann, John	1st NC Regiment	5/20/1781, a Private under Capt. Griffith John McRee. Deserted on 7/9/1781.	
McCann, John	6th NC Regiment	1775, a 2nd Lieutenant in the Wilmington District Minutemen. 4/17/1776, a 2nd Lieutenant under Capt. John James and Col. John Alexander Lillington. Also a Lieutenant under Capt. George Dougherty. Killed at the battle of Germantown on 10/4/1777. aka John McCanne, John McCan.	Germantown (PA).
McCarter, William	1st NC Regiment	9/8/1778, a known Private under Capt. Tilghman Dixon.	
McCarthur, Alexander	1st NC Regiment	3/10/1777, a Private under Capt. John Brown for three years.	
McCarthy, Florence	4th NC Regiment	5/1/1776, a Lieutenant under Capt. William Temple Coles. Dropped from the rolls in Jan. 1778.	
McCarthy, James	3rd NC Regiment	3/2/1782, a Private under Capt. Benjamin Bailey for 12 months.	
McCartney, Jeremiah	4th NC Regiment	5/8/1776, a Private under Capt. Robert Smith. Enlisted in Wilmington, NC. Discharged 9/1/1777 at Charleston, SC. S42947.	Ft. Moultrie #1 (SC).
McCartney, John	1st NC Regiment	5/26/1781, a Private under Capt. Alexander Brevard.	
McCauley, Matthew	10th NC Regiment	11/25/1776, a 1st Lieutenant under Capt. Andrew Vanoy and Col. Abraham Sheppard in the newly-created 1st Battalion of Volunteers (Militia). 4/19/1777, a 1st Lieutenant under Capt. James Wilson (10th NC Regiment) and Capt. Andrew Vanoy. Reprimanded for allowing a prisoner to escape. Dropped from the rolls in June 1778. From Orange County, NC. Later, a Captain in NC Militia. aka Matthew McCalley, Matthew McColley. W17121.	
McCay, Richard	1st NC Regiment	1777, a Private under Capt. John Brown. Deserted on 2/11/1779. aka Richard McCoy.	
McClainey, William	2nd NC Regiment	5/15/1781, a Private under Capt. Tilghman Dixon. Discharged on 5/21/1782 (1st NC Regiment).	
McClammy, Joseph	2nd NC Regiment	10/20/1775, an Ensign. Died in July 1776. May have also been a 2nd Lieutenant. aka Joseph McLammy, McLemmy.	
McClaskey, Allen	1st NC Regiment	1781, a Private under Capt. Alexander Brevard. Discharged on 3/12/1782 (3rd NC Regiment).	
McClaskey, George	5th NC Regiment	6/23/1779, a Private under Capt. Joseph Montford for 18 months. Deserted in Sep. 1779. From Dobbs County, NC. aka George	

Name	1st Unit	Year / Rank / Served Under / Notes	Known Battles
		McClarkey.	
McClellan, Malcolm	1st NC Regiment	Oct. 1775, a Private under Capt. Robert Rowan for six months. From Cumberland County, NC. Born in the shire of Argyle in Scotland. S5070.	
McClelland, James	4th NC Regiment	5/1/1776, a Sergeant under Capt. John Nelson for three years. 6/1/1778, a Sergeant under Capt. Griffith John McRee (1st NC Regiment). Discharged on 5/1/1779. aka James McClellen, James McLelland.	
McClelland, Thomas	1st NC Regiment	May 1781, a Private under Capt. Elijah Moore for 12 months. Discharged 5/1/1782 near Bacon's Bridge, SC. Earlier in NC Militia. From Rowan County, NC. S2763.	
McClenahan, Malcome	3rd NC Regiment	8/20/1782, a Private under Capt. Benjamin Bailey for 12 months.	
McCleran, Daniel	1st NC Regiment	1782, a Private under Capt. Joshua Hadley for 18 months. Discharged at James Island, SC. From Cumberland County, NC. aka Daniel McCarran, Daniel MacLarrin. S41836.	
McCleyea, John	9th NC Regiment	7/28/1777, a Musician under Capt. Thomas McCrory. A Private in Aug. 1778. Back to Musician in Sep. 1778. 9/8/1778, a known Musician in the Lt. Colonel's Company (Lt. Col. Robert Mebane) (1st NC Regiment) led by Capt. Joshua Bowman. aka John Mickleya.	
McCloud, Alexander	2nd NC Regiment	1/5/1782, a Private under Capt. Benjamin Andrew Coleman for 12 months.	
McCloud, Daniel	4th NC Regiment	5/5/1776, a Private under Capt. William Temple Coles for three years. 9/8/1778, a known Private under Capt. John Sumner (1st NC Regiment). Discharged on 5/10/1779.	
McClure, Francis	9th NC Regiment	1777, a Private under Capt. Thomas McCrory. Deserted in Nov. 1777.	
McClure, Thomas	4th NC Regiment	1775, an Ensign in the Salisbury District Minutemen. 4/17/1776, an Ensign under Capt. Robert Smith and Col. Thomas Polk.	
McClure, William	6th NC Regiment	4/17/1776 or 5/1/1776 (two sources), a Surgeon. 6/7/1776 transferred to 2nd NC Regiment. 1780, in 1st NC Regiment. POW at the Fall of Charleston, exchanged 6/14/1781. 2/6/1782, assigned to 3rd NC Regiment. 4/24/1782, back in 2nd NC Regiment. Served to the end of the war.	Siege of Charleston 1780 (SC).
McCobb, James	1st NC Regiment	Nov. 1777, a Private, unit unknown.	
McCollister, John	10th NC Regiment	8/8/1777, a Private under Capt. James Wilson. Dropped from the rolls in Aug. 1778.	
McCollister, Joseph	10th NC Regiment	7/15/1777, a Private under Capt. James Wilson.	
McComber, Benjamin	3rd NC Regiment	7/20/1778, a Private under Capt. Michael Quinn. Discharged on 7/23/1778.	
McComber, Humphrey	3rd NC Regiment	7/20/1778, a Sergeant under Capt. Michael Quinn for nine months. 6/27/1779, a Sergeant under Capt. George "Gee" Bradley for 18	

Name	1st Unit	Year / Rank / Served Under / Notes	Known Battles
		months. aka Humph. McCumber.	
McConnel, Philip	2nd NC Regiment	1777, a Private under Capt. John Armstrong. Discharged 9/10/1778. From Dobbs County, NC.	
McConnough, Dougal	5th NC Regiment	6/23/1779, a Private under Capt. Joseph Montford for 18 months.	
McCormick, Archibald	3rd NC Regiment	8/20/1782, a Private under Capt. Benjamin Bailey for 12 months.	
McCoy, Daniel	1st NC Regiment	1777, a Private under Capt. Joshua Bowman.	
McCoy, Daniel	6th NC Regiment	1777, a Private under Capt. George Dougherty.	
McCoy, John	1st NC Regiment	Private under Capt. Robert Raiford. Killed at the battle of Eutaw Springs, SC on 9/8/1781.	Eutaw Springs (SC).
McCoy, John	5th NC Regiment	1777, a Private under Capt. Simon Alderson. Died on 3/10/1778.	
McCoy, John	6th NC Regiment	1777, a Private under Capt. Griffith John McRee.	
McCoy, Reuben	3rd NC Regiment	7/1/1779, a Private under Capt. George "Gee" Bradley for 18 months.	
McCreary, Archibald	4th NC Regiment	1776, a Private under Capt. John Nelson for three years. aka Archibald McCravy, McGreavy, McCrevy, McCrary.	
McCrory, Hugh	8th NC Regiment	May 1778, a Private under Capt. Robert Raiford. June 1778, this unit was in the 2nd NC Regiment. 1779, transferred to either 4th or 5th NC Regiment, unit unknown. 1780, in NC Militia. From Guilford County, NC. S46254.	Stono Ferry (SC).
McCrory, James	9th NC Regiment	4/15/1776 (?), a Sergeant under Capt. Richard D. Cook. 5/2/1777, an Ensign under Capt. Richard D. Cook. Later under Capt. Joseph John Wade. Dropped from the rolls in Jan. 1778. Then, in NC Militia. From Guilford County, NC. aka James McRory.	Brandywine Creek (PA), Germantown (PA).
McCrory, Thomas	9th NC Regiment	11/28/1776, a Captain under Col. John Williams. Died on 11/2/1777. From Salisbury District. aka Thomas McRory, Thomas McCrary.	Brandywine Creek (PA), Germantown (PA).
McCuller, Joseph	7th NC Regiment	1777, a Sergeant under Capt. Joseph Walker. Died on 4/3/1778.	
McCullers, Bryant	NC Light Dragoons	1780, a Sergeant under Capt. Solomon Wood. At this time, this unit was State Troops.	
McCulloch, James	1st NC Regiment	Sep. 1775, a Private under Capt. Alfred Moore for six months. Discharged 3/16/1776 in Wilmington, NC. Later in NC Militia. From Orange County, NC. S7201.	
McCullock, Alexander	1st NC Regiment	10/10/1777, a Private under Capt. James Read. 9/8/1778, in same unit. aka Alex McCulloch.	
McCullock, John	6th NC Regiment	Spring 1776, a Private under Capt. Archibald Lytle for 12 months. Enlisted at Hillsborough, NC. Discharged in June/July 1777 at Halifax, NC. From Orange County, NC. R6671.	
McCullough, Francis	3rd NC Regiment	1782, a Private under Capt. Alexander Brevard for 18 months. March 1783, transferred to ?	

Name	1ˢᵗ Unit	Year / Rank / Served Under / Notes	Known Battles
McCullough, James	2ⁿᵈ NC Regiment	Dec. 1775, a Private under Capt. William Knox. 1777, in NC Militia. From Rowan County, NC. S30570.	Ft. Moultrie #1 (SC).
McCullough, John	4ᵗʰ NC Regiment	2/8/1777, a Private under Capt. William Temple Coles for three years. 9/8/1778, a known Private under Capt. John Sumner (1st NC Regiment). POW on 4/14/1779 (?). Mustered again in November 1779. On some rolls as John McCullock. W9558.	
McCumber, Humpy	8ᵗʰ NC Regiment	A Private under Capt. Michael Quinn, dates unknown.	
McDaniel, Andrew	3ʳᵈ NC Regiment	10/1/1781, a Private under Capt. Samuel Jones for 12 months.	
McDaniel, Arthur	6ᵗʰ NC Regiment	1776, a Private under Capt. Arthur Council then Capt. Thomas White for 2-1/2 years. Re-enlisted for the duration of the war under Capt. Thomas Donoho (1st NC Regiment). From Chatham County, NC. W4732.	Brandywine Creek (PA), Germantown (PA), Monmouth (NJ), Stony Point (NY), Siege of Charleston 1780 (SC).
McDaniel, George	3ʳᵈ NC Regiment	5/4/1776, a Drummer under Capt. James Emmett for three years. Discharged on 5/1/1779 at Continental Village as a Drum Major. Later in NC Militia. Enlisted in Chatham County, NC. On the "official rolls" as George McDonald (incorrect). S36099.	Brandywine Creek (PA), Germantown (PA), Monmouth (NJ).
McDaniel, Hugh	4ᵗʰ NC Regiment	1777, a Sergeant under Capt. John Nelson. Dropped from the rolls in Feb. 1778.	
McDaniel, James	2ⁿᵈ NC Regiment	7/20/1778, a Private under Maj. Reading Blount for nine months. Later in NC Militia. From Granville County, NC. W8447.	
McDaniel, Joseph	10ᵗʰ NC Regiment	7/1/1777, a Private under Capt. Andrew Vanoy. 3/12/1779, re-enlisted for the duration of the war in the Colonel's Company (Col. Thomas Clark) (1st NC Regiment) led by Capt. John Gambier Scull. Dropped from the rolls in Nov. 1779.	
McDaniel, Thomas	2ⁿᵈ NC Regiment	9/10/1778, a known Private under Capt. Thomas Armstrong.	
McDaniel, Thomas	3ʳᵈ NC Regiment	5/1/1776, Private under Capt. James Emmett. Discharged on 5/1/1779 at North River, CT. aka Thomas McDonald (only on gov't lists).	Brandywine Creek (PA), Germantown (PA), Monmouth (NJ).
McDauval, Alexander	1ˢᵗ NC Regiment	1777, a Private under Capt. Joshua Bowman. Probably the same man as Alexander McDonald below.	
McDermid, Malcom	1ˢᵗ NC Regiment	7/1/1781, a Private under Capt. Anthony Sharpe. Discharged on 7/1/1782 (4th NC Regiment).	

Name	1st Unit	Year / Rank / Served Under / Notes	Known Battles
McDonald, Alexander	1st NC Regiment	9/8/1778, a known Private under Capt. Joshua Bowman.	
McDonald, Alexander	6th NC Regiment	A Private under Capt. George Dougherty. A Corporal on 5/20/1779. Discharged in Jan. 1780.	
McDonald, Arthur	1st NC Regiment	1776, a Private under Capt. Joshua Bowman. 9/8/1778, a known Private under Capt. Joshua Bowman.	
McDonald, Arthur	6th NC Regiment	1777, a Private under Capt. George Dougherty. A Corporal on 12/1/1778, regiment and unit unknown. Back to Private in 1782.	
McDonald, Benjamin	1st NC Regiment	8/1/1782, a Private under Capt. Joshua Hadley for 18 months. Deserted on 6/20/1783 (?).	
McDonald, Call	2nd NC Regiment	1/15/1782, a Private under Capt. Benjamin Andrew Coleman for 12 months.	
McDonald, Daniel	3rd NC Regiment	2/1/1782, a Private under Capt. Samuel Jones for 12 months.	
McDonald, Finlay	2nd NC Regiment	6/14/1781, a Sergeant under Capt. Joshua Hadley, then under Capt. Samuel Jones (1st NC Regiment). A Private in April 1782. Discharged in Dec. 1782. aka Findley McDonald. S41828.	
McDonald, Hugh	1st NC Regiment	9/8/1778, a known Private under Capt. Joshua Bowman.	
McDonald, Hugh	1st NC Regiment	2/2/1782, a Private under Capt. James Mills for 12 months. 2/6/1782, this unit was transferred to the 4th NC Regiment.	
McDonald, Hugh	6th NC Regiment	6/10/1776, a Private under Lt. Daniel Porterfield, Capt. Arthur Council, then Capt. Thomas White for 2-1/2 years. 1777, a Private under Capt. George Dougherty. Discharged from 1st NC Regiment in Nov. 1778 at Kings Ferry, NY. Enlisted at Cross Creek, NC. S41837.	Brandywine Creek (PA), Germantown (PA), Monmouth (NJ).
McDonald, James	2nd NC Regiment	1782, a Private under Capt. Benjamin Carter for 18 months. Deserted on 11/17/1782.	
McDonald, Jonathan	2nd NC Regiment	1778, a Private under Capt. Clement Hall. Died on 2/20/1778.	
McDonald, Joseph	1st NC Regiment	7/1/1777, a Private, unit unknown. 9/8/1778, a known Private in the Colonel's Company (Col. Thomas Clark) led by Capt. John Gambier Scull.	
McDonald, Larkins	1st NC Regiment	6/14/1781, a Private under Capt. Thomas Donoho. Discharged on 6/14/1782.	
McDonald, Malcolm	6th NC Regiment	1777, a Private under Capt. Griffith John McRee. Dropped from the rolls in June 1778.	
McDonald, Samuel	5th NC Regiment	6/12/1779, a Private under Maj. Reading Blount. Deserted in Oct. 1779.	
McDonald, Thomas	2nd NC Regiment	1777, a Private under Capt. Charles Allen.	
McDonnell, David	6th NC Regiment	1777, a Private under Capt. Thomas Donoho. Dropped from the rolls in Jan. 1778. aka David McDonel.	
McDonnell, Hugh	1st NC Regiment	1776, a Private under Capt. Joshua Bowman.	

Name	1st Unit	Year / Rank / Served Under / Notes	Known Battles
McDonnock, John	2nd NC Regiment	1782, a Private under Capt. Benjamin Carter for 18 months. Deserted on 5/18/1783 (?).	
McDougal, Dougal	4th NC Regiment	1781, a Private under Capt. George Dougherty. Discharged on 5/25/1782.	
McDougal, Peter	2nd NC Regiment	9/9/1778, a known Private under Capt. Clement Hall.	
McDouge, James	1st NC Regiment	Apr. 1778, a Private under Maj. Henry "Hal" Dixon. 9/8/1778, a known Private under Capt. Tilghman Dixon. Dropped from the rolls in March 1779. aka James McDoug, James McDowg.	
McDowell, David	6th NC Regiment	1777, a Private under Capt. Thomas Donoho.	
McDowell, George	2nd NC Regiment	1777, a Private under Capt. John Armstrong. Deserted on 3/8/1778.	
McDowell, Jesse	2nd NC Regiment	6/1/1777, a Private under Capt. Robert Fenner.	
McDowell, John	1st NC Regiment	5/14/1781, a Private under Capt. Griffith John McRee. Deserted on 6/10/1781.	
McDowell, Peter	5th NC Regiment	1777, a Private under Capt. Benjamin Stedman. Deserted on 3/1/1779.	
McElroy, Samuel	5th NC Regiment	1777, a Private under Capt. William Caswell. Dropped from the rolls in Feb. 1778.	
McElroy, William	6th NC Regiment	1777, a Private under Capt. Philip Taylor. Dropped from the rolls in August 1778.	
McElyea, William	3rd NC Regiment	Late summer 1782, enlisted under Capt. Elijah Moore (1st NC Regiment) for 18 months, quickly transferred to Capt. Alexander Brevard. Then, under Capt. Joseph T. Rhodes (4th NC Regiment). Living in Caswell County, NC when he enlisted. Discharged at James Island, SC. S33084.	
McFadden, Adam	3rd NC Regiment	1775, an Ensign in the Salisbury District Minutemen. 4/17/1776, an Ensign under Capt. James Cook and Col. Jethro Sumner.	
McFarlane, Morgan	3rd NC Regiment	1/12/1782, a Private under Capt. Samuel Jones for 12 months.	
McFarlin, Alexander	10th NC Regiment	11/4/1777, a Private under Capt. James Wilson for three years. 9/8/1778, a known Tailor in the Major's Company (Maj. Griffith John McRee) (1st NC Regiment) - stationed at Lancaster, PA on that date. Deserted in Jan. 1780. aka Alexander McFailin.	
McFashin, Caleb	3rd NC Regiment	7/20/1778, a Private under Capt. John Baker. Died on 11/4/1778.	
McFatter, Daniel	6th NC Regiment	1777, a Private under Capt. Griffith John McRee. Deserted on 5/17/1778. Rejoined in 1781, regiment and unit unknown. aka Daniel McFalter.	
McGaunds, John	1st NC Regiment	4/15/1781, a Private under Capt. Anthony Sharpe. Discharged on 4/15/1782 (4th NC Regiment).	
McGaw, Neil	9th NC Regiment	1777, a Private under Capt. Thomas McCrory. Deserted in Nov. 1777.	

500

Name	1st Unit	Year / Rank / Served Under / Notes	Known Battles
McGee, Peter	6th NC Regiment	May 1778, a Private under Capt. Francis Child. 6/1/1778, a Private under Capt. Griffith John McRee (1st NC Regiment). A Corporal in March 1779. A Sergeant in Nov. 1779.	
McGee, Thomas	2nd NC Regiment	5/28/1781, a Private under Capt. Tilghman Dixon. Discharged on 6/1/1782 (1st NC Regiment). Born in Orange County, lived in Anson County when he enlisted. On the official rolls as Thomas McGehee. S5071.	
McGibbon, Neil	1st NC Regiment	1777, a Private under Capt. John Brown. Dropped from the rolls in Aug. 1778.	
McGibbony, Patrick	4th NC Regiment	11/27/1776, an Ensign under Capt. John Nelson. 12/9/1776, a Lieutenant under Capt. Thomas Harris. Dropped from the rolls in June 1778. Re-enlisted again in the 4th NC Regiment in Jan. 1779.	
McGill, James	4th NC Regiment	1777, a Private under Capt. Thomas Harris. Discharged on 7/28/1777.	
McGinnis, Daniel	2nd NC Regiment	5/12/1781, a Private under Capt. Tilghman Dixon. 2/7/1782, transferred to the Pennsylvania Line.	
McGinnis, John	3rd NC Regiment	1782, a Private under Capt. Alexander Brevard for 18 months. Deserted in March 1783 (?). aka John McGennis.	
McGlaughan, John	7th NC Regiment	11/28/1776, a Captain under Col. James Hogun. Resigned on 10/12/1777. From Hertford County, NC. aka John McGlanhan, John McGlaughon, John Glaughan.	Brandywine Creek (PA), Germantown (PA).
McGlaughlin, John	4th NC Regiment	5/6/1776, a Private under Capt. Robert Smith. Discharged on 5/14/1779.	
McGraw, Joseph	2nd NC Regiment	June 1778, a known Private in the Lt. Colonel's Company (Lt. Col. Selby Harney). Dropped from the rolls in Oct. 1778.	
McGraw, Roger	2nd NC Regiment	12/25/1781, a Private under Capt. Benjamin Andrew Coleman for 12 months. Sep. 1782, re-enlisted for the duration of the war.	
McGuire, Michael	5th NC Regiment	1777, a Private under Capt. Benjamin Stedman. Discharged on 4/25/1778.	
McGuire, Silas	2nd NC Regiment	1777, a Private under Capt. Edward Vail, Jr. Died on 7/1/1778.	
McIlwaine, Samuel Stringer	2nd NC Regiment	1777, a 2nd Lieutenant under Capt. John Armstrong. Resigned on 10/24/1777. Later, a Captain and a Major in the NC Militia. aka Mackilwean, McIlwane, McKlewaine.	
McIntire, Charles	3rd NC Regiment	8/20/1782, a Private under Capt. Benjamin Bailey for 12 months.	
McIntire, Gilbert	3rd NC Regiment	8/20/1782, a Private under Capt. Benjamin Bailey for 12 months.	
McIntire, James	2nd NC Regiment	1782, a Sergeant under Capt. Robert Raiford for 18 months.	
McIntire, William	6th NC Regiment	1777, a Private under Capt. Thomas Donoho.	
McIntosh, Murdock	1st NC Regiment	8/1/1782, a Private under Capt. Joshua Hadley for 18 months.	

Name	1ˢᵗ Unit	Year / Rank / Served Under / Notes	Known Battles
McKabe, Joshua	7ᵗʰ NC Regiment	1777, a Private under Capt. Joseph Walker. Died in Feb. 1778.	
McKay, Alexander	1ˢᵗ NC Regiment	A Sergeant under Capt. James Pearl and Capt. James Campbell for two years, dates unknown. Earlier in NC Militia, unit and dates unknown. From Rowan County, NC. aka Alexander McKoy.	
McKay, Daniel	1ˢᵗ NC Regiment	9/8/1778, a known Private under Capt. Joshua Bowman.	
McKay, Dougal	1ˢᵗ NC Regiment	A QM Sergeant under Capt. Samuel Jones. Discharged 2/1/1783. One source claims he died around August 1782 while in service. aka Dougal McKey.	
McKay, John	1ˢᵗ NC Regiment	9/8/1778, a known Private under Capt. Joshua Bowman.	
McKay, John	1ˢᵗ NC Regiment	5/4/1781, a Private under Capt. Robert Raiford. Killed at the battle of Eutaw Springs, SC on 9/8/1781.	Eutaw Springs (SC).
McKay, Richard	1ˢᵗ NC Regiment	9/8/1778, a known Private under Capt. Joshua Bowman.	
McKay, Robert	5ᵗʰ NC Regiment	A Private for nine months - Captain not named. Discharged 8/10/1779 by Lt. Col. James Thackston. Then in NC Militia. From Rowan County, NC. R6745.	
McKay, William	6ᵗʰ NC Regiment	1776, a Private under Capt. John Griffin McRee for six months. Later, in NC Militia in Rowan County. From Bladen County, NC. W7429.	
McKean, John	5ᵗʰ NC Regiment	7/1/1779, a Private under Maj. Reading Blount. Died on 10/15/1779.	
McKee, John	2ⁿᵈ NC Regiment	1/1/1782, a Private under Capt. Benjamin Andrew Coleman for 12 months.	
McKee, William	2ⁿᵈ NC Regiment	5/16/1781, a Private under Capt. Benjamin Andrew Coleman for 12 months.	
McKeel, Michael	2ⁿᵈ NC Regiment	5/10/1776, a Private, unit unknown. 9/9/1778, a known Private in the Lt. Colonel's Company (Lt. Col. Selby Harney). Discharged on 8/1/1779. From Hertford County, NC.	
McKeithan, John	1ˢᵗ NC Regiment	12/20/1781, a Private under Capt. James Mills for 12 months. 2/6/1782, this unit was transferred to the 4th NC Regiment. Enlisted in Duplin County, NC. Discharged at Wilmington, NC. S41841.	
McKenny, James	5ᵗʰ NC Regiment	1775, an Ensign in the New Bern District Minutemen. 4/17/1776, an Ensign under Capt. Simon Alderson and Col. Edward Buncombe. aka James McKinnie.	
McKenny, Robert	1ˢᵗ NC Regiment	4/28/1781, a Private under Capt. Griffith John McRee. Discharged on 4/28/1782 (3rd NC Regiment). Sep. 1782, re-enlisted for the duration of the war.	
McKenny, Samuel	2ⁿᵈ NC Regiment	1782, a Private under Capt. Robert Raiford for 18 months. Deserted on 6/11/1783 (?).	
McKensey, James	1ˢᵗ NC Regiment	8/1/1782, a Private under Capt. Joshua Hadley for 18 months. Deserted on 6/24/1783 (?).	

Name	1st Unit	Year / Rank / Served Under / Notes	Known Battles
McKenzie, William	1st NC Regiment	8/20/1782, a Private under Capt. Joshua Hadley for 12 months. Re-enlisted and served a total of 19 months. From Cumberland (what is now Moore) County, NC. aka William McKinsey. R6755.	
McKey, John	1st NC Regiment	8/1/1782, a Private under Capt. Joshua Hadley for 18 months.	
McKiel, Thomas	2nd NC Regiment	Jan. 1778, a Private under Capt. Clement Hall. Dropped from the rolls in June 1778.	
McKinley, Daniel	9th NC Regiment	1777, a Sergeant under Capt. Thomas McCrory. Dropped from the rolls in Jan. 1778.	
McKinley, John	1st NC Regiment	7/9/1777, a Private under Capt. Micajah Lewis for 2-1/2 years. Jan. 1779, a Private under Capt. Philip Taylor (5th NC Regiment). Discharged in April of 1779 at the Black Swamp, SC. Later in NC Militia, unit unknown. S38184.	
McKinney, William	1st NC Regiment	August 1782, a Private under Lt. Thomas Pasteur, Capt. Benjamin Carter. Then, under Capt. Robert Raiford (2nd NC Regiment). From Franklin County, NC. Born 1764 in Louisa County, VA. S9017.	
McKinsey, Alexander	4th NC Regiment	1782, a Private under Capt. Thomas Evans for 18 months.	
McKinsey, Hugh	2nd NC Regiment	1/4/1782, a Private under Capt. Benjamin Andrew Coleman for 12 months.	
McKinsey, William	1st NC Regiment	2/1/1782, a Private under Capt. James Mills for 12 months. On 2/6/1782, this unit was transferred to the 4th NC Regiment.	
McKissack, Thomas	3rd NC Regiment	A Private under Capt. Kedar Ballard, dates unknown. aka Thomas McKissick. S164.	
McKithen, Duncan	2nd NC Regiment	12/26/1781, a Private under Capt. Benjamin Andrew Coleman for 12 months.	
McKithen, John	2nd NC Regiment	12/20/1781, a Private under Capt. Benjamin Andrew Coleman for 12 months.	
McKnight, Andrew	2nd NC Regiment	1781, a Corporal under Capt. Tilghman Dixon. Discharged on 5/21/1782 (1st NC Regiment). Received clothing on 5/24/1782. From Caswell County.	
McLain, Hugh	3rd NC Regiment	8/20/1782, a Private under Capt. Benjamin Bailey for 12 months.	
McLain, William		1/1/1783, a Sergeant, unit unknown.	
McLammy, Mark	4th NC Regiment	1775, a 2nd Lieutenant in the Wilmington District Minutemen. 4/17/1776, a 2nd Lieutenant under Capt. John Ashe, Jr. and Col. Thomas Polk. aka Mark McLainy, Mark McLamy.	
McLamore, John	2nd NC Regiment	12/15/1781, a Private under Capt. Benjamin Andrew Coleman for 12 months.	
McLane, John	4th NC Regiment	Earlier a Captain in the Edenton District Minutemen. 4/16/1776, a Captain under Col. Thomas Polk. Left the service in Dec. 1779. aka Jerome McLean, Jerome McLaine, Jerome MacLaine, Jeremiah McClane.	Stono Ferry (SC).
McLaughlan,	1st NC	5/6/1776, a Lieutenant. Some claim he was later	

503

Name	1st Unit	Year / Rank / Served Under / Notes	Known Battles
John	Regiment	a Captain, but probably confused with John McGlaughan.	
McLaughlin, Alexander	2nd NC Regiment	2/5/1782, a Private under Capt. Benjamin Andrew Coleman. Died 10/1/1782.	
McLaughlin, John	4th NC Regiment	5/6/1776, a Private under Capt. Robert Smith for three years. 9/8/1778, a known Private in the Colonel's Company (Col. Thomas Clark) (1st NC Regiment) led by Capt. John Gambier Scull. Then, in NC Militia. aka John McLaughlan. W174.	Ft. Moultrie #1 (SC), Brandywine Creek (PA), Germantown (PA).
McLean, Charles	4th NC Regiment	1775, a Lt. Colonel in NC Militia. 4/16/1776, a Major under Col. Thomas Polk. Resigned in March or April 1777 to take his seat in the NC Senate. 1779, a Colonel in NC Militia. From Tryon (would soon become Lincoln) County, NC.	
McLeland, William	1st NC Regiment	4/28/1781, a Private under Capt. Griffith John McRee. Discharged on 4/28/1782 (3rd NC Regiment).	
McLeod, John	2nd NC Regiment	1782, a Private under Capt. Benjamin Carter for 18 months. aka John McLoud.	
McLeod, John	3rd NC Regiment	9/4/1782, a Private under Capt. Benjamin Bailey for 12 months.	
McMahan, Barnet	3rd NC Regiment	1782, a Private under Capt. Alexander Brevard. Deserted on 3/25/1783 (?).	
McMullen, James	3rd NC Regiment	5/10/1776, a Musician under Capt. Thomas Granbury. Discharged on 11/10/1778.	
McMullen, Jerome	4th NC Regiment	1777, a Private under Capt. William Temple Coles. Dropped from the rolls in April 1778.	
McMullen, Michael	5th NC Regiment	Jan. 1779, a Private under Capt. Philip Taylor.	
McMullin, Michael	5th NC Regiment	6/2/1779, a Corporal under Capt. Joseph Montford for three years. aka Michael McMullen.	
McNalty, John	8th NC Regiment	1777, a Private under Capt. John Walsh. Dropped from the rolls in Jan. 1778.	
McNaughton, John	8th NC Regiment	11/28/1776, a 2nd Lieutenant under Capt. Henry Pope. 1/16/1777, under Capt. Francis Tartanson. A 1st Lieutenant on 8/5/1777. Retired on 6/1/1778. From Dobbs County, NC.	
McNeal, Archibald	1st NC Regiment	A Private under Capt. Henry "Hal" Dixon. Deserted on 1/1/1777.	
McNees, John	5th NC Regiment	3/8/1777, a 2nd Lieutenant under Capt. John Pugh Williams. A 1st Lieutenant on 11/20/1777. 1779, a Lieutenant under Capt. Michael Quinn (3rd NC Regiment). POW at the Fall of Charleston, exchanged 6/14/1781. Transferred to 1st NC Regiment on 1/1/1781. 2/6/1782, in 3rd NC Regiment. 11/2/1782, promoted to Captain. Mostly a recruiter located in the town of Halifax, NC. Retired 1/1/1783. aka John McKees.	Siege of Charleston 1780 (SC).
McNeill, Hector	1st NC Regiment	9/1/1775, a 1st Lieutenant. Deserted on 2/3/1776. A Loyalist.	

504

Name	1st Unit	Year / Rank / Served Under / Notes	Known Battles
McNeill, Hector	1st NC Regiment	April 1781, a Private under Capt. William Lytle, then Capt. Elijah Moore. 6/16/1782, a Private under Capt. Benjamin Bailey (3rd NC Regiment) for 12 months. From Cumberland County, NC. Born in Scotland. aka Hector McNeal. W4285.	
McOllister, Daniel	4th NC Regiment	1777, a Private under Capt. Robert Smith. Discharged on 8/11/1777.	
McPherson, Abel	2nd NC Regiment	1777, a Sergeant under Capt. Robert Fenner. 9/9/1778, a known Sergeant in the Lt. Colonel's Company (Lt. Col. Selby Harney). A QM Sergeant on 12/20/1779.	
McPherson, Abel	2nd NC Regiment	9/9/1778, a known Private in the Lt. Colonel's Company (Lt. Col. Selby Harney). Probably the same man as directly above.	
McPherson, Othmiel	5th NC Regiment	8/5/1779, a Private under Maj. Reading Blount. Deserted in Oct. 1779.	
McPherson, William	5th NC Regiment	8/5/1779, a Private under Maj. Reading Blount. Deserted in Oct. 1779.	
McQuillin, Walter	1st NC Regiment	1781, a Private under Capt. Anthony Sharpe. Died on 12/1/1781.	
McRay, John	3rd NC Regiment	3/24/1781, a Sergeant under Capt. Samuel Jones for 12 months.	
McRee, John Griffith	6th NC Regiment	4/16/1776, a Captain under Col. John Alexander Lillington. 6/1/1778, a Captain under Col. Thomas Clark (1st NC Regiment). POW at the Fall of Charleston, exchanged 2/27/1781. 1781, a Captain under Lt. Col. John Baptiste Ashe (1st NC Regiment). Promoted to Major in 3rd NC Regiment on 9/11/1781. One source asserts this promotion was into the 6th NC Regiment in 1781 (?) (Not true). In April of 1782, his Major's commission was back-dated to 3/1/1779. Served to the end of the war. Earlier in NC Militia. Born on 2/1/1758. Enlisted in Bladen County, NC. After the war, lived in Brunswick and New Hanover Counties. W4731.	Brandywine Creek (PA), Germantown (PA), Monmouth (NJ), Siege of Charleston 1780 (SC), Guilford Court House, Hobkirk's Hill (SC), Eutaw Springs (SC).
McReynolds, Robert	10th NC Regiment	4/19/1777, an Ensign under Capt. James Wilson. Dropped from the rolls in June 1778. aka Robert McRevels.	
McSheehy, Miles	9th NC Regiment	2/12/1777, an Adjutant. Dropped from the rolls in Jan. 1778. aka Miles McSheby.	
McSwain, McAm.	1st NC Regiment	Oct. 1782, a Private under Capt. James Mills for 12 months.	
McSwain, William	3rd NC Regiment	1782, a Private under Capt. Alexander Brevard for 18 months. March 1783, transferred to ? W2409.	
McVay, Eli	4th NC Regiment	2/17/1782, a Private under Capt. James Mills for 12 months. Sep. 1782, re-enlisted for the duration of the war. Enlisted in Orange County, NC. Discharged at James Island, SC on 7/4/1783. W964.	
McVay, John	2nd NC Regiment	1/14/1782, a Private under Capt. Benjamin Andrew Coleman. Died on 9/6/1782.	

Name	1st Unit	Year / Rank / Served Under / Notes	Known Battles
McWhirter, James	1st NC Regiment	1775, an Orderly Sergeant under Capt. George Lee Davidson for six months. Later in NC Militia. From Rowan County, NC. R6818.	Great Cane Brake (SC), Snow Campaign (SC).
Meacon, James	3rd NC Regiment	1777, a Private under Capt. Jacob Turner. Dropped from the rolls in Sep. 1777.	
Meacon, William	3rd NC Regiment	1777, a Private under Capt. Jacob Turner. Dropped from the rolls in Sep. 1777.	
Meadows, Abraham	6th NC Regiment	1777, a Private under Capt. Thomas Donoho. 9/8/1778, a known Private under Capt. Griffith John McRee (1st NC Regiment) - sick on that date at Valley Forge. Deserted on 2/18/1780. aka Abraham Medows.	
Meadows, John	1st NC Regiment	Jan. 1781, a Private under Lt. Elijah Moore for 4 months. Earlier and later in NC Militia. From Caswell County, NC.	Guilford Court House.
Measley, Josiah	3rd NC Regiment	4/23/1779, a known Private in the Lt. Colonel's Company (Lt. Col. Robert Mebane) led by Capt. George "Gee" Bradley. Died at Philadelphia Hospital.	
Mebane, Robert	7th NC Regiment	11/27/1776, a Lt. Colonel in the NC 7th Regiment under Col. James Hogun. Transferred to 1st NC Regiment on 6/1/1778 thru Jan. 1779. 1/9/1779, commanded the 3rd NC Regiment (should have been promoted to full Colonel, why not unknown). Surrendered 162 men at the Fall of Charleston – he was a POW. After his exchange, he acted as a Colonel of NC Militia; killed in Oct. 1781 by Loyalists.	Brandywine Creek (PA), Germantown (PA), Monmouth (NJ), Siege of Charleston 1780 (SC).
Meck, John	3rd NC Regiment	8/1/1782, a Private under Capt. Benjamin Bailey for 12 months.	
Medearis, John	6th NC Regiment	1775, a 2nd Lieutenant in the Hillsborough District Minutemen. 4/17/1776, a 2nd Lieutenant under Capt. James Emmett and Col. John Alexander Lillington. 4/15/1777, a 1st Lieutenant under Capt. Pinketham Eaton (3rd NC Regiment). 12/23/1777, a Captain in the 3rd NC Regiment. Reprimanded for unintentional forgery. At some time, in charge of the Public Factory at Harrisburg (Granville County) under Col. Nicholas Long (DQMG). Also Ass't QM General stationed at Wake County, NC. Transferred to 1st NC Regiment on 2/6/1782. March 1782, said he would not return to service. Born 2/22/1744 in Essex County, VA. aka John Madaris. S2823.	
Medgett, William	1st NC Regiment	5/17/1781, a Private under Capt. Benjamin Bailey. Discharged on 5/17/1782 (3rd NC Regiment). aka William Midjett.	
Medici, Cosmo	NC Light Dragoons	4/16/1776, a Lieutenant under Capt. James Jones as Provincial troops. Oct. 25, 1776, Acting Captain of the 3rd Company, due to the resignation of Capt. James Jones. Commissioned as Captain on 3/7/1777 - this is the date	Brandywine Creek (PA), Germantown (PA).

Name	1st Unit	Year / Rank / Served Under / Notes	Known Battles
		when the NC Light Dragoons were placed on the Continental Line. September 1778, attached to 7th NC Regiment under Col. James Hogun. Jan. 1779, a Major under Col. Francois DeMalmedy (NC State Troops). aka Cosmo de Medici, Cosmode Medici, Cosimo Madacy, Cosimo De Medici.	
Medlin, Shadrack	3rd NC Regiment	1777, a Private under Capt. Jacob Turner, then Capt. Kedar Ballard. Served 20 months. Discharged at Valley Forge, PA. 4/5/1781, a Corporal under Capt. Edward Yarborough for 12 months. Discharged 4/22/1782 at Bacon's Bridge, SC. Enlisted in Franklin County, NC. S42869.	Germantown (PA), Eutaw Springs (SC).
Medlock, Nathaniel	1st NC Regiment	6/6/1781, a Private under Capt. William Lytle. Dropped from the rolls sometime during 1781.	
Medum, John	4th NC Regiment	7/28/1776, a Private under Capt. William Goodman. Dropped from the rolls in Dec. 1777.	
Meeks, Robert	5th NC Regiment	12/8/1776, a Corporal under Capt. Simon Alderson. A Private in June 1778 in the Colonel's Company (Col. John Patten) (2nd NC Regiment) led by Capt. John Craddock. Discharged on 3/1/1780.	
Meeks, William	1st NC Regiment	1782, a Corporal under Capt. Peter Bacot for 18 months.	
Meeks, William	5th NC Regiment	5/3/1776, a Private under Capt. Simon Alderson for 2-1/2 years. 9/9/1778, a known Private in the Colonel's Company (Col. John Patten) (2nd NC Regiment) led by Capt. John Craddock. Discharged on 11/30/1778.	
Meggs, James	1st NC Regiment	5/15/1781, a Private under Capt. Griffith John McRee. Discharged on 5/15/1782 (3rd NC Regiment).	
Meigs, Thomas	3rd NC Regiment	7/20/1778, a Private under Lt./Capt. Joseph Montford for nine months.	
Melton, Benjamin	2nd NC Regiment	1781, a Private under Capt. Tilghman Dixon. Discharged on 5/21/1782 (1st NC Regiment). Earlier in NC Militia. From Caswell County, NC. W2227.	Eutaw Springs (SC), Raid on St. John's Island (SC).
Melton, Jonathan	6th NC Regiment	4/16/1776, a Private under Capt. George Mitchell, then Capt. Thomas Donoho for 2-1/2 years. 9/8/1778, a known Private under Capt. Griffith John McRee (1st NC Regiment) - sick on that date at Valley Forge. Enlisted in Onslow County, NC. Discharged on 11/10/1778 at Kings Ferry, NJ. S4186?.	Brandywine Creek (PA), Germantown (PA).
Melton, William	1st NC Regiment	Summer of 1776, a Private under Capt. Henry "Hal" Dixon, then under Capt. James Read. A Corporal on 11/1/1777. POW at the Fall of Charleston, taken to Nova Scotia and held until the end of the war. S36117.	Brandywine Creek (PA), Germantown (PA), Monmouth (NJ), Siege of Charleston 1780 (SC).

Name	1st Unit	Year / Rank / Served Under / Notes	Known Battles
Menius, Frederick	4th NC Regiment	1782, recruited by Capt. Edward Yarborough (3rd NC Regiment) for 18 months and transferred after drilling for a month to Capt. Anthony Sharpe. From Rowan County, NC. Born in Germany. W3848.	
Mercer, John	7th NC Regiment	11/28/1776, an Ensign under Capt. John Poynter then Capt. Joseph Walker. Resigned on 11/22/1777. From Edenton District.	
Merchant, Caleb	1st NC Regiment	9/10/1777, a Private under Capt. Howell Tatum. 9/8/1778, a known Private under Capt. Howell Tatum. aka Caleb Marchant.	
Merchant, John	2nd NC Regiment	1777, a Private under Capt. William Fenner. Died on 4/20/1778. aka John Marchant.	
Meredith, William	4th NC Regiment	1775, an Ensign in the Salisbury District Minutemen. 4/17/1776, an Ensign under Capt. Joseph Phillips and Col. Thomas Polk. From Surry County.	
Merrian, Philip	1st NC Regiment	A Private under Capt. Henry "Hal" Dixon. Dropped from the rolls in Feb. 1779. aka Philip Merriam. Probably the same man as Philip Marion above.	
Merridith, William	3rd NC Regiment	9/18/1782, a Corporal under Capt. Benjamin Bailey for 18 months. A Private in Dec. 1782. aka William Merredeth.	
Merrit, Joel	3rd NC Regiment	7/20/1778, a Private under Lt./Capt. Joseph Montford for nine months.	
Merritt, Drury	4th NC Regiment	1782, a Private under Capt. Anthony Sharpe for 18 months.	
Merritt, Thomas	1st NC Regiment	7/1/1781, a Private under Lt./Capt. Benjamin Bailey. Discharged on 7/1/1782 (3rd NC Regiment) at Bacon's Bridge, SC. Earlier in NC Militia. From Warren County, NC. aka Thomas Merit. S1233.	Eutaw Springs (SC).
Meryman, William	1st NC Regiment	May 1781, a Private under Capt. James Campbell (?) for about 7 months. Got sick, then furloughed. Earlier in NC Militia. From Granville County, NC. R7136.	Hobkirk's Hill (SC).
Mesick, Jacob	8th NC Regiment	4/24/1777, a Private under Capt. John Walsh. Died on 12/11/1777.	
Messer, Benjamin	2nd NC Regiment	6/1/1777, a Private in the Colonel's Company (Col. Alexander Martin). 9/9/1778, a known Private in the Colonel's Company (Col. John Patten) led by Capt. John Craddock. Transferred to the "Invalids" in Nov. 1779.	
Messer, Jeremiah	1st NC Regiment	4/15/1781, a Private under Capt. Anthony Sharpe. Discharged in May of 1782 (4th NC Regiment) near Dorchester, SC. Earlier in NC Militia. From Pitt County, NC. S8893.	Eutaw Springs (SC).
Messer, John	4th NC Regiment	1781, a Private under Capt. George Dougherty. Discharged on 7/20/1782.	
Messey, Joseph	4th NC Regiment	1782, a Private under Capt. Anthony Sharpe. Died on 6/22/1783.	
Messey, Philip	4th NC Regiment	1782, a Private under Capt. Anthony Sharpe for 18 months.	

508

Name	1st Unit	Year / Rank / Served Under / Notes	Known Battles
Messick, Aaron	4th NC Regiment	2/6/1782, a Private under Capt. James Mills for 12 months.	
Messick, Jacob	8th NC Regiment	11/28/1776, an Ensign under Capt. Robert Raiford. 4/24/1777, a Lieutenant under Capt. John Walsh. Died 12/11/1777. aka Jacob Mezick.	
Messick, Joseph	2nd NC Regiment	1777, a Private under Capt. Edward Vail, Jr. 9/9/1778, a known Private in the Colonel's Company (Col. John Patten) led by Capt. John Craddock. Deserted on 7/10/1779.	
Messley, Josiah	3rd NC Regiment	7/20/1778, a known Private in the Lt. Colonel's Company (Lt. Col. William Lee Davidson) led by Lt./Capt. George "Gee" Bradley for nine months.	
Metchler, John	4th NC Regiment	1782, a Private under Capt. Anthony Sharpe for 18 months.	
Metissick, Thomas	3rd NC Regiment	4/16/1776, a Corporal under Capt. Jacob Turner. A Private in June 1778. 9/9/1778, a known Private in the Major's Company (Maj. Hardy Murfree) (2nd NC Regiment). Discharged on 10/30/1778. aka Thomas Metisuck.	
Metters, Jethro	1st NC Regiment	5/19/1781, a Private under Capt. Robert Raiford. Discharged on 5/19/1782 (2nd NC Regiment).	
Mexico, Abraham	2nd NC Regiment	1777, a Corporal under Capt. John Armstrong. A Private in June 1778. Died on 6/20/1778. aka Albue Mexico, Abue Mexico.	
Michum, Paul	3rd NC Regiment	7/20/1778, a Private under Lt./Capt. Joseph Montford for nine months. aka Paul Micham.	
Middleton, Daniel	5th NC Regiment	1777, a Private under Capt. Simon Alderson. Dropped from the rolls in Feb. 1778.	
Middleton, Samuel	8th NC Regiment	1777, a Sergeant under Capt. John Walsh. POW in Feb. 1778 (?). Dropped from the rolls in June 1778.	
Middleton, Solomon	1st NC Regiment	1781, a Private under Capt. William Armstrong.	
Miers, George	4th NC Regiment	1782, a Corporal under Capt. William Lytle for 18 months.	
Mileborn, Robert		3/18/1777, rank and unit unknown. 9/8/1778, a known Corporal under Capt. Howell Tatum (1st NC Regiment).	
Miles, Joseph	1st NC Regiment	1777, a Sergeant under Capt. John Brown. A Private in Jan. 1778. Dropped from the rolls in Feb. 1778. aka Joseph Mills.	
Millen, Martin	1st NC Regiment	1781, a Private under Capt. Anthony Sharpe. Discharged on 8/1/1782 (4th NC Regiment).	
Miller, Abel	3rd NC Regiment	7/20/1778, a Private under Maj. Thomas Hogg for nine months.	
Miller, Benedict	1st NC Regiment	4/28/1781, a Private under Capt. Alexander Brevard. Discharged on 4/28/1782 (3rd NC Regiment). aka Bernidic Miller.	
Miller, Christopher	2nd NC Regiment	1782, a Private under Capt. Benjamin Carter for 18 months.	

509

Name	1st Unit	Year / Rank / Served Under / Notes	Known Battles
Miller, Conrad	4th NC Regiment	1782, a Private under Capt. William Lytle for 18 months.	
Miller, Daniel	10th NC Regiment	8/14/1777, a Private under Capt. Armwell Herron. 9/9/1778, a known Private in the Lt. Colonel's Company (Lt. Col. Selby Harney) (2nd NC Regiment).	
Miller, George	3rd NC Regiment	8/1/1782, a Private under Capt. Edward Yarborough for 18 months. One of MG Nathaniel Greene's Lifeguards. W4293.	
Miller, George	4th NC Regiment	1782, a Private under Capt. Anthony Sharpe for 18 months.	
Miller, Gilbert	9th NC Regiment	1777, a Private under Capt. Richard D. Cook. Dropped from the rolls in Sep. 1777.	
Miller, Henry	2nd NC Regiment	9/9/1778, a known Private in the Lt. Colonel's Company (Lt. Col. Selby Harney.	
Miller, Henry	5th NC Regiment	3/8/1777, a Drum Major. Dropped from the rolls sometime between January and September of 1779.	
Miller, Henry	5th NC Regiment	A Private under Capt. Reading Blount. A Corporal in Feb. 1780. A Sergeant in 1782.	
Miller, Jacob	3rd NC Regiment	1778, an Orderly Sergeant under Lt./Capt. Christopher Goodwin for nine months - 11/5/1778 to 8/5/1779. Earlier and later in NC Militia. From Mecklenburg County, NC.	Briar Creek (GA), Stono Ferry (SC).
Miller, James	NC Artillery	2/6/1778, a Matross under Capt. Thomas Clark. Also on 9/9/1778.	
Miller, James	2nd NC Regiment	1777, a Private under Capt. James Martin. Dropped from the rolls in Feb. 1778.	
Miller, James	2nd NC Regiment	11/22/1776, a 1st Lieutenant under Capt. Joseph Hardin. From Tryon (what is now Rutherford) County, NC.	
Miller, John	3rd NC Regiment	6/30/1779, a Private under Capt. George "Gee" Bradley for 18 months.	
Miller, John	3rd NC Regiment	1781, a Musician under Capt. Clement Hall. Discharged on 7/10/1782 (2nd NC Regiment).	
Miller, John	7th NC Regiment	1777, a Corporal under Capt. Thomas Brickell. Died on 3/4/1778.	
Miller, John	10th NC Regiment	5/8/1777, a Private under Capt. John Jarvis. Discharged on 9/1/1778.	
Miller, Joseph	1st NC Regiment	2/26/1778, a known Private under Capt. Howell Tatum.	
Miller, Josiah	4th NC Regiment	7/20/1776, a Private under Capt. William Goodman for three years. 9/8/1778, a known Private in the Colonel's Company (Col. Thomas Clark) (1st NC Regiment) led by Capt. John Gambier Scull. Dropped from the rolls in Nov. 1779.	
Miller, Martin	9th NC Regiment	12/22/1776, a Private under Capt. Richard D. Cook for three years. A Musician in Sep. 1777. Back to Private in Feb. 1778. 9/8/1778, a known Private in the Lt. Colonel's Company (Lt. Col. Robert Mebane) (1st NC Regiment) led by Capt. Joshua Bowman. Discharged on 1/27/1780. From Granville County, NC.	Germantown (PA).

Name	1st Unit	Year / Rank / Served Under / Notes	Known Battles
		W7453.	
Miller, Peter	3rd NC Regiment	8/9/1782, a Private under Capt. Benjamin Bailey for 12 months.	
Miller, Richard	1st NC Regiment	Jan. 1776, a Private under Capt. George Davidson for nine months. From Guilford County, NC. S23808.	Ft. Moultrie #1 (SC).
Miller, William	2nd NC Regiment	Dec. 1778, a Musician, unit unknown.	
Miller, William	3rd NC Regiment	12/20/1778, a Private under Capt. John Medearis.	
Milligan, James	1st NC Regiment	3/28/1777, an Ensign under Capt. Thomas Hogg. 8/29/1777, a Lieutenant under Capt. Thomas Hogg then Capt. Howell Tatum. Court-martialed, cashiered on 7/10/1778. aka James Mellegan, James Millegan.	
Mills, Benjamin	8th NC Regiment	11/28/1776, a 2nd Lieutenant under Capt. Thomas Nixon. Resigned 7/12/1777. Reenlisted in the NC Light Dragoons as a 1st Lieutenant on 7/15/1777, served until Jan. 1781.	
Mills, Daniel	1st NC Regiment	1781, a Private under Capt. William Armstrong. Discharged on 1/17/1782.	
Mills, Elisha	10th NC Regiment	6/9/1777, a Private under Capt. Silas Stevenson. 9/9/1778, a known Private in the Major's Company (Maj. Hardy Murfree) (2nd NC Regiment).	
Mills, Jacob	1st NC Regiment	8/1/1782, a Private under Capt. Joshua Hadley for 18 months.	
Mills, James	8th NC Regiment	11/28/1776, a 1st Lieutenant under Capt. Thomas Nixon. Transferred to 1st NC Regiment on 6/1/1778. 1/9/1779, a Captain under Col. Thomas Clark in the 5th NC Regiment. Spring of 1781, a Captain in the 1st NC Regiment. One source claims he was killed in a skirmish in March of 1781. Many sources show him alive well into 1782. 2/6/1782, transferred to 4th NC Regiment. Resigned on 1/1/1783. From Brunswick County, NC.	Stono Ferry (SC), Eutaw Springs (SC).
Mills, John	2nd NC Regiment	5/12/1781, a Sergeant under Capt. Benjamin Carter. Discharged on 5/2/1782. From Franklin County, NC. Died 5/1/1815.	
Mills, John	3rd NC Regiment	7/20/1778, a Musician under Capt. Francis Child for nine months. Later in NC Militia. From Pitt County, NC. S7231.	
Milton, John	8th NC Regiment	Nov. 1777, a Private under Capt. John Walsh. Dropped from the rolls in Jan. 1778.	
Mingo, ?	1st NC Regiment	6/10/1776, an Assistant Armourer under Capt. Henry "Hal" Dixon. Dropped from the rolls in Sep. 1777.	
Minnis, John	1st NC Regiment	1775, a Sergeant under Capt. John Walker for six months. Later in NC Militia. From Orange County, NC. S9413.	
Minns, Joseph	3rd NC Regiment	A Private under Capt. Edward Yarborough for 18 months. Discharged 10/28/1782 at Salisbury, NC. Retained at the Laboratory in Salisbury,	

Name	1st Unit	Year / Rank / Served Under / Notes	Known Battles
		NC for the duration of his service. From Rowan County, NC. aka Joseph Minzes. W2148.	
Minshew, John	1st NC Regiment	Apr. 1778, a Private in the Colonel's Company (Col. Thomas Clark). Died on 5/14/1778.	
Minson, Mas.	5th NC Regiment	1779, a Private under Maj. Reading Blount for nine months. Dropped from the rolls in Oct. 1779.	
Minyard, John	1st NC Regiment	5/20/1781, a Private under Capt. Griffith John McRee. Deserted in July 1781. Aug. 1781, re-enlisted. Discharged on 5/9/1782 (3rd NC Regiment).	
Mires, John	10th NC Regiment	8/21/1777, a Private under Capt. Andrew Vanoy for three years. Early 1778, a Private under Capt. John Craddock (2nd NC Regiment). POW at the Fall of Charleston (SC), escaped after two months. Discharged in Halifax County, NC. Then, in NC Militia. S35002.	Monmouth (NJ), Stony Point (NY), Siege of Charleston 1780 (SC).
Mitchell, Abner	2nd NC Regiment	1782, a Private under Capt. Benjamin Carter for 18 months.	
Mitchell, Abraham	6th NC Regiment	5/13/1776, a Private under Lt./Capt. Francis Child for 2-1/2 years. 9/8/1778, a known Private under Capt. Griffith John McRee (1st NC Regiment) - sick on that date. Discharged on 11/1/1778.	
Mitchell, Arthur	4th NC Regiment	1777, a Private under Capt. John Nelson. Dropped from the rolls in Feb. 1778.	
Mitchell, Beth'w	2nd NC Regiment	Jan. 1778, a Private under Capt. Clement Hall. Dropped from the rolls in March 1778. Probably Bartholomew Mitchell.	
Mitchell, Charles	3rd NC Regiment	12/25/1781, a Private under Capt. Samuel Jones for 12 months.	
Mitchell, Ezekiel	1st NC Regiment	6/15/1781, a Private under Capt. Robert Raiford. Deserted on 8/30/1781. aka Ezekiel Michel.	
Mitchell, Frederick	4th NC Regiment	1777, a Private under Capt. William Temple Coles. Discharged on 8/10/1777.	
Mitchell, George	3rd NC Regiment	10/1/1781, a Private under Capt. Samuel Jones for 12 months. Discharged 10/4/1782 (1st NC Regiment) at Ashley Hill, SC. From Wayne County, NC. W4031.	
Mitchell, George	6th NC Regiment	1775, a Captain in the Salisbury District Minutemen. Lived in the Wilmington District. 4/17/1776, a Captain in the 6th NC Regiment. Resigned in April of 1777, and his unit was taken over by Capt. Benjamin Pike. Later a Captain and a Colonel in NC Militia. From Onslow County, NC.	
Mitchell, Isham	3rd NC Regiment	1776, a Private for 2-1/2 years under Capt. James Emmett, Col. Jethro Sumner. From Granville County, NC. W18510.	Brandywine Creek (PA), Germantown (PA).
Mitchell, Jacob	3rd NC Regiment	5/25/1778, a Private under Lt./Capt. George "Gee" Bradly for nine months. Discharged 5/25/1779 at Philadelphia, PA. S38217.	

Name	1ˢᵗ Unit	Year / Rank / Served Under / Notes	Known Battles
Mitchell, James	3ʳᵈ NC Regiment	6/2/1779, a Private under Capt. George "Gee" Bradley for 18 months.	
Mitchell, Jesse	1ˢᵗ NC Regiment	4/15/1781, a Private under Capt. Tilghman Dixon. Discharged on 4/25/1782.	
Mitchell, Jesse	5ᵗʰ NC Regiment	8/5/1779, a Private under Maj. Reading Blount. Deserted in Oct. 1779.	
Mitchell, Job	1ˢᵗ NC Regiment	1777, a Private under Capt. Micajah Lewis. Dropped from the rolls in Sep. 1777.	
Mitchell, John	NC Artillery	1/1/1777, a Matross under Capt. Thomas Clark as NC Provincial Troops. 7/10/1777, on Continental Line. Also on 9/9/1778.	
Mitchell, John	1ˢᵗ NC Regiment	5/15/1781, a Private under Capt. Griffith John McRee. Discharged on 5/15/1782 (3rd NC Regiment).	
Mitchell, John	1ˢᵗ NC Regiment	4/12/1781, a Sergeant under Capt. William Lytle. A Private in Jan. 1782. Discharged on 4/12/1782 (4th NC Regiment)	
Mitchell, John	4ᵗʰ NC Regiment	5/6/1776, a Private under Capt. John Nelson. Discharged on 5/14/1779.	
Mitchell, John	10ᵗʰ NC Regiment	5/18/1777, a Private under Capt. Abraham Sheppard, Jr. Dropped from the rolls in June 1778.	
Mitchell, John	10ᵗʰ NC Regiment	8/15/1777, a Private under Capt. Abraham Sheppard, Jr.	
Mitchell, Joshua	4ᵗʰ NC Regiment	5/6/1776, a Private under Capt. John Nelson for three years. 9/8/1778, a known Private in the Colonel's Company (Col. Thomas Clark) (1st NC Regiment) led by Capt. John Gambier Scull. Discharged on 5/14/1779. aka Joseph Mitchell.	
Mitchell, Nathaniel	3ʳᵈ NC Regiment	Regimental QM, start date unknown. Dismissed in Oct. 1779.	
Mitchell, Oliver	1ˢᵗ NC Regiment	9/10/1782, a Private under Capt. Joshua Hadley for 18 months.	
Mitchell, Oliver	3ʳᵈ NC Regiment	7/20/1778, a Private under Maj. Thomas Hogg for nine months.	
Mitchell, Theophilus	1ˢᵗ NC Regiment	4/12/1781, a Private under Capt. William Lytle. Confined four nights for desertion during July 1781. Dead by Apr. 1782.	
Mitchell, William		4/25/1776, a Private, regiment and unit unknown. 1778, a Private under Capt. John Baker (3rd NC Regiment). Dropped from the rolls in Nov. 1779. From Bertie County, NC. R7281.	
Mitchell, William	1ˢᵗ NC Regiment	4/12/1781, a Private under Lt./Capt. Benjamin Bailey. Discharged on 4/12/1782 (3rd NC Regiment).	
Mitchell, William	1ˢᵗ NC Regiment	4/15/1781, a Private under Capt. Robert Raiford. Discharged on 4/15/1782 (2nd NC Regiment). aka William Michel.	
Mitchell, William	2ⁿᵈ NC Regiment	6/2/1777, a Private under Capt. James Martin. A Musician in Feb. 1778. A Private in June 1778. 9/9/1778, a known Private in the Major's Company (Maj. Hardy Murfree). A Musician again in July 1779.	

Name	1st Unit	Year / Rank / Served Under / Notes	Known Battles
Mitchell, William	2nd NC Regiment	1782, a Private under Capt. Benjamin Carter for 18 months.	
Mixon, Charles	6th NC Regiment	4/2/1777, an Ensign under Capt. Philip Taylor. Dropped from the rolls in Sep. 1777. aka Charles Mixom.	
Modglin, Truman	1st NC Regiment	1779, a Private under Capt. Joshua Hadley. From Chatham County, NC. W1057.	Stono Ferry (SC).
Modlin, Benjamin	7th NC Regiment	1777, a Private under Capt. Thomas Brickell. 2/26/1778, a known Private under Capt. Howell Tatum (1st NC Regiment). 9/8/1778, a known Private under Capt. Howell Tatum. aka Benjamin Modling.	
Modlin, Elisha	10th NC Regiment	5/3/1777, a Private under Capt. Isaac Moore for three years. 9/8/1778, a known Private in the Lt. Colonel's Company (Lt. Col. Robert Mebane) (1st NC Regiment) led by Capt. Joshua Bowman. Re-enlisted on 3/27/1780.	
Modlin, Ezekiel	10th NC Regiment	12/1/1777, a Private under Capt. Isaac Moore. Died on 4/20/1778.	
Modlin, Jeremiah	7th NC Regiment	1777, a Private under Capt. Thomas Brickell. 2/26/1778, a known Private under Capt. Howell Tatum (1st NC Regiment).	
Modlin, Miles	10th NC Regiment	5/17/1777, a Private under Capt. Isaac Moore for three years. 9/8/1778, a known Private in the Lt. Colonel's Company (Lt. Col. Robert Mebane) (1st NC Regiment) led by Capt. Joshua Bowman - sick on that date at Trenton. Dropped from the rolls in Sep. 1778. aka Miller Modlin, Miles Modling.	
Modlin, Thomas	10th NC Regiment	5/17/1777, a Private under Capt. Isaac Moore for three years. A Corporal in Aug. 1778. 9/8/1778, a known Corporal in the Lt. Colonel's Company (Lt. Col. Robert Mebane) (1st NC Regiment) led by Capt. Joshua Bowman. Back to Private in March 1779. aka Thomas Modling.	
Modlin, Zebulon	10th NC Regiment	5/17/1777, a Private under Capt. Isaac Moore for three years. 9/8/1778, a known Private in the Lt. Colonel's Company (Lt. Col. Robert Mebane) (1st NC Regiment) led by Capt. Joshua Bowman.	
Mogar, Timothy	3rd NC Regiment	4/23/1779, a known Private in the Lt. Colonel's Company (Lt. Col. Robert Mebane) led by Capt. George "Gee" Bradley.	
Moglin, Freeman	2nd NC Regiment	Feb. 1779, a Private in the Colonel's Company (Col. John Patten) led by Capt. John Craddock.	
Molbone, Malachi	2nd NC Regiment	1777, a Private under Capt. James Gee. 9/9/1778, a known Private under Capt. John Ingles. Deserted on 7/10/1779.	
Mollet, Thomas	5th NC Regiment	1779, a Private under Maj. Reading Blount. Deserted in Sep. 1779.	
Money, John	1st NC Regiment	10/16/1775, a Private under Capt. William Davis for six months. From Bladen County, what is now Columbus County, NC.	
Moneyham,	2nd NC	11/27/1781, a Private under Capt. Benjamin	

Name	1st Unit	Year / Rank / Served Under / Notes	Known Battles
Thomas	Regiment	Andrew Coleman for 12 months.	
Monger, Robert	3rd NC Regiment	7/20/1778, a Private in the Lt. Colonel's Company (Lt. Col. William Lee Davidson) led by Lt./Capt. George "Gee" Bradley for nine months. 4/23/1779, a known Private in the Lt. Colonel's Company (Lt. Col. Robert Mebane) led by Capt. George "Gee" Bradley. Died at New Windsor Hospital.	
Monk, Israel	7th NC Regiment	1777, a Private under Capt. John McGlaughan. Deserted in Apr. 1777.	
Monk, James	2nd NC Regiment	1782, a Private under Capt. Benjamin Carter for 18 months. aka James Munk. S41905.	
Monk, Nottingham	7th NC Regiment	1/15/1777 or 6/13/1777 (two sources), a Private under Capt. John McGlaughan for three years. 2/26/1778, a known Private under Capt. Howell Tatum (1st NC Regiment). 9/8/1778, a known Private under Capt. Howell Tatum. Discharged on 1/19/1780. From Hertford County, NC. aka Nollingham Mont.	
Monnyhan, John	3rd NC Regiment	7/20/1778, a Private under Capt. John Baker for nine months. aka John Monnyham. Could be Moneyham, see above.	
Montague, Bryan	2nd NC Regiment	1777, a Private under Capt. Charles Allen. Dropped from the rolls in Jan. 1778.	
Montague, Samuel	2nd NC Regiment	1777, a Private under Capt. Charles Allen. Dropped from the rolls in Jan. 1778.	
Montcrief, Maxwell	3rd NC Regiment	7/20/1778, a Private under Lt./Capt. Joseph Montford for nine months.	
Montford, Joseph	3rd NC Regiment	1775, an Ensign in the Halifax District Minutemen. 4/17/1776, an Ensign under Capt. Pinketham Eaton – OR – 4/17/1776, a 1st Lieutenant under Capt. Thomas Granbury (two different sources). 1/9/1779, a Captain in the 5th NC Regiment. Spring of 1780, would be in 1st NC Regiment. Wounded and taken prisoner at the Fall of Charleston, paroled. Not exchanged until 11/26/1782. Resigned 1/1/1783.	Briar Creek (GA), Stono Ferry (SC), Siege of Charleston 1780 (SC).
Monto, Frederick	5th NC Regiment	7/25/1779, a Private under Maj. Reading Blount. Deserted on 12/17/1779.	
Moody, Thomas	4th NC Regiment	April 1781, a Private under Capt. George Dougherty, then under Capt. Samuel Jones (3rd NC Regiment). Discharged on 5/25/1782 (1st NC Regiment) at Bacon's Bridge, SC. Then joined SC unit. From Onslow County, enlisted at Duplin Court House, NC. S41892.	Eutaw Springs (SC).
Moon, Sampson	2nd NC Regiment	1782, a Private under Capt. Benjamin Carter for 18 months.	
Moon, Sampson	3rd NC Regiment	7/20/1778, a Private under Capt. Francis Child for nine months.	
Mooney, Thomas	1st NC Regiment	A Private under Capt. Thomas Hogg. Deserted in Jan. 1777.	
Mooney, William	2nd NC Regiment	5/15/1781, a Corporal under Capt. Tilghman Dixon. A Sergeant by Jan. 1782. Discharged on 5/21/1782 (1st NC Regiment). Received clothing	Eutaw Springs (SC).

Name	1st Unit	Year / Rank / Served Under / Notes	Known Battles
		on 5/24/1782. Enlisted in Caswell County. From Guilford County, NC. S41885.	
Moons, Shadrack	5th NC Regiment	1777, a Private under Capt. Simon Alderson. Died on 10/5/1777.	Germantown (PA).
Moore, Alfred	1st NC Regiment	9/1/1775, a Captain under Col. James Moore. Resigned 3/8/1777. Later, a Colonel in NC Militia. From Brunswick County, NC.	Moore's Creek Bridge [4], Ft. Johnston #4, Ft. Johnston #5, Breech Inlet Naval Battle (SC).
Moore, Cuffee	5th NC Regiment	1779, a Private under Maj. Reading Blount. Died on 8/17/1779.	
Moore, Daniel	1st NC Regiment	6/6/1781, a Private under Capt. William Lytle for 12 months. Discharged on 6/6/1782 (4th NC Regiment). Earlier in NC Militia. From Burke County, NC. S7249.	
Moore, Dempsey	6th NC Regiment	1775, a 2nd Lieutenant in the Hillsborough District Minutemen. 4/17/1776, a 2nd Lieutenant under Capt. Philip Taylor and Col. John Alexander Lillington. 10/28/1776, a 1st Lieutenant under Capt. Thomas Donoho. Resigned 8/27/1777. Later a Captain of NC Militia. From Caswell County, NC.	
Moore, Elijah	4th NC Regiment	1782, a Private under Capt. Thomas Evans for 18 months.	
Moore, Elijah	10th NC Regiment	10/12/1777, a 1st Lieutenant. Transferred to 1st NC Regiment on 6/1/1778. Promoted to Captain on 10/13/1781. Transferred to 4th NC Regiment on 2/6/1782. Retired on 1/1/1783. From Granville County, NC. aka Elizah Moore. W7469.	Guilford Court House, Siege of Ninety-Six 1781 (SC), Eutaw Springs (SC).
Moore, Frederick	5th NC Regiment	A Private under Capt. Reading Blount, dates unknown. 9/9/1778, a known Private under Capt. John Ingles (2nd NC Regiment).	
Moore, George	2nd NC Regiment	10/18/1781, a Private under Capt. Benjamin Carter for 12 months. Discharged on 10/18/1782. From Rutherford County, NC. Enlisted at Charlotte, NC. Born on 11/13/1763 in Queen Anne County, MD. aka George Moor. S21382.	
Moore, Isaac	10th NC Regiment	4/19/1777, a Captain under Col. Abraham Sheppard. Transferred to 1st NC Regiment on 6/1/1778. Died 7/10/1778.	Monmouth (NJ).
Moore, Jacob	5th NC Regiment	A Private under Capt. Reading Blount. Died on 4/28/1778.	
Moore, James	1st NC Regiment	1780, an Ensign. 7/1/1781, a Lieutenant under Capt. William Lytle. Wounded at Eutaw Springs, SC on September 8, 1781. Did not rejoin regiment.	Eutaw Springs (SC).
Moore, James	1st NC Regiment	8/21/1775, Colonel over 1st NC Regiment (Provincial Troops). 11/28/1775, Colonel over 1st NC Regiment (Continental Troops). 4/10/1776, a Brigadier General. Died from gout	Brunswick Town #1.

Name	1st Unit	Year / Rank / Served Under / Notes	Known Battles
		on 4/15/1777. Another source says he died on 4/22/1777. From Brunswick County, NC. Born in 1737 in New Hanover (what would become Brunswick) County, NC.	
Moore, James	2nd NC Regiment	5/2/1776, a Private, unit unknown. 9/9/1778, a known Private in the Lt. Colonel's Company (Lt. Col. Selby Harney).	
Moore, James	4th NC Regiment	7/20/1782, a Private under Capt. Thomas Evans for 18 months, then Capt. Benjamin Andrew Coleman. Enlisted at Duplin Court House, NC. Discharged at Wilmington, NC. S37263.	
Moore, James	5th NC Regiment	5/2/1776, a Corporal under Capt. Reading Blount. A Private in Sep. 1777. Discharged in Oct. 1778. aka Joseph Moore.	
Moore, Jesse	1st NC Regiment	4/15/1781, a Private under Capt. Anthony Sharpe. Discharged on 4/5/1782 (4th NC Regiment).	
Moore, Jesse	5th NC Regiment	6/20/1779, a Private under Capt. Joseph Montford for 18 months. aka James Moore.	
Moore, John	2nd NC Regiment	Apr. 1782, a Private under Capt. Clement Hall. Dropped from the rolls in Sep. 1782.	
Moore, John	3rd NC Regiment	7/20/1778, a Private under Maj. Thomas Hogg for nine months.	
Moore, John	4th NC Regiment	1779, a Private under Capt. John McLane for six months. Earlier and later in NC Militia. From Granville County, NC. W7472.	Stono Ferry (SC).
Moore, John	7th NC Regiment	12/17/1776, a 1st Lieutenant under Capt. Lemuel Ely. Dropped from the rolls in Nov. 1777.	
Moore, John	8th NC Regiment	2/21/1777, a Private under Capt. Robert Raiford. Dec. 1777, a Private under Capt. Benjamin Williams (2nd NC Regiment) taking the place of Malachai Jolly. Died on 12/31/1778.	
Moore, Joseph	2nd NC Regiment	Jan. 1778, a Musician under Capt. Robert Fenner. Died 3/16/1778.	
Moore, Lemuel	1st NC Regiment	4/15/1781, a Private under Capt. Anthony Sharpe. Discharged on 4/15/1782 (4th NC Regiment).	
Moore, Lemuel	5th NC Regiment	1777, a Private under Capt. Simon Alderson. A Musician in Nov. 1777. Back to Private in Jan. 1778. Back to Musician in Feb. 1778. Died on 4/26/1778.	
Moore, Marmaduke	2nd NC Regiment	11/1/1777, a Private in the Colonel's Company (Col. Alexander Martin). 9/9/1778, under Capt. Benjamin Andrew Coleman (2nd NC Regiment). 3/12/1779, re-enlisted under Capt. Benjamin Andrew Coleman. From Hertford County, NC.	
Moore, Matthew	3rd NC Regiment	7/20/1778, a Private under Maj. Thomas Hogg for nine months.	
Moore, Maurice Jr.	1st NC Regiment	9/1/1775, an Ensign. 1/4/1776, a 2nd Lieutenant. Killed on 1/18/1776. (?)	
Moore,	4th NC	1777, a Private under Capt. Wiliam Temple	

Name	1st Unit	Year / Rank / Served Under / Notes	Known Battles
Nathaniel	Regiment	Coles. Discharged on 8/10/1777.	
Moore, Ralph	2nd NC Regiment	6/1/1777, a Private under Capt. James Martin for three years. Dropped from the rolls in Nov. 1777. Re-enlisted in Oct. 1778. Died on 12/2/1778. Last name might be Moon (?).	
Moore, Reuben	3rd NC Regiment	7/20/1778, a Private under Lt./Capt. Joseph Montford for nine months.	
Moore, Robert	9th NC Regiment	11/28/1776, an Ensign under Capt. Hezekiah Rice. Later, a Captain in the "New Levies." From Caswell County.	
Moore, Roger	4th NC Regiment	1775, a Captain in the Edenton District Minutemen. 4/17/1776, a Captain in 4th NC Regiment. Resigned in Nov. 1776. His unit taken over by Capt. William Goodman.	
Moore, Shadrack	3rd NC Regiment	1781, a Private under Capt. Clement Hall for 12 months. Discharged on 10/1/1782 (2nd NC Regiment).	
Moore, Simeon	4th NC Regiment	1782, a Private under Capt. Thomas Evans for 18 months. Discharged near Charleston, SC. From Craven County, NC. S41960.	
Moore, Thomas	1st NC Regiment	1781, a Private under Capt. Alexander Brevard. Discharged on 6/7/1782 (3rd NC Regiment).	
Moore, Thomas	4th NC Regiment	11/1/1776, a Private under Capt. William Goodman for three years. 9/8/1778, a known Private in the Colonel's Company (Col. Thomas Clark) (1st NC Regiment) led by Capt. John Gambier Scull. Discharged on 11/10/1778.	
Moore, Thomas	5th NC Regiment	A Private under Capt. Reading Blount. 9/9/1778, a known Private under Capt. John Ingles (2nd NC Regiment). Discharged on 11/10/1778.	
Moore, William	3rd NC Regiment	7/20/1778, a Private in the Lt. Colonel's Company (Lt. Col. William Lee Davidson) led by Lt./Capt. George "Gee" Bradley for nine months. 4/23/1779, a known Private in the Lt. Colonel's Company (Lt. Col. Robert Mebane) led by Capt. George "Gee" Bradley.	
Moore, William	3rd NC Regiment	May 1781, a Private, unit unknown. Wounded in the knee at the battle of Eutaw Springs, SC. Discharged 1/31/1782. From Duplin County, NC.	Eutaw Springs (SC).
Moore, William	3rd NC Regiment	4/2/1782, a Private under Capt. Benjamin Bailey for 12 months.	
Moore, William	3rd NC Regiment	7/20/1778, a Private under Maj. Thomas Hogg for nine months.	
Moore, William	4th NC Regiment	1781, a Private under Capt. George Dougherty. Discharged on 1/31/1782.	
Moore, William	4th NC Regiment	9/20/1776, a Sergeant under Capt. William Temple Coles. Dropped from the rolls in Feb. 1778. Said to be promoted, rank and date unknown.	
Moore, William	5th NC Regiment	1777, a Private under Capt. Henry Darnell. Deserted in Aug. 1777.	
Moore,	10th NC	1/19/1778, a Surgeon's Mate. Resigned in May	

Name	1st Unit	Year / Rank / Served Under / Notes	Known Battles
William	Regiment	1778.	
Moore, Wyllis	2nd NC Regiment	11/8/1781, a Private under Capt. Benjamin Andrew Coleman for 12 months.	
Moran, William	1st NC Regiment	1781, a Private under Capt. Anthony Sharpe for 12 months. Discharged on 4/12/1782 (4th NC Regiment). From Halifax County, NC. W17167.	
Morehead, James	1st NC Regiment	3/23/1779, a Lieutenant under Capt. William Lytle.	
Morehead, James	5th NC Regiment	Jan. 1779, a Captain under Col. Thomas Clark. Left the service in Dec. 1779. One source claims he was also a Captain in the 10th NC Regiment earlier (?).	Stono Ferry (SC).
Moreland, Bartlet	3rd NC Regiment	7/20/1778, a Private under Lt./Capt. Joseph Montford for nine months.	
Morgan, Benjamin	1st NC Regiment	4/5/1781, a Private under Capt. Griffith John McRee. Discharged on 9/1/1782 (3rd NC Regiment).	
Morgan, Benjamin	3rd NC Regiment	1775, an Ensign in the Halifax District Minutemen. 4/17/1776, an Ensign under Capt. Jacob Turner and Col. Jethro Sumner.	
Morgan, Bennett	2nd NC Regiment	9/9/1778, under Capt. Clement Hall. 3/12/1779, re-enlisted under Capt. Clement Hall.	
Morgan, Bennett	2nd NC Regiment	11/7/1776, a Sergeant under Lt./Capt. Clement Hall for three years. 9/9/1778, a known Sergeant under Capt. Clement Hall. 3/12/1779, in same unit.	
Morgan, Charles	5th NC Regiment	5/14/1776, a Private under Capt. Reading Blount. A Sergeant in Nov. 1777. Discharged on 10/25/1778.	
Morgan, Charles	5th NC Regiment	1777, a Corporal under Capt. John Pugh Williams. A Sergeant in Nov. 1777. A Private in June 1778. Probably the same man as directly above.	
Morgan, Isaac	1st NC Regiment	1782, a Private under Capt. Peter Bacot for 18 months.	
Morgan, James	2nd NC Regiment	12/18/1777, a Private under Maj. Hardy Murfree. 9/8/1778, a known Private under Capt. Tilghman Dixon (1st NC Regiment). From Hertford County, NC.	
Morgan, James	7th NC Regiment	12/18/1776, a Private under Capt. Joseph Walker. A Corporal in Dec. 1776. Back to Private in June 1778. Discharged on 1/29/1780. aka Joseph Morgan.	
Morgan, John	1st NC Regiment	5/19/1781, a Private under Capt. Robert Raiford. Discharged on 4/19/1782 (2nd NC Regiment).	
Morgan, John	1st NC Regiment	6/14/1781, a Private under Capt. Thomas Donoho. Discharged on 6/14/1782. From Onslow County, NC. Earlier in Chatham County in the NC Militia.	Eutaw Springs (SC).
Morgan, John	6th NC Regiment	4/26/1776, a Private under Lt./Capt. Thomas White for three years. 9/8/1778, a known Private under Capt. John Sumner (1st NC Regiment). Discharged on 5/10/1779. From	

Name	1st Unit	Year / Rank / Served Under / Notes	Known Battles
		Edgecombe (what is now Nash) County, NC. W18528.	
Morgan, John	9th NC Regiment	1777, a Private under Capt. Joseph J. Wade. A Musician in Feb. 1778. Died on 7/10/1778.	
Morgan, Reuben	1st NC Regiment	4/12/1781, a Private under Capt. Alexander Brevard. Discharged on 4/12/1782 (3rd NC Regiment).	
Morgan, Richard	10th NC Regiment	7/26/1777, a Private under Capt. Armwell Herron. 6/26/1778, re-enlisted as a Private under Capt. Clement Hall (2nd NC Regiment). Died on 9/23/1778.	
Morgan, Sampson	1st NC Regiment	4/12/1781, a Private under Capt. William Lytle. Deserted on 7/6/1781. Re-enlisted in Jan. 1782 for the duration of the war.	
Morgan, Sampson	3rd NC Regiment	1781, a Private under Capt. Clement Hall for 12 months. Discharged on 11/1/1782 (2nd NC Regiment).	
Morgan, Timothy	3rd NC Regiment	7/20/1778, a known Private in the Lt. Colonel's Company (Lt. Col. William Lee Davidson) led by Lt./Capt. George "Gee" Bradley for nine months.	
Morgan, William	1st NC Regiment	1776, a Private under Capt. Joshua Bowman. 9/8/1778, a known Private under Capt. Joshua Bowman. A Sergeant for some time. Wounded at the battle of Stony Point (NY). POW at the Fall of Charleston (SC). Enlisted at Brunswick Town, NC. Discharged in Wilmington, NC. From Brunswick County, NC. S41886.	Brandywine Creek (PA), Germantown (PA), Monmouth (NJ), Stony Point (NY), Siege of Charleston 1780 (SC).
Morgan, William	1st NC Regiment	1777, a Corporal under Capt. Lawrence Thompson.	
Morgan, William	10th NC Regiment	July 1777, a Private under Capt. Armwell Herron for three years. 6/6/1779, a Private under Capt. Michael Quinn (3rd NC Regiment). POW at the Fall of Charleston (SC), held for 14 months. S41895.	Siege of Charleston 1780 (SC).
Moring, Maurice	1st NC Regiment	Jan. 1782, a Private under Capt. William Armstrong for the duration of the war. 2/6/1782, this unit was transferred to the 3rd NC Regiment.	
Morning, John	2nd NC Regiment	1777, Private under Capt. Benjamin Williams. Dropped from the rolls in Jan. 1778.	
Morphis, John	3rd NC Regiment	1775, an Ensign in the Hillsborough District Minutemen. 4/17/1776, an Ensign under Capt. James Emmett and Col. Jethro Sumner. 1777, a 2nd Lieutenant under Capt. Thomas Granbury, then under Capt. Matthew Wood. Mostly served as a recruiter in NC. aka John Morphes, John Morpis. S41884.	Ft. Moultrie #1 (SC).
Morris, Abraham	1st NC Regiment	4/15/1781, a Musician under Capt. Thomas Donoho. Discharged on 4/15/1782.	
Morris,	3rd NC	7/20/1778, a Private under Capt. Francis Child	

Name	1st Unit	Year / Rank / Served Under / Notes	Known Battles
Benjamin	Regiment	for nine months.	
Morris, Benjamin	5th NC Regiment	1777, a Private under Capt. Henry Darnell. Dropped from the rolls in Feb. 1778.	
Morris, Edward	4th NC Regiment	7/20/1778, a Private under Lt. (maybe Capt.) Kedar Parker for nine months. From Nash County, NC. Born 10/22/1767 in Halifax County, NC. R7401.	Stono Ferry (SC).
Morris, Edward	9th NC Regiment	1777, a Sergeant under Capt. Joel Brevard. Reduced in rank on 6/3/1778. Deserted on 6/15/1778.	
Morris, Griffin	1st NC Regiment	4/12/1781, a Private under Capt. William Lytle. Deserted on 7/6/1781. Re-enlisted in Jan. 1782 for the duration of the war.	
Morris, James	5th NC Regiment	1777, a Corporal under Capt. Henry Darnell. A Private in Jan. 1778. Dropped from the rolls in Feb. 1778.	
Morris, John	4th NC Regiment	8/21/1781, a Private under Capt. Anthony Sharpe for 18 months. Per the official records, he deserted on 4/19/1783 (?). He claims he was honorably discharged at Charleston, SC. R7405.	
Morris, John	5th NC Regiment	A Private under Capt. John Pugh Williams. Discharged on 6/16/1778.	
Morris, John	10th NC Regiment	7/15/1777, a Private under Capt. Dempsey Gregory. 9/8/1778, a known Private under Capt. Howell Tatum (1st NC Regiment).	
Morris, Nathan	4th NC Regiment	1782, a Private under Capt. Thomas Evans for 18 months.	
Morris, Philemon	1st NC Regiment	1/11/1778, a Private under Capt. Howell Tatum for three years. 9/8/1778, a known Private under Capt. Howell Tatum.	
Morris, Richard	5th NC Regiment	8/17/1776, a Private under Capt. John Pugh Williams. Discharged in Oct. 1778.	
Morris, Shadrack	5th NC Regiment	1777, a Private under Capt. Simon Alderson. Died on 10/5/1777, most likely from wounds received at the battle of Germantown, PA.	Germantown (PA).
Morris, William	1st NC Regiment	Aug. 1781, a Private under Capt. Alexander Brevard. Wounded at the battle of Eutaw Springs (SC). Discharged on 6/9/1782 (3rd NC Regiment). W5147.	Siege of Ninety-Six 1781 (SC), Eutaw Springs (SC).
Morris, William	1st NC Regiment	6/6/1781, a Private under Capt. William Lytle. Dropped from the rolls sometime during 1781.	
Morris, William	2nd NC Regiment	12/1/1779, a Private in the Colonel's Company (Col. John Patten) led by Capt. John Craddock.	
Morris, William	3rd NC Regiment	7/20/1778, a Private under Capt. John Baker. Died on 11/24/1778.	
Morris, William	4th NC Regiment	1782, a Sergeant under Capt. Anthony Sharpe. Deserted on 4/19/1783 (?).	
Morris, Witt	4th NC Regiment	1782, a Private under Capt. Anthony Sharpe for 18 months.	
Morrisett, Henry	7th NC Regiment	1777, Private under Capt. Joseph Walker. Died on 3/28/1778.	
Morrisett, Peter	4th NC Regiment	5/21/1778, a Corporal under Capt. Benjamin Carter.	

Name	1st Unit	Year / Rank / Served Under / Notes	Known Battles
Morrison, Alexander	1st NC Regiment	1777, a Sergeant under Capt. Howell Tatum. A Private on 8/14/1777. Back to Sergeant in Oct. 1777. 9/8/1778, a known Private under Capt. Joshua Bowman. Discharged in May 1783.	
Morrison, Isaac	7th NC Regiment	3/8/1777, a Private under Capt. John Poynter. Deserted on 12/5/1777. Rejoined in Sep. 1778. Deserted again in Nov. 1778.	
Morrison, John	1st NC Regiment	5/25/1781, a Private under Lt./Capt. Benjamin Bailey. Discharged on 5/25/1782 (3rd NC Regiment).	
Morrison, Robert	NC Artillery	8/26/1776, a Bombardier under Capt. John Vance as NC Provincial Troops. 7/10/1777, on Continental Line. 11/16/1777, under Capt. John Kingsbury. 5/1/1778, in same unit. A Sergeant in July 1778. 9/10/1778, in same unit.	
Morrison, Thomas	NC Artillery	8/12/1776, a Matross under Capt. John Vance as NC Provincial Troops. 7/10/1777, on Continental Line. 11/16/1777, under Capt. John Kingsbury. 5/1/1778, in same unit. Mustered out in May 1778, not fit for duty.	
Morrow, Samuel	4th NC Regiment	5/1/1776, a Corporal under Capt. Robert Smith for three years. A Private in June 1778. 9/8/1778, a known Private in the Colonel's Company (Col. Thomas Clark) (1st NC Regiment) led by Capt. John Gambier Scull. Discharged on 5/14/1779. W7482.	Brandywine Creek (PA), Germantown (PA), Monmouth (NJ).
Morse, Farrell	6th NC Regiment	1777, a Private under Capt. Philip Taylor. Died on 3/13/1778.	
Morse, Francis	10th NC Regiment	4/3/1778, a Private under Capt. James Wilson. Deserted on 4/20/1778.	
Morton, Jacob	3rd NC Regiment	1779, a Private under Capt. Kedar Ballard. Discharged on 12/1/1779.	
Morton, William	4th NC Regiment	1782, a Sergeant under Capt. Thomas Evans for 18 months.	
Morton, William	6th NC Regiment	A Private under Capt. Thomas Donoho. Deserted in Aug. 1777.	
Moseley, John	8th NC Regiment	2/21/1777, a Private under Capt. Francis Tartanson. 9/9/1778, a known Private under Capt. Robert Fenner (2nd NC Regiment). POW at Ft. Lafayette, NY on 6/1/1779. Discharged on 2/20/1780.	Ft. Lafayette (NY).
Moseley, Thomas	5th NC Regiment	1777, a Private under Capt. Simon Alderson. Dropped from the rolls in March 1778.	
Moseley, William	3rd NC Regiment	7/20/1778, a Private under Capt. Francis Child for nine months.	
Moseley, William	6th NC Regiment	12/11/1776, a Paymaster. Resigned in May 1777.	
Moses, Abraham	1st NC Regiment	5/18/1781, a Private under Capt. Robert Raiford. Discharged on 5/18/1782 (2nd NC Regiment).	
Mosier, Francis	4th NC Regiment	1779, a Private under Capt. Micajah Lewis for 13 months. Then, in NC Militia. From Surry County, NC. W25719.	
Moss, Joseph	NC Light	1777, a Private under Capt. John Dickerson,	Germantown

Name	1st Unit	Year / Rank / Served Under / Notes	Known Battles
	Dragoons	Capt. Samuel Ashe. 3/7/1777, this unit was placed on the NC Continental Line. From Granville County, NC. W9204.	(PA).
Moss, Richard	3rd NC Regiment	1779, a Private under Capt. Kedar Ballard.	
Moss, Robert	7th NC Regiment	1777, a Private under Capt. John McGlaughan. 2/26/1778, a known Private under Capt. Howell Tatum (1st NC Regiment).	
Mossam, Richard	2nd NC Regiment	9/4/1778, an Ensign under Capt. Clement Hall. aka Richard Mossom.	
Mosslander, Abel	4th NC Regiment	1775, an Ensign in the Edenton District Minutemen. 4/17/1776, an Ensign under Capt. Roger Moore and Col. Thomas Polk. 1/25/1777, a Lieutenant under Capt. James Williams. Dropped from the rolls in Jan. 1778. aka Abel Moslander.	
Mott, Benjamin	NC Artillery	7/19/1776, a Drummer under Capt. John Vance as NC Provincial Troops. 7/10/1777, on Continental Line. 11/16/1777, under Capt. John Kingsbury. 5/1/1778, in same unit. 9/16/1778, in same unit.	
Mott, Benjamin	3rd NC Regiment	2/1/1780, a Corporal under Lt./Capt. Samuel Jones. A Sergeant in April 1782 under Capt. Clement Hall (2nd NC Regiment). From New Hanover County, NC. S46327.	
Mott, Daniel	1st NC Regiment	1777, a Private under Capt. John Brown. 9/8/1778, a known Private under Capt. Joshua Bowman. Dropped from the rolls in July 1779. aka Daniel Motte.	
Mott, Edgerton	1st NC Regiment	1776, a Private under Capt. John Walker. 1777, a Private under Capt. John Brown. 9/8/1778, a known Private under Capt. Joshua Bowman. A Corporal in Nov. 1779. POW at the Fall of Charleston, escaped. 1781, under Capt. Robert Raiford. Back to Private in 1782 (2nd NC Regiment). aka Edge Motte. W7466.	Moore's Creek Bridge, Brandywine Creek (PA), Siege of Charleston 1780 (SC).
Mount, Jeremiah	3rd NC Regiment	7/20/1778, a Private under Capt. Francis Child for nine months.	
Mount, Richard	6th NC Regiment	5/31/1776, a Private under Capt. Archibald Lytle, then Capt. Griffith John McRee, then Capt. Thomas White for 2-1/2 years. Unit consolidated into the company led by Capt. Tilghman Dixon (1st NC Regiment) in June 1778. 9/8/1778, a known Private under Capt. Joshua Bowman (1st NC Regiment). Discharged at Paramus, NJ. Dropped from the rolls in March 1779. S43021.	Brandywine Creek (PA), Germantown (PA), Monmouth (NJ).
Moye, Gardner	10th NC Regiment	5/22/1777, a Musician under Capt. Armwell Herron for three years. A Private in June 1778 under Capt. Benjamin Andrew Coleman (2nd NC Regiment). A Corporal in Nov. 1778. POW at Ft. Lafayette, NY on 6/1/1779 for 11 months. Exchanged, discharged at Morristown, NY. aka Gardner Moy, Gardner May. S41815.	Monmouth (NJ), Ft. Lafayette (NY).

Name	1st Unit	Year / Rank / Served Under / Notes	Known Battles
Moye, George	5th NC Regiment	5/11/1776, a Private under Capt. Reading Blount for 2-1/2 years. 9/9/1778, a known Private in the Colonel's Company (Col. John Patten) (2nd NC Regiment) led by Capt. John Craddock. Discharged on 11/10/1778.	
Mucilyea, John	1st NC Regiment	7/28/1777, a Private, unit unknown, enlisted for three years. 9/8/1778, a known Drummer in the Lt. Colonel's Company (Lt. Col. Robert Mebane) led by Capt. Joshua Bowman. 3/12/1779, re-enlisted for the duration of the war in the same unit. On some rolls as John Midsleya, John Michleya.	
Mullen, Michael	4th NC Regiment	1782, a Private under Capt. Anthony Sharpe. Died on 12/8/1782.	
Mullen, Richard	10th NC Regiment	8/11/1777, a Private under Capt. Isaac Moore for three years. 9/8/1778, a known Private in the Lt. Colonel's Company (Lt. Col. Robert Mebane) (1st NC Regiment) led by Capt. Joshua Bowman - sick on that date. aka Richard Mullin.	
Mullen, Thomas	1st NC Regiment	5/25/1781, a Private under Capt. Alexander Brevard. Deserted on 7/1/1781. aka Thomas Mullin.	
Mullen, William	10th NC Regiment	8/15/1777, a Corporal under Capt. Isaac Moore for three years. A Private in June 1778. 9/8/1778, a known Private in the Lt. Colonel's Company (Lt. Col. Robert Mebane) (1st NC Regiment) led by Capt. Joshua Bowman. aka William Mullin.	
Mullins, Malone	3rd NC Regiment	4/10/1776, a Private under Capt. William Brinkley. 9/9/1778, a known Private in the Lt. Colonel's Company (Lt. Col. Selby Harney) led by Capt. Joshua Bowman. Discharged on 10/10/1778. From Bute County, NC. aka Melone Mullen, Malone Mullin.	Monmouth (NJ).
Mumford, Charles	2nd NC Regiment	2/11/1782, a Private under Capt. Benjamin Andrew Coleman for 12 months.	
Mundin, Joseph	10th NC Regiment	5/17/1777, a Private under Capt. Isaac Moore. Died on 12/20/1777.	
Mungoe, Jesse	1st NC Regiment	4/12/1781, a Private under Capt. William Lytle. Discharged on 4/12/1782 (4th NC Regiment).	
Murfree, Hardy	2nd NC Regiment	9/1/1775, a Captain under Col. Robert Howe and Col. Alexander Martin. A Major from 2/1/1777 to 11/24/1778. Mostly a recruiter from his home in Hertford County, NC. 4/1/1778, a Lt. Colonel in the 2nd NC Regiment. His promotion to Lt. Colonel was clearly back-dated since so many records show him as a Major until 1782. After the Fall of Charleston, a Lt. Colonel of 1st NC Regiment. Assumed command of the 2nd NC Regiment in early 1782 (after Feb. 6), when Lt. Col. Reading Blount took leave. Active until June 1782 or Jan. 1, 1783 (two sources)	Great Bridge (VA), Ft. Moultrie #1 (SC), Brandywine Creek (PA), Germantown (PA), Monmouth (NJ), Stony Point (NY), Siege of Charleston

Name	1st Unit	Year / Rank / Served Under / Notes	Known Battles
			1780 (SC).
Murphy, Archibald	2nd NC Regiment	12/18/1781, a Private under Capt. Benjamin Andrew Coleman for 12 months.	
Murphy, Daniel	3rd NC Regiment	7/20/1778, a Private under Maj. Thomas Hogg for nine months.	
Murphy, James	1st NC Regiment	4/28/1781, a Private under Capt. Griffith John McRee. Died in Oct. 1781.	
Murphy, James	4th NC Regiment	1782, a Private under Capt. William Lytle for 18 months.	
Murphy, Moses	5th NC Regiment	8/5/1779, a Private under Maj. Reading Blount. Deserted in Oct. 1779.	
Murphy, Patrick	3rd NC Regiment	5/3/1779, a Private under Capt. George "Gee" Bradley for 18 months. Discharged 1/6/1783.	
Murphy, Solomon	5th NC Regiment	8/5/1779, a Private under Maj. Reading Blount. Deserted in Oct. 1779.	
Murphy, Thomas	5th NC Regiment	1777, a Private under Capt. William Caswell. Died on 2/3/1778.	
Murphy, William	5th NC Regiment	6/24/1779, a Private under Capt. Joseph Montford. Deserted on 11/3/1779.	
Murray, Barnabas	1st NC Regiment	1775, a Private under Capt. Robert Rowan. Later in NC Militia. From Orange County, NC. S30611.	Moore's Creek Bridge, Fort Moultrie #1 (SC).
Murray, Charles	4th NC Regiment	5/1/1776, a Sergeant under Capt. Robert Smith for three years. A Private in Oct. 1777. 9/8/1778, a known Private in the Colonel's Company (Col. Thomas Clark) (1st NC Regiment) led by Capt. John Gambier Scull - sick at Valley Forge on that date. Discharged on 11/10/1778.	
Murray, John	4th NC Regiment	1777, a Private under Capt. Robert Smith. A Sergeant in Oct. 1777.	
Murray, L. Alexander	1st NC Regiment	5/2/1781, a Sergeant under Lt./Capt. Benjamin Bailey. Discharged on 5/2/1782 (3rd NC Regiment).	
Murray, Morgan	4th NC Regiment	1781, a Private under Capt. Joseph T. Rhodes. Discharged on 4/1/1782.	
Murray, William	4th NC Regiment	4/1/1777, an Ensign under Capt. James Williams. Dropped from the rolls in Jan. 1778. Rejoined in Jan. 1779.	
Murrell, Barnabas	3rd NC Regiment	7/20/1778, a Private in the Lt. Colonel's Company (Lt. Col. William Lee Davidson) led by Lt./Capt. George "Gee" Bradley for nine months. 4/23/1779, a known Private in the Lt. Colonel's Company (Lt. Col. Robert Mehane) led by Capt. George "Gee" Bradley.	
Murrell, Matthew	3rd NC Regiment	7/20/1778, a Sergeant in the Lt. Colonel's Company (Lt. Col. William Lee Davidson) led by Capt. George "Gee" Bradley for nine months. Probably the same man as directly below.	
Murrill, Matthew	3rd NC Regiment	4/23/1779, a known Private in the Lt. Colonel's Company (Lt. Col. Robert Mebane) led by Capt. George "Gee" Bradley. Died at Philadelphia	

Name	1st Unit	Year / Rank / Served Under / Notes	Known Battles
		Hospital.	
Mushaw, John	3rd NC Regiment	7/20/1778, a Private under Maj. Thomas Hogg for nine months. Died on 10/23/1778.	
Muskinock, George	2nd NC Regiment	6/5/1781, a Private under Capt. Benjamin Carter. Discharged on 6/6/1782.	
Muster, John	1st NC Regiment	1781, a Private under Capt. Robert Raiford. Dropped from the rolls sometime during 1781.	
Myers, Henry	1st NC Regiment	7/1/1778, a Private in the Colonel's Company (Col. Thomas Clark) led by Capt. John Gambier Scull. aka Henry Mines, Henry Mires, Henry Myre. Deserted in July 1779.	
Myers, Jacob	5th NC Regiment	June 1777, a Private under Capt. William Lytle. Discharged in Sep. 1779. Then, in NC Militia. From Guilford County, NC. S35533.	Briar Creek (GA), Stono Ferry (SC).
Myers, John	2nd NC Regiment	8/21/1777, a Private, unit unknown. 9/9/1778, a known Private in the Colonel's Company (Col. John Patten) led by Capt. John Craddock.	
Myers, Philip	3rd NC Regiment	6/6/1779, a Private under Capt. Michael Quinn for nine months. Discharged in Dec. 1779.	
Myers, William	5th NC Regiment	1779, a Private under Maj. Reading Blount for nine months. Dropped from the rolls in Oct. 1779.	
Myhan, William	2nd NC Regiment	A Private under Capt. Robert Fenner. Died on 7/18/1778.	
Myres, David	1st NC Regiment	5/9/1781, a Private under Capt. Griffith John McRee. Deserted on 7/2/1781. Re-enlisted in Jan. 1782. Discharged in May 1782 (3rd NC Regiment).	
Myrick, James	7th NC Regiment	11/28/1776, an Ensign under Capt. Bennett Wood. 12/11/1776, a Lieutenant under Capt. John Macon. Resigned prior to 12/18/1776. From Bute County, NC.	
Myson, Zach'l	3rd NC Regiment	12/1/1781, a Private under Capt. Clement Hall for 12 months.	
Nall, Thomas	1st NC Regiment	4/25/1781, a Private under Capt. Alexander Brevard. aka Thomas Noll.	
Nash, Clement	2nd NC Regiment	5/3/1776, a 1st Lieutenant. Resigned 2/1/1777. Then a Captain in GA Continentals - POW at Briar Creek (GA).	
Nash, Francis	1st NC Regiment	9/1/1775, a Lt. Colonel under Col. James Moore. 4/10/1776, promoted to Colonel when James Moore promoted to Brigadier General. A Brigadier General on Feb. 5, 1777. Mortally wounded at Germantown on Oct. 4, 1777, died on Oct. 7th. From Orange County, NC.	Moore's Creek Bridge [4], Ft. Moultrie #1 (SC), Brandywine Creek (PA), Germantown (PA).
Nash, Francis	5th NC Regiment	1777, Private under Capt. William Caswell. Died on 3/1/1778.	
Nash, John	4th NC Regiment	11/9/1776, a Private under Capt. John Nelson for three years. 6/1/1778, a Private under Capt. Griffith John McRee (1st NC Regiment). A Corporal in Dec. 1778. A Sergeant in May 1779. Discharged in Nov. 1779.	

Name	1st Unit	Year / Rank / Served Under / Notes	Known Battles
Nash, Joseph	2nd NC Regiment	1777, a Private under Capt. Edward Vail, Jr. 9/9/1778, a known Private in the Colonel's Company (Col. John Patten) (2nd NC Regiment) led by Capt. John Craddock. Deserted on 3/15/1779.	
Nash, Michael	NC Artillery	8/12/1776, a Gunner under Capt. John Vance as NC Provincial Troops. 7/10/1777, on Continental Line. 11/16/1777, under Capt. John Kingsbury. 5/1/1778, in same unit. 9/16/1778, in same unit. Deserted on 4/1/1779.	
Nash, Michael	3rd NC Regiment	1776, a Private under Capt. James Emmett. Then in SC Continental unit. From Guilford County, NC. Born on 2/14/1758. W4042.	
Nasworthy, Samuel	4th NC Regiment	2/27/1782, a Private under Capt. James Mills.	
Neal, Christopher	1st NC Regiment	1781, a Private under Capt. William Walton.	
Neal, Thomas	DQMG	1780, a Gunstocker on the roll of Capt. Solomon Wood (NC Light Dragoons) - this seems to be for convenience only. 8/23/1781, an Artificer under Col. Nicholas Long (Deputy QM General). Made Gunstocks.	
Neckins, Malachi	2nd NC Regiment	1781, a Private under Capt. Benjamin Carter.	
Needham, John	4th NC Regiment	6/1/1777, a Private under Capt. William Goodman for three years. A Private in Oct. 1777. 9/8/1778, a known Private in the Colonel's Company (Col. Thomas Clark) (1st NC Regiment) led by Capt. John Gambier Scull. 3/12/1779, re-enlisted for the duration of the war in the same unit.	
Needham, Thomas	1st NC Regiment	1777, a Sergeant under Capt. Howell Tatum. A Private in Sep. 1777. Back to Sergeant in Dec. 1777. Dropped from the rolls in Jan. 1778.	
Negroe, Benjamin	2nd NC Regiment	1777, a Musician under Capt. John Armstrong. Discharged in Dec. 1777.	
Negroe, Frederick	2nd NC Regiment	1777, a Musician under Capt. William Fenner. Dropped from the rolls in Jan. 1778. aka Frederick Negrove.	
Neil, Daniel	8th NC Regiment	2/24/1777, a Private under Capt. Robert Raiford. Dropped from the rolls in March 1778. aka Daniel Niel.	
Neil, John	3rd NC Regiment	1777, a Private under Capt. Jacob Turner. Died in Nov. 1777.	
Neil, John	4th NC Regiment	1782, a Private under Capt. William Lytle. aka John Niel.	
Neil, John	8th NC Regiment	1777, a Private under Capt. Francis Tartanson. Dropped from the rolls in Jan. 1778. aka John Niel.	
Neil, Philip	1st NC Regiment	4/5/1781, a Sergeant under Capt. Anthony Sharpe. Discharged on 4/5/1782 (4th NC Regiment).	
Neill, Henry	1st NC Regiment	9/1/1775, an Ensign. 1/4/1776, a 2nd Lieutenant. 3/28/1776, a 1st Lieutenant.	Moore's Creek Bridge [4].

Name	1st Unit	Year / Rank / Served Under / Notes	Known Battles
		2/5/1777, a Captain. Resigned 4/3/1777. aka Henry Neale.	
Neill, William	9th NC Regiment	11/28/1776, a 2nd Lieutenant under Capt. Joel Brevard. Dropped from the rolls in Jan. 1778. Later, in NC Militia. From Burke County, NC. aka William Niel, William Neal.	
Neithercutt, William	4th NC Regiment	5/25/1781, a Private under Capt. George Dougherty. Discharged on 5/25/1782. Earlier, served five or six tours in NC Militia, unit(s) unknown. aka William Nithercut. S35539.	Eutaw Springs (SC).
Nelson, Alexander	4th NC Regiment	1775, an Ensign in the Salisbury District Minutemen. 4/17/1776, an Ensign under Capt. John Nelson and Col. Thomas Polk. 7/1/1777, an Ensign under Capt. James Smith. Dropped from the rolls in Jan. 1778. Jan. 1779, re-enlisted into the 4th NC Regiment again.	
Nelson, Arthur	8th NC Regiment	7/20/1777, a Private under Lt./Capt. Michael Quinn. Died 10/24/1778.	
Nelson, George	6th NC Regiment	5/15/1776, a Private under Capt. Arthur Council for 12 months. 1777, re-enlisted under Capt. Matthew Ramsey (9th NC Regiment) for the duration of the war. Enlisted first time at Hillsborough, NC. R21891.	Stono Ferry (SC).
Nelson, Giles	5th NC Regiment	1776, a Private under Capt. John Enloe for 2-1/2 years. Under other officers in other regiments, not noted which. Discharged on 1/17/1782. From Pitt County, NC. S7263.	
Nelson, Jesse	10th NC Regiment	5/12/1777, a Private under Capt. Abraham Sheppard, Jr. 9/9/1778, a known Private under Capt. Robert Fenner (2nd NC Regiment). 3/12/1779, re-enlisted under Capt. Robert Fenner.	
Nelson, John	4th NC Regiment	1775, a Captain in the Salisbury District Minutemen. 4/17/1776, a Captain in 4th NC Regiment. A Major in the 1st NC Regiment on 2/3/1778. POW at the Fall of Charleston. Finally exchanged on 11/26/1782. Retired 1/1/1783. aka John Neilson. R20131.	Brandywine Creek (PA), Germantown (PA), Monmouth (NJ), Siege of Charleston 1780 (SC).
Nelson, Robert	4th NC Regiment	5/2/1776, a Private under Capt. John Nelson for three years. 6/1/1778, a Wagoner under Capt. Griffith John McRee (1st NC Regiment). Discharged on 5/1/1779.	
Nelson, Robert	6th NC Regiment	1/1/1777, a QM Sergeant for 2-1/2 years. Dropped from the rolls in Jan. 1778. Probably from Orange County, NC (married in 1781 at Hillsborough). W26571.	
Nelson, William	5th NC Regiment	1777, a Private under Capt. John Enloe. Died on 8/15/1778.	
Nettles, Jesse	1st NC Regiment	7/9/1781, a Private under Capt. William Lytle. Dropped from the rolls sometime during 1781.	
Nettles, Shadrack	1st NC Regiment	7/9/1781, a Private under Capt. William Lytle. Discharged on 6/26/1782.	

Name	1st Unit	Year / Rank / Served Under / Notes	Known Battles
Nevill, George	4th NC Regiment	2/27/1782, a Private under Capt. William Lytle. Deserted on 3/16/1783 (?).	
Nevy, Frederick	4th NC Regiment	1777, a Private under Capt. William Temple Coles. Dropped from the rolls in Jan. 1778.	
New, William	4th NC Regiment	1776, a Private under Capt. James Williams for 18 months. Discharged 11/9/1777. Earlier and later in NC Militia. From New Hanover County, NC. S7267.	Germantown (PA).
Newark, Nicholas	2nd NC Regiment	11/1/1781, a Private under Capt. Benjamin Andrew Coleman.	
Newbern, Thomas	4th NC Regiment	4/22/1776, a Private under Capt. Micajah Lewis for 2-1/2 years. A Private in Oct. 1777. 9/8/1778, a known Private in the Colonel's Company (Col. Thomas Clark) (1st NC Regiment) led by Capt. John Gambier Scull. Discharged on 11/10/1778. aka Thomas Newburn.	
Newby, Francis	3rd NC Regiment	Spring/Summer 1781, a Private under Capt. Edward Yarborough for 12 months. Discharged on 2/25/1782. Wounded at the battle of Eutaw Springs, SC. Enlisted in Franklin County, NC.	Eutaw Springs (SC).
Newby, Matthew	5th NC Regiment	Jan. 1779, a Private under Capt. Philip Taylor.	
Newell, John	3rd NC Regiment	7/20/1778, a Private under Lt./Capt. George "Gee" Bradley for nine months.	
Newell, Nathan	10th NC Regiment	8/19/1777, a Private under Capt. Abraham Sheppard, Jr. Dropped from the rolls in Jan. 1778.	
Newham, Francis	5th NC Regiment	7/1/1779, a Private under Capt. Joseph Montford. Deserted on 10/22/1779.	
Newham, Francis	4th NC Regiment	1782, a Private under Capt. Thomas Evans. Deserted on 4/20/1783 (?).	
Newly, Matthew	2nd NC Regiment	3/12/1782, a Sergeant under Capt. Clement Hall.	
Newman, Edward	1st NC Regiment	2/4/1782, a Private under Capt. James Mills. 2/6/1782, this unit was transferred to the 4th NC Regiment. aka Edward Newsom.	
Newman, Joseph	2nd NC Regiment	2/9/1782, a Private under Capt. Benjamin Andrew Coleman.	
Newman, Reuben	6th NC Regiment	5/1/1776, a Private under Capt. William Glover, then Capt. Benjamin Pike until he died in 1777. 9/8/1778, a known Private under Capt. James Read (1st NC Regiment). Discharged on 11/10/1778 at Paramus, NJ. From Granville County, NC. W10812.	Monmouth (NJ).
Newport, James	4th NC Regiment	1777, a Private under Capt. John Nelson. Deserted on 9/16/1777.	
Newsom, Aaron	3rd NC Regiment	7/20/1778, a Private under Lt./Capt. George "Gee" Bradley for nine months. Died on 10/30/1778.	
Newsom, Boothe	3rd NC Regiment	7/20/1778, a Private in the Lt. Colonel's Company (Lt. Col. William Lee Davidson) led by Lt./Capt. George "Gee" Bradley for nine months. 4/23/1779, a known Private in the Lt.	

Name	1st Unit	Year / Rank / Served Under / Notes	Known Battles
		Colonel's Company (Lt. Col. Robert Mebane) led by Capt. George "Gee" Bradley.	
Newsom, Natheldred	3rd NC Regiment	6/24/1779, a Private under Capt. Michael Quinn. From Dobbs County, NC. aka Nathelrid Newsom, Etheldred Newsom.	
Newsom, Randolph	5th NC Regiment	1777, a Musician under Capt. William Caswell. Dropped from the rolls in Jan. 1778. Jan. 1779, a Musician under Capt. Philip Taylor. A resident of Sussex County, VA, while visiting, he enlisted at Wilmington, NC. aka Randle Newson. S14019.	Brandywine Creek (PA), Germantown (PA), Stono Ferry (SC).
Newsom, Robert	3rd NC Regiment	5/31/1779, a Private under Capt. Michael Quinn.	
Newsom, Thomas	1st NC Regiment	4/12/1781, a Private under Capt. Alexander Brevard. Discharged on 3/12/1782 (3rd NC Regiment). aka Thomas Nusum.	
Newton, Edward	3rd NC Regiment	1782, a Private under Capt. Alexander Brevard. Died on 6/25/1783.	
Newton, Edward	4th NC Regiment	2/7/1782, a Private under Capt. James Mills then Capt. Robert Raiford. From New Hanover County, NC. R20410.	
Newton, Jesse	2nd NC Regiment	7/20/1778, a Private under Maj. Reading Blount for nine months.	
Newton, Joseph	4th NC Regiment	2/7/1782, a Private under Capt. James Mills.	
Newton, Levy	2nd NC Regiment	5/15/1781, a Private under Capt. Tilghman Dixon. Discharged on 5/21/1782 (1st NC Regiment). Received clothing on 5/24/1782. From Caswell County. aka Levi Newton.	
Newton, Patrick	4th NC Regiment	1781, a Sergeant under Capt. George Dougherty. Dropped from the rolls in April 1782.	
Nicholas, George	2nd NC Regiment	1777, a Private under Capt. John Armstrong. Deserted on 3/1/1778. Rejoined in May 1778 under Capt. Robert Fenner. Deserted again on 3/17/1779. aka George Nichols.	
Nicholas, Hancock	NC Artillery	8/12/1776, a Matross under Capt. John Vance as NC Provincial Troops. 7/10/1777, on Continental Line. 11/16/1777, under Capt. John Kingsbury. 5/1/1778, in same unit. 9/16/1778, in same unit. aka Hancock Nicklls.	
Nicholas, James	2nd NC Regiment	4/15/1776, a Private, unit unknown. 9/9/1778, a known Private in the Colonel's Company (Col. John Patten) led by Capt. John Craddock.	
Nicholas, John	1st NC Regiment	3/17/1777, a Private under Capt. Thomas Hogg.	
Nicholas, John	2nd NC Regiment	1777, a Private under Capt. Clement Hall. Dropped from the rolls in Jan. 1778.	
Nicholas, John	4th NC Regiment	2/6/1782, a Private under Capt. James Mills.	
Nicholas, Samuel	2nd NC Regiment	1777, a Private under Capt. James Gee. Dropped from the rolls in Jan. 1778.	
Nicholas, Samuel	2nd NC Regiment	1777, a Sergeant under Capt. James Gee. Died on 7/22/1777.	

Name	1ˢᵗ Unit	Year / Rank / Served Under / Notes	Known Battles
Nicholas, William	1ˢᵗ NC Regiment	1781, a Private under Capt. Anthony Sharpe. Discharged on 5/23/1782 (4th NC Regiment).	
Nicholas, William	10ᵗʰ NC Regiment	11/4/1777, a Private under Capt. Isaac Moore. POW at Ft. Lafayette, NY on 6/1/1779.	Ft. Lafayette (NY).
Nichols, Henry	1ˢᵗ NC Regiment	4/15/1781, a Private under Capt. Robert Raiford. Discharged on 4/15/1782 (2nd NC Regiment).	
Nicholas, James	5ᵗʰ NC Regiment	4/15/1776, a Private under Capt. Simon Alderson for 2-1/2 years. Discharged on 10/30/1778.	
Nichols, Jacob	3ʳᵈ NC Regiment	7/20/1778, a Sergeant under Capt. Kedar Ballard for nine months.	
Nichols, John	7ᵗʰ NC Regiment	3/11/1776, a Private under Capt. John McGlaughan.	
Nichols, Joseph	3ʳᵈ NC Regiment	1781, a Private under Capt. Clement Hall. Discharged on 8/1/1782 (2nd NC Regiment).	
Nichols, Julius Jr.	DQMG	1780, a Wagoner under Col. Nicholas Long (Deputy QM General).	
Nichols, William	4ᵗʰ NC Regiment	8/1/1782, a Private under Capt. Joseph T. Rhodes for 18 months. Enlisted while living in Anson County, NC. R7654.	
Nichols, William	10ᵗʰ NC Regiment	11/4/1777, a Private under Capt. Isaac Moore. 9/9/1778, a known Private in the Lt. Colonel's Company (Lt. Col. Selby Harney - 2nd Regiment). POW at Ft. Lafayette, NY on 6/1/1779.	Ft. Lafayette (NY).
Nicholson, Isaac	1ˢᵗ NC Regiment	4/16/1781, a Sergeant under Capt. Robert Raiford. Dec. 1781, a Sergeant Major. Discharged on 4/12/1782 (2nd NC Regiment).	
Nicholson, Isaac	1ˢᵗ NC Regiment	1781, a Commissary. Mentioned in his son's pension application - James Nicholson (S8918).	
Nicholson, Isaac	4ᵗʰ NC Regiment	1777, a Private under Capt. Joseph Phillips. 9/8/1778, a known Private under Capt. James Read (1st NC Regiment). Deserted on 6/24/1779.	
Nicholson, James	1ˢᵗ NC Regiment	1781, a Private under Capt. Robert Raiford for 15 months. From Surry County, what is now Stokes County, NC. Enlisted in Duplin County, NC. His father, Isaac Nicholson, was a Commissary. S8918.	
Nicholson, John	1ˢᵗ NC Regiment	7/20/1777, a Private under Capt. Thomas Hogg for nine months.	
Nicholson, Robert	10ᵗʰ NC Regiment	4/19/1777, a 1st Lieutenant under Capt. Isaac Moore. Transferred to 1st NC Regiment on 6/1/1778 in the Lt. Colonel's Company (Lt. Col Robert Mebane) led by Capt. Joshua Bowman. Resigned 7/4/1779. He claims he was discharged on 6/25/1779. From Perquimans County, NC. S38263.	
Nickens, Malachi	2ⁿᵈ NC Regiment	5/19/1781, a Private under Capt. Benjamin Carter. Discharged on 5/19/1782. Enlisted in Hertford County, NC. S41925.	Siege of Ninety-Six (SC), Eutaw Springs (SC).
Night,	5ᵗʰ NC	6/23/1779, a Private under Maj. Reading	

Name	1st Unit	Year / Rank / Served Under / Notes	Known Battles
Absalom	Regiment	Blount. Deserted in Oct. 1779.	
Night, Jesse	3rd NC Regiment	5/24/1777, a Private under Lt./Capt. Joseph Montford.	
Nikins, Edward	3rd NC Regiment	Jan. 1779, a Private in the Lt. Colonel's Company (Lt. Col. Robert Mebane) led by Capt. George "Gee" Bradley.	
Nisco, Nicholas	1st NC Regiment	1781, a Private under Capt. William Armstrong. Discharged on 4/25/1782 (3rd NC Regiment).	
Nixon, John	10th NC Regiment	5/13/1778, a Corporal under Capt. Isaac Moore for three years. 9/8/1778, a known Corporal under Capt. John Sumner (1st NC Regiment). A Private in March 1779. Deserted on 4/20/1779.	
Nixon, Thomas	8th NC Regiment	11/28/1776, a Captain under Col. James Armstrong. Resigned 9/20/1777. Later, a Captain in the NC Militia under Col. Enoch Ward (Carteret County Regiment).	Brandywine Creek (PA).
Noah, James	2nd NC Regiment	11/7/1776, a Corporal under Lt./Capt. John Ingles.	
Noble, William	6th NC Regiment	May 1776, a Sergeant under Capt. George Mitchell, then Capt. Thomas Donoho for 2-1/2 years. Then, a Sergeant Major and an Adjutant. Regiment dissolved in June 1778. April 1779, re-enlisted in 4th NC Regiment, unit and rank unknown. Discharged in Oct. 1779 at Halifax, NC. S38962.	Brandywine Creek (PA), Germantown (PA), Stono Ferry (SC).
Noble, William	7th NC Regiment	11/28/1776, a 1st Lieutenant under Capt. Henry Dawson. 1778, a Lieutenant under Capt. Philip Taylor (6th NC Regiment). From Halifax County, NC. aka William Noblin.	
Nobles, Benjamin	1st NC Regiment	5/15/1781, a Private under Lt./Capt. Benjamin Bailey. Discharged on 5/15/1782 (3rd NC Regiment).	
Nobles, Drury	1st NC Regiment	4/15/1781, a Private under Capt. Anthony Sharpe. Discharged on 4/15/1782 (4th NC Regiment).	
Nobles, Ezekiel	1st NC Regiment	1781, a Private under Capt. William Walton.	
Nobles, Hezekiah	5th NC Regiment	5/5/1776, a Musician under Capt. John Pugh Williams. A Private in Sep. 1777. Discharged in Oct. 1778. W6844.	
Nobles, James	3rd NC Regiment	7/20/1778, a Private under Capt. Francis Child for nine months.	
Nobles, John	4th NC Regiment	Aug. 1782, a Private under Capt. Thomas Evans, then Capt. Benjamin Coleman for 12 months. Earlier in NC Militia. From Pitt County, NC. S8922.	
Nolley, Dixon	8th NC Regiment	1777, a Private under Capt. John Walsh. Died on 1/10/1778.	
Nookes, Asahel	2nd NC Regiment	1782, a Private under Capt. Benjamin Carter. Deserted on 6/3/1783 (?).	
Nooning, William	4th NC Regiment	1777, a Private under Capt. Micajah Lewis. Died on 6/2/1778.	
Norkett, William	6th NC Regiment	1777, a Private under Capt. Griffith John McRee. Deserted on 11/1/1777. aka William	

Name	1st Unit	Year / Rank / Served Under / Notes	Known Battles
		Norkell.	
Norman, Thomas	10th NC Regiment	6/17/1777, a Private under Capt. Isaac Moore for three years. 9/8/1778, a known Private in the Lt. Colonel's Company (Lt. Col. Robert Mebane) (1st NC Regiment) led by Capt. Joshua Bowman - sick on that date at the Flying Hospital.	
Norris, Thomas	7th NC Regiment	1777, a Private under Capt. Joseph Walker. Deserted on 7/28/1778.	
Norsworthy, James	7th NC Regiment	Jan. 1777, a Sergeant under Capt. Lemuel Ely, then Capt. John Macon for 18 months. From Bute (what is now Warren) County, NC. Later an Adjutant in NC Militia. S38961.	Brandywine Creek (PA), Germantown (PA).
North, James	3rd NC Regiment	6/20/1779, a Private under Capt. Kedar Ballard. Dropped from the rolls in Oct. 1779.	
Northern, Solomon	1st NC Regiment	4/28/1781, a Private under Capt. Alexander Brevard. Discharged on 4/8/1782 (3rd NC Regiment). aka Solomon Nothern. S38965.	
Northgroves, William	7th NC Regiment	1/19/1777, a Private under Capt. John Poynter. Deserted on 5/9/1777.	
Norton, Jacob	1st NC Regiment	1777, a Private under Capt. Joshua Bowman.	
Norton, Jacob	1st NC Regiment	1777, a Musician under Capt. Thomas Hogg. A Private in June 1778. Died on 7/28/1778.	
Norton, William	1st NC Regiment	1777, a Musician under Capt. Joshua Bowman. A Private in Feb. 1778. 9/8/1778, a known Private under Capt. Griffith John McRee - sick on that date at Valley Forge. Died in Sep. 1778.	
Norton, William	3rd NC Regiment	1777, a Private under Capt. Pinketham Eaton. Died in Jan. 1778.	
Norvel, Enos	3rd NC Regiment	7/20/1778, a Private under Capt. Kedar Ballard for nine months.	
Norwood, John	3rd NC Regiment	7/20/1778, a Private in the Lt. Colonel's Company (Lt. Col. William Lee Davidson) led by Lt./Capt. George "Gee" Bradley for nine months. 4/23/1779, a known Private in the Lt. Colonel's Company (Lt. Col. Robert Mebane) led by Capt. George "Gee" Bradley. Discharged at Halifax, NC in July of 1779. From Northampton County, NC. W4300.	
Norwood, William	8th NC Regiment	7/20/1777, a Private under Lt./Capt. Michael Quinn. Dropped from the rolls on 10/24/1778 (3rd NC Regiment).	
Nosworthy, Samuel	7th NC Regiment	1777, a Private under Capt. John Macon. Dropped from the rolls in Jan. 1778. Probably the same man as Samuel Nasworthy above.	
Nowell, Josiah	2nd NC Regiment	Jan. 1782, a Private under Capt. Benjamin Carter, then Capt. Clement Hall. Discharged on 1/6/1783 in Wilmington, NC. Enlisted in Bertie County, NC. S38971.	
Nowles, Richard	3rd NC Regiment	7/20/1778, a Sergeant under Capt. George "Gee" Bradley for nine months.	
Nube, Francis	3rd NC Regiment	1781, a Private under Capt. Edward Yarborough. Discharged on 2/25/1782.	

Name	1st Unit	Year / Rank / Served Under / Notes	Known Battles
Nunnery, Anderson	4th NC Regiment	Jan. 1782, a Private under Maj. George Dougherty. aka Anderson Nonnery.	
Nunnery, Henry	3rd NC Regiment	5/5/1776, a Private under Capt. Thomas Granbury. Discharged in Oct. 1778.	
Nuthall, Nathaniel	9th NC Regiment	5/20/1777, a Regimental QM and an Ensign. 5/26/1777, an Adjutant. 7/9/1778, an Ensign and QM for the new 7th NC Regiment. Winter 1778, found guilty of "behaving in an infamous manner unbecoming an Officer and a Gentlemen," and also for embezzling stores. Dismissed on 11/4/1778.	
O'Banion, William	3rd NC Regiment	7/20/1778, a Private under Lt./Capt. George "Gee" Bradley. Discharged on 11/6/1778.	
O'Barr, Daniel	1st NC Regiment	1777, a Private under Capt. Henry "Hal" Dixon. 9/8/1778, a known Wagoner under Capt. James Read. aka Daniel O'Bar.	
O'Barr, Michael	1st NC Regiment	1777, a Private under Capt. Henry "Hal" Dixon. Dropped from the rolls in Jan. 1778. aka Michael O'Bar.	
O'Barr, Robert	1st NC Regiment	1777, a Drummer under Capt. Henry "Hal" Dixon for 12 months. 9/8/1778, a known Wagoner under Capt. James Read. From Caswell County, NC. aka Robert Ober, O'Bar. S38973.	Brandywine Creek (PA), Germantown (PA), Monmouth (NJ), Siege of Charleston (SC).
O'Bryan, Dennis	9th NC Regiment	1777, a Private under Capt. Richard D. Cook. Drummed out of the Regiment in July 1777 for desertion. Court-Martial found him to be unfit for duty and of a simple mind.	
O'Bryan, Richard	4th NC Regiment	4/12/1781, a Sergeant under Capt. George Dougherty. 10/13/1781, transferred to Capt. William Lytle. Discharged on 5/25/1782.	
O'Bryan, William	2nd NC Regiment	Nov. 1778, a Private under Capt. Benjamin Andrew Coleman for three years. Summer of 1781, under Capt. Joshua Hadley. Discharged in Nov. or Dec. 1781 in SC. Enlisted in Dobbs County, NC - from Jones County, NC. Born 8/19/1757 in Craven (would become Jones) County, NC. S7277.	Briar Creek (GA), Guilford Court House, Rockfish Creek.
O'Bryant, John	1st NC Regiment	Dec. 1782, a Private under Capt. Peter Bacot for 18 months.	
Odam, Aaron	3rd NC Regiment	7/20/1778, a Private under Maj. Thomas Hogg for nine months. Discharged at Halifax, NC, after serving one year. On the official rolls as Aaron Odum. S38975.	
Odder, Peter	1st NC Regiment	5/25/1781, a Private under Lt./Capt. Benjamin Bailey. Discharged on 5/25/1782 (2nd NC Regiment).	
Odin, Robert	7th NC Regiment	1777, a Corporal under Capt. John McGlaughan. A Private in Sep. 1777. Died on 12/25/1777.	
O'Donnelly,	3rd NC	6/7/1779, a Private under Capt. Michael Quinn.	

Name	1st Unit	Year / Rank / Served Under / Notes	Known Battles
Benjamin	Regiment	Dropped from the rolls in Oct. 1779.	
O'Donnelly, Daniel	3rd NC Regiment	6/24/1779, a Private under Capt. Michael Quinn. Deserted in Dec. 1779.	
O'Donnelly, Hugh	1st NC Regiment	4/15/1781, a Private under Capt. William Lytle. Discharged or died on 1/24/1782. aka Hugh O'Donnally.	
Odum, Lewis	5th NC Regiment	8/9/1779, a Private under Capt. Joseph Montford. Dropped from the rolls in Oct. 1779.	
Ogelbie, Thomas	NC Artillery	12/24/1776, a Matross under Capt. John Vance as NC Provincial Troops. 7/10/1777, on Continental Line. 11/16/1777, under Capt. John Kingsbury. Deserted on 1/16/1778. aka Francis Ogeline (?)	
O'Given, John	5th NC Regiment	1777, a Private under Capt. Henry Darnell. Deserted in Aug. 1777. aka John O'Guien.	
Oiler, John	1st NC Regiment	2/14/1777, a Private, unit unknown, enlisted for three years. 9/8/1778, a known Private under Capt. Griffith John McRee (1st NC Regiment). 3/12/1779, re-enlisted for the duration of the war under Capt. Griffith John McRee (1st NC Regiment). aka John Oyler.	
O'Kelly, Patrick	8th NC Regiment	1777, a Private under Capt. Francis Tartanson. Dropped from the rolls in Sep. 1778.	
Oldridge, William		4/19/1776, a Private, regiment and unit unknown. Discharged on 10/22/1778.	
Oligood, Henry		Jan. 1778, a Private, regiment and unit unknown. Dropped from the rolls in Feb. 1778.	
Oliver, Abisha	1st NC Regiment	1777, a Private under Capt. Lawrence Thompson. Dropped from the rolls in Jan. 1778.	
Oliver, George	2nd NC Regiment	Oct. 1778, a Private under Capt. Robert Raiford for nine months. Later in NC Militia. From Guilford County, NC. S8906.	
Oliver, John	2nd NC Regiment	9/1/1775, an Ensign.	
Oliver, John	4th NC Regiment	4/12/1781, a Private under Capt. George Dougherty. 10/13/1781, transferred to Capt. William Lytle. Discharged on 5/25/1782.	
Oliver, John	10th NC Regiment	4/22/1777, a Private under Capt. Silas Stevenson. Discharged on 6/6/1778. Apparently re-enlisted, date unknown. 3/12/1779, a known Private under Capt. Griffith John McRee (1st NC Regiment).	
Oliver, Rhesa	4th NC Regiment	Oct. 1778, a Private under Capt. George Dougherty. Discharged in August 1780. Earlier and later in NC Militia. From Cumberland County, NC. aka Ricey Oliver. S32420.	Stono Ferry (SC).
Oliver, William	1st NC Regiment	8/1/1782, a Private under Capt. Joshua Hadley for 18 months.	
Oller, Francis	4th NC Regiment	1782, a Private under Capt. Anthony Sharpe for 18 months. aka Francis Oiler.	
O'Merry, Jacob	2nd NC Regiment	6/3/1781, a Private under Capt. Benjamin Carter. Discharged on 6/12/1782. Sick in Camden (SC) Hospital during battle of Eutaw Springs, SC. From Beaufort County, NC.	

Name	1ˢᵗ Unit	Year / Rank / Served Under / Notes	Known Battles
		S4592.	
O'Neal, Benjamin	1ˢᵗ NC Regiment	1782, a Private under Capt. Peter Bacot for 18 months.	
O'Neal, Charles	3ʳᵈ NC Regiment	4/18/1777, an Ensign under Capt. Thomas Granbury. 7/20/1777, a 2nd Lieutenant under Capt. Thomas Granbury. Retired 7/1/1778.	
O'Neal, Isom	3ʳᵈ NC Regiment	7/20/1778, a Private under Maj. Thomas Hogg for nine months.	
O'Neal, James	4ᵗʰ NC Regiment	5/12/1777, a Private under Capt. James Williams. 9/8/1778, a known Private under Capt. Joshua Bowman (1st NC Regiment).	
O'Neal, John	5ᵗʰ NC Regiment	2/18/1777 (?), a Private under Capt. Benjamin Andrew Coleman. Sentenced to receive 225 lashes for forging and selling discharges. 9/8/1778, in 2nd NC Regiment, unit unknown.	
O'Neal, William	3ʳᵈ NC Regiment	7/20/1778, a Private under Capt. Kedar Ballard for nine months.	
Oram, John	3ʳᵈ NC Regiment	1777, a Private under Capt. Thomas Granbury. Died on 3/11/1778.	
Orange, William	2ⁿᵈ NC Regiment	6/14/1781, a Private under Capt. Tilghman Dixon. At some time, transferred to Capt. Robert Raiford. Discharged 12/14/1782.	
Orange, William	3ʳᵈ NC Regiment	7/20/1778, a Private under Lt./Capt. Joseph Montford for nine months.	
Order, Peter	4ᵗʰ NC Regiment	1782, a Private under Capt. Thomas Evans for 18 months.	
Organ, William		8/8/1777, a Private under Capt. Williams. Discharged on 8/21/1778.	
Orr, ?	3ʳᵈ NC Regiment	1777, a Private under Capt. James Emmett. Dropped from the rolls in Sep. 1777.	
Orr, Charles	1ˢᵗ NC Regiment	1777, a Private under Capt. John Brown. A Corporal on 9/1/1777. Died on 6/20/1778.	
Orrell, Thomas	10ᵗʰ NC Regiment	3/14/1778, an Ensign. Retired 6/1/1778.	
Osborne, Benjamin	1ˢᵗ NC Regiment	1782, a Private under Capt. Peter Bacot. Deserted on 6/19/1783 (?). aka Benjamin Osborn.	
Osborne, Jesse	4ᵗʰ NC Regiment	8/1/1782, a Private under Capt. Elijah Moore, then transferred to Capt. Joshua Hadley (1st NC Regiment) for 18 months. Furloughed after 11 months near Charleston, SC. Enlisted in Wake County, NC. aka Jesse Osborn, Jesse Osbourn, Jesse Osburne. `S41930.	
Osborne, John	3ʳᵈ NC Regiment	7/20/1778, a Private under Capt. John Baker for nine months.	
Osborne, Joseph	2ⁿᵈ NC Regiment	1777, a Private under Capt. James Gee. Deserted on 8/10/1778.	
Osborne, Morgan	4ᵗʰ NC Regiment	1782, a Private under Capt. William Lytle. Discharged on 12/31/1782. aka Morgan Osborn.	
Osborne, Squire	1ˢᵗ NC Regiment	4/28/1781, a Private under Capt. Alexander Brevard. Discharged on 4/28/1782 (3rd NC Regiment). aka Squire Osborn.	
Osteen, William	4ᵗʰ NC Regiment	1782, a Private under Capt. Thomas Evans for 18 months.	

Name	1st Unit	Year / Rank / Served Under / Notes	Known Battles
Outlaw, Alexander	10th NC Regiment	1777, a Quarter Master. As QM, he was charged with misconduct and deposed. Was a Captain of Militia. From Duplin County, NC. He moved to Washington County, NC and joined Militia there.	
Outlaw, Edward	6th NC Regiment	1775, an Ensign in the Wilmington District Minutemen. 4/17/1776, an Ensign under Capt. John James and Col. John Alexander Lillington. From Duplin County.	
Outlaw, James	2nd NC Regiment	4/25/1781, a Private under Capt. Benjamin Carter. Discharged on 4/25/1782 at Wilmington, NC. S41929.	
Outlaw, James	2nd NC Regiment	1781, a Lieutenant under Capt. Clement Hall. Earlier in NC Militia as a Sergeant and a Lieutenant. From Duplin County, NC.	
Outlaw, Lewis	7th NC Regiment	1777, a Private under Capt. Thomas Brickell. Dropped from the rolls in Oct. 1777.	
Overstreet, Henry	DQMG	1780, a Canteen Maker on the roll of Capt. Solomon Wood (NC Light Dragoons) - this seems to be for convenience only. An Artificer under Col. Nicholas Long (Deputy QM General). Made Gunstocks. A Canteen Maker on 8/23/1781.	
Overton, Caleb	10th NC Regiment	6/30/1777 or 7/15/1777 (two sources), a Private under Capt. Isaac Moore for three years. 9/8/1778, a known Private in the Lt. Colonel's Company (Lt. Col. Robert Mebane) (1st NC Regiment).	
Overton, Daniel	2nd NC Regiment	6/20/1779, a Private under Capt. Robert Raiford.	
Overton, James	5th NC Regiment	3/1/1779, a Private under Capt. Joseph Montford for three years. Wounded at the Fall of Charleston, SC. Discharged 10/25/1782 near Charleston, SC. S41927.	Stono Ferry (SC), Siege of Charleston 1780 (SC).
Overton, Joab	7th NC Regiment	1/14/1777, a Corporal under Capt. John Poynter. A Private in June 1778. 9/8/1778, a known Private under Capt. Tilghman Dixon (1st NC Regiment). Died on 4/29/1779.	
Overton, John	1st NC Regiment	1/7/1782, a Private under Capt. James Mills. 2/6/1782, this unit was transferred to the 4th NC Regiment. Died on 9/9/1782.	
Overton, Jonathan	3rd NC Regiment	1780, a Private under Capt. George "Gee" Bradley. POW at the Fall of Charleston, paroled. 11/17/1781, a Private under Capt. Samuel Jones for 12 months. Earlier and later in NC Militia. From Chowan County, NC. S8915.	Siege of Charleston 1780 (SC).
Overton, Samuel	10th NC Regiment	6/30/1777 or 7/18/1777 (two sources), a Private under Capt. Isaac Moore for three years. 9/8/1778, a known Private in the Lt. Colonel's Company (Lt. Col. Robert Mebane) (1st NC Regiment) led by Capt. Joshua Bowman. Wounded at the battle of Germantown, PA. A free man of color. aka Lemuel Overton. S41928.	Germantown (PA), Siege of Charleston 1780 (SC).
Overturfe,	1st NC	6/6/1781, a Private under Capt. William Lytle.	

Name	1st Unit	Year / Rank / Served Under / Notes	Known Battles
John	Regiment	Discharged on 6/6/1782 (4th NC Regiment). aka John Overturie.	
Owen, David	6th NC Regiment	1777, a Private under Capt. Griffith John McRee. Died on 4/28/1778.	
Owen, Enoch	4th NC Regiment	4/12/1781, a Private under Capt. George Dougherty. 10/13/1781, transferred to Capt. William Lytle. Discharged on 4/12/1782.	
Owen, Etheldred	1st NC Regiment	5/4/1781, a Private under Capt. Robert Raiford. Discharged on 5/4/1782 (2nd NC Regiment). Born 1742 in Edgecombe County, NC. aka Etheldred Owens.	
Owen, Francis	6th NC Regiment	1777, a Private under Capt. Griffith John McRee. Dropped from the rolls in Nov. 1778.	
Owen, Omery	3rd NC Regiment	A Private under Capt. Jacob Turner. Died in Jan. 1778.	
Owens, Bailey	3rd NC Regiment	1779, a Private under Capt. Kedar Ballard. Discharged on 12/1/1779.	
Owens, Daniel	6th NC Regiment	1777, a Private under Capt. Thomas Donoho. Deserted in Aug. 1777.	
Owens, Francis	1st NC Regiment	9/8/1778, a known Private under Capt. Joshua Bowman.	
Owens, Jacob	8th NC Regiment	1777, a Private under Capt. Robert Raiford. 9/9/1778, a known Private under Capt. Clement Hall (2nd NC Regiment). Dropped from the rolls in Feb. 1779.	
Owens, James	8th NC Regiment	1777, a Private under Capt. John Walsh. Dropped from the rolls in Feb. 1777. aka James Oram.	
Owens, John	1st NC Regiment	3/29/1777, a Private, unit unknown. 9/8/1778, a known Tailor under Capt. James Read - stationed at Lancaster, PA.	
Owens, John	3rd NC Regiment	6/10/1779, a Private under Capt. George "Gee" Bradley for 18 months.	
Owens, John	3rd NC Regiment	2/12/1782, a Private under Capt. Samuel Jones for 12 months.	
Owens, John	5th NC Regiment	1777, a Private under Capt. William Caswell. Died on 2/2/1778.	
Owens, John	6th NC Regiment	5/7/1776, a Lieutenant. Earlier in NC Militia.	
Owens, Stephen	8th NC Regiment	Jan. 1777, an Ensign. 8/15/1777, a Lieutenant under Capt. Robert Raiford. Retired in June 1778.	
Owens, Thomas	3rd NC Regiment	6/20/1779, a Private under Capt. George "Gee" Bradley for 18 months. Discharged at Charleston, SC. R16882.	
Owens, Thomas	3rd NC Regiment	1777, a Private under Capt. Kedar Ballard. Discharged on 12/1/1779.	
Owles, Piram	3rd NC Regiment	Feb. 1779, a Private under Capt. John Medearis.	
Paden, Thomas	10th NC Regiment	5/20/1777, a Private under Capt. James Wilson for three years. 9/8/1778, a known Private in the Major's Company (Maj. John Baptiste Ashe) (1st NC Regiment). aka Thomas Peddan.	
Padget, John	1st NC	5/2/1781, a Corporal under Lt./Capt. Benjamin	

Name	1st Unit	Year / Rank / Served Under / Notes	Known Battles
	Regiment	Bailey for 12 months. Discharged on 5/2/1782.	
Padget, Solomon	5th NC Regiment	1777, a Private under Capt. Henry Darnell. Deserted in Aug. 1777.	
Pafford, William	1st NC Regiment	1781, a Drummer under Capt. William Armstrong. Enlisted at Salisbury, NC. W5483.	Eutaw Springs (SC).
Page, Abraham	3rd NC Regiment	7/20/1778, a Private under Lt./Capt. George "Gee" Bradley for nine months. Died on 9/26/1778.	
Page, Benjamin	1st NC Regiment	6/14/1781, a Corporal under Capt. Thomas Donoho. A Private in Jan. 1782. Discharged on 6/14/1782.	
Page, Solomon	3rd NC Regiment	9/10/1782, a Corporal under Capt. Benjamin Bailey. A Private in Jan. 1783.	
Pair, William	10th NC Regiment	12/26/1776 (?), a Private under Capt. John Jarvis.	
Palmer, Joseph	5th NC Regiment	6/6/1776, an Ensign under Capt. William Caswell.	
Palmer, Robert	8th NC Regiment	1777, a Private under Capt. Francis Tartanson. Dropped from the rolls in Feb. 1778.	
Palmer, Thomas	3rd NC Regiment	9/13/1782, a Private under Capt. Benjamin Bailey for 12 months.	
Pander, Thomas	4th NC Regiment	Summer of 1782, a Private under Capt. Elijah Moore for 18 months. Furloughed near Charleston, SC. Earlier in NC Militia. From Caswell County, NC. Born on 3/22/1765 in PA. aka Thomas Ponder. W21906.	
Paramore, Amos	5th NC Regiment	1777, a Corporal under Capt. John Enloe.	
Paramore, James	10th NC Regiment	5/5/1777, a Private under Capt. Abraham Sheppard, Jr. 9/9/1778, a known Private under Capt. Robert Fenner (2nd NC Regiment). Died on 10/20/1778.	
Pardmore, John	3rd NC Regiment	7/20/1778, a Private under Capt. Francis Child for nine months.	
Pardon, Jeremiah		5/27/1777, a Private, regiment and unit unknown. 9/8/1778, a known Private under Capt. John Sumner (1st NC Regiment).	
Parham, Drury	3rd NC Regiment	7/20/1778, a Private under Lt./Capt. Joseph Montford for nine months. Later in NC Militia. From Halifax County, NC. S9452.	
Parham, Thomas	1st NC Regiment	1781, a Private under Capt. Robert Smith, then Capt. William Lytle. Earlier in NC Militia. From Granville County, NC. W5524.	Fort Motte (SC), Siege of Ninety-Six 1781 (SC).
Parham, William	3rd NC Regiment	7/20/1778, a Private under Lt./Capt. Joseph Montford for nine months.	
Parish, Edward	1st NC Regiment	8/1/1782, a Private under Capt. Joshua Hadley for 18 months.	
Parish, John	5th NC Regiment	9/1/1776, a Private under Capt. William Caswell. 9/9/1778, a known Private in the Major's Company (Maj. Hardy Murfree) (2nd NC Regiment). Deserted on 11/20/1779 - per official records. From Bute County, NC. aka John Parrish. R7930.	

Name	1st Unit	Year / Rank / Served Under / Notes	Known Battles
Parker, Abraham	4th NC Regiment	8/20/1782, a Private under Capt. Elijah Moore then under Capt. Joseph T. Rhodes for 18 months. Furloughed on 7/5/1783 at the 10-Mile House, SC. Earlier in NC Militia. From Orange County, NC. S3640.	
Parker, Amos	2nd NC Regiment	1/13/1782, a Private under Capt. Benjamin Andrew Coleman for 12 months.	
Parker, Arthur	3rd NC Regiment	7/1/1782, a Sergeant under Capt. Benjamin Bailey for 12 months.	
Parker, Arthur	5th NC Regiment	4/16/1776, a Private under Capt. William Caswell. 9/9/1778, a known Private under Capt. Robert Fenner (2nd NC Regiment). Discharged on 11/10/1778.	
Parker, Daniel	3rd NC Regiment	7/20/1778, a Private in the Lt. Colonel's Company (Lt. Col. William Lee Davidson) led by Lt./Capt. George "Gee" Bradley for nine months. 4/23/1779, a known Private in the Lt. Colonel's Company (Lt. Col. Robert Mebane) led by Capt. George "Gee" Bradley.	
Parker, Hillery	10th NC Regiment	5/17/1777, a Private under Capt. John Jarvis for three years. 9/8/1778, a known Private in the Major's Company (Maj. John Baptiste Ashe) (1st NC Regiment) - sick in camp on that date. Died on 11/3/1778. aka Hillory Parker.	
Parker, James	1st NC Regiment	5/9/1776, a Private under Capt. John Brown. 9/8/1778, a known Private under Capt. Tilghman Dixon. Deserted on 9/10/1778. Re-enlisted in Nov. 1778. Deserted again on 6/28/1779.	
Parker, Jeptha		4/22/1776, regiment, unit, and rank unknown, enlisted for three years. 9/8/1778, a known Private under Capt. John Sumner (1st NC Regiment). 3/12/1779, re-enlisted for the duration of the war in the same unit.	
Parker, Jesse	6th NC Regiment	4/26/1776, a Private under Capt. Philip Taylor. A Corporal in Jan. 1779. A Sergeant in Nov. 1779.	
Parker, John	6th NC Regiment	1776, a Private under Capt. Griffith John McRee for seven months. Earlier and later in NC Militia. From Bladen County, NC. W10856.	
Parker, Joseph	3rd NC Regiment	7/20/1778, a Private under Lt./Capt. George "Gee" Bradley for nine months.	
Parker, Kadar	6th NC Regiment	1776, an Ensign. 5/7/1776, a 2nd Lieutenant. 9/19/1776, a 1st Lieutenant under Capt. John Griffith McRee. Dropped from the rolls in Dec. 1777. June 1778, joined the 4th NC Regiment. Mortally wounded at the battle of Camden, SC, died a few days later.	Stono Ferry (SC), Camden (SC).
Parker, Leonard	2nd NC Regiment	5/15/1781, a Sergeant under Capt. Tilghman Dixon. Dropped from the rolls during 1781. Received clothing on 5/24/1782. From Caswell County.	
Parker, Samuel	1st NC Regiment	12/1/1776, a Private under Capt. Henry "Hal" Dixon. 9/8/1778, a known Private under Capt.	

Name	1st Unit	Year / Rank / Served Under / Notes	Known Battles
		Tilghman Dixon. Dropped from the rolls in March 1779.	
Parker, Thomas	4th NC Regiment	7/30/1776, a Private under Capt. Roger Moore, then Capt. William Goodman for 2-1/2 years. 9/8/1778, a known Private in the Colonel's Company (Col. Thomas Clark) (1st NC Regiment) led by Capt. John Gambier Scull. Discharged on 7/31/1779.	
Parker, William	DQMG	1780, a Wagoner under Col. Nicholas Long (Deputy QM General).	
Parker, William	7th NC Regiment	1777, a Sergeant Major. POW on 9/11/1777 at the battle of Brandywine Creek, PA. Later, joined 5th NC Regiment as a Private. Deserted in May 1779.	Brandywine Creek (PA).
Parkerson, Drury	1st NC Regiment	6/14/1781, a Private under Capt. Thomas Donoho. Dropped from the rolls sometime during 1781. aka Drury Perkerson.	
Parkerson, Jacob	2nd NC Regiment	7/1/1779, a Private under Capt. John Craddock. Earlier had been a Private in the 3rd VA Regiment, but since John Parkerson was his brother, he convinced everyone to trade places with a John Lynch - who left the 2nd NC Regiment and joined the 3rd VA Regiment in his place. Sick during the Siege of Charleston (SC), so was not captured. Joined NC Militia. aka Jacob Parkinson. S31902.	Stony Point (NY).
Parkerson, John	3rd NC Regiment	4/16/1776, a Corporal under Capt. Pinketham Eaton. A Sergeant on 8/1/1777. Back to Corporal in June 1778 under Capt. Robert Fenner (2nd NC Regiment). 3/12/1779, re-enlisted under Capt. Benjamin Williams. A Private on 7/15/1779.	
Parkinson, James	2nd NC Regiment	May 1777, a 1st Lieutenant under Capt. Benjamin Williams. Died on 3/26/1778. aka James Parkerson.	
Parks, Andrew	3rd NC Regiment	1781, a Private under Capt. Edward Yarborough for 12 months. Dropped from the rolls on 4/1/1782.	
Parks, Hugh	1st NC Regiment	1781, a Sergeant under Capt. William Lytle. Discharged on 6/10/1782 (4th NC Regiment).	
Parks, Hugh	4th NC Regiment	5/20/1776, a Private under Capt. Roger Moore, then Capt. William Goodman for three years. 9/8/1778, a known Private in the Colonel's Company (Col. Thomas Clark) (1st NC Regiment) led by Capt. John Gambier Scull. Discharged on 5/20/1779 at Paramus, NJ. From Orange County, NC. W9591.	Brandywine Creek (PA), Germantown (PA).
Parks, James	2nd NC Regiment	1782, a Private under Capt. Benjamin Carter for 18 months.	
Parks, James	4th NC Regiment	4/12/1781, a Private under Capt. Joseph T. Rhodes. Discharged on 4/8/1782 as a Sergeant at Bacon's Bridge, SC. From Northampton County, NC. Born in February of 1753 in Northampton County, NC. S17000.	Eutaw Springs (SC).

Name	1st Unit	Year / Rank / Served Under / Notes	Known Battles
Parks, John	1st NC Regiment	5/25/1781, a Private under Capt. Thomas Donoho. Discharged on 5/25/1782.	
Parks, John	5th NC Regiment	A Private under Lt. Col. Henry "Hal" Dixon. Deserted on 1/7/1780.	
Parks, Peter	3rd NC Regiment	1780, a Private under Capt. Edward Yarborough, Capt. William Bush, and Capt. Thomas Donoho. Discharged on 5/1/1782. From Northampton County, NC. S35546.	Camden (SC), Eutaw Springs (SC).
Parks, Samuel	7th NC Regiment	1777, a Private under Capt. Joseph Walker. Died on 11/27/1777.	
Parks, William	1st NC Regiment	1781, a Private under Capt. William Armstrong for 12 months. Discharged on 10/1/1782 (3rd NC Regiment).	
Parks, William	2nd NC Regiment	1782, a Private under Capt. Benjamin Carter for 18 months.	
Parks, William	3rd NC Regiment	4/29/1777, a Private under Lt./Capt. George "Gee" Bradley. Deserted on 10/15/1779.	
Parks, William	4th NC Regiment	1781, a Private under Capt. Joseph T. Rhodes.	
Parmer, John	5th NC Regiment	3/1/1779, a Private under Capt. Joseph Montford for nine months. Discharged on 12/1/1779.	
Parnel, Abraham	2nd NC Regiment	Jan. 1779, a Private in the Major's Company (Maj. Hardy Murfree) for the duration of the war.	
Parr, Isaiah	2nd NC Regiment	1775, a Private under Capt. James Blount for six months. 5/20/1776, a Private under Capt. Roger Moore (4th NC Regiment). 12/24/1776, a Sergeant under Capt. William Goodman (4th NC Regiment) for 2-1/2 years. 9/8/1778, a known Sergeant in the Colonel's Company (Col. Thomas Clark) (1st NC Regiment) led by Capt. John Gambier Scull. Discharged on 11/10/1778. Later, a Major in NC Militia. From Currituck County, NC. On some rolls as Isaiah Pare. S41939.	Great Bridge (VA), Brandywine Creek (PA), Germantown (PA), Monmouth (NJ), Stony Point (NY).
Parr, Noah	2nd NC Regiment	1777, a Musician under Capt. Edward Vail, Jr. Aug. 1778, a Private. From Pasquotank County, NC. R1960.	Brandywine Creek (PA).
Parr, William		12/25/1776, a Private, regiment and unit unknown, enlisted for three years. 6/1/1778, a Private under Capt. Griffith John McRee (1st NC Regiment).	
Parrish, Abraham	3rd NC Regiment	1/22/1780, a Private under Capt. George "Gee" Bradley.	
Parrish, Jacob	3rd NC Regiment	7/20/1778, a Private under Lt./Capt. George "Gee" Bradley for nine months.	
Parrott, Nathaniel	1st NC Regiment	6/14/1781, a Private under Capt. Thomas Donoho. Discharged on 6/14/1782.	
Parsons, James	2nd NC Regiment	5/15/1781, a Corporal under Capt. Tilghman Dixon. Discharged on 5/21/1782 (1st NC Regiment). Received clothing on 5/24/1782. From Caswell County. aka James Persons.	
Parsons,	3rd NC	6/22/1779, a Private under Capt. Kedar Ballard.	

Name	1st Unit	Year / Rank / Served Under / Notes	Known Battles
James	Regiment	Deserted in Oct. 1779.	
Parsons, Jesse	8th NC Regiment	1777, a Private under Capt. John Walsh. POW on 10/4/1777 at the battle of Germantown, PA.	Germantown (PA).
Parsons, Nathan	8th NC Regiment	1777, a Private under Capt. John Walsh. POW on 10/4/1777 at the battle of Germantown, PA.	Germantown (PA).
Parsons, Roger	8th NC Regiment	1777, a Private under Capt. John Walsh. 9/9/1778, a known Private under Capt. Robert Fenner (2nd NC Regiment). Dropped from the rolls in Feb. 1779. aka Roger Parson.	
Parsons, Samuel	8th NC Regiment	1777, a Sergeant under Capt. John Walsh. A Private in Jan. 1778. Died on 3/19/1778.	
Parthis, Hardy	10th NC Regiment	A Private in the Lt. Colonel's Company. Deserted on 7/29/1778.	
Partin, Benjamin	3rd NC Regiment	7/20/1778, a Private under Lt./Capt. Joseph Montford for nine months.	
Partree, Emanuel	4th NC Regiment	1777, a Private under Capt. William Goodman. Died on 10/4/1777 at the battle of Germantown, PA.	Germantown (PA).
Parum, William	1st NC Regiment	4/5/1781, a Private under Capt. William Lytle. Discharged on 4/5/1782 (4th NC Regiment).	
Pass, William	NC Light Dragoons	Oct.-Dec. 1777, a known Corporal under Capt. Martin Phifer in the 2nd Company of Light Horse.	
Passmore, Amos	2nd NC Regiment	10/24/1776, a Private, unit unknown. 9/10/1778, a known Private under Capt. Thomas Armstrong.	
Passmore, David	10th NC Regiment	5/15/1777 or 8/6/1777 (two sources), a Private under Capt. James Wilson. May 1778, under Capt. James Verner (1st NC Regiment). 9/8/1778, a known Private under Capt. John Gambier Scull. POW at the Fall of Charleston (SC), exchanged at Jamestown, VA in July 1781. 12/2/1781, re-enlisted as a Private under Capt. Robert Raiford (1st NC Regiment), then under Capt. Samuel Jones (1st NC Regiment) for 12 months. From Orange County, NC. S1924.	Monmouth (NJ), Siege of Charleston (SC).
Passmore, Joseph	10th NC Regiment	6/21/1777, a Private under Capt. Dempsey Gregory. 9/8/1778, a known Private under Capt. Howell Tatum (1st NC Regiment) - sick on that date at Yellow Springs. Died on 7/13/1778 (?). aka Joseph Palmore, Joseph Pasmore.	
Pasteur, John	6th NC Regiment	7/2/1776, a 2nd Lieutenant under Capt. George Mitchell.	
Pasteur, Thomas	4th NC Regiment	7/15/1777, an Ensign under Capt. Thomas Harris. 6/1/1778, transferred to the 1st NC Regiment under Capt. Joshua Bowman. 12/29/1778, a 2nd Lieutenant. 6/26/1779, an Adjutant. 11/20/1779, a 1st Lieutenant. POW at the Fall of Charleston, exchanged in Dec. of 1780. 1781, a Captain in Dobbs County Militia. 10/19/1782, a Paymaster in the 4th NC Regiment. aka Thomas Pasture.	Siege of Charleston 1780 (SC).
Pasteur, William	2nd NC Regiment	9/1/1775, a Surgeon. Transferred to 4th NC Regiment on 12/12/1776 - one source claims he	

Name	1st Unit	Year / Rank / Served Under / Notes	Known Battles
		was then a Paymaster. Another says the Surgeon was William Patten, not Pasteur. Beats me.	
Pate, Cordie	1st NC Regiment	5/4/1781, a Private under Capt. Robert Raiford. Discharged on 5/4/1782 (2nd NC Regiment).	
Pate, Edward	1st NC Regiment	5/4/1781, a Private under Capt. Robert Raiford. Discharged on 5/4/1782 (2nd NC Regiment).	
Pate, William	8th NC Regiment	6/29/1777, a Corporal under Capt. John Walsh. Deserted on 10/17/1777. Rejoined on 12/1/1777 as a Private. 9/9/1778, a known Private under Capt. Robert Fenner (2nd NC Regiment). A Corporal again in Feb. 1779. Discharged on 1/31/1780.	
Patrick, Andrew	4th NC Regiment	4/1/1777, a Private under Capt. Joseph Phillips. Discharged on 11/10/1778.	
Patrick, Benjamin	1st NC Regiment	A Musician under Capt. James Read. Dropped from the rolls in June 1778.	
Patrick, Daniel	2nd NC Regiment	9/11/1778, a Private under Capt. Robert Raiford.	
Patrick, John	4th NC Regiment	1777, a Private under Capt. Joseph Phillips. Deserted on 10/26/1777.	
Patrick, Spencer	1st NC Regiment	1782, a Private under Capt. Peter Bacot.	
Patrick, William	4th NC Regiment	1777, a Private under Capt. Joseph Phillips for 2-1/2 years. The official records indicate that he deserted on 10/26/1777. He claims he started much earlier and was honorably discharged. From Surry County, NC. R7999.	Brandywine Creek (PA), Germantown (PA).
Patrie, Peter	3rd NC Regiment	1782, a Private under Capt. Alexander Brevard for 18 months.	
Patten, John	2nd NC Regiment	9/1/1775, a Major under Col. Robert Howe. 4/10/1776, a Lt. Colonel. Summer of 1776, marched his men towards Charlestown, halted at Little River Neck. 11/22/1777, a full Colonel when Col. Alexander Martin resigned. Early 1778, the 4th NC Regiment was folded into 2nd NC Regiment. Surrendered 301 men at the Fall of Charleston. POW at the Fall of Charleston, held until 11/26/1782. March 1782, on paper as the leader of the 2nd NC Regiment, even though still in captivity. Retired 1/1/1783.	Brandywine Creek (PA), Germantown (PA), Monmouth (NJ), Near West Point (NY), Siege of Charleston 1780 (SC).
Patterson, Duncan	2nd NC Regiment	1/15/1782, a Private under Capt. Benjamin Andrew Coleman. aka Duncan Petterson.	
Patterson, John	2nd NC Regiment	1777, a Private under Capt. James Gee. 9/9/1778, a known Private under Capt. John Ingles. Deserted on 5/1/1779.	
Patterson, John	5th NC Regiment	1777, a Private under Capt. Benjamin Andrew Coleman. Jan. 1779, in the 4th NC Regiment, unit unknown.	
Patterson, Tilmon	1st NC Regiment	11/1/1778, a Sergeant under Capt. Anthony Sharpe for 12 months. Discharged in August 1779. From what is now Franklin County. NC. 1780, in NC Militia. aka Tilman Patterson. S41942.	
Patterson,	3rd NC	1781, a Private under Capt. Edward Yarborough	

Name	1st Unit	Year / Rank / Served Under / Notes	Known Battles
William	Regiment	for 12 months. Discharged on 2/25/1782.	
Pattin, John	3rd NC Regiment	1782, a Private under Capt. Alexander Brevard for 18 months.	
Patton, Joseph	4th NC Regiment	1775, an Ensign in the Salisbury District Minutemen. 4/17/1776, an Ensign under Capt. William Temple Coles and Col. Thomas Polk. aka Joseph Patten.	
Patton, William	3rd NC Regiment	1782, a Private under Capt. Edward Yarborough for 18 months, hired a substitute (Michael Hinnings) after serving one month. Earlier in NC and GA Militias. From Rowan County, NC. W4307.	
Paul, Philip	1st NC Regiment	5/20/1781, a Private under Capt. Griffith John McRee. Discharged on 5/25/1782.	
Paul, Stephen	5th NC Regiment	1777, a Private under Capt. Benjamin Stedman. Died on 9/20/1777.	
Pavey, Nehemiah	4th NC Regiment	2/6/1782, a Private under Capt. James Mills for 12 months. Sep. 1782, re-enlisted for the duration of the war.	
Pavey, Samuel	1st NC Regiment	8/10/1781, a Private under Capt. William Lytle for 12 months. Discharged in Oct. 1782 at James Island, SC. Born 1761 in Accomack County, VA. From Guilford County, NC. R8017.	
Pavy, Thomas	5th NC Regiment	6/24/1779, a Private under Capt. Joseph Montford for nine months. Probably Thomas Pavey.	
Payford, William	2nd NC Regiment	1782, a Musician under Capt. Benjamin Carter for 18 months.	
Payne, Michael	2nd NC Regiment	9/1/1775, a Captain under Col. Robert Howe. Left the service before 6/1/1776.	
Payne, Thomas	3rd NC Regiment	8/30/1779, a Private under Capt. Kedar Ballard. Deserted in Oct. 1779.	
Peacock, John	10th NC Regiment	5/11/1778, a Private, unit unknown. 9/9/1778, a known Private in the Colonel's Company (Col. John Patten) (2nd NC Regiment) led by Capt. John Craddock.	
Peal, Daniel	7th NC Regiment	12/26/1776, a Private under Capt. Thomas Brickell for three years. 9/8/1778, a known Private under Capt. Howell Tatum (1st NC Regiment). 3/12/1779, re-enlisted for the duration of the war in the same unit. aka Daniel Peale.	
Peal, Pearson	10th NC Regiment	6/22/1777, a Private, unit unknown. A Corporal in Aug. 1778. 9/9/1778, a known Corporal in the Major's Company (Maj. Hardy Murfree) (2nd NC Regiment). 3/12/1779, re-enlisted in the Major's Company (Maj. Hardy Murfree). A Sergeant on 2/1/1780.	
Pearce, George	9th NC Regiment	11/28/1776, an Ensign under Capt. Thomas McCrory. From Salisbury District.	
Pearce, Israel	2nd NC Regiment	5/2/1781, a Private under Capt. William Goodman, then under Capt. Benjamin Bailey (1st NC Regiment). Discharged on 5/2/1782	Eutaw Springs (SC).

Name	1st Unit	Year / Rank / Served Under / Notes	Known Battles
		(3rd NC Regiment) at High Hills, SC. Earlier in NC Navy. From Tyrrell County, NC when he enlisted. On official rolls as Israel Pearse. S3660.	
Pearce, Jacob	4th NC Regiment	Oct. 1777, a Private under Capt. James Williams. Dropped from the rolls in Jan. 1778. 9/8/1778, a known Private in the Colonel's Company (Col. Thomas Clark) (1st NC Regiment) led by Capt. John Gambier Scull.	
Pearce, William	4th NC Regiment	1777, a Private under Capt. William Goodman for 18 months. Drafted in Hertford, NC (Perquimans County). Discharged in SC. Born 12/9/1752 in Perquimans (what is now Gates) County, NC. W3590.	Stono Ferry (SC).
Pearl, James	8th NC Regiment	Earlier a Sergeant in the NC Militia. 11/28/1776, an Ensign under Capt. John Walsh. 10/26/1777, a Lieutenant under Capt. William Dennis. Transferred to the 1st NC Regiment on 6/1/1778 under Capt. Anthony Sharpe. Promoted to Captain on 7/17/1782. Retired 1/1/1783. From Cumberland County.	
Pearse, Abner	4th NC Regiment	1782, a Private under Capt. Thomas Evans for 18 months. Dec. 1782, transferred - to where unknown.	
Pearson, Jonathan	7th NC Regiment	May 1777, a Private under Col. James Hogun for eleven months, unit unknown. 1778, in NC Militia. From Johnston County, NC. Enlisted in Edgecombe County, NC. W10876.	
Pearson, Thomas	3rd NC Regiment	7/20/1778, a Private under Capt. John Baker for nine months.	
Peavey, Thomas	1st NC Regiment	1777, a Private under Capt. Henry "Hal" Dixon. Dropped from the rolls in Jan. 1778.	
Peck, Frederick	9th NC Regiment	12/1/1777, a Private under Capt. Anthony Sharpe.	
Peck, Joseph	1st NC Regiment	4/28/1781, a Private under Capt. Griffith John McRee. Aug. 1781, transferred to the Legion (State or Lee's? - Unknown).	
Pee, Jonathan	3rd NC Regiment	7/20/1778, a Private under Capt. John Baker for nine months.	
Peevel, John	3rd NC Regiment	1779, a Private under Capt. Kedar Ballard. Dropped from the rolls in Oct. 1779.	
Pell, Gilbert	3rd NC Regiment	1779, a Private under Capt. Michael Quinn. Deserted in Sep. 1779.	
Pemel, John	4th NC Regiment	1777, a Private under Capt. James Williams. Died in Nov. 1777.	
Pendergrass, David	6th NC Regiment	4/20/1776, a Private under Capt. Philip Taylor for 2-1/2 years. 6/1/1778, a Private under Capt. Griffith John McRee (1st NC Regiment). Discharged on 11/10/1778. Later in NC Militia. From Granville County, NC. R8086.	
Pendergrass, Job	4th NC Regiment	5/6/1776, a Private under Capt. Roger Moore for three years. Apr. 1779, a known Private under Capt. Joseph T. Rhodes. Discharged on 5/6/1779 in Chatham County, NC. Later in NC	

Name	1ˢᵗ Unit	Year / Rank / Served Under / Notes	Known Battles
		Militia, unit(s) unknown. Enlisted at Hillsborough, NC. S41504.	
Pendergrass, John	4ᵗʰ NC Regiment	5/20/1776, a Private under Capt. Roger Moore for three years. 9/8/1778, a known Private in the Colonel's Company (Col. Thomas Clark - 1st NC Regiment) led by Capt. John Gambier Scull - sick at Valley Forge on that date. Discharged on 5/20/1779. Later in NC Militia. From Orange County, NC. W18730.	
Pendleton, Benjamin	1ˢᵗ NC Regiment	5/9/1781, a Private under Capt. Alexander Brevard.	
Pendleton, Edmund	6ᵗʰ NC Regiment	1777, a Sergeant under Capt. Philip Taylor. Dropped from the rolls in Feb. 1778.	
Pendleton, Hiram	7ᵗʰ NC Regiment	5/22/1778, a Private under Lt. Benjamin Bailey, who was soon transferred to the 1st NC Regiment. Then joined NC Militia. From Pasquotank County, NC when he enlisted.	Stono Ferry (SC).
Penniger, Martin	1ˢᵗ NC Regiment	4/28/1781, a Private under Capt. Griffith John McRee, then Capt. Elijah Moore (4th NC Regiment). Discharged on 4/28/1782. Enlisted in Rowan County, NC. Later, lived in Cabarrus County, NC. aka Martin Penigar, Martin Peniger. S41951.	Eutaw Springs (SC).
Pennington, William	NC Artillery	3/7/1777, a Sergeant under Capt. Thomas Clark. Also on 9/9/1778.	
Penrice, Francis	3ʳᵈ NC Regiment	1781, a Private under Capt. Clement Hall for 12 months. Discharged on 8/16/1782.	
Penrice, Francis	3ʳᵈ NC Regiment	1/7/1782, a Private under Capt. Benjamin Bailey. Discharged on 1/7/1783. aka Francis Penris.	
Penrice, Samuel	3ʳᵈ NC Regiment	1781, a Sergeant under Capt. Clement Hall for 12 months. Discharged on 8/16/1782 (2nd NC Regiment).	
Penticost, Dancey	3ʳᵈ NC Regiment	4/20/1776, a Sergeant, unit unknown. A QM Sergeant in Nov. 1777. Dropped from the rolls in Sep. 1778.	
Peoples, William	5ᵗʰ NC Regiment	4/1/1776, a Private under Capt. William Caswell for 2-1/2 years. 9/9/1778, a known Private under Capt. Robert Fenner (2nd NC Regiment). Discharged on 10/1/1778.	
Perdue, Caleb	3ʳᵈ NC Regiment	7/30/1778, a Private under Maj. Thomas Hogg for nine months.	
Perkins, Abraham	9ᵗʰ NC Regiment	1777, a Private under Capt. Matthew Ramsey. Died on 3/5/1778.	
Perkins, Adam	3ʳᵈ NC Regiment	Jan. 1779, a Private in the Lt. Colonel's Company (Lt. Col. Robert Mebane) led by Capt. George "Gee" Bradley.	
Perkins, Adam	10ᵗʰ NC Regiment	4/17/1777, a Lt. Colonel under Col. Abraham Sheppard. Resigned on 6/1/1778. Then, a Colonel in the Edenton District Regiment of Militia.	
Perkins, David	4ᵗʰ NC Regiment	2/6/1782, a Sergeant under Capt. James Mills. A Private in Apr. 1782.	
Perkins,	2ⁿᵈ NC	1781, a Private under Capt. Benjamin Carter.	Eutaw Springs

Name	1st Unit	Year / Rank / Served Under / Notes	Known Battles
Ephraim	Regiment	Transferred to Capt. Clement Hall (3rd NC Regiment/2nd NC Regiment). Earlier in NC Militia.	(SC).
Perkins, Isaac	10th NC Regiment	5/16/1777, a Private under Capt. Silas Stevenson. Transferred to 2nd NC Regiment under Capt. Clement Hall. POW at the Fall of Charleston (SC), escaped. Then in NC Militia, unit(s) unknown. S41953.	Siege of Charleston 1780 (SC).
Perkins, John	4th NC Regiment	1782, a Private under Capt. Elijah Moore, then Capt. Joseph T. Rhodes, and finally Capt. Alexander Brevard (3rd NC Regiment) for 18 months. Discharged after serving 12 or 13 months at 10-Mile House, SC. Earlier in VA Militia. 1782, moved to, and living in, Caswell County, NC when he was drafted. On the official rolls as Thomas Cayson. Raised by his mother as Thomas Carson - but his real name was John Perkins. During the war, he was known as Thomas Carson. W2640.	
Perkins, Richard	3rd NC Regiment	6/24/1779, a Private under Capt. Kedar Ballard.	
Perkins, Thomas	1st NC Regiment	4/28/1781, a Private under Capt. Alexander Brevard. Discharged on 4/28/1782 (3rd NC Regiment) at Bacon's Bridge, SC. From Lincoln County, NC. Born on 3/31/1757 in Orange County, NC. S9455.	Siege of Ninety-Six 1781 (SC), Eutaw Springs (SC).
Perrit, Needham	6th NC Regiment	March 1777, a Private under Capt. George Mitchell. 1778, a Private under Capt. Kedar Ballard for nine months (3rd NC Regiment). aka Needham Perrett. S38998.	
Perry, Jeremiah	3rd NC Regiment	4/29/1776, a Private under Capt. Pinketham Eaton. A Corporal from Feb. 1778 to June 1778. 9/9/1778, a known Private under Capt. John Ingles (2nd NC Regiment). Discharged on 11/10/1778. aka Jeremiah Perrey, aka Jerry Perry.	
Perry, John	1st NC Regiment	May 1781, a Private under Capt. Thomas Donoho, then Capt. Edward Yarborough (3rd NC Regiment) for 12 months. Discharged on 5/17/1782 at Bacon's Bridge, SC. Enlisted at Hillsborough, NC. aka John Parry. W975.	
Perry, John	6th NC Regiment	4/16/1776, a Private under Capt. Thomas Donoho for 2-1/2 years. 6/1/1778, a Private under Capt. Griffith John McRee (1st NC Regiment). Discharged on 11/10/1778. aka John Perrey.	
Perry, John	6th NC Regiment	1777, a Private under Capt. Philip Taylor. Dropped from the rolls in Sep. 1777.	
Perry, Robert	1st NC Regiment	Jan. 1782, a Private under Capt. William Armstrong. 2/6/1782, this unit was transferred to the 3rd NC Regiment.	
Perry, William	6th NC Regiment	1777, a Private under Capt. Francis Child. Died on 3/13/1778.	
Person,	3rd NC	7/30/1778, a Private under Maj. Thomas Hogg	

Name	1st Unit	Year / Rank / Served Under / Notes	Known Battles
Jonathan	Regiment	for nine months.	
Pervas, Tiberius	1st NC Regiment	5/10/1781, a Corporal under Capt. Robert Raiford. Discharged on 5/18/1782 (2nd NC Regiment).	
Pervers, William		5/13/1777, a Private, regiment and unit unknown. 9/8/1778, a known Private in the Major's Company (Maj. John Baptiste Ashe) (1st NC Regiment).	
Peters, Charles	2nd NC Regiment	1778, a Private under Capt. Benjamin Andrew Coleman.	
Peters, John	3rd NC Regiment	6/18/1779, a Private under Capt. Kedar Ballard. Deserted in Feb. 1780.	
Peterson, James	6th NC Regiment	March of 1776, a Private under Capt. Archibald Lytle for 2-1/2 years. Discharged in September of 1778 in Wilmington, NC. From Orange (what would become Caswell) County, NC. W4050.	
Pethosell, Thomas	1st NC Regiment	5/2/1781, a Private under Capt. Anthony Sharpe. Dropped from the rolls sometime during 1781.	
Petigrew, Ance	3rd NC Regiment	9/15/1776 (?), a Private under Lt./Capt. Kedar Ballard for 3 years. Discharged on 12/1/1779.	
Petree, Peter	4th NC Regiment	1782, a Private under Capt. William Lytle for 18 months. From Granville County, NC. W4310.	
Pettaway, Micajah	3rd NC Regiment	4/20/1776, a Private under Capt. William Brinkley, then under Capt. James Bradley, then under Capt. Thomas Granbury for 2-1/2 years. Transferred to 2nd NC Regiment under Capt. Benjamin Williams. Discharged in Oct. 1778 near West Point, NY. 1779, in NC Militia. From Edgecombe County, NC. On the official rolls as Micaja Pataway and/or Macaja Potaway.	Brandywine Creek (PA), Monmouth (NJ).
Petteway, James	2nd NC Regiment	4/25/1781, a Private under Capt. Benjamin Carter for 12 months. Discharged on 5/25/1782.	
Pettiford, Elias	1st NC Regiment	6/14/1781, a Private under Capt. Thomas Donoho. Discharged on 6/14/1782.	
Pettiford, George	4th NC Regiment	1776, a Private under Capt. Roger Moore, Capt. William Goodman for nine months. Enlisted in Caswell County, NC. Probably from Granville County, NC. W9223.	
Pettiford, Philip	1st NC Regiment	6/14/1781, a Private under Capt. Thomas Donoho, then Capt. William Walton. Discharged on 6/14/1782. From Granville County, NC. Brother of William below, S41952.	Eutaw Springs (SC).
Pettiford, William	1st NC Regiment	6/14/1781, a Private under Capt. Thomas Donoho, then Capt. William Saunders. Discharged on 6/14/1782 (4th NC Regiment). From Granville County, NC. Brother of Philip above. S41948.	
Pettijohn, Abraham	1st NC Regiment	4/24/1781, a Private under Lt./Capt. Benjamin Bailey. Discharged on 4/24/1782 (3rd NC Regiment).	

Name	1st Unit	Year / Rank / Served Under / Notes	Known Battles
Pettis, James	1st NC Regiment	6/11/1781, a Private under Capt. Griffith John McRee. A Corporal in Aug. 1781. Discharged on 6/11/1782. aka James Pittia.	
Pettis, Stephen	3rd NC Regiment	7/20/1778, a Private under Lt./Capt. George "Gee" Bradley for nine months.	
Pettit, Gideon	8th NC Regiment	4/5/1777, a Musician under Capt. Simon Jones, then Capt. Robert Raiford. Dropped from the rolls in Jan. 1778. May 1779, joined the 5th NC Regiment, unit unknown. Discharged on 4/11/1780. From Pitt County, NC.	Brandywine Creek (PA), Germantown (PA), Stono Ferry (SC).
Petty, John	3rd NC Regiment	9/17/1782, a Private under Capt. Benjamin Bailey for 18 months. Earlier in SC units. S39007.	
Pettyjohn, Thomas	10th NC Regiment	5/6/1777, a Private under Capt. Isaac Moore for three years. 9/8/1778, a known Corporal in the Lt. Colonel's Company (Lt. Col. Robert Mebane) (1st NC Regiment) led by Capt. Joshua Bowman - sick on that date. Died on 1/19/1779. aka Thomas Pittyjohn, Thomas Petyjohn.	
Pevier, James	6th NC Regiment	1777, a Private under Capt. Griffith John McRee. Dropped from the rolls in June 1778.	
Pevy, Samuel	4th NC Regiment	1782, a Musician under Capt. William Lytle for 18 months. Deserted on 3/16/1783 (?).	
Pharas, Absalom	1st NC Regiment	5/17/1781, a Private under Lt./Capt. Benjamin Bailey. Discharged on 5/17/1782 (3rd NC Regiment).	
Phelps, James	10th NC Regiment	5/4/1777, a Private under Capt. Abraham Sheppard, Jr. 9/9/1778, a known Private in the Colonel's Company (Col. John Patten) (2nd NC Regiment) led by Capt. John Craddock. A Musician in Nov. 1779.	
Phelps, Keeder	10th NC Regiment	5/12/1777, a Private under Capt. Abraham Sheppard, Jr. A Musician in June 1778. 9/9/1778, a known Private under Capt. Clement Hall (2nd NC Regiment). aka Kador Phelps, Kader Phelps.	
Phifer, Martin	NC Light Dragoons	4/16/1776, a Captain of the 2nd Company of Light Horse until April of 1780. 3/7/1777, on Continental Line. Jan. 1779, in State Troops under Col. Francois DeMalmedy. From Mecklenburg (what is now Cabarrus) County, NC. Brother to Caleb and John, both in NC Militia of Mecklenburg County. aka Martin Pfifer.	Brandywine Creek (PA), Germantown (PA), Monmouth (NJ).
Philip, William	1st NC Regiment	8/1/1782, a Private under Capt. Joshua Hadley. Died on 6/6/1783. [same man as William Phillips below]	
Phillips, Aaron	3rd NC Regiment	1782, a Private under Capt. Alexander Brevard for 18 months.	
Phillips, Andrew	4th NC Regiment	4/1/1777, a Private under Capt. Joseph Phillips for 3 years. 1/8/1778, transferred as a Private under Capt. James Read (1st NC Regiment). Discharged on 4/20/1780. S32442.	

550

Name	1st Unit	Year / Rank / Served Under / Notes	Known Battles
Phillips, Bush	5th NC Regiment	1777, a Private under Capt. Benjamin Andrew Coleman. Dropped from the rolls in Sep. 1777.	
Phillips, David	2nd NC Regiment	4/7/1781, a Private under Capt. Benjamin Carter for 12 months. Discharged on 4/2/1782.	
Phillips, David	3rd NC Regiment	4/16/1776, a Private under Capt. Jacob Turner. Discharged in Oct. 1778.	
Phillips, George	2nd NC Regiment	1777, a Private under Capt. Charles Allen. 9/10/1778, a known Private under Capt. Thomas Armstrong.	
Phillips, Henry	3rd NC Regiment	1779, a Private under Capt. Kedar Ballard for nine months. Died on 8/19/1779.	
Phillips, John	3rd NC Regiment	1778, a Private under Capt. Kedar Ballard for nine months.	
Phillips, John	10th NC Regiment	9/1/1777, a Private under Capt. Abraham Sheppard, Jr. 6/1/1778, a Private under Maj. Hardy Murfree (2nd NC Regiment). Discharged on 9/11/1778 at White Plains, CT. S39010.	
Phillips, Joseph	4th NC Regiment	1775, a Captain in the Salisbury District Minutemen. 4/16/1776, a Captain under Col. Thomas Polk. Dropped from the rolls in Jan. 1778. 1779, a Captain of NC Militia under Col. Martin Armstrong (Surry County Regiment).	Brandywine Creek (PA), Germantown (PA).
Phillips, Joseph	10th NC Regiment	7/1/1777, a Private, unit unknown. 9/9/1778, a known Private in the Lt. Colonel's Company (Lt. Col. Selby Harney) (2nd NC Regiment). POW at Ft. Lafayette, NY on 6/1/1779.	Ft. Lafayette (NY).
Phillips, Lovin	1st NC Regiment	5/19/1781, a Private under Capt. Robert Raiford. Oct. 1781, transferred to the SC Line.	
Phillips, Mitchell	1st NC Regiment	9/9/1777, a Private under Capt. Tilghman Dixon for three years. 9/8/1778, known a Private under Capt. Tilghman Dixon. POW at the Fall of Charleston (SC), exchanged at Jamestown, VA. From Camden County, NC. S41956.	Siege of Charleston 1780 (SC).
Phillips, Richard	4th NC Regiment	5/10/1776, a Private under Capt. Joseph Phillips for 3 years. 9/8/1778, a known Private under Capt. James Read (1st NC Regiment). Discharged on 5/20/1779.	
Phillips, Thomas	1st NC Regiment	5/20/1781, a Private under Capt. Griffith John McRee. Deserted on 6/1/1781.	
Phillips, William	1st NC Regiment	8/1/1782, a Private under Capt. Joshua Hadley for 18 months. Died on 6/6/1783.	
Phillips, William	3rd NC Regiment	June 1778, a Private under Lt./Capt. Joseph Montford. Dropped from the rolls in July 1778.	
Phillips, Zachariah	1st NC Regiment	5/25/1781, a Private under Capt. Thomas Donoho, then under Capt. William Walton. Discharged on 5/25/1782 at Bacon's Bridge, SC. S35559.	
Phillips, Zachariah	1st NC Regiment	8/1/1782, a Private under Capt. Joshua Hadley. Died on 1/16/1783.	
Phips, John	1st NC Regiment	11/10/1778, a Private under Capt. Anthony Sharpe for 12 months.	
Pickett, Thomas	1st NC Regiment	10/20/1775 to Jan. 1776, an Ensign.	
Pickett,	4th NC	1775, a 1st Lieutenant in NC Militia. 4/17/1776,	

Name	1st Unit	Year / Rank / Served Under / Notes	Known Battles
Thomas	Regiment	a 1st Lieutenant under Capt. Thomas Harris and Col. Thomas Polk. From Anson County.	
Pickett, William	1st NC Regiment	9/1/1775, a Captain under Col. James Moore. This company was broken up on 1/4/1776 and he joined the local Militia as a Captain, a Major, then a Lt. Colonel. From Anson County, NC. aka William Packett.	Great Cane Brake (SC), Snow Campaign (SC).
Pierce, Edward	2nd NC Regiment	1781, a Private under Capt. Benjamin Carter for 12 months. Discharged on 4/25/1782. First name might be Edmund - seen both.	
Pierce, Ephraim	2nd NC Regiment	5/12/1781, a Sergeant under Capt. Benjamin Carter for 12 months. Discharged on 5/2/1782.	
Pierce, Hardy	2nd NC Regiment	6/1/1778, a Private under Capt. Clement Hall. Died in Oct. 1778.	
Pierce, Israel	3rd NC Regiment	6/15/1779, a Private under Capt. Kedar Ballard for 18 months.	
Pierce, James	1st NC Regiment	1781, a Private under Capt. William Lytle. Discharged 4/12/1782 (4th NC Regiment).	
Pierce, James	5th NC Regiment	8/24/1777, a Private under Capt. Benjamin Andrew Coleman. 9/9/1778, a known Private under Capt. Robert Fenner (2nd NC Regiment). 3/12/1779, re-enlisted under Capt. Benjamin Andrew Coleman. From Hertford County, NC. aka James Pearce.	
Pierce, John		A Private in NC Continental Line, regiment, unit, and dates unknown. S7320.	Eutaw Springs (SC).
Pierce, Lewis	1st NC Regiment	4/12/1781, a Private under Capt. William Lytle. Deserted on 7/7/1781.	
Pierce, Reuben	1st NC Regiment	4/15/1781, a Private under Capt. Anthony Sharpe. Dropped from the rolls during 1781.	
Pierce, Theophilus	6th NC Regiment	A Private under Capt. Thomas White. Died on 5/21/1778.	
Pierce, Thomas	2nd NC Regiment	1777, a Private under Capt. Benjamin Williams. Died on 1/2/1778. One source claims this man's name was Thomas Price - so he's listed below under that name as well.	
Pierce, Thomas	5th NC Regiment	1777, a Private under Capt. John Pugh Williams. 9/9/1778, a known Private in the Major's Company (Maj. Hardy Murfree) (2nd NC Regiment). Died in Oct. 1778. From Hertford County, NC.	
Pierce, William	4th NC Regiment	1777, a Private under Capt. William Temple Coles. Aug. 1777, in the "Invalids."	
Pierce, William	5th NC Regiment	1777, a Private under Capt. John Pugh Williams. Dropped from the rolls in Feb. 1778.	
Pierce, William	7th NC Regiment	1777, a Private under Capt. Thomas Brickell. Deserted in Apr. 1777.	
Pierson, Richard	1st NC Regiment	5/24/1781, a Private under Capt. Alexander Brevard. Discharged on 5/24/1782 (3rd NC Regiment). aka Richard Pearson.	
Pierson, Thomas	4th NC Regiment	1781, a Private under Capt. George Dougherty. Discharged on 5/25/1782.	
Pierson, Thomas	6th NC Regiment	A Private under Capt. Thomas Donoho. Dropped from the rolls in Sep. 1777.	

Name	1st Unit	Year / Rank / Served Under / Notes	Known Battles
Pike, Benjamin	6th NC Regiment	1775, a 2nd Lieutenant under Capt. George Mitchell and Col. Thomas Wade in the Salisbury District Minutemen. Lived in the Wilmington District. 4/17/1776, a 2nd Lieutenant under Capt. George Mitchell and Col. John Alexander Lillington. 6/6/1776, a 1st Lieutenant. 4/28/1777, a Captain who took over for Capt. George Mitchell who had resigned. Died 10/11/1777 at Alexandria, VA on the Potomac River from Smallpox inoculation. From Onslow County, NC.	
Pilchard, John	5th NC Regiment	1777, a Private under Capt. John Enloe. Dropped from the rolls in Jan. 1778.	
Pilley, John	2nd NC Regiment	12/11/1776, an Ensign under Capt. Edward Vail, Jr.	
Pinkstone, William	1st NC Regiment	5/12/1781, a Private under Capt. Alexander Brevard. Discharged on 2/20/1782 (3rd NC Regiment). aka William Pinkston.	
Pinkum, Philip	10th NC Regiment	8/12/1777, a Corporal under Capt. Abraham Sheppard, Jr. A Private in June 1778. 9/9/1778, a known Private under Capt. John Ingles (2nd NC Regiment). 3/12/1779, re-enlisted under Capt. John Ingles. POW at Ft. Lafayette, NY on 6/1/1779. Deserted on 12/6/1779.	Ft. Lafayette (NY).
Pipkin, William	4th NC Regiment	2/6/1782, a Private under Capt. James Mills. Died 8/9/1782.	
Pitchet, Oliver	6th NC Regiment	A Private under Capt. Thomas Donoho. Deserted in Aug. 1777.	
Pitman, John	1st NC Regiment	1781, a Private under Capt. William Walton. Discharged on 6/9/1782.	
Pitt, Thomas	3rd NC Regiment	7/20/1778, a Private under Capt. John Baker for nine months.	
Pitt, James	2nd NC Regiment	1782, a Private under Capt. Benjamin Carter for 18 months. Earlier in NC Militia. From Franklin County, NC. S7313.	
Pivikins, Isaac	2nd NC Regiment	5/16/1777, a Private under Capt. Clement Hall. 9/9/1778, a known Private under Capt. Clement Hall.	
Platt, John	9th NC Regiment	4/10/1778, a Private under Capt. Anthony Sharpe.	
Platt, Samuel	7th NC Regiment	3/16/1777, a Sergeant Major. Dropped from the rolls in Dec. 1777.	
Player, Stephen	1st NC Regiment	1775, a Private under Capt. Alfred Moore [4].	Moore's Creek Bridge [4].
Plumley, George	3rd NC Regiment	7/20/1778, a Private under Lt./Capt. George "Gee" Bradley for nine months.	
Plumpus, Timothy	6th NC Regiment	1777, a Private under Capt. Francis Child. Dropped from the rolls in Nov. 1777.	
Poe, David	3rd NC Regiment	5/15/1776, a Private under Capt. James Emmett. 9/9/1778, a known Private in the Colonel's Company (Col. John Patten - 2nd NC Regiment) led by Capt. John Craddock. Discharged on 11/10/1778. Enlisted in Chatham County, NC. S41962.	

Name	1st Unit	Year / Rank / Served Under / Notes	Known Battles
Poe, Henry W.	2nd NC Regiment	Sep. 1782, a Private under Capt. Clement Hall. Deserted on 11/30/1782. Earlier in NC Militia, deserted there, too. From Randolph County, NC. R8204.	
Poe, John	1st NC Regiment	5/9/1781, a Private under Capt. Alexander Brevard.	
Poe, Simeon	3rd NC Regiment	1782, a Private under Capt. Alexander Brevard for 18 months.	
Polk, Thomas	4th NC Regiment	9/9/1775, Colonel of Mecklenburg County Regiment of Militia. 4/15/1776, commander of 4th NC Regiment. 6/1/1778, it was folded into the 2nd NC Regiment, and Col. Thomas Polk sent back to NC to aid in recruiting - he resigned on 6/26/1778. Later appointed as Commissary General of the Southern Department, resigned late 1780.	Great Cane Brake (SC), Snow Campaign (SC), Moore's Creek Bridge [4], Ft. George - Bald Head Island, Germantown (PA).
Polk, William	9th NC Regiment	1775, a Lieutenant in SC unit - wounded at Great Cane Brake on 12/22/1775. 11/27/1776, a Major in the 9th NC Regiment under Col. John Williams. Badly wounded at Germantown, PA. Discharged Summer of 1779. July 1780, a Lt. Colonel as an Aide to Maj. Gen. Richard Caswell – NC Militia. Then under Col. Robert Irwin. April 1781, created a regiment of SC State Troops as a Lt. Colonel under BG Thomas Sumter for ten months - commissioned by SC Governor John Rutledge. S3706.	Brandywine Creek (PA), Germantown (PA), Beaver Creek Ford (SC), Camden (SC), Cowan's Ford.
Pollard, Matthew	3rd NC Regiment	7/20/1778, a Private under Lt./Capt. George "Gee" Bradley for nine months.	
Pollard, William	2nd NC Regiment	1777, a Private under Capt. James Martin. Dropped from the rolls in Sept. 1777.	
Pollock, Jacob	4th NC Regiment	1775, a 1st Lieutenant in the Edenton District Minutemen. 4/17/1776, a 1st Lieutenant under Capt. John McLane. Died in 1777.	
Pollock, Jesse	4th NC Regiment	1782, a Private under Capt. Thomas Evans for 18 months.	
Polmore, Elijah	4th NC Regiment	1782, a Private under Capt. Thomas Evans for 18 months.	
Polson, John	3rd NC Regiment	5/11/1776, a Corporal under Capt. James Emmett. A Sergeant in Oct. 1777. 9/9/1778, a known Sergeant in the Major's Company (Maj. Hardy Murfree) (2nd NC Regiment). Discharged on 10/16/1778. aka John Poulson, John Paulson.	
Pond, John	2nd NC Regiment	1777, a Private under Capt. John Armstrong. 9/9/1778, a known Private under Capt. Robert Fenner. Deserted on 6/28/1779. Rejoined in Nov. 1779. Deserted again on 2/5/1780.	
Ponder, Thomas	3rd NC Regiment	1782, a Sergeant under Capt. Alexander Brevard for 18 months.	
Ponder, William	5th NC Regiment	6/30/1777, a Private under Capt. John Pugh Williams. A Musician in Sep. 1777. 9/9/1778, a	

Name	1st Unit	Year / Rank / Served Under / Notes	Known Battles
		known Drummer in the Major's Company (Maj. Hardy Murfree) (2nd NC Regiment). A Private again in Sep. 1778. aka William Pouder.	
Pool, James	5th NC Regiment	6/29/1779, a Private under Capt. Joseph Montford. Deserted on 11/22/1779. From Dobbs County, NC. aka James Poole.	
Poore, Thomas	1st NC Regiment	September 1775, a Private under Capt. Henry "Hal" Dixon. Wounded at the battle of Ft. Moultrie (SC). POW at the Fall of Charleston (SC), exchanged in 1781. Then in NC Militia, unit unknown. S39024.	Ft. Moultrie #1 (SC), Siege of Charleston 1780 (SC).
Poore, William	10th NC Regiment	6/23/1777, a Private under Capt. Andrew Vanoy for three years. 9/8/1778, a known Private in the Lt. Colonel's Company (Lt. Col. Robert Mebane) (1st NC Regiment) led by Capt. Joshua Bowman. aka William Poor.	
Pope, Henry	1st NC Regiment	9/1/1775, an Ensign. 11/28/1776, a Captain in the 8th NC Regiment under Col. James Armstrong. Resigned in Jan. 1777. From Dobbs County, NC.	
Pope, Samuel	5th NC Regiment	1777, a Private under Capt. Simon Alderson.	
Pope, Samuel	10th NC Regiment	5/18/1777, a Private under Capt. Abraham Sheppard, Jr.	
Pope, Samuel Sr.	10th NC Regiment	5/5/1777, a Sergeant under Capt. Abraham Sheppard, Jr. A Private in June 1778. 9/9/1778, a known Private under Capt. John Ingles (2nd NC Regiment). Discharged on 6/30/1779.	
Pope, William	10th NC Regiment	5/15/1777, a Sergeant under Capt. Abraham Sheppard, Jr. A Private in June 1778 in the Lt. Colonel's Company (Lt. Col. Selby Harney) (2nd NC Regiment). POW at the Fall of Charleston (SC), escaped after 12 days. Then joined SC Militia. S35031.	Monmouth (NJ), Siege of Charleston 1780 (SC).
Pope, Willis	5th NC Regiment	1775, a 2nd Lieutenant in the Salisbury District Minutemen. Lived in the Hillsborough District. 4/17/1776, a 2nd Lieutenant under Capt. William Ward and Col. Edward Buncombe. Later a Lieutenant under Capt. Philip Taylor. From Wake County.	
Porch, Henry	1st NC Regiment	1781, a Private under Capt. Anthony Sharpe, Capt. William Bush, Capt. William Walton. Discharged on 6/2/1782. Earlier in NC Militia. From Franklin County, NC. aka Henry Porks. W9234.	
Porch, James	1st NC Regiment	11/1/1778, a Private under Capt. Anthony Sharpe for 12 months.	
Porter, Charles	1st NC Regiment	Aug. or Sep. 1780, a Private under Capt. James Verner. Stationed at Halifax, NC making stuff for Col. Nicholas Long. Captured by British, paroled. Enlisted in Edgecombe County, NC, where he was born in 1745. S7327.	Halifax.
Porter, James	3rd NC Regiment	5/24/1779, a Private under Capt. George "Gee" Bradley.	

Name	1st Unit	Year / Rank / Served Under / Notes	Known Battles
Porter, Joshua	1st NC Regiment	4/15/1781, a Private under Capt. Anthony Sharpe. Dropped from the rolls sometime during 1781.	
Porter, William	1st NC Regiment	1777, a Private under Capt. John Brown. Died on 3/5/1778.	
Porter, William	1st NC Regiment	4/15/1781, a Private under Capt. Anthony Sharpe. Dropped from the rolls sometime during 1781.	
Porterfield, Dennis	6th NC Regiment	1775, an Ensign in the NC Militia. 4/17/1776, an Ensign undr Capt. Arthur Council and Col. John Alexander Lillington. 4/2/1777, a Lieutenant under Capt. Francis Child. Dropped from the rolls in Jan. 1778. Re-enlisted into the 1st NC Regiment on 6/1/1778. Jan. 1779, a Lieutenant in the 5th NC Regiment. 2/1/1779, a Captain in the 5th NC Regiment. Spring of 1781, in the 3rd NC Regiment under Maj. John Armstrong. Killed at the battle of Eutaw Springs, SC on September 8, 1781. From Cumberland County. aka Dennis Potterfield, Denny Porterfield.	Eutaw Springs (SC).
Portiss, Hardy	3rd NC Regiment	7/20/1778, a Private in the Lt. Colonel's Company (Lt. Col. William Lee Davidson) led by Lt./Capt. George "Gee" Bradley for nine months. 4/23/1779, a known Private in the Lt. Colonel's Company (Lt. Col. Robert Mebane) led by Capt. George "Gee" Bradley. aka Hardy Porthis.	
Portiss, Lewis	2nd NC Regiment	5/15/1781, a Private under Capt. Tilghman Dixon. Discharged on 5/25/1782 (1st NC Regiment).	
Portlock, Caleb	7th NC Regiment	9/1/1777, a Private under Capt. John Poynter. 9/8/1778, a known Private under Capt. Tilghman Dixon (1st NC Regiment).	
Portress, John	3rd NC Regiment	1777, a Private under Capt. Pinketham Eaton. Died on 5/1/1778.	
Potter, Daniel	1st NC Regiment	1776, a Private under Capt. Joshua Bowman. 9/8/1778, a known Private under Capt. Joshua Bowman.	
Potter, Daniel	2nd NC Regiment	1782, a Corporal under Capt. Benjamin Carter for 18 months. A Sergeant in Dec. 1782.	
Potter, Daniel	6th NC Regiment	A Private under Capt. George Dougherty. A Corporal in Nov. 1777. A Sergeant in May 1778. Discharged on 3/21/1779.	
Potter, Edward	2nd NC Regiment	6/3/1781, a Private under Capt. Benjamin Carter for 12 months. POW at the battle of Eutaw Springs, SC on 9/8/1781.	Eutaw Springs (SC).
Potter, John	3rd NC Regiment	4/27/1776, a Private under Capt. Thomas Granbury for 2-1/2 years. Discharged in Oct. 1778.	
Potter, Peleg	3rd NC Regiment	7/30/1778, a Private under Capt. Michael Quinn for nine months.	
Potter, Samuel	8th NC Regiment	1777, a Private under Capt. Robert Raiford. Died in Sep. 1777.	

Name	1st Unit	Year / Rank / Served Under / Notes	Known Battles
Potter, Thomas	10th NC Regiment	5/18/1777, a Private under Capt. Abraham Sheppard, Jr.	
Potts, Jesse	DQMG	1779, Adjutant QM General under Col. Nicholas Long (Deputy QM General), with rank equal to a Captain. Born 10/4/1754 in Prince George's County, VA. S47664.	
Pough, Stephen	2nd NC Regiment	Sep. 1782, a Private under Capt. Clement Hall for the duration of the war. Deserted on 12/10/1782.	
Poulston, Jonas	1st NC Regiment	1781, a Private under Capt. William Lytle. Discharged on 10/1/1782 (4th NC Regiment).	
Pound, Samuel	7th NC Regiment	1777, a Private under Capt. John Macon. Deserted in Aug. 1777.	
Powell, Exum	1st NC Regiment	5/2/1781, a Private under Capt. Robert Raiford. Discharged on 5/2/1782 (2nd NC Regiment). From Hertford County, NC. aka Axom Powell.	
Powell, George	1st NC Regiment	4/28/1781, a Private under Capt. Alexander Brevard. Discharged on 4/25/1782 (3rd NC Regiment).	
Powell, Jacob	1st NC Regiment	11/1/1778, a Corporal under Capt. Anthony Sharpe for 12 months.	
Powell, James	3rd NC Regiment	7/20/1778, a Private under Lt./Capt. Joseph Montford for nine months. From what is now Warren County, NC. W17472.	Briar Creek (GA).
Powell, Jesse	1st NC Regiment	2/14/1777, a Private, unit unknown. 9/8/1778, a known Private under Capt. Tilghman Dixon.	
Powell, John	3rd NC Regiment	4/16/1776, a Corporal under Capt. Jacob Turner. A Private in June 1778. Discharged in Oct. 1778. From Warren County, NC. W17471.	
Powell, Joseph	3rd NC Regiment	7/20/1778, a Private under Lt./Capt. Joseph Montford.	
Powell, Lewis	1st NC Regiment	11/25/1780, a Private under Capt. William Lytle. Wounded at the Siege of Ninety-Six (SC). At the battle of Eutaw Springs, SC under Capt. Edward Yarborough (3rd NC Regiment). Dropped from the rolls sometime during 1781. Earlier in NC Militia. From Franklin County, NC. W4055.	Guilford Court House, Siege of Augusta (GA), Siege of Ninety-Six 1781 (SC), Eutaw Springs (SC).
Powell, Lewis	1st NC Regiment	9/10/1782, a Private under Capt. Joshua Hadley for 18 months. Deserted on 6/10/1783 (?).	
Powell, Stephen	1st NC Regiment	8/1/1782, a Private under Capt. Joshua Hadley for 18 months. Died on 5/18/1783.	
Powell, Thomas	10th NC Regiment	8/31/1777, a Private, unit unknown. A Corporal on 6/1/1779.	
Powell, William	3rd NC Regiment	8/9/1779, a Private under Capt. Kedar Ballard. Deserted in Oct. 1779.	
Powell, William	3rd NC Regiment	2/4/1782, a Private under Capt. Samuel Jones for 12 months. From Orange County, NC. S21427.	
Powell, William	10th NC Regiment	10/5/1777, a Private, unit unknown. 9/9/1778, a known Private in the Major's Company (Maj. Hardy Murfree) (2nd NC Regiment) assigned to the QM General's Department in Halifax, NC	

557

Name	1st Unit	Year / Rank / Served Under / Notes	Known Battles
		under Col. Nicholas Long. Discharged on 3/29/1782. From Halifax County, NC. R8392.	
Powers, Absalom	1st NC Regiment	4/12/1781, a Private under Capt. Alexander Brevard. Possibly the same man as below.	
Powers, Absalom	1st NC Regiment	1781, a Sergeant under Capt. Alexander Brevard. Discharged on 5/12/1782 (3rd NC Regiment).	
Powers, Absalom	3rd NC Regiment	7/20/1778, a Corporal under Lt./Capt. Joseph Montford for nine months.	
Powers, David	2nd NC Regiment	1777, a Private under Capt. William Fenner. Died on 5/3/1778.	
Powers, James	3rd NC Regiment	1781, a Private under Capt. Clement Hall for 12 months. Discharged on 7/10/1782 (2nd NC Regiment) at Bacon's Bridge, SC. Enlisted in Currituck County, NC. S38315.	
Powers, James	7th NC Regiment	11/28/1776, a 2nd Lieutenant under Capt. John McGlaughan. 4/20/1777, a 1st Lieutenant under Capt. Thomas Brickell. Transferred to 3rd NC Regiment on 6/1/1778. Dropped from the rolls between January and September of 1779. From Edenton District.	
Powers, Jesse	1st NC Regiment	4/12/1781 Private under Capt. Alexander Brevard. Discharged on 5/12/1782 (3rd NC Regiment).	
Powers, Moses	1st NC Regiment	4/12/1781, a Private under Capt. Robert Smith, then Capt. Alexander Brevard. Discharged on 4/12/1782 (3rd NC Regiment) at Bacon's Bridge, SC. S41963.	Siege of Augusta (GA), Raid on John's Island (SC).
Powers, William	1st NC Regiment	5/13/1777, a Private, unit unknown, enlisted for three years. 9/8/1778, a known Private under Maj. John Baptiste Ashe. Discharged on 11/30/1778. On some rolls as William Power.	
Powers, William	5th NC Regiment	June 1779, a Private under Capt. William Lytle.	
Powers, William	3rd NC Regiment	June 1779, a Private under Capt. Kedar Ballard. Discharged on 8/1/1779.	
Poyner, Peter	10th NC Regiment	5/9/1777, a Private under Capt. John Jarvis. 9/8/1778, a known Private under Capt. Howell Tatum (1st NC Regiment). Dropped from the rolls in Nov. 1779. aka Peter Pyner.	
Poynter, John	7th NC Regiment	11/28/1776, a Captain under Col. James Hogun. Dropped from the rolls in Jan. 1778. 1778, a Major in NC Militia. From Currituck County, NC. aka John Pointer.	Brandywine Creek (PA), Germantown (PA).
Pratt, Thomas	1st NC Regiment	1781, a Private under Capt. Alexander Brevard, then Capt. James Mills. Discharged on 5/28/1782 (4th NC Regiment) at Bacon's Bridge, SC. From Guilford (what would become Rockingham) County, NC. W1075.	
Pratt, Zebulon	10th NC Regiment	5/6/1777, a Private under Capt. Isaac Moore for three years. 9/8/1778, a known Private in the Lt. Colonel's Company (Lt. Col. Robert Mebane) (1st NC Regiment) led by Capt. Joshua Bowman. Discharged 3/27/1780 at Charleston,	

Name	1st Unit	Year / Rank / Served Under / Notes	Known Battles
		SC. S41969.	
Prescott, Aaron	4th NC Regiment	1777, a Private under Capt. Micajah Lewis. Died on 11/4/1777.	
Prescott, Austin	NC Artillery	8/17/1776, a Matross under Capt. John Vance as NC Provincial Troops. 7/10/1777, on Continental Line. 11/16/1777, under Capt. John Kingsbury. 5/1/1778, in same unit. 9/16/1778, in same unit. Sent to Georgetown for supplies when Charleston fell, therefore not taken prisoner. aka Oston Rescod, Oston Prescott. S41967.	
Prescott, Charles	4th NC Regiment	1777, a Private under Capt. Micajah Lewis. Died on 8/15/1777.	
Prescott, Thomas	10th NC Regiment	4/21/1777, a Private under Capt. Silas Stevenson. Died on 3/20/1778 from his Smallpox inoculation. Col. Abraham Sheppard wrote on 4/7/1778 that he was a Sergeant when he died.	
Prescott, Willoughby	6th NC Regiment	May 1776, a Private under Capt. George Mitchell, then Capt. Thomas Donoho for three years. 6/1/1778, a Private under Capt. Griffith John McRee (1st NC Regiment). POW at the Fall of Charleston, paroled, but not exchanged until near the end of the war. Enlisted in Onslow County, NC. aka Willobey Prescote. S41966.	Brandywine Creek (PA), Germantown (PA), Monmouth (NJ), Siege of Charleston 1780 (SC).
Prevat, Isaac	3rd NC Regiment	9/9/1775, a 1st Lieutenant in the Halifax District Minutemen. 4/17/1776, a 1st Lieutenant under Capt. William Brinkley. aka Isaac Privat.	
Prewitt, Joshua	4th NC Regiment	6/1/1776, a Private under Capt. John Nelson for three years. 6/1/1778, a known Private under Capt. Griffith John McRee (1st NC Regiment). Discharged on 6/1/1779 at West Point, NY. aka Joshua Prewet, Joshua Pruett. S39027.	
Prewitt, Ransom	4th NC Regiment	6/1/1776, a Private under Capt. John Nelson for three years. 6/1/1778, a known Private under Capt. Griffith John McRee (1st NC Regiment). Discharged on 6/1/1779 at West Point, NY. aka Ransom Prewet, Ransom Pruett. S39029.	Brandywine Creek (PA), Germantown (PA), Monmouth (NJ).
Price, Edward	1st NC Regiment	1781, a Private under Capt. William Walton. Discharged on 7/1/1782. From Johnston County, NC. W4769.	
Price, Humphrey	6th NC Regiment	Aug. 1777, hired by George Baker to finish his term of service under Capt. George Dougherty. 6/1/1778, this unit was transferred to the 4th NC Regiment. Discharged by Maj. John Armstrong.	
Price, James	3rd NC Regiment	7/20/1778, a Private under Capt. Francis Child for nine months.	
Price, James	10th NC Regiment	7/25/1777, a Private under Capt. Andrew Vanoy. Taken away by his master on 4/12/1778. aka Joseph Price.	
Price, Lewis	2nd NC Regiment	4/15/1781, a Private under Capt. Benjamin Carter for 12 months. Discharged on 4/25/1782.	

Name	1st Unit	Year / Rank / Served Under / Notes	Known Battles
Price, Matthew	3rd NC Regiment	7/30/1778, a Private under Capt. Michael Quinn for nine months.	
Price, Micajah	7th NC Regiment	1777, a Private under Capt. John McGlaughan. Died on 11/15/1777.	
Price, Samuel	9th NC Regiment	11/15/1777, a Private under Capt. Anthony Sharpe for three years. 9/8/1778, a known Private in the Lt. Colonel's Company (Lt. Col. Robert Mebane) (1st NC Regiment) led by Capt. Joshua Bowman.	
Price, Thomas	2nd NC Regiment	1777, a Private under Capt. Benjamin Williams. Died on 1/2/1778. Another source claims this man's name was Thomas Pierce - so he's listed above under that name as well.	
Price, Thomas	10th NC Regiment	5/18/1777, a Private under Capt. Abraham Sheppard, Jr.	
Price, William	1st NC Regiment	1782, a Private under Capt. Peter Bacot.	
Price, William	3rd NC Regiment	7/20/1778, a Private under Capt. Francis Child for nine months.	
Prichard, Edward	4th NC Regiment	1777, a Private under Capt. James Williams. 3/12/1779, re-enlisted for the duration of the war under Capt. Griffith John McRee (1st NC Regiment). Later, in NC Militia. From Wake County, NC. aka Edward Pritchett, Edward Prichet. W8536.	Brandywine Creek (PA), Monmouth (NJ).
Prichel, John	3rd NC Regiment	1777, a Private under Capt. Thomas Granbury. Dropped from the rolls on 9/7/1777.	
Pridgeon, Francis	1st NC Regiment	12/1/1781, a Private under Capt. James Mills for 12 months. Discharged Dec. 1782 (4th NC Regiment). From Bladen County, NC when he enlisted. Born on 12/15/1760 in Duplin County, what is now Sampson County, NC. aka Francis Pridgen, Francis Pridgion. W6880.	
Pridgion, Thomas	8th NC Regiment	1777, a Corporal under Capt. Robert Raiford. A Private in Feb. 1778. 9/9/1778, a known Private in the Major's Company (Maj. Hardy Murfree) (2nd NC Regiment). Died in Oct. 1778. aka Thomas Pridgen.	
Priest, William	3rd NC Regiment	7/20/1778, a Private under Capt. John Baker for nine months.	
Primm, James	4th NC Regiment	7/20/1778, a Private under Lt. Kadar Parker for nine months. Might have been a Corporal. Later in NC Militia. From what is now Franklin County, NC.	Stono Ferry (SC).
Prior, Thomas	3rd NC Regiment	7/30/1778, a Private under Capt. Michael Quinn for nine months.	
Prise, Samuel	6th NC Regiment	10/4/1777, a Private under Ensign Joseph Richardson.	
Pritchard, Jesse	1st NC Regiment	1777, a Private under Capt. Joshua Bowman.	
Pritchard, Jesse	6th NC Regiment	1777, a Sergeant under Capt. Francis Child. Died in Feb. 1778. aka Jese Prichard.	
Pritchett, Joshua	3rd NC Regiment	7/30/1778, a Private under Maj. Thomas Hogg for nine months.	

Name	1st Unit	Year / Rank / Served Under / Notes	Known Battles
Privat, Peter	4th NC Regiment	1781, a Private under Capt. Joseph T. Rhodes. Discharged on 4/1/1782.	
Privat, William	3rd NC Regiment	1782, a Private under Capt. Alexander Brevard for 18 months. aka William Prival.	
Private, Miles	5th NC Regiment	11/15/1776, a Private under Capt. Simon Alderson. Dropped from the rolls in Feb. 1778. 9/9/1778, a known Private in the Colonel's Company (Col. John Patten) (2nd NC Regiment) led by Capt. John Craddock. aka Miles Privett.	
Privit, John	2nd NC Regiment	5/12/1781, a Private under Capt. Tilghman Dixon, then Capt. Joshua Hadley, then Capt. Benjamin Bailey (3rd NC Regiment). Discharged on 5/26/1782 at Bacon's Bridge, SC. aka John Prebit. S41968.	
Proctor, Aaron	3rd NC Regiment	2/1/1782, a Private under Capt. Samuel Jones for 12 months.	
Proctor, Francis	1st NC Regiment	Dec. 1782, a Private under Capt. Peter Bacot for 12 months.	
Proctor, Joshua	8th NC Regiment	1777, a Private under Capt. Robert Raiford. Dropped from the rolls in March 1778. aka Joshua Procter.	
Proctor, William	3rd NC Regiment	1778, a Private under Capt. Kedar Ballard for nine months.	
Proctor, William	5th NC Regiment	5/15/1776, a Private under Capt. Reading Blount. 9/9/1778, a known Private under Capt. John Ingles (2nd NC Regiment). Discharged on 11/10/1778.	
Proudfoot, John	4th NC Regiment	5/28/1777, a Private under Capt. William Temple Coles for three years. 9/8/1778, a known Private under Capt. John Sumner (1st NC Regiment). 3/12/1779, re-enlisted for the duration of the war in the same unit. aka John Proudford.	
Prozer, John	4th NC Regiment	1782, a Private under Capt. Anthony Sharpe for 18 months.	
Pucket, Solomon	1st NC Regiment	6/15/1781, a Private under Capt. Griffith John McRee. Deserted on 8/1/1781.	
Pudney, Jeremiah	2nd NC Regiment	1782, a Private under Capt. Robert Raiford. Deserted on 6/11/1782.	
Pugh, Arthur	1st NC Regiment	2/20/1778, a Private under Capt. Howell Tatum. 9/8/1778, a known Private under Capt. Howell Tatum - sick at Valley Forge on that date. aka Arthur Pew.	
Pugh, David	DQMG	1780, a Saddler on the roll of Capt. Solomon Wood (NC Light Dragoons) - this seems to be for convenience only. 8/23/1781, a Leather Worker under Col. Nicholas Long (Deputy QM General), making saddles, harnesses, caps, etc.	
Pugh, Shadrack	1st NC Regiment	8/15/1781, a Private under Lt./Capt. William Walton. Earlier in NC Militia. From Bertie County, NC. R8514.	
Pugh, Thomas	5th NC Regiment	9/9/1775, a 1st Lieutenant in the Edenton District Minutemen. 4/17/1776, a 1st Lieutenant	

Name	1st Unit	Year / Rank / Served Under / Notes	Known Battles
Whitmell		under Capt. John Pugh Williams and Col. Edward Buncombe. From Bertie County.	
Pugh, Whitmell	2nd NC Regiment	9/1/1775, an Ensign. Resigned in October 1775. aka Whitmill Pugh.	
Pulley, Isom	3rd NC Regiment	5/5/1776, a Private under Capt. Thomas Granbury for 2-1/2 years. 9/9/1778, a known Private under Capt. John Ingles (2nd NC Regiment). Discharged in Oct. 1778.	
Pulley, James	3rd NC Regiment	5/12/1776, a Musician under Capt. Thomas Granbury for 2-1/2 years. A Private in June 1778. 9/9/1778, a known Private in the Major's Company (Maj. Hardy Murfree) (2nd NC Regiment). Discharged on 11/12/1778.	
Pully, Wasdon	3rd NC Regiment	7/20/1778, a Private under Lt./Capt. Joseph Montford for nine months.	
Punal, Abraham	3rd NC Regiment	11/5/1778, a Private under Lt./Capt. Joseph Montford.	
Purdy, James	10th NC Regiment	5/24/1777, a Private, unit unknown. 9/9/1778, a known Private in the Lt. Colonel's Company (Lt. Col. Selby Harney) (2nd NC Regiment). aka James Purdie.	
Purse, William	NC Artillery	1780, served under Capt. John Kingsbury. POW at the Fall of Charleston, retained for fifteen months. Earlier in SC unit. S18171.	Siege of Charleston 1780 (SC).
Purser, Joseph	1st NC Regiment	4/15/1781, a Private under Capt. Anthony Sharpe. Dropped from the rolls sometime during 1781.	
Purvis, James	4th NC Regiment	1782, a Private under Capt. Thomas Evans for 18 months. Deserted on 6/21/1783 (?). Earlier in NC Militia. From Pitt and Martin Counties in NC. R8529.	
Pyatt, Peter	2nd NC Regiment	3/30/1782, a Lieutenant under Capt. Tilghman Dixon. One source claims it was 1781. aka Peter Pyeatt.	
Pyatt, Peter	9th NC Regiment	1777, a Sergeant under Capt. Richard D. Cook. A QM Sergeant on 6/15/1778. Discharged on 6/15/1779. Possibly the same man as above.	
Pyland, Peter	3rd NC Regiment	9/17/1782, a Private under Capt. Benjamin Bailey for 18 months.	
Pyot, Thomas	2nd NC Regiment	1777, a Private under Capt. William Fenner. Dropped from the rolls in Jan. 1778.	
Quilina, Shadrack	2nd NC Regiment	1781, a Private under Capt. Benjamin Carter. Discharged on 7/20/1782.	
Quinby, Eleazor	2nd NC Regiment	5/4/1776, a Private, unit unknown. 9/9/1778, a known Private under Capt. Clement Hall. Discharged on 7/30/1779. aka Eleamus Quinby.	
Quinn, David	4th NC Regiment	5/25/1781, a Private under Capt. Joseph T. Rhodes. Wounded at the battle of Eutaw Springs, SC. Earlier in NC Militia. From Duplin County, NC. W4771.	Eutaw Springs (SC).
Quinn, David	4th NC Regiment	1781, a Corporal under Capt. George Dougherty. Discharged on 5/25/1782.	
Quinn, Francis	1st NC Regiment	1782, a Private under Capt. Peter Bacot. Dec. 1782, transferred to the Pennsylvania Line.	

Name	1st Unit	Year / Rank / Served Under / Notes	Known Battles
Quinn, Michael	NC Artillery	6/13/1776, a Lt. Fireworker under Capt. John Vance. 11/28/1776, a 2nd Lieutenant under Capt. Frederick Hargett (8th NC Regiment), then Capt. John Walsh. Promoted to Captain on 8/1/1777 under Col. James Armstrong. 6/1/1778, a Captain in the 3rd NC Regiment. Resigned on 12/14/1779, then became a traitor and joined the British cause. He was captured in 1781 in Edenton, NC and was executed. From Craven County, NC.	Edenton.
Quinn, Thomas	10th NC Regiment	8/29/1777, a Private under Capt. Abraham Sheppard, Jr. 9/9/1778, a known Private under Capt. John Ingles (2nd NC Regiment). POW at Ft. Lafayette, NY on 6/1/1779. Rejoined in Nov. 1779.	Ft. Lafayette (NY).
Raby, Adam	4th NC Regiment	A Private under Capt. Micajah Lewis. Dropped from the rolls in Sep. 1777.	
Raby, Cader	4th NC Regiment	A Private under Capt. Micajah Lewis. Deserted on 10/26/1777.	
Rackley, Micajah	2nd NC Regiment	1781, a Private under Capt. Thomas Evans, then under Capt. Edward Yarborough (3rd NC Regiment) for 12 months. Discharged on 4/22/1782 at Bacon's Bridge, SC. Earlier in NC Militia. On the official rolls a Micajah Rittey. W26396.	
Ragains, Thomas	1st NC Regiment	1775, a Sergeant under Capt. Robert Rowan. Wounded in a skirmish at Charleston, SC lighthouse just prior to the battle of Breech Inlet Naval Battle (SC) on June 28, 1776. Re-enlisted under Capt. Henry "Hal" Dixon. Discharged at Wilmington, NC. Later in NC Militia. From Cumberland County, NC. Moved to Orange County, NC. W4502.	Florida Expedition 1776.
Ragly, Blake	2nd NC Regiment	7/20/1778, a Private under Maj. Reading Blount for nine months. aka Blake Rayly.	
Ragsdale, Benjamin	3rd NC Regiment	June/July 1781, a Private under Capt. Edward Yarborough for 18 months. May have only served three or four months. Earlier in NC Militia. From Chatham County, NC. W1079.	
Raifield, Spencer	3rd NC Regiment	5/10/1776, a Private under Capt. Pinketham Eaton. 9/9/1778, a known Private in the Major's Company (Maj. Hardy Murfree) (2nd NC Regiment). Discharged on 11/10/1778. aka Spinencoy Raifield.	
Raiford, Caleb	1st NC Regiment	4/12/1781, a Private under Capt. William Lytle. Confined four nights for desertion during July 1781. Discharged on 4/12/1782 (4th NC Regiment). aka Caleb Rafle.	
Raiford, John	1st NC Regiment	1777, a 2nd Lieutenant under Capt. Clement Hall. Resigned 2/1/1778. aka John Radford.	
Raiford, Peter	1st NC Regiment	A Captain in 1779, nothing more known.	
Raiford, Robert	8th NC Regiment	1775, in NC Militia. 11/28/1776, a Captain under Col. James Armstrong. Transferred to 2nd	Brandywine Creek (PA),

Name	1st Unit	Year / Rank / Served Under / Notes	Known Battles
		NC Regiment on 6/1/1778. Mid-1781, a Captain under Lt. Col. John Baptiste Ashe (1st NC Regiment). 2/6/1782, moved back to 2nd NC Regiment. Served to the end of the war. From Cumberland County, NC.	Germantown (PA), Monmouth (NJ), Eutaw Springs (SC), Bladen County Court House.
Railey, Edmond	2nd NC Regiment	2/1/1782, a Private under Capt. Benjamin Andrew Coleman for 12 months.	
Railey, Isaac	1st NC Regiment	11/17/1778, a Private under Capt. Anthony Sharpe.	
Rainey, James	4th NC Regiment	4/26/1776, a Sergeant under Capt. William Goodman, then under Capt. Roger Moore. A Private in June 1778. 9/8/1778, a known Private under Capt. Joshua Bowman (1st NC Regiment). Discharged on 5/10/1779. S35599.	
Rainey, James	9th NC Regiment	4/26/1776, a Private under Capt. Hezekiah Rice for three years. 9/8/1778, a known Wagoner in the Colonel's Company (Col. Thomas Clark) (1st NC Regiment) led by Capt. John Gambier Scull. Dropped from the rolls in Nov. 1779. aka James Raney.	
Rainey, Peter	1st NC Regiment	6/23/1777, unit and rank unknown. 9/8/1778, a known Sergeant in the Lt. Colonel's Company (Lt. Col. Robert Mebane) led by Capt. Joshua Bowman. aka Peter Raney.	
Raintree, Reuben	10th NC Regiment	4/19/1777, a Lieutenant under Capt. Armwell Herron. Dropped from the rolls in June 1778. 1779, a Lietuenant in the NC State Regiment (State Troops). aka Ruben Raindtree, Rountree.	
Rakes, James	3rd NC Regiment	6/24/1779, a Sergeant under Capt. Michael Quinn. Deserted in Sep. 1779.	
Rall, James	1st NC Regiment	6/14/1781, a Private under Capt. Thomas Donoho. Discharged on 5/19/1782.	
Ralph, John	7th NC Regiment	A Private under Capt. Ely. Died on 4/4/1778.	
Ralph, Lewis	4th NC Regiment	2/18/1777, a Sergeant under Capt. James Smith for 2-1/2 years. A Private in Oct. 1777. A Private in Feb. 1778. 9/8/1778, a known Private in the Colonel's Company (Col. Thomas Clark) (1st NC Regiment) led by Capt. John Gambier Scull. Dropped from the rolls in Nov. 1779.	
Ralph, Thomas	1st NC Regiment	5/9/1781, a Private under Capt. Griffith John McRee then Capt. William Goodman, then Capt. Elijah Moore for 12 months. Discharged on 5/9/1782 at Bacon's Bridge, SC. Earlier in NC Militia. From Guilford County, NC. S38323.	Eutaw Springs (SC).
Ralsby, Richard		2/14/1776, a Private, regiment and unit unknown. 6/1/1778, a Private under Capt. Griffith John McRee (1st NC Regiment). aka Richard Rabsby.	
Ralston, Isaac	2nd NC Regiment	1775, a Captain of NC Militia. 6/8/1776, an Ensign under Capt. Armstrong. Jan. 1777, a 1st	

Name	1st Unit	Year / Rank / Served Under / Notes	Known Battles
		Lieutenant under Capt. Clement Hall. Retired 6/1/1778. Later, a Captain in NC Militia. From Guilford County, NC. aka Isaac Rolstone, Isaac Ralston. W26406.	
Ralston, Robert	1st NC Regiment	9/1/1775, an Ensign. 1/4/1776, a 2nd Lieutenant. 3/28/1776, a 1st Lieutenant. 3/8/1777, a Captain. Resigned on 8/29/1777. Later, a Major in the NC Militia. From Guilford County, NC. aka Robert Rolston, Robert Rolestone.	Moore's Creek Bridge [4].
Ram, Jacob	5th NC Regiment	6/2/1779, a Private under Capt. Joseph Montford. Deserted in Sep. 1779.	
Ramage, Alexander	9th NC Regiment	1/1/1777, a Corporal under Capt. Richard D. Cook. A Sergeant in Jan. 1778. A Private in Feb. 1778. 9/8/1778, a known Private under Capt. Howell Tatum (1st NC Regiment). Died on 3/19/1779. aka Alexander Rammage.	
Ramage, Thomas	2nd NC Regiment	1781, a Private under Capt. Benjamin Carter. Died on 10/15/1781.	
Ramsay, Allen	7th NC Regiment	12/18/1776, a Lieutenant under Capt. James Vaughan. Dropped from the rolls in Jan. 1778.	
Ramsay, Daniel	1st NC Regiment	5/25/1781, a Private under Capt. Griffith John McRee. Died in Oct. 1781.	
Ramsay, Mills	7th NC Regiment	1/1/1777, a Private under Capt. James Vaughan. Died on 1/2/1778. However, found on the roll of Capt. Howell Tatum (1st NC Regiment) on 2/26/1778. (?).	
Ramsey, Joel	4th NC Regiment	5/20/1776, a Private under Capt. William Goodman for three years. 9/8/1778, a known Private in the Colonel's Company (Col. Thomas Clark) (1st NC Regiment) led by Capt. John Gambier Scull. Discharged on 5/20/1779. S39031.	Brandywine Creek (PA), Germantown (PA), Monmouth (NJ).
Ramsey, John	4th NC Regiment	1782, a Private under Capt. Anthony Sharpe. Transferred to ? on 12/1/1782. aka John Ramey.	
Ramsey, Matthew	9th NC Regiment	11/28/1776, a Captain under Col. John Williams. 6/1/1778, a Captain under Col. James Armstrong (4th NC Regiment). Resigned in Nov. 1781. aka Mathew Ramsay.	Stono Ferry (SC), Siege of Savannah (GA), Guilford Court House.
Ramsey, William	6th NC Regiment	5/10/1776, a Private under Capt. Philip Taylor. Deserted in Aug. 1777.	
Randall, Andrew	10th NC Regiment	5/15/1777, a Sergeant under Capt. James Wilson for three years. A Private on 7/1/1778. 9/8/1778, a known Private in the Major's Company (Maj. Griffith John McRee) (1st NC Regiment) - sick on that date near Cranberry. Back to Sergeant on 1/1/1779. aka Andruss Randall, Andrews Randall, Andrew Randell.	
Rape, F. John	5th NC Regiment	6/4/1779, a Private under Capt. Joseph Montford. Deserted in Sep. 1779.	
Raper, Caleb	2nd NC Regiment	1777, a Private under Capt. Edward Vail, Jr. Dropped from the rolls in Oct. 1777.	
Raper, John	2nd NC	12/22/1776, a Private under Capt. William	

Name	1st Unit	Year / Rank / Served Under / Notes	Known Battles
	Regiment	Fenner for three years. 9/9/1778, a known Private in the Lt. Colonel's Company (Lt. Col. Selby Harney). A Musician in July 1779. Discharged on 2/1/1780. aka John Raiper.	
Raper, Robert	2nd NC Regiment	12/22/1776, a Private under Capt. William Fenner. 9/9/1778, a known Private in the Lt. Colonel's Company (Lt. Col. Selby Harney). POW at the Fall of Charleston, SC - escaped after two months. aka Robert Raiper. W4569.	Brandywine Creek (PA), Germantown (PA), Monmouth (NJ), Siege of Charleston 1780 (SC).
Rasher, Hardy	2nd NC Regiment	1782, a Private under Capt. Robert Raiford for 18 months.	
Rasko, Tettle	7th NC Regiment	1/14/1777, a Private under Capt. James Vaughan. A Corporal in Jan. 1778. Died on 2/24/1778. aka Tetkle Rasko.	
Rason, John	1st NC Regiment	3/12/1779, re-enlisted under Capt. James Read for the duration of the war. Earlier, unit and dates unknown.	
Ratcliff, William	7th NC Regiment	1778, a Private under Capt. John Baker. Deserted on 7/14/1778.	
Ratley, Benjamin	1st NC Regiment	6/6/1781, a Private under Capt. William Lytle. Discharged on 6/6/1782 (4th NC Regiment).	
Ratley, John	3rd NC Regiment	1777, a Private under Capt. Jacob Turner. Died 7/30/1778.	
Ravell, Nathaniel	3rd NC Regiment	6/24/1779, a Private under Michael Quinn. Deserted in Sep. 1779.	
Raws, Lawrence	3rd NC Regiment	7/1/1779, a Private under Capt. Kedar Ballard.	
Rawson, Daniel	3rd NC Regiment	1781, a Sergeant under Capt. Edward Yarborough for 12 months. Discharged on 4/27/1782.	
Ray, Archibald	2nd NC Regiment	1/4/1782, a Private under Capt. Benjamin Andrew Coleman for 12 months.	
Ray, Benjamin	6th NC Regiment	1776, a Private under Capt. John Baptiste Ashe and Capt. George Dougherty. 6/1/1778, a Private under Capt. Griffith John McRee (1st NC Regiment). POW at the Fall of Charleston, held 14 months. W26355.	Brandywine Creek (PA), Germantown (PA), Monmouth (NJ), Siege of Charleston 1780 (SC).
Ray, Daniel	7th NC Regiment	1778, a Private under Capt. John Baker. Deserted on 7/9/1778.	
Ray, Stephen	7th NC Regiment	1777, a Private under Capt. John McGlaughan. 2/26/1778, a known Private under Capt. Howell Tatum (1st NC Regiment). Died on 3/31/1778. From Hertford County, NC.	
Rayburn, George	4th NC Regiment	7/25/1776, a Private under Capt. William Goodman for three years. 9/8/1778, a known Private in the Colonel's Company (Col. Thomas Clark) (1st NC Regiment) led by Capt. John Gambier Scull. Discharged on 7/25/1779. aka	

566

Name	1st Unit	Year / Rank / Served Under / Notes	Known Battles
		George Raibourn.	
Raymond, Daniel	1st NC Regiment	Jan. 1782, a Private under Capt. Alexander Brevard. Deserted on 6/23/1783 (3rd NC Regiment).	
Razor, Christopher	1st NC Regiment	4/28/1781, a Private under Capt. Griffith John McRee. Discharged on 4/28/1782.	
Read, Duncan	NC Artillery	11/19/1776, a Matross under Capt. John Vance as NC Provincial Troops. 7/10/1777, on Continental Line. 11/16/1777, under Capt. John Kingsbury. Deserted on 1/18/1778.	
Read, James	1st NC Regiment	1/4/1776, an Ensign. 7/6/1776, a 2nd Lieutenant. 7/7/1776, a 1st Lieutenant under Capt. Henry "Hal" Dixon. 7/8/1777, a Captain under Col. Thomas Clark. 6/1/1778, also regimental Paymaster. POW at the Fall of Charleston. 1781, a Continental Captain acting as a full Colonel of NC State Troops - POW taken at Hillsborough, not exchanged until 11/26/1782. aka James Reed.	Moore's Creek Bridge [4], Brandywine Creek (PA), Germantown (PA), Monmouth (NJ), Siege of Charleston 1780 (SC), Hillsborough.
Read, James	2nd NC Regiment	9/14/1777, a Private, unit unknown. 9/9/1778, a known Private in the Colonel's Company (Col. John Patten) led by Capt. John Craddock. 3/12/1779, re-enlisted in the Colonel's Company (Col. John Patten) led by Capt. John Craddock. aka James Reade.	
Read, Jesse	5th NC Regiment	10/20/1776, a 2nd Lieutenant under Capt. Benjamin Stedman. 8/31/1777, left in NC to recruit new men for the 5th NC Regiment. 10/25/1777, a 1st Lieutenant. Transferred to 2nd NC Regiment on 6/1/1778 under Capt. Clement Hall. POW at the Fall of Charleston, exchanged 6/14/1781. POW at the battle of Eutaw Springs, SC on 9/8/1781. Promoted to Captain on 10/15/1782. Still considered a POW as of 11/26/1782. Retired 1/1/1783. aka Jese Reid, Reed.	Siege of Charleston 1780 (SC), Eutaw Springs (SC).
Reames, Joshua	3rd NC Regiment	4/23/1779, a known Private in the Lt. Colonel's Company (Lt. Col. Robert Mebane) led by Capt. George "Gee" Bradley. aka Joshua Remes.	
Reams, William	2nd NC Regiment	1782, a Private under Capt. Benjamin Carter for 18 months.	
Reardon, Dudley	5th NC Regiment	8/25/1777, a Private under Capt. Benjamin Andrew Coleman. 9/8/1778, in 2nd NC Regiment. Discharged on 12/4/1778.	
Reardon, Jeremiah	4th NC Regiment	5/27/1777, a Private under Capt. William Temple Coles for three years. 9/8/1778, a known Private under Capt. John Sumner (1st NC Regiment). On some rolls as Jeremiah Rardon.	
Reasoner, John	1st NC Regiment	1781, a Private under Capt. Anthony Sharpe. Transferred to ? before Apr. 1782.	
Reasoner, William	DQMG	1780, a Wagoner under Col. Nicholas Long (Deputy QM General). Said to be an ex-	

Name	1st Unit	Year / Rank / Served Under / Notes	Known Battles
		Continental soldier (?).	
Reasons, Thomas	10th NC Regiment	8/15/1777, a Private under Capt. Abraham Sheppard, Jr. 9/9/1778, a known Private under Capt. Benjamin Andrew Coleman (2nd NC Regiment).	
Reasons, William	5th NC Regiment	9/10/1776, a Musician under Capt. Reading Blount. A Private in Jan. 1778. 9/9/1778, a known Private in the Lt. Colonel's Company (Lt. Col. Selby Harney) (2nd NC Regiment). Deserted in June 1779. 7/1/1779, a known Private under Capt. George "Gee" Bradley (3rd NC Regiment) for 18 months. aka William Reason.	
Reaves, Zachariah	1st NC Regiment	1775, a Private under Capt. Thomas Allen for nine months. 1776, re-enlisted for 2-1/2 years and made a Sergeant under Capt. Griffith John McRee (6th NC Regiment). Discharged early in 1777 at Wilmington, NC due to illness. Enlisted in Bladen County, NC. Later in NC Militia. S41973.	
Recford, Morris	5th NC Regiment	1777, a Private under Capt. Benjamin Andrew Coleman. A Corporal in Oct. 1777. Dropped from the rolls in Jan. 1778.	
Rector, Lewis	4th NC Regiment	1782, a Private under Capt. Anthony Sharpe for 18 months. From Surry County, NC when he enlisted. Discharged at Salisbury, NC in 1783. W45.	
Redd, William	4th NC Regiment	1781, a Private under Capt. George Dougherty for 12 months. Discharged on 5/25/1782 at Salisbury, NC. From Onslow County, NC. Aka William Red, William Read. S7373.	
Reddick, Abraham	3rd NC Regiment	1781, a Private under Capt. Clement Hall for 12 months. Discharged 8/16/1782 (2nd NC Regiment).	
Reddick, Isaac	10th NC Regiment	6/7/1777, a Private under Capt. Isaac Moore for three years. 9/8/1778, a known Private in the Lt. Colonel's Company (Lt. Col. Robert Mebane) (1st NC Regiment) led by Capt. Joshua Bowman.	
Reddie, John	3rd NC Regiment	1778, a Sergeant, unit and dates unknown.	
Redding, John	5th NC Regiment	Jan. 1779, a Private under Capt. Philip Taylor for 2-1/2 years – later would be 3rd NC Regiment. Earlier in NC Militia. From Halifax County. On the official rolls as John Reading. S41971.	
Reddit, Constant	2nd NC Regiment	7/20/1778, a Corporal under Maj. Reading Blount. A Sergeant on 10/25/1778.	
Redley, Hardy	3rd NC Regiment	6/24/1779, a Private under Michael Quinn. Dropped from the rolls in Oct. 1779.	
Redner, George	7th NC Regiment	1777, a Musician under Capt. Thomas Brickell. Died on 11/4/1777. aka George Rednor.	
Redpeth, John	4th NC Regiment	8/20/1777, a Lieutenant under Capt. William Temple Coles. Died on 10/13/1777 from	Germantown (PA).

Name	1st Unit	Year / Rank / Served Under / Notes	Known Battles
		wounds received at the battle of Germantown, PA on 10/4/1777. aka John Redpith.	
Reed, Benjamin	1st NC Regiment	6/14/1781, a Private under Capt. Thomas Donoho. Discharged on 6/14/1782 in Hertford County, NC. The preceeding is per official records. Per his pension application, he enlisted much earlier and was in the key northern battles, Brandywine, Germantown, and Monmouth, as well as a POW at the Fall of Charleston, SC. Apparently from Gates County, NC. S41976.	Eutaw Springs (SC).
Reed, Frederick	3rd NC Regiment	7/20/1778, a Private under Capt. John Baker for nine months. Discharged in May 1779 at Philadelphia, PA. From Nash County, NC. R8689.	
Reed, James	3rd NC Regiment	7/20/1778, a Private under Capt. Michael Quinn for nine months. Most likely from Mecklenburg County, NC. R8655.	
Reed, James	5th NC Regiment	9/10/1777, a Private under Capt. Benjamin Andrew Coleman.	
Reed, Joseph	7th NC Regiment	1/20/1777, a Sergeant under Capt. Thomas Brickell. Died in Aug. 1777.	
Reed, Moses	5th NC Regiment	5/4/1777, a Private under Capt. Benjamin Andrew Coleman. 9/9/1778, in 2nd NC Regiment. Dropped from the rolls in Feb. 1779.	
Reed, Samuel	3rd NC Regiment	7/20/1778, a Sergeant under Capt. Michael Quinn for nine months.	
Reed, Saul	3rd NC Regiment	1778, a Sergeant, unit and dates unknown.	
Reed, William	4th NC Regiment	1777, a Private under Capt. William Temple Coles. 9/8/1778, a known Private under Capt. John Sumner (1st NC Regiment). Dropped from the rolls in Nov. 1779.	
Reeks, William	1st NC Regiment	6/14/1781, a Private under Capt. Thomas Donoho. Discharged on 5/2/1782.	
Reel, Joshua	4th NC Regiment	1782, a Private under Capt. Thomas Evans for 18 months.	
Rees, John	5th NC Regiment	Jan. 1779, a Private under Capt. John Medearis.	
Rees, Roger	5th NC Regiment	Nov. 1779, a Private under Capt. John Medearis for three years. Most likely from Wake County, NC. R8672.	
Reese, George	9th NC Regiment	11/28/1776, a Lieutenant.	
Reeves, Frederick	4th NC Regiment	1781, a Private under Capt. Joseph T. Rhodes for 12 months. Discharged on 1/23/1782. On official rolls as Frederick Reves. Most likely from Wake County, NC. W18801.	
Reeves, Jesse	3rd NC Regiment	7/20/1778, a Private in the Lt. Colonel's Company (Lt. Col. William Lee Davidson) led by Lt./Capt. George "Gee" Bradley for nine months. A Corporal in Oct. 1778.	
Reeves, Samuel	4th NC Regiment	5/10/1776, a Private under Capt. Joseph Phillips for 2-1/2 years. Transferred to His Excellency's	Brandywine Creek (PA),

Name	1st Unit	Year / Rank / Served Under / Notes	Known Battles
		Guards in 1778. 9/8/1778, listed under Capt. James Read (1st NC Regiment), although still identified as in His Excy's Guards. Married in Wake County, NC in 1785. W56.	Germantown (PA).
Reff, Charles	2nd NC Regiment	1777, a Sergeant under Capt. Benjamin Williams. Deserted in Nov. 1777.	
Reinhart, Jacob	1st NC Regiment	1781, a Private under Capt. Alexander Brevard. Discharged 10/12/1782. From Lincoln County, NC. aka Jacob Rinehart. R8695.	
Reizer, John	4th NC Regiment	1776, a Private under Capt. Joseph Philips. Then, under Capt. James Read (1st NC Regiment). 3/29/1778, a Private under Capt. Isaac Moore (10th NC Regiment). POW on 4/14/1779. aka John Razor, Razon, Raissor, Reisser. S39038.	Brandywine Creek (PA), Germantown (PA), Monmouth (NJ).
Renney, Peter	9th NC Regiment	6/23/1777, a Sergeant under Capt. Hezekiah Rice.	
Respess, John	8th NC Regiment	11/28/1776, an Ensign under Capt. Frederick Hargett. Resigned on 4/24/1777. From Beaufort County, NC.	
Respess, Richard	8th NC Regiment	11/28/1776, a 1st Lieutenant under Capt. Henry Pope. 1/16/1777, under Capt. Francis Tartanson. From Beaufort County, NC.	
Revell, Lazarus	1st NC Regiment	4/2/1781, a Private under Capt. William Lytle. Deserted on 7/5/1781. Re-enlisted in Jan. 1782. Deserted again on 10/10/1782 (4th NC Regiment).	
Reynolds, Ephraim	3rd NC Regiment	A Private under Capt. Samuel Jones for nine months, dates unknown. From Carteret County, NC. S38328.	
Reynolds, George	NC Artillery	11/17/1776, a Sergeant under Capt. John Vance as NC Provincial Troops. 7/10/1777, on Continental Line. 11/16/1777, under Capt. John Kingsbury. 5/1/1778, in same unit. 9/16/1778, in same unit.	
Reynolds, James	3rd NC Regiment	5/26/1778, a Private under Lt./Capt. Joseph Montford. 1780, in 1st NC Regiment. POW at the Fall of Charleston 1780 (SC) until the end of the war. From Perquimans County, NC. S7370.	Stono Ferry (SC), Siege of Charleston 1780 (SC).
Reynolds, Joseph	1st NC Regiment	6/1/1778, a Private under Capt. Griffith John McRee.	
Reynolds, William	1st NC Regiment	1782, a Private under Capt. Peter Bacot. Died on 11/28/1782.	
Rhein, Peter	8th NC Regiment	2/10/1777, a Sergeant under Capt. John Walsh. Nov. 1777, a QM Sergeant. Back to Sergeant in Jan. 1778. 9/9/1778, a Sergeant under Capt. Benjamin Andrew Coleman (2nd NC Regiment). A Private on 7/4/1779. Discharged on 2/10/1780. aka Peter Rhem.	
Rhinehart, Jacob	3rd NC Regiment	8/1/1782, a Private under Capt. Benjamin Bailey for 12 months.	
Rhodes, Charles	5th NC Regiment	5/14/1776, a Sergeant under Capt. John Pugh Williams for 2-1/2 years. Discharged on 10/25/1778. 1779, a Captain in the NC Militia.	Brandywine Creek (PA), Germantown

Name	1st Unit	Year / Rank / Served Under / Notes	Known Battles
		From Bertie County, NC. S7386.	(PA).
Rhodes, Elisha	5th NC Regiment	1775, an Ensign in the Edenton District Minutemen. 4/17/1776, an Ensign under Capt. John Pugh Williams and Col. Edward Buncombe. 1780, a Captain in NC Militia. From Bertie County.	
Rhodes, Ephraim	3rd NC Regiment	1779, a Private under Lt. Samuel Jones. Sick, discharged early. From Carteret County, NC.	
Rhodes, Henry	8th NC Regiment	1777, a Private under Capt. John Walsh. Dropped from the rolls in Jan. 1778.	
Rhodes, Isaac	5th NC Regiment	4/28/1776, a Private under Capt. John Pugh Williams for 2-1/2 years. 9/9/1778, a known Private in the Major's Company (Maj. Hardy Murfree) (2nd NC Regiment). Discharged on 10/28/1778. aka Isaac Rhoads.	
Rhodes, Joseph	8th NC Regiment	11/28/1776, a 1st Lieutenant under Capt. Thomas Nixon, then Capt. John Walsh. 8/5/1777, a Captain. Retired on 6/1/1778.	
Rhodes, Joseph	10th NC Regiment	8/1/1777, a Private under Capt. Joseph T. Rhodes.	
Rhodes, Joseph Thomas	10th NC Regiment	8/1/1777, a Captain under Col. Abraham Sheppard. 6/1/1778, a Captain under Col. James Armstrong (4th NC Regiment). Wounded at Stono Ferry. Spring of 1781, in the rebuilding 1st NC Regiment. Late Summer of 1781, back in 4th NC Regiment. 2/6/1782, a known Captain in the 4th NC Regiment. From Duplin County, NC. aka Joseph J. Rhodes.	Stono Ferry (SC), Siege of Augusta (GA), Eutaw Springs (SC).
Rhodes, Nathaniel	3rd NC Regiment	8/1/1781, a Private under Capt. Clement Hall. Discharged on 8/1/1782 (2nd NC Regiment) at Bacon's Bridge, SC. Enlisted at Edenton, NC. S41981.	Eutaw Springs (SC).
Rhodes, William	3rd NC Regiment	7/20/1778, a Private under Capt. John Baker for nine months.	
Rhodes, William	8th NC Regiment	1777, a Sergeant under Capt. John Walsh. A Private in Feb. 1778. Dropped from the rolls in Feb. 1778.	
Rice, Benjamin	5th NC Regiment	6/23/1779, a Private under Capt. Joseph Montford. Deserted in Sep. 1779.	
Rice, Hezekiah	1st NC Regiment	9/1/1775, a Lieutenant. Resigned on 11/20/1775. Then a Sergeant in NC Militia. 11/28/1776, a Captain in the 9th Regiment under Col. John Williams. From Dobbs County, NC.	Brandywine Creek (PA), Germantown (PA).
Rice, Hezekiah	9th NC Regiment	1777, a Private under Capt. Richard D. Cook. Dropped from the rolls in Jan. 1778.	
Rice, Jeptha	9th NC Regiment	11/28/1776, a QM Sergeant. 3/15/1777, an Ensign under his father, Capt. Hezekiah Rice. 5/15/1781, a QM Sergeant again, unit unknown. Per his pension statement, he was promoted to Lieutenant, and ultimately to Captain, and was in the battles of Guilford Court House and Eutaw Springs, SC. Received clothing on 5/24/1782. From Caswell County, NC. aka	Brandywine Creek (PA), Germantown (PA).

Name	1st Unit	Year / Rank / Served Under / Notes	Known Battles
		Jeptha Ricely. W5700.	
Rice, John	1st NC Regiment	Sep. 1775, a Private under Capt. Henry Dixon. 12/10/1776, an Adjutant. 3/28/1777, an Ensign under Capt. John Walker. 4/8/1777, a 2nd Lieutenant under Capt. John Brown. Discharged in June 1778. Later, in NC Militia, unit and dates unknown. W2003.	Brandywine Creek (PA), Germantown (PA).
Rice, Thomas	1st NC Regiment	1777, a Sergeant under Capt. Henry "Hal" Dixon. Died on 9/5/1777.	
Rice, Thomas	1st NC Regiment	7/10/1777, an Ensign under Capt. Tilghman Dixon.	
Rich, Timothy	10th NC Regiment	10/10/1777, a Corporal under Capt. James Wilson. A Private in June 1778. 9/8/1778, a known Private under Capt. Joshua Bowman (1st NC Regiment). Dropped from the rolls in June 1779. aka Timothy Rice.	
Richards, Charles	4th NC Regiment	1777, a Private under Capt. James Williams. Discharged in Aug. 1777.	
Richards, Charles	4th NC Regiment	1777, a Private under Capt. John Nelson. Dropped from the rolls in Jan. 1778.	
Richards, Curtis	1st NC Regiment	5/18/1781, a Private under Capt. Robert Raiford. Discharged on 5/18/1782 (2nd NC Regiment).	
Richards, George	1st NC Regiment	A Private under Capt. Joshua Bowman, dates unknown.	
Richards, George	1st NC Regiment	1777, a Private under Capt. Henry "Hal" Dixon. Dropped from the rolls in April 1778.	
Richards, Jacob	6th NC Regiment	1777, a Private under Capt. Thomas White. A Sergeant in Oct. 1777. A Sergeant Major in Nov. 1777. Dropped from the rolls in Jan. 1778.	
Richards, James	9th NC Regiment	4/23/1777, a Private under Capt. Richard D. Cook. Deserted in Aug. 1777. Rejoined in 1778. 9/9/1778, under Capt. Benjamin Andrew Coleman (2nd NC Regiment). Discharged on 11/10/1778.	
Richards, Jonathan	10th NC Regiment	5/10/1777, a Private under Capt. James Wilson. Dropped from the rolls in June 1778.	
Richards, Joseph	3rd NC Regiment	4/25/1776, a Sergeant under Capt. Jacob Turner. POW at Germantown, PA on 10/4/1777.	Germantown (PA).
Richards, Levy		A Private, regiment, unit, and dates unknown.	
Richards, Lewis	4th NC Regiment	Jan. 1782, a Private under Maj. George Dougherty. Deserted on 3/1/1782.	
Richards, Lewis	5th NC Regiment	Jan. 1779, a Private under Maj. Pinketham Eaton.	
Richards, Nicholas	2nd NC Regiment	1/8/1782, a Private under Capt. Benjamin Andrew Coleman for 12 months.	
Richards, William	2nd NC Regiment	1777, a Private under Capt. James Martin. 9/9/1778, a known Private under Capt. Benjamin Andrew Coleman.	
Richardson, Andrew	4th NC Regiment	1782, a Sergeant under Capt. Thomas Evans for 18 months.	
Richardson, Ellis	1st NC Regiment	5/9/1781, a Private under Capt. Alexander Brevard. Deserted before Apr. 1782.	

Name	1st Unit	Year / Rank / Served Under / Notes	Known Battles
Richardson, James	3rd NC Regiment	7/20/1778, a Private under Capt. John Baker for nine months.	
Richardson, John	1st NC Regiment	6/10/1781, a Private under Capt. Robert Raiford. Discharged on 6/10/1782 (2nd NC Regiment). From Johnston County, NC. R8769.	
Richardson, John	2nd NC Regiment	1777, a Private under Capt. Charles Allen. A Corporal in July 1778 under Capt. Thomas Armstrong. Deserted on 4/30/1779.	
Richardson, John	10th NC Regiment	10/1/1777, an Ensign under Capt. Dempsey Gregory. Dropped from the rolls in June 1778.	
Richardson, Joseph	6th NC Regiment	Jan. 1777, an Ensign. 8/27/1777, a 2nd Lieutenant. Retired on 6/1/1778.	
Richardson, Lewis	3rd NC Regiment	1779, a Private under Capt. Kedar Ballard.	
Richardson, Richard	1st NC Regiment	5/19/1781, a Private under Capt. Robert Raiford. Discharged on 5/19/1782 (2nd NC Regiment).	
Richardson, William	1st NC Regiment	8/1/1782, a Private under Capt. Joshua Hadley. Deserted on 4/18/1783 (?).	
Richardson, William	2nd NC Regiment	1781, a Private under Capt. Benjamin Carter. Discharged on 4/25/1782.	
Richmond, John	5th NC Regiment	6/1/1779, a Private under Maj. Reading Blount.	
Ricketson, Jesse	5th NC Regiment	1776, a Private under Capt. William Caswell for one year. 3/27/1777, a Private under Capt. William Caswell for three years. 9/9/1778, a known Private under Capt. Robert Fenner (2nd NC Regiment). Then under Capt. Joshua Bowman and Capt. John Craddock. POW at the Fall of Charleston, SC. 1775, in New Bern District Minutemen. Later, in NC Militia. From Craven County, NC. aka Jesse Rickerson. W26382.	Brandywine Creek (PA), Germantown (PA), Monmouth (NJ), Stony Point (NY), Siege of Charleston 1780 (SC).
Ricketts, Reason	9th NC Regiment	1/6/1777, a Private under Capt. Richard D. Cook. A Corporal in Jan. 1778. Back to Private in June 1778. Hanged 11/21/1779.	
Ricketts, Thomas	9th NC Regiment	1777, a Musician under Capt. Richard D. Cook. 1779, in the 5th NC Regiment, unit and dates unknown.	
Ricks, Benjamin	1st NC Regiment	4/15/1781, a Sergeant Major. Discharged on 4/15/1782.	
Riddle, James	2nd NC Regiment	5/15/1781, a Private under Capt. Tilghman Dixon. Discharged on 5/21/1782 (1st NC Regiment). Received clothing on 5/24/1782. From Caswell County. aka James Riddell.	
Ridgeway, John	2nd NC Regiment	1777, a Private under Capt. James Gee. 9/9/1778, a known Private under Capt. John Ingles. Deserted on 12/6/1779.	
Ridgeway, Joseph	3rd NC Regiment	7/20/1778, a Private under Capt. Michael Quinn for nine months.	
Ridley, William	3rd NC Regiment	4/21/1777, a Surgeon. AWOL 11/21/1777.	
Riel, John	1st NC Regiment	4/28/1781, a Private under Capt. Griffith John McRee. Aug. 1781, transferred to Lee's Legion	Eutaw Springs (SC) (in Lee's

Name	1st Unit	Year / Rank / Served Under / Notes	Known Battles
		(VA). aka John Reel. W9619.	Legion).
Riggin, John	6th NC Regiment	1777, a Private under Capt. Philip Taylor. Dropped from the rolls in June 1778.	
Riggin, William	1st NC Regiment	4/12/1781, a Private under Lt./Capt. Benjamin Bailey. Discharged on 4/12/1782 (3rd NC Regiment).	
Riggins, James	3rd NC Regiment	3/1/1782, a Private under Capt. Samuel Jones for 12 months.	
Riggins, Joel	NC Light Dragoons	1778, Private under Lt. Edmund Gamble, Capt. Cosmo Medici. Later joined SC unit and became a POW. W4322.	
Riggins, John	1st NC Regiment	9/8/1778, a known Private under Capt. Joshua Bowman.	
Riggins, Powell	4th NC Regiment	5/20/1776, a Private under Capt. William Goodman. 9/8/1778, a known Wagoner in the Colonel's Company (Col. Thomas Clark) (1st NC Regiment) led by Capt. John Gambier Scull. Discharged on 5/20/1779. 5/25/1781, a Private under Capt. Thomas Donoho (1st NC Regiment). Discharged on 5/25/1782. aka Powell Riggans.	
Right, Levi	5th NC Regiment	5/7/1777, a Private under Capt. Benjamin Andrew Coleman. 9/9/1778, a known Private under Capt. Clement Hall (2nd NC Regiment).	
Rigsby, Frederick	4th NC Regiment	5/9/1776, a Private under Capt. Joseph Phillips. A Corporal in Oct. 1777. Back to Private in June 1778. 9/8/1778, a known Private under Capt. James Read (1st NC Regiment). Discharged on 5/10/1779. Enlisted in Surry County, NC. W1490.	Brandywine Creek (PA), Germantown (PA), Monmouth (NJ).
Rigsby, James	2nd NC Regiment	1/10/1782, a Private under Capt. Benjamin Andrew Coleman for 12 months (per DAR and NC State Records). In his pension statement, he claims he served under Capt. James Mills. From Duplin (what would become Sampson) County, NC. S9060.	
Riles, William	1st NC Regiment	4/28/1781, a Private under Lt./Capt. Elijah Moore. Discharged on 4/28/1782 (4th NC Regiment).	
Riley, William	3rd NC Regiment	1782, a Private under Capt. Alexander Brevard for 18 months. A Sergeant in March 1783.	
Riley, William	1st NC Regiment	Feb. 1780, a Sergeant under Capt. William Lytle. POW at the Fall of Charleston, paroled. Earlier and later, in NC Militia. 1782, a Sergeant under Capt. Elijah Moore (4th NC Regiment), then under Capt. Joseph T. Rhodes. From Orange County, NC. W1083.	Siege of Charleston 1780 (SC).
Rinefield, Henry	4th NC Regiment	1777, a Private under Capt. Thomas Harris. Discharged on 10/18/1777.	
Ring, James	2nd NC Regiment	1777, a Musician under Capt. Benjamin Williams. Died on 9/13/1777.	
Ring, James Sr.	2nd NC Regiment	1777, a Private under Capt. Benjamin Williams. Died on 12/1/1777.	
Riseing,	3rd NC	1/4/1782, a Private under Capt. Samuel Jones	

Name	1st Unit	Year / Rank / Served Under / Notes	Known Battles
David	Regiment	for 12 months.	
Risk, William	2nd NC Regiment	June 1778, a Private under Capt. Benjamin Andrew Coleman. Dropped from the rolls in Aug. 1778.	
Riskey, David	2nd NC Regiment	8/9/1777, a Private, unit unknown. 9/9/1778, a known Private under Capt. Benjamin Andrew Coleman. 3/12/1779, re-enlisted under Capt. Benjamin Andrew Coleman.	
Ritto, Josiah	3rd NC Regiment	7/20/1778, a Private under Lt./Capt. George "Gee" Bradley for nine months.	
Ritto, Peter	3rd NC Regiment	6/22/1779, a Musician under Capt. Kedar Ballard. A Private in Oct. 1779. Deserted on 1/4/1780.	
Rivers, Benjamin	2nd NC Regiment	1782, a Private under Capt. Robert Raiford.	
Roark, James	1st NC Regiment	9/9/1776, a Private under Capt. Robert Ralston for three years. 9/8/1778, a known Private under Capt. John Sumner.	
Roark, Nicholas	1st NC Regiment	Dec. 1781, a Private under Capt. James Mills for 12 months.	
Roark, Nicholas	5th NC Regiment	1/1/1777, a Private under Capt. Benjamin Andrew Coleman. POW at Ft. Lafayette, NY on 6/1/1779. Rejoined in Nov. 1779. Discharged on 1/31/1780.	Ft. Lafayette (NY).
Roback, William	1st NC Regiment	A Musician under Capt. Robert Ralston. Dropped from the rolls in July 1778.	
Robb, William	6th NC Regiment	4/24/1776, a Corporal under Lt./Capt. Thomas White for 2-1/2 years. A Private in Nov. 1777. 9/8/1778, a known Wagoner under Capt. John Sumner (1st NC Regiment). Dropped from the rolls in Nov. 1778. aka William Robbs.	
Roberds, ?	DQMG	1780, a Wagoner under Col. Nicholas Long (Deputy QM General). Said to be an ex-Continental soldier from Lee's Legion (VA).	
Roberson, Mark	1st NC Regiment	6/14/1781, a Private under Capt. Thomas Donoho. Discharged on 6/14/1782.	
Roberts, Edmund	1st NC Regiment	9/1/1775, a Private under Lt. Lawrence Thompson, Capt. Alfred Moore for six months. Later, in NC Militia as a Sergeant. From what is now Caswell County, NC. S1715.	Moore's Creek Bridge.
Roberts, Isaac	1st NC Regiment	5/5/1781, a Private under Capt. Anthony Sharpe. Dropped from the rolls during 1781.	
Roberts, Ishmael	10th NC Regiment	6/3/1777, a Private under Capt. Capt. Abraham Sheppard, Jr. Dropped from the rolls in June 1778.	
Roberts, James	3rd NC Regiment	7/20/1778, a Private in the Lt. Colonel's Company (Lt. Col. William Lee Davidson) led by Lt./Capt. George "Gee" Bradley for nine months. 4/23/1779, a known Private in the Lt. Colonel's Company (Lt. Col. Robert Mebane) led by Capt. George "Gee" Bradley. Later, in NC Militia. From Surry County, NC. W4063.	
Roberts, James	10th NC Regiment	5/2/1777, a Private under Capt. Armwell Herron. 9/9/1778, a known Private in the	

575

Name	1st Unit	Year / Rank / Served Under / Notes	Known Battles
		Major's Company (Maj. Hardy Murfree) (2nd NC Regiment). aka James Robets. S4147.	
Roberts, John	1st NC Regiment	1777, a Private under Capt. Robert Ralston. 9/8/1778, a known Private under Capt. John Sumner. 3/12/1779, re-enlisted for the duration of the war in the same unit. Born in Northampton County, lived in Chatham County, NC when enlisted. S7402.	Briar Creek (GA), Stono Ferry (SC), Guilford Court House.
Roberts, John	5th NC Regiment	3/28/1777, a Lieutenant under Capt. William Caswell. Retired on 6/1/1778. Joined VA unit as a Captain.	
Roberts, Kinchin	3rd NC Regiment	1777, a Private under Capt. William Brinkley. Died on 3/10/1778. aka Kitchin Roberts.	
Roberts, Moses	1st NC Regiment	5/21/1781, a Private under Capt. Anthony Sharpe. Transferred to Capt. Alexander Brevard. Discharged on 5/21/1782 (3rd NC Regiment).	
Roberts, Reuben	6th NC Regiment	1776, a Private under Capt. Thomas White. Wounded at Germantown, PA. Dropped from the rolls in June 1778. Later in NC Militia, unit and regiment unknown. 1781, served in Lee's Legion (VA) under a Capt. Amis till right after Cornwallis surrendered. W1492.	Brandywine Creek (PA), Germantown (PA).
Roberts, Richard	2nd NC Regiment	7/10/1777, a Private under Capt. Clement Hall for three years. POW at Ft. Lafayette, NY on 6/1/1779. S38339.	Ft. Lafayette (NY).
Roberts, Richard	2nd NC Regiment	1/22/1782, a Corporal under Capt. Benjamin Andrew Coleman for 12 months. Dec. 1782, re-enlisted as a Private for the duration of the war.	
Roberts, Richard	10th NC Regiment	7/12/1777, a Private under Capt. Abraham Sheppard, Jr. 9/9/1778, a known Wagoner in the Major's Company (Maj. Hardy Murfree) (2nd NC Regiment).	Ft. Lafayette (NY).
Roberts, Samuel	1st NC Regiment	A Musician under Capt. Howell Tatum. Died on 4/3/1778.	
Roberts, Thomas	3rd NC Regiment	6/2/1779, a Private under Capt. George "Gee" Bradley for 18 months.	
Roberts, Thomas	3rd NC Regiment	7/20/1778, a Sergeant Major for nine months.	
Roberts, Thomas	5th NC Regiment	1777, a Sergeant under Capt. Reading Blount. Re-enlisted as a Private in 1779 as Thomas Robison under Capt. Philip Taylor.	
Roberts, Vincent	9th NC Regiment	1777, a Private under Capt. Richard D. Cook.	
Roberts, William	1st NC Regiment	1/1/1777, a Private under Capt. John Brown. 9/8/1778, a known Private under Capt. John Sumner (1st NC Regiment). Deserted in 1779. aka William Robarts.	
Roberts, William	3rd NC Regiment	1782, a Private under Capt. Alexander Brevard for 18 months. March 1783, transferred - to what unknown.	
Roberts, William	9th NC Regiment	11/10/1777, a Private under Capt. Anthony Sharpe. 9/8/1778, a known Private in the Lt. Colonel's Company (Lt. Col. Robert Mebane)	

576

Name	1st Unit	Year / Rank / Served Under / Notes	Known Battles
		led by Capt. Joshua Bowman.	
Robertson, Benjamin	5th NC Regiment	8/17/1776, a Private under Capt. Reading Blount. A Musician in Nov. 1778. Dropped from the rolls in June 1779.	
Robertson, David	4th NC Regiment	A Private under Capt. William Goodman for nine months. Earlier and later in NC Militia. From Mecklenburg County, NC. S31333.	Stono Ferry (SC).
Robertson, Edward	6th NC Regiment	A Private under Capt. George Dougherty. A Sergeant in Feb. 1778. Died on 5/8/1778.	
Robertson, Henry	7th NC Regiment	1777, a Musician under Capt. Henry Dawson. Died on 2/6/1778.	
Robertson, Jacob	5th NC Regiment	1777, a Sergeant under Capt. Reading Blount. A Private in Sep. 1777. Dropped from the rolls in Dec. 1777.	
Robertson, James	1st NC Regiment	6/13/1781, a Private under Capt. Robert Raiford. Discharged on 6/13/1782 (2nd NC Regiment).	
Robertson, Jesse	6th NC Regiment	5/24/1776 or 10/24/1776 (two sources), a Private under Capt. Archibald Lytle, then Capt. Thomas White for three years. 9/8/1778, a known Private under Capt. John Sumner (1st NC Regiment). Discharged 10/24/1779 at West Point, NY. Enlisted at Halifax, NC. aka Jesse Robinson. S39049.	Brandywine Creek (PA), Germantown (PA).
Robertson, John	NC Artillery	8/1/1777, a Matross under Capt. John Vance. 11/16/1777, under Capt. John Kingsbury. Died on 2/12/1778. aka John Robison.	
Robertson, John	1st NC Regiment	A Private under Capt. James Read. Dropped from the rolls in Feb. 1778.	
Robertson, John	4th NC Regiment	2/6/1782, a Private under Capt. James Mills for 12 months.	
Robertson, John	4th NC Regiment	1782, a Corporal under Capt. Thomas Evans for 18 months.	
Robertson, Peter	DQMG	1780, a Gunstocker on the roll of Capt. Solomon Wood (NC Light Dragoons) - this seems to be for convenience only. An Artificer under Col. Nicholas Long (Deputy QM General). Made Gunstocks. Also on 8/23/1781. aka Peter Roberson.	
Robertson, Thomas	2nd NC Regiment	5/15/1781, a Private under Capt. Tilghman Dixon. Discharged on 5/21/1782 (1st NC Regiment). Received clothing on 5/24/1782. From Caswell County, NC. Born 7/11/1762. Claims to have also served earlier - no official record. aka Thomas Robinson. R8890.	Eutaw Springs (SC).
Robertson, Thomas	5th NC Regiment	Jan. 1779, a Private under Capt. Phillip Taylor.	
Robertson, Upsher	3rd NC Regiment	1781, a Private under Capt. Edward Yarborough for 12 months. Discharged on 6/1/1782.	
Robeson, Joseph	5th NC Regiment	Spring of 1778, a Private under Lt./Capt. William Lytle for two years. Later in NC Militia. From Caswell County, NC. aka Joseph Robertson. S4158.	Briar Creek (GA), Stono Ferry (SC).
Robeson,	1st NC	4/28/1781, a Private under Capt. Griffith John	

Name	1st Unit	Year / Rank / Served Under / Notes	Known Battles
Mark	Regiment	McRee. Discharged on 4/28/1782.	
Robeson, William	10th NC Regiment	4/21/1777, a Private under Capt. Silas Stevenson. Deserted in Apr. 1778. Rejoined in June 1778, unit unknown. A Sergeant in Aug. 1778. Deserted again in 1779.	
Robido, Peter		1779, a Private, regiment and unit unknown. Deserted in 1779.	
Robins, James	7th NC Regiment	1/1/1777, a Private under Capt. Henry Dawson. 9/8/1778, a known Private under Capt. James Read (1st NC Regiment). Discharged on 2/1/1780.	
Robins, John	1st NC Regiment	Apr. 1782, a Private under Capt. James Mills for 12 months. Discharged on 4/1/1783.	
Robins, John	7th NC Regiment	1777, a Private under Capt. Henry Dawson. Dropped from the rolls in Jan. 1778.	
Robinson, Benjamin	5th NC Regiment	7/17/1776, a Private under Capt. Reading Blount. 1778, served under Capt. Benjamin Williams (2nd NC Regiment), then under Capt. John Craddock. Discharged 2/8/1780. Born in Onslow County, NC. S41996.	
Robinson, Edward	1st NC Regiment	1776, a Private under Capt. Joshua Bowman.	
Robinson, Hanibal	NC Artillery	1/2/1777, a Gunner under Capt. Thomas Clark. Also on 9/9/1778. aka Hamblen Robinson.	
Robinson, Hardy	2nd NC Regiment	7/20/1778, a Private under Maj. Reading Blount until 7/5/1779, when he was discharged at Halifax, NC. From Bertie County, NC. S41992.	
Robinson, Hugh	4th NC Regiment	1777, a Private under Capt. Joseph Phillips. A Corporal in Sep. 1777. Deserted on 10/6/1777.	
Robinson, Jacob	4th NC Regiment	5/16/1776, a Private under Capt. William Temple Coles for three years. 9/8/1778, a known Private under Capt. John Sumner (1st NC Regiment) - sick at Valley Forge on that date. Discharged on 5/1/1779. On some rolls as Jarod or Jared Robinson.	
Robinson, John	4th NC Regiment	1782, a Musician under Capt. Thomas Evans for 18 months.	
Robinson, John	5th NC Regiment	1779, a Private under Maj. Reading Blount. Deserted in Dec. 1779.	
Robinson, Reuben	3rd NC Regiment	1777, a Private under Capt. James Emmett. Died on 9/4/1777.	
Robinson, Septimus	1st NC Regiment	3/28/1776, an Ensign. 7/7/1776, a 2nd Lieutenant. Died on 12/10/1776. One source asserts that he resigned on 10/10/1776.	
Robinson, William	2nd NC Regiment	9/2/1777, a Private, unit unknown. 9/9/1778, a known Private in the Lt. Colonel's Company (Lt. Col. Selby Harney).	
Robinson, Willoughby	1st NC Regiment	5/17/1781, a Private under Lt./Capt. Benjamin Bailey. Discharged on 5/17/1782 (3rd NC Regiment).	
Robison, John	1st NC Regiment	4/12/1781, a Private under Capt. William Lytle. Dropped from the rolls sometime during 1781.	
Robison, Noah	3rd NC Regiment	7/20/1778, a Private under Maj. Thomas Hogg for nine months.	

Name	1st Unit	Year / Rank / Served Under / Notes	Known Battles
Robison, Thomas	5th NC Regiment	Jan. 1779, a Private under Capt. Philip Taylor. Earlier a Sergeant using the name of Thomas Roberts. Later, in NC Militia. From Caswell County, NC. aka Thomas Robertson, Thomas Robinson. R8892.	
Rochelle, Amos	2nd NC Regiment	12/18/1782, a Private under Capt. Benjamin Andrew Coleman for 12 months.	
Rochelle, George	3rd NC Regiment	1777, a Private under Capt. Nicholas Edmunds. Died in 1779 in SC while in service. From Hertford County, NC.	
Rochelle, John	9th NC Regiment	11/28/1776, a Private under Capt. Richard D. Cook. Dropped from the rolls in Jan. 1778.	
Rochelle, John	9th NC Regiment	11/28/1776, a Captain under Col. John Williams. Another source claims he was a Captain in 3rd NC Regiment at this time (wrong). Earlier, a Captain in NC Militia. W8567.	
Rochelle, Lodowick	9th NC Regiment	11/28/1776, a 1st Lieutenant under Capt. John Rochelle. One source claims he was in the 3rd NC Regiment at this time. Resigned in Nov. 1777. From Hillsborough District. aka Lovick Rochel, Louise Rochel.	
Rochelle, Stokes	3rd NC Regiment	A Private under Capt. Nicholas Edmunds. Died in NC while in service, date unknown. From Hertford County, NC.	
Rochester, Nathaniel	6th NC Regiment	4/17/1776, PM for 6th NC Regiment. Rescinded 4/18/1776. Then, Deputy Commissary General. Resigned on 11/23/1776.	
Rochester, Nicholas	6th NC Regiment	5/10/1776, a Private under Capt. Philip Taylor. Also a Sergeant at some point in time. Discharged 1/8/1778 due to his loss of his right eye - unstated when and where it happened. W8565.	
Rochester, William	1st NC Regiment	6/14/1781, a Corporal under Capt. Thomas Donoho. Dropped from the rolls during 1781.	
Rochester, William	6th NC Regiment	5/10/1776, a Private under Capt. Philip Taylor for 2-1/2 years. Dropped from the rolls in Sep. 1777. Sep. 1778, re-enlisted, regiment and unit unknown. Discharged on 3/21/1779.	
Rock, Jack	5th NC Regiment	6/18/1779, a Private under Capt. Joseph Montford.	
Rodgers, Arthur	1st NC Regiment	5/24/1776, a Private under Lt./Capt. John Brown for 2-1/2 years. 9/8/1778, a known Private in the Lt. Colonel's Company (Lt. Col. Robert Mebane) (1st NC Regiment) led by Capt. Joshua Bowman - sick on that date. Died on 10/22/1778. aka Arthur Rogers.	
Rodgers, Daniel	4th NC Regiment	1782, a Private under Capt. William Lytle and then Capt. Elijah Moore. Living in Granville County, NC when he enlisted. Originally from SC. S1871.	
Roe, Jesse	1st NC Regiment	1781, a Musician under Capt. Anthony Sharpe. Discharged on 8/15/1782 (4th NC Regiment).	
Roe, Jesse	1st NC	8/1/1782, a Private under Capt. Joshua Hadley	

Name	1st Unit	Year / Rank / Served Under / Notes	Known Battles
	Regiment	for 18 months. A Musician in Dec. 1782.	
Roe, Lemuel	7th NC Regiment	1/4/1777, a Corporal under Capt. John Poynter for 3 years. A Private in Nov. 1777. Discharged on 2/1/1780.	
Roe, Samuel	2nd NC Regiment	4/9/1776, a Private under Lt./Capt. James Gee for 2-1/2 years. Discharged on 11/10/1778.	
Roebuck, George	1st NC Regiment	1775, a Private under Capt. Henry Dixon for six months. Re-enlisted for another twelve months. Enlisted in Orange County, NC. Then moved to Spartanburg District, SC and joined SC Militia. Born on 3/15/1757 in Orange County, VA. S9467.	Moore's Creek Bridge, Ft. Moultrie #1 (SC).
Rogers, Daniel	3rd NC Regiment	1782, a Private under Capt. Alexander Brevard for 18 months.	
Rogers, David	1st NC Regiment	11/10/1778, a Private under Capt. Anthony Sharpe for nine months.	
Rogers, Dunson	4th NC Regiment	1781, a Private under Capt. Joseph T. Rhodes for 12 months. Discharged on 12/1/1782.	
Rogers, Eli	5th NC Regiment	8/12/1777, a Private under Capt. Benjamin Andrew Coleman. 9/9/1778, a known Private in the Colonel's Company (Col. John Patten) (2nd NC Regiment) led by Capt. John Craddock. A Corporal on 3/1/1780.	
Rogers, James	1st NC Regiment	4/28/1781, a Private under Capt. Griffith John McRee. Discharged on 4/28/1782 at Camden, SC. Enlisted in Anson County, NC. W2168.	
Rogers, John	10th NC Regiment	5/4/1777, a Private under Capt. Isaac Moore for three years. 9/8/1778, a known Private in the Lt. Colonel's Company (Lt. Col. Robert Mebane) (1st NC Regiment) led by Capt. Joshua Bowman - sick on that date. 3/12/1779, re-enlisted for the duration of the war in the same unit. Hanged for desertion in 1781. aka John Rodgers.	
Rogers, John Jr.	5th NC Regiment	12/11/1776, a Paymaster.	
Rogers, Parker	1st NC Regiment	5/1/1781, a Musician under Capt. Robert Raiford. Discharged on 5/1/1782 (2nd NC Regiment). May have rejoined in late 1782.	
Rogers, Patrick	1st NC Regiment	11/3/1776, a Regimental QM. 3/28/1777, an Ensign. 4/3/1777, a 2nd Lieutenant under Capt. Howell Tatum. Died on 4/19/1778.	
Rogers, Silvester	3rd NC Regiment	6/24/1779, a Private under Michael Quinn.	
Rogers, Stephen	5th NC Regiment	8/17/1777, a Private under Capt. Benjamin Andrew Coleman. 9/9/1778, a known Private under Capt. Robert Fenner (2nd NC Regiment).	
Rogers, Thomas	1st NC Regiment	10/9/1775, a Private under Capt. John Walker [4].	Moore's Creek Bridge.
Rogers, William	1st NC Regiment	11/10/1778, a Private under Capt. Anthony Sharpe for nine months.	
Rogers, William	2nd NC Regiment	Nov. 1779, a Private under Capt. Clement Hall.	
Rogers,	3rd NC	1/1/1782, a Private under Capt. Samuel Jones.	

Name	1st Unit	Year / Rank / Served Under / Notes	Known Battles
William	Regiment	Died on 8/29/1782 (1st NC Regiment).	
Rogers, Willoughby	3rd NC Regiment	10/3/1781, a Corporal under Capt. Samuel Jones for 12 months. Discharged on 10/1/1782 (1st NC Regiment).	
Rogers, Wilson	6th NC Regiment	1776, a Private under Capt. William Glover for 2-1/2 years. Later, in NC Militia. From Granville County, NC. R8964.	
Rogers, Zachariah	9th NC Regiment	1777, a Sergeant under Capt. Richard Donaldson Cook. Wounded at the battle of Brandywine Creek (PA) and at the battle of Germantown (PA). Earlier in SC Continental Line. From Richmond County, NC. R8965.	Brandywine Creek (PA), Germantown (PA).
Rogerson, John	10th NC Regiment	5/4/1777, a Private under Capt. Isaac Moore. On 6/1/1778, this unit was transferred to the 1st NC Regiment. POW at the Fall of Charleston, SC. From Perquimans County, NC. S41988.	Monmouth (NJ), Siege of Charleston 1780 (SC).
Roland, Godfrey	10th NC Regiment	9/4/1777, a Private under Capt. John Jarvis. Dropped from the rolls in June 1778.	
Rollin, Robert	8th NC Regiment	1777, a Sergeant under Capt. Francis Tartanson. Dropped from the rolls in Nov. 1777.	
Roman, Thomas	4th NC Regiment	1782, a Corporal under Capt. Anthony Sharpe for 18 months.	
Rooks, Hardiman	5th NC Regiment	8/10/1779, a Private under Capt. Joseph Montford. Deserted in Sep. 1779.	
Roper, David	1st NC Regiment	9/16/1775, a Private under Capt. John Walker for six months. 1777, re-enlisted under Capt. Andrew Vanoy (10th NC Regiment) for six months. Discharged at Camden, SC. From Orange County, NC. S30683.	
Roper, George	1st NC Regiment	Feb. 1781, a Private under Capt. Anthony Sharpe. Discharged on 6/6/1782 (4th NC Regiment) at Ashley Old Fields, SC. S36261.	Guilford Court House, Eutaw Springs (SC).
Roper, James	2nd NC Regiment	4/7/1777, a Private under Lt./Capt. John Craddock. A resident of Northampton County, NC when he enlisted. Discharged at Wilmington, NC on 11/22/1780. Soon thereafter, joined the NC Militia. S7413.	Monmouth (NJ), Siege of Charleston 1780 (SC).
Roper, James	3rd NC Regiment	4/7/1777, a Private under Capt. William Brinkley for three years. 9/9/1778, a known Private under Capt. John Ingles (2nd NC Regiment). aka James Rooper.	
Roper, James	3rd NC Regiment	1781, a Private under Capt. Edward Yarborough for 12 months. Dropped from the rolls sometime during 1782.	
Rose, John	6th NC Regiment	5/10/1776, a Private under Capt. Philip Taylor. Deserted in Aug. 1777.	
Rose, John	7th NC Regiment	1777, a Private under Capt. John Poynter. Deserted on 4/16/1777.	
Rose, William	4th NC Regiment	4/23/1776, a Private under Capt. John Nelson for three years. A Sergeant in May 1778. Back to Private in June 1778. 6/1/1778, a known Private under Capt. Griffith John McRee (1st NC Regiment).	
Roser, David	1st NC	8/1/1782, a Private under Capt. Joshua Hadley	

Name	1st Unit	Year / Rank / Served Under / Notes	Known Battles
	Regiment	for 18 months.	
Roser, John	2nd NC Regiment	1782, a Private under Capt. Robert Raiford for 18 months.	
Ross, Benjamin	1st NC Regiment	8/1/1782, a Corporal under Capt. Joshua Hadley for 18 months. Deserted on 6/18/1783 (?).	
Ross, Charles	3rd NC Regiment	7/20/1778, a Private under Capt. Michael Quinn for nine months.	
Ross, Francis	9th NC Regiment	11/28/1776, a 1st Lieutenant under Capt. Richard Donaldson Cook. From Hillsborough District.	
Ross, James	NC Light Dragoons	1777, a Private under Capt. Samuel Ashe, Jr. Jan. 1779, hired a substitute to serve his remaining four months. From Granville County, NC. S35639.	Brandywine Creek (PA), Germantown (PA).
Ross, James	1st NC Regiment	1781, a Private under Capt. William Lytle. Discharged on 8/1/1782 (4th NC Regiment).	
Ross, John	NC Light Dragoons	Earlier a Corporal in the 2nd Salisbury District Minutemen. Oct.-Dec. 1777, a known Corporal under Capt. Martin Phifer.	
Ross, John	1st NC Regiment	April 1776, a Private under Capt. John Ashe, Jr., then under Capt. Griffith John McRee. POW at the Fall of Charleston, retained until the end of the war. Earlier in NC Militia. Born 1760 in Scotland. Lived in New Hanover County (Wilmington), NC when he enlisted. R9023.	Brandywine Creek (PA), Germantown (PA), Monmouth (NJ), Siege of Charleston 1780 (SC).
Ross, John	4th NC Regiment	9/16/1776, a Private under Capt. James Williams. 9/8/1778, a known Private in the Colonel's Company (Col. Thomas Clark) (1st NC Regiment) led by Capt. John Gambier Scull.	
Ross, Nathaniel	NC Artillery	1/1/1777, a Bombardier under Capt. Thomas Clark as NC Provincial Troops. 7/10/1777, on Continental Line. Also on 9/9/1778. A Private on 4/30/1779.	
Ross, Thomas	5th NC Regiment	3/1/1779, a Private under Capt. Joseph Montford and Capt. Samuel Chapman for nine months. Discharged on 12/1/1779 in Charleston, SC. 1780, in NC Miltia. From Wake County, NC. Born 9/1/1760 in Granville County, NC. S4126.	Siege of Savannah (GA).
Rotley, John	3rd NC Regiment	1777, a Private under Capt. Jacob Turner. Died on 7/30/1778.	
Rough, Peter	4th NC Regiment	1777, a Private under Capt. William Temple Coles. Died on 3/15/1778.	
Roundtree, Jesse	4th NC Regiment	1782, a Private under Capt. Thomas Evans for 18 months.	
Routledge, William	4th NC Regiment	1/25/1777, a 1st Lieutenant under Capt. James Williams. Resigned on 8/20/1777. aka William Roulledge.	
Rowan, Jesse	DQMG	1780, a Timbergetter (for wagons, etc.) on the roll of Capt. Solomon Wood (NC Light Dragoons) - this seems to be for convenience only. 8/23/1781, a Timber Getter under Col.	

Name	1st Unit	Year / Rank / Served Under / Notes	Known Battles
		Nicholas Long (Deputy QM General) - for the making of Wagons, Gunstocks, etc.	
Rowan, John	1st NC Regiment	Mar. 1776, a Private under Capt. George Davidson for nine months. Spring of 1777, a Lieutenant under Capt. William Temple Cole (4th NC Regiment). Spent most of his time in Salisbury as a recruiter. From Bute County, NC. R9038.	
Rowan, Robert	1st NC Regiment	9/1/1775, a Captain under Col. James Moore. Feb. 1776, joined Col. James Moore at Rockfish Creek with 60 men. He and some of his men were in battle of Moore's Creek Bridge [4]. Resigned on 6/29/1776. Later, a Commissary and a Colonel in NC Militia. From Cross Creek, Cumberland County, NC.	Moore's Creek Bridge [4], Breech Inlet Naval Battle (SC).
Rowe, Charles	3rd NC Regiment	1779, a Private under Capt. Kedar Ballard for nine months. Discharged on 12/9/1779.	
Rowe, George	8th NC Regiment	1777, a Private under Capt. John Walsh. Dropped from the rolls in Jan. 1778.	
Rowe, James	NC Artillery	8/17/1776, a Fifer under Capt. John Vance as NC Provincial Troops. 7/10/1777, on Continental Line. 11/16/1777, under Capt. John Kingsbury. 5/1/1778, in same unit. 9/16/1778, in same unit. POW at the Fall of Charleston, escaped. Enlisted in Craven County, NC. aka James Roe. S41933.	Monmouth (NJ), Stony Point (NY), Siege of Charleston 1780 (SC).
Rowe, Jesse	8th NC Regiment	1777, a Musician under Capt. John Walsh. Dropped from the rolls in Jan. 1778.	
Rowe, Samuel	1st NC Regiment	9/8/1778, a known Private under Capt. Joshua Bowman.	
Rowe, Samuel	2nd NC Regiment	9/9/1778, a Private under Capt. John Ingles.	
Rowell, Andrew	3rd NC Regiment	7/20/1778, a Private in the Lt. Colonel's Company (Lt. Col. William Lee Davidson) led by Lt./Capt. George "Gee" Bradley for nine months. 4/23/1779, a known Private in the Lt. Colonel's Company (Lt. Col. Robert Mebane) led by Capt. George "Gee" Bradley. Died at Philadelphia Hospital.	
Rowell, Isaac	3rd NC Regiment	7/20/1778, a Private and a Sergeant in the Lt. Colonel's Company (Lt. Col. William Lee Davidson) led by Lt./Capt. George "Gee" Bradley for nine months. Discharged 5/15/1779 in NY. Later joined VA Militia. W9634.	
Rowell, Jesse	1st NC Regiment	1776, a Private under Capt. Thomas Allen, Capt. Lawrence Thompson, and Capt. Joshua Bowman. POW at the Fall of Charleston (SC), never exchanged until Peace was made. From Franklin County, NC. S38337.	Brandywine Creek (PA), Germantown (PA), Siege of Charleston 1780 (SC).
Rowell, Jesse	1st NC Regiment	1777, a Private under Capt. Lawrence Thompson.	
Rowland, Daniel	2nd NC Regiment	5/12/1781, a Private under Capt. Benjamin Carter for 12 months. Discharged on 4/25/1782.	

583

Name	1st Unit	Year / Rank / Served Under / Notes	Known Battles
		aka Daniel Rowlang.	
Rowland, Frederick	3rd NC Regiment	1779, a Corporal under Capt. Kedar Ballard for nine months. Discharged on 12/9/1779.	
Rowland, John	1st NC Regiment	6/5/1781, a Private under Capt. William Lytle.	
Rowland, William	3rd NC Regiment	1781, a Private under Capt. Edward Yarborough for 12 months. Dropped from the rolls sometime during 1782.	
Rowland, William	9th NC Regiment	1777, a Private under Capt. Richard D. Cook. Died on 3/11/1778.	
Rown, Henry	4th NC Regiment	1782, a Private under Capt. Anthony Sharpe for 18 months. Deserted on 6/24/1783 (?).	
Royal, James	2nd NC Regiment	1777, a Corporal under Capt. William Fenner. Died on 3/6/1778.	
Royal, William	2nd NC Regiment	6/26/1777, a Private under Capt. John Armstrong. Dropped from the rolls in April 1778.	
Royals, Joseph	1st NC Regiment	1777, a Private under Capt. John Brown. Died on 3/6/1778.	
Royer, John		None of the officers he names are on any official rolls - NC Continentals or Militia. Either his recall is terrible or everything is made up for his pension application.	Brandywine Creek (PA) (wounded), Germantown (PA).
Rozer, Charles	1st NC Regiment	3/9/1777, a Private under Capt. Lawrence Thompson for three years. 9/8/1778, a known Private in the Lt. Colonel's Company (Lt. Col. Robert Mebane) (1st NC Regiment) led by Capt. Joshua Bowman. Deserted on 3/28/1783 (?).	
Rozer, Jordan	1st NC Regiment	3/19/1777, a Private under Capt. Joshua Bowman, then Capt. Lawrence Thompson. 9/8/1778, a known Private under Capt. Tilghman Dixon. Deserted on 2/1/1780.	
Rue, Charles	5th NC Regiment	1777, a Private under Capt. Benjamin Stedman. Dropped from the rolls in Dec. 1777.	
Ruff, Robert	3rd NC Regiment	7/20/1778, a Private under Maj. Thomas Hogg for nine months.	
Rule, James	6th NC Regiment	A Private under Capt. George Dougherty. Missing on 10/4/1777 at the battle of Germantown, PA.	Germantown (PA).
Rumer, Cornelius	2nd NC Regiment	1777, a Sergeant under Capt. James Martin. A Corporal in Oct. 1777. Died on 4/29/1778. One source claims he was only a Private and a Corporal, not a Sergeant. aka Cornelius Runner, Corn Runner.	
Runnals, Joseph	3rd NC Regiment	A Private under Capt. Francis Child. 11/8/1779, a Corporal.	
Runnels, Ephraim	3rd NC Regiment	9/23/1781, a Corporal under Capt. Samuel Jones for 12 months. A Private in April 1782 (1st NC Regiment).	
Rush, Absalom	1st NC Regiment	6/5/1781, a Private under Capt. William Lytle. Deserted on 7/1/1781.	
Rush,	8th NC	1777, a Lieutenant.	

Name	1st Unit	Year / Rank / Served Under / Notes	Known Battles
William	Regiment		
Russ, George	9th NC Regiment	11/28/1776, a 2nd Lieutenant under Capt. Michael Henderson. From Salisbury District.	
Russ, John	1st NC Regiment	1781, a Private under Capt. Alexander Brevard. Discharged on 4/28/1782 (3rd NC Regiment).	
Russell, James	5th NC Regiment	5/1/1779, a Sergeant under Maj. Reading Blount for 2-1/2 years. This regiment soon became the new 3rd NC Regiment under Lt. Col. Robert Mebane. POW at the Fall of Charleston, SC. From Orange County, NC. W5167.	Briar Creek (GA), Stono Ferry (SC), Siege of Charleston 1780 (SC).
Russell, John	1st NC Regiment	A Private under Capt. Robert Raiford. Killed at the battle of Eutaw Springs, SC on 9/8/1781.	Eutaw Springs (SC).
Russell, John	5th NC Regiment	1777, a Private under Capt. Reading Blount. Died on 1/8/1778.	
Russell, John	6th NC Regiment	A Private under Capt. Daniel Williams. Dropped from the rolls in Feb. 1778.	
Russell, Major	5th NC Regiment	12/6/1776, a Private under Capt. Reading Blount. 9/9/1778, a known Private in the Lt. Colonel's Company (Lt. Col. Selby Harney) (2nd NC Regiment).	
Russell, Malachi	NC Artillery	9/17/1777, a Bombardier under Capt. John Vance. 11/16/1777, under Capt. John Kingsbury. 5/1/1778, in same unit. 9/16/1778, in same unit - sick in camp. Deserted on 4/1/1779. aka Malicah Rasil, Mabakee Russell, Malaca Rusil.	
Russell, Urias	1st NC Regiment	5/4/1781, a Private under Capt. Robert Raiford. Died in Oct. 1781.	
Russell, William	3rd NC Regiment	7/20/1778, a Private under Lt./Capt. George "Gee" Bradley for nine months.	
Russell, William	3rd NC Regiment	6/24/1779, a Private under Michael Quinn.	
Russell, William	5th NC Regiment	5/1/1779, a Sergeant under Maj. Reading Blount.	
Russworm, William	3rd NC Regiment	4/16/1776, a 2nd Lieutenant under Capt. Pinketham Eaton. 1778, a Cornet in the NC Light Dragoons. aka William Rushworm. W3390.	
Rutherford, Thomas	3rd NC Regiment	1782, a Private under Capt. Alexander Brevard then Capt. Joseph T. Rhodes (4th NC Regiment) for 18 months. Discharged in March 1783. From Orange County, NC. R9114.	
Rutland, Randolph	1st NC Regiment	5/2/1781, a Private under Capt. Robert Raiford. Discharged on 5/2/1782 (2nd NC Regiment).	
Rutland, Reading	1st NC Regiment	5/2/1781, a Private under Capt. Robert Raiford. Discharged on 5/2/1782 (2nd NC Regiment). aka Reding Rutland.	
Rutor, Lewis	1st NC Regiment	1778, a Private under Capt. Anthony Sharpe for 18 months.	
Rutter, Joseph	10th NC Regiment	8/25/1777, a Private under Capt. Capt. Abraham Sheppard, Jr. Died on 5/28/1778.	
Ryall, William	2nd NC Regiment	6/1/1782, a Private under Capt. Clement Hall. Enlisted by Capt. James Mills in Rutherford	

Name	1st Unit	Year / Rank / Served Under / Notes	Known Battles
		County, NC. aka William Royal, William Royall. W6108.	
Ryan, Cornelius	4th NC Regiment	Jan. 1782, a Private under Maj. George Dougherty. 8/1/1782, a Private under Capt. Joshua Hadley (1st NC Regiment).	
Ryan, Hercules	4th NC Regiment	5/1/1777, a Private under Capt. William Goodman. Died on 11/24/1777.	
Ryan, Patrick	4th NC Regiment	6/29/1777, a Private under Capt. William Temple Coles for three years. 9/8/1778, a known Private under Capt. John Sumner (1st NC Regiment). 3/12/1779, re-enlisted for the duration of the war in the same unit. A Corporal in April 1779. A Sergeant in July 1779. Died 9/6/1782.	
Ryan, Thomas	1st NC Regiment	4/28/1781, a Private under Capt. Griffith John McRee. Deserted on 6/1/1781.	
Ryan, Thomas	5th NC Regiment	10/1/1776, a Musician under Capt. John Pugh Williams. Discharged on 10/30/1778.	
Ryan, William	5th NC Regiment	6/7/1779, a Private under Maj. Reading Blount. Deserted in Oct. 1779.	
Ryles, David	3rd NC Regiment	7/20/1778, a Private under Maj. Thomas Hogg for nine months.	
Sailor, George	1st NC Regiment	1781, a Private under Capt. Alexander Brevard. Discharged on 11/29/1782 (3rd NC Regiment).	
Salisbury, Benjamin	3rd NC Regiment	10/28/1776, a Private under Capt. Jacob Turner. Discharged in Oct. 1778. On the official rolls as Benjamin Solsberry.	
Salmon, Vincent	2nd NC Regiment	1781, a Private under Capt. Clement Hall, then under Capt. Joseph Thomas Rhodes and Maj. George Dougherty (4th NC Regiment) Furloughed in Charleston, SC after the British evacuated (12/14/1782). Some records indicate that he was probably also a Corporal at some point in time. From Johnston County, NC. R9156.	
Salomon, Lazarus	4th NC Regiment	1781, a Private under Capt. Joseph T. Rhodes.	
Salter, James	2nd NC Regiment	12/18/1776, a Commissary.	
Salter, John	7th NC Regiment	May 1777, a Private under Capt. Joseph Walker. A Musician in Dec. 1777. 9/8/1778, a known Musician (Drummer) under Capt. John Sumner (1st NC Regiment). Deserted in Jan. 1780.	
Salter, Robert	2nd NC Regiment	4/23/1776, a Commissary. Resigned 12/1/1776.	
Salyers, Dunn	1st NC Regiment	1780, a Private under Capt. William Lytle for 18 months. Earlier in SC Continental Line. W4795.	
Salyers, Martin	1st NC Regiment	6/6/1781, a Private under Capt. William Lytle. Dropped from the rolls sometime during 1781.	
Samples, William	2nd NC Regiment	1778, a Private under Capt. Benjamin Andrew Coleman. Deserted on 8/20/1778.	
Sampson, Isaac	1st NC Regiment	4/25/1781, a Private under Capt. Alexander Brevard. Discharged on 4/28/1782 (3rd NC	Eutaw Springs (SC).

Name	1st Unit	Year / Rank / Served Under / Notes	Known Battles
		Regiment) at Wilmington, NC. Enlisted in Carteret County, NC. aka Isaac Samson. S41999.	
Sanderlin, Isaac	10th NC Regiment	5/22/1777, a Private under Capt. Dempsey Gregory. 9/8/1778, a known Private under Capt. Howell Tatum (1st NC Regiment). aka Isaac Sanderlind.	
Sanderlin, John	2nd NC Regiment	1777, a Private under Capt. James Gee. Deserted on 12/25/1777.	
Sanderlin, Josiah	1st NC Regiment	5/17/1781, a Private under Lt./Capt. Benjamin Bailey. Discharged on 5/17/1782 (3rd NC Regiment).	
Sanderlin, Levy	2nd NC Regiment	Private under Capt. Clement Hall. Deserted on 12/25/1777. Rejoined 5th NC Regiment in Jan. 1779. A Corporal in June 1779.	
Sanderlin, Robert	2nd NC Regiment	1782, a Private under Capt. Robert Raiford for 18 months.	
Sanders, Andrew	2nd NC Regiment	2/1/1777, a Private under Capt. Benjamin Williams for three years. 9/9/1778, a known Private in the Major's Company (Maj. Hardy Murfree) (2nd NC Regiment). A Corporal on 11/13/1778. POW at Ft. Lafayette, NY on 6/1/1779. Discharged on 2/1/1780. aka Andrew Saunders.	Ft. Lafayette (NY).
Sanders, Benjamin	3rd NC Regiment	7/20/1778, a Private under Capt. Francis Child. Died in Sep. 1778.	
Sanders, Cornelius	2nd NC Regiment	May 1781, a Drummer under Capt. Joshua Hadley and Capt. William Lytle (4th NC Regiment) for 12 months. Earlier in NC Militia. From Nash County, NC. S2019.	Siege of Ninety-Six 1781 (SC).
Sanders, Duss	5th NC Regiment	1777, a Private under Capt. Benjamin Stedman. Missing on 9/11/1777 at the battle of Brandywine Creek, PA.	Brandywine Creek (PA).
Sanders, Henry	3rd NC Regiment	1782, a Musician under Capt. Alexander Brevard for 18 months.	
Sanders, Isaac	7th NC Regiment	1777, a Private under Capt. Joseph Walker. Died in May 1778.	
Sanders, James	5th NC Regiment	Dec. 1777, a Private under Capt. John Pugh Williams. Dropped from the rolls in Jan. 1778.	
Sanders, James	5th NC Regiment	A Private under Capt. John Pugh Williams. Died on 9/17/1778.	
Sanders, Job	3rd NC Regiment	7/20/1778, a Private under Maj. Thomas Hogg for nine months.	
Sanders, John	10th NC Regiment	A Private under Capt. Abraham Sheppard, Jr. for nine months. Earlier and later in NC Militia. From Dobbs County, NC. W3874.	
Sanders, Joseph	5th NC Regiment	3/1/1779, a Corporal under Maj. Reading Blount.	
Sanders, Joseph	7th NC Regiment	1777, a Private under Capt. Joseph Walker. Dropped from the rolls in Oct. 1777.	
Sanders, Robert	1st NC Regiment	5/5/1781, a Musician under Capt. Robert Raiford for two years or the duration of the war. A Private in Sep. 1782.	
Sanders,	4th NC	1782, a Private under Capt. William Lytle for	

Name	1st Unit	Year / Rank / Served Under / Notes	Known Battles
Samuel	Regiment	18 months.	
Sanders, Thomas	2nd NC Regiment	5/19/1781, a Private under Capt. Benjamin Carter. Discharged on 5/19/1782 at Wilmington, NC. From Hertford County, NC. S42000.	Eutaw Springs (SC).
Sanders, William	2nd NC Regiment	2/1/1777, a Private under Capt. Benjamin Williams for 3 years. Discharged on 2/1/1780.	
Sanderson, Caleb	10th NC Regiment	5/6/1777, a Corporal under Capt. John Jarvis for three years. A Private in June 1778. 9/8/1778, a known Private in the Major's Company (Maj. John Baptiste Ashe) (1st NC Regiment). Died on 12/2/1778. aka Caleb Saunderson.	
Sandiford, Amos	2nd NC Regiment	5/19/1781, a Private under Capt. Benjamin Carter. Died in Sep. 1781.	
Sandiford, Robert	3rd NC Regiment	5/28/1779, a Private under Capt. Michael Quinn for 18 months. Dropped from the rolls in Oct. 1779.	
Sanford, Samuel	10th NC Regiment	5/18/1777, a Private under Capt. Abraham Sheppard, Jr.	
Santee, Caesar	3rd NC Regiment	2/22/1777, a Private under Capt. Pinketham Eaton for three years. 9/9/1778, a known Private under Capt. Clement Hall (2nd NC Regiment). 3/12/1779, re-enlisted under Capt. Clement Hall. POW at Ft. Lafayette, NY on 6/1/1779. Served until the end of the war. aka Sesar Santee, Caesar Santy.	Ft. Lafayette (NY).
Santee, Michael	1st NC Regiment	5/9/1781, a Private under Lt./Capt. Benjamin Bailey. Discharged on 5/9/1782 (3rd NC Regiment).	
Saunders, James	2nd NC Regiment	9/9/1778, a known Private under Capt. Clement Hall.	
Saunders, Jesse	6th NC Regiment	1775, a Captain in the Hillsborough District Minutemen. 4/17/1776, a Captain in the 6th NC Regiment. Resigned in May of 1776.	
Saunders, John	1st NC Regiment	4/12/1781, a Private under Capt. William Lytle. Discharged on 4/12/1782 (4th NC Regiment).	
Saunders, Joshua	4th NC Regiment	Mar. 1779, a Corporal under Capt. George Dougherty.	
Saunders, William	6th NC Regiment	4/2/1777, an Ensign under Capt. Thomas Donoho. Transferred to 1st NC Regiment on 6/1/1778. 2/8/1779, a Lieutenant. Then a Captain. However, the 4/24/1782 roll claims he was still a Lieutenant. Resigned on 1/1/1783. aka William Sanders. R20211.	
Saunderson, William	2nd NC Regiment	2/1/1777, a Private, unit unknown. 9/9/1778, a known Private in the Major's Company (Maj. Hardy Murfree).	
Savage, Micajah	1st NC Regiment	1782, a Private under Capt. Peter Bacot for 18 months.	
Savage, Michael	3rd NC Regiment	Apr. 1776, a Private under Capt. Jacob Turner for 2-1/2 years. Discharged in Oct. 1778.	
Savage, Moses	2nd NC Regiment	5/19/1781, a Private under Capt. Benjamin Carter. Discharged on 5/19/1782.	
Savage, Ransom	2nd NC Regiment	6/2/1777, a Private, unit unknown. A Sergeant in Feb. 1778. 9/9/1778, a known Sergeant under	

Name	1st Unit	Year / Rank / Served Under / Notes	Known Battles
		Capt. John Ingles. aka Savage Ransom.	
Savage, Thomas	2nd NC Regiment	1782, a Private under Capt. Robert Raiford for 18 months.	
Savory, James	3rd NC Regiment	7/1/1779, a Private under Capt. Kedar Ballard for 18 months.	
Sawyer, Henry	1st NC Regiment	A Private under Capt. Howell Tatum. Died in Aug. 1778.	
Sawyer, Levi	2nd NC Regiment	Sep. 1777, a 2nd Lieutenant under Capt. John Armstrong. Resigned on 3/16/1778. One source asserts this man is the same as William Sawyer, previously identified as an Ensign under Capt. Edward Vail, Jr.	
Sawyer, Miller	7th NC Regiment	12/16/1776, a Musician under Capt. Joseph Walker for three years. 9/8/1778, a known Musician under Capt. Tilghman Dixon (1st NC Regiment). 3/12/1779, re-enlisted for the duration of the war in the same unit. aka Milton Sawyer.	
Sawyer, Thomas	6th NC Regiment	4/24/1777, a Private under Capt. George Dougherty. 9/8/1778, a known Private under Capt. Joshua Bowman (1st NC Regiment). Deserted on 2/6/1780.	
Sawyer, William	2nd NC Regiment	5/15/1776, an Ensign under Capt. Edward Vail, Jr. Dropped from the rolls in Sept. 1777. One source asserts that in Sep. 1777 he was a 2nd Lieutenant under Capt. Thomas Armstrong using the name of Levi Sawyer - who resigned 3/1/1778.	
Sawyer, Willis	7th NC Regiment	1/13/1777, a Private under Capt. John Poynter. Died in May 1778.	
Sawyers, Joseph	1st NC Regiment	4/28/1781, a Private under Capt. Alexander Brevard. Wounded at the battle of Eutaw Springs, SC on 9/8/1781. Discharged on 4/1/1782 (3rd NC Regiment). Born 1765 and enlisted from Rowan County, NC. S9470.	Siege of Ninety-Six 1781 (SC), Eutaw Springs (SC).
Saxton, James	4th NC Regiment	5/7/1777, a Sergeant under Capt. William Temple Coles for three years. A Private in Jan. 1778. 9/8/1778, a known Private under Capt. John Sumner (1st NC Regiment). POW on 4/14/1779 (?).	
Saxton, Jeremiah	1st NC Regiment	1777, a Private under Capt. Joshua Bowman. Died on 4/25/1779.	
Saxton, William		4/5/1778, a Private, regiment and unit unknown. POW at Ft. Lafayette, NY on 6/1/1779.	Ft. Lafayette (NY).
Saylers, Josiah		NC Continental. Sentenced to be hanged, friends saved him. Nothing more known.	
Scaff, Joseph	4th NC Regiment	1782, a Private under Capt. William Lytle. Jan. 1783, transferred to SC Line.	
Scalf, John	10th NC Regiment	5/30/1777, a Corporal under Capt. Dempsey Gregory. A Private in June 1778. 9/8/1778, a known Private under Capt. Howell Tatum (1st NC Regiment) - sick at Yellow Springs on that date. Badly wounded in unnamed skirmish. Enlisted from Johnston County, NC. W9280.	Brandywine Creek (PA), Germantown (PA), Monmouth (NJ).

Name	1st Unit	Year / Rank / Served Under / Notes	Known Battles
Scandling, Michael	9th NC Regiment	1777, a Musician under Capt. Richard D. Cook. A Private in Nov. 1777. 9/8/1778, a known Private in the Lt. Colonel's Company (Lt. Col. Robert Mebane) (1st NC Regiment) led by Capt. Joshua Bowman - sick on that date. Deserted in Feb. 1779. aka Michael Scantling.	
Scandrett, James	2nd NC Regiment	8/10/1776, a Sergeant under Capt. John Armstrong for 2-1/2 years. 9/9/1778, a known Sergeant under Capt. Robert Fenner. Dropped from the rolls in Feb. 1779.	
Scanthen, William	6th NC Regiment	A Private under Capt. Thomas Donoho. Dropped from the rolls in Nov. 1778.	
Scantling, Patrick	4th NC Regiment	4/26/1776, a Private under Capt. Robert Smith for three years. 9/8/1778, a known Private in the Colonel's Company (Col. Thomas Clark) (1st NC Regiment) led by Capt. John Gambier Scull. Discharged on 5/1/1779. aka Patrick Scanthing.	
Scarborough, John	1st NC Regiment	4/12/1781, a Private under Capt. Alexander Brevard.	
Scarborough, Nathaniel	4th NC Regiment	1782, a Private under Capt. Joseph T. Rhodes for 18 months. Dec. 1782, transferred to Capt. Thomas Evans.	
Scarborough, Samuel	1st NC Regiment	4/12/1781, a Private under Capt. Alexander Brevard. Discharged on 4/12/1782 (3rd NC Regiment).	
Scarborough, Shadrack	3rd NC Regiment	1781, a Private under Capt. Clement Hall. Discharged on 4/12/1782 (2nd NC Regiment).	
Scarlet, James	3rd NC Regiment	11/13/1781, a Private under Capt. Samuel Jones. Died on 9/20/1782 (1st NC Regiment).	
Scarlet, Thomas	2nd NC Regiment	11/13/1781, a Private under Capt. Benjamin Andrew Coleman for 12 months. From Orange County, NC. W17784.	
Scarlet, William	3rd NC Regiment	2/1/1782, a Private under Capt. Samuel Jones for 12 months.	
Scarsey, Asiah	4th NC Regiment	1781, a Private under Capt. Joseph T. Rhodes. Discharged on 5/24/1782.	
Scews, William	4th NC Regiment	1782, a Private under Capt. William Lytle for 18 months.	
Schaw, Daniel	6th NC Regiment	4/2/1777, an Ensign under Capt. Daniel Williams. Transferred to 1st NC Regiment on 6/1/1778 under Capt. Griffith John McRee. Regimental QM on 6/1/1778. A 1st Lieutenant on 10/1/1779. POW at the Fall of Charleston, exchanged 6/14/1781. Served until the end of the war. Another source claims he retired on 1/1/1783. aka Daniel Shaw.	Siege of Charleston 1780 (SC).
Schoolfield, Benjamin	7th NC Regiment	1/15/1777, a Private under Capt. John Poynter. Died on 1/27/1778.	
Schultz, Lewis		1/22/1777, a Private, regiment and unit unknown. aka Lewis Shultz.	
Scipio, Hill	3rd NC Regiment	1781, a Private under Capt. Edward Yarborough. Discharged on 4/22/1782.	
Scollar, Isaac	5th NC Regiment	A Private under Capt. John Pugh Williams. Killed at the battle of Germantown, PA on	Germantown (PA).

Name	1st Unit	Year / Rank / Served Under / Notes	Known Battles
		10/4/1777.	
Scott, Abraham	4th NC Regiment	1782, a A Private under Capt. Joseph T. Rhodes for 18 months. Dec. 1782, transferred to Capt. Thomas Evans.	
Scott, Adam	2nd NC Regiment	Apr. 1778, a Private under Capt. Clement Hall. Died in Oct. 1778.	
Scott, David	2nd NC Regiment	9/25/1775, a Private under Capt. Hardy Murfree for 12 months. Later in SC Continental Line. S9473.	
Scott, Dennis	2nd NC Regiment	1782, a Private under Capt. Benjamin Carter for 18 months.	
Scott, Dennis	3rd NC Regiment	1781, a Private under Capt. Edward Yarborough for twelve months. Discharged on 5/1/1782 at James Island, SC. Wounded in the ankle at the battle of Eutaw Springs, SC. S39063.	Eutaw Springs (SC).
Scott, Drewry	2nd NC Regiment	8/1/1782, a Private under Capt. Benjamin Andrew Coleman.	
Scott, Emanuel	1st NC Regiment	4/25/1781, a Private under Capt. Robert Raiford. Discharged on 4/25/1782 (2nd NC Regiment).	
Scott, Isham	DQMG	1780, a Timber Getter (for wagons, etc.) on the roll of Capt. Solomon Wood (NC Light Dragoons) - this seems to be for convenience only. 8/23/1781, a Timber Getter under Col. Nicholas Long (Deputy QM General) - for the making of Wagons, Gunstocks, etc.	
Scott, Isham	3rd NC Regiment	April 1781, a Private under Capt. Edward Yarborough for 12 months. Dropped from the rolls on 4/1/1782. From Halifax County, NC. aka Isom Scott. S42004.	
Scott, Isaac	1st NC Regiment	1782, a Private under Capt. Peter Bacot for 18 months.	
Scott, Israel	3rd NC Regiment	7/20/1778, a Private in the Colonel's Company (Col. Jethro Sumner) for nine months.	
Scott, James	1st NC Regiment	Aug. 1782, a Private under Capt. Peter Bacot for 18 months. Furloughed after about 12 months of service at James Island, SC. From Halifax County, NC. Born on 1/10/1764 in Isle of Wight County, VA. S3864.	
Scott, James	2nd NC Regiment	1777, a Private under Capt. Edward Vail, Jr. Dropped from the rolls in Nov. 1777.	
Scott, James	3rd NC Regiment	A Private under Capt. William Barret for 2-1/2 years. From Northampton County, NC. Later in SC Militia. S39064.	
Scott, James	3rd NC Regiment	8/1/1781, a Private under Capt. Benjamin Bailey for 12 months.	
Scott, John	3rd NC Regiment	1777, a Private under Capt. Pinketham Eaton. Dropped from the rolls in June 1778. In Jan. 1779, joined the 4th NC Regiment.	
Scott, John	6th NC Regiment	1776, a Sergeant under Ensign/Lt./Capt. Joshua Hadley. 6/1/1778, this unit was transferred to the 1st NC Regiment. In 1781, this unit was transferred to the 2nd NC Regiment. Severely wounded at the battle of Eutaw Springs, SC.	Brandywine Creek (PA), Stony Point (NY), Eutaw Springs (SC).

591

Name	1st Unit	Year / Rank / Served Under / Notes	Known Battles
		X926.	
Scott, Michael	3rd NC Regiment	7/20/1778, a Private under Capt. Kedar Ballard for nine months.	
Scott, Nathaniel	3rd NC Regiment	7/20/1778, a Private under Capt. Kedar Ballard for nine months.	
Scott, Philip	5th NC Regiment	6/11/1779, a Private under Maj. Reading Blount for 18 months.	
Scott, Samuel	1st NC Regiment	1781, a Private under Capt. William Lytle. Dropped from the rolls sometime during 1781.	
Scott, Samuel	3rd NC Regiment	1781, a Private under Capt. Clement Hall. Discharged on 12/13/1782 (2nd NC Regiment).	
Scott, Sterling	3rd NC Regiment	7/20/1778, a Private in the Lt. Colonel's Company (Lt. Col. William Lee Davidson) led by Lt./Capt. George "Gee" Bradley for nine months. 4/23/1779, a known Waiter in the Lt. Colonel's Company (Lt. Col. Robert Mebane) led by Capt. George "Gee" Bradley.	
Scott, Thomas	2nd NC Regiment	6/16/1777, a Private under Capt. Benjamin Williams for three years. A Musician in Jan. 1778. 9/9/1778, a known Private in the Major's Company (Maj. Hardy Murfree).	
Scott, Thomas	4th NC Regiment	1782, a Private under Capt. Joseph T. Rhodes for 18 months. Dec. 1782, transferred to Capt. Thomas Evans.	
Scott, William	2nd NC Regiment	5/3/1777, a Private, unit unknown. 9/9/1778, a known Private in the Major's Company (Maj. Hardy Murfree).	
Scott, William	3rd NC Regiment	7/20/1778, a Private in the Lt. Colonel's Company (Lt. Col. William Lee Davidson) led by Lt./Capt. George "Gee" Bradley for nine months. 4/23/1779, a known Pioneer in the Lt. Colonel's Company (Lt. Col. Robert Mebane) led by Capt. George "Gee" Bradley.	
Scott, William	3rd NC Regiment	7/20/1778, a Private under Capt. Kedar Ballard for nine months.	
Screw, Joseph	3rd NC Regiment	2/3/1782, a Private under Capt. Samuel Jones for 12 months.	
Scriggs, Richard	1st NC Regiment	1782, a Private under Capt. Peter Bacot for 18 months.	
Scrimshear, John	3rd NC Regiment	1781, a Private under Capt. Alexander Brevard for 18 months. The official records indicate that he deserted on 11/27/1782. He asserts that he was furloughed early - after twelve months of service. Earlier in NC Militia. Living in Rowan County, NC when he enlisted, earlier in Anson County, NC. On the official rolls as John Scrimshire. aka John Scimshire. R9274.	Eutaw Springs (SC).
Scudder, Abner	1st NC Regiment	1781, a Private under Capt. Alexander Brevard for twelve months. Discharged on 4/28/1782 (3rd NC Regiment). Wounded at the battle of Eutaw Springs, SC. From Rowan County, NC. Born on 6/17/1754 in Essex County, NJ. S32510.	Siege of Ninety-Six 1781 (SC), Eutaw Springs (SC).
Scudder,	NC	1/7/1777, a Bombardier under Capt. Thomas	

Name	1st Unit	Year / Rank / Served Under / Notes	Known Battles
Major	Artillery	Clark as NC Provincial Troops. 7/10/1777, on Continental Line. Also on 9/9/1778. A Private on 10/31/1778.	
Scull, Alexander	2nd NC Regiment	4/21/1777, a Private, unit unknown. 9/9/1778, a known Private in the Colonel's Company (Col. John Patten) led by Capt. John Craddock. Discharged on 10/30/1778.	
Scull, John Gambier	1st NC Regiment	6/1/1776, an Ensign. 11/21/1776, a 2nd Lieutenant. 4/26/1777, a 1st Lieutenant under Capt. John Brown. Many references indicate that he was most likely a Capt.-Lt. on 6/1/1778. 9/8/1778, a known Captain-Lieutenant. A Captain in Spring of 1780 leading the Colonel's Company.	Monmouth (NJ).
Scurlock, George	NC Light Dragoons	Oct.-Dec. 1777, a known Private under Capt. Martin Phifer. Not on any official rolls.	
Scurlock, James	3rd NC Regiment	7/20/1778, a Private in the Colonel's Company (Col. Jethro Sumner) for nine months. 9/1/1781, a Lieutenant under Capt. Benjamin Carter. Wounded at Eutaw Springs (SC). 9/11/1781, a Captain in the 4th NC Regiment – however, he's still identified as a Lieutenant on the 4/24/1782 roll. Resigned on 1/1/1783. BLWt2048-200.	Eutaw Springs (SC).
Scurlock, James	3rd NC Regiment	5/22/1782, a Private under Capt. Benjamin Bailey for 12 months.	
Scypeart, Robert	3rd NC Regiment	5/15/1776, a Private under Capt. James Emmett for 2-1/2 years. Discharged on 10/31/1778 in New Windsor, NY. Enlisted in Chatham County, NC. Born 9/5/1755. On the official rolls as Robert Sypress. aka Robert Seypeart. S39066.	Brandywine Creek (PA), Germantown (PA), Monmouth (NJ).
Seaborn, Joseph	2nd NC Regiment	2/1/1777, a Private under Capt. Benjamin Williams for three years. 9/9/1778, a known Private in the Major's Company (Maj. Hardy Murfree). Discharged in Nov. 1778, unfit for service. 10/12/1781, a Private under Capt. Benjamin Carter for 18 months. Discharged on 4/1/1783. aka Joseph Sebron, Joseph Seeburn.	
Seaborn, William	2nd NC Regiment	9/9/1778, a known Private under Capt. John Ingles.	
Seagraves, Jacob	4th NC Regiment	1779, a Private under Capt. Joseph Thomas Rhodes for 2-1/2 years. From Granville County, NC. S39067.	Eutaw Springs (SC).
Seagraves, John	3rd NC Regiment	1782, a Private under Capt. Alexander Brevard for 18 months.	
Seagraves, John	3rd NC Regiment	1777, a Private under Capt. William Ward for three years. Re-enlisted for the duration of the war and remained in service until the cessation of arms. Probably the same man as directly above. S42005.	Stono Ferry (SC), Siege of Ninety-Six 1781 (SC), Eutaw Springs (SC).
Seagrove, John	6th NC Regiment	5/9/1776, a Private under Capt. Philip Taylor for 2-1/2 years. 9/8/1778, a known Private under Capt. John Sumner (1st NC Regiment).	Brandywine Creek (PA), Germantown

Name	1st Unit	Year / Rank / Served Under / Notes	Known Battles
		Discharged on 11/17/1778 in New York. On the offical rolls as John Seagroves. S49300.	(PA), Monmouth (NJ).
Seagroves, Thomas	3rd NC Regiment	1781, a Private under Capt. Edward Yarborough. Discharged on 4/22/1782.	
Seals, John	7th NC Regiment	1777, a Private under Capt. Henry Dawson. Died in Oct. 1777.	
Searcey, Asa	4th NC Regiment	1781, a Private under Capt. Joseph T. Rhodes for 12 months. Discharged on 5/24/1782. From Granville County, NC. W8992.	
Searcey, Luke	2nd NC Regiment	Jan. 1779, a Private in the Colonel's Company (Col. John Patten) led by Capt. John Craddock. Died in May 1779. On the official rolls as Luke Sersy. His widow submitted a totally incorrect pension application and was therefore rejected. R9340.	
Searles, Thomas	1st NC Regiment	4/28/1781, a Private under Capt. Griffith John McRee. Discharged on 4/28/1782.	
Searles, Thomas	4th NC Regiment	1779, a Private under Capt. Matthew Ramsey. Died in Sep. 1779.	
Sears, David	4th NC Regiment	1779, a Private under Capt. Matthew Ramsey for nine months. Dropped from the rolls in Oct. 1779.	
Sears, John	10th NC Regiment	8/5/1777, a Private under Capt. Isaac Moore. Dropped from the rolls in Sep. 1778.	
Seawell, Zaddock	1st NC Regiment	1/8/1777, a Private, unit unknown. 9/8/1778, a known Private under Capt. James Read (1st NC Regiment). 3/12/1779, re-enlisted for the duration of the war in the same unit. aka Zedekia Sewell, Zaddock Sewell. See Zadock Sowell below, probably the same man.	
Seayers, Robert	2nd NC Regiment	8/22/1782, a Private under Capt. Clement Hall.	
Sebril, Joshua	4th NC Regiment	1781, a Private under Capt. Joseph T. Rhodes. Discharged on 5/24/1782.	
Seers, Asa	2nd NC Regiment	5/12/1781, a Private under Capt. Tilghman Dixon. Discharged on 5/21/1782 (1st NC Regiment).	
Segraves, Jacob	4th NC Regiment	1781, a Private under Capt. Joseph T. Rhodes. Discharged on 4/24/1782.	
Sellers, Daniel	1st NC Regiment	9/8/1778, a known Private under Capt. Joshua Bowman.	
Sellers, Daniel	6th NC Regiment	A Private under Capt. Griffith John McRee, dates unknown.	
Sellers, Henry	4th NC Regiment	5/1/1776, a Sergeant under Capt. Joseph Phillips for three years. 9/8/1778, a known Sergeant under Capt. James Read (1st NC Regiment). 3/12/1779, re-enlisted for the duration of the war in the same unit. Deserted on 12/25/1779.	
Sellers, James	4th NC Regiment	Nov. 1778, a Private under Capt. Matthew Ramsey for nine months. From Chatham County, NC. S3872.	Stono Ferry (SC).
Sellers, John	3rd NC Regiment	12/15/1781, a Private under Capt. Samuel Jones for 12 months.	

Name	1st Unit	Year / Rank / Served Under / Notes	Known Battles
Sellers, Jordan	3rd NC Regiment	Dec. 1781, a Private under Capt. Samuel Jones for 12 months. Discharged in Wilmington, NC around 1/1/1783 (1st NC Regiment). From Bladen County, NC. W25437.	
Sellinger, Absalom	5th NC Regiment	1777, a Private under Capt. Henry Darnell. Died on 5/3/1778.	
Selves, David	3rd NC Regiment	7/20/1778, a Private under Capt. Michael Quinn for nine months.	
Semons, Ismael	10th NC Regiment	5/18/1777, a Private under Capt. Abraham Sheppard, Jr.	
Sentell, Samuel	3rd NC Regiment	7/20/1778, a Private in the Colonel's Company (Col. Jethro Sumner) for nine months. 1780, a Sergeant under Capt. John Pitts (Halifax County Regiment). 1781, a Private and a Sergeant under Capt. Robert Raiford (1st NC Regiment) for 12 months. Wounded at the battle of Eutaw Springs, SC on 9/8/1781. Discharged on 4/26/1782 (2nd NC Regiment). From Halifax County, NC. aka Samuel Sentez, Samuel Senter. W6017.	Siege of Ninety-Six 1781 (SC), Eutaw Springs (SC).
Serratt, Samuel	10th NC Regiment	5/12/1777, a Private under Capt. James Wilson for three years. 9/8/1778, a known Private in the Major's Company (Maj. John Baptiste Ashe) (1st NC Regiment) - sick in camp on that date. aka Samuel Saratt.	
Sessions, John	2nd NC Regiment	9/24/1775, a Private under Capt. Simon Bright for 12 months. 11/7/1776, re-enlisted as a Private under Capt. John Herrigate, then under Capt. Clement Hall for three years. Discharged on 11/7/1779 at Charleston, SC. S38362.	
Sessoms, Abel	1st NC Regiment	1/4/1782, a Private under Capt. James Mills. Died on 8/21/1782. aka Abel Sessons.	
Sewalls, Daniel	2nd NC Regiment	1777, a Private under Capt. James Martin. Died on 4/14/1778. aka Daniel Sewells.	
Sexton, Jeremiah	1st NC Regiment	9/8/1778, a known Private under Capt. Tilghman Dixon - enlisted for one year.	
Sexton, John	1st NC Regiment	5/25/1781, a Private under Capt. Alexander Brevard. Deserted on 7/1/1781.	
Sexton, William	2nd NC Regiment	9/9/1778, a Private in the Colonel's Company (Col. John Patten) led by Capt. John Craddock.	
Seymore, Phelix	5th NC Regiment	11/26/1776, a Private under Capt. William Caswell for 3 years. Discharged on 2/8/1780.	
Seymore, Solomon	4th NC Regiment	5/1/1776, a Corporal under Capt. James Williams for 2-1/2 years. A Private in Oct. 1777. A Private in June 1778. 9/8/1778, a known Private in the Colonel's Company (Col. Thomas Clark) (1st NC Regiment) led by Capt. John Gambier Scull. Discharged on 11/10/1778. From Chatham County, NC. aka Solomon Seymour. W19314.	Germantown (PA).
Seymore, William	9th NC Regiment	12/1/1776, a Private under Capt. Richard D. Cook for three years. 9/8/1778, a known Private in the Lt. Colonel's Company (Lt. Col. Robert Mebane) (1st NC Regiment) led by Capt.	

Name	1st Unit	Year / Rank / Served Under / Notes	Known Battles
		Joshua Bowman - sick on that date at Valley Forge. Discharged on 1/28/1780. aka William Seamore.	
Shabshaw, Peter	4th NC Regiment	1779, a Private under Capt. Matthew Ramsey. Died in Sep. 1779.	
Shackler, Philip	2nd NC Regiment	1775, a Private under Capt. John White. 3/23/1776, a Corporal under Capt. William Fenner. A Private again in Jan. 1778. 9/9/1778, a known Private in the Lt. Colonel's Company (Lt. Col. Selby Harney) (2nd NC Regiment). POW at the Fall of Charleston, SC. aka Philip Shacklar, Philip Shackly. S39068.	Brandywine Creek (PA), Germantown (PA), Monmouth (NJ), Siege of Charleston 1780 (SC).
Shaddock, Charles		1779, a Private, regiment and unit unknown.	
Shadforth, Whittier	3rd NC Regiment	7/20/1778, a Private under Capt. Michael Quinn for nine months. aka Wittica Shadforth.	
Shanks, James	3rd NC Regiment	7/20/1778, a Private in the Colonel's Company (Col. Jethro Sumner) for nine months.	
Sharp, Benjamin	6th NC Regiment	5/13/1776, a Private under Lt./Capt. Thomas White for three years. 9/8/1778, a known Private under Capt. John Sumner (1st NC Regiment). A Sergeant in Sep. 1778. 3/12/1779, re-enlisted for the duration of the war as a Sergeant under Capt. John Sumner. Back to Private in 1782.	
Sharpe, Anthony	9th NC Regiment	11/28/1776, a 1st Lieutenant under Capt. Thomas McCrory. 8/24/1777, a Captain under Col. John Williams. Transferred to 1st NC Regiment on 6/1/1778. Transferred to 4th NC Regiment on 2/6/1782. Served until the end of the war. Earlier a Major in NC Militia. From Guilford County, NC. aka Anthony Sharp. R5366.	Brandywine Creek (PA), Germantown (PA), Monmouth (NJ), Stony Point (NY), Eutaw Springs (SC).
Sharpe, Joseph	2nd NC Regiment	Sept. 1775, a Private under Capt. George Davidson, Lt. Col. Alexander Martin for 12 months. After serving six months, he hired a substitute for the remainder. Later in NC Militia. From Rowan County, NC. S7482.	Great Cane Brake (SC), Snow Campaign (SC).
Sharpley, John	2nd NC Regiment	Jan. 1778, a Private under Capt. Clement Hall.	
Shavers, John	2nd NC Regiment	2/1/1780, a Private in the Colonel's Company (Col. John Patten) for 28 months.	
Shaw, Duncan	2nd NC Regiment	1/1/1782, a Private under Capt. Benjamin Andrew Coleman for 12 months.	
Shaw, Robert	4th NC Regiment	1776, a Private under Capt. Robert Smith. Discharged on 8/10/1777. Later, in NC Militia. From Guilford County, NC. W6006.	
Sheard, William	NC Artillery	4/17/1777, a Matross under Capt. John Vance as NC State Troops. 7/10/1777, on Continental Line. 11/16/1777, under Capt. John Kingsbury. 9/16/1778, in same unit. aka William Swords.	
Sheets,	4th NC	1782, a Private under Capt. Anthony Sharpe.	

Name	1st Unit	Year / Rank / Served Under / Notes	Known Battles
David	Regiment	Deserted on 6/23/1783 (?).	
Sheffield, George	2nd NC Regiment	1781, a Private and a Sergeant under Capt. Benjamin Coleman. Earlier in NC Militia. From Wilkes County, NC. W3611.	
Sheffield, William	2nd NC Regiment	1782, a Private under Capt. Clement Hall for 12 months.	
Shehorn, William	3rd NC Regiment	7/20/1778, a Private under Capt. Francis Child for nine months. aka William Sheborn.	
Shelton, James	2nd NC Regiment	5/12/1781, a Private under Capt. Tilghman Dixon. Discharged on 5/26/1782 (1st NC Regiment). aka Joseph Shelton.	
Shepard, Bird	4th NC Regiment	1782, a Private under Capt. Anthony Sharpe for 18 months.	
Shepard, John	2nd NC Regiment	1777, a Private under Capt. James Gee. 9/9/1778, a known Private under Capt. John Ingles.	
Shepard, William	4th NC Regiment	5/20/1776, a Private under Capt. Joseph Phillips. Dropped from the rolls in April 1778.	
Shepard, William	4th NC Regiment	1781, a Sergeant under Capt. George Dougherty. Discharged 5/25/1782.	
Shephard, Valentine	2nd NC Regiment	1782, a Private under Capt. Robert Raiford for 18 months. Earlier a British soldier under Cornwallis, deserted and joined the Patriots. Born in Germany. Later in Wayne County and Johnston County, NC. W6032.	
Shepherd, James	4th NC Regiment	1775, a 1st Lieutenant in the Salisbury District Minutemen. 4/17/1776, a 1st Lieutenant under Capt. Joseph Phillips and Col. Thomas Polk. From Surry County.	
Shepherd, William	3rd NC Regiment	1777, a Private under Capt. Curtis Ivey. Soon, a 1st Lieutenant in the 10th NC Regiment. 1/20/1778, a Captain under Col. Abraham Sheppard. Dropped from the rolls in June 1778. From Duplin County, NC. aka William Sheppard. R9479.	
Sheppard, Abraham	10th NC Regiment	4/17/1777, Colonel/Commandant of the 10th NC Regiment. Retired on 6/1/1778. Some pension statements indicate that he remained the Commandant of the 10th NC Regiment until the end of the war. However, most historians agree that he retired in 1778. aka Abraham Shepard.	
Sheppard, Abraham Jr.	10th NC Regiment	4/19/1777, a Captain under Col. Abraham Sheppard (his father). 1780, a Major in NC Militia. aka Abram Sheppard, Jr.	Brandywine Creek (PA), Germantown (PA).
Sheppard, Benjamin	10th NC Regiment	1777, a Paymaster. Discharged 12/11/1777.	
Sheppard, John	1st NC Regiment	1777, a Private under Capt. Robert Ralston. 9/8/1778, a known Private under Capt. John Sumner. aka John Shepherd.	
Sheppard, John	10th NC Regiment	1777, a Major under Col. Abraham Sheppard.	
Sheppard, Willoughby	4th NC Regiment	1782, a Private under Capt. Joseph T. Rhodes for 18 months. Dec. 1782, transferred to Capt.	

Name	1st Unit	Year / Rank / Served Under / Notes	Known Battles
		Thomas Evans.	
Sherly, Thomas	1st NC Regiment	5/15/1781, a Private under Capt. Anthony Sharpe. A Sergeant in Jan. 1782. Discharged on 4/15/1782 (4th NC Regiment). Probably same man as Thomas Shurley below.	
Sherrard, Edward	3rd NC Regiment	7/20/1778, a Private under Capt. John Baker for nine months.	
Sherrard, Richard	5th NC Regiment	6/7/1779, a Private under Maj. Reading Blount.	
Sherrin, Jacob	3rd NC Regiment	1777, a Private under Capt. Jacob Turner. A Corporal on 11/7/1777. Died on 5/20/1778.	
Sherrod, Benjamin	1st NC Regiment	4/10/1781, a Private under Lt./Capt. Elijah Moore. Discharged on 2/1/1783 (4th NC Regiment).	
Sherrod, Jordan	3rd NC Regiment	7/20/1778, a Private under Capt. John Baker for nine months. Discharged 5/9/1779 at Winton, NC. Later in NC Militia. From Nash County, NC. On the official rolls as Jordan Sherrard. S7489.	
Sherwood, Jordan	1st NC Regiment	4/12/1781, a Private under Capt. William Lytle. Deserted on 7/6/1781.	
Shevers, William	1st NC Regiment	4/12/1781, a Private under Capt. Alexander Brevard.	
Shields, William	1st NC Regiment	7/1/1777, a Wagon Maker under Capt. Robert Ralston. Dropped from the rolls in Sep. 1777.	
Shipman, Asa	3rd NC Regiment	7/20/1778, a Private under Capt. Michael Quinn for nine months.	
Shipman, Jacob	3rd NC Regiment	7/20/1778, a Private under Capt. Michael Quinn for nine months. From Tryon (soon to become Rutherford) County, NC. Born 1744 in either Brunswick or Lunenburg County, VA [45]. The same source also says he was born 1746 in Bladen County, NC.	
Shipman, Toney	3rd NC Regiment	7/20/1778, a Private under Capt. Michael Quinn for nine months.	
Shivers, James	3rd NC Regiment	6/24/1779, a Private under Michael Quinn for three years.	
Shivers, Jesse	3rd NC Regiment	7/20/1778, a Musician under Capt. Francis Child for nine months. Discharged around 5/1/1779 in Halifax, NC. From Pitt County, NC. S42010.	
Shivers, Joseph	3rd NC Regiment	7/24/1779, a Private under Capt. Michael Quinn.	
Shockley, Isaac	5th NC Regiment	A Private under Capt. Reading Blount. Died on 11/5/1777.	
Shoemaker, John	1st NC Regiment	4/28/1781, a Private under Capt. Alexander Brevard. Mortally wounded at the battle of Eutaw Springs, SC, taken to Camden Hospital where he died. Brother of Corporal Randal Shoemaker.	Eutaw Springs (SC).
Shoemaker, Randal	1st NC Regiment	4/28/1781, a Corporal under Capt. Alexander Brevard. A Sergeant for some unknown length of time under Capt. Alexander Brevard. Discharged on 4/28/1782 (3rd NC Regiment) in	Eutaw Springs (SC).

Name	1st Unit	Year / Rank / Served Under / Notes	Known Battles
		Mecklenburg County, NC. aka Randle Shoemaker, Randel Shoemaker, Randolph Shoemaker. S42007.	
Shoementon, Hezekiah	3rd NC Regiment	12/20/1776, a Private under Capt. Thomas Granbury. 9/9/1778, a known Private under Capt. Clement Hall (2nd NC Regiment). Discharged in Nov. 1778. aka Hezekiah Shirmentine, Hezekiah Shermentine.	
Shores, David	6th NC Regiment	5/9/1776, a Private under Capt. Philip Taylor for 2-1/2 years. Dropped from the rolls in Nov. 1777. 9/8/1778, a known Private under Capt. John Sumner (1st NC Regiment) - sick in camp on that date.	
Short, Charles	3rd NC Regiment	6/24/1779, a Musician under Capt. Michael Quinn.	
Short, Hardy	3rd NC Regiment	7/20/1778, a Private in the Lt. Colonel's Company (Lt. Col. William Lee Davidson) led by Lt./Capt. George "Gee" Bradley for nine months. 4/23/1779, a known Private in the Lt. Colonel's Company (Lt. Col. Robert Mebane) led by Capt. George "Gee" Bradley.	
Short, Henry	3rd NC Regiment	7/20/1778, a Private in the Lt. Colonel's Company (Lt. Col. William Lee Davidson) led by Lt./Capt. George "Gee" Bradley. Died on 11/27/1778 at Roberdson's Hospital.	
Shoulder, William	4th NC Regiment	1779, a Private under Capt. Matthew Ramsey. Deserted in Sep. 1779.	
Shoulders, William	1st NC Regiment	10/21/1778, a Private under Capt. Anthony Sharpe.	
Shrode, Adam	3rd NC Regiment	1781, a Private under Capt. Clement Hall. Discharged on 12/27/1782 (2nd NC Regiment).	
Shropshire, William	2nd NC Regiment	September 1775, served under Capt. John Armstrong for 12 months. Later in NC Militia. From Guilford County, NC. W7180.	
Shurer, Frederick	2nd NC Regiment	1782, a Private under Capt. Robert Raiford for 18 months.	
Shurley, Thomas	3rd NC Regiment	7/20/1778, a Private under Capt. Francis Child for nine months.	
Shute, Jesse	2nd NC Regiment	12/2/1777, a Private, unit unknown. A Musician in Feb. 1778. Back to Private in June 1778 in the Lt. Colonel's Company (Lt. Col. Selby Harney). 3/12/1779, re-enlisted under Capt. Benjamin Williams.	
Shute, Thomas	10th NC Regiment	4/19/1777, an Ensign under Capt. Armwell Herron. Due to the breakup of the regiment he retired on 6/1/1778. Then, a Lieutenant and Captain in NC Militia. From Dobbs (what would soon become Wayne) County, NC. S42009.	
Shute, William	10th NC Regiment	5/1/1777, a Sergeant under Capt. Silas Stevenson. A Corporal in June 1778. A Private in Oct. 1778. Dropped from the rolls on 2/7/1779.	
Shy, Jesse	1st NC	Dec. 1779, a Private under Capt. William Lytle.	Guilford Court

Name	1st Unit	Year / Rank / Served Under / Notes	Known Battles
	Regiment	Then served under Capt. Elijah Moore. 6/5/1782, a Private under Capt. Benjamin Bailey (3rd NC Regiment) for 12 months. Enlisted in Orange County, NC. aka Jesse Sky. S31369.	House, Eutaw Springs (SC).
Siborn, William	2nd NC Regiment	1777, a Private under Capt. James Gee.	
Siddle, Jesse	1st NC Regiment	1781, a Private under Capt. William Walton.	
Sikes, James	4th NC Regiment	2/6/1782, a Sergeant under Capt. James Mills for 12 months. A Sergeant Major on 9/1/1782. Born on 7/25/1752 in Edgecombe County, NC. Lived in New Hanover County, NC when he enlisted. Later lived and died in Brunswick County, NC. On the official rolls as James Sykes. W9653.	
Silas, Thomas	1st NC Regiment	8/1/1782, a Private under Capt. Joshua Hadley for 18 months.	
Sill, Thomas	4th NC Regiment	1777, a Private under Capt. James Williams. Dropped from the rolls in Sep. 1777.	
Sillards, Thomas	10th NC Regiment	5/3/1777, a Private under Capt. Andrew Vanoy. 9/8/1778, a known Private under Capt. Tilghman Dixon (1st NC Regiment). Discharged on 6/1/1779. aka Thomas Sillard.	
Silverthorn, Robert	4th NC Regiment	3/10/1782, a Private under Capt. James Mills for 12 months. Furloughed at Wilmington, NC. From Hyde County, NC. Born on 1/22/1763 in Hyde County, NC. On the official rolls as Robert Silverthan. W4802.	
Silvester, Luke	10th NC Regiment	5/5/1777, a Private under Capt. John Jarvis for three years. 9/8/1778, a known Private in the Major's Company (Maj. Griffith John McRee) (1st NC Regiment) - sick on that date at Valley Forge. Died in Dec. 1778. aka Luke Sylvester.	
Silvester, Nathaniel	4th NC Regiment	12/1/1782, a Private under Capt. Joseph T. Rhodes for 18 months. Dec. 1782, transferred to Capt. Thomas Evans.	
Simkins, John	4th NC Regiment	1782, a Private under Capt. Joseph T. Rhodes for 18 months. Dec. 1782, transferred to Capt. Thomas Evans.	
Simkins, Joseph	4th NC Regiment	1779, a Private under Capt. Matthew Ramsey for nine months. Dropped from the rolls in Oct. 1779.	
Simmons, Anthony	7th NC Regiment	2/14/1777, a Private under Capt. John Poynter. Dropped from the rolls in Sep. 1777.	
Simmons, Benjamin	2nd NC Regiment	9/9/1778, a known Private in the Lt. Colonel's Company (Lt. Col. Selby Harney).	
Simmons, Benjamin	4th NC Regiment	1777, a Private under Capt. Robert Smith. Dropped from the rolls in Jan. 1778.	
Simmons, Benjamin	8th NC Regiment	1777, a Private under Capt. Michael Quinn. Oct. 1779, a Sergeant in the 3rd NC Regiment.	
Simmons, Gideon	10th NC Regiment	5/2/1777, a Corporal under Capt. Andrew Vanoy. A Private in June 1778. 9/9/1778, a known Private under Capt. John Ingles (2nd NC	

Name	1st Unit	Year / Rank / Served Under / Notes	Known Battles
		Regiment).	
Simmons, Isham	1st NC Regiment	1776, served under Capt. Henry "Hal" Dixon. Later in NC Militia. From Guilford County, NC. W8725.	Brunswick Town #1.
Simmons, Isler	4th NC Regiment	10/1/1776, a Sergeant under Capt. William Goodman for 3 years. A Private on 8/16/1778. 9/8/1778, a known Private in the Colonel's Company (Col. Thomas Clark) (1st NC Regiment) led by Capt. John Gambier Scull. Discharged on 11/10/1779. One source claims he joined on 5/7/1776, probably as a Private. aka Isle Simmons.	
Simmons, James	2nd NC Regiment	A Private under Capt. James Martin. 9/9/1778, a known Private in the Colonel's Company (Col. John Patten) led by Capt. John Craddock. 3/12/1779, re-enlisted in the Colonel's Company (Col. John Patten) led by Capt. John Craddock. aka James Simons.	
Simmons, James	3rd NC Regiment	7/20/1778, a Private under Maj. Thomas Hogg for nine months. Deserted on 7/21/1778 (the next day after enlisting).	
Simmons, Jeremiah	1st NC Regiment	12/25/1781, a Private under Capt. James Mills for 12 months. Discharged at Wilmington, NC. Enlisted in Bladen County, NC. Born on 1/9/1761 in Duplin (what is now Sampson) County, NC. W4803.	
Simmons, John	1st NC Regiment	4/6/1781, a Private under Capt. William Lytle. Discharged on 4/12/1782 (4th NC Regiment). From Chatham County, NC. W60.	Siege of Augusta (GA).
Simmons, John	1st NC Regiment	5/17/1781, a Private under Lt./Capt. Benjamin Bailey. Discharged on 5/17/1782 (3rd NC Regiment).	
Simmons, John	2nd NC Regiment	12/18/1781, a Private under Capt. Benjamin Andrew Coleman for 12 months.	
Simmons, John Sr.	10th NC Regiment	8/15/1777, a Private under Capt. James Wilson for 3 years. Discharged on 8/21/1778.	
Simmons, John	10th NC Regiment	8/15/1777, a Sergeant under Capt. James Wilson. Discharged on 8/21/1778.	
Simmons, Malachi	2nd NC Regiment	1777, a Private under Capt. James Martin. Died on 5/1/1778.	
Simmons, Peter	10th NC Regiment	5/11/1777, a Private under Capt. Isaac Moore. Died on 8/15/1777.	
Simmons, Philip	4th NC Regiment	1782, a Private under Capt. William Lytle for 18 months.	
Simmons, Richard	NC Light Dragoons	1777, a Cornet under Capt. Martin Phifer.	
Simmons, Samuel	10th NC Regiment	5/9/1777, a Corporal under Capt. John Jarvis. A Private in June 1778. 9/8/1778, a known Private under Capt. Joshua Bowman (1st NC Regiment). aka Samuel Simmonds.	
Simmons, Sanders	1st NC Regiment	12/25/1781, a Private under Capt. James Mills for 12 months. Discharged at Wilmington, NC. Living in Duplin County when he enlisted in Bladen County, NC. Born on 1/18/1763 in	

NC Patriots 1775-1783: Their Own Words

Name	1st Unit	Year / Rank / Served Under / Notes	Known Battles
		Duplin (what would become Sampson) County, NC. S7516.	
Simmons, Willis	4th NC Regiment	1781, a Private under Capt. George Dougherty. Discharged on 5/25/1782.	
Simon, Peter	5th NC Regiment	1775, a Captain in the Edenton District Minutemen. 4/17/1776, a Captain in the 5th NC Regiment. aka Peter Simons.	
Simons, John	10th NC Regiment	6/7/1777, a Private under Capt. John Jarvis. Discharged on 9/1/1778.	
Simons, Felix	2nd NC Regiment	9/9/1778, a known Private under Capt. Robert Fenner.	
Simpkins, Joshua	4th NC Regiment	1782, a Private under Capt. Anthony Sharpe for 18 months.	
Simpson, Andrew	7th NC Regiment	5/21/1777, a Private under Capt. Joseph Walker. A Corporal in June 1778. 9/8/1778, a known Corporal under Capt. Tilghman Dixon (1st NC Regiment). A Sergeant in July 1779.	
Simpson, Benjamin	6th NC Regiment	A Private under Capt. George Dougherty. Dropped from the rolls in April 1778.	
Simpson, John	1st NC Regiment	1777, a Private under Capt. Henry "Hal" Dixon. 9/8/1778, a known Private under Capt. James Read. aka John Simson.	
Simpson, Joseph	5th NC Regiment	1777, a Private under Capt. Henry Darnell. Deserted in Aug. 1777.	
Simpson, Moses	3rd NC Regiment	7/20/1778, a Private under Capt. Michael Quinn for nine months. Discharged on 9/7/1778.	
Simpson, Richard	4th NC Regiment	2/6/1782, a Private under Capt. James Mills for 12 months.	
Simpson, Samuel	3rd NC Regiment	1777, a Private under Capt. Pinketham Eaton for 2-1/2 years. 9/9/1778, a known Private under Capt. Clement Hall (2nd NC Regiment) - sick at Valley Forge. A Corporal on 4/1/1779. Back to Private in 1782. From Chowan County, NC. R9603.	
Simpson, Smith	4th NC Regiment	1777, a Private under Capt. William Goodman. Dropped from the rolls in June 1778.	
Simpson, William	4th NC Regiment	2/6/1782, a Private under Capt. James Mills for 12 months.	
Sinclair, William	1st NC Regiment	5/5/1781, a Private under Capt. Anthony Sharpe. A Sergeant in Jan. 1782. Discharged on 4/5/1782 (4th NC Regiment).	
Singletary, Richard	6th NC Regiment	1775, an Ensign in the Wilmington District Minutemen. 4/17/1776, an Ensign under Capt. Griffith John McRee and Col. John Alexander Lillington.	
Singletary, William	8th NC Regiment	11/28/1776, a 1st Lieutenant under Capt. Robert Raiford. Resigned on 10/26/1777.	
Singleton, Henry	8th NC Regiment	2/22/1777, a Private under Capt. John Walsh. 9/9/1778, a known Private in the Colonel's Company (Col. John Patten) (2nd NC Regiment) led by Capt. John Craddock. 3/12/1779, re-enlisted under Capt. Benjamin Williams.	
Singleton,	4th NC	Spring of 1776, a Private under Capt. John	

Name	1st Unit	Year / Rank / Served Under / Notes	Known Battles
Robert	Regiment	Nelson. 1777, an Ensign under Capt. Andrew Vanoy (10th NC Regiment). In his pension application he states that he was taken sick in 1779 and given a leave of absence. From Guilford County, NC. S39072.	
Sirks, James	1st NC Regiment	10/24/1776, a Private, unit unknown. 9/10/1778, a known Private under Capt. Thomas Armstrong.	
Sirmon, Levy	3rd NC Regiment	7/20/1778, a Private under Capt. Francis Child for nine months. aka Levy Sirmore.	
Sisk, James		10/1/1776, a Private, regiment and unit unknown. A Corporal in Nov. 1779.	
Sitgreaves, John	5th NC Regiment	9/9/1775, a 2nd Lieutenant in the New Bern District Minutemen. 4/17/1776, a 2nd Lieutenant under Capt. William Caswell and Col. Edward Buncombe. From Craven County.	
Sivett, Allen	1st NC Regiment	1782, a Private under Capt. Peter Bacot for 18 months.	
Skeen, John	10th NC Regiment	7/24/1777, a Private under Capt. Armwell Herron. 9/9/1778, a known Private in the Major's Company (Maj. Hardy Murfree) (2nd NC Regiment). 3/12/1779, re-enlisted in the Major's Company (Maj. Hardy Murfree). POW at the Fall of Charleston (SC), escaped. From Craven County, NC. aka John Skean, John Skien, John Skeene.	Monmouth (NJ), Stony Point (NY), Siege of Charleston 1780 (SC).
Skeets, William	3rd NC Regiment	7/20/1778, a Private under Capt. Kedar Ballard for nine months.	
Sketo, Joseph	3rd NC Regiment	7/20/1778, a Private under Lt./Capt. George "Gee" Bradley for nine months.	
Skinner, Evan	3rd NC Regiment	1781, a Private under Capt. Clement Hall. Discharged on 4/21/1782 (2nd NC Regiment). aka Evan Skinners.	
Skinner, John	1st NC Regiment	1782, a Private under Capt. Peter Bacot for 18 months.	
Skinner, John	3rd NC Regiment	5/1/1776, a Corporal under Capt. Pinketham Eaton for 2-1/2 years. A Private in June 1778. 9/9/1778, a known Private in the Major's Company (Maj. Hardy Murfree) (2nd NC Regiment). Discharged on 11/1/1778.	
Skinner, Thomas	2nd NC Regiment	7/20/1778, a Private under Maj. Reading Blount for nine months.	
Skinner, William	2nd NC Regiment	7/20/1778, a Private under Maj. Reading Blount for nine months.	
Skipper, George	4th NC Regiment	Jan. 1779, a Private under Capt. George Dougherty.	
Skipper, James	1st NC Regiment	12/18/1781, a Private under Capt. James Mills for 12 months.	
Skipper, James	2nd NC Regiment	9/16/1775, a Private under Capt. Simon Bright. Discharged on 5/1/1776. Then in NC Militia. From Dobbs County, NC. R9639.	
Skipper, Joseph	8th NC Regiment	A Private under Capt. John Walsh. Died on 12/19/1777.	
Skipper,	4th NC	Jan. 1779, a Private under Capt. George	

Name	1st Unit	Year / Rank / Served Under / Notes	Known Battles
Joshua	Regiment	Dougherty.	
Skipper, Nathan	8th NC Regiment	1777, a Private under Capt. Frederick Hargett for three years. S39074.	
Slade, Frederick	2nd NC Regiment	3/1/1782, a Private under Capt. Clement Hall for 12 months.	
Slade, Nathaniel	4th NC Regiment	August 1782, a Private under Capt. Elijah Moore, Capt. Joseph T. Rhodes, and Capt. Alexander Brevard (3rd NC Regiment) until July 1783. Earlier in NC Militia. From Caswell County, NC. W6071.	
Slade, Stephen	2nd NC Regiment	5/12/1776, a QM Sergeant. Regimental QM on 1/1/1778. 9/5/1778, an Ensign in the Lt. Colonel's Company (Lt. Col. Selby Harney) led by Capt. Charles Stewart. 1/23/1780, a 2nd Lieutenant. POW at the Fall of Charleston, exchanged 6/14/1781. Promoted while in captivity to 1st Lieutenant on 1/23/1781. Retired on 1/1/1783.	Siege of Charleston 1780 (SC).
Slade, William	4th NC Regiment	1/2/1777, an Ensign. 4/26/1777, a 2nd Lieutenant. Transferred to 1st NC Regiment on 6/1/1778 under Capt. Joseph Phillips. Regimental Adjutant on 6/1/1778. 9/8/1778, a 2nd Lieutenant under Capt. John Gambier Scull. 6/25/1779, a 1st Lieutenant. Resigned 2/18/1780. From Martin County, NC.	
Slater, James	1st NC Regiment	1781, a Private under Capt. William Walton. Discharged in Dec. 1782.	
Slaughter, John	3rd NC Regiment	1/1/1782, a Private under Capt. Samuel Jones for 12 months.	
Slaughter, John	10th NC Regiment	A Captain in the 10th NC Regiment, dates unknown. 1779, a Captain under Col.Thomas Clark in the 5th NC Regiment. S42312.	Stono Ferry (SC).
Slaughter, Robert	3rd NC Regiment	1/1/1782, a Private under Capt. Samuel Jones for 12 months.	
Slaven, Samuel	6th NC Regiment	A Musician under Capt. Griffith John McRee. Died on 4/13/1778.	
Sledge, Arthur	7th NC Regiment	12/18/1776, an Ensign under Capt. John Macon to replace James Myrick, who resigned.	
Sloan, Samuel	4th NC Regiment	Nov. 1778, a Private under Capt. Matthew Ramsey for nine months. Discharged on 8/5/1779 at Stono River, SC. R9661.	Stono Ferry (SC).
Sloan, William	1st NC Regiment	11/10/1778, a Private under Capt. Anthony Sharpe for nine months.	
Slocum, John	1st NC Regiment	5/9/1781, a Private under Capt. Alexander Brevard. Deserted on 6/3/1781. aka John Slocorn.	
Small, James	1st NC Regiment	4/14/1777, a Private under Capt. Tilghman Dixon. 9/8/1778, a known Private under Capt. Tilghman Dixon.	
Smart, John	4th NC Regiment	1781, a Private under Capt. Joseph T. Rhodes. Discharged on 4/12/1782.	
Smethers, Garet	4th NC Regiment	1779, a Private under Capt. Matthew Ramsey. Deserted in Sep. 1779.	
Smiter,	4th NC	1777, a Private under Capt. William Temple	

Name	1st Unit	Year / Rank / Served Under / Notes	Known Battles
Valente	Regiment	Coles. Deserted on 10/12/1777.	
Smith, Aaron	1st NC Regiment	6/6/1781, a Private under Capt. William Lytle for 12 months. 7/28/1781, under Capt. Michael Rudolph in Lt. Col. Henry "Light Horse Harry" Lee's Legion Infantry (VA). Severely wounded at the battle of Eutaw Springs (SC). Discharged on 6/28/1782 at the High Hills of the Santee, SC by Maj. John Armstrong (4th NC Regiment). From Burke County, NC. Born 4/5/1765. R9681.	Eutaw Springs (SC).
Smith, Benjamin	1st NC Regiment	5/25/1781, a Private under Lt./Capt. Benjamin Bailey for 12 months. Discharged on 5/25/1782 (3rd NC Regiment). From Franklin County, NC. Died on 3/15/1785. W17138.	
Smith, Benjamin	4th NC Regiment	5/20/1776, a Sergeant under Capt. Joseph Phillips for 3 years. A Private in June 1778. 9/8/1778, a known Private under Capt. Joshua Bowman (1st NC Regiment). (Another source asserts he was under Capt. James Read on 9/8/1778.) Discharged on 5/25/1779.	
Smith, Benjamin	10th NC Regiment	8/20/1777 or 9/17/1777 (two sources), a Private under Capt. Abraham Sheppard, Jr. 9/9/1778, a known Private under Capt. John Ingles (2nd NC Regiment). POW at the Fall of Charleston (SC), exchanged 7/2/1781 at Jamestown, VA. From Dobbs (what would become Wayne) County, NC. S7541.	Monmouth (NJ), Siege of Charleston 1780 (SC).
Smith, Benjamin	10th NC Regiment	6/3/1777, a Private under Capt. Isaac Moore. Died on 11/20/1778.	
Smith, Bryant	10th NC Regiment	Spring 1778, a Private under Capt. Abraham Sheppard, Jr. 9/9/1778, a known Wagoner in the Major's Company (Maj. Hardy Murfree) (2nd NC Regiment). 1781, in NC Militia. From Randolph County, NC. aka Brien Smith. R9699.	
Smith, Burrell	1st NC Regiment	1782, a Sergeant under Capt. Benjamin Carter. Died on 1/26/1783.	
Smith, Caleb	2nd NC Regiment	1776, a Private under Capt. James Gee. Upon the death of Capt. Gee, he was placed under Capt. John Ingles. 9/9/1778, a known Private under Capt. John Ingles. Badly wounded at the Siege of Charleston, in hospital when taken POW - escaped. Living in Henry County, VA when he enlisted. S39083.	Brandywine Creek (PA), Germantown (PA), Monmouth (NJ), Siege of Charleston 1780 (SC).
Smith, Charles	4th NC Regiment	7/20/1778, a Private in the Colonel's Company (Col. James Armstrong) for nine months. Discharged at Moncks Corner, SC. From Pitt County, NC. Born 1758 in Craven County, NC. S45777.	Stono Ferry (SC).
Smith, Clement	4th NC Regiment	7/25/1776, a Private under Capt. William Goodman for three years. A Private in Oct. 1777. 9/8/1778, a known Private in the Colonel's Company (Col. Thomas Clark) (1st	

Name	1st Unit	Year / Rank / Served Under / Notes	Known Battles
		NC Regiment) led by Capt. John Gambier Scull. Discharged on 7/20/1779.	
Smith, David	4th NC Regiment	1781, a Private under Capt. Joseph T. Rhodes for 18 months. After the battle of Eutaw Springs (SC), he was under Capt. Anthony Sharpe. Discharged at Haddrell's Point, SC. S42016.	
Smith, David	5th NC Regiment	11/20/1776, a Private under Capt. Henry Darnell. 9/9/1778, a known Private under Capt. Benjamin Andrew Coleman (2nd NC Regiment). 3/12/1779, re-enlisted under Capt. Benjamin Andrew Coleman.	
Smith, Drewry	4th NC Regiment	1782, a Private under Capt. William Lytle. Deserted on 12/10/1782.	
Smith, Drury	7th NC Regiment	1777, a Private under Capt. Henry Dawson. After the battle of Germantown (PA), he was transferred to Capt. John Macon. The official rolls state that he deserted on 10/25/1777. In his pension application, he asserts that he was maliciously accused of disobedience and sentenced to the lash, to escape which he left the service and furnished a substitute, James McMullen, who was received by Maj. Patrick Lockard [Samuel Lockhart]. From Halifax County, NC. aka Drew Smith. R9713.	Germantown (PA).
Smith, Elias	3rd NC Regiment	7/20/1778, a Private under Maj. Thomas Hogg for the duration of the war.	
Smith, Ezekiel	4th NC Regiment	Nov. 1781, a Private under Capt. Joseph T. Rhodes for 18 months. Dec. 1782, transferred to Capt. Thomas Evans. Discharged on 7/1/1783 at James Island, SC. Earlier in NC Militia. From Wayne County, NC. W25480.	
Smith, Frederick	2nd NC Regiment	12/5/1776, a Private, unit unknown. 9/9/1778, under Capt. Benjamin Andrew Coleman.	
Smith, George	DQMG	1780, an Artificer under Col. Nicholas Long (Deputy QM General). Made Canteens.	
Smith, George	1st NC Regiment	10/6/1777, a Private under Maj. Henry "Hal" Dixon for three years. 9/8/1778, a known Private under Capt. Tilghman Dixon. A Sergeant in Nov. 1778. 3/12/1779, re-enlisted for the duration of the war in the same unit.	
Smith, Henry	1st NC Regiment	1777, a Private under Capt. Howell Tatum. 9/8/1778, a known Private under Capt. Howell Tatum - sick at Valley Forge on that date.	
Smith, Henry	1st NC Regiment	6/14/1781, a Private under Capt. Thomas Donoho. Discharged in June 1782.	
Smith, Henry	1st NC Regiment	1782, a Corporal under Capt. William Walton for 12 months. Discharged on 6/15/1783.	
Smith, Henry	3rd NC Regiment	7/20/1778, a Private under Maj. Thomas Hogg for nine months.	
Smith, Isaac	1st NC Regiment	5/7/1781, a Private under Lt./Capt. Benjamin Bailey. Discharged on 5/7/1782 (3rd NC Regiment). S42017.	
Smith, Jabez	5th NC Regiment	Jan. 1777, an Ensign. 9/1/1777, a 2nd Lieutenant. Dropped from the rolls in Jan. 1778.	

Name	1st Unit	Year / Rank / Served Under / Notes	Known Battles
		aka Jaly Smith.	
Smith, Jacob	2nd NC Regiment	1782, a Private under Capt. Benjamin Carter for 18 months.	
Smith, Jacob	3rd NC Regiment	1/1/1782, a Private under Capt. Samuel Jones for 12 months.	
Smith, James	1st NC Regiment	5/9/1781, a Private under Capt. Alexander Brevard.	
Smith, James	1st NC Regiment	1/1/1782, a Private under Capt. James Mills.	
Smith, James	3rd NC Regiment	12/1/1781, a Private under Capt. Clement Hall for 12 months. Discharged on 12/1/1782 (2nd NC Regiment).	
Smith, James	3rd NC Regiment	7/29/1779, a Private under Capt. Kedar Ballard. Deserted on 8/22/1779. aka Joseph Smith.	
Smith, James	3rd NC Regiment	6/22/1780, a Private under Capt. George "Gee" Bradley.	
Smith, James	3rd NC Regiment	7/20/1778, a Corporal under Capt. Francis Child for nine months. Discharged on 7/20/1779 at Halifax, NC. Enlisted at Williamston in Martin County, NC. S42018.	
Smith, James	4th NC Regiment	Jan. 1779, a Private under Capt. William Goodman.	
Smith, James	10th NC Regiment	6/17/1777, a Private under Capt. John Jarvis for three years. 9/8/1778, a known Private in the Major's Company (Maj. John Baptiste Ashe) (1st NC Regiment). 3/12/1779, re-enlisted for the duration of the war in the same unit.	
Smith, Jeremiah	2nd NC Regiment	1777, a Private under Capt. Charles Allen. 9/10/1778, a known Private under Capt. Thomas Armstrong. Discharged on 1/30/1780. From Lincoln County, NC. Born on 3/8/1752. R9794.	
Smith, Jeremiah	3rd NC Regiment	1/1/1782, a Private under Capt. Samuel Jones. Died on 9/14/1782 (1st NC Regiment).	
Smith, Joab	3rd NC Regiment	1/1/1782, a Private under Capt. Samuel Jones for 12 months.	
Smith, Job	6th NC Regiment	A Private under Capt. George Dougherty. A Sergeant in Sep. 1777. Dropped from the rolls in Jan. 1778	
Smith, John		6/4/1776, regiment, unit, and rank unknown, enlisted for three years. 9/8/1778, a known Private under Capt. John Sumner (1st NC Regiment).	
Smith, John	NC Light Dragoons	Oct.-Dec. 1777, a known Private under Capt. Martin Phifer. Not on any official rolls.	
Smith, John	1st NC Regiment	2/1/1782, a Private under Capt. James Mills, Died on 9/19/1782.	
Smith, John	1st NC Regiment	8/1/1782, a Corporal under Capt. Joshua Hadley for 18 months.	
Smith, John	2nd NC Regiment	7/17/1776, a Private under Capt. Charles Allen for three years or the duration of the war. 9/9/1778, a known Private under Capt. Clement Hall. POW at Ft. Lafayette, NY on 6/1/1779.	Ft. Lafayette (NY).
Smith, John Jr.	2nd NC Regiment	11/7/1776, a Private under Capt. Clement Hall for 2-1/2 years. Deserted on 2/17/1780.	

Name	1st Unit	Year / Rank / Served Under / Notes	Known Battles
Smith, John Sr.	2nd NC Regiment	1777, a Private under Capt. Clement Hall. Died on 2/27/1778.	
Smith, John	2nd NC Regiment	4/25/1781, a Private under Capt. Tilghman Dixon. Discharged on 4/25/1782.	
Smith, John	4th NC Regiment	1782, a Private under Capt. Anthony Sharpe for 18 months.	
Smith, John	4th NC Regiment	Jan. 1778, a Private under Capt. John Nelson. Dropped from the rolls in June 1778.	
Smith, John	5th NC Regiment	6/27/1779, a Private under Maj. Reading Blount for 18 months.	
Smith, John	6th NC Regiment	A Private under Capt. Philip Taylor. Dropped from the rolls in Sep. 1778.	
Smith, John	7th NC Regiment	Nov. 1777, a Musician under Capt. Joshua Dayley. Died on 2/24/1778.	
Smith, John	9th NC Regiment	11/28/1776, an Ensign under Capt. Michael Henderson. From Salisbury District.	
Smith, John	10th NC Regiment	7/12/1777, a Private under Capt. Andrew Vanoy. 9/9/1778, a known Private under Capt. Robert Fenner (2nd NC Regiment). 3/12/1779, re-enlisted under Capt. Benjamin Williams.	
Smith, John	10th NC Regiment	7/25/1777, a Private under Capt. Abraham Sheppard, Jr. 9/10/1778, a known Private under Capt. Thomas Armstrong (2nd NC Regiment).	
Smith, Joseph	1st NC Regiment	1777, a Corporal under Capt. Henry "Hal" Dixon. Deserted on 3/24/1777. Re-enlisted as a Private in May 1778. 9/8/1778, a known Private under Capt. James Read - sick on that date.	
Smith, Joshua	3rd NC Regiment	Jan. 1779, a Private in the Lt. Colonel's Company (Lt. Col. Robert Mebane) led by Capt. George "Gee" Bradley.	
Smith, Malachi	2nd NC Regiment	1781, a Private under Capt. Tilghman Dixon. Discharged on 4/25/1782.	
Smith, Malachi	7th NC Regiment	1777, a Private under Capt. John McGlaughan. Deserted in Apr. 1777.	
Smith, Mitchell	NC Artillery	6/2/1776, a Gunner under Capt. John Vance as NC Provincial Troops. 7/10/1777, on Continental Line. 11/16/1777, under Capt. John Kingsbury. 5/1/1778, in same unit. 9/16/1778, in same unit. aka Michael Smith.	
Smith, Nehemiah	3rd NC Regiment	7/20/1778, a Musician under Capt. John Baker for nine months.	
Smith, Owen	1st NC Regiment	A Private under Capt. Henry "Hal" Dixon. Died on 8/17/1777.	
Smith, Peter	1st NC Regiment	Sep. 1775, a Private under Capt. Henry "Hal" Dixon for one year. From Orange (what is now Caswell) County, NC. S42015.	
Smith, Peter	2nd NC Regiment	1782, a Private under Capt. Benjamin Carter for 18 months.	
Smith, Peter	3rd NC Regiment	12/1/1781, a Private under Capt. Clement Hall for 12 months. Discharged on 12/1/1782 (2nd NC Regiment).	
Smith, Peter	4th NC Regiment	1782, a Private under Capt. William Lytle. Deserted on 12/10/1782.	
Smith, Platt	3rd NC	7/20/1778, a Private under Capt. Michael Quinn	

Name	1st Unit	Year / Rank / Served Under / Notes	Known Battles
	Regiment	for nine months.	
Smith, Reddick	2nd NC Regiment	12/5/1776, a Musician under Capt. James Martin. A Private in June 1778. A Corporal in July 1779. aka Redick Smith.	
Smith, Reuben	5th NC Regiment	Jan. 1779, a Private under Maj. Pinketham Eaton for nine months.	
Smith, Richard	1st NC Regiment	5/5/1781, a Private under Capt. Robert Raiford. Discharged on 5/3/1782 (2nd NC Regiment).	
Smith, Richard	1st NC Regiment	1/1/1782, a Private under Capt. James Mills. Died on 9/10/1782 (4th NC Regiment).	
Smith, Richard	1st NC Regiment	8/1/1782, a Private under Capt. Joshua Hadley for 18 months.	
Smith, Richard	2nd NC Regiment	4/25/1781, a Private under Capt. Benjamin Carter. Died on 9/16/1781.	
Smith, Robert	1st NC Regiment	Sep. 1775, a Private under Capt. John Walker for six months. April 1776, a Private under Capt. John Ashe, Jr. (4th NC Regiment) for 18 months. Said his friends "procured him a 2nd Lieutenancy in the 3rd Regiment" - not on any official rolls thusly. From Johnston County, NC. W1504.	
Smith, Robert	1st NC Regiment	Newly-recreated 1st NC Regiment in April of 1781. Took over this unit when Maj. Thomas Pinketham Eaton was captured/killed at Ft. Grierson (Siege of Augusta, GA). Resigned soon thereafter.	Fort Motte (SC), Siege of Augusta (GA).
Smith, Robert	2nd NC Regiment	9/1/1775, a 1st Lieutenant. Resigned 10/21/1775. 12/21/1775, a Captain in NC Militia (2nd Salisbury District Minutemen). 4/16/1776, a Captain in the 4th NC Regiment. 1/9/1777, transferred to 3rd Continental Dragoons (VA), retired on 11/4/1778. 1780, a Lt. Colonel in Lincoln County Regiment of Militia. Aug. 1781, a Colonel in the newly-created NC State Legion.	Ft. Moultrie #1 (SC), Ft. George - Bald Head Island.
Smith, Samuel	2nd NC Regiment	5/3/1776, an Ensign.	
Smith, Samuel	4th NC Regiment	5/20/1776, a Private under Capt. Roger Moore, then under Capt. William Goodman for 3 years. 9/8/1778, a known Private under Capt. Joshua Bowman (1st NC Regiment). A Corporal on 12/1/1778. Discharged on 5/20/1779 at Paramus (NJ). From Orange County, NC. S39082.	Brandywine Creek (PA), Monmouth (NJ).
Smith, Samuel	4th NC Regiment	Dec. 1782, a Private under Capt. Anthony Sharpe. From Bladen County, NC. R9815.	
Smith, Samuel	7th NC Regiment	1777, a Private under Capt. Thomas Brickell.	
Smith, Simon	3rd NC Regiment	4/20/1776, a Private under Capt. Thomas Granbury for 2-1/2 years. 9/10/1778, a known Private under Capt. Thomas Armstrong (2nd NC Regiment). Wounded at the battle of Brandywine Creek (PA). Discharged on 11/10/1778. S39079.	Brandywine Creek (PA).
Smith,	4th NC	1782, a Private under Capt. Joseph T. Rhodes	

Name	1st Unit	Year / Rank / Served Under / Notes	Known Battles
Stephen	Regiment	for 18 months. Dec. 1782, transferred to Capt. Thomas Evans. Died 6/3/1783 while in service. From Dobbs (what is now Greene) County, NC.	
Smith, Thomas	1st NC Regiment	6/10/1776, an Assistant Armourer under Lt./Capt. Robert Ralston. Dropped from the rolls in Sep. 1777.	
Smith, Thomas	1st NC Regiment	5/9/1781, a Private under Capt. Griffith John McRee. Dropped from the rolls in Jan. 1782-sick. Received clothing on 5/24/1782. From Caswell County.	
Smith, Thomas	2nd NC Regiment	11/26/1776, a Corporal under Capt. William Caswell. A Sergeant in Aug. 1778 under Capt. Robert Fenner (2nd NC Regiment). A Private on 11/19/1779. Discharged on 2/8/1780.	
Smith, Thomas	2nd NC Regiment	5/15/1781, a Private under Capt. Tilghman Dixon. Discharged on 5/21/1782 (1st NC Regiment). Wounded at the battle of Eutaw Springs (SC) - lost his right leg below the knee. From Cumberland County, NC. S10019.	Eutaw Springs (SC).
Smith, Thomas	3rd NC Regiment	1777, a Private under Capt. Thomas Granbury. Deserted in Aug. 1777.	
Smith, Thomas	3rd NC Regiment	7/20/1778, a Corporal in the Colonel's Company (Col. Jethro Sumner) for nine months.	
Smith, Thomas	4th NC Regiment	7/25/1776, a Private under Capt. William Goodman for three years. 9/8/1778, a known Private in the Colonel's Company (Col. Thomas Clark) (1st NC Regiment) led by Capt. John Gambier Scull. Discharged on 7/25/1779.	
Smith, Thomas	5th NC Regiment	10/24/1776, a Private under Capt. John Enloe. 9/10/1778, a known Private under Capt. Thomas Armstrong (2nd NC Regiment). 3/12/1779, re-enlisted under Capt. Thomas Armstrong.	
Smith, Thomas	5th NC Regiment	11/26/1776, a Corporal under Capt. William Caswell. A Sergeant in Aug. 1778. A Private on 11/19/1779. Discharged on 2/8/1780.	
Smith, Thomas	6th NC Regiment	A Private under Capt. George Dougherty. Dropped from the rolls in Jan. 1778.	
Smith, William	1st NC Regiment	8/1/1777, a Sergeant under Capt. John Brown.	
Smith, William	1st NC Regiment	9/8/1778, a known Private under Capt. Joshua Bowman.	
Smith, William	1st NC Regiment	5/15/1781, a Private under Capt. Anthony Sharpe. Discharged on 4/15/1782 (4th NC Regiment).	
Smith, William	1st NC Regiment	4/15/1781, a Sergeant under Lt./Capt. Benjamin Bailey. A Private on 2/26/1782. Discharged on 4/15/1782 (3rd NC Regiment).	
Smith, William	2nd NC Regiment	12/18/1776, a Private under Capt. Benjamin Williams for 3 years. 9/9/1778, a known Private in the Lt. Colonel's Company (Lt. Col. Selby Harney). Discharged on 1/30/1780.	
Smith, William	2nd NC Regiment	1777, a Private under Capt. James Gee. Died on 2/28/1778.	
Smith,	2nd NC	5/13/1777, a Private, unit unknown. 9/9/1778,	

Name	1st Unit	Year / Rank / Served Under / Notes	Known Battles
William	Regiment	under Capt. Benjamin Andrew Coleman. 3/12/1779, re-enlisted under Capt. Benjamin Andrew Coleman.	
Smith, William	2nd NC Regiment	12/7/1776, a Sergeant under Capt. William Fenner. A Private in Aug. 1778. 9/8/1778, a known Private in the Lt. Colonel's Company (Lt. Colonel Selby Harney). 3/12/1779, a known Private under Capt. Benjamin Andrew Coleman.	
Smith, William	2nd NC Regiment	7/20/1778, a Private under Maj. Reading Blount for nine months.	
Smith, William	2nd NC Regiment	March 1781, a Private under Lt. Richard Andrews and Lt. Thomas Finney. After the battle of Eutaw Springs, he was placed under Capt. Benjamin Bailey (1st NC Regiment). Discharged from the 3rd NC Regiment on 6/1/1782 at Bacon's Bridge, SC. Earlier in NC Militia. From Bertie County, NC. W17828.	Eutaw Springs (SC).
Smith, William	2nd NC Regiment	1782, a Private under Capt. Benjamin Andrew Coleman for 3 months (?). Earlier in VA Militia and NC Militia. From Northampton Co. S4853.	
Smith, William	3rd NC Regiment	12/22/1776, a Private under Capt. James Emmett. Discharged on 2/1/1780.	
Smith, William	3rd NC Regiment	1777, a Private under Capt. Pinketham Eaton. Died on 3/31/1778.	
Smith, William	3rd NC Regiment	7/20/1778, a Private under Capt. Kedar Ballard for nine months. Dropped from the rolls in Oct. 1778	
Smith, William	3rd NC Regiment	7/20/1778, a Private in the Lt. Colonel's Company (Lt. Col. William Lee Davidson) led by Lt./Capt. George "Gee" Bradley for nine months. 4/23/1779, a known Private in the Lt. Colonel's Company (Lt. Col. Robert Mebane) led by Capt. George "Gee" Bradley.	
Smith, William	3rd NC Regiment	7/1/1779, a Private under Capt. Kedar Ballard. Deserted on 10/19/1779.	
Smith, William	3rd NC Regiment	1781, a Private under Capt. Edward Yarborough. Discharged on 5/1/1782.	
Smith, William	4th NC Regiment	1779, a Private under Capt. Matthew Ramsey for nine months. Dropped from the rolls in Oct. 1779.	
Smith, William	5th NC Regiment	1777, a Private under Capt. Henry Darnell. Deserted in Aug. 1777.	
Smith, William	5th NC Regiment	1777, a Private under Capt. Simon Alderson. Dropped from the rolls in Feb. 1778.	
Smith, William	5th NC Regiment	3/1/1779, a Private under Capt. Joseph Montford for nine months. Discharged on 12/1/1779.	
Smith, William	7th NC Regiment	1777, a Private under Capt. John McGlaughan. Deserted in Apr. 1777.	
Smith, William	7th NC Regiment	2/20/1777, a Sergeant under Capt. John Macon. Died on 4/9/1778.	
Smith, William	10th NC Regiment	5/13/1777, a Private under Capt. Silas Stevenson.	

Name	1st Unit	Year / Rank / Served Under / Notes	Known Battles
Smithers, Garnet	1st NC Regiment	5/9/1781, a Private under Capt. Alexander Brevard.	
Smithwick, Edward	5th NC Regiment	1777, a Private under Capt. Henry Darnell. Dropped from the rolls in Feb. 1778.	
Smithwick, William	3rd NC Regiment	7/20/1778, a Sergeant under Capt. Francis Child for nine months.	
Smithwick, William	5th NC Regiment	1777, a Corporal under Capt. Henry Darnell. A Sergeant in Oct. 1777. Back to Corporal in Jan. 1778. Back to Sergeant in Nov. 1779.	
Snead, William	2nd NC Regiment	1781, a Private under Capt. Benjamin Carter. Deserted on 9/15/1781. aka William Sneed.	
Snead, Zadock	2nd NC Regiment	4/25/1781, a Private under Capt. Benjamin Carter. Discharged on 4/25/1782.	
Sneet, George	3rd NC Regiment	7/20/1778, a Private in the Colonel's Company (Col. Jethro Sumner) for nine months.	
Snell, James	7th NC Regiment	4/14/1777, a Private under Capt. Joseph Walker. 9/8/1778, a known Private under Capt. Tilghman Dixon (1st NC Regiment). Born on 5/20/1759. S42020.	Brandywine Creek (PA), Germantown (PA), Monmouth (NJ), Siege of Charleston 1780 (SC).
Sniles, Anthony	4th NC Regiment	2/7/1782, a Private under Capt. James Mills. Died on 8/7/1782.	
Snipes, William	3rd NC Regiment	1781, a Private under Capt. Clement Hall. Discharged on 4/1/1782 (2nd NC Regiment).	
Snow, Spencer	DQMG	1780 a Tailor under Col. Nicholas Long (Deputy QM General).	
Snowden, Nathaniel		6/5/1778, a Private, regiment and unit unknown.	
Snowden, William	7th NC Regiment	11/28/1776, a 1st Lieutenant under Capt. John Poynter. Resigned prior to 12/18/1776. From Edenton District.	
Snowden, Zebulon	10th NC Regiment	5/22/1777, a Private under Capt. Isaac Moore. Deserted in Apr. 1778.	
Snutman, William	4th NC Regiment	1781, a Private under Capt. Joseph T. Rhodes. Discharged on 4/25/1782.	
Snyder, Christopher	1st NC Regiment	6/1/1781, a Private under Capt. William Lytle. Discharged on 6/1/1782 (4th NC Regiment).	
Soddin, John	7th NC Regiment	1777, a Private under Capt. Thomas Brickell. Sep. 1777, a Private under Capt. Dempsey Gregory (10th NC Regiment).	
Solomon, Lazarus	4th NC Regiment	1781, a Private under Capt. Joseph T. Rhodes. Discharged on 4/25/1782.	
Solomon, William	1st NC Regiment	5/21/1781, a Private under Capt. Anthony Sharpe. Discharged on 5/21/1782 (4th NC Regiment).	
Sorrell, Lewis	2nd NC Regiment	2/12/1781, a Private under Capt. Benjamin Carter. Dropped from the rolls sometime prior to 1782.	
Sorrell, Thomas	2nd NC Regiment	7/20/1778, a Private under Maj. Reading Blount for nine months. Died on 9/16/1778.	
Southall,	1st NC	4/25/1781, a Private under Capt. Robert	

Name	1st Unit	Year / Rank / Served Under / Notes	Known Battles
Furney	Regiment	Raiford. Discharged on 4/26/1782 (2nd NC Regiment).	
Southall, Stephen	2nd NC Regiment	4/1/1777, an Ensign. 4/1/1778, a Lieutenant under Capt. Benjamin Andrew Coleman. Resigned on 10/4/1778.	
Southerland, Daniel	NC Artillery	1/2/1777, a Matross under Capt. Thomas Clark as NC Provincial Troops. 7/10/1777, on Continental Line. Also on 9/9/1778. aka Daniel Sutherland, Daniel Sullivan.	
Southerland, Ransom	4th NC Regiment	4/23/1776, a Paymaster.	
Soward, Isaac	1st NC Regiment	5/9/1781, a Private under Capt. Alexander Brevard.	
Sowell, Isaac	1st NC Regiment	A Private under Capt. Anthony Sharpe then under Capt. Elijah Moore. Died in the General Hospital, probably in 1781, and buried at Ashley Hill, SC.	
Sowell, Isaac	4th NC Regiment	1782, a Private under Capt. William Lytle. Deserted on 11/25/1782.	
Sowell, William	3rd NC Regiment	9/10/1782, a Private under Capt. Benjamin Bailey for 18 months.	
Sowell, Zadock	7th NC Regiment	1/8/1777, a Private under Capt. Henry Dawson. June 1778, under Capt. James Read (1st NC Regiment). Avoided being captured during the Fall of Charleston, SC. S38394.	Siege of Charleston 1780 (SC).
Spain, Augustin	5th NC Regiment	1777, a Sergeant under Capt. John Enloe. Dropped from the rolls in Feb. 1778. 1779, a Captain in NC Militia. From Pitt County, NC.	
Spain, Epps	2nd NC Regiment	1777, a Corporal under Capt. Edward Vail, Jr. A Sergeant on 12/1/1777. A Private in June 1778 in the Colonel's Company (Col. John Patten) led by Capt. John Braddock. Back to Sergeant in Oct. 1778. Back to Private on 1/1/1780.	
Spain, Thomas	1st NC Regiment	8/1/1782, a Musician under Capt. Joshua Hadley for 18 months. Probably the same man as directly below.	
Spain, Thomas	8th NC Regiment	2/10/1777, a Musician under Capt. James May, then under Capt. Francis Tartanson for three years. A Private in June 1778. 9/9/1778, a known Private under Capt. John Ingles (2nd NC Regiment). Back to Musician in Nov. 1778. POW at the Fall of Charleston, SC. From Pitt County, NC. R9949.	Brandywine Creek (PA), Germantown (PA), Siege of Charleston 1780 (SC).
Spain, William	8th NC Regiment	3/10/1777, a Fifer under Capt. James May, then under Capt. Francis Tartanson. 9/9/1778, a known Private in the Lt. Colonel's Company (Lt. Col. Selby Harney) (2nd NC Regiment). POW at the Fall of Charleston, SC. From Pitt County, NC. Born on 9/28/1763. W6148.	Brandywine Creek (PA), Germantown (PA), Monmouth (NJ), Siege of Charleston 1780 (SC).
Spann, James	NC Light Dragoons	April 1776, a Private under Capt. James Jones, then under Capt. Cosmo Medici for 2-1/2 years. On 3/7/1777, this unit was placed on NC	

Name	1ˢᵗ Unit	Year / Rank / Served Under / Notes	Known Battles
		Continental Line. Enlisted at Halifax, NC. 1779, in SC Militia. S9484.	
Spear, David	2ⁿᵈ NC Regiment	12/26/1776, a Sergeant under Capt. James Gee for 3 years. A Sergeant Major on 6/1/1778 in the Colonel's Company (Col. John Patten) led by Capt. John Craddock. Back to Sergeant on 2/1/1779. aka David Spiers.	
Spear, Joseph	3ʳᵈ NC Regiment	7/20/1778, a Private in the Colonel's Company (Col. Jethro Sumner) for nine months. See Joseph Spears below, may be the same man.	
Spear, Samuel	3ʳᵈ NC Regiment	7/20/1778, a Private in the Colonel's Company (Col. Jethro Sumner) for nine months. Probably the same man as Samuel Spears below.	
Spear, Spencer	1ˢᵗ NC Regiment	Jan. 1782, a Private under Capt. Anthony Sharpe. Deserted on 6/13/1783 (4th NC Regiment) (?).	
Spearman, George	2ⁿᵈ NC Regiment	1782, a Private under Capt. Robert Raiford for 18 months.	
Spearpoint, Joseph	1ˢᵗ NC Regiment	5/9/1781, a Private under Capt. Alexander Brevard. 3/26/1782, transferred to the Artificers.	
Spearpoint, Joseph	4ᵗʰ NC Regiment	1777, a Private under Capt. William Temple Coles. Dropped from the rolls in March 1778. Probably the same man as directly above.	
Spears, Joseph	1ˢᵗ NC Regiment	5/9/1781, a Private under Capt. Griffith John McRee. Deserted on 6/1/1781.	
Spears, Joseph	1ˢᵗ NC Regiment	5/28/1781, a Private under Capt. Alexander Brevard. Discharged on 5/25/1782 (3rd NC Regiment) near Charleston, SC. Enlisted at Salisbury, NC. S39086.	Eutaw Springs (SC).
Spears, Kindred	1ˢᵗ NC Regiment	4/12/1781, a Private under Capt. William Lytle. Discharged on 4/12/1782 (4th NC Regiment).	
Spears, Samuel	3ʳᵈ NC Regiment	May 1778, a Private under Lt./Capt. George "Gee" Bradley for nine months - served twelve months. Discharged May 25, 1779 at Halifax, NC. Enlisted in Halifax County, NC. S39085.	
Spears, Willis	1ˢᵗ NC Regiment	1782, a Corporal under Capt. Peter Bacot for 18 months.	
Speer, John	3ʳᵈ NC Regiment	7/20/1778, a Private under Capt. Kedar Ballard for nine months. Dropped from the rolls in Oct. 1778. aka John Spreer.	
Spellman, Asa	3ʳᵈ NC Regiment	7/20/1778, a Private under Capt. Michael Quinn for nine months. Discharged at Halifax, NC. S42022.	Near West Point (NY).
Spellman, Simon	3ʳᵈ NC Regiment	6/28/1779, a Private under Capt. George "Gee" Bradley.	
Spellmore, Aaron	1ˢᵗ NC Regiment	5/5/1781, a Private under Capt. Anthony Sharpe. Discharged on 4/5/1782 (4th NC Regiment) at Wilmington, NC. aka Aaron Spelmore. S42023.	Siege of Ninety-Six 1781 (SC), Eutaw Springs (SC).
Spellmore, Jacob	1ˢᵗ NC Regiment	5/15/1781, a Private under Capt. Anthony Sharpe. Dropped from the rolls sometime during 1781. aka Jacob Spelmore.	
Spellmore,	2ⁿᵈ NC	4/3/1781, a Private under Capt. Benjamin	

Name	1st Unit	Year / Rank / Served Under / Notes	Known Battles
Jacob	Regiment	Carter. Discharged on 4/25/1782. aka Jacob Spelmore.	
Spells, Henry	3rd NC Regiment	5/5/1776, a Private under Capt. Pinketham Eaton for 2-1/2 years. Discharged on 12/1/1778.	
Spence, Incell	3rd NC Regiment	7/20/1778, a Private under Lt./Capt. George "Gee" Bradley for nine months.	
Spence, Jabez	7th NC Regiment	1777, a Private under Capt. John Poynter. Dropped from the rolls in Oct. 1777. aka Jabez Spense.	
Spence, James	NC Light Dragoons	May 1776, a Private under Capt. James Jones, then Capt. Cosmo Medici for 2-1/2 years. On 3/7/1777, this unit was placed on the NC Continental Line. Discharged in the Fall of 1778. S36782.	Ft. Moultrie #1 (SC).
Spencer, Robert	1st NC Regiment	5/15/1781, a Private under Capt. Anthony Sharpe. Discharged on 4/15/1782 (4th NC Regiment). aka Robert Spenser.	
Spencer, Solomon	2nd NC Regiment	7/20/1778, a Private under Maj. Reading Blount for nine months.	
Spenney, William		5/13/1777, a Private, regiment and unit unknown, enlisted for three years. 9/8/1778, a known Private under Capt. John Sumner (1st NC Regiment).	
Spicer, James	5th NC Regiment	1777-1778, a Paymaster.	
Spicer, John	2nd NC Regiment	1777, a Private under Capt. John Armstrong. Dropped from the rolls in Nov. 1777. A black man.	
Spicer, John	2nd NC Regiment	12/11/1776, a Paymaster. Later, a Colonel in NC Militia. From Onslow County, NC.	
Spiers, Absalom	2nd NC Regiment	11/20/1776, a Private under Capt. William Fenner for three years. 9/9/1778, a known Private in the Lt. Colonel's Company (Lt. Col. Selby Harney). Discharged in the Spring of 1783 at Halifax, NC. Born on 11/1/1760. On the official rolls as Absalom Spires. W17860.	
Spights, Joseph	1st NC Regiment	9/8/1778, an Artificer under Capt. James Read.	
Spikes, Joseph	1st NC Regiment	1776, a Private under Capt. Joshua Bowman.	
Spikes, Joseph	1st NC Regiment	1777, a Private under Capt. Lawrence Thompson. Deserted on 9/17/1777. Rejoined in Nov. 1777.	
Spill, Henry	2nd NC Regiment	9/9/1778, a known Private under Capt. Robert Fenner.	
Spilliards, Jesse	1st NC Regiment	1777, a Private under Capt. John Brown. Deserted in March 1783 (?).	
Spindler, Boston	4th NC Regiment	10/20/1777, a Private under Capt. William Temple Coles for three years. 9/8/1778, a known Private under Capt. John Sumner (1st NC Regiment). 3/12/1779, re-enlisted for the duration of the war in the Colonel's Company (Col. Thomas Clark) (1st NC Regiment) led by Capt. John Gambier Scull.	

Name	1ˢᵗ Unit	Year / Rank / Served Under / Notes	Known Battles
Spires, Thomas	1ˢᵗ NC Regiment	5/17/1781, a Private under Capt. Robert Raiford. Discharged on 5/17/1782 (2nd NC Regiment).	
Spittards, Jesse	1ˢᵗ NC Regiment	9/8/1778, a known Private under Capt. Joshua Bowman.	
Sport, William	2ⁿᵈ NC Regiment	1782, a Private under Capt. Benjamin Carter. Deserted on 4/29/1783 (?).	
Sportman, William	1ˢᵗ NC Regiment	4/28/1781, a Private under Capt. Griffith John McRee. Transferred to the Legion in Aug. 1781 (State or Lee's-unknown).	
Spratt, Thomas	9ᵗʰ NC Regiment	11/28/1776, a 1st Lieutenant under Capt. Michael Henderson. From Salisbury District.	
Sprewell, Godfrey	1ˢᵗ NC Regiment	5/3/1781, a Private under Lt./Capt. Benjamin Bailey. Discharged on 5/3/1782 (3rd NC Regiment).	
Springer, Levi	4ᵗʰ NC Regiment	7/18/1777, a known Private under Capt. John Nelson. Court-martialed for deserting his company and enlisting in a VA unit. Found guilty and sentenced to receive 50 lashes.	
Springfield, Aaron	1ˢᵗ NC Regiment	1782, a Private under Capt. Alexander Brevard for 18 months. aka Aaron Stringfield.	
Springs, Micajah	4ᵗʰ NC Regiment	March 1781, a Private under Capt. George Dougherty, then under Capt. Joseph T. Rhodes. Discharged on 5/25/1782 at Wilmington, NC. From Duplin County, NC. W1327.	Eutaw Springs (SC).
Springs, Sedgewick	1ˢᵗ NC Regiment	6/10/1776, an Assistant Armourer under Lt./Capt. Robert Ralston. Promoted to Superintendent of Artificers after the battle of Germantown, PA. Dropped from the rolls in Nov. 1777 (?). From Wilmington, NC. Born on 4/2/1756 in NC. W6147.	Germantown (PA), Monmouth (NJ).
Squares, Thomas	1ˢᵗ NC Regiment	8/25/1778, a Private under Capt. Anthony Sharpe.	
Squires, Andrew	1ˢᵗ NC Regiment	1781, a Private under Capt. Anthony Sharpe. Discharged on 12/16/1782 (4th NC Regiment).	
Squires, John	2ⁿᵈ NC Regiment	5/22/1777, a Private under Capt. James Martin for 3 years. 9/9/1778, a known Private under Capt. Benjamin Andrew Coleman. aka John Squares.	
Squires, Skidmore	2ⁿᵈ NC Regiment	11/20/1777, a Private under Capt. Charles Allen for three years. 9/10/1778, a known Private under Capt. Thomas Armstrong. Deserted on 2/14/1779.	
Sriven, James	3ʳᵈ NC Regiment	7/20/1778, a Private under Maj. Thomas Hogg for nine months.	
Stacey, John	1ˢᵗ NC Regiment	6/14/1781, a Private under Capt. Thomas Donoho. Discharged on 6/14/1782. aka John Stacy.	
Stafford, John	6ᵗʰ NC Regiment	A Private under Capt. Griffith John McRee. Dropped from the rolls in Nov. 1778.	
Stafford, Josiah	10ᵗʰ NC Regiment	7/5/1777, a Private under Capt. Abraham Sheppard, Jr. for three years. 9/9/1778, a known Private under Capt. John Ingles (2nd NC Regiment). POW at the Fall of Charleston, SC -	Monmouth (NJ), Siege of Charleston 1780 (SC).

Name	1st Unit	Year / Rank / Served Under / Notes	Known Battles
		escaped. Enlisted in Dobbs County, NC. S39091.	
Stallings, Moses	1st NC Regiment	4/6/1781, a Corporal under Capt. William Lytle. Discharged on 4/6/1782 (4th NC Regiment). Earlier in NC Militia. From Franklin County, NC. On the official rolls as Moses Stallions. S31997.	Eutaw Springs (SC).
Stamey, John	1st NC Regiment	August 1782, a Private under Capt. Peter Bacot for 18 months. Discharged in July 1783 at 10-Mile House, SC. From Lincoln County. Earlier in SC unit. On the official rolls as John Staymay. aka John Stayway. S7611.	
Standen, Jim	1st NC Regiment	2/26/1778, a known Private under Capt. Howell Tatum.	
Standfast, William	4th NC Regiment	1777, a Sergeant under Capt. James Williams. A QM Sergeant on 9/11/1777. Back to Sergeant in Aug. 1778. A Private in Oct. 1777. 9/8/1778, a known Private in the Colonel's Company (Col. Thomas Clark) (1st NC Regiment) led by Capt. John Gambier Scull. A Private on 4/1/1779. Deserted on 1/1/1780.	
Standing, Thomas	2nd NC Regiment	10/20/1775, an Ensign. 5/3/1776, a Lieutenant. Jan. 1777, a Captain. Resigned on 5/15/1777. aka Thomas Standiss, Thomas Standin.	
Standley, James	2nd NC Regiment	1782, a Private under Capt. Robert Raiford for 18 months.	
Standley, James	8th NC Regiment	1777, a Private under Capt. John Walsh. Dropped from the rolls in Jan. 1778. aka Joseph Standley.	
Standley, Jonathan	5th NC Regiment	1779, a Private under Capt. Joseph Montford. Discharged in Sep. 1779.	
Stanfield, James	2nd NC Regiment	7/18/1781, a Corporal and a Sergeant under Capt. Benjamin Andrew Carter for 12 months. Discharged on 6/20/1782. From Rowan County, NC. Born on 2/4/1753 in Edgecombe County, NC. aka James Stanphill. W158.	Eutaw Springs (SC).
Stanfield, Thomas	4th NC Regiment	7/18/1780, a Private under Capt. Benjamin Carter for 12 months. Served nine months, contracted Smallpox, furloughed. Later joined NC Militia. From Rowan County, NC. R10047.	
Stanley, Robert	8th NC Regiment	1777, a Sergeant under Capt. John Walsh. A Private in Jan. 1778. Dropped from the rolls in Feb. 1778.	
Stanly, Hugh		An Invalid Pensioner since the Revolutionary War. 1821, living in Jones County. S14594.	
Stanmul, Peter	3rd NC Regiment	1/22/1780, a Private under Capt. George "Gee" Bradley.	
Stansberry, Luke	5th NC Regiment	6/12/1779, a Private under Maj. Reading Blount for 3 years. 1780, this unit was in the 3rd NC Regiment. POW at the Fall of Charleston, SC - escaped after being held about a year. From Caswell County, NC. aka Luke Stansbury. W165.	Siege of Charleston 1780 (SC).
Stanton, John	1st NC	1777, a Sergeant under Capt. Howell Tatum. A	

Name	1st Unit	Year / Rank / Served Under / Notes	Known Battles
	Regiment	Private in June 1778. 9/8/1778, a known Private under Capt. Howell Tatum. Back to Sergeant in March 1780. aka John Standen.	
Stanton, John	3rd NC Regiment	7/20/1778, a Private under Capt. Michael Quinn for nine months. Discharged on 7/14/1778 (?).	
Staples, Robert	6th NC Regiment	A Musician under Capt. George Dougherty. Dropped from the rolls in Jan. 1778. Jan. 1779, in the 5th NC Regiment, unit unknown.	
Starke, Henry	2nd NC Regiment	5/2/1781, a Private under Capt. Robert Raiford. Discharged on 5/2/1782 (2nd NC Regiment).	
Starritt, James	4th NC Regiment	1775, a 2nd Lieutenant in the Salisbury District Minutemen. 4/17/1776, a 2nd Lieutenant under Capt. John Nelson and Col. Thomas Polk. Got very sick, resigned. 1781, a Private in the NC Militia. From Guilford County, NC. aka James Starrat, James Sarrat. R10084.	
Stearn, Moses	10th NC Regiment	2/1/1778, a Private under Capt. James Wilson for three years. 9/8/1778, a known Private in the Major's Company (Maj. John Baptiste Ashe) (1st NC Regiment). 3/12/1779, re-enlisted for the duration of the war in the same unit. aka Moses Stern.	
Stedman, Benjamin	5th NC Regiment	1775, a Captain in the New Bern District Minutemen. 4/16/1776, a Captain in the 5th NC Regiment. Late Sep. 1777, in NC as a recruiter for the 5th NC Regiment. Dropped from the rolls in Jan. 1778. One source says he was from Hyde County, NC.	Brandywine Creek (PA).
Steed, Jesse	4th NC Regiment	1777, a Sergeant under Capt. James Williams. Dropped from the rolls in Jan. 1778.	
Steed, Jesse	4th NC Regiment	6/1/1781, an Ensign under Capt. Mathew Ramsey. 7/13/1781, Regimental QM. 9/8/1781, a Lieutenant under Capt. Matthew Ramsey. Transferred to 1st NC Regiment on 2/6/1782. Retired on 1/1/1783. From Franklin County, NC. R11616.	
Steel, Anthony		Aug. 1778, a Private, regiment and unit unknown. Dropped from the rolls in Sep. 1778.	
Steel, William	1st NC Regiment	1778, a Corporal under Capt. Thomas Donoho for 2 years. W6196.	Briar Creek (GA), Stono Ferry (SC).
Steel, William	3rd NC Regiment	3/6/1782, a Private under Capt. Samuel Jones for 12 months.	
Steeley, Jeremiah	4th NC Regiment	May 1778, a Private under Capt. William Goodman for nine months. S42028.	
Steelman, John	2nd NC Regiment	1777, a Private under Capt. Clement Hall. Deserted in Aug. 1777.	
Steelman, William	3rd NC Regiment	3/6/1782, a Private under Capt. William Armstrong for 12 months. Earlier in NC Militia. From Rowan County, NC. W8888.	
Steem, William	1st NC Regiment	1/7/1777, a Private under Lt./Capt. Anthony Sharpe. Dropped from the rolls in Feb. 1779.	
Steigerwaldt, Frederick	1st NC Regiment	1781, a Private under Lt./Capt. Elijah Moore for 12 months. From Rowan County, NC. Born on	Siege of Ninety-Six

618

Name	1st Unit	Year / Rank / Served Under / Notes	Known Battles
		8/10/1762 in Germany. S7647.	1781 (SC), Eutaw Springs (SC).
Stellard, Peter	4th NC Regiment	1782, a Private under Capt. Anthony Sharpe for 18 months.	
Step, John	1st NC Regiment	6/14/1781, a Private under Capt. Thomas Donoho. Dropped from the rolls sometime during 1781.	
Stephens, Henry	1st NC Regiment	6/14/1781, a Private under Capt. Thomas Donoho. Discharged on 6/14/1782. On the official rolls as Henry Stevens. Earlier and later in NC Militia. From Orange County, NC. W6189.	Eutaw Springs (SC).
Stephens, John	5th NC Regiment	1776, a Private under Captain Simon Alderson for 2-1/2 years. 9/9/1778, a known Private under Capt. John Ingles (2nd NC Regiment). POW at the Fall of Charleston, SC - a prisoner for 14 months. Earlier in NC Militia. From Pitt County, NC. On the official rolls as John Stevens. S42025.	Brandywine Creek (PA), Germantown (PA), Monmouth (NJ), Siege of Charleston 1780 (SC).
Stephens, Richard	DQMG	1780, a Wagoner under Col. Nicholas Long (Deputy QM General).	
Stephenson, William	DQMG	1780, a Saddler on the roll of Capt. Solomon Wood (NC Light Dragoons) - this seems to be for convenience only. 8/23/1781, a Super-intendent of Leather Workers under Col. Nicholas Long (Deputy QM General), making saddles, harnesses, caps, etc. aka William Stephinson.	
Steptoe, John	3rd NC Regiment	7/20/1778, a Sergeant in the Colonel's Company (Col. Jethro Sumner) for nine months.	
Steptoe, Thomas	1st NC Regiment	1782, a Musician under Capt. Peter Bacot. Deserted on 6/18/1783 (?).	
Sterling, Elisha	4th NC Regiment	1781, a Private under Capt. Joseph T. Rhodes. Discharged on 6/4/1782.	
Sterling, Isaac	2nd NC Regiment	1777, a Private under Capt. Edward Vail, Jr. A Sergeant on 12/5/1777. Died on 4/5/1778.	
Sterling, Robert	4th NC Regiment	A Private under Capt. Joseph T. Rhodes. Also under Capt. William Armstrong (1st NC Regiment). Discharged on 4/25/1782. Earlier in NC Militia. From Wayne County, NC. S7637.	Eutaw Springs (SC).
Sterling, Seth	1st NC Regiment	1/10/1782, a Private under Capt. James Mills for 12 months. Furloughed on 1/6/1783 at Wilmington, NC. Earlier in NC Militia. From Duplin County, NC. R10118.	
Stevens, Benjamin	1st NC Regiment	A Private under Capt. Joshua Bowman, dates unknown.	
Stevens, Benjamin	2nd NC Regiment	5/19/1781, a Private under Capt. Benjamin Carter. Discharged on 5/19/1782.	
Stevens, Henry	4th NC Regiment	1/5/1782, a Private under Capt. Joseph T. Rhodes. Discharged on 1/5/1783.	
Stevens, Hugh	2nd NC Regiment	4/25/1781, a Private under Capt. Benjamin Carter. Discharged on 4/25/1782.	

619

Name	1st Unit	Year / Rank / Served Under / Notes	Known Battles
Stevens, James	4th NC Regiment	1/5/1782, a Private under Capt. Joseph T. Rhodes. Discharged on 1/5/1783.	
Stevens, John	3rd NC Regiment	7/1/1779, a Corporal under Capt. Michael Quinn for 18 months.	
Stevens, Joseph	1st NC Regiment	3/5/1777, a Private under Lt./Capt. Howell Tatum. 9/8/1778, a known Private under Capt. Howell Tatum.	
Stevens, Lewis	3rd NC Regiment	5/5/1776, a Private under Capt. Thomas Granbury for 2-1/2 years. Discharged on 11/10/1778.	
Stevens, Thomas	1st NC Regiment	1777, a Private under Capt. Joshua Bowman. Deserted in Aug. 1777.	
Stevens, Thomas	4th NC Regiment	1782, a Private under Capt. William Lytle for 18 months.	
Stevenson, Benjamin	6th NC Regiment	A Private under Capt. George Dougherty. 9/8/1778, a known Private under Capt. John Sumner (1st NC Regiment) - sick on that date at Valley Forge. Died in Feb. 1779.	
Stevenson, Hugh	10th NC Regiment	4/25/1777, a Private under Capt. Abraham Sheppard, Jr. 9/9/1778, a known Private in the Colonel's Company (Col. John Patten) (2nd NC Regiment) led by Capt. John Craddock. Transferred to the "Invalids" in Nov. 1779. aka Hugh Stephenson.	
Stevenson, James	8th NC Regiment	1777, a Sergeant under Capt. Francis Tartanson. Died on 2/12/1778. aka Joseph Stevenson.	
Stevenson, John	3rd NC Regiment	6/21/1779, a Private under Capt. Kedar Ballard for 18 months. Dropped from the rolls in Oct. 1779.	
Stevenson, Silas		11/28/1776, a 1st Lieutenant, unit unknown. 4/19/1777, a Captain under Col. Abraham Sheppard (10th NC Regiment). Retired on 6/1/1778. His name was Silas Ayres Stevenson, but many referred to him as Sears Stevenson. Earlier and later a Captain in NC Miltia. From Craven County, NC.	
Stevenson, William	2nd NC Regiment	1/1/1777, a Private under Capt. Benjamin Williams for 3 years.	
Steward, Daniel	1st NC Regiment	5/15/1781, a Private under Capt. Anthony Sharpe. Discharged on 4/15/1782 (4th NC Regiment).	
Steward, John	10th NC Regiment	8/20/1777, a Private under Capt. Andrew Vanoy. 9/9/1778, a known Private under Capt. Clement Hall (2nd NC Regiment). 3/12/1779, re-enlisted under Capt. Clement Hall. aka John Stewart.	
Steward, William	2nd NC Regiment	6/27/1777, a Musician under Capt. John Armstrong for three years. A Private in March 1778. Deserted on 1/1/1780.	
Stewart, Charles	1st NC Regiment	1777, a Sergeant under Capt. Lawrence Thompson. Dropped from the rolls in Jan. 1778.	
Stewart, Charles	4th NC Regiment	Dec. 1782, a Private under Capt. Anthony Sharpe. Furloughed on 5/26/1783. From Bladen County, NC. Born on 1/16/1761 in Bladen	

Name	1st Unit	Year / Rank / Served Under / Notes	Known Battles
		(what is now Robeson) County, NC. W6171.	
Stewart, Charles	5th NC Regiment	1775, an Ensign in the New Bern District Minutemen. 4/17/1776, an Ensign under Capt. Benjamin Stedman and Col. Edward Buncombe. 7/23/1777, a 1st Lieutenant under Capt. William Caswell. Transferred to the 2nd NC Regiment on 6/1/1778. 1/1/1779, a Captain-Lieutenant under Col. John Patten. POW at the Fall of Charleston, exchanged on 6/14/1781 (another source claims he was not exchanged until 11/26/1782). A full Captain on 5/18/1781 in the 2nd NC Regiment. Several sources claim he was killed at the battle of Eutaw Springs, SC – but other records indicate he was alive and on active duty in 1782. aka Charles Steward. BLWt2228-300.	Siege of Charleston 1780 (SC), Eutaw Springs (SC).
Stewart, Coldwell	1st NC Regiment	4/2/1781, a Private under Capt. William Lytle. Deserted on 7/5/1781. Re-enlisted in Jan. 1782.	
Stewart, Daniel	3rd NC Regiment	1/4/1782, a Private under Capt. Samuel Jones. Died on 10/4/1782 (1st NC Regiment).	
Stewart, Dempsey	4th NC Regiment	1782, a Private under Capt. Joseph T. Rhodes for 18 months. Dec. 1782, transferred to Capt. Thomas Evans. From Northampton County, NC. W3734.	
Stewart, George	2nd NC Regiment	11/28/1776, a 2nd Lieutenant under Capt. Thomas McCrory. From Salisbury District.	
Stewart, George	8th NC Regiment	1777, a Sergeant under Capt. Francis Tartanson. Dropped from the rolls in Sep. 1777.	
Stewart, James	2nd NC Regiment	7/24/1777, a Private, unit unknown. 9/9/1778, a known Private in the Lt. Colonel's Company (Lt. Col. Selby Harney). 3/12/1779, re-enlisted in the Lt. Colonel's Company (Lt. Col. Selby Harney).	
Stewart, James	4th NC Regiment	1782, a Private under Capt. William Lytle for 18 months.	
Stewart, James	9th NC Regiment	1777, a Private under Capt. Thomas McCrory. Discharged on 11/20/1777. aka Joseph Stewart.	
Stewart, James	10th NC Regiment	7/24/1777, a Private under Capt. Armwell Herron. aka Joseph Stewart.	
Stewart, John	3rd NC Regiment	7/20/1778, a Private under Maj. Thomas Hogg for nine months.	
Stewart, Joseph	9th NC Regiment	11/28/1776, a 1st Lieutenant under Capt. Matthew Ramsey. From Hillsborough District.	
Stewart, Nicholas	2nd NC Regiment	4/10/1777, a Lieutenant.	
Stewart, Samuel	1st NC Regiment	5/26/1781, a Private under Capt. Griffith John McRee. Deserted the same day - 5/26/1781.	
Stewart, Thomas	1st NC Regiment	Sep. 1775, a Private under Capt. George Lee Davidson for six months - served ten months. Then in NC Militia. From Rowan County, NC. R10172.	Great Cane Brake (SC), Snow Campaign (SC), Moore's Creek Bridge.
Stewart,	NC	12/1/1776, a Matross under Capt. John Vance as	

Name	1st Unit	Year / Rank / Served Under / Notes	Known Battles
William	Artillery	NC Provincial Troops. 7/10/1777, on Continental Line. 11/16/1777, under Capt. John Kingsbury. 5/1/1778, in same unit. May 1778, at Lancaster, PA. 9/10/1778, in same unit. Deserted on 4/1/1779. One source says he enlisted on 4/17/1777. aka William Stuard.	
Stewart, William	1st NC Regiment	1777, a Private under Capt. Robert Ralston. Dropped from the rolls in Sep. 1777.	
Stewart, William	2nd NC Regiment	6/27/1777, a Private under Capt. Robert Fenner for three years. 9/9/1778, a known Private under Capt. Robert Fenner. 3/12/1779, re-enlisted under Capt. Robert Fenner. Discharged in June 1780. The official rolls assert that he deserted in January 1780. A colored man from Northampton County, NC. R10173.	Monmouth (NJ).
Still, James	1st NC Regiment	5/17/1781, a Private under Lt./Capt. Benjamin Bailey. Discharged on 5/17/1782 (3rd NC Regiment).	
Still, John	1st NC Regiment	8/1/1782, a Sergeant under Capt. Joshua Hadley for 18 months.	
Stiller, Peter	4th NC Regiment	1782, recruited by Capt. Edward Yarborough (3rd NC Regiment) for 18 months and transferred after drilling for a month to Capt. Anthony Sharpe. From Rowan County, NC.	
Stillwell, David	1st NC Regiment	5/26/1777, a Private under Capt. Robert Ralston, soon transferred to Capt. John Sumner for three years. 9/8/1778, a known Private under Capt. John Sumner. POW/wounded at the Fall of Charleston, exchanged in summer of 1781 at Jamestown, VA. Discharged when he reached Halifax, NC. Enlisted in Guilford County, NC. Born on 10/29/1755. aka David Stilwell. S36816.	Monmouth (NJ), Siege of Charleston 1780 (SC).
Stillwell, Jacob	1st NC Regiment	1776, a Fife Major under Capt. Henry "Hal" Dixon, then under Capt. Tilghman Dixon. Discharged on 2/1/1778. 5/15/1781, a Musician again under Capt. Tilghman Dixon (2nd NC Regiment). A Private on 1/1/1782. Discharged on 5/21/1782 (1st NC Regiment). Received clothing on 5/24/1782. From Caswell County. Born on 1/25/1755 in Bedford County, VA. S31993.	Ft. Moultrie #1 (SC), Brandywine Creek (PA), Germantown (PA), Eutaw Springs (SC).
Stocks, Joshua	1st NC Regiment	5/15/1781, a Private under Capt. Anthony Sharpe. Dropped from the rolls sometime during 1781.	
Stokeley, Peter	3rd NC Regiment	3/1/1782, a Private under Capt. Samuel Jones for 12 months. A Corporal in Sep. 1782 (1st NC Regiment).	
Stokeley, Thomas	4th NC Regiment	2/6/1782, a Private under Capt. James Mills for 12 months.	
Stokes, Drury	4th NC Regiment	1777, a Private under Capt. Thomas Harris. Discharged on 10/31/1777.	
Stokes, Henry	3rd NC Regiment	7/20/1778, a Private under Capt. Kedar Ballard for nine months. Dropped from the rolls in Oct.	

Name	1st Unit	Year / Rank / Served Under / Notes	Known Battles
		1778.	
Stokes, Joel	10th NC Regiment	5/6/1777, a Musician under Capt. James Wilson for three years. A Private in June 1778. 9/8/1778, a known Private in the Major's Company (Maj. John Baptiste Ashe) (1st NC Regiment). A Corporal on 3/20/1779. Back to Private in Nov. 1779.	
Stokes, Richard	3rd NC Regiment	Oct. 1781, a Private under Capt. Samuel Jones for 12 months. Served nine months then got very sick, hired a substitute for remaining three months. From Franklin County, NC. S42026.	
Stokes, Young	4th NC Regiment	1777, a Private under Capt. Thomas Harris. Discharged on 10/31/1777.	
Stollings, James	5th NC Regiment	1777, a Private under Capt. John Pugh Williams. Dropped from the rolls in Feb. 1778.	
Stone, Benjamin	2nd NC Regiment	7/20/1778, a Private under Maj. Reading Blount for nine months.	
Stone, John	1st NC Regiment	4/28/1781, a Private under Capt. Griffith John McRee. Discharged on 4/28/1782.	
Storry, William	8th NC Regiment	1777, a Private under Capt. Francis Tartanson. Dropped from the rolls in Sep. 1777.	
Story, Caleb	5th NC Regiment	4/5/1778, a Private under Capt. Benjamin Andrew Coleman. Died on 6/16/1778 (2nd NC Regiment)	
Stove, Warren	4th NC Regiment	1781, a Private under Capt. Joseph T. Rhodes. Discharged on 5/14/1782.	
Strader, George	1st NC Regiment	1776, a Private under Capt. Henry "Hal" Dixon. Deserted in 1776.	
Strader, George	4th NC Regiment	May 1776, a Private under Capt. John Nelson for three years. June 1778, in 1st NC Regiment under Capt. Griffith John McRee. Wounded/POW at the Fall of Charleston, escaped after two months. Later, in NC Militia. From Guilford County, NC. R10253.	Monmouth (NJ), Siege of Charleston 1780 (SC).
Stradford, John	1st NC Regiment	9/8/1778, a known Private under Capt. Joshua Bowman.	
Stradley, Edward	2nd NC Regiment	1777, a Corporal under Capt. Charles Allen. 9/10/1778, under Capt. Thomas Armstrong. A Private on 5/15/1779. POW at Ft. Lafayette, NY on 6/1/1779.	Ft. Lafayette (NY).
Stradley, James	10th NC Regiment	5/4/1777, a Private under Capt. Abraham Sheppard, Jr. POW at Ft. Lafayette, NY on 6/1/1779. Rejoined in Nov. 1779. aka Joseph Stradley.	Ft. Lafayette (NY).
Stranfield, William	2nd NC Regiment	1782, a Private under Capt. Benjamin Carter. Deserted on 12/7/1782.	
Strange, Ephraim	3rd NC Regiment	6/24/1779, a Private under Capt. Michael Quinn for 18 months. Deserted in Dec. 1779.	
Strange, James	1st NC Regiment	5/15/1777, a Private under Capt. Joshua Bowman for three years. 9/8/1778, a known Private in the Major's Company (Maj. John Baptiste Ashe).	
Strange, William	3rd NC Regiment	4/2/1782, a Private under Capt. Benjamin Bailey for 12 months.	

Name	1st Unit	Year / Rank / Served Under / Notes	Known Battles
Stranges, James	6th NC Regiment	1777, a Musician under Capt. Thomas Donoho. A Private in June 1778. 1779, a Private under Maj. Reading Blount (5th NC Regiment). aka James Stranger.	
Strawn, Richard	2nd NC Regiment	Dec. 1782, a Private under Capt. Clement Hall. Deserted on 5/1/1783 (?).	
Street, John	4th NC Regiment	1777, a Sergeant under Capt. Thomas Harris. Discharged 10/31/1777.	
Strickland, John	1st NC Regiment	4/12/1781, a Private under Capt. William Lytle. Confined four nights for desertion during July 1781. Discharged on 4/12/1782 (4th NC Regiment).	
Strickland, Marmaduke	1st NC Regiment	4/12/1781, a Private under Capt. William Lytle. Confined four nights for desertion during July 1781. Dropped from the rolls sometime during 1781. aka Marmaduke Strickley.	
Strickler, John	3rd NC Regiment	3/15/1777, a Private under Capt. Thomas Granbury for 2-1/2 years. Discharged on 11/10/1778.	
Stricklin, Frederick	2nd NC Regiment	5/12/1781, a Private under Capt. Tilghman Dixon for 12 months. Mustered at Hillsborough, NC. Discharged on 5/26/1782 (1st NC Regiment) at Guilford, NC. S39092.	Eutaw Springs (SC).
Striker, John	2nd NC Regiment	5/10/1776, a Private, unit unknown. 9/9/1778, a known Private in the Colonel's Company (Col. John Patten) led by Capt. John Craddock.	
Stringer, Hezekiah	2nd NC Regiment	1782, a Private under Capt. Benjamin Andrew Coleman for 18 months.	
Stringer, John	4th NC Regiment	2/8/1782, a Corporal under Capt. James Mills. A Private in Dec. 1782.	
Stringer, John	10th NC Regiment	6/3/1777, a Musician under Capt. Abraham Sheppard, Jr. 9/9/1778, a known Private in the Major's Company (Maj. Hardy Murfree) (2nd NC Regiment). 3/12/1779, re-enlisted in the Major's Company (Maj. Hardy Murfree).	
Stringer, Josiah	5th NC Regiment	12/1/1776, a Private under Capt. Reading Blount for 3 years. 9/9/1778, a known Private in the Lt. Colonel's Company (Lt. Col. Selby Harney) (2nd NC Regiment). A Corporal in Nov. 1778. A Sergeant in June 1779. Discharged on 2/1/1780.	
Stringer, Minger	1st NC Regiment	5/5/1781, a Private under Capt. Anthony Sharpe. Discharged on 4/5/1782 (4th NC Regiment).	
Stringer, Noah	1st NC Regiment	1781, a Private under Capt. Anthony Sharpe. Discharged on 10/28/1782 (4th NC Regiment).	
Stringer, Samuel	5th NC Regiment	5/11/1776, a Sergeant under Capt. William Caswell for 2-1/2 years. 9/9/1778, a known Sergeant in the Major's Company (Maj. Hardy Murfree) (2nd NC Regiment). Discharged on 10/1/1778.	
Stringer, William	1st NC Regiment	1781, a Private under Capt. Anthony Sharpe. Discharged on 4/5/1782 (4th NC Regiment). (Might be mixed up with Minger Stringer above	

Name	1st Unit	Year / Rank / Served Under / Notes	Known Battles
		- seen both names for same man.)	
Stroud, John	9th NC Regiment	5/15/1777, a Private under Lt./Capt. Anthony Sharpe for three years. 9/8/1778, a known Private in the Major's Company (Maj. John Baptiste Ashe) (1st NC Regiment) - sick in camp on that date. 3/12/1779, re-enlisted for the duration of the war in the same unit.	
Stroud, Lott	10th NC Regiment	5/12/1777, a Private under Capt. Andrew Vanoy for three years. 9/8/1778, a known Private in the Major's Company (Maj. John Baptiste Ashe) (1st NC Regiment) - sick in the flying hospital on that date.	
Stuart, John	2nd NC Regiment	12/10/1781, a Private under Capt. Benjamin Coleman then under Capt. Samuel Jones (1st NC Regiment) for 12 months. Earlier in NC Militia. From Duplin County, NC. On the official rolls as John Stewart. S7615.	
Stunn, William		1/17/1777, regiment, unit and rank unknown, enlisted for three years. 9/8/1778, a known Private in the Lt. Colonel's Company (Lt. Col. Robert Mebane) (1st NC Regiment) led by Capt. Joshua Bowman - sick on that date at Valley Forge. aka William Stumm.	
Sturdivant, Charles	1st NC Regiment	May 1782, a Sergeant under Capt. Peter Bacot for 18 months. Discharged in July or August 1783 in Wilmington, NC. On the official rolls as Charles Sturtevant. S36326.	
Sturt, Henry	3rd NC Regiment	5/15/1776, a Private under Capt. Thomas Granbury for 2-1/2 years. Discharged on 11/10/1778.	
Styles, John	1st NC Regiment	4/12/1781, a Private under Capt. William Lytle. Deserted on 7/6/1781.	
Styrewall, Frederick	1st NC Regiment	4/28/1781, a Private under Capt. Griffith John McRee. Discharged on 4/28/1782.	
Suddell, Richard	10th NC Regiment	5/18/1777, a Private under Capt. Abraham Sheppard, Jr.	
Suet, Samuel	1st NC Regiment	4/2/1781, a Private under Capt. William Lytle. Deserted on 7/6/1781.	
Sugg, John	5th NC Regiment	6/16/1779, a Private under Capt. Joseph Montford for three years. From Dobbs County, NC.	
Suggs, Eligood	2nd NC Regiment	1/1/1782, a Private under Capt. Benjamin Andrew Coleman for 12 months.	
Suggs, Ezekiel	2nd NC Regiment	1/1/1782, a Private under Capt. Benjamin Andrew Coleman for 12 months.	
Suggs, George	5th NC Regiment	1775, a 1st Lieutenant in the New Bern District Minutemen. 4/17/1776, a 1st Lieutenant under Capt. John Enloe and Col. Edward Buncombe.	
Sugins, Joseph	4th NC Regiment	1779, a Private under Capt. Matthew Ramsey. Died in Sep. 1779.	
Sullanaver, John	NC Artillery	5/9/1776, a Gunner under Capt. John Vance as NC Provincial Troops. 7/10/1777, on Continental Line. 11/16/1777, under Capt. John Kingsbury. 5/1/1778, in same unit. May 1778,	

Name	1ˢᵗ Unit	Year / Rank / Served Under / Notes	Known Battles
		sick in camp. 9/16/1778, in same unit. ska John Silanavar, John Sullinavis, John Silvanovas.	
Sullivan, Barnabas	10ᵗʰ NC Regiment	8/31/1777, a Private under Capt. Andrew Vanoy for three years. In June of 1778, under Capt. Clement Hall (2nd NC Regiment). Dropped from the rolls in June 1779. Rejoined in Nov. 1779. POW at the Fall of Charleston, SC - exchanged after 18 months. Enlisted in Edgecombe County, NC. On the official rolls as Barnabas Stertevant. W20077.	Monmouth (NJ), Siege of Charleston 1780 (SC).
Sullivan, James	1ˢᵗ NC Regiment	1781, a Corporal under Capt. William Walton. Discharged on 5/25/1782.	
Sullivan, John	1ˢᵗ NC Regiment	1781, a Private under Capt. Robert Raiford. Charged with desertion, claimed he was an indentured servant. Died on 4/3/1783.	
Sullivan, John	4ᵗʰ NC Regiment	1782, a Private under Capt. Joseph T. Rhodes for 18 months. Dec. 1782, transferred to Capt. Thomas Evans. Deserted on 6/21/1783 (?).	
Sullivan, Timothy	1ˢᵗ NC Regiment	Nov. 1779, a Private under Capt. Howell Tatum. aka Tenig Sullivan.	
Sullivant, Owen	4ᵗʰ NC Regiment	2/7/1782, a Private under Capt. James Mills for 12 months. Discharged in January 1783 at Wilmington, NC. From Wayne County, NC. On the official rolls as Owen Sullivan. W11580.	
Summers, George	2ⁿᵈ NC Regiment	5/15/1781, a Sergeant under Capt. Tilghman Dixon for 12 months. Discharged on 5/21/1782 (1ˢᵗ NC Regiment) at Bacon's Bridge, SC. Received clothing on 5/24/1782. Enlisted in Caswell County, NC. W6606.	Eutaw Springs (SC).
Summers, James	1ˢᵗ NC Regiment	1777, a Musician under Capt. Henry "Hal" Dixon. A Fife Major on 6/1/1778. A Private on 12/1/1778. A Sergeant on 2/1/1780. POW at the Fall of Charleston, escaped. From Caswell County, NC. W2192.	Monmouth (NJ), Siege of Charleston 1780 (SC), Eutaw Springs (SC).
Summers, Leven	5ᵗʰ NC Regiment	Jan. 1779, a Private under Maj. Pinketham Eaton. Died on 5/20/1779.	
Sumner, Francis	8ᵗʰ NC Regiment	5/15/1777, a Private under Capt. Michael Quinn. 9/9/1778, a known Private in the Major's Company (Maj. Hardy Murfree) (2nd NC Regiment). Dec. 1782, a Private under Capt. Benjamin Carter (2nd NC Regiment).	
Sumner, James	NC Light Dragoons	4/16/1776, a Lieutenant under Capt. Martin Phifer as Provincial troops. 3/7/1777, this unit placed on the NC Continental Line.	
Sumner, Jethro	3ʳᵈ NC Regiment	4/15/1776, Colonel/Commandant of the 3ʳᵈ NC Regiment. 9/3/1776, leave of absence, duration unknown. Early 1778, the 5th NC Regiment was folded into the 3rd NC Regiment, Jethro Sumner commanded. Promoted to Brigadier General on 1/9/1779. Sick and absent during the Siege of Charleston, SC. In the Fall of 1780, he was pursuaded to take over most of the NC Militia, reporting to Maj. Gen. Richard Caswell.	Ft. Moultrie #1 (SC), Brandywine Creek (PA), Germantown (PA), Monmouth (NJ), Stono Ferry (SC),

Name	1st Unit	Year / Rank / Served Under / Notes	Known Battles
		When Caswell was dismissed in favor of BG William Smallwood (MD), he soon resigned (Mid-Oct. 1780). In early 1781, Maj. Gen. Nathanael Green convinced him to ressurrect the NC Continentals, which he then led. Served to the end of the war. Was a Major in the Halifax District Minutemen 1775-1776. Originally from Edgecombe County, then lived in Warren County, NC.	Eutaw Springs (SC).
Sumner, John	1st NC Regiment	3/28/1776, an Ensign. 7/7/1776, a 2nd Lieutenant. 2/5/1777, a 1st Lieutenant under Capt. Henry "Hal" Dixon. 7/10/1778, a Captain under Col. Thomas Clark. During 1779, this unit was in the 5th NC Regiment. POW at Williamson's Plantation on 7/12/1780 until 11/26/1782. Retired on 1/1/1783. aka John Summers.	Monmouth (NJ), Briar Creek (GA), Stono Ferry (SC), Siege of Charleston 1780 (SC), Williamson's Plantation (SC).
Sumner, Richard	3rd NC Regiment	7/20/1778, a Private in the Lt. Colonel's Company (Lt. Col. William Lee Davidson) led by Lt./Capt. George "Gee" Bradley for nine months. 4/23/1779, a known Private in the Lt. Colonel's Company (Lt. Col. Robert Mebane) led by Capt. George "Gee" Bradley.	
Surls, Robert	3rd NC Regiment	7/20/1778, a Private under Lt./Capt. George "Gee" Bradley for nine months. Earlier in NC Militia. From Dobbs (Wayne) County, NC. On the official rolls as Robert Surles. S7659.	
Sutherland, George	1st NC Regiment	Sep. 1775, a Drummer under Capt. Henry "Hal" Dixon for three years. A Sergeant in Oct. 1777. Dropped from the rolls in Jan. 1778. From Caswell County, NC. Moved to Albemarle County, VA, joined VA unit. aka George Southerland. S7667.	
Sutherland, James	10th NC Regiment	6/1/1777, a Private under Capt. Isaac Moore for three years. 9/8/1778, a known Artificer in the Lt. Colonel's Company (Lt. Col. Robert Mebane) (1st NC Regiment) led by Capt. Joshua Bowman.	
Sutherland, John	6th NC Regiment	April 1776, a Private under Lt. Thomas White and Capt. Archibald Lytle. Dropped from the rolls in Oct. 1777. Later in NC Militia, unit(s) unknown. S39098.	Brandywine Creek (PA), Germantown (PA).
Sutherland, William	1st NC Regiment	1777, a Private under Capt. Henry "Hal" Dixon. Dropped from the rolls in Sep. 1777. aka William Southerland.	
Sutton, James	2nd NC Regiment	12/16/1776, a 2nd Lieutenant. Resigned on 3/10/1778.	
Sutton, James	5th NC Regiment	8/1/1779, a Private under Maj. Reading Blount for 12 months. Deserted in Oct. 1779. aka Joseph Sutton.	
Sutton, Jeremiah	NC Artillery	8/12/1776, a Sergeant under Capt. John Vance as NC Provincial Troops. 7/10/1777, on Continental Line. 11/16/1777, under Capt. John	

Name	1st Unit	Year / Rank / Served Under / Notes	Known Battles
		Kingsbury. 5/1/1778, in same unit. 9/16/1778, in same unit.	
Sutton, Ralph	3rd NC Regiment	7/20/1778, a Private under Lt./Capt. George "Gee" Bradley for nine months.	
Swales, Enoch	3rd NC Regiment	1778, a Private under Capt. Kedar Ballard. Deserted on 7/15/1778.	
Swan, Nimrod	5th NC Regiment	6/18/1777, a Regimental QM. Dropped from the rolls in Jan. 1778. aka Nimrod Swann.	
Swanson, John	1st NC Regiment	5/12/1781, a Private under Capt. Tilghman Dixon. After the battle of Eutaw Springs, attached to serve under Lt. Col. William Washington's 3rd Regiment of Light Dragoons. Discharged on 5/26/1782 (1st NC Regiment). Earlier in NC Militia. From Wake County, NC. W1900.	Eutaw Springs (SC).
Swearing-ham, Van	4th NC Regiment	1777, a Private under Capt. Thomas Harris. Discharged on 10/31/1777.	
Sweat, Abraham	1st NC Regiment	4/25/1781, a Private under Capt. Robert Raiford. Discharged on 4/25/1782 (2nd NC Regiment).	
Sweat, David	10th NC Regiment	7/12/1777, a Private under Capt. Abraham Sheppard, Jr. 9/9/1778, a known Private under Capt. Benjamin Andrew Coleman (2nd NC Regiment). 3/12/1779, re-enlisted under Capt. Benjamin Andrew Coleman. S42031.	Monmouth (NJ), Stony Point (NY).
Sweat, William	3rd NC Regiment	4/20/1776, a Private under Capt. Pinketham Eaton for 2-1/2 years. 9/9/1778, a known Private in the Major's Company (Maj. Hardy Murfree) (2nd NC Regiment). Discharged on 10/20/1778.	
Sweatman, William	4th NC Regiment	1781, a Private under Capt. Joseph Thomas Rhodes for 12 months. Discharged at Bacon's Bridge, SC. From Duplin County, NC. W6116.	Eutaw Springs (SC).
Sweeny, Thomas	3rd NC Regiment	1781, a Private under Capt. Edward Yarborough. Discharged on 5/2/1782.	
Sweet, George		7/20/1778, a Private in the Colonel's Company. Either the 2nd or 3rd NC Regiment.	
Swenet, James	3rd NC Regiment	1777, a Private under Capt. Thomas Granbury. Deserted in Aug. 1777.	
Swett, Allen	1st NC Regiment	June 1782, a Private under Capt. Peter Bacot for 18 months. Enlisted in Halifax County, NC. Discharged in July 1783 at Haddrell's Point, SC. aka Allen Sweat. W16.	
Swindle, Jesse	5th NC Regiment	1777, a Private under Capt. Simon Alderson. Dropped from the rolls in March 1778.	
Swindle, Solomon	1st NC Regiment	1781, a Private under Capt. Alexander Brevard. Discharged on 7/11/1782 (3rd NC Regiment).	
Swink, John	1st NC Regiment	11/1/1781, a Private under Capt. William Armstrong for 12 months, principally engaged at Salisbury, NC repairing wagons, shoeing horses for the army, and guarding the stores. After about four weeks, he was transferred to Capt. Edward Yarborough (3rd NC Regiment). From Rowan County, NC. W2022.	

Name	1st Unit	Year / Rank / Served Under / Notes	Known Battles
Swinney, Jesse	8th NC Regiment	Nov. 1776, a Private under Capt. Frederick Hargett for three years. 6/1/1778, under Capt. Robert Raiford (2nd NC Regiment). POW at the Fall of Charleston, SC, escaped after six months. Rejoined - unit not known. From Craven County, NC. R10364.	Brandywine Creek (PA), Germantown (PA), Monmouth (NJ), Siege of Charleston 1780 (SC).
Swinson, Richard	5th NC Regiment	April 1776, a Private under Capt. Benjamin Stedman for 12 months. Discharged on 4/24/1777. From Tyrrell County, NC. S42033.	
Swinson, William	2nd NC Regiment	2/1/1777, a Private, unit unknown. 9/9/1778, a known Private in the Major's Company (Maj. Hardy Murfree). 3/12/1779, re-enlisted in the Major's Company (Maj. Hardy Murfree).	
Syas, Jesse	1st NC Regiment	6/1/1781, a Private under Capt. William Lytle. Discharged on 6/1/1782 (4th NC Regiment).	
Sykes, Adam	5th NC Regiment	1777, a Private under Capt. John Pugh Williams. Dropped from the rolls in Feb. 1778.	
Sykes, Dempsey	1st NC Regiment	5/25/1781, a Musician under Capt. Thomas Donoho. Discharged on 5/25/1782.	
Sykes, Henry	1st NC Regiment	5/17/1781, a Private under Lt./Capt. Benjamin Bailey. Discharged on 5/17/1782 (3rd NC Regiment).	
Sykes, James	DQMG	1780, an Artificer under Col. Nicholas Long (Deputy QM General). Made Gunstocks.	
Sykes, James	1st NC Regiment	July 1782, a Private under Capt. Peter Bacot, then under Capt. Robert Raiford (2nd NC Regiment) for 18 months. Furloughed after 12 months. Living in Halifax County, NC when he enlisted. Born in August of 1760 or 1762 in Norfolk County, VA. S1892.	
Sykes, Sampson	1st NC Regiment	4/12/1781, a Private under Capt. William Lytle. Found guilty of forging a pass, received 100 lashes.	
Sykes, Sampson	3rd NC Regiment	7/20/1778, a Private under Capt. John Baker. Deserted three days later on 7/23/1778.	
Sykes, William	DQMG	1780, a Saddler on the roll of Capt. Solomon Wood (NC Light Dragoons) - this seems to be for convenience only. 8/23/1781, a Leather worker under Col. Nicholas Long (Deputy QM General), making saddles, harnesses, caps, etc. aka William Sikes.	
Sykes, Zedekiah	7th NC Regiment	2/4/1777, a Private under Capt. John Poynter for 3 years. 9/8/1778, a known Private under Capt. Tilghman Dixon (1st NC Regiment). Discharged on 2/8/1780.	
Sypress, Robert	3rd NC Regiment	5/15/1776, a Sergeant under Capt. James Emmett. Discharged in Oct. 1778.	
Syrus, James	4th NC Regiment	A Private under Capt. John Nelson. Discharged on 10/13/1777.	
Taborn, Joel	2nd NC Regiment	1776, served under Lt./Capt. Manlove Tarrant as a "servant." 6/14/1781, a Private under Capt. Thomas Donoho (1st NC Regiment). Jan. 1782,	Siege of Charleston 1780 (SC),

Name	1st Unit	Year / Rank / Served Under / Notes	Known Battles
		re-enlisted for the duration of the war. A free man of color from Nash County, later in Northampton County, NC. aka Joel Taburn, Joel Tabourn. S42037.	Siege of Ninety-Six 1781 (SC), Eutaw Springs (SC).
Tabourne, Burrell	1st NC Regiment	4/5/1781, a Private under Capt. William Lytle. Discharged on 4/5/1782 (4th NC Regiment). From Nash County, NC. S7694.	
Taburn, William	6th NC Regiment	1776, a Private under Capt. Jesse Saunders, Lt. Col. William Taylor, traded his wagon and team of horses to tend the crops of another man. Later in NC Militia. From Granville County, NC. On the official rolls as William Tayburn. A free man of color. aka William Taborn. W18115.	
Tailor, William	1st NC Regiment	1777, a Private under Capt. Howell Tatum. Deserted on 7/25/1777.	
Talbert, John	4th NC Regiment	1782, a Private under Capt. Thomas Evans for 18 months.	
Talton, James	1st NC Regiment	1781, a Private under Capt. Robert Raiford. Discharged on 9/13/1782 (2nd NC Regiment).	
Talton, James	2nd NC Regiment	1777, a Private under Capt. Clement Hall. Dropped from the rolls in Jan. 1778.	
Talton, Josiah	1st NC Regiment	6/1/1781, a Private under Capt. William Lytle. Discharged on 6/1/1782 (4th NC Regiment).	
Talton, William	5th NC Regiment	1777, a Private under Capt. Benjamin Andrew Coleman. Dropped from the rolls in Jan. 1778.	
Tankesley, William	2nd NC Regiment	5/15/1781, a Private under Capt. Tilghman Dixon for 12 months. Dropped from the rolls sometime during 1781. Received clothing on 5/24/1782. From Caswell County. aka William Tanksly.	
Tann, Drewry	1st NC Regiment	8/1/1782, a Private under Capt. Joshua Hadley for 18 months. From Wake County, NC. A free man of color. aka Drewry Tan. S19484.	
Tann, Ephraim	3rd NC Regiment	7/20/1778, a Private under Capt. John Baker for nine months.	
Tann, James	3rd NC Regiment	7/20/1778, a Private under Capt. Michael Quinn. Dropped from the rolls sometime during 1779.	
Tanner, Jennings	1st NC Regiment	6/14/1781, a Private under Capt. Thomas Donoho. Discharged on 6/14/1782.	
Tapley, Thomas	1st NC Regiment	5/26/1781, a Private under Capt. Alexander Brevard.	
Tapp, George	1st NC Regiment	1777, a Private under Capt. Howell Tatum. Discharged on 12/10/1778.	
Tarbarra, Samuel	1st NC Regiment	8/1/1782, a Private under Capt. Joshua Hadley for 18 months.	
Tarlton, John	3rd NC Regiment	4/1/1782, a Private under Capt. Samuel Jones. Deserted on 9/1/1782 (1st NC Regiment).	
Tarlton, Josiah	3rd NC Regiment	9/13/1782, a Private under Capt. Benjamin Bailey for 18 months.	
Tarlton, William	5th NC Regiment	5/4/1776, a Private under Capt. William Ward, enlisted for 12 months - served 20 months, being retained until Xmas of 1777. 4/30/1777,	Brandywine Creek (PA), Germantown

Name	1st Unit	Year / Rank / Served Under / Notes	Known Battles
		under Capt. Benjamin Andrew Coleman. From Johnston County, NC, where he enlisted. S7693.	(PA).
Tarrant, Manlove	2nd NC Regiment	5/3/1776, an Ensign under Capt. John Heritage. 6/8/1776, a 2nd Lieutenant under Capt. John Heritage. 5/15/1777, a 1st Lieutenant under Capt. Edward Vail, Jr. 10/24/1777, a Captain. Sep. 1777, left in NC to continue recruiting for 2nd NC Regiment. Retired 6/1/1778.	Ft. Moultrie #1 (SC).
Tart, Thomas	2nd NC Regiment	7/20/1778, a Private under Capt. Reading Blount for nine months. From Bertie County, NC. S7676.	
Tartanson, Francis	8th NC Regiment	1/16/1777, a Captain under Col. James Armstrong. June 1778, in 3rd NC Regiment. Resigned on 9/19/1778. aka Francis Tartarson.	Brandywine Creek (PA), Germantown (PA), Monmouth (NJ).
Tarver, Samuel	4th NC Regiment	1781, a Private under Capt. Joseph T. Rhodes for 18 months. Discharged in 1782 at Charleston, SC. W11594.	
Tate, James	1st NC Regiment	10/13/1775, a Chaplain. Brigade Chaplain for all NC Troops in the Northern Department on 6/1/1778. Served to the end of the war.	Moore's Creek Bridge [4].
Tate, Joseph	2nd NC Regiment	9/1/1775, a 1st Lieutenant under Capt. John Armstrong. 5/16/1776, a Captain under Col. Alexander Martin. Died on 6/2/1777.	Ft. Moultrie #1 (SC).
Tate, William	NC Light Dragoons	April 1776, a trooper in the 3rd Company of Light Horse under Capt. James Jones then Capt. Cosmo Medici for 2-1/2 years. This unit was placed on the Continental Line on 3/7/1777 until Jan. 1779. His term expired on 12/9/1778 and he was discharged. Enlisted while living in Wake County, NC. S3751.	
Tatum, Absalom	1st NC Regiment	9/1/1775, a Lieutenant first under Capt. John Walker. 6/29/1776, a Captain. Resigned on 9/19/1776. 1779, a Major in NC Militia - Hillsborough District Brigade. One source claims his first name was Abraham.	Moore's Creek Bridge [4].
Tatum, Howell	1st NC Regiment	9/1/1775, an Ensign. 1/4/1776, a 2nd Lieutenant. 3/28/1776, a 1st Lieutenant. 4/3/1777, a Captain under Col. Thomas Clark. POW at the Fall of Charleston, exchanged on 6/14/1781. Resigned 5/20/1782. R2027.	Moore's Creek Bridge, Brandywine Creek (PA), Germantown (PA), Monmouth (NJ), Near West Point (NY), Siege of Charleston 1780 (SC).
Tatum, James	9th NC Regiment	8/12/1777, an Ensign under Capt. Joel Brevard. 1/1/1778, a 2nd Lieutenant. Transferred to 3rd NC Regiment on 6/1/1778 under Capt. John Rochelle. 12/14/1779, a 1st Lieutenant. POW at	Siege of Charleston 1780 (SC).

Name	1st Unit	Year / Rank / Served Under / Notes	Known Battles
		the Fall of Charleston. On parole until his exchange, finally, on 11/26/1782. Resigned 1/1/1783. Brother of Capt. Howell Tatum. S39102.	
Tatum, John	7th NC Regiment	5/24/1777, a Private under Capt. Lemuel Ely. 9/8/1778, a known Private under Capt. Tilghman Dixon (1st NC Regiment). Later in NC Militia, unit and dates unknown. Enlisted in Granville County, NC. W999.	Monmouth (NJ), Siege of Charleston 1780 (SC).
Taunt, Jesse	10th NC Regiment	4/26/1777, a Private under Capt. Armwell Herron. 9/9/1778, a known Private under Capt. Robert Fenner (2nd NC Regiment).	
Taunt, Thomas	10th NC Regiment	4/15/1777, a Private under Capt. Armwell Herron. A Fifer in June 1778 under Capt. Robert Fenner (2nd NC Regiment). POW at the Fall of Charleston, held for 13 months and exchanged in Jamestown, VA. Discharged at Richmond, VA. From Craven County, NC. S42036.	Siege of Charleston 1780 (SC).
Taunt, William	10th NC Regiment	4/26/1777, a Sergeant under Capt. Armwell Herron. A Private in June 1778 under Capt. Robert Fenner (2nd NC Regiment).	
Tayburn, Allen	3rd NC Regiment	7/20/1778, a Private under Capt. John Baker. Deserted three days later on 7/23/1778.	
Taylor, Aaron	10th NC Regiment	4/1/1778, a Musician under Capt. Andrew Vanoy.	
Taylor, Abel	4th NC Regiment	1782, a Private under Capt. William Lytle for 18 months.	
Taylor, Abraham	2nd NC Regiment	9/9/1778, a known Private under Capt. Robert Fenner.	
Taylor, Abraham	3rd NC Regiment	3/1/1782, a Private under Capt. Samuel Jones for 12 months.	
Taylor, Abraham	5th NC Regiment	3/27/1777, a Private under Capt. William Caswell for 3 years.	
Taylor, Benjamin	2nd NC Regiment	1781, a Private under Capt. Benjamin Carter, then under Capt. Clement Hall (3rd NC Regiment) for 12 months. Discharged on 11/1/1782. Earlier in NC Militia. From Lincoln County, NC. S16000.	Eutaw Springs (SC).
Taylor, Benjamin	2nd NC Regiment	6/3/1781, a Corporal under Capt. Benjamin Carter.	
Taylor, Benjamin	4th NC Regiment	1782, a Corporal under Capt. Anthony Sharpe for 18 months. Deserted on 4/19/1783 (?).	
Taylor, Caleb	2nd NC Regiment	1778, a Private under Capt. Benjamin Andrew Coleman. Dropped from the rolls in Feb. 1779.	
Taylor, Charles	4th NC Regiment	1782, a Sergeant under Capt. Anthony Sharpe for 18 months. Deserted on 4/19/1783 (?).	
Taylor, Elias	10th NC Regiment	7/25/1777, a Musician under Capt. Armwell Herron. A Private in June 1778. Deserted on 8/25/1778.	
Taylor, Emanuel	1st NC Regiment	1781, a Private under Capt. Alexander Brevard. Discharged on 8/14/1782 (3rd NC Regiment).	
Taylor, Jacob	1st NC Regiment	8/1/1782, a Private under Capt. Joshua Hadley for 18 months.	

Name	1st Unit	Year / Rank / Served Under / Notes	Known Battles
Taylor, James	2nd NC Regiment	9/9/1778, a known Private under Capt. Robert Fenner.	
Taylor, James	4th NC Regiment	1782, a Private under Capt. William Lytle for 18 months.	
Taylor, James Jr.	5th NC Regiment	3/27/1777, a Private under Capt. William Caswell for 3 years.	
Taylor, James Sr.	5th NC Regiment	1777, a Private under Capt. William Caswell. Dropped from the rolls in Feb. 1778.	
Taylor, James	5th NC Regiment	3/28/1777, a Sergeant Major. Dropped from the rolls in Jan. 1778.	
Taylor, Jesse	5th NC Regiment	3/1/1779, a Private under Maj. Reading Blount for nine months. Discharged on 12/1/1779.	
Taylor, Jesse	10th NC Regiment	5/5/1777, a Private under Capt. Abraham Sheppard, Jr. Died on 3/20/1778. aka Jese Talor.	
Taylor, John	1st NC Regiment	7/4/1781, a Private under Capt. Robert Raiford. Discharged on 7/4/1782 (2nd NC Regiment).	
Taylor, John	1st NC Regiment	9/1/1775, an Ensign. Resigned in October 1775.	
Taylor, John	2nd NC Regiment	1777, a Private under Capt. James Gee. 9/9/1778, a known Private under Capt. John Ingles. Claims to have enlisted in Oct. 1775, but officers' names don't work out. From Camden County, NC. Enlisted at Jonesburgh, NC. S42038.	Brandywine Creek (PA), Germantown (PA), Monmouth (NJ), Stony Point (NY), Siege of Charleston 1780 (SC).
Taylor, John	4th NC Regiment	1777, a Musician under Capt. Joseph Phillips. Dropped from the rolls in June 1778.	
Taylor, John	4th NC Regiment	1781, under Capt. Benjamin Andrew Coleman (?), then soon transferred to Capt. William Lytle for 18 months. Discharged in the Spring of 1783. From Craven County, NC. S7688.	
Taylor, John	5th NC Regiment	6/30/1779, a Private under Capt. Joseph Montford. Deserted in Sep. 1779.	
Taylor, John	8th NC Regiment	7/24/1777, a Lieutenant and a Paymaster. Dropped from the rolls in Jan. 1778. Later, a QM, Lieutenant, and a Captain in NC Militia. From Orange County, NC. W18114.	
Taylor, Joseph	5th NC Regiment	A Private under Capt. Reading Blount. 9/9/1778, a known Private under Capt. John Ingles (2nd NC Regiment). Discharged on 1/30/1779.	
Taylor, Lewis	1st NC Regiment	10/22/1781, a Private under Capt. James Mills for 12 months.	
Taylor, Philip	6th NC Regiment	1775, a Captain in the Hillsborough District Minutemen. 4/17/1776, a Captain in 6th NC Regiment. Retired on 6/1/1778. Joined the 5th NC Regiment in early 1779. Early 1780, in 3rd NC Regiment under Lt. Col. Robert Mebane. POW at the Fall of Charleston, released fairly soon thereafter. Later in NC Militia as a	Brandywine Creek (PA), Germantown (PA), Stono Ferry (SC), Siege of Charleston

Name	1st Unit	Year / Rank / Served Under / Notes	Known Battles
		Colonel. From Granville County, NC. W18100.	1780 (SC).
Taylor, Sampson	1st NC Regiment	11/10/1778, a Private under Capt. Anthony Sharpe for nine months.	
Taylor, Samuel	DQMG	1780, an Express Rider under Col. Nicholas Long (Deputy QM General).	
Taylor, Samuel	1st NC Regiment	6/5/1781, a Private under Capt. Griffith John McRee. Discharged on 6/5/1782.	
Taylor, Thomas	7th NC Regiment	3/14/1777, a Private under Capt. James Vaughan. Deserted in Aug. 1777.	
Taylor, William	4th NC Regiment	1782, a Private under Capt. Thomas Evans for 18 months.	
Taylor, William	6th NC Regiment	4/15/1776, a Lt. Colonel under Col. John Alexander Lillington. Resigned on 2/2/1777.	
Taylor, William	10th NC Regiment	8/12/1777, a Private under Capt. Abraham Sheppard, Jr. Dropped from the rolls in June 1778. 1780, a Wagoner under Col. Nicholas Long (Deputy QM General).	
Tayner, Arthur	2nd NC Regiment	11/15/1776, a Private, unit unknown. 9/9/1778, a known Private in the Colonel's Company (Col. John Patten) led by Capt. John Craddock.	
Teal, Emanuel	3rd NC Regiment	7/20/1778, a Private under Capt. Francis Child for nine months. Enlisted while living in Pitt County, NC. Later lived in Anson County, NC. R10440.	
Teaner, James	1st NC Regiment	1781, a Private under Capt. William Walton. Discharged on 5/25/1782.	
Tear, William	NC Artillery	5/9/1776, a Gunner under Capt. John Vance as NC Provincial Troops. 7/10/1777, on Continental Line. 11/16/1777, under Capt. John Kingsbury. 5/1/1778, in same unit. 9/16/1778, in same unit. aka William Fear.	
Teder, Thomas	3rd NC Regiment	7/20/1778, a Private under Lt./Capt. George "Gee" Bradley for nine months.	
Tellet, Avery	2nd NC Regiment	1777, a Private under Capt. James Gee. POW at Ft. Lafayette on 6/1/1779. Rejoined in Nov. 1779.	Ft. Lafayette (NY).
Templeton, Thomas	9th NC Regiment	1777, a Sergeant, unit unknown. Dropped from the rolls in Jan. 1778. May 1779, joined the 5th NC Regiment, unit and rank unknown.	
Tennison, Absalom	3rd NC Regiment	1781, a Private under Capt. Edward Yarborough for 12 months. Discharged on 4/22/1782.	
Tennison, Matthew	3rd NC Regiment	9/10/1782, a Private under Capt. Benjamin Bailey for 18 months. Deserted on 6/21/1783 (?).	
Terrell, James		12/15/1777, a Private, unit unknown, enlisted for three years. 9/8/1778, a known Private in the Lt. Colonel's Company (Lt. Col. Robert Mebane) (1st NC Regiment) led by Capt. Joshua Bowman. aka James Terrill.	
Terrell, John	1st NC Regiment	6/14/1781, a Private under Capt. Thomas Donoho. Dropped from the rolls sometime during 1781.	
Terrell, Richmond	6th NC Regiment	A Private under Capt. Griffith John McRee, dates unknown. 9/8/1778, a known Private in	

Name	1st Unit	Year / Rank / Served Under / Notes	Known Battles
		the Colonel's Company (Col. Thomas Clark) (1st NC Regiment) led by Capt. John Gambier Scull. aka Richmond Terryl, Richmond Terrall.	
Terrell, Simon	4th NC Regiment	1777, a Private under Lt. Col. James Thackston, Captain unknown. Later in NC Militia. From Chatham County, NC. S32008.	
Terrell, William	2nd NC Regiment	9/9/1778, a Lieutenant under Capt. John Craddock in the Colonel's Company (Col. John Patten).	
Terry, David	3rd NC Regiment	7/20/1778, a Private under Lt./Capt. Joseph Montford for nine months.	
Terry, Pompey	1st NC Regiment	1782, a Private under Capt. Alexander Brevard for 18 months. Mar. 1783, transferred to ?	
Tesley, John	3rd NC Regiment	7/20/1778, a Private in the Lt. Colonel's Company (Lt. Col. William Lee Davidson) led by Lt./Capt. George "Gee" Bradley for nine months. Died on 10/24/1778.	
Thackston, James	4th NC Regiment	1775, a Colonel/Commandant of the Hillsborough District Minutemen. 4/15/ 1776, a Lt. Colonel under Col. Thomas Polk. Had a finger shot off at the battle of Stono Ferry (SC). Late 1779, in NC recruiting. Retired on 1/1/1781 with 1/2 pay. aka James Thaxton.	Brandywine Creek (PA), Germantown (PA), Stono Ferry (SC).
Tharp, Bishop	5th NC Regiment	1777, a Private under Capt. Simon Alderson. Dropped from the rolls in March 1778.	
Tharp, Charles	5th NC Regiment	6/1/1779, a Private under Capt. Joseph Montford. Deserted on 11/22/1779.	
Tharp, Eleazor	5th NC Regiment	6/1/1779, a Private under Maj. Reading Blount for nine months. Deserted in Oct. 1779.	
Tharp, James	3rd NC Regiment	7/20/1778, a Private in the Lt. Colonel's Company (Lt. Col. William Lee Davidson) led by Lt./Capt. George "Gee" Bradley for nine months. 4/23/1779, a known Corporal in the Lt. Colonel's Company (Lt. Col. Robert Mebane) led by Capt. George "Gee" Bradley.	
Tharp, John	5th NC Regiment	6/1/1779, a Private under Capt. Joseph Montford. Deserted on 11/22/1779.	
Thatcher, David	2nd NC Regiment	Jan. 1779, a Private in the Colonel's Company (Col. John Patten).	
Thaxton, William	3rd NC Regiment	1781, a Private under Capt. Edward Yarborough for 12 months. Discharged on 5/1/1782. Received clothing on 5/24/1782. Guarded the baggage during battle of Eutaw Springs (SC). Earlier in NC Militia. From Caswell County, NC. On the official rolls as William Thexton. R10483.	
Theames, Jonathan	3rd NC Regiment	5/25/1781, a Sergeant under Capt. Dennis Porterfield, then under Capt. Benjamin Bailey (1st NC Regiment) for 12 months. Discharged on 5/25/1782 (3rd NC Regiment) at Bacon's Bridge, SC. From Cumberland County, NC. On the official rolls as Jonathan Tims. S42042.	Eutaw Springs (SC).
Themnel, William	1st NC Regiment	1776, a Private under Capt. Joshua Bowman.	

Name	1st Unit	Year / Rank / Served Under / Notes	Known Battles
Therrell, Abraham	2nd NC Regiment	7/2/1777, a Private, unit unknown. 9/9/1778, a Private in the Major's Company (Maj. Hardy Murfree).	
Thom, Thomas	2nd NC Regiment	1777, a Private under Capt. James Martin. Died on 7/20/1778. aka Thomas Thow.	
Thomas, Abisha	1st NC Regiment	5/1/1777, the Deputy Muster Master General. Dropped from the rolls in Nov. 1777. 1780, a Lt. Colonel in NC Militia supporting Col. Nicholas Long (DQMG). From Orange County, NC.	
Thomas, Amos	1st NC Regiment	4/15/1781, a Private under Capt. Robert Raiford. Discharged on 4/25/1782 (2nd NC Regiment).	
Thomas, Amos	2nd NC Regiment	7/20/1778, a Private under Maj. Reading Blount for nine months. Discharged at Halifax, NC. From Bertie County, NC. S42041.	
Thomas, Asa	5th NC Regiment	4/29/1776, a Private under Capt. John Pugh Williams for 2-1/2 years. 9/9/1778, a known Private under Capt. Clement Hall (2nd NC Regiment). Discharged on 11/10/1778. From Wake County, NC. On the official rolls as Ashia Thomas. R10494.	
Thomas, Benjamin	9th NC Regiment	1777, a Private under Capt. Thomas McCrory. Dropped from the rolls in Jan. 1778.	
Thomas, Caleb	4th NC Regiment	Dec. 1776, a Private under Capt. William Goodman. 5/1/1777, a Private under Capt. Andrew Vanoy (10th NC Regiment). A Musician on 1/1/1778. 9/8/1778, a known Musician in the Colonel's Company (Col. Thomas Clark) (1st NC Regiment) led by Capt. John Gambier Scull. 3/12/1779, re-enlisted for the duration of the war in the same unit. POW at the Fall of Charleston, SC under Capt. Thomas Callendar. After being exchanged in August of 1781, a Drummer under Capt. Clement Hall. Back to a Private in Dec. 1782. Discharged in June 1783. BLWt1274-100, S46474.	Monmouth (NJ), Siege of Charleston 1780 (SC).
Thomas, James	1st NC Regiment	5/2/1781, a Private under Capt. Thomas Donoho. Discharged on 5/2/1782.	
Thomas, Jeremiah	3rd NC Regiment	7/20/1778, a Corporal under Capt. John Baker for nine months.	
Thomas, John	1st NC Regiment	11/10/1778, a Private under Capt. Anthony Sharpe for nine months.	
Thomas, John	2nd NC Regiment	3/3/1777, a Private under Capt. John Armstrong. 9/9/1778, a known Private under Capt. Robert Fenner.	
Thomas, John	2nd NC Regiment	9/9/1778, a known Private in the Lt. Colonel's Company (Lt. Col. Selby Harney).	
Thomas, John	5th NC Regiment	3/3/1777, a Musician under Capt. Reading Blount. A Private in Dec. 1777. Then a Private under Capt. Charles Stewart (2nd NC Regiment). Enlisted in Craven County, NC. Discharged at Charleston, SC just prior to its Fall in May 1780. Joined NC Militia, unit	Brandywine Creek (PA), Germantown (PA), Stony Point (NY), Monmouth

Name	1st Unit	Year / Rank / Served Under / Notes	Known Battles
		unknown - POW at the Fall of Charleston as Militiaman. S42040.	(NJ).
Thomas, John	9th NC Regiment	11/28/1776, an Ensign under Capt. Joel Brevard. From Salisbury District.	
Thomas, Lemuel	1st NC Regiment	1777, a Private under Capt. Henry "Hal" Dixon. 9/8/1778, a known Private under Capt. James Read. aka Samuel Thomas.	
Thomas, Philemon	1st NC Regiment	5/25/1781, a Sergeant under Capt. Robert Raiford. Discharged on 5/18/1782 (2nd NC Regiment). Earlier and later in NC Militia. From Guilford County, NC. S31417.	
Thomas, Philip	4th NC Regiment	May 1781, a Sergeant under Capt. George Dougherty for 12 months. Discharged on 5/10/1782. Wounded at the battle of Eutaw Springs (SC). From Duplin County, NC. R10509.	Eutaw Springs (SC).
Thomas, Philip	6th NC Regiment	A Private under Capt. Philip Taylor. Dropped from the rolls in Sep. 1777.	
Thomas, Richard	6th NC Regiment	June 1776, a Private under Capt. Thomas White. Discharged on 6/7/1778. From Orange County, NC. S14688.	
Thomas, Samuel	1st NC Regiment	9/8/1778, a known Wagoner under Capt. James Read.	
Thomas, Samuel	1st NC Regiment	5/19/1781, a Private under Capt. Robert Raiford. Discharged on 5/19/1782 (2nd NC Regiment).	
Thomas, Stephen	1st NC Regiment	5/2/1781, a Private under Capt. Anthony Sharpe. Wounded at the battle of Eutaw Springs (SC). Discharged on 2/1/1782. From Richmond County, NC. S289.	Eutaw Springs (SC).
Thomas, Thomas	1st NC Regiment	4/15/1781, a Musician under Capt. Robert Raiford. Discharged on 4/15/1782 (2nd NC Regiment).	
Thomas, Thomas	5th NC Regiment	5/14/1776, a Private under Capt. John Pugh Williams for 2-1/2 years. 9/9/1778, under Capt. Clement Hall (2nd NC Regiment). Discharged on 11/10/1778.	
Thomas, William	2nd NC Regiment	June 1778, a Private in the Lt. Colonel's Company (Lt. Col. Selby Harney) (2nd NC Regiment).	
Thomas, William	9th NC Regiment	1777, a Private under Capt. Richard D. Cook. Died in Aug. 1777.	
Thomason, John	NC Artillery	3/30/1777, a Corporal under Capt. John Vance as NC State Troops. 7/10/1777, on Continental Line. 11/16/1777, under Capt. John Kingsbury. 5/1/1778, in same unit. 9/16/1778, in same unit. aka John Thompson, John Tomison, John Thomison.	
Thomaston, Charles	1st NC Regiment	5/21/1781, a Sergeant under Capt. Anthony Sharpe. Dropped from the rolls during 1781.	
Thompkins, Jordan	3rd NC Regiment	1779, a Private under Capt. Kedar Ballard for nine months. Discharged on 12/1/1779. aka Jordan Thomkins.	
Thompson,	3rd NC	7/20/1778, a Private in the Lt. Colonel's	

Name	1st Unit	Year / Rank / Served Under / Notes	Known Battles
Charles	Regiment	Company (Lt. Col. William Lee Davidson) led by Lt./Capt. George "Gee" Bradley for nine months. 4/23/1779, a known Private in the Lt. Colonel's Company (Lt. Col. Robert Mebane) led by Capt. George "Gee" Bradley. Died at New Windsor Hospital.	
Thompson, Daniel	4th NC Regiment	2/14/1777, a Musician under Capt. John Nelson for three years. 6/1/1778, a Fifer under Capt. Griffith John McRee (1st NC Regiment). A Private in Feb. 1779. Discharged in Feb. 1779.	
Thompson, Edward	7th NC Regiment	1777, a Private under Capt. Joseph Walker. Died on 2/3/1778.	
Thompson, George	2nd NC Regiment	1782, a Private under Capt. Clement Hall for 12 months. Discharged on 1/15/1783.	
Thompson, Goodwin	5th NC Regiment	1777, a Private under Capt. Henry Darnell. Died on 8/22/1777.	
Thompson, Jesse	1st NC Regiment	4/15/1781, a Private under Lt./Capt. Benjamin Bailey. Discharged on 4/15/1782 (3rd NC Regiment).	
Thompson, John	1st NC Regiment	1781, a Sergeant under Capt. Alexander Brevard for 12 months. Discharged on 7/21/1782.	
Thompson, John	3rd NC Regiment	1782, a Private under Capt. Alexander Brevard for 18 months.	
Thompson, John	4th NC Regiment	April 1776, a Private under Capt. John Ashe, Jr. for three years. Enlisted at Hillsborough, NC. Wounded at battle of Germantown (PA). Discharged at Trenton, NJ. Moved to Augusta County VA, joined unit there. S41239.	Germantown (PA).
Thompson, John	4th NC Regiment	1777, a Private under Capt. James Williams. Discharged in Aug. 1777.	
Thompson, John	4th NC Regiment	1777, a Private under Capt. William Temple Coles. Discharged on 8/10/1777.	
Thompson, John	4th NC Regiment	1782, a Private under Capt. Anthony Sharpe for 18 months.	
Thompson, Lawrence	1st NC Regiment	1776, a Sergeant under Capt. Alfred Moore for six months. From Rowan County, enlisted at Hillsborough, NC. Born 1758 in Dunmore County, VA. S32554.	
Thompson, Lawrence	1st NC Regiment	9/1/1775, a 1st Lieutenant under Capt. Alfred Moore. 8/15/1776, a Captain when Thomas Allen resigned. Resigned/retired on 6/1/1778. From Orange County, NC. R10546A.	Moore's Creek Bridge, Breech Inlet Naval Battle (SC), Brandywine Creek (PA), Germantown (PA).
Thompson, Nathaniel	10th NC Regiment	5/20/1777, a Private under Capt. James Wilson for three years. 9/8/1778, a known Private in the Major's Company (Maj. John Baptiste Ashe) (1st NC Regiment). POW on 4/14/1779 (?). aka Nathaniel Thomson.	
Thompson, Nicholas	1st NC Regiment	1781, a Private under Capt. Robert Raiford. Discharged by Capt. Benjamin Andrew	

Name	1st Unit	Year / Rank / Served Under / Notes	Known Battles
		Coleman in Sep. 1782 (2nd NC Regiment). R10530A.	
Thompson, Richard	DQMG	1780, a Wagon Maker on the roll of Capt. Solomon Wood (NC Light Dragoons) - this seems to be for convenience only. 8/23/1781, a Wagon Maker under Col. Nicholas Long (Deputy QM General).	
Thompson, Robert	DQMG	1780, a Shoemaker on the roll of Capt. Solomon Wood (NC Light Dragoons) - this seems to be for convenience only. 8/23/1781, a Shoemaker under Col. Nicholas Long (Deputy QM General).	
Thompson, Samuel	1st NC Regiment	Sep. 1775, a Private under Capt. Alfred Moore for six months. Later in NC Militia. From Orange County, NC. W4605.	
Thompson, Samuel	6th NC Regiment	4/17/1776, a 2nd Lieutenant under Capt. Archibald Lytle and Col. John Alexander Lillington. Resigned in June 1776.	
Thompson, Samuel	4th NC Regiment	1781, a Corporal under Capt. Joseph T. Rhodes for 12 months. Discharged on 4/12/1782.	
Thompson, Uriah	3rd NC Regiment	1778, a Private under Lt./Capt. Joseph Montford for nine months.	
Thompson, William	2nd NC Regiment	4/26/1776, a Private, unit unknown. 9/9/1778, a known Private under Capt. John Ingles (2nd NC Regiment). Discharged on 11/10/1778.	
Thompson, William	2nd NC Regiment	1782, a Private under Capt. Benjamin Carter for 18 months.	
Thompson, William	3rd NC Regiment	1782, a Private under Capt. Alexander Brevard for 18 months.	
Thompson, William	6th NC Regiment	1776, a Private for six months under Capt. Arthur Council. Then, in NC Militia. From Chatham County, NC. S30731.	
Thompson, William	10th NC Regiment	5/5/1777, a Sergeant under Capt. John Jarvis for three years. A Private in June 1778 (1st NC Regiment). 9/8/1778, a known Private in the Major's Company (Maj. John Baptiste Ashe) (1st NC Regiment) - sick in camp on that date.	
Thompson, Willis	10th NC Regiment	7/12/1777, a Private under Capt. Abraham Sheppard, Jr. for three years. 9/9/1778, a known Private under Capt. Clement Hall (2nd NC Regiment). Died in Oct. 1778.	
Thompson, Willoughby	10th NC Regiment	12/12/1777, a Private under Capt. John Jarvis for three years. 9/8/1778, a known Private in the Major's Company (Maj. John Baptiste Ashe) (1st NC Regiment). Died on 1/12/1779. aka Willobey Thompson.	
Thomson, Andrew	7th NC Regiment	1777, a Private under Capt. John McGlaughan. Dropped from the rolls in Oct. 1778 - said to be transferred - where unknown.	
Thomson, Benjamin	1st NC Regiment	1777, a Private under Capt. Joshua Bowman.	
Thomson, James		1782-1783, a Commissary, regiment unknown. Earlier in NC Militia. From Duplin County, NC.	
Thomson,	9th NC	1777, a Private under Capt. Richard D. Cook.	

Name	1st Unit	Year / Rank / Served Under / Notes	Known Battles
Thomas	Regiment	Deserted in Aug. 1777.	
Thomson, Tickle	1st NC Regiment	2/26/1778, a known Private under Capt. Howell Tatum.	
Thornhill, Benjamin	1st NC Regiment	1/1/1782, a Private under Capt. James Mills for 12 months.	
Thorogood, Francis	2nd NC Regiment	1777, a Private under Capt. Charles Allen. 9/10/1778, a known Private under Capt. Thomas Armstrong. A Corporal on 7/15/1779.	
Threat, Frederick	3rd NC Regiment	5/5/1776, a Private under Capt. Jacob Turner for 2-1/2 years. Discharged in Oct. 1778.	
Thrift, Abraham	9th NC Regiment	1/17/1777, a Private under Capt. Richard D. Cook for three years. 9/8/1778, a known Private under Capt. John Sumner (1st NC Regiment) - sick in camp on that date. aka Abram Thrift.	
Thrift, Miles	3rd NC Regiment	1778, a Private under Capt. Francis Child. 6/1/1778, a Private under Capt. Griffith John McRee (1st NC Regiment). Died in May 1779.	
Thrift, Solomon	9th NC Regiment	1777, a Private under Capt. Richard D. Cook. Died on 6/15/1778.	
Throp, Adam	NC Light Dragoons	Oct.-Dec. 1777, a known Private under Capt. Martin Phifer. Not on any official rolls.	
Thurrell, Abraham	8th NC Regiment	7/2/1777, a Private under Capt. John Walsh. Died in Jan. 1779.	
Thursnell, John	6th NC Regiment	A Private under Capt. George Dougherty. 9/8/1778, a known Private under Capt. Tilghman Dixon (1st NC Regiment). Died in Nov. 1778. aka John Thurnell.	
Thurston, William	3rd NC Regiment	4/16/1776, a Private under Capt. James Emmett for 2-1/2 years. 9/9/1778, a known Private in the Major's Company (Maj. Hardy Murfree) (2nd NC Regiment). Discharged on 10/16/1778.	
Thurston, William	3rd NC Regiment	9/10/1782, a Private under Capt. Benjamin Bailey for 18 months.	
Tiack, Thomas	2nd NC Regiment	9/9/1778, a Fife Major in the Colonel's Company (Col. John Patten).	
Tice, Henry	3rd NC Regiment	1781, a Private under Capt. Clement Hall for 12 months. Discharged on 4/15/1782 (2nd NC Regiment).	
Tice, James	3rd NC Regiment	1781, a Private under Capt. Clement Hall for 12 months. Discharged on 4/15/1782 (2nd NC Regiment).	
Tice, Thomas	3rd NC Regiment	3/1/1782, a Private under Capt. Samuel Jones for 12 months. A Sergeant in Sep. 1782 (1st NC Regiment).	
Tiffin, Thomas	2nd NC Regiment	Oct. 1775, a Private under Capt. Charles Crawford for six months. 10/26/1776, a Sergeant under Capt. Benjamin Williams. Back to Private on 1/1/1778. 9/9/1778, a known Private under Capt. Robert Fenner. Discharged on 1/31/1780. Rejoined. POW at the Fall of Charleston, exchanged after nine months. 5/15/1781, a Private under Capt. Tilghman Dixon. Discharged on 5/21/1782 (1st NC Regiment). Received clothing on 5/24/1782.	Great Bridge (VA), Brandywine Creek (PA), Germantown (PA), Monmouth (NJ), Siege of Charleston 1780 (SC),

Name	1st Unit	Year / Rank / Served Under / Notes	Known Battles
		From Caswell County. S38444.	Eutaw Springs (SC).
Tiller, Thomas	2nd NC Regiment	7/31/1781, a Private under Capt. Benjamin Carter for 12 months. Discharged on 7/28/1782.	
Tillery, John	3rd NC Regiment	A QM. April 1777, a Lieutenant under Capt. Pinketham Eaton. Dropped from the rolls in Jan. 1778.	
Tillet, Avery	2nd NC Regiment	1777, a Private under Capt. James Gee. 9/9/1778, a known Private under Capt. John Ingles. Probably the same man as directly below.	
Tillet, Avery	6th NC Regiment	1777, a Private under Capt. Thomas Donoho. Deserted in Aug. 1777. aka Avery Tilley.	
Tilley, Jacob	1st NC Regiment	6/20/1781, a Private under Capt. Alexander Brevard. Discharged on 6/21/1782 (3rd NC Regiment). May be the same man as directly below. aka Jacob Tilly.	
Tilley, Jacob	4th NC Regiment	1782, a Private under Capt. William Lytle for 18 months.	
Tilley, Lewis	4th NC Regiment	4/1/1777, a Private under Capt. Joseph Phillips. 9/8/1778, a known Private under Capt. James Read (1st NC Regiment).	
Tilman, Aaron	1st NC Regiment	1781, a Private under Capt. Elijah Moore. Discharged on 5/10/1782 (4th NC Regiment). aka Aaron Tillman.	
Tilman, Belitha	2nd NC Regiment	6/2/1777, a Private under Capt. Clement Hall. 6/10/1777, a Private under Capt. Armwell Herron (10th NC Regiment). 9/9/1778, a known Private in the Major's Company (Maj. Hardy Murfree) (2nd NC Regiment). A Corporal on 10/10/1778. 3/12/1779, re-enlisted in the Major's Company (Maj. Hardy Murfree). Back to Private on 6/1/1779. Deserted on 7/3/1779. Re-enlisted in Nov. 1779. aka Balitha Tilmon, Belisha Tilman, Belitha Tillman.	
Tilman, John	10th NC Regiment	7/1/1777, a Private under Capt. Armwell Herron. 9/9/1778, a known Private in the Major's Company (Maj. Hardy Murfree) (2nd NC Regiment). aka John Tilmon.	
Tilman, William	10th NC Regiment	7/1/1777, a Private under Capt. Armwell Herron. 9/9/1778, a known Private in the Major's Company (Maj. Hardy Murfree) (2nd NC Regiment). aka William Tilmon.	
Timbrell, John	4th NC Regiment	1777, a Private under Capt. James Williams. Dropped from the rolls in Sep. 1777.	
Timer, Daniel	1st NC Regiment	8/1/1782, a Private under Capt. Joshua Hadley for 18 months.	
Tiner, Jesse	1st NC Regiment	11/10/1778, a Private under Capt. Anthony Sharpe for nine months. Discharged on 5/13/1779.	
Tiney, James	3rd NC Regiment	1779, a Private under Capt. Kedar Ballard for nine months. Discharged on 12/1/1779.	
Tinker, John	1st NC Regiment	6/6/1781, a Private under Capt. Griffith John McRee. Died in Oct. 1781.	

Name	1st Unit	Year / Rank / Served Under / Notes	Known Battles
Tinnen, James	1st NC Regiment	5/20/1781, a Private under Capt. Thomas Donoho then Capt. William Walton. Discharged 7/5/1782. Earlier in NC Militia. From Orange County, NC. S3814.	Eutaw Springs (SC).
Tinney, John	5th NC Regiment	3/1/1779, a Private under Maj. Reading Blount for nine months. Discharged on 12/1/1779.	
Tinney, Samuel	4th NC Regiment	1782, a Private under Capt. William Lytle for 18 months. Dropped from the rolls in Jan. 1783.	
Tinsley, Charles	3rd NC Regiment	7/20/1778, a Private under Capt. Francis Child for nine months.	
Tipper, John	4th NC Regiment	5/10/1776, a Private under Capt. James Williams for 2-1/2 years. 9/8/1778, a known Private in the Colonel's Company (Col. Thomas Clark) (1st NC Regiment) led by Capt. John Gambier Scull - assigned to His Excy's Guard. Discharged on 11/10/1778.	
Tipper, William	2nd NC Regiment	5/12/1781, a Private under Capt. Tilghman Dixon. Discharged on 5/25/1782 (1st NC Regiment) at Salisbury, NC. S39109.	Eutaw Springs (SC).
Tippett, Erastus	3rd NC Regiment	7/20/1778, a Musician under Lt./Capt. Joseph Montford for nine months. 1782, a Musician under Capt. Peter Bacot (1st NC Regiment) for 18 months. Enlisted in Halifax County, NC. S38108.	
Tippett, George	3rd NC Regiment	1782, a Private under Capt. Alexander Brevard for 18 months.	
Tippett, Rasper	NC Light Dragoons	Oct.-Dec. 1777, a known Corporal under Capt. Martin Phifer. Possibly the same man as Erastus Tippett above. aka Rasper Tippit.	
Tise, Daniel	1st NC Regiment	2/26/1778, a known Private under Capt. Howell Tatum.	
Titterson, John	4th NC Regiment	1782, a Private under Capt. Thomas Evans for 18 months.	
Tobin, William	2nd NC Regiment	1782, a Private under Capt. Benjamin Carter. Deserted on 3/28/1782.	
Toby, William	3rd NC Regiment	5/4/1776, a Private under Capt. Pinketham Eaton. A Corporal in Oct. 1777. Back to Private in June 1778. POW at Ft. Lafayette, NY on 6/1/1779.	Ft. Lafayette (NY).
Tocksey, William	2nd NC Regiment	5/3/1776, an Ensign. aka William Toschey.	
Todd, Ephraim	7th NC Regiment	1777, a Private under Capt. John McGlaughan. 2/26/1778, a known Private under Capt. Howell Tatum (1st NC Regiment).	
Todd, James	7th NC Regiment	1777, a Private under Capt. John McGlaughan. Died on 9/29/1777.	
Todd, John	3rd NC Regiment	7/20/1778, a Private under Capt. John Baker for nine months.	
Todd, Josiah	3rd NC Regiment	7/20/1778, a Private under Capt. John Baker for nine months.	
Todd, Thomas	4th NC Regiment	6/3/1779, a Private under Lt. David Cowan. Later in NC Militia. From Rowan County, NC. S17736.	Stono Ferry (SC).
Todd,	7th NC	1777, a Musician under Capt. John	

Name	1ˢᵗ Unit	Year / Rank / Served Under / Notes	Known Battles
Thomas	Regiment	McGlaughan. Died in Sep. 1777.	
Todd, William	7ᵗʰ NC Regiment	1/1/1777, a Private under Capt. John McGlaughan for three years. 2/26/1778, a known Private under Capt. Howell Tatum (1st NC Regiment). 3/12/1779, re-enlisted for the duration of the war in the Lt. Colonel's Company (Lt. Col. Robert Mebane - 1st NC Regiment) led by Capt. Joshua Bowman. A Corporal on 2/1/1780.	
Todwine, Coleman	5ᵗʰ NC Regiment	1777, a Sergeant under Capt. William Caswell. Dropped from the rolls in Jan. 1778.	
Tolar, Daniel	2ⁿᵈ NC Regiment	Sep. 1775, a Private under Capt. Charles Crawford for 12 months. Discharged in SC, then joined SC Continentals. S42043.	
Toliver, James	NC Artillery	8/26/1777, a Matross under Capt. John Vance. 11/16/1777, under Capt. John Kingsbury. 9/16/1778, in same unit. Deserted on 12/18/1778.	
Tomblin, John	5ᵗʰ NC Regiment	6/7/1779, a Private under Maj. Reading Blount for nine months. Deserted in Oct. 1779.	
Tomlinson, Aaron	1ˢᵗ NC Regiment	1/3/1782, a Private under Capt. James Mills for 12 months.	
Toney, Arthur	5ᵗʰ NC Regiment	Spring of 1779, a Private under Capt. William Lytle. From Halifax County, NC. W4835.	
Toney, John	3ʳᵈ NC Regiment	1780, a Private under Capt. Edward Yarborough for 12 months. Dropped from the rolls on 4/1/1781. From Halifax County, NC.	Guilford Court House.
Toole, Henry Irwin	2ⁿᵈ NC Regiment	9/1/1775, a Captain under Col. Robert Howe. Resigned in April of 1776. One source claims he later became Lt. Colonel in the 5th NC Regiment. From Edgecombe County, NC.	Great Bridge (VA).
Toomer, Henry	NC Artillery	5/9/1777, recommended by NC Senate as Commissary. Placed on Continental Line on 7/10/1777. Earlier a Commissary in NC Militia.	
Topp, George	1ˢᵗ NC Regiment	Spring of 1776, a Private under Capt. Caleb Grainger. 2/26/1778, a known Private under Capt. Howell Tatum. 9/8/1778, a known Private under Capt. Howell Tatum. Discharged in Nov. 1778 due to sickness and infirmity. Enlisted in Halifax County, NC. S42044.	Brandywine Creek (PA), Germantown (PA).
Tottevaine, Winder	5ᵗʰ NC Regiment	A Private under Capt. Joseph Montford. Deserted in Sep. 1779.	
Tow, Christopher	7ᵗʰ NC Regiment	1777, a Corporal under Capt. Thomas Brickell. Deserted on 9/1/1777. Rejoined in Feb. 1778. Died on 4/1/1778.	
Towel, Abraham	5ᵗʰ NC Regiment	8/5/1779, a Private under Maj. Reading Blount for nine months. Deserted in Oct. 1779.	
Towning, James	8ᵗʰ NC Regiment	12/15/1776, a Private under Capt. John Walsh. 9/9/1778, a known Private in the Colonel's Company (Col. John Patten) (2nd NC Regiment) led by Capt. John Craddock. aka James Townen.	
Townley, Philemon	4ᵗʰ NC Regiment	2/7/1782, a Private under Capt. James Mills for 12 months.	

Name	1st Unit	Year / Rank / Served Under / Notes	Known Battles
Townley, William	1st NC Regiment	1777, a Private under Capt. John Brown. Dropped from the rolls in Feb. 1778.	
Toxa, John	2nd NC Regiment	9/9/1778, a known Private under Capt. John Ingles.	
Toxey, Nathaniel	1st NC Regiment	5/17/1781, a Private under Lt./Capt. Benjamin Bailey. Discharged on 5/17/1782 (3rd NC Regiment).	
Tracey, John	10th NC Regiment	6/24/1777, a Private under Capt. Andrew Vanoy. Dropped from the rolls in June 1778.	
Trader, George		5/20/1776, a Private, regiment and unit unknown, enlisted for three years. 9/8/1778, a known Private under Capt. Griffith John McRee (1st NC Regiment) - sick on that date in Valley Forge. A Corporal in July 1779. aka George Tradder.	
Trader, John	3rd NC Regiment	9/17/1782, a Private under Capt. Benjamin Bailey for 18 months. Deserted on 6/21/1783.	
Trader, Jonathan	2nd NC Regiment	5/19/1781, a Private under Capt. Benjamin Carter for 12 months. Discharged on 5/19/1782.	
Trainer, Arthur	5th NC Regiment	11/15/1776, a Sergeant under Capt. Henry Darnell. Dropped from the rolls in Sep. 1777. Jan. 1778, rejoined as a Private. POW at Ft. Lafayette, NY on 6/1/1779. aka Arthur Tainer.	Ft. Lafayette (NY).
Trantham, Martin	1st NC Regiment	1777, a Private under Capt. Joshua Bowman. Dropped from the rolls in Dec. 1777 - sick.	
Tranton, John	3rd NC Regiment	9/10/1782, a Private under Capt. Benjamin Bailey for 18 months.	
Trapp, Elijah	2nd NC Regiment	Apr. 1782, a Musician under Capt. Clement Hall.	
Trapp, Martin	1st NC Regiment	5/9/1781, a Private under Capt. Alexander Brevard.	
Trapp, Martin	3rd NC Regiment	Apr. 1782, a Private under Capt. William Armstrong. Deserted on 12/10/1782. Rejoined on 12/14/1782. Deserted again on 5/28/1783.	
Travathan, William	DQMG	1780, a Shoemaker on the roll of Capt. Solomon Wood (NC Light Dragoons) - this seems to be for convenience only. 8/23/1781, a Shoemaker under Col. Nicholas Long (Deputy QM General). aka William Trewathan.	
Trent, Stephen	2nd NC Regiment	3/12/1779, re-enlisted under Capt. Benjamin Andrew Coleman.	
Trent, William	4th NC Regiment	1782, a Sergeant under Capt. Anthony Sharpe for 18 months.	
Trewhitt, Stephen	10th NC Regiment	7/1/1777, a Private under Capt. Armwell Herron. 9/9/1778, under Capt. Benjamin Andrew Coleman (2nd NC Regiment). POW at the Fall of Charleston, escaped after 48 days. From Dobbs County, NC. aka Stephen Truhitt, Trewhit, Truit, Trewit. S45451.	Monmouth (NJ), Stony Point (NY), Siege of Charleston 1780 (SC).
Triplett, Charles	1st NC Regiment	9/19/1776, an Ensign. Died in Dec. of 1776.	
Trotman, Thomas	2nd NC Regiment	5/19/1781, a Private under Capt. Benjamin Carter for 12 months. Discharged on 5/19/1782.	
Trowal,	1st NC	3/1/1777, a Musician under Capt. Joshua	Brandywine

Name	1st Unit	Year / Rank / Served Under / Notes	Known Battles
William	Regiment	Bowman. Enlisted at Cross Creek, NC. Wounded twice at the battle of Brandywine Creek (PA) - placed in hospital until next Spring. A Private in June of 1778. 9/8/1778, a known Private under Capt. John Sumner - sick on that date. POW at the Fall of Charleston (SC) - held until peace declared. Per the official records, he deserted on 6/13/1783 (?). On the official rolls as William Trowell. aka William Trowall. R10714.	Creek (PA), Siege of Charleston 1780 (SC).
Trowell, John	10th NC Regiment	1/12/1778, a Private under Capt. Andrew Vanoy for three years. 9/8/1778, a known Private under Capt. John Sumner (1st NC Regiment) - sick at Valley Forge on that date. Deserted on 3/8/1779. aka John Trawl.	
Troy, James	7th NC Regiment	1777, a Private under Capt. Joseph Walker. Dropped from the rolls in April 1778.	
Truelock, Sutton	5th NC Regiment	8/12/1776, a Private under Capt. Reading Blount for 3 years. 9/9/1778, a known Private in the Lt. Colonel's Company (Lt. Col. Selby Harney) (2nd NC Regiment). aka Sutton Trueheek.	
Truett, William	4th NC Regiment	1782, a Private under Capt. Thomas Evans. Deserted on 6/8/1783 (?).	
Truit, Franklin	2nd NC Regiment	1777, a Private under Capt. Clement Hall.	
Truit, Stephen	2nd NC Regiment	7/1/1777, a Private under Capt. John Armstrong for three years.	
Tryer, William	2nd NC Regiment	5/3/1777, a Private, unit unknown. 9/9/1778, a known Private under Capt. John Ingles.	
Tucker, Carrel	3rd NC Regiment	1781, a Private under Capt. Edward Yarborough for 12 months. Discharged on 4/22/1782.	
Tucker, Curl	3rd NC Regiment	6/7/1779, a Private under Capt. Michael Quinn for 18 months. A Sergeant in Jan. 1780. A Corporal in March 1780.	
Tucker, Gray	1st NC Regiment	Jan. 1782, a Private under Capt. William Armstrong. Earlier in NC Militia. From Halifax County, NC. W9867.	
Tucker, James	1st NC Regiment	1779, a Private under Capt. Anthony Sharpe. On leave when battle of Guilford Court House happened. Separated from his unit, he joined NC Militia. From Randolph County, NC. His pension application was rejected–probably accused of desertion. R10735.	
Tucker, James	4th NC Regiment	July 1782, a Private under Capt. William Lytle for 18 months. Enlisted in Randolph County, NC. Deserted on 12/10/1782. Rejoined in Jan. 1783 for the duration of the war. Furloughed at Charleston in July 1783. He does not mention the desertion in his pension application, but the authorities do. R10736.	
Tucker, John	2nd NC Regiment	1782, a Private under Capt. Benjamin Andrew Coleman for 18 months. Discharged in July 1783 at Charleston, SC. In a skirmish on James	

Name	1st Unit	Year / Rank / Served Under / Notes	Known Battles
		Island - date not noted. Claims to have been in battle of Eutaw Springs (SC) (9/8/1781), must've been in NC Militia.	
Tucker, John	3rd NC Regiment	1/8/1781, a Corporal under Capt. Clement Hall for 12 months. Discharged on 8/16/1782 (2nd NC Regiment). R10738.	
Tucker, John	4th NC Regiment	1782, a Private under Capt. Thomas Evans for 18 months.	
Tucker, John	4th NC Regiment	1782, a Private under Capt. William Lytle. Deserted on 12/10/1782.	
Tucker, Richard	4th NC Regiment	7/25/1776, a Private under Capt. William Goodman for 2-1/2 years. 9/8/1778, a known Private in the Colonel's Company (Col. Thomas Clark) (1st NC Regiment) led by Capt. John Gambier Scull.	
Tucker, Thomas	DQMG	1780, a Saddler on the roll of Capt. Solomon Wood (NC Light Dragoons) - this seems to be for convenience only. A Tailor under Col. Nicholas Long (Deputy QM General). An invalid. Said to be an ex-Continental soldier (?). 8/23/1781, a Leather Worker, making saddles, harnesses, caps, etc. aka Thomas Tuchor.	
Tucker, Thomas	9th NC Regiment	1777, a Corporal under Capt. Richard D. Cook. Dropped from the rolls in Jan. 1778. Probably the same man as directly above.	
Tue, Alexander	2nd NC Regiment	11/8/1781, a Private under Capt. Benjamin Andrew Coleman for 12 months.	
Tulston, William	3rd NC Regiment	1777, a Private under Capt. James Emmett. Deserted in Aug. 1777.	
Tunk, Robert	5th NC Regiment	5/30/1779, a Private under Maj. Reading Blount for nine months. A Corporal on 12/1/1779.	
Turbee, William	3rd NC Regiment	7/6/1777, a Lieutenant. In service during Jan. of 1780.	
Turnage, George	10th NC Regiment	5/18/1777, a Private under Capt. Abraham Sheppard, Jr.	
Turner, Adam	2nd NC Regiment	Jan. 1779, a Private in the Major's Company (Maj. Hardy Murfree).	
Turner, Adam	4th NC Regiment	1782, a Private under Capt. Thomas Evans for 18 months.	
Turner, Arthur	1st NC Regiment	7/26/1781, a Private under Lt./Capt. Benjamin Bailey. Discharged on 7/26/1782 (3rd NC Regiment).	
Turner, Benajah	4th NC Regiment	9/9/1775, a 2nd Lieutenant in the Edenton District Minutemen. 4/17/1776, a 2nd Lieutenant under Capt. Roger Moore and Col. Thomas Polk.	
Turner, Benjamin	2nd NC Regiment	1777, a Private under Capt. Benjamin Williams. Died on 12/1/1777.	
Turner, Berryman	1st NC Regiment	9/1/1775, an Ensign. Resigned in October 1775. Later a Captain in the NC Militia. From Caswell County, NC.	
Turner, Bryan	3rd NC Regiment	4/22/1777, a Sergeant under Capt. Jacob Turner. Deserted on 10/15/1777.	
Turner,	8th NC	1777, a Corporal under Capt. Robert Raiford. A	

Name	1st Unit	Year / Rank / Served Under / Notes	Known Battles
Daniel	Regiment	Private in Nov. 1777. Died in Jan. 1778.	
Turner, David	1st NC Regiment	1781, a Private under Capt. William Armstrong.	
Turner, Jacob	3rd NC Regiment	4/17/1776, a Captain under Col. Jethro Sumner. Distinguished himself at the battle of Brandywine Creek (PA). Killed at Germantown, PA on 10/4/1777. From Bertie County, NC.	Ft. Moultrie #1 (SC), Brandywine Creek (PA), Germantown (PA).
Turner, James	DQMG	1780, a Shoemaker on the roll of Capt. Solomon Wood (NC Light Dragoons) - this seems to be for convenience only. 8/23/1781, a Shoemaker under Col. Nicholas Long (Deputy QM General).	
Turner, John	1st NC Regiment	8/1/1777, a Sergeant under Capt. John Brown. A Private in June 1778. 9/8/1778, a known Private under Capt. Joshua Bowman. From Surry (what is now Stokes) County, NC. W8792.	
Turner, John	7th NC Regiment	2/13/1777, a Private under Capt. James Vaughan. Deserted in Oct. 1777.	
Turner, Mathias	8th NC Regiment	1777, a Corporal under Capt. Robert Raiford. A Private in Jan. 1778. Dropped from the rolls in Feb. 1779.	
Turner, Robert	5th NC Regiment	1775, a 1st Lieutenant in the New Bern District Minutemen. 4/17/1776, a 1st Lieutenant under Capt. Benjamin Stedman and Col. Edward Buncombe. Feb. 1778, a Lieutenant under Capt. Silas Stevenson (10th NC Regiment). Retired on 6/1/1778. From Craven County.	
Turner, Thomas	3rd NC Regiment	7/20/1778, a Private under Lt./Capt. Joseph Montford for nine months.	
Turner, Titus Jennings	5th NC Regiment	May 1776, a Private under Capt. William Ward. Discharged after 12 months due to illness. Later in NC Militia. From Johnston County, NC. R20187.	
Turner, William	1st NC Regiment	1777, a Private under Capt. John Brown. Died on 5/24/1778.	
Turner, William	3rd NC Regiment	7/20/1778, a Private under Capt. John Baker for nine months. Discharged in April 1779. Later in NC Militia. From Nash County, NC. W4089.	
Turner, William	5th NC Regiment	6/7/1779, a Private under Maj. Reading Blount for nine months. Deserted in Oct. 1779.	
Turpin, William	1st NC Regiment	4/5/1781, a Private under Capt. William Lytle. Dropped from the rolls sometime during 1781.	
Tutson, Thomas	2nd NC Regiment	July 1778, a Private under Capt. Benjamin Andrew Coleman. Deserted on 8/15/1778.	
Twigg, Daniel	4th NC Regiment	Jan. 1779, a Musician under Capt. William Goodman. Sometime in 1781, this unit was transferred to the 2nd NC Regiment. After the battle of Eutaw Springs, this unit was taken over by Capt. Benjamin Bailey (1st NC Regiment). Jan. 1782, a known Musician under Capt. Benjamin Bailey. aka Daniel Twig. S38449.	Eutaw Springs (SC).

Name	1st Unit	Year / Rank / Served Under / Notes	Known Battles
Tyack, D. Thomas	5th NC Regiment	6/21/1777, the Regimental Fife Major.	
Tycer, Ellis	1st NC Regiment	1782, a Private under Capt. Peter Bacot for 18 months. Earlier in NC Militia. From Halifax County, NC. aka Ellis Tyson, Ellis Tyse. S6291.	
Tyler, Moses	6th NC Regiment	1777, a Private under Capt. Daniel Williams for three years. Jan. 1779, a Musician under Capt. Philip Taylor (5th NC Regiment). 1782, a Private under Capt. Peter Bacot (1st NC Regiment) for 18 months. From Bladen County (what is now Columbus County), NC. W4090.	Stono Ferry (SC).
Tyler, Owen	2nd NC Regiment	1782, a Private under Capt. Robert Raiford.	
Tyler, William	10th NC Regiment	10/1/1777, a Private under Capt. James Wilson for three years. 9/8/1778, a known Private in the Major's Company (Maj. John Baptiste Ashe) (1st NC Regiment). Deserted in Jan. 1780.	
Tyner, Arthur	5th NC Regiment	Jan. 1779, a Corporal under Capt. Philip Taylor. Discharged in Apr. 1779.	
Tyner, Nicholas	3rd NC Regiment	May 1776, a Private under Capt. William Barret for three years. Jan. 1779, a Corporal under Capt. Philip Taylor (5th NC Regiment). Discharged in Apr. 1779. Later in NC Militia. Enlisted in Northampton County, NC. S7773.	Ft. Moultrie #1 (SC).
Tyner, William	2nd NC Regiment	1782, a Private under Capt. Robert Raiford for 18 months.	
Tysinger, Ad.	1st NC Regiment	4/28/1781, a Private under Capt. Griffith John McRee. Deserted in May 1781.	
Tyson, Aaron	4th NC Regiment	1782, a Private under Capt. Thomas Evans for 18 months.	
Tyson, Abraham	8th NC Regiment	1777, a Sergeant under Capt. Francis Tartanson. A Private in June 1778 under Capt. Thomas Armstrong (2nd NC Regiment). Dropped from the rolls in Feb. 1779. aka Abraham Tison.	
Tyson, Henry	5th NC Regiment	12/19/1776, a Corporal under Capt. Simon Alderson. A Private in June 1778 in the Colonel's Company (Col. John Patten) (2nd NC Regiment) led by Capt. John Craddock. Discharged on 1/30/1780. aka Henry Tison.	Ft. Lafayette (NY).
Tyson, James	5th NC Regiment	12/9/1776, a Private and a Corporal under Capt. Simon Alderson for three years. 9/9/1778, a known Corporal in the Colonel's Company (Col. John Patten - 2nd NC Regiment) led by Capt. John Craddock. Discharged at Halifax, NC. aka James Tisen. S38442.	Brandywine Creek (PA), Germantown (PA), Monmouth (NJ).
Uell, William	4th NC Regiment	1781, a Sergeant under Capt. Joseph T. Rhodes. Discharged on 5/2/1782. Probably William Ewell.	
Underdown, Stephen	1st NC Regiment	Sep. 1775, a Private under Capt. Alfred Moore for six months. From Caswell County, NC. Moved to Rutherford County and joined the NC Militia. S30760.	
Underdew, Dempsey	10th NC Regiment	6/17/1777, a Private under Capt. John Jarvis for three years. 9/8/1778, a known Private in the	

Name	1ˢᵗ Unit	Year / Rank / Served Under / Notes	Known Battles
		Major's Company (Maj. John Baptiste Ashe) (1st NC Regiment). 3/12/1779, re-enlisted for the duration of the war in the same unit. aka Dempsey Underdue, Underden.	
Underhill, James	10ᵗʰ NC Regiment	5/12/1777, a Private under Capt. Silas Stevenson for 3 years. 9/9/1778, a known Private in the Colonel's Company (Col. John Patten) (2nd NC Regiment) led by Capt. John Craddock.	
Underwood, Shadrack	3ʳᵈ NC Regiment	7/20/1778, a Private under Capt. John Baker for nine months.	
Unger, Lorentz	1ˢᵗ NC Regiment	1781, a Private under Capt. Anthony Sharp for 18 months. Earlier in NC Militia. From Rowan County, NC. aka Lawrence Unger. W3891.	
Upchurch, Charles	NC Light Dragoons	May 1776, a Private under Capt. James Jones, then Capt. Cosmo Medici. On 3/7/1777, this unit was placed on the NC Continental Line until Jan. 1779. Discharged 2/1/1779. Then in NC Militia. From Wake County, NC. S16562.	Brandywine Creek (PA).
Upton, John	2ⁿᵈ NC Regiment	12/14/1776, a Private under Capt. Charles Crawford. 9/10/1778, a known Private under Capt. Thomas Armstrong. A Corporal in Feb. 1779. 3/12/1779, re-enlisted under Capt. Thomas Armstrong. POW at the Fall of Charleston (SC) - taken to Nova Scotia never to return home. From Norfolk, VA, where he enlisted while NC Regiment was marching northwards. R10811.	Brandywine Creek (PA), Germantown (PA), Monmouth (NJ), Siege of Charleston 1780 (SC).
Upton, Josiah	7ᵗʰ NC Regiment	2/4/1777, a Private under Capt. John Poynter. Dropped from the rolls in April 1778. Father of John and Willis. From Norfolk, VA.	
Upton, Willie	2ⁿᵈ NC Regiment	A Private, unit unknown. Died from fatigue at the battle of Monmouth, NJ on 6/28/1778.	Monmouth (NJ).
Upton, Willis	7ᵗʰ NC Regiment	2/14/1777, a Private under Capt. John Poynter. Died on 7/1/1778. Brother of John Upton above. From Norfolk, VA.	
Usher, William	3ʳᵈ NC Regiment	12/4/1776, a Surgeon. Transferred to 4th NC Regiment on 4/24/1777. Resigned on 11/1/1777.	
Vail, Edward Jr.	2ⁿᵈ NC Regiment	9/1/1775, a 1st Lieutenant. 8/21/1776, a Captain. Tried for cowardice at the battle of Germantown, convicted. Cashiered 12/21/1777.	Brandywine Creek (PA), Germantown (PA).
Vaison, Lemuel	2ⁿᵈ NC Regiment	1782, a Private under Capt. Benjamin Carter for 18 months.	
Vaisy, Nathaniel	3ʳᵈ NC Regiment	7/20/1778, a Sergeant under Maj. Thomas Hogg for nine months.	
Valentine, Daniel	3ʳᵈ NC Regiment	6/7/1779, a Private under Capt. George "Gee" Bradley for 18 months. Probably died while in service. Not clear. Brother of Peter Valentine. R10820.	
Valentine, Peter	3ʳᵈ NC Regiment	7/20/1778, a Private in the Lt. Colonel's Company (Lt. Col. William Lee Davidson) led by Lt./Capt. George "Gee" Bradley for nine	

Name	1st Unit	Year / Rank / Served Under / Notes	Known Battles
		months. 4/23/1779, a known Private in the Lt. Colonel's Company (Lt. Col. Robert Mebane) led by Capt. George "Gee" Bradley. Died at Philadelphia Hospital. Brother of Daniel Valentine. R10820.	
Van, Nathaniel	2nd NC Regiment	7/20/1778, a Private under Maj. Reading Blount for nine months.	
Vance, David	2nd NC Regiment	1782, a Private under Capt. Benjamin Carter for 18 months.	
Vance, David	2nd NC Regiment	4/20/1776, an Ensign under Capt William Fenner. 6/8/1776, a 1st Lieutenant under Capt. Clement Hall. Retired on 6/1/1778. Later, a Captain in NC Militia. From Burke County, NC.	
Vance, David	5th NC Regiment	4/29/1776, a Private under Capt. John Pugh Williams. 9/9/1778, a known Private under Capt. Clement Hall (2nd NC Regiment) - sick at Yellow Swamp. Discharged on 11/10/1778.	
Vance, Elijah	5th NC Regiment	5/12/1776, a Private under Capt. John Pugh Williams. 9/9/1778, a known Private under Capt. Clement Hall (2nd NC Regiment) - sick at Yellow Swamp. Discharged on 11/10/1778.	
Vance, James	3rd NC Regiment	7/20/1779, a Private under Capt. Francis Child for nine months. 9/9/1778, under Capt. Clement Hall (2nd NC Regiment). Died on 11/15/1778.	
Vance, John	NC Artillery	1775, a Captain in the New Bern District Minutemen. 5/9/1776, a Captain of NC State Troops. As an Independent Artillery Company, this unit was placed on the Continental Line 7/10/1777, not to be attached to any regiment. Resigned in Nov. 1777 because the NC General Assembly deemed he was unworthy of being an officer. Replaced by John Kingsbury.	
Vance, John	1st NC Regiment	5/25/1781, a Private under Capt. Alexander Brevard. Deserted on 7/1/1781.	
Vance, John Carlow	NC Artillery	11/16/1777, a 2nd Lieutenant under Capt. John Kingsbury. POW at the Fall of Charleston, exchanged on 6/14/1781. aka John Curton Vance, aka John Curlew Vance.	Siege of Charleston 1780 (SC).
Vance, William Ross	NC Artillery	6/10/1777, a Corporal under Capt. John Vance as NC State Troops for three years. 7/10/1777, on Continental Line. 11/16/1777, under Capt. John Kingsbury. 5/1/1778, in same unit. 9/16/1778, in same unit. Discharged on 3/11/1779.	
Vandeford, Noah	7th NC Regiment	1777, a Private under Capt. Joseph Walker. Died on 3/5/1778.	
Vandergrift, Leonard	5th NC Regiment	1779, a Private under Maj. Reading Blount. Deserted in Oct. 1779.	
Vandiver, Matthew	2nd NC Regiment	1776, a Private under Capt. William Knox for six months. Later in NC Militia. From Rowan County, NC. S9500.	Moore's Creek Bridge.
Van Duyck, John	NC Artillery	2/1/1777, a 1st Lieutenant under Capt. Thomas Clark. aka John Van Dyk.	
Vandyke,	9th NC	1777, a Private under Capt. Richard D. Cook.	

Name	1st Unit	Year / Rank / Served Under / Notes	Known Battles
Charles	Regiment	Died on 4/3/1778.	
Vanoy, Andrew	10th NC Regiment	11/25/1776, a Captain in the 1st Battalion of Volunteers under Col. Abraham Sheppard (Militia). 4/19/1777, a Captain in the 10th NC Regiment under Col. Abraham Sheppard. Retired on 6/1/1778. 1778, a Captain in the Rowan County Regiment of Militia under Col. Francis Locke.	Brandywine Creek (PA), Germantown (PA).
Vanpelt, Peter	6th NC Regiment	1777, a Private under Capt. Thomas Donoho. Deserted in Aug. 1777.	
Varcaze, James	10th NC Regiment	3/17/1778, a Lieutenant under Capt. Silas Stevenson. Retired on 6/1/1778.	
Varder, David	3rd NC Regiment	1781, a Private under Capt. Clement Hall for 12 months. Discharged on 8/1/1782 (2nd NC Regiment).	
Varey, Benjamin	8th NC Regiment	1777, a Private under Capt. Williams (?). Deserted on 10/1/1777. aka Benjamin Varry.	
Varner, Robert	1st NC Regiment	3/8/1777, a Private under Capt. Henry "Hal" Dixon.	
Varner, Robert	1st NC Regiment	3/28/1776, an Ensign under Capt. Robert Rowan. 7/7/1776, a 2nd Lieutenant. 3/8/1777, a 1st Lieutenant under Capt. Henry "Hal" Dixon. Cashiered on 10/1/1779. aka Robert Varnell.	
Vaugh, Richard	6th NC Regiment	A Private under Capt. Francis Child. Died on 6/2/1778.	
Vaughan, Abraham	4th NC Regiment	1782, a Private under Capt. William Lytle for 18 months.	
Vaughan, Daniel	2nd NC Regiment	5/19/1781, a Corporal under Capt. Benjamin Carter. Died on 9/26/1781.	
Vaughan, James	7th NC Regiment	11/28/1776, a 1st Lieutenant under Capt. Josiah Cotton. 12/18/1776, a Captain when Josiah Cotton resigned. Resigned on 8/27/1777. From Northampton County, NC.	
Vaughan, West	7th NC Regiment	1777, a Private under Capt. Joshua Dayley. Died on 2/20/1778.	
Vaughan, Vincent	3rd NC Regiment	7/20/1778, a Private under Lt./Capt. Joseph Montford for nine months. Served almost a full year. He claims he was a Sergeant, but not found in official records except as a Private. Earlier and later in NC Militia. From Halifax County, NC. W4366.	
Vaughan, William	1st NC Regiment	5/9/1781, a Private under Capt. Alexander Brevard. Discharged on 5/9/1782 (3rd NC Regiment). aka William Vaughn.	
Vaughn, James	1st NC Regiment	1777, a Private under Capt. John Brown. 9/8/1778, a known Private under Capt. Tilghman Dixon.	
Vaughn, John	5th NC Regiment	Mar. 1779, a Private under Capt. Christopher Goodwin.	
Vaughn, William	1st NC Regiment	5/9/1781, a Private under Capt. Griffith John McRee. Deserted on 7/1/1781.	
Venters, Daniel	10th NC Regiment	9/12/1777, a Private under Capt. Silas Stevenson. 9/9/1778, a known Private in the Colonel's Company (Col. John Patten) (2nd NC	

Name	1st Unit	Year / Rank / Served Under / Notes	Known Battles
		Regiment) led by Capt. John Craddock.	
Venters, Moses	7th NC Regiment	1/8/1777, a Private under Capt. John Poynter. 9/8/1778, a known Private under Capt. Tilghman Dixon (1st NC Regiment). Discharged on 1/28/1780.	
Ventress, Lemuel	1st NC Regiment	12/25/1777, a Private under Capt. Howell Tatum. Discharged 9/1/1778.	
Vermillion, Jesse	1st NC Regiment	1776, a Private under Capt. Alfred Moore. From Caswell County, NC. Moved to Washington County, NC, joined Militia there.	
Verner, James	1st NC Regiment	5/8/1777, a Captain-Lieutenant. In service Jan. 1780.	Monmouth (NJ).
Verrier, James	5th NC Regiment	10/1/1776, an Ensign and an Adjutant. June 1778, a Lieutenant under Capt. Thomas Armstrong (2nd NC Regiment). Found guilty of beating the regiment's Fife Major, but not "cruelly." Resigned 11/22/1778. A Quarter Master in the 5th NC Regiment from Apr. 1779 to 9/10/1779 (resigned).	
Vessells, James	1st NC Regiment	5/9/1781, a Private under Capt. Alexander Brevard. Deserted on 6/20/1781.	
Vicas, Thomas	4th NC Regiment	1782, a Private under Capt. William Lytle for 18 months. A Musician on 12/1/1782.	
Vick, Isaac	2nd NC Regiment	9/16/1777, a Private under Capt. Clement Hall for three years. 9/9/1778, a known Private under Capt. Robert Fenner. aka Isaiah Vick.	
Vick, Jacob	2nd NC Regiment	1782, a Sergeant under Capt. Benjamin Carter for 18 months.	
Vick, Jesse	3rd NC Regiment	7/20/1778, a Sergeant under Maj. Thomas Hogg for nine months.	
Vick, Joseph	4th NC Regiment	1781, a Private under Capt. Joseph T. Rhodes. Discharged on 7/16/1782. Earlier in NC Militia. From Duplin (what is now Sampson) County, NC. W6364.	
Vickers, Riley		A Private, unit and dates unknown. Either from Granville or Orange County, NC. R10941.	
Vickery, Marmaduke	4th NC Regiment	1782, a Private under Capt. William Lytle. Died on 12/14/1782.	
Vickory, Luke	1st NC Regiment	8/9/1781, a Private under Lt./Capt. Elijah Moore, then under Capt. Alexander Brevard (3rd NC Regiment), then under Capt. Joseph T. Rhodes (4th NC Regiment). Wounded at the battle of Eutaw Springs, SC. July 1782, furloughed at 10-Mile, SC. Earlier in NC Militia. From Randolph County, NC. On the official rolls as Luke Vickery. S1782.	Eutaw Springs (SC).
Vickry, John	1st NC Regiment	Jan. 1782, a Private under Capt. William Armstrong.	
Vincent, Benjamin	3rd NC Regiment	7/20/1778, a Private under Capt. Kedar Ballard for nine months.	
Vincent, David	1st NC Regiment	5/18/1781, a Private under Capt. Robert Raiford. Died in Oct. 1781. aka David Vincen.	
Vincent, Henry	3rd NC Regiment	4/16/1776, a 2nd Lieutenant. aka Harry Vincents.	

652

Name	1st Unit	Year / Rank / Served Under / Notes	Known Battles
Vines, John	1st NC Regiment	12/19/1781, a Private under Capt. James Mills for 12 months. From New Hanover County, NC.	
Vines, John	1st NC Regiment	4/15/1781, a Corporal under Capt. Anthony Sharpe. Discharged on 4/15/1782 (4th NC Regiment).	
Vines, Samuel	1st NC Regiment	12/19/1781, a Private under Capt. James Mills for 12 months. From New Hanover County, NC.	
Vining, Keedar	3rd NC Regiment	7/20/1778, a Private under Capt. Michael Quinn for nine months.	
Visson, Henry	2nd NC Regiment	9/1/1775, an Ensign. aka Henry Vipon, Henry Vipson.	Moore's Creek Bridge [4].
Vize, Henry	6th NC Regiment	5/2/1776, a Private under Lt./Capt. Francis Child for 2-1/2 years. 9/8/1778, a known Private under Capt. Griffith John McRee (1st NC Regiment) - sick at Valley Forge on that date. 3/12/1779, re-enlisted for the duration of the war under Capt. Griffith John McRee (1st NC Regiment). aka Henry Vire, Henry Voze.	
Vollow, Nicholas	4th NC Regiment	1781, a Private under Capt. George Dougherty for 12 months. Discharged on 5/25/1782.	
Vose, Joseph	1st NC Regiment	5/25/1781, a Private under Capt. Alexander Brevard. Died on 7/10/1783.	
Vowell, William	6th NC Regiment	5/1/1776, a Private under Lt./Capt. Thomas White for three years. 9/8/1778, a known Private under Capt. John Sumner (1st NC Regiment). 3/12/1779, re-enlisted for the duration of the war in the same unit.	
Waddle, James	4th NC Regiment	1781, a Corporal under Capt. George Dougherty. Discharged on 5/25/1782.	
Wade, Andrew	6th NC Regiment	4/25/1776, a Private under Capt. Philip Taylor for 2-1/2 years. 9/8/1778, a known Private under Capt. John Sumner (1st NC Regiment) - sick in camp on that date. Discharged in Nov. 1778. aka Andrew Waid.	
Wade, Daniel	4th NC Regiment	1777, a Musician under Capt. James Williams. Killed while in service, when and where unknown. Dropped from the rolls in Feb. 1778. From Northampton County, NC. W18267.	
Wade, Elisha	2nd NC Regiment	1782, a Private under Capt. Benjamin Carter for 18 months.	
Wade, John	4th NC Regiment	1782, a Private under Capt. William Lytle for 18 months.	
Wade, Joseph John	9th NC Regiment	11/28/1776, a Captain under Col. John Williams. Dropped from the rolls in Jan. 1778. From Salisbury District. aka I. Joseph Wade.	
Wade, William	1st NC Regiment	5/14/1781, a Private under Capt. Thomas Donoho for 12 months.	
Wadkins, Benjamin	1st NC Regiment	8/1/1782, a Private under Capt. Joshua Hadley for 18 months. aka Benjamin Watkins.	
Wadkins, John	3rd NC Regiment	7/20/1778, a Private under Capt. John Baker for nine months. From Guilford County, NC. W6415.	
Wadsworth, William	4th NC Regiment	Dec. 1782, a Private under Capt. Joseph T. Rhodes for 18 months. Enlisted in Craven	

Name	1st Unit	Year / Rank / Served Under / Notes	Known Battles
		County, NC. Discharged after about 11 months of service when peace announced. aka William Wardsworth. S7807.	
Waggoner, James	2nd NC Regiment	1781, a Private under Capt. Benjamin Carter. Died on 2/15/1782.	
Wainwright, Obediah	1st NC Regiment	8/1/1782, a Private under Capt. Joshua Hadley for 18 months. Died on 6/13/1783.	
Wakefield, William	7th NC Regiment	1/23/1777, a Musician under Capt. John Poynter for 3 years. A Private in Nov. 1777. 9/8/1778, a known Private under Capt. Tilghman Dixon (1st NC Regiment). Discharged in 1/28/1780.	
Walden, David	1st NC Regiment	1777, a Private under Capt. Tilghman Dixon. Then, under Capt. Anthony Sharp (10th NC Regiment) - discharged in Sep. 1779. 5/2/1781, a Private under Capt. Anthony Sharpe (1st NC Regiment). Dropped from the rolls sometime during 1781. From Mecklenburg County, NC. S32570.	Florida Expedition 1778, Briar Creek (GA).
Walden, John	4th NC Regiment	1781, a Private under Capt. George Dougherty. Discharged on 5/25/1782. Earlier in NC Militia. From Warren County, NC. W4374.	
Waldnan, Thomas	2nd NC Regiment	Dec. 1776, a Musician under Capt. Edward Vail, Jr. for three years. A Private in June 1778 in the Colonel's Company (Col. John Patten) led by Capt. John Craddock. POW at the Fall of Charleston (SC), escaped in March 1781. From Pasquotank County, NC. aka Thomas Waldren, Thomas Waldron. S42057.	Brandywine Creek (PA), Germantown (PA), Siege of Charleston 1780 (SC).
Walker, James	5th NC Regiment	8/5/1779, a Private under Maj. Reading Blount. Deserted in Oct. 1779.	
Walker, Jeremiah	4th NC Regiment	1778-1779, in the "New Levies." Early 1779, a Private under Col. James Armstrong, Captain not named. Fall of 1780 in NC Militia. 4/7/1781, a Sergeant under Capt. Robert Smith (1st NC Regiment) and Capt. William Lytle. Discharged on 4/7/1782 (4th NC Regiment). From Franklin County, NC. S31457.	Stono Ferry (SC), Camden (SC), Fort Motte (SC), Siege of Augusta (GA), Eutaw Springs (SC).
Walker, John	1st NC Regiment	4/12/1781, a Private under Capt. William Lytle. Discharged on 4/5/1782 (4th NC Regiment). Earlier in NC Militia. From Warren County, NC. S7796.	
Walker, John	1st NC Regiment	9/1/1775, a Captain under Col. James Moore. Aide-de-Camp to Maj. Gen. George Washington on 2/17/1777. A Major from 4/26/1777 until 12/22/1777, when he resigned. Very early 1775, a Colonel of NC Militia. From Tryon (later Rutherford) County, NC. aka Jack Walker.	Moore's Creek Bridge [4], Breech Inlet Naval Battle (SC), Brandywine Creek (PA), Germantown (PA).
Walker, John	2nd NC Regiment	9/1/1775, a Captain under Col. Robert Howe. Resigned 10/21/1775. From New Hanover Co.	
Walker, John	3rd NC	1775, a 2nd Lieutenant in the Salisbury District	

Name	1ˢᵗ Unit	Year / Rank / Served Under / Notes	Known Battles
Jr.	Regiment	Minutemen. 4/17/1776, a 2ⁿᵈ Lieutenant under Capt. James Cook and Col. Jethro Sumner. From Tryon County, NC.	
Walker, John	9ᵗʰ NC Regiment	1/20/1777, a Sergeant under Capt. Thomas McCrory then under Capt. Richard D. Cook for 12 months. A QM Sergeant on 9/20/1777. Dropped from the rolls in Jan. 1778. From Guilford County, NC. W64.	
Walker, Joseph	7ᵗʰ NC Regiment	11/28/1776, a Captain under Col. James Hogun. Dropped from the rolls in Jan. 1778. From Hertford County, NC.	Brandywine Creek (PA), Germantown (PA).
Walker, Moses	6ᵗʰ NC Regiment	Oct. 1777, a Private under Capt. Griffith John McRee. Dropped from the rolls in Feb. 1778.	
Walker, S. Richard		6/7/1779, a Sergeant Major - regiment unknown.	
Walker, Solomon	3ʳᵈ NC Regiment	6/18/1782, a Private under Capt. Benjamin Bailey for 12 months.	
Walker, Solomon	6ᵗʰ NC Regiment	1775, an Ensign in the Hillsborough District Minutemen. 4/17/1776, an Ensign under Capt. Philip Taylor and Col. John Alexander Lillington. 4/20/1777, a 2ⁿᵈ Lieutenant under Capt. Benjamin Pike. Resigned on 8/28/1777.	
Walker, Thomas	1ˢᵗ NC Regiment	4/5/1777, a Wagoner and a Wagon Master. Discharged 10/19/1777 in Pennsylvania after the battle of Germantown. From Mecklenburg County, NC. W6397.	
Walker, Thomas	5ᵗʰ NC Regiment	7/1/1779, a Private under Capt. Joseph Montford. Deserted on 10/21/1779.	
Walker, William	2ⁿᵈ NC Regiment	1782, a Private under Capt. Robert Raiford for 18 months.	
Walker, William	2ⁿᵈ NC Regiment	A Lieutenant, unit and dates unknown. POW at the Fall of Charleston, exchanged on 6/14/1781.	Siege of Charleston 1780 (SC).
Walker, William	5ᵗʰ NC Regiment	8/3/1779, a Private under Maj. Reading Blount for 3 years.	
Walker, William	10ᵗʰ NC Regiment	9/4/1777, a Private under Capt. Abraham Sheppard, Jr. for three years. 9/8/1778, a known Private under Capt. Howell Tatum (1st NC Regiment). 3/12/1779, re-enlisted for the duration of the war under Capt. Tilghman Dixon (1st NC Regiment). Deserted on 3/24/1779.	
Wall, David	2ⁿᵈ NC Regiment	9/9/1778, a known Private in the Major's Company (Maj. Hardy Murfree).	
Wall, James	NC Artillery	11/16/1777, a 3rd Lieutenant under Capt. John Kingsbury. 9/10/1778, a known 1st Lieutenant under Capt. John Kingsbury. Resigned on 7/20/1779.	
Wall, Joel	10ᵗʰ NC Regiment	8/7/1777, a Private under Capt. Andrew Vanoy. A Sergeant in Apr. 1778. 9/9/1778, a known Sergeant in the Lt. Colonel's Company (Lt. Col. Selby Harney) (2nd NC Regiment). Back to Private in June 1778. 3/12/1779, re-enlisted in the Lt. Colonel's Company (Lt. Col. Selby	Brandywine Creek (PA), Monmouth (NJ).

Name	1st Unit	Year / Rank / Served Under / Notes	Known Battles
		Harney). From Pitt or Beaufort County, NC. W4095.	
Wall, John	1st NC Regiment	4/15/1781, a Private under Capt. Anthony Sharpe. Dropped from the rolls sometime during 1781.	
Wall, Jonathan	1st NC Regiment	Aug. 1781, a Private under Capt. Alexander Brevard. 1782, a Private under Capt. William Lytle (4th NC Regiment) for 18 months. Earlier in NC Militia. From Wilkes County, NC. S9569.	
Wall, Richard	1st NC Regiment	1/4/1782, a Private under Capt. James Mills for 12 months. 2/6/1782, this unit was transferred to the 4th NC Regiment. S42054.	
Wallace, Aaron	1st NC Regiment	4/28/1781, a Private under Capt. Alexander Brevard. Deserted on 5/7/1781. Probably the same man as directly below.	
Wallace, Aaron	4th NC Regiment	1782, a Private under Capt. Benjamin Coleman (2nd NC Regiment), then soon transferred to Capt. William Lytle (4th NC Regiment). He claims to have been discharged. Official records indicate that he deserted on 5/15/1783 (?). Enlisted in Wayne County, NC. R11062.	
Wallace, George	8th NC Regiment	4/1/1777, a Musician under Capt. James May, then transferred to Capt. Francis Tartanson. 3/12/1779, re-enlisted under Capt. Benjamin Andrew Coleman (2nd NC Regiment). A Regimental Fife Major in Dec. 1782. From Pitt County, NC. W11741.	Brandywine Creek (PA), Siege of Charleston 1780 (SC), Eutaw Springs (SC).
Wallace, James		11/30/1778, a Lieutenant, regiment and unit unknown. Dropped from the rolls sometime between Jan. 1779 and Sep. 1779.	
Wallace, John	8th NC Regiment	Private under Capt. Joseph T. Rhodes. July 1778, under Capt. Charles Stewart (2nd NC Regiment). 1779, under Capt. Thomas Armstrong (2nd NC Regiment). POW at Ft. Lafayette, NY on 6/1/1779 for 11 months. Enlisted in Duplin County, NC. Probably the same man as the two id'd below. W25897.	Ft. Lafayette (NY).
Wallace, John	10th NC Regiment	6/4/1777, a Private, unit unknown. 9/9/1778, a known Private in the Lt. Colonel's Company (Lt. Col. Selby Harney) (2nd NC Regiment). 3/12/1779, re-enlisted in the Lt. Colonel's Company (Lt. Col. Selby Harney). POW at Ft. Lafayette, NY on 6/1/1779.	Ft. Lafayette (NY).
Wallace, John	10th NC Regiment	6/4/1777, a Private under Capt. Andrew Vanoy. 9/9/1778, a known Private under Capt. Robert Fenner (2nd NC Regiment). POW at Ft. Lafayette, NY on 6/1/1779. Probably the same man as directly above. aka John Wallis.	Ft. Lafayette (NY).
Wallace, Richard	3rd NC Regiment	7/20/1778, a Private under Capt. Francis Child for nine months.	
Wallace, Thomas	1st NC Regiment	4/15/1781, a Private under Capt. Griffith John McRee. Died in Oct. 1781.	

656

Name	1st Unit	Year / Rank / Served Under / Notes	Known Battles
Wallace, Thomas	3rd NC Regiment	4/1/1782, a Sergeant under Capt. Benjamin Bailey for 12 months.	
Wallace, Thomas	5th NC Regiment	4/19/1776, a Private under Capt. William Caswell for 12 months. Discharged on 4/19/1777 in Halifax County, NC. S39116.	
Waller, Nathaniel	2nd NC Regiment	1782, a Private under Capt. Benjamin Carter for 18 months. S42051.	
Wallis, James	1st NC Regiment	5/25/1781, a Private under Capt. Thomas Donoho. Jan. 1782, a Sergeant. Discharged on 5/20/1782.	
Wallis, James	3rd NC Regiment	11/30/1778, an Ensign.	
Wallis, John	1st NC Regiment	5/25/1781, a Private under Capt. Thomas Donoho. Discharged on 5/25/1782. From Wake County, NC. aka John Wallace. W6410.	
Wallis, Matthew	1st NC Regiment	March 1781, a Fifer in VA unit at the battle of Guilford Court House. Soon thereafter, he enlisted as a Fifer under Capt. Thomas Donoho. Discharged at Charlotte, NC in August 1782. Later lived in Wake County, NC. From Amelia County, VA. R11087.	Siege of Ninety-Six 1781 (SC), Eutaw Springs (SC).
Wallron, Archibald	1st NC Regiment	4/12/1781, a Private under Capt. Alexander Brevard.	
Walsh, John	8th NC Regiment	11/28/1776, a Captain under Col. James Armstrong. Dropped from the rolls in Jan. 1778. Earlier in 1776, a Captain from Wake County, attached to Col. Ebenezer Folsome (Cumberland County).	Brandywine Creek (PA), Germantown (PA).
Walsh, Robert	8th NC Regiment	2/16/1777, a Private under Capt. Robert Raiford. Dropped from the rolls in Feb. 1778.	
Walter, Dempsey	7th NC Regiment	1777, a Private under Capt. Thomas Brickell. Missing on 10/4/1777 at the battle of Germantown, PA.	Germantown (PA).
Walter, Jeremiah	4th NC Regiment	1782, a Private under Capt. Thomas Evans for 18 months. Deserted in Jan. 1783.	
Walter, John	1st NC Regiment	10/13/1777, a Private under Capt. James Read. 9/8/1778, in same unit.	
Walter, William	7th NC Regiment	1777, a Private under Capt. Thomas Brickell. Dropped from the rolls in Oct. 1777.	
Walters, John	1st NC Regiment	1777, a Musician under Capt. Thomas Hogg. 9/8/1778, a known Private under Capt. Joshua Bowman. A Drum Major in July 1779. aka John Waters.	
Walters, Walter	5th NC Regiment	1779, a Private under Maj. Reading Blount. Died on 8/30/1779.	
Walton, Richard	1st NC Regiment	1776, a Private under Capt. Joshua Bowman. Dropped from the rolls in Sep. 1778.	
Walton, William	7th NC Regiment	4/17/1777, a 2nd Lieutenant under Capt. John Poynter. Transferred to 1st NC Regiment on 6/1/1778. 8/15/1778, a 1st Lieutenant under Capt. Howell Tatum. POW at the Fall of Charleston, escaped. 10/13/1781, a Captain - took over the company previously led by Capt. Thomas Donoho. In April 1782, his commission	Siege of Charleston 1780 (SC).

Name	1st Unit	Year / Rank / Served Under / Notes	Known Battles
		was back-dated to 9/8/1781. Retired on 1/1/1783. From Hertford County, NC.	
Wamble, Benjamin	5th NC Regiment	4/16/1776, a Private under Capt. William Caswell for 2-1/2 years. Discharged on 11/10/1778.	
Warburton, Solomon	3rd NC Regiment	1781, a Private under Capt. Clement Hall for 12 months. Discharged on 4/21/1782 (2nd NC Regiment).	
Warburton, Thomas	3rd NC Regiment	8/1/1782, a Private under Capt. Benjamin Bailey for 18 months.	
Ward, Benjamin	1st NC Regiment	1781, a Private under Capt. Robert Raiford. Died in Nov. 1781.	
Ward, Drewry	4th NC Regiment	5/16/1776, a Private under Capt. John Nelson for three years. 6/1/1778, a Private under Capt. Griffith John McRee (1st NC Regiment). Discharged on 5/15/1779. aka Drury Ward.	
Ward, Edward	8th NC Regiment	11/28/1776, a Captain under Col. James Armstrong. Resigned on 8/1/1777. From Wilmington District.	
Ward, Elijah	3rd NC Regiment	7/20/1778, a Private under Capt. Kedar Ballard for nine months.	
Ward, Elijah	4th NC Regiment	1782, a Private under Capt. Thomas Evans for 18 months.	
Ward, Isaac	3rd NC Regiment	7/1/1779, a Private under Capt. Kedar Ballard. Deserted in March 1780.	
Ward, James	1st NC Regiment	A Surgeon's Mate. Resigned 7/14/1777.	
Ward, James	6th NC Regiment	1777, a Private under Capt. Thomas Donoho. Deserted in Aug. 1777.	
Ward, Job	5th NC Regiment	1777, a Private under Capt. Henry Darnell. Dropped from the rolls in Feb. 1778.	
Ward, John	1st NC Regiment	1781, a Private under Capt. William Lytle.	
Ward, John	4th NC Regiment	4/16/1776, a Private under Capt. John Nelson for three years. 9/8/1778, a known Private under Capt. Griffith John McRee (1st NC Regiment) - sick on that date. 3/12/1779, re-enlisted for the duration of the war in the same unit.	
Ward, John	10th NC Regiment	5/18/1777, a Private under Capt. Abraham Sheppard, Jr.	
Ward, Joseph	3rd NC Regiment	7/20/1778, a Private in the Lt. Colonel's Company (Lt. Col. William Lee Davidson) led by Lt./Capt. George "Gee" Bradley for nine months. 4/23/1779, a known Private in the Lt. Colonel's Company (Lt. Col. Robert Mebane) led by Capt. George "Gee" Bradley. Died at New Windsor Hospital.	
Ward, Ludwick	3rd NC Regiment	6/29/1779, a Private under Capt. Kedar Ballard. Deserted on 8/5/1779.	
Ward, Richard	5th NC Regiment	3/1/1779, a Private under Capt. Joseph Montford. Discharged on 12/1/1779.	
Ward, Richard	10th NC Regiment	4/28/1777, a Sergeant under Capt. Andrew Vanoy. Dropped from the rolls in June 1778.	
Ward,	1st NC	1777, a Private under Capt. Joshua Bowman.	

Name	1ˢᵗ Unit	Year / Rank / Served Under / Notes	Known Battles
Thomas	Regiment		
Ward, Thomas	1ˢᵗ NC Regiment	1777, a Private under Capt. Henry "Hal" Dixon. Dropped from the rolls in June 1778.	
Ward, Thomas	5ᵗʰ NC Regiment	1777, a Private under Capt. Benjamin Andrew Coleman. Deserted on 7/22/1777.	
Ward, William	4ᵗʰ NC Regiment	1782, a Private under Capt. Anthony Sharpe for 18 months.	
Ward, William	5ᵗʰ NC Regiment	1775, a Captain in the Salisbury District Minutemen. 4/17/1776, a Captain in the 5th NC Regiment. Resigned in early 1777.	
Ward, William	6ᵗʰ NC Regiment	1777, a Private under Capt. Daniel Williams. Earlier and later in NC Militia. From Duplin County, NC. S7809.	Brandywine Creek (PA).
Ward, William	7ᵗʰ NC Regiment	1777, a Private under Capt. Thomas Brickell. Deserted in Apr. 1777.	
Ward, Willis	1ˢᵗ NC Regiment	4/2/1781, a Private under Lt./Capt. Benjamin Bailey. Discharged on 4/2/1782 (3rd NC Regiment). From Nash County, NC. W18255.	
Ware, George	DQMG	1780, a Tailor on the roll of Capt. Solomon Wood (NC Light Dragoons) - this seems to be for convenience only. A Tailor under Col. Nicholas Long (Deputy QM General). Said to be an ex-Continental soldier (?). Also on 8/23/1781.	
Ware, William	4ᵗʰ NC Regiment	Spring of 1776, a Private under Capt. Roger Moore for 13 months. 1779, in NC Militia. From Caswell County, NC. W6386.	
Warf, George	1ˢᵗ NC Regiment	6/14/1781, a Private under Capt. Thomas Donoho. Discharged on 6/14/1782.	
Warner, Hardin	5ᵗʰ NC Regiment	10/1/1779, a Private under Maj. Reading Blount. W18253.	
Warner, John	5ᵗʰ NC Regiment	4/6/1776, a Private under Capt. Reading Blount for 2-1/2 years. 9/9/1778, a known Private in the Lt. Colonel's Company (Lt. Col. Selby Harney - 2nd NC Regiment). Discharged in Oct. 1778.	
Warren, Archibald	1ˢᵗ NC Regiment	1781, a Private under Capt. Alexander Brevard. Discharged on 4/12/1782 (3rd NC Regiment).	
Warren, Edward	5ᵗʰ NC Regiment	1777, a Private under Capt. Henry Darnell. Discharged in Aug. 1777.	
Warren, John	1ˢᵗ NC Regiment	4/12/1781, a Private under Capt. Alexander Brevard. Discharged on 4/12/1782 (3rd NC Regiment) at Pon Pon, SC. Earlier in NC Militia. From Northampton County, NC. S3457.	Siege of Augusta (GA), Eutaw Springs (SC).
Warren, Matthew	6ᵗʰ NC Regiment	A Private under Capt. Thomas White. Died on 2/9/1778.	
Warren, Samuel	1ˢᵗ NC Regiment	8/1/1782, a Private under Capt. Joshua Hadley for 18 months.	
Warren, William	5ᵗʰ NC Regiment	5/11/1776, a Private under Capt. Peter Simon, then Capt. Henry Darnell. June 1778, under Capt. Benjamin Andrew Coleman (2nd NC Regiment). Discharged at Valley Forge on 4/29/1779. S42052.	Brandywine Creek (PA), Germantown (PA).
Warren, Zebulon	5ᵗʰ NC Regiment	1777, a Musician under Capt. Benjamin Andrew Coleman. Died on 2/15/1778.	

Name	1st Unit	Year / Rank / Served Under / Notes	Known Battles
Warwick, John	3rd NC Regiment	7/20/1778, a Private under Capt. Michael Quinn for nine months.	
Warwick, Shadrach	3rd NC Regiment	11/1/1778, a Corporal under Lt./Capt. Joseph Montford.	
Warwick, Thomas	9th NC Regiment	1777, a Private under Capt. Thomas McCrory. Dropped from the rolls in Jan. 1778.	
Warwick, Wyatt	4th NC Regiment	1781, a Private under Capt. George Dougherty for 12 months. Discharged on 5/25/1782 at Wilmington, NC. Joined at Tarborough, NC (Edgecombe County). W3898.	
Washington, Etheldred	7th NC Regiment	7/12/1777, a Musician under Capt. James Vaughan for three years. 2/26/1778, a known Private under Capt. Howell Tatum (1st NC Regiment). 9/8/1778, a known Musician under Capt. Howell Tatum. 3/12/1779, re-enlisted for the duration of the war in the same unit.	
Washington, Robert	3rd NC Regiment	4/15/1776, an Adjutant. From Halifax County.	
Washington, William	2nd NC Regiment	1777, a Sergeant under Capt. Charles Allen. Dropped from the rolls in Nov. 1777.	
Washington, William	9th NC Regiment	8/15/1777, an Ensign under Capt. Joseph J. Wade. Retired on 1/1/1778.	
Waters, Isaac	4th NC Regiment	1777, a Private under Capt. James Williams. Discharged in Nov. 1777.	
Waters, James	1st NC Regiment	12/24/1776, an Ensign. 3/29/1777, a 2nd Lieutenant under Capt. Robert Ralston. Resigned on 4/23/1777.	
Waters, John	6th NC Regiment	1777, a Private under Capt. Thomas Donoho. Deserted in Aug. 1777.	
Waters, John	10th NC Regiment	11/15/1777, a Private under Capt. Andrew Vanoy. 3/12/1779, re-enlisted for the duration of the war under Capt. Griffith John McRee (1st NC Regiment). Discharged on 2/1/1780.	
Waters, Samuel	1st NC Regiment	12/24/1776, an Ensign. 3/29/1777, a 2nd Lieutenant under Capt. Robert Ralston. Resigned on 4/23/1777. aka Samuel Walters.	
Waters, Solomon	4th NC Regiment	2/6/1782, a Musician under Capt. James Mills. A Private in Sep. 1782.	
Waters, William	1st NC Regiment	1776, a Private under Capt. Joshua Bowman.	
Watford, William	2nd NC Regiment	7/20/1778, a Private under Maj. Reading Blount for nine months. Discharged in April 1779 at Halifax, NC. From Bertie County, NC. S3463.	
Watkins, Shadrack	1st NC Regiment	1777, a Private under Capt. Henry "Hal" Dixon. 9/8/1778, a known Private under Capt. James Read.	
Watson, Alexander	3rd NC Regiment	3/12/1782, a Private under Capt. Benjamin Bailey for 12 months.	
Watson, Ephraim	3rd NC Regiment	7/20/1778, a Private under Maj. Thomas Hogg for nine months. aka Ephraim Whatson.	
Watson, James	4th NC Regiment	1777, a Private under Capt. William Temple Coles. Deserted on 9/22/1777.	
Watson, Lott	2nd NC	8/1/1782, a Private under Capt. Clement Hall.	

Name	1st Unit	Year / Rank / Served Under / Notes	Known Battles
	Regiment		
Watson, Micajah	5th NC Regiment	11/26/1777, a Private under Capt. William Caswell. 9/9/1778, a known Private under Capt. Robert Fenner (2nd NC Regiment). POW at the Fall of Charleston, SC. On some muster rolls as Michael Watson. From Hertford County, NC. W4096.	Siege of Charleston 1780 (SC).
Watson, Miles	3rd NC Regiment	7/20/1778, a Private under Lt./Capt. Joseph Montford. Died on 9/12/1778.	
Watson, Neal	3rd NC Regiment	8/1/1782, a Private under Capt. Benjamin Bailey for 12 months.	
Watson, Neal	3rd NC Regiment	7/20/1778, a Private under Capt. Michael Quinn for nine months. S42056.	
Watson, Philip	9th NC Regiment	1/16/1777, a Private under Capt. Richard D. Cook for three years. 9/8/1778, a known Wagoner in the Lt. Colonel's Company (Lt. Col. Robert Mebane) (1st NC Regiment) led by Capt. Joshua Bowman. Discharged on 1/27/1780 in Halifax, NC. Enlisted in Granville County, NC. W6413.	Brandywine Creek (PA), Germantown (PA), Monmouth (NJ).
Watson, Robert	5th NC Regiment	5/16/1776, a Private under Capt. Benjamin Stedman. 9/9/1778, a known Private under Capt. Clement Hall (2nd NC Regiment). Deserted on 4/29/1779.	
Watson, Solomon	3rd NC Regiment	7/20/1778, a Private under Maj. Thomas Hogg for nine months.	
Watson, Thomas	2nd NC Regiment	1777, a Sergeant under Capt. Clement Hall. Dropped from the rolls in Jan. 1778.	
Watson, Thomas	7th NC Regiment	11/28/1776, a 1st Lieutenant under Capt. John McGlaughan. Resigned on 8/12/1777. From Edenton District.	
Watson, William	DQMG	1780, a Saddler on the roll of Capt. Solomon Wood (NC Light Dragoons) - this seems to be for convenience only. 8/23/1781, a Leather Worker under Col. Nicholas Long (Deputy QM General), making saddles, harnesses, caps, etc.	
Watson, William	5th NC Regiment	A Private, unit and dates unknown. Deserted five times.	
Watters, John	NC Artillery	4/13/1778, a Matross under Capt. John Kingsbury for three years. 5/1/1778, in same unit. 9/16/1778, in same unit. aka John Walters, John Warters, John Worters.	
Watters, William	1st NC Regiment	9/19/1776, an Ensign. 2/5/1777, a 2nd Lieutenant under Capt. Lawrence Thompson. Transferred to the NC Light Dragoons on 6/1/1778. From Orange County, NC. aka William Walters, William Waters. W3897.	Germantown (PA).
Watts, Andrew	4th NC Regiment	1777, a Private under Capt. Thomas Harris. Died on 2/19/1778.	
Watts, John	1st NC Regiment	1781, a Private under Capt. William Walton for 12 months. Discharged on 6/14/1782.	
Watts, Peter	4th NC Regiment	May 1776, a Private under Capt. John Nelson. In service about one year. Enlisted from Guilford County, NC where he lived until	

661

Name	1st Unit	Year / Rank / Served Under / Notes	Known Battles
		around 1779 - moved to Kentucky. Born 1756 in Culpeper County, VA. S30765.	
Watts, William	9th NC Regiment	1777, a Private under Capt. Richard D. Cook. Died on 9/9/1777.	
Waycroft, Mark	2nd NC Regiment	6/13/1777, a Private, unit unknown. 9/9/1778, a known Private in the Major's Company (Maj. Hardy Murfree).	
Waymouth, Corbin	2nd NC Regiment	12/18/1776, a Private under Capt. James Gee. 9/9/1778, a known Private under Capt. John Ingles (2nd NC Regiment). A Corporal in Nov. 1778. POW at Ft. Lafayette, NY on 6/1/1779. Discharged on 1/1/1780.	Ft. Lafayette (NY).
Weaks, Dixon	1st NC Regiment	1781, a Private under Capt. Alexander Brevard for 12 months. Discharged on 6/11/1782 (3rd NC Regiment).	
Weaks, Lewis	3rd NC Regiment	1/1/1782, a Sergeant under Capt. Samuel Jones for 12 months.	
Wearing, James	1st NC Regiment	6/30/1777, a Private under Capt. Joshua Bowman. Deserted on 7/2/1777.	
Weather, John	3rd NC Regiment	7/20/1778, a Private under Capt. Kedar Ballard for nine months.	
Weathers, Philip	3rd NC Regiment	1781, a Private under Capt. Clement Hall.	
Weathers, Willis	1st NC Regiment	1781, a Private under Capt. Griffith John McRee, then under Capt. Clement Hall (3rd NC Regiment). Discharged on 4/12/1782 (2nd NC Regiment). Earlier, in NC Militia. Enlisted while living in Franklin County, NC. S7862.	
Weather-spoon, Lawrence	6th NC Regiment	1777, a Private under Capt. Philip Taylor. Deserted on 7/5/1777.	
Weaver, Benjamin	1st NC Regiment	4/25/1781, a Private under Capt. Robert Raiford. Discharged on 4/25/1782 (2nd NC Regiment).	
Weaver, Daniel	1st NC Regiment	6/26/1781, a Private under Capt. Robert Raiford. Discharged on 6/26/1782 (2nd NC Regiment).	
Weaver, Edward	1st NC Regiment	1781, a Private under Capt. Anthony Sharpe. Discharged on 5/15/1782 (4th NC Regiment).	
Weaver, John	10th NC Regiment	5/18/1777 or 7/3/1777 (two sources), a Private under Capt. Abraham Sheppard, Jr. 9/9/1778, a known Private under Capt. Clement Hall (2nd NC Regiment). POW at the Fall of Charleston (SC), exchanged. S42161.	Monmouth (NJ), Siege of Charleston 1780 (SC).
Weaver, Lewis	4th NC Regiment	1777, a Corporal under Capt. William Temple Coles. Dropped from the rolls in Sep. 1777.	
Weaver, William	1st NC Regiment	5/2/1781, a Corporal under Capt. Alexander Brevard.	
Webb, Charles	2nd NC Regiment	1777, a Corporal under Capt. Charles Allen. 9/10/1778, a known Corporal under Capt. Thomas Armstrong. A Private in Feb. 1779.	
Webb, Elisha	7th NC Regiment	11/28/1776, an Ensign under Capt. Josiah Cotton then under Capt. James Vaughan. From Northampton County, NC.	

Name	1st Unit	Year / Rank / Served Under / Notes	Known Battles
Webb, Jacob	1st NC Regiment	4/12/1781, a Private under Lt./Capt. Benjamin Bailey. Discharged on 4/12/1782 (3rd NC Regiment).	
Webb, James	3rd NC Regiment	7/20/1778, a Fifer under Lt./Capt. George "Gee" Bradley for nine months. Discharged at Halifax, NC in May 1779. Enlisted in April 1778 in Dobbs County, NC. 1776, in Dobbs County Militia.	
Webb, Jesse	1st NC Regiment	1781, a Private for seven months under Capt. Robert Smith. Hired a substitute for remaining five months. Earlier in NC Militia. From Franklin County, NC. W18333.	Siege of Augusta (GA).
Webb, John	2nd NC Regiment	1777, a Private in the Colonel's Company as a 3-year man. Probably at the Fall of Charleston, SC in May 1780. From Wilkes County, NC.	
Webb, John	3rd NC Regiment	4/23/1776, a Commissary.	
Webb, John	4th NC Regiment	1777, a Private under Capt. Robert Smith. Discharged on 8/10/1777.	
Webb, John	10th NC Regiment	9/1/1777, a Private under Capt. Silas Stevenson. 9/10/1778, a known Private under Capt. Thomas Armstrong (2nd NC Regiment).	
Webb, Joseph	5th NC Regiment	1777, a Private under Capt. Henry Darnell. Dropped from the rolls in Feb. 1778.	
Webb, Joseph	10th NC Regiment	5/20/1777, a Private under Capt. Silas Stevenson. Dropped from the rolls in June 1778.	
Webb, Joshua	2nd NC Regiment	5/20/1777, a Private under Capt. William Fenner for 3 years. 9/10/1778, a known Private under Capt. Thomas Armstrong.	
Webb, Lewis	2nd NC Regiment	1782, a Musician under Capt. Benjamin Carter for 18 months.	
Webb, Rice	1st NC Regiment	4/12/1781, a Private under Lt./Capt. Benjamin Bailey. Discharged on 4/12/1782 (3rd NC Regiment).	
Webb, Samuel	1st NC Regiment	8/1/1782, a Private under Capt. Joshua Hadley for 18 months.	
Weble, John	1st NC Regiment	1/20/1782, a Private under Capt. James Mills for 12 months. On 2/6/1782, this unit was transferred to the 4th NC Regiment.	
Webley, Samuel	6th NC Regiment	A Private under Capt. George Dougherty. Died on 12/8/1777.	
Webster, Richard	2nd NC Regiment	12/23/1776, a Private under Capt. William Fenner for 3 years. 9/9/1778, a known Private in the Lt. Colonel's Company (Lt. Col. Selby Harney).	
Weeks, Cornelius	6th NC Regiment	1777, a Sergeant under Capt. Francis Child. One source claims he was dropped from the rolls in Dec. 1777. Another source claims he was discharged in April 1779.	
Weeks, Hardy	2nd NC Regiment	1777, a Private under Capt. James Martin. Deserted in Aug. 1777.	
Weeks, Levi	6th NC Regiment	5/3/1776, a Private under Capt. George Mitchell, then Capt. Benjamin Pike, then Capt. Thomas Donoho for 2-1/2 years. 6/1/1778, a	Brandywine Creek (PA), Germantown

NC Patriots 1775-1783: Their Own Words

Name	1st Unit	Year / Rank / Served Under / Notes	Known Battles
		Private under Capt. Griffith John McRee (1st NC Regiment). Also a Life Guard to General George Washington. Discharged on 11/10/1778. Drafted again in 1781 to serve under Capt. Samuel Jones (3rd NC Regiment). From Carteret County, NC.	(PA), Monmouth (NJ).
Weeks, Silas	6th NC Regiment	1777, a Private under Capt. Thomas Donoho. Died on 5/22/1778.	
Weeks, Sylvanus	1st NC Regiment	1777, a Private under Capt. Henry "Hal" Dixon. Died on 3/15/1778.	
Weeks, Theophilus	6th NC Regiment	5/20/1776, a Private under Capt. George Mitchell, then Capt. Thomas Donoho for 2-1/2 years. Deserted in Aug. 1777. Rejoined in Jan. 1778. 6/1/1778, a Private under Capt. Griffith John McRee (1st NC Regiment). Discharged on 11/10/1778. Born 10/21/1760. W22579.	
Welch, Basil	3rd NC Regiment	11/1/1776, a Private under Capt. Pinketham Eaton. 9/9/1778, a known Private under Capt. Robert Fenner (2nd NC Regiment). Discharged on 12/1/1778. aka Brazil Welsh.	
Welch, C. Noah	1st NC Regiment	8/1/1782, a Private under Capt. Joshua Hadley for 18 months. Died on 4/21/1783.	
Welch, William		Two tours in Militia, then a Continental under Capt. Lytle. From Orange County, NC.	Brandywine Creek (PA).
Welch, William	1st NC Regiment	Jan. 1782, a Private under Capt. Alexander Brevard. Probably from Carteret County, NC.	
Welch, William	1st NC Regiment	1777, a Corporal under Capt. John Brown. Deserted on 9/28/1777.	
Weldon, Samuel	DQMG	1780, a Blacksmith under Col. Nicholas Long (Deputy QM General). Also on 8/23/1781.	
Wells, Isaac	1st NC Regiment	5/15/1781, a Private under Lt./Capt. Benjamin Bailey. Discharged on 5/15/1782 (3rd NC Regiment).	
Wells, Isaac	5th NC Regiment	1779, a Private under Maj. Reading Blount. Deserted in Sep. 1779.	
Wells, Jesse	2nd NC Regiment	9/1/1775, a Private under Ens. William Caswell, Lt. John Herritage, Capt. Simon Bright for six months. Served eight months. Later in NC Militia. Enlisted in Dobbs County, NC. S3499.	
Wells, John	1st NC Regiment	Jan. 1782, a Private under Capt. Anthony Sharpe. 2/6/1782, this unit was transferred to the 4th NC Regiment.	
Wells, Uriah	3rd NC Regiment	6/8/1778, a Private under Lt./Capt. George "Gee" Bradley for 18 months. Dropped from the rolls in Oct. 1779.	
Wells, Willis	4th NC Regiment	1777, a Private under Capt. Micajah Lewis. Died on 11/16/1777. aka Willis Wills.	
Welsh, Thomas	4th NC Regiment	1781, a Private under Capt. George Dougherty. Discharged on 5/25/1782.	
West, Ciprian	3rd NC Regiment	7/20/1778, a Private under Lt./Capt. George "Gee" Bradley for nine months.	
West, James	4th NC Regiment	1782, a Private under Capt. Anthony Sharpe for 18 months.	
West, Joseph	5th NC	5/12/1776, a Sergeant under Capt. John Pugh	

Name	1ˢᵗ Unit	Year / Rank / Served Under / Notes	Known Battles
	Regiment	Williams for 2-1/2 years. A Private in Nov. 1777. Back to Sergeant in Jan. 1778. Back to Private on 5/20/1778. Discharged in Oct. 1778.	
West, Levy	6ᵗʰ NC Regiment	May 1776, a Drummer under Capt. George Mitchell, then Capt. Benjamin Pike. A Drum Major in Sep. 1777. Oct. 1777, a Musician under Capt. Thomas Donoho. Dropped from the rolls in Jan. 1778. He claims to have served a full three years and was discharged in 1779. S39122.	Brandywine Creek (PA), Germantown (PA).
West, Meredith	1ˢᵗ NC Regiment	12/22/1781, a Private under Capt. James Mills for 12 months. On 2/6/1782, this unit was transferred to the 4th NC Regiment.	
West, Nathaniel	5ᵗʰ NC Regiment	1777, a Private under Capt. Simon Alderson. Died on 11/30/1777. aka Nath. Weat.	
West, Samuel	2ⁿᵈ NC Regiment	1782, a Private under Capt. Robert Raiford for 18 months.	
West, William	1ˢᵗ NC Regiment	5/18/1781, a Private under Capt. Robert Raiford. Discharged on 5/18/1782 (2nd NC Regiment). W18304.	
Westbrook, William	1ˢᵗ NC Regiment	1777, a Private under Capt. John Brown. 9/8/1778, a known Private under Capt. Tilghman Dixon. Deserted on 2/12/1779.	
Westbrook, William	1ˢᵗ NC Regiment	6/14/1781, a Private under Capt. Thomas Donoho. Discharged on 6/14/1782.	
Westerdale, Francis	2ⁿᵈ NC Regiment	3/30/1776, a Musician under Lt./Capt. William Fenner. A Private in June 1778 in the Lt. Colonel's Company (Lt. Col. Selby Harney) (2nd NC Regiment).	
Weston, Amos	2ⁿᵈ NC Regiment	7/20/1778, a Private under Maj. Reading Blount for nine months.	
Weston, John	3ʳᵈ NC Regiment	9/24/1781, a Private under Capt. Samuel Jones for 12 months.	
Westray, Daniel	4ᵗʰ NC Regiment	1778, a Private under Capt. William Temple Coles for nine months. Sick during the battle of Stono Ferry, SC. From Franklin County, NC. S7851.	
Whaley, Ezekiel	10ᵗʰ NC Regiment	7/20/1777, a Private under Capt. Andrew Vanoy. A Musician in Sep. 1778. 9/9/1778, a known Fifer in the Major's Company (Maj. Hardy Murfree) (2nd NC Regiment). 3/12/1779, re-enlisted in the Major's Company (Maj. Hardy Murfree). POW at the Fall of Charleston. Discharged on 7/4/1783. Enlisted in Duplin County, NC. aka Ezekiel Wheely. S42064.	Siege of Charleston 1780 (SC).
Whaley, Francis	3ʳᵈ NC Regiment	7/20/1778, a Musician under Capt. Michael Quinn for nine months.	
Whaley, John	3ʳᵈ NC Regiment	7/20/1778, a Musician under Capt. Michael Quinn for nine months.	
Wharton, James	7ᵗʰ NC Regiment	4/6/1777, a Private under Capt. John McGlaughan. 2/26/1778, a known Private under Capt. Howell Tatum (1st NC Regiment).	

Name	1st Unit	Year / Rank / Served Under / Notes	Known Battles
Whedbee, Richard	7th NC Regiment	11/28/1776, a 2nd Lieutenant under Capt. Thomas Brickell. 8/15/1777, a 1st Lieutenant. Dismissed on 1/15/1778. From Edenton District. aka Richard Whedbey.	
Wheeler, Asa	2nd NC Regiment	1/10/1782, a Private under Capt. Benjamin Andrew Coleman. A Corporal in Sep. 1782.	
Wheeler, Benjamin	4th NC Regiment	1781, a Private under Capt. Joseph T. Rhodes. Discharged on 5/14/1782. aka Benjamin Wheelor.	
Wheeler, David	2nd NC Regiment	1781, a Corporal under Capt. Benjamin Carter. Died on 5/29/1783.	
Wheeler, David	3rd NC Regiment	5/23/1779, a Musician under Capt. Michael Quinn for 18 months. aka David Wheelor.	
Wheeler, Emperor		1779, a Private, regiment, unit, and dates unknown.	
Wheeler, Samuel	3rd NC Regiment	4/18/1776, a Private under Capt. Jacob Turner. 9/9/1778, a known Private under Capt. Robert Fenner (2nd NC Regiment). Discharged on 11/10/1778. aka Samuel Whelor.	
Wheelis, Sion	3rd NC Regiment	7/20/1778, a Private under Lt./Capt. Joseph Montford for nine months.	
Wheelow, H. Edward	1st NC Regiment	4/2/1781, a Private under Capt. William Lytle. Deserted on 7/12/1781.	
Whilley, Arthur	2nd NC Regiment	5/2/1776, a Private, unit unknown. 9/9/1778, a known Private in the Major's Company (Maj. Hardy Murfree).	
Whitaker, Hudson	7th NC Regiment	12/22/1776, an Ensign under Capt. Henry Dawson. 10/21/1777, a Captain when Henry Dawson resigned. Wounded at Hickory Hill on 6/24/1779 – regiment unknown.	
Whitaker, Robert L.	1st NC Regiment	Jul. 1782, under Lt. Robert Bell, then under Capt. Benjamin Carter (2nd NC Regiment). Furloughed in July 1783 at James Island, SC. Enlisted in Franklin County, NC. W10276.	
White, Benjamin	2nd NC Regiment	Apr. 1782, a Private under Capt. Clement Hall.	
White, Benjamin	4th NC Regiment	May 1776, a Private under Capt. Robert Smith for 12 months. Enlisted in Mecklenburg County. Discharged in May 1777 at Wilmington, NC. 1779, a Sergeant under Capt. Joseph T. Rhodes (4th NC Regiment) for nine months. Then, in NC Miltia. S39123.	Ft. George - Bald Head Island.
White, Benjamin	4th NC Regiment	1782, a Private under Capt. Thomas Evans. Died in Jan. 1783.	
White, Burrall	2nd NC Regiment	7/20/1778, a Private under Maj. Reading Blount for nine months. Dropped from the rolls in Oct. 1778.	
White, Christopher	2nd NC Regiment	5/9/1781, a Private under Capt. Griffith John McRee. July 1781, transferred to the Legion (State or Lee's - unknown).	
White, Churchill	2nd NC Regiment	5/16/1781, a Private under Capt. Benjamin Carter. Discharged on 5/16/1782. 1782, a Private under Capt. Thomas Evans (4th NC Regiment) for 18 months. aka Church White.	

Name	1st Unit	Year / Rank / Served Under / Notes	Known Battles
White, Daniel	1st NC Regiment	1775, a Private under Capt. William Pickett for one year. Capt. Pickett resigned. He then joined as a Private under Capt. Richard D. Cook (9th NC Regiment) for two years. He was denied a pension by the War Department because he was considered to be a deserter. He was from Anson County, NC. R11405.	Great Cane Brake (SC), Snow Campaign (SC), Moore's Creek Bridge, Brandywine Creek (PA).
White, Daniel	5th NC Regiment	10/24/1776, a Musician under Capt. John Enloe for three years. A Private in Oct. 1777. Back to Musician in Jan. 1778. Back to Private in Apr. 1778. 9/10/1778, a Private under Capt. Thomas Armstrong (2nd NC Regiment). Discharged on 11/10/1778. From Edgecombe County, NC. W6479.	
White, Daniel	9th NC Regiment	12/24/1776, a Corporal under Capt. Richard D. Cook. Deserted on 10/10/1777.	
White, David	4th NC Regiment	1782, a Private under Capt. Thomas Evans for 18 months.	
White, Dempsey	2nd NC Regiment	3/20/1776, a Private under Capt. James Martin for 2-1/2 years. Deserted on 11/1/1779 (?).	
White, Edward	3rd NC Regiment	4/1/1782, a Private under Capt. Samuel Jones for 12 months.	
White, Elisha	3rd NC Regiment	6/29/1779, a Private under Capt. Kedar Ballard. Dropped from the rolls in Oct. 1779.	
White, Ezekiel	4th NC Regiment	5/4/1776, a Private under Capt. John McLane, then Capt. Micajah Lewis for three years. 9/8/1778, a known Private in the Colonel's Company (Col. Thomas Clark) (1st NC Regiment) led by Capt. John Gambier Scull. Discharged on 5/14/1779 at Paramus, NJ. Enlisted at Windsor, NC in Bertie County, his home. S42070.	Brandywine Creek (PA), Germantown (PA), Monmouth (NJ).
White, George	1st NC Regiment	9/10/1782, a Private under Capt. Joshua Hadley for 18 months.	
White, George	4th NC Regiment	1777, a Private under Capt. James Williams. 9/8/1778, a known Private in the Colonel's Company (Col. Thomas Clark) (1st NC Regiment) led by Capt. John Gambier Scull.	
White, George	5th NC Regiment	1779, a Private under Maj. Reading Blount. Deserted in Sep. 1779.	
White, Haines	3rd NC Regiment	7/20/1778, a Private under Capt. Kedar Ballard for nine months. Deserted on 8/30/1778. Rejoined in Nov. 1778 for the duration of the war.	
White, Hampton	1st NC Regiment	1/81, a Private under Capt. William Walton for 12 months. Discharged on 6/14/1782.	
White, Henry	1st NC Regiment	5/9/1776, a Private under Ens./Lt./Capt. James Read. 9/8/1778, a known Private under Capt. James Read. Discharged on 11/10/1778.	
White, Henry	1st NC Regiment	5/14/1781, a Private under Capt. Thomas Donoho. Discharged on 6/14/1782. Originally from Halifax County, NC. From Granville County when he enlisted. Philip White was his	Eutaw Springs (SC).

Name	1st Unit	Year / Rank / Served Under / Notes	Known Battles
		brother. R11410.	
White, Jacob Jr.	10th NC Regiment	4/21/1777, a Musician under Capt. Silas Stevenson. 9/9/1778, in the Lt. Colonel's Company (Lt. Col. Selby Harney) (2nd NC Regiment). Jan. 1782, re-enlisted for the duration of the war.	
White, Jacob Sr.	10th NC Regiment	4/21/1777, a Private under Capt. Silas Stevenson. 9/9/1778, a known Private in the Lt. Colonel's Company (Lt. Col. Selby Harney) (2nd NC Regiment).	
White, James	2nd NC Regiment	7/20/1778, a Private under Maj. Reading Blount for nine months.	
White, James	7th NC Regiment	1777, a Private under Capt. John McGlaughan. Died on 1/27/1778.	
White, John	1st NC Regiment	1782, a Private under Capt. Peter Bacot for 18 months.	
White, John	2nd NC Regiment	1777, a Private under Capt. James Gee. Died on 5/16/1778.	
White, John (Dr.)	2nd NC Regiment	9/1/1775, a Captain and an Adjutant under Col. Robert Howe.	
White, John	2nd NC Regiment	4/10/1776 to 2/1/1777, a Major in 2nd NC Regiment. Then, commanded a regiment in Georgia as Colonel.	
White, John	3rd NC Regiment	1777, a Private under Capt. James Emmett. Died on 4/12/1778.	
White, John	6th NC Regiment	1777, a Sergeant under Capt. Griffith John McRee. Died on 1/6/1778.	
White, John	7th NC Regiment	1/4/1777, a Private under Capt. John McGlaughan. 2/26/1778, a known Private under Capt. Howell Tatum (1st NC Regiment). 9/8/1778, a known Private under Capt. Howell Tatum - sick on that date in Princeton. Died in Aug. 1778 (?) (probably Sept.)	
White, John	7th NC Regiment	3/6/1777, a Private under Lt./Capt. John Baker for 3 years. Dropped from the rolls sometime during 1779. From Bertie County, NC. S42067.	
White, Joseph	10th NC Regiment	4/21/1777, a Private under Capt. Silas Stevenson. POW at Ft. Lafayette, NY on 6/1/1779. Discharged on 3/1/1780.	Ft. Lafayette (NY).
White, Joseph	10th NC Regiment	8/13/1777, a Cadet under Capt. Andrew Vanoy. Dropped from the rolls in Feb. 1778.	
White, Malachi	5th NC Regiment	1777, a Private under Capt. Henry Darnell. Dropped from the rolls in July 1779. Rejoined in Nov. 1779.	
White, Matthew	6th NC Regiment	11/2/1776, a Lieutenant, unit unknown. 4/1/1777, a Lieutenant under Capt. Daniel Williams. Killed at the battle of Germantown, PA on 10/4/1777.	Germantown (PA).
White, Peter	5th NC Regiment	Feb. 1779, a Private under Maj. Reading Blount for nine months. Served 12-1/2 months. Discharged at Halifax, NC. From Bertie County, NC. S42066.	
White, Philip	1st NC Regiment	5/14/1781, a Private under Capt. Thomas Donoho. Discharged on 6/14/1782. Originally	Eutaw Springs (SC).

Name	1st Unit	Year / Rank / Served Under / Notes	Known Battles
		from Halifax County, NC. From Granville County when he enlisted. In the Granville County Regiment (Militia) prior to this service. Henry White was his brother. W6478.	
White, Richard	2nd NC Regiment	10/2/1776, a Private under Capt. John Armstrong for 2-1/2 years. 9/9/1778, a known Private under Capt. Robert Fenner. 3/12/1779, re-enlisted under Capt. Robert Fenner. POW at Ft. Lafayette, NY on 6/1/1779. Rejoined in Nov. 1779.	Ft. Lafayette (NY).
White, Stephen	1st NC Regiment	April 1781, a Private under Capt. William Armstrong for 12 months. Soon thereafter, assigned to QM and Capt. Edmund Gamble at Salisbury (Militia), finished his term of service and was discharged. From Granville County, NC. Earlier in Granville County Regiment (Militia). War Department did not consider any of this to be on the Continental Line. S3542.	
White, Stephen	1st NC Regiment	A Sergeant under Capt. James Read. Died from fatigue at Monmouth, NJ on 6/28/1778.	Monmouth (NJ).
White, Thomas	NC Light Dragoons	April 1776, a Private under Capt. John Dickerson (Provincial Troops). 3/7/1777, this unit was placed on the NC Continental Line, and he was then under Capt. Samuel Ashe as a Corporal. Discharged in October 1778. Then, in NC Militia. W1521.	Germantown (PA).
White, Thomas	1st NC Regiment	4/28/1781, a Private under Capt. Griffith John McRee. Dropped from the rolls in Jan. 1782 - sick.	
White, Thomas	6th NC Regiment	1775, a 1st Lieutenant in NC Militia. 4/17/1776, a 1st Lieutenant under Capt. Arthur Council and Col. John Alexander Lillington (6th NC Regiment). Also a Lieutenant under Capt. Archibald Lytle. 1/20/1777, a Captain. Retired on 6/1/1778. Jan. 1779, a Captain in the 5th NC Regiment. Left the service in Dec. 1779. From Cumberland County.	Brandywine Creek (PA), Germantown (PA).
White, Timothy	1st NC Regiment	1779, a Private under Capt. Anthony Sharpe. Discharged on 3/20/1779.	
White, Wallace	2nd NC Regiment	9/9/1778, a Private under Capt. Benjamin Andrew Coleman.	
White, William	1st NC Regiment	A Private under Capt. James Read. Died on 3/31/1778.	
White, William	1st NC Regiment	2/26/1778, a known Private under Capt. Howell Tatum.	
White, William	1st NC Regiment	8/1/1782, a Private under Capt. Joshua Hadley for 18 months. Died on 5/26/1783.	
White, William	2nd NC Regiment	7/20/1778, a Private under Maj. Reading Blount for nine months.	
White, William	3rd NC Regiment	10/22/1782, a Private under Capt. Benjamin Bailey.	
White, William	7th NC Regiment	12/10/1776, a Sergeant under Capt. John McGlaughan for three years. 9/8/1778, a known Sergeant under Capt. Howell Tatum (1st NC	Brandywine Creek (PA), Germantown

Name	1st Unit	Year / Rank / Served Under / Notes	Known Battles
		Regiment). Discharged on 1/27/1780. From Bertie County, NC when he enlisted. S42071.	(PA), Monmouth (NJ), Near West Point (NY).
White, William	7th NC Regiment	4/17/1777, an Ensign under Capt. John Poynter. Dropped from the rolls in Nov. 1777.	
White, William	10th NC Regiment	1/1/1778, a Private under Capt. Andrew Vanoy for three years. 9/8/1778, a known Private under Capt. John Sumner (1st NC Regiment) - sick in camp on that date. Deserted on 3/8/1779. 3/12/1779, re-enlisted for the duration of the war in the same unit.	
Whitehead, Daniel	NC Artillery	1/1/1777, a Gunner under Capt. Thomas Clark as NC Provincial Troops. 7/10/1777, on Continental Line. Also on 9/9/1778. aka Daniel Whithead.	
Whitehead, John	1st NC Regiment	1782, a Private under Capt. Elijah Moore, then Capt. Alexander Brevard (1st NC Regiment) for 18 months. Entered the service in Hillsborough, NC. W6495.	
Whitehead, John	5th NC Regiment	3/1/1776, a Private later assigned to Capt. William Caswell for 12 months. Discharged on 7/12/1777 at Halifax, NC. Possibly also served as a Corporal, if not for all his time, at least for part of it. Later in NC Militia, unit unknown. From Craven County, NC. S42065.	
Whitehead, William	2nd NC Regiment	Feb. 1779, a Private in the Colonel's Company (Col. John Patten) led by Capt. John Craddock for 2-1/2 years.	
Whitehouse, Anthony	4th NC Regiment	1782, a Private under Capt. Thomas Evans for 18 months.	
Whitehouse, Joel	8th NC Regiment	1777, a Private under Capt. Robert Raiford. POW at Ft. Lafayette, NY on 6/1/1779. Rejoined in Nov. 1779.	Ft. Lafayette (NY).
Whitely, Micajah	1st NC Regiment	1781, a Private under Capt. William Armstrong.	
Whites, Batson	3rd NC Regiment	7/20/1778, a Private under Maj. Thomas Hogg for nine months.	
Whitfield, Willis	2nd NC Regiment	1782, a Private drafted under Capt. Peter Bacot (1st NC Regiment) for 18 months, quickly transferred to Capt. Robert Raiford. Earlier in NC Militia. From Nash County, NC. W1013.	
Whitley, Arthur	5th NC Regiment	5/2/1776, a Private under Capt. John Pugh Williams for 2-1/2 years. Discharged on 11/10/1778.	
Whitley, Haniford	3rd NC Regiment	4/22/1776, a Private under Capt. Pinketham Eaton for 2-1/2 years. 9/9/1778, a known Private under Capt. Robert Fenner (2nd NC Regiment). Discharged on 11/10/1778. aka Hansford Whitley.	
Whitley, John	5th NC Regiment	1775, a 1st Lieutenant in the Salisbury District Minutemen. Lived in the Hillsborough District. 4/17/1776, a 1st Lieutenant under Capt. William Ward and Col. Edward Buncombe.	

Name	1st Unit	Year / Rank / Served Under / Notes	Known Battles
Whitley, Micajah	1st NC Regiment	1781, a Private under Capt. Peter Bacot for 18 months. Served as a substitute for last seven months of Lawrence Killebrew's 18-month tour.	
Whitley, Micajah	1st NC Regiment	1781, a Private under Capt. William Armstrong. Discharged on 4/23/1782 (3rd NC Regiment). Possibly same man as directly above. S42068.	
Whitley, Samuel	1st NC Regiment	A Private under Capt. Joshua Bowman, dates unknown.	
Whitley, Thomas	3rd NC Regiment	7/20/1778, a Musician under Lt./Capt. George "Gee" Bradley for nine months.	
Whitley, William	5th NC Regiment	1777, a Private under Capt. John Pugh Williams. Died on 11/2/1777.	
Whitman, Frederick	4th NC Regiment	1782, a Private under Capt. Anthony Sharpe for 18 months.	
Whitmill, Thomas Blount	4th NC Regiment	4/17/1776, a 2nd Lieutenant under Capt. John McLane and Col. Thomas Polk. 11/20/1776, a Lieutenant under Capt. Robert Smith. Wounded at the battle of Brandywine Creek (PA). Dropped from the rolls in Jan. 1778. From Bertie County, NC. aka Blunt Whitmel. W1522.	Brandywine Creek (PA).
Whitson, Benjamin	2nd NC Regiment	1781, a Private under Capt. Benjamin Carter. Deserted on 9/15/1781.	
Whittaker, Robert	2nd NC Regiment	1782, a Private under Capt. Benjamin Carter for 18 months.	
Whorton, Jacob	2nd NC Regiment	7/20/1778, a Private under Maj. Reading Blount for nine months.	
Whorton, Samuel	1st NC Regiment	12/1/1776, a Private under Capt. Henry "Hal" Dixon. 9/8/1778, known a Private under Capt. Tilghman Dixon. aka Lemuel Wharton.	
Wicker, Willis	3rd NC Regiment	Jan. 1779, a Sergeant in the Lt. Colonel's Company (Lt. Col. Robert Mebane) led by Capt. George "Gee" Bradley.	
Widener, Samuel	4th NC Regiment	1782, a A Sergeant under Capt. William Lytle. One source claims he was only a Corporal. Unknown which is correct.	
Wiggins, Absalom	2nd NC Regiment	1777, a Private under Capt. James Gee. Dropped from the rolls in Jan. 1778.	
Wiggins, Arthur	3rd NC Regiment	9/10/1782, a Private under Capt. Benjamin Bailey for 18 months. Earlier in NC Militia. From Bertie County, NC. Brother of Matthew Wiggins below - both joined at same time. S7952.	
Wiggins, Charles	5th NC Regiment	6/1/1779, a Private under Capt. Joseph Montford. Deserted on 11/12/1779.	
Wiggins, Edward	2nd NC Regiment	7/20/1778, a Private under Maj. Reading Blount for nine months.	
Wiggins, Elisha	4th NC Regiment	1782, a Private under Capt. William Lytle for 18 months.	
Wiggins, George	1st NC Regiment	11/10/1778, a Private under Capt. Anthony Sharpe for nine months.	
Wiggins, Henry	3rd NC Regiment	1777, a Private under Capt. James Emmett. Dropped from the rolls in June 1778.	
Wiggins, James	1st NC Regiment	1781, a Private under Capt. William Lytle for 12 months. Discharged on 4/12/1782 (4th NC	

Name	1st Unit	Year / Rank / Served Under / Notes	Known Battles
		Regiment).	
Wiggins, James	2nd NC Regiment	9/10/1778, a known Private under Capt. Thomas Armstrong. 3/12/1779, re-enlisted under Capt. Thomas Armstrong.	
Wiggins, James	3rd NC Regiment	7/20/1778, a Private under Maj. Thomas Hogg for nine months.	
Wiggins, James	7th NC Regiment	1/1/1777, a Sergeant under Capt. James Vaughan. Deserted on 9/19/1777.	
Wiggins, James	10th NC Regiment	8/12/1777, a Private under Capt. Silas Stevenson for three years.	
Wiggins, Levy	4th NC Regiment	Jan. 1782, a Musician under Capt. George Dougherty. A Private in Apr. 1782.	
Wiggins, Malachi	10th NC Regiment	10/10/1777, a Private under Capt. Andrew Vanoy. 9/10/1778, a known Private under Capt. Thomas Armstrong (2nd NC Regiment). aka Moloha Wiggins.	
Wiggins, Matthew	3rd NC Regiment	9/10/1782, a Private under Capt. Benjamin Bailey for 18 months. Brother of Arthur Wiggins above - both joined at same time.	
Wiggins, Noah	3rd NC Regiment	1777, a Private under Capt. James Emmett. Discharged on 5/11/1778.	
Wiggins, Thomas	3rd NC Regiment	7/20/1778, a Private in the Lt. Colonel's Company (Lt. Col. William Lee Davidson) led by Lt./Capt. George "Gee" Bradley for nine months. 4/23/1779, a known Private in the Lt. Colonel's Company (Lt. Col. Robert Mebane) led by Capt. George "Gee" Bradley. 6/26/1779, a Private under Capt. Michael Quinn for 18 months.	
Wiggins, Thomas	5th NC Regiment	A Private under Capt. John Enloe. Died on 4/27/1778.	
Wiggins, William	2nd NC Regiment	1/1/1782, a Private under Capt. Benjamin Andrew Coleman for 12 months.	
Wiggins, William	7th NC Regiment	1777, a Private under Capt. Thomas Brickell. Deserted in Apr. 1777.	
Wiggins, Willis	3rd NC Regiment	4/11/1776, a Corporal under Capt. James Emmett for 2-1/2 years. A Sergeant in Oct. 1777. Back to Corporal in June 1778. 9/9/1778, a known Corporal in the Major's Company (Maj. Hardy Murfree) (2nd NC Regiment). Discharged on 10/17/1778.	
Wigley, Thomas	10th NC Regiment	9/30/1777, a Sergeant under Capt. Dempsey Gregory. A Private in June 1778. 9/8/1778, a known Private under Capt. Howell Tatum (1st NC Regiment).	
Wilbourne, Robert	7th NC Regiment	3/18/1777, a Private under Capt. James Vaughan. 2/26/1778, a known Private under Capt. Howell Tatum (1st NC Regiment). A Corporal in March 1778. 9/8/1778, a known Corporal under Capt. Howell Tatum. aka Robert Wileborn, Robert Welburne.	
Wilbourne, Zachariah	1st NC Regiment	4/5/1781, a Private under Capt. William Lytle. Discharged on 4/5/1782 (4th NC Regiment). aka Zach. Wilburne.	

Name	1st Unit	Year / Rank / Served Under / Notes	Known Battles
Wilcox, Benjamin	1st NC Regiment	1781, a Private under Capt. Anthony Sharpe. Discharged on 5/20/1782 (4th NC Regiment).	
Wilcox, David	2nd NC Regiment	10/10/1782, a Private under Capt. Clement Hall. Deserted on 6/9/1783 (?).	
Wilcox, David	5th NC Regiment	6/15/1779, a Private under Capt. Joseph Montford. Dropped from the rolls in Oct. 1779.	
Wilcox, George	5th NC Regiment	1777, a Corporal under Capt. Reading Blount. Died on 11/4/1777.	
Wilcox, John	3rd NC Regiment	Jan. 1782, a Private under Capt. Clement Hall. Deserted on 6/9/1783 (2nd NC Regiment) (?).	
Wilday, Absalom	2nd NC Regiment	7/20/1778, a Private under Maj. Reading Blount for nine months. 6/3/1779, re-enlisted as a Corporal for 18 months. 1780, under Capt. George "Gee" Bradley (3rd NC Regiment). POW at the Fall of Charleston, escaped after 31 days. 5/6/1781, a known Private under Capt. Robert Raiford (1st NC Regiment). Wounded at the battle of Eutaw Springs, SC. Discharged on 4/16/1782 (2nd NC Regiment). aka Absalom Wildie, Absalom Wiley. S38473.	Siege of Charleston 1780 (SC), Eutaw Springs (SC).
Wilder, William	4th NC Regiment	1781, a Private under Capt. Joseph T. Rhodes. Discharged on 5/16/1782. Living in Wake County, NC when he joined the service. Born in Edgecombe County, NC in 1749. S7948.	Eutaw Springs (SC).
Wile, Martin	4th NC Regiment	1777, a Private under Capt. Joseph Phillips. Deserted on 10/26/1777.	
Wiles, Anthony	6th NC Regiment	9/3/1777, a Private under Ensign Joseph Richardson.	
Wiley, James		5/21/1777, a Private, regiment and unit unknown. 9/8/1778, a known Private in the Lt. Colonel's Company (Lt. Col. Robert Mebane) (1st NC Regiment) led by Capt. Joshua Bowman.	
Wiley, James	2nd NC Regiment	5/2/1781, a Private under Capt. William Goodman, then Capt. Benjamin Bailey (1st NC Regiment). Discharged on 5/2/1782 (3rd NC Regiment) at High Hills of Santee, SC. Earlier in NC Militia. aka James Willey. S42075.	Eutaw Springs (SC).
Wiley, Stephen	5th NC Regiment	1777, a Private under Capt. Henry Darnell. Dropped from the rolls in Sep. 1777.	
Wilford, Archibald	4th NC Regiment	1782, a Private under Capt. William Lytle for 18 months.	
Wilford, Lewis	2nd NC Regiment	8/25/1777, a Private under Capt. Hardy Murfree. 9/9/1778, a known Private under Capt. Benjamin Andrew Coleman. 3/12/1779, re-enlisted under Capt. Benjamin Andrew Coleman. POW at the Fall of Charleston, SC. aka Lewis Willford, Williford. W6548.	Siege of Charleston 1780 (SC).
Wilkerson, John	1st NC Regiment	9/8/1778, a known Private under Capt. Joshua Bowman.	
Wilkerson, John	3rd NC Regiment	1781, a Private under Capt. Edward Yarborough for 12 months. Discharged on 5/25/1782.	
Wilkerson, John	10th NC Regiment	5/29/1777, a Sergeant under Capt. James Wilson for three years. A Private in June 1778.	

673

Name	1st Unit	Year / Rank / Served Under / Notes	Known Battles
		3/12/1779, re-enlisted for the duration of the war under Capt. Griffith John McRee (1st NC Regiment). Deserted in Apr. 1779. aka John Wilkinson.	
Wilkerson, Reuben	4th NC Regiment	12/20/1776, a Lieutenant under Capt. Micajah Lewis. He and Lt. Edward Yarborough fought a duel - he was wounded in left arm. Retired on 6/1/1778. From Johnston County, NC. aka Reuben Wilkinson.	
Wilkerson, William	3rd NC Regiment	7/20/1778, a Private in the Lt. Colonel's Company (Lt. Col. William Lee Davidson) led by Lt./Capt. George "Gee" Bradley for nine months. 4/23/1779, a known Private in the Lt. Colonel's Company (Lt. Col. Robert Mebane) led by Capt. George "Gee" Bradley. aka William Wilkinson.	
Wilkerson, William	3rd NC Regiment	1781, a Corporal under Capt. Edward Yarborough for 12 months. Discharged on 5/1/1782.	
Wilkerson, William	10th NC Regiment	5/29/1777, a Private under Capt. James Wilson for 3 years. 6/1/1778, a Private under Capt. Joshua Bowman (1st NC Regiment). POW at the Fall of Charleston (SC), escaped after about a month. From Caswell County, NC. aka William Wilkinson. S1937.	Monmouth (NJ), Siege of Charleston 1780 (SC).
Wilkins, Andrew	10th NC Regiment	5/2/1777, a Private under Capt. Andrew Vanoy. 9/9/1778, a known Private in the Major's Company (Maj. Hardy Murfree) (2nd NC Regiment). 3/12/1779, re-enlisted in the Major's Company (Maj. Hardy Murfree). Deserted on 3/15/1779.	
Wilkins, Burrel	1st NC Regiment	4/25/1781, a Private under Capt. Robert Raiford. Died in Nov. 1781.	
Wilkins, Elijah	1st NC Regiment	5/14/1781, a Private under Capt. Thomas Donoho. A Corporal in Jan. 1782. Discharged on 4/25/1782.	
Wikins, Elisha	3rd NC Regiment	7/20/1778, a Private under Lt./Capt. George "Gee" Bradford for nine months. Jan. 1779, under Capt. Joseph Montford (5th NC Regiment). Discharged 5/14/1779 from the Philadelphia Hospital, a month after his term expired due to illness. Earlier and later in NC Militia. From Halifax County, NC.	
Wilkins, George	3rd NC Regiment	Dec. 1782, a Private under Capt. John McNees, then Capt. Clement Hall (2nd NC Regiment). Discharged on 12/13/1783 (2nd NC Regiment). Enlisted while living in Orange County, NC. Born on 3/6/1758 in Philadelphia County, PA. S32605.	
Wilkins, Jordan	3rd NC Regiment	7/20/1778, a Corporal under Capt. Kedar Ballard for nine months.	
Wilkins, Joshua	1st NC Regiment	8/15/1777, a Private under Capt. Howell Tatum for three years. 9/8/1778, in same unit. 3/12/1779, re-enlisted for the duration of the	

Name	1st Unit	Year / Rank / Served Under / Notes	Known Battles
		war in the same unit.	
Wilkins, Kinchen	2nd NC Regiment	11/27/1781, a Private under Capt. Benjamin Andrew Coleman for 12 months.	
Wilkins, Thomas	1st NC Regiment	4/15/1781, a Private under Capt. Anthony Sharpe. Discharged on 4/15/1782 (4th NC Regiment).	
Wilkins, Thomas	1st NC Regiment	8/1/1782, a Private under Capt. Joshua Hadley for 18 months.	
Wilkins, William	3rd NC Regiment	8/12/1779, a Private under Capt. Kedar Ballard. Dropped from the rolls in Oct. 1780.	
Wilkinson, John	NC Artillery	8/13/1776, a Matross under Capt. John Vance as NC Provincial Troops. 7/10/1777, on Continental Line. 11/16/1777, under Capt. John Kingsbury. 5/1/1778, in same unit. 9/16/1778, in same unit.	
Wilkinson, Reuben	3rd NC Regiment	5/1/1779, an Ensign. 1/9/1779, a 2nd Lieutenant in the Lt. Colonel's Company (Lt. Col. Robert Mebane) led by Capt. George "Gee" Bradley. Retired on 7/21/1782.	
Will, John	1st NC Regiment	4/19/1781, Lt. Col. John Baptiste Ashe asks HQ for a certificate of commission for this man as a Lieutenant.	
Willard, Major	4th NC Regiment	5/16/1776, a Private under Capt. John Nelson for three years. 9/8/1778, a known Private under Capt. Griffith John McRee (1st NC Regiment) - sick on that date. 3/12/1779, re-enlisted for the duration of the war under Capt. Griffith John McRee (1st NC Regiment).	
Willford, Lewis	10th NC Regiment	8/25/1777, a Private under Capt. Andrew Vanoy. 3/12/1779, re-enlisted under Capt. Benjamin Andrew Coleman (2nd NC Regiment).	
Williams, Alexander	3rd NC Regiment	April 1778 or 7/20/1778 (two sources), a Private under Lt./Capt. George "Gee" Bradley, Maj. Thomas Hogg for nine months. Discharged in December 1779 at Philadelphia, PA. S39130.	
Williams, Allenby	1st NC Regiment	6/1/1781, a Private under Capt. William Lytle. Discharged on 6/6/1782 (4th NC Regiment).	
Williams, Benjamin	1st NC Regiment	1782, a Private under Capt. Peter Bacot for 18 months.	
Williams, Benjamin	2nd NC Regiment	9/1/1775, a 1st Lieutenant under Capt. Nathaniel Keais. 7/19/1776, a Captain. Resigned on 1/1/1779 (?). Several lists claim that men re-enlisted under him on 3/12/1779 (?). Later, a Captain and a Lt. Col./Colonel of NC Militia and NC State Troops. From Johnston County, NC.	Brandywine Creek (PA), Germantown (PA), Monmouth (NJ).
Williams, Benjamin	7th NC Regiment	2/6/1777, a Private under Capt. John Poynter for 3 years. 9/8/1778, a known Private under Capt. James Read (1st NC Regiment). A Sergeant on 5/1/1779.	
Williams, Charles	2nd NC Regiment	1777, a Private under Capt. Benjamin Williams. Died on 3/15/1778.	
Williams,	1st NC	1782, a Private under Capt. Peter Bacot for 18	

Name	1st Unit	Year / Rank / Served Under / Notes	Known Battles
Coleden	Regiment	months.	
Williams, Daniel	6th NC Regiment	1775, a 1st Lieutenant in the Wilmington District Minutemen. 4/17/1776, a 1st Lieutenant under Capt. John James and Col. John Alexander Lillington. 4/1/1777, a Captain - took over the company of Capt. William Glover. Retired on 6/1/1778. A Captain in the Militia 1778-1781. From Duplin County, NC.	Brandywine Creek (PA), Germantown (PA).
Williams, David	1st NC Regiment	1777, a Sergeant under Capt. Henry "Hal" Dixon. Discharged on 9/27/1777.	
Williams, David	2nd NC Regiment	1/10/1782, a Private under Capt. Benjamin Andrew Coleman for 12 months.	
Williams, Dudley	4th NC Regiment	1782, a Private under Capt. William Lytle. Died in Jan. 1783.	
Williams, Edward	1st NC Regiment	1/25/1782, a Private under Capt. James Mills. On 2/6/1782, this unit was transferred to the 4th NC Regiment. Died on 3/28/1783.	
Williams, Elisha	5th NC Regiment	12/18/1776, a Private under Capt. Simon Alderson. 9/9/1778, a known Private in the Colonel's Company (Col. John Patten) (2nd NC Regiment) led by Capt. John Craddock. Discharged on 5/20/1779.	
Williams, Francis	2nd NC Regiment	1777, a Private under Capt. Edward Vail, Jr. 9/9/1778, a known Private in the Colonel's Company (Col. John Patten) led by Capt. John Craddock. POW at Ft. Lafayette, NY on 6/2/1779. 8/1/1782, a Private under Capt. Joshua Hadley (1st NC Regiment) for 18 months. aka Francis William.	Ft. Lafayette (NY).
Williams, George	1st NC Regiment	5/1/1777, a Private under Capt. Joshua Bowman. 9/8/1778, a known Private under Capt. Tilghman Dixon.	
Williams, George	2nd NC Regiment	6/1/1779, a Sergeant in the Colonel's Company (Col. John Patten) for 18 months.	
Williams, George	6th NC Regiment	6/28/1776, a Corporal under Capt. George Dougherty for 2-1/2 years. A Private in June 1778 (4th NC Regiment). Discharged on 1/14/1779.	
Williams, Gilstrap	3rd NC Regiment	6/22/1779, a Corporal under Capt. Michael Quinn. A Private in March 1779.	
Williams, Hickman	3rd NC Regiment	May 1776, a Private under Capt. Jacob Turner for 2-1/2 years. Discharged in August 1777 at Halifax, NC. Enlisted in Wake County, NC. Married in Franklin County, NC. R11629.	Ft. Moultrie #1 (SC) (a guard).
Williams, James	1st NC Regiment	6/11/1777, a Sergeant under Capt. Isaac Moore. A Corporal in June 1778. 9/8/1778, a known Corporal in the Lt. Colonel's Company (Lt. Col. Robert Mebane) (1st NC Regiment) led by Capt. Joshua Bowman. Died on 9/24/1778. Apparently enlisted on 5/25/1777 for three years, probably as a Private.	
Williams, James	4th NC Regiment	6/7/1776, a 1st Lieutenant under Capt. John Ashe. 4/3/1777, a Captain. Died on 5/2/1778.	Brandywine Creek (PA), Germantown

Name	1st Unit	Year / Rank / Served Under / Notes	Known Battles
			(PA).
Williams, James	5th NC Regiment	6/8/1779, a Private under Maj. Reading Blount for 18 months. POW at the Fall of Charleston, escaped after three months. Joined NC Militia. From Burke County, NC. S31487.	Siege of Charleston 1780 (SC).
Williams, Jeremiah	4th NC Regiment	1782, a Private under Capt. William Lytle and Capt. Joseph Thomas Rhodes for 18 months. S42077.	
Williams, John	1st NC Regiment	Fall of 1776, a Private under Ensign Edmund Gamble, Capt. Lawrence Thompson. 6/1/1778, a Private under Lt. Edmund Gamble and Capt. Cosmo Medici in the NC Light Dragoons, which were removed from the Continental Line in January 1779. Then, in NC State Troops. From Warren County, NC. W177.	
Williams, John	1st NC Regiment	5/9/1781, a Private under Capt. Alexander Brevard.	
Williams, John	2nd NC Regiment	7/20/1778, a Private under Maj. Reading Blount for nine months.	
Williams, John	2nd NC Regiment	9/1/1775, a Lieutenant. Resigned in October of 1775.	
Williams, John	2nd NC Regiment	4/21/1777, a 1st Lieutenant under Capt. James Martin. Retired on 6/1/1778.	
Williams, John	3rd NC Regiment	1/10/1782, a Private under Capt. Samuel Jones for 12 months.	
Williams, John	7th NC Regiment	1777, a Private under Capt. Henry Dawson. Dropped from the rolls in Jan. 1778.	
Williams, John	7th NC Regiment	2/21/1777, a Private under Capt. James Vaughan for 3 years. 2/26/1778, a known Private under Capt. Howell Tatum (1st NC Regiment). 9/8/1778, a known Private under Capt. Howell Tatum. Discharged on 3/1/1780. From Hertford County, NC. W9017.	Brandywine Creek (PA), Germantown (PA), Monmouth (NJ).
Williams, John	9th NC Regiment	11/26/1776, Colonel/Commandant of the 9th NC Regiment. Regiment disbanded on 6/1/1778. 1778, he returned to Caswell County to assist the Militia there. From Caswell County, NC. W9147.	Brandywine Creek (PA), Germantown (PA).
Williams, John Pugh	5th NC Regiment	1775, a Captain in the Edenton District Minutemen. 4/17/1776, a Captain in the 5th NC Regiment. Dropped from the rolls in Jan. 1778. Later, a Colonel and a Brigadier General (3 days-declined) in NC Militia. From Bertie County, NC.	Brandywine Creek (PA), Germantown (PA).
Williams, Joseph	10th NC Regiment	6/10/1777, a Private under Capt. Isaac Moore for three years. 9/8/1778, a known Private in the Lt. Colonel's Company (Lt. Col. Robert Mebane) (1st NC Regiment) led by Capt. Joshua Bowman. POW 4/14/1779 (?). Rejoined in Nov. 1779. 3/27/1780, re-enlisted.	
Williams, Michael	3rd NC Regiment	1781, a Private under Capt. Clement Hall. Deserted on 4/1/1782 (2nd NC Regiment).	
Williams, Morson	10th NC Regiment	June 1778, a Private under Capt. Andrew Vanoy. 9/9/1778, a known Private in the	

Name	1st Unit	Year / Rank / Served Under / Notes	Known Battles
		Major's Company (Maj. Hardy Murfree) (2nd NC Regiment). Discharged on 10/30/1778.	
Williams, Nathaniel	3rd NC Regiment	Jan. 1782, a Private under Capt. Clement Hall (2/6/1782 - 2nd NC Regiment).	
Williams, Nathaniel Brice	8th NC Regiment	11/28/1776, a 2nd Lieutenant under Capt. Edward Ward and then Capt. John Walsh. Retired 6/1/1778. 1/23/1781, re-enlisted as a 1st Lieutenant, regiment and unit unknown. 2/6/1782 he was in the 4th NC Regiment. Resigned on 1/1/1783. aka Brice Nathaniel Williams.	
Williams, Nicholas	4th NC Regiment	Dec. 1782, a Private under Capt. Anthony Sharpe for 18 months. Deserted on 3/29/1783 (?).	
Williams, Nicholas	4th NC Regiment	1781, a Corporal under Capt. George Dougherty. Discharged on 5/25/1782.	
Williams, Peter	10th NC Regiment	6/30/1777 or 7/5/1777 (two sources), a Private under Capt. Isaac Moore for three years. 9/8/1778, a known Private in the Lt. Colonel's Company (Lt. Col. Robert Mebane) (1st NC Regiment) led by Capt. Joshua Bowman. A Corporal in March 1779. A Sergeant on 2/1/1780. Jan. 1782, a Sergeant under Capt. William Armstrong (1st NC Regiment) for the duration of the war.	
Williams, Ralph	9th NC Regiment	11/28/1776, a Lieutenant under Capt. Hezekiah Rice then Capt. Joseph J. Wade. Dropped from the rolls in Jan. 1778. 1778, a Captain of "New Levies." From Granville County, NC.	
Williams, Robert	1st NC Regiment	5/25/1781, a Private under Capt. James Mills. On 2/6/1782, this unit was transferred to the 4th NC Regiment.	
Williams, Robert	3rd NC Regiment	1/1/1782, a Private under Capt. Clement Hall (2/6/1782 - 2nd NC Regiment). Discharged on 1/1/1783.	
Williams, Robert	3rd NC Regiment	1781, a Surgeon. Earlier a Private, Surgeon's Mate and Surgeon in NC Militia.	
Williams, Robert	8th NC Regiment	Feb. 1777, a Private under Capt. James May, Jr. August 1777, a Sergeant under Capt. Francis Tartanson. A Private in April 1778. A Corporal in June 1778 in 2nd NC Regiment. 9/9/1778, a known Private in the Major's Company (Maj. Hardy Murfree) (2nd NC Regiment). Discharged on 2/1/1780 at Halifax, NC. S39129.	Brandywine Creek (PA), Germantown (PA).
Williams, Samuel	DQMG	1780, a Blacksmith under Col. Nicholas Long (Deputy QM General). Also on 8/23/1781.	
Williams, Samuel	3rd NC Regiment	Mid-1781, a Private under Capt. Clement Hall for 12 months. Discharged at Ashley Ferry, SC. Earlier in NC Militia. From Gates County, NC. S7957.	
Williams, Samuel	4th NC Regiment	1781, a Private under Capt. George Dougherty. Discharged on 5/25/1782.	
Williams,	5th NC	11/10/1776, a Musician under Capt. Henry	

Name	1st Unit	Year / Rank / Served Under / Notes	Known Battles
Samuel	Regiment	Darnell. A Private in June 1778. 9/9/1778, under Capt. Benjamin Andrew Coleman (2nd NC Regiment).	
Williams, Seth	2nd NC Regiment	1782, a Private under Capt. Benjamin Carter. Deserted on 1/20/1783.	
Williams, Solomon	6th NC Regiment	1777, a Corporal under Capt. Thomas Donoho. Dropped from the rolls in Sep. 1777.	
Williams, Spencer	10th NC Regiment	6/20/1777, a Sergeant under Capt. Isaac Moore. Deserted in Apr. 1778.	
Williams, Stephen	2nd NC Regiment	1782, a Private under Capt. Robert Raiford for 18 months. Earlier in NC Militia. From Duplin County, NC where he enlisted. Born in Edgecombe County, NC. W9897.	
Williams, Stephen	3rd NC Regiment	March 1781 - April 22, 1782, a Sergeant under Capt. Edward Yarborough. Earlier in NC Militia. From Franklin County, NC. S36846.	Eutaw Springs (SC).
Williams, Theophilus	6th NC Regiment	4/2/1777, an Ensign under Capt. Philip Taylor. Dropped from the rolls in Jan. 1778.	
Williams, Theophilus	7th NC Regiment	A Private under Capt. Joseph Walker. A Corporal in Sep. 1777. A Sergeant in Nov. 1777. Died in March 1778. aka Thophis Williams.	
Williams, Thomas	1st NC Regiment	1777, a Private under Capt. Howell Tatum. 9/8/1778, a known Private under Capt. Howell Tatum (1st NC Regiment) - a baggage guard at Lancaster, PA on that date.	
Williams, Thomas	5th NC Regiment	1777, a Private under Capt. John Pugh Williams. Died on 7/20/1777.	
Williams, Thomas	5th NC Regiment	1777, a Private under Capt. William Caswell. Dropped from the rolls in June 1778.	
Williams, Thomas	10th NC Regiment	12/8/1777 and 5/1/1778, a known Commissary.	
Williams, William	DQMG	1780, a Wagoner under Col. Nicholas Long (Deputy QM General). Said to be an ex-Continental soldier (?).	
Williams, William	2nd NC Regiment	5/5/1776, a Private, unit unknown for 2-1/2 years. 9/9/1778, a known Private under Capt. John Ingles (2nd NC Regiment). Discharged on 11/10/1778.	
Williams, William	2nd NC Regiment	6/1/1779, a Private in the Colonel's Company (Col. John Patten) led by Capt. John Craddock for 18 months.	
Williams, William	2nd NC Regiment	4/25/1781, a Private under Capt. Tilghman Dixon. Dropped from the rolls during 1781.	
Williams, William	2nd NC Regiment	1782, a Private under Capt. Benjamin Carter for 18 months.	
Williams, William	2nd NC Regiment	12/11/1776, an Ensign under Capt. Benjamin Williams.	
Williams, William	4th NC Regiment	9/1/1775, a 1st Lieutenant and Adjutant under Capt. Thomas Harris. Wounded at Germantown, PA on 10/4/1777. 4/1/1778, a Captain in the Invalids Regiment (National - known as the Continental Corps of Invalids from 1777 to 1783) and served until 4/23/1783.	Germantown (PA).

Name	1st Unit	Year / Rank / Served Under / Notes	Known Battles
Williams, William	7th NC Regiment	5/16/1776, a Private under Capt. John McGlaughan. Aug. 1777, furloughed due to illness, rejoined in Jan. 1778. 9/8/1778, a known Private under Capt. Tilghman Dixon (1st NC Regiment). Discharged in Nov. 1778. From Orange County, NC. W3907.	Monmouth (NJ).
Williams, William	10th NC Regiment	6/10/1777, a Private under Capt. Isaac Moore for three years. 9/8/1778, a known Private in the Lt. Colonel's Company (Lt. Col. Robert Mebane) (1st NC Regiment) led by Capt. Joshua Bowman. While out on a scouting party, taken prisoner for four months, exchanged on 4/14/1779. POW also at the Fall of Charleston (SC), retained a little over a year. Enlisted at Perquimans County, NC. Born 1/30/1755 in Perquimans County, NC. S46082.	Monmouth (NJ), Siege of Charleston 1780 (SC).
Williams, William B.	1st NC Regiment	9/1/1775, an Adjutant. 6/13/1776, a Major. In Philadelphia during 1779 under BG James Hogun.	Moore's Creek Bridge [4], Brandywine Creek (PA), Germantown (PA).
Williams, Willoughby	10th NC Regiment	1777, a Private under Col. Abraham Sheppard, unit unknown. From Dobbs (what would become Wayne) County, NC. His widow claimed he rose to Major and Colonel, but no records exist to substantiate this. 1779-1780, an Ensign in NC Militia. 1780, a Captain in NC Militia from Wayne County. W36.	
Williams, Zadock	7th NC Regiment	12/23/1776, a Private under Capt. Joseph Walker for three years. 9/8/1778, a known Private under Capt. Tilghman Dixon (1st NC Regiment). Discharged on 1/29/1780. aka Zeddock Williams, Zaddock Williams.	
Williams, Zebedee	10th NC Regiment	5/29/1777, a Private under Capt. Dempsey Gregory. 9/8/1778, a known Private under Capt. Howell Tatum (1st NC Regiment). POW at the Fall of Charleston, SC, released in 1781. aka Zebediah Williams, Zebede Williams. S39131.	Siege of Charleston 1780 (SC).
Williamson, Adam	4th NC Regiment	2/6/1782, a Corporal under Capt. James Mills for 12 months.	
Williamson, Charles	5th NC Regiment	11/26/1776, a Private under Capt. William Caswell. 9/9/1778, a known Private under Capt. Robert Fenner (2nd NC Regiment). Official records indicate he was a POW at Ft. Lafayette, NY on 6/1/1779. In in own pension application, he does not mention Ft. Lafayette, but asserts he was taken prisoner at the battle of Stono Ferry, SC on 6/20/1779. From Rowan County, NC. S7939.	Ft. Lafayette (NY) or Stono Ferry (SC).
Williamson, George	6th NC Regiment	1777, a Private under Capt. Francis Child. Deserted on 9/3/1778. 9/8/1778, a known Private under Capt. Griffith John McRee (1st NC Regiment) - sick on that date at E. Town.	

680

Name	1st Unit	Year / Rank / Served Under / Notes	Known Battles
Williamson, Henry	1st NC Regiment	5/20/1776, a Private under Ens./Lt./Capt. James Read. 9/8/1778, a known Private under Capt. James Read (1st NC Regiment). Discharged on 5/27/1779.	
Williamson, Isaac	4th NC Regiment	1778, nine months as a Sergeant in the "New Levies." Discharged in August 1779 by Maj. John Armstrong. Born on 3/15/1747. W6522.	
Williamson, Jacob	3rd NC Regiment	7/20/1778, a Private under Lt./Capt. Joseph Montford for nine months. aka Jacob Williams.	
Williamson, John	5th NC Regiment	1777, a Private under Capt. Simon Alderson. Dropped from the rolls in Feb. 1778.	
Williamson, Robert	5th NC Regiment	April 1778, a Private under Capt. Simon Alderson for the duration of the war. Dropped from the rolls in Feb. 1778 (?). From New Hanover County, NC. Born 1750 in England. R11636.	Guilford Court House, Eutaw Springs (SC).
Williamson, William	3rd NC Regiment	4/16/1776, a Private under Capt. Jacob Turner for 2-1/2 years. 9/10/1778, a known Private under Capt. Thomas Armstrong (2nd NC Regiment). Discharged on 11/10/1778. From Bute (what would become Warren) County, NC. W18356.	Brandywine Creek (PA), Germantown (PA), Monmouth (NJ).
Williamson, William	3rd NC Regiment	1781, a Private under Capt. Edward Yarborough for 12 months. Discharged on 5/16/1782.	
Williamson, William	4th NC Regiment	March 1776, a Private under Capt. John Ashe, Jr. then Capt. William Goodman for 18 months. Served five months additional. From New Hanover County, NC. W1686.	Brandywine Creek (PA), Germantown (PA).
Williamson, William	4th NC Regiment	1777, a Private under Capt. James Williams. Discharged in Nov. 1777.	
Willibough, John	6th NC Regiment	6/12/1777, a Private under Ensign Joseph Richardson.	
Williford, Archibald	1st NC Regiment	9/10/1782, a Private under Capt. Joshua Hadley for 18 months.	
Williford, James	1st NC Regiment	1782, a Private under Capt. Joshua Hadley for 18 months.	
Williford, Theo.	1st NC Regiment	1781, a Private under Capt. Anthony Sharpe. Discharged on 6/24/1782 (4th NC Regiment).	
Williford, Willis	3rd NC Regiment	7/20/1778, a Private under Capt. Kedar Ballard for nine months. Discharged on 4/21/1779 at Halifax, NC. From Edgecombe County, NC. S42074.	
Willis, Augustor	3rd NC Regiment	9/24/1776, a Sergeant under Capt. Pinketham Eaton. Dropped from the rolls in June 1778.	
Willis, George	2nd NC Regiment	10/10/1776, a Private under Capt. William Fenner for three years. 9/9/1778, a known Private in the Lt. Colonel's Company (Lt. Col. Selby Harney). 3/12/1779, re-enlisted in the Lt. Colonel's Company (Lt. Col. Selby Harney). POW at Ft. Lafayette, NY on 6/1/1779. Rejoined in Nov. 1779.	Ft. Lafayette (NY).
Willis, Robert	2nd NC Regiment	1775, a Sergeant under Capt. Armstrong. Got sick, requested help from the Provincial Congress.	

681

Name	1st Unit	Year / Rank / Served Under / Notes	Known Battles
Willoughby, James	5th NC Regiment	6/24/1779, a Private under Capt. Joseph Montford.	
Willoughby, John	5th NC Regiment	6/24/1779, a Private under Capt. Joseph Montford. A Musician on 11/1/1779.	
Willowby, John	8th NC Regiment	1777, a Private under Capt. Francis Tartanson. Died on 2/14/1778.	
Wills, John	1st NC Regiment	Jan. 1782, a Private under Capt. Anthony Sharpe.	
Wilson, Aaron	2nd NC Regiment	1777, a Private under Capt. William Fenner. POW at Brandywine Creek, PA in Sep. 1777. Rejoined in June 1778. 9/9/1778, a known Private under Capt. Robert Fenner. Deserted on 6/15/1779.	Brandywine Creek (PA).
Wilson, Augustin	2nd NC Regiment	Sep. 1775, a Private under Capt. Simon Bright for six months. Later in NC Militia. From Dobbs County, NC. S7920.	Great Bridge (VA).
Wilson, Edward	2nd NC Regiment	7/20/1778, a Private under Maj. Reading Blount for nine months.	
Wilson, George	4th NC Regiment	1777, a Private under Capt. Robert Smith. Dropped from the rolls in Jan. 1778.	
Wilson, Henry	3rd NC Regiment	7/1/1779, a Private under Capt. Kedar Ballard. Deserted in Aug. 1779.	
Wilson, James	2nd NC Regiment	6/1/1781, a Private under Capt. Benjamin Andrew Coleman for 12 months.	
Wilson, James	10th NC Regiment	4/19/1777, a Captain under Col. Abraham Sheppard. Resigned on 5/20/1778. Later a Captain in NC Militia. From Caswell County, NC. W9008.	
Wilson, John	1st NC Regiment	1777, a Private under Capt. Henry "Hal" Dixon. Died on 2/21/1778.	
Wilson, John	2nd NC Regiment	1778, a Private under Capt. Thomas Armstrong. Discharged on 3/4/1782 near Greenville, NC. Earlier in NC Militia. From Pitt County, NC.	
Wilson, John	3rd NC Regiment	7/20/1778, a Private under Capt. Francis Child for nine months.	
Wilson, John	3rd NC Regiment	7/20/1778, a Private in the Lt. Colonel's Company (Lt. Col. William Lee Davidson) led by Lt./Capt. George "Gee" Bradley for nine months. 4/23/1779, a known Private in the Lt. Colonel's Company (Lt. Col. Robert Mebane) led by Capt. George "Gee" Bradley.	
Wilson, John	4th NC Regiment	1782, a Private under Capt. Anthony Sharpe for 18 months.	
Wilson, John	8th NC Regiment	1/1/1777, a Private under Capt. John Walsh for three years. A Corporal in Nov. 1778 – unit unknown. From Johnston County, NC. R11680.	
Wilson, Joshua	4th NC Regiment	1778, a Private under Capt. Joseph T. Rhodes for 12 months. Earlier and later in NC Militia. From Warren County, NC. S32599.	Stono Ferry (SC).
Wilson, Josiah	1st NC Regiment	5/17/1781, a Private under Capt. Robert Raiford. Discharged on 5/15/1782 (2nd NC Regiment). Earlier in NC Militia. From Bertie County, NC. On some rolls as Joseph Wilson. S14855.	Eutaw Springs (SC).

Name	1st Unit	Year / Rank / Served Under / Notes	Known Battles
Wilson, Robert	1st NC Regiment	6/20/1781, a Wagoner under Capt. Alexander Brevard. Discharged on 5/20/1782 (3rd NC Regiment) in Mecklenburg County, NC. S38476.	Siege of Ninety-Six 1781 (SC), Eutaw Springs (SC).
Wilson, Robert	4th NC Regiment	1782, a Private under Capt. William Lytle. Deserted on 11/25/1782.	
Wilson, Robert	6th NC Regiment	6/8/1776 or 4/16/1776 (two sources), a Surgeon. Died on 10/28/1777.	
Wilson, Thomas	1st NC Regiment	6/11/1781, a Private under Capt. Griffith John McRee. Discharged on 5/11/1782.	
Wilson, Thomas	3rd NC Regiment	6/15/1779, a Sergeant under Capt. Kedar Ballard. A Private in Oct. 1779. Deserted in March 1780.	
Wilson, Thomas	4th NC Regiment	1782, a Private under Capt. Anthony Sharpe. 2/8/1783, transferred to Pennsylvania Line.	
Wilson, Whitfield	3rd NC Regiment	4/24/1777, a Regimental QM. Resigned on 10/1/1777.	
Wilson, William	1st NC Regiment	4/15/1781, a Private under Capt. Anthony Sharpe. Discharged on 4/15/1782 (4th NC Regiment).	
Wilson, William	4th NC Regiment	1781, a Private under Capt. Joseph T. Rhodes. Discharged on 4/25/1782.	
Wilson, William	5th NC Regiment	1777, a Private under Capt. Simon Alderson for three years. Dropped from the rolls in Feb. 1778. From Johnston County, NC. W18352.	
Wilton, James	4th NC Regiment	1782, a Private under Capt. William Lytle for 18 months.	
Winbern, Philip	1st NC Regiment	5/19/1781, a Private under Capt. Robert Raiford. Discharged on 5/19/1782 (2nd NC Regiment).	
Winborn, John		1779, a Private, regiment and unit unknown. Deserted in 1779.	
Winborne, Henry	7th NC Regiment	5/24/1777, a Private under Capt. Joseph Walker for 3 years. 9/8/1778, a known Private under Capt. Tilghman Dixon (1st NC Regiment). From Hertford County, NC. aka Henry Winburn.	
Winborne, John	7th NC Regiment	11/28/1776, a 2nd Lieutenant under Capt. Joseph Walker. Reported as dead in Nov. 1777 - died as a result of being inoculated for Smallpox at Alexandria, VA. From Hertford County, NC. aka John Winburn.	
Windham, Obediah	NC Artillery	5/20/1776, a Gunner under Capt. John Vance as NC Provincial Troops. 7/10/1777, on Continental Line. 11/16/1777, under Capt. John Kingsbury. 5/1/1778, in same unit. 9/16/1778, in same unit - Sick at Fish Kills. Dropped from the rolls in Jan. 1779. From Craven County, NC. His sister, Sally Windham Baker, claims he was killed at the battle of Monmouth, NJ on 6/28/1778 (?). aka Obadia Winnom, Obediah Wynnon.	Monmouth (NJ) (?).
Windslow,	6th NC	1777, a Private under Capt. Thomas Donoho.	

Name	1st Unit	Year / Rank / Served Under / Notes	Known Battles
Silvester	Regiment	Deserted in Aug. 1777.	
Winham, John	10th NC Regiment	6/30/1777, a Private under Capt. Isaac Moore. Deserted in Apr. 1778.	
Winkles, James	4th NC Regiment	Aug. 1781, a Private under Capt. Joseph T. Rhodes for 18 months. From Onslow County, NC. Born on 10/26/1758 in Edgecombe County, NC. R11717.	
Winley, James	2nd NC Regiment	4/15/1781, a Sergeant under Capt. Benjamin Carter. Discharged 4/25/1782.	
Winn, Zachariah	4th NC Regiment	1782, a Private under Capt. Anthony Sharp for twelve months. Living in Anson County, NC when he enlisted. Born 1761 in VA. On the official rolls as Zachariah Wynn. S18286.	
Winters, Moses	1st NC Regiment	4/12/1781, a Private under Capt. Alexander Brevard. Discharged on 4/12/1782 (3rd NC Regiment).	
Wise, Jesse	1st NC Regiment	1781, a Private under Capt. Robert Raiford. Discharged on 4/1/1782 (2nd NC Regiment).	
Wise, John	5th NC Regiment	June 1776, a Private under Capt. William Ward for one year. Dec. 1777, a Private under Capt. Benjamin Andrew Coleman. A Corporal in Jan. 1779 under Capt. Philip Taylor. Discharged at Stono, SC. S36395.	Brandywine Creek (PA), Germantown (PA).
Wise, John	8th NC Regiment	1777, a Musician under Capt. Robert Raiford. Died on 3/6/1777.	
Wiseheart, William	8th NC Regiment	1/8/1777, a Private under Capt. Robert Raiford. Dropped from the rolls in March 1778.	
Wiset, James	10th NC Regiment	10/5/1777, a Private under Capt. James Wilson. Dropped from the rolls in June 1778.	
Witherington, Joseph	7th NC Regiment	5/6/1777, a Private under Capt. Joseph Walker and Capt. John Baker. June 1778, a Private under Capt. Tilghman Dixon (1st NC Regiment). POW at the Fall of Charleston, SC - held 13 months, then escaped. Earlier in NC Militia. From Hertford County, NC. S1938.	Siege of Charleston 1780 (SC).
Witherington, William	7th NC Regiment	6/13/1777, a Sergeant under Capt. Henry Dawson. A Private in June 1778. 9/8/1778, a known Private under Capt. James Read (1st NC Regiment). Discharged on 2/1/1780. aka William Withrington.	
Witherspoon, James	NC Brigade	As a Major, an Aide-de-Camp to BG Francis Nash. Killed at the battle of Germantown, PA on Oct. 4, 1777.	Brandywine Creek (PA), Germantown (PA).
Witt, Burgess	4th NC Regiment	1782, a Private under Capt. William Lytle for 18 months. Discharged on 5/4/1782 near Charleston, SC. Earlier in NC Militia. From Guilford County, NC. Born 1765 in VA. aka Berge Witt. W54.	
Witty, James	9th NC Regiment	5/21/1777, a Private under Capt. Thomas McCrory for three years. Deserted in Nov. 1777. Rejoined in May 1778 under Capt. Joshua Bowman (1st NC Regiment). 9/8/1778, a known Private in the Lt. Colonel's Company (Lt. Col.	Monmouth (NJ), Siege of Charleston 1780 (SC).

Name	1st Unit	Year / Rank / Served Under / Notes	Known Battles
		Robert Mebane) (1st NC Regiment) led by Capt. Joshua Bowman. POW at the Fall of Charleston (SC), held fourteen months. From Guilford County, NC. On some rolls as James Wittey. S18662.	
Witwell, Thomas	2nd NC Regiment	1782, a Private under Capt. Benjamin Carter for 18 months.	
Wodle, Jacob	3rd NC Regiment	6/24/1779, a Sergeant under Capt. Michael Quinn. Dropped from the rolls in Oct. 1779.	
Woesley, Bryan	5th NC Regiment	4/15/1777, a Private under Capt. Simon Alderson.	
Wollard, Jesse	2nd NC Regiment	9/9/1778, a Private under Capt. Benjamin Andrew Coleman.	
Wolton, Christopher	1st NC Regiment	1777, a Private under Capt. Howell Tatum.	
Womack, William	1st NC Regiment	Jan. 1778, a Regimental QM. Retired on 6/1/1778.	
Womble, Benjamin	2nd NC Regiment	1782, a Private under Capt. Robert Raiford. Deserted on 6/11/1783 (?).	
Womble, Benjamin	2nd NC Regiment	9/9/1778, a known Private under Capt. Robert Fenner.	
Womble, Dempsey	2nd NC Regiment	4/25/1781, a Private under Capt. Tilghman Dixon. 1782, a Musician under Capt. William Walton (1st NC Regiment).	
Womble, John	3rd NC Regiment	6/1/1779, a Private under Capt. Michael Quinn. Then, under Capt. John Campbell (4th NC Regiment). POW at the Fall of Charleston, paroled. From Edgecombe County, NC. S42083.	Siege of Savannah (GA), Siege of Charleston 1780 (SC).
Wood, Aaron	3rd NC Regiment	7/20/1778, a Private under Capt. Michael Quinn for nine months.	
Wood, Bennett	1st NC Regiment	Dec. 1782, a Private under Capt. Peter Bacot. Discharged on 12/13/1783.	
Wood, Bennett	7th NC Regiment	11/28/1776, appointed a Captain under Col. James Hogun, refused his commission. From Bute County, NC.	
Wood, Charles	6th NC Regiment	May 1776, a Private under Capt. Philip Taylor. 9/8/1778, a known Private under Capt. John Sumner (1st NC Regiment) - sick at Valley Forge on that date. A Corporal in May 1779. POW at the Fall of Charleston, held for 14 months. Back to Private in 1782, unit unknown. Enlisted in Wake County, NC. S42084.	Brandywine Creek (PA), Germantown (PA), Monmouth (NJ), Siege of Charleston 1780 (SC).
Wood, Edward	10th NC Regiment	6/1/1777, a Private under Capt. Isaac Moore. Discharged on 8/1/1778.	
Wood, Isaac	3rd NC Regiment	1781, a Private under Capt. Edward Yarborough for 12 months. Discharged on 4/22/1782. From Pasquotank County, NC. R3530.	
Wood, James	2nd NC Regiment	3/20/1780, a Private under Capt. Benjamin Andrew Coleman till the end of the war. From Johnston County, NC. W6571.	
Wood, Jesse	5th NC Regiment	8/14/1779, a Private under Maj. Reading Blount. Deserted in Oct. 1779.	

Name	1st Unit	Year / Rank / Served Under / Notes	Known Battles
Wood, John	1st NC Regiment	4/4/1777, a Private under Capt. Lawrence Thompson for three years. A Sergeant in Jan. 1778. Back to Private in June 1778. 6/1/1778, a Private under Capt. Griffith John McRee.	
Wood, John	1st NC Regiment	4/28/1781, a Private under Capt. William Armstrong, then under Capt. Griffith John McRee. Official rolls assert that he deserted on 6/13/1781. From Surry County, NC. R11792.	Siege of Ninety-Six 1781 (SC).
Wood, John	1st NC Regiment	1781, a Wagon Conductor under Capt. Anthony Sharpe. Discharged on 4/25/1782 (4th NC Regiment).	
Wood, John	2nd NC Regiment	10/20/1776, a Private, unit unknown. 9/9/1778, a known Private in the Lt. Colonel's Company (Lt. Col. Selby Harney).	
Wood, John	4th NC Regiment	1781, a Private under Capt. Joseph T. Rhodes. Discharged on 4/1/1782.	
Wood, John	5th NC Regiment	10/20/1776, a Sergeant under Capt. Simon Alderson. 1/1/1779, a QM Sergeant. 12/10/1779, a Wagon Master.	
Wood, John	5th NC Regiment	6/27/1776, a 2nd Lieutenant under Capt. William Ward.	
Wood, Joseph	5th NC Regiment	1779, a Private under Maj. Reading Blount. Deserted in Sep. 1779.	
Wood, Matthew	3rd NC Regiment	1775, a 2nd Lieutenant in the Halifax District Minutemen. 4/17/1776, a 1st Lieutenant under Capt. John Gray, then under Capt. Jacob Turner. 11/22/1777, a Captain. After the battle of Monmouth (NJ), was sent back to NC as a recruiter for about a year, then retired. From Halifax County, NC. 1781, a Major in the NC Militia. S39135.	Ft. Moultrie #1 (SC), Brandywine Creek (PA), Germantown (PA), Monmouth (NJ).
Wood, Matthew	5th NC Regiment	1776, an Ensign under Capt. William Ward.	
Wood, Sampson	1st NC Regiment	5/25/1781, a Private under Capt. Thomas Donoho. Discharged on 5/25/1782 at Bacon's Bridge, SC. Enlisted in Orange County, NC. S42079.	Eutaw Springs (SC).
Wood, Solomon	8th NC Regiment	11/28/1776, a 2nd Lieutenant under Capt. William Gurley. Refused to serve. From Johnston County, NC.	
Wood, Thomas	5th NC Regiment	8/14/1779, a Private under Maj. Reading Blount. Deserted in Oct. 1779.	
Wood, William	1st NC Regiment	1777, a Private under Capt. Joshua Bowman.	
Wood, William	1st NC Regiment	Dec. 1775, a Sergeant under Capt. Alfred Moore for 12 months. Discharged in Dec. 1776. Later, in NC Militia. From Orange County, NC. S7971.	Moore's Creek Bridge.
Wood, Willis	4th NC Regiment	8/1/1782, a Private under Capt. Thomas Evans for 18 months.	
Woodard, John	1st NC Regiment	1777, a Private under Capt. Robert Ralston. 9/8/1778, a known Private under Capt. John Sumner (1st NC Regiment). aka John Woodward.	

Name	1st Unit	Year / Rank / Served Under / Notes	Known Battles
Woodert, Henry	1st NC Regiment	6/6/1781, a Private under Capt. William Lytle. Discharged on 6/6/1782 (4th NC Regiment).	
Woodhouse, John	2nd NC Regiment	9/1/1775, an Ensign.	
Woodill, John	1st NC Regiment	8/1/1782, a Private under Capt. Joshua Hadley for 18 months. Earlier in NC Militia. From Johnston County, NC. aka John Woodell. W3911.	
Woodle, Jeremiah	4th NC Regiment	1782, a Private under Capt. Joseph T. Rhodes. Discharged on 7/21/1782.	
Woodle, Joseph	4th NC Regiment	1782, a Private under Capt. Joseph T. Rhodes. Discharged on 7/21/1782.	
Woodley, Thomas	10th NC Regiment	5/17/1777, a Private under Capt. Isaac Moore. Dropped from the rolls in June 1778.	
Woodman, Edward	6th NC Regiment	4/28/1776, a Private under Lt./Capt. Thomas White and Capt. Archibald Lytle for 2-1/2 years. 1/8/1778, a Private under Lt./Capt. John Sumner (1st NC Regiment). 9/8/1778, in same unit. Discharged on 11/18/1778. W2893.	Brandywine Creek (PA), Germantown (PA), Monmouth (NJ).
Woodrow, H. Edward	1st NC Regiment	1781, a Private under Capt. William Lytle.	
Woodruff, John	1st NC Regiment	5/5/1781, a Private under Capt. Robert Raiford. Killed on 9/8/1781 at the battle of Eutaw Springs, SC.	Eutaw Springs (SC).
Woods, William	3rd NC Regiment	3/6/1782, a Private under Capt. Samuel Jones for 12 months.	
Woods, William	7th NC Regiment	1777, a Fifer under Capt. Joseph Walker. Deserted on 9/17/1777.	
Woodside, William	4th NC Regiment	1779, a Private under Capt. Matthew Ramsey for a short while. Earlier and later in NC Militia. From Rowan (what is now Iredell) County, NC.	Stono Ferry (SC).
Woodward, Caleb	3rd NC Regiment	7/20/1778, a Private in the Lt. Colonel's Company (Lt. Col. William Lee Davidson) led by Lt./Capt. George "Gee" Bradley. Died in Sep. 1778 at Roberdson's Hospital.	
Woodward, David	2nd NC Regiment	1782, a Private under Capt. Benjamin Carter for 18 months.	
Woodward, Edward	3rd NC Regiment	8/27/1782, a Private under Capt. Benjamin Bailey for 18 months.	
Woodward, John	1st NC Regiment	1777, a Private under Capt. Robert Ralston.	
Woolard, James	3rd NC Regiment	7/20/1778, a Private under Capt. Francis Child for nine months. Discharged at Philadelphia, PA. Enlisted in Martin County, NC. aka James Wallard, James Woollard. S42082.	
Woolard, Jesse	5th NC Regiment	1777, a Private under Capt. Henry Darnell. 6/1/1778, in 2nd NC Regiment, unit unknown. POW at Ft. Lafayette, NY on 6/1/1779. Rejoined 11/1779.	Ft. Lafayette (NY).
Wooten, Christopher	1st NC Regiment	1777, a Private under Capt. Howell Tatum. 2/26/1778, a known Private under Capt. Howell Tatum. 9/8/1778, a known Private under Capt. Howell Tatum. aka Christopher Wotton.	

Name	1st Unit	Year / Rank / Served Under / Notes	Known Battles
Wooten, Jesse	2nd NC Regiment	4/4/1776, a Private, unit unknown for 2-1/2 years. 9/9/1778, a known Private in the Colonel's Company (Col. John Patten) led by Capt. John Craddock. Discharged on 10/30/1778.	
Wooten, Joel	DQMG	1780, a Tailor on the roll of Capt. Solomon Wood (NC Light Dragoons) - this seems to be for convenience only. 8/23/1781, a Tailor under Col. Nicholas Long (Deputy QM General), to make 60 hats within three months.	
Wooten, Shadrack	5th NC Regiment	1775, an Ensign in the New Bern District Minutemen. 4/17/1776, an Ensign under Capt. John Enloe and Col. Edward Buncombe. Born in Edgecombe County, but living in Pitt County, NC when he enlisted. Later, settled in Columbus County, NC.	
Wooten, William	2nd NC Regiment	1777, a Private under Capt. Charles Allen. Died on 4/21/1778. aka William Wooton.	
Woreley, John	10th NC Regiment	8/1/1777, a Musician under Capt. Silas Stevenson. A Drum Major on 8/6/1778. A Drummer in Sep. 1778. aka John Wareley.	
Workman, Peter	1st NC Regiment	4/28/1781, a Private under Capt. Alexander Brevard. Discharged on 4/28/1782 (3rd NC Regiment) at Camden, SC. S39136.	
Worley, Matthew	3rd NC Regiment	7/20/1778, a Private under Lt./Capt. Joseph Montford for nine months.	
Worneck, William	9th NC Regiment	1777, a Sergeant under Capt. Joseph J. Wade. QM on 1/14/1778. Dropped from the rolls in June 1778.	
Worrell, John	2nd NC Regiment	1782, a Private under Capt. Benjamin Carter for 18 months.	
Worsley, Bryant	2nd NC Regiment	4/15/1777, a Private under Capt. Simon Alderson for 3 years. 9/9/1778, a known Private in the Colonel's Company (Col. John Patten) led by Capt. John Craddock. 3/12/1779, re-enlisted under Capt. Benjamin Williams. aka Bryan Worsley.	
Worsley, John	5th NC Regiment	6/28/1777, a Drummer, unit unknown. 9/9/1778, a known Drummer in the Colonel's Company (Col. John Patten) (2nd NC Regiment) led by Capt. John Craddock.	
Worsley, John	3rd NC Regiment	7/20/1778, a Private under Capt. Francis Child for nine months.	
Worsley, Leman	1st NC Regiment	1782, a Private under Capt. Peter Bacot for 18 months.	
Worsley, Thomas	3rd NC Regiment	7/10/1778, a Private under Capt. Michael Quinn for nine months. Discharged 6/1/1779 at Halifax, NC. From Beaufort County, NC. S42081.	
Worsley, Thomas	3rd NC Regiment	7/20/1778, a Corporal under Capt. Michael Quinn for nine months.	
Worth, Joseph	2nd NC Regiment	10/20/1775, an Ensign. 5/3/1776, a 1st Lieutenant. Died on 4/6/1777. From Edenton, NC.	

Name	1st Unit	Year / Rank / Served Under / Notes	Known Battles
Wotton, William	8th NC Regiment	1777, a Sergeant under Capt. Michael Quinn. Died on 5/1/1778.	
Wren, William	4th NC Regiment	5/13/1776, a Private under Capt. William Temple Coles for three years. 9/8/1778, a known Private under Capt. John Sumner (1st NC Regiment). 3/12/1779, re-enlisted for the duration of the war in the same unit. A Corporal on 2/10/1780. aka William Wrenn.	
Wright, Abraham	2nd NC Regiment	12/1/1781, a Sergeant under Capt. Benjamin Andrew Coleman. A Private in Apr. 1782.	
Wright, Adam	4th NC Regiment	1777, a Musician under Capt. Thomas Harris. Dropped from the rolls in March 1778. Jan. 1779, re-enlisted.	
Wright, Asa	4th NC Regiment	5/16/1778, a Private under Capt. William Goodman. Wounded at the battle of Stono Ferry, SC. Later in NC Militia. From Caswell County, NC. S18292.	Stono Ferry (SC).
Wright, David	10th NC Regiment	4/19/1777, an Ensign under Capt. Isaac Moore. 2/15/1778, a Lieutenant. 6/1/1778, transferred to 1st NC Regiment under Maj. John Baptiste Ashe. Resigned on 2/5/1780. S6448.	
Wright, Ewell	2nd NC Regiment	1782, a Private under Capt. Benjamin Carter for 18 months.	
Wright, John	4th NC Regiment	1777, a Private under Capt. Robert Smith. Dropped from the rolls in Sep. 1777.	
Wright, Levi	2nd NC Regiment	3/12/1779, re-enlisted under Capt. Clement Hall.	
Wright, Micajah	5th NC Regiment	6/22/1779, a Private under Maj. Reading Blount. Deserted in Oct. 1779.	
Wright, O. Prince	3rd NC Regiment	7/20/1778, a Private under Capt. Francis Child for nine months. Dropped from the rolls sometime during 1779.	
Wright, Thomas	4th NC Regiment	4/29/1776, a Private under Capt. Thomas Harris for 3 years. 9/8/1778, a known Private under Capt. John Sumner (1st NC Regiment). Discharged on 5/10/1779.	
Wyatt, James	10th NC Regiment	10/2/1777, a Private under Capt. Andrew Vanoy. 9/8/1778, a known Private under Capt. Tilghman Dixon (1st NC Regiment). A Corporal in Apr. 1783. Deserted on 6/15/1783 (?).	
Wyatt, John	7th NC Regiment	A Sergeant under Capt. Lemuel Ely. Died on 4/29/1777.	
Wynn, Ezekiel	4th NC Regiment	1782, a Private under Capt. Anthony Sharpe for 18 months.	
Wynne, Jones	1st NC Regiment	1777, a Private under Capt. Henry "Hal" Dixon. 9/8/1778, a known Wagoner under Capt. James Read. aka Jones Wynn.	
Wynne, Knibb	1st NC Regiment	1777, a Sergeant under Capt. Henry "Hal" Dixon. Dropped from the rolls in Jan. 1778.	
Wynne, William	1st NC Regiment	1777, a Private under Capt. Henry "Hal" Dixon. Dropped from the rolls in Jan. 1778.	
Yancey, Charles	9th NC Regiment	11/28/1776, a 2nd Lieutenant under Capt. Richard Donaldson Cook. From Hillsborough	

Name	1st Unit	Year / Rank / Served Under / Notes	Known Battles
		District.	
Yarborough, David	1st NC Regiment	6/18/1782, a Private under Capt. Benjamin Bailey for 12 months.	
Yarborough, Davis	4th NC Regiment	May 1782, a Private under Capt. William Lytle, then under Capt. Elijah Moore. Furloughed Feb. 1783 at Wilmington, NC. From Randolph County, NC. S1606.	
Yarborough, Edward	3rd NC Regiment	5/8/1776, an Ensign under Capt. Jacob Turner. 4/16/1776, a 1st Lieutenant under Capt. Jacob Turner. Promoted to Captain-Lieutenant on 1/9/1777. 5/10/1779, a full Captain. Retired on 1/1/1783.	Little Lynches Creek (SC), Camden (SC), Guilford Court House, Hobkirk Hill (SC), Eutaw Springs (SC).
Yarborough, James		Shows up dead in 1779. Duh (?)	
Yarborough, Reuben	3rd NC Regiment	4/25/1776, a Sergeant under Capt. Jacob Turner for 2-1/2 years. 9/9/1778, a known Sergeant in the Colonel's Company (2nd NC Regiment - Col. John Patten) led by Capt. John Craddock. Discharged on 10/30/1778. aka Reuben Yerberry.	
Yarborough, Reuben	3rd NC Regiment	4/14/1777, a known Ensign under Capt. Daniel Jones.	
Yarborough, Richard	3rd NC Regiment	7/20/1778, a Private under Lt./Capt. Joseph Montford for nine months.	
Yates, David	4th NC Regiment	1782, a Private under Capt. William Lytle for 18 months.	
Yates, John	6th NC Regiment	A Private under Capt. Thomas White. Dropped from the rolls in Feb. 1778.	
Yates, Samuel	3rd NC Regiment	7/20/1778, a Private under Capt. Kedar Ballard for nine months.	
Yates, Thomas	1st NC Regiment	1782, a Private under Capt. Peter Bacot for 18 months.	
Yates, William	1st NC Regiment	5/9/1781, a Private under Capt. Griffith John McRee. Dropped from the rolls in Aug. 1781 - sick.	
Yeates, Thomas	1st NC Regiment	1776, a Private under Lt. Absalom Tatum and Capt. John Walker for six months. Later in NC Militia. From what is now Caswell County, NC. W7335.	
Yeoman, Harris	3rd NC Regiment	7/20/1778, a Private under Capt. Michael Quinn for nine months. 1782, rejoined under Capt. Robert Raiford (2nd NC Regiment). Deserted on 6/11/1783 (?).	
Yewman, Christopher	1st NC Regiment	5/25/1781, a Private under Capt. Thomas Donoho for 12 months.	
Yordon, Philip	2nd NC Regiment	1782, a Private under Capt. Benjamin Carter for 18 months.	
York, William	1st NC Regiment	Sep. 1775, a Private under Capt. Henry "Hal" Dixon. 9/8/1778, a known Private under Capt. James Read. POW at the Fall of Charleston (SC). S38481.	Moore's Creek Bridge, Brandywine Creek (PA),

Name	1st Unit	Year / Rank / Served Under / Notes	Known Battles
			Germantown (PA), Monmouth (NJ), Siege of Charleston 1780 (SC).
Young, James	1st NC Regiment	1777, a Private under Capt. Joshua Bowman. 9/8/1778, a known Private under Capt. Joshua Bowman. Dropped from the rolls in July 1779.	
Young, Jesse	6th NC Regiment	A Private under Capt. Francis Child. Died on 2/13/1778.	
Young, John	3rd NC Regiment	8/1/1776, a Corporal under Capt. Jacob Turner for 2-1/2 years. A Private in June 1778. 9/9/1778, a known Private under Capt. John Ingles (2nd NC Regiment). Discharged on 10/31/1778.	
Young, John	3rd NC Regiment	1779, a Private under Capt. Kedar Ballard for three years.	
Young, Michael	4th NC Regiment	1782, a Private under Capt. Anthony Sharpe for 18 months - per official records. Per his own pension statement of 1830, he claims that he was first under Capt. Edward Yarborough (3rd NC Regiment) in March or April of 1782 at Salisbury for four weeks. He was then transferred to Capt. Robert Raiford (2nd NC Regiment) for twelve months and marched to SC. S35758.	
Young, William	6th NC Regiment	A Private under Capt. Francis Child. Died on 2/28/1778.	
Zacha, Jackson	1st NC Regiment	6/30/1777, a Private unit unknown. 9/8/1778, a Private under Capt. Tilghman Dixon.	
Zakel, James	1st NC Regiment	4/2/1776, a Private under Capt. Thomas Granbury. POW on 6/1/1779 at Ft. Lafayette, NY.	Ft. Lafayette (NY).

Sources

Ashe, Samuel A'Court, *History of North Carolina, Volume I From 1584 to 1783*, Greensboro, NC, Charles L. Van Noppen, Publisher, 1908.

Babits, Lawrence E. & Howard, Joshua B., *Long, Obstinate and Bloody – the Battle of Guilford Courthouse*, Chapel Hill, NC, The University of North Carolina Press, 2009.

Buchanan, John, *The Road to Guilford Courthouse*, New York, NY, John Wiley & Sons, Inc., 1997.

Carrington, Henry B., M.A., LL.D., *Battles of the American Revolution 1775-1781*, New York, NY, A.S. Barnes & Company, 1876.

Clark, Walter, *The State Records of North Carolina, Volumes XI-XVII, XIX, XXIV*, Winston, NC, M.I. & J.C. Stewart, Printers to the State, 1895.

Davis, Charles L., *A Brief History of the North Carolina Troops on the Continental Establishment in the War of the Revolution*, Philadelphia, PA, 1896.

Daughters of the American Revolution, *Pierce's Register*, Washington, DC, Senate Documents, Vol. 9, No. 988, 63d Congress, 3d Session, 1915.

Emmet, Dr. Thomas Addis, *Original Papers Relating to The Siege of Charleston 1780,* Charleston, SC, Walker, Evans & Cogswell & Co., 1898.

Glasson, William Henry, Ph.B., *History of Military Pension Legislation*, New York, NY, Columbia University Doctoral Thesis, 1900.

Heitman, F.B., *Historical Register of Officers of the Continental Army*, Washington, DC, The Rare Book Publishing Co., Inc., 1914.

Hough, Franklin Benjamin, *The Siege of Charleston by the British Fleet and Army under the Command of Admiral Arbuthnot and Sir Henry Clinton*, Albany, NY, J. Munsell Co., 1867.

Koontz, Russell, *An Angel Has Fallen! The Glasgow Land Frauds and the Establishment of the North Carolina Supreme Court*, Raleigh, NC, North Carolina State University Master's Thesis, 1995

Lossing, Benson J., *The Pictorial Field-Book of the Revolution*, New York, NY, Harper & Brothers, 1850.

Moss, Bobby Gilmer, *Roster of the Patriots in the Battle of Moore's Creek Bridge*, Blacksburg, SC, Scotia-Hibernia Press, 1992

Rankin, Hugh F., *The North Carolina Continentals*, Chapel Hill, NC, The University of North Carolina Press, 1971.

Robinson, Blackwell P., *William R. Davie*, Chapel Hill, NC, The

University of North Carolina Press, 1957.

Rodenbough, Charles D., *Governor Alexander Martin*, Jefferson, NC, McFarland & Company, Inc., Publishers, 1932.

Saunders, William L. (editor), *The Colonial Records of North Carolina, Volume X*, Raleigh, NC, Josephus Daniels, Printer to the State, 1890.

Schenck, David, LL.D, *North Carolina 1780-1781*, Raleigh, NC, Edwards & Broughton, Publishers, 1889.

Troiani, Don & Kochan, James L., *Soldiers of the American Revolution*, Mechanicsburg, PA, Stackpole Books, 2007

U.S. National Archives & Records Administration (NARA), *Microfilm Records M246, Roll 79*–Revolutionary War Rolls 1775-1783 (NC).

U.S. National Archives & Records Administration (NARA), *Microfilm Records M804* – Revolutionary War Pension & Bounty Land Warrant Application Files (thousands of documents).

U.S. National Archives & Records Administration (NARA), *Microfilm Records M853* – Numbered Record Books Concerning Military Operataions and Service, Pay, and Settlement of Accounts and Supplies (thousands of documents).

U.S. National Archives & Records Administration (NARA), *Microfilm Records M859*–Miscellaneous Numbered Records in the War Department (The Manuscript Files), Collection of Revolutionary War Records (thousands of documents).

Wheeler, Col. John H., *Historical Sketches of North Carolina from 1584 to 1851*, New York, NY, Frederick H. Hitchcock, Publisher, 1925

Whitaker, Harriett Reed & Hay, Gertrude Sloan, *Roster of Soldiers from North Carolina in the American Revolution*, Durham, NC, The North Carolina Daughters of the American Revolution, 1932.

Index

Lamb, Abner – 149
Lamb, Gideon – 20, 22, 25, 37, 41, 43,
    49, 55, 60, 74, 77, 78, 94, 108, 116,
    143, 144, 233, 236
Lancaster (PA) – 49
Laurens, John (SC) – 155, 156, 157,
    169, 170, 238, 243
Leak, John – 64, 239
Lawrence, Nathaniel – 82
Lee, Henry (VA) – 124, 134, 136, 137,
    139, 149, 153, 154, 155, 156, 163
Lee, Charles (VA) – 23, 24, 25, 27, 28,
    67, 68, 69
Lenud's Ferry (SC) – 100
Leslie, Alexander (British) – 95, 119,
    157, 158, 166, 176
Lewis, Joel – 86, 166
Lewis, Micajah – 55, 60, 63, 66, 72, 78,
    116, 124, 232, 234
Lewis, William – 64
Lewis, William Terrell – 185
Lillington, John Alexander – 10, 12,
    20, 22, 25, 33, 36, 43, 97, 133
Lincoln, Benjamin (MA) – 73, 74,
    77, 79, 85, 86, 87, 88, 89, 90, 91,
    96, 97, 98, 102, 108, 151
Lincoln County – 102, 139
Linton, William Thomas – 60, 66, 72,
    132, 237
Linzee, John (British) – 29
Little River (SC) – 23, 35
Locke, Francis – 102, 187
Lockhart, Samuel – 20, 21, 25, 33, 37,
    41, 43, 56, 101, 232, 235
Lockwood's Folly – 35
Log Town (SC) – 104
Long, Nicholas – 4, 23, 132, 143, 167
Lossing, Benson J. – 148
Ludwig, Christopher – 57
Luttrell, John – 33, 34, 37, 41, 44, 55
Luzerne, Chevalier La – 135
Lynch, Charles (VA) – 128
Lytle, Archibald – 20, 22, 25, 33, 37,
    40, 41, 43, 55, 60, 63, 74, 77, 78,
    79, 80, 81, 88, 89, 94, 97, 125, 130,
    149, 151, 159, 160, 171, 173, 174,
    175, 177, 233, 236, 238, 239, 243
Lytle, William – 63, 78, 81, 89, 91,
    93, 99, 101, 104, 118, 130, 134,
    140, 145, 159, 163, 173, 174, 177,

238, 239, 240, 241, 242

MacLaine, Archibald – 109, 179
Macon, John – 37, 41, 55, 60, 234, 236
Maitland, John (British) – 87
Majoribanks, John (British) – 148
Maples, Marmaduke – 151, 243
Marion, Francis (SC) – 134, 136, 137,
    147, 149, 153, 154
Martin, Alexander – 3, 4, 20, 23, 25,
    26, 32, 33, 39, 41, 44, 48, 49, 55, 56,
    57, 109, 112, 155, 164, 165, 170,
    171, 172, 174, 175, 177, 178, 179,
    180, 231, 232, 235
Martin, Henry – 130
Martin, James (Lt. Col.) – 11, 13
Martin, James (Captain) – 41, 55, 60,
    230, 232, 235
Martin, Josiah (Royal Governor) – 1, 2,
    5, 6, 7, 8, 9, 10, 12, 14, 15, 30, 100,
    111
Martin, Samuel – 118
Mason, Richard – 159
Matson's Ford (PA) – 57, 66
Matthews, Giles – 4
Matthews, John (SC) – 176
Matthews, Joseph – 149
Maxwell, William – 46, 48, 51, 52, 67
May, James – 33, 34, 37, 41
McBride, James – 26
McCartney, Jeremiah – 26
McCauley, Matthew – 64, 89, 238, 239
McCrory, Thomas – 33, 34, 37, 41, 55,
    234, 236
McDonald, Donald (Loyalist) – 7, 8,
    9, 10, 12, 14
McDougall, Alexander – 51, 52, 57, 70,
    84
McGlaughan, John – 33, 37, 41, 233,
    236
McIntosh, George (British) – 17
McIntosh, Lachlan (GA) – 58, 60, 65
McLane, John – 20, 21, 25, 33, 37, 41,
    55, 60, 66, 72, 78, 89, 233, 235, 239
McLean, Alexander – 10
McLean, Charles – 20, 21, 25, 33, 37
McLeod, Donald (Loyalist) – 7, 10, 11,
    15
McLeod, John (British) – 129
McNairy, John (TN) – 187

www.ingramcontent.com/pod-product-compliance
Lightning Source LLC
Chambersburg PA
CBHW071906090426
42811CB00004B/763